# Internet Marketing

Strategy, Implementation and Practice

Visit the *Internet Marketing, Strategy, Implementation and Practice*, Fourth Edition Companion Website at **www.pearsoned.co.uk/chaffey** to find valuable **student** learning material including:

- Multiple choice questions for every chapter
- Links to video material, on YouTube and FT.com, that demonstrates marketing theory
- Annotated weblinks which provide examples for further study
- A comprehensive online glossary and flashcards which help define key terms and phrases

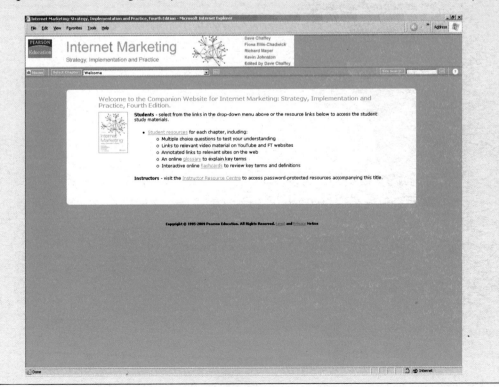

Fourth Edition

# Internet
# Marketing

Strategy, Implementation and Practice

Dave Chaffey
Fiona Ellis-Chadwick
Richard Mayer
Kevin Johnston

Edited by Dave Chaffey

**FT** Prentice Hall
FINANCIAL TIMES

*An imprint of* **Pearson Education**
Harlow, England • London • New York • Boston • San Francisco • Toronto
Sydney • Tokyo • Singapore • Hong Kong • Seoul • Taipei • New Delhi
Cape Town • Madrid • Mexico City • Amsterdam • Munich • Paris • Milan

**Pearson Education Limited**
Edinburgh Gate
Harlow
Essex CM20 2JE
England

and Associated Companies throughout the world

*Visit us on the World Wide Web at*:
www.pearsoned.co.uk

First published 2000
Second edition published 2003
Third edition published 2006
**Fourth edition published 2009**

ISBN-13: 978-0-273-71740-9

**British Library Cataloguing-in-Publication Data**
A catalogue record for this book is available from the British Library

**Library of Congress Cataloging-in-Publication Data**
A catalog record for this book is available from the Library of Congress

10 9 8 7 6 5 4
12 11

Typeset in 10/12pt Minion by 30
Printed and bound by Rotolito Lombarda, Italy

# Brief contents

# Contents

## Supporting resources

Visit **www.pearsoned.co.uk/chaffey** to find valuable online resources:

### Companion Website for students

- Multiple choice questions for every chapter
- Links to video material, on YouTube and FT.com, that demonstrates marketing theory
- Annotated weblinks which provide examples for further study
- A comprehensive online glossary and flashcards which help define key terms and phrases

### For instructors

- A complete, downloadable Instructor's Manual
- PowerPoint slides which are downloadable and available to use for teaching
- A Testbank of question material, which you can use to test your students

**Also:** The Companion Website also provides the following features:

- Search tool to help locate specific items of content
- E-mail results and profile tools to send results of quizzes to instructors
- Online help and support to assist with website usage and troubleshooting

For more information please contact your local Pearson Education sales representative or visit **www.pearsoned.co.uk/chaffey**

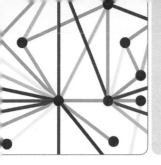

# Preface

## The Internet – opportunity and treat

The Internet and other digital media have transformed marketing. For customers, they give a much wider choice of products, services and prices from different suppliers and the means to select and purchase items more readily. For organisations marketing these products and services it gives the opportunity to expand into new markets, offer new services, apply new online communications techniques and compete on a more equal footing with larger businesses. For those working within these organisations it gives the opportunity to develop new skills and to use the Internet to improve the competitiveness of the company.

At the same time, the Internet gives rise to many threats to organisations. For example, start-up companies such as Amazon (books) (www.amazon.com), Expedia (travel) (www.expedia.com), AutoByTel (cars) (www.autobytel.com) and CDWOW (CDs) (www.cdwow.com) have captured a significant part of their market and struck fear into the existing players. Indeed the phrase 'amazoning a market sector' has become a frequently used expression among marketers.

## The Internet – management issues

With the success stories of companies capturing market share together with the rapidly increasing adoption of the Internet by consumers and business buyers has come a fast-growing realisation that all organisations must have an effective Internet presence to prosper, or possibly even survive! Michael Porter has said:

> *The key question is not whether to deploy Internet technology – companies have no choice if they want to stay competitive – but how to deploy it.*

What are these challenges of deploying Internet and digital technology? Figure P.1 gives an indication of the marketing activities that need to be managed effectively and which are covered in this book.

The figure shows the range of different marketing activities or operating processes needed to support acquiring new customers through communicating with them on third-party websites, attracting them to a company website, converting website visits into sales and then using online media to encourage further sales. Applying the Internet as part of multichannel marketing to support customer journeys through different media is also a major theme throughout this text. Management processes related to Internet marketing include planning how Internet marketing can be best resourced to contribute to the organisation and integrate with other marketing activities. The increased adoption of Internet marketing also implies a significant programme of change that needs to be managed. New objectives need to be set, new communications strategies developed and staff developed through new responsibilities and skills.

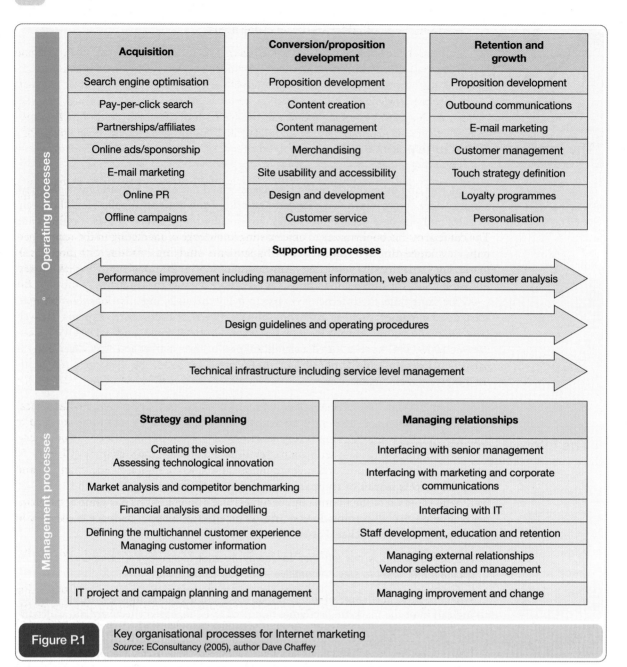

| Figure P.1 | Key organisational processes for Internet marketing<br>*Source*: EConsultancy (2005), author Dave Chaffey |
|---|---|

# The Internet – new skills required?

The aim of this text is to provide you with a comprehensive guide to the concepts, techniques and best practice to support all the digital marketing processes shown in Figure P.1. This book is based on emerging academic models together with best practice from leading adopters of digital media. The practical knowledge developed through reviewing these concepts and best practice is intended to enable graduates entering employment and marketing professionals to exploit the opportunities of marketing using the Internet while minimising the risks.

Specifically, this book addresses the following needs:

- There is a need to know to what extent the Internet changes existing marketing models and whether new models and strategies can be applied to exploit the medium effectively.
- Marketing practitioners need practical Internet marketing skills to market their products effectively. Knowledge of the new jargon – terms such as 'portal', 'click-through', 'cookie', 'hits' and 'page impressions'– and of effective methods of site design and promotion such as search engine marketing will be necessary, either for direct 'hands-on' development of a site or to enable communication with other staff or agencies that are implementing and maintaining the site.
- Given the rapidly changing market characteristics and best practices of Internet marketing, web-based information sources are needed to update knowledge regularly. This text and the supporting companion website contain extensive links to websites to achieve this.

The content of this book assumes some existing knowledge of marketing in the reader, perhaps developed through experience or by students studying introductory modules in marketing fundamentals, marketing communications or buyer behaviour. However, the text outlines basic concepts of marketing, communications theory, buyer behaviour and the marketing mix.

## Changes for the fourth edition of *Internet Marketing*

The acclaimed structure of previous editions has been retained since this provides a clear sequence to the stages of strategy development and implementation which are required to plan successfully for Internet marketing in existing and start-up companies. The fourth edition is a significant update with many revisions including a new chapter (Chapter 9) detailing best practice in marketing communications using digital media channels and nearly 100 new figures to better explain Internet marketing concepts.

Note that the use of the terms 'digital marketing', 'digital media' and 'digital media channels' has been increased in this edition, consistent with the use of these terms in industry in the US, UK, Europe and Asia.

The main changes for the fourth edition, based on feedback from reviews and prompted by continued innovation in the use of the web for marketing, are:

1 **Social networking and online PR**. Increased emphasis is given to the role of marketing and public relations through social media and word-of-mouth marketing, given popularity of social networks such as MySpace, Facebook with change in media consumption (Chapters 1, 2, 5 and 9).

2 **Web 2.0**. Higher broadband penetration has facilitated use of Web 2.0 applications and use of Rich Internet Applications and media such as video streaming. The marketing potential for different Web 2.0 and Web 3.0 applications such as blogs, feeds, mashups, IPTV and widgets are reviewed and illustrated through companies who have successfully applied them.

   Since students are now more likely to be familiar with introductory concepts of Internet technology, this content has been reduced and moved from the end of Chapter 1 to within Chapter 3.

3 **Case studies enhanced**. The main case studies have been updated and extended including new in-depth cases on Dell, Facebook and Google. More European and Asian case studies have been included, particularly through the new 'Digital Marketing in Practice' case studies at the start of each chapter which are based on interviews with leading US and European e-commerce managers.

4   **Practical details on web design and digital communications**. Since the text is already widely used by students who work or will go onto to work in digital marketing, both on the agency and client side, we have incorporated even more practical details on website design, e-retail merchanding and managing digital campaigns. This is achieved through restructuring Chapter 8 to be based around the stages involved in managing an integrated digital campaign and a new chapter on digital media channels in Chapter 9. Chapter 9 covers practical aspects of traffic building such as search engine marketing, affiliate marketing, online advertising, etc. For each digital media channel, we explain its applications, advantages and disadvantages and success factors which need to be considered by marketers to make it successful.

5   **Academic references and website links**. We have incorporated references to the most significant recent academic research papers into each chapter. Website links for each chapter have been reviewed to include the top ten or so most useful sites for students and professionals researching these areas.

6   **Consumer buyer behaviour and customer-centric marketing models**. In Chapter 2, five different perspectives to assessing consumer behaviour have been incorporated together with the latest references. Also there is more detail in Chapter 7 on models for assessing consumer experience.

New marketing models to approach new consumers have also been incorporated including coverage of Net Promoter Score (Chapter 6), online customer engagement (Chapter 7) and word-of-mouth marketing (Chapter 9).

7   **Specialist digital marketing techniques**. Content on these areas has been revised and extended:
   - Mobile marketing (Chapter 3)
   - IPTV (Chapter 3)
   - Business-to-consumer and e-retailing (Chapter 11)
   - Business-to-business (Chapter 12)

8   **Budgeting models for digital marketing**. We have incorporated practical budget models of revenue sources for a startup business (Chapter 2) and creating a digital communications or campaign budget (Chapter 8). The intention is to equip students with the practical financial skills needed to work in digital agencies and digital marketing teams. For example, the text is used by professionals studying for professional qualifications such as the Chartered Institute of Marketing E-marketing award; the Institute of Direct Marketing Diploma in Digital Marketing and MSc in Digital Marketing Communications from Manchester Metropolitan University and EConsultancy.

9   **Marketplace analysis**. Instructions on how best to complete a marketplace analysis as part of developing an Internet marketing strategy or campaign plan, including a new directory of online resources and tools that students can use when performing company case studies (Chapter 2).

10  **Internet marketing strategy**. The frameworks for developing a strategy and setting goals for digital channels in Chapter 4 have been retained with additional examples of goal-setting and planning activities based on the latest EConsultancy Managing Digital Channels research completed by Dave Chaffey.

11  **Privacy, brand protection and other legal developments**. Increased clarity on legal requirements and security for online marketers through revision of structure and content in Chapter 3 including a new summary table.

12  **Integration with online rich media to enhance learning**. Video cases from FT.com have been incorporated and links to online resources to help with case studies, e.g. how to create a digital marketing budget, tutorials on keyword analysis for Search Engine Marketing, completing a case-study-based assignment and how to perform an Internet SWOT analysis are included.

| Table P.1 | In-depth case studies in *Internet Marketing*, 4th edition |
| --- | --- |

| Chapter | Case study | Themes |
| --- | --- | --- |
| 1 Introduction | eBay thrives in the global marketplace | Business and revenue model, proposition, competition, objectives and strategies, risk management |
| 2 Micro-environment | Zopa launches a new lending model | Assessing a consumer market, business models, marketing communications |
| 3 Macro-environment | Boo hoo – learning from the largest European dot-com failure | Companion vision, branding, target market, communicating the proposition, challenges and reasons for failure |
| 4 Internet marketing strategy | Tesco.com uses the Internet to support its diversification strategy | Business models, proposition and online product range, target market strategy |
| 5 Internet marketing mix | The re-launched Napster changes the music marketing mix | Peer-to-peer services, revenue models, proposition design, strategy, competition, risk factors |
| 6 Relationship marketing | Dell gets closer to its customers online | Influence of website design on conversion, retention marketing, personalisation, e-CRM, RFM analysis |
| 7 Online customer experience | Refining the online customer experience at dabs.com | Strategy, proposition, site design, on-site search capabilities |
| 8 Campaign planning | A short history of Facebook | Ad revenue models, privacy |
| 9 Digital media channels | Innovation at Google | Technology, ad revenue models, innnovation |
| 10 Evaluation and improvement of digital channel performance | Learning from Amazon's culture of metrics | Strategy, measurement, online marketing communications, personalisation approach |
| 11 Business-to-consumer marketing | lastminute.com: establishing and maintaining a competitive position | Online consumer profiles, purchasing behaviour and expectations and e-retailing |
| 12 Business-to-business marketing | Growth, volume and dispersion of electronic markets | B2B trading environment, business markets, trading partnerships and digital marketing strategies |

A new series of cases 'Digital Marketing in Practice – The EConsultancy interview' are included at the start of each chapter. These are presented in question and answer format and focus on the practical challenges and opportunities facing practitioners working in digital media:

- *Chapter 1* Ted Speroni, Director, EMEA (Europe-Middle East and Asia), HP.com
- *Chapter 2* Martin Newman, Head of E-commerce at fashion chain Ted Baker
- *Chapter 3* Mike Clark, Managing Director of GD Worldwide, supplier to the social network bands
- *Chapter 4* Sharon Shaw, Standard Life, on strategy and planning
- *Chapter 5* William Reeve, Chief Operating Officer, Online DVD retailer LOVEFiLM
- *Chapter 6* Timo Soininen, CEO, Sulake (Habbo Hotel)
- *Chapter 7* Steve Nicholas, Assistant Director of E-commerce at Guess
- *Chapter 8* Matt Finch of Warner Breaks on silver surfers
- *Chapter 9* Nick Robertson, CEO, ASOS, on the tension between affiliate and brand marketing
- *Chapter 10* Justin Basini, Head of Brand Marketing, Capital One.

## The structure and content of this book

The book is divided into three parts, each covering a different aspect of how organisations use the Internet for marketing to help them achieve competitive advantage. Table P.2 shows how the book is related to established marketing topics.

### Part 1 Internet marketing fundamentals (Chapters 1–3)

Part 1 relates the use of the Internet to traditional marketing theories and concepts, and questions the validity of existing models given the differences between the Internet and other media.

- Chapter 1 *Introducing Internet marketing* introduces using the Internet as part of customer-centric, multichannel marketing; it also reviews the relationship between Internet marketing, digital marketing, e-commerce and e-business, and the benefits the Internet can bring to adopters, and outlines differences from other media and briefly introduces the technology.

**Table P.2**  Coverage of marketing topics in different chapters

| Topic | 1 | 2 | 3 | 4 | 5 | 6 | 7 | 8 | 9 | 10 | 11 | 12 |
|---|---|---|---|---|---|---|---|---|---|---|---|---|
| Advertising | | | | | | | | ✓ | | ✓ | | |
| Branding | | | | ✓ | ✓ | ✓ | | | | ✓ | ✓ | |
| Consumer behaviour | ✓ | ✓ | | | | | ✓ | ✓ | ✓ | ✓ | ✓ | ✓ |
| Channel and market structure | ✓ | ✓ | | ✓ | | | | | | ✓ | ✓ | ✓ |
| Communications mix | | | | ✓ | | | | ✓ | ✓ | | | |
| Communications theory | ✓ | | | | | | | ✓ | ✓ | | | |
| Customer service quality | | | | | | ✓ | ✓ | ✓ | | | ✓ | ✓ |
| Direct marketing | | | | | | ✓ | | ✓ | ✓ | | | |
| International marketing | | ✓ | ✓ | ✓ | | | ✓ | | | | ✓ | ✓ |
| Marketing mix | | ✓ | | ✓ | ✓ | | | ✓ | | | | |
| Marketing research | ✓ | ✓ | ✓ | | | | | | | ✓ | | |
| Evaluation and measurement | ✓ | | | ✓ | | | ✓ | ✓ | ✓ | ✓ | | |
| Pricing strategy | | ✓ | | ✓ | ✓ | | | | | | | |
| Promotion | ✓ | ✓ | | ✓ | | | | ✓ | ✓ | | | |
| Public relations | | | | | | | | ✓ | ✓ | | | |
| Relationship marketing | | | | | | ✓ | ✓ | | | | | |
| Segmentation | | ✓ | | ✓ | ✓ | ✓ | | ✓ | | ✓ | | |
| Services marketing | | | | | ✓ | | ✓ | | | | | |
| Strategy and planning | ✓ | ✓ | ✓ | ✓ | ✓ | ✓ | ✓ | ✓ | ✓ | ✓ | ✓ | ✓ |
| Technology background including Web 2.0 | ✓ | | ✓ | | | | | | | ✓ | ✓ | |

Note: A large, bold tick ✓ indicates fairly detailed coverage; a smaller tick ✓ indicates a brief direct reference or indirect coverage.

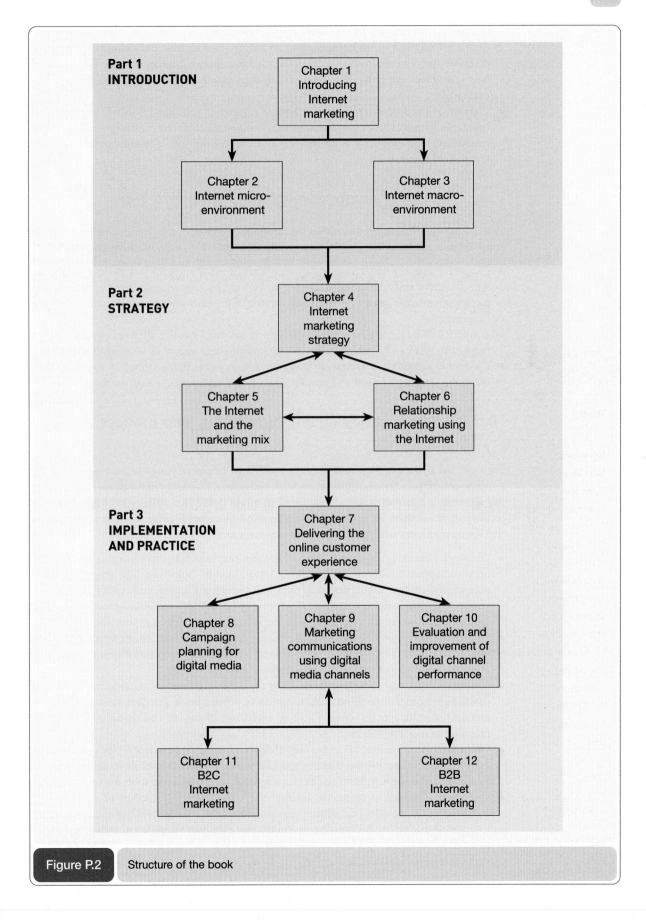

**Part 1**
**INTRODUCTION**

Chapter 1
Introducing Internet marketing

Chapter 2
Internet micro-environment

Chapter 3
Internet macro-environment

**Part 2**
**STRATEGY**

Chapter 4
Internet marketing strategy

Chapter 5
The Internet and the marketing mix

Chapter 6
Relationship marketing using the Internet

**Part 3**
**IMPLEMENTATION AND PRACTICE**

Chapter 7
Delivering the online customer experience

Chapter 8
Campaign planning for digital media

Chapter 9
Marketing communications using digital media channels

Chapter 10
Evaluation and improvement of digital channel performance

Chapter 11
B2C Internet marketing

Chapter 12
B2B Internet marketing

| Figure P.2 | Structure of the book |

- Chapter 2 *The Internet micro-environment* reviews how the Internet changes the immediate environment of an organisation, including marketplace and channel structure. It describes the type of situation analysis needed to support Internet strategy by examining how customers, competitors and intermediaries and the interplay between them can be evaluated.
- Chapter 3 *The Internet macro-environment* reviews the impact of social, technological, economic, political and legal environmental influences on Internet strategy and its implementation. The emphasis is on privacy and data protection regulations and managing technology innovation.

## Part 2 Internet strategy development (Chapters 4–6)

Part 2 describes the emerging models for developing strategy and provides examples of the approaches companies have used to integrate the Internet into their marketing strategy.

- Chapter 4 *Internet marketing strategy* considers how the Internet strategy can be aligned with business and marketing strategies and describes a generic strategic approach with phases of situation review, goal setting, strategy formulation and resource allocation and monitoring.
- Chapter 5 *The Internet and the marketing mix* assesses how the different elements of the marketing mix can be varied in the online environment as part of strategy formulation.
- Chapter 6 *Relationship marketing using the Internet* details the strategies and tactics for using the Internet to build and sustain 'one-to-one' relationships with customers.

## Part 3 Internet marketing: implementation and practice (Chapters 7–11)

Part 3 of the book explains practical approaches to implementing an Internet marketing strategy. Techniques for communicating with customers, building relationships and facilitating electronic commerce are all reviewed in some detail. Knowledge of these practical techniques is essential for undergraduates on work placements involving a website, and for marketing managers who are dealing with suppliers such as design agencies.

- Chapter 7 *Delivering the online customer experience* explains how an online presence is developed to support branding and customer service quality objectives. The stages, including analysis of customer needs, design of the site structure and layout, and creating the site, are covered together with key techniques such as user-centred design, usability and accessibility design. It also covers different service quality models used to assess experience.
- Chapter 8 *Campaign planning for digital media* describes the novel characteristics of digital media, and then goes on to different aspects of marketing communications which then need to be considered for a successful online campaign.
- Chapter 9 *Marketing communications using digital media channels*. Among the techniques covered are banner advertising, affiliate networks, promotion in search engines, co-branding and sponsorship, e-mail, online PR, viral and word-of-mouth marketing with particular reference to social networks.
- Chapter 10 *Evaluation and improvement of digital channel performance* reviews methods for assessing and improving the effectiveness of a site and communications in delivering business and marketing benefits. The chapter briefly covers process and tools for updating sites.
- Chapter 11 *Business-to-consumer Internet marketing* examines models of marketing to consumers and provides case studies of how retail businesses are tackling such marketing.
- Chapter 12 *Business-to-business Internet marketing* examines the different area of marketing to other businesses and provides many examples of how companies are achieving this to support international marketing.

## Who should use this book?

### Students

This book has been created primarily as the main student text for undergraduate and post-graduate students taking specialist marketing courses or modules which cover e-marketing, Internet and digital marketing, electronic commerce and e-business. The book is relevant to students who are:

- *undergraduates on business programmes* which include modules on the use of the Internet and e-commerce. This includes specialist degrees such as Internet marketing, electronic commerce, marketing, tourism and accounting or general business degrees such as business studies, business administration and business management;
- *undergraduate project students* who select this topic for final-year projects or dissertations – this book is an excellent supporting text for these students;
- *undergraduates completing a work placement* in a company using the Internet to promote its products;
- *students at college aiming for vocational qualifications* such as the HNC or HND in Business Management or Computer Studies;
- *postgraduate students* taking specialist masters degrees in electronic commerce or Internet marketing, generic MBAs and courses leading to qualifications such as the Certificate in Management or Diploma in Digital Marketing or Management Studies which involve modules on electronic commerce and digital marketing.

### Practitioners

Previous editions have been widely used by digital marketing practitioners including:

- *marketing managers or specialists such as e-commerce managers or e-marketing managers* responsible for defining an Internet marketing strategy and implementing and maintaining the company website;
- *senior managers and directors* wishing to understand the potential of Internet marketing for a company and who need practical guidelines on how to exploit this potential;
- *technical project managers or webmasters* who may understand the technical details of building a site, but have a limited knowledge of marketing fundamentals and how to develop an Internet marketing strategy.

### What does the book offer to lecturers teaching these courses?

The book is intended to be a comprehensive guide to all aspects of using the Internet and other digital media to support marketing. The book builds on existing marketing theories and concepts, and questions the validity of models in the light of the differences between the Internet and other media. The book references the emerging body of literature specific to Internet marketing. It can therefore be used across several modules. Lecturers will find the book has a good range of case studies, activities and exercises to support their teaching. Website links are given in the text and at the end of each chapter to provide important information sources for particular topics.

## Student learning features

A range of features has been incorporated into this book to help the reader get the most out of it. Each feature has been designed to assist understanding, reinforce learning and help readers find information easily, particularly when completing assignments and preparing for exams. The features are described in the order in which you will find them in each chapter.

### At the start of each chapter

The 'Chapter at a glance' page provides easy navigation for each chapter. It contains:

- *Main topics*: the main topics and their page numbers.
- *Case studies*: the main cases and their page numbers.
- *Learning objectives*: a list describing what readers can learn through reading the chapter and completing the exercises.
- *Questions for marketers*: explaining the relevance of the chapter for practitioners.
- *Links to other chapters*: a summary of related information in other chapters.

### In each chapter

- *Definitions*: when significant terms are first introduced the main text contains succinct definitions in the margin for easy reference.
- *Web references*: where appropriate, web addresses are given to enable readers to obtain further information. They are provided in the main text where they are directly relevant as well as at the end of the chapter.
- *Case studies*: real-world examples of how companies are using the Internet for marketing. Questions at the end of the case study are intended to highlight the main learning points from the example.
- *Mini case studies*: short features which give a more detailed example, or explanation, than is practical in the main text. They do not contain supplementary questions.
- *Activities*: exercises in the main text which give readers the opportunity to practise and apply the techniques described in the text.
- *Chapter summaries*: intended as revision aids to summarise the main learning points from the chapter.

### At the end of each chapter

- *Self-assessment exercises*: short questions which will test understanding of terms and concepts described in the chapter.
- *Essay questions*: conventional essay questions.
- *Discussion questions*: these require longer essay-style answers discussing themes from the chapter. They can be used either as topics for individual essays or as the basis for seminar discussion.
- *Examination questions*: typical short-answer questions of the type that are encountered in exams. These can also be used for revision.
- *References*: these are references to books, articles or papers referred to within the chapter.
- *Further reading*: supplementary texts or papers on the main themes of the chapter. Where appropriate, a brief commentary is provided on recommended supplementary reading on the main themes of the chapters.

- *Web links*: these are significant sites that provide further information on the concepts and topics of the chapter. This list does not repeat all the website references given within the chapter, for example company sites. For clarity, the website address prefix 'http://' is generally omitted.

## At the end of the book

- *Glossary*: comprehensive definitions of all key terms and phrases used within the main text, cross-referenced for ease of use.
- *Index*: all key words and abbreviations referred to in the main text.

## Support material

Free supplementary materials are available via the Pearson Education companion website at www.pearsoned.co.uk/chaffey and Dave Chaffey's website at www.davechaffey.com to support all users of the book. This regularly updated website contains advice, comment, support materials and hyperlinks to reference sites relevant to the text. There is a password-protected area for lecturers only to discuss issues arising from using the text; additional examination-type questions and answers; a multiple-choice question bank with answers; additional cases with suggestions for discussion; and a downloadable version of the Lecturer's Guide and OHP Masters.

## References

EConsultancy (2005) Managing an e-commerce team. Integrating digital marketing into your organisation. 60-page report. Author: Dave Chaffey. Available from www.e-consultancy.com.

EConsultancy (2008) Managing digital channels. Integrating digital marketing into your organisation (190-page report). Author: Dave Chaffey. Available from www.e-consultancy.com.

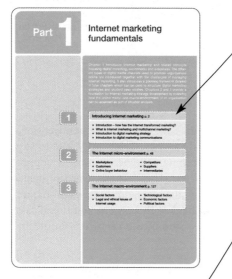

**Part openers** summarise the main themes with brief chapter contents.

**Chapter openers** help you structure your reading.

**Learning objectives** enable you to focus on what you can gain from reading the chapter.

The chapters' **main topics** are listed for quick and easy reference.

**Questions for marketers** will stimulate further reading and thought.

**Links to other chapters** help you to integrate your reading.

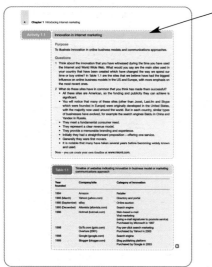

**Activities** give readers the opportunity to practise and apply the techniques described in the text.

**Mini case studies** encourage debate and classroom discussion.

**Margin definitions** help emphasise the concepts covered in the body of the text.

**Case studies** are positioned at the end of each section, showcasing relevant theories and themes.

**Figures** and **tables** illustrate key concepts and processes, visually reinforcing your learning.

**Full-colour screenshots** from genuine websites help to connect theory with real-life practical examples.

Each chapter ends with a number of **Exercises**, designed for use in class, as essay questions, and in exams.

**Summaries** clinch the important concepts that have been presented in each section.

At the end of each chapter you will also find a full list of **References**.

Suggested articles and texts for your **Further reading** are listed, as are a number of useful **Web links**.

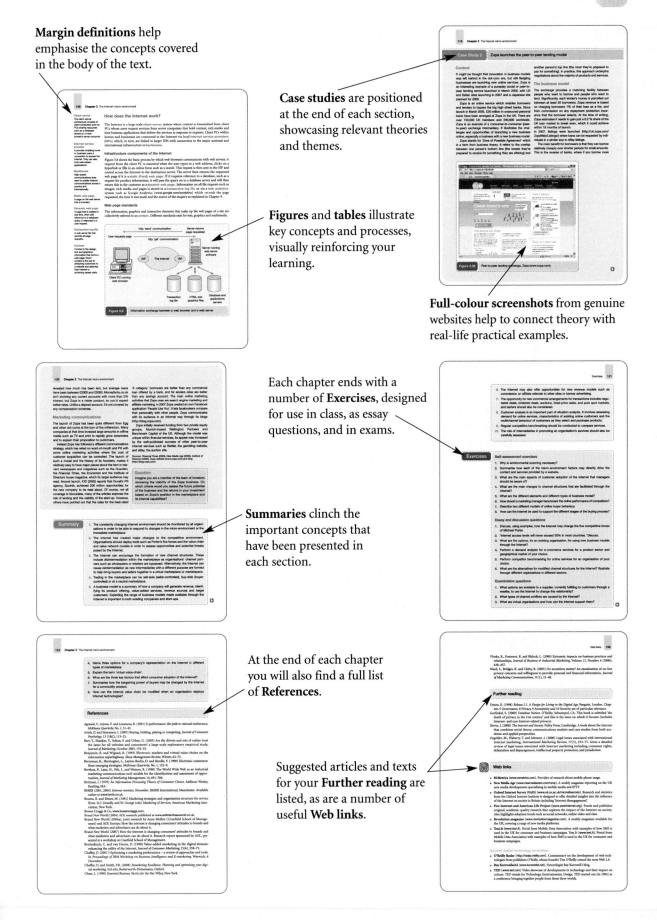

# About the authors

### Dave Chaffey BSc, PhD, FCIM, MIDM

Dave Chaffey (www.davechaffey.com) is an independent Internet marketing trainer and consultant for Marketing Insights Limited. He is a lecturer on e-marketing courses at Cranfield and Warwick Universities and the Institute of Direct Marketing, for which he is a tutor and Senior Examiner for the Diploma in Digital Marketing. Author of several best-selling texts, he has also written the in-depth Best Practice Guides to Managing Digital Channels, Paid Search Marketing, Search Engine Optimisation (SEO) and Website design for EConsultancy (www.e-consultancy.com/research) He also works as consultant in the cScape Customer Engagement Unit (www.cscape.com). Dave has been recognised by the CIM as one of 50 marketing 'gurus' worldwide who have shaped the future of marketing. He is also proud to have been recognised by the Department of Trade and Industry as one of the leading individuals who have provided input and influence on the development and growth of e-commerce and the Internet in the UK over the last 10 years. Dave is an active blogger and posts updates to help readers of this text at www.davechaffey.com/Internet-Marketing.

### Fiona Ellis-Chadwick PhD, BSc, Dip Sys Prac, PGCCE

Fiona Ellis-Chadwick is a lecturer in Marketing at the Business School at Loughborough University and is a member of the Marketing and Retailing Research Group. Fiona had a successful commercial career in retail management and development before joining the Business School in 2000 following completion of her PhD thesis titled 'An Empirical Study of Internet Adoption Among Leading United Kingdom Retailers'. Currently, her research interests focus on e-strategy from an organisational perspective and she has published and presented widely in the areas of retail Internet adoption and Internet marketing. Her work on these topics has been published in *Journal of Business Research, International Journal of Retail Distribution and Management, European Journal of Marketing, Internet Research, Managing Service Quality* plus additional texts and practitioner journals.

### Richard Mayer MA, DipM, MCIM

Richard Mayer is a Senior Lecturer in Marketing at the University of Derby and Director of his own Marketing Training Company specialising in Strategic Marketing, Business to Business Marketing and Marketing Communications. He is programme manager for the Chartered Institute of Marketing qualifications at the University of Derby. He has co-authored and contributed chapters to several marketing publications, including *Marketing – An Active Learning Approach* and *The Practice of Advertising*.

### Kevin Johnston BSc, MBA

Kevin Johnston is a Senior Lecturer in marketing, strategy and e-commerce at Liverpool John Moores University and is the programme leader for the BSc (Hons) E-Business Technology and Enterprise programme. He previously lectured at the University of Derby where he created one of the UK's first e-commerce degree programmes. He has published papers in a number of marketing, management and e-commerce journals such as the *International Journal of Internet Research* and the *International Journal of Networking and Virtual Organisations* and presented papers at international conferences such as the *European Conference on Knowledge Management*.

# Acknowledgements

I am fortunate to have shared my journey of understanding how the Internet can be harnessed for marketing with thousands of students and marketing professionals and I thank you for sharing your experiences with me. I have also been fortunate to work with many e-marketing and e-commerce specialists to support them and their organisations on their journeys. These have been important in highlighting the success factors for digital marketing. So, thanks to Pip Chesters and David Grant at 3M, Matthew Clarke and Piers Dickinson at BP, Julian Brewer at Barclays, Vincent Coyle at Euroffice, Matt Dooley and Paul Say at HSBC, Eileen Pevreall and David Hedges at CIPD, Martyn Etherington and Mike Rizzo at Tektronix, and fellow 'e-consultants' Ashley Friedlein, Jim Sterne, Neil Mason, Richard Sedley, Lucy Conlan and Richard Coombes.

The authors would like to thank the team at Pearson Education in Harlow for their help in the creation of this book, especially David Cox (Aquisitions Editor) and Philippa Fiszzon who managed the book through the production process.

As always, especial thanks go to my family for supporting me in the ongoing updates.

*Dave Chaffey*

I'd like to acknowledge my parents by way of a dedication: 'For Ivan and Janet Johnston'.

*Kevin Johnston*

## Publisher's Acknowledgements

The publishers are grateful to the reviewers of this book for their valuable comments.

The publishers are grateful to the following for permission to reproduce copyright material:

Figures P.1, 4.3, 4.26, 4.28, 4.29 and Table 1.3 from Managing an E-commerce team. Integrating digital marketing into your organization, author: Dave Chaffey, reprinted by permission of E Consultancy.com Ltd. (EConsultancy 2005); Figure 1.1 screenshot of Google (circa 1998) from http://web.archive.org/web/19981111183552/google.stanford.edu reprinted by permission of Wayback Machine Archive; Figures 1.1, 1.2, 1.3, 1.6, 1.10, 1.15, 2.6, 2.13, 2.16, 2.17, 2.22, 2.23, 2.24, 2.27, 2.30, 2.35, 2.36, 3.2, 3.3, 3.6, 3.9, 3.16, 3.18, 4.9, 4.13, 4.14, 4.16, 4.20, 4.21, 4.22, 5.2, 5.4, 5.6, 5.7, 5.10, 5.11, 5.15, 6.3, 6.17, 7.5, 7.9, 7.11, 7.12, 7.13, 7.15, 8.1, 8.21, 8.23, 9.2, 9.5, 9.6, 9.7, 9.8, 9.13, 9.14, 9.16, 9.17, 9.18, 9.19, 10.11, 10.12, 11.2, 11.3, 11.6, 12.2, 12.3 and 12.4 screenshot frames reprinted with permission from Microsoft Corporation; Figures 1.2, 5.4 and 9.18 from www.firstdirect.com reprinted by permission of First Direct Bank; Table 1.2 was published in *Emarketing Excellence. Planning and Optimising Your Digital Marketing, 3rd Edition* by P. R. Smith and D. Chaffey, Copyright Elsevier 2008, reprinted with permission; Figure 1.3 from www.willitblend.com reprinted by permission of BLENDTEC; Figure 1.4 from http://novaspivack.typepad.com/nova_spivacks_weblog/2007/02/steps_towards_a.html reprinted by permission of Nova Spivack; Figure 1.15 from www.travelrepublic.co.uk reprinted by permission of Travel Republic Ltd.; Table 2.2 from www.hitwise.com reprinted by permission of Hitwise UK Ltd.; Table 2.4 from Michael De Kare-Silver, *e-Shock 2000*, published 1999, Macmillan, reproduced with permission of Palgrave Macmillan; Figure 2.6 from www.i-to-i.com reprinted by permission of i-to-i on behalf of TUI Travel PLC; Figure 2.7 from http://www.oecd.org/sti/ict/broadband reprinted by permission of OECD; Table 2.7 reprinted by permission from Macmillan Publishers Ltd: JOURNAL OF DIRECT DATA AND DIGITAL MARKETING PRACTICE (then called *Interactive Marketing*), H. Menteth et al., Multi-channel experience consistency : evidence from Lexus, vol. 6, Issue 4, pp. 317–25, copyright 2005, published by Palgrave Macmillan; Figure 2.8 and Table 3.4 from http://www.mmetrics.com reprinted by permission of M:Metrics; Table 2.8 from Understanding influence and making it work for you, CNET.com, 2007, reproduced with permission; Figure 2.11 from UK Statistics (2006), Report from the UK National Statistics Omnibus Survey. Published online at www.statistics.gov.uk. Crown Copyright material is reproduced with the permission of the Controller, Office of Public Sector Information (OPSI); Figure 2.13 from www.dulux.co.uk Dulux is a trademark of ICI, © ICI, reprinted by permission of ICI; Figures 2.14 and 3.22 and Table 2.5 from http://ec.europa.eu/information_society/eeurope/i2010/ index_en.htm; (c) European Communities, 2007, Source: Annual Information Society Report 2007, A European Information Society for Growth and Employment; Figures 2.16, 5.15 and 9.2 from www.google.co.uk/search reprinted by permission of Google, Inc. Google™ search engine is a trademark of Google, Inc.; Figure 2.17 from www.comet.co.uk/cometbrowse reprinted by permission of Comet Group plc; Figure 2.20 from www.bowencraggs.com reprinted by permission of Bowen Craggs; Figure 2.21 from www.gomez.com reprinted by permission of Gomez Europe Ltd.; Figure 2.22 from www.allthingsgreen.net reprinted by permission of All Things Green; Figure 2.26 from www.kelkoo.co.uk reprinted by permission of Kelkoo.com (UK) Ltd.; Figure 2.27 from http://shop.lonelyplanet.com reproduced with permission from the Lonely Planet website www.lonelyplanet.com © 2008 Lonely Planet Publications Pty Ltd; Figure 2.28 from Deise et al. (2000) Executive's Guide to E-business. From Tactics to Strategy. Copyright © John Wiley & Sons, Inc. 2000. This material is used by permission of John Wiley & Sons, Inc.; Figure 2.30 from www.screentrade.co.uk reprinted by permission of Lloyds TSB Insurance Services Limited; Figure 2.35 from www.e-consultancy.com/publications reprinted by permission of E Consultancy.com Ltd.; Figure 2.36 from www.zopa.com reprinted by permission of Zopa Limited; Figures 3.3 and 7.5 from www.hsbc.co.uk reprinted by permission of HSBC Bank PLC; Figure 3.6 from www.cruises.co.uk reprinted by permission of cruise.co.uk; Figure 3.7 from www.blogpulse.com reprinted by permission of Nielsen Buzzmetrics; Figure 3.12 from Mobile Data Association reprinted by permission of Mobile Data Association; Figure 3.13 from http://www.giagia.co.uk/?cat=63 reprinted by permission of Twentieth Century Fox; Figure 3.14 from http://dotMobi.mobi/emulator.php reproduced with special permission of dotMobi (mTLD Top Level Domain Ltd.); Figure 3.15 from www.hypertag.com reprinted by permission of Hypertag Limited; Table 4.2 from Managing digital channels research report, author: Dave Chaffey, available from www.e-consultancy.com, reprinted by permission of E Consultancy.com Ltd.; Figure 4.9 from www.arenaflowers.com reprinted by permission of Arena Flowers (www.arenaflowers.com); Table 4.9 reprinted by permission of Neil Mason, Applied Insights; Figure 4.13 from www.smile.co.uk reprinted by permission of The Co-operative Financial Services; Figure 4.14 from www.ideastorm.com reprinted by permission of Dell Inc., © 2008 Dell Inc. All Rights Reserved; Figure 4.16 from www.ap.dell.com/content/ default.aspx?c=sg&1=en&s=gen reprinted by permission of Dell Inc., © 2008 Dell Inc. All Rights Reserved; Figures 4.18 and 8.14 from Euroffice, www.euroffice.co.uk, reprinted by permission of Euroffice Limited; Figure 4.21 from www.firebox.com reprinted with permission from Firebox.com; Figure 4.22 from www.britishairways.com reprinted by permission of British Airways plc; Table 5.2 from A comparison of time-varying online price and price dispersion between multichannel and dotcom DVD retailers in *Journal of Interactive Marketing*, 20 (2), 3–20, John Wiley & Sons, Inc., reprinted with permission of John Wiley & Sons, Inc. (Xing, X., Yang, S. and Tang, F. 2006); Figure 5.3 www.osselect.co.uk reprinted by permission of Ordnance Survey on behalf of HMSO; Figure 5.6 from www.dorsetcereals.co.uk reprinted by permission of Dorset Cereals Ltd.; Figures 5.8, 5.9 and 9.1 from Brand New World: Anne Mollen (Cranfield School of Management)/AOL Europe, 2004 reprinted by permission of AOL Europe and Anne Mollen; Figure 5.11 from www.mysupermarket.co.uk reprinted by permission of mySupermarket

Limited; Figure 6.3 from www.feefo.com showing independent feedback for www.ctshirts.co.uk reprinted by permission from Feefo Limited and Charles Tyrwhitt LLP; Figure 6.7 screenshot of Thomson opt-in customer profiling form reprinted by permission of Thomson (TUI UK); Figures 6.11 and 6.18 from www.cipd.co.uk reprinted by permission of Chartered Institute of Personnel and Development (CIPD); Figure 6.16 Reprinted by permission from Macmillan Publishers Ltd: JOURNAL OF DIRECT DATA AND DIGITAL MARKETING PRACTICE (then called *Interactive Marketing*), Mark Patron, Case Study: Applying RFM Segmentation to the SilverMinds catalogue vol. 5, issue 3, 9 January, copyright 2004, published by Palgrave Macmillan; Figure 6.19 from www-03.ibm.com/press/us/en/photo/22427.wss, Reprint Courtesy of International Business Machines Corporation, copyright 2007 © International Business Machines Corporation; visual elements in Figure 6.19 from Second Life virtual world in which Linden Research, Inc. owns a copyright, reproduced with permission from Linden Research, Inc.; Second Life is a trademark of Linden Research, Inc. Certain materials have been reproduced with the permission of Linden Research, Inc. COPYRIGHT © 2001-2008 LINDEN RESEARCH, INC. ALL RIGHTS RESERVED; NF 7.1 Reprinted by permission of Macmillan Publishers Ltd.: *Journal of Brand Management*, based on a diagram in de Chernatony, L. (2001) Succeeding with brands on the internet, 8 (3), pp.186-95, copyright 2001, published by Palgrave Macmillan; Table 7.2 adapted from Benchmarks – UK 100 Report, week starting 6 October 2005, reprinted by permission of Site Confidence, UK's leading website monitoring company; Table 7.4 from www.w3schools.com/browsers/browsers_stats.asp, Jan. 2007, reprinted by permission of Refsnes Data; Table 7.8 from D. Chaffey and M. Edgar, Measuring online service quality in *Journal of Targeting, Analysis and Measurement for Marketing*, 8 (4), May 2000, Macmillan, reproduced with permission of Palgrave Macmillan; Figure 7.11 from www.sainsburys.com reprinted by permission of J. Sainsbury plc; Figure 7.13 from www.wine.com reprinted by permission of Wine.com, Inc.; Figure 7.14 from Scene7 on demand survey: Web 2.0 experience 2008 and beyond, January 2008, http://www.scene7.com/survey/Scene7_2008_Survey_Report.pdf, © 2008 Adobe Systems Incorporated. All rights reserved. Adobe is/are either (a) registered trademark(s) or a trademark(s) of Adobe Systems Incorporated in the United States and/or other countries, reprinted by permission; Figure 8.1 from www.threadless.com reprinted by permission of Skinnycorp LLC; Figure 8.4 used with permission from Millward Brown UK Ltd.; Table 8.6 reprinted by permission of the Interactive Advertising Bureau; Figure 8.12 from http://weblogs.hitwise.com/sandra-hanchard/2007/10/ reprinted by permission of Hitwise UK Ltd.; Figure 8.13 from Hitwise posting: http://weblogs.hitwise.com/robin-goad/2008/01/longhaul_travel_searches_incre.html reprinted by permission of Hitwise UK Ltd.; Figure 8.15 from www.centreforintegratedmarketing.com CODAR is a registered trademark of Stepping Stones Consultancy Ltd.; Figure 8.23 from www.tourismirelandtaxichallenge.com reprinted by permission of Laughlin Rigby at tourismireland.com; Table 9.2 from http://blog.efrontier.com/insights/2008/02/average-cpcs.html reprinted by permission of Efficient Frontier; Table 9.4 from National Email Benchmarking Survey, Q4, 2006, published at www.dma.org.uk reprinted by permission of The Direct Marketing Association (DMA); Figure 9.5 from www.responsesource.com reprinted by permission of Daryl Wilcox Publishing Ltd.; Figure 9.6 from www.e-consultancy.com/newsblog reprinted by permission of E Consultancy.com Limited; Figure 9.7 from http://del.icio.us/search/?fr=del_icio_us&p=technology+innovation&type=all reproduced with permission of Yahoo! Inc. ® 2008 by Yahoo! Inc. Yahoo! and the Yahoo! logo are trademarks of Yahoo! Inc.; Figure 9.8 from www.feedjit.com/stats/davechaffey.com/map reprinted by permission of Feedjit Inc.; Figure 9.10 from www.adtech.info/archive2007_1/pr-070510.htm reprinted by permission of ADTECH; Figure 9.13 from www.bannerblog.com.au reprinted by permission of SOAP Creative; Figure 9.15 from National Client Email Marketing Survey 2007 published at www.dma.org.uk reprinted by permission of The Direct Marketing Association (DMA); Figure 9.16 from www.emailreaction.com reprint permission given by: SMARTFOCUS GROUP PLC; Figure 9.17 from admin.emailreaction.com reproduced by kind permission of smartFOCUS DIGITAL; Figure 9.20 from The Hitwise UK Media Impact Report, September 2006 reprinted by permission of Hitwise UK Ltd.; Table 10.1 from ABCe, www.abce.org.uk, reprinted by permission of ABC Electronic; Figure 10.5 was published in *The Multichannel Challenge: Integrating Customer Experiences for Profit*, edited by H. Wilson et al, fig. 8.5, c187, Copyright Elsevier (2008), reprinted by permission; Test reports for Figures 10.7 and 10.8 courtesy of Maxymiser Content Intelligence, www.maxymiser.com; Figure 10.11 from www.davechaffey.com, reproduced with permission from Google, Inc.; Table 11.5 from JOURNAL OF URBAN TECHNOLOGY by J. Weltevreden et al., Copyright 2005 by Taylor & Francis Informa UK Ltd – Journals. Reproduced with permission of Taylor & Francis Informa UK Ltd – Journals in the format Other book via Copyright Clearance Center; Figure 11.6 reprinted by permission of McArthurGlen Designer Outlets, Fox Kalomaski Ltd – Destination Marketing and Adam B. Colour Services Ltd. – Photography; Table 11.6 reprinted by permission of Allegra Strategies Ltd. (Allegra 2005); Table 12.1 from INTERNET RESEARCH by G. Gunawan, F. Ellis-Chadwick, M. King. Copyright 2008 by Emerald Group Publishing Limited. Reproduced with permission of Emerald Group Publishing Limited in the format Textbook via Copyright Clearance Center.; Figure 12.5 from INTERNATIONAL JOURNAL OF RETAIL AND DISTRIBUTION MANAGEMENT by A. Nicholls and A. Watson. Copyright 2005 by Emerald Group Publishing Limited in the format Textbook via Copyright Clearance Center.

Chapter 1, The EConsultancy Interview with Ted Speroni (http://www.e-consultancy.com/news-blog/newsletter/3200/interview-ted-speroni-director-emea-hp-com.html; Chapter 2, The EConsultancy Interview with Martin Newman (http://www.e-consultancy.com/news-blog/newsletter/3379/ted-baker-s-martin-newman-on-multi--channel-retail.html); Mini Case Study 2.2 from Agency.com available through the IAB (www.iabuk.net) and presented at Engage 2007, reprinted by permission of Agency.com; Chapter 3, The EConsultancy interview with Mike Clark (http://www.e-consultancy.com/news-blog/newsletter/ 3229/interview-with-mike-clark-of-gd-worldwide.html); Chapter 4, The EConsultancy interview with Sharon Shaw (From www.e-consultancy.com/news-blog/newsletter/3504/interview-with-standard-life-s-sharon-shaw.html); Mini Case Study 4.1 from EConsultancy, E-business Briefing (2008) Arena Flowers' Sam Barton on web design and development, E-newsletter interview, 12th March, 2008; Chapter 5, EConsultancy interview with William Reeve (http://www.e-consultancy.com/news-blog/newsletter/3540/interview-with-lovefilm-coo-william-reeve.html); Chapter 6, EConsultancy interview with Timo Soininen (http://www.e-consultancy.com/news-blog/newsletter/3450/sulake-ceo-timo-soininen-discusses-habbo-hotel.html); Chapter 7, EConsultancy interview with Steve Nicholas (http://www.e-consultancy.com/news-blog/newsletter/3415/steve-nicholas-assistant-director-of-e--commerce-at-guess.html); Chapter 8, EConsultancy interview with Matthew Finch (http://www.e-consultancy.com/news-blog/ newsletter/3361/warner-breaks-mat-finch-on-silver-surfers.html#1); Chapter 9, EConsultancy interview with Nick Robertson (http://www.e-consultancy.com/news-blog/newsletter/3223/asos-ceo-speaks-out-on-grubbygate.html); and Chapter 10, EConsultancy interview with Justin Basini (http://www.e-consultancy.com/news-blog/newsletter/3440/q-amp-a-with-capital-one-s-head-of-brand-marketing-justin-basini.html); reprinted by permission of EConsultancy.com Ltd.; Mini Case Study 1.2 written by Peter Davies, eCommerce adviser at Menter Mon (www.menter.mon) for the Opportunity Wales project (www.opportunitywales.co.uk) reprinted by permission of the author; Mini Case Study 1.4 from TravelRepublic Press release, 2nd December 2007, Travel Republic is the UK's Fastest Growing Private Company (http://www.travelrepublic.co.uk/help/pressRelease_003.aspx) reprinted by permission of Travel Republic Ltd.; Mini Case Study 2.2 developed and presented by Agency.com at Engage 2007 (www.iabuk.net) reprinted by permission of Agency.com; Mini Case Study 3.2 reprinted by permission of HSBC Bank plc; Chapter 3 extracts from Data Protection Act 1984, 1998 (DPA) AND EXTRACTS FROM Privacy and Electronics Communications Regulation (PECR) Act 2003, Crown copyright material is reproduced with the permission of the Controller of HMSO and the Queen's printer for Scotland; Mini Case Study 3.5 from www.blog.ericgoldman.org/archives/2007/05/broad_matching.htm reprinted by permission of Eric `Goldman; Box 3.3 from www.mattcutts.com/blog/seo-glossary-url-definitions/ reprinted by permission of Matt Cutts; Box 3.4 from specialist website security consultants Watson Hall (www.watsonhall.com) reprinted by permission of Watson Hall Ltd.; Mini Case Study 3.8 adapted from case study Comet: The Price is Right Promotion from http://www.virginradio.co.uk/sales/case_studies/25.html reprinted by permission of Virgin Radio; Mini Case Study 4.2 reprinted by permission of Euroffice Ltd.; Chapter 4, extract adapted from Customer Promise from http://www.virginwines.com reprinted by permission of Virgin Wines; Mini Case Study 4.3 print ad copy for Have you clicked yet? campaign reprinted by permission of British Airways plc; Chapter 5 definition of prosumer from http://www.wordspy.com/words/prosumer.asp, Copyright © 1995–2006 Paul McFedries and Logophilia Limited, reprinted by permission of Paul McFedries; Mini Case Study 6.3 from article Interactive Being in *Computer Weekly*, 2 May, reprinted by permission of Computer Weekly (Nicolle, L. 2001); Chapter 7 extract from How do people evaluate a web site's credibility?, a Consumer WebWatch research report, prepared by Stanford Persuasive Technology Lab., reprinted by permission of Consumers Reports WebWatch; Mini Case Study 7.1 reprinted by permission of Bazaarvoice © 2008 Bazaarvoice; Mini Case Study 8.2 extract from article The medium is part of the message, published in the proceedings of the ARF/ESOMAR Publications Series, vol. 241, reprinted by permission of the author (Branthwaite, A. 2000); Mini Case study 8.4 from DEC Tsunami 2004/5, www.dec.org.uk, reprinted by permission of Disasters Emergency Committee; Box 8.1 adapted from IPA, *Econometrics Explained* by Louise Cook and Mike Holmes, edited by Les Binet, 2004, reprinted by permission of IPA; Mini Case Study 8.6, extracts from New Media Age reprinted by permission of Centaur Media; Extract in Chapter 9 adapted from How the internet is changing consumers' attitudes to brands and what marketers and advertisers can do about it, Brand New World: Anne Mollen (Cranfield School of Management)/AOL Europe, 2004 reprinted by permission of AOL Europe and Anne Mollen; Mini Case Study 12.1 Reprinted by permission of Harvard Business Review. Excerpt from Transforming Strategy One Customer at a Time by R. Harrington and A. Tjan, March 2008. Copyright © 2008 by The Harvard Business School Publishing Corporation; all rights reserved.

We are grateful to the Financial Times Limited for permission to reprint the following material:

Figure 1.10 Nick Robertson on *Ft.com* video, © *FT.com*; Figure 2.23 Jack Ma on *FT.com*/View from the Top, © *FT.com*; Figure 3.2 Prof. Donald Sull of London Business School talking about strategic agility on *FT.com*/Business School, © *FT.com*; Figure 4.24 Flow chart for deciding on the significance of the Internet to a business, Kumar, N. (1999) Internet distribution strategies: dilemmas for the incumbent, *Financial Times*, Special Issue on Mastering Information Management, no. 7. Electronic Commerce.

In some instances we have been unable to trace the owners of copyright material, and we would appreciate any information that would enable us to do so.

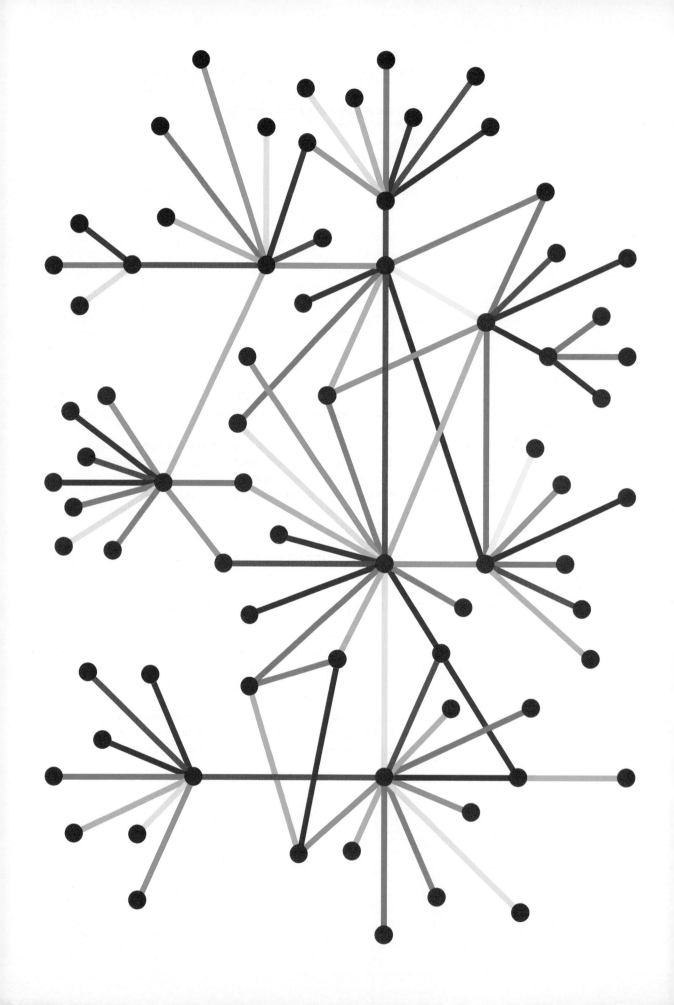

# Part 1

# Internet marketing fundamentals

Chapter 1 introduces Internet marketing and related concepts including digital marketing, e-commerce and e-business. The different types of digital media channels used to promote organisations online are introduced together with the challenges of managing Internet marketing. It also introduces a planning framework detailed in later chapters which can be used to structure digital marketing strategies and student case studies. Chapters 2 and 3 provide a foundation for Internet marketing strategy development by reviewing how the online micro- and macro-environment of an organisation can be assessed as part of situation analysis.

## 1 Introducing Internet marketing p. 2

- Introduction – how has the Internet transformed marketing?
- What is Internet marketing and multichannel marketing?
- Introduction to digital marketing strategy
- Introduction to digital marketing communications

## 2 The Internet micro-environment p. 48

- Marketplace
- Customers
- Online buyer behaviour
- Competitors
- Suppliers
- Intermediaries

## 3 The Internet macro-environment p. 127

- Social factors
- Legal and ethical issues of Internet usage
- Technological factors
- Economic factors
- Political factors

# 1

# Introducing Internet marketing

## Learning objectives

After reading this chapter, the reader should be able to:

- Evaluate the relevance of the Internet to the customer-centric, multichannel marketing concept
- Distinguish between Internet marketing, e-marketing, digital marketing, e-commerce and e-business
- Evaluate the advantages and challenges of digital media
- Identify the key differences between Internet marketing and traditional marketing
- Assess how the Internet can be used in different marketing functions

## Questions for marketers

Key questions for marketing managers related to this chapter are:

- How significant is the Internet as a marketing tool?
- How does Internet marketing relate to e-marketing, e-commerce and e-business?
- What are the key benefits of Internet marketing?
- What differences does the Internet introduce in relation to existing marketing communications models?

## Links to other chapters

This chapter provides an introduction to Internet marketing, and the concepts introduced are covered in more detail later in the book, as follows:

- Chapters 2 and 3 explain how situation analysis for Internet marketing planning can be conducted
- Chapters 4, 5 and 6 in Part 2 describe how Internet marketing strategy can be developed
- Chapters 7, 8, 10 and 11 in Part 3 describe strategy implementation
- Chapters 11 and 12 in Part 3 describe B2C and B2B applications

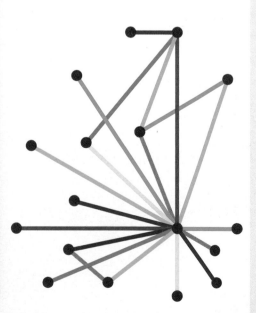

# Introduction – how has the Internet transformed marketing?

The Internet has transformed marketing and business since the first website (http://info.cern.ch) went live in 1991. With over one billion people around the world regularly using the web to find products, entertainment and soulmates, consumer behaviour and the way companies market to both consumers and businesses have changed dramatically.

To succeed in the future, organisations will need marketers, strategists and agencies with up-to-date knowledge of how to apply digital media such as the web, e-mail, mobile and interactive TV. The aim of *Internet Marketing: Strategy, Implementation and Practice* is to support students and professionals in gaining and developing this knowledge. In the text, we will show how traditional marketing models and concepts can be applied to help develop Internet marketing strategies and plans and where new models are appropriate. We will also give many practical examples and tips of best practice in applying online communications tools to effectively market an organisation's products and services using the Internet and other digital media.

For the authors of this book, Internet marketing is an exciting area to be involved with, since it poses many new opportunities and challenges yearly, monthly and even daily. Innovation is a given with the continuous introduction of new technologies, new business models and new communications approaches. For example, Google innovates relentlessly. Its service has developed a long way since 1998 (Figure 1.1) with billions of pages now indexed and other services such as web mail, pay-per-click adverts, analytics and social networks all part of its offering. Complete Activity 1.1 or view Table 1.1 to see other examples of the rate at which new innovations occur.

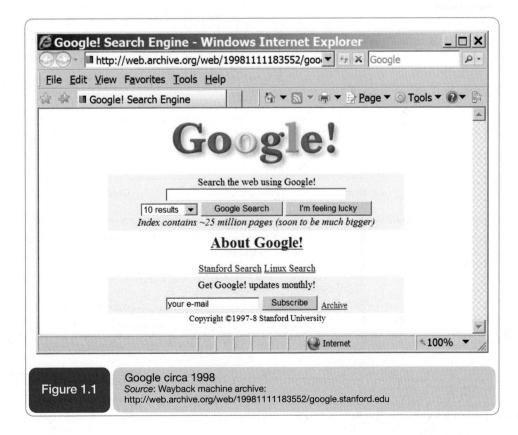

| Figure 1.1 | Google circa 1998<br>*Source*: Wayback machine archive:<br>http://web.archive.org/web/19981111183552/google.stanford.edu |
| --- | --- |

| Activity 1.1 | Innovation in Internet marketing |
|---|---|

**Purpose**

To illustrate innovation in online business models and communications approaches.

**Questions**

1 Think about the innovation that you have witnessed during the time you have used the Internet and World Wide Web. What would you say are the main sites used in your country that have been created which have changed the way we spend our time or buy online? In Table 1.1 are the sites that we believe have had the biggest influence on online business models in the US and Europe, with more emphasis on the most recent ones.

2 What do these sites have in common that you think has made them successful?
   • All these sites are American, so the funding and publicity they can achieve is significant.
   • You will notice that many of these sites (other than Joost, Last.fm and Skype which were founded in Europe) were originally developed in the United States, with the majority now used around the world. But in each country, similar types of businesses have evolved, for example the search engines Baidu in China and Yandex in Russia.
   • They meet a fundamental consumer need.
   • They represent a clear revenue model.
   • They provide a memorable branding and experience.
   • Initially they had a straightforward proposition – offering one service.
   • Generally they were first movers.
   • It is notable that many have taken several years before becoming widely known and used.

Note – you can create your own timeline at **www.miomi.com**.

| Table 1.1 | Timeline of websites indicating innovation in business model or marketing communications approach |
|---|---|

| Year founded | Company/site | Category of innovation |
|---|---|---|
| 1994 | Amazon | Retailer |
| 1995 (March) | Yahoo! (yahoo.com) | Directory and portal |
| 1995 (September) | eBay | Online auction |
| 1995 (December) | Altavista (altavista.com) | Search engine |
| 1996 | Hotmail (hotmail.com) | Web-based e-mail<br>Viral marketing<br>(using e-mail signatures to promote service)<br>Purchased by Microsoft in 1997 |
| 1998 | GoTo.com (goto.com)<br>Overture (2001) | Pay-per-click search marketing<br>Purchased by Yahoo! in 2003 |
| 1998 | Google (google.com) | Search engine |
| 1999 | Blogger (blogger.com) | Blog publishing platform<br>Purchased by Google in 2003 |

| Year founded | Company/site | Category of innovation |
|---|---|---|
| 1999 | Alibaba (alibaba.com) | B2B marketplace with $1.7 billion IPO on Hong Kong stock exchange in 2007. See case in Chapter 2, p. **93** |
| 1999 | MySpace (myspace.com) Formerly eUniverse | Social network Purchased by News Corp in 2005 |
| 2001 | Wikipedia (wikipedia.com) | Open Encyclopedia |
| 2002 | Last.fm | A UK-based Internet radio and music community website, founded in 2002. On 30 May 2007, CBS Interactive acquired Last.fm for £140m (US$280m) |
| 2003 | Skype (skype.com) | Peer-to-peer Internet telephony VOIP – Voice over Internet Protocol Purchased by eBay in 2005 |
| 2003 | Second Life (secondlife.com) | Immersive virtual world |
| 2004 | Facebook (facebook.com) | Social network applications and groups |
| 2005 | YouTube (youtube.com) | Video sharing and rating |
| 2007 | Joost (joost.com) | Quality video broadcast service IP TV – Internet Protocol TV |
| ? | The future | ? |

The challenge for marketers is to assess which innovations are most relevant to their organisation and to seek to gain advantage through introducing them to a company such that the digital marketing techniques integrate effectively with traditional marketing communications.

The chapters of this book will take you through the questions to ask and potential solutions step by step to enable you to develop appropriate strategies. In this introductory chapter, after an initial scoping of what is involved with Internet marketing, we review two main aspects of managing Internet marketing.

In the first part of this chapter, we review the main strategic challenges of Internet marketing and digital channels that must be managed by organisations and secondly we introduce the opportunities for promoting companies online through digital media communications such as Search Engine Marketing (SEM), social networking and display advertising.

## Digital marketing in practice    The EConsultancy interview

### Ted Speroni, Director, EMEA (Europe-Middle East and Asia), HP.com

#### Overview and main concepts covered

This practitioner interview highlights some of the challenges and opportunities for a traditional organisation in marketing its products online. It also introduces some of the important online marketing communications techniques such as search engine marketing, affiliate marketing, social media and widget marketing. Ted Speroni heads the European operations of HP.com, as well as the tech giant's regional preferred online partner programme – an interesting case study in how to incentivise resellers via the web and drive sales through third parties.

## The interview

*Q*: **Can you briefly summarise your role at HP.com?**

*Ted Speroni*: I look after HP.com for the EMEA region. We have around 40 country websites throughout the region in something like 28 languages, so that's my responsibility. I'm also responsible for all of our electronic content management across Europe, which is where we intersect with the online retail community.

At HP, we have a clear strategy of making our products available wherever our customers want to buy them – through high street shops, proximity resellers, online retailers, e-resellers and direct through HP.

We only sell direct through HP.com in five countries in Europe – the UK, France, Germany, Switzerland and Spain. So in most countries, we connect in with the leading e-tailers.

We get daily feeds from all of them on their product availability and pricing, and we display them on HP.com. We then deep link into the shopping basket on each e-tailer, so we're generating leads for them.

It's just like an affiliate programme [a commission-based sales arrangement covered in Chapter 9], but we don't get a commission because it's for our own products. We track the number and quality of leads we are sending each retailer and their conversion rates. We have all the data on which products sell and which cross-sell.

It's a pretty big programme - we have about 150 partners in Europe that are part of it and we generate quite a considerable number of leads and traffic for them. You have to qualify to be part of it – there are certain criteria you have to meet.

*Q*: **What are you doing at the moment to drive more traffic to these e-tailers?**

*Ted Speroni*: The first thing is the integrated marketing approach we have. Search engine marketing (SEM) and search engine optimisation (SEO) are probably the two biggest areas we are working on.

The fundamental principle is that we want to drive all that traffic to pages where we give the customer choice. All the marketing traffic drives people to landing pages that give people a choice about where to purchase the product.

Our investment in SEM is probably in line with the growth we see overall in the industry. We're also making quite heavy investments internally in SEO, because a much higher percentage of our traffic comes from natural search and the conversion rate is not that dissimilar to SEM.

Natural search is a big area of focus for us at the moment. With SEM, we always get people to the right page, to specific landing pages. With natural search, we're not as convinced we're always getting people to the correct page.

For that, we're analysing where the traffic is going from natural search results so that we can give the customer choice on those pages, and also looking at how to make sure people go to the pages they want to go to.

*Q*: **Do you have any challenges in terms of funnelling search traffic – whether natural or paid – through your site, rather than straight to e-tailers? Do you allow brand bidding, for example?**

*Ted Speroni*: We are currently assessing what we will do in this area from both a technical perspective and from a commercial perspective as part of our co-op marketing programme with the channel. I would anticipate that we will do some limited pilots as part of this assessment.

**Q: How difficult is it to maintain communication with partners across multiple channels?**

*Ted Speroni*: We're pretty happy with the multichannel approach we have taken. Encompassing all the different ways customers want to buy products is the most important thing.

We've struggled with that for a long time and we're just trying to make each channel as efficient as possible. We still have a way to go – I'm still working on a number of projects to optimise the different channels.

One thing is the question of high street retailers and the question of integration of inventory. When a customer wants to buy a specific camera they want to know whether it is in stock today, and I don't want the site to send them to the wrong place.

**Q: How are you managing the syndication of your product content to your partners in the programme? How challenging is that?**

*Ted Speroni*: My team syndicates [electronically distributes] out all the content to our resellers. What this is all about is we want to control the HP brand in relation to our products. We produce electronic content feeds in 28 languages of all the product information – pictures, marketing messaging, specifications, everything.

Whenever a customer anywhere in Europe is seeing information about an HP product, there's a very high probability that that will be content we have created. The picture is the picture we want people to see. We feel it's been very successful for us – not only in terms of controlling our brand, but also in terms of cutting costs for our partners. They don't need to do content acquisition.

We'll either syndicate the content via XML feeds, or sometimes the resellers are buying the content through content aggregators. And this extends beyond simple product information – we also syndicate out our recommended cross-sell products. If you buy a HP printer, we have a list of recommended accessories.

This is a key thing – similar to what Dell have talked about in terms of increasing the average shopping basket. Our top priority partners are partners that sell complete HP solutions, so this tool helps them sell complete HP solutions. Resellers can't say they don't know which products sell well with others, because we are telling them.

I should also mention another component – we're not just syndicating content, we also syndicate a configurator for configuring PCs.

We feed all the data into the configurator about the different configurations you can build. You as a customer configure the PC and the information goes into the shopping basket of the retailer, as well as coming through to the HP factory so we can build the configuration. We then match up the order when the retailer passes the order through to us, and we ship it.

It goes beyond syndicating content – you're syndicating widgets, real web apps that can be integrated into websites.

**Q: How else are you looking to use widgets?**

*Ted Speroni*: Another area is product advisors. We have product advisors on HP.com and we would like to syndicate them out. The principle behind this is that we don't want to provide a link on retailers' websites to HP.com, we want to keep the customers on their sites.

As we move HP.com to a more modular, Web 2.0-type approach, we'll see which components we can syndicate out. We also have flash demos so there's an opportunity for resellers to have them on their website, although the resellers do have to have some merchandising people that know about the products. Their sites also have to be Web 2.0-enabled.

**Q: What are you doing in terms of social media and social shopping?**

*Ted Speroni*: We're starting to pilot some social tagging concepts on our product pages, so that people can easily embed our product pages into different sites, like Myspace profiles for example.

It's at a very early stage but it's about the whole concept of exporting our stuff onto the social networking sites, as opposed to trying to get people onto our sites. We haven't implemented it in Europe, but in the US we have started some pilots.

For a while now, we have also had RSS links on promotions from our site – we've had some uptake of that, but it's not a killer app I would say. We're basically looking at how we can help people who want to create content around our products, and facilitate that.

There's a lot of HP content on YouTube – lots of people make videos about how to make the new HP printer, for example. So our approach is 'if people want to do this, let's help them and let's benefit from it'. If we can get user generated linkage to our products, it's incredibly powerful.

**Q: Have you looked at user-generated reviews?**

*Ted Speroni*: We're doing a pilot in the US with user-generated reviews. We haven't started that yet in Europe – I'm trying to work out a scaleable model with all the language issues.

We have to have some quality control on the user reviews – we can't depend completely on community policing. We need some proactive moderation – since it's on our website, we can't take risks with legal issues and so on.

You can say our products aren't good but you have to use appropriate language. Also, we don't want you to be able to comment on our competitors' products. You can say what you want about our products but you can't push competitors' products.

We've been runnning this for about six months in the US and there's been good uptake, and we haven't had big issues with appropriateness. In Europe, I am looking to deploy something and looking into the multi-language issues.

*Source*: http://www.e-consultancy.com/news-blog/newsletter/3200/interview-ted-speroni-director-emea-hp-com.html. E-consultancy.com provides information, training and events on best practice in online marketing and e-commerce management.

## Definitions – what is Internet marketing and multichannel marketing?

**Digital media**
Communications are facilitated through content and interactive services delivered by different digital technology platforms including the Internet, web, mobile phone, interactive TV, IPTV and digital signage.

The use of the Internet and other **digital media** to support marketing has given rise to a bewildering range of labels and jargon created by both academics and professionals. In this section we briefly review some of the different definitions to help explain the scope and applications of this new form of marketing. Before we start by defining these terms, complete Activity 1.2 which considers the relative popularity of these terms.

| Activity 1.2 | What's in a term – what do we call this 'e-thing'? |
|---|---|

**Purpose**

To illustrate how different marketers perceive Internet marketing. There is a range of terms used to describe Internet marketing – it is called different things by different people. It is important that within companies and between agency and client there is clarity on the scope of Internet marketing, so the next few sections explore alternative definitions.

**Question**

One simple, but revealing, method of assessing how commonly these terms are used is to use the Google syntax 'intitle:' which returns the number of pages which contain a particular phrase in their body or title when this is typed into the search box together with the phrase. For example: intitle: "digital marketing" shows the number of pages containing this expression in the title.

Type into Google the following phrases in double quotes or use intitle: "phrase" and note the number of pages (at the top right-hand of the results page):

- "Internet marketing"
- "E-marketing"
- "Digital marketing"
- "E-business"
- "E-commerce"

**Internet marketing**
The application of the Internet and related digital technologies in conjunction with traditional communications to achieve marketing objectives.

**Internet marketing** can be simply defined as:

*Achieving marketing objectives through applying digital technologies.*

This succinct definition helps remind us that it is the results delivered by technology that should determine investment in Internet marketing, not the adoption of the technology! These digital technologies include Internet media such as websites and e-mail as well as other digital media such as wireless or mobile and media for delivering digital television such as cable and satellite.

In practice, Internet marketing will include the use of a company website in conjunction with online promotional techniques introduced later in this chapter and detailed in Chapter 9 such as search engine marketing, interactive advertising, e-mail marketing and partnership arrangements with other websites. These techniques are used to support the objectives of acquiring new customers and providing services to existing customers that help develop the customer relationship. However, for Internet marketing to be successful there is still a necessity for integration of these techniques with traditional media such as print, TV and direct mail as part of multichannel marketing communications.

## E-marketing defined

**E-marketing**
Achieving marketing objectives through use of electronic communications technology.

The term 'Internet marketing' tends to refer to an external perspective of how the Internet can be used in conjunction with traditional media to acquire and deliver services to customers. An alternative term is **e-marketing** or electronic marketing (*see* for example McDonald and Wilson (1999) and Chaffey and Smith (2008)) which can be considered to have a broader scope since it refers to digital media such as web, e-mail and wireless media, but also includes management of digital customer data and electronic customer relationship management systems (e-CRM systems).

The role of e-marketing in supporting marketing is suggested by applying the definition of marketing by the Chartered Institute of Marketing (www.cim.co.uk):

*Marketing is the management process responsible for identifying, anticipating and satisfying customer requirements profitably.*

This definition emphasises the focus of marketing on the customer, while at the same time implying a need to link to other business operations to achieve this profitability. Chaffey and Smith (2008) note that e-marketing can be used to support these aims as follows:

- *Identifying* – the Internet can be used for marketing research to find out customers' needs and wants (Chapters 7 and 10).
- *Anticipating* – the Internet provides an additional channel by which customers can access information and make purchases – evaluating this demand is key to governing resource allocation to e-marketing as explained in Chapters 2, 3 and 4.
- *Satisfying* – a key success factor in e-marketing is achieving customer satisfaction through the electronic channel, which raises issues such as: is the site easy to use, does it perform adequately, what is the standard of associated customer service and how are physical products dispatched? These issues of customer relationship management are discussed further in Chapters 6 and 7.

A broader definition of marketing has been developed by Dibb, Simkin, Pride and Ferrell (Dibb *et al.*, 2001):

*Marketing consists of individual and organisational activities that facilitate and expedite satisfying exchange relationships in a dynamic environment through the creation, distribution, promotion and pricing of goods, services and ideas.*

This definition is useful since it highlights different marketing activities necessary to achieve the 'exchange relationship', namely product development, pricing, promotion and distribution. We will review the way in which the Internet affects these elements of the marketing mix in Chapter 5.

## Digital marketing defined

**Digital marketing**

This has a similar meaning to 'electronic marketing' – both describe the management and execution of marketing using electronic media such as the web, e-mail, interactive TV, IPTV and wireless media in conjunction with digital data about customers' characteristics and behaviour.

**Digital marketing** is yet another term similar to Internet marketing. We use it here because it is a term increasingly used by specialist e-marketing agencies in recruitment of specialist staff and the new media trade publications such as *New Media Age* (www.nma.co.uk) and *Revolution* (www.revolutionmagazine.com). The Institute of Direct Marketing (IDM) has also adopted the term to refer to its specialist professional qualifications.

To help explain the scope and approaches used for digital marketing the IDM has developed a more detailed explanation of digital marketing:

*Digital marketing involves:*

*Applying these technologies which form online channels to market:*
- *web, e-mail, databases, plus mobile/wireless and digital TV.*

*To achieve these objectives:*
- *support marketing activities aimed at achieving profitable acquisition and retention of customers . . . within a multichannel buying process and customer lifecycle.*

*Through using these marketing tactics:*
- *recognising the strategic importance of digital technologies and developing a planned approach to reach and migrate customers to online services through e-communications and traditional communications. Retention is achieved through improving our customer knowledge (of their profiles, behaviour, value and loyalty drivers), then delivering integrated, targeted communications and online services that match their individual needs.*

**Blog**

Personal online diary, journal or news source compiled by one person, an internal team or external guest authors. Postings are usually in different categories. Typically comments can be added to each blog posting to help create interactivity and feedback.

**Feed or RSS feed**

Blog, news or other content is published by an XML standard and syndicated for other sites or read by users in RSS reader services such as Google Reader, personalised home pages or e-mail systems. RSS stands for Really Simple Syndication.

**Podcast**

Individuals and organisations post online media (audio and video) which can be viewed in the appropriate players (including the iPod which first sparked the growth in this technique). The latest podcast updates can be automatically delivered by RSS.

**Social network**

A site that facilitates peer-to-peer communication within a group or between individuals through providing facilities to develop user-generated content (UGC) and to exchange messages and comments between different users.

Let's now look at each part of this description in more detail. The first part of the description illustrates the range of access platforms and communications tools that form the online channels which e-marketers use to build and develop relationships with customers, including PCs, PDAs, mobile phones, interactive digital TV and radio.

Different access platforms deliver content and enable interaction through a range of different online communication tools or media channels. Some are well established techniques which will be familiar to you like websites, search engines, e-mail and text messaging. One of the most exciting things about working in digital media is the introduction of new tools and techniques which have to be assessed for their relevance to a particular marketing campaign. For example, recent innovations, which we discuss further in Chapters 8 and 9, include **blogs**, **feeds**, **podcasts** and **social networks**. The growth of social networks has been documented by Boyd and Ellison (2007) who describe social networking sites (SNS) as:

*Web-based services that allow individuals to (1) construct a public or semi-public profile within a bounded system, (2) articulate a list of other users with whom they share a connection, and (3) view and traverse their list of connections and those made by others within the system.*

The interactive capabilities to post comments or other content and rate content are surprisingly missing from this definition.

For example, an online bank can potentially use many of these technologies to communicate with its customers according to the customers' preferences – some prefer to use the web, others mobile or SMS, others wireless or interactive TV and others traditional channels. Bank First Direct (www.firstdirect.com) has a strategy of innovation and showcases its latest approaches in First Direct Interactive (Figure 1.2). It uses SMS short codes as direct response from TV or print advertising to integrate traditional and digital media channels and also uses SMS periodically to deliver relevant related product offers to customers.

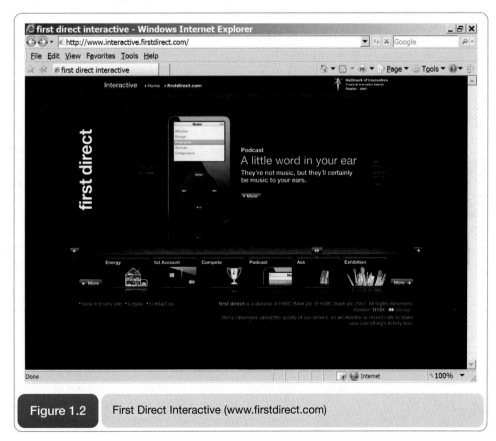

| Figure 1.2 | First Direct Interactive (www.firstdirect.com) |

The second part of the definition of digital marketing shows that it should not be the technology that drives digital marketing, but the business returns from gaining new customers and maintaining relationships with existing customers. It also emphasises how digital marketing does not occur in isolation, but is most effective when it is integrated with other communications channels such as phone, direct mail or face-to-face. As we have said, the role of the Internet in supporting multichannel marketing is another recurring theme in this book and Chapters 5 and 6 in particular explain its role in supporting different customer communications channels and distribution channels. Online channels should also be used to support the whole buying process from pre-sale to sale to post-sale and further development of customer relationships.

The final part of the description summarises approaches to customer-centric e-marketing. It shows how success online requires a planned approach to migrate existing customers to online channels and acquire new customers by selecting the appropriate mix of e-communications and traditional communications. Retention of online customers needs to be based on developing customer insight by researching their characteristics, behaviour, what they value and what keeps them loyal, and then delivering tailored, relevant web and e-mail communications.

## Web 2.0

Since 2004, the Web 2.0 concept has increased in prominence among website owners and developers. The main technologies and principles of Web 2.0 have been explained in an influential article by Tim O'Reilly (O'Reilly, 2005). Behind the label, Web 2.0, lies a bewildering range of interactive tools and social communications techniques like those we have just mentioned such as blogs, podcasts and social networks which have engaged many web users. These are aimed at increasing user participation and interaction on the web. With the widespread adoption of high-speed broadband in many countries, rich media experiences are increasingly used to engage customers with the hope they will have a *viral effect*, i.e. they will be discussed online or offline and more people will become aware of or interact with the brand campaign. Mini case study 1.1 on WillItBlend gives one successful example which helped sell products.

**Multichannel marketing**
Customer communications and product distribution are supported by a combination of digital and traditional channels at different points in the buying cycle.

**Customer insight**
Knowledge about customers' needs, characteristics, preferences and behaviours based on analysis of qualitative and quantitative data. Specific insights can be used to inform marketing tactics directed at groups of customers with shared characteristics.

**Web 2.0 concept**
A collection of web services that facilitate interaction of web users with sites to create user-generated content and encourage behaviours such as community or social network participation, mashups, content rating, use of widgets and tagging.

| Mini Case Study 1.1 | Blendtec uses rich media and viral marketing to grow awareness and sales |
|---|---|

This example shows how an engaging idea can be discussed initially online and then in traditional media to help increase the awareness of a brand. On the WillItBlend campaign microsite (www.willitblend.com, Figure 1.3) a blender designed for making smoothies has blended an iPhone, an iPod, golf balls, glow sticks and a video camera and more. It's only meant to make smoothies and milkshakes! As well as the microsite for the viral campaign, there is also a brand channel on YouTube (http://www.youtube.com/user/blendtec) where different ads received several million views. There is also a blog (http://blog.blendtec.com) for new announcements and to provide information for journalists. The blender has also been extensively featured on traditional media such as TV, newspapers, magazine and radio, showing that traditional media are important in increasing awareness further after the initial impact.

The viral idea was developed by Blendtec employee George Wright who came up with it and announced that in 2007 sales increased tremendously: 'because we're a smaller company, we were able to put out something edgy and fun. In terms of the product you see on YouTube, our sales have gone up by 500%'.

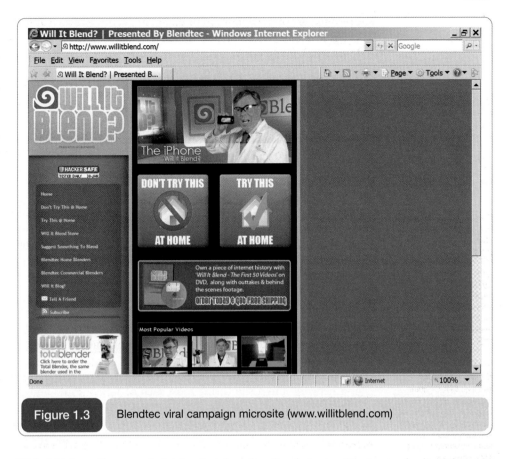

**Figure 1.3**  Blendtec viral campaign microsite (www.willitblend.com)

Web 2.0 also references methods of exchanging data between sites in standardised formats, such as the feeds merchants use to supply shopping comparison sites with data about products offered and their prices.

The main characteristics of Web 2.0 are that it typically involves:

- Web services or interactive applications hosted on the web such as Flickr (www.flickr.com), Google Maps™ (http://maps.google.com) or blogging services such as Blogger.com or Typepad (www.typepad.com).
- Supporting participation – many of the applications are based on altruistic principles of community participation.
- Encouraging creation of user-generated content – blogs are the best example of this. Another example is the collaborative encyclopedia Wikipedia (www.wikipedia.com).
- Enabling rating of content and online services – services such as delicious (http://del.icio.us) and traceback comments on blogs support this. These services are useful given the millions of blogs that are available – rating and tagging (categorising) content help indicate the relevance and quality of the content.
- Ad funding of neutral sites – web services such as Google Mail/GMail™ and many blogs are based on contextual advertising such as Google Adsense™ or Overture/Yahoo! Content Match.
- Data exchange between sites through XML-based data standards. RSS is based on XML, but has relatively little semantic markup to describe the content. An attempt by Google to facilitate this which illustrates the principle of structured information exchange and searching is Google Base™ (http://base.google.com). This allows users to upload data about particular services, such as training courses, in a standardised format based on XML. New classes of content can also be defined.
- Use of rich media or creation of rich internet applications (RIA) which provide for a more immersive, interactive experience. These may be integrated into web browsers or may be separate applications like that downloaded for Second Life (www.secondlife.com).

- Rapid application development using interactive technology approaches known as 'Ajax' (Asynchronous JavaScript and XML). The best-known Ajax implementation is Google Maps which is responsive since it does not require refreshes to display maps.

Participation and interaction is at the heart of Web 2.0 with site users encouraged to create their own 'user generated content' whether this is a guest blog posting, a comment or a product rating. Web 2.0 techniques include blogs, communities, mashups, RSS feeds, podcasts, tagging, social networks, video streams, virtual worlds, widgets and Wikis.

Figure 1.4 summarises the evolution of digital and web-related technologies. Not all terms are explained at this point in the book, but the majority are included in the Glossary (see page **668**). The terms related to technology are explained further in Chapter 3 and Web 2.0 in the online PR section of Chapter 9.

### Web 3.0

**Web 3.0 concept**

Next generation web incorporating high-speed connectivity, complex cross-community interactions and an intelligent or semantic web where automated applications can access data from different online services to assist searchers perform complex tasks of supplier selection.

Since the Web 2.0 concept has been widely applied, it is natural that commentators would try to evolve the concept to **Web 3.0**, although the term has not been widely applied to date. We can suggest that, as web functionality evolves, these approaches which could be deemed 'Web 3.0' will become more important:

- *Web applications.* Usage of web-based applications and services (like Google word processor and spreadsheets) using the web in this way is sometimes termed '*cloud computing*' where all that is really needed for many activities is a computer with a web browser with local software applications used less widely.
- *Syndication.* Increased incorporation of syndicated content and services from other sites or a network into a site (using tools such as Yahoo! Pipes and XML exchange between widgets). We refer to this concept as 'atomisation' in Chapter 9.
- *Streamed video or IPTV.* Increased use of streamed video from existing TV providers and user-generated content (as suggested by use of YouTube and IPTV services such as Joost).

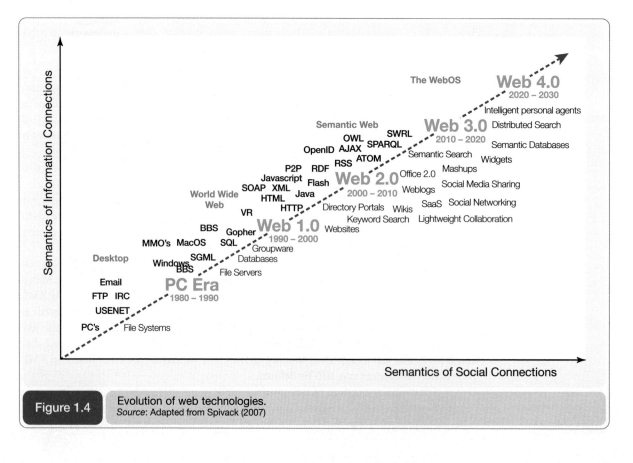

| Figure 1.4 | Evolution of web technologies. |
| --- | --- |
| | *Source*: Adapted from Spivack (2007) |

**Electronic commerce**

All financial and informational electronically mediated exchanges between an organisation and its external stakeholders.

**Sell-side e-commerce**

E-commerce transactions between a supplier organisation and its customers.

**Buy-side e-commerce**

E-commerce transactions between a purchasing organisation and its suppliers.

**Electronic business**

All electronically mediated information exchanges, both within an organisation and with external stakeholders, supporting the range of business processes.

- *Virtual worlds.* Increased use of immersive virtual environments such as Second Life.
- *Personal data integration.* Increased exchange of data between social networks fulfilling different needs (as indicated by the recent Google development of OpenSocial).
- *The semantic web.* Increased use of semantic markup leading to the semantic web envisioned by Tim Berners-Lee over 10 years ago. It seems semantic markup will be needed to develop artificial intelligence applications which recommend content and services to web users without them actively having to seek them and apply their own judgement as to the best products and brands (i.e. an automated shopping comparison service) (as suggested by the use of standardised data feeds between shopping comparison sites and Google Base).

## E-commerce and e-business defined

To complete our coverage of definitions, the terms 'e-commerce' and 'e-business' are often used in a similar context to 'Internet marketing' but their scope is different. **Electronic commerce (e-commerce)** refers to *both financial and informational* electronically mediated transactions between an organisation and any third party it deals with (Chaffey, 2006). So e-commerce involves management not only online of sales transactions, but also of non-financial transactions such as inbound customer service enquiries and outbound e-mail broadcasts.

E-commerce is often further subdivided into a **sell-side e-commerce** perspective which refers to transactions involved with selling products to an organisation's customers and a **buy-side e-commerce** perspective which refers to business-to-business transactions to procure resources needed by an organisation from its suppliers. This is shown in Figure 1.5.

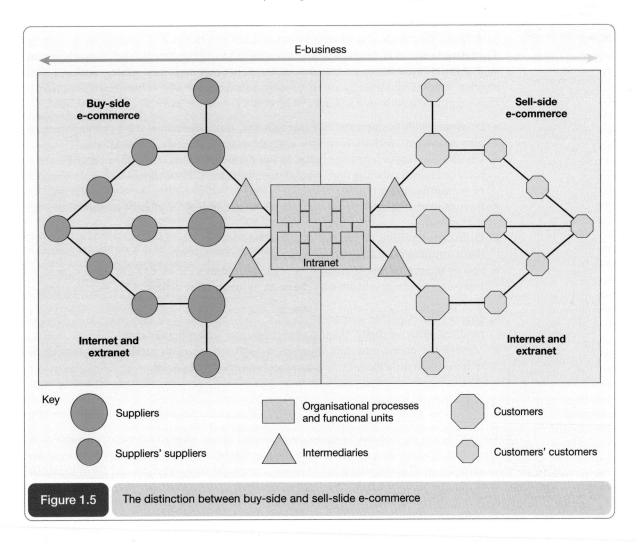

| Figure 1.5 | The distinction between buy-side and sell-slide e-commerce |

Finally, **e-business** is similar to e-commerce but broader in scope and refers to using digital technology to manage a range of business processes incorporating the sell-side and buy-side e-commerce shown in Figure 1.5, and also other key supporting business processes including research and development, marketing, manufacturing and inbound and outbound logistics.

## Introduction to digital marketing strategy

**Positioning**
Customers' perception of the product and brand offering relative to those of competitors.

**Target marketing strategy**
Evaluation and selection of appropriate customer segments and the development of appropriate offers.

**Online value proposition**
A statement of the benefits of online services that reinforces the core proposition and differentiates from an organisation's offline offering and those of competitors.

The key strategic decisions for Internet marketing are in common with traditional business and marketing strategy decisions. As we will see in Chapter 4, which defines a process for developing an Internet marketing strategy, customer segmentation, targeting and **positioning** are all key to effective digital marketing. These familiar **target marketing strategy** approaches involve selecting target customer groups and specifying how to deliver value to these groups as a proposition of services and products. As we will see in Chapter 7, as well as positioning of the core product or brand proposition, online development of a compelling **extended product** or **online value proposition (OVP)** is also important, which defines the online experience of a brand is delivered through content, visual design, interactivity and rich media. All of the companies referenced in Table 1.1 have a clear, compelling OVP. Strategic decisions about the future OVP of a company offers is a key part of Internet marketing strategy.

### Key features of Internet marketing strategy

The interaction and integration between Internet channels and traditional channels is a key part of Internet marketing strategy development. Internet marketing strategy is essentially a **channel marketing strategy** and it needs to be integrated with other channels as part of **multichannel marketing**. It follows that an effective Internet marketing strategy should:

- Be aligned with business strategy (for example, many companies use a rolling three-year plan and vision), with more specific annual business priorities and initiatives.
- Use clear objectives for business and brand development and the online contribution of leads and sales for the Internet or other digital channels. These should be based on models of the number using the channels.
- Be consistent with the types of customers who use and can be effectively reached through the channel.
- Define a compelling, differential **value proposition** for the channel which must be effectively communicated to customers.
- Specify the mix of online and offline communication tools used to attract visitors to the company website or interact with the brand through other digital media such as e-mail or mobile.
- Support the customer journey through the buying process as they select and purchase products using the digital channel in combination with other channels.
- Manage the online customer lifecycle through the stages of attracting visitors to the website, converting them to customers and retention and growth.

### Applications of Internet marketing

For established multichannel organisations, digital media offer a range of opportunities for marketing products and services across the purchase cycle which companies need to review as part of their digital strategy. For example, companies such as easyJet and BP illustrate the applications of Internet marketing since they show how organisations can use online communications such as their website, third-party websites and e-mail marketing as:

- An *advertising medium*. For example, BP plc and its subsidiary companies, such as Castrol Limited, use large-format display or interactive ads on media sites to create awareness of brands and products such as fuels and lubricants.
- A *direct-response medium*. For example, easyJet uses sponsored links when a user is researching a flight using a search engine to prompt them to directly visit the easyJet site by clicking through to it. Similarly the easyJet e-mail newsletter sent to customers can encourage them to click through to a website to generate sales.
- A *platform for sales transactions*. For example, easyJet sells flights online to both consumers and business travellers.
- A *lead-generation method*. For example, BP offers content to business car managers about selecting the best fuel for company cars in order to identify interest from a car fleet manager.
- A *distribution channel*. For example, for distributing digital products. This is often specific to companies with digital products to sell such as online music resellers such as Napster (www.napster.com) and Apple iTunes (www.itunes.com) or publishers of written or video content.
- A *customer service mechanism*. For example, customers serve themselves on easyJet.com by reviewing frequently asked questions.
- A *relationship-building medium* where a company can interact with its customers to better understand their needs and publicise relevant products and offers. For example, easyJet uses its e-mail newsletter and tailored alerts about special deals to help keep its customers and engage them in a dialogue to understand their needs through completing surveys and polls.

## Digital marketing benefits

In Chapter 4, we show how to quantify different goals as part of developing digital marketing strategy. To introduce the typical types of goals for digital marketing, see Table 1.2 which gives a basic framework for reviewing the types of goals based on the 5 Ss of Chaffey and Smith (2008).

| Table 1.2 | The 5 Ss of Internet marketing | |
|---|---|---|
| **Benefit of e-marketing** | **How benefit is delivered** | **Typical objectives** |
| Sell – Grow sales | Includes direct online sales and sales from offline channels influenced online. Achieved through wider distribution to customers you cannot readily service offline or perhaps through a wider product range than in-store, or lower prices compared to other channels | • Achieve 10% of sales online in market <br> • Increase online sales for product by 20% in year |
| Serve – Add value | Achieved through giving customers extra benefits online or inform product development through online dialogue and feedback | • Increase interaction with different content on site <br> • Increase dwell-time duration on site by 10% (sometimes known as 'stickiness') <br> • Increasing number of customers actively using online services (at least once per month) to 30% |

| Benefit of e-marketing | How benefit is delivered | Typical objectives |
|---|---|---|
| Speak – Get closer to customers | Creating a two-way dialogue through web interactions like forums and surveys and conducting online market research through formal surveys and informally monitoring chat rooms to learn about them | • Grow e-mail coverage to 50% of current customer database<br>• Survey 1000 customers online each month<br>• Increase visitors to community site section by 5% |
| Save – Save costs | Achieved through online e-mail communications, sales and service transactions to reduce staff, print and postage costs. Savings also accrue through 'web self-service' where customers answers queries through online content | • Generate 10% more sales for same communications budget<br>• Reduce cost of direct marketing by 15% through e-mail<br>• Increase web self-service to 40% of all service enquiries and reduce overall cost-to-serve by 10% |
| Sizzle – Extend the brand online | Achieved through providing new propositions, new offers and new experiences online while at the same time appearing familiar | • Improve branding metrics such as brand awareness, reach, brand favourability and purchase intent |

*Source*: Chaffey and Smith, 2008

A powerful method of evaluating the strategic marketing opportunities of using the Internet is to apply the strategic marketing grid of Ansoff (1957) as discussed in the strategy formulation section of Chapter 4 (Figure 4.10). This shows how the Internet can potentially be used to achieve four strategic directions:

1 *Market penetration.* The Internet can be used to sell more existing products into existing markets.
2 *Market development.* Here the Internet is used to sell into new geographical markets, taking advantage of the low cost of advertising internationally without the necessity for a supporting sales infrastructure in the customers' countries.
3 *Product development.* New products or services are developed which can be delivered by the Internet. These are typically digital products.
4 *Diversification.* In this sector, the Internet supports selling new products which are developed and sold into new markets.

More recently, Geyskens *et al.* (2002), have suggested in an alternative perspective that there are three main forms of demand expansion for an existing company when they adopt direct Internet channels, these are (1) *Market expansion* which occurs when new segments of customers are reached who did not previously buy in a category – they give the example of Estée Lauder who hopes that the Clinique.com site will attract customers who avoid buying at a cosmetics counter because they find the experience intimidating; (2) *Brand switching* which is by winning customers from competitors; and (3) *Relationship deepening* which is selling more to existing customers. For well established brands with a loyal customer-base price reduction relative to other channels is not necessarily essential or some web-channel price reductions can be used, but they note that often competitive pressures may require lower online prices. These authors also note the potential benefits of reduction in transactional and distribution costs through introducing a direct Internet channel once initial startup costs are incurred.

As well as assisting large corporate organisations develop their markets, perhaps the most exciting potential of the Internet is to help existing small and medium enterprises (SMEs) expand. Read Mini case study 1.2 'North West Supplies extends its reach online' which also illustrates some of the challenges of managing an online business and highlights the need for continual review and investment in functionality.

---

**Mini Case Study 1.2**    North West Supplies extends its reach online

NWS commenced operations in March 1999 when Andrew Camwell, a member of the RAF Volunteer Reserve at the time, spotted a gap in the UK market for mail-order supplies of military garments to people active in the Volunteer Reserve and the Air Cadet Force. Andrew, his wife Carys and her sister Elaine Hughes started running a mail-order business out of shop premises in the village of Cemaes Bay.

The web store (www.northwestsupplies.co.uk, Figure 1.6) has been online since November 2002. As it can take several months for a website to be indexed by search engines, NWS used pay-per-click advertising (PPC – see Chapter 8) as a method of very quickly increasing the website's presence in the major search engines. This marketing method proved successful. The directors were pleasantly surprised as they had previously been somewhat dubious about the prospect of the Internet generating sales in their sector. Within six months of running the website, the company had increased turnover by £20,000, but further advances would incur a high advertising cost. Following an eCommerce Review by Opportunity Wales, the company decided to tackle the issues by implementing search engine optimisation (SEO – see Chapter 9) and a site re-design which included:

- *Improved graphic design* – this was to be changed to a more professional and up-to-date look.
- *Best, featured and latest products* – the introduction of a dynamic front page to entice customers to re-visit the site on a regular basis. The contents of this page would feature the best sellers, and latest or featured products.
- *Reviews and ratings* – to provide confidence to consumers and allow some kind of interaction with them, which would allow users to review products they have purchased and give them a star rating.
- *Cross-selling* – when customers view a product there may be other products or categories that may be of interest or be complementary, hence there was a proposal to allow staff to link products and categories so that these would be displayed.
- *Segmentation* – the site would be split into two sections emphasising the segmentation of product lines into military wear and outdoor wear, thus being less confusing and easier to use for the respective users.
- *Navigation by sub-categories* – as the product range had expanded, the additional pages created in each category made it harder for customers to find specific items or have to browse many pages before finding a suitable product. The introduction of sub-categories would provide a clear link to the areas of interest and contain fewer pages to browse thus helping the customer to make a choice more easily and more quickly.

### Benefits

The owners describe the benefits of the improvements to their multichannel business as follows:

- *Increased direct sales* – '*The new launch increased sales and appealed to a broader audience – young and old*'. The annual turnover of the business has increased from £250,000 to £350,000 and this is mainly attributable to the new website. The high profile launch aimed at existing customers, the greater visibility in search engines, and the greater usability of the site have all contributed to this.
- *Improved promotion of the whole range of stock* – '*We started selling stuff that we hadn't sold before*'. The changes in navigation, particularly division into two market segments (military and outdoors) and greater use of sub-categories, meant that products were easier to find and hence easier to buy, leading to increased sales of products that had previously been slow sellers.

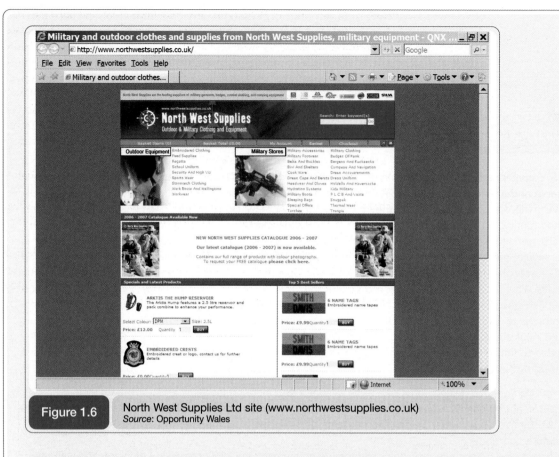

| Figure 1.6 | North West Supplies Ltd site (www.northwestsupplies.co.uk)<br>*Source*: Opportunity Wales |

- *New customers – 'We now send more items abroad'*. The better performance of the site in search engines has led to an increase in orders from new customers and from abroad. The company now has regular sales to Canada, Australia, New Zealand and various European states. Some 60% of orders are from new customers – not bad for a business that initially set up on the premise of a niche market for UK-based cadet forces.
- *Adding value to the brand – 'New corporate clients could look at our website and see we weren't fly-by-night and that we meant business'*. Improvements to the design have raised confidence levels in visitors and this has led to increased sales. But perhaps more significantly, the professional image of the site was a good boost to confidence for potential business partners in the emerging business-to-business division that started to trade as North Star Contracts.

## Alternative digital business models

As part of strategy development, organisations require clarity on the type of business model they will develop.

### Business and consumer business models

**Business-to-consumer**
Commercial transactions between an organisation and consumers.

**Business-to-business**
Commercial transactions between an organisation and other organisations (inter-organisational marketing).

A fundamental aspect of the business model is whether the proposition developed appeals to consumers or business. So Internet marketing opportunities are described in terms of the extent to which an organisation is transacting with consumers (**business-to-consumer – B2C**) or other businesses (**business-to-business – B2B**).

Reference to the well-known online companies in Table 1.1 initially suggests these companies are mainly focused on B2C markets. However, B2B communications are still important for many of these companies since business transactions may occur, as for example with eBay

**Consumer-to-consumer**
Informational or financial transactions between consumers, but usually mediated through a business site.

**Consumer-to-business**
Consumers approach the business with an offer.

**E-government**
The use of Internet technologies to provide government services to citizens.

Business (http://business.ebay.com/), or the B2C service may need to be sustained through advertising provided through B2B transactions, for example Google's revenue is largely based on its B2B AdWords (http://adwords.google.com/). Advertising service and advertising-based revenue is also important to sites such as YouTube, MySpace and Facebook.

Figure 1.7 gives examples of different companies operating in the business-to-consumer (B2C) and business-to-business (B2B) spheres. Often companies such as easyJet and BP will have products that appeal to both consumers and businesses, so will have different parts of their site to appeal to these audiences. Figure 1.7 also presents two additional types of transaction – those where consumers transact directly with other consumers (**C2C**) and where they initiate trading with companies (**C2B**). Common C2C interactions include transactional exchange (e.g eBay, www.ebay.com), financial services (e.g. Zopa, www.zopa.com) and betting (e.g. Betfair, www.betfair.com) Hoffman and Novak (1996) suggested that C2C interactions are a key characteristic of the Internet that it is important for companies to consider, but their assertion has only been borne out more recently by the growth of the social networks), as is shown by Activity 1.3.

The diagram also includes government and public services organisations which deliver online or **e-government** services. As well as the models shown in Figure 1.7, it has also been suggested that employees should be considered as a separate type of consumer through the use of intranets, which is referred to as employee-to-employee or E2E.

| | From: Supplier of content/service | |
|---|---|---|
| ***Consumer or citizen*** | ***Business (organisation)*** | ***Government*** |
| **Consumer-to-Consumer (C2C)**<br>• eBay<br>• Peer-to-peer (Skype)<br>• Blogs and communities<br>• Product recommendations<br>Social network (Bebo, Facebook MySpace) | **Business-to-Consumer (B2C)**<br>• Transactional: Amazon<br>• Relationship-building: BP<br>• Brand-building: Unilever<br>• Media owner – News Corp<br>• Comparison intermediary: Kelkoo, Pricerunner | **Government-to-Consumer (G2C)**<br>• National government transactional: Tax – Inland Revenue<br>• National government information<br>• Local government information<br>• Local government services |
| **Consumer-to-Business (C2B)**<br>• Priceline<br>• Consumer-feedback, communities or campaigns | **Business-to-Business (B2B)**<br>• Transactional: Euroffice<br>• Relationship-building: BP<br>• Media owned: Emap business productions<br>• B2B marketplaces: EC21<br>Social network (Linked-in, Plaxo) | **Government-to-Business (B2B)**<br>• Government services and transactions: tax<br>• Legal regulations |
| **Consumer-to-Government (C2G)**<br>• Feedback to government through pressure group or individual sites | **Business-to-Government (B2G)**<br>• Feedback to government businesses and non-governmental organisations | **Government-to-government (G2G)**<br>• Inter-government services<br>• Exchange of information |

To: Consumer of content/service — Consumer or citizen / Business (organisation) / Government

**Figure 1.7** Summary and examples of transaction alternatives between businesses, consumers and governmental organisations

| Activity 1.3 | Why are C2C interactions important? |
|---|---|

**Purpose**

To highlight the relevance of C2C transactions to B2C companies.

**Activity**

Consult with fellow students and share experience of C2C interactions online. Think of C2C on both independent sites and organisational sites. How can C2C communications assist these organisations?

## Different forms of online presence

The form of digital strategy developed by a company will also depend on the nature of a business. Chaffey (2006) identifies different types of online presence which each have different objectives and are appropriate for different markets. Note that these are not clear-cut categories of websites since any company may combine these types as part of their business model, but with a change in emphasis according to the market they serve. As you review websites, note how organisations have different parts of the site focusing on these functions of sales transactions, services, relationship-building, brand-building and providing news and entertainment. The five main types of site are as follows.

### 1 Transactional e-commerce site

Enables purchase of products online. The main business contribution of the site is through sale of these products. The sites also support the business by providing information for consumers who prefer to purchase products offline.

- Visit these examples: an end-product manufacturer such as Vauxhall (www.vauxhall.co.uk) or an online retailer such as Amazon (www.amazon.com).

### 2 Services-oriented relationship-building website

Provides information to stimulate purchase and build relationships. Products are not typically available for purchase online. Information is provided through the website and e-newsletters to inform purchase decisions. The main business contribution is through encouraging offline sales and generating enquiries or leads from potential customers. Such sites also add value to existing customers by providing them with detailed information to help support them in their lives at work or at home.

- Visit these examples: B2B management consultants such as PricewaterhouseCooper (www.pwcglobal.com) and Accenture (www.accenture.com), B2C portal for energy supplier British Gas (www.house.co.uk).

### 3 Brand-building site

Provides an experience to support the brand. Products are not typically available for online purchase. Their main focus is to support the brand by developing an online experience of the brand. They are typical for low-value, high-volume fast-moving consumer goods (FMCG) brands for consumers.

- Visit these examples: Tango (www.tango.com), Guinness (www.guinness.com).

## 4 Portal or media site

**Brochureware site**
A simple site with limited interaction with the user that replicates offline marketing literature.

Provides information or news about a range of topics. 'Portal' refers to a gateway of information. This is information both on the site and through links to other sites. Portals have a diversity of options for generating revenue including advertising, commission-based sales, sale of customer data (lists).

- Visit these examples: Yahoo! (www.yahoo.com) (B2C) and Silicon (www.silicon.com) (B2B).

**Stage models**
Models for the development of different levels of Internet marketing services.

Each of these different types of sites tend to increase in sophistication as organisations develop their Internet marketing. Many organisations began the process of Internet marketing with the development of websites in the form of brochureware sites or electronic brochures introducing their products and services, but are now enhancing them to add value to the full range of marketing functions. In Chapters 2 and 4 we look at stage models of the development of Internet marketing services, from static brochureware sites to dynamic transactional sites that support interactions with customers.

**Transactional sites**
Sites that support online sales.

## 5 Social network or community site

These sites or parts of sites focus on enabling community interactions between different consumers (C2C model). Typical interactions include posting comments and replies to comments, sending messages, rating content and tagging content in particular categories.

Well-known examples include Bebo, Facebook, MySpace and Linked-In. Other startups also have a social network element such as Delicious (social bookmarking or rating web pages), Digg (comment on blog postings), Flickr (image tagging), Technorati (blog postings) and YouTube (videos). B2B social networks to keep business professionals in contact include Linked-in and Plaxo although some are turning to Facebook for this function. (Large social networks such as Facebook or MySpace are effectively media owners and this is their main revenue source and in previous editions of this book were included in that category.) In addition to distinct social network sites such as these, social networks can also be integrated into other site types. For example, travel and insurance company Saga Group, which provides products primarily to the over-50s market, has developed Saga Zone (www2.saga.co.uk/sagazone) where users can chat or post photos.

## Challenges in developing and managing Internet marketing strategy

Some of the challenges in managing Internet marketing strategy which are commonly seen in many organisations (and should be managed) include:

- *Unclear responsibilities* for the many different Internet marketing activities shown in Figure P. 1 in the Preface.
- *No specific objectives* are set for Internet marketing.
- *Insufficient budget* is allocated for Internet marketing because *customer demand for online services is underestimated* and *competitors potentially gain market share* through superior online activities.
- *Budget is wasted* as different parts of an organisation experiment with using different tools or suppliers without achieving economies of scale.
- *New online value propositions for customers* are not developed since the Internet is treated as 'just another channel to market' without review of opportunities to offer improved, differentiated online services.
- *Results from digital marketing are not measured or reviewed* adequately, so actions cannot be taken to improve effectiveness.
- *An experimental rather than planned approach* is taken to using e-communications with *poor integration between online and offline marketing* communications.

Research by EConsultancy (2008) investigated the challenges of managing Internet marketing. The research found that many companies were experiencing problems of deploying the right resources for Internet marketing. Challenges were rated by respondents as follows:

- Gaining senior management buy-in or resource (67% agreed)
- Gaining buy-in or resource from traditional marketing functions or brands (66% agreed)
- Gaining IT resource or technical support (61% agreed)
- Finding suitable staff (75% agreed)
- Finding suitable digital media agencies (54% agreed)

You can see that there are challenges both in managing different types of internal resources and finding suitable staff. The main challenges mentioned included gaining buy-in and budget along with conflicts of ownership and tensions between a digital marketing team and other teams such as traditional marketing, IT, finance and senior management. Co-ordination with different channels in conjunction with teams managing marketing programmes elsewhere in the business was also challenging.

### Applying the 7 Ss

The 7 Ss are a useful framework for reviewing an organisation's existing and future capabilities to meet the challenges posed by the new digital channels and some of the aspects of this are shown in Table 1.3.

You may have encountered the 7 S framework, summarised by Waterman *et al.* (1980) and developed by McKinsey consultants in the 1980s. It is often referenced when referring to the management of a business. EConsultancy (2005) has summarised some of the strategic resource management issues that require consideration, as shown in Table 1.3.

| Table 1.3 | Summary of some of the organisational challenges of digital marketing that need to be managed in the context of the 7 S framework. |
|---|---|

| Element of 7 S model | Application to digital marketing strategy | Key issues from practice and literature |
|---|---|---|
| Strategy | The significance of digital marketing in influencing and supporting the organisation's strategy | Gaining appropriate budgets and demonstrating /delivering value and ROI from budgets. Annual planning approach. Techniques for using digital marketing to impact organisation strategy. Techniques for aligning digital strategy with organisational and marketing strategy. |
| Structure | The modification of organisational structure to support digital marketing | Integration of team with other management, marketing (corporate communications, brand marketing, direct marketing) and IT staff. Use of cross-functional teams and steering groups. Insourcing vs outsourcing. |
| Systems | The development of specific processes, procedures or information systems to support digital marketing | Campaign planning approach–integration. Managing/sharing customer information. Managing content quality. Unified reporting of digital marketing effectiveness. In-house vs external best-of-breed vs external integrated technology solutions. |

| Element of 7 S model | Application to digital marketing strategy | Key issues from practice and literature |
|---|---|---|
| Staff | The breakdown of staff in terms of their background and characteristics such as IT vs marketing, use of contractors/ consultants, age and sex | Insourcing vs outsourcing. Achieving senior management buy-in/ involvement with digital marketing. Staff recruitment and retention. Virtual working. Staff development and training. |
| Style | Includes both the way in which key managers behave in achieving the organisation's goals and the cultural style of the organisation as a whole | Relates to role of digital marketing team in influencing strategy – it is it dynamic and influential or conservative and looking for a voice. |
| Skills | Distinctive capabilities of key staff, but can be interpreted as specific skill sets of team members | Staff skills in specific areas: supplier selection, project management, content management, specific e-marketing approaches (SEO, PPC, affiliate marketing, e-mail marketing, online advertising). |
| Superordinate goals | The guiding concepts of the digital marketing organisation which are also part of shared values and culture. The internal and external perception of these goals may vary | Improving the perception of the importance and effectiveness of the digital marketing team among senior managers and staff it works with (marketing generalists and IT). |

*Source*: EConsultancy (2005)

## A strategic framework for developing Internet marketing strategy

To realise the benefits of Internet marketing and avoid the pitfalls that we have described, an organisation needs to develop a planned, structured approach. Consequently, this book defines a strategic approach to Internet marketing which is intended to manage these risks and deliver the opportunities available from online channels. In Figure 1.8 we suggest a process for developing and implementing an Internet marketing plan which is based on our experience of strategy definition in a wide range of companies. This diagram highlights the key activities and their dependencies which are involved for the creation of a typical Internet marketing strategy and relates them to coverage in different chapters in this book:

### A: Defining the online opportunity

Setting objectives to define the potential is the core of this phase of strategy development. Key activities are:

- *1 Set e-marketing objectives (Chapter 4 and 8).* Companies need to set specific numerical objectives for their online channels and then resource to deliver these objectives. These objectives should be informed by and influence the business objectives and also the following two activities.
- *1a Evaluate e-marketing performance (Chapters 4 and 10).* Apply web analytics tools to measure the contribution of leads, sales and brand involvement currently delivered by online communications such as search engine marketing, online advertising and e-mail marketing in conjunction with the website.
- *1b Assess online marketplace (Chapters 2, 3 and 4).* Situation analysis review of the micro-environment (customers, competitors, intermediaries, suppliers and internal capabilities and resources) and the broader macro-environment which influences strategy such as legal requirements and technology innovation.

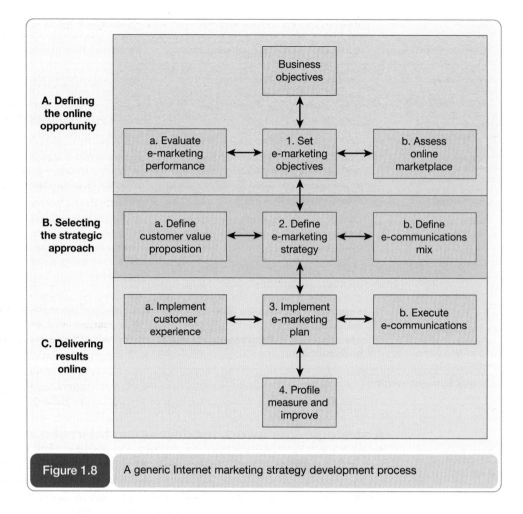

| Figure 1.8 | A generic Internet marketing strategy development process |

## B: Selecting the strategic approach

- *2 Define e-marketing strategy (Chapter 4).* Select appropriate strategies to achieve the objectives set at stage A1.
- *2a Define customer value proposition (Chapters 4 to 7).* Define the value proposition available through the online channel and how it relates to the core proposition delivered by the company. Reviewing the marketing mix and brand values to evaluate how they can be improved online.
- *2b Define e-communications mix (Chapters 4, 8 and 9).* Select the offline and online communications tools to encourage usage of an organisation's online services and to generate leads and sales. Develop new outbound communications and event-triggered touch strategies to support customers through their relationship with the company.

## C: Delivering results online

- *3 Implement e-marketing plan (Part 3).* This details the implementation of the strategy.
- *3a Implement customer experience (Chapter 7).* Build the website and create the e-mail marketing communications which form the online interactions customers make with a company. Create online customer relationship management capabilities to understand customers' characteristics, needs and behaviours and to deliver targeted, personalised value (Chapter 6).
- *3b Execute e-communications (Chapter 8).* Manage the continuous online marketing communications such as search engine marketing, partnerships, sponsorships and affiliate arrangements, and campaign-based e-marketing communications such as online adver-

**Digital media channels**

Online communications techniques used to achieve goals of brand awareness, familiarity, favourability and to influence purchase intent by encouraging users of digital media to visit a website to engage with the brand or product, and ultimately to purchase online or offline through traditional media channels such as by phone or in-store.

tising, e-mail marketing and microsites to encourage usage of the online service and to support customer acquisition and retention campaigns. Integrate the digital media channels with traditional marketing.

- *4 Customer profiling (Chapter 6), monitoring and improving online activities and maintaining the online activities (Chapter 9).* Capture profile and behavioural data on customer interactions with the company and summarise and disseminate reports and alerts about performance compared with objectives in order to drive performance improvement.

You will see that in the process diagram, Figure 1.8, many double-headed arrows are used, since the activities are often not sequential but rather inform each other, so activity 1, set e-marketing objectives, is informed by the activities around it but may also influence them. Similarly, activity 4, profile, measure and improve, is informed by the execution of online activities but there should be a feedback loop to update the tactics and strategies used.

## Introduction to digital marketing communications

**Pay-per-click search marketing**

PPC refers to when a company pays for text ads to be displayed on the search engine results pages as a sponsored link (typically above, to the right of or below the natural listings) when a specific keyphrase is entered by the search users. It is so called because the marketer pays each time the hypertext link in the ad is clicked on. If a link is clicked repeatedly, then this will be detected by the search engine as click fraud and the marketer will not be charged.

**Search engine optimisation**

A structured approach used to increase the position of a company or its products in search engine natural or organic results listings (the main body of the search results page) for selected keywords or phrases.

**Display ads (advertising)**

Use of graphical or *rich media ad units* within a web page to achieve goals of delivering brand awareness, familiarity, favourability and purchase intent. Many ads encourage interaction through prompting the viewer to *rollover* to play videos, complete an online form or to view more details before clicking through to a site.

For many years, marketing campaigns were based on traditional media including TV, print and radio ads, and direct mail supported by public relations. But, in a few short years, since the web concept was first proposed in the late 1980s by Sir Tim Berners-Lee, there have been great changes in marketing communications. The digital equivalents of these traditional media, which are known as digital media channels, are vital components of most marketing campaigns. For example, in an online campaign, marketers can deploy display ads, the familiar banner and skyscraper ads seen on many online publisher sites; pay-per-click (PPC) ads such as the Sponsored Links in Google; search engine optimisation (SEO) to gain higher positions in the natural listings of Google; affiliate marketing where sites which generate a sale for a merchant gain commission and e-mail marketing, which is most effective when messages are sent to an existing customer base, i.e. customers who have given their permission to receive them. Many of these digital communications techniques are analogous to their traditional equivalents, for example, display ads are broadly equivalent to print or display ads and e-mail marketing is equivalent to direct mail.

But the approaches used to target the online audience are potentially very different with personalisation based on the customer profile and previous interactions with communications giving many options to deliver more timely, relevant messages. (Personalised communications are also effective on the website where landing pages are commonly used to make the page more relevant to what the customer is seeking.) Leading websites also provide great opportunities to engage the visitor through in-depth text content, rich media such as video and audio and participation in customer communities.

## The relationship between digital and traditional communications

It is helpful to understand the relationship between the new digital communications techniques and traditional communications, in order that new opportunities are not missed and campaigns can be planned in an integrated fashion. As Jenkinson and Sain (2001) explain:

*A variety of concepts and terms are used across both academics and practitioners. For example, within our research into media neutral planning, some people referred to media, some to contact points or channels as methods of distributing communication. Similarly, some referred to tools and others to channels, disciplines or methods as the techniques by which the media could be used.*

To illustrate the relationship between different levels of marketing communications consider Table 1.4 which is based on terminology introduced by Jenkinson and Sain (2001) and increasingly adopted by practiioners and academics.

**Affiliate marketing**
A commission-based arrangement where referring sites (publishers) receive a commission on sales or leads by merchants (retailers). Commission is usually based on a percentage of product sale price or a fixed amount for each sale, but may also be based on a per-click basis, for example when an aggregator refers visits to merchants.

**E-mail marketing**
Typically applied to outbound communications from a company to prospects or customers to encourage purchase or branding goals. E-mail marketing is most commonly used for mailing to existing customers on a house-list, but can also be used for mailing prospects on a rented or co-branded list. E-mails may be sent as part of a one-off campaign or can be automated event-based triggered e-mails such as a welcome strategy which can be broadcast based on rules about intervals and customer characteristics.

| Table 1.4 | Key marketing communications concepts |
|---|---|

| Marketing communications term | Definition | Examples from traditional and digital media |
|---|---|---|
| Medium (media) | '*Anything that conveys a message*' The carrier of the message or method of transmission. Can be conceived as the touchpoint with the customer | Broadcast (television, radio), press, direct mail, cinema, poster, digital (web, e-mail, mobile) |
| Discipline | '*A body of craft technique biased towards a facet of marketing communication*' These are traditionally known as 'promotion tools' or the different elements of the communications mix | Advertising, direct marketing, public relations, market research, personal selling, sales promotion, sponsorship, packaging, exhibitions and trade shows. All are also used online |
| Channel (tools) | The combination of a discipline with a medium | Direct mail, direct response TV, television brand advertising. Digital channels: different forms of search marketing, affiliate marketing, display advertising, e-mail marketing, social media, blogs and feeds |
| Vehicle | A specific channel used to reach a target audience | TV (ITV, Channel 4), newspaper (Sun, Metro, Times), magazine (Economist, Radio Times), radio (Virgin Radio, BBC Radio 5) and their website equivalents. Different search engines such as Google fit, or aggregators of product from other suppliers such as Moneysupermarket, also fit here |

| Activity 1.4 | Innovation in Internet marketing |
|---|---|

**Landing page**
A destination page when a user clicks on an ad or other form of link from a *referring site*. It can be a home page but more typically and desirably, a landing page is a page with the messaging focused on the offer in the ad. This will maximise conversion rates and brand favourability.

**Purpose**

To illustrate similarities and differences between digital and traditional media.

**Instruction**

Make two columns. On the left, write down different digital media channels and, on the right, the corresponding communications disciplines such as advertising, direct marketing or PR which are most appropriate.

**Rich media**
Advertisements or site content that are not static, but provide animation, sound or interactivity. An example of this would be a display advertisement for a loan in which a customer can type in the amount of loan required, and the cost of the loan is calculated immediately.

## The key types of digital media channels

There are many online communications tools which marketers must review as part of their communications strategy or as part of planning an online marketing campaign. To assist with planning, Chaffey and Smith (2008) recommend that these online marketing tools are divided into the six main groups shown in Figure 1.9.

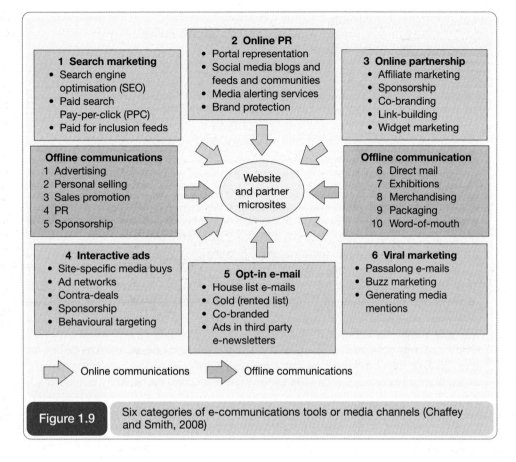

**Figure 1.9**    Six categories of e-communications tools or media channels (Chaffey and Smith, 2008)

In Chapters 8 and 9, we review these tools in detail, but this is the essence of each digital media channel:

1 *Search engine marketing.* Placing messages on a search engine to encourage click-through to a website when the user types a specific keyword phrase. Two key search marketing techniques are paid placements or sponsored links using pay-per-click, and placements in the natural or organic listings using search engine optimisation (SEO).

2 *Online PR.* Maximising favourable mentions of your company, brands, products or websites on third-party websites such as social networks or blogs that are likely to be visited by your target audience. Also includes responding to negative mentions and conducting public relations via a site through a press centre or blog, for example.

3 *Online partnerships.* Creating and managing long-term arrangements to promote your online services on third-party websites or through e-mail communications. Different forms of partnership include link building, affiliate marketing, aggregators such as price comparison sites like Moneysupermarket (www.moneysupermarket.com), online sponsorship and co-branding.

4 *Interactive advertising.* Use of online ads such as banners and rich media ads to achieve brand awareness and encourage click-through to a target site.

5 *Opt-in e-mail marketing.* Renting e-mail lists or placing ads in third-party e-newsletters or the use of an in-house list for customer activation and retention.

6 *Viral marketing.* Viral marketing is effectively online word of mouth – messages are forwarded to help achieve awareness and, in some cases, drive response.

**Viral marketing**
A marketing message is communicated from one person to another, facilitated by different media, such as word of mouth, e-mail or websites, in particular social network or blog sites. Viral marketing implies rapid transmission of messages is intended.

| Mini Case Study 1.3 | ASOS taps into fashion online |
| --- | --- |

ASOS (www.asos.com), a fashion e-tailer was launched in 2000 as As Seen On Screen. By 2007, it was a profitable business with revenues increasing by 83% year-on-year. The name originally referred to fashions worn by celebrities such as the Beckhams, but today the site offers a wider range of the latest fashions for men and women.

You can hear CEO and co-founder Nick Robertson explaining his strategy for growing the online brand and success with the business using the FT.com video shown in Figure 1.10.

When speaking to NMA, Nick Robertson explained his communications strategy as follows: 'We had £2.3m at start-up, which really isn't much, so we did the same cheap and dirty things that everyone at the time did, starting with affiliate marketing and PR. We then ran full pages in magazines like *Heat* and *Grazia*. Although we have good brand awareness now, it has taken six years to get to that stage. Ironically, we've gone from being an online-only brand to moving away from online marketing. For example, we canned our affiliate marketing campaign three months ago [although there are plans to restart the affiliate programme].

ASOS recently sponsored America's Next Top Model on UK Living, the first TV spot ASOS has ever run. This includes an SMS campaign, where viewers can text to ASOS and receive a unique discount voucher. Nick Robertson justifies the move as follows: 'TV sponsorship is cut-through. It's establishing ASOS as THE online fashion retailer. You're not going to do that with a few banners going around the web. You have to get to critical mass'. Robertson still believes in the power of magazine and content sites online, indeed the blog (http://blog.asos.com) was established to rival big publishing houses, such as Condé Nast, who are increasingly pushing their brands on the web. However, ASOS will partner where appropriate and ASOS was one of the brands to partner Condé Nast within Stylefinder.com, the celebrity fashion site.

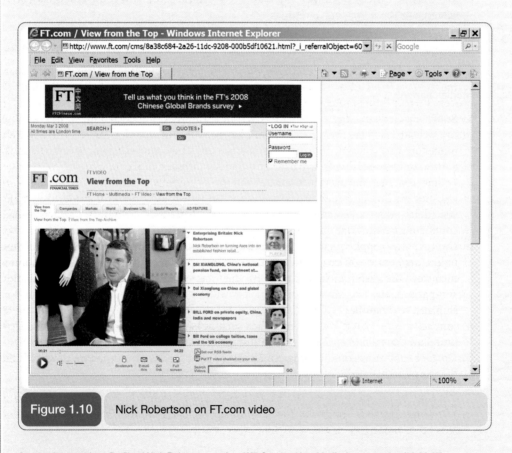

| Figure 1.10 | Nick Robertson on FT.com video |
| --- | --- |

*Source*: Adapted from Profile of Nick Robertson; author: Will Cooper, *New Media Age* magazine (08.03.07)

## What benefits do digital media provide for the marketer?

In the section on digital marketing strategy, we described some of the applications of Internet marketing to support communications with customers across the purchase cycle from generating awareness, achieving direct response for lead generation or sale and supporting customer service and relationship marketing.

Internet marketing communications differs significantly from conventional marketing communications because digital media enable new forms of interaction and new models for information exchange. A useful summary of the differences between these new media and traditional media has been developed by McDonald and Wilson (1999) – they describe the '6 Is of the e-marketing mix'. Note that these can be used as a strategic analysis tool, but they are not used in this context here. The six Is are useful since they highlight factors that apply to practical aspects of Internet marketing such as personalisation, direct response and marketing research, but also strategic issues of industry restructuring and integrated channel communications.

### 1 Interactivity

John Deighton was one of the first authors to summarise this key characteristic of the Internet. He identified the following characteristics inherent in a digital medium (Deighton, 1996) which are true for much online marketing activity:

- the customer initiates contact;
- the customer is seeking information or an experience (*pull*);
- it is a high-intensity medium – the marketer will have 100% of the individual's attention when he or she is viewing a website;
- a company can gather and store the response of the individual;
- individual needs of the customer can be addressed and taken into account in future *dialogues*.

Figure 1.11(a) shows how traditional media are predominantly *push media* where the marketing message is broadcast from company *to* customer and other stakeholders. During this process, there is limited interaction with the customer, although interaction is encouraged in some cases such as the direct-response advert or mail-order campaign. On the Internet it is often the customer who initiates contact and is *seeking* information through researching information on a website. In other words it is a '*pull*' mechanism where it is particularly important to have good visibility in search engines such as Google, Yahoo! and MSN when customers are entering search terms relevant to a company's products or services. Note though that outbound e-mail marketing and online advertising can be considered as 'push' broadcast techniques. Figure 1.11(b) shows how the Internet should be used to encourage two-way communications, which may be extensions of the direct-response approach. For example, FMCG suppliers such as Nestlé (www.nescafe.co.uk) use their website as a method of generating interaction by providing incentives such as competitions and sales promotions to encourage the customer to respond with their names, addresses and profile information such as age and sex.

Hoffman and Novak (1997) believe that digital media represent such a shift in the model of communication that it is a new model or paradigm for marketing communications. They suggest that the facilities of the Internet represent a computer-mediated environment in which the interactions are not between the sender and receiver of information, but with the medium itself. They say:

> *consumers can interact with the medium, firms can provide content to the medium and, in the most radical departure from traditional marketing environments, consumers can provide commercially-oriented content to the media.*

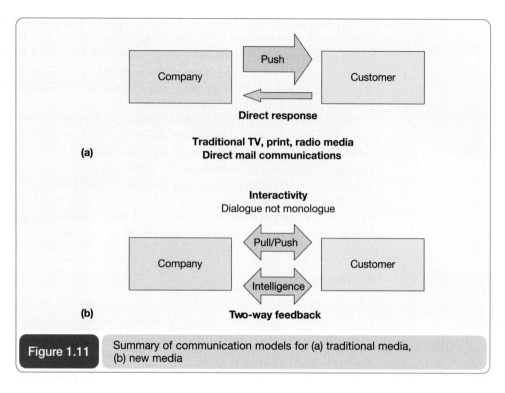

**Figure 1.11** Summary of communication models for (a) traditional media, (b) new media

It has taken ten years of the growth in use of individual recommendations, auction sites, community sites and more recently blogs and **podcasts** for the full extent of this shift to become apparent. In 2005, a *Business Week* cover feature article referred to the 'Power of us' to explain this change and showed that although relatively few consumers are creating blogs (low single-figure percentages), a large proportion of Internet users are accessing them.

### 2 Intelligence

The Internet can be used as a relatively low-cost method of collecting marketing research, particularly about customer perceptions of products and services. In the competitions referred to above, Nestlé are able to profile their customers' characteristics on the basis of questionnaire response.

A wealth of marketing research information is also available from the website itself. Marketers use the **web analytics** approaches described in Chapter 9 to build their knowledge of customer preferences and behaviour according to the types of sites and content which they consume when online. Every time a website visitor downloads content, this is recorded and analysed as 'site statistics' as described in Chapter 9 in order to build up a picture of how consumers interact with the site.

### 3 Individualisation

Another important feature of the interactive marketing communications is that they can be tailored to the individual (Figure 1.12(b)) at relatively low costs, unlike in traditional media where the same message tends to be broadcast to everyone (Figure 1.12(a)). Importantly, this individualisation can be based on the intelligence collected about site visitors and then stored in a database and subsequently used to target and personalise communications to customers to achieve *relevance* in all media. The process of tailoring is also referred to as **personalisation** – Amazon is the most widely known example where the customer is greeted by name on the website and receives recommendations on site and in their e-mails based on previous purchases. This ability to deliver '**sense and respond communications**' is another key feature of Internet marketing.

**Podcasts**

Individuals and organisations post online media (audio and video) which can be viewed in the appropriate players including the iPod which first sparked the growth in this technique.

**Web analytics**

Techniques used to assess and improve the contribution of e-marketing to a business, including reviewing traffic volume, referrals, clickstreams, online reach data, customer satisfaction surveys, leads and sales.

**Personalisation**

Delivering individualised content through web pages or e-mail.

**Sense and respond communications**

Customer behaviour is monitored at an individual level and the marketer responds with communications tailored to the individual's need.

Another example of personalisation is that achieved by business-to-business e-tailer RS Components (www.rswww.com). Every customer who accesses their system is profiled according to their area of product interest and information describing their role in the buying unit. When they next visit the site information will be displayed relevant to their product interest, for example office products and promotions if this is what was selected. This is an example of what is known as **mass customisation** where generic customer information is supplied for particular segments, i.e. the information is not unique to individuals, but is relevant to those with a common interest. Personalisation and mass customisation concepts are explored further in Chapter 6.

**Mass customisation**
Delivering customised content to groups of users through web pages or e-mail.

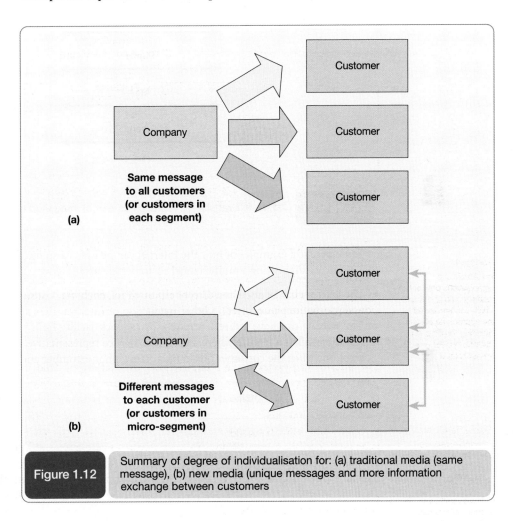

**Figure 1.12**  Summary of degree of individualisation for: (a) traditional media (same message), (b) new media (unique messages and more information exchange between customers

## 4 Integration

**Outbound Internet-based communications**
The website and e-mail marketing are used to send personalised communications to customers.

**Inbound Internet-based communications**
Customers enquire through web-based forms and e-mail.

The Internet provides further scope for integrated marketing communications. Figure 1.13 shows the role of the Internet in multichannel marketing. When assessing the marketing effectiveness of a website, the role of the Internet in communicating with customers and other partners can best be considered from two perspectives. First, there is **outbound Internet-based communications** from *organisation to customer*. We need to ask how does the Internet complement other channels in communicating the proposition for the company's products and services to new and existing customers with a view to generating new leads and retaining existing customers? Second, **inbound Internet-based communications** from *customer to organisation*: how can the Internet complement other channels to deliver customer service to these customers? Many companies have now integrated e-mail response and website callback into their existing call centre or customer service operation.

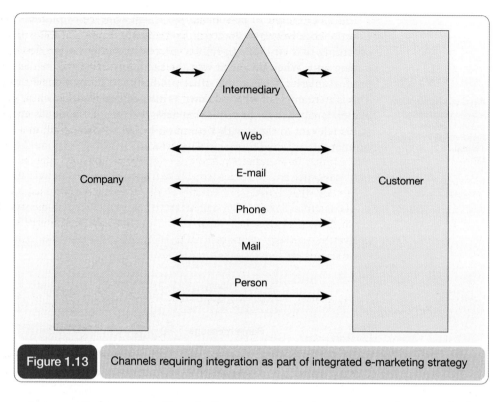

Figure 1.13   Channels requiring integration as part of integrated e-marketing strategy

Some practical examples of how the Internet can be used as an integrated communications tool as part of supporting a multichannel customer journey (Figure 1.14) are the following:

- The Internet can be used as a direct-response tool, enabling customers to respond to offers and promotions publicised in other media.
- The website can have a direct response or callback facility built into it. The Automobile Association has a feature where a customer service representative will contact a customer by phone when the customer fills in their name, phone number and a suitable time to ring.

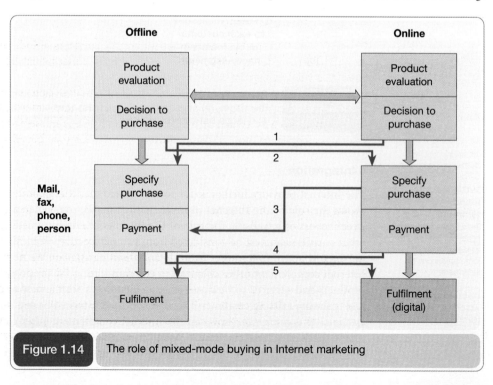

Figure 1.14   The role of mixed-mode buying in Internet marketing

- The Internet can be used to support the buying decision even if the purchase does not occur via the website. For example, Dell has a prominent web-specific phone number on their website that encourages customers to ring a representative in the call centre to place their order. This has the benefits that Dell is less likely to lose the business of customers who are anxious about the security of online ordering and Dell can track sales that result partly from the website according to the number of callers on this line. Considering how a customer changes from one channel to another during the buying process, this is referred to as **mixed-mode buying**. It is a key aspect of devising online marketing communications since the customer should be supported in changing from one channel to another.
- Customer information delivered on the website must be integrated with other databases of customer and order information, such as those accessed via staff in the call centre to provide what Seybold (1999) calls a '360 degree view of the customer'.
- The Internet can be used to support customer service. For example easyJet (www.easyjet.com), which receives over half of its orders electronically, encourages users to check a list of frequently asked questions (FAQ) compiled from previous customer enquiries before contacting customer support by phone.

**Mixed-mode buying**
The process by which a customer changes between online and offline channels during the buying process.

---

**Activity 1.5** | **Integrating online and offline communications**

**Purpose**

To highlight differences in marketing communications introduced through the use of the Internet as a channel and the need to integrate these communications with existing channels.

**Activity**

List communications between a PC vendor and a home customer over the lifetime of a product such as a PC. Include communications using both the Internet and traditional media. Refer to channel-swapping alternatives in the buying decision in Figure 1.13 to develop your answer.

---

## 5 Industry restructuring

**Disintermediation**
The removal of intermediaries such as distributors or brokers that formerly linked a company to its customers.

**Disintermediation** and **reintermediation** are key concepts of industry restructuring that should be considered by any company developing an e-marketing strategy and are explored in more detail in Chapters 2, 4 and 5.

For the marketer defining their company's communications strategy it becomes very important to consider the company's representation on these intermediary sites by answering questions such as 'Which intermediaries should we be represented on?' and 'How do our offerings compare to those of competitors in terms of features, benefits and price?'

## 6 Independence of location

**Reintermediation**
The creation of new intermediaries between customers and suppliers providing services such as supplier search and product evaluation.

Electronic media also introduce the possibility of increasing the reach of company communications to the global market. This gives opportunities to sell into international markets which may not have been previously possible. The Internet makes it possible to sell to a country without a local sales or customer service force (although this may still be necessary for some products). In such situations and with the restructuring in conjunction with disintermediation and reintermediation, strategists also need to carefully consider channel conflicts that may arise. If a customer is buying direct from a company in another country rather than via the agent, this will marginalise the business of the local agent who may want some recompense for sales efforts or may look for a partnership with competitors.

Kiani (1998) has presented a useful perspective to differences between the old and new media, which are shown as a summary to this section in Table 1.5.

| Table 1.5 | An interpretation of the differences between the old and digital media |
| --- | --- |

| Old media | Digital media | Comment |
| --- | --- | --- |
| One-to-many communication model | One-to-one or many-to-many communication model | Hoffman and Novak (1996) state that theoretically the Internet is a many-to-many medium, but for company-to-customer organisation(s) communications it is best considered as one-to-one or one-to-many |
| Mass-marketing push model | Individualised marketing or mass customisation. Pull model for web marketing | Personalisation possible because of technology to monitor preferences and tailor content (Deighton, 1996). Pull occurs through targeted search engine marketing which tends to have lower wastage. Personalised e-mails used for push communications |
| Monologue | Dialogue | Indicates the interactive nature of the World Wide Web, with the facility for feedback and participation through social networks and forums. |
| Branding | Communication | Increased involvement of customer in defining brand characteristics. Opportunities for adding value to brand |
| Supply-side thinking | Demand-side thinking | Customer pull becomes more important |
| Customer as a target | Customer as a partner | Customer has more input into products and services required, particularly through surveys and product ratings |
| Segmentation | Communities | Aggregations of like-minded consumers rather than arbitrarily defined target segments |

*Source*: After Kiani (1998)

| Mini Case Study 1.4 | Travel Republic achieves growth through taking advantage of benefits of digital marketing |
| --- | --- |

Online travel agent Travel Republic topped The Sunday Times Virgin Fast Track 100 list just four years after the company was launched. The company was the UK's fastest growing privately owned company boasting 284.23% annual sales growth. The Kingston-upon-Thames based business was set up in 2003 and is the brainchild of three university friends – Paul Furner, managing director, Chris Waite, IT director and Kane Pirie, finance and operations director.

Since its launch, TravelRepublic.co.uk's sales have increased from £2.8 million to £108 million, with the business on track for turnover of more than £200 million in the current financial year. The company employs more than 150 staff. TravelRepublic.co.uk appears in the IMRG-Hitwise Hot Shops List which ranks the UK's top 50 most popular internet retailers, across all sectors (ranked by number of web visitors). In the online travel agency sector TravelRepublic.co.uk is more popular than the likes of Opodo and ebookers.com. Only Expedia.co.uk and lastminute.com rank higher.

A major reason for the growth of Travel Republic is that it has taken advantage of the 'pull' effect of web communications. Through using sponsored links in search networks such as Google AdWords it has been able to target its offering precisely to an online audience looking for a competitive price on a holiday or a flight to a particular destination. Of course, this has to be backed up by a strong proposition, an easy to use, high performance website and trust in the brand indicated by user reviews and holiday guarantees (Figure 1.15).

| Figure 1.15 | Travel Republic (www.travelrepublic.co.uk) |

TravelRepublic.co.uk caters for a broad range of customers including families, couples and groups. The website offers charter, low-cost and scheduled airlines, powerful rate shopping technology for hotel rooms and apartments, plus hotel reviews and resort guides written by its customers.

Customers can save up to 50% on the price of a comparable package holiday purchased online or on the high street. TravelRepublic.co.uk works with over 100 different flight operators and offers flights to more than 200 destinations. The website also offers over 30,000 discounted hotels, apartments and villas plus a wide range of other services such as taxi transfers, airport parking and car hire. The website gives customers complete flexibility with flights, hotels and durations.

Paul Furner, managing director of TravelRepublic.co.uk explains:

*Chris, Kane and I met at university but then followed very different careers – Chris in software development, Kane in corporate finance/private equity and me in software quality assurance. These differing backgrounds, all outside of the travel industry, have allowed us to take a fresh new look at the sector and become one of its leading innovators.*

*However, equally important has been our commitment, from the outset, to deliver gold standard customer service to our customers. At a time when it is often said that there is no loyalty on the web we would beg to differ. Our levels of repeat and recommended business suggest that we have a real affinity with our customers which we plan to build upon in the coming months.*

*Source*: Travel Republic press release, 2 December 2007, Travel Republic is the UK's Fastest Growing Private Company, http://www.travelrepublic.co.uk/help/pressReplace_003.aspx

In terms of deploying campaigns, there are other key differences and benefits of digital media which we can illustrate through the Google AdWords (http://adwords.google.com) paid search advertising programme or similar programmes from Microsoft, Yahoo! and Ask which we will reference in more detail in Chapter 9:

- *Accountability*. Digital media are potentially more accountable through the use of measurement systems known collectively as **web analytics**. Google provides a free tool known as Google Analytics (www.google.com/analytics) to enable its advertisers to test the value generated from its ads.
- *Testing*. Potentially, testing becomes more straightforward at a lower cost with the option to trial alternative creative executions, messaging or offers. Google offers another free tool – the Website Optimiser – to test alternative landing pages.
- *Flexibility*. Campaigns can be more flexible with the capability to change, copy or offers during a campaign. Alternative ads can be served within Google to evaluate which works best. Google AdWords also offers dayparting where ads can be displayed at different times of the day.
- *Micro-targeting*. Alternative messages can be delivered for different audiences according to what they are searching for. Potentially a company can show a different advert in Google AdWords for each term searched on.
- *Cost-control*. Costs can be controlled for each group of search terms entered by customers through the search engine, managed collectively, and bids made can be increased or decreased with the aid of software.

## Key challenges of digital communications

It is sometimes suggested by some suppliers of digital media that they are 'quick, cheap and easy' to deploy. This is a great misconception since there are many challenges which need to be overcome when managing digital campaigns. Again referring to a Google AdWords campaign as an example, these include:

- *Complexity*. To enable the benefits we have mentioned above – such as personalisation, testing and dynamic variation in ads through time – time has to go into configuring the campaign although the search engines provide defaults to enable easy setup. This requires specialist expertise either in-house or at an agency to manage the campaign.
- *Responding to competitors*. Since competitors can also change their approach readily, more resource has to be used to monitor competitor activity. Automated tools known as bid management tools can assist with this – they will automatically check amounts competitors are paying and then adjust them according to pre-defined rules.
- *Responding to changes in technology*. Google and the other ad-serving companies innovate to offer better capabilities for their customers. This means that staff managing campaigns need training to keep up-to-date. Google offers 'Adwords Qualified Professionals' so that companies can be certain of a minimum skills level.
- *Cost*. Although costs can be readily controlled, in competitive categories, the costs can be high, exceeding €10 per click.
- *Attention*. While online paid search ads are highly targeted and there is arguably little wastage, not everyone will view paid adverts, indeed there is a phenomenon known as 'banner blindness' where web users ignore online ads (see Chapter 9 for more details). Engaging with the audience with advertising is also a problem in social networks and other publisher sites which can lead to a very low rate of people clicking on ads.

### Customer engagement

This difficulty in gaining attention online on all types of sites has led to the emergence of the concept of **customer engagement** as a key challenge with which digital marketers are increasingly concerned. cScape (2008) describe customer engagement as:

*Repeated interactions that strengthen the emotional, psychological or physical investment a customer has in a brand.*

while for Haven (2007) customer engagement is:

*the level of involvement, interaction, intimacy, and influence an individual has with a brand over time.*

Arguably, the biggest difference in communications introduced by the growth of digital media and the web is the capability, or many would say necessity, to include customer's conversations as an integral part of communications. Today, proactively managing consumer participation which occurs through social networks such as Bebo, MySpace and Facebook, video postings and comments on YouTube and myriad blogs and forums is essential since, when a positive sentiment is expressed by a real person independent from a company this confers credibility on the company.

Equally, there are negative sentiments or comments made by consumers on the web that need to be managed. For example, on one site (www.haveyoursay.com) a purchaser of a car was highly critical about a make of car and the comments appeared near the top of the Google search results page when someone searched for the brand, yet for several years the manufacturer did nothing to manage this.

This was well expressed in the ground-breaking *Cluetrain Manifesto* (www.cluetrain.net, Levine *et al.*, 2000) which will remain equally or even more valid as we approach 2020. The Cluetrain Manifesto suggests that marketers shouldn't conceive the Internet as an impassive network of hardware and software, but as a means of creating global conversations within markets – a new dynamic dialogue. These conversations take the form of discussion of the merits of products or brands in social networks or forums, blog comments or ratings on retailer sites. To illustrate the danger of ignoring this potential for dialogue and participation, the authors say:

*Conversations among human beings sound human. They are conducted in a human voice.*

*Most corporations, on the other hand, only know how to talk in the soothing, humorless monotone of the mission statement, marketing brochure, and your-call-is-important-to-us busy signal. Same old tone, same old lies. No wonder networked markets have no respect for companies unable or unwilling to speak as they do.*

*Corporate firewalls have kept smart employees in and smart markets out. It's going to cause real pain to tear those walls down. But the result will be a new kind of conversation. And it will be the most exciting conversation business has ever engaged in.*

To conclude this chapter, read Case study 1 for the background on the success factors which have helped build one of the biggest online brands.

| Case Study 1 | eBay thrives in the global marketplace |
|---|---|

## Context

It's hard to believe that one of the most well-known dot-coms has now celebrated its tenth birthday. Pierre Omidyar, a 28-year-old French-born software engineer living in California, coded the site while working for another company, eventually launching the site for business on Monday, 4 September 1995 with the more direct name 'Auction Web'. Legend reports that the site attracted no visitors in its first 24 hours. The site became eBay in 1997.

## Mission

eBay describes their purpose as to 'pioneer new communities around the world built on commerce, sustained by trust, and inspired by opportunity'.

At the time of writing eBay comprises three major businesses:

1 *The eBay Marketplaces (approximately 70% of net revenues in 2007)*. The mission for the core eBay business is to 'create the world's online marketplace'.The marketplace platforms include an average of 100 million products for sale each day! eBay's SEC filing notes some of the success factors for this business for which eBay seeks to manage the functionality, safety, ease-of-use and reliability of the trading platform.

2 *PayPal (approximately 25% of net revenues in 2007)*. The mission is to 'create the new global standard for online payments'. This company was acquired in 2003.

3 *Skype Internet telephony (5% of net revenues in 2007)*. This company was acquired in 2005. eBay has suffered an 'impairment charge' from valuing the company too highly, but more recently it has started to provide the service for MySpace users.

Advertising and other net revenues represented 4% of total net revenues during 2007.

This case focuses on the best known eBay business, the eBay Marketplace.

## Revenue model

The vast majority of eBay's revenue is for the listing and commission on completed sales. For PayPal purchases an additional commission fee is charged. The margin on each transaction is phenomenal since once the infrastructure is built, incremental costs on each transaction are tiny – all eBay is doing is transmitting bits and bytes between buyers and sellers.

Advertising and other non-transaction net revenues represent a relatively small proportion of total net revenues and the strategy is that this should remain the case. Advertising and other net revenues totalled $94.3 million in 2004 (just 3% of net revenue).

## Proposition

The eBay marketplace is well known for its core service which enables sellers to list items for sale on an auction or fixed-price basis giving buyers the opportunity to bid for and purchase items of interest. At the end of 2007, there were over 532,000 online storefronts established by users in locations around the world.

Software tools are provided, particularly for frequent traders, including Turbo Lister, Seller's Assistant, Selling Manager and Selling Manager Pro, which help automate the selling process, the Shipping Calculator, Reporting tools, etc. Today over 60% of listings are facilitated by software, showing the value of automating posting for frequent trading.

Fraud is a significant risk factor for eBay. BBC (2005) reported that around 1 in 10,000 transactions within the UK were fraudulent. 0.0001% is a small percentage, but scaling this up across the number of transactions makes a significant volume.

eBay has developed 'Trust and Safety Programs' which are particularly important to reassure customers since online services are prone to fraud. For example, the eBay feedback forum can help establish credentials of sellers and buyers. Every registered user has a feedback profile that may contain compliments, criticisms and/or other comments by users who have conducted business with that user. The Feedback Forum requires feedback to be related to specific transactions. There is also a Safe Harbor data protection method and a standard purchase protection system.

According to the SEC filing, eBay summarises the core messages to define its proposition as follows:

*For buyers*:

● selection
● value
● convenience
● entertainment.

In 2007, as part of the social media revolution eBay introduced Neighbourhoods (http://neighborhoods.ebay.com) where groups can discuss brands and products they have a high involvement with.

*For sellers*:

● access to broad markets
● cost effective marketing and distribution
● access to large buyer base
● good conversion rates.

In January 2008, eBay announced significant changes to its Marketplaces business in three major areas: fee structure, seller incentives and standards, and feedback. These changes have been controversial with some sellers, but are aimed at improving the quality of experience. Detailed Seller Ratings (DSRs) enable sellers to be reviewed in four areas: (1) item as described, (2) communication, (3) delivery time, and (4) postage and packaging charges. This is part of a move to help increase conversion rate by increasing positive shopping experiences, for example by including more accurate descriptions with better pictures and avoiding excessive shipping charges. Powersellers with positive DSRs will be featured more favourably in the search results pages and will gain additional discounts.

## Competition

Although there are now few direct competitors of online auction services in many countries, there are many indirect competitors. SEC (2008) describes competing channels as including online and offline retailers, distributors, liquidators, import and export companies, auctioneers, catalogue and mail-order companies, classifieds, directories, search engines, products of search engines, virtually all online and offline commerce participants (consumer-to-consumer, business-to-consumer and business-to-business) and online and offline shopping channels and networks.

BBC (2005) reports that eBay is not complacent about competition. It has already pulled out of Japan due to competition from Yahoo! and within Asia and China is also facing tough competition by Yahoo! which has a portal with a broader range of services more likely to attract subscribers.

Before the advent of online auctions, competitors in the collectibles space included antique shops, car boot sales and charity shops. Anecdotal evidence suggests that all of these are now suffering at the hands of eBay. Some have taken the attitude of 'if you can't beat 'em, join 'em'. Many smaller traders who have previously run antique or car boot sales are now eBayers. Even charities such as Oxfam now have an eBay service where they sell high-value items contributed by donors. Other retailers such as Vodafone have used eBay as a means to distribute certain products within their range.

## Objectives and strategy

The overall eBay aims are to increase the gross merchandise volume and net revenues from the eBay Marketplace. More detailed objectives are defined to achieve these aims, with strategies focusing on:

1 *Acquisition* – increasing the number of newly registered users on the eBay Marketplace.
2 *Activation* – increasing the number of registered users that become active bidders, buyers or sellers on the eBay Marketplace.
3 *Activity* – increasing the volume and value of transactions that are conducted by each active user on the eBay Marketplace. eBay had approximately 83 million active users at the end of 2007, compared to approximately 82 million at the end of 2006. An active user is defined as any user who bid on, bought or listed an item during the most recent 12-month period.

The focus on each of these three areas will vary according to strategic priorities in particular local markets.

eBay Marketplace growth is also driven by defining approaches to improve performance in these areas. First, category growth is achieved by increasing the number and size of categories within the marketplace, for example: Antiques, Art, Books and Business & Industrial. Second, formats for interaction. The traditional format is auction listings, but it has been refined now to include the 'Buy-It-Now' fixed price format. Another format is the 'Dutch Auction' format, where a seller can sell multiple identical items to the highest bidders. eBay Stores was developed to enable sellers with a wider range of products to showcase their products in a more traditional retail format. eBay say they are constantly exploring new formats, often through acquisition of other companies, for example through the acquisition in 2004 of mobile.de in Germany and Marktplaats.nl in the Netherlands, as well as investment in craigslist, the US-based classified ad format. Another acquisition is Rent.com, which enables expansion into the online housing and apartment rental category. In 2007, eBay acquired StubHub, an online ticket marketplace, and it also owns comparison marketplace Shopping.com. Finally Marketplace growth is achieved through delivering specific sites localised for different geographies as follows. You can see there is still potential for greater localisation, for example in parts of Scandinavia, Eastern Europe and Asia.

Localised eBay marketplaces:

| | | |
|---|---|---|
| • Australia | • India | • South Korea |
| • Austria | • Ireland | • Spain |
| • Belgium | • Italy | • Sweden |
| • Canada | • Malaysia | • Switzerland |
| • China | • The Netherlands | • Taiwan |
| • France | • New Zealand | • United Kingdom |
| • Germany | • The Philippines | • United States |
| • Hong Kong | • Singapore | |

In its SEC filing, success factors eBay believes are important to enable it to compete in its market include:

- ability to attract buyers and sellers;
- volume of transactions and price and selection of goods;
- customer service;
- brand recognition.

eBay stresses the importance of developing its 'Value-Added Tools and Services' which are 'pre-trade' and 'post-trade' tools and services to enhance the user experience and to make trading faster, easier and safer. It also notes that in the context of its competitors, other factors it believes are important are:

- community cohesion, interaction and size;
- system reliability;
- reliability of delivery and payment;
- website convenience and accessibility;
- level of service fees;
- quality of search tools.

This implies that eBay believes it has optimised these factors, but its competitors still have opportunities for improving performance in these areas which will make the market more competitive.

| | Year ended December 31, 2005 | Change from 2005 to 2006 | Year ended December 31, 2006 | Change from 2006 to 2007 | Year ended December 31, 2007 |
|---|---|---|---|---|---|
| | | (in thousands, except per cent changes) | | | |
| **Net revenues by type:** | | | | | |
| Net transaction revenues | | | | | |
| Marketplaces | $ 3,402,301 | 24% | $ 4,203,340 | 22% | $ 5,135,363 |
| Payments | 1,001,915 | 40% | 1,401,824 | 31% | 1,838,539 |
| Communications | 24,809 | 677% | 192,756 | 95% | 376,715 |
| Total net transaction revenues | 4,429,025 | 31% | 5,797,920 | 27% | 7,350,617 |
| Advertising and other net revenues | 123,376 | 39% | 171,821 | 87% | 321,712 |
| Total net revenues | $ 4,552,401 | 31% | $ 5,969,741 | 29% | $ 7,672,329 |
| **Net revenues by segment:** | | | | | |
| Marketplaces | $ 3,499,137 | 24% | $ 4,334,290 | 24% | $ 5,363,891 |
| Payments | 1,028,455 | 40% | 1,440,530 | 34% | 1,926,616 |
| Communications | 24,809 | 686% | 194,921 | 96% | 381,822 |
| Total net revenues | $ 4,552,401 | 31% | $ 5,969,741 | 29% | $ 7,672,329 |
| **Net revenues by geography:** | | | | | |
| US | $ 2,471,273 | 26% | $ 3,108,986 | 20% | $ 3,742,670 |
| International | 2,081,128 | 37% | 2,860,755 | 37% | 3,929,659 |
| Total net revenues | $ 4,552,401 | 31% | $ 5,969,741 | 29% | $ 7,672,329 |

| | Year ended December 31, | | |
|---|---|---|---|
| | **2005** | **2006** | **2007** |
| | | (in millions) | |
| **Supplemental operating data:** | | | |
| *Marketplaces Segment(1):* | | | |
| Active users(2) | 71.8 | 81.8 | 83.2 |
| Number of listings(3) | 1,876.8 | 2,365.3 | 2,340.5 |
| Gross merchandise volume(4) | $ 44,299 | $ 52,474 | $ 59,353 |
| *Payments Segment:* | | | |
| Active registered accounts(5) | 41.3 | 49.4 | 57.3 |
| Net total payment volume(6) | $ 26,066 | $ 35,800 | $ 47,470 |
| *Communications Segment:* | | | |
| Registered users(7) | 74.7 | 171.2 | 276.3 |

Notes on supplemental operating data.
1   Rent.com, Shopping.com and our classified websites are not included in these metrics.
2   All users, excluding users of Half.com, StubHub and Internet Auction Co., our Korean subsidiary, who bid on, bought, or listed an item within the previous 12-month period. Users may register more than once and as a result may have more than one account.
3   Listings on eBay Marketplaces trading platforms during the period, regardless of whether the listing subsequently closed successfully.
4   Total value of all successfully closed items between users on eBay Marketplaces trading platforms during the period, regardless of whether the buyer and seller actually consummated the transaction.
5   All registered accounts that successfully sent or received at least one payment or payment reversal through the PayPal system within the previous 12-month period.
6   Total dollar volume of payments, net of payment reversals, successfully completed through the PayPal system during the period, excluding the payment gateway business.
7   Cumulative number of unique user accounts, which includes users who may have registered via non-Skype based websites, as of the end of the period. Users may register more than once and as a result may have more than one account.

*Sources*: BBC (2005), SEC (2008)

## Risk management

The SEC filing lists the risks and challenges of conducting business internationally as follows:

- regulatory requirements, including regulation of auctioneering, professional selling, distance selling, banking and money transmitting;
- legal uncertainty regarding liability for the listings and other content provided by users, including uncertainty as a result of less Internet-friendly legal systems, unique local laws and lack of clear precedent or applicable law;
- difficulties in integrating with local payment providers, including banks, credit and debit card associations, and electronic fund transfer systems;
- differing levels of retail distribution, shipping and communications infrastructures;
- different employee/employer relationships and the existence of workers' councils and labour unions;
- difficulties in staffing and managing foreign operations;
- longer payment cycles, different accounting practices and greater problems in collecting accounts receivable;
- potentially adverse tax consequences, including local taxation of fees or of transactions on websites;
- higher telecommunications and Internet service provider costs;
- strong local competitors;
- different and more stringent consumer protection, data protection and other laws;
- cultural ambivalence towards, or non-acceptance of, online trading;
- seasonal reductions in business activity;
- expenses associated with localising products, including offering customers the ability to transact business in the local currency;
- laws and business practices that favour local competitors or prohibit foreign ownership of certain businesses;
- profit repatriation restrictions, foreign currency exchange restrictions and exchange rate fluctuations;
- volatility in a specific country's or region's political or economic conditions;
- differing intellectual property laws and taxation laws.

## Results

eBay's community of confirmed registered users has grown from around two million at the end of 1998 to more than 94 million at the end of 2003 and to more than 135 million at 31 December 2004. It is also useful to identify active users who contribute revenue to the business as a buyer or seller. eBay had 56 million active users at the end of 2004 who they define as any user who has bid, bought, or listed an item during a prior 12-month period.

Financial results are presented in the table on page 42.

### Question

Assess how the characteristics of the digital media and the Internet, together with strategic decisions taken by its management team, have supported eBay's continued growth.

---

### Summary

1. Internet marketing refers to the use of Internet technologies, combined with traditional media, to achieve marketing objectives. E-marketing and digital marketing have a broader perspective and imply the use of other technologies, such as databases, and approaches, such as customer relationship management (e-CRM).

2. A customer-centric approach to digital marketing considers the needs of a range of customers using techniques such as persona and customer scenarios (Chapter 2) to understand customer needs in a multichannel buying process. Tailoring to individual customers may be practical using personalisation techniques.

3. Electronic commerce refers to both electronically mediated financial and informational transactions.

4. Sell-side e-commerce involves all electronic business transactions between an organisation and its customers, while buy-side e-commerce involves transactions between an organisation and its suppliers.

5. 'Electronic business' is a broader term referring to how technology can benefit all internal business processes and interactions with third parties. This includes buy-side and sell-side e-commerce and the internal value chain.

6. E-commerce transactions include business-to-business (B2B), business-to-consumer (B2C), consumer-to-consumer (C2C) and consumer-to-business (C2B) transactions.

7. The Internet is used to develop existing markets through enabling an additional communications and/or sales channel with potential customers. It can be used to develop new international markets with a reduced need for new sales offices and agents. Companies can provide new services and possibly products using the Internet.

8. The Internet can support the full range of marketing functions and in doing so can help reduce costs, facilitate communication within and between organisations and improve customer service.

9. Interaction with customers, suppliers and distributors occurs across the Internet. The web and e-mail are particularly powerful if they can be used to create *relevant, personalised communications*. These communications are also interactive. If access is restricted to favoured third parties this is known as an *extranet*. If Internet technologies are used to facilitate internal company communications this is known as an *intranet* – a private company internet.

10. The marketing benefits the Internet confers are advantageous both to the large corporation and to the small or medium-sized enterprise. These include:
    - a new medium for advertising and PR;
    - a new channel for distributing products;
    - opportunities for expansion into new markets;
    - new ways of enhancing customer service;
    - new ways of reducing costs by reducing the number of staff in order fulfilment.

## Exercises

### Self-assessment exercises

1. Which measures can companies use to assess the significance of the Internet to their organisation?

2. Why did companies only start to use the Internet widely for marketing in the 1990s, given that it had been in existence for over 30 years?

3. Distinguish between Internet marketing and e-marketing.

4. Explain what is meant by electronic commerce and electronic business. How do they relate to the marketing function?

5. What are the main differences and similarities between the Internet, intranets and extranets?

6. Summarise the differences between the Internet and traditional media using the 6 Is.

7. How is the Internet used to develop new markets and penetrate existing markets? What types of new products can be delivered by the Internet?

### Essay and discussion questions

1. The Internet is primarily thought of as a means of advertising and selling products. What are the opportunities for use of the Internet in other marketing functions?

2. 'The World Wide Web represents a *pull* medium for marketing rather than a *push* medium.' Discuss.

3. You are a newly installed marketing manager in a company selling products in the business-to-business sector. Currently, the company has only a limited website containing electronic versions of its brochures. You want to convince the directors of the benefits of investing in the website to provide more benefits to the company. How would you present your case?

4. Explain the main benefits that a company selling fast-moving consumer goods could derive by creating a website.

## Examination questions

1. Contrast electronic commerce to electronic business.

2. Internet technology is used by companies in three main contexts. Distinguish between the following types and explain their significance to marketers.
   (a) intranet;
   (b) extranet;
   (c) Internet.

3. An Internet marketing manager must seek to control and accommodate all the main methods by which consumers may visit a company website. Describe these methods.

4. Imagine you are explaining the difference between the World Wide Web and the Internet to a marketing manager. How would you explain these two terms?

5. What is the relevance of 'conversion marketing' to the Internet?

6. Explain how the Internet can be used to increase market penetration in existing markets and develop new markets.

## References

Ansoff, H. (1957) Strategies for diversification, *Harvard Business Review*, September–October, 113–24.

BBC (2005) eBay's 10-year rise to world fame. Robert Plummer story from BBC News, 2 September. http://news.bbc.co.uk/go/pr/fr/-/1/hi/business/4207510.stm. Published: 2005/09/02.

Boyd, D. and Ellison, N. (2007) Social network sites: definition, history and scholarship, *Journal of Computer-Mediated Communication*, 13(1), 210–230.

*Business Week* (2005) The Power of Us. Mass collaboration on the Internet is shaking up business. Feature, June 20, 2005. http://www.businessweek.com/magazine/content/05_25/63938601.htm.

Chaffey, D. (2006) *E-Business and E-Commerce Management*, 3rd edn. Financial Times/Prentice Hall, Harlow.

Chaffey, D. and Smith, P.R. (2008) *Emarketing Excellence, Planning and optimising your digital marketing*, 3rd edn. Butterworth-Heinemann, Oxford. Copyright Elsevier.

cScape (2008) Second Annual Online Customer Engagement Report 2008. Produced by EConsultancy in association with cScape. Published online at www.e-consultancy.com.

Deighton, J. (1996) The future of interactive marketing, *Harvard Business Review*, November–December, 151–62.

Dibb, S., Simkin, S., Pride, W. and Ferrell, O. (2001) *Marketing. Concepts and Strategies*, 4th European edn. Houghton Mifflin, New York. See Chapter 1, An overview of the marketing concept.

EConsultancy (2005) Managing an e-commerce team: integrating digital marketing into your organisation. Author: Dave Chaffey. Available from www.e-consultancy.com.

EConsultancy (2008) Managing Digital Channels Research Report. Author: Dave Chaffey. Available from www.e-consultancy.com.

EIAA (2005) European Advertising Association. European media research, October 2004. Research conducted by Millward Brown. Published at www.eiaa.net in 2005.

Geyskens, I., Gielens, K. and Dekimpe, M. (2002) The market valuation of internet channel additions, *Journal of Marketing*, Vol. 66 (April 2002), 102–119.

Haven, B. (2007) Marketing's new key metric: Engagement, 8 August, Forrester.

Hoffman, D.L. and Novak, T.P. (1996) Marketing in hypermedia computer-mediated environments: conceptual foundations, *Journal of Marketing*, 60 (July), 50–68.

Hoffman, D.L. and Novak, T.P. (1997) A new marketing paradigm for electronic commerce. *The Information Society*, Special issue on electronic commerce, 13 (January–March), 43–54.

Jenkinson, A. and Sain, B. (2001) *Getting words clear – Marketing needs a clear and consistent terminology*. White paper available from Centre for Integrated Marketing, (www.integratedmarketing.org.uk).

Kiani, G. (1998) Marketing opportunities in the digital world, *Internet Research: Electronic Networking Applications and Policy*, 8(2), 185–94.

Levine, R., Locke, C., Searls, D. and Weinberger, D. (2000) *The Cluetrain Manifesto*. Perseus Books, Cambridge, MA.

McDonald, M. and Wilson, H. (1999) *E-Marketing: Improving Marketing Effectiveness in a Digital World*. Financial Times/Prentice Hall, Harlow.

O'Reilly, T. (2005) What Is Web 2? Design Patterns and Business Models for the Next Generation of Software. Web article, 30 September. O'Reilly Publishing, Sebastopol, CA.

SEC (2008) United States Securities and Exchange Commission submission Form 10-K. eBay submission for the fiscal year ended December 31, 2007.

Seybold, P. (1999) *Customers.com*. Century Business Books, Random House, London.

Spivack (2007) Nova Spivack blog posting. How the WebOS Evolves? 9 February 2007, http://novaspivack.typepad.com/nova_spivacks_weblog/2007/02/steps_towards_a.html.

Waterman, R.H., Peters, T.J. and Phillips, J.R. (1980) Structure is not organisation. *McKinsey Quarterly in-house journal*. McKinsey & Co., New York.

## Further reading

Deighton, J. (1996) The future of interactive marketing, *Harvard Business Review*, November–December, 151–62. One of the earliest articles to elucidate the significance of the Internet for marketers. Readable.

Hoffman, D.L. and Novak, T.P. (1997) A new marketing paradigm for electronic commerce, *The Information Society*, Special issue on electronic commerce, 13 (Jan.–Mar.), 43–54. This was the seminal paper on Internet marketing when it was published, and is still essential reading for its discussion of concepts. Available online at Vanderbilt University (http://ecommerce.vanderbilt.edu/papers.html).

Smith, P.R. and Chaffey, D. (2005) *E-Marketing Excellence: at the Heart of E-Business*, 2nd edn. Butterworth-Heinemann, Oxford. Chapter 1 gives more details on the benefits of Internet marketing.

**Web links**

Web links

Leading portals and blogs covering digital marketing developments

- **ClickZ Experts** (www.clickz.com/experts). An excellent collection of articles on online marketing communications. US-focused.
- **ClickZ Stats** (www.clickz.com/stats). The definitive source of news on Internet developments, and reports on company and consumer adoption of the Internet and characteristics in Europe and worldwide. A searchable digest of most analyst reports.
- **DaveChaffey.com** (www.davechaffey.com/Internet-Marketing, case dependent). A blog containing updates and articles on all aspects of digital marketing structured according to the chapters in this *Internet Marketing* book.
- **Direct Marketing Association UK** (www.dma.org.uk). Source of up-to-date data protection advice and how-to guides about online direct marketing.
- **EConsultancy.com** (www.e-consultancy.com). UK-focused portal with extensive supplier directory, best-practice white papers and forum.
- **eMarketer** (www.emarketer.com). Includes reports on media spend based on compilations of other analysts. Fee-based service.
- **iMediaConnection** (www.imediaconnection.com). Articles covering best practice in digital media channels.
- **Interactive Advertising Bureau** (www.iab.net). Best practice on interactive advertising. See also www.iabuk.net.
- **The Interactive Media in Retail** (www.imrg.org). Trade body for e-retailers reporting on growth and practice within UK and European e-commerce.
- **Journal of Computer Mediated Communications** (http://www.blackwell-synergy.com/loi/jcmc). A free online peer-reviewed journal describing developments in interactive communications.
- **Marketing Sherpa** (www.marketingsherpa.com). Case studies and news about online marketing.
- **Marketing Vox** (www.marketingvox.com). Covers news and developments in digital media channels.

Print trade publications with online resources

- **New Media Age** (www.newmediazero.com/nma). A weekly magazine reporting on the UK new media interest. Full content available online.
- **Revolution magazine** (www.revolutionmagazine.com). A monthly magazine on UK new media applications and approaches. Partial content available online.

# 2

# The Internet micro-environment

## Learning objectives

After reading this chapter, the reader should be able to:

- Identify the different elements of the Internet environment that impact on an organisation's Internet marketing strategy
- Complete an online marketplace analysis to assess customer, intermediary and competitor use of the Internet as part of strategy development
- Evaluate the relevance of changes in trading patterns and business models enabled by digital channels

## Questions for marketers

Key questions for marketing managers related to this chapter are:

- How do I complete a situation analysis as part of planning for digital marketing?
- How are the competitive forces and value chain changed by the Internet?
- How do I assess the demand for Internet services and customer behaviour?
- How do I compare our online marketing with that of competitors?
- What is the relevance of the new intermediaries?

## Links to other chapters

This chapter, together with the following one, provides a foundation for later chapters on Internet marketing strategy and implementation:

- Chapter 3, The Internet macro-environment, complements this chapter
- Chapter 4, Internet marketing strategy, explains how environment analysis is used as part of strategy development
- Chapter 5, The Internet and the marketing mix, considers the role of 'Place' in the online marketing mix

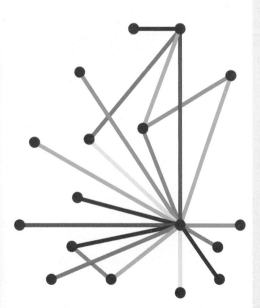

# Introduction

**Situation analysis**
Collection and review of information about an organisation's external environment and internal processes and resources in order to inform its strategies.

**Environmental scanning and analysis**
The process of continuously monitoring the environment and events and responding accordingly.

**Micro-environment**
Specific forces on an organisation generated by its stakeholders.

**Macro-environment**
Broader forces affecting all organisations in the marketplace including social, technological, economic, political and legal aspects.

All organisations operate within an environment that influences the performance of their business. Organisations that monitor, understand and respond appropriately to changes in the environment have the greatest opportunities to compete effectively in the competitive marketplace. Understanding an organisation's environment is a key part of **situation analysis** for the Internet marketing strategy development process introduced in Figure 1.8 and covered further in Chapter 4. There is also the need for a process to continually monitor the environment, which is often referred to as **environmental scanning**.

In the next two chapters we look specifically at how organisations can assess and understand changes to the digital environment they operate in. The need to 'sense and respond' is particularly important for online marketers because of the rapid changes in customer behaviour we introduced in the first chapter.

## Different environment components

The Internet introduces new facets to the environment that must be considered by marketers since strategy development is strongly influenced by considering the environment the business operates in. Figure 2.1 illustrates the key elements of a business's environment that will influence the organisation. Many authors such as Porter (1980) on corporate strategy or Kotler *et al.* (2001) on marketing strategy make the distinction between **micro-environment** and **macro-environment**. The micro-environment, sometimes known as '*the operating environment*', is the immediate marketplace of an organisation. For development of Internet marketing strategy, the most significant influences are arguably those of the micro-environment. This is shaped by the needs of customers and how services are provided to them through the competitors,

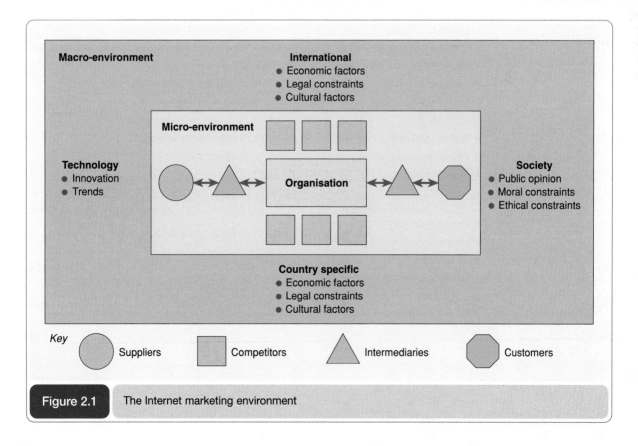

| Figure 2.1 | The Internet marketing environment |

intermediaries and upstream suppliers within the marketplace. The Internet and electronic communications have major implications for organisations and these must inform their Internet marketing strategy.

The macro-environment is sometimes known as '*the remote environment*'; its influences, which we study in Chapter 3, are broader being provided by local and international economic conditions and legislation together with acceptable business practices. The Internet and electronic communications have also introduced major changes to the macro-environment. Reviewing the relevance of technological innovations to an organisation is vital in providing opportunities for superior services to competitors and to changing the shape of the marketplace. Another significant macro-environment influence is legal – specific laws have been enacted to control online marketing and of course the influence of new technologies.

In this chapter, the impact of the Internet on the different elements of the micro-environment illustrated in Table 2.1 will be reviewed in turn. In the next chapter we then review the constraints and opportunities of the Internet macro-environment. For each of these elements we will highlight the issues that a marketing or Internet marketing manager needs to consider when developing e-marketing plans.

| Table 2.1 | Factors in the macro- and micro-environment of an organisation and Internet marketing related issues |
| --- | --- |

| **Micro-environment** | **Macro-environment** |
| --- | --- |
| *The marketplace* | *Social* |
| ● Online marketplace analysis | ● Privacy |
| ● Competitive forces | ● Acceptable usage |
| ● Value chain analysis | ● Internet culture |
| ● New channel structures | *Technological* |
| ● Location of trading | ● Selecting new technologies |
| ● Commercial arrangements for transactions | ● Coping with technological change |
| ● New business and revenue models | *Economic* |
| *The organisation* | ● The current and future economic situation |
| ● Adaptability to change | *Political, legal, ethical and taxation* |
| *Its customers* | ● Legal and tax constraints |
| ● Access levels to the Internet | ● Government incentives |
| ● Propensity to use and buy | ● Internet governance |
| ● Buyer behaviour | |
| *Its suppliers* | |
| ● Access levels to the Internet | |
| ● Propensity to use | |
| ● Integration with existing systems | |
| *Its competitors* | |
| ● Competitor capabilities | |
| *Intermediaries* | |
| ● New capabilities | |
| ● New intermediaries | |

## Internal organisation characteristics and capabilities

A review of the suitability of the characteristics and capabilities of an organisation to make increased use of electronic communications should occur as part of developing Internet marketing plans. This is sometimes known as the 'internal environment' of the organisation. The role of internal audits to assess the organisation as part of situation analysis for strategy development is illustrated by discussion of the 7 S framework in Chapter 1 (Table 1.3).

| Digital marketing in practice | The EConsultancy interview |
| --- | --- |

### Martin Newman, Head of E-commerce at fashion chain Ted Baker

#### Overview and main concepts covered

Martin Newman is the Head of E-commerce at fashion chain Ted Baker and is one of the few UK retailers to have been selling on the web since 1996. He has experience across all aspects of e-commerce, as well as retail, direct mail, web kiosks and mobile.

Martin explains the opportunities for retailers in the multichannel arena, as well as challenges such as integration and conversion tracking.

#### The interview

**Q: Can you quickly summarise 'where you are' as an online/multichannel retailer?**

*Martin Newman*: We are a multichannel retailer but not fully integrated yet, selling in-store and online.

We are currently developing web kiosks for testing in a few retail environments for deployment from September. This obviously has the potential to increase conversion rates from in-store footfall as, in some cases, the web kiosks will have a wider range to choose from and customers will also benefit from being able to buy a product even if it's out of stock in the store.

We are also introducing a gift catalogue that we will distribute through our stores, direct mail and electronically. This is just the beginning for us as we move our model towards true integration, enabling customers to enjoy the same experience through all channels and all touchpoints with the brand.

**Q: Do you think multichannel integration is being driven by e-commerce? Do all retailers need a transactional store online?**

*Martin Newman*: I believe that multichannel integration should be driven by e-commerce as e-commerce is a driver for both online and offline purchases. And therefore the customer experience has to correlate with this multichannel approach for example; buy online, pick up in-store, buy in-store, have delivered to your home, buy through direct mail, have delivered to your home or pick up in-store etc.

Also, those driving e-commerce tend to be closer to customer insight as they have the most detailed view of customer behaviour and therefore know how best to influence this through an integrated multichannel marketing communications approach.

We all know that multichannel customers can be up to ten times the value of a single channel customer, but you need to know the customer's behaviour in the first instance in order to understand how to influence it.

**Q: Do all retailers need a transactional store online?**

*Martin Newman*: It's only a few years ago that many people said footwear and apparel would never work online. This is now the fastest growing category in e-commerce.

So irrespective of the product, the answer for all must surely be yes. Smaller and larger retailers both benefit from extended reach, but the key driver is convenience, and customers want to be able to buy from you when and through whatever channel they choose.

There is also a huge amount of 'channel hopping' now among consumers, as well as 'brand switching', therefore if you don't enable them to buy from you online, they will simply buy from one of your competitors.

**Q: How important and difficult is it to measure the influence of offline and online channels in the product selection and purchase process?**

*Martin Newman*: It's vitally important to measure the influence of all channels on product selection and on the purchase process, as doing so successfully will enable you to increase sell-through, drive sales and margin, maximise customer retention and the lifetime value of customers, while continually driving down costs related to acquiring customers and writing-off stock.

Product selection should be driven by a number of factors . . .

- The role the e-commerce channel has in driving sales in-store.
- The website is a showcase for any business and therefore an opportunity to promote the whole range of products or services on offer.
- Effective merchandising will determine whether or not the business model lends itself to the 'long tail' as this is not necessarily the case in all sectors.
- There is a data capture opportunity through all channels – retail, e-commerce, direct mail, mobile, web kiosks – this can provide useful analysis when it comes to product selection across channels.
- Customer profiles vary by channel but it's still hugely important to have a single customer database with a single customer view, and this in turn should feed into the range planning process for each channel.

Integrated multichannel marketing communications will enable you to measure the value of one channel to the other in terms of its influence on the customer base.

**Q: What can you do to limit cannibalisation of other sales channels by online? Or do you really need to?**

*Martin Newman*: All channels complement each other. Forrester suggests that a purchase made in store that was first researched online has a 45% higher average transaction value. All channels should be used and viewed as an opportunity to also drive sales through all other channels.

**Q: What's the point of in-store web kiosks, and what are the challenges associated with introducing them?**

*Martin Newman*: As above, to maximise demand in-store when out of a size, style, model or colourway, or when the range is narrow due to limited shelf space. The challenges come down to:

- Building a robust business case for developing in the first place and justifying the ROI.
- Ensuring the kiosks are developed with a focus on durability.
- The ability to edit and update remotely without impinging on the retail team.

- Deciding where to put the kiosks in-store to maximise demand without detracting from the retail experience.
- Creating compelling content that drives sales.
- Ensuring the web store has sufficient stock to deal with the uplift in demand driven by web kiosks.

**Q: What's your opinion of the web as a customer retention tool?**

*Martin Newman*: The web lends itself well to customer retention due to the ability to understand customer behaviour better than in a bricks and mortar retail environment. It therefore creates the opportunity to target customers more cost effectively with highly relevant promotional offers.

Some retailers can track purchase behaviour but on the web you can also track the behaviour pre-purchase and when no purchase is made.

Personalisation and targeted content also enable you to increase the retention of customers, albeit as I pointed out previously, channel hopping is becoming more and more prevalent and therefore customer retention strategy needs to have a true multi-channel approach.

Segmentation by recency, frequency and value will help to sort out the wheat from the chaff, while also enabling you to target those customers who lend themselves best to being multichannel customers with the greatest lifetime value.

**Q: What are your opinions on using mobile to acquire or retain customers?**

*Martin Newman*: Mobile will undoubtedly be a key channel moving forward but the reality is, at present, that for most multichannel businesses, it's a more effective marketing communications channel than a customer recruitment tool or sales channel.

Source: http://www.e-consultancy.com/news-blog/newsletter/3379/ted-baker-s-martin-newman-on-multi--channel-retail.html

## Online marketplace analysis

Analysis of the online marketplace or 'marketspace' is a key part of developing a long-term Internet marketing plan or creating a shorter-term digital marketing campaign. Completing a marketplace analysis helps to define the main types of online presence that are part of a 'click ecosystem' which describes the consumer behaviour or flow of online visitors between search engines, media sites, other intermediaries to an organisation and its competitors. Prospects and customers in an online marketplace will naturally turn to search engines to find products, services, brands and entertainment. Search engines act as a distribution system which connects searchers to sites for different phrases. So, organisations need to analyse consumer use of key phrases entered from generic searches for products or services, more specific phrases and brand phrases incorporating their brand and competitor names (see Chapter 9 for an explanation of tools to gain this information).

To help understand and summarise the online linkages between online businesses and traffic flows it is worthwhile producing an online marketplace map as shown in Figure 2.2. This shows the relative importance of different online intermediaries in the marketplace and the flow of clicks between your different customer segments, your company site(s) and different competitors via the intermediaries.

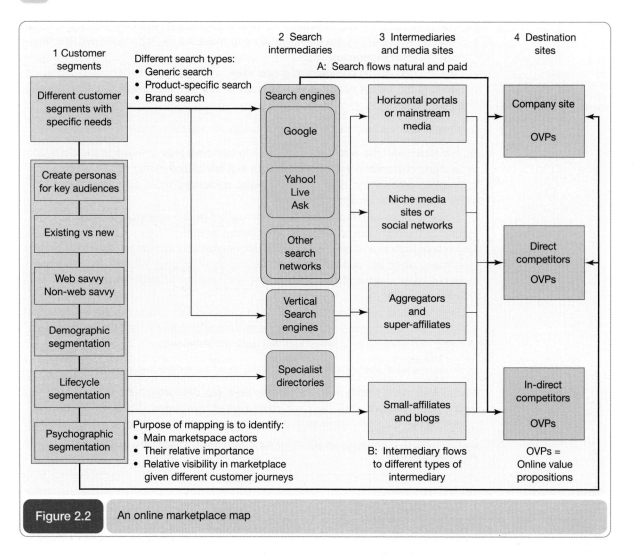

| Figure 2.2 | An online marketplace map |
|---|---|

The main elements of the online marketplace map presented in Figure 2.2 are:

1 *Customer segments.* The marketplace analysis should identify and summarise different target segments for an online business in order to then understand their online media consumption, buyer behaviour and the type of content and experiences they will be looking for from intermediaries and your website. In a campaign or website design project, personas are used to understand the preferences, characteristics and online behaviours of different groups as described in the section on online buyer behaviour later in this chapter.

2 *Search intermediaries.* These are the main search engines in each country. Typically Google, Yahoo!, Microsoft Live Search and Ask but others are important in some markets such as China (Baidu), Russia (Yandex) and South Korea (Naver). You can use audience panel data from Comscore (www.comscore.com), Hitwise (www.hitwise.com), Nielsen Netratings (www.nielsennetratings.com) to find out their relative importance in different countries country.

Companies need to know which sites are effective in harnessing search traffic and either partner with them or try to obtain a share of the search traffic using the search engine marketing and affiliate marketing techniques explained in Chapter 9. Well known, trusted brands which have developed customer loyalty are in a good position to succeed online since a common consumer behaviour is to go straight to the site through entering a URL or from a bookmark or e-mail. Alternatively they may search for the brand or URL.

Hitwise provides this type of insight, as shown in Table 2.2. By evaluating the type and volume of phrases used to search for products in a given market, it is possible to calculate the total potential opportunity and the current share of search terms for a company. 'Share of search' can be determined from web analytics reports from the company site which indicate the precise key phrases used by visitors to actually reach a site from different search engines.

**Share of search**
The audience share of Internet searchers achieved by a particular audience in a particular market.

| Table 2.2 | Top 10 generic and branded search terms sending traffic to a custom category of the top 25 flower websites in the UK over the four weeks ending 1 March 2008 |
|---|---|

| | Branded term popularity | Generic term popularity |
|---|---|---|
| 1 | Interflora | flowers |
| 2 | Flying flowers | mothers day flowers |
| 3 | Tesco | flower delivery |
| 4 | Interflora uk | mothers day |
| 5 | Tesco flowers | flowers delivered |
| 6 | Next flowers | mothers day gifts |
| 7 | Flowers by post | florists |
| 8 | Next | flowers for mothers day |
| 9 | Asda | valentines flowers |
| 10 | Asda flowers | send flowers |

*Source*: Hitwise UK press release: UK Internet visits to flower websites at highest ever peak in February; London, 6 March 2008

**Affiliate**
A company promoting a merchant typically through a commission-based arrangement either direct or through an affiliate network.

**Aggregators**
An alternative term to price comparison sites. Aggregators include product, price and service information comparing competitors within a sector such a financial services, retail or travel. Their revenue models commonly include affiliate revenues (CPA), pay-per-click advertising (CPC) and display advertising (CPM).

3 *Intermediaries and media sites.* Media sites and other intermediaries such as **aggregators** and **affiliates** are often successful in attracting visitors via search or direct since they are mainstream brands. Companies need to assess potential online media and distribution partners in the categories shown in Figure 2.2 such as:

- *Mainstream news media sites or portals.* These include traditional, for example, FT.com or Times or Pureplay, e.g. Google news an aggregator.
- *Niche/vertical media sites.* For example EConsultancy, ClickZ.com in B2B.
- *Price comparison sites* (also known as aggregators). For example, Moneysupermarket, Kelkoo, Shopping.com, uSwitch, etc.
- *Superaffiliates.* Affiliates gain revenue from a merchant they refer traffic to by being paid commission based on a proportion of the sale or a fixed amount. They are important in e-retail markets, accounting for tens of % of sales.
- *Niche affiliates or bloggers.* These are often individuals but they may be important, for example, in the UK Martin Lewis of Moneysavingexpert.com receives millions of visits every month. smaller affiliates and bloggers can be important collectively.

4 *Destination sites.* These are the sites that the marketer is trying to generate visitors to, whether these are transactional sites, like retailers, financial services or travel companies or manufacturers or brands. Figure 2.2 refers to OVP or 'online value proposition' which is a summary of the unique features of the site which are described in more detail in Chapter 4. The OVP is a key aspect to consider within planning – marketers should evaluate their OVPs against competitors and think about how they can refine them to develop a unique online experience.

## Resources for analysing the online marketplace

**Unique visitors**

Individual visitors to a site measured through cookies or IP addresses on an individual computer.

To effectively plan digital marketing based on the actual marketplace characteristics rather than intuition, it is useful to tap into the wealth of research about current Internet usage and future trends. In Table 2.3, we summarise a selection of free and paid-for services which can be used for online marketplace analysis. These resources can be used to assess the number of people searching for information and the popularity of different types of sites measured by the number of **unique visitors**.

EConsultancy (www.e-consultancy.com) provide a summary of much of the latest research from these sources together with their own reports, such as the Internet Statistics compendium.

| Table 2.3 | Research tools for assessing your e-marketplace |
| --- | --- |

| Service | Usage |
| --- | --- |
| 1 **Alexa** (www.alexa.com) Free tool, see also www.compete.com. Also use the Google syntax related:domain.com to find related sites | Free service owned by Amazon which provides traffic ranking of individual sites compared to all sites. Works best for sites in top 100,000. Sample dependent on users of the Alexa toolbar |
| 2 **Hitwise** (www.hitwise.com) Paid tool, but free research available at http://weblogs.hitwise.com | Paid service available in some countries to compare audience size and search/site usage. Works through monitoring IP traffic to different sites through ISPs |
| 3 **Netratings** (www.netratings.com) Paid tool. Free data on search engines and intermediaries available from press release section | Panel service based on at-home and at-work users who have agreed to have their web usage tracked by software. Top rankings on site gives examples of most popular sites in several countries |
| 4 **Comscore** (www.comscore.com) Paid tool. Free data on search engines and intermediaries available from press release section | A similar panel service to Netratings, but focusing on the US and UK. A favoured tool for media planners |
| 5 **ABCE Database** (www.abce.org.uk) Free tool. (Choose ABCE Database.) | The Audit Bureau of Circulation (Electronic) gives free access to its database of portals (not destination sites) who have agreed to have their sites audited to prove traffic volumes to advertisers |
| 6 **Search key phrase analysis tools** Compilation available from www.davechaffey.com/seo-keyword-tools | Tools such as the Google Keyword tool and Google Traffic Estimator can be used to assess the popularity of brands and their products reflected by the volume of search terms typed into Google and other search engines. The Yahoo! Site Explorer can be used to assess links between sites |
| 7 **Forrester** (www.forrester.com) Paid research service. Some free commentary and analysis within blogs (http://blogs.forrester.com) | Offers reports on Internet usage and best practice in different vertical sectors such as financial services, retail and travel. Free research summaries available in press release section and on its Marketing blog (http://blogs.forrester.com) |

| Service | Usage |
|---------|-------|
| 8  Gartner (www.gartner.com) | Another research service in this case focusing on technology adoption. See also Jupiter research (www.jupiterresearch.com) who often have good reports on e-mail marketing best practice |
| 9  Internet or Interactive Advertising Bureau (IAB) US: www.iab.net UK: www.iabuk.net Europe: www.europe.uk.net (see also www.eiaa.net) | Rresearch focusing on investment in different digital media channels, in particular display ads and search marketing |
| 10  Internet Media in Retail Group (IMRG) (www.imrg.org) | The IMRG has compilations on online e-commerce expenditure and most popular retailers in the UK |

In the next sections, we will show how the different members of the online marketplace should be assessed.

## Customer analysis and consumer behaviour

**Consumer behaviour**
Research into the motivations, media consumption preferences and selection processes used by consumers as they use digital channels together with traditional channels to purchase online products and use other online services.

**Customer insight**
Knowledge about customers' needs, characteristics, preferences and behaviours based on analysis of qualitative and quantitative data. Specific insights can be used to inform marketing tactics directed at groups of customers with shared characteristics.

**Customer segments**
Groups of customers sharing similar characteristics, preferences and behaviours who are targeted with different propositions as part of *target marketing strategy*.

Situation analysis related to customers is very important to setting realistic objectives, estimates for volumes of online customers and developing appropriate propositions for customers online. Customer-related analysis can be divided into two. Firstly, demand analysis, which involves understanding the potential and actual volume of visitors to a site and the extent to which they convert to outcomes on the site such as leads and sales (conversion modelling). Secondly, we need to understand the needs, characteristics and consumer behaviour of users of digital channels, often collectively referred to as customer insight. As a result of this analysis, customer segments will be created which will be used to develop targeting approaches as part of the strategy development described in Chapters 4 onwards.

### Demand analysis and conversion modelling

It is essential for Internet marketing and e-marketing managers to understand the current levels and trends in usage of the Internet for different services and the factors that affect how many people actively use these services. This evaluation process is demand analysis. If customer usage of online media is evaluated for customers in a target market, companies can identify the opportunity for influencing and delivering sales online. They can also understand the drivers to usage and barriers to increased usage and so encourage adoption of online channels by emphasising the benefits in their communications and explaining why some of the barriers may not be valid. For example, marketing communications can be used to explain the value proposition and reduce fears of complexity and security.

Surveys reported in the social factors section of the next chapter show that the following are important factors in governing adoption and usage of the Internet:

- cost of access
- value proposition
- perception of ease of use
- perception of security.

**Demand analysis**
Quantitative
determination of the
potential usage and
business value achieved
from online customers of
an organisation.
Qualitative analysis of
perceptions of online
channels is also
assessed.

## Assessing demand for digital services

To set realistic strategic objectives such as leads or sales levels for each customer segment companies need to assess their volume and share of customers who:

- have access to the digital channel;
- are influenced by using the digital channel but purchase using another channel as part of the multichannel buyer behaviour;
- purchase or use other services using the digital channel.

This can be simplified to the ratios: 'Access : Choose : Transact'. This information can be gathered as secondary research by the researcher by accessing published research for different sectors such as that shown in Table 2.3. Primary research can be used to better understand these characteristics in the target market.

## Conversion models

As part of situation analysis and objective setting, experienced online marketers build conversion or waterfall models of the efficiency of their web marketing. Using this approach, the total online demand for a service in a particular market can be estimated and then the success of the company in achieving a share of this market determined. **Conversion marketing** tactics can then be used to convert as many *potential* site visitors into *actual* visitors and then convert these into leads, customers and repeat customers.

**Conversion
marketing**
Using marketing
communications to
maximise conversion of
potential customers to
actual customers.

A widely quoted conceptual measurement framework based on the industrial marketing concepts of purchasing decision processes and hierarchy of effects models, which can be applied for conversion marketing, was proposed by Berthon *et al.* (1998). The model assesses efficiency of offline and online communications in drawing the prospect through different stages of the buying decision. The main measures defined in the model are the following ratios:

- *Awareness efficiency*: target web users/all web users.
- *Locatability or attractability efficiency*: number of individual visits/number of seekers.
- *Contact efficiency*: number of active visitors/number of visits.
- *Conversion efficiency*: number of purchases/number of active visits.
- *Retention efficiency*: number of re-purchases/number of purchases.

This model is instructive for improving Internet marketing within an organisation since these different types of conversion efficiency are key to understanding how effective online and offline marketing communications are in achieving marketing outcomes. Figure 2.3 is an adaptation of the original model of Berthon *et al.* (1998) from Chaffey (2001), which highlights the key conversion metrics of attraction efficiency and conversion efficiency. It shows key traffic or audience measures ($Q_0$ to $Q_4$), first-time visitors ($Q_2$) and repeat visitors ($Q_{2R}$) and key conversion efficiency ratios. E-marketers need to know how conversion effectiveness differs between first-time users and repeat users. An additional important aspect of online buyer behaviour not shown in the figure is the site path or **clickstream** for different audience types or segments.

**Clickstream**
The sequence of clicks
made by a visitor to the
site to make a purchase.

Figure 2.4 shows an example of how measuring conversion rates can be used to improve web marketing. Numbers are across a fixed time period of one month. If for a particular market there is a potential audience (market) of 200,000 ($Q_1$), then if online and offline promotion techniques (Chapter 8) achieve 100,000 visitors to the site ($Q_2$), marketers have achieved an impressive conversion rate of 50%. The online marketers are then looking to convert these visitors to action. Before this is achieved, the visitors must be engaged. Data from log files show that many visitors leave when they first visit the home page of a site if they do not find the site acceptable or they are not happy with the experience. The number of visitors engaged ($Q_3$) is 50,000, which is half of all visitors. For the visitors that are engaged, the next step is to convert them to action. This is achieved for 500 visitors ($Q_4$), giving a conversion rate ($Q_4/Q_3$) of 1%. If what is calculated (as is most common) is ($Q_4/Q_2$), this gives a conversion rate of 0.5%.

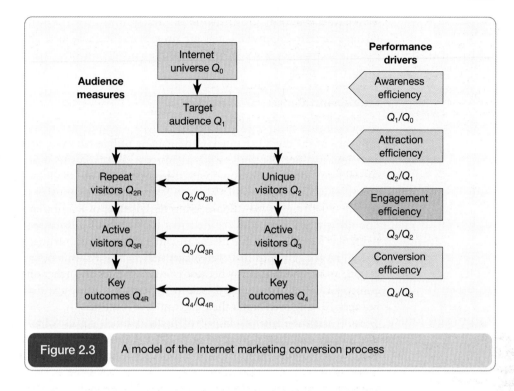

**Figure 2.3**    A model of the Internet marketing conversion process

In this example, the organisation seems highly efficient in attracting visitors to the site, but less efficient at converting them to action – future marketing improvements could be directed at improving this. Some organisations will measure different conversion rates for different segments and for different conversion goals such as generating new leads, responding to a sales promotion or signing up for a seminar. We discuss different types of conversion goals as part of describing communications goals in Chapter 8.

Analysis by Agrawal *et al.* (2001) suggested that the strongest sites may have conversion rates from visit to sale for e-commerce sites as high as 12%, as against 2.5% for average sites and 0.4% for poorly performing ones. For the latest compilations of conversion rates, see

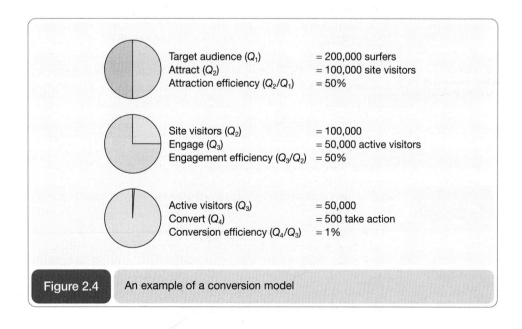

**Figure 2.4**    An example of a conversion model

www.davechaffey.com/conversion-rates. Clearly, measurement of the conversion rate and taking actions to improve this rate are key e-marketing activities. The marketing communications techniques used to increase these conversion rates are considered further in Chapters 7 and 8.

### Multichannel conversion models

Models such as that presented in Figure 2.3 are a simplification, since they do not take the influence of the digital channel in influencing offline sales into account. For example, an advertiser may use Google Adwords to promote their product, but some visitors to the website will not convert online and will instead prefer to use the phone to order if they have questions to answer or will buy in-store. Referring to an example in the travel industry, Revolution (2008) quotes Matt Rooke, e-business director of Kuoni who says: 'There is probably nobody who is happy with their current look-to-book conversion rates. Even if the best figure was 5 to 10%, that still means around 95% are not converting. Where are those people going?' he asks. He adds that even bigger sites such as Expedia have made the call to offline action far more visible, partly because conversion rates are higher offline and because of the complexity of the consumer decision: 'Expedia five years ago didn't even have a phone number. Now it's even bigger than the "continue" button'.

So, to assess the potential impact of digital channels it is useful to put in place tracking or research which assesses the cross-channel conversions at different stages in the buying process. For example, phone numbers which are unique to the website can be used as an indication of the volume of callers to a contact centre influenced by the website. This insight can then be built into budget models of sales levels such as that shown in Figure 2.5. This shows that of the 100,000 unique visitors in a period we can determine that 5000 (5%) may actually become offline leads. Figure 2.6 gives an example of a company that uses prominent tailored phone numbers to encourage offline leads and then tracks inbound phone activity by country and product.

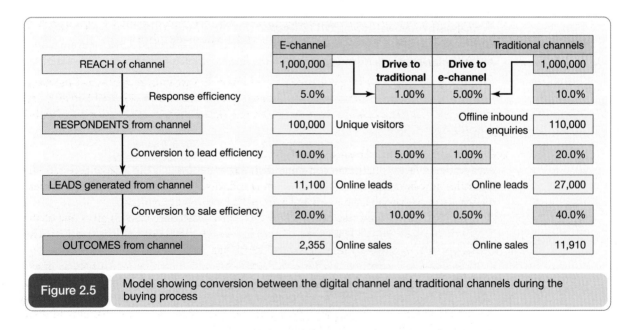

| | E-channel | | | Traditional channels | |
|---|---|---|---|---|---|
| REACH of channel | 1,000,000 | | Drive to traditional | Drive to e-channel | 1,000,000 |
| Response efficiency | 5.0% | → | 1.00% | 5.00% | 10.0% |
| RESPONDENTS from channel | 100,000 | Unique visitors | | Offline inbound enquiries | 110,000 |
| Conversion to lead efficiency | 10.0% | | 5.00% | 1.00% | 20.0% |
| LEADS generated from channel | 11,100 | Online leads | | Online leads | 27,000 |
| Conversion to sale efficiency | 20.0% | | 10.00% | 0.50% | 40.0% |
| OUTCOMES from channel | 2,355 | Online sales | | Online sales | 11,910 |

**Figure 2.5** Model showing conversion between the digital channel and traditional channels during the buying process

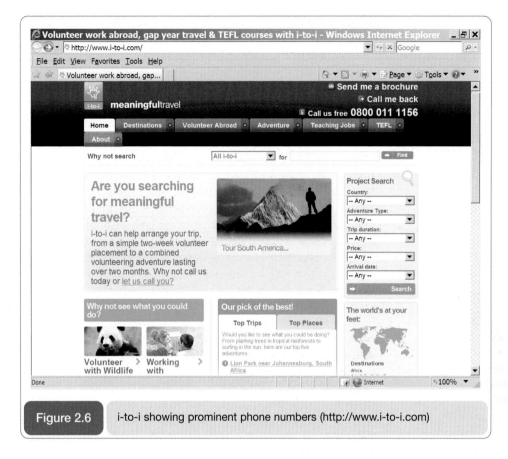

**Figure 2.6**    i-to-i showing prominent phone numbers (http://www.i-to-i.com)

## Evaluating demand levels

We will now review each of the following three factors that affect demand for digital services in a little more detail, starting with consumers in the B2C marketplace.

### 1 Internet access

E-commerce provides a global marketplace, and this means we must review access and usage of the Internet channel at many different geographic levels: worldwide and between and within continents and countries. See www.internetworldstats.com for a compilation of global statistics from different sources.

*Type of access including broadband and mobile access*
An additional factor relating to consumer digital channel usage is the type of access. Some countries now have significant levels of high-speed, always-on, broadband access but there are still many who don't have access and a dramatic variation by country.

The OECD broadband research (http://www.oecd.org/sti/ict/broadband) gives one of the most reliable sources on usage of broadband across different countries (Figure 2.7). The data shows that many consumers are still not using high-speed Internet services.

Broadband access permits more sophisticated sites and streaming media such as music and video. Usage of the Internet also tends to increase with broadband because of the 'always-on' connection. Data on usage of mobile channels is available from M:Metrics (www.mmetrics.com). Such research providers show how consumers are changing in their usage of mobile phones. Figure 2.8 shows a snapshot.

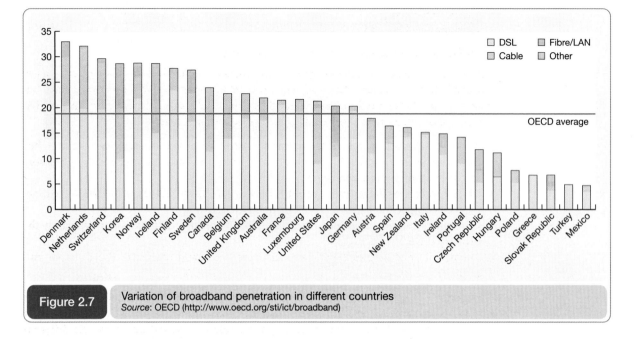

**Figure 2.7** Variation of broadband penetration in different countries
*Source*: OECD (http://www.oecd.org/sti/ict/broadband)

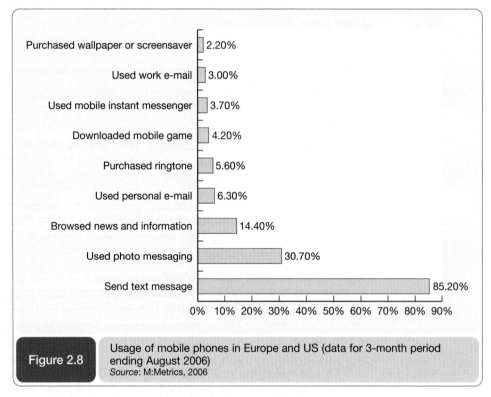

**Figure 2.8** Usage of mobile phones in Europe and US (data for 3-month period ending August 2006)
*Source*: M:Metrics, 2006

Gaining the latest research insights is important since with digital technology, there can be major differences in adoption in different cultures. For example, the research on short code response from M:Metrics found that a sizable percentage of mobile subscribers are responding to short codes placed in advertisements or in other media:

- Spain – 29.1%
- UK – 18.5%
- France – 10.1%

- United States – 7%
- Germany – 3.4%

### 2 Consumers influenced by using the online channel

Next we must look at the extent to which consumers are influenced by online media – a key aspect of consumer buyer behaviour. Many Internet users now research products online, but they may buy through offline channels such as phone or in-store. Research summarised in the AOL-sponsored BrandNewWorld II (2007) study showed that:

- The Internet is a vital part of the research process, with Internet users agreeing that they now spend longer researching products. The purchase process is generally now more considered and is more convoluted.
- The Internet is used at every stage of the research process from the initial scan to the more detailed comparison and final check before purchase.
- Consumers are more informed from a multiplicity of sources; price is not exclusively the primary driver.
- Online information and experience (and modified brand opinions) also translate into offline purchase.

An understanding of the information sources used for making decisions about which sites are used to purchase products and use other services is useful as part of planning so that companies can make sure they achieve a favourable representation across the different sources. Figure 2.9, taken from cross-European research, indicates some of the main online and offline information sources.

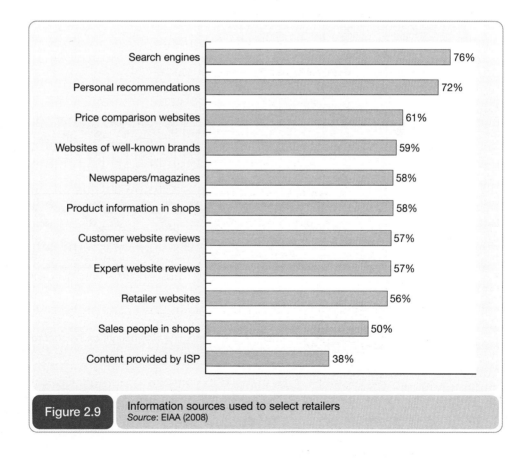

| Figure 2.9 | Information sources used to select retailers |
|---|---|
| | *Source:* EIAA (2008) |

There is also a wide variation in influence according to type of product, so it is important to assess the role of the web in supporting buying decisions for a particular market. Understanding the potential reach of a website and its role in influencing purchase is clearly important in setting e-marketing budgets. A different perspective on this is indicated by Figure 2.10 which shows the proportion of people who purchase online after online research (for product categories where online purchase is lower, the audience is researching online, but then transacting offline).

The range of different ways in which consumers use the Internet to research or transact are provided by Figure 2.11. It can be seen that male and female usage of the Internet for different activities is now very similar, but with downloading of different types of digital content generally more popular among males.

The amount of Internet usage also appears to increase with familiarity. BMRB (2001) reports that those using the Internet for more than two years spent an average of 20 hours online per month. This compares to 14 hours for those who had been using the Internet for less than two years. Similarly, the activities that consumers get involved with increase in depth of involvement and risk through time. Figure 2.12 shows that initially Internet users may restrict themselves to searching for information or using e-mail. As their confidence grows their use of the Internet for purchase is likely to increase with a move to higher-value items and more frequent purchases. This is often coupled with the use of broadband. For this reason, there is still good potential for e-retail sales, even if the percentage of the population with access to the Internet flattens off.

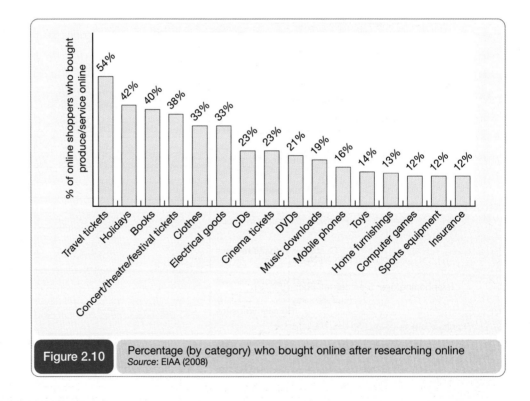

**Figure 2.10**

Percentage (by category) who bought online after researching online
*Source:* EIAA (2008)

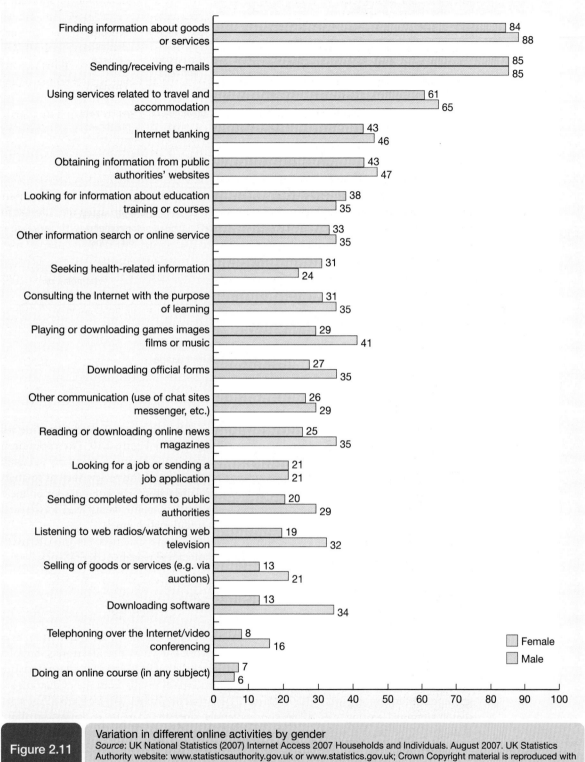

**Figure 2.11**

Variation in different online activities by gender

*Source*: UK National Statistics (2007) Internet Access 2007 Households and Individuals. August 2007. UK Statistics Authority website: www.statisticsauthority.gov.uk or www.statistics.gov.uk; Crown Copyright material is reproduced with the permission of the Controller, Office of Public Sector Information (OPSI).

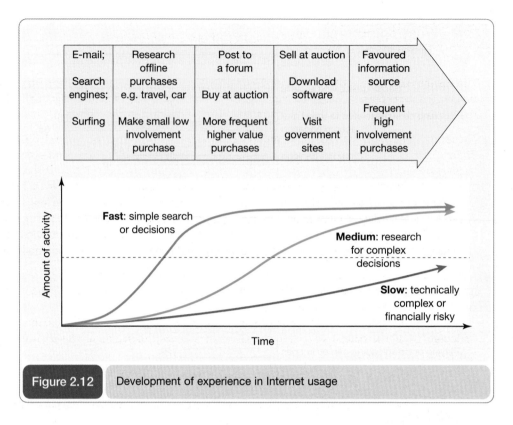

| E-mail;<br><br>Search engines;<br><br>Surfing | Research offline purchases e.g. travel, car<br><br>Make small low involvement purchase | Post to a forum<br><br>Buy at auction<br><br>More frequent higher value purchases | Sell at auction<br><br>Download software<br><br>Visit government sites | Favoured information source<br><br>Frequent high involvement purchases |

**Figure 2.12**    Development of experience in Internet usage

### 3 Transact online

The proportion of Internet users who will purchase different types of product online will vary dramatically according to product type as suggested by Figure 2.10. The variation in Figure 2.10 shows that there are still significant barriers to purchasing, particularly in certain categories of higher value, complex products or products requiring review such as financial services, sports and travel equipment. This partly explains why conversion rates for online e-commerce sites are so low in many categories – the sites are mainly being used for research into products, brands and prices before purchase in traditional channels.

A substantial proportion of people simply prefer traditional channels. For the UK, over a quarter of all consumers still do not shop online, stating these reasons (UK Statistics, 2006):

- Have no need – 28%
- Prefer to shop in person/like to see the product – 24%
- Security concerns – 25%

The factors which affect the propensity to purchase can be estimated for different types of products. De Kare-Silver (2000) developed a framework known as The Electronic Shopping Test in which he suggests that the criteria for purchase include product characteristics, familiarity and confidence and consumer attributes. Typical results from the evaluation are: groceries (27/50), mortgages (15/50), travel (31/50) and books (38/50). De Kare-Silver states that any product scoring over 20 has good potential, since the score for consumer attributes is likely to increase through time. Given this, he suggests companies will regularly need to review the score for their products. The effectiveness of this test is now demonstrated by data for online purchases in different product categories (see Figure 2.10, page **64**).

| Mini Case Study 2.1 | The Electronic Shopping or ES Test |
|---|---|

The ES Test was developed by de Kare-Silver (2000) to assess the extent to which consumers are likely to purchase a retail product using the Internet. De Kare-Silver suggests factors that should be considered in the ES Test:

1 *Product characteristics*. Does the product need to be physically tried, or touched, before it is bought?
2 *Familiarity and confidence*. Considers the degree to which the consumer recognises and trusts the product and brand.
3 *Consumer attributes*. These shape the buyer's behaviour – is he or she amenable to online purchases (i.e. in terms of access to the technology and skills available) and does he or she no longer wish to shop for a product in a traditional retail environment? For example, a student familiar with technology may buy a CD online because they are comfortable with the technology. An elderly person looking for a classical CD would probably not have access to the technology and might prefer to purchase the item in person.

In his book, de Kare-Silver describes a method for ranking products. Product characteristics and familiarity and confidence are marked out of 10, and consumer attributes are marked out of 30. Using this method, he scores products as shown in Table 2.4.

De Kare-Silver states that any product scoring over 20 has good potential, since the score for consumer attributes is likely to increase through time. Given this, he suggests companies will regularly need to review the score for their products.

| Table 2.4 | Product scores in de Kare-Silver's (2000) Electronic Shopping (ES) potential test |
|---|---|

| Product | Product characteristics (10) | Familiarity and confidence (10) | Consumer attributes (30) | Total |
|---|---|---|---|---|
| Groceries | 4 | 8 | 15 | 27 |
| Mortgages | 10 | 1 | 4 | 15 |
| Travel | 10 | 6 | 15 | 31 |
| Books | 8 | 7 | 23 | 38 |

### Customer characteristics

Understanding the nature of customers is fundamental to marketing practice and it is equally important online. We will see in Chapter 4 on strategy development that traditional segmentation approaches can be used successfully to understand the range of audiences. A further technique that can be used as part of situation analysis is customer persona and scenario analysis which is an online technique for user- or customer-centric website design. This is an extension of the traditional marketing approach of **psychographic segmentation**. See Box 2.1 'Psychographic segmentation for transactional e-commerce' for an example of this type of segmentation applied to online purchase behaviour. Which profile do you fit?

**Psychographic segmentation**
A breakdown of customers according to different characteristics.

| Box 2.1 | Psychographic segmentation for transactional e-commerce |
| --- | --- |

Market research firm BMRB (2004) has developed this segmentation which is used to represent different attitudes to purchasing online.

1  *Realistic enthusiasts* (14% 2004, 15% 1999) – characterised by an enthusiastic approach toward e-commerce but they typically like to see the product in real life before making a purchase and they often consider that finding the product to purchase is a difficult process. Examples of this include a willingness to use the Internet for purchases in excess of £500; they are prepared to purchase products from an unknown company and consider the convenience of Internet shopping to be more important than price.

2  *Confident brand shoppers* (18% 2004, 16% 1999) – members of this group are happy to use the Internet the next time they want to make a purchase in excess of £500, with this confidence stemming from the importance they lay on purchasing well-known brands and the necessity to shop around.

3  *Carefree spenders* (19% 2004, 15% 1999) – these consumers are prepared to purchase from unknown companies and do not consider that purchases should be restricted to well-known brands. Furthermore, they are willing to make the purchase without seeing the product first.

4  *Cautious shoppers* (14% 2004, 20% 1999) – these shoppers are not likely to purchase goods through an online auction, have concerns over the quality of products they purchase and would like to see the product prior to making a purchase.

5  *Bargain hunters* (21% 2004, 16% 1999) – this group would buy from an unknown company or any website as long as it was the cheapest and are driven not by the convenience of the medium but by price.

6  *Unfulfilled* (14% 2004, 17% 1999) – this group finds it too difficult to find the products they wish to purchase on the Internet. They would not buy from any website or through an auction and they think it takes too long for products purchased online to be delivered.

### Demographic characteristics

**Demographic characteristics**
Variations in attributes of the populations such as age, sex and social class.

Within each country, adoption of the Internet also varies significantly according to individual **demographic characteristics** such as sex, age and social class or income. This analysis is important as part of the segmentation of different groups within a target market. Since these factors will vary throughout each country there will also be regional differences. Access is usually much higher in capital cities.

To fully understand online customer access we also need to consider the user's access location, access device and 'webographics', all of which are significant for segmentation and constraints on site design. '*Webographics*' is a term coined by Grossnickle and Raskin (2001). According to these authors webographics includes:

- *Usage location.* In most countries, many users access either from home or from work, with home being the more common location. Work access places constraints on Internet marketers since firewalls will not permit some plug-ins or rich e-mail to be accepted.
- *Access device.* For example, browser type, screen resolution and computer platform (available from web analytics services as described in Chapter 9), digital TV or mobile phone access.
- *Connection speed* – dial-up or different choice of broadband speed.
- *ISP* – a portal-based ISP such as AOL or Wanadoo, or an ISP which does not provide any additional content.

- *Experience level* – length of time using the web and their familiarity with online purchase.
- *Usage type* – mode of usage, for example work, social, entertainment.

### Usage level – frequency of use and length of sessions giving total usage level in minutes per month. Customer persona and scenario analysis

**Personas**
A thumbnail summary of the characteristics, needs, motivations and environment of typical website users.

Creating **personas** for typical site visitors is a powerful technique for influencing the planning of online campaigns and the usability and customer centricity of a website.

Personas are essentially a 'thumbnail' description of a type of person. They have been used for a long time in research for segmentation and advertising, but in recent years have also proved effective for improving website design by companies that have applied the technique.

**Customer scenarios (user journeys)**
Alternative tasks or outcomes required by a visitor to a website. Typically accomplished in a series of stages of different tasks involving different information needs or experiences.

**Customer scenarios** are developed for different personas. Patricia Seybold, in her book with Ronni Marshak, *The Customer Revolution* (2001), explains them as follows:

> A customer scenario is a set of tasks that a particular customer wants or needs to do in order to accomplish his or her desired outcome.

You will see that scenarios can be developed for each persona. For an online bank, scenarios might include:

- New customer – opening an online account.
- Existing customer – transferring an account online.
- Existing customer – finding an additional product.

Each scenario is split up into a series of steps or tasks before the scenario is completed. These steps can be best thought of as a series of questions a visitor asks. By identifying questions, website designers identify the different information needs of different customer types at different stages in the buying process.

The use of scenarios is a simple, but very powerful, web design technique that is still relatively rare in website design. They can also be used when benchmarking competitor sites as part of situation analysis.

Here are two simple examples of a commercial bank offering business services which show an experienced user (persona 1) and less experienced user (persona 2).

#### Online banking persona 1 – Switcher

Chris Barber owns a top-quality restaurant, and in the long term would like to build up a small chain of country hotels and restaurants. As the owner–manager, Chris currently uses a competitor (Barclays) for his business banking. He is thinking of moving to business Internet banking since he has used Barclays Internet banking for his personal banking. He will use the Internet to select the best offering for his needs. His main interest is to minimise bank charges by switching. Chris has been using the Internet for five years.

#### Online banking persona 2 – Start-up

John Smith has just registered Gifts-R-Us as a new business. The company will be a wholesale gift supplier selling a range of imported gift products, such as candles and decorations to small shops and stores. He has worked as a marketing director in a similar business previously, but is now seeking to start up his own business with the operations manager of the other company as his partner. John is selecting a business bank, but is not sure whether to use Internet banking or not. He wants to assess the benefits. He has no preferences for a business bank – he wants to review all the options and find the easiest to use. He also wants one with favourable banking rates. He is not an experienced Internet user since previously his secretary accessed the Internet for him.

The customer persona/scenario approach has the following benefits:

- fostering customer-centricity;
- identifies detailed information needs and steps required by customers;
- can be used to test existing website designs or prototypes and to devise new designs;

- can be used to compare and test the strength and clarity of communication of proposition on different websites;
- can be linked to specific marketing outcomes required by site owners.

Here are some guidelines and ideas on what can be included when developing a persona. The start or end point is to give each persona a name. The detailed stages are:

1 Build personal attributes into personas:
   - demographic: age, sex, education, occupation and, for B2B, company size, position in buying unit;
   - psychographic: goals, tasks, motivation;
   - webographics: web experience (months), usage location (home or work), usage platform (dial-up, broadband), usage frequency, favourite sites.

2 Remember that personas are only models of characteristics and environment:
   - design targets;
   - stereotypes;
   - three or four usually suffice to improve general usability, but more may be needed for specific behaviours;
   - choose one **primary persona** whom, if satisfied, means others are likely to be satisfied.

**Primary persona**
A representation of the typical site user.

3 Different scenarios can be developed for each persona as explained further below. Write three or four, for example:
   - information-seeking scenario (leads to site registration);
   - purchase scenario – new customer (leads to sale);
   - purchase scenario – existing customer (leads to sale).

Once different personas have been developed that are representative of key site-visitor types or customer types, a primary persona is sometimes identified. Wodtke (2002) says:

> *Your primary persona needs to be a common user type who is both important to the business success of the product and needy from a design point of view – in other words, a beginner user or a technologically challenged one.*

She also says that secondary personas can also be developed, such as super-users or complete novices. Complementary personas are those that don't fit into the main categories and which display unusual behaviour. Such complementary personas help 'out-of-box thinking' and offer choices or content that may appeal to all users.

For another example of the application of personas, see Mini case study 2.2 about paint manufacturer, Dulux, which uses personas to design its site and to integrate with offline media campaigns.

---

| Mini Case Study 2.2 | Dulux paint a picture of consumers with personas |

### Campaign aims

The aims behind this brand initiative were to reposition Dulux from a paint brand to a colour help brand by meeting customer needs, in a way competitors don't, to help differentiate the Dulux brand. The aim was to position Dulux.co.uk (Figure 2.13) as 'the online destination for colour scheming and visualisation to help you achieve your individual style from the comfort of your home'. Specific outcomes on the site are to browse colours, add colours to a personal scrapbook, use the paint calculator and find a stockist. Further aims were to 'win the war before the store', i.e. to provide colour help tools that can develop a preference for Dulux before consumers are in-store and to prompt other ideas to sell more than one colour at a time.

Specific SMART objectives were to increase the number of unique visitors from 1 million p.a. in 2003 to 3.5 million p.a. in 2006 and to drive 12% of visitors to a desired outcome (e.g. ordering swatches).

## Target audience

Based on research, it was found that the main audience for the site was female with these typical demographics and psychographics:

- would be adventurous 25–44 women, online;
- lack of confidence with previous site:
  - gap between inspiration (TV, magazines, advertising) and lived experience (DIY sheds, nervous discomfort);
  - no guidance or reassurance previously available currently on their journey;
- colours and colour combining is key;
- online is a well-used channel for help and guidance on other topics;
- twelve-month decorating cycle;
- propensity to socialise;
- quality, technical innovation and scientific proficiency of Dulux is a given.

Specific personas were developed as follows:

- *First time buyer*. Penny Edwards, age: 27; partner: Ben; location: north London; occupation: sales assistant.
- *Part-time mum*. Jane Lawrence, age: 37; husband: Joe; location: Manchester; occupation: part-time PR consultant.
- *Single mum*. Rachel Wilson, age: 40; location: Reading; occupation: business analyst.

Each has a different approach to interacting with the brand, for Penny it is summarised by the statement:

*I've got loads of ideas and enthusiasm, I just don't know where to start.*

Each persona was also characterised by their media consumption and preferences such as types of websites, TV, magazines and radio channels and their favourite hobbies and socialising activities.

A storyboard was developed which illustrates the typical 'customer journey' for each persona and these informed the final site design (Figure 2.13).

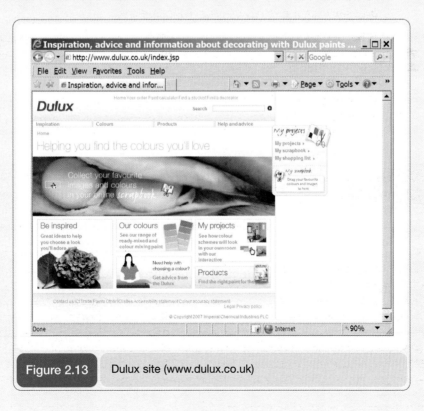

**Figure 2.13**    Dulux site (www.dulux.co.uk)

**Brand campaign**

To support the relaunch of the site, digital channels such as online banner advertising and interactive TV were used, with traditional channels such as press, in-store and PR. The main theme of the ads was 'colour chemistry' which was developed through featuring personas in the ads such as Candy Love, Forest Lake and Treacle Tart. The ads had a clear call-to-action to visit the website to find the right match for the consumer's personality and style.

*Source*: Case study developed by Agency.com; available through the IAB (www.iabuk.net) and presented at Engage 2007.

## Online demand for business services

We now turn our attention to how we assess online customer demand and characteristics for business services. The B2B market is more complex than that for B2C in that variation in online demand or research in the buying process will occur according to different types of organisation and people within the buying unit in the organisation. We need to profile business demand according to:

Variation in organisation characteristics:

- size of company – employees or turnover;
- industry sector and products;
- organisation type – private, public, government, not-for-profit;
- application of service – which business activities do purchased products and services support?
- country and region.

Individual role:

- role and responsibility from job title, function or number of staff managed;
- role in buying decision – purchasing influence;
- department;
- product interest;
- demographics – age, sex and possibly social group.

For generating demand estimates, we can also profile business users of the Internet in a similar way to consumers by assessing the following three factors.

### 1 The percentage of companies with access

In the business-to-business market, Internet access levels are higher than for business-to-consumer. In Europe, research completed for the i2010 initiative monitored usage of the Internet by business (European Commission, 2007) and it found that around 95% of businesses in the majority of countries surveyed have Internet access although this figure masks lower levels of access for SMEs (small and medium-sized enterprises) and particularly micro-businesses (Figure 2.14).

Understanding access for different members of the organisational buying unit among their customers is also important for marketers. Although the Internet seems to be used by many companies we also need to ask whether it reaches the right people in the buying unit. The answer is 'not necessarily' – access is not available to all employees. This can be an issue if marketing to particular types of staff who have shared PC access, such as healthcare professionals for example.

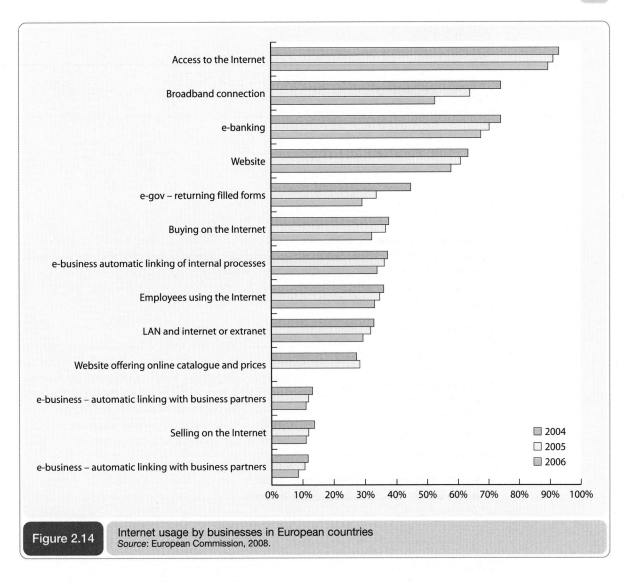

**Figure 2.14**  Internet usage by businesses in European countries
*Source*: European Commission, 2008.

## 2 Influenced online

In B2B marketing, the high level of access is consistent with a high level of using the Internet to identify suppliers, but there are surprisingly few companies offering transactional services (Figure 2.14).

Research into the reasons limiting this adoption are shown in Table 2.5. You can see that the perceived cost of complexity of implementing technology are the most important across companies of different sizes, with security and legal issues also significant.

| Table 2.5 | Reasons for limited adoption of e-business services in Europe | | | | |
|---|---|---|---|---|---|
| **Barrier to e-business adoption (size of company)** | **Total** | **1–9** | **10–49** | **50–249** | **250+** |
| Company too small | 68 | 75 | 54 | 36 | 19 |
| e-Business technologies too expensive | 40 | 46 | 30 | 37 | 40 |
| Technology too complicated | 35 | 37 | 31 | 33 | 13 |
| Compatibility problems with partners | 26 | 31 | 19 | 34 | 20 |
| Security issues | 33 | 36 | 25 | 31 | 35 |
| Legal challenges | 21 | 25 | 17 | 23 | 24 |
| Reliability of IT suppliers | 22 | 22 | 24 | 30 | 19 |

*Source*: European Commission, 2007

### 3 Transact online

The European Commission (2007) research also reveals that there is a large variation between how businesses in different countries order online with the figure substantially higher in some countries such as Sweden and Germany in comparison to Italy and France for example. This shows the importance of understanding differences in the environment for e-commerce in different countries since this will dramatically affect the volume of leads and orders.

Across all 25 countries surveyed in 2006, the average levels of Internet transactions, which show the potential for future growth in business-to-business e-commerce, are:

- 11.7% e-commerce as a percentage of total turnover of enterprises;
- 13.9% enterprises receiving Internet orders;
- 37.9% enterprises purchasing on the Internet.

## Online consumer behaviour

As part of situation analysis, either for a campaign or a longer-term digital plan, it is important that marketers gain an appreciation of online consumer behaviour for their audiences including the combination of web and mobile media with other channels.

For the Internet marketer, a review of the factors influencing behaviour is especially important since a single website may need to accommodate consumers with different needs at different stages of the buying process. Users will also have different levels of experience of using different web services.

In this section we will review different models of online buyer behaviour that have been developed to help marketers develop online services and communications compatible with this behaviour:

1 Information/experience seeking behaviour models.
2 Hierarchy of response buying process models.
3 Multichannel buying models.
4 Trust-based models.
5 Social interaction communication models.

## 1 Information/experience seeking behaviour models

Standard models of consumer buyer behaviour have been developed by Bettman (1979) and Booms and Bitner (1981). In these models, consumers process and interpret marketing stimuli such as the 4 Ps (page 276) and environmental stimuli according to their personal characteristics such as their culture, social group and personal and psychological make-up. Together these characteristics will affect the consumers' response to marketing messages.

Specific behavioural traits are evident on the Internet. Studies show that the World Wide Web is used quite differently by different groups of people. Lewis and Lewis (1997) identified five different types of web users or rather modes of usage of the Internet which remain valid today:

1 *Directed information-seekers.* These users will be looking for product, market or leisure information such as details of their football club's fixtures. They are not typically planning to buy online.
2 *Undirected information-seekers.* These are the users, usually referred to as 'surfers', who like to browse and change sites by following hyperlinks. Members of this group tend to be novice users (but not exclusively so) and they may be more likely to click on banner advertisements.
3 *Directed buyers.* These buyers are online to purchase specific products online. For such users, brokers or cybermediaries that compare product features and prices will be important locations to visit.
4 *Bargain hunters.* These users (sometimes known as 'compers') want to find the offers available from sales promotions such as free samples or competitions. For example, the MyOffers site (www.myoffers.co.uk) is used by many brands to generate awareness and interest from consumers.
5 *Entertainment seekers.* These are users looking to interact with the web for enjoyment through entering contests such as quizzes, puzzles or interactive multi-player games.

Styler (2001) describes four consumer buying behaviours derived from in-depth home interviews researching behaviour across a range of media, including the Internet. These behaviours are brand-focused, price-sensitive, feature-savvy and advice-led. As Moe (2003) has pointed out, in the bricks-and-mortar environment, stores employ sales people who can distinguish between shoppers based on their in-store behaviour. Some shoppers appear to be very focused in looking for a specific product. In those cases, sales people may try to help the shopper find what they are looking for. In other cases, the shopper is just browsing or 'window shopping'. The experienced sales person can identify these shoppers and either ignore them and let them continue or can try to stimulate a purchase. Although there is no sales person to perform this role online, Moe and Fader (2004) believe that through analysing clickstream behaviour and patterns of repeated visits, it may be possible to identify directed buying, browsing or searching behaviour and make prompts accordingly online.

The revised Web Motivation Inventory (WMI) identified by Rodgers *et al.* (2007) is a useful framework for understanding different motivations for using the web which will differ for different parts of a web session. The four motives which cut across cultures are research (information acquisition), communicate (socialisation), surf (entertainment) and shop and these are broken down further below.

1 *Community*
   - Get to know other people
   - Participate in an online chat
   - Join a group.
2 *Entertainment*
   - Amuse myself
   - Entertain myself
   - Find information to entertain myself.

3 *Product trial*
  - Try on the latest fashions
  - Experience a product
  - Try out a product.

4 *Information*
  - Do research
  - Get information I need
  - Search for information I need.

5 *Transaction*
  - Make a purchase
  - Buy things
  - Purchase a product I've heard about.

6 *Game*
  - Play online games
  - Entertain myself with internet games
  - Play online games with individuals from other countries.

7 *Survey*
  - Take a survey on a topic I care about
  - Fill out an online survey
  - Give my opinion on a survey.

8 *Downloads*
  - Download music
  - Listen to music
  - Watch online videos.

9 *Interaction*
  - Connect with my friends
  - Communicate with others
  - Instant message others I know.

10 *Search*
  - Get answers to specific questions
  - Find information I can trust.

11 *Exploration*
  - Find interesting web pages
  - Explore new sites
  - Surf for fun.

12 *News*
  - Read about current events and news
  - Read entertainment news.

Web advertisers and site owners can use this framework to review the suitability of facilities to meet these needs. In a report on benchmarking the user experience of UK retail sites, EConsultancy (2004) identified a useful classification of online shopping behaviour to test how well website design matches different consumer behaviours. In a similar way to previous studies, three types of potential behaviour were identified which are trackers, hunters and explorers. Note that these do not equate to different people, since according to the type of product or occasion, the behaviour of an individual may differ.

1 *Tracker*

Knows exactly which product they wish to buy and uses an online shopping site to track it down and check its price, availability, delivery time, delivery charges or after-sales support.

That is, the tracker is looking for specific information about a particular product. The report says:

> *If they get the answers they are seeking they need little further persuasion or purchase-justification before completing the purchase.*

While this may not be true since they may compare on other sites, this type of shopper will be relatively easy to convert.

2 *Hunter*

> Doesn't have a specific product in mind but knows what type of product they are looking for (e.g. digital camera, cooker) and probably has one or more product features they are looking for. The hunter uses an online shopping site to find a range of suitable products, compare them and decide which one to buy. The hunter needs more help, support and guidance to reach a purchasing decision.

The report says:

> *Once a potential purchase is found, they then need to justify that purchase in their own minds, and possibly to justify their purchase to others. Only then will confirmation of the purchase become a possibility.*

3 *Explorer*

> Doesn't even have a particular type of product in mind. They may have a well-defined shopping objective (buying a present for someone or treating themselves), a less-resolved shopping objective (buying something to 'brighten up' the lounge) or no shopping objective at all (they like the high street store and thought they would have a look at the online site).

The report suggests that the explorer has a range of possible needs and many uncertainties to be resolved before committing to purchase, but the following may be helpful in persuading these shoppers to convert:

> *Certain types of information, however, are particularly relevant. Suggested gift ideas, guides to product categories, lists of top selling products and information-rich promotions (What's New? What's Hot?) – these could all propel them towards a purchasing decision.*

From this brief review of online buyer behaviours, we can suggest that online marketers need to take into account the range of behaviours shown in Table 2.6 both when developing an Internet marketing strategy and when executing it through site design.

| Table 2.6 | Alternative perspectives on online buyer behaviours |
| --- | --- |

| Range of behavioural traits | Sources referred to |
| --- | --- |
| Directed to undirected information-seekers | Lewis and Lewis (1997), Kothari *et al.* (2001) |
| Brand-knowledgeable to not knowledgeable | Kothari *et al.* (2001), Styler (2001) |
| Feature-led to not feature-led | Styler (2001) |
| Price-led to not price-led | Styler (2001) |
| Service-quality-led to not service-quality-led | — |
| Require advice to do not require advice | Styler (2001) |
| Brand-loyal to opportunistic | Clemons and Row (2000), Styler (2001) |

## 2 Hierarchy of response buying process models

An alternative view of consumer behaviour in using the Internet during different stages of the buying process relates to the well-documented 'hierarchy of response model', summarised for example by Kotler *et al.* (2001), as made up of the following stages:

- awareness;
- interest;
- evaluation;
- trial;
- adoption.

Breitenbach and van Doren (1998) also suggest that audience members of an individual website tend to pass through these stages, while Chaffey and Smith (2008) describe them as:

1 Problem recognition
2 Information search
3 Evaluation
4 Decision
5 Action (sale or usage of online service)
6 Post purchase.

Figure 2.15 indicates how a summary of how the Internet can be used to support the different stages in the buying process. The boxes on the left show the typical stages that a new prospect passes through, according to, for example, Robinson *et al.* (1967). A similar analysis was performed by Berthon *et al.* (1998), who speculated that the relative communications effectiveness of using a website in this process gradually increased from 1 to 6.

It is worthwhile reviewing each of the stages in the buying process referred to in Figure 2.15 in order to highlight how effective the Internet can be when used at different stages to support the marketing communications objectives. Of course, the exact stage of the buying decision varies for different products and different types of customers, so an alternative approach is to develop channel chains (Figure 2.32) which reflect these differences. In general, digital media support the consumer buying process as follows.

### 1 Consumer: unaware. Company: generates awareness (of need, product or service)

Generating awareness of need is conventionally achieved principally through the mass media used in offline advertising. The Internet is relatively ineffective at this since it tends to have a more limited impact and reach than television, radio or print media. However, display advertising or paid search marketing can be used to supplement offline awareness-building as explained in Chapter 8. Online equivalents of word-of-mouth or recommendations from friends or colleagues, perhaps influenced by a viral marketing campaign, can also create awareness of need. Some companies such as Zopa (see Case Study 2 p.118) have effectively developed brand awareness by means of PR and media mentions concerning their success on the Internet, with the result that even if a customer does not have a current need for a product, that customer may be aware of the source when the need develops.

### 2 Consumer: aware of need, develops specification. Company: position features, benefits and brand

Once a consumer is aware of a need and is considering what features and benefits he or she requires from a product or online service, then they may turn straight to the web to start identifying the range of features available from a particular type of product through using a generic search using search engines such as Google, MSN and Yahoo! So influencing consumers through search engine marketing and affiliate marketing is important at this stage.

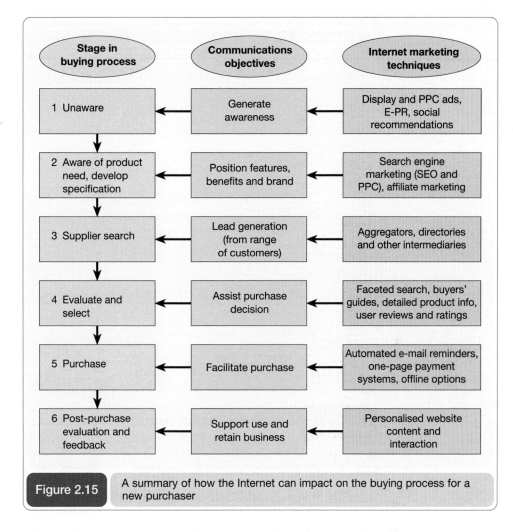

| Stage in buying process | Communications objectives | Internet marketing techniques |
|---|---|---|
| 1 Unaware | Generate awareness | Display and PPC ads, E-PR, social recommendations |
| 2 Aware of product need, develop specification | Position features, benefits and brand | Search engine marketing (SEO and PPC), affiliate marketing |
| 3 Supplier search | Lead generation (from range of customers) | Aggregators, directories and other intermediaries |
| 4 Evaluate and select | Assist purchase decision | Faceted search, buyers' guides, detailed product info, user reviews and ratings |
| 5 Purchase | Facilitate purchase | Automated e-mail reminders, one-page payment systems, offline options |
| 6 Post-purchase evaluation and feedback | Support use and retain business | Personalised website content and interaction |

**Figure 2.15**   A summary of how the Internet can impact on the buying process for a new purchaser

Specification development effectively happens at the same time as supplier search and more suppliers can be evaluated in greater depth than traditionally. For example, Figure 2.16 shows e-retailers available in paid search for an initial product search on fridges. Retailers such as Comet are displayed in the natural listings (see Chapter 8) while others such as Tesco are displayed in the sponsored links.

Intermediaries well known within a sector, such as Kelkoo (www.kelkoo.com), are quite important in supplier search and can also help in evaluation. For example, aggregators Kelkoo, Pricerunner and Ciao appear in Figure 2.16. It can be difficult for these aggregators or manufacturers such as Whirlpool to afford to feature high in the paid listings. On the web, if companies have the right permission marketing incentives described in Chapter 6, such as an opt-in e-newsletter or coupon discount, then they may effectively gain interest earlier in the lifecycle in comparison with traditional channels.

### 3 Consumer: supplier search. Company: generate leads (engage and capture interest)

Once customers are actively searching for products (the directed information-seeker of Lewis and Lewis, 1997), the web provides an excellent medium to help them do this. It also provides a good opportunity for companies to describe the benefits of their websites and obtain qualified leads. The Internet marketer must consider the methods that a customer will choose for searching and then ensure that the company or its product is featured prominently on these sites whether they are search engines, aggregators or affiliate intermediaries.

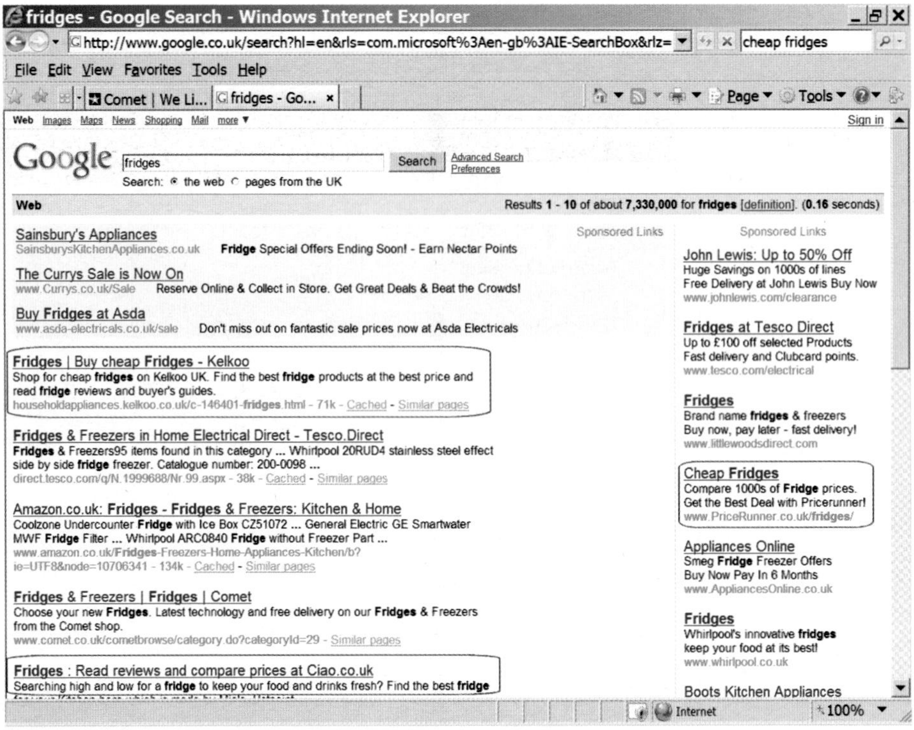

**Figure 2.16** Initial product search showing e-retailers available

### 4 Consumer: evaluate and select. Supplier: assist purchase decision

One of the most powerful features of websites is their facility to carry a large amount of content at relatively low cost. This can be turned to advantage when customers are looking to identify the best product. By providing relevant information in a form that is easy to find and digest, a company can use its website to help in persuading the customer. For example, the Comet site (Figure 2.17) enables customers to readily compare product features side-by-side, so they can decide on the best products for them. Thanks to the web, this stage can now overlap with earlier stages. Brand issues are important here, as proved by research in the branding section of Chapter 5, since a new buyer naturally prefers to buy from a familiar supplier with a good reputation – it will be difficult for a company to portray itself in this way if it is unknown and has a slow, poorly designed or shoddy website.

### 5 Consumer: purchase. Company: facilitate purchase

Once a customer has decided to purchase, then the company will not want to lose the custom at this stage! The website should enable standard credit-card payment mechanisms with the option to place the order by phone or mail. Online retailers pay great attention to identifying factors that encourage customers to convert once they have added a product to their 'shopping basket'. Security guarantees, delivery choices and free delivery offers, for example, can help increase conversion rates.

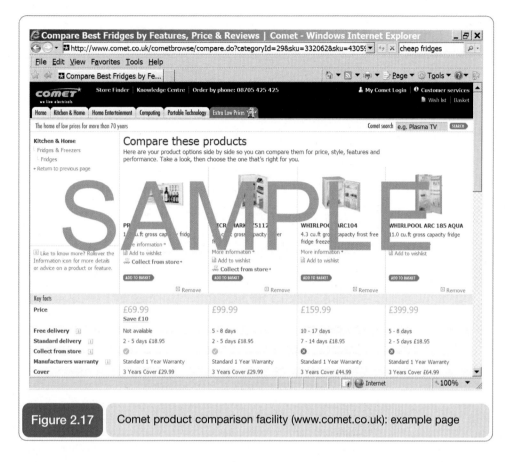

**Figure 2.17**   Comet product comparison facility (www.comet.co.uk): example page

### 6 Consumer: post-purchase evaluation and feedback. Company: support product use and retain business

The Internet also provides great potential for retaining customers, as explained in Chapter 6 since:

- value-added services such as free customer support can be provided by the website and these encourage repeat visits and provide value-added features;
- feedback on products can be provided to customers; the provision of such information will indicate to customers that the company is looking to improve its service;
- e-mail can be used to give regular updates on products and promotions and encourage customers to revisit the site;
- repeat visits to sites provide opportunities for cross-selling and repeat selling through personalised sales promotions messages based on previous purchase behaviour.

In this section we have reviewed simple models of the online buying process that can help Internet marketers convert more site visitors to lead and sale; however, in many cases the situation is not as simple as the models. Mini case study 2.4 'Multi-site online car purchase behaviour' indicates the complexity of online buyer behaviour, suggesting that it is difficult to develop general models that define online buyer behaviour.

Activity 2.1

### Changes in consumer buyer behaviour caused by digital channels

Although the model shown in Figure 2.15 provides a useful starting point for assessing buyer behaviour, it is right to remember that the Internet has changed behaviour and in some ways the model is not an accurate reflection of reality. What do you think are its main weaknesses? We would suggest:

- Process not necessarily sequential.
- Process compressed – for low involvement products, the decision can be made straightaway. Process will often start with a search and is mediated through search engines throughout, with the searches refined iteratively from generic to specific plus brand, for example 'fridge', 'upright fridge', 'comets fridge', 'whirlpool fridge', 'whirlpool 20TB L4'.
- The participation on the web and the creation of user-generated content (UGC), such as reviews and ratings on the retail site and comparison intermediaries such as Revoo (www.revoo.com), are important in the decision process.
- Viral marketing, and online PR, can be important for generating awareness (see Mini case study 1.1 on page **12** on Blendtec). In a virtual environment, trust becomes important, as we will see below, so the strength and familiarity of brands will be important.

## 3 Multichannel buying models

Remember that the customer scenario or user journey on the website is only part of a wider customer experience which involves multiple channels. The importance of multichannel strategies should also be built into assessing customer behaviour and their perception of the online customer experience. The importance of digital channels in influencing the overall customer experience is indicated in Mini case study 2.3 'Lexus assesses multichannel experience consistency'.

Mini Case Study 2.3

### Lexus assesses multichannel experience consistency

The luxury car brand Lexus has worked with the Multichannel Marketing Best Practice Club at the Cranfield School of Management, UK to assess the relative importance of consistency between channels. The pertinent results of this study are presented in Table 2.7. It can be seen that, as might be expected, the showroom experience is very important to the overall attitude towards the brand and purchase intent. The importance of the website experience quality is also notable and especially its role in the propensity to recommend – the Lexus customer can readily recommend the website to a friend or a colleague. So, it is the interactive channels that deliver the best experience, as would be expected.

| Table 2.7 | The impact of channel experience on customer relationship | | |
|---|---|---|---|

| Lexus communication channel | Attitude towards the brand | Future purchase intention | Propensity to recommend |
|---|---|---|---|
| TV experience quality | 0.362** | 0.360** | 0.185 |
| Print experience quality | 0.203 | 0.133 | 0.023 |
| Direct mail experience quality | 0.343* | 0.204 | 0.072 |
| Showroom experience quality | 0.447** | 0.292* | 0.217 |
| Contact centre experience quality | 0.431* | 0.566 | 0.147 |
| website experience quality | 0.452** | 0.315* | 0.309* |

*Source*: Menteth *et al*. (2005)
\* Correlation is significant at the 0.05 level
\*\* Correlation is significant at the 0.01 level

*Source*: Menteth *et al*, 2005. Reprinted by permission of Macmillan Publishers Ltd: *Interactive Marketing*, 6(4) 317–25, copyright 2005, published by Palgrave Macmillan. (The new name of this journal is *Journal of Direct Data and Digital Marketing Practice*).

| Mini Case Study 2.4 | Multi-site online car purchase behaviour |
|---|---|

Forrester Research (2002) has analysed online buyer behaviour in the car industry in detail. They estimate that different sites such as car manufacturers, dealers and independent auto sites collectively invest more than $1 billion each year trying to turn online auto shoppers into buyers. They recommend that to effectively identify serious car buyers from the millions of site visitors, auto site owners must correlate car buyers' *multi-site* behaviour to near-term (within three months) vehicle purchases. In the research, Forrester analysed behaviour across sites from three months of continuous online behaviour data and buyer-reported purchase data provided by comScore Networks, extracted from comScore's Global Network of more than 1.5 million opt-in Internet users. To find the correlation between online shopping behaviour and car buying, Forrester observed 78,000 individual consumers' paths through 170 auto sites and interviewed 17 auto site owners and software providers. Behaviour patterns like frequency and intensity of online research sessions and cross-site comparison-shopping were strong purchase predictors.

By researching user paths from site to site, Forrester found that:

- Online auto marketing and retailing continues to see strong growth despite weak demand in 2001 from the car market. While independent sites remain popular with consumers, manufacturer sites saw a 59% increase in traffic in 2001.
- Site owners currently lack the data and software tools to know where they fit in the online auto-retail landscape – or even how individual customers use their sites.
- Roughly one in four auto site visitors buys a car within three months.
- Repeat visitors are rare. 64% of all buyers complete their research in five sessions or fewer.
- Auto shoppers' web research paths predict their probability of vehicle purchase; on some paths, 46% are near-term buyers.
- The theory of a 'marketing funnel' doesn't map to actual car-buyer behaviour. Conventional wisdom suggests that shoppers first visit information sites, then manufacturer, then e-retailer or dealer sites, as they go from awareness to interest, desire and action. Mapping consumer data reveals a messier, more complex consideration process.

Summarising the research Mark Dixon Bünger, senior analyst at Forrester Research, says:

> Common assumptions about customer behavior when shopping for vehicles online are wrong. For example, loyalty and repeat visits are actually an anti-predictor of purchase. Most people who buy come in short, intense bursts, and don't hang out on auto sites. Single-site traffic analysis is not enough to understand and influence multi-site, multi-session auto shoppers. Today's website analysis tools weren't created to measure the complex nature of online auto shopping, which involves many sites over several episodes.

### A segmentation of car buying profiles

Forrester developed what they call a 'site owner road map' to help car site owners better understand their customers and segment them into four distinct car buying profiles. Since this segmentation is not predictive, Forrester suggest that to sell more cars through a better site experience, companies need to help each type of buyer reach its different goals. The four types are:

- *Explorers*. Forrester suggest that car buying is a 'journey of discovery' for these users, so suggest giving them a guide tour or user guides. This should lead them through a convenient, explicit buying process.
- *Offroaders*. These perform detailed research before visiting showrooms, but often leave without purchasing. If dealers can identify these visitors through the number of configurations, comparisons and number of page views they have, then dealers should quickly respond to the number of quotes they require.
- *Drive-bys*. These are the largest segment of car site visitors. They visit four sites or fewer, but only 20% buy online. Forrester suggest profiling these customers by incentivising them in order to better understand their purchase intentions.
- *Cruisers*. Frequent visitors, but only 15% buy a car in the short term. These are influencers who have a great interest in cars, but are not necessarily interested in purchase.

Since online interactions on a website often happen with limited consumer experience of a site, site owners and designers need to understand how they can develop trust with the audience.

## 4 Trust-based models

Online, purchasers lack the physical reassurance we have when purchasing from a store or talking to someone over a phone. This is compounded because of stories of fraud and security problems. It follows that consumers are looking for cues of trust when they are on a site and marketers need to understand the nature of these. These cues can include brand familiarity, site design, the type of content, accreditation and recommendations by other customers.

Bart *et al.* (2005) have developed a useful, widely referenced conceptual model that links website and consumer characteristics, online trust and behaviour based on 6,831 consumers across 25 sites from eight website categories including retail, travel, financial services, portals and community sites. We have summarised the eight main drivers of trust from the study in Figure 2.18 and have added some details about how these elements of trust can be substantiated or proved on the website.

The model of Bart *et al.* (2005) and similar models are centred on a site, but perceptions of trust are also built from external sources indicated by the research shown in Figure 2.9. Research by Brand New World (2004a) ranked the following information sources in order of importance when researching or considering a product or service:

- 71%: search engines
- 67%: personal recommendations
- 57%: websites of well-known retailers
- 56%: price-comparison websites
- 50%: reviews/opinions on the internet written by experts

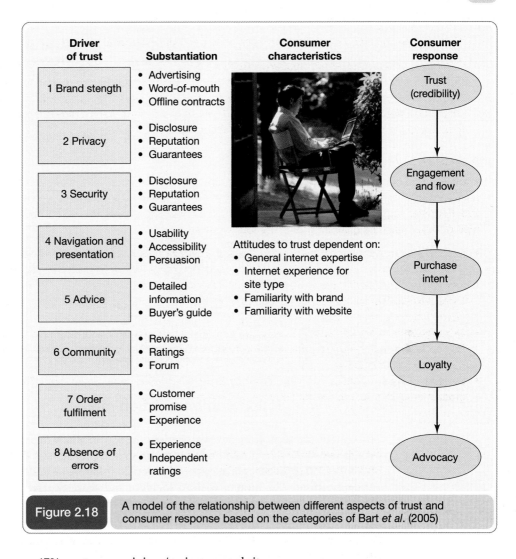

| Driver of trust | Substantiation | Consumer characteristics | Consumer response |
|---|---|---|---|
| 1 Brand stength | • Advertising<br>• Word-of-mouth<br>• Offline contracts | | Trust (credibility) |
| 2 Privacy | • Disclosure<br>• Reputation<br>• Guarantees | | Engagement and flow |
| 3 Security | • Disclosure<br>• Reputation<br>• Guarantees | | |
| 4 Navigation and presentation | • Usability<br>• Accessibility<br>• Persuasion | Attitudes to trust dependent on:<br>• General internet expertise<br>• Internet experience for site type<br>• Familiarity with brand<br>• Familiarity with website | Purchase intent |
| 5 Advice | • Detailed information<br>• Buyer's guide | | |
| 6 Community | • Reviews<br>• Ratings<br>• Forum | | Loyalty |
| 7 Order fulfilment | • Customer promise<br>• Experience | | |
| 8 Absence of errors | • Experience<br>• Independent ratings | | Advocacy |

**Figure 2.18**   A model of the relationship between different aspects of trust and consumer response based on the categories of Bart *et al.* (2005)

- 47%: customer opinions/reviews on websites
- 46%: product information in shops
- 38%: content provided by your internet service provider
- 34%: television
- 34%: newspapers/magazines
- 24%: salespeople in shops

When reviewing products on a destination site, web users will differ in their decision-making style which will vary according to their knowledge of the web and their attitude to risk and trust. To evaluate these issues, a useful framework has been developed by Forrester for the financial services market to segment customers. This is summarised in Figure 2.19. It shows how customers will generally fall into four groups, first based on those who gather detailed information and those who rely on less information and then based on those those who value advice from advisers.

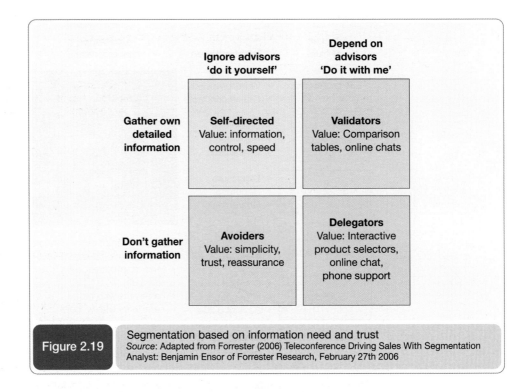

| Figure 2.19 | Segmentation based on information need and trust<br>*Source*: Adapted from Forrester (2006) Teleconference Driving Sales With Segmentation<br>Analyst: Benjamin Ensor of Forrester Research, February 27th 2006 |

## 5 Social interaction communication models

Throughout this section we have emphasised the way in which digital media have dramatically increased the role of recommendations from other consumers. We have seen that many of the Web 2.0 approaches involve participation and sharing of information between different applications. The human wish to socialise and share experiences is the real reason behind the popularity of Web 2.0 sites, such as the social network. Research by Microsoft (2007) based on interviews and surveys with social networkers found these human motivations for using social networks:

- 59% – to keep in touch with friends and family;
- 57% – I like looking at other people's spaces;
- 47% – I want to meet people with similar interests;
- 46% – to express my opinions and views on topics;
- 20% – it is a good way to date;
- 17% – using it for a specific reason, e.g. wedding, job networking.

Members of a community or social network will differ in the extent to which they are connected with others. The most influential network members will be highly connected and will discuss issues of interests with a wider range of contacts than those who are less connected (Table 2.8).

| Table 2.8 | Variations in number of connections in a sample |
|-----------|------------------------------------------------|

| Mean number of people communicated with monthly by each method | Less connected 10 or fewer connections | Moderately connected 11 to 99 connections | Highly connected 100+ or fewer connections |
|---|---|---|---|
| E-mail | 5 | 21 | 84 |
| See in person | 4 | 20 | 88 |
| Talk on the phone | 4 | 14 | 46 |
| Instant message | 1 | 5 | 16 |
| Text message | 1 | 4 | 15 |

*Source*: Understanding Influence, and Making It Work For You: A CNET Networks Study, Published 2007

It is generally believed by PR professionals seeking to influence marketplace perceptions that it is important to target the highly connected individuals since they are typically trusted individuals who other members of the community may turn to for advice. But there is much discussion about the influence of the influencers online. Researchers of community interactions believe that is the collective interaction between typical network members (known as the 'moderately connected majority') that are equally important. For example, Watts and Dodds (2007) argue that the 'influentials hypothesis' is based on untested assumptions and in most cases does not match how diffusion operates in the real world. They comment that 'most social change is driven not by influentials, but by easily influenced individuals influencing other easily influenced individuals'.

Although there is a clear wish to socialise online, site owners need to remember that it is not straightforward to engage an online audience as they move between different sites. Only a relatively small proportion will engage. Mini case study 2.5 on the '90:9:1' rule shows that only a relatively small number of site visitors will actively participate.

| Mini Case Study 2.5 | Nielsen's 90:9:1 rule of participation inequality: encouraging more users to contribute |
|---------------------|------------------------------------------------------------------------------------------|

To encourage online community participation is a challenge since the majority of visitors to a community lurk or don't participate. Usability expert Jakob Nielsen gives examples of participation on Wikipedia (just 0.2% of visitors are active) and Amazon (fewer than 1% post reviews). He says that 'in most online communities, 90% of users are lurkers who never contribute, 9% of users contribute a little and 1% of users account for almost all the action'. He explains:

● 90% of users are lurkers (i.e. read or observe, but don't contribute).
● 9% of users contribute from time to time, but other priorities dominate their time.
● 1% of users participate a lot and account for most contributions: it can seem as if they don't have lives because they often post just minutes after whatever event they're commenting on occurs.

While 'lurking' or passive consumption of community content is a natural consumer behaviour it is possible to encourage participation. Nielsen suggests some participation strategies. First, there should be easy methods for a visitor to contribute, clicking a rating or commenting without registering. Second, automate contributions, but showing related recommendations or the most read articles. Third, provide templates for response. Fourth, reward users by giving them accolades for contribution and finally promote participation through design or featuring top reviewers.

## Competitors

**Competitor analysis**
Review of Internet marketing services offered by existing and new competitors and adoption by their customers.

**Competitor analysis** and benchmarking of competitor use of Internet marketing for acquisition and retention of customers is especially important because of the dynamic nature of the Internet medium. As Porter (2001) has pointed out, this dynamism enables new services to be launched and elements of the marketing mix, such as price and promotion, changed much more frequently than was traditionally the case. Copying of concepts and approaches within sectors is rife, but can sometimes be controlled through patenting. For example, Amazon.com has patented the 'One Click' approach to purchase, so this term and approach is not seen on other sites. The implications of this dynamism are that competitor benchmarking is not a one-off activity while developing a strategy, but needs to be continuous.

**Competitor benchmarking**
A structured analysis of the online services, capabilities and performance of an organisation within the areas of customer acquisition, conversion, retention and growth.

'**Competitor benchmarking**' is the term used for structured comparison of digital marketing approaches of an organisation's services within a market. Its purpose is to identify threats posed by changes to competitor offerings, but also to identify opportunities for enhancing a company's own web services through looking at innovative approaches in non-competing companies. Competitor benchmarking is closely related to developing the customer proposition and brand experience and is informed by understanding the requirements of different customer personas, as introduced earlier in this chapter.

Benchmarking of services has different perspectives which serve different purposes:

1 *Internal capabilities* such as resourcing, structure and processes vs *external customer facing* features of the sites.
2 *Different aspects of the customer lifecycle*: customer acquisition, conversion to retention. Capabilities are benchmarked in all the activities of each shown in Figure P. 1 in the Preface.
3 *Qualitative to quantitative*: from qualitative assessments by customers through surveys and focus groups through to quantitative analysis by independent auditors of data across customer acquisition (e.g. number of site visitors or reach within market, cost of acquisition, number of customers, sales volumes and revenues and market share); conversion (average conversion rates) and retention such as repeat conversion and number of active customers.
4 *In-sector and out-of-sector*: benchmarking against similar sites within sector and reviewing out-of-sector to sectors which tend to be more advanced, e.g. online publishers, social networks and brand sites. Benchmarking services are available for this type of comparison from analysts such as Bowen Craggs & Co (www.bowencraggs.com). An example of one of their benchmark reports is shown in Figure 2.20. You can see that this is based on the expert evaluation of the suitability of the site for different audiences as well as measures under the overall construction (which includes usability and accessibility), message (which covers key brand messages and suitability for international audiences) and contact (which shows integration between different audiences). Although some research into site types is based on the presence or absence of a feature, but Figure 2.20 is based on an expert review taking ten hours. The methodology states: 'it is not "tick box": every metric is judged by its existence, its quality and its utility to the client, rather than "Is it there or is it not?"'
5 *Financial to non-financial measures*. Through reviewing competitive intelligence sources such as company reports or tax submissions additional information may be available on turnover and profit generated by digital channels. But other forward-looking aspects of the company's capability which are incorporated on the balanced score measurement framework (see Chapter 4) should also be considered, including resourcing, innovation and learning.
6 *From user experience to expert evaluation*. Benchmarking research should take two alternative perspectives, from actual customer reviews of usability to expert evaluations.

| Pos | Company | Construction | Message | Contact | Serving society | Serving investors | Serving the media | Serving job seekers | Serving customers | Total | URL | Country |
|-----|---------|--------------|---------|---------|-----------------|-------------------|-------------------|---------------------|-------------------|-------|-----|---------|
|  | maximum score | 60 | 48 | 12 | 32 | 32 | 32 | 32 | 32 | 280 | | |
| 1 | Siemens | 47 | 40 | 10 | 27 | 21 | 28 | 24 | 24 | 221 | www.siemens.com | Germany |
| 2 | Royal Dutch Shell | 46 | 41 | 7 | 26 | 22 | 21 | 24 | 22 | 209 | www.shell.com | Netherlands |
| 3 | BP | 41 | 39 | 10 | 28 | 27 | 18 | 19 | 25 | 207 | www.bp.com | UK |
| 4 | Nokia | 44 | 36 | 8 | 26 | 24 | 24 | 16 | 25 | 203 | www.nokia.com | Finland |
| 5 | AstraZeneca | 48 | 33 | 9 | 20 | 20 | 27 | 16 | 27 | 200 | www.astrazeneca.com | France |
|  | Total | 44 | 39 | 11 | 25 | 27 | 12 | 22 | 21 | 200 | www.total.com | UK/Sweden |
| 7 | IBM | 41 | 36 | 11 | 23 | 26 | 26 | 12 | 24 | 199 | www.ibm.com | US |
| 8 | ING | 43 | 40 | 8 | 22 | 25 | 21 | 16 | 22 | 197 | www.ing.com | Netherlands |
| 9 | UBS | 37 | 36 | 6 | 20 | 27 | 22 | 26 | 20 | 194 | www.ubs.com | Switzerland |
| 10 | General Electric | 42 | 37 | 10 | 25 | 17 | 19 | 17 | 24 | 191 | www.ge.com | US |

**Figure 2.20**  Benchmark comparison of corporate websites
*Source*: Bowen Craggs & Co (www.bowencraggs.com)

Traditionally competitors will be well known. With the Internet and the global marketplace there may be new entrants that have the potential to achieve significant market share. This is particularly the case with retail sales. For example, successful new companies have developed on the Internet that sell books, music, CDs and electronic components. As a consequence, companies need to review the Internet-based performance of both existing and new players. Companies should review:

● well-known local competitors (for example, UK or European competitors for British companies);
● well-known international competitors;
● new Internet companies local and worldwide (within sector and out of sector);
● Chase (1998) advocates that when benchmarking, companies should review competitors' sites identifying best practices, worst practices and 'next practices'. Next practices are where a company looks beyond its industry sector at new approaches from innovative Internet companies such as Amazon (www.amazon.com) or Apple (www.apple.com) in business-to-consumer and Cisco (www.cisco.com) in business-to-business. For example, Cisco was one of the first business-to-business sites to take advantage of Web 2.0 approaches when it launched its Innovation network which features BizWize TV, Audio podcasts and interactive forums.

As well as assessing competitors on performance criteria, it is also worthwhile categorising them in terms of their capability to respond. Deise *et al.* (2000) suggest an equation that can be used in combination to assess the capability of competitors to respond:

$$Competitive\ capability = \frac{agility \times reach}{time\text{-}to\text{-}market}$$

'Agility' refers to the speed at which a company is able to change strategic direction and respond to new customer demands. 'Reach' is the ability to connect to or to promote products and generate new business in new markets. 'Time-to-market' is the product lifecycle from concept through to revenue generation. Companies with a high competitive capability within their market and competitive markets are arguably the most important ones to watch.

Companies can also turn to performance-benchmarking organisations such as Gomez (www.gomez.com). For example, Figure 2.21 shows a comparison of Canadian banks according to their speed of response and availability.

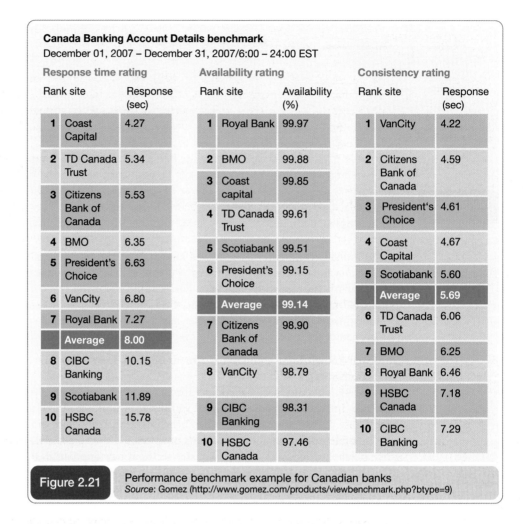

**Canada Banking Account Details benchmark**
December 01, 2007 – December 31, 2007/6:00 – 24:00 EST

| Response time rating | | Availability rating | | Consistency rating | |
|---|---|---|---|---|---|
| Rank site | Response (sec) | Rank site | Availability (%) | Rank site | Response (sec) |
| 1 Coast Capital | 4.27 | 1 Royal Bank | 99.97 | 1 VanCity | 4.22 |
| 2 TD Canada Trust | 5.34 | 2 BMO | 99.88 | 2 Citizens Bank of Canada | 4.59 |
| 3 Citizens Bank of Canada | 5.53 | 3 Coast capital | 99.85 | 3 President's Choice | 4.61 |
| | | 4 TD Canada Trust | 99.61 | | |
| 4 BMO | 6.35 | 5 Scotiabank | 99.51 | 4 Coast Capital | 4.67 |
| 5 President's Choice | 6.63 | 6 President's Choice | 99.15 | 5 Scotiabank | 5.60 |
| 6 VanCity | 6.80 | Average | 99.14 | Average | 5.69 |
| 7 Royal Bank | 7.27 | 7 Citizens Bank of Canada | 98.90 | 6 TD Canada Trust | 6.06 |
| Average | 8.00 | | | | |
| 8 CIBC Banking | 10.15 | 8 VanCity | 98.79 | 7 BMO | 6.25 |
| 9 Scotiabank | 11.89 | 9 CIBC Banking | 98.31 | 8 Royal Bank | 6.46 |
| 10 HSBC Canada | 15.78 | | | 9 HSBC Canada | 7.18 |
| | | 10 HSBC Canada | 97.46 | 10 CIBC Banking | 7.29 |

**Figure 2.21**    Performance benchmark example for Canadian banks
*Source*: Gomez (http://www.gomez.com/products/viewbenchmark.php?btype=9)

In some sectors, such as banking, competitors share data with a benchmarking organisation enabling them to see their relative performance (without knowing actual sales or efficiency levels). An example is eBenchmarkers, which in the UK produces reports for different financial services markets. Performance criteria are related to the conversion efficiency – companies are ranked relative to each other on their capacity to attract, convert and retain customers to use their e-commerce services.

We revisit competitor benchmarking in more detail in Chapters 4, 7 and 10.

# Suppliers

The most significant aspect of monitoring suppliers in the context of Internet marketing is with respect to the effect suppliers have on the value of quality of product or service delivered to the end customer. Key issues include the effect of suppliers on product price, availability and features. This topic is not discussed further since it is less significant than other factors in an Internet marketing context.

## Intermediaries

**Marketing intermediaries**

Firms that can help a company to promote, sell and distribute its products or services.

**Destination sites**

Sites typically owned by merchants, product manufacturers or retailers providing product information.

**Online intermediary sites**

Websites that facilitate exchanges between consumer and business suppliers.

**Marketing intermediaries** are firms that can help a company to promote, sell and distribute its products or services. In the Internet context, online intermediaries can be contrasted with destination sites which are typically merchant sites owned by manufacturers or retailers which offer information and products (in reality any type of site can be a **destination site**, but the term is generally used to refer to merchant and brand sites).

**Online intermediary sites** provide information about destination sites and provide a means of connecting Internet users with product information. The best known online intermediaries are the most popular sites such as Google, MSN and Yahoo! These are known as 'portals' and are described further below. Other consumer intermediaries such as Kelkoo (www.kelkoo.com) and Bizrate (www.bizrate.com) provide price comparison for products, as described earlier in this chapter. Most newspaper and magazine publishers, such as VNU (www.vnu.com) and Emap (www.emap.com), now provide online versions of their publications. These are as important in the online world in promoting products as newspapers and magazines are in the offline world.

There is a trend to more specialist intermediaries such as All Things Green (see Mini case study 2.6).

---

| Mini Case Study 2.6 | All Things Green creates an ethical marketplace |

Owner James Collins explains the growth of All Things Green.

*AllThingsGreen (Figure 2.22) was created in July 2006, as an online marketing and e-commerce resource for green companies.*

*As a subscription 'added value' e-commerce service, we have been adding services to our marketplace and associated 'Trader panel' ever since.*

*It now includes automatic Amazon listings, direct links with popular shopping comparison sites, an independent affiliate network and a growing number of green companies using its services.*

*Since we started developing the system, over 100 green companies have signed up and successfully used the service.*

*Our aim is to provide more and more green companies with online marketing services, the continuous development of the product allows us to ensure that all of our green traders have access to as much exposure for their products across the internet.*

*Our re-launch in July 2008 will be our first major re-structure of the consumer marketplace since launched, and will include feature upgrades that have been identified through our use of detailed analytic collection since its inception.*

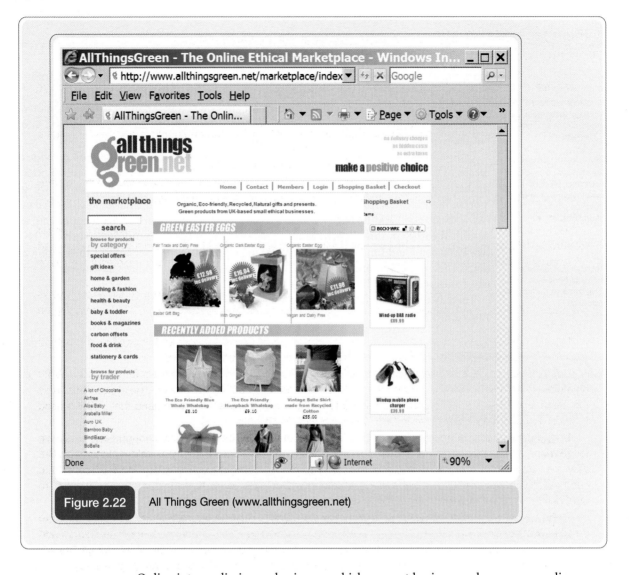

| Figure 2.22 | All Things Green (www.allthingsgreen.net) |
| --- | --- |

**Online social network**

A service facilitating the connection, collaboration and exchange of information between individuals.

Online intermediaries are businesses which support business and consumer audiences, so they can serve both B2B and B2C information exchanges. Auction sites are another type of online intermediary that support the B2B and the C2C exchanges introduced in Chapter 1. Online intermediaries sometimes support **online social networks** which are a form of online community described in more detail in the section on virtual communities at the end of Chapter 6. The Google Orkut service (www.orkut.com) is an example of a personal social network, while Linked In (www.linkedin.com) and Ecademy (www.ecademy.com) are examples of business networks. A business-to-business community serving the interest of Internet marketers is the EConsultancy forums (www.e-consultancy.com/forum).

Online intermediaries are typically independent of merchants and brands, but can be owned by brands. In business-to-business marketing, examples of such intermediaries include Clearly Business (www.clearlybusiness.com) from Barclays or bCentral (www.bcentral.co.uk) from Microsoft which has now been incorporated into the main Microsoft site at it's small-business centre (www.microsoft.com/uk/smallbusiness/). These are examples of 'countermediaries' referred to earlier in the chapter which are created by a service provider to provide valuable content or services to their audience with a view to enhancing their brand, so they are not truly independent.

Alibaba.com is one of the leading B2B e-commerce companies in China. It provides a marketplace connecting small and medium-sized buyers and suppliers from China and around the world. Its web presence includes an international marketplace (www.alibaba.com) which focuses on global importers and exporters and a China marketplace (www.alibaba.com.cn) which focuses on suppliers and buyers trading domestically in China.

From a launch in 1999 the marketplaces have a community of more than 24 million registered users and over 255,000 paying members. In November 2007, Alibaba launched on the Hong Kong stock exchange and raised HK$13.1 billion (US$1.7 billion) in gross proceeds before offering expenses making it the largest Internet IPO in Asia and the second largest globally.

Jack Ma, the founder of Alibaba, first saw the Internet in 1995 when he went to Seattle as an interpreter for a trade delegation and a friend showed him the Internet. They searched for the word 'beer' on Yahoo and discovered that there was no data about China. He decided to launch a website and registered the name China Pages.

He borrowed $2000 to set up his first company and at the time knew nothing about personal computers or e-mails and had never touched a keyboard before. He described the experience as a 'blind man riding on the back of a blind tiger'.

Initially, the business did not fare well, since it was a part of China Telecom and Jack Ma reflects that: 'everything we suggested, they turned us down, it was like an elephant and an ant'.

He resigned, but in 1999 he gathered 18 people in his apartment and spoke to them for two hours about his vision. Everyone put their money on the table, and he got $60,000 to start Alibaba. He chose Alibaba as the name since it was easy to spell and associated with 'Open Sesame', the command that AliBaba used to open doors to hidden treasures in *One Thousand and One Nights*.

During the dot-com bubble there were layoffs, such that by 2002 there was only enough cash to survive for 18 months. We had a lot of free members using our site, and we didn't know how we'd make money. But they then developed a product for China exporters to meet US buyers online which Ma said saved the company. By the end of 2002, Alibaba made $1 in profits! Each year since it has improved in profitability to the position where it was launched on the stock market.

Today, Jack Ma's vision is to build an e-commerce ecosystem that allows consumers and businesses to do all aspects of business online. They are partnering with Yahoo and have launched an online auction and payment businesses. His vision is expansive, he says: 'I want to create one million jobs, change China's social and economic environment, and make it the largest Internet market in the world' (Figure 2.23).

*Source*: You can view the video of CEO Jack Ma talking about the business on FT.com (search on Jack Ma), http://www.ft.com/cms/8a38c684-2a26-11dc-9208-000b5df1062.html

Ali Baba Press releases, Alibaba.com Limited Trading Debut, 7 November 2007, http://resources.alibaba.com/article/225276/ Alibaba_com_Limited_Trading_Debut_.htm

Riding the Blind Tiger: The Unlikely Rise of Alibaba CEO, Jack Ma, 8 January 2008, http://resources.alibaba.com/article/246718/ Riding_the_Blind_Tiger_The_Unlikely_Rise_of_Alibaba_CEO_Jack_MA.htm

| Figure 2.23 | Jack Ma, CEO of Alibaba, explains his business strategy |

Sarkar *et al.* (1996) identified many different types of potential online intermediaries (mainly from a B2C perspective) which they refer to as 'cybermediaries'. Some of the main intermediaries identified by Sarkar *et al.* (1996), listed with current examples, are:

- Directories (such as Yahoo! directory, Open Directory, Business.com).
- Search engines (Google, Yahoo! Search).
- Malls (now replaced by comparison sites such as Kelkoo and Pricerunner).
- Virtual resellers (own inventory and sells direct, e.g. Amazon, CDWOW).
- Financial intermediaries (offering digital cash and payment services such as PayPal which is now part of eBay).
- Forums, fan clubs and user groups (referred to collectively as 'virtual communities' or social networks such as HabboHotel for youth audiences).
- Evaluators (sites which act as reviewers or comparison of services such as Kelkoo).

At the time that Sarkar *et al.* (1996) listed the different types of intermediaries given above, there were many separate websites offering these types of services. For example, AltaVista (www.altavista.com) offered **search engine** facilities and Yahoo! (www.yahoo.com) offered a **directory** of different websites. Since this time, such sites have diversified the services offered. Yahoo! now offers all these services and additional types such as dating, communi-

**Search engines, spiders and robots**
Automatic tools known as 'spiders', crawlers or 'robots' index registered sites. Users search by typing keywords and are presented with a list of pages.

**Directories or catalogues**
Structured listings of registered sites in different categories.

ties and auctions. Diversification has occurred through the introduction of new intermediaries that provide services to other intermediaries and also through acquisition and merger. Since Google issued shares it has increasingly acquired or developed new services in its Google Labs (http://labs.google.com) to integrate into its services, as Yahoo! has done throughout its history. For example, it has purchased provider Blogger (www.blogger.com) and introduced the Gmail e-mail service and Orkut social networking service.

Activity 2.2 highlights the alternative revenue models available to these new intermediaries, in this case an evaluator, and speculates on their future.

---

**Activity 2.2** | **Kelkoo.com, an example of revenue models for new intermediaries**

### Purpose

To provide an example of the services provided by cybermediaries and explore their viability as businesses.

### Questions

1  Visit the Kelkoo website (www.kelkoo.com) shown in Figure 2.24 and search for this book, a CD or anything else you fancy. Explain the service that is being offered to customers.

2  Write down the different revenue opportunities for this site (some may be evident from the site, but others may not); write down your ideas also.

3  Given that there are other competing sites in this intermediary category, such as Shopsmart (www.shopsmart.com), assess the future of this online business using press releases and comments from other sites such as Moreover (www.moreover.com).

**Figure 2.24** | Kelkoo.com, a European price comparison site

**Infomediary**
An intermediary business whose main source of revenue derives from capturing consumer information and developing detailed profiles of individual customers for use by third parties.

Hagel and Rayport (1997) use 'infomediary' specifically to refer to the sale of customer information, although it is sometimes used more widely to refer to sites offering detailed information about any topic. Traditional infomediaries are Experian (www.experian.com) and Claritas (www.claritas.com) which provide customer data for direct marketing or credit scoring. Such companies now use the web to collect additional customer information from prize draw sites such as Email Inform (www.emailinform.com). An example of an infomediary providing detailed information about a sector, in this case e-marketing topics, is EConsultancy (www.e-consultancy.com).

A further type of intermediary is the *virtual marketplace* or virtual B2B trading community mentioned earlier in the chapter.

## Portals

**Portal**
A website that acts as a gateway to information and services available on the Internet by providing search engines, directories and other services such as personalised news or free e-mail.

An Internet portal is a website that acts as a gateway to information and services available on the Internet. Essentially, it is an alternative term for online intermediary, but the main emphasis is on providing access to information on the portal site and other sites.

Portals are important to Internet marketers since portals are where users spend the bulk of their time online when they are not on merchant or brand sites. Situation analysis involves assessing which portals target customers with different demographics and psychographics use. It also relates to competitor benchmarking, since the sponsorship deals and co-branding arrangements set up by competitors should also be reviewed.

For marketers to extend the visibility or reach of their company online, they need to be well represented on a range of portals through using sponsorships, online adverts and search marketing, as explained in Chapter 8. Portals also enable targeted communications. Specialist portals enable markets to target a particular audience through advertising, sponsorship and PR, while general portals often have sections or 'channels' which indicate a particular product interest. For example, financial services provider Alliance and Leicester uses a Loan calculator to sponsor the Money, Loans channel on ISP portal Wanadoo (www.wanadoo.com.uk) and web measurement company NetIQ sponsors the relevant channel on ClickZ (www.clickz.com) to reach their target audiences. Main portals such as newspapers and trade magazines also have registration, so can provide options for delivering messages via e-mail also.

| Activity 2.3 | Which are the top portals? |
| --- | --- |

To see the most important portals in your region, visit Nielsen//NetRatings (www.netratings.com) and choose 'Top Rankings'. This gives the top ten most popular sites in the countries listed. You will see that the largest portals, such as MSN and Google, can be used to reach over 50% of the Internet audience in a country. The pattern of top sites is different in each country, so international marketers need to ensure they are equally visible in different countries.

Many portals are related to Internet service providers – ISPs such as AOL (www.aol.com) and Wanadoo (www.wandadoo.com) have created a portal as the default home page for their users. The Microsoft Network (www.msn.com) is a popular portal since when users install the Internet Explorer browser it will be set up so that the home page is a Microsoft page.

### Types of portals

Portals vary in scope and in the services they offer, so naturally terms have evolved to describe the different types of portals. It is useful, in particular, for marketers to understand these terms since they act as a checklist that companies are represented on the different types of portals. Table 2.9 shows different types of portals. It is apparent that there is overlap between the different types of portal. Yahoo! for instance is a horizontal portal since it offers a range of services, but it has also been developed as a geographical portal for different countries and, in the USA, even for different cities. Many vertical and marketplace portals such as Chemdex and many Vertical Net sites (now VertMarkets (www.vertmarkets.com)) which were created at the height of the dot-com boom proved unsustainable and have largely been replaced by online versions of trader magazines for these markets.

| Table 2.9 | Portal characteristics |
| --- | --- |

| Type of portal | Characteristics | Example |
| --- | --- | --- |
| Access portal | Associated with ISP or telco | Orange (www.orange.co.uk)<br>AOL (www.aol.com) |
| Horizontal or functional portal | Range of services: search engines, directories, news recruitment, personal information management, shopping, etc. | Yahoo! (www.yahoo.com)<br>MSN (www.msn.com)<br>Lycos (www.lycos.com) |
| Vertical | A vertical portal covers a particular market, such as construction, with news and other services | Construction Plus (www.constructionplus.co.uk)<br>Chem Industry (www.chemindustry.com) |
| Media portal | Main focus is on consumer or business news or entertainment | BBC (www.bbc.co.uk)<br>Guardian (www.guardian.co.uk)<br>ITWeek (www.itweek.co.uk) |
| Geographical (region, country, local) | May be:<br>• horizontal<br>• vertical | Yahoo! country and city versions<br>Countyweb (www.countyweb.com) |
| Marketplace | May be:<br>• horizontal<br>• vertical<br>• geographical | Alibaba (www.alibaba.com)<br>EC21 (www.ec21.com)<br>eBay (www.eBay.com) |
| Search portal | Main focus is on search<br>Ask Jeeves (www.ask.com) | Google (www.google.com) |
| Media type | May be:<br>• voice<br>• video<br>Delivered by streaming media or downloads of files | BBC (www.bbc.co.uk)<br>Silicon (www.silicon.com) |

## Marketplace models

In this section we review how existing business model marketplaces can be applied to assist with developing digital strategies and understanding the changes introduced by the advent of the digital channels. The main marketplace models we will review are:

- competitive forces
- value chain creation and analysis
- new channel structures
- location of trading
- business models
- revenue models.

## Competitive forces

After the different customers, competitors and intermediaries have been identified through the approach suggested in Figure 2.2, the strategist needs to assess the relative strength and balance of power between customers, intermediaries and competitors. Michael Porter's classic 1980 model of the five main competitive forces that impact a company is one framework that can be used. Table 2.10 summarises the main impacts of the Internet on the five competitive forces affecting an organisation. Note that this form of analysis does not directly emphasise the importance of neutral intermediaries and strategic partnerships in affecting the visibility of an organisation within the online marketplace. Intermediaries such as search engines, aggregators and even blogs often have a strong influence on the balance between the bargaining power of buyers and suppliers and tend to intensify rivalry between existing competitors.

| Table 2.10 | Impact of the Internet on the five competitive forces |
|---|---|

| Bargaining power of buyers | Bargaining power of suppliers | Threat of substitute products and services | Barriers to entry | Rivalry between existing competitors |
|---|---|---|---|---|
| • The power of online buyers is increased since they have a wider choice and prices are likely to be forced down through increased customer knowledge and price transparency (see Chapter 5) | • When an organisation purchases, the bargaining power of its suppliers is reduced since there is wider choice and increased commoditisation due to e-procurement and e-marketplaces | • Substitution is a significant threat since new digital products or extended products can be readily introduced | • Barriers to entry are reduced, enabling new competitors, particularly for retailers or service organisations that have traditionally required a high-street presence or a mobile sales force | • The Internet encourages commoditisation which makes it less easy to differentiate products |
| • For a B2B organisation, forming electronic links with customers may deepen a relationship and it may increase switching costs, leading to 'soft lock-in' | • The reverse arguments regarding bargaining power of buyers | • The introduction of new substitute products and services should be carefully monitored to avoid erosion of market share<br>• Internet technology enables faster introduction of products and services<br>• This threat is related to new business models which are covered in a later section in this chapter | • New entrants must be carefully monitored to avoid erosion of market share<br>• Internet services are easier to imitate than traditional services, making it easy for 'fast followers' | • Rivalry becomes more intense as product lifecycles decrease and lead times for new product development decrease<br>• The Internet facilitates the move to the global market, increasing the number of competitors |

| Activity 2.4 | Assessing the impact of the Internet on competitive forces in different industries |

**Purpose**

To assess how some of the changes to the competitive forces caused by electronic communications impact particular industries.

**Activity**

Referring to Table 2.2, assess the impact of the Internet on a sector you select from the options below. State which you feel are the most significant impacts.

1　Banking.
2　Grocery retail.
3　Book retail.
4　B2B engineering component manufacturer.
5　B2B software services company selling customer relationship management software.
6　Not-for-profit organisation such as hospital, local government or charity.

### Examples of changes to the five forces

In this section further examples are given of changes to the five competitive forces.

#### Bargaining power of buyers

The increase in customer power and knowledge is perhaps the single biggest threat posed by electronic trading. The bargaining power of customers is greatly increased when they are using the Internet to evaluate products and compare prices. This is particularly true for standardised products for which offers from different suppliers can be readily compared through online intermediaries such as search engines and price comparison sites such as Kelkoo (www.kelkoo.com) or Pricerunner (www.pricerunner.com). For commodities, auctions on business-to-business exchanges can also have a similar effect of driving down price. Purchase of some products that have not traditionally been thought of as commodities, may become more price-sensitive. This process is known as **commoditisation**. Examples of goods that are becoming commoditised include electrical goods and cars.

In the business-to-business arena, a further issue is that the ease of use of the Internet channel makes it potentially easier for customers to swap between suppliers – switching costs are lower. With the Internet, which offers a more standard method for purchase through web browsers, the barriers to swapping to another supplier will be lower. With a specific EDI (electronic data interchange) link that has to be set up between one company and another, there may be reluctance to change this arrangement (**soft lock-in** due to switching costs). Commentators often glibly say 'online, your competitor is only a mouse click away', but it should be remembered that soft lock-in still exists on the web – there are still barriers and costs to switching between suppliers since, once a customer has invested time in understanding how to use a website to select and purchase a particular type of products, they may not want to learn another service.

A significant downstream channel threat is the potential loss of partners or distributors if there is a channel conflict resulting from disintermediation (see the sections on new channel structures, pages **106** and **310**). For example, a car distributor could switch to an alternative manufacturer if its profitability were threatened by direct sales from the manufacturer. The *Economist* (2000) reported that to avoid this type of conflict, Ford US are now using dealerships as part of the e-commerce solution and are still paying commission when sales are achieved online. This also helps protect their revenue from the lucrative parts and services market.

**Commoditisation**
The process whereby product selection becomes more dependent on price than on differentiating features, benefits and value-added services.

**Soft lock-in**
Electronic linkages between supplier and customer increase switching costs.

### Bargaining power of suppliers

**Internet EDI**
Use of electronic data interchange standards delivered across non-proprietary Internet protocol networks.

This can be considered as an opportunity rather than a threat. Companies can insist, for reasons of reducing cost and increasing supply chain efficiency, that their suppliers use electronic links such as EDI or **Internet EDI** to process orders. Additionally, the Internet tends to reduce the power of suppliers since barriers to migrating to a different supplier are reduced, particularly with the advent of **business-to-business exchanges**. However, if suppliers insist on proprietary technology to link companies, then this creates soft lock-in due to the cost or complexity of changing supppliers.

**Business-to-business exchanges or marketplaces**
Virtual intermediaries with facilities to enable trading between buyers and sellers.

### Threat of substitute products and services

This threat can occur from established or new companies. The Internet is particularly good as a means of providing information-based services at a lower cost. The greatest threats are likely to occur where digital product and/or service fulfilment can occur over the Internet. These substitutes can involve the new online channel essentially replicating an existing service as is the case with online banking or e-books. But, often, online can involve adding to the proposition. For example, compared to traditional music retailers, online legal subscription music services such as Napster (www.napster.com) offer a much wider choice of products with different delivery modes (real-time streaming to a PC or the capability to burn onto a CD or download to a portable music device such as an MP3 player). In banking, new facilities have been developed to help customers manage their finances online by aggregating services from different providers into one central account. Such added-value digital services can help lock customers into a particular supplier.

### Barriers to entry

For traditional companies, new online entrants have been a significant threat for retailers selling products such as books and financial services. For example, for the banking sector in Europe, traditional banks were threatened by the entry of completely new start-up competitors, such as First-e (www.first-e.com) (which later became financially unviable), or of traditional companies from one country that use the Internet to facilitate their entry into another country. US company Citibank (www.citibank.com) and ING Direct (www.ingdirect.co.uk) from the Netherlands used the latter approach. New companies were also created by traditional competitors – for example, Prudential created Egg (www.egg.com), Abbey National created Cahoot (www.cahoot.com), and the Co-operative bank created Smile (www.smile.co.uk). ING Direct has acquired millions of customers in new markets such as Canada, Australia and the UK through a combination of offline advertising, online advertising and an online or phone application process and account servicing.

These new entrants have been able to enter the market rapidly since they do not have the cost of developing and maintaining a distribution network to sell their products and these products do not require a manufacturing base.

However, to succeed, new entrants need to be market leaders in executing marketing and customer service. These are sometimes described as *barriers to success* or '*hygiene factors*' rather than barriers to entry. The costs of achieving these will be high, for example First-e has not survived as an independent business. This competitive threat is less common in vertical business-to-business markets involving manufacture and process industries such as the chemical or oil industries since the investment barriers to entry are much higher.

## Value creation and value chain analysis

How businesses create value within their markets is fundamental to their success. Digital technologies have a significant role in changing the balance of value creation within a market, so the extent of this change and how well it has been implemented must be evaluated as part of environment analysis. Value delivered is dependent on the difference between the consumer benefit created by the business and the costs incurred in producing or delivering the value as suggested by Figure 2.25. You can see that, arguably, the biggest impact of the Internet is the capability to reduce costs through reducing intermediaries such as physical stores and also through changing the intangible benefits. Together, these combine to form the online value proposition, as explained in Chapter 4. To pass on the reduced costs of dealing direct to the customer it will be necessary for retailers, banks and other companies to change their structure and accounting practices to isolate online channels as a separate profit centre.

**Value chain**

A model that considers how supply chain activities can add value to products and services delivered to the customer.

Michael Porter's **value chain** (VC) is a well-established concept for considering key activities that an organisation can perform or manage with the intention of creating value for customers (Porter, 1980). We can identify an *internal* value chain within the boundaries of an organisation and an *external* value chain, where activities are performed by partners. By analysing the different parts of the value chain, managers can redesign internal and external processes to improve their efficiency and effectiveness. Traditional value chain analysis (Figure 2.26(a)) of the internal value chain distinguishes between *primary activities* which contribute directly to getting goods and services to the customer (such as inbound logistics, including procurement, manufacturing, marketing and delivery to buyers, support and servicing after sale) and *support activities* which provide the inputs and infrastructure that allow the primary activities to take place.

Value chain analysis generally involves these steps:

1 Identify the organisation's main activities or processes using Porter's framework.
2 For each activity, identify changes to the current process with the potential to create value through means of introducing a cost advantage or differentiation compared to competitors.
3 Review the suitability of enhancement to processes with a view to their capability to create a sustained competitive advantage.

For Internet marketers, reviewing the technologies available to enhance customer value is a useful activity as part of situation analysis. This can involve both upstream value chain analysis of partners and downstream value chain analysis of channel partners (intermediaries) used to reach audiences online. Table 2.11 indicates some typical examples of how the Internet can be used to generate value within the context of the value chain framework given in Figure 2.26(a).

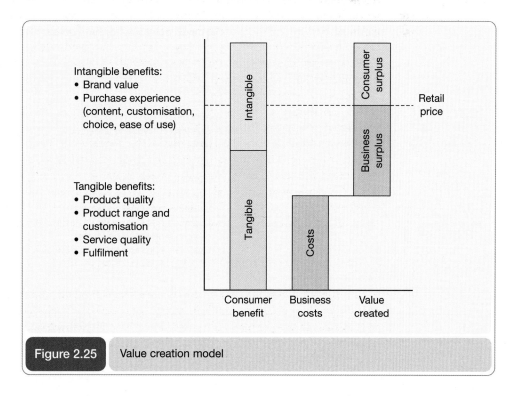

**Figure 2.25** Value creation model

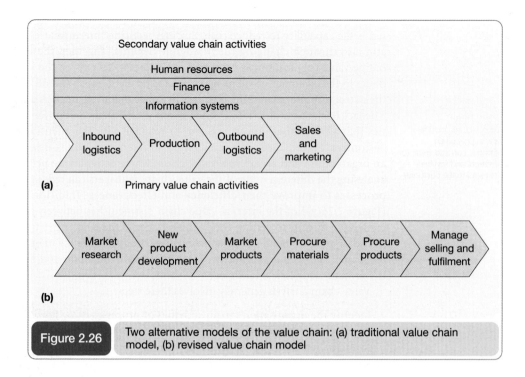

**Figure 2.26** Two alternative models of the value chain: (a) traditional value chain model, (b) revised value chain model

Figure 2.27 gives one example of a publisher who has innovated their value chain online. Lonely Planet has new options to buy individual chapters and to 'pick and mix' chapters. It also involves its customers in shaping future guides such as the Blue Guides.

**Table 2.11** Example of digital value-adding activities in the value chain

| | **Examples of Internet-based value-adding activities** |
|---|---|
| Market research and new product development | • Encourage customer feedback on new products (see for example Dell IdeaStorm (www.ideastorm.com).<br>• Monitor marketplace trends through social networks<br>• Use search engine keyphrase analysis to understand the demand for new products or content<br>• Use web analytics to understand the popularity of different products |
| Market products | • Attract new customers at lower cost through online marketing techniques (e.g. affiliate marketing, paid search marketing)<br>• Use aggregators (price comparison sites) to make products available to a wider audience<br>• Use customer communities (reviews and ratings) to encourage other customers to purchase<br>• Customise product options or bundles online |

| | **Examples of Internet-based value-adding activities** |
|---|---|
| Procure materials and products | • Review options for buying direct from suppliers (disintermediation)<br>• Options for buying from online auctions and marketplaces |
| Manage selling and fulfilment | • Use web self-service or online chat to reduce cost-to-sale<br>• Offer choice in delivery (for example weekend or evening deliveries or deliveries to work) |

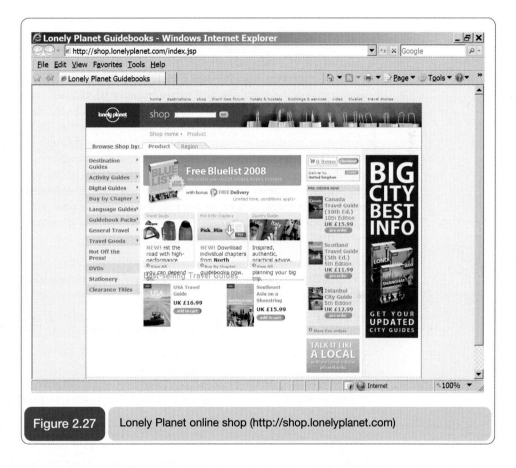

**Figure 2.27**     Lonely Planet online shop (http://shop.lonelyplanet.com)

Value can be created for the customer by reducing the costs of providing goods and services *and* adding benefits for customers:

- *within each* element of the value chain such as procurement, manufacture, sales and distribution;
- *at the interface between* elements of the value chain such as between sales and distribution. In equation form this is:

  *Value = (Benefit of each VC activity − its cost) + (Benefit of each interface between VC activities − its cost)*

Rayport and Sviokla (1996) contend that the Internet enables value to be created by gathering, organising, selecting, synthesising and distributing information. They refer to a separate parallel *virtual value chain* mirroring the physical value chain. The virtual value chain involves electronic commerce used to mediate traditional value chain activities such as market research, procurement, logistics, manufacture, marketing and distributing. Michael Porter (2001)also stresses the importance of information:

> *because every [value chain] activity involves the creation, processing and communication of information, information technology has a pervasive influence on the value chain.*

Understanding how Internet technologies can be used to process, transfer and share market-ing-related information is vital to help Internet marketers evaluate and revise value chain activities. For example, if a grocery retailer shares information electronically with its suppli-ers about demand for its products, this can enhance the value chain of both parties since the cycle time for ordering can be reduced resulting in lower inventory holding, and hence lower costs for both. The retailer can also set up links between its online product catalogues and all appropriate comparison intermediaries for products using data transfer technologies such as XML. This is the mechanism used by shopping comparison sites such as Kelkoo and Pricerunner, so it is important for online retailers to evaluate this integration. If this work is not seen as important since it is not a traditional marketing activity, then the opportunities of increased online visibility, and hence number of visitors and sales, will be reduced. Retailer Tesco has created its Price Check initiative (www.tesco.com/pricecheck) to highlight its competitiveness by making its competitor price survey available online. Of course, the most obvious examples of value creation occur directly through the interface between the website and the customer, for example through detailed product information, product selec-tion guides, personalised product recommendations and online customer support facilities which involve reducing cost to serve and may have intangible benefits for the customer such as improved recommendations or decreasing the purchase time.

### Restructuring the internal value chain

Traditional models of the value chain (such as Figure 2.26(a)) have been re-evaluated with the advent of global electronic communications. It can be suggested that there are some key weaknesses in the traditional value chain model:

- It is most applicable to manufacturing of physical products as opposed to services.
- It is a one-way chain involving pushing products to the customer; it does not highlight the importance of understanding customer needs through market research and responsive-ness through innovation and new product development.
- The internal value chain does not emphasise the importance of value networks (although Porter (1980) did produce a diagram that indicated network relationships).

A revised form of the value chain has been suggested by Deise *et al.* (2000); an adaptation of this model is presented in Figure 2.26(b). This digital value chain starts with the market research process, emphasising the importance of real-time environment scanning for deci-sion making. For each of the different types of organisation site introduced in Chapter 1, there are opportunities to create value by processing information in new ways:

1 Customer information collected on a *transactional e-commerce site* can develop greater understanding of the purchasing behaviour of its target customers, which can also be analysed in terms of demographic profiles through tracking online shopping preferences and sequences.
2 *Service-oriented relationship-building sites* can collect information as part of creating a dialogue using profiling forms, feedback forms and forums on the site enabling their owners to better understand customer characteristics and purchasing behaviour.
3 *Brand-building sites* also have opportunities to collect information about the profiles and preferences of their site visitors or those in their target market using third-party sites.

4 *Portal or media sites* can potentially use visitors to contribute content. Think of the BBC website which now has feedback on its news, sport and entertainment sites, so adding value to its visitors. Even well-known media owner Rupert Murdoch has suggested that online newspapers consider recruiting bloggers to add value to their audiences (Murdoch, 2005).

5 *Social networking sites* can summarise conversations to show trends in topics of interest, the 'zeitgeist'.

### External value chains and value networks

**Value network**
The links between an organisation and its strategic and non-strategic partners that form its external value chain.

Reduced time to market and increased customer responsiveness can be achieved through reviewing the efficiency of internal processes and how information systems are deployed. However, these goals are also achieved through consideration of how partners can be involved to outsource some processes that have traditionally been considered to be part of the internal value chain of a company. Porter's original work considered both the internal value chain and the external value chain or network. Since the 1980s there has been a tremendous increase in outsourcing of both core value-chain activities and support activities. As companies outsource more and more activities, management of the links between the company and its partners becomes more important. Deise *et al.* (2000) describe value network management as:

> the process of effectively deciding what to outsource in a constraint-based, real-time environment based on fluctuation.

Electronic communications have facilitated this shift to outsourcing, enabling the transfer of information necessary to create, manage and monitor partnerships. These links are not necessarily mediated directly through the company, but can take place through intermediaries known as value-chain integrators or directly between partners. In addition to changes in the efficiency of value-chain activities, electronic commerce also has implications for whether these activities are achieved under external control or internal control. These changes have been referred to as value-chain *disaggregation* (Kalakota and Robinson, 2000) or *deconstruction* (Timmers, 1999), and value-chain *reaggregation* (Kalakota and Robinson, 2000) or *reconstruction* (Timmers, 1999). Value-chain disaggregation can occur through deconstructing the primary activities of the value chain and then outsourcing as appropriate. Each of the elements can be approached in a new way, for instance by working differently with suppliers. In value-chain reaggregation the value chain is streamlined to increase efficiency between each of the value-chain stages.

The value network offers a different perspective which is intended to emphasise:

- the electronic interconnections between partners and the organisation and directly between partners that potentially enable real-time information exchange between partners;
- the dynamic nature of the network. The network can be readily modified according to market conditions or in response to customer demands. New partners can readily be introduced into the network and others removed if they are not performing well;
- different types of links can be formed between different types of partners. For example, EDI links may be established with key suppliers, while e-mail links may suffice for less significant suppliers.

Figure 2.28, which is adapted from the model of Deise *et al.* (2000), shows some of the partners of a value network that characterises partners as:

1 supply-side partners (upstream supply chain) such as suppliers, business-to-business exchanges, wholesalers and distributors;

2 partners who fulfil primary or core value-chain activities. The number of core value-chain activities that will have been outsourced to third parties will vary with different companies and the degree of virtualisation of an organisation which involves outsourcing non-core services;

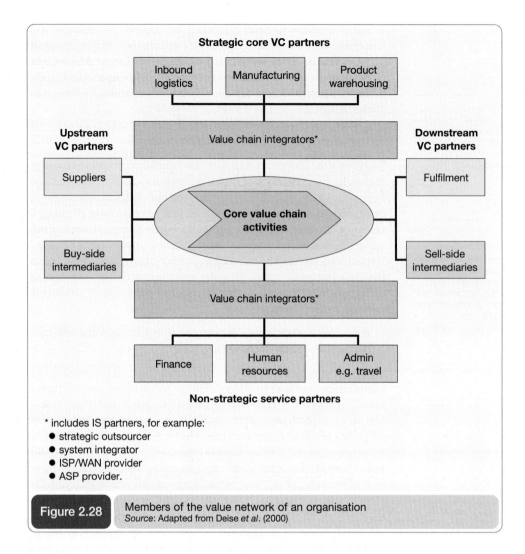

| Figure 2.28 | Members of the value network of an organisation |
| --- | --- |
| | *Source*: Adapted from Deise *et al*. (2000) |

**3** sell-side partners (downstream supply chain) such as business-to-business exchanges, wholesalers, distributors and customers (not shown, since they perceived as distinct from other partners);

**4** value chain integrators or partners who supply services that mediate the internal and external value chain. These companies typically provide the electronic infrastructure for a company and include strategic outsourcing partners, system integrators, ISPs and application service providers (ASPs).

Examples which illustrate the importance of value networks to Internet marketing are the affiliate networks and ad networks described in Chapter 8. Rather than working directly with individual publishers to drive visitors to a site, an online merchant will work with an affiliate network provider such as Commission Junction (www.cj.com) or ad network such as Miva (www.miva.com) which manages the links with the third parties.

## New channel structures

**Channel structure**
The configuration of partners in a distribution channel.

**Channel structures** describe the way a manufacturer or selling organisation delivers products and services to its customers. The distribution channel will consist of one or more intermediaries such as wholesalers and retailers. For example, a music company is unlikely to distribute its CDs directly to retailers, but will use wholesalers that have a large warehouse of titles that are then distributed to individual branches according to demand. A company selling business products may have a longer distribution channel involving more intermediaries.

The relationship between a company and its channel partners can be dramatically altered by the opportunities afforded by the Internet. This occurs because the Internet offers a means of bypassing some of the channel partners. This process is known as **disintermediation** or, in plainer language, 'cutting out the middleman'.

Figure 2.29 illustrates disintermediation in a graphical form for a simplified retail channel. Further intermediaries, such as additional distributors, may occur in a business-to-business market. Figure 2.29(a) shows the former position where a company marketed and sold its products by 'pushing' them through a sales channel. Figures 2.29(b) and (c) show two different types of disintermediation in which the wholesaler (b) or the wholesaler and retailer (c) are bypassed, allowing the producer to sell and promote direct to the consumer. The benefits of disintermediation to the producer are clear – it is able to remove the sales and infrastructure cost of selling through the channel. Benjamin and Weigand (1995) calculate that, using the sale of quality shirts as an example, it is possible to make cost savings of 28% in the case of (b) and 62% for case (c). Some of these cost savings can be passed on to the customer in the form of cost reductions.

**Disintermediation**
The removal of intermediaries such as distributors or brokers that formerly linked a company to its customers.

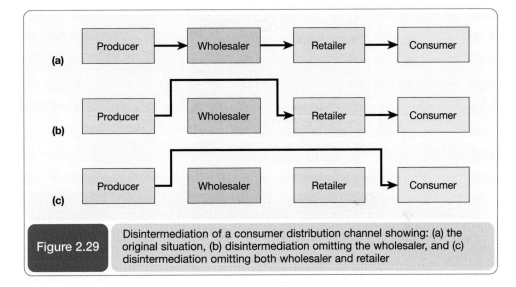

| Figure 2.29 | Disintermediation of a consumer distribution channel showing: (a) the original situation, (b) disintermediation omitting the wholesaler, and (c) disintermediation omitting both wholesaler and retailer |

At the start of business hype about the Internet in the mid-1990s there was much speculation that widespread disintermediation would see the failure of many intermediary companies as direct selling occurred. While many companies have taken advantage of disintermediation, the changes have not been as significant as predicted. Since purchasers of products still require assistance in the selection of products, this led to the creation of new intermediaries, a process referred to as **reintermediation**. In the UK Screentrade (www.screentrade.co.uk, Figure 2.30) was established as a broker to enable different insurance companies to sell direct. While it was in business for several years, it eventually failed as online purchasers turned to established brands. However, it was sold to an existing bank (Lloyds TSB) which continues to operate it as an independent intermediary.

Figure 2.31 shows the operation of reintermediation in a graphical form. Following disintermediation, where the customer goes direct to different suppliers to select a product, this becomes inefficient for the consumer. Take, again, the example of someone buying insurance – to decide on the best price and offer, they would have to visit say five different insurers and then return to the one they decide to purchase from. Reintermediation removes this inefficiency by placing an intermediary between the purchaser and seller. This intermediary performs the price evaluation stage of fulfilment since its database has links updated from prices contained within the databases of different suppliers.

**Reintermediation**
The creation of new intermediaries between customers and suppliers providing services such as supplier search and product evaluation.

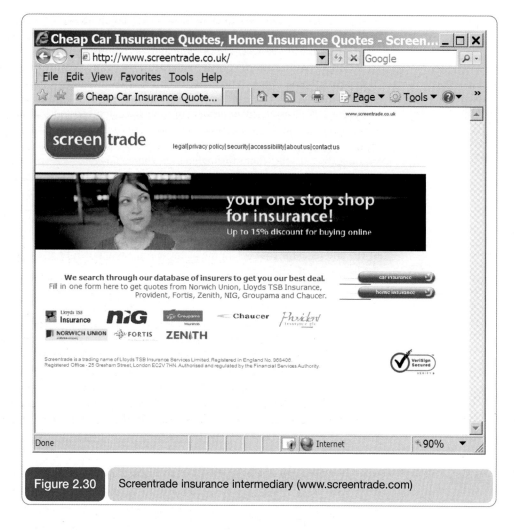

| Figure 2.30 | Screentrade insurance intermediary (www.screentrade.com) |

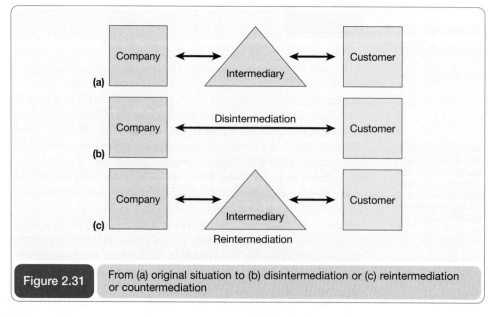

| Figure 2.31 | From (a) original situation to (b) disintermediation or (c) reintermediation or countermediation |

What are the implications of reintermediation for the Internet marketer? First, it is necessary to make sure that a company, as a supplier, is represented with the new intermediaries operating within your chosen market sector. This implies the need to integrate, using the Internet, databases containing price information with that of different intermediaries. Secondly, it is important to monitor the prices of other suppliers within this sector (possibly by using the intermediary website for this purpose). Thirdly, long-term partnering arrangements such as sponsorships need to be considered. Finally, it may be appropriate to create your own intermediary to compete with existing intermediaries or to pre-empt similar intermediaries. For example, the Thomson Travel Group set up Latedeals.com (www.latedeals.com) in direct competition with Lastminute.com (www.lastminute.com). A further example is that, in the UK, Boots the Chemist set up its own intermediaries Handbag (www.handbag.com) and Wellbeing (www.wellbeing.com). This effectively created barriers to entry for other new intermediaries wishing to operate in this space. Such tactics to counter or take advantage of reintermediation are sometimes known as **countermediation**.

Market mapping and developing channel chains is a powerful technique recommended by McDonald and Wilson (2002) for analysing the changes in a marketplace introduced by the Internet. A market map can be used to show the flow of revenue between a manufacturer or service provider and its customers through traditional intermediaries and new types of intermediaries. For example, Thomas and Sullivan (2005) give the example of a US multi-channel retailer that used cross-channel tracking of purchases through assigning each customer a unique identifier to calculate channel preferences as follows: 63% bricks-and-mortar store only, 12.4% Internet-only customers, 11.9% catalogue-only customers, 11.9% dual-channel customers and 1% three-channel customers.

A channel chain is similar – it shows different customer journeys for customers with different channel preferences. It can be used to assess the current and future importance of these different customer journeys. An example of a channel chain is shown in Figure 2.32.

**Countermediation**
Creation of a new intermediary by an established company.

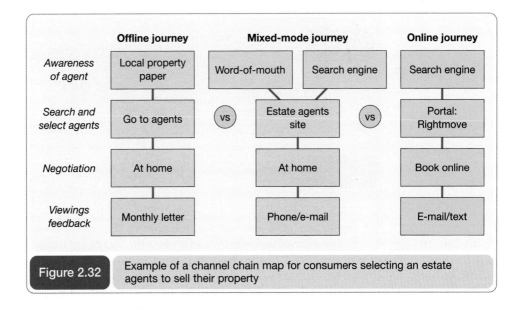

**Figure 2.32**    Example of a channel chain map for consumers selecting an estate agents to sell their property

## Location of trading

**Electronic marketspace**
A virtual marketplace such as the Internet in which no direct contact occurs between buyers and sellers.

While traditional marketplaces have a physical location, Internet-based markets have no physical presence – it is a virtual marketplace. Rayport and Sviokla (1996) used this distinction to coin the new term **electronic marketspace**. This has implications for the way in which the relationships between the different actors in the marketplace occur.

**Representation**
The locations on the Internet where an organisation is located for promoting or selling its services.

The new electronic marketspace has many alternative virtual locations where an organisation needs to position itself to communicate and sell to its customers. Thus, one tactical marketing question is 'What representation do we have on the Internet?' A particular aspect of **representation** that needs to be reviewed is the different types of marketplace location. Berryman *et al.* (1998) have identified a simple framework for this. They identify three key online locations for promotion of services and for performing e-commerce transactions with customers (Figure 2.33). The three options are:

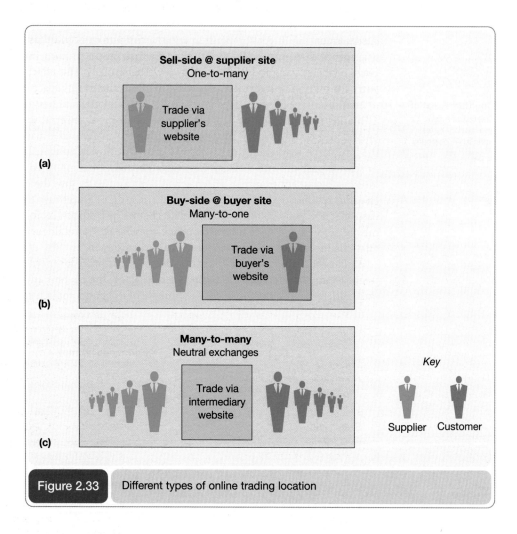

| Figure 2.33 | Different types of online trading location |

(a) *Supplier-controlled sites (sell-side at supplier site, one supplier to many customers)*. This is the main website of the company and is where the majority of transactions take place. Most e-tailers such as Amazon (www.amazon.com) or Dell (www.dell.com) fall into this category.

(b) *Buyer-controlled sites (buy-side at buyer site, many suppliers to one customer)*. These are intermediaries that have been set up so that it is the buyer that initiates the market-making. This can occur through procurement posting where a purchaser specifies what they wish to purchase, it is sent by e-mail to suppliers registered on the system and then offers are awaited. Aggregators involve a group of purchasers combining to purchase a multiple order, thus reducing the purchase cost. General Electric Trading Post Network was the first to set up this type of arrangement (http://tpn.geis.com, although this site is site no longer available) but it remains uncommon in comparison to the other two alternatives.

(c) *Neutral sites or intermediaries (neutral location – many suppliers to many customers).* For consumers, evaluator intermediaries that enable price and product comparison have become commonplace as we have seen. B2B intermediaries are known as *trading exchanges, marketplaces* or *hubs.* Examples of independent B2B exchanges mentioned in the previous edition are Vertical Net (www.vertical.net), Commerce One Marketsite (www.commerceone.com) and Covisint (www.covisint.net), none of which now exist in their original form. While some B2B intermediaries remain for some commodities or simple services (for example, EC21 (www.ec21.com), Elance (www.elance.com), eBay Business (http://business.ebay.com)) the new trading arrangements have not developed as predicted by many analysts due to the complexity of business purchase decisions and negotiations and their destabilising nature on markets.

## Commercial arrangement for transactions

Markets can also be considered from another perspective – that of the type of commercial arrangement that is used to agree a sale and price between the buyer and supplier. The main alternative commercial arrangements are shown in Table 2.12.

| Table 2.12 | Commercial mechanisms and online transactions |
| --- | --- |
| **Commercial (trading) mechanism** | **Online transaction mechanism of Nunes *et al*. (2000)** |
| 1 **Negotiated deal**<br>Example: can use similar mechanism to auction as on<br>Commerce One (www.ec21.com) | • Negotiation – bargaining between single seller and buyer<br>• Continuous replenishment – ongoing fulfilment of orders under preset terms |
| 2 **Brokered deal**<br>Example: intermediaries such as Screentrade (www.screentrade.co.uk) | • Achieved through online intermediaries offering auction and pure markets online |
| 3 **Auction**<br>C2C: eBay (www.ebay.com)<br>B2B: eBay business<br>(http://business.ebay.com) | • Seller auction – buyers' bids determine final price of sellers' offerings<br>• Buyer auction – buyers request prices from multiple sellers<br>• Reverse – buyer posts desired price for seller acceptance |
| 4 **Fixed price sale**<br>Example: all e-tailers | • Static call – online catalogue with fixed prices<br>• Dynamic call – online catalogue with continuously updated prices and features |
| 5 **Pure markets**<br>Example: electronic share dealing | • Spot – buyers' and sellers' bids clear instantly |
| 6 **Barter**<br>Example: www.intagio.com | • Barter – buyer and seller exchange goods |

It can be seen from Table 2.12 that each of these commercial arrangements is similar to a traditional arrangement. Although the mechanism cannot be considered to have changed, the relative importance of these different options has changed with the Internet. Owing to the ability to rapidly publish new offers and prices, auction has become an important means of selling on the Internet. A turnover of billions of dollars has been achieved by eBay from consumers offering items ranging from cars to antiques. Many airlines have successfully trialled auctions to sell seats remaining on an aircraft just before a flight.

Research suggests that participants in auctions do not necessarily behave rationally. In a study of the consumer approach to auctions which assessed the type of value assessments and decision dynamics made at each stage of the auction, Ariely and Simonson (2003) suggested that participants in auctions do not always get the bargain they may be looking for – their study of purchases of DVDs and electronic equipment found that:

> *(a) due to a focus on the narrow auction context, consumers under-search and, consequently, overpay for widely available commodities (CDs, DVDs) and (b) higher auction starting prices tend to lead to higher winning bids, particularly when comparable items are not available in the immediate context.*

## Business models in e-commerce

**Business model**
A summary of how a company will generate revenue, identifying its product offering, value-added services, revenue sources and target customers.

A consideration of the different business models made available through e-commerce is of particular importance to both existing and start-up companies. Venkatraman (2000) points out that existing businesses need to use the Internet to build on current business models while at the same time experimenting with new business models. New business models may be important to gain a competitive advantage over existing competitors and at the same time head off similar business models created by new entrants. For start-ups or dot-coms the viability of a business model will be crucial to funding from venture capitalists. But what is a business model? Timmers (1999) defines a 'business model' as:

> *an architecture for product, service and information flows, including a description of the various business actors and their roles; and a description of the potential benefits for the various business actors; and a description of the sources of revenue.*

It can be suggested that a business model for e-commerce requires consideration of the marketplace from several different perspectives:

- Does the company operate in the B2B or B2C arena, or a combination?
- How is the company positioned in the value chain between customers and suppliers?
- What is its value proposition and for which target customers?
- What are the specific revenue models that will generate different income streams?
- What is its representation in the physical and virtual world, i.e. high-street presence, online only, intermediary, mixture?

Timmers (1999) identifies no fewer than eleven different types of business model that can be facilitated by the web as follows:

1 *e-shop* – marketing of a company or shop via the web;
2 *e-procurement* – electronic tendering and procurement of goods and services;
3 *e-mall* – a collection of e-shops such as BarclaySquare (www.barclays-square.com);
4 *e-auctions* – these can be for B2C, e.g. eBay (www.ebay.com), or B2B, e.g. QXL (www.qxl.com);
5 *virtual communities* – these can be B2C communities such as Habbo Hotel for teenagers (www.habbo.com) or B2B communities such as Clearlybusiness (www.clearlybusiness.com/community) which are both important for their potential in e-marketing and are described in the virtual communities section in Chapter 6;
6 *collaboration platforms* – these enable collaboration between businesses or individuals, e.g. E-groups (www.egroups.com), now part of Yahoo! (www.yahoo.com) services;
7 *third-party marketplaces* – marketplaces are intermediaries that facilitate online trading by putting buyers and sellers in contact. They are sometimes also referred to as 'exchanges' or 'hubs';
8 *value-chain integrators* – offer a range of services across the value chain;

9 *value-chain service providers* – specialise in providing functions for a specific part of the value chain such as the logistics company UPS (www.ups.com);

10 *information brokerage* – providing information for consumers and businesses, often to assist in making the buying decision or for business operations or leisure;

11 *trust and other services* – examples of trust services include Internet Shopping is Safe (ISIS) (www.imrg.org/isis) or TRUSTe (www.truste.org) which authenticate the quality of service and privacy protection provided by companies trading on the web.

Figure 2.34 suggests a different perspective for reviewing alternative business models. There are three different perspectives from which a business model can be viewed. Any individual organisation can operate in different categories, as the examples below show, but most will focus on a single category for each perspective. Such a categorisation of business models can be used as a tool for formulating e-business strategy. The three perspectives, with examples are:

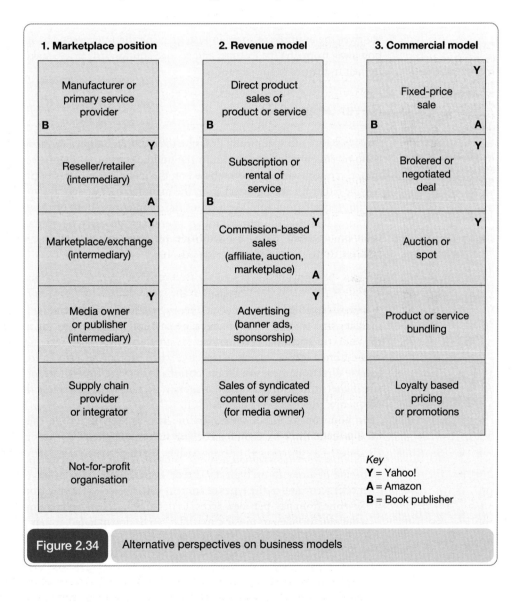

Figure 2.34    Alternative perspectives on business models

1 *Marketplace position perspective.* The book publisher is the manufacturer, Amazon is a retailer and MSN is a retailer, marketplace intermediary and media owner.
2 *Revenue model perspective.* The book publisher can use the web to sell direct and MSN and Amazon can take commission-based sales. Yahoo! also has advertising as a revenue model.
3 *Commercial model perspective.* All three companies offer fixed-price sales, but in its place as a marketplace intermediary, MSN also offers other alternatives.

Michael Porter (2001) urges caution against overemphasis on new business or revenue models and attacks those who have suggested that the Internet invalidates his well-known strategy models. He says:

*many have assumed that the Internet changes everything, rendering all the old rules about companies and competition obsolete. That may be a natural reaction, but it is a dangerous one . . . [companies have taken] decisions that have eroded the attractiveness of their industries and undermined their own competitive advantages.*

He gives the example of some industries using the Internet to change the basis of competition away from quality, features and service and towards price, making it harder for anyone in their industries to turn a profit.

## Revenue models

**Revenue models**
Describe methods of generating income for an organisation.

**Revenue models** specifically describe different techniques for generation of income. The main revenue models are shown in the middle column of Figure 2.34. For existing companies, revenue models have been based on the income from sales of products or services. This may be either for selling direct from the manufacturer or supplier of the service, or through an intermediary that will take a cut of the selling price. Both of these revenue models are, of course, still crucial in online trading. There may, however, be options for other methods of generating revenue: perhaps a manufacturer may be able to sell advertising space or sell digital services that were not previously possible.

### Types of revenue model

A knowledge of the range of options for generating revenue online is useful, both for intermediary sites such as media owners, portals and affiliates, and for transactional sites where the main transactional revenue may be supplemented by ad revenue, for example. It is also useful from a media-buying perspective when promoting a site, since when viewed from the reverse direction, these are all the options for paying for visitors, either when approaching site owners direct or via a media agency. So you need to review the options and select a media mix which delivers the best ROI.

In addition to direct selling online and brokering online sales through an auction arrangement, there are eight main online ad revenue models.

1 *Revenue from subscription access to content.* A range of documents can be accessed for a period of a month or, typically, a year. For example, FT.com has a three tier subscription model according to the types of content you can access varying from £100 to £400 per year.
2 Revenue from pay-per-view access to documents. Here payment occurs for single access to a document, video or music clip which can be downloaded. It may or may not be protected with a password or digital rights management. For example, we pay to access detailed best practice guides on Internet marketing from Marketing Sherpa.
3 *Revenue from CPM display advertising on site* (e.g. banners ads, skyscrapers or rich media). CPM stands for 'cost per thousand' where M denotes 'mille'. The site owner such as FT.com charges advertisers a rate card price (for example €50 CPM) according to the number of its ads shown to site visitors. Ads may be served by the site owner's own ad server or more commonly through a third-party ad network service. With display ad networks, space can be bought a lower rate because it is known as a blind ad buy – CPM rates are lower because it is not known where the ads will be placed.

4  *Revenue from CPC advertising on site (pay-per-click text ads).* CPC stands for 'cost per click'. Advertisers are charged not simply for the number of times their ads are displayed, but according to the number of times they are clicked. These are typically text ads similar to sponsored links within a search engine but delivered over a network of third-party sites such as Google Adsense (www.google.com/adsense), Yahoo! Content Match (http://searchmarketing. yahoo.com/srch/contentmatch.php), Microsoft content ads (http://advertising.microsoft. com/advertise/search/content-advertising) or MIVA (www.miva.com). For example, Dave Chaffey's site (www.davechaffey.com) uses Google Adsense by inserting Javascript at different points in the page to automatically serve contextual ads related to the content, so a page about e-mail marketing has ads about e-mail services which can be bought on a CPM (site targeted) or cost-per-click basis. For us, the search content networks are one of the biggest secrets in online marketing with search engines such as Google generating over a third of their revenue from the network, but some advertisers do not realise their ads are being displayed beyond search engines and so are not served for this purpose. Google is the innovator and offers options for different formats of ad units including text ads, display ads, streamed videos and now even cost per action as part of its pay-per-action scheme.

5  *Revenue from sponsorship of site sections or content types (typically fixed fee for a period) – fixed price deal, CPA or CPC deal.* A company can pay to advertise a site channel or section. For example, bank HSBC sponsors the Money section on the Orange portal. This type of deal is often struck for a fixed amount per year. It may also be part of a reciprocal arrangement, sometimes known as a 'contra-deal' where neither party pays. However, it is a negotiated deal, so may also have CPA or CPC elements. A fixed-fee sponsorship approach was famously used by Alex Tew in 2005, a 21-year-old considering going to university in the UK, who was concerned about paying off his university debts. This is no longer a concern since he earned $1,000,000 in 4 months when he set up his Million Dollar Homepage (www.milliondollarhomepage.com).

6  *Affiliate revenue (typically CPA, but could be CPC).* Affiliate revenue is commission based, for example if you display links to Amazon books on your site, you can receive around 5% of the cover price as a fee from Amazon. Such an arrangement is sometimes known as cost per acquisition (CPA). Amazon, and others, offer a tiered scheme where the affiliate is incentivised to gain more revenue the more they sell. Hence this is often called a pay-per-performance ad deal. Increasingly this approach is replacing CPM or CPC approaches where the advertiser has more negotiating power. For example, in 2005 manufacturing company Unilever negotiated CPA deals with online publishers where it paid for every e-mail address captured by a campaign rather than a traditional CPM deal. However, it depends on the power of the publisher who will often receive more revenue overall for CPM deals. After all, the publisher cannot influence the quality of the ad creative or the incentivisation to click which will affect the click-through rate on the ad and so the CPM.

7  *Subscriber data access for e-mail marketing.* The data a site owner has about its customers is also potentially valuable since it can send different forms of e-mail to its customers if they have given their permission that they are happy to receive e-mail either from the publisher or third parties. The site owner can charge for adverts placed in its newletter or can deliver a separate message on behalf of the advertiser (sometimes known as list rental). A related approach is to conduct market research with the site customers.

8  *Access to customers for online research.* An example of a company that uses this approach to attract revenue from surveys is the teen site Dubit.

### Assessing the best form of revenue model

Considering all of these approaches to revenue generation together, the site owner will seek to use the best combination of techniques to maximise the revenue. To assess how effective different pages or sites in their portfolio are at generating revenue, they will use two approaches.

The first is **eCPM**, or **effective cost per thousand**. This is a measure of the total revenue the site owner can generate every time 1000 pages are served. By increasing the number of ad units on each page this value will increase. This is why you will see some sites which are cluttered with ads. The other alternative to assess page or site revenue generating effectiveness is revenue per click (RPC) and the similar **earnings per click** (**EPC**), actually based on one hundred clicks to make it more meaningful for affiliates who will only generate revenue for a small percentage of clicks out from their sites. Basic revenue model evaluation spreadsheets based on these variables are available from www.marketing-insights.co.uk/spreadsheet.htm.

Activity 2.5 explores some of the revenue models that are possible.

---

**Activity 2.5** | **Revenue models at Yahoo!**

### Purpose

To illustrate the range of revenue generating opportunities for a company operating as an Internet pure-play. Yahoo! (www.yahoo.com) is a well-known intermediary with local content available for many countries.

### Activity

Visit the local Yahoo! site for your region, e.g. www.yahoo.co.uk, and explore the different site services which generate revenue. Reference the investor relations reports to gain an indication of the relative importance of these revenue sources.

---

**Activity 2.6** | **Revenue models at online marketing portals**

### Purpose

To illustrate the range of revenue-generating opportunities for online publishers. This activity shows how ad-based revenue models are calculated and indicates the amount of revenue generated by looking at three alternative approaches for publishing referencing three different types of portal.

### Question

Visit each of the sites in this category. You should:

1  Summarise the revenue models which are used for each site by looking at the information for advertisers and affiliates.

2  What are the advantages and disadvantages of the different revenue models for the site audience and the site owner?

3  Given an equivalent audience, which of these sites do you think would generate the most revenue? You could develop a simple spreadsheet model based on the following figures:
   - *monthly site visitors*: 100,000 – 0.5% of these visitors click-through to affiliate sites where 2% go on to buy business reports or services at an average order value of €100;
   - *monthly page views*: 1,000,000 – average of three ads are displayed for different advertisers at €20 CPM (we are assuming all ad inventory is sold, this is rarely true in reality);

- *Subscribers to weekly newsletter*: 50,000 – each newsletter broadcast four times per month has four advertisers each paying at a rate of €10 CPM.

Note: These are not actual figures for any of these sites. Go to www.marketing-insights.co.uk/spreadsheet.htm to obtain the revenue model.

The sites are:

- EConsultancy (www.e-consultancy.com), Figure 2.35.
- iMediaConnection (www.imediaconnection.com)
- Marketing Sherpa (www.marketingsherpa.com)

Answers to activities can be found at www.booksites.net/chaffey.

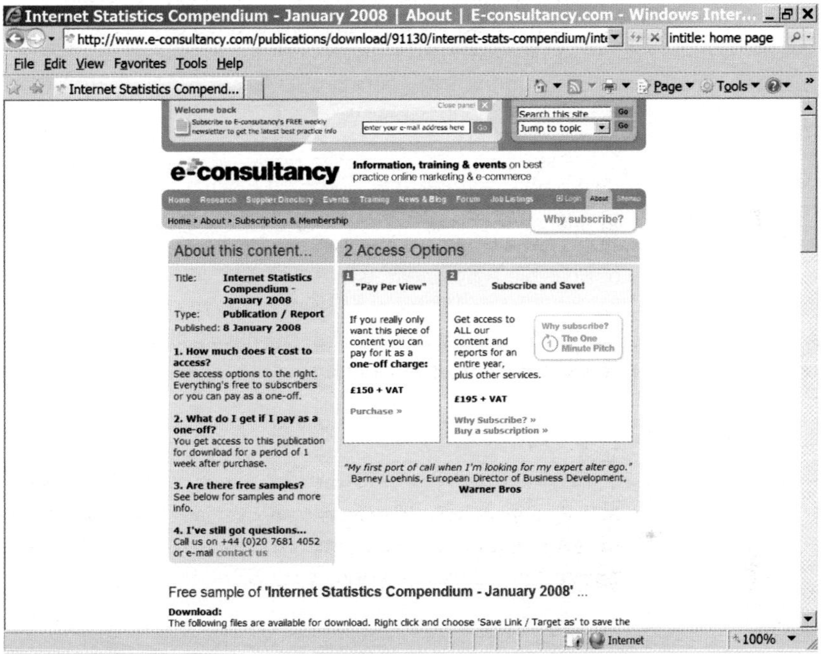

| Figure 2.35 | Business-to-business publisher EConsultancy (www.e-consultancy.com) |

The main case study for this chapter is an example of a new business model and gives you an opportunity to review the marketplace for this product.

| Case Study 2 | Zopa launches the peer-to-peer lending model |
| --- | --- |

## Context

It might be thought that innovation in business models was left behind in the dot-com era, but still fledgling businesses are launching new online services. Zopa is an interesting example of a pureplay social or peer-to-peer lending service launched in March 2005, with US and Italian sites launching in 2007 and a Japanese site planned for 2008.

Zopa is an online service which enables borrowers and lenders to bypass the big high street banks. Since launch in March 2005, £20 million in unsecured personal loans have been arranged at Zopa in the UK. There are over 150,000 UK members and 200,000 worldwide. Zopa is an example of a consumer-to-consumer (peer-to-peer) exchange intermediary. It illustrates the challenges and opportunities of launching a new business online, especially a business with a new business model.

Zopa stands for 'Zone of Possible Agreement' which is a term from business theory. It refers to the overlap between one person's bottom line (the lowest they're prepared to receive for something they are offering) and another person's top line (the most they're prepared to pay for something). In practice, this approach underpins negotiations about the majority of products and services.

## The business model

The exchange provides a matching facility between people who want to borrow and people who want to lend. Significantly, each lender's money is parcelled out between at least 50 borrowers. Zopa revenue is based on charging borrowers 1% of their loan as a fee, and from commission on any repayment protection insurance that the borrower selects. At the time of writing, Zopa estimates it needs to gain just a 0.2 % share of the UK loan market to break even, which it could achieve within 18 months of launch.

In 2007, listings were launched (http://uk.zopa.com/ZopaWeb/Listings/) where loans can be requested by individuals in a similar way to eBay listings.

The main benefit for borrowers is that they can borrow relatively cheaply over shorter periods for small amounts. This is the reverse of banks, where if you borrow more

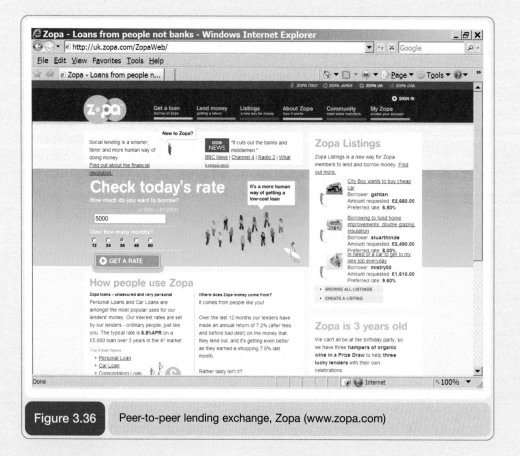

| Figure 3.36 | Peer-to-peer lending exchange, Zopa (www.zopa.com) |
| --- | --- |

and for longer it gets cheaper. The service will also appeal to borrowers who have difficulty gaining credit ratings from traditional financial services providers.

For lenders, higher returns are possible than through traditional savings accounts if there are no bad debts. These are in the range of 20 to 30% higher than putting money in a deposit account, but of course there is the risk of bad debt. Lenders choose the minimum interest rate that they are prepared to accept after bad debt has been taken into account for different markets within Zopa. Borrowers are placed in different risk categories with different interest rates according to their credit histories (using the same Equifax-based credit ratings as used by the banks) and lenders can decide which balance of risk against return they require.

Borrowers who fail to pay are pursued through the same mechanism as banks use and also get a black mark against their credit histories. But for the lender, their investment is not protected by any compensation scheme, unless they have been defrauded.

The *Financial Times* reported that banks don't currently see Zopa as a threat to their high street business. One financial analyst said Zopa was 'one of these things that could catch on but probably won't'.

Zopa does not have a contact centre. According to its website, enquiries to Zopa are restricted to e-mail in order to keep its costs down. However, there is a service promise of answering e-mails within three hours during working hours.

Although the service was launched initially in the UK in 2005, *Financial Times* (2005) reported that Zopa has 20 countries where people want to set up franchises. Other countries include China, New Zealand, India and South American countries.

The peer-to-peer lending marketplace now has several providers. For example, the social lending site Kiva allows lenders to give to a specific entrepreneur in a poor or developing world country. In the US, Prosper (www.prosper.com) has over 600,000 members and uses a loan listing model.

## About the founders

The three founders of Zopa are chief executive Richard Duvall, chief financial officer James Alexander and David Nicholson. All were involved with Egg, with Richard Duvall creating the online bank for Prudential in 1998. Mr Alexander had been strategy director at Egg after joining in 2000, and previously had written the business plan for Smile, another online bank owned by the Co-operative. The founders were also joined by Sarah Matthews, who was Egg's brand development director.

## Target market

The idea for the business was developed from market research that showed there was a potential market of 'freeformers' to be tapped.

Freeformers are typically not in standard employment, rather they are self-employed or carry out work that is project-based or freelance. Examples include consultants and entrepreneurs. Consequently, their incomes and lifestyles may be irregular, although they may still be assessed as creditworthy. According to James Alexander, 'they're people who are not understood by banks, which value stability in people's lives and income over everything else'. The Institute of Directors (IOD) (2005) reported that the research showed that freeformers had 'much less of a spending model of money and much more of an asset model'.

Surprisingly, the research indicated a large number of freeformers. New Media Age reported Duvall as estimating that in the UK there may be around six million freeformers (of a population of around 60 million). Duvall is quoted as saying: 'it's a group that's growing really quickly. I think that in 10 or 15 years time most people will work this way. It's happening right across the developing world. We've been doing some research in the US and we think there are some 30 or 40 million people there with these attitudes and behaviours'.

Some of the directors see themselves as freeformers, they have multiple interests and do not only work for Zopa; James Alexander works for one day a week in a charity and Sarah Matthews works just three days a week for Zopa. You can see example personas of typical borrowers and lenders on the website: www.zopa.com/ZopaWeb/public/how/zopamembers.shtml.

From reviewing the customer base, lenders and borrowers are often united by a desire to distance themselves from conventional institutions. James Alexander says: 'I spend a lot of time talking to members and have found enormous goodwill towards the idea, which is really like lending to family members or within a community'. But he also says that some of the lenders are simply entrepreneurs who have the funds, understand portfolio diversification and risk and are lending on Zopa alongside other investments.

## Business status

The *Financial Times* (2005) reported that Zopa had just 300 members at launch, but within four months it had 26,000 members. According to James Alexander, around 35% are lenders, who between them have £3m of capital waiting to be distributed. The company has not, to date, revealed how much has been lent, but average loans have been between £2000 and £5000. Moneyfacts.co.uk isn't showing any current accounts with more than 5% interest, but Zopa is a riskier product, so you'd expect better rates. Unlike a deposit account, it's not covered by any compensation schemes.

## Marketing communications

The launch of Zopa has been quite different from Egg and other dot-coms at the turn of the millennium. Many companies at that time invested large amounts in offline media such as TV and print to rapidly grow awareness and to explain their proposition to customers.

Instead Zopa has followed a different communications strategy, which has relied on word-of-mouth and PR with some online marketing activities where the cost of customer acquisition can be controlled. The launch of such a model and the history of its founders, makes it relatively easy to have major pieces about the item in relevant newspapers and magazines such as the *Guardian*, the *Financial Times*, the *Economist* and the Institute of Directors house magazine, which its target audience may read. Around launch, IOD (2005) reports that Duvall's PR agency, Sputnik, achieved 200 million opportunities for the new company to be read about. Of course, not all coverage is favourable, many of the articles explored the risk of lending and the viability of the start-up. However, others have pointed out that the rates for the best-rated

'A category' borrowers are better than any commercial loan offered by a bank, and for lenders rates are better than any savings account. The main online marketing activities that Zopa uses are search engine marketing and affiliate marketing. In 2007 Zopa created an own Facebook application 'People Like You', it lets facebookers compare their personality with other people. Zopa communicates with its audience in an informal way through its blogs (http://blog.zopa.com).

Zopa initially received funding from two private equity groups, Munich-based Wellington Partners and Benchmark Capital of the US. Although the model was unique within financial services, its appeal was increased by the well-publicised success of other peer-to-peer Internet services such as Betfair, the gambling website, and eBay, the auction site.

*Sources: Financial Times (2005), New Media Age (2005), Institute of Directors (2005), Zopa website (www.zopa.com) and blog (http://blog.zopa.com).*

### Question

Imagine you are a member of the team of investors reviewing the viability of the Zopa business. On which criteria would you assess the future potential of the business and the returns in your investment based on Zopa's position in the marketplace and its internal capabilities?

## Summary

1. The constantly changing Internet environment should be monitored by all organisations in order to be able to respond to changes in the micro-environment or the immediate marketplace.

2. The Internet has created major changes to the competitive environment. Organisations should deploy tools such as Porter's five forces and the value chain and value network models in order to assess opportunities and potential threats posed by the Internet.

3. The Internet can encourage the formation of new channel structures. These include *disintermediation* within the marketplace as organisations' channel partners such as wholesalers or retailers are bypassed. Alternatively, the Internet can cause *reintermediation* as new intermediaries with a different purpose are formed to help bring buyers and sellers together in a *virtual marketplace* or *marketspace*.

4. Trading in the marketplace can be sell-side (seller-controlled), buy-side (buyer-controlled) or at a neutral marketplace.

5. A business model is a summary of how a company will generate revenue, identifying its product offering, value-added services, revenue sources and target customers. Exploiting the range of business models made available through the Internet is important to both existing companies and start-ups.

6. The Internet may also offer opportunities for new revenue models such as commission on affiliate referrals to other sites or banner advertising.

7. The opportunity for new commercial arrangements for transactions includes negotiated deals, brokered deals, auctions, fixed-price sales, and pure spot markets; and barters should also be considered.

8. Customer analysis is an important part of situation analysis. It involves assessing demand for online services, characteristics of existing online customers and the multichannel behaviour of customers as they select and purchase products.

9. Regular competitive benchmarking should be conducted to compare services.

10. The role of intermediaries in promoting an organisation's services should also be carefully assessed.

## Exercises

### Self-assessment exercises

1. Why is environmental scanning necessary?

2. Summarise how each of the micro-environment factors may directly drive the content and services provided by a website.

3. What are the main aspects of customer adoption of the Internet that managers should be aware of?

4. What are the main changes to channel structures that are facilitated through the Internet?

5. What are the different elements and different types of business model?

6. How should a marketing manager benchmark the online performance of competitors?

7. Describe two different models of online buyer behaviour.

8. How can the Internet be used to support the different stages of the buying process?

### Essay and discussion questions

1. Discuss, using examples, how the Internet may change the five competitive forces of Michael Porter.

2. 'Internet access levels will never exceed 50% in most countries.' Discuss.

3. What are the options, for an existing organisation, for using new business models through the Internet?

4. Perform a demand analysis for e-commerce services for a product sector and geographical market of your choice.

5. Perform competitor benchmarking for online services for an organisation of your choice.

6. What are the alternatives for modified channel structures for the Internet? Illustrate through different organisations in different sectors.

### Examination questions

1. What options are available to a supplier, currently fulfilling to customers through a reseller, to use the Internet to change this relationship?

2. What types of channel conflicts are caused by the Internet?

3. What are virtual organisations and how can the Internet support them?

4. Name three options for a company's representation on the Internet in different types of marketplace.

5. Explain the term 'virtual value-chain'.

6. What are the three key factors that affect consumer adoption of the Internet?

7. Summarise how the bargaining power of buyers may be changed by the Internet for a commodity product.

8. How can the internal value chain be modified when an organisation deploys Internet technologies?

## References

Agrawal, V., Arjona, V. and Lemmens, R. (2001) E-performance: the path to rational exuberance, *McKinsey Quarterly*, No. 1, 31–43.

Ariely, D. and Simonson, I. (2003) Buying, bidding, playing or competing, *Journal of Consumer Psychology*, 13 (1&2), 113–23.

Bart, Y., Shankar, V., Sultan, F. and Urban, G. (2005) Are the drivers and role of online trust the same for all websites and consumers? a large-scale exploratory empirical study, *Journal of Marketing*, October 2005, 133–52.

Benjamin, R. and Wigand, R. (1995) Electronic markets and virtual value-chains on the information superhighway, *Sloan Management Review*, Winter, 62–72.

Berryman, K., Harrington, L., Layton-Rodin, D. and Rerolle, V. (1998) Electronic commerce: three emerging strategies, *McKinsey Quarterly*, No. 1, 152–9.

Berthon, P., Lane, N., Pitt, L. and Watson, R. (1998) The World Wide Web as an industrial marketing communications tool: models for the identification and assessment of opportunities, *Journal of Marketing Management*, 14, 691–704.

Bettman, J. (1979) *An Information Processing Theory of Consumer Choice*. Addison-Wesley, Reading, MA.

BMRB (2001, 2004) *Internet monitor, November*. BMRB International, Manchester. Available online at www.bmrb.co.uk.

Booms, B. and Bitner, M. (1981) Marketing strategies and organisation structure for service firms. In J. Donelly and W. George (eds) *Marketing of Services*. American Marketing Association, New York.

Bowen Craggs & Co, www.bowencraggs.com.

Brand New World (2004) AOL research published at www.aolbrandnewworld.co.uk.

Brand New World (2004a), joint research by Anne Mollen (Cranfield School of Management) and AOL Europe: How the internet is changing consumers' attitudes to brands and what marketers and advertisers can do about it.

Brand New World (2007) How the Internet is changing consumers' attitudes to brands and what marketers and advertisers can do about it. Research report sponsored by AOL, presented at a workshop at Cranfield School of Management.

Breitenbach, C. and van Doren, D. (1998) Value-added marketing in the digital domain: enhancing the utility of the Internet, *Journal of Consumer Marketing*, 15(6), 559–75.

Chaffey, D. (2001) Optimising e-marketing performance – a review of approaches and tools. In *Proceedings of IBM Workshop on Business Intelligence and E-marketing*. Warwick, 6 December.

Chaffey, D. and Smith, P.R. (2008) *Emarketing Excellence. Planning and optimising your digital marketing*, 3rd edn, Butterworth-Heinemann, Oxford.

Chase, L. (1998) *Essential Business Tactics for the Net*. Wiley, New York.

Clemons, E. and Row, M. (2000) Behaviour is key to web retailing. *Financial Times*, Mastering Management Supplement, 13 November.

Deise, M., Nowikow, C., King, P. and Wright, A. (2000) *Executive's Guide to E-Business. From Tactics to Strategy*. Wiley, New York.

de Kare-Silver, M. (2000) *EShock 2000. The Electronic Shopping Revolution: Strategies for Retailers and Manufacturers*. Macmillan, London.

*Economist* (2000) Enter the ecosystem, *Economist*, 11 November.

EConsultancy (2004) Online Retail 2004, benchmarking the user experience of UK retail sites. Report, July, London. Available online from www.e-consultancy.com.

EIAA Online Shoppers (2008) Mediascope Europe report into online consumer behaviour. Source: http://www.eiaa.net/research/research.asp.

European Commission (2007) i2010 Annual Information Society Report 2007, published at: http://ec.europa.eu/information_society/eeurope/i2010/index_en.htm.

*Financial Times* (2005) Lending exchange bypasses high street banks. Paul J. Davies, *Financial Times*, 22 August.

Forrester Research (2002) Mapping customer paths across multiple sites helps site owners predict which consumers are likely to buy and when. Forrester Research Press Release, Cambridge, MA, 19 February.

Forrester (2007a) Consumer Trends Survey North America – leveraging user generated content. January 2007. Brian Haven.

Forrester (2007b) North American Consumer Technographics research report, published February 2007

Grossnickle, J. and Raskin, O. (2001) *The Handbook of Online Marketing Research: Knowing your Customer Using the Net*. McGraw-Hill, New York.

Hagel, J. III and Rayport, J. (1997) The new infomediaries, *McKinsey Quarterly*, No. 4, 54–70.

Institute of Directors (2005) Profile – Richard Duvall, *Director*, September, 51–5.

Kalakota, R. and Robinson, M. (2000) *E-Business. Roadmap for Success*. Addison-Wesley, Reading, MA.

Kothari, D., Jain, S., Khurana, A. and Saxena, A. (2001) Developing a marketing strategy for global online customer management, *International Journal of Customer Relationship Management*, 4(1), 53–8.

Kotler, P., Armstrong, G., Saunders, J. and Wong, V. (2001) *Principles of Marketing*, 3rd European edn. Financial Times/Prentice Hall, Harlow.

Lewis, H. and Lewis, R. (1997) Give your customers what they want, selling on the Net. *Executive Book Summaries*, 19(3), March.

McDonald, M. and Wilson, H. (2002) *New Marketing: Transforming the Corporate Future*. Butterworth-Heinemann, Oxford.

Menteth, H., Arbuthnot, S. and Wilson, H. (2005) Multi-channel experience consistency: evidence from Lexus, *Interactive Marketing*, 6 (4) 317–25.

M:Metrics (2006) M:metrics unveils industry's first definitive mobile marketing metrics, 3 October 2006, http://www.mmetrics.com/press/PressRelease.aspx?article=20061003-sms-shorttext.

Microsoft (2007) Word of the web guidelines for advertisers. Understanding trends and monetising social networks. Research report.

Moe, W. (2003) Buying, searching, or browsing: differentiating between online shoppers using in-store navigational clickstream, *Journal of Consumer Psychology*, 13 (1/2), 29.

Moe, W. and Fader, P. (2004) Dynamic conversion behavior at e-commerce sites. *Management Science*, 50 (3), 326–35.

Murdoch, R. (2005) Speech to the American Society of Newspaper editors, 13 April. Available online at www.newscorp.com.

*New Media Age* (2005) Personal Lender, Dominic Dudley, 18 August.

Nielsen (2007) Participation Inequality: encouraging more users to contribute, AlertBox, October 9, 2006, www.useit.com/alertbox/participation_inequality.html.

Nunes, P., Kambil, A. and Wilson, D. (2000) The all in one market, *Harvard Business Review*, May–June, 2–3.

Porter, M. (1980) *Competitive Strategy*. Free Press, New York.

Porter, M. (2001) Strategy and the Internet, *Harvard Business Review*, March, 62–78.

Rayport, J. and Sviokla, J. (1996) Exploiting the virtual value-chain, *McKinsey Quarterly*, No. 1, 20–32.

Revolution (2008) Roundtable: Travel brands seek new online models. 28 January 2008. Online article published at: http://www.brandrepublic.com/News/778745/Roundtable-Travel-brands-seek-new-online-models/.

Robinson, P., Faris, C. and Wind, Y. (1967) *Industrial Buying and Creative Marketing*. Allyn and Bacon, Boston.

Rodgers, S., Chen, Q., Wang, Y. Rettie, R. and Alpert, F. (2007) The Web Motivation Inventory, *International Journal of Advertising*, 2007, Vol. 26, Issue 4, p447–476.

Sarkar, M., Butler, B. and Steinfield, C. (1996) Intermediaries and cybermediaries. A continuing role for mediating players in the electronic marketplace, *Journal of Computer Mediated Communication*, issue 1.

Seybold, P. and Marshak, R. (2001) *The Customer Revolution*. Crown Business, New York.

Styler, A. (2001) Understanding buyer behaviour in the 21st century, *Admap*, September, 23–6.

Thomas, J. and Sullivan, U. (2005) Managing marketing communications with multichannel customers, *Journal of Marketing*, 69 (October), 239–51.

Timmers, P. (1999) *Electronic Commerce Strategies and Models for Business-to-Business Trading*. Wiley, Chichester.

UK Statistics (2007) Individuals accessing the Internet – Report from the UK National Statistics Omnibus Survey. Published online at www.statistics.gov.uk.

Venkatraman, N. (2000) Five steps to a dot-com strategy: how to find your footing on the web, *Sloan Management Review*, Spring, 15–28.

Watts, D. and Dodds, S. (2007) Influentials, networks, and public opinion formation, *Journal of Consumer Research*, 34, 4 (2007): 441–58.

Wodtke, C. (2002) *Information Architecture: Blueprints for the Web*. New Riders, IN.

## Further reading

Dibb, S., Simkin, S., Pride, W. and Ferrel, O. (2001) *Marketing. Concepts and Strategies*, 4th European edn. Houghton Mifflin, New York. *See* Chapter 2, The marketing environment.

Kotler, P., Armstrong, G., Saunders, J. and Wong, V. (2001) *Principles of Marketing*, 3rd European edn. Financial Times/Prentice Hall, Harlow. *See* Chapter 4, The marketing environment.

Porter, M. (2001) Strategy and the Internet, *Harvard Business Review*, March, 62–78. A retrospective assessment of how the Internet has changed Porter's model, first proposed in the 1980s.

Timmers, P. (1999) *Electronic Commerce Strategies and Models for Business-to-Business Trading*. Wiley, Chichester. Detailed descriptions of different B2B models are available in this book.

**Web links**

A directory of Internet marketing links, including sources for statistics from the Internet environment, is maintained by Dave Chaffey at www.davechaffey.com.

### Sources for Internet adoption statistics

#### Online research aggregators and publishers

- **ClickZ Internet research** (www.clickz.com/stats).
- **EConsultancy** (www.e-consultancy.com). See their Internet statistics compendium. Fee-based service with some free data available.
- **eMarketer** (www.emarketer.com). Includes reports on media spend based on compilations of other analysts. Fee-based service with some free data available.
- **Internet World Stats** (www.internetworldstats.com). Compiles global statistics by region country from other sources on this list.
- **Marketing Charts** (www.marketingcharts.com). Has an online media section with visual summaries of reports mainly from the audience media panels.

#### Government sources on Internet usage and adoption

- **European government** (http://europa.eu.int/comm/eurostat).
- **OECD** (www.oecd.org). OECD broadband research (http://www.oecd.org/sti/ict/broadband).
- **UK government** (wwww.statistics.gov.uk).
- **Ofcom** (www.ofcom.org.uk). Ofcom is the independent regulator and competition authority for the UK communications industries, with responsibilities across television, radio, telecommunications and wireless communications services and has in-depth reports on communications markets.
- **US government** (www.stat-usa.gov).

#### Online audience panel media consumption and usage data

These are fee-based data, but contain useful free data within press release sections.

- **Comscore** (www.comscore.com).
- **Hitwise** (www.hitwise.com). Hitwise blog (http://weblogs.hitwise.com). Sample reports from Hitwise on consumer search behaviour and importance of different online intermediaries. Netratings (www.netratings.com).

#### Other major online research providers

- **The European Interactive Advertising Association** (www.eiaa.net). The EIAA is a pan-European trade organisation with surveys of media consumption and usage across Europe.
- **The Pew Internet & American Life Project** (www.pewinternet.org), produces reports that explore the impact of the internet on families, communities, work and home, daily life, education, healthcare, and civic and political life.

### Business model development

- **Business 2** (http://money.cnn.com/magazines/business2). Also covers the development of business models with a US focus.
- **FastCompany** (www.fastcompany.com). Also covers the development of business models with a US focus.
- **Ghost sites** (www.disobey.com/ghostsites). Steve Baldwin's compilation of failed e-businesses, including the Museum of E-failure!
- **Paid Content** (www.paidcontent.org). Covers the development of revenue models for publishers
- **Paid Content UK** (www.paidcontent.co.uk). Covers developments in startup companies within the UK.

# The Internet macro-environment

## Learning objectives

After reading this chapter, the reader should be able to:

- Identify the different elements of the Internet macro-environment that impact on an organisation's Internet marketing strategy and execution
- Assess the impact of legal, moral and ethical constraints and opportunities on an organisation and devise solutions to accommodate them
- Evaluate the significance of other macro-factors such as economics, taxation and legal constraints

## Questions for marketers

Key questions for marketing managers related to this chapter are:

- How do I complete a situation analysis as part of planning for digital marketing?
- Which factors affect the environment for online trading in a country?
- How do I make sure my online marketing is consistent with evolving online culture and ethics?
- How do I assess new technological innovations?
- Which laws am I subject to when trading online?

## Links to other chapters

Like the previous chapter, this one provides a foundation for later chapters on Internet marketing strategy and implementation:

- Chapter 4, Internet marketing strategy
- Chapter 5, The Internet and the marketing mix
- Chapter 6, Relationship marketing using the Internet
- Chapter 7, Delivering the online customer experience
- Chapter 8, Campaign planning for digital media

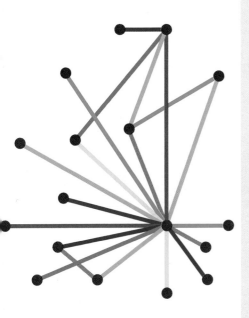

## Introduction

In the previous chapter we reviewed the influence of the immediate marketplace that an organisation must consider in order to assess the impact of the Internet. In this chapter, we will review how the macro-economic factors can influence the way in which the Internet is used to support marketing.

We present the macro-environment factors using the widely used SLEPT framework. SLEPT stands for Social, Legal, Economic, Political and Technological factors. Often, these factors are known as the PEST factors, but we use SLEPT since it is useful to stress the importance of the law in influencing Internet marketing practices. The SLEPT factors are:

- *Social factors* – these include the influence of consumer perceptions in determining usage of the Internet for different activities.
- *Legal and ethical factors* – determine the methods by which products can be promoted and sold online. Governments, on behalf of society, seek to safeguard individuals' rights to privacy.
- *Economic factors* – variations in the economic performance in different countries and regions affect spending patterns and international trade.
- *Political* – national governments and transnational organisations have an important role in determining the future adoption and control of the Internet and the rules by which it is governed.
- *Technological factors* – changes in technology offer new opportunities to the way products can be marketed.

For the digital marketer, it is useful to focus on the SLEPT factors which are most relevant to creating a digital strategy and managing online marketing activities. This is the approach we will use in this chapter, with the main focus on the legal and technological factors. The influence of society and culture is also important, but we considered these issues in Chapter 2 as part of the customer analysis.

While it can be considered that the macro-economic factors will influence all competitors in a marketplace, this doesn't mean that the macro-environment factors are unimportant. Changes in the macro-environment such as changes in social behaviour, new laws and the introduction of new technologies can all present opportunities or threats. Organisations that monitor and respond best to their macro-environment can use it as a source of differentiation and competitive advantage.

## Digital marketing in practice    The EConsultancy interview

### Mike Clark, Managing Director of GD Worldwide, supplier to the social network bands

#### Overview and main concepts covered

GD Worldwide is an online resource for independent bands to help establish an Internet presence and manage the distribution of their material. It also allows bands to create a 'backstage area' via its Usync tool. It highlights the innovation made possible by digital technology and how one web startup business has taken advantage of them. We caught up with UK MD Mark Clark to discuss plans and progress to date.

## The interview

**Q: When, how and why was the company formed?**

*Mike Clark*: The company is called GD Worldwide and was formed in 2001 by the Australian band Gabriel's Day – a touring, working band. They're relatively small in the global scale of artists, but in Australia have got a core following and a sustainable fan base.

The music business in Australia has, to an extent, been overlooked by the big record labels, at least relative to other markets, so it has spawned more of an independent, self-managed environment. The artists have much more of a sense of community about them.

So the idea behind GD Worldwide was to take the experiences of Gabriel's Day and give other artists the tools they need to create self-sustaining careers outside of the traditional, major label system. It gives them an alternative route to market – they don't have to go through the existing model.

In that model, the creative group behind a band have to go through a series of gatekeepers in order to reach their audience – the distribution, the rights organisations, the retailers and so on.

There's a whole load of people that get in between the artist and the audience and they are taking meat off the table. Those people aren't really adding a tremendous amount of value – they are normally taking it away – so the artists find it difficult to reach their audience in a sustainable way.

The other side of it is that the gatekeeper model represents only what we estimate to be 3% of the total music marketplace. It's the short tail and the market is set up to create and feed that, rather like the Hollywood star model. There is the other 97% of the market – the long tail – and we are a company set up to operate there. We put the artist at the centre of things and reorientate the resources around them.

The other thing is that it's no secret that record sales are declining, and while the music is predicting that there is huge growth to be had in the future, nobody seems to know how to get their hands on it.

**Q: What do you offer over the likes of Bebo and Myspace?**

*Mike Clark*: In Myspace, there are up to three million artists but very few have worked out how to monetise their presence or commercialise the interest they have created.

We think of our Usync product as the next step on from Myspace, where an artist can interact, manage and learn from their audiences, as well as commercialising them.

Bands need a Myspace profile – it's a great way to attract interest – but once you have brought people into your space, how many of those are true fans? You want to take the 20% of those that are and bring them into the backstage area we create for you, where they get treated to exclusive content and so on.

In any business, you segment your high value customers and you treat them accordingly, but in the music business that doesn't really seem to happen at the moment.

In terms of visibility, we are looking to build this as a strategic business and we know we are not for everyone. We are in that long tail and finding those people is going to be important. We are looking for other alternative communities. Our marketing will take a kind of grassroots approach, in the venues themselves.

**Q: How do you earn your money?**

*Mike Clark*: We don't want to be in the business of horse-trading an artist's audience as that's the most valuable thing the artist has, so we create an audience community but don't hit them with advertising or sponsorship.

We take a 20% cut of every transaction that happens in the Usync channel – which is a recognition that we give the artist as much money back as we can, so they can decide how to reinvest it.

We don't ask for exclusive rights deals or touch their copyright and don't ask for a share of future earnings, and don't ask for a cut of sales outside of Usync. They can also set the prices they want to. If they want to give their material away for free, that's fine by us.

**Q: How much have you generated in sales so far?**

*Mike Clark*: I don't have specific figures I can share at the moment, but the situation we are at as an organisation is that we have around 30 artists that are either active or building their backstage areas with us.

We've only just enabled people to come to the site remotely and sign up, and we're signing up around two or three people a day at the moment. And we haven't really started any heavy promotion of that yet. We've started to work with companies like Sonic Bids [which allows musicians to produce electronic press kits] to promote ourselves to the artists in their database.

But we're also not overly aggressive in terms of acquisition – we don't want the three million Myspace artists, we want the hardworking, independently-minded artists who want to put the effort in to make it work.

**Q: What's your position on DRM [digital rights management]?**

*Mike Clark*: We use MP3. Everyone's started to talk about it but we've heard from various people over the last few months that DRM is dead, and that consumers are starting to vote with their feet. DRM has definitely run its course and I don't think it has a future. There will be much more sophisticated non-DRM models that will emerge in the future.

**Q: How can bands get access to financing outside of the label system?**

*Mike Clark*: We are looking at different tools that we can use to support artists from a financial perspective.

We feel that copyright needs to be supplemented by some other device or right, and we are looking at ways we can employ those tools. We have looked at Creative Commons and it is interesting, but it is focused on bringing flexibility to current copyright law. We feel that there is another step we could take that is completely outside of copyright, and we are talking with some top entertainment lawyers here in the UK and in the US to help us develop that, and we will probably bring that to market in around a year's time.

In terms of financing, for a small band getting money together is difficult. So we are working on how to solve that problem. We are thinking that in an artist community, other artists may be willing to put up some money to help other artists, maybe in the form of a levy on some of the transactions.

**Q: How can a band use the site as a marketing tool?**

*Mike Clark*: The fact is that 45% of new music is discovered through personal recommendation – word of mouth. It isn't about watching TV ads or looking at who has bought the front window of HMV this week. If you look at the online communities and sites like last.fm and Pandora, there is a lot to be said for recommendation as a means of discovery.

What we've done on the site is to help you develop your fan base. There are tools to allow you to share tracks and you can give fans rewards for doing so. I think it's a far smarter way of marketing artists and creating that buzz.

Very often, marketing money is spent against things that are certain. With a new album, people will say 'let's do a huge advertising splurge' across the UK but no one will get fired as they know that album will be successful. They very rarely use those tools unless the artist has already become a success and they want to sustain that success.

**Q: Why have you gone down the route of e-commerce rather than ad-supported content?**

*Mike Clark*: In some ways, you need to have an integrity in the relationship between the artist and audience, but at a certain stage an artist may say that he or she is prepared to work with a brand or brand owner if I think they can add value to my community.

For example, if a brand does want to sponsor an artist, he or she can talk to the audience and ask what they think. They have much more commercial control over those relationships.

For us, we haven't ruled out the advertising route but we would never do it exclusively inside the artists' backstage areas. Where we might do it is in the Usync community itself – if a last.fm or Pandora wanted to create a Usync radio with Usync artists, we may look at a sponsor to bring that to market.

*Source*: http://www.e-consultancy.com/news-blog/newsletter/3229/interview-with-mike-clark-of-gd-worldwide.html

## The rate of environment change

An indication of the challenge of assessing the macro-environment factors is presented in Figure 3.1. This figure of the 'waves of change' shows how fluctuations in the characteristics of different aspects of the environment vary at different rates through time. The manager has to constantly scan the environment and assess which changes are relevant to their sphere of influence. Changes in social culture and particularly pop culture (what's 'hot' and what's not) tend to be very rapid. Introduction of new technologies and changes in their popularity tend to be frequent too and need to be assessed. Government and legal changes tend to happen over longer time scales, although since this is only a generalisation new laws can be introduced relatively quickly. The trick for Internet marketers is to identify those factors which are important in the context of Internet marketing that are critical to competitiveness and service delivery and monitor these. We believe it is the technological and legal factors which are most important to the Internet marketer, so we focus on these.

**Strategic agility**
The capability to innovate and so gain competitive advantage within a marketplace by monitoring changes within an organisation's marketplace, and then to efficiently evaluate alternative strategies, and then select, review and implement appropriate candidate strategies.

### Strategic agility

The capacity to respond to these environmental opportunities and threats is commonly referred to as **strategic agility**. Strategic agility is a concept strongly associated with knowledge management theory and is based on developing a sound process for reviewing marketplace opportunities and threats and then selecting the appropriate strategy options.

See Mini case study 3.1 for an excellent video introduction to the principles of strategic agility.

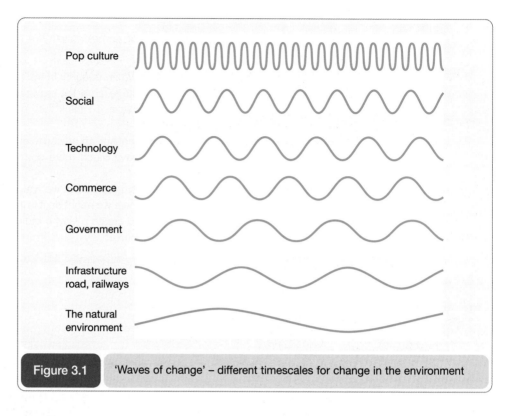

| Figure 3.1 | 'Waves of change' – different timescales for change in the environment |

---

**Mini Case Study 3.1**    The Marine Corps demonstrate strategic agility

Professor Donald N. Sull is an Associate Professor of Management Practice in the Strategy and International Management faculty at the London Business School.

In the first video tutorial (Figure 3.2, go to www.ft.com/video and search for London Business School) on strategic agility, he asserts that traditional management models of creating a long-term vision are flawed since our knowledge of the future is always imperfect and marketplace conditions are changing continuously. Rather than being the captain of a ship surveying the far horizon, analogous with the top-down model of strategy, the reality for managers is that their situation is more akin to a racing car drive on a foggy day, constantly looking to take the right decisions based on the mass of information about their surroundings coming through the fog. He believes that having a clear long-term vision, particularly where it isn't based on environment analysis, isn't practical in most industries. Instead he says that companies should '*Keep vision fuzzy but current priorities clear*'. He gives the example of the failure of Microsoft to respond sufficiently fast to the growth of the Internet.

In the second video tutorial he explains the basis for strategic agility. He explains that all knowledge of the future is based on uncertainty, but that managers must act now so they need to put in place US Marine Corps-style reconnaissance missions as an army would in order to make their battle plans. He gives the example of Dell, explaining how they spend relatively little in research and development, but are instead constantly probing the marketplace, trialling new ideas with multiple probes into the approach. He stresses the importance of finding anomalies in the marketplace where it doesn't appear as expected and these may represent learnings or opportunities. Detailed customer insights and business performance is necessary to identify these anomalies. Finally he makes the point of the need to act rapidly to have scalability to 'swarm the gap in the defences of the enemy' where there is a strong opportunity.

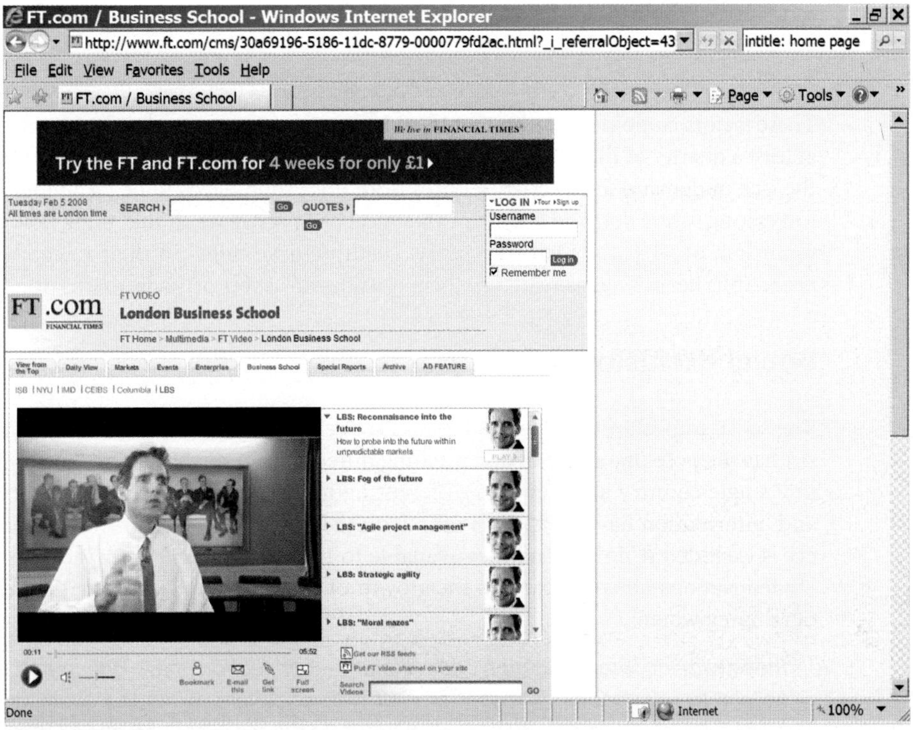

**Figure 3.2**    Professor Donald Sull of London Business School talking about strategic agility

In a digital marketing context, we can see that strategic agility requires these characteristics and requirements for an organisation to be successful in its strategy development:

1 Efficient collection, dissemination and evaluation of different information sources from the micro- and macro-environment.
2 Having effective processes for generating and reviewing the relevance of new strategies based on creating new value for customers.
3 Efficient research into potential customer value against the business value generated.
4 Efficient implementation of prototypes of new functionality to deliver customer value.
5 Efficient measurement and review of results from prototypes to revise further to improve proposition or to end a trial.

## Social factors

In the previous chapter, in the sections on customer adoption of Internet technology, we looked at how Internet usage varies across different countries in terms of levels of access, amount of usage, its influence on offline purchase and the proportion of online purchases. These variations are in part dependent on how the Internet is perceived in society. We saw that social barriers to adoption of the Internet include:

- no perceived benefit
- lack of trust
- security problems
- lack of skills
- cost.

These factors combine to mean that there is a significant group in each national population of at least a quarter of the adult population that does not envisage ever using the Internet. Clearly, the lack of demand for Internet services from this group needs to be taken into account when forecasting future demand and from an ethical perspective we should think how to avoid social exclusion, or what the Oxford Internet Institute have called in their research into Internet usage 'Internet disengagement' or others consider an aspect of 'social exclusion'.

## Social exclusion

**Social exclusion**

Part of society is excluded from the facilities available to the remainder.

The social impact of the Internet has also concerned many commentators because the Internet has the potential effect of accentuating differences in quality of life, both within a society in a single country and between different nations, essentially creating 'information haves' and 'information have-nots'. This may accentuate social exclusion where one part of society is excluded from the facilities available to the remainder and so becomes isolated. The United Nations noted, as early in the growth of the Internet as 1999, that parallel worlds are developing where:

> those with income, education and – literally – connections have cheap and instantaneous access to information. The rest are left with uncertain, slow and costly access . . . the advantage of being connected will overpower the marginal and impoverished, cutting off their voices and concerns from the global conversation.

Developed countries with the economies to support it are promoting the use of IT and the Internet through social programmes such as the UK government's UK Online initiative, which operated between 2000 and 2004 to promote the use of the Internet by business and consumers. The European Commission (2007) believe that '*e-Inclusion policies and actions have made significant progress in implementing the goal of an inclusive knowledge-based society (Europa (2007))*'. They recommend that governments should focus on three aspects of e-Inclusion:

1 The access divide (or 'early digital divide') which considers the gap between those with and those without access. Governments will encourage competition to reduce costs and give a wider choice of access through different platforms (e.g. mobile phone or interactive TV access in addition to fixed PC access).
2 The usage divide ('primary digital divide') concentrating on those who have access but are non-users. Governments promote learning of basic Internet skills through ICT courses to those with the highest risks of disengagement.
3 The divide stemming from quality of use ('secondary digital divide') focusing on differentials in participation rates of those people who have access and are users. Training can also be used to reduce this divide.

To assist with social exclusion due to lack of technology, The One Laptop Per Child initiative (OLPC, www.laptop.org) was founded as a non-profit organisation in 2005. The original concept was to offer a $100 laptop in developed and developing countries. The first, low-power XO which has WiFi, a Linux operating system and an Advanced Micro Devices chip, is closer to $200 in US.

Like other innovations, such as mechanised transport, electricity or the phone, the Internet has been used to support social progress. Those with special needs and interests can now communicate on a global basis and empowering information sources are readily available to all. For example, visually impaired people are no longer restricted to Braille books but can use screen readers to hear information available to sighted people on the web. The use of social networks and virtual worlds may also appeal to those who are disabled, although some of the social networks have been criticised for not being easy to access for the visually impaired. As we will see, this has implications for disability discrimination laws which impact accessibility. However, these same technologies, including the Internet, can have negative social impacts such as changing traditional social ideals and being used as a conduit for crime. The Internet has facilitated the publication of and access to information, which has led to many benefits, but it has also led to publication of and access to information which most in society would deem inappropriate. Well-known problems include the use of the Internet to incite racial hatred and terrorism, support child pornography and for identity theft. Such social problems can have implications for marketers who need to respond to laws or the morals established by society and respond to the fears generated. For example, portals such as MSN (www.msn.com) and Yahoo! (www.yahoo.com) discontinued their use of unmoderated chatrooms in 2003 since paedophiles were using them to 'groom' children for later real-world meetings.

## Cultural factors

The local language and culture of a country or region can dramatically affect the requirements of users of a web service. We discuss this issue further in Chapter 7 on website design. The types of sites used (media consumption) and search engines used can also vary dramatically by country as discussed in Chapter 9. So it is important for situation analysis to review country differences.

## Environmental and green issues related to Internet usage

The future state of our planet is a widely held social concern that is closely related to economic issues. Although technology is generally seen as detrimental to the environment – think long- and short-haul flights, TVs and electronic gadgets burning fuel when left on standby – there are some arguments that e-commerce and digital communications can have environment benefits. These benefits are also often beneficial to companies in that they can make cost-savings while positioning themselves as environmentally concerned – see Mini case study 3.2 'HSBC customers plant Virtual Forest'.

| Mini Case Study 3.2 | HSBC customers plant Virtual Forest |

HSBC has committed to improving the environment since it became a climate-neutral company globally in November 2005. Through the use of green technologies and emission-offset trading, HSBC counteracts all $CO_2$ emissions generated by its building operations and corporate travel. In 2006, 35% of operations in North America were offset by investments in Renewable Energy Certificates from wind power alone.

Another aspect of its green policy is its online banking service, where it encourages paperless billing. For example, in the UK in 2007 over 400,000 customers switched from paper statements to online delivery, creating a virtual tree each time (Figure 3.3), and for every 20 virtual trees HSBC promised to plant a real one.

Potentially, online shopping through transactional e-commerce can also have environment benefits. Imagine a situation where we no longer travelled to the shops, and 100% of items were efficiently delivered to us at home or at work. This would reduce traffic considerably! Although this situation is inconceivable since most of us enjoy shopping in the real world too much, online shopping is growing considerably and it may be having an impact. Research by the Internet Media in Retail Group (www.imrg.org) shows the growing importance of e-commerce in the UK where over 10% of retail sales are now online. In 2007 it launched a Go Green, Go Online campaign where it identified six reasons why it believes e-commerce is green. They are:

1 *Fewer vehicle miles*. Shopping is the most frequent reason for car travel in Great Britain, accounting for 20% of all trips, and for 12% of mileage. A study by the Swiss Online Grocer LeShop.ch calculated that each time a customer decides to buy online rather than go shopping by car, 3.5 kg of $CO_2$ emissions are saved.

2 *Lower inventory requirements*. The trend towards pre-selling online – i.e. taking orders for products before they are built, as implemented by Dell – avoids the production of obsolete goods that have to be disposed of if they don't sell, with associated wastage in energy and natural resources.

3 *Fewer printed materials*. Online e-newsletters and brochures replace their physical equivalent so saving paper and distribution costs. Data from the Direct Mail Information Service (www.dmis.co.uk) shows that direct mail volumes have fallen slightly in the last two years reversing an upward trend in the previous 10 years. This must be partly due to marketing e-mails, which the DMA e-mail benchmarks (www.dma.org.uk) show number in their billions in the UK alone.

4 *Less packaging*. Although theoretically there is less need for fancy packaging if an item is sold online this argument is less convincing, since most items like software or electronic items still come in packaging to help convince us we have brought the right thing – to reduce post-purchase dissonance. At least those billions of music tracks downloaded from iTunes and Napster don't require any packaging or plastic.

5 *Less waste*. Across the whole supply chain of procurement, manufacturing and distribution, the Internet can help reduce product and distribution cycles. Some even claim that auction services like eBay and Amazon Marketplace which enable redistribution of second-hand items can promote recycling.

6 *Dematerialisation*. Better known as digitisation, this is the availability of products like software, music and video in digital form.

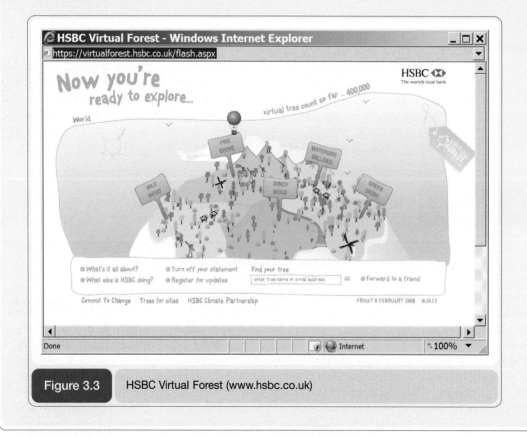

| Figure 3.3 | HSBC Virtual Forest (www.hsbc.co.uk) |

If companies trading online can explain these benefits to their customers effectively, as HSBC have done, then this can benefit these online channels.

But what does the research show about how much e-shopping reduces greenhouse gas emissions? A study by Finnish researchers Siikavirta *et al.* (2003), limited to e-grocery shopping, has suggested that, depending on the home delivery model used, it is theoretically possible to reduce the greenhouse gas emissions generated by grocery shopping by 18% to 87% compared with the situation in which household members go to the store. Some of the constraints that were used in the simulation model include: maximum of 60 orders per route, maximum of 3000 L per route, working time maximum 11 hr per van, working time maximum 5 hr per route, loading time per route 20 min, drop-off time per customer 2 min. The researchers estimated that this would lead to a reduction of all Finland's greenhouse gas emissions by as much as 1%, but in reality the figure is much lower since only 10% of grocery shopping trips are online. Cairns (2005) has completed a study for the UK which shows the importance of grocery shopping – she estimates that car travel for food and other household items represents about 40% of all UK shopping trips by car, and about 5% of all car use. She considers that a direct substitution of car trips by van trips could reduce vehicle-km by 70% or more. A broader study by Ahmed and Sharma (2006) has used value-chain analysis to assess the role of the Internet in changing the amount of energy and materials consumed by businesses for each part of the supply chain. However, no estimates of savings are made.

## Legal and ethical issues of Internet usage

**Ethical standards**
Practices or behaviours which are morally acceptable to society.

**Ethical standards** are personal or business practices or behaviours which are generally considered acceptable by the norms of society.

Ethical issues and the associated laws developed to try to ensure an ethical approach to Internet marketing is an important consideration of the Internet business environment for marketers. Many laws have been enacted to prevent unethical marketing practice, so marketers have to understand and work within this regulatory framework. Which online marketing activities do you think are controlled through law? We have grouped the six most important legal issues for marketers to consider in Table 3.1. This section is structured according to these six areas.

| Table 3.1 | Significant laws which control digital marketing |
| --- | --- |

| Legal issue | Digital marketing activities affected |
| --- | --- |
| 1 Data protection and privacy law | • Collection, storage, usage and deletion of personal information directly through data capture on forms and indirectly through tracking behaviour through web analytics<br>• E-mail marketing and SMS mobile marketing<br>• Use of viral marketing to encourage transmission of marketing messages between consumers<br>• Use of cookies and other techniques for personalising content and tracking on site<br>• Use of cookies for tracking between sites, for example for advertising networks<br>• Use of digital assets installed on a user's PC for marketing purposes, e.g. toolbars or other downloadable utilties sometimes referred to as 'malware' |

| Legal issue | Digital marketing activities affected |
|---|---|
| 2 Disability and discrimination law | • Accessibility of content such as images for the visually impaired within different digital environments:<br>  – website<br>  – e-mail marketing<br>  – mobile marketing<br>  – IPTV<br>• Accessibility affecting other forms of disability including hearing difficulties and motor impairment |
| 3 Brand and trademark protection | • Use of trademarks and brand names within:<br>  – domain names<br>  – content on site (for search engine optimisation)<br>  – paid search advertising campaigns (e.g. Google AdWords)<br>• Representation of a brand on third-party sites including partners, publishers and social networks<br>• Defamation of employees |
| 4 Intellectual property rights | • Protection of digital assets such as text content, images, audio and sounds through digital rights management (DRM) |
| 5 Contract law | • Validity of electronic contracts relevant to:<br>  – cancellations<br>  – returns<br>  – errors in pricing<br>• Distance selling law<br>• International taxation issues where the e-commerce service provider is under a different tax regime to the purchaser |
| 6 Online advertising law | • Similar issues to traditional media:<br>  – representation of offer<br>  – causing offence (e.g. viral marketing) |

## Legal activities can be considered unethical

It is not always sufficient for marketers to be compliant with the law since the rate of innovation may mean that the law is unclear through lack of case law or because no law has been enacted to govern a certain activity. In this case, marketers need to tread very carefully since unethical action can result in serious damage to the reputation of a company and negative sentiment can result in a reduction in online audience or sales.

One the first examples of this risk was in 1999–2001 when privacy groups complained about how ad-serving companies such as Doubleclick could use cookies to track the behaviour of customers between sites without their explicit permission. At the time this forced a move away from ad-serving networks to ad technology. More recently, social network Facebook has had users complain vehemently against the sharing of data on their purchases and Google has had privacy campaigners complain about:

- collection of data via the Google toolbar;
- the release of three million customer searches via AOL, who use the Google search technology
- the length for which data about searches completed were kept (18 months).

### 1 Data protection and privacy law

**Privacy**
A moral right of individuals to avoid intrusion into their personal affairs.

**Identity theft**
The misappropriation of the identity of another person, without their knowledge or consent.

**Privacy** refers to a moral right of individuals to avoid intrusion into their personal affairs by third parties. Privacy of personal data, such as our identities, likes and dislikes, is a major concern to consumers, particularly with the dramatic increase in **identity theft**.

Yet for marketers to better understand their customers' needs this type of information is very valuable. Through collecting such information it will also be possible to use more targeted communications and develop products that are more consistent with users' needs. How should marketers respond to this dilemma? An obvious step is to ensure that marketing activities are consistent with the latest data protection and privacy laws. Although compliance with the laws may sound straightforward, in practice different interpretations of the law are possible and since these are new laws they have not been tested in court. As a result, companies have to make their own business decisions based on the business benefits of applying particular marketing practices against the financial and reputational risks of less strict compliance.

Effective e-commerce requires a delicate balance to be struck between the benefits the individual customer will gain to their online experience through providing personal information and the amount and type of information that they are prepared for companies to hold about them.

What are the main information types used by the Internet marketer which are governed by ethics and legislation? The main information needs are:

1 *Contact information.* This is the name, postal address, e-mail address and, for B2B companies, website address.
2 *Profile information.* This is information about a customer's characteristics that can be used for segmentation. They include age, sex and social group for consumers, and company characteristics and individual role for business customers. The specific types of information and how they are used are referenced in Chapters 2 and 6. The willingness of consumers to give this information and the effectiveness of incentives have been researched for Australian consumers by Ward *et al.* (2005). They found that consumers are willing to give non-financial data if there is an appropriate incentive.
3 *Platform usage information.* Through web analytics systems it is possible to collect information on type of computer, browser and screen resolution used by site users (see Chapter 7).
4 *Behavioural information (on a single site).* This is purchase history, but also includes the whole buying process. Web analytics (Chapter 9) can be used to assess the web and e-mail content accessed by individuals.
5 *Behavioural information (across multiple sites).* This can potentially show how a user accesses multiple sites and responds to ads across sites. Typically this data is collected and used through an anonymous profile based on cookie or IP addresses which is not related to an individual.

Table 3.2 summarises how these different types of customer information are collected and used through technology. The main issue to be considered by the marketer is *disclosure* of the types of information collection and tracking data used. The first two types of information in the table are usually readily explained through a privacy statement at the point of data collection and, as we will see, this is usually a legal requirement. However, with the other types of information, users would only know they were being tracked if they have cookie monitoring software installed or if they seek out the privacy statement of a publisher which offers advertising.

| Table 3.2 | Types of information collected online and the related technologies |
| --- | --- |

| Type of information | Approach and technology used to capture and use information |
| --- | --- |
| 1 Contact information | • *Online forms* – online forms linked to a customer database<br>• Cookies – are used to remember a specific person on subsequent visits |
| 2 Profile information including personal information | • *Online forms*<br>• Cookies can be used to assign a person to a particular segment by linking the cookie to a customer database record and then offering content consistent with their segment |
| 3 Access platform usage | • Web analytics system – identification of computer type, operating system and screen characteristics based on http attributes of visitors |
| 4 Behavioural information on a single site | • Purchase histories are stored in the sales order database<br>• Webbase analytics store details of IP addresses against clickstreams of the sequence of web pages visited<br>• Web beacons in e-mail marketing – a single pixel GIF is used to assess whether a reader opened an e-mail<br>• First-party cookies are also used for monitoring visitor behaviour during a site visit and on subsequent visits<br>• Malware can collect additional information such as passwords |
| 5 Behavioural information across multiple sites | • Third-party cookies used for assessing visits from different sources such as online advertising networks or affiliate networks (Chapter 9)<br>• Search engines such as Google use cookies to track advertising through its AdWords Pay-Per-Click programme<br>• Services such as Hitwise (www.hitwise.com) monitor IP traffic to assess site usage of customer groups within a product category |

**Malware**
Malicious software or toolbars, typically downloaded via the Internet, which act as a 'trojan horse' by executing unwanted activites such as keylogging of user passwords or viruses which may collect e-mail addresses.

Ethical issues concerned with personal information ownership have been usefully summarised by Mason (1986) into four areas:

1  *Privacy* – what information is held about the individual?
2  *Accuracy* – is it correct?
3  *Property* – who owns it and how can ownership be transferred?
4  *Accessibility* – who is allowed to access this information, and under what conditions?

Fletcher (2001) provides an alternative perspective, raising these issues of concern for both the individual and the marketer:

• *Transparency* – who is collecting what information, how do they disclose the collection of data and how it will be used?
• *Security* – how is information protected once it has been collected by a company?
• *Liability* – who is responsible if data are abused?

All of these issues arise in the next section which reviews actions that marketers should take to achieve privacy and trust.

### Data protection law

**Personal data**
Any information about an individual stored by companies concerning their customers or employees.

Data protection legislation is enacted to protect the individual, to protect their privacy and to prevent misuse of their personal data. Indeed, the first article of the European Union Directive 95/46/EC (see http://ec.europa.eu/justice_home/fsi/pricacy/) on which legislation in individual European countries is based, specifically refers to **personal data**. It says:

> *Member states shall protect the fundamental rights and freedoms of natural persons [i.e. a named individual at home or at work], and in particular their right to privacy with respect to the processing of personal data.*

In the UK, the enactment of the European legislation is the Data Protection Act 1984, 1998 (DPA), which is managed by the legal requirements of the 1998 UK Data Protection Act and summarised at www.informationcommissioner.gov.uk. This law is typical of laws that have evolved in many countries to help protect personal information. Any company that holds personal data on computers or on file about customers or employees must be registered with a data protection registrar (although there are some exceptions which may exclude small businesses). This process is known as **notification**.

**Notification**
The process whereby companies register with the data protection registrar to inform about their data holdings.

The guidelines on the eight data protection principles which marketers need to consider are produced by Information Commissioner (1998) on which this overview is based. These principles state that personal data should be:

#### 1 Fairly and lawfully processed
In full:

> *Personal data shall be processed fairly and lawfully and, in particular, shall not be processed unless at least one of the conditions in Schedule 2 is met; and in the case of sensitive personal data, at least one of the conditions in Schedule 3 is also met.*

The Information Commissioner has produced a 'fair processing code' which suggests how an organisation needs to achieve 'fair and lawful processing' under the details of Schedules 2 and 3 of the Act. This requires:

**Data controller**
Each company must have a defined person responsible for data protection.

- Appointment of a **data controller** who is the person with defined responsibility for data protection within a company.

- Clear details in communications such as on a website or direct mail of how a '**data subject**' can contact the data controller or a representative.

**Data subject**
The legal term to refer to the individual whose data are held.

- Before data processing 'the data subject has given his consent' or the processing must be *necessary* either for a 'contract to which the data subject is a party' (for example, as part of a sale of a product) or because it is required by other laws. Consent is defined in the published guidelines as 'any freely given specific and informed indication of his wishes by which the data subject signifies his agreement to personal data relating to him being processed'.

- Sensitive personal data requires particular care, this includes:
  - the racial or ethnic origin of the data subject;
  - political opinions;
  - religious beliefs or other beliefs of a similar nature;
  - membership of a trade union;
  - physical or mental health or condition;
  - sexual life;
  - the commission or alleged commission or proceedings of any offence.

- No other laws must be broken in processing the data.

### 2 Processed for limited purposes
In full:

> *Personal data shall be obtained only for one or more specified and lawful purposes, and shall not be further processed in any manner incompatible with that purpose or those purposes.*

This implies that the organisation must make it clear why and how the data will be processed at the point of collection. For example, an organisation has to explain how your data will be used if you provide your details on a website when entering a prize draw. You would also have to agree (give consent) for further communications from the company.

Figure 3.4 suggests some of the issues that should be considered when a data subject is informed of how the data will be used. Important issues are:

- whether future communications will be sent to the individual (explicit consent is required for this in online channels; this is clarified by the related Privacy and Electronic Communications Regulation Act which is referred to below);
- whether the data will be passed on to third parties (again explicit consent is required);
- how long the data will be kept.

### 3 Adequate, relevant and not excessive
In full:

> *Personal data shall be adequate, relevant and not excessive in relation to the purpose or purposes for which they are processed.*

This specifies that the minimum necessary amount of data is requested for processing. There is difficulty in reconciling this provision between the needs of the individual and the needs of the company. The more details that an organisation has about a customer, then the better they can understand that customer and so develop products and marketing communications specific to that customer which they are more likely to respond to.

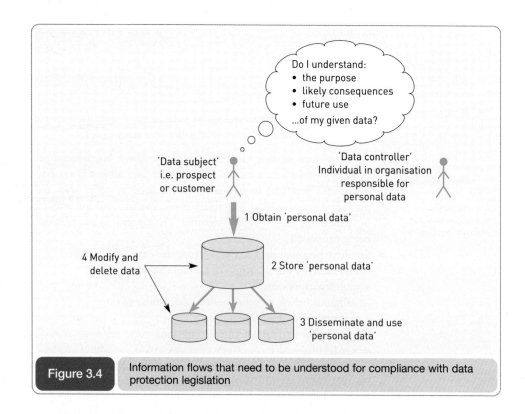

| Figure 3.4 | Information flows that need to be understood for compliance with data protection legislation |

*4 Accurate*

In full:

> *Personal data shall be accurate and, where necessary, kept up to date.*

It is clearly also in the interest of an organisation in an ongoing relationship with a partner that the data be kept accurate and up-to-date. The guidelines on the Act suggest that additional steps should be taken to check data are accurate, in case they are in error, for example due to mis-keying by the data subject or the organisation or for some other reason. Inaccurate data are defined in the guidelines as 'incorrect or misleading as to any matter of fact'.

The guidelines go on to discuss the importance of keeping information up-to-date. This is only necessary where there is an ongoing relationship and the rights of the individual may be affected if they are not up-to-date. This implies, for example, that a credit-checking agency should keep credit scores up-to-date.

*5 Not kept longer than necessary*

In full:

> *Personal data processed for any purpose or purposes shall not be kept for longer than is necessary for that purpose or those purposes.*

The guidelines state:

> *To comply with this Principle, data controllers will need to review their personal data regularly and to delete the information which is no longer required for their purposes.*

It might be in a company's interests to 'clean data' so that records that are not relevant are archived or deleted, for example if a customer has not purchased for ten years. However, there is the possibility that the customer may still buy again, in which case the information would be useful.

If a relationship between the organisation and the data subject ends, then data should be deleted. This will be clear in some instances, for example when an employee leaves a company. With a consumer who has purchased products from a company this is less clear since frequency of purchase will vary, for example a car manufacturer could justifiably hold data for several years.

*6 Processed in accordance with the data subject's rights*

In full:

> *Personal data shall be processed in accordance with the rights of data subjects under this Act.*

**Subject access request**
A request by a data subject to view personal data from an organisation.

One aspect of the data subject's rights is the option to request a copy of their personal data from an organisation; this is known as a '**subject access request**'. For payment of a small fee, such as £10 or £30, an individual can request information which must be supplied by the organisation within 40 days. This includes all information on paper files and on computer. If you requested this information from your bank there might be several boxes of transactions!

Other aspects of a data subject's rights which the law upholds are designed to prevent or control processing which:

- causes damage or distress (for example, repeatedly sending mailshots to someone who has died);
- is used for direct marketing (for example, in the UK consumers can subscribe to the mail, e-mail or telephone preference services to avoid unsolicited mailings, e-mails or phone calls). This invaluable service is provided by the Direct Marketing Association (www.dmaconsumers.org). If you subscribe to these services, organisations must check against these 'exclusion lists' before contacting you. If they don't, and some don't, they are breaking the law;
- is used for automatic decision making – automated credit checks, for example, may result in unjust decisions on taking a loan. These can be investigated if you feel the decision is unfair.

*7 Secure*

In full:

> *Appropriate technical and organisational measures shall be taken against unauthorised or unlawful processing of personal data and against accidental loss or destruction of, or damage to, personal data.*

This guideline places a legal imperative on organisations to prevent unauthorised internal or external access to information and also its modification or destruction. Of course, most organisations would want to do this anyway since the information has value to the organisation and the reputational damage of losing customer information or being subject to a hack attack can be severe. For example in late 2006, online clothing retail group TJX Inc. (owner of TK Maxx) was hacked resulting in loss of credit card details of over 45 million customer in the US and Europe. TJX later said in its security filing that its potential liability (loss) from the computer intrusion(s) was $118 million.

Of course, the cost of security measures will vary according to the level of security required. The Act allows for this through this provision:

> *(i) Taking into account the state of technological development at any time and the cost of implementing any measures, the measures must ensure a level of security appropriate to: (a) the harm that might result from a breach of security; and (b) the nature of the data to be protected. (ii) The data controller must take reasonable steps to ensure the reliability of staff having access to the personal data.*

*8  Not transferred to countries without adequate protection*

In full:

> *Personal data shall not be transferred to a country or territory outside the European Economic Area, unless that country or territory ensures an adequate level of protection of the rights and freedoms of data subjects in relation to the processing of personal data.*

Transfer of data beyond Europe is likely for multinational companies. This principle prevents export of data to countries that do not have sound data processing laws. If the transfer is required in concluding a sale or contract, or if the data subject agrees to it, then transfer is legal. Data transfer with the US is possible through companies registered through the Safe Harbor scheme (www.export.gov/safeharbor).

### Anti-spam legislation

**Spam**
Unsolicited e-mail (usually bulk-mailed and untargeted).

Laws have been enacted in different countries to protect individual privacy and with the intention of reducing spam or unsolicited commercial e-mail (UCE). Originally, the best-known 'spam' was tinned meat (a contraction of 'spiced ham'), but a modern version of this acronym is '*sending persistent annoying e-mail*'. Spammers rely on sending out millions of e-mails in the hope that even if there is only a 0.01% response they may make some money, if not get rich.

**Cold list**
Data about individuals that are rented or sold by a third party.

**House list**
Data about existing customers used to market products to encourage future purchase.

Anti-spam laws do not mean that e-mail cannot be used as a marketing tool. As explained below, permission-based e-mail marketing based on consent or opt-in by customers, and the option to unsubscribe or opt-out is the key to successful e-mail marketing. E-mail lists can also be rented where customers have opted in to receive e-mail. This is known as a cold list, so called because the company that purchases the data from a third party does not know you. Your name will also potentially be stored on an opt-in house list within companies you have purchased from where you have given your consent to be contacted by the company or given additional consent to be contacted by its partners.

### European regulations on privacy and electronic communications

While the Data Protection Directive 95/46 and Data Protection Act afford a reasonable level of protection for consumers, they were quickly superseded by advances in technology and the rapid growth in spam. As a result, in 2002 the European Union passed the '2002/58/EC

Directive on Privacy and Electronic Communications' to complement previous data protection law. This Act is significant for marketers since it applies specifically to electronic communications such as e-mail and the monitoring of websites.

Clauses 22 to 24 are the main clauses relevant to e-mail communications.

---

### Box 3.1 — Privacy and Electronic Communications Regulations Act

**Opt-in**
A customer proactively agrees to receive further information.

**Opt-out**
A customer declines the offer to receive further information.

This is a law intended to control the distribution of e-mail and other online communications including cookies.

As with other European laws, this law was implemented differently in different countries. Some countries considered infringements more seriously. A company which is in breach of the directive in Italy is threatened by fines of up to €66,000 while in the UK the maximum fine is £5000. It is clearly important for managers to have access to legal advice which applies not only to their own country, but also to other European countries.

---

### Mini Case Study 3.3 — UK and European e-mail marketing law

As an example of European privacy law which covers use of e-mail, SMS and cookies for marketing, we review the implications for managers of the UK enactment of 2002/58/EC Directive on Privacy and Electronic Communications. We will contrast this with the law in other European countries. This came into force in the UK on 11 December 2003 as the **Privacy and Electronic Communications Regulations (PECR) Act**. The law is published at: www.hmso.gov.uk/si/si2003/20032426.htm. Consumer marketers in the UK also need to heed the Code of Advertising Practice from the Advertising Standards Agency (ASA CAP code, www.asa.org.uk/the_codes). This has broadly similar aims and places similar restrictions on marketers to the PECR law.We will summarise the main implications of the law by picking out key phrases. The new PECR law:

#### 1 Applies to consumer marketing using e-mail or SMS text messages

22(1) applies to *individual subscribers*. 'Individual subscribers' means consumers, although the Information Commissioner has stated that this may be reviewed in future to include business subscribers, as is the case in some other countries such as Italy and Germany.

Although this sounds like great news for business-to-business (B2B) marketers – and some take the view 'great, the new law doesn't apply to us' – this could be dangerous. There has been adjudication by the Advertising Standards Agency which found against a B2B organisation that had unwittingly e-mailed consumers from what they believed was an in-house list of B2B customers.

#### 2 Is an 'opt-in' regime

The new law applies to '*unsolicited communications*' (22(1)). It was introduced with a view to reducing spam, although we all know its impact will be limited on spammers beyond Europe. The relevant phrase is part of 22(2) where the recipient must have 'previously notified the sender that he consents' or has proactively agreed to receiving commercial e-mail. This is **opt-in**. Opt-in can be achieved online or offline through asking people whether they want to receive e-mail. Online this is often done through a tick box.

The main options are shown in Figure 3.5. Figure 3.5 (a) is opt-out and it can be considered to be against the spirit of the law since someone may sign up to receive e-mail communications without realising it. Figure 3.5(b) is opt-in since the subscriber has to explicitly check the box. Figure 3.5 (c) is also opt-in, but this is a more subtle approach. The consumer cannot enter the prize draw unless they complete the form. In fact, the PECR law does not mandate a tick-box option provided consent is clearly indicated.

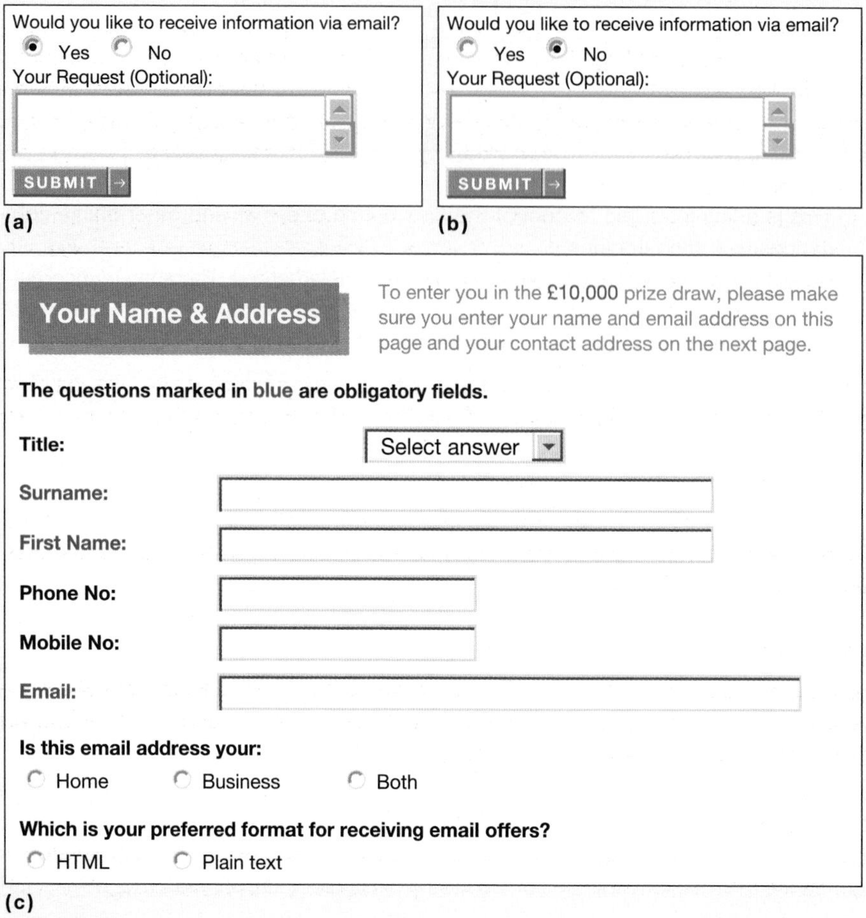

Would you like to receive information via email?
⦿ Yes  ○ No
Your Request (Optional):
[                    ]
SUBMIT →

**(a)**

Would you like to receive information via email?
○ Yes  ⦿ No
Your Request (Optional):
[                    ]
SUBMIT →

**(b)**

**Your Name & Address**

To enter you in the £10,000 prize draw, please make sure you enter your name and email address on this page and your contact address on the next page.

The questions marked in blue are obligatory fields.

Title:          Select answer ▾

Surname:        [                    ]

First Name:     [                    ]

Phone No:       [            ]

Mobile No:      [            ]

Email:          [                    ]

**Is this email address your:**
○ Home      ○ Business      ○ Both

**Which is your preferred format for receiving email offers?**
○ HTML      ○ Plain text

**(c)**

**Figure 3.5**    Online forms: (a) opt-out, (b) opt-in, (c) implicit opt-in

The approach required by the law has, in common with many aspects of data protection and privacy law, been used by many organisations for some time. In other words, sending unsolicited e-mails was thought to be unethical and also not in the best interests of the company because of the risk of annoying customers. In fact, the law conforms to an established approach known as 'permission marketing', a term coined by US commentator Seth Godin (1999, Chapter 6 – first four chapters available free from www.permission.com).

**Viral marketing**

One widespread business practice that is not covered explicitly in the PECR law is 'viral marketing' (Chapter 9). In the guidelines for marketers for the law, the commissioner states that it 'takes a dim view' of viral marketing, especially when it is incentivised and the marketer needs to be careful that consent of the friend is agreed.

### 3 Requires an opt-out option in all communications

An opt-out or method of 'unsubscribing' is required so that the recipient does not receive future communications. In a database this means that a 'do not e-mail' field must be created to avoid e-mailing these customers. The law states that a 'simple means of refusing' future communications is required both when the details were first collected and in each subsequent communication.

### 4 Does not apply to existing customers when marketing similar products

This common-sense clause (22(3)(a)) states that previous opt-in is not required if the contact details were obtained during the course of the sale or negotiations for the sale of a product or service. This is sometimes known as the 'soft or implied opt-in exception'. This key soft opt-in caveat is interpreted differently in different European countries, with seven countries, Italy, Denmark, Germany, Austria, Greece, Finland and Spain not including it. The differences mean that marketers managing campaigns across Europe need to take the differences in different countries into account.

Clause 22(3)(b) adds that when marketing to existing customers, the marketer may market 'similar products and services only'. Case law will help in clarifying this. For example, for a bank, it is not clear whether a customer with an insurance policy could be targeted for a loan.

### 5 Requires contact details must be provided

It is not sufficient to send an e-mail with a simple sign-off from 'the marketing team' or 'the web team' with no further contact details. The law requires a name, address or phone number to whom a recipient can complain.

### 6 Requires the 'from' identification of the sender to be clear

Spammers aim to disguise the e-mail originator. The law says that the identity of the person who sends the communication must not be 'disguised or concealed' and that a valid address to 'send a request that such communications cease' should be provided.

### 7 Applies to direct marketing communications

The communications that the legislation refers to are for 'direct marketing'. This suggests that other communications involved with customer service, such as an e-mail about a monthly phone statement, are not covered, so the opt-out choice may not be required here.

### 8 Restricts the use of cookies

Some privacy campaigners consider that the user's privacy is invaded by planting cookies or electronic tags on the end-user's computer. The concept of the cookie and its associated law is not straightforward, so it warrants separate discussion.

---

| Box 3.2 | Understanding cookies |
| --- | --- |

**Permission marketing**
Customers agree (opt-in) to be involved in an organisation's marketing activities, usually as a result of an incentive

**Viral marketing**
A marketing message is communicated from one person to another, facilitated by different media, such as word of mouth, e-mail or websites. It implies rapid transmission of messages is intended.

A cookie is a data file placed on your computer that identifies that individual computer. 'Cookie' derives from the Unix operating system term 'magic cookie' which meant something passed between routines or programs that enables the receiver to perform some operation.

### Types of cookies

The main cookie types are:

- **Persistent cookies** – these stay on a user's computer between multiple sessions and are most valuable for marketers to identify repeat visits to sites;
- Temporary or **session cookies** (single session) – useful for tracking within pages of a session such as on an e-commerce site.
- **First-party cookies** – served by the site currently in use, typically for e-commerce sites. These can be persistent or session cookies;
- **Third-party cookies** – served by another site to the one being viewed, typically for portals where an ad network will track remotely or where the web analytics software places a cookie. These are typically persistent cookies.

## Cookies

Cookies are small text files stored on an end-user's computer to enable websites to identify the user.

## Persistent cookies

Cookies that remain on the computer after a visitor session has ended. Used to recognise returning visitors.

## Session cookies

A cookie used to manage a single visitor session.

## First-party cookies

Served by the site currently in use – typically for e-commerce sites.

## Third-party cookies

Served by another site to the one being viewed – typically for portals where an ad network will track remotely or where the web analytics software places a cookie.

Cookies are stored as individual text files in a directory on a personal computer. There is usually one file per website. For example: dave_chaffey@british-airways.txt. This file contains encoded information as follows:

*FLT_VIS |K:bapzRnGdxBYUU|D:Jul-25-1999| british-airways.com/ 0 425259904 29357426 1170747936 29284034 \**

The information in the cookie file is essentially just an identification number and the date of the last visit, although other information can be stored.

Cookies are specific to a particular browser and computer, so if a user connects from a different computer, such as at work or starts using a different browser, the website will not identify him or her as a similar user.

### What are cookies used for?

Common marketing applications of cookies include:

- *Personalising a site for an individual*. Cookies are used to identify individual users and retrieve their preferences from a database according to an identifier stored in the cookie. For example, I subscribe to the EConsultancy service (www.e-consultancy. com) for the latest information about e-business; each time I return I do not have the annoyance of having to log in because it remembers my previous visit. Many sites feature a 'Remember Me' option which implies using a cookie to recognise a returning visitor. Retailers such as Amazon can use cookies to recognise returning visitors and can recommend related books purchased by other readers. This approach generally has good benefits for both the individual (it is a hassle to sign in again and relevant content can be delivered) and the company (tailored marketing messages can be delivered).
- *Online ordering systems*. This enables a site such as Tesco.com to track what is in your basket as you order different products.
- *Tracking within a site*. Web analytics software such as Webtrends (www.webtrends.com) or analyses statistics on visitors to websites and relies on persistent cookies to find the proportion of repeat visitors to a website. Webtrends and other tools increasingly use first-party cookies since they are more accurate and less likely to be blocked. Marketers should check whether use of first-party cookies is possible on their site.
- *Tracking across sites*. Advertising networks use cookies to track the number of times a particular computer user has been shown a particular banner advertisement; they can also track adverts served on sites across an ad network. There was an individual rights outcry in the late 1990s since Doubleclick was using this to profile customers. Doubleclick no longer operates an ad network, partly due to this.

Affiliate networks and pay-per-click ad networks such as Google Adwords and Yahoo! Search services (Overture) may also use cookies to track through from a click on a third-party site to a sale or lead being generated on a destination or merchant site. These approaches tend to use third-party cookies. For example, if conversion tracking is enabled in Google Adwords, Google sets a cookie when a user clicks through on an ad. If this user buys the product, then the purchase confirmation page will include script code supplied by Google to make a check for a cookie placed by Google. If there is a match, the sale is attributed to Adwords. An alternative approach using third-party tracking is that different online campaigns have different tracking parameters or codes within the links through to the destination site, and when the user arrives on a site from a particular source (such as Google Adwords) this is identified and a cookie set. When purchase confirmation occurs, this can then be attributed back to the original source, e.g. Google Adwords, and the particular referrer.

Owing to the large investments made now in pay-per-click marketing and affiliate marketing by many companies, this is the area of most concern for marketers since the tracking can become inaccurate. However, a sale should still occur even if the cookies are blocked or deleted, so the main consequence is that the ROI (return on investment) of online advertising or pay-per-click marketing may look lower than expected. In affiliate marketing, this phenomenon may benefit the marketer in that payment may not need to be made to the third party if a cookie has been deleted (or blocked) between the time of original click-through and sale.

## Privacy issues with cookie use

The problem for Internet marketers is that, despite these important applications, blocking by browsers, such as Internet Explorer, or security software and deletion by users has increased dramatically. In 2005 Jupiter Research claimed that 39% of online users may be deleting cookies from their primary computer monthly, although this is debated.

Many distrust cookies since they indicate a 'big brother' is monitoring their actions. Others fear that their personal details or credit card details may be accessed by other websites. This is very unlikely since all the cookies contain is a short identifier or number that is used to link you to your record in a database. Anyone who found the cookie wouldn't be able to log on to the database without your password. Cookies do not contain passwords, credit card information or any personal details as many people seem to think. These are held on the site servers, protected by firewalls and usernames and passwords. In most cases, the worst that someone can do who gets access to your cookies is to find out which sites you have been visiting.

It is possible to block cookies if the user finds out how to block them, but this is not straightforward and many customers either do not know how or do not mind that their privacy may be infringed. In 2003 an interesting survey on the perception and behaviour with regards to cookies was conducted on cookie use in the UK (RedEye, 2003). Of the 1000 respondents:

- 50% had used more than one computer in the last three months;
- 70% said that their computer was used by more than one person;
- 94% said they either accepted cookies or did not know what they were, although 20% said they only accepted session cookies;
- 71% were aware of cookies and accepted them – of these only 18% did not know how to delete cookies, and 55% of them were deleting them on a monthly basis;
- 89% knew what cookies were and how to delete them and said that they had deleted them once in the last three months.

## Legal constraints on cookies

The new PECR law limits the use of cookies. It states:

*a person shall not use an electronic communications network to store information, or to gain access to information stored, in the terminal equipment of a subscriber or user unless the following requirements are met.*

The requirements are:

(a) the user is provided with clear and comprehensive information about the purposes of the storage of, or access to, that information; and
(b) is given the opportunity to refuse the storage of or access to that information.

(a) suggests that it is important that there is a clear **privacy statement** and (b) suggests that opt in to cookies is required. In other words, on the first visit to the site, a box would have to be ticked to agree to the use of cookies. This was thought

**Privacy statement**
Information on a website explaining how and why individuals' data are collected, processed and stored.

by many commentators to be a curious provision since this facility is already available in the web browser. A further provision clarifies this. The law states: 'where such storage or access is strictly necessary for the provision of an information society service requested by the subscriber or user'. This indicates that for an e-commerce service session cookies are legitimate without the need for opt-in. It is arguable whether the identification of return visitors is 'strictly necessary' and this is why some sites have a 'remember me' tick box next to the log-in. Through doing this they are compliant with the law. Using cookies for tracking return visits alone would seem to be outlawed, but we will have to see how case law develops over the coming years before this is resolved.

### Worldwide regulations on privacy and electronic communications

In the US in January 2004, a new federal law known as the CAN-SPAM Act (www.ftc.gov/spam) was introduced to assist in the control of unsolicited e-mail. CAN-SPAM stands for 'Controlling the Assault of Non-Solicited Pornography and Marketing' (an ironic juxtaposition between pornography and marketing). This harmonised separate laws in different US states, but was less strict than in some states such as California. The Act requires unsolicited commercial e-mail messages to be labelled (though not by a standard method) and to include opt-out instructions and the sender's physical address. It prohibits the use of deceptive subject lines and false headers in such messages. Anti-spam legislation in other countries can be accessed at:

- www.privacy.gov.au (Australia enacted a SPAM act in 2003)
- www.privcom.gc.ca (Canada has a privacy act)
- www.privacy.org.nz (New Zealand Privacy Commissioner)
- www.spamlaws.com (summary for all countries)

We conclude this section on privacy legislation with a checklist summary of the practical steps that are required to audit a company's compliance with data protection and privacy legislation. Companies should:

1 Follow privacy and consumer protection guidelines and laws in all local markets. Use local privacy and security certification where available.
2 Notify or inform the site visitor before asking for information on:
   – who the company is;
   – what personal data are collected, processed and stored;
   – the purpose of collection;
   – how the site visitor can opt-out (be unsubscribed from e-mail lists or cookies);
   – how the site visitor can obtain information held about them.
3 Ask for consent for collecting sensitive personal data, and it is good practice to ask before collecting any type of data.
4 Reassure customers by providing clear and effective privacy statements and explaining the purpose of data collection.
5 Let individuals know when 'cookies' or other covert software are used to collect information about them.
6 Never collect or retain personal data unless it is strictly necessary for the organisation's purposes. For example, a person's name and full address should not be required to provide an online quotation. If extra information is required for marketing purposes this should be made clear and the provision of such information should be optional.
7 Amend incorrect data when informed and tell others. Enable correction on site.
8 Only use data for marketing (by the company or third parties) when a user has been informed this is the case and has agreed to this. (This is opt-in.)
9 Provide the option for customers to stop receiving information. (This is opt-out.)
10 Use appropriate security technology to protect the customer information on your site.

## 2 Disability and discrimination law

**Accessibility legislation**

Legislation intended to protect users of websites with disabilities including visual disability.

Laws relating to discriminating against disabled users who may find it more difficult to use websites because of audio, visual or motor impairment are known as **accessibility legislation**. This is often contained within disability and discrimination acts. In the UK, the relevant act is the Disability and Discrimination Act 1995.

Web accessibility refers to enabling all users of a website to interact with it regardless of disabilities they may have or the web browser or platform they are using to access the site. The visually impaired or blind are the main audience that designing an accessible website can help. Coverage of the requirements that accessibility places on web design are covered in Chapter 7.

## 3 Brand and trademark protection

Online brand and trademark protection covers several areas, including use of a brand name within domain names and use of trademarks within other websites and in online adverts.

**Domain name registration**

The process of reserving a unique web address that can be used to refer to the company website.

### Domain name registration

Most companies are likely to own several domains, perhaps for different product lines or countries or for specific marketing campaigns. Domain name disputes can arise when an individual or company has registered a domain name which another company claims they have the right to. This is sometimes referred to as 'cybersquatting'.

One of the best-known cases was brought in 1998 by Marks and Spencer and other high street retailers, since another company, 'One In a Million Limited', had registered names such as marks&spencer.com, britishtelecom.net and sainsbury.com. It then tried to sell these names for a profit. The companies already had sites with more familiar addresses, such as marksandspencers.co.uk, but had not taken the precaution of registering all related domains with different forms of spelling and different top-level domains, such as .net. Unsurprisingly, an injunction was issued against One in a Million which was no longer able to use these names.

The problem of companies' names being misappropriated was common during the 1990s, but companies still need to be sure to register all related domain names for each brand since new top-level domain names are created through time, such as .biz and .eu.

If you are responsible for websites, you need to check that domain names are automatically renewed by your hosting company (as most are today). For example, the .co.uk domain must be renewed every two years. Companies that don't manage this process potentially risk losing their domain name since another company could potentially register it if the domain name lapsed. A further option with domain registration is to purchase generic domain names of established sites which may perform well in the search engines.

---

| Mini Case Study 3.4 | How much is a domain worth? |
|---|---|

One of the highest values attached to a domain in Europe was paid in 2008 when the website cruise.co.uk paid the German travel company Nees Reisen £560,000 for the rival name cruises.co.uk (Figure 3.6). *Guardian* (2008) reported the new owner of cruises.co.uk as saying that he hopes to use the new domain differently – by turning the site into an online intermediary or community for cruising enthusiasts while its existing cruise.co.uk will concentrate on offering the best deals for voyages. Explaining the valuation, cruise.co.uk's managing director, Seamus Conlon stated:

> 'Cruises' is consistently ranked first on Google, with 'cruise' just behind. We wanted the top positions so that when Internet users are searching for cruise deals, reviews or news we are the first port of call. The cruise market is one of the fastest and most consistently growing sectors in the travel industry.

Figure 3.6 Cruises.co.uk

In the US, the record domain values are higher from when they were exchanged in the late 1990s including:

- sex.com for $12m
- business.com for $7.5m
- beer.com for $7m in 1999.

### Using competitor names and trademarks in meta-tags (for search engine optimisation)

Meta-tags, which are part of the HTML code of a site, are used to market websites by enabling them to appear more prominently in search engines as part of search engine optimisation (SEO) (see Chapter 8). Some companies have tried putting the name of a competitor company within the meta-tags. This is not legal since case law has found against companies that have used this approach. A further issue of marketing-related law is privacy law for e-mail marketing which was considered in the previous section.

### Using competitor names and trademarks in pay-per-click advertising

A similar approach can potentially be used in **pay-per-click marketing** (explained in Chapter 9) to advertise on competitors' names and trademarks. For example, if a search user types 'Dell laptop' can an advertiser bid to place an ad offering an 'HP laptop'? There is less case law in this area and differing findings have occurred in the US and France (such advertising is not permitted in France). One example of the types of issues that can arise is highlighted in Mini case study 3.5. Who owns the term 'Sport Court'?'

**Pay-per-click search marketing**

Refers to when a company pays for text ads to be displayed on the search engine results pages when a specific keyphrase is entered by the search users. It is so called since the marketer pays for each time the hypertext link in the ad is clicked on.

| Mini Case Study 3.5 | Who owns the term 'Sport Court'? |
|---|---|

This case involved two competitors who manufacture synthetic sports flooring. In 2002, Sport Court sued Rhino Sports for trademark infringement, and the parties settled with a permanent injunction restricting Rhino Sports from 'directly or indirectly using in commerce the mark SPORT COURT'. This injunction listed the digital assets or advertising where this might occur: '...on or in connection with the Internet, such as in an Internet domain name, as a sponsored link, in connection with an Internet web page, or as HTML code for an Internet website in any manner, such as the title or keyword portions of a metatag, or otherwise'.

However, because of broadmatching facility in Google AdWords this didn't cover another activity which arose in 1996. Sport Court discovered that Rhino Sports' ad appeared as a sponsored link in response to the search term 'sport court' (without quotes) and went to court claiming that Rhino Sport was in contempt of the original injunction. However, the ad copy didn't contain the phrase 'sport court,' and Rhino Sports said it bought the broad-matched keyword terms 'court' and 'basketball court'. which triggered the ad. As a result, the complaint was rejected. Goldman explains:

> First, the literal terms of the injunction only restrict using the term 'Sport Court' as a sponsored link. Arguably, invisible keyword triggering using 'Sport Court' wouldn't violate this provision. Second, Rhino Sports didn't buy the keyword 'Sport Court,' and the injunction doesn't restrict Rhino Sports' purchase of generic terms like 'court' or 'basketball court'.
>
> This court's reasoning is solid, but I'm interested by the fact that the court didn't discuss Rhino Sports' ability to negative keyword match the phrase 'sport court'. This would be easy for Rhino Sports to do and it would appear to solve Sport Court's problem. Given that the court didn't bail the plaintiff out here, plaintiffs drafting injunctions may need to update their boilerplate injunction language to contemplate the different technologies offered by the ad networks, both now and in the future.

Finally, since it was in court anyway, Rhino Sports took a stab at trying to modify the injunction to let it buy the keyword 'sport court', like numerous other Sport Court competitors are doing. Because the injunction was stipulated, the court wasn't that excited about disturbing the initial agreement. Further, although there have been some important developments about keyword advertising and trademark use in commerce in other circuits (such as the Rescuecom and JG Wentworth cases), the court repeatedly notes the unsettled nature of Ninth Circuit law as another reason not to change the initial deal. 'I don't blame the court for not wanting to touch the Ninth Circuit's hairball jurisprudence with a ten foot pole, but I think this reinforces how important it is that the Ninth Circuit fix its mess'.

*Source*: Goldman (2007)

### Reputational damage in advertising

Companies fear reputational damage through advertising on sites with which they wouldn't want their brand associated because of ad buys on social networks or ad networks (Chapter 9) where it was not clear what content their ads would be associated with. For example, Vodafone removed all its advertising from the social network Facebook after its ads appeared on the group profile for the British National Party. Many other advertisers withdrew their advertising as a result.

### Monitoring brand conversations in social networks and blogs

Online brand reputation management and alerting software tools offer real-time alerts when comments or mentions about a brand are posted online in different locations, including blogs and social networks. Some basic tools are available including:

- Googlealert (www.googlealert.com) and Google Alerts (www.google.com/alerts) which will alert companies when any new pages appear that contain a search phrase such as your company or brand names.
- Nielsen BuzzMetrics' BlogPulse (www.blogpulse.com) gives trends and listings of any phrase (see the example in Figure 3.7) and individual postings can be viewed.

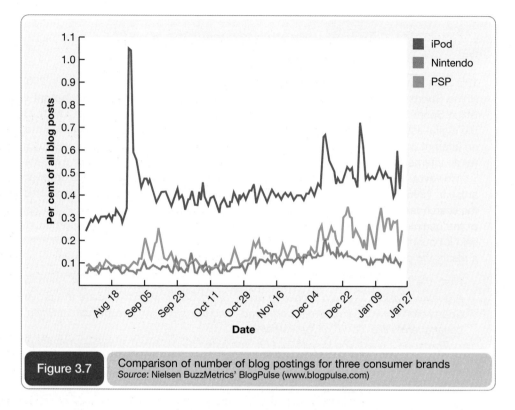

| Figure 3.7 | Comparison of number of blog postings for three consumer brands |
|---|---|
| | *Source*: Nielsen BuzzMetrics' BlogPulse (www.blogpulse.com) |

There are also more sophisticated online reputation-management services which offer more in-depth analysis on whether the sentiment is positive or negative and cover other issues such as unauthorised use of logos and use of trademarks. Examples documented at http://www.davechaffey.com/online-reputation-management-tools include Mark Monitor, Reputation Intelligence, Brand Intelligence, Big Mouth Media and Market Sentinel.

The challenges of policing online trademark infringement, given the range of opportunities for this and the lag between what the law stipulates and what is possible through the technology, is evident from Mini case study 3.5.

## 4 Intellectual property rights

**Intellectual property rights**
Protect the intangible property created by corporations or individuals that is protected under copyright, trade secret and patent laws.

**Intellectual property rights (IPRs)** protect designs, ideas and inventions and include content and services developed for e-commerce sites. Closely related is copyright law which is designed to protect authors, producers, broadcasters and performers by ensuring they see some returns from their works every time they are experienced. The European Directive of Copyright (2001/29/EC) came into force in many countries in 2003. This is a significant update to the law which covers new technologies and approaches such as streaming a broadcast via the Internet.

IP can be misappropriated in two senses online.

**Trademark**
A trademark is a unique word or phrase that distinguishes your company. The mark can be registered as plain or designed text, artwork or a combination. In theory, colours, smells and sounds can also be trademarks.

First, an organisation's IP may be misappropriated and you need to protect against this. For example, it is relatively easy to copy web content and re-publish on another site, and this practice is not unknown among smaller businesses. Reputation management services can be used to assess how an organisation's content, logos and **trademarks** are being used on other websites.

Secondly, an organisation may misappropriate content inadvertently. Some employees may infringe copyright if they are not aware of the law. Additionally, some methods of designing transactional websites have been patented. For example, Amazon has patented its 'One-click' purchasing option which is why you do not see this labelling and process on other sites.

## 5 Contract law

We will look at two aspects of forming an electronic contract – the country of origin principle and distance selling laws.

### Country of origin principle

The contract formed between a buyer and a seller on a website will be subject to the laws of a particular country. In Europe, many such laws are specified at the regional (European Union) level, but are interpreted differently in different countries. This raises the issue of the jurisdiction in which law applies – is it that for the buyer, for example located in Germany, or the seller (merchant) whose site is based in France? Although this has been unclear, in 2002 attempts were made by the EU to adopt the '*country of origin principle*'. This means that the law for the contract will be that where the merchant is located. The Out-Law site produced by lawyers Pinsent Mason gives more information on jurisdiction (http://www.out-law.com/page-479).

### Distance-selling law

Sparrow (2000) advises different forms of disclaimers to protect the retailer. For example, if a retailer made an error with the price or the product details, then the retailer is not bound to honour a contract, since it was only displaying the products as 'an invitation to treat', not a fixed offer.

A well-known case was when an e-retailer offered televisions for £2.99 due to an error in pricing a £299 product. Numerous purchases were made, but the e-retailer claimed that a contract had not been established simply by accepting the online order, although the customers did not see it that way! Unfortunately, no legal precedent was established in this case since the case did not come to trial.

Disclaimers can also be used to limit liability if the website service causes a problem for the user, such as a financial loss resulting from an action based on erroneous content. Furthermore, Sparrow suggests that terms and conditions should be developed to refer to issues such as timing of delivery and damage or loss of goods.

The distance-selling directive also has a bearing on e-commerce contracts in the European Union. It was originally developed to protect people using mail order (by post or phone). The main requirements, which are consistent with what most reputable e-retailers would do anyway, are that e-commerce sites must contain easily accessible content which clearly states:

- the company's identity including address;
- the main features of the goods or services;
- price information, including tax and, if appropriate, delivery costs;
- the period for which the offer or price remains valid;
- payment, delivery and fulfilment performance arrangements;
- right of the consumer to withdraw, i.e. cancellation terms;
- the minimum duration of the contract and whether the contract for the supply of products or services is to be permanent or recurrent, if appropriate;
- whether an equivalent product or service might be substituted, and confirmation as to whether the seller pays the return costs in this event.

After the contract has been entered into, the supplier is required to provide written confirmation of the information provided. An e-mail confirmation is now legally binding provided both parties have agreed that e-mail is an acceptable form for the contract. It is always advisable to obtain an electronic signature to confirm that both parties have agreed the contract, and this is especially valuable in the event of a dispute. The default position for services is that there is no cancellation right once services begin.

The Out-Law site produced by lawyers Pinsent Mason gives more information on distance selling (http://www.out-law.com/page-430).

### 6 Online advertising law

Advertising standards that are enforced by independent agencies such as the UK's Advertising Standards Authority Code also apply in the Internet environment (although they are traditionally less strongly policed, leading to more 'edgy' creative executions online which are intended to have a viral effect).

The Out-Law site produced by lawyers Pinsent Mason gives more information on online advertising law (www.out-law.com/page-5604).

## Technological factors

**Internet**
The physical network that links computers across the globe. It consists of the infrastructure of network servers and communication links between them that are used to hold and transport the vast amount of information on the Internet.

**World Wide Web**
The World Wide Web is a medium for publishing information and providing services on the Internet. It is accessed through **web browsers**, which display site *content* on different **web pages**. The content making up **websites** is stored on **web servers**.

**Web server**
Used to store the web pages accessed by web browsers. They may also contain databases of customer or product information, which can be queried and retrieved using a browser.

**Web browser**
Browsers such as Mozilla Firefox and Microsoft Internet Explorer provide an easy method of accessing and viewing information stored as HTML web documents on different web servers.

**Streaming media**
Sound and video that can be experienced within a web browser before the whole clip is downloaded.

Marketers require a basic understanding of Internet technology and terminology so they can discuss with agencies or technical staff how customer behaviour can be evaluated online through web analytics as customers respond to different messages on third-party sites such as affiliates or adverts on publisher sites. They will also need to discuss with agencies, or an internal IT team, the technologies for running campaigns, building sites or managing customer data. So, in this section, we give a brief outline of Internet and web technology, including security, before going on to digital TV and mobile marketing. Further information on designing sites is given in Chapter 7.

Equally importantly, as suggested by the section on strategic agility at the start of the chapter, marketers need to stay up-to-date on the latest technologies to evaluate the relevance of them to new ways of delivering value to customers. So at the end of this section we will also discuss how decisions can be taken about which technologies to adopt.

## A short introduction to Internet technology

The **Internet** has existed since the late 1960s when a limited number of computers were connected for military and research purposes in the United States to form the ARPAnet.

The recent dramatic growth in the use of the Internet has occurred because of the development of the **World Wide Web**. This became a commercial proposition in 1993 after development of the original concept by Tim Berners-Lee, a British scientist working at CERN in Switzerland in 1989. Today, the main principles of web technology hold true. Web content is stored on **web server** computers and then accessed by users who run **web browser** software such as Microsoft Internet Explorer, Apple Safari or Mozilla Firefox which display the information and allow users to interact and select links to access other websites. Rich media, such as Flash applications, audio or video content, can also be stored on a web server, or a specialist **streaming media server**.

Promoting website addresses is important to marketing communications. The technical name for web addresses is **uniform** or **universal resource locators (URLs)**. URLs can be thought of as a standard method of addressing, similar to postal codes, that make it straightforward to find the name of a site.

Web addresses are structured in a standard way as follows:

*http://www.domain-name.extension/filename.html*

The 'domain-name' refers to the name of the web server and is usually selected to be the same as the name of the company, and the extension will indicate its type. The 'extension' is also commonly known as the generic top-level domain (gTLD). Note that gTLDs are currently under discussion and there are proposals for adding new types such as .store and .firm.

Common gTLDs are:

- **.com** represents an international or American company (e.g. www.travelocity.com)
- **.org** are not-for-profit organisations (e.g. www.greenpeace.org)

**Streaming media server**

A specialist server used to broadcast audio (e.g. podcasts) or video (e.g. IPTV or webcast presentations). Served streams can be unicast (a separate copy of stream is served for each recipient), multicast (recipients share streams) or peer-to-peer where the media is shared between different recipient's computers using a Bitorrent or Kontiki approach favoured by distributors of TV programmes such as the BBCs iPlayer.

**Uniform (universal) resource locator (URL)**

A web address used to locate a web page on a web server.

- **.mobi** was introduced in 2006 for sites configured for mobile phones
- **.net** is a network provider such as www.demon.net

There are also specific country code top-level domains (ccTLDs):

- **.co.uk** represents a company based in the UK (e.g. www.thomascook.co.uk)
- **.au**, **.ca**, **.de**, **.es**, **fi**, **.fr**, **.it**, **nl**, etc. represent other countries (the co.uk syntax is an anomaly!)
- **.ac.uk** is a UK-based university or other higher education institution (e.g. www.cranfield.ac.uk)
- **.org.uk** is for an organisation focusing on a single country (e.g. www.mencap.org.uk)

The 'filename.html' part of the web address refers to an individual web page, for example 'products.html' for a web page summarising a company's products. When a web address is typed in without a filename, for example www.bt.com, the browser automatically assumes the user is looking for the home page, which by convention is referred to as index.html. When creating sites, it is therefore vital to name the home page index.html (or an equivalent such as index.asp or index.php). The file index.html can also be placed in sub-directories to ease access to information. For example, to access a support page a customer would type www.bt.com/support rather than www.bt.com/support/index.htm. In offline communications sub-directories are publicised as part of a company's URL strategy (see Chapter 8).

As we stressed in the section on law for Internet marketing, it is important to protect brand abuse of domains by other companies through registering the variants possible for a company through a domain registration registrar. These are companies accredited by the Internet Corporation for Assigned Names and Numbers (ICANN) and/or by a national ccTLD authority to register domains.

There is further terminology associated with a URL, which will often be required when discussing a campaign, shown in Box 3.3 'What's in a URL?'

---

| Box 3.3 | What's in a URL? |
|---|---|

A great example is provided by Google engineer Matt Cutts (Cutts, 2007):

http://video.google.co.uk:80/videoplay?docid=7246927612831078230&hl=en#00h02m30s

Here are some of the components of the url:

- The *protocol* is http. Other protocols are https, ftp, etc
- The *host* or *hostname* is video.google.co.uk
- The *sub-domain* is video
- The *domain name* is google.co.uk
- The *top-level domain* or TLD is uk [also known as gTLD]. The uk domain is also referred to as a country-code top-level domain or ccTLD. For google.com, the TLD would be com
- The *second-level domain* (SLD) is co.uk
- The *port* is 80, which is the default port for web servers (not usually used in URLs when it is the default, although all web servers broadcast on ports)
- The *path* is /videoplay. Path typically refers to a file or location on the web server, e.g. /directory/file.html:
- An example of the URL parameter is docid and the value of that parameter is: -7246927612831078230. These are often called a name-value pair. URLs often have lots of parameters. Parameters start with a question mark (?) and are separated with an ampersand (&)
- The *anchor* or fragment is '#00h02m30s'

**Client–server**

The client–server architecture consists of client computers such as PCs sharing resources such as a database stored on a more powerful server computer.

**Internet service provider**

A provider enabling home or business users a connection to access the Internet. They can also host web-based applications.

**Backbones**

High-speed communications links used to enable Internet communications across a country and internationally.

**Static web page**

A page on the web server that is invariant.

**Dynamic web page**

A page that is created in real time, often with reference to a database query, in response to a user request.

**Transaction log file**

A web server file that records all page requests.

**Content**

Content is the design, text and graphical information that forms a web page. Good content is the key to attracting customers to a website and retaining their interest or achieving repeat visits.

# How does the Internet work?

The Internet is a large-scale **client–server** system where content is transmitted from client PCs whose users request services from server computers that hold content, rich media and host business applications that deliver the services in response to requests. Client PCs within homes and businesses are connected to the Internet via local **Internet service providers (ISPs)** which, in turn, are linked to larger ISPs with connection to the major national and international infrastructure or **backbones**.

## Infrastructure components of the Internet

Figure 3.8 shows the basic process by which web browsers communicate with web servers. A request from the client PC is executed when the user types in a web address, clicks on a hyperlink or fills in an online form such as a search. This request is then sent to the ISP and routed across the Internet to the destination server. The server then returns the requested web page if it is a **static (fixed) web page**. If it requires reference to a database, such as a request for product information, it will pass the query on to a database server and will then return this to the customer as a **dynamic web page**. Information on all file requests such as images, rich media and pages is stored in a **transaction log file** or via a **web analytics** system such as Google Analytics (www.google.com/analytics) which records the page requested, the time it was made and the source of the enquiry as explained in Chapter 9.

## Web page standards

The information, graphics and interactive elements that make up the web pages of a site are collectively referred to as **content**. Different standards exist for text, graphics and multimedia.

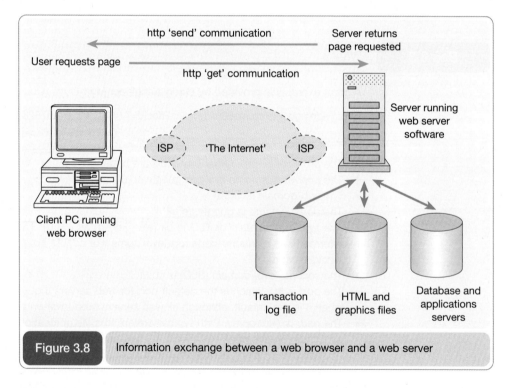

| Figure 3.8 | Information exchange between a web browser and a web server |

**HTML (Hypertext Markup Language)**
A standard format used to define the text and layout of web pages. HTML files usually have the extension .HTML or .HTM.

## Text information – HTML (Hypertext Markup Language)

Web page content is formatted and rendered by the browser software using **HTML** (or XHTML) **Hypertext Markup Language**. HTML is an international standard established by the World Wide Web Consortium (published at www.w3.org) intended to ensure that any web page written according to the definitions in the standard will appear the same in any web browser.

A simple example of HTML is given for a simplified home page for a B2B company in Figure 3.9. The HTML code used to construct pages has codes or instruction tags, such as <TITLE>, to indicate to the browser what is displayed. The <TITLE> tag indicates what appears at the top of the web browser window. Each starting tag has a corresponding end tag, usually marked by a '/', for example <B>plastics</B> is used to embolden 'plastics'.

## Text information and data – XML (eXtensible Markup Language)

**Metadata**
Literally, data about data – a format describing the structure and content of data.

**XML or eXtensible Markup Language**
A standard for transferring structured data, unlike HTML which is purely presentational.

When the early version of HTML was designed by Tim Berners-Lee at CERN, he based it on the existing standard for representation of documents. This standard was SGML, the Standard Generalised Markup Language, which was ratified by the ISO in 1986. SGML uses tags to identify the different elements of a document such as title and chapters. While HTML proved powerful in providing a standard method of displaying information that was easy to learn, it was purely presentational. It lacked the ability to describe the data on web pages. A metadata language providing data about data contained within pages is much more powerful and is provided by **XML** or **eXtensible Markup Language**, produced in February 1998. This is also based on SGML. The key word describing XML is 'extensible'. This means that new markup tags can be created that facilitate the searching and exchange of information. For example, product information on a web page could use the XML tags <NAME>, <DESCRIPTION>, <COLOUR> and <PRICE>. The tags can effectively act as a standard set of database field descriptions so that data can be exchanged through price comparison sites.

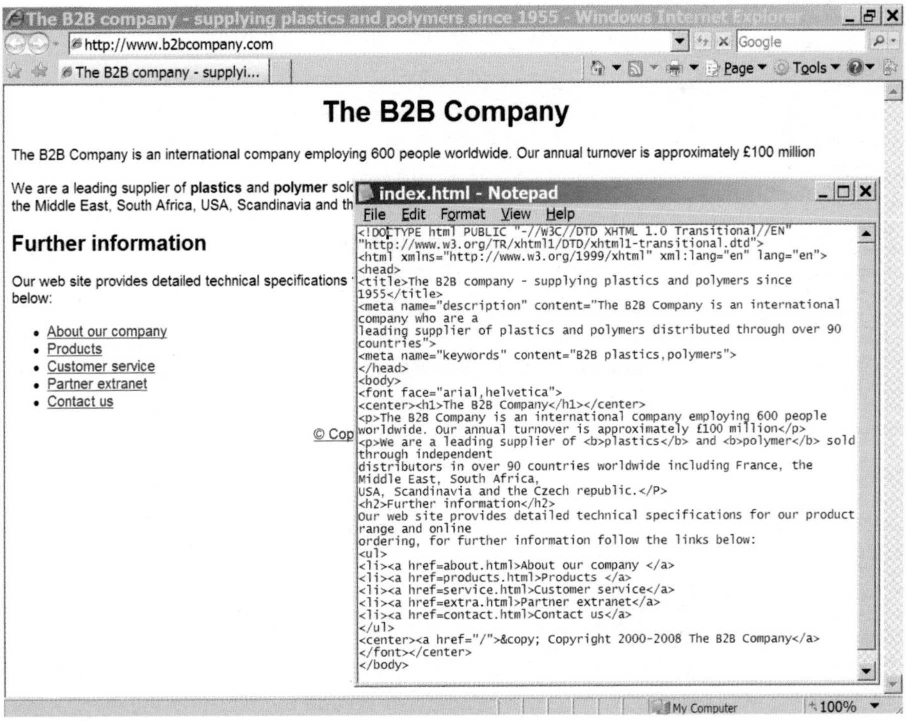

**Figure 3.9** Basic home page index.html for The B2B Company in a web browser showing the HTML source in a text editor

The importance of XML for data integration is indicated by its incorporation by Microsoft into its BizTalk server for B2B integration and the creation of the ebXML (electronic business XML) standard by their rival Sun Microsystems. We will see in Chapter 9 that the basic meta-data that each page of a website can use is important for search engine optimisation (SEO).

### Graphical images (GIF, JPEG and PNG files)

**GIF (Graphics Interchange Format)**
A graphics format and compression algorithm best used for simple graphics.

**JPEG (Joint Photographic Experts Group)**
A graphics format and compression algorithm best used for photographs.

Graphics produced by graphic designers or captured using digital cameras can be readily incorporated into web pages as images. **GIF (Graphics Interchange Format)** and **JPEG (Joint Photographic Experts Group)** refer to two standard file formats most commonly used to present images on web pages. GIF files are limited to 256 colours and are best used for small, simple graphics, such as banner adverts, while JPEG is best used for larger images where image quality is important, such as photographs. Both formats use image compression technology to minimise the size of downloaded files. Portable Network Graphics (.PNG) is growing in popularity since it is a patent and licence-free standard file format approved by the World Wide Web Consortium to replace the GIF file format.

### Animated graphical information (Flash and plug-ins)

**Plug-in**
An add-on program to a web browser providing extra functionality such as animation.

**Plug-ins** are additional programs, sometimes referred to as 'helper applications', and work in association with the web browser to provide features not present in the basic web browser. The best-known plug-ins are probably that for Adobe Acrobat which is used to display documents in .pdf format (www.adobe.com) and the Macromedia Flash and Shockwave products for producing interactive graphics (www.macromedia.com). Silverlight (www.silverlight.com) is a similar service introduced by Microsoft in 2007 for delivery of applications and streamed media.

### Audio and video standards

Traditionally, sound and video or 'rich media' have been stored as the Microsoft standards .WMA and .AVI. Alternative standards are RM3, MP3 MPEG.

## From the Internet to intranets and extranets

**Intranet**
A network within a single company that enables access to company information using the familiar tools of the Internet such as e-mail and web browsers. Only staff within the company can access the intranet, which will be password-protected.

**Extranet**
Formed by extending the intranet beyond a company to customers, suppliers, collaborators or even competitors. This is again password-protected to prevent access by general Internet users.

'Intranet' and 'extranet' are two terms that arose in the 1990s to describe applications of Internet technology with specific audiences, rather than anyone with access to the Internet. They are commonly used for marketing. Access to an intranet is limited by username and password to company staff, while an extranet can only be accessed by authorised third parties such as registered customers, suppliers and distributors. This relationship between the Internet, intranets and extranets is indicated by Figure 3.10. You can see that an intranet is effectively a private company internet with access available to staff only. An extranet permits access to trusted third parties, and the Internet provides global access.

Extranets such as Dell's Premier Pages provide exciting opportunities to communicate with major customers since tailored information such as special promotions, electronic catalogues and order histories can be provided on a web page personalised for each customer. Vlosky *et al.* (2000) examine in more detail how extranets impact business practices and relationships.

## Web security

We now focus on security technology, which is, like privacy, a major concern for Internet users that needs to be understood and managed by site owners and marketers to ensure sites are secure and that consumers are reassured about security. From a customer or merchant point of view, these are the main security risks involved in an e-commerce transaction:

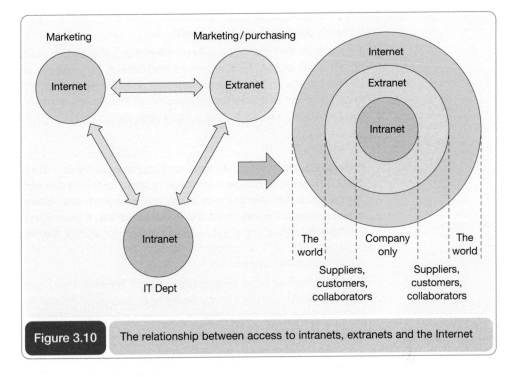

| Figure 3.10 | The relationship between access to intranets, extranets and the Internet |

- Customer details or passwords accessed on user's computer, e.g. through keylogging software or malware.
- Transaction or credit card details stolen in transit, e.g. through 'packet sniffing' software.
- Customer's credit card details stolen from merchant's server, for example through hacking.
- Customer's details accessed by company staff (or through a hacker who is in the building and has used 'social engineering' techniques to find information).
- Merchant or customer are not who they claim to be.

In this section we assess the measures that can be taken to reduce the risk of these breaches of e-commerce security. We start by reviewing some of the theory of online security and then review the techniques used.

For a summary of the main security risks for a website owner that must be managed within the design, see the summary in Box 3.4.

| Box 3.4 | The main website security risks |

This summary is provided by specialist website security consultants Watson Hall (www.watsonhall.com). They consider the top ten Internet security risks to be:

### 1 Validation of input and output data

All data used by the website (from users, other servers, other websites and internal systems) must be validated for type (e.g. numeric, date, string), length (e.g. 200 characters maximum, or a positive integer), syntax (e.g. product codes begin with two letters and are followed by five digits) and business rules (e.g. televisions can only cost between £100 and £2000, an order can contain at most 20 items, daily credit limit must not be exceeded). All data written as output (displayed) needs to be safe to view in a browser, e-mail client or other software and the integrity of any data that is returned must be checked. Utilising Asynchronous JavaScript and XML (AJAX) or Adobe Flex increases complexity and the possible attack vectors.

## 2 Direct data access (and theft)

If data exist, they can potentially be viewed or extracted. Avoid storing data that you do not need on the website and its database(s), for example some data relating to payment cards should never be stored. Poorly developed systems may allow access to data through SQL injection compromises, insufficient input and output data validation (see item 1 above) or poor system security.

## 3 Data poisoning

If users can amend or delete data inappropriately and this is then used to update your internal systems, business information is being lost. This can be hard to detect and it is important that the business rules are examined and enforced to validate data changes to ensure that poisoning is not occurring. If poisoning is not detected until well after it has occurred, it may be impossible to recover the original data.

## 4 Malicious file execution

Uploaded files or other data feeds may not be what they seem. Never allow user-supplied input to be used in any file name or path (e.g. URLs or file system references). Uploaded files may also contain a malicious payload so should not be stored in web accessible locations.

## 5 Authentication and session management

Websites rely on identifying users to provide access permissions to data and functions. If authentication (verification of identity, registration and logging in), authorisation (granting access rights) and session management (keeping track of the identity of a logged in user while they browse a website) can be circumvented or altered, then a user could access resources they are not allowed to. Beware especially of how password reminders, remember-me, change password, log out and updating account details are handled, how session tokens are used and always have login forms on dedicated and encrypted (SSL) pages.

## 6 System architecture and configuration

The information system architecture model should address the sensitivity of data identified during the requirements and specification phase of a website project. This may entail having separate web, application and database servers or involve clustering, load balancing or virtualisation. Additional security issues can be created through the way the live environment is configured. Sufficient and safe logging, monitoring and alerting facilities need to be built in to allow audit.

## 7 Phishing

Phishing, where users are misled into believing some other entity is or belongs to an own organisation (e-mail messages and websites are the most common combination), is best tackled through user education, but the way the website is designed, its architecture and how it communicates with users can reduce the risk.

*Commentary*: Phishing (pronounced 'fishing') is a specialised form of online identity theft. The most common form of 'phishing' is where a spam e-mail is sent out purporting to be from an organisation such as a bank or payment service. In 2004, the sites barclaysprivate.com and eurocitibank.com – neither of them anything to do with existing banks – were shut down, having been used to garner ID details for fraud. Recipients are then invited to visit a website to update their details after entering their username and password. The web address directs them to a false site very similar in

**Phishing**
Obtaining personal details online through sites and e-mails masquerading as legitimate businesses.

appearance to the organisation's site. When the username and password are entered these are then collected and used for removing money from the recipient's real account. Such scams are a modern version of the scam devised by criminals where they install a false ATM in a wall with a card reader to access someone's account details. This form of scam is difficult to counter since the e-mail and website can be made to appear identical to those of the organisation through copying. The main countermeasure is education of users, so banks for instance will tell their customers that they would never send this form of e-mail. However, this will not eradicate the problem since with millions of online customers some will always respond to such scams. A further approach is the use of multiple passwords, such that when an account is first accessed from a new system an additional password is required which can only be obtained through mail or by phone. Of course, this will only work if identity theft hasn't occurred. So, for organisations subject to phishing attacks, options for e-mail marketing are limited.

Phishing involves 'spoofing' where one party masquerades as someone else. Spoofing can be of two sorts:

- IP spoofing is used to gain access to confidential information by creating false identification data such as the originating network (IP) address. The objective of this access can be espionage, theft or simply to cause mischief, generate confusion and damage corporate public image or political campaigns. Firewalls can be used to reduce this threat.
- Site spoofing, i.e. fooling the organisation's customers using a similar URL such as www.amazno.com, can divert customers to a site which is not the bona fide retailer.

Firewalls can be used to minimise the risk of security breaches by hackers and viruses. Firewalls are usually created as software mounted on a separate server at the point the company is connected to the Internet. Firewall software can then be configured to accept only links from trusted domains representing other offices in the company or key account customers.

## 8 Denial of service

While malicious users might try to swamp the web server with a vast number of requests or actions that degrade its performance (filling up logs, uploading large files, undertaking tasks that require a lot of memory repeatedly), denial of service attacks include locking out valid user accounts or those caused by coding problems (e.g. memory leaks, resources not being released).

*Commentary*: The risk to companies of these attacks was highlighted in the spring of 2000, when the top websites were targeted. The performance of these sites, such as Yahoo! (www.yahoo.com) and eBay (www.ebay.com), was severely degraded as millions of data packets flooded the site from a number of servers. This was a distributed attack where the sites were bombarded from rogue software installed on many servers, so it was difficult for the e-tailers to counter. Since then fraudsters have attempted to blackmail online merchants at critical times, for example online betting companies before a major sporting event or e-retailers before Christmas. These are often very sophisticated attacks which involve using viruses to compromise many 'zombie' computers around the world forming a botnet – these are not adequately protected by firewalls and are then subsequently used to broadcast messages. Such attacks are very difficult to counter.

### Firewall

A specialised software application mounted on a server at the point where the company is connected to the Internet. Its purpose is to prevent unauthorised access into the company from outsiders.

### Denial of service attack

Also known as a distributed denial of service (DDOS) attack, these involve a hacker group taking control of many 'zombie' computers attached to the Internet whose security has been compromised. This 'botnet' is then used to make many requests to a target server, so overloading it and preventing access to other visitors.

### Botnet

Independent computers, connected to the Internet, are used together, typically for malicious purposes through controlling software. For example, they may be used to send out spam or for a denial of service attack where they repeatedly access a server to degrade its software. Computers are often initially infected through a virus when effective anti-virus measures are not in place.

> ### 9 System information leakage
>
> Web servers, errors, staff, partner organisations, search engines and rubbish can all be the source of important information about your website – its technologies, business logic and security methods. An attacker can use such information to their advantage so it is important to avoid system information leakage as far as possible.
>
> ### 10 Error handling
>
> Exceptions such as user data validation messages, missing pages and server errors should be handled by the code so that a custom page is displayed that does not provide any system information to the user (see item 9 above). Logging and alerting of unusual conditions should be enabled and these should allow subsequent audit.

## Principles of secure systems

Before we look at the principles of secure systems, it is worth reviewing the standard terminology for the different parties involved in the transaction:

- *Purchasers* – the consumers buying the goods.
- *Merchants* – the retailers.
- *Certification authority (CA)* – a body that issues digital certificates that confirm the identity of purchasers and merchants. The best known are Verisign and Thawte.
- *Banks* – traditional banks.
- *Electronic token issuer* – a virtual bank that issues digital currency.

The basic requirements for security systems from these different parties to the transaction are as follows:

1 *Authentication* – are parties to the transaction who they claim to be?
2 *Privacy and confidentiality* – is the transaction data-protected? The consumer may want to make an anonymous purchase. Are all non-essential traces of a transaction removed from the public network and all intermediary records eliminated?
3 *Integrity* – is the message sent complete, i.e. it isn't corrupted.
4 *Non-repudiability* – ensures sender cannot deny sending message.
5 *Availability* – how can threats to the continuity and performance of the system be eliminated?

## Approaches to developing secure systems

### Digital certificates

**Digital certificates (keys)**

Consist of keys made up of large numbers that are used to uniquely identify individuals.

**Symmetric encryption**

Both parties to a transaction use the same key to encode and decode messages.

There are two main methods of encryption using **digital certificates** or 'keys':

1 Secret-key **(symmetric) encryption**. This involves both parties having an identical (shared) key that is known only to them. Only this key can be used to encrypt and decrypt messages. The secret key has to be passed from one party to the other before use, in much the same way that a copy of a secure attaché case key would have to be sent to a receiver of information. This approach has traditionally been used to achieve security between two separate parties, such as major companies conducting EDI. Here the private key is sent out electronically or by courier to ensure it is not copied.

This method is not practical for general e-commerce since it would not be safe for a purchaser to give a secret key to a merchant because control of it would be lost and it could not then be used for other purposes. A merchant would also have to manage many customer keys.

**Asymmetric encryption**
Both parties use a related but different key to encode and decode messages.

2 **Public-key (asymmetric) encryption.** Asymmetric encryption is so called since the keys used by the sender and receiver of information are different. The two keys are related by a numerical code, so only the *pair* of keys can be used in combination to encrypt and decrypt information. Figure 3.11 shows how public-key encryption works in an e-commerce context. A customer can place an order with a merchant by automatically looking up the public key of the merchant and then using this key to encrypt the message containing their order. The scrambled message is then sent across the Internet and on receipt by the merchant is read using the merchant's private key. In this way only the merchant who has the only copy of the private key can read the order. In the reverse case the merchant could confirm the customer's identity by reading identity information such as a digital signature encrypted with the private key of the customer using their public key.

### Digital signatures

**Digital signature**
A method of identifying individuals or companies using public-key encryption.

**Digital signatures** can be used to create commercial systems by using public-key encryption to achieve authentication: the merchant and purchaser can prove they are genuine. The purchaser's digital signature is encrypted before sending a message using their private key, and on receipt the public key of the purchaser is used to decrypt the digital signature. This proves the customer is genuine. Digital signatures are not widely used currently due to the difficulty of setting up transactions, but will become more widespread as the public-key infrastructure (PKI) stabilises and the use of certificate authorities increases.

### The public-key infrastructure (PKI) and certificate authorities

**Certificate and certificate authorities**
A certificate is a valid copy of a public key of an individual or organisation together with identification information. It is issued by a trusted third party (TTP) or certificate authority (CA). CAs make public keys available and also issue private keys.

In order for digital signatures and public-key encryption to be effective it is necessary to be sure that the public key intended for decryption of a document actually belongs to the person you believe is sending you the document. The developing solution to this problem is the issuance by a trusted third party (TTP) of a message containing owner identification information and a copy of the public key of that person. The TTPs are usually referred to as **certificate authorities (CAs)** – an example is Verisign (www.verisign.com). The message is called a **certificate**. In reality, as asymmetric encryption is rather slow, it is often only a sample of the message that is encrypted and used as the representative digital signature.

Examples of certificate information are:

- user identification data;
- issuing authority identification and digital signature;
- user's public key;
- expiry date of this certificate;
- class of certificate;
- digital identification code of this certificate.

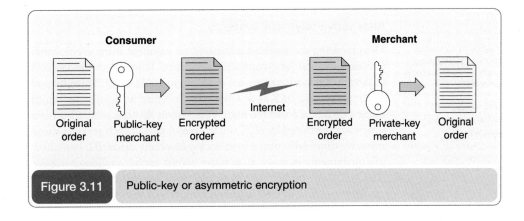

**Consumer** ... Original order ... Public-key merchant ... Encrypted order ... Internet ... Encrypted order ... Private-key merchant ... Original order ... **Merchant**

**Figure 3.11** Public-key or asymmetric encryption

### Virtual private networks

**Virtual private network**
Private network created using the public network infrastructure of the Internet.

A **virtual private network** (VPN) is a private wide-area network (WAN) that runs over the public network, rather than a more expensive private network. The technique by which a VPN operates is sometimes referred to as *tunnelling*, and involves encrypting both packet headers and content using a secure form of the Internet protocol known as IPSec. VPNs enable the global organisation to conduct its business securely, but using the public Internet rather than more expensive proprietary systems.

### Current approaches to e-commerce security

In this section we review the approaches used by e-commerce sites to achieve security using the techniques described above.

### Secure Sockets Layer protocol (SSL)

SSL is the most common security mechanism used on transactional websites in association with CAs like Verisign who issue an SSL certificate that verifies the identity of the certificate owner. The SSL approach enables encryption of sensitive information during online transactions using PKI and digital certificates to ensure privacy and authentication. In practice, transaction information is transferred by TCP/IP (Transmission Control Protocol/Internet Protocol) broken into packets, numbered sequentially with an error control attached. Individual packets are sent by different routes. The detailed stages of SSL are as follows:

1  Client browser sends request for a secure connection.
2  Server responds with a digital certificate which is sent for authentication.
3  Client and server negotiate *session keys*, which are symmetrical keys used only for the duration of the transaction.
4  Encryption is used to scramble the details of an e-commerce transaction as it is passed between the sender and receiver.

SSL is more widely used than the rival S-HTTP method. Here, when encryption is occurring they will see that the web address prefix in the browser changes from 'http://' to 'https://' and a padlock appears at the bottom of the browser window.

### Secure Electronic Transaction (SET)

**Secure Electronic Transaction**
A standard for public-key encryption intended to enable secure e-commerce transactions, lead-developed by Mastercard and Visa.

**Secure Electronic Transaction (SET)** was once touted as the way forward for increasing Internet security, but adoption was limited due to the difficulty of exchanging keys and the time of transaction, with most e-commerce sites still using SSL. SET is a security protocol based on digital certificates, originally developed by a consortium led by Mastercard and Visa, which allows parties to a transaction to confirm each other's identity. Due to complexity of implementation, SET is not widely used and SSL has become the de facto standard.

### Alternative payment systems

**Payment system**
Method of transferring funds from a customer to a merchant.

**Micropayment**
Small-denomination payment.

The preceding discussion has focused on payment using credit card systems since this is the prevalent method for e-commerce purchases. Throughout the 1990s there were many attempts to develop alternative **payment systems** to credit cards. These focused on **micropayments** or electronic coinage such as downloading an online newspaper, for which the overhead and fee of using a credit card was too high. One system that has succeeded is PayPal (www.paypal.com) which was purchased by eBay and is a major part of their revenue stream since it is used for payment by those who don't have access to credit cards. BT launched BT 'Click and Buy' for micropayments in the UK. A more recent service is Google Checkout (www.google.com/checkout) which has proved popular with smaller merchants because of introductory discounted transaction prices based on the level of use of Google AdWords.

### Reassuring the customer

Once the security measures are in place, content on the merchant's site can be used to reassure the customer, for example Amazon (www.amazon.com) takes customer fears about security seriously judging by the prominence and amount of content it devotes to this issue. Some of the approaches used indicate good practice in allaying customers' fears. These include:

- use of customer guarantee to safeguard purchase;
- clear explanation of SSL security measures used;
- highlighting the rarity of fraud ('ten million customers have shopped safely without credit card fraud');
- the use of alternative ordering mechanisms such as phone or fax;
- the prominence of information to allay fears – the guarantee is one of the main menu options.

Companies can also use independent third parties that set guidelines for online privacy and security. The best-known international bodies for privacy are TRUSTe (www.truste.org) and Verisign for payment authentication (www.verisign.com). Within particular countries there may be other bodies such as, in the UK, ISIS (www.imrg.oeg.uk/isis). For security, 'Hacker Safe' accreditation is available from Scan Alert (www.scanalert.com) who are owned by McAfee security products. This involves automated daily scans to test site security.

## Alternative digital technologies

**Access platform**
A method for customers to access digital media.

In this section we introduce three alternative or complementary digital media access platforms to PC or Apple-based fixed Internet access, which provide many similar advantages. These access platforms, or environments, are mobile or wireless, interactive digital TV and digital radio.

### Mobile or wireless access devices

Important mobile access devices that site owners and e-mail marketers need to consider support for in their communications include:

1 Mobile phones using short-code response to campaigns or interactive sites based on WAP or use of rich media streaming supported by broadband 3G technology.
2 Personal Digital Assistants or smart phones such as the Blackberry and Windows mobile 'Pocket PC' phones.
3 Traditional PCs accessing the web over Wi-Fi.
4 Gaming platforms with a lower screen resolution accessing the web via Wi-Fi such as the Nintendo DS Lite or Sony PlayStation Plus (PSP).

Mobile technologies have been touted for many years as the future for Internet access. They are widely used, but primarily for text messaging within Europe and the US (see Figure 2.8). However, in some countries, such as Japan and China, the majority of web access is via mobile phone and we can expect to see increased mobile use in all countries. In China there are more mobile subscribers than the whole US population (Belic, 2007) and according to the regularly updated Comscore panel data (www.comscore.com) use of the web by mobile devices in Japan is equal to that of traditional computer access.

Mobile phones are important in terms of paid content services due to their popularity in countries such as Japan. They distribute more content ($31 billion) than the total global content on the Internet ($25 billion led by pornography and gambling) and more than Hollywood box office's annual $30 billion (Ahonen and Moore, 2007).

The benefits that mobile or wireless connections offer to their users are ubiquity (can be accessed from anywhere), reachability (their users can be reached when not in their normal location) and convenience (it is not necessary to have access to a power supply or fixed-line connection). In addition to these obvious benefits, there are additional benefits that are less obvious: they provide security – each user can be authenticated since each wireless device has a unique identification code; their location can be used to tailor content; and they provide a degree of privacy compared with a desktop PC – looking for jobs on a wireless device might be better than under the gaze of a boss. An additional advantage is that of instant access or 'always-on' where there is no need to dial up a wireless connection. Table 3.3 provides a summary of the mobile or wireless Internet access proposition. There are considerable advantages in comparison to PC-based Internet access, but it is still limited by the display limitations such as small screen size and limited graphics.

| Table 3.3 | Summary of mobile or wireless Internet access consumer proposition |
|---|---|

| Element of proposition | Evaluation |
|---|---|
| Not fixed location | The user is freed from the need to access via a desktop, making access possible when commuting for example |
| Location-based services | Mobiles can be used to give geographically based services, e.g. an offer in a particular shopping centre. Future mobiles will have global positioning services integrated |
| Instant access/convenience | The latest GPRS and 3G services are always on, avoiding the need for lengthy connection (see section on alternative digital technologies) |
| Privacy | Mobiles are more private than desktop access, making them more suitable for social use or for certain activities such as an alert service for looking for a new job |
| Personalisation | As with PC access, personal information and services can be requested by the user, although these often need to be set up via PC access |
| Security | In the future mobile may become a form of wallet, but thefts of mobiles make this a source of concern |

### Technology convergence

**Technology convergence**
A trend in which different hardware devices such as TVs, computers and phones merge and have similar functions.

**Technology convergence** is an important phenomenon as digital marketers consider how they can evolve their propositions for consumers. As you know, today a mobile phone is not just a phone, it is likely also a text messaging system, music playing system, e-mail reading platform, camera, personal organiser, Internet access device and global positioning system (GPS). Of course, just because a technology is possible does not mean it is widely used. So, for marketers it is important to assess new technologies and support them once they reach critical mass, or if there is a niche which can be exploited. For example, Mintel reported in 2005 that the downloadable content for ringtones and games had passed $1 billion in the UK. Many users now use phones or PDAs for accessing e-mails, so it is important that marketers ensure their messages are received on these devices.

### SMS messaging

**Short Message Service**
The formal name for text messaging.

In addition to offering voice calls and data transfer, mobile phones have increasingly been used for e-mail and the **Short Message Service (SMS)**, commonly known as 'texting' (Figure 3.12). SMS is, of course, a simple form of e-mail that enables messages to be transferred between mobile phones.

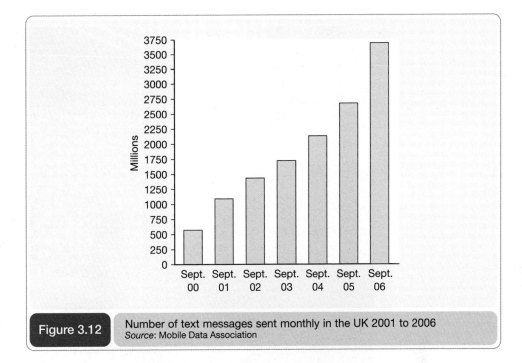

| Figure 3.12 | Number of text messages sent monthly in the UK 2001 to 2006 |
| --- | --- |
| | *Source*: Mobile Data Association |

Texting has proved useful for business in some niche applications. For example, banks now notify customers when they approach an overdraft balance and provide weekly statements using SMS. Text has also been used by consumer brands to market their products, particularly to a younger audience as the case studies at text agency Flytxt (www.flytxt.com) and Text.It, the organisation promoting text messaging (www.text.it), show. Texting can also be used in supply chain management applications for notifying managers of problems or deliveries.

### SMS applications

For the creative marketer who respects opt-in and privacy legislation, SMS has proved a great way to get closer to customers, particularly those in the youth market who are difficult to reach with other media. These are some of the applications showcased on Text.it (www.text.it):

1 *Database building/direct response to ads/direct mail or on-pack.* This is one of the most significant applications. For example, Ford engaged its audience when promoting the Ford Ka by offering consumers to text in a unique code printed on their postcard for entry into a prize draw.

2 *Location-based services.* Text for the nearest pub, club, shop or taxi. In London you can now text for the nearest available taxi, and pay the congestion charge through texting, once accounts are set up via the web!

3 *Sampling/trial.* Nestlé used an opt-in SMS database to offer samples for a new chocolate bar to consumers in its target group.

4 *Sales promotions.* Timed e-coupons can be sent out to encourage footfall in real and virtual stores. Drinks brand WKD offered its consumers 'Peel Off and Win' on its bottles. The competition offered prizes of 3000 football club shirts, mini footballs, 10,000 referee cards, and 1m exclusive ringtones and logos designed by WKD. Half a million people played the game, a campaign response rate of 3%. A 3000-strong opt-in database of the company's 18–24-year-old customer base was created. The company plans to use this database to trial new WKD variety Silver.

5 *Rewarding with offers for brand engagement.* Valuable content on mobiles can be offered via SMS, for example free ringtones, wallpaper, Java games or credits can be offered to consumers via text.

| Figure 3.13 | Use of QR code for promotion of film 28 days later<br>*Source*: http://www.giagia.co.uk/?cat=63, created by http://www.giagia.co.uk/?page_id=2<br>blog |
| --- | --- |

**Short code**

Five-digit number combined with text that can be used by advertisers or broadcasters to encourage consumers to register their interest. They are typically followed-up by an automated text message from the advertiser with the option to opt-in to further information by e-mail or to link through to a WAP site.

**Quick Response code**

A-two-dimensional matrix bar code. QR codes were invented in Japan where they are a popular type of two-dimensional code used for direct response.

6  *Short codes.* Short codes are easy-to-remember 5-digit numbers combined with text that can be used by advertisers or broadcasters to encourage consumers to register their interest. A similar approach is Quick Response (QR) code which is a kind of barcode published in newspapers or billboards which can be scanned by a mobile phone camera and then linked directly through to a website. It does require specific software. Figure 3.13 shows an example.

7  *Offering paid for WAP services and content.* Any service such as a ringtone delivered by WAP can be invoked from a text message. For example, Parker's Car Guides now prints ad text 'go parkers' to 89080 (a short code) for quick access to the Parker's WAP site which provides car prices on-the-go, at £1 for 10 minutes.

SMS messaging has recently been augmented by Picture Messaging or Multimedia Messaging Services (MMS). While volumes have been relatively low initially, the overlap between text messaging and e-mail marketing will decrease as there are more handsets with larger screens.

### Mobile services

Mobile services can be delivered over a bewildering number of protocols. Initially, in 2001, new services became available on GPRS (General Packet Radio Service) which was around five times faster than GSM (Global System for Mobile Communications) and is an 'always-on' service which is charged according to usage. Display is still largely text-based and based on WAP. In 2003, a completely new generation (3G) of services became available delivered over UMTS (Universal Mobile Telecommunications System); with delivery of audio and video possible, enabling continuous, 'always on' instant access to the Internet.

**GPRS (General Packet Radio Service)**
This is approximately five times faster than GSM and is an 'always-on' service which is charged according to usage. Display is still largely text-based and based on the WAP protocol.

**GSM (Global System for Mobile Communications)**
GSM is the digital transmission technique standard used widely for mobile voice data.

**WAP (Wireless Application Protocol)**
WAP is a technical standard for transferring information to wireless devices, such as mobile phones.

**3G**
Third generation of mobile phone technology

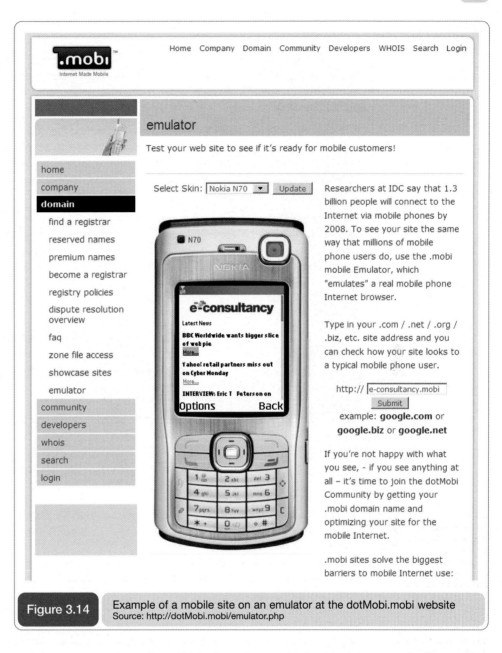

| Figure 3.14 | Example of a mobile site on an emulator at the dotMobi.mobi website |
|---|---|
| | Source: http://dotMobi.mobi/emulator.php |

Mobile sites are now made available through a .mobi domain (Figure 3.14) where a WAP site is available for download of content.

The services delivered for consumers, to date, have included transactional and informational. Consumer applications to date include retail (WH Smith Online books, the Carphone Warehouse), ticketing (lastminute.com), brokering, banking (the Woolwich), gambling (Ladbrokes), bill payment and job searching. Some informational services based on personalisation, such as those of Excite UK and Yahoo!, have also been launched. These include information such as sports news, stock prices, news, cinemas, weather, horoscopes and reminders. Mobile is also a natural application for social networking as Box 3.5, 'Social networking sites turn to mobile', shows.

| Box 3.5 | Social networking sites turn to mobile |
|---------|----------------------------------------|

Much social networking is already completed via mobiles, despite the relative new immaturity of social networks. Mark Donovan, senior analyst at M:Metrics says (M:Metrics, 2007):

> Nearly every online social networking site has added the ability to connect to these communities with a mobile phone, allowing people to access profiles and share content while they're on the go. With the mobile phone playing a central role in people's social lives, it's only natural that social networking sites are working to bridge the gap between the online and mobile worlds.

MySpace and Facebook are the top two social networking sites accessed via mobile in both the US and UK (see Table 3.4). MySpace attracts 3.7 million US and 440,000 UK mobile users. In America, Facebook's mobile audience is about two million, and in Britain about 307,000. Number 3 is YouTube in the US with 901,000 mobile visitors and Bebo in the UK with 288,000.

NMA (2008) reports how important the owner of MySpace considers mobile access to social networks to be; he says:

> Over half of the site's traffic will be from mobile within five years, We're pushing aggressively to enable us to capitalise on that. We don't see ourselves as a website: we're a set of tools and a service for people to connect with other people.

| Table 3.4 | Social network access via mobile in Europe and the US (June 2007) |
|-----------|-------------------------------------------------------------------|

|  | France | Germany | Italy | Spain | UK | US |
|--|--------|---------|-------|-------|-----|-----|
| Almost every day | 0.8% | 0.5% | 1.5% | 0.7% | 0.3% | 0.7% |
| At least once each week | 0.2% | 0.4% | 0.4% | 0.6% | 0.7% | 1.1% |
| Once to three times throughout the month | 0.7% | 1.0% | 0.9% | 1.0% | 1.4% | 1.8% |
| Ever in month | 1.7% | 1.9% | 2.8% | 2.3% | 2.5% | 3.5% |

*Source*: M:Metrics (2007)

Services for businesses delivered by WAP are currently less developed, but are forecast to centre on supply-chain integration where there will be facilities to place orders, check stock availability, notify of dispatch and track orders.

### Wi-Fi

**Wi-Fi (wireless fidelity)**

A high-speed wireless local-area network enabling wireless access to the Internet for mobile, office and home users.

Wi-Fi ('wireless fidelity') is the shorthand often used to describe a high-speed wireless local area network. Wi-Fi can be deployed in an office or home environment where it removes the need for cabling and adds flexibility. However, it has attracted most attention for its potential for offering wireless access in cities and towns without the need for a fixed connection. The Intel Centrino mobile chip launched in 2003 offers facilities to make Wi-Fi access easier for laptop users.

For example, in 2002 some airports, cafés and hotels started offering Wi-Fi 'hotspots' which allowed customers access to the Internet from their laptops or other mobile devices without the need to connect using a wire. This helped differentiate themselves from other services without this facility. Such hot spots have now become widespread.

### Bluetooth wireless applications

**Bluetooth**
A wireless standard for transmission of data between devices over short ranges (less than 10m).

**Proximity marketing**
Marketing messages are delivered in real-time according to customers' presence based on the technology they are carrying, wearing or have embedded. Bluecasting is the best known example.

**Bluecasting**
Involves messages being automatically pushed to a consumer's bluetooth-enabled phone or they can pull or request audio, video or text content to be downloaded from a live advert. In the future, ads will be able to respond to those who view them.

**Bluetooth technology** has potential for different forms of local marketing campaigns known as **proximity marketing**: (1) viral communication; (2) community activities (dating or gaming events); (3) location-based services – electronic coupons as you pass a store. It is currently in its infancy, but some trials of bluecasting, such as that shown in Figure 3.15, where sample music tracks are downloaded, and the Mini case study 3.6 have been successful.

| Figure 3.15 | Using a proximity device, such as a Hypertag, to download music tracks |

| Mini Case Study 3.6 | Bluecasting encourages trial of new album |
|---|---|

One of the early commercial uses of bluecasting was to support the launch of the Coldplay *X&Y* album where a London-based campaign involved 13,000 fans downloading free pre-release video clips, never-before seen interviews, audio samples and exclusive images onto their mobiles via Bluetooth from screens at mainline train stations. In this campaign, 87,000 unique handsets were 'discovered' and 13,000 people opted in to receive the material, a response rate of 15%. The busiest day was two days before the official album launch date – when over 8000 handsets were discovered and over 1100 users opted in to receive a video file. The BlueCast systems can deliver time-sensitive contextual content, so, for example, in the morning the user would get an audio clip of the tracks 'Fix You' and be prompted to tune in to Radio 1; in the afternoon the clip would be the same but the user would be prompted to watch Jonathan Ross on BBC One.

*Source*: www.mobileburn.com/pressrelease.jsp?Id=1557

**Bluejacking**

Sending a message from a mobile phone or transmitter to another mobile phone which is in close range via **bluetooth** technology.

Bluecasting has also caused concern where the user has not proactively agreed to receive communications, as with the examples above, but instead the message is sent to any local mobile where bluetooth is set up to detect connections. **Bluejacking** involves sending a message from a mobile phone (or other transmitter) to another mobile phone which is in close range and set up to connect with other bluetooth devices, such as from a store to customers.

Bank HSBC used this approach in a 2007 trial to offer one of its investment products to people passing its Canary Wharf branch who had their phones set to receive bluetooth messages. The risks of this approach can be seen from the write-up in *Finextra* which was headlined 'HSBC spams passersby in mobile marketing ploy'. Although the UK Information Commissioner has acknowledged that the technique isn't covered adequately by privacy rules, obviously care needs to be taken since this technique could be seen as intrusive.

Google is also innovating in this area. You may have read of its first forays into Google Classifieds where ads are placed in newspapers and magazines, or Google Audio ads where you can place ads across US radio stations. But did you read about the trial of an interactive billboard where eyetracking technology was used to measure the number of eyeballs viewing the ad? You can see the next steps could be iris recognition technology identifying the passer-by from a global consumer database and then tailoring ads.

### Current levels of usage of mobile commerce

**Mobile commerce (m-commerce)**

The use of wireless devices such as mobile phones for informational or monetary transactions.

**Mobile commerce (m-commerce)** refers to the use of wireless devices such as mobile phones for informational or monetary transactions. Levels of product purchase by mobile phone have proved very low in comparison with the Internet, even for standardised products such as books and CDs. Many m-commerce providers such as Sweden's M-box went into receivership at the turn of the millennium. However, analysts expect that with new access platforms, such as 3G (third-generation mobile devices which will have higher access speeds offering video transmissions), this will change. Consider the example of travel, which is the leading e-commerce category in Europe by revenue for the fixed Internet.

**i-Mode**

A mobile access platform that enables display of colour graphics and content subscription services.

The Japanese experience with **i-Mode** suggests that with suitable access devices, coupled with the right content and services that support colour images, the impact of 3G could be significant. Mobile phone ringtones and other music downloads are the most popular i-Mode purchase, followed by other paid-for information services. The strength of the proposition is indicated by the fact that over 30 million Japanese were using this service despite a launch less than two years previously. The i-Mode service has now been launched in Europe.

## IPTV (Internet TV)

**IPTV (Internet Protocol Television)**
Digital television service is delivered using Internet Protocol, typically by a broadband connection. IPTV can be streamed for real-time viewing or downloaded before playback.

The growth in popularity of **IPTV**, or 'Internet TV', where streamed TV and video is tranmitted via broadband across the Internet, is one of the most exciting developments in recent years. In 2007, services offering streamed viewing of hundreds of channels from providers such as the European-based Joost (Figure 3.16, www.joost.com) and the US service Hulu (www.hulu.com) launched and there are many competitors such as Babelgum, Vuze and Veoh. IPTV is sometimes referred to as non-linear TV or on-demand broadcasting to contrast it with the traditional broadcasting to schedule.

IPTV will also be used to deliver standard channels available on satellite – in the UK for example BT Vision and Tiscali TV offer Freeview channels. Then there is also the IPTV option of digital TV downloaded before playback, as is possible with many traditional broadcasters such as the BBC, Sky and ITV, using peer-to-peer distribution from technology providers such as Kontiki (a commercial version of Bit Torrent, where many users download and share small chunks of the programme).

It will be essential for marketers and ad agencies to learn how to exploit the new IPTV in order to reach these audiences online who may be forsaking traditional media for ever – already some digital technophiles have, and will, never own a conventional TV – all TV is delivered via Internet Protocol!

Providers of IPTV services such as Joost are experimenting with new ad formats because the days of the 30-second TV spot are gone forever. Research by Moorey-Denholm and Green (2007) has shown that effective video ads are substantially shorter with brief pre-rolls and that interstitial ads between shots are the order of the day. A further challenge is that advertisers will only want their ads associated with certain types of content for targeting purposes and to avoid reputational damage to their brand by association. IPTV also offers opportunities for programme makers to involve more interaction with their audiences

**Figure 3.16**    Joost (www.joost.com)

through chat and channel forums. Of course, brands can provide their own channels, such as the brand channels available on YouTube (www.youtube.com/advertise).

Brand advertisers also have the opportunity to develop their own brief IPTV viral clips to spread their message – witness the 2007 video viral clips from Cadbury and a follow-up spoof from Wonderbra which gained millions of views on YouTube. Because of limits in the amount of video that can be uploaded and control of the environment, some subscription payment video hosting services such as MyDeo (www.mydeo.com) emerging.

### Interactive digital television

**Interactive digital TV**
Television displayed using a digital signal delivered by a range of media – cable, satellite, terrestrial (aerial). Interactions can be provided through phone line or cable service.

**Interactive digital television (iDTV)** delivered by satellite, cable or digital broadcasts has now been used in Europe for nearly 20 years. With many countries such as the UK ending non-digital analogue broadcasts, it will be the most popular digital platform in many countries after mobile and with more users than fixed Internet access.

Interactive digital TV offers similar e-commerce facilities to the Internet, but due to a lower resolution and bandwidth it is provided with a simpler interface with more limited content that can be operated from a remote control.

Table 3.5 summarises the proposition for interactive digital TV. It is evident that it is more similar to PC-based Internet access than to mobile access. A key difference is that TV viewing is more likely to involve several members of a family while PC usage is more individual. This may cause conflict in the use of some individualised iDTV services.

| Table 3.5 | Summary of interactive digital TV consumer proposition |
|---|---|
| **Element of proposition** | **Evaluation** |
| Instant access/convenience | Interactive services are available quite rapidly, but return path connections using phone lines for purchase are slower |
| Personalisation | This is less practical for PC and mobile since there are usually several viewers |
| Security | Credit card details can be held by the iDTV provider making it theoretically unnecessary to repeatedly enter personal details |

Curry (2001) has proposed three alternative types of interactivity that online marketers can exploit:

1 *Distribution interactivity*. Here the user controls when the content is delivered. Video-on-demand is an example of this. Using personal video recorders such as Sky+ or TiVO is a further example, since users can choose to watch content at a later time and possibly omit adverts.

2 *Information interactivity*. Here the user can select different information. Curry gives the example of teletext and games which are, together, the most popular interactive TV activity. A further example is where a viewer of an advert can access a microsite with further information on the advert (known as 'red button advertising' in the UK). Information can be exchanged via a **return path** such as entering a competition. This provides an improved option for direct response advertising in comparison to traditional TV. An example is given in Mini case study 3.7: 'Volvo encourages viewers to 'Press Red' for their 'Mystery of Dalaro' campaign'. Interaction with interactive TV is often combined with text messaging in quiz and reality TV programmes.

**Return path**
An interaction where the customer sends information to the iDTV provider using a phone line or cable.

3  *Participation activity*. This is where the user can select different options during a programme, such as choosing a different camera angle in a football match or different news stories. There is no return path in this case.

---

| Mini Case Study 3.7 | Volvo encourages viewers to 'Press Red' for their 'Mystery of Dalaro' campaign |
| --- | --- |

This innovative campaign, supporting the launch of the Volvo S40, was shot in the style of a documentary purporting to be a real account of the Swedish village Dalaro where 32 people all bought a new Volvo S40 on the same day.

But Volvo has now revealed that it was Spike Jonze, the director of the films *Being John Malkovich* and *Adaptation*, as well as the legendary Beastie Boys video *Sabotage*, who made the documentary. However, it has stated that the characters in the campaign are real residents of Dalaro and not actors.

This campaign shows how offline ad executions naturally drive visitors online. During the campaign, visits to the Volvo UK website doubled and 435,000 digital viewers of the ad selected the red button option to view the documentary via interactive TV.

Those pressing red on iTV saw a longer eight-minute version of the documentary, made by director Spike Jonze, featuring interviews with residents of Dalaro talking about the spooky phenomenon and had the opportunity to download brochures, thus interacting much more closely with the brand than was possible before the advent of iTV. The documentary was also available from the website which received 96,000 visits with 64% accessing the video and several thousand requesting a brochure.

*Source: Revolution Magazine*, 19 March 2004 (www.revolutionmagazine.com)

---

### How does interactive digital TV work?

Figure 3.17 shows that a set-top box is an important component of the interactive digital TV system. This is used to receive and decode the message from a satellite dish or cable that is then displayed on a conventional TV. The set-top box also includes a modem that is used to pass back selections made on the interactive shopping channel to the company across the Internet using standard phone lines for the connection. For digital cable connections, there is a continuous connection between the set-top box and the provider which means that more detailed information on customer behaviour is available. The image displayed is lower-resolution than that on a PC and each supplier uses a different display standard. This means that HTML web content cannot readily be transferred to iDTV and needs to be repurposed.

**Repurposing**
Developing for a new access platform content that was previously used for a different platform such as the web.

Sky interactive services have previously been limited to a small number of e-commerce sites such as Domino Pizza and BlueSquare paying premium fees.

When a company decides how to respond to iDTV, several levels of commitment can be identified:

- *promotion* – using interactive ads linked to a microsite as with the Volvo example – this is the main application for most brands;
- *content* – repurposing website for interactive TV;
- *content* – new interactive services;
- *e-commerce* – transactional services typically for low value, relatively simple products such as pizzas or betting, or for a retailer – for a limited range of products.

Another service often made available through iDTV is digital home storage, which has been described as 'the biggest change in conventional broadcasting since the industry began'. Variously referred to as 'personal video recorders', 'home media servers' or 'content refrigerators', they all involve recording a TV programme direct to a magnetic disk which gives many hours of recording time. Examples are Sky+ and TiVo. These offer the opportunity to pause a pro-

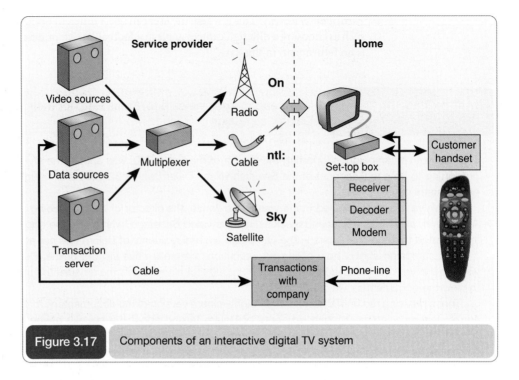

| Figure 3.17 | Components of an interactive digital TV system |

gramme while it is being transmitted, record it and return to it later. It may also be possible to filter out adverts. There is likely to be convergence of these devices with the PC. Home entertainment PCs running Windows MediaCenter are gradually growing in importance.

As a conclusion to this section complete Activity 3.1, which illustrates the type of technology dilemma marketers face as new technologies are introduced.

### Out of home TV and interactive signage

**Digital signage**
The use of interactive digital technologies within billboard and point of sale ads. For example, videos and bluetooth interaction.

A further nascent category of digital TV media is referred to as 'out-of-home TV', as is used in shopping centres, individual stores or ad displays related to public places or public transport. Interactive or **digital signage** will often be set up to integrate with the mobile Bluetooth, shortcode and QR code interactions mentioned in the section on mobile and proximity marketing.

| Activity 3.1 | Assessing new technology options |

#### Purpose

To illustrate the process for reviewing the relevance of new technology options.

#### Activity

You work for an FMCG (fast-moving consumer goods) brand and are attending an industry trade show where you see a presentation about the next-generation (3G) mobile phones which are due to launch in your country in one year's time. You need to decide whether your organisation adopts the new phone and if so when. Complete the following:

1  How would you assess the significance of this new technology?
2  Summarise the proposition of the new access devices for both consumers and your organisation.
3  What recommendations would you make about when to adopt and which services to offer?

### Digital radio

We can identify two types of digital radio – digital radio and web radio. Both are interactive. Digital radio is also available through interactive TV, mobile and in-car.

**Digital radio** requires buying a new digital radio although it can be streamed just like a 'traditional analogue web radio'. Digital radio is often accompanied by a big liquid crystal 4" × 5" display and is transactional 2-way. Digital radio is now widely known as **digital audio broadcasting (DAB) radio**.

**Web radio** or Internet radio is when existing broadcasts are streamed via the Internet and listened to using plug-ins such as Real Media or Windows Media Player. This is an important trend, with radio-listener auditing service Rajar reporting that in the UK in 2008 that nearly 20% of all radio listening is via a digital platform with:

- 9.9% via DAB
- 3.1% via DTV and
- 1.9% via the Internet.

It can be seen that a relatively small amount of radio listening is web-based and this is likely to be representative of other countries.

For many web radio users, logging on to a web radio station and leaving it to play as you work is the main application. You can order a particular track or broadcast feature you can order it there and then or promotions on behalf of advertisers by radio stations can be redeemed from a microsite. Perhaps the most important innovation the web can offer is to support community interactions with presenters and other listeners as the Virgin Radio offering fan forums show (Figure 3.18).

**Figure 3.18**   Virgin Radio community forums (www.virginradio.co.uk)

A variant of web radio is that provided by music downloading services such as iTunes and Napster. Here, listeners can define their own sequence of tracks to listen to, or listen to prepared selections of tracks – currently without presenters, so there are limited opportunities for advertising between tracks.

According to the World DAB Forum (www.worlddab.org), the trade association promoting DAB, the benefits of DAB for the consumer are:

> Aside from distortion-free reception digital sound quality, DAB offers further advantages as it has been designed for the multimedia age. DAB can carry not only audio, but also text, pictures, data and even videos – all on your radio at home and on the move!

One of the limitations of DAB is that a 'return path' isn't available, so a direct response has to be achieved through other e-tools such as a website or SMS.

Web radio can be used successfully for integrated campaigns. Listeners may first see an ad in the newspaper or on TV, register it, but not respond. When they then hear about it online, response is more seamless – they just type in the company or campaign code into their browser. For example, for Christmas 2004 eBay UK ran a treasure hunt to showcase the range of products on sale through clues on the home page which prompted a search. It was advertised both in print and on streaming radio stations.

---

| Mini Case Study 3.8 | Comet uses Virgin Radio for positioning and response |

In 2004, Virgin Radio was the most popular commercial radio station in the UK. Its website receives over 1,000,000 unique visitors per month. The Comet campaign is a typical cross-media campaign that uses on-air and website messaging and interaction.

**Campaign objectives**

- Support awareness of Comet's Price Promise that they provide low prices all year round.
- Communicate that Comet has great Christmas gifts for all the family.
- Drive traffic to Comet's gift finder at comet.co.uk.
- Create competitive standout through engaging activity.

**Implementation**

Listeners were invited to play 'The Price is Right' with Comet in a week-long Drivetime Show promotion. Each day, a prize package demonstrating Comet's wide product range was up for grabs with a higher than normal starting price. Two listeners then guessed ever-decreasing prices to guess the package's true low Comet price. The first listener to get the price right won, or the first to get the price too low lost (and the other won by default). On-air mentions directed listeners to Comet's Gift Finder which was built into a co-branded micro-site on virginradio.co.uk.

Banner ads and a competitions area on the website were used to direct visitors to Gift Finder.

*Source*: Virgin Radio (www.virginradio.co.uk)

---

## Assessing the marketing value of technology innovation

One of the great challenges for Internet marketers is to be able to successfully assess which new technological innovations can be applied to give competitive advantage. For example, personalisation technology (Chapter 6) is intended to enhance the customer's online experience and increase their loyalty. However, a technique such as personalisation may require a large investment in proprietary software and hardware technology to be able to implement it effectively. How does the manager decide whether to proceed and which solution to adopt? In addition to technologies deployed on the website, the suitability of new approaches for attracting visitors to the site must be evaluated – for example, should registration at a paid-for search engine, or new forms of banner adverts or e-mail marketing be used? Decisions on strategy are covered in Chapter 4 and decisions on the best mix of digital media channels is discussed further in Chapter 8.

The manager may have read articles in the trade and general press or spoken to colleagues which have highlighted the potential of a new technology-enabled marketing technique. They then face a difficult decision as to whether to:

- ignore the use of the technique completely, perhaps because it is felt to be too expensive or untried, or because they simply don't believe the benefits will outweigh the costs;
- ignore the technique for now, but keep an eye on the results of other companies that are starting to use it;
- evaluate the technique in a structured manner and then make a decision whether to adopt it according to the evaluation;
- enthusiastically adopt the technique without a detailed evaluation since the hype alone convinces the manager that the technique should be adopted.

Depending on the attitude of the manager, this behaviour can be summarised as:

1 cautious, a 'wait and see' approach;
2 intermediate approach, sometimes referred to as 'fast-follower'. Let others take the majority of the risk, but if they are proving successful then rapidly adopt the technique, i.e. copy them;
3 risk-taking, an early-adopter approach.

**Early adopters**
Companies or departments that invest in new technologies and techniques.

Different behaviours by different adopters will result in different numbers of adopters through time. This diffusion–adoption process (represented by the bell curve in Figure 3.19) was identified by Rogers (1983) who classified those trialling new products as being innovators, **early adopters**, early majority, late majority, through to the laggards.

Figure 3.19 can be used in two main ways as an analytical tool to help managers. First, it can be used to understand the stage at which customers are in adoption of a technology, or any product. For example, the Internet is now a well-established tool and in many developed countries we are into the late majority phase of adoption with large numbers of users of

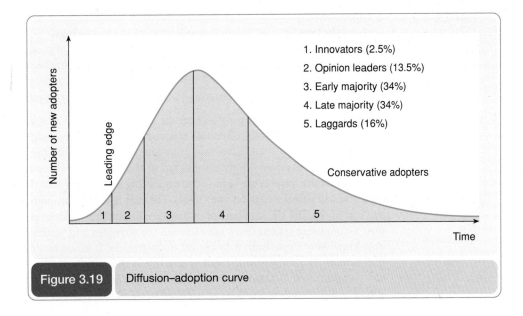

1. Innovators (2.5%)
2. Opinion leaders (13.5%)
3. Early majority (34%)
4. Late majority (34%)
5. Laggards (16%)

Conservative adopters

Number of new adopters

Leading edge

Time

**Figure 3.19**    Diffusion–adoption curve

services. This suggests it is essential to use this medium for marketing purposes. But if we look at WAP technology (see below) it can be seen that we are in the innovator phase, so investment now may be wasted since it is not clear how many will adopt the product. Secondly, managers can look at adoption of a new technique by other businesses – from an organisational perspective. For example, an online supermarket could look at how many other e-tailers have adopted personalisation to evaluate whether it is worthwhile adopting the technique.

Trott (1998) looks at this organisational perspective to technology adoption. He identifies different requirements that are necessary within an organisation to be able to respond effectively to technological change or innovation. These are:

- growth orientation – a long- rather than short-term vision;
- vigilance – the capability of environment scanning;
- commitment to technology – willingness to invest in technology;
- acceptance of risk – willingness to take managed risks;
- cross-functional cooperation – capability for collaboration across functional areas;
- receptivity – the ability to respond to externally developed technology;
- slack – allowing time to investigate new technological opportunities;
- adaptability – a readiness to accept change;
- diverse range of skills – technical and business skills and experience.

**Hype cycle**
A graphic representation of the maturity, adoption and business application of specific technologies.

A commercial application of the diffusion of innovation curve was developed by technology analyst Gartner and has been applied to different technologies since 1995. They describe a **hype cycle** as a graphic representation of the maturity, adoption and business application of specific technologies.

Gartner (2005) recognises the following stages within a hype cycle, an example of which is given for current trends in 2005 (Figure 3.20):

1 *Technology trigger* – The first phase of a hype cycle is the 'technology trigger' or breakthrough, product launch or other event that generates significant press and interest.

2 *Peak of inflated expectations* – In the next phase, a frenzy of publicity typically generates over-enthusiasm and unrealistic expectations. There may be some successful applications of a technology, but there are typically more failures.

3 *Trough of disillusionment* – Technologies enter the 'trough of disillusionment' because they fail to meet expectations and quickly become unfashionable. Consequently, the press usually abandons the topic and the technology.

4 *Slope of enlightenment* – Although the press may have stopped covering the technology, some businesses continue through the 'slope of enlightenment' and experiment to understand the benefits and practical application of the technology.

5 *Plateau of productivity* – A technology reaches the 'plateau of productivity' as the benefits of it become widely demonstrated and accepted. The technology becomes increasingly stable and evolves in second and third generations. The final height of the plateau varies according to whether the technology is broadly applicable or benefits only a niche market.

The problem with being an early adopter (as an organisation) is that being at the leading edge of using new technologies is often also referred to as the 'bleeding edge' due to the risk of failure. New technologies will have bugs, may integrate poorly with the existing systems or the marketing benefits may simply not live up to their promise. Of course, the reason for risk taking is that the rewards are high – if you are using a technique that your competitors are not, then you will gain an edge on your rivals. For example, RS Components (www.rswww.com) was one of the first UK suppliers of industrial components to adopt personalisation as part of their e-commerce system. They have learned the strengths and weaknesses of the product and now know how to position it to appeal to customers. It offers facilities such as customised pages, access to previous order history and the facility to place repeat orders or modified rebuys. This has enabled them to build up a base of customers who are familiar with using the RS Components online services and are then less likely to swap to rival services in the future.

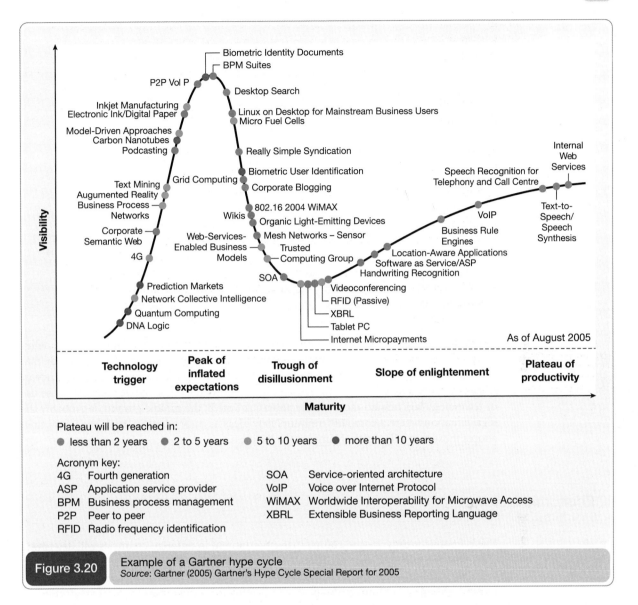

**Plateau will be reached in:**
● less than 2 years   ● 2 to 5 years   ● 5 to 10 years   ● more than 10 years

Acronym key:
| | | | |
|---|---|---|---|
| 4G | Fourth generation | SOA | Service-oriented architecture |
| ASP | Application service provider | VoIP | Voice over Internet Protocol |
| BPM | Business process management | WiMAX | Worldwide Interoperability for Microwave Access |
| P2P | Peer to peer | XBRL | Extensible Business Reporting Language |
| RFID | Radio frequency identification | | |

**Figure 3.20**   Example of a Gartner hype cycle
*Source*: Gartner (2005) Gartner's Hype Cycle Special Report for 2005

It may also be useful to identify how rapidly a new concept is being adopted. When a product or service is adopted rapidly this is known as *rapid diffusion*. The access to the Internet is an example of this. In developed countries the use of the Internet has become widespread more rapidly than the use of TV, for example. It seems that interactive digital TV and Internet-enabled mobile phones are relatively slow-diffusion products! Activity 3.1, page **178**, considers this issue further.

So, what action should e-commerce managers take when confronted by new techniques and technologies? There is no straightforward rule of thumb, other than that a balanced approach must be taken. It would be easy to dismiss many new techniques as fads, or classify them as 'not relevant to my market'. However, competitors are likely to be reviewing new techniques and incorporating some, so a careful review of new techniques is required. This indicates that benchmarking of 'best of breed' sites within a sector and in different sectors is essential as part of environmental scanning. However, by waiting for others to innovate and review the results on their website, a company has probably already lost 6 to 12 months. Figure 3.21 summarises the choices. The stepped curve I shows the variations in technology through time. Some changes may be small incremental ones such as a new operating system;

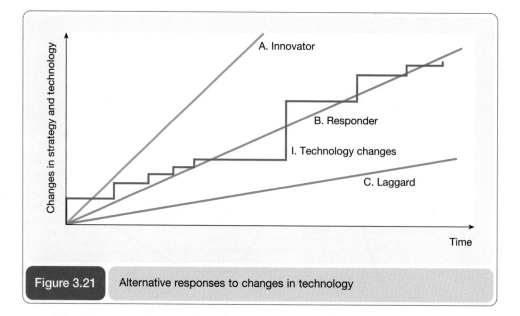

| Figure 3.21 | Alternative responses to changes in technology |

others, such as the introduction of personalisation technology, are more significant in delivering value to customers and so improving business performance. Line A is a company that is using innovative business techniques, adopts technology early, or is even in advance of what the technology can currently deliver. Line C shows the conservative adopter whose use of technology lags behind the available potential. Line B, the middle ground, is probably the ideal situation where a company monitors new ideas as early adopters, trials them and then adopts those that will positively impact the business.

## Economic factors

The economic prosperity and competitive environment in different countries will determine the e-commerce potential of each country. Managers developing e-commerce strategies will target the countries that are most developed in the use of the technology. Knowledge of different economic conditions is also part of budgeting for revenue from different countries.

The trend to globalisation can arguably insulate a company, to some extent, from fluctuations in regional markets, but is, of course, no protection from a global recession. Managers can also study e-commerce in leading countries to help predict future e-commerce trends in their own country.

In Chapter 2 we saw that there is wide variation in the level of use of the Internet in different continents and countries, particularly for consumer use. According to Roussel (2000), economic, regulatory and cultural issues are among the factors affecting use of the Internet for commercial transactions. The role of government policies and local economic issues in enabling commercial developments is suggested by Figure 3.22 which shows the variation in broadband penetration through Europe.

### Globalisation

**Globalisation**

The increase of international trading and shared social and cultural values.

**Globalisation** refers to the move towards international trading in a single global marketplace and the blurring of social and cultural differences between countries. Some perceive it as 'Westernisation' or even 'Americanisation'.

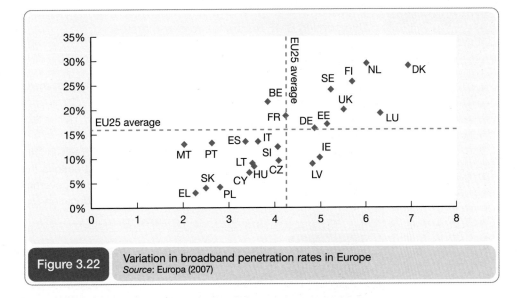

| Figure 3.22 | Variation in broadband penetration rates in Europe
Source: Europa (2007) |

Quelch and Klein (1996) point out some of the consequences for organisations that wish to compete in the global marketplace. They say a company must have:

- a 24-hour order-taking and customer service response capability;
- regulatory and customs-handling experience to ship internationally;
- in-depth understanding of foreign marketing environments to assess the advantages of its own products and services.

Language and cultural understanding may also present a problem, and a small or medium-sized company is unlikely to possess the resources to develop a multi-language version of its site or employ staff with language skills. On the other hand, Quelch and Klein (1996) note that the growth of the use of the Internet for business will accelerate the trend of English becoming the lingua franca of commerce.

Hamill and Gregory (1997) highlight the strategic implications of e-commerce for business-to-business exchanges conducted internationally. They note that there will be increasing standardisation of prices across borders as businesses become more aware of price differentials. Secondly, they predict that the importance of traditional intermediaries such as agents and distributors will be reduced by Internet-enabled direct marketing and sales.

Larger organisations typically already compete in the global marketplace, or have the financial resources to achieve this. But what about the smaller organisation? Most governments are looking to encourage SMEs to use electronic commerce to tap into the international market. Advice from governments must reassure SMEs wishing to export. Hamill and Gregory (1997) identify the barriers to SME internationalisation in Table 3.6. Complete Activity 3.2 to look at the actions that can be taken to overcome these barriers.

| Activity 3.2 | Overcoming SME resistance to e-commerce |

**Purpose**

To highlight barriers to exporting among SMEs and suggest measures by which they may be overcome by governments.

**Activity**

For each of the four barriers to internationalisation given in Table 3.6, suggest the management reasons why the barriers may exist and actions that governments can take to overcome these barriers. Evaluate how well the government in your country communicates the benefits of e-commerce through education and training.

| Table 3.6 | Issues in SME resistance to exporting (barriers from Hamill and Gregory (1997) and Poon and Jevons (1997)) |

| Barrier | Management issues | How can barrier be overcome? |
| --- | --- | --- |
| Psychological | | |
| Operational | | |
| Organisational | | |
| Product/market | | |

# Political factors

The political and regulatory environment is shaped by the interplay of government agencies, public opinion and consumer pressure groups such as CAUCE (the coalition against unsolicited e-mail) which were active in the mid-1990s and helped in pressurising for laws (www.cauce.org), and industry-backed organisations such as TRUSTe (www.truste.org) that promote best practice among companies. The political environment is one of the drivers for establishing the laws to ensure privacy and to collect taxes, as described in previous sections.

Political action enacted through government agencies to control the adoption of the Internet can include:

- promoting the benefits of adopting the Internet for consumers and business to improve a country's economic prosperity;
- sponsoring research leading to dissemination of best practice among companies, for example the DTI international benchmarking survey;
- enacting legislation to regulate the environment, for example to protect privacy or control taxation;
- setting up international bodies to co-ordinate the Internet such as ICANN (the Internet Corporation for Assigned Names and Numbers, www.icann.com) which has introduced new domains such as .biz and .info.

Some instances of the role of government organisations in promoting and regulating e-commerce is given by these examples from the European Commission:

- In 1998 new data protection guidelines were enacted, as described in the section on privacy, to help protect consumers and increase the adoption of e-commerce by reducing security fears.
- In May 2000 the e-Europe Action Plan was launched with objectives of 'a cheaper, faster, more secure Internet; investing in people's skills and access; and stimulating the use of the Internet'. The Commission intends to increase Internet access relative to the USA in order to make Europe more competitive.
- Also in May 2000 the Commission announced that it wants the supply of local loops, the copper cables that link homes to telephone exchanges, to be unbundled so that newer companies can compete with traditional telecommunications suppliers. The objective here is the provision of widespread broadband services as a major aim of the EU.
- In June 2000 an e-commerce directive was adopted by the European Union. Pullen and Robinson (2001) note that the most fundamental provision of the Act is in Article 3 which defines the principles of country of origin and mutual recognition. This means that any company trading in an EU member state is subject in that country to the laws of that country and not those of the other member states. This prevents the need for companies to adhere to specific advertising or data protection laws in the countries in which they operate.

**E-government**
The use of Internet technologies to provide government services to citizens.

The type of initiative launched by governments is highlighted by the launch in the UK in September 1999 of a new 'UK online' campaign, a raft of initiatives and investment aimed at moving people, business and government itself online (**e-government**). E-envoy posts and an e-minister have also been appointed. The prime minister said in 1999:

> There is a revolution going on in our economy. A fundamental change, not a dot.com fad, but a real transformation towards a knowledge economy. So, today, I am announcing a new campaign. Its goal is to get the UK online. To meet the three stretching targets we have set: for Britain to be the best place in the world for e-commerce, with universal access to the Internet and all Government services on the net. In short, the UK online campaign aims to get business, people and government online.

Specific targets have been set for the proportion of people and businesses that have access, including public access points for those who cannot currently afford the technology. Managers who are aware of these initiatives can tap into sources of funding for development or free training to support their online initiatives.

## Political control of online comparison intermediaries

Another area where government action can have a significant impact on the online marketplace is control of intermediaries. This depends on the amount of regulation in a given country and in individual markets. Taking the UK as example, regulation of different marketplaces occurs through these groups:

- Financial Services Authority – controls providers of banking products such as current accounts, savings and loans.
- Ofgen – controls provision of energy such as electricity and gas.
- Ofcom – controls providers of mobile phone and broadband services.

In the financial services market it is not necessary for a price comparison intermediary to show all providers, so, for example, one major insurance provider, Direct Line, has decided not to be included. However, in the energy industry it is required that all providers are to be included due to the industry regulators, although links between the intermediary and the suppliers do not.

## Internet governance

**Internet governance**
Control of the operation
and use of the Internet.

**Internet governance** describes the control put in place to manage the growth of the Internet and its usage. Governance is traditionally undertaken by government, but the global nature of the Internet makes it less practical for a government to control cyberspace. Dyson (1998) says:

> *Now, with the advent of the Net, we are privatising government in a new way – not only in the traditional sense of selling things off to the private sector, but by allowing organisations independent of traditional governments to take on certain 'government' regulatory roles. These new international regulatory agencies will perform former government functions in counterpoint to increasingly global large companies and also to individuals and smaller private organisations who can operate globally over the Net.*

The US approach to governance, formalised in the Framework for Global Electronic Commerce in 1997, is to avoid any single country taking control.

Dyson (1998) describes different layers of jurisdiction. These are:

- physical space comprising each individual country where their own laws such as those governing taxation, privacy and trading and advertising standards hold;
- ISPs – the connection between the physical world and the virtual world;
- domain name control (www.icann.net) and communities;
- agencies such as TRUSTe (www.truste.org).

## Taxation

How to change tax laws to reflect the globalisation through the Internet is a problem that many governments are grappling with. The fear is that the Internet may cause significant reductions in tax revenues to national or local governments if existing laws do not cover changes in purchasing patterns. In Europe, the use of online betting in lower-tax areas such as Gibraltar has resulted in lower revenues to governments in the countries where consumers would have formerly paid gaming tax to the government via a betting shop. Large UK bookmakers such as William Hill and Victor Chandler are offering Internet-based betting from 'offshore' locations such as Gibraltar. The lower duties in these countries offer the companies the opportunity to make betting significantly cheaper than if they were operating under a higher-tax regime. This trend has been dubbed LOCI or Location Optimised Commerce on the Internet by Mougayer (1998). Meanwhile, the government of the country from which a person places the bet will face a drop in its tax revenues. In the UK the government has sought to reduce the revenue shortfall by reducing the differential between UK and overseas costs.

The extent of the taxation problem for governments is illustrated by the US ABC News (2000) reporting that between $300 million and $3.8 billion of potential tax revenue was lost by authorities in 2000 in the USA as more consumers purchased online. The revenue shortfall occurs because online retailers need to impose sales or use tax only when goods are being sent to a consumer who lives in a state (or country) where the retailer has a bricks-and-mortar store. Buyers are supposed to voluntarily pay the appropriate sales taxes when buying online, but this rarely happens in practice. This makes the Internet a largely tax-free area in the USA.

Since the Internet supports the global marketplace it could be argued that it makes little sense to introduce tariffs on goods and services delivered over the Internet. Such instruments would, in any case, be impossible to apply to products delivered electronically. This position is currently that of the USA. In the document 'A Framework for Global Electronic Commerce', former President Clinton stated that:

> *The United States will advocate in the World Trade Organisation (WTO) and other appropriate international fora that the Internet be declared a tariff-free zone.*

## Tax jurisdiction

Tax jurisdiction determines which country gets the tax income from a transaction. Under the current system of international tax treaties, the right to tax is divided between the country where the enterprise that receives the income is resident ('residence' country) and that from which the enterprise derives that income ('source' country). Laws on taxation are rapidly evolving and vary dramatically between countries. A proposed EU directive intends to deal with these issues by defining the place of establishment of a merchant as where they pursue an economic activity from a fixed physical location. At the time of writing, the general principle that is being applied is that tax rules are similar to those for a conventional mail-order sale; for the UK, the tax principles are as follows:

(a) if the supplier (residence) and the customer (source) are both in the UK, VAT will be chargeable;
(b) exports to private customers in the EU will attract either UK VAT or local VAT;
(c) exports outside the EU will be zero-rated (but tax may be levied on import);
(d) imports into the UK from the EU or beyond will attract local VAT, or UK import tax when received through customs;
(e) services attract VAT according to where the supplier is located. This is different from products and causes anomalies if online services are created. For example, a betting service located in Gibraltar enables UK customers to gamble at a lower tax rate than with the same company in the UK.

---

## Case Study 3    Boo hoo – learning from the largest European dot-com failure

### Context

'Unless we raise $20 million by midnight, boo.com is dead.' So said Boo.com CEO Ernst Malmsten, on 18 May 2000. Half the investment was raised, but this was too little, too late, and at midnight, less than a year after its launch, Boo.com closed. The headlines in the *Financial Times* the next day read: 'Boo.com collapses as investors refuse funds. Online Sports retailer becomes Europe's first big Internet casualty.'

The Boo.com case remains a valuable case study for all types of businesses, since it doesn't only illustrate the challenges of managing e-commerce for a clothes retailer, but rather highlights failings in e-commerce strategy and management that can be made in any type of organisation.

### Company background

Boo.com was a European company founded in 1998 and operating out of a London head office. It was founded by three Swedish entrepreneurs, Ernst Malmsten, Kajsa Leander and Patrik Hedelin. Malmsten and Leander had previous business experience in publishing where they created a specialist publisher and had also created an online bookstore, bokus.com, which in 1997 became the world's third largest book e-retailer behind Amazon and Barnes & Noble. They became millionaires when they sold the company in 1998. At Boo.com, they were joined by Patrik Hedelin who was also the financial director at bokus, and at the time they were perceived as experienced European Internet entrepreneurs by the investors who backed them in their new venture.

### Company vision

The vision for Boo.com was for it to become the world's first online global sports retail site. It would be a European brand, but with a global appeal. Think of it as a sports and fashion retail version of Amazon. At launch it would open its virtual doors in both Europe and America with a view to 'amazoning the sector'. Note though that, in contrast, Amazon did not launch simultaneously in all markets. Rather it became established in the US before providing local European distribution through acquisition and re-branding of other e-retailers in the United Kingdom for example.

### The boo.com brand name

According to Malmsten *et al.* (2001), the Boo brand name originated from film star Bo Derek, best known for her role in the movie *10*. The domain name 'Bo.com' was unavailable, but adding an 'o' they managed to procure the domain 'Boo.com' for $2500 from a domain name dealer. According to Rob Talbot, director of marketing for Boo.com, Boo were 'looking for a name that was easy to spell across all the different countries and easy to remember . . . something that didn't have a particular meaning'.

## Target market

The audience targeted by Boo.com can be characterised as 'young, well-off and fashion-conscious' 18-to-24-year-olds. The concept was that globally the target market would be interested in sports and fashion brands stocked by Boo.com.

The market for clothing in this area was viewed as very large, so the thought was that capture of only a small part of this market was required for Boo.com to be successful. The view at this time on the scale of this market and the basis for success is indicated by *New Media Age* (1999) where it was described:

> The $60b USD industry is dominated by Gen X'ers who are online and, according to market research, in need of knowing what is in, what is not and a way to receive such goods quickly. If boo.com becomes known as the place to keep up with fashion and can supply the latest trends then there is no doubt that there is a market, a highly profitable one at that, for profits to grow from.

The growth in market was also supported by retail analysts, with Verdict predicting online shopping in the United Kingdom to grow from £600 million in 1999 to £12.5 billion in 2005.

However, *New Media Age* (1999) does note some reservations about this market, saying:

> Clothes and trainers have a high rate of return in the mail order/home shopping world. Twenty year olds may be online and may have disposable income but they are not the main market associated with mail order. To date there is no one else doing anything similar to boo.com.

## The Boo.com proposition

In their proposal to investors, the company stated that 'their business idea is to become the world-leading Internet-based retailer of prestigious brand leisure and sportswear names'. They listed brands such as Polo, Ralph Lauren, Tommy Hilfiger, Nike, Fila, Lacoste and Adidas. The proposition involved sports and fashion goods alongside each other. The thinking was that sports clothing has more standardised sizes with less need for a precise fit than designer clothing.

The owners of Boo.com wanted to develop an easy-to-use experience which re-created the offline shopping experience as far as possible. As part of the branding strategy, an idea was developed of a virtual salesperson, initially named Jenny and later Miss Boo. She would guide users through the site and give helpful tips. When selecting products, users could drag them on to models, zoom in and rotate them in 3D to visualise them from different angles. The technology to achieve this was built from scratch along with the stock control and distribution software. A large investment was required in technology with several suppliers being replaced before launch, which was six months later than promised to investors, largely due to problems with implementing the technology.

Clothing the mannequin and populating the catalogue was also an expensive challenge. During 2000, about $6 million was spent on content about spring/summer fashionwear. It cost $200 to photograph each product, representing a monthly cost of more than $500,000.

Although the user experience of Boo.com is often criticised for its speed, it does seem to have had that wow factor that influenced investors. Analyst Nik Margolis, writing in *New Media Age* (1999), illustrates this by saying:

> What I saw at boo.com is simply the most clever web experience I have seen in quite a while. The presentation of products and content are both imaginative and offer an experience. Sure everything loads up fast in an office but I was assured by those at boo.com that they will keep to a limit of 8 seconds for a page to download. Eight seconds is not great, but the question is will it be worth waiting for?

Of course, today the majority of European users have broadband but in the late 1990s the majority were on dial-up and had to download the software to view products.

## Communicating the Boo.com proposition

Early plans referred to extensive 'high-impact' marketing campaigns on TV and in newspapers. Public relations were important in leveraging the novelty of the concept and human side of the business – Leander was previously a professional model and had formerly been Malmsten's partner. This PR was initially focused within the fashion and sportswear trade and then rolled out to publications likely to be read by the target audience. The success of this PR initiative can be judged by the 350,000 e-mail pre-registrations who wanted to be notified of launch. For the launch Malmsten *et al.* (2001) explains that 'with a marketing and PR spend of only $22.4 million we had managed to create a world-wide brand'.

To help create the values of the Boo.com brand, Boom, a lavish online fashion magazine, was created, which required substantial staff for different language versions. The magazine wasn't a catalogue which directly supported sales, rather it was a publishing venture competing with established fashion titles. For existing customers the *Look Book*, a 44-page print catalogue, was produced which showcased different products each month.

## The challenges of building a global brand in months

The challenges of creating a global brand in months are illustrated well by Malmsten *et al.* (2001). After an initial round of funding, including investment from JP Morgan, LMVH Investment and the Benetton family, which generated around $9 million, the founders planned towards launch by identifying thousands of individual tasks, many of which needed to be completed by staff yet to be recruited. These tasks were divided into twenty-seven areas of responsibility familiar to many organisations including office infrastructure, logistics, product information, pricing, front-end applications, call centres, packaging, suppliers, designing logos, advertising/PR, legal issues and recruitment. At its zenith, Boo.com had 350 staff, with over 100 in London and new offices in Munich, New York, Paris and Stockholm. Initially, Boo.com was available in UK English, US English, German, Swedish, Danish and Finnish with localised versions for France, Spain and Italy added after launch. The website was tailored for individual countries using the local language and currency, and also local prices. Orders were fulfilled and shipped out of one of two warehouses: one in Louisville, Kentucky and the other in Cologne, Germany. This side of the business was relatively successful with on-time delivery rates approaching 100% achieved.

Boo possessed classic channel conflicts. Initially, it was difficult getting fashion and sports brands to offer their products through Boo.com. Manufacturers already had a well-established distribution network through large high-street sports and fashion retailers and many smaller retailers. If clothing brands permitted Boo.com to sell their clothes online at discounted prices, then this would conflict with retailers' interests and would also portray the brands in a negative light if their goods were in an online 'bargain bucket'. A further pricing issue is where local or *zone pricing* in different markets exists, for example lower prices often exist in the US than Europe and there are variations in different European countries.

## Making the business case to investors

Today it seems incredible that investors were confident enough to invest $130 million in the company and that at the high point the company was valued at $390 million. Yet much of this investment was based on the vision of the founders to be a global brand and achieve 'first-mover advantage'. Although there were naturally revenue projections, these were not always based on an accurate detailed analysis of market potential. Immediately before launch, Malmsten *et al.* (2001) explains a meeting with would-be investor Pequot Capital, represented by Larry Lenihan who had made successful investments in AOL and Yahoo! The Boo.com management team were able to provide revenue forecasts, but were unable to answer fundamental questions for modelling the potential of the business, such as How many visitors are you aiming for? What kind of conversion rate are you aiming for? How much does each customer have to spend? What's your customer acquisition cost? And what's your payback time on customer acquisition cost? When these figures were obtained, the analyst found them to be 'far-fetched' and reputedly ended the meeting with the words, 'I'm not interested. Sorry for my bluntness, but I think you're going to be out of business by Christmas'.

When the site launched on 3 November 1999, around 50,000 unique visitors were achieved on the first day, but only 4 in 1000 placed orders (a 0.25% conversion rate), showing the importance of modelling conversion rate accurately in modelling business potential. This low conversion rate was also symptomatic of problems with technology. It also gave rise to negative PR. One reviewer explained how he waited:

*eighty-one minutes to pay too much money for a pair of shoes that I still have to wait a week to get.*

These rates did improve as problems were ironed out – by the end of the week 228,848 visits had resulted in 609 orders with a value of $64,000. In the six weeks from launch, sales of $353,000 were made and conversion rates had more than doubled to 0.98% before Christmas. However, a re-launch was required within six months to cut download times and to introduce a 'low-bandwidth version' for users using dial-up connections. This led to conversion rates of nearly 3% on sales promotion. Sales results were disappointing in some regions, with US sales accounting for 20% compared to the planned 40%.

The management team felt that further substantial investment was required to grow the business from a presence in 18 countries and 22 brands in November to 31 countries and 40 brands the following spring. Turnover was forecast to rise from $100 million in 2000/01 to $1350 million by 2003/4, which would be driven by $102.3 million in marketing in 2003/4. Profit was forecast to be $51.9 million by 2003/4.

## The end of Boo.com

The end of Boo.com came on 18 May 2000, when investor funds could not be raised to meet the spiralling marketing, technology and wage bills.

### Questions

1 Which strategic marketing assumptions and decisions arguably made Boo.com's failure inevitable? Contrast these with other dot-com era survivors that are still in business, for example, Lastminute.com, Egg.com and Firebox.com.

2 Using the framework of the marketing mix, appraise the marketing tactics of Boo.com in the areas of product, pricing, place, promotion, process, people and physical evidence.

3 In many ways, the vision of Boo's founders were 'ideas before their time'. Give examples of e-retail techniques used to create an engaging online customer experience which Boo adopted that are now becoming commonplace.

*Source*: Prepared by Dave Chaffey from original sources including Malmsten *et al.* (2001) and *New Media Age* (1999)

## Summary

1. Environmental scanning and analysis of the macro-environment are necessary in order that a company can respond to environmental changes and act on legal and ethical constraints on its activities.

2. Social factors include variation in usage of the Internet while ethical issues include the need to safeguard consumer privacy and security of details. Privacy issues include collection and dissemination of customer information, cookies and the use of direct e-mail. Marketers must act within current law, reassure customers about their privacy and explain the benefits of collection of personal information.

3. Rapid variation in technology requires constant monitoring of adoption of the technology by customers and competitors and appropriate responses.

4. Economic factors considered in this chapter include the regional differences in the use of the Internet for trade. Different economic conditions in different markets are considered in developing e-commerce budgets.

5. Political factors involve the role of governments in promoting e-commerce, but also in trying to restrict it.

6. Legal factors to be considered by e-commerce managers include privacy and data protection, distance-selling rules, taxation, brand reputation protection including domain name registration and copyright.

## Exercises

### Self-assessment exercises

1. Summarise the key elements of the macro-environment that should be scanned by an e-commerce manager.

2. Give an example of how each of the macro-environment factors may directly drive the content and services provided by a website.

3. What actions should e-commerce managers take to safeguard consumer privacy and security?

4. Give three examples of techniques websites can use to protect the user's privacy.

5. How do governments attempt to control the adoption of the Internet?

6. Suggest approaches to managing technological innovation.

## Essay and discussion questions

1. You recently started a job as e-commerce manager for a bank. Produce a checklist of all the different legal and ethical issues that you need to check for compliance on the existing website of the bank.

2. How should the e-commerce manager monitor and respond to technological innovation?

3. Benchmark different approaches to achieving and reassuring customers about their privacy and security using three or four examples for a retail sector such as travel, books, toys or clothing.

4. Select a new Internet-access technology (such as phone, kiosks or TV) that has been introduced in the last two years and assess whether it will become a significant method of access.

## Examination questions

1. Explain the different layers of governance of the Internet.

2. Summarise the macro-environment variables a company needs to monitor when operating an e-commerce site.

3. Explain the purpose of environmental scanning in an e-commerce context.

4. Give three examples of how websites can use techniques to protect the user's privacy.

5. Explain the significance of the diffusion–adoption concept to the adoption of new technologies to:
   (a) consumers purchasing using technological innovations;
   (b) businesses deploying technological innovations.

6. What action should an e-commerce manager take to ensure compliance with ethical and legal standards of their site?

## References

ABC News (2000) *Ecommerce Causes Tax Shortfall in US*. News story on ABC.com. 27/07/00, http://abcnews.go.com/sections/business/DailyNews/internettaxes000725.html.

Ahmed, N.U. and Sharma, S.K. (2006) 'Porter's value chain model for assessing the impact of the internet for environmental gains', *Int. J. Management and Enterprise Development*, Vol. 3, No. 3, 278–295.

Ahonen, T. and Moore, A. (2007) *Communities Dominate Brands*, Future Text, London Supported by blog: http://communities-dominate.blogs.com/.

Belic, D. (2007) China Mobile Subscribers surpass total population of the United States, *IntoMobile*, 7 April.

Cairns, S. (2005) Delivering supermarket shopping: more or less traffic? *Transport Reviews*, Vol. 25, No. 1, 51–84, January 2005.

Curry, A. (2001) What's next for interactive television?, *Interactive Marketing*, 3(2), October/December, 114–28.

Cutts, M. (2007) Talk like a Googler: parts of a url, Blog posting, August 14, 2007, http://www.mattcutts.com/blog/seo-glossary-url-definitions/.

Dyson, E. (1998) *Release 2.1. A Design for Living in the Digital Age*. Penguin, London.

European Commission (2007) i2010 Annual Information Society Report 2007, published at: http://ec.europa.eu/information_society/eeurope/i2010/index_en.htm.

Fisher, A. (2000) Gap widens between the 'haves' and 'have-nots', *Financial Times*, 5 December.

Fletcher, K. (2001) Privacy: the Achilles heel of the new marketing, *Interactive Marketing*, 3(2), October/December, 128–41.

Gartner (2005) Gartner's Hype Cycle Special Report for 2005. Report summary available at www.gartner.com: ID Number: G00130115.

Godin, S. (1999) *Permission Marketing*. Simon and Schuster, New York.

Goldman, E. (2007) Eric Goldman Technology and Marketing Law blog. Rhino Sports, Inc. v. Sport Court, Inc., 8 May 2007, http://blog.ericgoldman.org/archives/2007/05/broad_matching.htm.

*Guardian* (2008) Porn? Sex? Britons value cruises much more, *The Guardian*, Richard Wray, Wednesday, 6 February 2008.

Hamill, J. and Gregory, K. (1997) Internet marketing in the internationalisation of UK SMEs, *Journal of Marketing Management*, Special edition on internationalisation, J. Hamill (ed.), 13 (1–3).

Information Commissioner (1998) *Legal guidelines on the 1998 UK Data Protection Act.* Available from: www.informationcommissioner.gov.uk.

IMRG (2006) Valuing home delivery – a cost-benefit analysis.

Malmsten, E., Portanger, E. and Drazin, C. (2001) *Boo Hoo. A Dot.com Story from Concept to Catastrophe.* Random House, London.

Mason, R. (1986) Four ethical issues of the information age, *MIS Quarterly*, March.

M:Metrics (2007) M:Metrics Press Release, Mobile social networking has 12.3 million friends in the US and Western Europe, 15 August 2007.

Moorey-Denholm, S. and Green, A. (2007) The effectiveness of online video advertising. *AdMap*, March 2007, 45–7.

Mougayer, W. (1998) *Opening Digital Markets – Battle Plans and Strategies for Internet Commerce*, 2nd edn. CommerceNet Press, McGraw-Hill, New York.

*New Media Age* (1999) Will boo.com scare off the competition? Budd Margolis, 22 July.

NMA (2008) Profile – Travis Katz, Author: Luan Goldie, *New Media Age magazine*, published 31 January 2008.

Poon, S. and Jevons, C. (1997) Internet-enabled international marketing: a small business network perspective, *Journal of Marketing Management*, 13, 29–41.

Pullen, M. and Robinson, J. (2001) The e-commerce directive and its impact on pan-European interactive marketing, *Interactive Marketing*, 2(3), 272–5.

Quelch, J. and Klein, L. (1996) The Internet and international marketing, *Sloan Management Review*, Spring, 61–75.

RedEye (2003) A study into the accuracy of IP and cookie-based online management information, The RedEye Report, available online at www.redeye.com.

Rogers, E. (1983) *Diffusion of Innovations*, 3rd edn. Free Press, New York.

Roussel, A. (2000) Leaders and laggards in B2C commerce. Gartner Group report. 4 August. SPA-11-5334, www.gartner.com.

Siikavirta, H. Punakivi, M., Karkkainen, M. and Linnanen, L. (2003) Effects of e-commerce on greenhouse gas emissions: a case study of grocery home delivery in Finland. *Journal of Industrial Ecology*, Vol. 6, No. 2, 83–97.

Sparrow, A. (2000) *E-Commerce and the Law. The legal implications of doing business online.* Financial Times Executive Briefings.

Svennevig, M. (2004) The interactive viewer: reality or myth? *Interactive Marketing*, 6(2), 151–64.

Trott, P. (1998) *Innovation Management and New Product Development*. Financial Times/Prentice Hall, Harlow.

United Nations (1999) New technologies and the global race for knowledge. In *Human Development Report*. United Nations, New York.

Vlosky, R., Fontenot, R. and Blalock, L. (2000) Extranets: impacts on business practices and relationships, *Journal of Business & Industrial Marketing*, Volume 15, Number 6 (2000), 438–457.

Ward, S., Bridges, K. and Chitty, B. (2005) Do incentives matter? An examination of on-line privacy concerns and willingness to provide personal and financial information, *Journal of Marketing Communications*, 11(1), 21–40.

## Further reading

Dyson, E. (1998) *Release 2.1. A Design for Living in the Digital Age.* Penguin, London. Chapters 5 Governance, 8 Privacy, 9 Anonymity and 10 Security are of particular relevance.

Garfinkel, S. (2000) *Database Nation.* O'Reilly, Sebastopol, CA. This book is subtitled 'the death of privacy in the 21st century' and this is the issue on which it focuses (includes Internet- and non-Internet-related privacy).

Slevin, J. (2000) *The Internet and Society.* Polity Press, Cambridge. A book about the Internet that combines social theory, communications analysis and case studies from both academic and applied perspectives.

Zugelder, M., Flaherty, T. and Johnson, J. (2000) Legal issues associated with international Internet marketing, *International Marketing Review*, 17(3), 253–71. Gives a detailed review of legal issues associated with Internet marketing including consumer rights, defamation and disparagement, intellectual property protection, and jurisdiction.

## Web links

- **M:Metrics** (www.mmetrics.com). Provider of research about mobile phone usage.

- **New Media Age** (www.newmediazero.com/nma). A weekly magazine reporting on the UK new media developments specializing in mobile media and IPTV.

- **Oxford Internet Survey (OxIS)** (www.oii.ox.ac.uk/microsites/oxis). Research and statistics from the Oxford Internet Institute is designed to offer detailed insights into the influence of the Internet on society in Britain including 'Internet disengagement'.

- **Pew Internet and American Life Project** (www.pewinternet.org). Funds and publishes original, academic-quality research that explores the impact of the Internet on society. Also highlights adoption trends such as social networks, online video and chat.

- **Revolution magazine** (www.revolutionmagazine.com). A weekly magazine available for the UK, covering a range of new media platforms.

- **Text.It** (www.text.it). Portal from Mobile Data Association with examples of how SMS is used in the UK for consumer and business campaigns. Text.It (www.text.it). Portal from Mobile Data Association with examples of how SMS is used in the UK for consumer and business campaigns.

### General digital technology innovation

- **O'Reilly Radar** (http://radar.oreilly.com). Commentary on the development of web technologies from publishers O'Reilly, whose founder Tim O'Reilly coined the term Web 2.0.

- **Ray KurzweilaiAI** (www.kurzweilai.net). Futurologist Ray Kurzweil's blog.

- **TED** (www.ted.com) Video showcase of developments in technology and their impact on culture. TED stands for Technology, Entertainment, Design. TED started out (in 1984) as a conference bringing together people from those three worlds.

### New digital law developments

- **iCompli** (www.icompli.co.uk). Portal and e-newsletter concentrating on e-commerce law.
- **Marketing Law** (www.marketinglaw.co.uk). Up-to-date source on all forms of law related to marketing activities.
- **OUT-LAW** (www.out-law.com). This site has 8000 pages of free legal news and guidance, mostly on IT and e-commerce issues produced by UK Law firm Pinsent Masons.
- **Privacy International** (www.privacyinternational.org). Group campaigning for privacy which contains information on legal developments in different countries.

### Country-specific privacy laws

- Australia also enacted a SPAM act in 2003 (www.privacy.gov.au).
- Canada also has a privacy act (www.privcom.gc.ca).
- European Commission Data Protection and privacy legal resources (http://ec.europa.eu/justice_home/fsj/privacy).
- New Zealand Privacy Commissioner (www.privacy.org.nz).
- United States (CAN-SPAM Act, www.ftc.gov/spam).
- United Kingdom (Information Commissioner, www.ico.gov.uk).
- Summary of all countries (www.spamlaws.com).

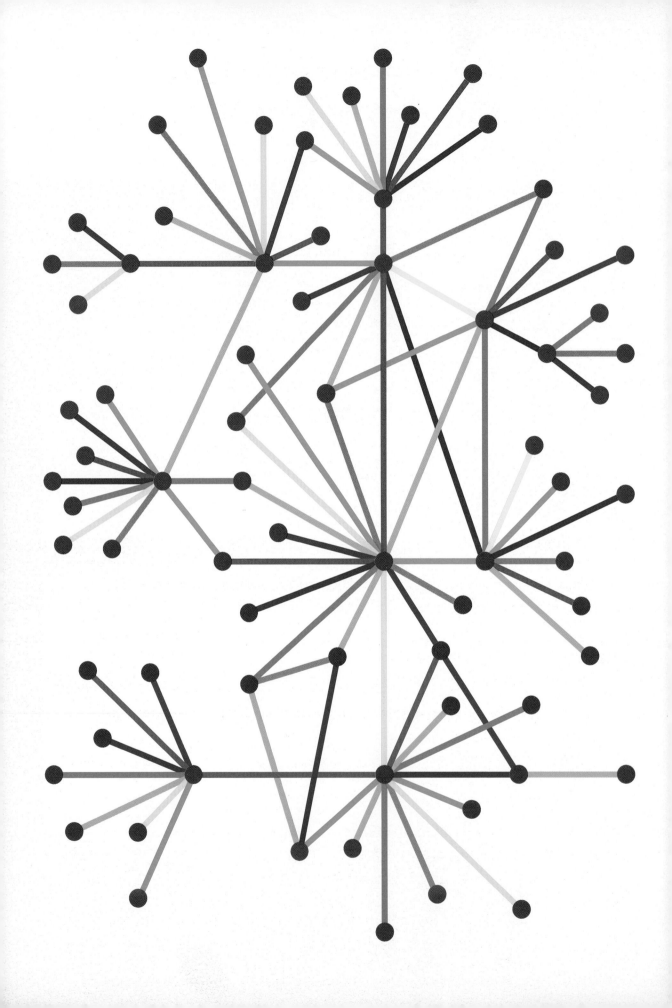

# Part 2

# Internet strategy development

In Part 2 approaches for developing an Internet marketing strategy are explored. These combine traditional approaches to strategic marketing planning with specific Internet-related issues that need to be considered by Internet marketers. In Chapter 4 a framework for developing digital marketing is described, Chapter 5 discusses the opportunities for varying the marketing mix online and Chapter 6 reviews strategies for online customer relationship management.

## 4 Internet marketing strategy  p 200

- An integrated Internet marketing strategy
- A generic strategic approach
- Situation review
- Strategic goal setting
- Strategy formulation
- Strategy implementation

## 5 The Internet and the marketing mix  p 275

- Product
- Price
- Place
- Promotion
- People, process and physical evidence

## 6 Relationship marketing using the Internet  p 329

- Key concepts of relationship marketing
- Key concepts of electronic customer relationship management (e-CRM)
- Customer lifecycle management
- Approaches to implementing e-CRM

# Internet marketing strategy

## Learning objectives

After reading this chapter, the reader should be able to:

- Relate Internet marketing strategy to marketing and business strategy
- Identify opportunities and threats arising from the Internet
- Evaluate alternative strategic approaches to the Internet

## Questions for marketers

Key questions for marketing managers related to this chapter are:

- What approaches can be used to develop Internet marketing strategy?
- How does Internet marketing strategy relate to other strategy development?
- What are the key strategic options for Internet marketing?

## Links to other chapters

This chapter is related to other chapters as follows:

- It builds on the evaluation of the Internet environment from Chapters 2 and 3
- Chapter 5 describes the potential for varying different elements of the marketing mix as part of Internet marketing strategy
- Chapter 6 describes customer relationship management strategies
- Options for segmenting online customers by activity levels are covered in Chapter 6. Options for segmenting site visitors through web analytics systems are covered in Chapter 10
- Chapter 8 gives examples of goal setting for digital campaigns and strategies for developing the right communications mix

## Introduction

The importance of the Internet to modern business strategy was underlined by Michael Porter (2001), who famously said:

*The key question is not whether to deploy Internet technology – companies have no choice if they want to stay competitive – but how to deploy it.*

**Internet marketing strategy**

Definition of the approach by which Internet marketing will support marketing and business objectives.

An **Internet marketing strategy** is needed to provide consistent direction for an organisation's e-marketing activities so that they integrate with its other marketing activities and support its overall business objectives. We can suggest that the Internet marketing strategy has many similarities to the typical aims of traditional marketing strategies, in that it will:

- provide a future direction to Internet marketing activities;
- involve analysis of the organisation's external environment, internal resources and capabilities to inform strategy;
- articulate Internet marketing objectives that support marketing objectives;
- involve selection of strategic options to achieve Internet marketing objectives and create sustainable differential competitive advantage;
- include strategy formulation to address typical marketing strategy options such as target markets, positioning and specification of the marketing mix;
- deciding which strategies NOT to pursue and which functionality is not suitable to implement;
- specify how resources will be deployed and how the organisation will be structured to achieve the strategy.

This chapter examines each of these elements of strategy. We start by considering, in more detail, an appropriate process for developing an Internet marketing strategy, and then consider the following aspects of strategy:

1 situation review (drawing on our coverage in Chapters 2 and 3);
2 goal setting;
3 strategy formulation.

Figure 4.1 indicates the context for Internet marketing strategy development. The internal influences include corporate objectives and strategy, and these in turn influence marketing strategy that should directly influence the Internet marketing strategy. Key external influences include the market structure and demand, competitor strategies and the current and evolving opportunities and threats, in particular those enabled by new digital technologies (for example, mobile marketing and IPTV) and marketing approaches (for example, search engine marketing and use of social media). Methods for monitoring the external environment to anticipate external opportunities and threats and competitors' actions have been introduced in Chapters 2 and 3, as were methods of assessing the demand of the market for Internet-delivered services.

**Channel marketing strategy**

Defines how a company should set specific objectives for a channel such as the Internet and vary its proposition and communications for this channel.

**Customer touchpoints**

Communications channels with which companies interact directly with prospects and customers. Traditional touchpoints include face-to-face (in-store or with sales representatives), phone and mail. Digital touchpoints include web services, e-mail and, potentially, mobile phone.

### Internet strategy is a channel marketing strategy

We need to remember that an Internet marketing strategy is a **channel marketing strategy** which defines how a company should set *channel-specific objectives* and develop a *differential channel-proposition* and *channel-specific communications* consistent with the characteristics of the channel and consumer usage of it. The Internet marketing strategy determines the strategic significance of the Internet relative to other communications channels which are used to communicate directly with customers at different **customer touchpoints**. Some organisations, such as low-cost airlines, will decide primarily to use virtual channels such as

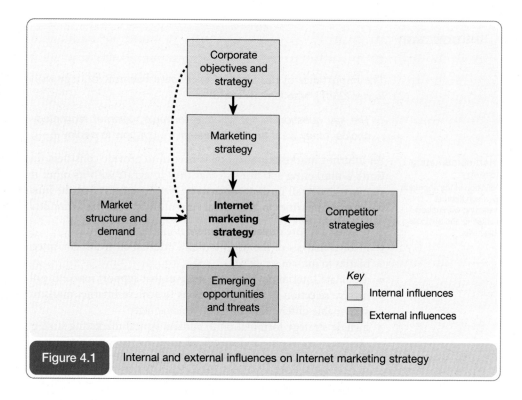

**Figure 4.1**    Internal and external influences on Internet marketing strategy

the website and e-mail marketing for delivering services and communicating with customers. Others may follow a strategy where the use of face-to-face, phone or direct mail communications remain important for the time being.

So the focus of Internet marketing strategy is decisions about how to use the channel to support existing marketing strategies, how to exploit its strengths and manage its weaknesses, and to use it in conjunction with other channels as part of a **multichannel marketing strategy**. This multichannel marketing strategy defines how different marketing channels should integrate and support each other in terms of their proposition development and communications based on their relative merits for the customer and the company.

**Multichannel marketing strategy**
Defines how different marketing channels should integrate and support each other in terms of their proposition development and communications based on their relative merits for the customer and the company.

## The scope of Internet marketing strategy

When reviewing options for Internet marketing strategy, it is useful to keep in mind that Internet strategy involves more than the narrow focus of a strategy to develop website functionality. Although this is a key part of Internet marketing strategy, marketers also examine broader issues of how to best partner with online intermediaries such as portals and social networks, how to best use e-mail and databases strategically as communications and relationship-building tools which must integrate with other marketing communications. Internet strategy may also involve redesigning business processes to integrate with partners such as suppliers and distributors in new ways. This point is made by Sultan and Rohm (2004) who, based on a study of three organisations, identify different forms of aligning Internet strategies with business goals, their framework identifying these strategic objectives:

- *Cost reduction and value chain efficiencies.* For example, B2B supplier AB Dick used the Internet to sell printer supplies via the Internet to reduce service calls.
- *Revenue generation.* Reebok uses the Internet for direct licensed sales of products such as treadmills which do not have strong distribution deals.
- *Channel partnership.* Partnering with distributors using extranets.
- *Communications and branding.* Car company Saturn developed the MySaturn site to foster close relationships with customers.

Figure P.1 in the Preface suggests the range of digital marketing activities that must be managed as part of an Internet marketing strategy. The figure shows that the operational activities which need to be implemented and managed as part of strategy can be usefully divided into those focusing on (1) customer acquisition, (2) customer conversion, proposition and experience development, and (3) customer retention and growth. Improving the capability to execute many of these activities will be decided upon through the review process of creating an Internet marketing strategy. An output from the digital strategy will be a series of strategic e-commerce initiatives in the areas of customer acquisition, conversion or retention such as those shown in Table 4.1. These e-commerce initiatives will typically be prioritised and placed as part of a long-term e-commerce 'roadmap' defining required developments over a longer period of 18 months to three years.

It is evident from Table 4.1 that Internet marketing strategy blends elements of marketing strategy and information technology strategy. In common with marketing strategy, Internet marketing strategy must determine the best value propositions to offer to online customers and how these integrate with other channels. But in common with IT strategy, many of the decisions of Internet marketing strategy involve selection of the most appropriate investments in software or functionality and hardware technology and resources to provide an improved customer experience and to provide an infrastructure to gain better results from digital channels.

| Table 4.1 | Summary of typical focus for main types of e-commerce-related strategic initiatives | |
|---|---|---|
| **Type of digital marketing strategy initiative** | **Commentary** | **Examples** |
| New customer proposition (product and pricing) | These are new site features or other online communications which are directly related to offering new products or services that will generate revenue | • Bank – introduce new product requiring different quotes<br>• Portal – introduce comparison service<br>• Service company – introduce new functionality acquired through takeover of company<br>• Magazine or music service offering new pricing options |
| Customer acquisition strategic initiatives | These are strategic projects to enhance a site's capability to deliver new prospects on a continuous basis through different online marketing techniques<br><br>They may involve investment in the site itself (e.g. SEO) or the back-end, integrating with affiliates | • SEO<br>• PPC<br>• Affiliate marketing<br>• Aggregators<br>• Enhance page type (to help increase conversion rate), e.g. category or product landing pages |
| Customer conversion and customer experience strategic initiatives | Investments in new customer features on the site. These will be based on a business case of increased conversion rate and average order value<br><br>May include major new functionality such as that for a new online store or more specific functionality integrated into existing site functionality<br><br>Many strategic initiatives are aimed at improving the customers' experience of a brand | • Implement online shop/secure payment<br>• Introduce customer reviews and ratings<br>• Merchandising capability to offer tailored promotions<br>• Interactive tools to help product selection<br>• Refine on-site search engine<br>• Buyers' guides consisting of in-depth content about products or rich media (e.g. videos showcasing products) |

| Type of digital marketing strategy initiative | Commentary | Examples |
| --- | --- | --- |
| Customer development and growth strategic initiatives | Investments to improve the experience and delivery of offers to existing customers | • Personalised recommendations for existing customers<br>• Development of e-mail welcome strategy for new online customers as part of development of an integrated contact or e-CRM strategy deliver through personalised web and e-mail messages and traditional direct communications<br>• Introduce blogs or RSS feeds to encourage return visitors<br>• Introduce more participation through customer communities |
| Enhance marketing capabilities through site infrastructure improvements | These typically involve 'back-end or back-office features' which won't be evident to users of the site, but will help in the management or administration of the site<br><br>Will often involve improving customer insight capabilities | • CRM or personalisation<br>• Content management system<br>• Performance improvement – improve management information, web analytics systems including systems for multivariate and AB testing<br>• Improve customer feedback facilities<br>• Update development approach for introducing new functionality |

## Digital marketing in practice — The EConsultancy interview

### Sharon Shaw, Standard Life, on strategy and planning

#### Overview and main concepts covered

Developing a new digital strategy can be a daunting experience, especially considering the lack of case studies and benchmarks.

In this interview, Sharon Shaw, e-commerce manager at Standard Life, talks about her experience of strategy creation including budgets, KPIs, incentives and structures.

#### The interview

*Q*: **When developing a new digital strategy, how do you start? What models are out there for you to base it on? We have developed a wheel framework for acquisition, conversion and retention, but what approach did you use?**

*Sharon Shaw*: Standard Life and Avenue A/Razorfish have used an Attract, Convert, Support, Extend model, which is very similar to the EConsultancy framework, though its meaning is evolving as the role of digital changes within the organisation. Measurement and optimisation are fundamentals in both.

Building the model, we combine existing business and brand strategies with primary and secondary customer research, competitor audits and innovation trends.

The customer research covers online attitudes and behaviours, and cross-channel preferences and needs. The competitor audit includes a SWOT analysis of our own site and an evaluation against business objectives and user expectations.

**Q: Someone said the evolution to digital is 'a bit like global warming' – we all know it's happening but fixed goalposts or yardsticks are hard to find. What references and benchmarks can you use for targets and comparisons?**

*Sharon Shaw:* The boon with digital is that it is so measurable. As such, setting financial targets and comparisons is easier than in traditional media. ROI stands out as the most obvious measure for individual projects, varying for brand campaigns and e-commerce builds (but always positive!).

Overall, we like to look at the percentage contribution digital makes to total sales volumes and we can set a benchmark target of around 15% for a mature multichannel retail business.

Strategically, the aim is to reference the customer experience online and across channels to make sure it is consistent and mutually constructive. This can be measured through online and offline surveys, and increasingly through 'buzz' metrics on the social web.

Standard Life is considering using services like eBenchmarkers to compare site performance with competitors. It provides metrics for our site in comparison to aggregated scores across all their registered sites.

**Q: What are the key success metrics and what reliable data is out there to compare 'like with like'?**

*Sharon Shaw:* Ultimately, success in e-commerce is measured through improved profits across sales and marketing activity.

Conversion rates and basket value are therefore the most important numbers for the site, followed by (and related to) campaign ROI and/or CPA. Natural and paid search performance are key traffic generation metrics.

Other measures include dwell time to evaluate customer engagement with rich media, and a recency–frequency model to score customer loyalty. For reliable data, we refer to the IMRG, Hitwise, comScore, Mintel, eMarketer and TGI.

**Q: What are the challenges and opportunities of moving towards multichannel measurement and integration?**

*Sharon Shaw:* Both the biggest opportunities and biggest challenges lie in the integration of online and offline systems and databases.

We know that allowing each channel the same view of the customer and their transactional history can drive KPIs up, through delivering a consistent and personalised customer experience at every touchpoint.

But it is rare that such integration can happen easily as most organisations have developed their online and offline architectures in isolation. Which leads us nicely on to the other key challenge – getting the budget, staff and (most importantly) board level buy-in to undertake the large-scale business change needed to deliver an effective multichannel proposition.

**Q: Where should e-commerce fit into the overall budget – should it have its own P&L, or is it a cost centre for other business units?**

*Sharon Shaw:* It really depends on the organisation, its objectives and how far it has already gone with e-commerce.

A dedicated P&L is great for new e-commerce ventures that don't rely too much on other channels. The autonomy and flexibility of financial control allow the channel to change and grow at pace.

A more mature online channel that has significant crossover with offline will at the very least need to share elements of their P&L with other business units. For instance, if an initial enquiry is made online and a sale is converted from the lead by telephone, who gets the credit?

A sensible approach would be to give the telephone centre 75% and the website 25%. If the telephone centre has a code to give customers when they go online, the reverse can be true. The point being, the P&L should be used to encourage a symbiotic relationship between channels.

If e-commerce is solely a cost centre for other units, decision making will be slow, political manoeuvring common and the team fragmented.

**Q: Where should e-commerce sit in the organisation and who should be the senior person responsible for it?**

*Sharon Shaw:* We strongly recommend a dedicated team runs e-commerce. The channel requires people with appropriate skills and experience to drive it forward and a mandate to give it their complete attention. The integration with the rest of the business should happen through collaboration on the ground and only through reporting lines at the most senior levels.

The organisation at the senior level is a point of some debate. It is fairly common in retail for a Commercial Director to take responsibility for e-commerce sales but the marketing team has a significant input and interest.

The online marketing budget to advertise and attract customers is growing all the time and there is a powerful need to integrate communications and the customer experience across channels.

One approach is to create a multichannel role responsible for all online activity and how it is integrated with the rest of the business. This role could report to the Sales & Marketing Director or directly to the MD.

In terms of incentive structures and targets, if each channel has its own target, how do you avoid channels competing with each other to the detriment of the overall organisation's goals?

The challenge here is to motivate and reward the team that is tasked with growing a new channel without upsetting other channels that may be experiencing slower growth. The P&L attribution is a key factor but incentives can also help.

Most companies reward on total business performance to target first, followed by an individual's performance.

One way to motivate a channel team might be to introduce a middle tier related to the channel performance to target, a factor that will give them a boost if they see strong growth in their area.

**Q: Do you have any tips on staff recruitment and retention – finding and retaining the right skills for a reasonable price?**

*Sharon Shaw:* The main issues for digital workers seem to be the environment in which they work, the variety of their work and their opportunities for personal development.

With a dedicated online team there is a great opportunity to create a fun and fast-paced workplace that feels dynamic and creative (even for the techies!). There is a risk of giving people repetitive work when administering a site so it is also important to make sure staff have a chance to try their hand at different tasks and project work. Back this up with the security of good HR and corporate benefits.

Finally, don't forget that the digital world doesn't stand still. Give all the team plenty of exposure to the latest research, emerging trends and breakthrough technologies.

**Q: When a large business is going through a major reorganisation, what are the main ways this can impact upon the e-commerce/digital marketing team? What types of demands are placed on the team by different business units?**

*Sharon Shaw:* The biggest problem tends to be a freeze on investment and/or significant change. Digital teams are expected to carry on delivering business as usual but won't be given the opportunities to make often long-awaited improvements until the reorganisation is complete.

Projects get put on hold and the team feel stuck in limbo. Strong leadership is needed to keep everyone on track.

*Source*: http://www.e-consultancy.com/news-blog/newsletter/3504/interview-with-standard-life-s-sharon-shaw.html. E-consultancy.com provides information, training and events on best practice in online marketing and e-commerce management

Internet marketing strategy also differs from marketing strategy in that media selection becomes a more strategic decision. In traditional marketing, media used are generally selected as suitable for each campaign. For Internet marketing, many media investments or techniques used to attract visitors to a website are *continuous* activities that continue year-round as explained in Chapter 8. For many online companies, search engine optimisation (SEO), pay-per-click (PPC) marketing, affiliates, aggregators and, for existing customers, e-mail marketing are continuous activities. Although the mix of these will be refined seasonally, Internet marketing strategy will define the level of investment in these media compared to traditional media and the average mix based on targets for visitor or sales volume and cost-per-acquisition (CPA) in order that these can be resourced through internal and agency resources managing these digital media channels.

## An integrated Internet marketing strategy

The integration of an Internet marketing strategy into business and marketing strategies represents a significant challenge for many organisations, in part because they may have traditionally considered the Internet in isolation and in part because of the profound implications of the Internet for change at an industry level and within organisations. The EConsultancy (2008) research highlighted the challenges of Internet marketing strategy. The research involved e-commerce managers at companies in markets where their products could be sold online – for example, mobile phones (Orange, Carphone Warehouse), travel (Tui and MyTravel), financial services (Lloyds TSB and Bradford & Bingley) and direct marketers such as BCA. Respondents were asked what their main challenges were and these highlighted the issues of gaining sufficient resource for Internet marketing. Challenges included:

- *gaining buy-in and budget* consistent with audience media consumption and value generated;
- *conflicts of ownership and tensions* between a digital marketing team and other teams such as traditional marketing, IT, finance and senior management;
- *coordination with different channels* in conjunction with teams managing marketing programmes elsewhere in the business;
- *managing and integrating customer information* about characteristics and behaviours collected online;
- *achieving consistent reporting*, review, analysis and follow-up actions of digital marketing results throughout the business;

- *structuring the specialist digital team* and integrating into the organisation by changing responsibilities elsewhere in the organisation;
- '*time to market*' for implementing new functionality on a site;
- insourcing vs outsourcing online marketing tactics, i.e. search, affiliate, e-mail marketing, PR;
- staff recruitment and retention.

## Is a separate Internet marketing plan needed?

Should an organisation have a separate e-marketing plan defining its strategic approach to the Internet, either for the organisation as a whole or for specific markets or brands? Consider Figure 4.2. You will be familiar with the hierarchy of plans for an organisation, from a corporate or business plan which informs a marketing plan which in turn informs a communications plan and campaign briefs for different markets or brands. But where does the e-marketing plan fit? Does the organisation need an e-marketing plan? Figure 4.2 suggests that an e-marketing plan may be useful to manage the 'e-campaign components', which refers to online communications tools such as online advertising or e-mail marketing or continuous e-marketing activities which may be conducted throughout the year to drive traffic, for example search engine marketing, affiliate marketing or online sponsorship.

You may be thinking that the marketer already has enough plans to deal with. Surely the practical approach for companies that are embracing e-marketing is to integrate e-marketing activities within their existing planning frameworks? But we believe that in many organisations, a distinct e-marketing plan is initially essential if the organisation is to effectively harness digital marketing. Since online channels are new, it is even more imperative to have clarity within the organisation. An e-marketing specialist can create an e-marketing plan to help inform and influence not only senior managers or directors and other non-marketing functions, but also to achieve buy-in from fellow marketers.

| Figure 4.2 | Hierarchy of organisation plans including e-marketing plans |

Our rationale is that online channels are still in their infancy, yet they have had and will have dramatic effects on how customers select and use products. We sometimes hear that the Internet is 'just another channel to market'. However, the potential significance of the Internet as an influencer and direct contributor to sales is such that often it does warrant separate attention. Strategies to increase the contribution of digital channels to a business are required and the e-marketing plan can help define these strategies.

In the longer term, once an organisation has successfully defined its approaches to Internet marketing, it is likely that a separate Internet marketing strategy or e-marketing plan *will not* need to be developed each year since the Internet can be considered as any other communications medium.

These problems are typical and commonplace when there is no clear planning or control for e-marketing:

1  Customer demand for online services will be underestimated if this has not been researched and it is under-resourced, and no or unrealistic objectives are set to achieve online marketing share.
2  Existing and start-up competitors will gain market share if insufficient resources are devoted to e-marketing and no clear strategies are defined.
3  Duplication of resources will occur, for example different parts of the marketing organisation purchasing different tools or different agencies for performing similar online marketing tasks.
4  Insufficient resource will be devoted to planning and executing e-marketing and there is likely to be a lack of specific specialist e-marketing skills, making it difficult to respond to competitive threats effectively.
5  Insufficient customer data are collected online as part of relationship building and these data are not integrated well with existing systems.
6  Efficiencies available through online marketing will be missed, for example lower communications costs and enhanced conversion rates in customer acquisition and retention campaigns.
7  Opportunities for applying online marketing tools, such as search marketing or e-mail marketing, will be missed or the execution may be inefficient if the wrong resources are used or marketers don't have the right tools.
8  Changes required to internal IT systems by different groups will not be prioritised accordingly.
9  The results of online marketing are not tracked adequately on a detailed or high-level basis.
10  Senior management support of e-marketing is inadequate to drive what often needs to be a major strategic initiative.

Furthermore, we can suggest that benefits of an e-marketing plan are in common with those of any marketing plan. McDonald (2003) describes the following reasons why a marketing plan is useful:

- for the marketer
- for superiors
- for non-marketing functions
- for subordinates
- to help identify sources of competitive advantage
- to force an organised approach
- to develop specificity
- to ensure consistent relationships
- to inform
- to get resources
- to get support
- to gain commitment
- to set objectives and strategies.

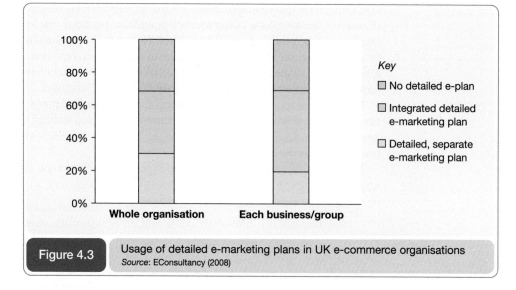

| Figure 4.3 | Usage of detailed e-marketing plans in UK e-commerce organisations |
| --- | --- |
| | Source: EConsultancy (2008) |

Managers responsible for a substantial investment in an Internet website and associated e-marketing communications will naturally want to ensure that the correct amount of money is invested and that it is used effectively. For these reasons and others given in this section, many leading adopters of e-commerce do have a distinct e-marketing plan, as the EConsultancy survey of UK e-commerce managers shows (Figure 4.3).

For smaller organisations, the digital plan need not be exhaustive – a two-page summary defining objectives and outlining strategies may be sufficient. The important thing is to set clear objectives and strategies showing how the digital presence should contribute to the sales and marketing process. Specific initiatives that are required such as search marketing, e-mail marketing or features of website redesign can be specified.

## A generic strategic approach

**Strategy process model**
A framework for approaching strategy development.

**Marketing planning**
A logical sequence and a series of activities leading to the setting of marketing objectives and the formulation of plans for achieving them.

A **strategy process model** provides a framework that gives a logical sequence to follow to ensure inclusion of all key activities of strategy development and implementation. In a marketing context, these strategy development and implementation activities are co-ordinated through a marketing plan, and the process of creating this is known as '**marketing planning**'. McDonald (2003) defines marketing planning simply as:

> the planned application of marketing resources to achieve marketing objectives ... Marketing planning is simply a logical sequence and a series of activities leading to the setting of marketing objectives and the formulation of plans for achieving them.

McDonald (2003) distinguishes between strategic marketing plans which cover a period beyond the next financial year (typically three to five years) and tactical marketing plans which cover detailed actions over a shorter time period of one year or less.

For Internet marketing, a similar distinction is useful. We suggest that a longer-term strategic Internet marketing plan should be developed in large organisations, which places emphasis on three key areas. First, early identification of changes to competitive forces in the micro-environment and significant changes in the macro-environment which will influence customer demand for online experiences and products. Second, developing value propositions for customers using online services as part of their buying process. Third, definition of the technology infrastructure and information architecture to deliver these value propositions as a customer experience. This long-term plan provides an eighteen-month to three-year roadmap of the infrastructure for e-commerce as noted by some interviewees in EConsultancy (2008) research. Many also noted that although there were often longer-term three- to five-year plans, quarterly revision of strategy into operational plans was also typical to promote strategic agility (see Chapter 3).

Figure 4.4 shows an overall strategy process model for strategic Internet marketing by Chaffey and Smith (2008). An alternative perspective was presented in Figure 1.8 in order to introduce the role of strategy development into the first three chapters. SOSTAC® stands for Situation, Objectives and Strategy, Tactics, Action and Control. Chaffey and Smith (2008) note that each stage is not discrete, rather there is some overlap during each stage of planning – previous stages may be revisited and refined, as indicated by the reverse arrows in Figure 4.4. The elements of SOSTAC® planning in the context of how they are described in this text with respect to digital marketing strategy are:

1 *Situation analysis means 'where are we now?'* Planning activities involved at this stage include performing an Internet-specific SWOT analysis reviewing the different aspects of the micro-environment we reviewed in Chapter 2 including customers, competitors and intermediaries forming the online marketplace. Situation analysis also involves review of the SLEPT factors forming the macro-environment which we reviewed in Chapter 3.

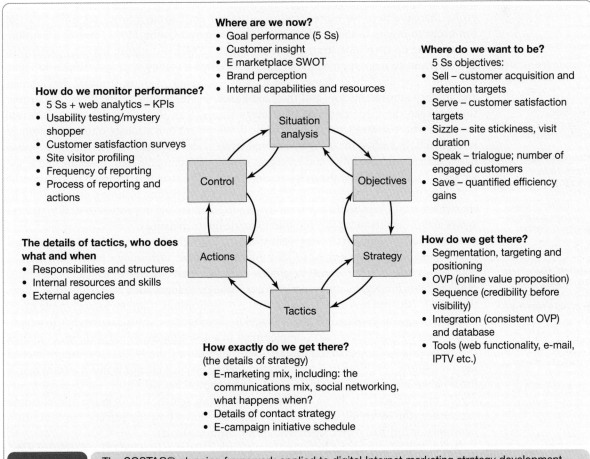

**Figure 4.4**    The SOSTAC® planning framework applied to digital Internet marketing strategy development
*Source*: Chaffey and Smith (2008)

**2** *Objectives means 'where do we want to be?'* This can include a vision for digital channels, and also specific numerical objectives for the digital channels such as projections of sales volumes and cost savings as explained in the section on objective setting in this chapter and with reference to communication objectives in Chapter 9.

**3** *Strategy means 'how do we get there?'* Strategy summarises how to achieve the objectives for the different decision points explained in this chapter including segmentation, targeting, proposition development (including the elements of the marketing mix described in more detail in Chapter 5 and e-CRM described in Chapter 6).

**4** *Tactics defines the usage of tactical digital communications tools.* This includes specific details of the marketing mix (Chapter 6), e-CRM (Chapter 7) and digital communications (Chapters 8 and 9) along with the details of the marketing mix which is covered in Chapter 2 and the communications mix which is covered in chapters 6 and 7; we won't address them in any detail in this introductory chapter.

**5** *Actions refers to action plans, change management and project management skills.* We refer to some of the issues of modifications to organisational roles and structures later in this chapter.

**6** *Control looks at the use of management information including web analytics to assess whether strategic and tactical objectives are achieved and how improvements can be made to enhance results further.* This is closely related to goal setting as described in this chapter and in Chapter 8, and also the coverage of web analytics and tracking in Chapter 9.

It can be argued, however, that with the pace at which markets and digital technologies evolve there is a need for more responsive strategy development processes where reaction can occur to events in the marketplace. Mintzberg and Quinn (1991) and other authors commenting on corporate strategy, such as Lynch (2000), distinguish between prescriptive and emergent strategy approaches. In the **prescriptive strategy** approach, similar to Figure 4.4, Lynch identifies three elements of strategy – strategic analysis, strategic development and strategy implementation, and these are linked together sequentially. Where the distinction between the three elements of strategy is less clear, this is the **emergent strategy** approach where strategic analysis, strategic development and strategy implementation are interrelated. In reality, most organisational strategy development and planning processes have elements of prescriptive and emergent strategy reflecting different planning and strategic review timescales. The prescriptive elements are the structured annual or six-monthly budgeting process or a longer-term three-year rolling marketing planning process. But on a shorter timescale, organisations naturally also need an emergent process to enable strategic agility and the ability to rapidly respond to marketplace dynamics.

It can be suggested that the emergent strategy approach is an essential part of any e-business strategy to enable response in a highly dynamic technology environment. This approach is best able to respond to sudden environmental changes which can open **strategic windows**. Strategic windows may occur through changes such as introduction of new technology (the Internet and different Web 2.0 applications is an obvious example here!), changes in regulation of an industry, changes to distribution channels in the industry (again the Internet has had this impact), development of a new segment or redefinitions of markets (an example is the growth in leisure and health clubs during the 1990s). The danger in creating a responsive capability to respond to technology-enabled change is that mistakes may be made either in evaluating the significance of new approaches (in which case strategic investments may be wasted) or in the implementation, which will degrade the customer experience (the Facebook case study in Chapter 8 shows how the privacy implications of new functionality had major repercussions for customer trust).

Based on preliminary findings by Brian Smith, Daniel *et al.* (2002) have suggested that planning styles adopted by organisations for e-commerce will be governed by a combination of market complexity, turbulence and the personal styles of company leaders. Smith identifies three main modes of strategy development:

**Prescriptive strategy**

The three core areas of strategic analysis, strategic development and strategy implementation are linked together sequentially.

**Emergent strategy**

Strategic analysis, strategic development and strategy implementation are interrelated and are developed together.

**Strategic windows**

Opportunities arising through a significant change in environment.

- *Logical rational planning.* Uses analytical tools and frameworks to formulate and implement strategy.
- *Pragmatic incremental.* Strategy develops in response to minor adjustments to the external environment.
- *Subjective visionary.* Strategy is the result of a leader, typically dominant or charismatic.

Daniel *et al.* (2002) suggest that in low-complexity, high-turbulence markets vision and incrementalism will be dominant, that in high-complexity, low-turbulence markets rational planning approaches are dominant, and that in highly complex, turbulent markets all three styles may be required.

EConsultancy (2008) has researched approaches used to encourage emergent strategies or strategic agility (see Chapter 3) based on interviews with e-commerce practitioners. Some of the approaches used by companies to support emergent strategy development are summarised in Table 4.2.

Kalakota and Robinson (2000) have also recommended a dynamic, emergent strategy process specific to e-business. The elements of this strategy approach are shown in Figure 4.5. The emphasis is on responsiveness with continuous review and prioritisation of investment in new Internet applications. Clearly, the quality of environment scanning and information collection, dissemination and analysis and the speed of response will be key for organisations following such a responsive, emergent approach. One example of an approach to collecting this market event data is **competitive intelligence** or **CI**.

**Competitive intelligence**
A process that transforms disaggregated information into relevant, accurate and usable strategic knowledge about competitors, position, performance, capabilities and intentions.

| Table 4.2 | Summary of approaches used to support emergent strategy |
|---|---|

| Aspect of emergent strategy | Approaches used to support emergent digital strategy |
|---|---|
| Strategic analysis | • Staff in different parts of organisation encouraged to monitor introduction of new approaches by competitors in-sector or out of sector<br>• Third-party benchmarking service report monthly or quarterly on new functionality introduced by competitors<br>• Ad-hoc customer panel used to suggest or review new ideas for site features<br>• Quarterly longitudinal testing of usability to complete key tasks (time intensive activities used by one large multinational direct retailer)<br>• Subscription to audience panel data (Comscore, Netratings, Hitwise) reviews changes in popularity of online services |
| Strategy formulation and selection | • Budget flexible to reassign priorities<br>• Dedicated or 'ring-fenced' IT budget up-to-agreed limits to reduce protracted review cycles<br>• Digital channel strategy group meets monthly – empowered to take decisions about which new web functionality to implement |
| Strategy implementation | • Use of agile development methodologies enable rapid development<br>• Area of site used to showcase new tools currently under trial (for example Google Labs (http:labs.google.com) |

*Source*: EConsultancy, 2008.

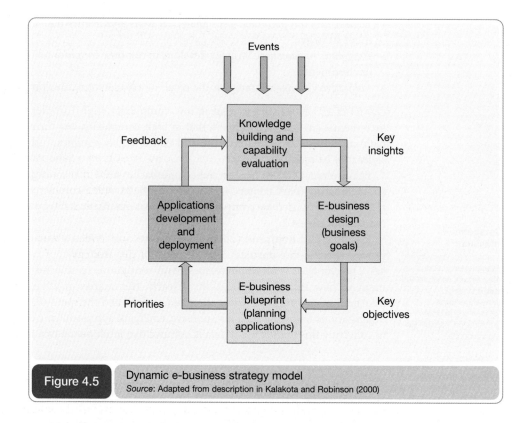

| Figure 4.5 | Dynamic e-business strategy model |
|---|---|
| | *Source*: Adapted from description in Kalakota and Robinson (2000) |

We will now start reviewing the four main stages of Internet marketing strategy development.

## Situation review

The situation review or analysis in classic marketing planning is best known as a marketing audit of the current effectiveness of marketing activities within a company, together with environmental factors outside the company that should govern the way the strategy is developed. These principles can be readily applied to reviewing online marketing effectiveness and internal capabilities. **Strategic analysis** or situation analysis involves review of:

**Strategic analysis**
Collection and review of information about an organisation's internal processes and resources and external marketplace factors in order to inform strategy definition.

- the internal capabilities, resources and processes of the company and a review of its activity in the marketplace (the 7 S framework introduced in Chapter 1 (Table 1.3) is a useful way of considering these internal capabilities to deliver strategy);
- the immediate competitive environment (micro-environment) including customer demand and behaviour, competitor activity, marketplace structure and relationships with suppliers and partners. These micro-environment factors were reviewed in Chapter 2 and are not considered in detail in this chapter;
- the wider environment (macro-environment) in which a company operates, which includes economic development and regulation by governments in the form of law and taxes together with social and ethical constraints such as the demand for privacy. These macro-environment factors including the social, legal, economic and political factors were reviewed in Chapter 3 and are not considered in detail in this chapter.

Now complete Activity 4.1, which illustrates the type of analysis that needs to be performed for an Internet marketing situation analysis.

| Activity 4.1 | Situation analysis for an e-commerce operation |
|---|---|

**Purpose**

To introduce the different types of Internet marketing analysis required as part of the situation review.

**Activity**

You are a newly incumbent e-commerce manager in an organisation that has operated a B2B e-commerce presence for two years in all the major European countries. The organisation sells office equipment and has been an established mail-order catalogue operation for 25 years. The UK, Germany, France and Italy each have their own localised content.

List the e-commerce-related questions you would ask of your new colleagues and the research you would commission under these headings:

- internal analysis;
- external analysis (micro-economic factors);
- external analysis (macro-economic factors).

## Internal audit or analysis

The internal audit will review the existing contribution that the Internet marketing channel is currently delivering in relation to other channels and in relation to the resources used.

### Assessing the current contribution of the Internet to the organisation

To assess the contribution and the effectiveness of Internet marketing involves the organisation in reviewing how well its online presence is meeting its goals. So this activity overlaps with that on strategic goal-setting discussed in the next section. Assessing effectiveness also requires a performance measurement or web analytics system to collect and report on data effectiveness. We cover this topic in more detail in Chapter 9. At this point, note that these different levels of measures can be usefully used to assess effectiveness:

#### 1 Business effectiveness

This will include the contribution of the site directly or indirectly to sales and how well it is supporting business objectives. The relative costs of producing, updating and promoting the site will also be reviewed as part of a cost–benefit analysis.

#### 2 Marketing effectiveness

These measures may include:

- leads (qualified enquiries);
- sales;
- customer retention and loyalty, including lifetime value;
- online market (or audience share);
- brand enhancement;
- customer service.

For large organisations, these measures can be assessed for each of the different markets a company operates in or for product lines produced on the website. The way in which the elements of the marketing mix are utilised will also be reviewed.

### 3 Internet effectiveness

These are specific measures that are used to assess the way in which the website is used, and the characteristics of the audience. They are described in more detail in Chapter 9. According to Chaffey and Smith (2008) key performance indicators (KPIs) for an online presence include:

- *unique visitors* – the number of separate, individual visitors to the site;
- total numbers of *sessions* or *visits* to the website;
- *repeat visits* – average number of visits per individual;
- *duration* – average length of time visitors spend on the site;
- *subscription rates* such as the number of visitors subscribing for services such as an opt-in e-mail and newsletters and the response rates for these e-newsletters;
- *conversion rates* – the percentage of visitors converting to subscribers (or becoming customers);
- *attrition rates* through the online buying process;
- *churn rates* – percentage of subscribers withdrawing or unsubscribing;
- *click-through rates (CTR)* from third-party sites to your own.

### Customer research

It is important that customer analysis is not restricted to quantitative demand analysis. Varianini and Vaturi (2000) point out that qualitative research about existing customers provides insights that can be used to inform strategy. They suggest using graphic profiling, which is an attempt to capture the core characteristics of target customers – not only demographics, but also their needs and attitudes and how comfortable they are with the Internet. In Chapter 2 we reviewed how customer **personas** and **customer scenarios** are developed to help inform understanding of online buyer behaviour.

More recently, Sam Decker, formerly e-commerce manager at Dell, who helped develop the customer-centric strategy for Dell's $8 billion US consumer business, has stressed the importance of this activity by referencing this approach as 'customer oxygen'. In EConsultancy (2008) he says:

> *Your company needs to breathe 'customer oxygen'. The word 'oxygen' is important, because it reflects the idea that the customer's perspective should infuse just about every business decision you make each day. This oxygen should flow from the CEO and beyond, as a customer-centric culture affects every division, department and function.*

He believes this is an ongoing activity rather than the sporadic customer insights collected by many organisations. He says:

> *Occasional research insights are important to guide the corporate ship like a compass, but not enough to sustain its course.*

Instead he advises:

> *For a corporate system to digest the perspective of the customer, a programme needs to integrate into processes, reporting, performance plans and other methods of day-to-day work and accountability. It becomes a programme that people in the company can continuously improve, which is something employees are good at doing. Your managers, colleagues and employees can feed on daily customer-focused tactics and metrics that can be part of their job and performance; weaving it into the overall fabric of your company.*

**Persona**

A thumbnail summary of the characteristics, needs, motivations and environment of a typical website user.

**Customer scenarios**

Alternative tasks or outcomes required by a visitor to a website. Typically accomplished in a series of stages of different tasks involving different information needs or experiences.

## Resource analysis

The internal audit will also include a **resource analysis**. This involves assessing the capabilities of the organisation to deliver its online services. The 7 S framework introduced in Chapter 1 in (Table 1.3) is a useful way of considering the suitability of interval capabilites to achieve strategic aims. Other aspects of resource analysis that can be reviewed include:

- *Financial resources* – the cost components of running an online presence, including site development, promotion and maintenance. Mismatch between current spend and required spend to achieve visibility within the online marketplace should be reviewed using tools such as Hitwise and Netratings which can be used to assess online market share.
- *Technology infrastructure resources* – availability and performance (speed) of website and service-level agreements with the ISP. The need for different applications to enhance the customer experience or increase conversion rates can be assessed (e.g. on-site search, customer review or customisation facilities). The infrastructure to manage sites such as content management, customer relationship management and web analytics should also be considered.
- *Human resources* – availability for an e-retailer includes service and fulfilment resources for answering customer queries and dispatching goods. For all companies there is a challenge of possibly recruiting new staff or re-skilling marketing staff to manage online marketing activities such as merchandising, search engine marketing, affiliate marketing and e-mail marketing. We return to this topic later in this chapter.
- *Structure* – what are the responsibilities and control mechanisms used to co-ordinate Internet marketing across different departments and business units? We again return to this topic later in the chapter.
- *Strengths and weaknesses* – SWOT analysis is referred to in the next section where generic strengths and weaknesses are summarised in Figure 4.7 and an example is given in Figure 4.8. Companies will also assess their distinctive competencies. Chaston (2000) suggests that a resource–advantage matrix should be produced which compares the costs of different online services against the value they provide to customers. These can then be evaluated to select strategic options. For example, a high-cost, low-value service might be terminated while a medium-cost, high-value service might be extended. This is a form of **portfolio analysis** where different e-commerce services are assessed for future potential. See also the strategy formulation section later in this chapter.

## Stage models of the Internet marketing capability

A further perspective on assessing current usage of the Internet channel is to assess the current level of Internet services and integration of Internet marketing with other marketing activities. Stage models of capability delivered through the online presence assist in this evaluation. Companies that operate in a particular market tend to follow a natural progression in developing their website to support their marketing activities. The following levels of Internet marketing can be identified:

- **Level 0.** No website or presence.
- **Level 1.** Company places an entry in a directory website that lists company names such as Yellow Pages (www.yell.co.uk) to make people searching the web aware of the existence of the company or its products. There is no website at this stage.
- **Level 2.** Simple static website created containing basic company contact and product information (sometimes referred to as 'brochureware').
- **Level 3.** Simple interactive site where users are able to search the site and make queries to retrieve information such as product availability and pricing. Enquiries submitted by a form and transmitted by e-mail may also be supported.

- **Level 4**. Interactive site supporting transactions with users. The functions offered will vary according to the company. If products can be sold direct then an electronic commerce or online store option for online sales will be available. Other functions might include an interactive customer-service helpdesk.
- **Level 5**. Fully interactive site providing relationship marketing with individual customers and facilitating the full range of marketing functions relevant for the sector.

A variety of online stage models have been produced since Quelch and Klein (1996) noted the sequence in which websites develop for different types of company. They distinguish between existing major companies (see Figure 4.6(a)) and start-up companies (see Figure 4.6(b)) that start as Internet companies. The main difference is that Internet start-ups are likely to introduce transaction facilities earlier than existing companies. However, they may take longer to develop suitable customer service facilities. Stage models can be usefully applied to SME businesses which, due to reasons of scale and resource, are less likely to have reached full digital capabilities. Levy and Powell (2003) have reviewed different adoption ladders which they classify as having four stages of (1) Publish, (2) Interact, (3) Transact and (4) Integrate.

Stage models have been criticised for a variety of reasons. First, as a generic model they typically apply to businesses that have products which are suitable for online sale, but may not apply to the full range of businesses such as the four types of online presence introduced in Chapter 1. Secondly, these stage models are externally focused and do not address the broader development of Internet marketing capabilities within an organisation. Dave Chaffey writing for EConsultancy (2008) has recently developed a framework for assessing internal digital marketing capabilities across a range of companies (Table 4.3). In the Internet marketing context, 'capabilities' refers to the processes, structures and skills adopted for planning and implementation of digital marketing. This was inspired by the capability maturity models devised by the Carnegie Mellon Software Engineering Institute (www.sei.cmu.edu/cmm/cmm.html) to help organisations improve their software development practices.

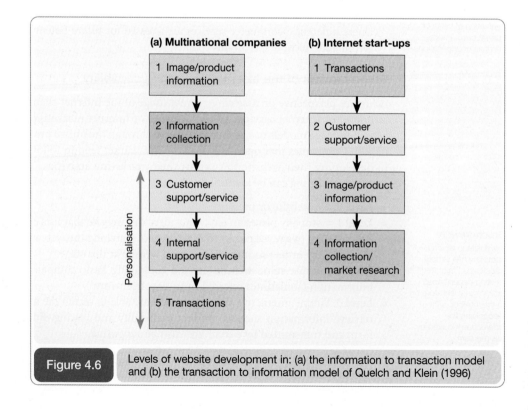

| Figure 4.6 | Levels of website development in: (a) the information to transaction model and (b) the transaction to information model of Quelch and Klein (1996) |

| Table 4.3 | Capability maturity model of e-commerce adoption based on EConsultancy (2008) research |

| Level | Strategy process and performance improvement | Structure: location of e-commerce | Senior management buy-in | Marketing integration | Online marketing focus |
|---|---|---|---|---|---|
| 1 Unplanned | *Limited*<br><br>Online channels not part of business planning process. Web analytics data collected, but unlikely to be reviewed or actioned | *Experimentation*<br><br>No clear centralised e-commerce resources in business. Main responsibility typically within IT | *Limited*<br><br>No direct involvement in planning and little necessity seen for involvement | *Poor integration*<br><br>Some interested marketers may experiment with e-communications tools | *Content focus*<br><br>Creation of online brochures and catalogues. Adoption of first style guidelines |
| 2 Diffuse management | *Low-level*<br><br>Online referenced in planning, but with limited channel-specific objectives. Some campaign analysis by interested staff | *Diffuse*<br><br>Small central e-commerce group or single manager, possibly with steering group controlled by marketing. Many separate websites, separate online initiatives, e.g. tools adopted and agencies for search marketing, e-mail marketing. E-communications funding from brands/businesses may be limited | *Aware*<br><br>Management becomes aware of expenditure and potential of online channels | *Separate*<br><br>Increased adoption of e-communications tools and growth of separate sites and microsites continues. Media spend still dominantly offline | *Traffic focus*<br><br>Increased emphasis on driving visitors to site through pay-per-click search marketing and affiliate marketing |
| 3 Centralised management | *Specific*<br><br>Specific channel objectives set. Web analytics capability not integrated to give unified reporting of campaign effectiveness | *Centralised*<br><br>Common platform for content management, web analytics. Preferred-supplier list of digital agencies. Centralised, independent e-commerce function, but with some digital-specific responsibilities by country/product/brand | *Involved*<br><br>Directly involved in annual review and ensures review structure involving senior managers from marketing, IT, operations and finance | *Arm's-length*<br><br>Marketing and e-commerce mainly work together during planning process. Limited review within campaigns. Senior e-commerce team-members responsible for encouraging adoption of digital marketing throughout organisation | *Conversion and customer experience focus*<br><br>Initiatives for usability, accessibility and revision of content management system (including search engine optimisation) are common at this stage |

| Level | Strategy process and performance improvement | Structure: Location of e-commerce | Senior management buy-in | Marketing integration | Online marketing focus |
|---|---|---|---|---|---|
| 4 Decentralised operations | *Refined*<br><br>Close cooperation between e-commerce and marketing. Targets and performance reviewed monthly. Towards unified reporting. Project debriefs | *Decentralised*<br><br>Digital marketing skills more developed in business with integration of e-commerce into planning and execution at business or country level. E-retailers commonly adopt direct-channel organisation of which e-commerce is one channel. Online channel profit and loss accountability sometimes controlled by businesses/brands, but with central budget for continuous e-communications spend (search, affiliates, e-communications) | *Driving performance*<br><br>Involved in review at least monthly | *Partnership*<br><br>Marketing and e-commerce work closely together through year. Digital media spend starts to reflect importance of online channels to business and consumers | *Retention focus*<br><br>Initiatives on analysis of customer purchase and response behaviour and implementation of well-defined touch strategies with emphasis on e-mail marketing. Loyalty drivers well known and managed |
| 5 Integrated and optimised | *Multichannel process*<br><br>The interactions and financial contribution of different channels are well understood and resourced and improved accordingly | *Integrated*<br><br>Majority of digital skills within business and e-commerce team commonly positioned within marketing or direct sales operation. 'Front-end' systems development skills typically retained in e-commerce team | *Integral*<br><br>Less frequent in-depth involvement required. Annual planning and six-monthly or quarterly review | *Complete*<br><br>Marketing has full complement of digital marketing skills, but calls on specialist resource from agencies or central e-commerce resource as required. Online potential not constrained by traditional budgeting processes | *Optimisation focus*<br><br>Initiatives to improve acquisition, conversion and retention according to developments in access platform and customer experience technologies. May use temporary multi-disciplinary team to drive performance |

Table 4.3 is intended to help:

1 review current approaches to digital marketing to identify areas for improvement;
2 benchmark with competitors who are in the same market sector or industry and in different sectors;
3 identify best practice from more advanced adopters;
4 set targets and develop strategies for improving capabilities.

Of the companies assessed within the research, the majority were at Level 3 or 4 overall, although companies may occupy different levels according to different criteria. We return to assessing capabilities using the 7 Ss to implement Internet marketing strategy at the end of the chapter.

### Competitor analysis

Competitor analysis or the monitoring of competitor use of e-commerce to acquire and retain customers is especially important in the e-marketplace due to the dynamic nature of the Internet medium. This enables new services to be launched and prices and promotions changed much more rapidly than through print communications. Activity 4.2 highlights some of the issues in competitor benchmarking, and this topic is referred to in more detail in Chapter 2.

### Intermediary analysis

Chapter 2 highlighted the importance of web-based intermediaries such as portals in driving traffic to an organisation's website. Situation analysis will also involve identifying relevant intermediaries for a particular marketplace and look at how the organisation and its competitors are using the intermediaries to build traffic and provide services. For example, an e-tailer needs to assess which comparison services such as Kelkoo (www.kelkoo.com) and Pricerunner (www.pricerunner.com) it and its competitors are represented on. Do competitors have any special sponsorship arrangements or microsites created with intermediaries? The other aspect of situation analysis for intermediaries is to consider the way in which the marketplace is operating. To what extent are competitors using disintermediation or reintermediation? How are existing channel arrangements being changed?

### Assessing opportunities and threats

Performing a structured SWOT analysis to summarise the external opportunities and threats that are presented by the Internet environment is a core activity for situation analysis.

---

**Activity 4.2**    **Competitor benchmarking**

#### Purpose

To understand the characteristics of competitor websites it is useful to know how to benchmark and to assess the value of benchmarking.

#### Activity

Choose a B2C industry sector such as airlines, book retailers, book publishers, CDs or clothing, or a B2B sector such as oil companies, chemical companies, construction industry companies or B2B exchanges. Work individually or in a group to identify the type of information that should be available from the website (and which parts of the site you will access it from) and will be useful in terms of competitor benchmarking. Once your criteria have been developed, you should then benchmark companies and summarise which you feel is making best use of the Internet medium.

Companies should also consider their own strengths and weaknesses in the Internet marketing environment. Summarising the results through Internet-specific SWOT analysis (internal Strengths and Weaknesses and external Opportunities and Threats) will clearly highlight the opportunities and threats. Appropriate planning to counter the threats and take advantage of the opportunities can then be built into the Internet marketing plan. An example of a typical SWOT analysis of Internet-marketing-related strengths and weaknesses is shown in Figure 4.7. As is often the case with SWOT analysis, the opportunities available to a company are the opposites of the threats presented by other companies. The strengths and weaknesses will vary according to the company involved, but many of the strengths and weaknesses are dependent on the capacity of senior management to acknowledge and act on change. The Internet SWOT can be reviewed in the main areas of online marketing activity, namely areas of customer acquisition, conversion, retention and growth.

This form of presentation of the Internet-specific SWOT shown in Figure 4.7 is a powerful technique since it not only indicates the SWOT, but can be used to generate appropriate strategies. Often, the most rewarding strategies combine Strengths and Opportunities or counter Threats through Strengths. Figure 4.8 gives an example of a typical Internet SWOT analytics for an established multichannel brand.

| The organisation | Stengths – S<br>1. Existing brand<br>2. Existing customer base<br>3. Existing distribution | Weaknesses – W<br>1. Brand perception<br>2. Intermediary use<br>3. Technology/skills<br>4. Cross-channel support |
|---|---|---|
| Opportunities – O<br>1. Cross-selling<br>2. New markets<br>3. New services<br>4. Alliances/co-branding | SO strategies<br>Leverage strengths to<br>maximise opportunities<br>= **Attacking strategy** | WO strategies<br>Counter weaknesses through<br>exploiting opportunities<br>= **Build strengths for<br>attacking strategy** |
| Threats – T<br>1. Customer choice<br>2. New entrants<br>3. New competitive products<br>4. Channel conflicts | ST strategies<br>Leverage strengths to<br>minimise threats<br>= **Defensive strategy** | WT strategies<br>Counter weaknesses and<br>threats<br>= **Build strengths for<br>defensive strategy** |

**Figure 4.7**    A generic Internet-specific SWOT analysis showing typical opportunities and threats presented by the Internet

## Strategic goal setting

Any marketing strategy should be based on clearly defined corporate objectives, but there has been a tendency for Internet marketing to be conducted separately from other business and marketing objectives. Porter (2001) has criticised the lack of goal setting when many organisations have developed Internet strategies. He notes that many companies, responding to distorted market signals, have used 'rampant experimentation' that is not economically sustainable. This resulted in the failure of many 'dot-com' companies and also poor investments by many established companies. He suggests that economic value or sustained profitability for a company is the final arbiter of business success.

It is best, of course, if the Internet marketing strategy is consistent with and aligns with business and marketing objectives. For example, business objectives such as increasing

| The organisation | Strengths – S<br>1 Existing brand<br>2 Existing customer base<br>3 Existing distribution | Weaknesses – W<br>1 Brand perception<br>2 Intermediary use<br>3 Technology/skills (poor web experience)<br>4 Cross-channel support<br>5 Churn rate |
|---|---|---|
| Opportunities – O<br>1 Cross-selling<br>2 New markets<br>3 New services<br>4 Alliances/co-branding | SO strategies<br>Leverage strengths to maximise opportunities = attacking strategy<br>**Examples:**<br>1 Migrate customers to web strategy<br>2 Refine customer contact strategy across customer lifecycle or commitment segmentation (e-mail, web)<br>3 Partnership strategy (co-branding, linking)<br>4 Launch new web-based products or value-adding experiences, e.g. video streaming | WO strategies<br>Counter weaknesses through exploiting opportunities = build strengths for attacking strategy<br>**Examples:**<br>1 Countermediation strategy (create or acquire)<br>2 Search marketing acquisition strategy<br>3 Affiliate-based acquisition strategy<br>4 Refine customer contact strategy (e-mail, web) |
| Threats – T<br>1 Customer choice (price)<br>2 New entrants<br>3 New competitive products<br>4 Channel conflicts<br>5 Social network | ST strategies<br>Leverage strengths to minimise threat = defensive strategy<br>**Examples:**<br>1 Introduce new Internet-only products<br>2 Add value to web services – refine OVP<br>3 Partner with complementary brand<br>4 Create own social network/customer reviews | WT strategies<br>Counter weaknesses and threats: = build strengths for defensive strategy<br>**Examples:**<br>1 Differential online pricing strategy<br>2 Acquire/create pure-play company with lower cost-base<br>3 Customer engagement strategy to increase conversion, average order value and lifetime value<br>4 Online reputation management strategy/E-PR |

| Figure 4.8 | An example of an Internet-specific SWOT for an established multi-channel brand showing how the elements of SWOT can be related to strategy formulation |
|---|---|

market share in an overseas market or introducing a new product to market can and should be supported by the Internet communications channel.

Goal setting for the Internet will be based on managers' view of the future relevance of the Internet to their industry. **Scenario-based analysis** is a useful strategic analysis approach to discussing alternative visions of the future prior to objective setting. Lynch (2000) explains that scenario-based analysis is concerned with possible models of the future of an organisation's environment. He says:

*The aim is not to predict, but to explore a set of possibilities; scenarios take different situations with different starting points.*

Lynch distinguishes qualitative scenario-based planning from quantitative prediction such as that of Activity 4.3 (page 227). In an Internet marketing perspective, scenarios that could be explored include:

**Scenario-based analysis**
Models of the future environment are developed from different starting points.

1  One player in our industry becomes dominant through use of the Internet ('Amazoning' the sector).
2  Major customers do not adopt e-commerce because of organisational barriers.
3  Major disintermediation (Chapter 2) occurs in our industry.
4  B2B marketplaces do or do not become dominant in our industry.
5  New entrants or substitute products change our industry.

Through performing this analysis, better understanding of the drivers for different views of the future will result, new strategies can be generated and strategic risks can be assessed. It is clear that the scenarios above will differ between worst-case and best-case scenarios.

As a starting point for setting specific objectives, it is useful to think through the benefits of the Internet channel so that these benefits can be converted into objectives. It is useful to identify both *tangible benefits*, for which monetary savings or revenues can be identified, and *intangible benefits*, for which it is more difficult to calculate financial benefits and costs, but are still important, for example customer service quality. Table 4.4 presents a summary of typical benefits of Internet marketing.

An alternative way of thinking through the benefits, is to review the 5 Ss of Chaffey and Smith (2008) who suggest there are five broad benefits of e-marketing:

- *Sell* – grow sales through wider distribution to customers you can't service offline, or perhaps through a wider product range than in-store, or better prices.
- *Serve* – add value by giving customers extra benefits online, or inform them of product development through online dialogue and feedback.
- *Speak* – get closer to customers by tracking them, asking them questions, conducting online interviews, creating a dialogue, monitoring chat rooms, learning about them.
- *Save* – save costs of service, sales transactions and administration, print and post. Can you reduce transaction costs and therefore either make online sales more profitable or use cost savings to enable you to cut prices, which in turn could enable you to generate greater market share?

| Table 4.4 | Tangible and intangible benefits from Internet marketing |
| --- | --- |

| Tangible benefits | Intangible benefits |
| --- | --- |
| Increased sales from new sales leads giving: <br> • new customers, new markets <br><br> • existing customers (repeat-selling) <br><br> • existing customers (cross-selling) <br> Cost reductions from: <br> • reduced time in customer service <br>   (customer self-service online) <br><br> • online sales <br> • reduced printing and distribution costs <br>   of marketing communications | Corporate image communication rise due to increased revenue from: <br><br> • Enhanced brand <br><br> • More rapid, more responsive marketing <br>   communications including PR <br><br> • Improved customer service <br><br> • Learning for the future <br><br> • Meeting customer expectations to have a <br>   website <br><br> • Identifying new partners, supporting existing <br>   partners better <br><br> • Better management of marketing information <br> and customer information <br><br> • Feedback from customers on products |

- *Sizzle* – extend the brand online. Reinforce brand values in a totally new medium. The web scores very highly as a medium for creating brand awareness, recognition and involvement, as explained further in Chapter 5.

Some examples of performance indicators of an online flower business are shown in Mini case study 4.1.

---

| Mini Case Study 4.1 | Arena Flowers controls its growth through key performance indicators |
| --- | --- |

Arena Flowers (Figure 4.9) is an online florist based in London. The business was incorporated in July 2006 and went live with a transactional website in September 2006. The company delivered £2 million net sales in year 1 and broke even within the first 12 months of trading. At the time of the interview they are forecasting sales of £4m in year 2 and make a healthy profit. The head of design and development, Sam Barton, explains how he sees opportunities to keep growing both sales and profitability at a similar rate going forward through various initiatives. For example, the company has developed a Facebook application that provides 15% of the site traffic – an opportunity that has been missed by many of its more established rivals.

Average order values (AOVs) have developed since the low £30 has grown month on month. The current level is £42. Ways of increasing AOV have included options to add a vase, make a deluxe bouquet and through selling Prestat's chocolates alongside the flowers.

The essence of the Arena Flowers' proposition is to cut out all middlemen and buy direct from growers, so they can get great prices and because the flowers are exceedingly fresh. 'There are no "relay" fees with

| Figure 4.9 | Arena Flowers (www.arenaflowers.com) |
| --- | --- |

us and, because of our high stock turnover, we get fresh flowers in daily and they go straight to the customer, rather than sitting in a hot shop window. Arena Flowers offer free delivery on all of our products and we were the first online florist in the UK to offer FFP-accredited, ethically sourced flowers.' That has been a good 'unique selling point' and enables Arena to offer something different from other suppliers such as supermarkets.

*Source*: EConsultancy E-business Briefing (2008) Arena Flowers' Sam Barton on web design and development, E-newsletter interview, 12 March 2008

### The online revenue contribution

**Online revenue contribution**

An assessment of the direct contribution of the Internet or other digital media to sales, usually expressed as a percentage of overall sales revenue.

A key objective for Internet marketing is the **online revenue contribution** since this gives a simple measure of the proportion of online sales achieved in different product categories. This is a measure of the extent to which a company's online presence directly impacts the sales revenue of the organisation, and scenarios in growth of contribution can be used to determine future resource allocation to the online channels. Online revenue contribution objectives can be specified for different types of products, customer segments and geographic markets. For example, in 1997 low-cost airline easyJet set an online contribution objective of 50% by the year 2000. This established a clear vision and resources could be put in place to achieve this. EasyJet now has an online revenue contribution of 95%. Forrester Research (2005) provides benchmark figures of direct online revenue contribution for different sectors in the US (forecasts for 2010 are in brackets):

- Services 15% (32%)
- Manufacturers 15% (32%)
- Financial services 15% (28%)
- Retail 14% (21%)
- Total 15% (29%).

**Allowable cost per acquisition**

A target maximum cost for generating leads or new customers profitably.

It is important that companies set sales and revenue goals for online channels for which costs are controlled through an **allowable cost per acquisition**. This takes into account the cost of attracting visitors through techniques such as affiliate marketing, paid search advertising or display advertising as explained in budget models presented in Chapter 8.

For some companies, such as an FMCG manufacturer, a beverage company or a B2B manufacturer, it is unrealistic to expect a direct online revenue contribution. In this case, an indirect online contribution can be stated. This considers the Internet as part of the promotional mix and its role in reaching and influencing a proportion of customers to purchase the product, generating trials, or in the case of a B2B company, leads. In this case a company could set an **online promotion contribution** or indirect online revenue contribution of 5% of its target market visiting the website and interacting with the brand. Bazett *et al.* (2005) give the example of a high-street chain that for every £1 of revenue it takes on the web, £3 is spent in the store after browsing online – so it has objectives for this and works equally hard to help these customers through such facilities as store locators and information on the nearest store with a particular product in stock. Complete Activity 4.3 to explore the factors that impact online revenue contribution in different markets.

**Online promotion contribution**

An assessment of the proportion of customers (new or retained) who are reached by online communications and are influenced as a result.

The contribution should also reference the contribution to customer service transaction as this reflects reduction in costs. Speaking to the EConsultancy Marketing Masterclass in November 2007, Paul Say, formerly head of e-marketing at First Direct explained how his vision for the bank had included clear targets for online acquisition, transactions and recommendations. These translated into the following results by November 2007:

- 40% of total sales now being through electronic channels;
- 71% of its customer base actively using electronic channels (measured as 90-day active);
- 72% of all customer transactions (e.g. bill payments) made electronically;
- 75% would recommend friends to use the service (compared to 30% UK banking average).

## Activity 4.3 — Assessing the significance of digital channels

### Purpose

To illustrate the issues involved with assessing the suitability of the Internet for e-commerce.

### Activity

For each of the products and services in Table 4.5, assess the suitability of the Internet for delivery of the product or service and position it on the grid in Figure 4.10 with justification. Make estimates in Table 4.5 for the direct and indirect online revenue contribution in 5 and 10 years' time for different products in your country. Choose specific products within each category shown.

**Table 4.5   Vision of online revenue contribution for different types of company**

| Products/services | Now | 2 years' time | 5 years' time | 10 years' time |
|---|---|---|---|---|
| **Example: Cars, US** | | | | |
| Direct online sales | 5% | 10% | 25% | 50% |
| Indirect online sales | 50% | 70% | 90% | 95% |
| **Financial services** | | | | |
| Direct online sales | | | | |
| Indirect online sales | | | | |
| **Clothing** | | | | |
| Direct online sales | | | | |
| Indirect online sales | | | | |
| **Business office supplies** | | | | |
| Direct online sales | | | | |
| Indirect online sales | | | | |

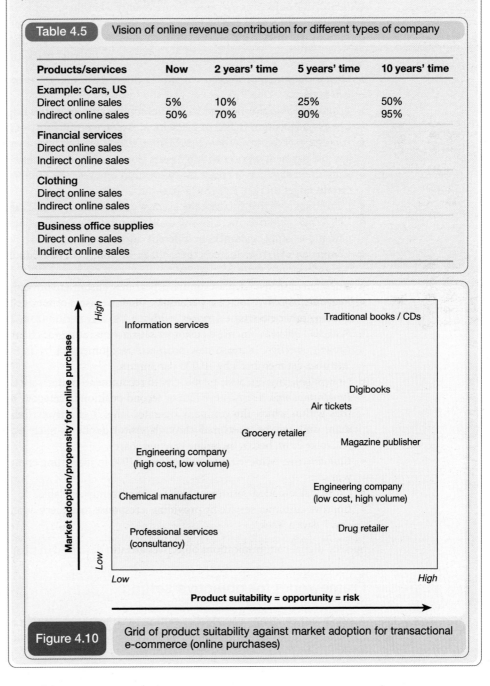

**Figure 4.10   Grid of product suitability against market adoption for transactional e-commerce (online purchases)**

### Setting SMART objectives

You have probably heard before that effective objectives and measures to assess performance are SMART. SMART is used to assess the suitability of objectives set to drive different strategies or the improvement of the full range of business processes.

- *Specific.* Is the objective sufficiently detailed to measure real-world problems and opportunities?
- *Measurable.* Can a quantitative or qualitative attribute be applied to create a metric?
- *Actionable.* Can the information be used to improve performance? If the objective doesn't change behaviour in staff to help them improve performance, there is little point in it!
- *Relevant.* Can the information be applied to the specific problem faced by the manager?
- *Time-related.* Can the information be constrained through time?

With SMART objectives everyone is sure exactly what the target is and progresses towards it and, if necessary, action can be taken to put the company back on target. Here are some typical examples of SMART objectives, including those to support goal-setting in customer acquisition, conversion and retention categories for Internet marketing strategy:

- *Digital channel contribution objective.* Achieve 10% online revenue contribution within two years.
- *Acquisition objective.* Acquire 50,000 new online customers this financial year at an average cost per acquisition (CPA) of £30 with an average profitability of £5.
- *Acquisition or conversion objective.* Migrate 40% of existing customers to using online 'paperless' bill payment services within 3 years (for example for a bank or utilities company).
- *Acquisition objective.* Increase by 20% within one year the number of sales arising from a certain target market, e.g. 18–25-year-olds.
- *Conversion objective.* Increase the average order value of online sales to £42 per customer.
- *Conversion objective.* Increase site conversion rate to 3.2% (would be based on model of new and existing customers in different categories).
- *Conversion objective.* Increase percentage of online service enquiries fulfilled online by 'web self-service' from 85% to 90%.
- *Retention objective.* Increase annual repeat new customer conversion rate by 20%.
- *Retention objective.* Increase percentage of active users of service transacting (purchasing or using other electronic services) within a 180-day period from 20% to 25%.
- *Retention objective.* Increase customer satisfaction rating for channel from 70% to 80%.
- *Growth objective.* Increase new prospects recommended by friends (viral marketing or 'member get member') by 10,000 per annum.
- *Growth objective.* Increase propensity to recommend online service from 60% to 70%.
- *Penetration objective.* Achieve first or second position in category penetration in the countries within which the company operates (this is effectively online audience or market share and can be measured through visitor rankings such as Hitwise or Netratings (Chapter 2) or, better, by online revenue share).
- *Cost objective.* Achieve a cost reduction of 10% in marketing communications within two years.
- Create value-added customer services not currently available.
- Improve customer service by providing a response to a query within 2 hours, 24 hours per day, 7 days a week.

Specific digital communications objectives are also described in Chapter 8.

## Frameworks for objective setting

A significant challenge of objective setting for Internet marketing is that there will potentially be many different measures such as those listed above and these will have be to grouped to be meaningful. Categorisation of objectives into groups is also useful since it can be used to identify suitable objectives. In this chapter, we have already seen two methods of categorising objectives. First, objectives can be set at the level of business effectiveness, marketing effectiveness and Internet marketing effectiveness as explained in the section on internal auditing as part of the situation analysis. Second, the 5 S framework of Sell, Speak, Serve, Save and Sizzle provides a simple framework for objective setting. A further five-part framework for goal setting and analysis is presented in Chapter 9.

## The balanced scorecard

Some larger companies will identify objectives for Internet marketing which are consistent with existing business measurement frameworks. Since the balanced business scorecard is a well-known and widely used framework it can be helpful to define objectives for Internet marketing in these categories.

**Balanced scorecard**
A framework for setting and monitoring business performance. Metrics are structured according to customer issues, internal efficiency measures, financial measures and innovation.

The **balanced scorecard**, popularised in a *Harvard Business Review* article by Kaplan and Norton (1993), can be used to translate vision and strategy into objectives and then, through measurement, assessing whether the strategy and its implementation are successful. In part, it was a response to over-reliance on financial metrics such as turnover and profitability and the tendency for these measures to be retrospective rather than looking at future potential, as indicated by innovation, customer satisfaction and employee development. In addition to financial data, the balanced scorecard uses operational measures such as customer satisfaction, efficiency of internal processes and also the organisation's innovation and improvement activities including staff development. It has since been applied to IT (Der Zee and De Jong, 1999), e-commerce (Hasan and Tibbits, 2000) and multichannel marketing (Bazett *et al.*, 2005).

**Efficiency**
Minimising resources or time needed to complete a process. 'Doing the thing right.'

**Effectiveness**
Meeting process objectives, delivering the required outputs and outcomes. 'Doing the right thing.'

Table 4.6 illustrates specific Internet marketing measures within the four main areas of organisational performance managed through the balanced scorecard. In our presentation we have placed objectives within the areas of **efficiency** ('doing the thing right') and **effectiveness** ('doing the right thing'). For example, efficiency involves increasing conversion rates and reducing costs of acquisition. Effectiveness involves supporting broader marketing objectives and often indicates the contribution of the online channel. It is useful to identify efficiency and effectiveness measures separately, since online marketing and web analytics often tend to focus on efficiency. Hasan and Tibbits (2000) note that the internal process measures in particular are concerned with the efficiency and the customer and business value perspectives are indicated with effectiveness, but these measures can be applied across all four areas as we have shown.

A further objective-setting or metrics framework, the online lifecycle management grid (Table 4.9), is presented at the end of the chapter (see page **266**) as a summary since this integrates objectives, strategies and tactics.

## Performance drivers

**Performance metrics**
Measures that are used to evaluate and improve the efficiency and effectiveness of business processes.

**Key performance indicators**
Metrics used to assess the performance of a process and/or whether set goals are achieved.

Specific **performance metrics** are used to evaluate and improve the efficiency and effectiveness of a process. **Key performance indicators (KPIs)** are a special type of performance metric which indicate the overall performance of a process or its sub-processes. An example of KPIs for an online electrical goods retailer is shown in Figure 4.11. Improving the results from the e-commerce site involves using the techniques on the left of the diagram to improve the performance drivers, and so the KPI. The KPI is the total online sales figure. For a traditional retailer, this could be compared as a percentage to other retail channels such as mail order or retail stores. It can be seen that this KPI is dependent on performance drivers such as number of site visits or average order value which combine to govern this KPI. Note that the definition of KPI is arbitrary and is dependent on scope. So, overall conversion rate could be a KPI and this is then supported by other performance drivers such as engagement rate, conversion to opportunity and conversion to sale.

| Table 4.6 | Example allocation of Internet marketing objectives within the balanced scorecard framework for a transactional e-commerce site | |
|---|---|---|

| Balanced scorecard sector | Efficiency | Effectiveness |
|---|---|---|
| Financial results (Business value) | • Channel costs<br>• Channel profitability | • Online contribution (direct)<br>• Online contribution (indirect)<br>• Profit contributed |
| Customer value | • Online reach (unique visitors as % of potential visitors)<br>• Cost of acquisition or cost per sale (CPA/CPS)<br>• Customer propensity to defect | • Sales and sales per customer<br>• New customers<br>• Online market share<br>• Customer satisfaction ratings<br>• Customer loyalty index |
| Operational processes | • Conversion rates<br>• Average order value<br>• List size and quality<br>• E-mail active % | • Fulfilment times<br>• Support response times |
| Innovation and learning (people and knowledge) | • Novel approaches tested<br>• Internal e-marketing education<br>• Internal satisfaction ratings | • Novel approaches deployed<br>• Performance appraisal review |

## Leading and lagging performance indicators

When developing goals and measurement systems used to review and improve performance of digital channels, it is also helpful to consider which are leading and lagging indicators of performance. Trends should be identified within these, for example are they increasing or decreasing year-on-year (often used as a good like-for-like comparison), or compared to the previous week, month or average for a recent period.

A leading performance indicator is a metric which is suggestive of future performance – think of the amber preceding the green light on traffic lights on a short timescale. The benefit of leading indicators is that they enable managers to be proactive in shaping future performance. There tend to be fewer leading performance indicators, but these can be applied to e-commerce:

- *Repeat sales metrics.* If repeat conversion rates are falling or the average time between sales (sales latency) is falling, then these are warning signs of future declining sales volume for which proactive action can be taken, for example through a customer e-mail marketing programme.
- *Customer satisfaction or advocacy ratings such as the Net Promoter Score.* If these are trending downwards or return rates are increasing, this may be a sign of a future decline in repeat sales since more customers are dissatisfied.
- *Sales trends compared to market audience trends.* If, for example, online sales are increasing at a lower rate than overall online audiences for a product category are indicated, for example through panel data, Hitwise or searches in particular categories, then this is a warning sign that needs to be acted upon.

**Leading performance indicator**
A measure which is suggestive of future performance and so can be used to take proactive action to shape future performance.

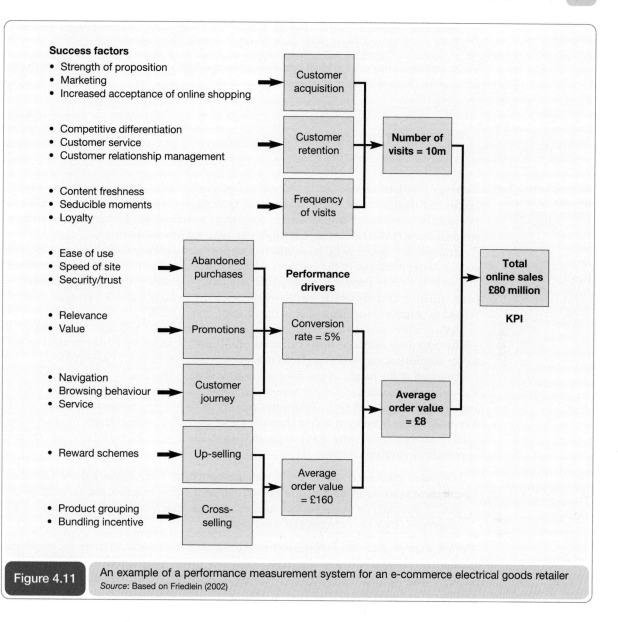

**Figure 4.11** An example of a performance measurement system for an e-commerce electrical goods retailer
*Source*: Based on Friedlein (2002)

The balanced scorecard has become a popular framework because it includes a combination of leading and lagging indicators rather than focusing on lagging indicators alone, as many performance dashboards do. The balanced scorecard seeks to measure innovation and learning as leading indicators and these can also be applied to e-commerce potentially, for example, time to implement new functionality, staff recruitment and development, although it is difficult to put hard and fast measures next to these.

A **lagging performance indicator** is one where the measure indicates past performance. Lagging indicators enable corrective action to be taken. Some also identify a coincident performance indicator which is more suggestive of current performance. Lagging performance indicators for a transactional retail site include:

**Lagging performance indicator**

A measure which indicates past performance. Corrective action can then be applied to improve performance.

- *Sales volume, revenue and profitability.* These are typically compared against target or previous periods.
- *Cost per acquisition (CPA).* The cost of gaining each new customer will also be compared against target. Variations in trends in CPA for different referrers (traffic sources) and between different product categories can potentially be used as leading indicators.

- *Conversion efficiency metrics.* For an e-commerce site these include process efficiency metrics such as conversion rate, average order and landing page bounce rates.

These lagging indicators are used operationally on a daily or weekly basis so that performance can be diagnosed and reviewed.

## Strategy formulation

**Strategy formulation**
Generation, review and selection of strategies to achieve strategic objectives.

**Strategy formulation** involves the identification of alternative strategies, a review of their merits and then selection of the best candidate strategies. Since the Internet is a relatively new medium, and many companies are developing a strategy for the first time, a range of strategic factors must be considered in order to make the best use of it.

Strategies are agreed to be most effective when they support specific business objectives such as those discussed in the previous section. A useful technique to help align strategies and objectives is to present them together in a table, together with the insight developed from situation analysis which may have informed the strategy. Table 4.7 gives an example related to examples provided earlier in this chapter, on page 228.

In this section we shall cover the main strategic options by defining eight key decisions. In addition to these decisions other examples of different strategic initiatives in areas of customer acquisition, conversion and retention are presented in Table 4.1 (page 203).

Although at the height of the dot-com bubble it was suggested by some commentators that companies should entirely re-invent themselves, for most companies Internet marketing strategy formulation typically involves making *adjustments* to marketing strategy to take advantage of the benefits of online channels rather than wholesale changes. Michael Porter (2001) attacks those who have suggested that the Internet invalidates well-known approaches to strategy. He says:

> Many have assumed that the Internet changes everything, rendering all the old rules about companies and competition obsolete. That may be a natural reaction, but it is a dangerous one . . . [resulting in] decisions that have eroded the attractiveness of their industries and undermined their own competitive advantages.

The key strategic decisions for e-marketing are the same as strategic decisions for traditional marketing. They involve selecting target customer groups and specifying how to deliver value to these groups. Segmentation, targeting, differentiation and positioning are all key to effective digital marketing.

For us, the main thrust of Internet marketing strategy is taking the right decisions on the selective targeting of customer groups and different forms of value delivery for online channels. But rather than selective development of online propositions, a common strategic option is to replicate existing offline segmentation, targeting, differentiation and positioning in the online channels. While this is a relatively easy strategic approach to implement, the company is likely to lose market share relative to more nimble competitors that modify their approach for online channels. An example of where companies have followed a 'do-nothing strategy' is grocery shopping where some have not rolled out home shopping to all parts of the country or do not offer the service at all. These supermarkets will lose customers to the most enthusiastic adopters of online channels such as Tesco.com and Sainsbury which will be difficult to win back in the future (see Case study 11, page 638 for examples).

As mentioned at the start of the chapter, we should remember that Internet marketing strategy is a channel marketing strategy and it needs to operate in the context of multichannel marketing. It follows that it is important that the Internet marketing strategy should:

- be based on objectives for online contribution of leads and sales for this channel;
- be consistent with the types of customers that use and can be effectively reached through the channel;

| Table 4.7 | An example of the relationship between objectives, strategies and performance indicators |
| --- | --- |

| Objectives | Substantiation (informed by situation analysis or insight, example) | Strategies to achieve goals | Key performance indicators (critical success factors) |
| --- | --- | --- | --- |
| 1 *Acquisition objective.* Acquire 50,000 new online customers this financial year at an average cost per acquisition (CPA) of £30 with an average profitability of 5% | Based on growth forecast based on current sales of 40,000 sales per year, but with incremental sales arising from new affiliate programme and SEO development | Start affiliate marketing programme and improve SEO. Existing media mix based on pay-per-click and display advertising supported by offline media | Overall CPA for online sales<br><br>Incremental number and % of sales from affiliate marketing programme<br><br>Number of strategic keywords ranked for in top positions in natural search results page |
| 2 *Acquisition (or conversion) objective.* Migrate 40% of existing customers to using online 'paperless' bill payment services services and e-mail communications within three years | Extrapolation of current natural migration coupled with increased adoption from offline direct marketing campaign | Direct marketing campaign using direct mail, phone prompts and online persuasion to encourage adoption. Use of incentive to encourage change | Number and percentage of existing customers registering to use online service<br><br>Number and percentage of customers actively using online services at different points after initially registering |
| 3 *Conversion objective.* Increase the average order value of online sales to £42 per customer | Growth estimated based on current AOV of £35 plus model suggesting 20% increase in AOV | Use of new merchandising system to show users related 'next best product' for different product categories | % of site visitors responding to merchandising/ cross-selling messages |
| 4 *Conversion objective.* Increase site conversion rate to 3.2% | Model showing separate increase in conversion for new and existing customers based on strategies shown right | Combination of strategies:<br>• Incentivised e-mail follow-up on checkout abandonments for new customers<br>• Introduction of more competitive pricing strategy on best sellers<br>• AB and multivariate messaging improvement of landing pages<br>• Refinement to quality of traffic purchased through pay-per-click programme | Variations in conversion rates for new and existing customers in different product categories |
| 5 *Retention objective.* Increase annual repeat new customer conversion rate by 20% | Business case based on limited personalisation of offers to encourage repeat purchases via e-mail | • Delivery of personalised product offers by e-mail<br>• 5% second purchase discount voucher | • Increased conversion rate of retention e-mail contact programme<br>• Conversion to sale for second purchase discount campaigns |
| 6 *Growth objective.* Increase new prospects recommended by friends (viral marketing or 'member get member') by 10,000 per annum | Model based on encouraging 2% of customers to recommend friends annually (based on trial scheme) | Supported by direct mail and e-mail recommendation programme | Response rate to direct mail campaign |

- support the customer journey as they select and purchase products using this channel in combination with other channels;
- define a unique, differential proposition for the channel;
- specify how we communicate this proposition to persuade customers to use online services in conjunction with other channels;
- manage the online customer lifecycle through the stages of attracting visitors to the website, converting them to customers and retention and growth.

This said, many of the decisions related to Internet marketing strategy development involve reappraising a company's approach to strategy based on familiar elements of marketing strategy. We will review these decisions:

- Decision 1: Market and product development strategies
- Decision 2: Business and revenue models strategies
- Decision 3: Target marketing strategy
- Decision 4: Positioning and differentiation strategy (including the marketing mix)
- Decision 5: Multichannel distribution strategy
- Decision 6: Multichannel communications strategy
- Decision 7: Online communications mix and budget
- Decision 8: Organisational capabilities (7 S framework).

The first four decisions are concerned with fundamental questions of how an organisation delivers value to customers online and which products are offered to which markets online. The next four decisions are more concerned with the mix of marketing communications used to communicate with customers across multiple channels.

## Decision 1: Market and product development strategies

In Chapter 1, we introduced the Ansoff matrix as a useful analytic tool for assessing online strategies for manufacturers and retailers. This tool is also fundamental to marketing planning and it should be the first decision point because it can help companies think about how online channels can support their marketing objectives, and also suggest innovative use of these channels to deliver new products and more markets (the boxes help stimulate 'out-of-box' thinking which is often missing with Internet marketing strategy). Fundamentally, the market and product development matrix (Figure 4.12) can help identify strategies to grow sales volume through varying what is sold (the product dimension on the horizontal axis of Figure 4.12) and who it is sold to (the market dimension on the vertical axis). Specific objectives need to be set for sales generated via these strategies, so this decision relates closely to that of objective setting. Let us now review these strategies in more detail.

### 1 Market penetration

This strategy involves using digital channels to sell more existing products into existing markets. The Internet has great potential for achieving sales growth or maintaining sales by the market penetration strategy. As a starting point, many companies will use the Internet to help sell existing products into existing markets, although they may miss opportunities indicated by the strategies in other parts of the matrix. Figure 4.12 indicates some of the main ways in which the Internet can be used for market penetration:

- *Market share growth* – companies can compete more effectively online if they have websites that are efficient at converting visitors to sale as explained in Chapter 7, and mastery of the online marketing communications techniques reviewed in Chapter 8, such as search engine marketing, affiliate marketing and online advertising.
- *Customer loyalty improvement* – companies can increase their value to customers and so increase loyalty by migrating existing customers online (see Mini case study 4.3 on page 249)

| | **Market development strategies** | **Diversification strategies** |
|---|---|---|
| **New markets** | Use the Internet for targeting:<br>• New geographic markets<br>• New customer segments | Using the Internet to support:<br>• Diversification into related businesses<br>• Diversification into unrelated businesses<br>• Upstream integration (with suppliers)<br>• Downstream integration (with intermediaries) |
| **Existing markets** | **Market penetration strategies**<br>Use the Internet for:<br>• Market share growth – compete more effectively online<br>• Customer loyalty improvement – migrate existing customers online and add value to existing products, services and brand<br>• Customer value improvement – increase customer profitability by decreasing cost to serve and increase purchase or usage frequency and quantity | **Product development strategies**<br>Use the Internet for:<br>• Adding value to existing products<br>• Developing digital products (new delivery/usage models)<br>• Changing payment models (subscription, per use, bundling)<br>• Increasing product range (especially e-retailers) |

*Market growth* (vertical axis)

*Existing products*                              *New products*

**Product growth**

**Figure 4.12**    Using the Internet to support different organisational growth strategies

by adding value to existing products, services and brand by developing their online value proposition (see Decision 4).

• *Customer value improvement* – the value delivered by customers to the company can be increased by increasing customer profitability by decreasing cost to serve (and so price to customers) and at the same time increasing purchase or usage frequency and quantity. These combined effects should drive up sales. Many companies will offer competitive online prices or discounts to help increase their market share. Approaches to specifying online pricing are covered in Chapter 5.

## 2 Market development

Here online channels are used to sell into new markets, taking advantage of the low cost of advertising internationally without the necessity for a supporting sales infrastructure in the customer's country. The Internet has helped low-cost airlines such as easyJet and Ryanair to enter new markets served by their routes cost-effectively. This is a relatively conservative use of the Internet but is a great opportunity for SMEs to increase exports at a low cost, though it does require overcoming the barriers to exporting.

Existing products can also be sold to new market segments or different types of customers. Virtual inventory enables new offerings to be made available to smaller segment sizes, an approach known as micro-targeting. This may happen simply as a by-product of having a website. For example, RS Components (www.rswww.com), a supplier of a range of MRO (maintenance, repair and operations) items, found that 10% of the web-based sales were to individual consumers rather than traditional business customers. It also uses the website to offer additional facilities for customers placing large orders online. The UK retailer Argos found the opposite was true with 10% of website sales being from businesses when their traditional market was consumer-based. EasyJet also has a section of its website to serve business customers. The Internet may offer further opportunities for selling to market sub-segments that have not been previously targeted. For example, a product sold to large businesses may also appeal to SMEs that they have previously been unable to serve because of the cost of sales via a specialist sales force. Alternatively a product targeted at young people could also appeal to some members of an older audience and vice versa. Many companies have found that the audience and customers of their website are quite different from their traditional audience.

### 3 Product development

The web can be used to add value to or extend existing products for many companies. For example, a car manufacturer can potentially provide car performance and service information via a website. Facilities can be provided to download tailored brochures, book a test drive or tailor features required from a car model. But truly new products or services that can be delivered only by the Internet apply for some types of products. These are typically digital media or information products – for example, online trade magazine *Construction Weekly* has diversified to a B2B portal Construction Plus (www.constructionplus.com) which has new revenue streams. Similarly, music and book publishing companies have found new ways to deliver products through the new development and usage model such as subscription and pay-per-use, as explained in Chapter 5 in the section on the product element of the marketing mix. Retailers can extend their product range and provide new bundling options online also.

### 4 Diversification

In this sector, new products are developed which are sold into new markets. The Internet alone cannot facilitate these high-risk business strategies, but it can facilitate them at lower costs than have previously been possible. The options include:

- *Diversification into related businesses* – for example, a low-cost airline can use the website and customer e-mails to promote travel-related services such as hotel booking, car rental or travel insurance at relatively low costs.
- *Diversification into unrelated businesses* – again the website can be used to promote less-related products to customers, which is the approach used by the Virgin brand, although it is relatively rare.
- *Upstream integration* with suppliers – achieved through data exchange between a manufacturer or retailer and its suppliers to enable a company to take more control of the supply chain.
- *Downstream integration* with intermediaries – again achieved through data exchange with distributors such as online intermediaries.

The benefits and risks of market and product development are highlighted by the creation of **smile** (Figure 4.13), an Internet-specific bank set up by The Co-operative Bank in the UK. **smile** opened for business in October 1999 and in its first year added 200,000 customers at a rate of 20,000 per month. Significantly, 80% of these customers were market development in the context of the parent, since they were not existing Co-operative Bank customers and typically belonged to a higher-income segment.

The risks of the new approach to banking were highlighted by the cost of innovation; with it being estimated that in its first year, the creation and promotion of **smile** increased overall costs at the Co-operative Bank by 5%. However, within five years **smile** was on target, profitable and growing strongly.

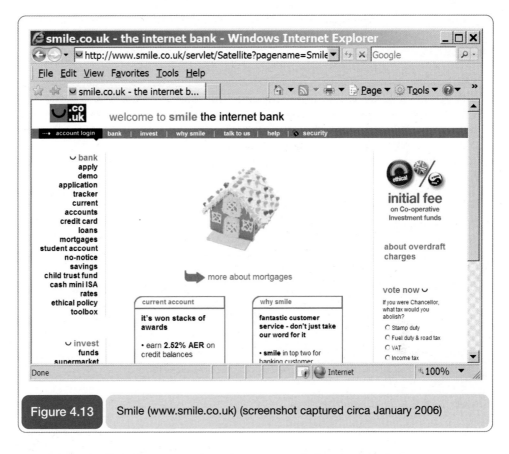

| Figure 4.13 | Smile (www.smile.co.uk) (screenshot captured circa January 2006) |

## Decision 2: Business and revenue models strategies

**Business model**
A summary of how a company will generate revenue, identifying its product offering, value-added services, revenue sources and target customers.

**Revenue model**
Describes methods of generating income for an organisation.

A further aspect of Internet strategy formulation closely related to product development options is the review of opportunities from new business models and revenue models, (first introduced in Chapter 2 and discussed further in the next chapter in the sections on product and price). Evaluating new models is important since if companies do not review opportunities to innovate then competitors and new entrants certainly will. Andy Grove of Intel famously said: 'Only the paranoid will survive', alluding to the need to review new revenue opportunities and competitor innovations. A willingness to test and experiment with new business models is also required. Dell is another example of a technology company that regularly reviews and modifies its business model as shown in Mini case study 4.1 'Innovation in the Dell business model'. Companies at the bleeding edge of technology such as Google and Yahoo! constantly innovate through acquiring other companies and internal research and development (witness Google Labs (http://labs.google.com) and Yahoo! Research (http://research.yahoo.com)). Case study 4 on Tesco.com at the end of this chapter also highlights innovation in the Tesco business model facilitated through online channels.

To sound a note of caution, flexibility in the business model should not be to the company's detriment through losing focus on the core business. A survey of CEOs of leading UK Internet companies such as Autonomy, Freeserve, NetBenefit and QXL (Durlacher, 2000) indicates that although flexibility is useful this may not apply to business models. The report states:

> A widely held belief in the new economy in the past has been that change and flexibility is good, but these interviews suggest that it is actually those companies who have stuck to a single business model that have been to date more successful . . . CEOs were not moving far from their starting vision, but that it was in the marketing, scope and partnerships where new economy companies had to be flexible.

| Mini Case Study 4.2 | Innovation in the Dell business model |
|---|---|

One example of how companies can review and revise their business model is provided by Dell Computers. Dell gained early-mover advantage in the mid-1990s when it became one of the first companies to offer PCs for sale online. Its sales of PCs and peripherals grew from the mid-1990s with online sales of $1 million per day to 2000 sales of $50 million per day. Based on this success it has looked at new business models it can use in combination with its powerful brand to provide new services to its existing customer base and also to generate revenue through new customers. In September 2000, Dell announced plans to become a supplier of IT consulting services through linking with enterprise resource planning specialists such as software suppliers, systems integrators and business consulting firms. This venture will enable the facility of Dell's PremierPages to be integrated into the procurement component of ERP systems such as SAP and Baan, thus avoiding the need for rekeying and reducing costs.

In a separate initiative, Dell launched a B2B marketplace (formerly www.dellmarketplace.com) aimed at discounted office goods and services procurements including PCs, peripherals, software, stationery and travel. This strategic option did not prove sustainable.

More recently, in 2007, Dell launched Ideastorm (www.ideastorm.com, see Figure 4.14), a site encouraging user participation where anyone can suggest new products and features which can be voted on, rather like the way stories are rated in Digg (www.digg.com). Importantly, Dell 'close the loop' through a separate *Ideas in Action* section where they update consumers on actions taken by the company. As well as improvements to customer service, they have explained how they have introduced systems with a non-Windows Linux operating system in response to suggestions on Ideastorm.

| Figure 4.14 | Dell Ideastorm (www.ideastorm.com) © 2008 Dell Inc. All Rights Reserved. |
|---|---|

Furthermore, where companies including transactional sites such as Amazon or Lastminute, have introduced advertising as part of their revenue model, the amount of revenue generated tends to be low compared to overall revenue (although it may be used as leverage for other co-branding work) or insight generated about customer response.

So with all strategy options, managers should also consider the 'do-nothing option'. Here, a company will not risk a new business model, but adopt a 'wait-and-see' or 'fast-follower' approach to see how competitors perform, and then respond rapidly if the new business model proves sustainable.

Finally, we can note that companies can make less radical changes to their revenue models through the Internet which are less far-reaching, but may nevertheless be worthwhile. For example:

- Transactional e-commerce sites (e.g. Tesco.com and Lastminute.com) can sell advertising space or run co-branded promotions on site or through their e-mail newsletters or lists to sell access to their audience to third parties.
- Retailers or media owners can sell-on white-labelled services through their online presence such as ISP, e-mail services or photo-sharing services.
- Companies can gain commission through selling products which are complementary (but not competitive to their own). For example, a publisher can sell its books through an affiliate arrangement through an e-retailer.

## Decision 3: Target marketing strategy

Deciding on which markets to target is a key strategic consideration for Internet marketing strategy in the same way it is key to marketing strategy. We will see that a company's web presence and e-mail marketing enables them to target more focused audiences than may be possible with other channels. **Target marketing strategy** involves the four stages shown in Figure 4.15, but the most important decisions are:

- *Segmentation/targeting strategy* – a company's online customers will often have different demographic characteristics, needs and behaviours from its offline customers. It follows that different approaches to segmentation may be required and specific segments may need to be selectively targeted through online media channels, the company website or e-mail communications. As we will see, persona development and lifecycle targeting are common approaches for online targeting.
- *Positioning/differentiation strategy* – competitors' product and service offerings will often differ in the online environment. Developing an appropriate online value proposition as described below is an important aspect of this strategy. However, there should also be clarity on the core brand proposition.

In an Internet context, organisations need to target those customer groupings with the highest propensity to access, choose and buy online.

The first stage in Figure 4.15 is **segmentation**. Segmentation involves understanding the groupings of customers in the target market in order to understand their needs and potential as a revenue source, so as to develop a strategy to satisfy these segments while maximising revenue. Dibb *et al.* (2001) say that:

> *market segmentation is the key of robust marketing strategy development . . . it involves more than simply grouping customers into segments . . . identifying segments, targeting, positioning and developing a differential advantage over rivals is the foundation of marketing strategy.*

In an Internet marketing planning context, market segments will be analysed to assess:

- their current market size or value, future projections of size and the organisation's current and future market share within the segment;

- competitor market shares within the segment;
- needs of each segment, in particular, unmet needs;
- organisation and competitor offers and propositions
- Is for each segment across all aspects of the buying process;
- usage of the site and conversion to action through web analytics. Options for segmenting online customers by activity levels are covered in Chapter 6.

Options for segmenting site visitors through web analytics systems are covered in Chapter 10. It is instructive to segment by referral source, first against returning visitors and the type of content accessed.

Stage 2 in Figure 4.15 is target marketing. Here we select segments for targeting online that are most attractive in terms of growth and profitability. These may be similar or different compared with groups targeted offline. Some examples of customer segments that are targeted online include:

- *the most profitable customers* – using the Internet to provide tailored offers to the top 20% of customers by profit may result in more repeat business and cross-sales;
- *larger companies (B2B)* – an extranet could be produced to service these customers and increase their loyalty;
- *smaller companies (B2B)* – large companies are traditionally serviced through sales representatives and account managers, but smaller companies may not warrant the expense of account managers. However, the Internet can be used to reach smaller companies more cost effectively. The number of smaller companies that can be reached in this way may be significant, so although the individual revenue of each one is relatively small, the collective revenue achieved through Internet servicing can be large;
- *particular members of the buying unit (B2B)* – the site should provide detailed information for different interests which supports the buying decision, for example technical docu-

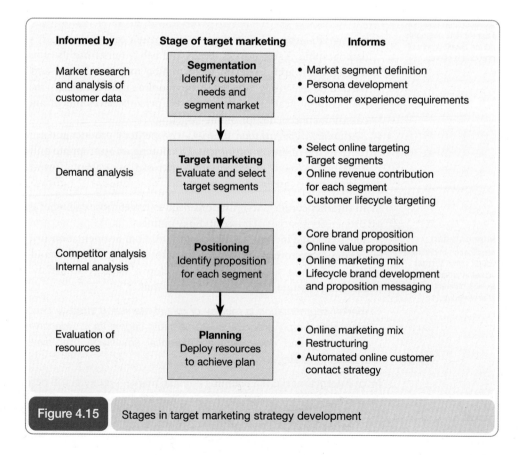

| Informed by | Stage of target marketing | Informs |
|---|---|---|
| Market research and analysis of customer data | **Segmentation** Identify customer needs and segment market | • Market segment definition<br>• Persona development<br>• Customer experience requirements |
| Demand analysis | **Target marketing** Evaluate and select target segments | • Select online targeting<br>• Target segments<br>• Online revenue contribution for each segment<br>• Customer lifecycle targeting |
| Competitor analysis Internal analysis | **Positioning** Identify proposition for each segment | • Core brand proposition<br>• Online value proposition<br>• Online marketing mix<br>• Lifecycle brand development and proposition messaging |
| Evaluation of resources | **Planning** Deploy resources to achieve plan | • Online marketing mix<br>• Restructuring<br>• Automated online customer contact strategy |

**Figure 4.15**    Stages in target marketing strategy development

mentation for users of products, information on savings from e-procurement for IS or purchasing managers, and information to establish the credibility of the company for decision makers;

- *customers that are difficult to reach using other media* – an insurance company looking to target younger drivers could use the web as a vehicle for this;
- *customers that are brand-loyal* – services to appeal to brand loyalists can be provided to support them in their role as advocates of a brand, as suggested by Aaker and Joachimsthaler (2000);
- *customers that are not brand-loyal* – conversely, incentives, promotion and a good level of service quality could be provided by the website to try and retain such customers.

Such groupings can be targeted online by using navigation options to different content groupings such that visitors *self-identify*. This is the approach used as the main basis for navigation on the Dell site (Figure 4.16) and has potential for subsidiary navigation on other sites. Dell targets by geography and then tailors the types of consumers or businesses according to country, the US Dell site having the most options. Other alternatives are to set up separate sites for different audiences – for example, Dell Premier is targeted at purchasing and IT staff in larger organisations. Once customers are registered on a site, profiling information in a database can be used to send tailored e-mail messages to different segments, as we explain in the Euroffice example in Mini case study 4.2 on page 243.

The most sophisticated segmentation and targeting schemes are often used by e-retailers, which have detailed customer profiling information and purchase history data and seek to increase customer lifetime value through encouraging increased use of online services through time. However, the general principles of this approach can also be used by other types of companies online. The segmentation and targeting approach used by e-retailers is

**Figure 4.16**    Dell Singapore site segmentation
*Source*: http://www.ap.dell.com/content/default.aspx?c=sg&1=en&s=gen. © 2008 Dell Inc. All Rights Reserved.

based on five main elements which in effect are layered on top of each other. The number of options used, and so the sophistication of the approach will depend on resources available, technology capabilities and opportunities afforded by the following.

### 1 Identify customer lifecycle groups

Figure 4.17 illustrates this approach. As visitors use online services they can potentially pass through seven or more stages. Once companies have defined these groups and set up the customer relationship management infrastructure to categorise customers in this way, they can then deliver targeted messages, either by personalised on-site messaging or through e-mails that are triggered automatically by different rules. First-time visitors can be identified by whether they have a cookie placed on their PC. Once visitors have registered, they can be tracked through the remaining stages. Two particularly important groups are customers that have purchased one or more times. For many e-retailers, encouraging customers to move from the first purchase to the second purchase and then on to the third purchase is a key challenge. Specific promotions can be used to encourage further purchases. Similarly, once customers become inactive (i.e. they have not purchased for a defined period such as three months) further follow-ups are required.

### 2 Identify customer profile characteristics

This is a traditional segmentation based on the type of customer. For B2C e-retailers this will include age, sex and geography. For B2B companies, it will include size of company and the industry sector or application they operate in.

### 3 Identify behaviour in response and purchase

As customers progress through the lifecycle shown in Figure 4.17, by analysis of their database the marketer will be able to build up a detailed response and purchase history which considers the details of recency, frequency, monetary value and category of products purchased. This approach, which is known as RFM or FRAC analysis, is reviewed in more detail in Chapter 6. See Case study 4 (page **267**) for how Tesco targets its online customers.

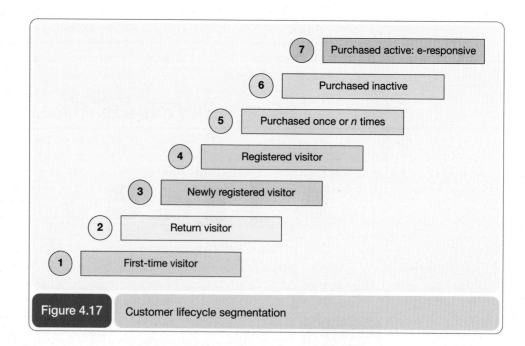

**Figure 4.17**   Customer lifecycle segmentation

## 4 Identify multichannel behaviour (channel preference)

Regardless of the enthusiasm of the company for online channels, some customers will prefer using online channels and others will prefer traditional channels. This will, to an extent, be indicated by RFM and response analysis since customers with a preference for online channels will be more responsive and will make more purchases online. Drawing a channel chain (Figure 2.32) for different customers is useful to help understand this. It is also useful to have a flag within the database which indicates the customer's channel preference and, by implication, the best channel to target them by. Customers who prefer online channels can be targeted mainly by online communications such as e-mail, while those who prefer traditional channels can be targeted by traditional communications such as direct mail or phone.

## 5 Tone and style preference

In a similar manner to channel preference, customers will respond differently to different types of message. Some may like a more rational appeal, in which case a detailed e-mail explaining the benefits of the offer may work best. Others will prefer an emotional appeal based on images and with warmer, less formal copy. Sophisticated companies will test for this in customers or infer it using profile characteristics and response behaviour and then develop different creative treatments accordingly. Companies that use polls can potentially use this to infer style preferences. To summarise this section, read Mini case study 4.3 which illustrates the combination of these different forms of communication.

| Mini Case Study 4.3 | Euroffice segment office supplies purchasers using a 'touch marketing funnel' approach |
| --- | --- |

Euroffice (www.euroffice.co.uk) targets small and medium-sized companies. According to George Karibian, CEO, 'getting the message across effectively required segmentation' to engage different people in different ways. The office sector is fiercely competitive with relatively little loyalty since company purchasers will often simply buy on price. However, targeted incentives can be used to reward or encourage buyers' loyalty. Rather than manually developing campaigns for each segment, which is time-consuming, Euroffice mainly uses an automated event-based targeting approach based on the system identifying the stage at which a consumer is in the lifecycle, i.e. how many products they have purchased and the types of product within their purchase history. Karibian calls this a '*touch marketing funnel*' approach, i.e. the touch strategy is determined by customer segmentation and response. Three main groups of customers are identified in the lifecycle and these are broken down further according to purchase category. Also layered on this segmentation is breakdown into buyer type – are they a small home-user, an operations manager at a mid-size company or a purchasing manager at a large company? Each will respond to different promotions.

The first group, at the top of the funnel and the largest, are '*Group 1: Trial customers*' who have made one or two purchases. For the first group, Euroffice believes that creating impulse buying through price promotions is most important. These will be based on categories purchased in the past. The second group, '*Group 2: The nursery*', have made three to eight purchases. A particular issue, as with many e-retailers, is encouraging customers from the third to fourth purchase – there is a more significant drop-out at this point which the company uses marketing to control. Karibian says: 'When they get to Group 2: it's about creating frequency of purchase to ensure they don't forget you'. Euroffice sends a printed catalogue to Group 2 separately from their merchandise as a reminder about the company. The final group, '*Group 3: Key accounts*', have made nine or more orders. They also tend to have a higher basket value. These people are 'the Crown Jewels' and will spend an average of £135 per order compared to an average of £55 for trial customers. They have a 90% probability of re-ordering within a six-month period. For this group, tools have been developed on the site to make it easier for them to shop. The intention is that these customers find these tools help them in making their orders and they become reliant on them, so achieving 'soft lock-in'.

| Figure 4.18 | Euroffice e-mail (www.euroffice.co.uk) |

*Source*: Adapted from the company website press releases and *Revolution* (2005a)

## Decision 4: Positioning and differentiation strategy (including the marketing mix)

**Positioning**

Customers' perception of the product offer relative to those of competitors.

Stage 3 in Figure 4.15 is **positioning**. Deise *et al.* (2000) suggest that in an online context, companies can position their products relative to competitor offerings according to four main variables: product quality, service quality, price and fulfilment time. They suggest it is useful to review these through an equation of how they combine to influence customer perceptions of value or brand:

$$Customer\ value\ (brand\ perception) = \frac{product\ quality \times service\ quality}{price \times fulfilment\ time}$$

Strategies should review the extent to which increases in product and service quality can be balanced against variations in price and fulfilment time. Chaston (2000) argues that there are four options for strategic focus to position a company in the online marketplace. It is evident that these are related to the different elements of Deise *et al.* (2000). He says that online these should build on existing strengths, and can use the online facilities to enhance the positioning as follows:

- *Product performance excellence.* Enhance by providing online product customisation.
- *Price performance excellence.* Use the facilities of the Internet to offer favourable pricing to loyal customers or to reduce prices where demand is low (for example, British Midland Airlines uses auctions to sell under-used capacity on flights).
- *Transactional excellence.* A site such as that of software and hardware e-tailer dabs.com offers transactional excellence through combining pricing information with dynamic availability information on products, listing number in stock, number on order and when they are expected.
- *Relationship excellence.* Personalisation features to enable customers to review sales order history and place repeat orders. An example is RS Components (www.rswww.com).

These positioning options have much in common with Porter's generic competitive strategies of cost leadership or differentiation in a broad market and a market segmentation approach focusing on a more limited target market (Porter, 1980). Porter has been criticised because many commentators believe that to remain competitive it is necessary to combine excellence in all of these areas. It can be suggested that the same is true for sell-side e-commerce. These are not mutually exclusive strategic options, rather they are prerequisites for success. Customers will be unlikely to judge on a single criterion, but on the balance of multiple criteria. This is the view of Kim *et al.* (2004) who concluded that for online businesses 'integrated strategies that combine elements of cost leadership and differentiation will outperform cost leadership or differentiation strategies'. It can be seen that Porter's original criteria are similar to the strategic positioning options of Chaston (2000) and Deise *et al.* (2000). Figure 4.19 summarises the positioning options described in this section, showing the emphasis on the three main variables for online differentiation – price, product and relationship-building services. The diagram can be used to show the mix of the three elements of positionings. EasyJet has an emphasis on price performance, but with a component of product innovation. Amazon is not positioned on price performance, but rather on relationship building and product innovation. We will see in Chapter 5, in the section on price, that although it would be expected that pricing is a key aspect determining online retail sales, there are other factors about a retail brand, such as familiarity, trust and service, which are also important.

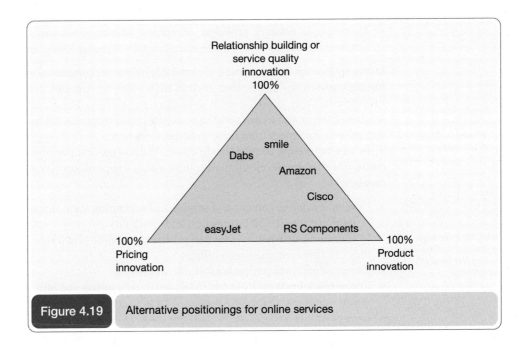

| Figure 4.19 | Alternative positionings for online services |

An alternative perspective on positioning strategies has been suggested by Picardi (2000). The three main approaches suggested are generic:

1 *Attack e-tailing.* As suggested by the name, this is an aggressive competitive approach that involves frequent comparison with competitors' prices and then matching or bettering them. This approach is important on the Internet because of the transparency of pricing and availability of information made possible through shopping comparison sites such as PriceRunner (www.pricerunner.com) and Kelkoo (www.kelkoo.com).

2 *Defend e-tailing.* This is a strategic approach that traditional companies can use in response to 'attack e-tailing'. It involves differentiation based on other aspects of brand beyond price. It will often be used by multichannel e-retailers such as Debenhams (www.debenhams.com) and John Lewis (www.johnlewis.com). Such retailers may not want to eat into sales from their high-street stores, or may believe that the strength of their brands is such that they do not need to offer differential online prices. They may use a mixed approach with some 'attack e-tailing' approaches such as competitive pricing on the most popular items or special promotions.

3 *E2E (end-to-end) integration.* This is an efficiency strategy that uses the Internet to decrease costs, and to increase product quality and shorten delivery times. This strategy is achieved by moving towards an automated supply chain and internal value chain. This approach is used by e-retailers such as dabs.com (www.dabs.com) and E-buyer (www.ebuyer.com).

## The online value proposition

The aim of positioning is to develop a **differential advantage** over rivals' products as perceived by the customer. Many examples of differentiated online offerings are based on the lower costs in acquiring and retaining online customers, which are then passed on to customers – to do this requires the creation of a different profit centre for e-commerce operations. Examples include:

- *Retailers* offering lower prices online. Examples: Tesco.com (price promotions on selected products), Comet (discounts relative to in-store pricing on some products).
- *Airlines* offering lower-cost flights for online bookings. Examples: easyJet, Ryanair, BA.
- *Financial services companies* offering higher interest rates on savings products and lower interest rates on credit products such as credit cards and loans. Examples: Nationwide, Alliance and Leicester.
- *Mobile phone* network providers or utilities offering lower-cost tariffs or discounts for customers accounts who are managed online without paper billing. Examples: $O_2$, British Gas.

Other options for differentiation are available online for companies where their products are not appropriate for sale online, such as high-value or complex products or FMCG (fast-moving consumer goods) brands sold through retailers. These companies can use online services, content and tools to add value to the brand or product through providing different services or experiences from those available elsewhere.

In an e-marketing context the differential advantage and positioning can be clarified and communicated by developing an **online value proposition (OVP)**. Developing an OVP, involves:

- Developing online content and service and explaining them through messages which:
  - reinforce core brand proposition and credibility
  - communicate what a visitor can get from an online brand that ...
- they can't get from the brand offline;
- they can't get from competitors or intermediaries.
- Communicating these messages to all appropriate online and offline customers with touch points in different levels of detail from straplines to more detailed content on the website or in print.

Communicating the OVP on the site can help create a customer-centric website. Look at how Autotrader does this for different types of visitors and services in Figure 4.20. Virgin Wines uses an OVP to communicate its service promise as follows:

- And what if . . . *You are out during the day*? We promise that our drivers will find a safe place to leave your wine; but if it does get stolen, we just replace it.
- *You find it cheaper elsewhere*? We will refund the difference if you are lucky enough to find a wine cheaper elsewhere.
- *You live somewhere obscure*? We deliver anywhere in the UK, including Northern Ireland, the Highlands and Islands, and the Scilly Isles for £5.99.
- *You are in a hurry*? We deliver within 7 days, or your delivery is free.

Many strategic planning decisions are based around the OVP and the quality of online customer experience delivered by a company. Interactive Web 2.0 features can be particularly important for transactional sites in that they may enhance the user's experience and so encourage conversion and repeat sales. Examples of how companies have developed their OVP through interactive features include customer reviews and ratings; podcast product

Figure 4.20    The Autotrader site (www.autotrader.co.uk) clearly communicates its proposition

reviews, a blog with customer comments enabled; buyers guide and video reviews. Figure 4.21 gives one example of a company that has put Web 2.0 customer reviews, including the capability for customers to upload videos and photos, at the heart of its OVP.

Mini case study 4.3 'BA asks 'Have you clicked yet?'[44] gives an example of an ad campaign to communicate an OVP. This is a good example since it explains the benefits of online services and e-mail communications and also positions these benefits within the customer buying process.

Varianini and Vaturi (2000) conducted a review of failures in B2C dot-com companies in order to highlight lessons that can be learned. They believe that many of the problems have resulted from a failure to apply established marketing orientation approaches. They summarise their guidelines as follows:

| Figure 4.21 | Firebox (www.firebox.com) proposition |

*First identify customer needs and define a distinctive value proposition that will meet them, at a profit. The value proposition must then be delivered through the right product and service and the right channels and it must be communicated consistently. The ultimate aim is to build a strong, long-lasting brand that delivers value to the company marketing it.*

Likewise, Agrawal *et al.* (2001) suggest that the success of leading e-commerce companies is often due to matching value propositions to segments successfully.

McDonald and Wilson (2002) suggest that to determine a value proposition, marketers should first assess changes in an industry's structure (see Chapter 2) since channel innovations will influence which proposition is possible. They then suggest sub-processes of first setting objectives for market share, volume or value by each segment and then defining the value to be delivered to the customer in terms of the marketing mix. They suggest starting with defining the price and value proposition using the 4 Cs and then defining marketing strategies using the 4 Ps (see Chapter 5).

| Mini Case Study 4.4 | BA asks 'Have you clicked yet?' |
| --- | --- |

In 2004, British Airways launched online services which allowed customers to take control of the booking process, so combining new services with reduced costs. BA decided to develop a specific online ad campaign to create awareness and encourage usage of its Online Value Proposition (Figure 4.22). BA's UK marketing manager said about the objective:

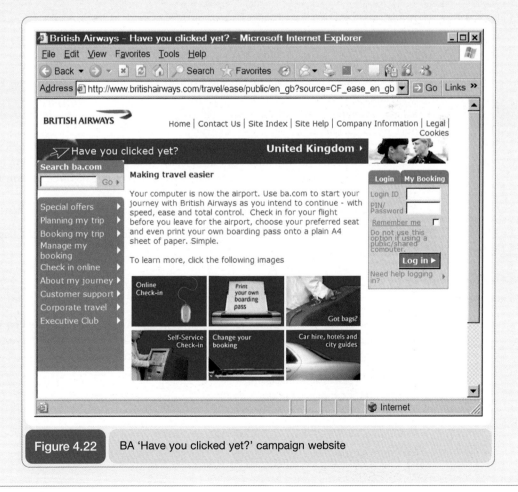

| Figure 4.22 | BA 'Have you clicked yet?' campaign website |
| --- | --- |

*British Airways is leading the way in innovating technology to simplify our customer's journey through the airport. The role of this campaign was to give a strong message about what is now available online, over and above booking tickets.*

The aim was to develop a campaign that educated and changed the way in which BA's customers behave before, during and after their travel. The campaign focused on the key benefits of the new online services – speed, ease and convenience – and promoted the ability to check in online and print out a boarding pass. The two main target audiences were quite different – early-adopters and those who use the web occasionally but don't rely on it. Early-adopters were targeted on sites such as T3.co.uk, Newscientist.com and DigitalHomeMag.com. Occasional users were reached through ads on sites such as JazzFM.com, Vogue.com and Menshealth.com.

Traditional media that were used to deliver the 'Have you clicked yet?' message included print, TV and outdoor media. The print ad copy, which details the OVP, was:

*Your computer is now the airport. Check in online, print your own boarding pass, choose your seat, change your booking card and even find hire cars and hotels. Simple.*

A range of digital media were used, including ATMs, outdoor LCD transvision screens such as those in London rail stations (which included Bluecasting where commuters could receive a video on their Bluetooth enabled mobile phone) and digital escalator panels. More than 650,000 consumers interacted with the ATM screen creative. Online ads included overlays and skyscrapers which showed a consumer at his computer, printing out a ticket and walking across the screen to the airport. Such rich-media campaigns generated 17% click-through and 15% interaction.

Source: *Revolution* (2005b)

Having a clear online value proposition has several benefits:

- it helps distinguish an e-commerce site from its competitors (this should be a website design objective);
- it helps provide a focus to marketing efforts so that company staff are clear about the purpose of the site;
- if the proposition is clear it can be used for PR, and word-of-mouth recommendations may be made about the company. For example, the clear proposition of Amazon on its site is that prices are reduced by up to 40% and that a wide range of three million titles are available;
- it can be linked to the normal product propositions of a company or its product.

We look further into options for varying the proposition and marketing mix in Chapter 5.

| Activity 4.4 | Online value proposition |
|---|---|

Visit the websites of the following companies and, in one or two sentences each, summarise their Internet value proposition. You should also explain how they use the content of the website to indicate their value proposition to customers.

- Tektronix (www.tektronix.com)
- Handbag.com (www.handbag.com)
- Harrods (www.harrods.com)
- Guinness (www.guinness.com)

# Decision 5: Multichannel distribution strategy

**Multichannel prioritisation**

Assesses the strategic significance of the Internet relative to other communications channels and then deploys resources to integrate with marketing channels.

**Customer communications channels**

The range of media used to communicate directly with a customer.

**Distribution channels**

The mechanism by which products are directed to customers either through intermediaries or directly.

**Clicks and mortar**

A business combining an online and offline presence.

**Clicks-only or Internet pureplay**

An organisation with principally an online presence. It does not operate a mail-order operation or promote inbound phone orders.

Decisions 5 and 6 relate to **multichannel prioritisation** which assesses the strategic significance of the Internet relative to other communications channels. In making this prioritisation it is helpful to distinguish between **customer communications channels** and **distribution channels**. Customer communications channels, which we review as Decision 6, refer to how an organisation influences its customers to select products and suppliers through the different stages of the buying process through inbound and outbound communications. For a retailer, it refers to selection of the mix of channels such as in-store, inbound contact-centre, web and outbound direct messaging used to communicate with prospects and customers.

'Distribution channels' refers to flow of products from a manufacturer or service provider to the end customer. These may be direct to consumer channels or, more often, intermediaries such as retailers are involved. Internet distribution channel priorities have been summarised by Gulati and Garino (2000) as 'getting the right mix of bricks and clicks'. This expression has been used to refer to traditional 'bricks and mortar' enterprises with a physical presence, but limited Internet presence. In the UK, an example of a 'bricks and mortar' store would be the bookseller Waterstones (www.waterstones.co.uk), which when it ventured online became '**clicks and mortar**'. It initially followed a strategy of creating its own online presence, but now delivers its online channel through a partnering arrangement based on the Amazon.com infrastructure, which is an example of the partnering strategy suggested by Gulati and Garino (2000). **Internet pureplays**, or 'e-businesses' such as dabs.com, which operate solely through their online representation are relatively rare. Dabs.com, which is featured in Case study 7 (page **436**), uses its website and e-mail marketing as the primary interactions with the customers. Other e-retailers such as Virgin Wines.com make more use of phone contact and physical mail with customers. Even dabs.com uses these channels where appropriate – for large-volume business customers.

The general options for the mix of 'bricks and clicks' are shown in Figure 4.23. The online revenue contribution estimate is informed by the customer demand analysis of propensity

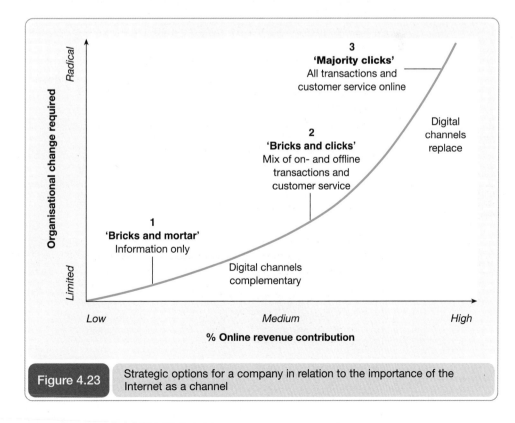

| Figure 4.23 | Strategic options for a company in relation to the importance of the Internet as a channel |

to purchase a particular type of product. A similar diagram was produced by de Kare-Silver (2000) who suggested that strategic e-commerce alternatives for companies should be selected according to the percentage of the target market using the channel and the commitment of the company. The idea is that the commitment should mirror the readiness of consumers to use the new medium. If the objective is to achieve a high online revenue contribution of greater than 70% then this will require fundamental change for the company to transform to a 'bricks and clicks' or 'clicks-only' company.

Kumar (1999) suggests that a company should decide whether the Internet will primarily *complement* the company's other channels or primarily *replace* other channels. Clearly, if it is believed that the Internet will primarily replace other channels, then it is important to invest in the promotion and infrastructure to achieve this. This is a key decision as the company is essentially deciding whether the Internet is 'just another communications and/or sales channel' or whether it will fundamentally change the way it communicates and sells to its customers.

Figure 4.24 summarises the main decisions on which a company should base its commitment to the Internet. Kumar (1999) suggests that replacement is most likely to happen when:

- customer access to the Internet is high;
- the Internet can offer a better value proposition than other media;
- the product can be delivered over the Internet (it can be argued that this condition is not essential for replacement, so it is not shown in the figure);
- the product can be standardised (the user does not usually need to view to purchase).

Only if all four conditions are met will there primarily be a replacement effect. The fewer conditions met, the more likely it is that there will be a complementary effect.

From an analysis such as that in Figure 4.24 it should be possible to state whether the company strategy should be directed as a complementary or as a replacement scenario. As mentioned in relation to the question of the contribution of the Internet to its business, the company should repeat the analysis for different product segments and different markets. It will then be possible to state the company's overall commitment to the Internet. If the future strategic importance of the Internet is high, with replacement likely, then a significant

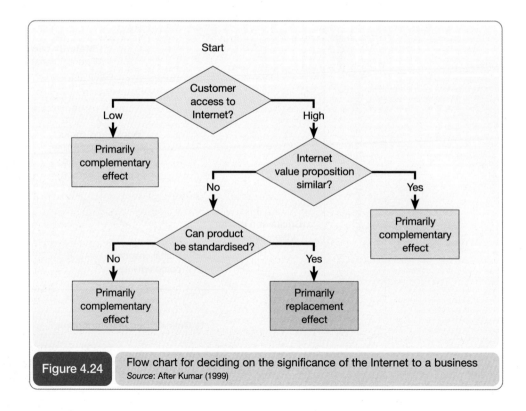

**Figure 4.24** — Flow chart for deciding on the significance of the Internet to a business
*Source*: After Kumar (1999)

investment needs to be made in the Internet, and a company's mission needs to be directed towards replacement. If the future strategic importance of the Internet is low then this still needs to be recognised and appropriate investment made.

Poon and Joseph (2000) have suggested that frameworks assessing the suitability of the Internet for sales, based solely on product characteristics are likely to be misleading. They surveyed Australian firms to assess the importance of product characteristics in determining online sales. They found that there was not a significant difference between physical goods and standardised digital goods such as software.

They conclude:

> *Although it is logical to believe that firms who are selling search goods of low tangibility have a natural advantage in Internet commerce, it is important to understand that all products have some degree of tangibility and a mixture of search and experience components. The only difference is the relative ratio of such characteristics. For example, a pair of jeans is an experience good with high tangibility, but the size and fit can be easily described using standard descriptions. Similarly, a piece of software is a search good with low tangibility, but the functionality of a software package cannot be fully appreciated without 'test-driving' a beta release.*

### Changes to marketplace structure

Strategies to take advantage of changes in marketplace structure should also be developed. These options are created through disintermediation and reintermediation (Chapter 2) within a marketplace. The strategic options for the sell-side downstream channels which have been discussed in Chapter 2 are:

- disintermediation (sell direct);
- create new online intermediary (countermediation);
- partner with new online or existing intermediaries;
- do nothing!

Prioritising strategic partnerships as part of the move from a value chain to a value network should also occur as part of this decision. For all options, tactics will be needed to manage the channel conflicts that may occur as a result of restructuring.

### Technological integration

To achieve strategic Internet marketing goals, B2B organisations will have to plan for integration with customers' and suppliers' systems. Chaffey (2008) describes how a supplier may have to support technical integration with a range of customer e-procurement needs, for example:

- *Links with single customers.* Organisations will decide whether a single customer is large enough to enforce such linkage. For example, supermarkets often insist that their suppliers trade with them electronically. However, the supplier may be faced with the cost of setting up different types of links with different supermarket customers.
- *Links with intermediaries.* Organisations have to assess which are the dominant intermediaries, such as B2B marketplaces or exchanges, and then evaluate whether the trade resulting from the intermediary is sufficient to set up links with this intermediary.

## Decision 6: Multichannel communications strategy

As part of creating an Internet marketing strategy, it is vital to define how the Internet integrates with other inbound communications channels used to process customer enquiries and orders and with outbound channels which use direct marketing to encourage retention and growth or deliver customer service messages. For a retailer, these channels include in-store, contact-centre, web and outbound direct messaging used to communicate with prospects and customers. Some of these channels may be broken down further into different media – for example, the contact-centre may involve inbound phone enquiries, e-mail enquiries or real-time chat. Outbound direct messaging may involve direct mail, e-mail media or web-based personalisation. Mini case study 2.3 'Lexus assesses multichannel experience consistency' on page 82 shows the importance of the quality of multiple channels in influencing customer experiences.

The multichannel communications strategy must review different types of customer contact with the company and then determine how online channels will best support these channels. The main types of customer contact and corresponding strategies will typically be:

- inbound sales-related enquiries (customer acquisition or conversion strategy);
- inbound customer-support enquiries (customer service strategy);
- outbound contact strategy (customer retention and development strategy).

For each of these strategies, the most efficient mix and sequence of media to support the business objectives must be determined. Typically the short-term objective will be conversion to outcome such as sale or satisfactorily resolved service enquiry in the shortest possible time with the minimum cost. However, longer-term objectives of customer loyalty and growth also need to be considered. If the initial experience is efficient, but unsatisfactory to the customer, then they may not remain a customer!

The multichannel communications strategy must assess the balance between:

- *customer channel preferences* – some customers will prefer online channels for product selection or making enquiries while others will prefer traditional channels;
- *organisation channel preferences* – traditional channels tend to be more expensive to service than digital channels for the company; however, they may not be as effective in converting the customer to sale (for example, a customer who responds to a TV ad to buy car insurance may be more likely to purchase if they enquire by phone in comparison to web enquiry) or in developing customer loyalty (the personal touch available through face-to-face or phone contact may result in a better experience for some customers which engenders loyalty).

Myers *et al.* (2004) say:

> customers may always be right, but allowing them to follow their own preferences often increases a company's costs while leaving untapped opportunities to boost revenues. Instead customers [segments with different characteristics and value] must be guided to the right mix of channels for each product or service.

They suggest companies need to use data to assess a mismatch between the company's actual customer channel preferences and those of the market at large. Thomas and Sullivan (2005) give the example of a US multichannel retailer that used cross-channel tracking of purchases through assigning each customer a unique identifier to calculate channel preferences as follow: 63% bricks-and-mortar store-only customers, 12.4% Internet-only customers, 11.9% catalogue-only customers, 11.9% dual-channel customers and 1% three-channel customers. This analysis shows the potential for multichannel sales since Myers *et al.* (2004) state that these multichannel customers spend 20 to 30% more.

So, the multichannel communications strategy needs to specify the extent of communications choices made available to customers and the degree to which a company persuades customers to use particular channels. Deciding on the best combination of channels is a complex challenge for organisations. Consider your mobile phone company – when purchasing you may make your decision about handset and network supplier in-store, on the web or through phoning the contact centre. Any of these contact points may either be direct with the network provider or through a retail intermediary. After purchase, if you have support questions about billing, handset upgrades or new tariffs you may again use any of these touch-points to resolve your questions. Managing this multichannel challenge is vital for the phone company for two reasons, both concerned with customer retention. First, the experience delivered through these channels is vital to the decision whether to remain with the network supplier when their contract expires – price is not the only consideration. Second, outbound communications delivered via website, e-mail, direct mail and phone are critical to getting the customer to stay with the company by recommending the most appropriate tariff and handset with appropriate promotions, but which is the most appropriate mix of channels for the company (each channel has a different level of cost-effectiveness for customers which contributes different levels of value to the customer) and the customer (each customer will have a preference for the combinations of channels they will use for different decisions)?

McDonald and Wilson (2002) suggest evaluating different distribution channels using the channel curve, which is a similar tool to the electronic shopping test of de Kare-Silver (2000) described in Chapter 2. For a particular product category they suggest evaluating the customer's preference for each channel against store, mail and phone ordering channels and in terms of cost, convenience, added-value, viewing and accessibility for the customer.

To review strategic options for the role of the Internet in multichannel marketing, the channel coverage map (Figure 4.25), popularised by Friedman and Furey (1999), is a useful tool. This model is best applied to a business-to-business context. Considering an organisation such as Dell, customers will vary by value within and between segments. Low-value segments will be smaller businesses and consumers, while large organisations placing many purchases will be higher-value. For consumers, Dell's preferred channel preference will be the low-cost online channel. For medium-sized companies, the preference will be a combination of desk-based sales agents in a call centre supported by the web. Through using phone contact, Dell can better explain the options available for multiple purchases. For the highest-value, large companies, the most important effective approach will be through field staff such as account managers. Specific web applications, such as the Dell Premier extranets, will form part of the strategy to support these customers. The model considers the different type of products a company sells from lower-cost standardised products through to higher-cost customised products and services such as network management.

We will return to this key decision about implementing customer contact strategies in later chapters in the book.

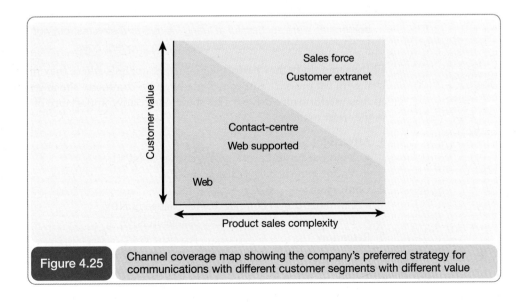

| Figure 4.25 | Channel coverage map showing the company's preferred strategy for communications with different customer segments with different value |

## Decision 7: Online communications mix and budget

The decision on the amount of spending on online communications and the mix between the different communications techniques such as search engine marketing, affiliate marketing, e-mail marketing and online advertising is closely related to the previous one.

Varianini and Vaturi (2000) suggest that many e-commerce failures have resulted from poor control of media spending. They suggest that many companies spend too much on poorly targeted communications. They suggest the communications mix should be optimised to minimise the cost of acquisition of customers. It can also be suggested that optimisation of the conversion to action on site is important to the success of marketing. The strategy will fail if the site design, quality of service and marketing communications are not effective in converting visitors to prospects or buyers.

A further strategic decision is the balance of investment between customer acquisition and retention. Many start-up companies will invest primarily on customer acquisition. This can be a strategic error since customer retention through repeat purchases will be vital to the success of the online service. For existing companies, there is a decision on whether to focus expenditure on customer acquisition or on customer retention or to use a balanced approach.

**Performance drivers**
Critical success factors that determine whether business and marketing objectives are met.

Agrawal *et al.* (2001) suggest that the success of e-commerce sites can be modelled and controlled based on the customer lifecycle of customer relationship management (Chapter 6). They suggest using a scorecard, assessed using a longitudinal study analysing hundreds of e-commerce sites in the USA and Europe. The scorecard is based on the **performance drivers** or critical success factors for e-commerce such as the costs for acquisition and retention, conversion rates of visitors to buyers to repeat buyers, together with churn rates. Note that to maximise retention and minimise churn (customers who don't continue to use the service) there will need to be measures that assess the quality of service including customer satisfaction ratings. These are discussed in Chapter 7. There are three main parts to their scorecard:

1 *Attraction.* Size of visitor base, visitor acquisition cost and visitor advertising revenue (e.g. media sites).
2 *Conversion.* Customer base, customer acquisition costs, customer conversion rate, number of transactions per customer, revenue per transaction, revenue per customer, customer gross income, customer maintenance cost, customer operating income, customer churn rate, customer operating income before marketing spending.
3 *Retention.* This uses similar measures to those for conversion customers.

The survey performed by Agrawal *et al.* (2001) shows that:

*companies were successful at luring visitors to their sites, but not at getting these visitors to buy or at turning occasional buyers into frequent ones.*

In the same study they performed a further analysis where they modelled the theoretical change in net present value contributed by an e-commerce site in response to a 10% change in these performance drivers. This shows the relative importance of these drivers, or 'levers' as they refer to them:

1 **Attraction**
   - Visitor acquisition cost: 0.74% change in NPV.
   - Visitor growth: 3.09% change in NPV.
2 **Conversion**
   - Customer conversion rate: 0.84% change in NPV.
   - Revenue per customer: 2.32% change in NPV.
3 **Retention**
   - Cost of repeat customer: 0.69% change in NPV.
   - Revenue per repeat customer: 5.78% change in NPV.
   - Repeat customer churn rate: 6.65% change in NPV.
   - Repeat customer conversion rate: 9.49% change in NPV.

This modelling highlights the importance of on-site marketing communications and the quality of service delivery in converting browsers to buyers and buyers into repeat buyers. It is apparent that marketing spend is large relative to turnover initially, to achieve customer growth, but is then carefully controlled to achieve profitability.

We will return to this topic in Chapter 8, where we will review the balance between **campaign-based e-communications** which are often tied into a particular event such as the launch or re-launch of a website or a product. For example, an interactive (banner) advert campaign may last for a period of two months following a site re-launch or for a five-month period around a new product launch.

In addition to campaign-based e-communications, we also need **continuous e-communications**. Organisations need to ensure that there is sufficient investment in continuous online marketing activities such as search marketing, affiliate marketing and sponsorship.

We observe that there is a significant change in mindset required to change budget allocations from a traditional campaign-based approach to an increased proportion of expenditure on continuous communications.

## Decision 8: Organisational capabilities (7 S framework)

A useful framework for reviewing an organisation's capabilities to implement Internet marketing strategy is shown in Table 1.3 (page 24) applied to Internet marketing. Which are the main challenges in implementing strategy? EConsultancy (2008) surveyed UK e-commerce managers to assess their views on the main challenges of managing e-commerce within an organisation. Their responses are summarised in Figure 4.26. In the context of the 7 Ss, we can summarise the main challenges as follows:

- *Strategy* – limited capabilities to integrate into Internet strategy within core marketing and business strategy as discussed earlier in this chapter is indicated by frustration on gaining appropriate budgets.
- *Structure* – structural and process issues are indicated by the challenges of gaining resource and buy-in from traditional marketing and IT functions.
- *Skills and staff* – these issues were indicated by difficulties in finding specialist staff or agencies.

To help manage the internal capabilities for improving the results from digital channels, EConsultancy (2008) has developed a useful checklist for auditing current internal capabilities, resources and processes and then putting in place a programme to improve results. EConsultancy (2008) recommends these steps in a digital channel performance audit and improvement plan:

- *Step 1 – Senior management commitment.* Assess and encourage senior management commitment. What is the level of understanding of digital channels and physical commitment and sponsorship among the senior management team? Develop a plan to educate and influence the senior management team.
- *Step 2 – Digital channel contribution.* What are the digital channels delivering across different markets and product categories now to support business goals in terms of sales, cost of acquisition, profitability and customer loyalty?
- *Step 3 – Brand alignment.* Reviewing how digital channels and website functionality can support traditional brand values but also enhance the brand through development of online value propositions (OVP).
- *Step 4 – Marketplace analysis.* Customer insight is key, i.e. qualitative and quantitative research of customer characteristics, behaviours and opinions. Also includes benchmarking of competitors' proposition, marketing communications and capabilities. Develop detailed understanding of online intermediaries, e.g. key portals, search engines and social networks which influence audience.

**Campaign-based e-communications**

E-marketing communications that are executed to support a specific marketing campaign such as a product launch, price promotion or a website launch.

**Continuous e-communications**

Long-term use of e-marketing communications for customer acquisition (such as, search engine and affiliate marketing) and retention (for example, e-newsletter marketing).

- *Step 5 – Technology infrastructure.* Review capability of technology infrastructure to support online marketing innovation. Is an acceptable 'time to market' for new functionality available dependent on legacy system integration, business case authorisation and prioritisation, dedicated development resource and agile technical development processes?
- *Step 6 – Vision and goals.* Develop a long-term vision for how digital channels will contribute to the development business. Set short-term goals for digital channels in areas of customer acquisition, conversion and customer experience, retention and growth.
- *Step 7 – Strategy and planning.* Ensure digital marketing is integrated into different planning cycles (i.e. long-term three to five-year plans, annual plans and quarterly/monthly operational planning reviews). Establish method and budget sources for identifying, reviewing business case and prioritisation for new site and campaign functionality.
- *Step 8 – Review capability of marketing resources to deliver efficient, integrated cross-channel communications.* Including organisation structure, staff roles and responsibilities, skills levels of staff, agency capability, marketing campaign management and review process.
- *Step 9 – Refine management information and reporting.* Ensure web analytics and other business reporting tools maximise understanding of the influence of different digital media

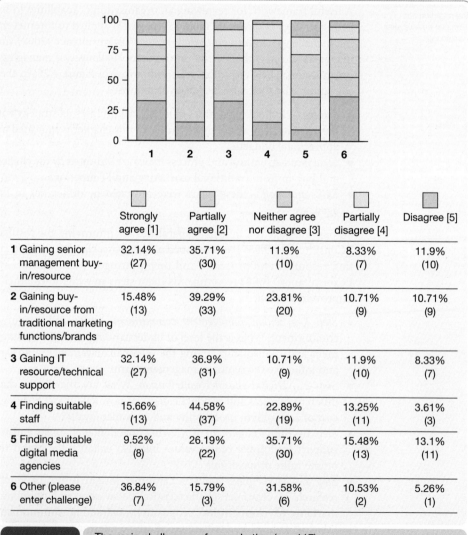

| | Strongly agree [1] | Partially agree [2] | Neither agree nor disagree [3] | Partially disagree [4] | Disagree [5] |
|---|---|---|---|---|---|
| **1** Gaining senior management buy-in/resource | 32.14% (27) | 35.71% (30) | 11.9% (10) | 8.33% (7) | 11.9% (10) |
| **2** Gaining buy-in/resource from traditional marketing functions/brands | 15.48% (13) | 39.29% (33) | 23.81% (20) | 10.71% (9) | 10.71% (9) |
| **3** Gaining IT resource/technical support | 32.14% (27) | 36.9% (31) | 10.71% (9) | 11.9% (10) | 8.33% (7) |
| **4** Finding suitable staff | 15.66% (13) | 44.58% (37) | 22.89% (19) | 13.25% (11) | 3.61% (3) |
| **5** Finding suitable digital media agencies | 9.52% (8) | 26.19% (22) | 35.71% (30) | 15.48% (13) | 13.1% (11) |
| **6** Other (please enter challenge) | 36.84% (7) | 15.79% (3) | 31.58% (6) | 10.53% (2) | 5.26% (1) |

**Figure 4.26**   The main challenges of e-marketing (*n* = 117)
*Source*: EConsultancy (2008)

channels on delivering leads or sales. Implement a culture and process for integrating review and action based on defined key performance indicators and structured tests.

- *Step 10 – Identify and implement 'quick wins'.* Based on strategic analysis performed, identify short-term projects to deliver business results across areas of customer acquisition (e.g. improvements to digital media channels such as search engine marketing, aggregators or affiliate marketing); conversion (improvements to landing page messaging and usability through small findability improvements to navigation or search labelling possibly based on AB or multivariate testing or customer journey improvements on home page, category, product or other landing pages and basket, registration or checkout process) or retention and growth (encouraging repeat site visits or purchases through e-mail marketing or on site merchandising).

Organisational structure decisions form two main questions. The first is 'How should internal structures be changed to deliver e-marketing?'; and the second 'How should the structure of links with partner organisations be changed to achieve e-marketing objectives?' Once structural decisions have been made attention should be focused on effective **change management**. Many e-commerce initiatives fail, not in their conceptualisation, but in their implementation. Chaffey (2008) describes approaches to change management and risk management in Chapter 10.

**Change management**

Controls to minimise the risks of project-based and organisational change.

## Internal structures

There are several alternative options for restructuring within a business such as the creation of an in-house digital marketing or e-commerce group. This issue has been considered by Parsons *et al.* (1996) from a sell-side e-commerce perspective. They recognise four stages in the growth of what they refer to as 'the digital marketing organisation' which are still useful for benchmarking digital marketing capabilities. A more sophisticated e-commerce capability assessment was presented earlier in this chapter in the section on situation review (Table 4.3). The stages are:

1 *Ad-hoc activity.* At this stage there is no formal organisation related to e-commerce and the skills are dispersed around the organisation. It is likely that there is poor integration between online and offline marketing communications. The website may not reflect the offline brand, and the website services may not be featured in the offline marketing communications. A further problem with ad-hoc activity is that the maintenance of the website will be informal and errors may occur as information becomes out-of-date.

2 *Focusing the effort.* At this stage, efforts are made to introduce a controlling mechanism for Internet marketing. Parsons *et al.* (1996) suggest that this is often achieved through a senior executive setting up a steering group which may include interested parties from marketing and IT and legal experts. At this stage the efforts to control the site will be experimental, with different approaches being tried to build, promote and manage the site.

3 *Formalisation.* At this stage the authors suggest that Internet marketing will have reached a critical mass and there will be a defined group or separate business unit within the company that will manage all digital marketing.

4 *Institutionalising capability.* This stage also involves a formal grouping within the organisation, but is distinguished from the previous stage in that there are formal links created between digital marketing and the company's core activities.

Although this is presented as a stage model with evolution implying that all companies will move from one stage to the next, many companies will find that true formalisation with the creation of a separate e-commerce or e-business department is unnecessary. For small and medium companies with a marketing department numbering a few people and an IT department perhaps consisting of two people, it will not be practical to have a separate group. Even large companies may find it is sufficient to have a single person or small team responsible for e-commerce with their role being to co-ordinate the different activities within the company using a matrix management approach.

Activity 4.5 reviews different types of organisational structures for e-commerce. Table 4.8 reviews some of the advantages and disadvantages of each.

| Table 4.8 | Advantages and disadvantages of the organisational structures shown in Figure 4.27 |
| --- | --- |

| Organisational structure | Circumstances | Advantages | Disadvantages |
| --- | --- | --- | --- |
| (a) No formal structure for e-commerce | Initial response to e-commerce or poor leadership with no identification of need for change | Can achieve rapid response to e-commerce | Poor-quality site in terms of content quality and customer service responses (e-mail, phone). Priorities not decided logically. Insufficient resources |
| (b) A separate committee or department manages and co-ordinates e-commerce | Identification of problem and response in (a) | Co-ordination and budgeting and resource allocation possible | May be difficult to get different departments to deliver their input because of other commitments |
| (c) A separate business unit with independent budgets | Internet contribution (Chapter 6) is sizeable (>20%) | As for (b), but can set own targets and not be constrained by resources. Lower-risk option than (d) | Has to respond to corporate strategy. Conflict of interests between department and traditional business |
| (d) A separate operating company | Major revenue potential or flotation. Need to differentiate from parent | As for (c), but can set strategy independently. Can maximise market potential | High risk if market potential is overestimated due to start-up costs |

| Activity 4.5 | Which is the best organisation structure for e-commerce? |
| --- | --- |

**Purpose**

To review alternative organisational structures for e-commerce.

**Activity**

1 Match the four types of companies and situations to the structures (a) to (d) in Figure 4.27.
   - A separate operating company. Example: Prudential and Egg (www.egg.com).
   - A separate business unit with independent budgets. Example: RS Components Internet Trading Channel (www.rswww.com).
   - A separate committee or department manages and co-ordinates e-commerce. Example: Derbyshire Building Society (www.derbyshire.co.uk).
   - No formal structure for e-commerce. Example: many small businesses.
2 Under which circumstances would each structure be appropriate?
3 Summarise the advantages and disadvantages of each approach.

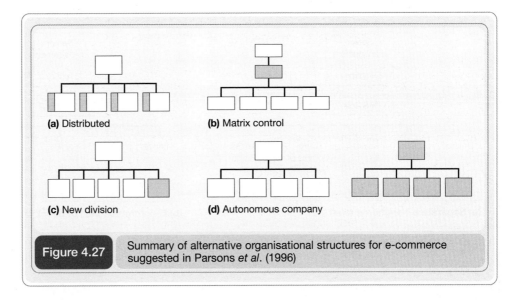

**(a)** Distributed

**(b)** Matrix control

**(c)** New division

**(d)** Autonomous company

| Figure 4.27 | Summary of alternative organisational structures for e-commerce suggested in Parsons *et al.* (1996) |

Where the main e-commerce function is internal, the EConsultancy (2008) research suggested that it was typically located in one of four areas (see Figure 4.28) in approximate decreasing order of frequency:

(a) Main e-commerce function in separate team.
(b) Main e-commerce function part of operations or direct channel.
(c) Main e-commerce function part of marketing, corporate communications or other central marketing function.
(d) Main e-commerce function part of information technology.

There is also often one or several secondary areas of e-commerce competence and resource. For example, IT may have a role in applications development and site build and each business, brand or country may have one or more e-commerce specialists responsible for managing e-commerce in their unit. Which was appropriate depended strongly on the market(s) the company operated in and their existing channel structures.

### Links with other organisations

Gulati and Garino (2000) identify a continuum of approaches from integration to separation for delivering e-marketing through working with outside partners. The choices are:

1 *In-house division (integration).* Example: RS Components Internet Trading Channel (www.rswww.com).
2 *Joint venture (mixed).* The company creates an online presence in association with another player.
3 *Strategic partnership (mixed).* This may also be achieved through purchase of existing dot-coms – for example, in the UK Great Universal Stores acquired e-tailer Jungle.com for its strength in selling technology products and strong brand, while John Lewis purchased Buy.com's UK operations.
4 *Spin-off (separation).* Example: Egg bank is a spin-off from Prudential Financial Services Company.

### Skills

There is a wide range of new skills required for e-commerce. Figure 4.29 gives an indication of typical roles within an e-commerce team, placed within a customer-lifecyle-based structure. Each grouping of roles is placed in a dotted box which indicates the other teams this

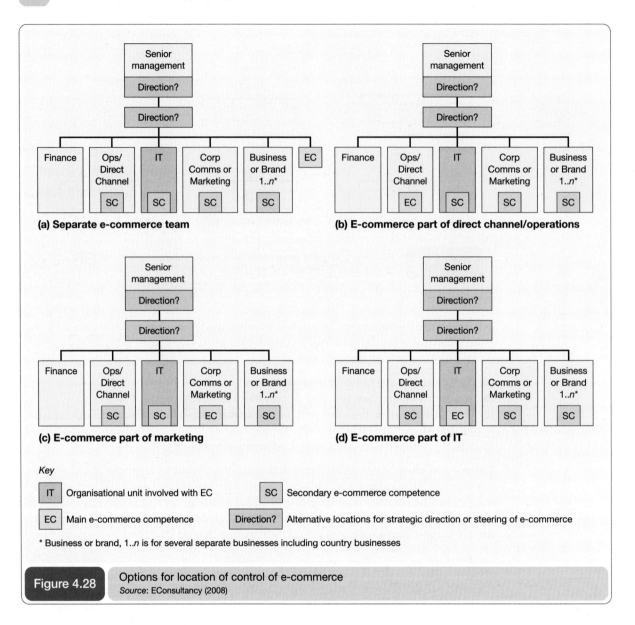

**Key**

| | |
|---|---|
| IT | Organisational unit involved with EC |
| EC | Main e-commerce competence |

| | |
|---|---|
| SC | Secondary e-commerce competence |
| Direction? | Alternative locations for strategic direction or steering of e-commerce |

\* Business or brand, 1..*n* is for several separate businesses including country businesses

| Figure 4.28 | Options for location of control of e-commerce<br>*Source*: EConsultancy (2008) |
|---|---|

group needs to work with, or potentially where in the organisation or outside this work is completed. For example, e-CRM activities such as e-mail marketing could be potentially undertaken in a particular business unit or country. Similarly, many activities of development planning and implementation can be completed within IT or a specialist agency.

For the skills indicated in Figure 4.29 it may be more efficient to outsource some skills. These are some of the main options for external suppliers for these Internet marketing skills:

1  Full-service digital agency.
2  Specialist digital agency.
3  Traditional agency.
4  In-house resource.

When deciding on supplier or resource, suppliers need to consider the level and type of marketing activities they will be covering. The level typically ranges through:

1  Strategy.
2  Analysis and creative concepts.

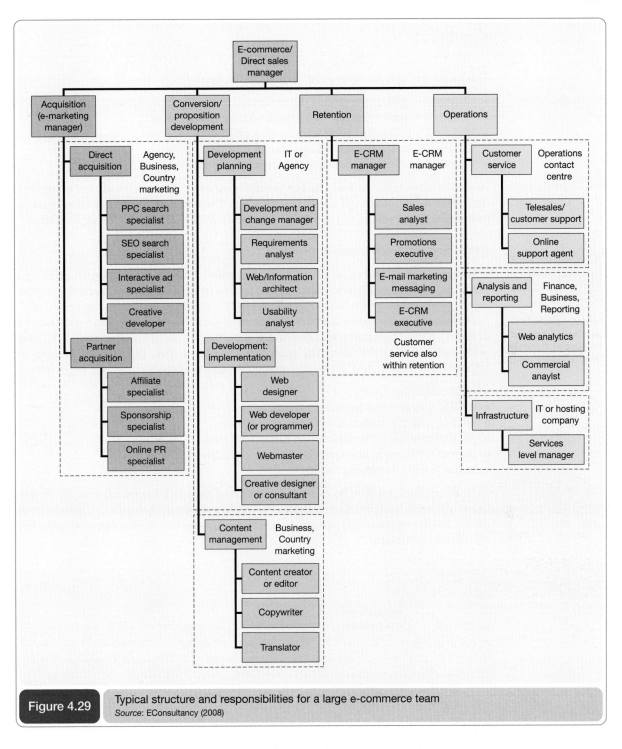

**Figure 4.29**    Typical structure and responsibilities for a large e-commerce team
*Source*: EConsultancy (2008)

3  Creative or content development.
4  Executing campaign, including reporting analysis and adjustment.
5  Infrastructure (e.g. web hosting, ad-serving, e-mail broadcasting, evaluation).

Options for outsourcing different e-marketing activities are reviewed in Activity 7.1 (page 395).

## Strategy implementation

This forms the topic for subsequent chapters in this book:

- Chapter 5 – options for varying the marketing mix in the Internet environment.
- Chapter 6 – implementing customer relationship management.
- Chapter 7 – delivering online services via a website.
- Chapter 8 – interactive marketing communications.
- Chapter 9 – monitoring and maintaining the online presence.

In each of these areas, such as CRM or development of website functionality, it is common that different initiatives will compete for budget. The next section reviews techniques for prioritising these projects and deciding on the best portfolio of e-commerce applications.

### Assessing different Internet projects

A further organisational capability issue is the decision about different information systems marketing applications. Typically, there will be a range of different Internet marketing alternatives to be evaluated. Limited resources will dictate that only some applications are practical.

**Portfolio analysis**

Identification, evaluation and selection of desirable marketing applications.

Portfolio analysis can be used to select the most suitable projects. For example, Daniel *et al.* (2001) suggest that potential e-commerce opportunities should be assessed for the value of the opportunity to the company against its ability to deliver. Typical opportunities for Internet marketing strategy for an organisation which has a brochureware site might be:

- online catalogue facility;
- e-CRM system – lead generation system;
- e-CRM system – customer service management;
- e-CRM system – personalisation of content for users;
- partner relationship management extranet for distributors or agents;
- transactional e-commerce facility.

Such alternatives can then be evaluated in terms of their risk against reward. Figure 4.30 shows a possible evaluation of strategic options. It is apparent that with limited resources, the e-CRM lead generation, partner extranet and customer services options offer the best mix of risk and reward.

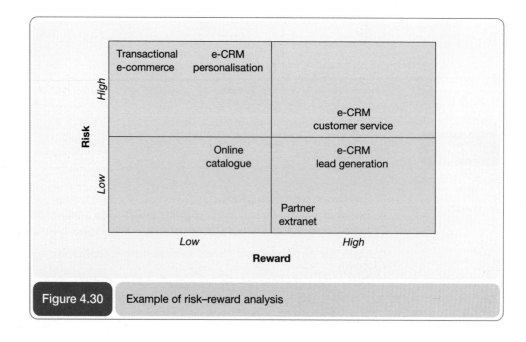

| **Figure 4.30** | Example of risk–reward analysis |

For information systems investments, the model of McFarlan (1984) has been used extensively to assess the future strategic importance applications in a portfolio. This model has been applied to the e-commerce applications by Daniel *et al.* (2008) and Chaffey (2006). Potential e-commerce applications can be assessed as:

- *Key operational* – essential to remain competitive. Example: partner relationship management extranet for distributors or agents.
- *Support* – deliver improved performance, but not critical to strategy. Example: e-CRM system – personalisation of content for users.
- *High-potential* – may be important for achieving future success. Example: e-CRM system – customer service management.
- *Strategic* – critical to future business strategy. Example: e-CRM system – lead generation system is vital to developing new business.

A further portfolio analysis suggested by McDonald and Wilson (2002) is a matrix of attractiveness to customer against attractiveness to company, which will give a similar result to the risk–reward matrix. Finally, Tjan (2001) has suggested a matrix approach of viability (return on investment) against fit (with the organisation's capabilities) for Internet applications. He presents five metrics for assessing viability and fit. Viability is ideally based on a quantitative business case assessment of the value of a new application that will be generated through increasing conversion and retention rates. Fit is a more subjective measure based on the ease of implementation given the fit of an application with an organisation's existing processes, capabilities and culture. Additional criteria are developed for viability and fit. For 'viability', the criteria used to assess the potential value of an investment are rated between 100 (positive) and 0 (unfavourable) in each of these areas:

- market value potential;
- time to positive cash flow;
- personnel requirement;
- funding requirement.

For 'fit', the criteria are rated as low to medium to high to assess the value of a potential investment:

- alignment with core capabilities;
- alignment with other company initiatives;
- fit with organisational structure;
- fit with company's culture and value;
- ease of technical implementation.

## The online lifecycle management grid

Earlier in the chapter, in the section on objective setting, we reviewed different frameworks for identifying objectives and metrics to assess whether they are achieved. We consider the online lifecycle management grid at this point since Table 4.9 acts as a good summary that integrates objectives, strategies and tactics.

The columns isolate the key performance areas of site visitor acquisition, conversion to opportunity, conversion to sale and retention. The rows isolate more detailed metrics such as the tracking metrics and performance drivers from higher-level metrics such as the customer-centric key performance indicators (KPIs) and business-value KPIs. In the bottom two rows we have also added in typical strategies and tactics used to achieve objectives which show the relationship between objectives and strategy. Note, though, that this framework mainly creates a focus on efficiency of conversion, although there are some effectiveness measures also.

These are some of the generic Internet marketing main strategies to achieve the objectives in the grid which apply to a range of organisations:

| Table 4.9 | Online performance management grid for an e-retailer |
| --- | --- |

| Metric and growth | Visitor acquisition | Conversion to opportunity | Conversion to sale | Customer retention |
| --- | --- | --- | --- | --- |
| Tracking metrics | • Unique visitors<br>• New visitors | • Opportunity volume | • Sales volume | • E-mail list quality<br>• E-mail response quality<br>• Transactions |
| Performance drivers (diagnostics) | • Bounce rate<br>• Conversion rate: new visit to start quote | • Macro-conversion rate to opportunity and micro-conversion efficiency | • Conversion rate to sale<br>• E-mail conversion rate | • Active customers %(site and e-mail active)<br>• Repeat conversion rate for different purchases |
| Customer centric KPIs | • Cost per click and per sale<br>• Brand awareness | • Cost per opportunity<br>• Customer satisfaction | • Cost per sale<br>• Customer satisfaction<br>• Average order value (AOV) | • Lifetime value<br>• Customer loyalty index<br>• Products per customer |
| Business value KPIs | • Audience share | • Online product requests (n, £, % of total) | • Online originated sales (n, £, % of total) | • Retained sales growth and volume |
| Strategy | • Online targeted reach strategy<br>• Offline targeted reach strategy | • Lead generation strategy | • Online sales generation strategy<br>• Offline sales impact strategy | • Retention and customer growth strategy |
| Tactics | • Continuous communications mix<br>• Campaign communications mix<br>• Online value proposition | • Usability<br>• Personalisation<br>• Inbound contact strategy (customer service) | • Usability<br>• Personalisation<br>• Inbound contact strategy (customer service)<br>• Merchandising<br>• Triggered e-mails | • Database/list quality<br>• Targeting<br>• Outbound contact strategy (e-mail)<br>• Personalisation |

*Source*: Adapted from Neil Mason's Applied Insights (www.applied-insights.co.uk) Acquisition, Conversion, Retention approach

- *Online value proposition strategy* – defining the value proposition for acquisition and retention to engage with customers online. Includes informational and promotional incentives used to encourage trial. Also defines programme of value creation through time, for example, business white papers published on partner sites.
- *Online targeted reach strategy* – the aim is to communicate with relevant audiences online to achieve communications objectives. The communications commonly include campaign communications such as online advertising, PR, e-mail, viral campaigns and continuous communications such as search engine marketing or sponsorship or partnership arrangements. The strategy may involve (1) driving new, potential customers to the company site, (2) migrating existing customers to online channels or (3) achieving reach to enhance brand awareness, favourability and purchase intent through ads and sponsorships on third-party sites. Building brand awareness, favourability and purchase intent on third-party sites may be a more effective strategy for low-involvement FMCG brands where it will be difficult to encourage visitors to the site.
- *Offline targeted reach strategy* – the objective is to encourage potential customers to use online channels, i.e. visit website and transact where relevant. The strategy is to communicate with selected customer segments offline through direct mail, media buys, PR and sponsorship.

- *Online sales efficiency strategy* – the objective is to convert site visitors to engage and become leads (for example, through registering for an e-newsletter or placing the first item in the shopping basket) to convert them to buy products and maximise the purchase transaction value.
- *Offline sales impact strategy* – the aim is to achieve sales offline from new or existing customers. Strategy defines how online communications through the website and e-mail can influence sales offline, i.e. by phone, mail-order or in-store.

## Case Study 4 | Tesco.com uses the Internet to support its diversification strategy

### Context

Tesco, well known as Britain's leading food retail group with a presence also in Europe and Asia, has also been a pioneer online. Tesco.com is generally recognised as the world's largest online grocer. By September 2007 online sales in the first half of the year were £748 million, a 35% year-on-year increase, and profit increased by 62% to £54.7 million. Tesco.com now receives over 300,000 orders each week.

In 2007, the company outlined a five point strategy for the future: to become an international retailer; maintain a strong core UK business; to be as strong in non-food as in food; to develop retailing services; and to put community at the heart of its offering. Its online strategy is aligned with this, with Tesco Direct now having 12,000 products online and expected to generate revenue in excess of £150m in the 2007/2008 financial year and within the top 10 UK strores.

### Product ranges

The Tesco.com site acts as a portal to most of Tesco's products, including various non-food ranges (for example books, DVDs and electrical items under the 'Extra' banner), Tesco Personal Finance and the telecoms businesses, as well as services offered in partnership with specialist companies such as dieting clubs, flights and holidays, music downloads, gas, electricity and DVD rentals. It does not currently sell clothing online but in May 2005 it introduced a clothing website (www.clothing_attesco.com), initially to showcase Tesco's clothing brands and link customers to their nearest store with this range.

### Competitors

Tesco currently leads the UK's other leading grocery retailers in terms of market share. This pattern is repeated online. The Nielsen/Netrating audience panel for September 2007 for the top UK supermarkets shows the lead of Tesco; the offline market share is in brackets and the data is from TNS which monitors the household grocery purchasing habits of 25,000 demographically representative households in the UK:

- Tesco.com (5.2. million unique users, September 2007, 30.9%)
- Asda (1.4 million, 16.9%)
- Sainsbury's (840,000, 16.4%)
- Waitrose (332,000)
- Morrisons (225,000).

Some companies are repeated since their main site and the online shopping site are reported on separately. Asda.com now seems to be performing in a consistent manner online to its offline presence. However, Sainsbury's online performance seems to be significantly lower compared to its offline performance. Some providers, such as Ocado which originally just operated within the London area, have a strong local performance.

Notably, some of Tesco.com's competitors are absent from the Hitwise listing since their strategy has been to focus on retail formats. These are Morrisons (12.5% retail share), Somerfield (5.5%) and Co-op (5.0%).

### Promotion of service

As with other online retailers, Tesco.com relies on in-store advertising and marketing to the supermarket's Clubcard loyalty scheme's customer base to persuade customers to shop online. *New Media Age* (2005) quotes Nigel Dodd, marketing director at Tesco.com, as saying: '*These are invaluable sources as we have such a strong customer base*'. However, for non-food goods the supermarket does advertise online using keyword targeted ads.

For existing customers, e-mail marketing and direct mail marketing to provide special offers and promotions to customers is important.

According to Humby and Hunt (2003), e-retailer Tesco.com uses what they describe as a 'commitment-based segmentation' or 'loyalty ladder' which is based on recency of purchase, frequency of purchase and value which is used to identify six lifecycle categories which are then further divided to target communications:

- 'Logged-on'
- 'Cautionary'
- 'Developing'
- 'Established'
- 'Dedicated'
- 'Logged-off' (the aim here is to win back).

Tesco then uses automated event-triggered messaging which can be created to encourage continued purchase. For example, Tesco.com has a touch strategy which includes a sequence of follow-up communications triggered after different events in the customer lifecycle. In the example given below, communications after event 1 are intended to achieve the objective of converting a website visitor to action; communications after event 2 are intended to move the customer from a first-time purchaser to a regular purchaser, and for event 3 to reactivate lapsed purchasers.

### Trigger event 1: Customer first registers on site (but does not buy)

Auto-response (AR) 1: Two days after registration e-mail sent offering phone assistance and £5 discount off the first purchase to encourage trial.

### Trigger event 2: Customer first purchases online

AR1: Immediate order confirmation.
AR2: Five days after purchase e-mail sent with link to online customer satisfaction survey asking about quality of service from driver and picker (e.g. item quality and substitutions).
AR3: Two weeks after first purchase – direct mail offering tips on how to use service and £5 discount on next purchases, intended to encourage re-use of online services.
AR4: Generic monthly e-newsletter with online exclusive offers encouraging cross-selling.
AR5: Bi-weekly alert with personalised offers for customer.
AR6: After two months – £5 discount for next shop.
AR7: Quarterly mailing of coupons encouraging repeat sales and cross-sales.

### Trigger event 3: Customer does not purchase for an extended period

AR1: Dormancy detected – reactivation e-mail with survey of how the customer is finding the service (to identify any problems) and a £5 incentive.
AR2: A further discount incentive is used in order to encourage continued usage to shop after the first shop after a break.

## Tesco's online product strategy

*New Media Age* (2005) ran a profile of Laura Wade-Gery, CEO of Tesco.com since January 2004, which provides an interesting insight into how the business has run. In her first year, total sales were increased 24% to £719 million. Laura is 40 years old, a keen athlete and has followed a varied career developing from a MA in History at Magdalen College, Oxford and an MBA from Insead; manager and partner in Kleinwort Benson; manager and senior consultant, Gemini Consulting; targeted marketing director (Tesco Clubcard), and group strategy director, Tesco Stores.

The growth overseen by Wade-Gery has been achieved through a combination of initiatives. Product range development is one key area. In early 2005, Tesco.com fulfilled 150,000 grocery orders a week but now also offers more intangible offerings, such as e-diets and music downloads.

Laura has also focused on improving the customer experience online – the time it takes for a new customer to complete their first order has been decreased from over an hour to 35 minutes through usability work culminating in a major site revision.

To support the business as it diversifies into new areas, Wade-Gery's strategy was 'to make home delivery part of the DNA of Tesco' according to *New Media Age* (2005). She continues: 'What we offer is delivery to your home of a Tesco service – it's an obvious extension of the home-delivered groceries concept.' By May 2005, Tesco.com had 30,000 customers signed up for DVD rental, through partner Video Island (which runs the rival Screenselect service). Over the next year, her target is to treble this total, while also extending home-delivery services to the likes of bulk wine and white goods.

Wade-Gery looks to achieve synergy between the range of services offered. For example, its partnership with e-Diets can be promoted through the Tesco Clubcard loyalty scheme, with mailings to 10m customers a year. In July 2004, Tesco.com Limited paid £2 million for the exclusive licence to eDiets.com in the UK and Ireland under the URLs www.eDietsUK.com and www.eDiets.ie. Through promoting these services through these URLs, Tesco can use the dieting business to grow use of the Tesco.com service and in-store sales.

To help keep focus on home retail-delivery, Wade-Gery sold women's portal iVillage (www.ivillage.co.uk) back to its US owners for an undisclosed sum in March 2004. She explained to *New Media Age*:

*It's a very different sort of product to the other services that we're embarking on. In my mind, we stand for providing services and products that you buy, which is slightly different to the world of providing information.*

The implication is that there was insufficient revenue from ad sales on iVillage and insufficient opportunities to promote Tesco.com sales. However, iVillage was a useful learning experience in that there are some parallels with iVillage, such as message boards and community advisers.

Wade-Gery is also director of Tesco Mobile, the joint 'pay-as-you-go' venture with O2 which is mainly serviced online, although promoted in-store and via direct mail. In 2008, Tesco has over 1.5 million mobile subscribers and of these 250,000 visit the mobile portal each month.

Tesco also offers broadband and dial-up ISP services, but believe the market for Internet telephony (provided through Skype and Vonage, for example) is not sufficiently developed. Tesco.com has concentrated on more traditional services which have the demand – for example, Tesco Telecom fixed-line services attracted over a million customers in their first year.

However, this is not to say that Tesco.com will not invest in relatively new services. In November 2004, Tesco introduced a music download service, and just six months later Wade-Gery estimates they have around 10% market share – one of the benefits of launching relatively early. Again, there is synergy, this time with hardware sales. *New Media Age* (2005) reported that as MP3 players were unwrapped, sales went up – even on Christmas Day! She says:

*The exciting thing about digital is where you can take it in the future. As the technology grows, we'll be able to turn Tesco.com into a digital download store of all sorts, rather than just music. Clearly, film [through video on demand] would be next.*

But it has to be based firmly on analysis of customer demand. She says:

*The number one thing for us is whether the product is something that customers are saying they want, has it reached a point where mass-market customers are interested?*

There also has to be scope for simplification. *New Media Age* (2005) notes that Tesco is built on a core premise of convenience and value, and Wade-Gery believes what it's already done with mobile tariffs, broadband packages and music downloads are good examples of the retailer's knack for streamlining propositions. She says: '*We've actually managed to get people joining broadband who have never even had a dial-up service.*'

Tesco uses affiliate marketing to help support the launch of new services online. According to Tradedoubler.com, Tesco.com used affiliates for different products with different commission as follows:

- e-diets commission from £12 on 1–9 sales to £20 on 61+ sales;
- wine at 2% on lowest tier to 3% on the Gold tier of sales of >£2500;
- grocery and utilities – flat fee of £5 for first time purchase only.

*Sources*: Humby and Hunt (2003), *New Media Age* (2005), Hitwise (2005), Wikipedia (2005), and Nielsen NetRating

### Question

Based on the case study and your own research on competitors, summarise the strategic approaches which have helped Tesco.com achieve success online.

### Summary

1. The development of the online presence follows stage models from basic static 'brochureware' sites through simple interactive sites with query facilities to dynamic sites offering personalisation of services for customers.

2. The Internet marketing strategy should follow a similar form to a traditional strategic marketing planning process and should include:
   - goal setting;
   - situation review;
   - strategy formulation;
   - resource allocation and monitoring.

   A feedback loop should be established to ensure the site is monitored and modifications are fed back into the strategy development.

3.  Strategic goal setting should involve:
    - setting business objectives that the Internet can help achieve;
    - assessing and stating the contribution that the Internet will make to the business in the future, both as a proportion of revenue and in terms of whether the Internet will complement or replace other media;
      - stating the full range of business benefits that are sought, such as improved corporate image, cost reduction, more leads and sales, and improved customer service.

4.  The situation review will include assessing internal resources and assets, including the services available through the existing website. External analysis will involve customer demand analysis, competitor benchmarking and review of the macro-environment SLEPT factors.

5.  Strategy formulation will involve defining a company's commitment to the Internet; setting an appropriate value proposition for customers of the website; and identifying the role of the Internet in exploiting new markets, marketplaces and distribution channels and in delivering new products and services. In summary:
    - Decision 1: Market and product development strategies
    - Decision 2: Business and revenue models strategies
    - Decision 3: Target market strategy
    - Decision 4: Positioning and differentiation strategy (including the marketing mix)
    - Decision 5: Multichannel distribution strategy
    - Decision 6: Multichannel communications strategy
    - Decision 7: Online communications mix and budget
    - Decision 8: Organisational capabilities (7 S framework)

## Exercises

### Self-assessment exercises

1.  Draw a diagram that summarises the stages through which a company's website may evolve.
2.  What is meant by the 'Internet contribution', and what is its relevance to strategy?
3.  What is the role of monitoring in the strategic planning process?
4.  Summarise the main tangible and intangible business benefits of the Internet to a company.
5.  What is the purpose of an Internet marketing audit? What should it involve?
6.  What does a company need in order to be able to state clearly in the mission statement its strategic position relative to the Internet?
7.  What are the market and product positioning opportunities offered by the Internet?
8.  What are the distribution channel options for a manufacturing company?

### Essay and discussion questions

1.  Discuss the frequency with which an Internet marketing strategy should be updated for a company to remain competitive.
2.  'Setting long-term strategic objectives for a website is unrealistic since the rate of change in the marketplace is so rapid.' Discuss.
3.  Explain the essential elements of an Internet marketing strategy.
4.  Summarise the role of strategy tools and models in formulating a company's strategic approach to the Internet.

## Examination questions

1. When evaluating the business benefits of a website, which factors are likely to be common to most companies?

2. Use Porter's five forces model to discuss the competitive threats presented to a company by other websites.

3. Which factors will affect whether the Internet has primarily a complementary effect or a replacement effect on a company?

4. Describe different stages in the sophistication of development of a website, giving examples of the services provided at each stage.

5. Briefly explain the purpose and activities involved in an external audit conducted as part of the development of an Internet marketing strategy.

6. What is the importance of measurement within the Internet marketing process?

7. Which factors would a retail company consider when assessing the suitability of its product for Internet sales?

8. Explain what is meant by the online value proposition, and give two examples of the value proposition for websites with which you are familiar.

## References

Aaker, D. and Joachimsthaler, E. (2000) *Brand Leadership.* Free Press, New York.

Agrawal, V., Arjona, V. and Lemmens, R. (2001) E-performance: the path to rational exuberance, *McKinsey Quarterly*, No. 1, 31–43.

Bazett, M., Bowden, I., Love, J., Street, R. and Wilson, H. (2005) Measuring multichannel effectiveness using the balanced scorecard. *Interactive Marketing*, 6(3) (January–March), 224–31.

Chaffey, D. (2006) *E-Business and E-Commerce Management*, 3rd edn. Financial Times/Prentice Hall, Harlow.

Chaffey, D. and Smith, P.R. (2008) *EMarketing Excellence: Planning and Optimizing Your Digital Marketing*, 3rd edn. Butterworth-Heinemann, Oxford.

Chaston, I. (2000) *E-Marketing Strategy.* McGraw-Hill, Maidenhead.

Daniel, E., Wilson, H., McDonald, M. and Ward, J. (2001) *Marketing Strategy in the Digital Age.* Financial Times/Prentice Hall, Harlow.

Daniel, E., Wilson, H., Ward, J. and McDonald, M. (2002) Innovation @nd integration: developing an integrated e-enabled business strategy. Preliminary findings from an industry-sponsored research project for the Information Systems Research Centre and the Centre for E-marketing. Cranfield University School of Management, January.

Deise, M., Nowikow, C., King, P. and Wright, A. (2000) *Executive's Guide to E-Business. From Tactics to Strategy.* Wiley, New York.

de Kare-Silver, M. (2000) *EShock 2000. The Electronic Shopping Revolution: Strategies for Retailers and Manufacturers.* Macmillan, London.

Der Zee, J. and De Jong, B. (1999) Alignment is not enough: integrating business and information technology management with the balanced business scorecard, *Journal of Management Information Systems*, 16(2), 137–57.

Dibb, S., Simkin, S., Pride, W. and Ferrell, O. (2001) *Marketing: Concepts and Strategies*, 4th European edn. Houghton Mifflin, New York.

Durlacher (2000) Trends in the UK new economy, *Durlacher Quarterly Internet Report*, November, 1–12.

EConsultancy (2008) Breathing customer oxygen: How to build a customer-centric-retail organization. Sam Decker, 14 March 2008, EConsultancy blog, http://www.e-consultacy.com/news-blog/365253/breathing-customer-oxygen-how-to-build-a-customer--centric-retail-organisation.html.

EConsultancy (2008) Managing Digital Channels Research Report. Author: Dave Chaffey. Available from www.e-consultancy.com.

Forrester Research (2005) Press release: Forrester research US eCommerce forecast: online retail sales to reach $329 billion by 2010. Cambridge, MA, 19 September.

Friedlein, A. (2002) *Maintaining and Evolving Successful Commercial Websites*. Morgan Kaufmann, San Francisco.

Friedman, L. and Furey, T. (1999) *The Channel Advantage*. Butterworth-Heinemann, Oxford.

Gulati, R. and Garino, J. (2000) Getting the right mix of bricks and clicks for your company, *Harvard Business Review*, May–June, 107–14.

Hasan, H. and Tibbits, H. (2000) Strategic management of electronic commerce: an adaptation of the balanced scorecard, *Internet Research*, 10(5), 439–50.

Hitwise (2005) Press release: The top UK grocery and alcohol websites week ending October 1st, ranked by market share of website visits, from Hitwise.co.uk. Press release available at www.hitwise.co.uk.

Humby, C. and Hunt, T. (2003) *Scoring points. How Tesco Is Winning Customer Loyalty*. Kogan Page, London.

Kalakota, R. and Robinson, M. (2000) *E-Business: Roadmap for Success*. Addison-Wesley, Reading, MA.

Kaplan, R.S. and Norton, D.P. (1993) Putting the balanced scorecard to work, *Harvard Business Review*, September–October, 134–42.

Kim, E., Nam, D. and Stimpert, D. (2004) The applicability of Porter's generic strategies in the digital age: assumptions, conjectures and suggestions, *Journal of Management*, 30(5).

Kumar, N. (1999) Internet distribution strategies: dilemmas for the incumbent, *Financial Times*, Special Issue on mastering information management, no 7. Electronic Commerce, (www.ftmastering.com).

Levy, M. and Powell, P. (2003) Exploring SME Internet adoption: towards a contingent model, *Electronic Markets*, 13 (2), 173–81, www.electronicmarkets.org.

Lynch, R. (2000) *Corporate Strategy*. Financial Times/Prentice Hall, Harlow.

McDonald, M. (2003) *Marketing Plans: How To Prepare Them, How To Use Them*, 5th edn. Butterworth-Heinemann, Oxford.

McDonald, M. and Wilson, H. (2002) *New Marketing: Transforming the Corporate Future*. Butterworth-Heinemann, Oxford.

McFarlan, F.W. (1984) Information technology changes the way you compete, *Harvard Business Review*, May–June, 54–61.

Mintzberg, H. and Quinn, J.B. (1991) *The Strategy Process*, 2nd edn. Prentice Hall, Upper Saddle River, NJ.

Myers, J., Pickersgill, A, and Van Metre, E. (2004) Steering customers to the right channels, *McKinsey Quarterly*, No. 4.

*New Media Age* (2005) Delivering the goods, *New Media Age*, Article by Nic Howell, 5 May.

Parsons, A., Zeisser, M. and Waitman, R. (1996) Organizing for digital marketing, *McKinsey Quarterly*, No. 4, 183–92.

Picardi, R. (2000) *EBusiness Speed: Six Strategies for ECommerce Intelligence*. IDC Research Report. IDC, Framlington, MA.

Poon, S. and Joseph, M. (2000) A preliminary study of product nature and electronic commerce, *Marketing Intelligence and Planning*, 19(7), 493–9.

Porter, M. (1980) *Competitive Strategy*. Free Press, New York.

Porter, M. (2001) Strategy and the Internet, *Harvard Business Review*, March, 62–78.

Quelch, J. and Klein, L. (1996) The Internet and international marketing, *Sloan Management Review*, Spring, 61–75.

*Revolution* (2005a) E-mail marketing report, by Justin Pugsley. *Revolution*, September, 58–60.

*Revolution* (2005b) Campaign of the month, by Emma Rigby, *Revolution*, October, p. 69.

Sultan, F. and Rohm, A. (2004) The evolving role of the Internet in marketing strategy. *Journal of Interactive marketing*, Volume 19, Number 2, Spring 2004.

Thomas, J. and Sullivan, U. (2005) Managing marketing communications with multichannel customers, *Journal of Marketing*, 69 (October), 239–51.

Tjan, A. (2001) Finally, a way to put your Internet portfolio in order, *Harvard Business Review*, February, 78–85.

Varianini, V. and Vaturi, D. (2000) Marketing lessons from e-failures, *McKinsey Quarterly*, No. 4, 86–97.

Wikipedia (2005). Tesco, *Wikipedia*, the free encyclopedia. http://en.wikipedia.org/wiki/Tesco.

## Further reading

Brassington, F. and Petitt, S. (2000) *Principles of Marketing*, 2nd edn. Financial Times/Prentice Hall, Harlow. *See* companion Prentice Hall website (www.booksites.net/brassington2). Chapters 10 and 11 describe pricing issues in much more detail than that given in this chapter. Chapters 20, Strategic management, and 21, Marketing planning, management and control, describe the integration of marketing strategy with business strategy.

Daniel, E., Wilson, H., McDonald, M. and Ward, J. (2001) *Marketing Strategy in the Digital Age*. Financial Times/Prentice Hall, Harlow. Clear guidelines on strategy development based on and including industry case studies.

Deise, M., Nowikow, C., King, P. and Wright, A. (2000) *Executive's Guide to E-Business: From Tactics to Strategy*. Wiley, New York. An excellent practitioners' guide.

Friedlein, A. (2002) *Maintaining and Evolving Successful Commercial Websites*. Morgan Kaufmann, San Francisco. An excellent book for professionals covering managing change, content, customer relationships and site measurement.

Ghosh, S. (1998) Making business sense of the Internet, *Harvard Business Review*, March–April, 127–35. This paper gives many examples of how US companies have adapted to the Internet and asks key questions that should govern the strategy adopted. It is an excellent introduction to strategic approaches.

Gulati, R. and Garino, J. (2000) Getting the right mix of bricks and clicks for your company, *Harvard Business Review*, May–June, 107–14. A different perspective on the six strategy decisions given in the strategic definition section with a roadmap through the decision process.

Hackbarth, G. and Kettinger, W. (2000) Building an e-business strategy, *Information Systems Management*, Summer, 78–93. An information systems perspective to e-business strategy.

Willcocks, L. and Sauer, C. (2000) Moving to e-business: an introduction. In L. Willcocks and C. Sauer (eds) *Moving to E-Business*, 1–18. Random House, London. Combines traditional IS-strategy-based approaches with up-to-date case studies.

## Web links

See Chapter 2 Web links which covers developments in business models, and Chapter 3 Web links for developments in technology.

- **CIO Magazine E-commerce resource centre** (www.cio.com/forum/ec_). One of the best online magazines from business technical perspective – see other research centres also, e.g. intranets, knowledge management.

- **DaveChaffey.com** (www.davechaffey.com). Updates about all aspects of digital marketing including strategy.
- **EConsultancy** (www.e-consultancy.com). Research on managing digital channels and e-commerce teams.
- **E-commerce Times** (www.ecommercetimes.com). An online newspaper specific to e-commerce developments.
- **EConsultancy.com** (www.e-consultancy.com). A good compilation of reports and white papers many of which are strategy-related.
- **Forrester Marketing Blog** (http://blogs.forrester.com/marketing/). Forrester analysts write about developments in technology.
- **Knowledge@Wharton Wharton** (http://knowledge.wharton.upenn.edu/www). Knowledge@Wharton is an online resource that offers the latest business insights, information, and research from a variety of sources.
- **Financial Times Digital Business** (http://news.ft.com/reports/digitalbusiness). Monthly articles based on case studies.
- **McKinseyQuarterly** (www.mckinseyquarter.com). Articles regularly cover digital marketing strategy.

# The Internet and the marketing mix

## Learning objectives

After reading this chapter, the reader should be able to:

- Apply the elements of the marketing mix in an online context
- Evaluate the opportunities that the Internet makes available for varying the marketing mix
- Assess the opportunities for online brand-building

## Questions for marketers

Key questions for marketing managers related to this chapter are:

- How are the elements of the marketing mix varied online?
- What are the implications of the Internet for brand development?
- Can the product component of the mix be varied online?
- How are companies developing online pricing strategies?
- Does 'place' have relevance online?

## Links to other chapters

This chapter is related to other chapters as follows:

- Chapter 2 introduces the impact of the Internet on market structure and distribution channels
- Chapter 4 describes how Internet marketing strategies can be developed
- Chapters 6 and 7 explain the service elements of the mix in more detail
- Chapter 7 explains site design can be used to support and enhance brand values
- Chapters 8 and 9 explain the promotion elements of the mix in more detail

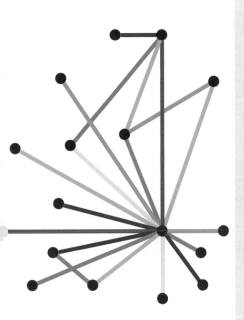

## Introduction

**Marketing mix**

The series of seven key variables – Product, Price, Place, Promotion, People, Process and Physical evidence – that are varied by marketers as part of the customer offering.

**Online branding**

How online channels are used to support brands that, in essence, are the sum of the characteristics of a product or service as perceived by a user.

This chapter shows how the well-established strategic framework of the **marketing mix** can be applied by marketers to inform their Internet marketing strategy. It explores this key issue of Internet marketing strategy in more detail than was possible in Chapter 4. As well as the marketing mix, **online branding** is another major topic covered in Chapter 5. As part of our discussion of product we will review how the Internet can be used to support and impact the way brands are developed.

The marketing mix – widely referred to as the 4 Ps of Product, Price, Place and Promotion – was originally proposed by Jerome McCarthy (1960) and is still used as an essential part of formulating and implementing marketing strategy by many practitioners. The 4 Ps have since been extended to the 7 Ps, which include three further elements that better reflect service delivery: People, Process and Physical evidence (Booms and Bitner, 1981), although others argue that these are subsumed within the 4 Ps. Figure 5.1 summarises the different sub-elements of the 7 Ps.

The marketing mix is applied frequently in discussion of marketing strategy since it provides a simple strategic framework for varying different elements of an organisation's product offering to influence the demand for products within target markets. For example, if the aim is to increase sales of a product, options include decreasing the price and changing the amount or type of promotion, or some combination of these elements.

Digital media provides many new opportunities for the marketer to vary the marketing mix, as suggested by Figure 5.1 and Activity 5.1. Digital media also have far-reaching implications for the relative importance of different elements of the mix for many markets, regardless of whether an organisation is involved directly in transactional e-commerce. Consequently, the marketing mix is a useful framework to inform strategy development. First, it gives a framework for comparing an organisation's existing services with competitors' in and out of sector as part of the benchmarking process described in Chapter 1. As well as a tool for benchmarking, it can also be used as a mechanism for generating alternative strategic approaches.

Given the potential implications of the Internet on the marketing mix, a whole chapter is devoted to examining its impact and strategies that companies can develop to best manage this situation.

| **Using the Internet to vary the marketing mix** | | | | | | |
|---|---|---|---|---|---|---|
| **Product** | **Promotion** | **Price** | **Place** | **People** | **Process** | **Physical evidence** |
| • Quality | • Marketing | • Positioning | • Trade | • Individuals | • Customer | • Sales/staff |
| • Image | communications | • List | channels | on marketing | focus | contact |
| • Branding | • Personal | • Discounts | • Sales | activities | • Business-led | experience |
| • Features | promotion | • Credit | support | • Individuals | • IT-supported | of brand |
| • Variants | • Sales | • Payment | • Channel | on customer | • Design | • Product |
| • Mix | promotion | methods | number | contact | features | packaging |
| • Support | • PR | • Free or | • Segmented | • Recruitment | • Research | • Online |
| • Customer | • Branding | value- | channels | • Culture/ | and | experience |
| service | • Direct | added | | image | development | |
| • Use | marketing | elements | | • Training | | |
| occasion | | | | and skills | | |
| • Availability | | | | • Remuneration | | |
| • Warranties | | | | | | |

| Figure 5.1 | The elements of the marketing mix |
|---|---|

| Activity 5.1 | How can the Internet be used to vary the marketing mix? |

**Purpose**

An introductory activity which highlights the vast number of areas which the Internet impacts.

**Activity**

Review Figure 5.1 and select the *two* most important ways in which the Internet gives new potential for varying the marketing mix for *each* of product, price, promotion, place, people and processes. State:

- new opportunities for varying the mix;
- examples of companies that have achieved this;
- possible negative implications (threats) for each opportunity.

The key issues related to different elements of the marketing mix that are discussed in this chapter are:

- *Product* – are there opportunities for modifying the core or extended product online?
- *Price* – the implications of the Internet for pricing and the adoption of new pricing models or strategies.
- *Place* – the implications for distribution.
- *Promotion* (what new promotional tools can be applied) – this is only discussed briefly in this chapter since it is described in more detail in Chapters 8 and 9.
- *People, process and physical evidence* – these are not discussed in detail in this chapter since their online application is covered in more detail in Chapters 6, 7 and 10 in connection with customer-relationship management and managing and maintaining the online presence.

Before embarking on a review of the role of the Internet on each of the 7 Ps, it is worth briefly restating some of the well-known criticisms of applying the marketing mix as a solitary tool for marketing strategy. First and perhaps most importantly, the marketing mix, because of its origins in the 1960s, is symptomatic of a push approach to marketing and does not explicitly acknowledge the needs of customers. As a consequence, the marketing mix tends to lead to a product orientation rather than customer orientation – a key concept of market orientation and indeed a key Internet marketing concept. To mitigate this effect, Lautenborn (1990) suggested the 4 Cs framework which considers the 4 Ps from a customer perspective. In brief, the 4 Cs are:

- Customer needs and wants (from the product)
- Cost to the customer (price)
- Convenience (relative to place)
- Communication (promotion).

This customer-centric approach also lends itself well online, since the customer is often in an active comparison mode rather than a passive media consumption mode.

It follows that the selection of the marketing mix should be based on detailed knowledge of buyer behaviour collected through market research. Furthermore, it should be remembered that the mix is often adjusted according to different target markets or segments to better meet the needs of these customer groupings.

As you read this chapter, you should consider which are the key elements of the mix which can be varied online for the different types of online presence introduced in Chapter 1, i.e. transactional e-commerce, relationship-building, brand-building, media owner portals and social networks. Allen and Fjermestad (2001) and Harridge-March (2004) have reviewed how the Internet has impacted the main elements of the marketing mix, particularly for digital products. There is no denying that all of the elements are still important, but Chaffey and Smith (2008) have said that, online, partnerships is the eighth P because this is so important in achieving reach and affiliation. In this text, though, partnerships will be considered as part of Place and Promotion.

---

| Digital marketing in practice | The EConsultancy interview |
| --- | --- |

### Chief Operating Officer, William Reeves, online DVD retailer LOVEFiLM

### Overview and main concepts covered

LOVEFiLM founder and COO William Reeve explains how the company uses a technique known as 'Hackathons' to develop their online proposition.

### The interview

**Q: We see you recently held a Hackathon to generate new ideas for the business. How did it go?**

*William Reeve:* It went really well. I read something about Facebook doing a Hackathon and looked up what it was on Wikipedia, and we invented a way of doing it ourselves. We had to debate a couple of things – whether to open it up to the whole business – and we had to come up with some rules so that the whole tech development team didn't have to down tools for the day.

We ended up with a decent level of participation – around a dozen people worked on creating ideas during the day and another four or five people assessing them in the evening. Everyone was really enthusiastic about it. It got people thinking outside the box.

**Q: Do you have any tips on making Hackathons effective?**

*William Reeve:* The real trick is how you follow through with ideas. We had two people working on one idea – a mobile feature – and they integrated it with our website and made it customer-ready in one day.

It pretty much worked and we liked the idea but we still haven't gone live with it. Obviously, if you have 500,000 customers you have to carefully think through the marketing. My tips would be to make sure you get senior business people involved at some point in the process – probably, like we did, as the audience. We had about half our total tech and web team in the UK there, as well as people from customer services and marketing.

Also, think about how you support the winning ideas in taking them forward, and design it in a way that suits your business.

**Q: When do you plan to hold the next one?**

*William Reeve:* We have a code freeze at Christmas and we're going to use that time to do another one. I think we'll aim to do it roughly quarterly from then on. We got some really good quality ideas and everyone that did it enjoyed it.

**Q: Where are you at now with the mobile service?**

*William Reeve:* I think we haven't quite decided whether the market demand is at a level that we would need to support a rollout of it. It's with the marketing folks at the moment – the issue being that mobile interfaces are so crap that you haven't got that many customers who would be prepared to put up with it. And this one's based on text, not for smartphones or anything.

It looks great and functions well but we would need to see *x*% of our customer base being prepared to use it before we got too excited about it, and we're not sure that's the case yet.

**Q: How is your download service going, in terms of subscribers?**

*William Reeve*: It's going. The issue is that we're not offering as good value on it as we'd like to. We're all about convenience and good value. Although it's competitively priced, it's not something I could tell my friends they should use.

Buying a download of something like King Kong for £20 when you can buy the DVD for £15 – why would you do that? We would love to offer it more competitively but our hands are tied by the studios on this stuff.

The studios vary in their stance, but on things like King Kong they want to make sure nobody in their retail supply chain grumbles about downloads. By pricing downloads more expensively they feel no one can complain because even if we steal a retail sale, they are making more money out of a download.

Other studios are a bit more enlightened than that, and understand that there are a lot of costs that come out of the retail chain when you download, and those savings should be passed on to consumers. But . . . there's a situation where different studios have different policies, there isn't consistency in pricing and there isn't a range of content we would be proud of.

We have some good titles – a few thousand – but our DVD service has almost 70,000 titles.

**Q: How long are these issues going to take to sort out?**

*William Reeve*: It's not going to be solved at the rate the media think it is. Two years ago, people thought piracy and DRM was an issue, but one of the things we have helped to prove is that is not an issue. We have had King Kong from the day of release but no one has been pirating it from our downloads.

We have helped to demonstrate the technology, because we believe it will become a huge business for us. But the proposition's not competitive with buying or renting DVDs or other ways to consume entertainment.

**Q: How many users of the service are there?**

*William Reeve*: It's growing and the customers that do use it like it. I'm not going to give you the exact user numbers. It's a small percentage of our business and it is not growing any faster than DVDs for us. But it is growing in line with our business.

**Q: Have you looked at ad-supported downloads?**

*William Reeve*: Yes, we're quite excited about doing that – that gets round some of the value for money issues. There's still the convenience issue – people still have to watch it on their laptops, but they are happy to do that.

**Q: How is advertising within your parcels developing as a revenue stream?**

*William Reeve*: It's growing quite well for us. Our post is popular post, if you see what I mean. Most of our customers say the envelopes they receive the DVDs in are their most popular bit of post, so it's a great opportunity if we can put relevant offers inside them. Nobody is complaining about that stuff – things like chocolate bars and cinema vouchers are going down really well.

We have 500,000 subs in the UK and they know their way around films, as well as knowing how to buy online and trying new things. That's an audience that's worth quite a bit. How big is it? It's bigger than our digital business.

**Q: Can you tell us a bit about customer retention – the techniques you use to segment and prioritise customers?**

*William Reeve:* We manage churn more carefully, if anything, than customer acquisition. There are a range of techniques we use – many of them not yet at anything like the level of sophistication we would like them to be at.

There are lots of things that affect churn that we aren't yet acting on internally, for example. But we are trying to act on them where we know about them. If we can predict you are about to churn then we can take proactive steps to stop you churning.

**Q: Are there many customers that you don't mind if they churn?**

*William Reeve:* There are a few but not very many – generally ones that try to take repeated trials out of us or always wait for our special offers, so much so that they are taking the mick.

**Q: What about high usage customers?**

*William Reeve:* We're generally all right about them – they may not be that profitable for us, but we value them anyway. Those customers will often be the ones that are shouting at the rooftops loudest about us. You have to be an absolute monster for us to decide we don't want your business. What you are probably doing is claiming you have lost so many discs it is costing us more in new stock than postage.

We have got the technique to prioritise certain customers against others, but we don't use it. We try and keep everyone at a level of service where they will rave about us to their friends.

*Source:* http://www.e-consultancy.com/news-blog/newsletter/3540/interview-with-lovefilm-coo-william-reeve.html.

## Product

**Product variable**

The element of the marketing mix that involves researching customers' needs and developing appropriate products.

**Core product**

The fundamental features of the product that meet the user's needs.

**Extended product**

Additional features and benefits beyond the core product.

The **Product** element of the marketing mix refers to characteristics of a product, service or brand. Product decisions should be informed by market research where customers' needs are assessed and the feedback is used to modify existing products or develop new products. There are many alternatives for varying the product in the online context when a company is developing its online strategy. Internet-related product decisions can be usefully divided into decisions affecting the **core product** and the **extended product**. The core product refers to the main product purchased by the consumer to fulfil their needs, while the extended or augmented product refers to additional services and benefits that are built around the core of the product.

The main implications of the Internet for the product aspect of the mix, which we will review in this section, are:

1 options for varying the core product;
2 options for offering digital products;
3 options for changing the extended product;
4 conducting research online;
5 velocity of new product development;
6 velocity of new product diffusion.

There is also a subsection which looks at the implications for migrating a brand online.

## 1 Options for varying the core product

For some companies, there may be options for new digital products which will typically be information products that can be delivered over the web. Ghosh (1998) talks about developing new products or adding 'digital value' to customers. The questions he posed still prove useful today:

- *Can I offer additional information or transaction services to my existing customer base?* For example, for a bookseller, providing reviews of customer books, previews of books or selling books online. For a travel company, providing video tours of resorts and accommodation.
- *Can I address the needs of new customer segments by repackaging my current information assets or by creating new business propositions using the Internet?* For an online bookseller, creating an electronic book service, or a DVD rental service as has been achieved by Amazon.
- *Can I use my ability to attract customers to generate new sources of revenue such as advertising or sales of complementary products?* Lastminute.com which sells travel-related services has a significant advertising revenue; it can also sell non-travel services.
- *Will my current business be significantly harmed by other companies providing some of the value I currently offer?* Considers the consequences if other companies use some of the product strategies described above.

Of course, the markets transformed most by the Internet are those where products themselves can be transformed into digital services. Such products include music (download or streaming of digital tracks – see the Napster case study at the end of the chapter), books (electronic books), newspaper and magazine publishing (online access to articles) and software (digital downloads and online subscription services).

Rayport and Sviokla (1994) describe transactions where the actual product has been replaced by information about the product, for example a company providing oil drilling equipment focusing instead on analysis and dissemination of information about drilling.

**Mass customisation**

Using economies of scale enabled by technology to offer tailored versions of products to individual customers or groups of customers.

The Internet also introduces options for **mass customisation** of products, particularly digital products digital or products that can be specified online. Levis provide a truly personal service that dates back to 1994, when Levi Strauss initiated its 'Personal Pair' programme. Women who were prepared to pay up to $15 more than the standard price and wait for delivery could go to Levi's stores and have themselves digitised – that is, have their measurements taken and a pair of custom jeans made, and then have their measurements stored on a database for future purchases. Today this option is no longer available, but Levis are involving consumers in 'co-creation' of products through competitions such as 'Project Runway' to submit and judge new jean designs.

**Prosumer**

'Producer + consumer'. The customer is closely involved in specifying their requirements in a product.

Mass customisation or personalisation of products in which a customer takes a more active role in product design is part of the move to the **prosumer**. Examples are provided in Figures 5.2 and 5.3. Further details on the prosumer concept are given in Box 5.1.

**Figure 5.2**     Pearson Custom Publishing (www.pearsoncustom.com)

---

**Box 5.1**     The prosumer

The prosumer concept was introduced in 1980 by futurist Alvin Toffler in his book *The Third Wave*. According to Toffler, the future would once again combine production with consumption. In *The Third Wave*, Toffler saw a world where interconnected users would collaboratively 'create' products. Note that he foresaw this over 10 years before the web was invented!

Alternative notions of the prosumer, all of which are applicable to e-marketing, are catalogued at Logophilia WordSpy (www.wordspy.com):

1   A consumer who is an amateur in a particular field, but who is knowledgeable enough to require equipment that has some professional features: ('professional' + 'consumer').
2   A person who helps to design or customise the products they purchase: ('producer' + 'consumer').
3   A person who creates goods for their own use and also possibly to sell: ('producing' + 'consumer').
4   A person who takes steps to correct difficulties with consumer companies or markets and to anticipate future problems: ('proactive' + 'consumer').

An example of the application of the prosumer is provided by BMW who used an interactive website prior to launch of their Z3 roadster where users could design their own preferred features. The information collected was linked to a database and as BMW had previously collected data on its most loyal customers, the database could give a very accurate indication of which combinations of features were the most sought after and should therefore be put into production.

Dominos Pizza provide a further example of supporting the Prosumer. They have introduced an online promotion called BFD, or *Big Fantastic Deal*, which lets pizza lovers ornament a pizza any way they like through a Flash-based microsite.

Users can specify crust type, amount of sauce and cheese, and any number of a series of toppings. Users can also name and register their pizzas for other users to try. Dominos report that over 12,000 pizzas have been registered, some with names like 'Happy Birthday Aaron' and 'Rhonda Half Doug Half,' according to Springwise. The most popular custom pizza is 'Ciao Bella,' which has been ordered 83,000 times.

**1 Select your map scale**

Choose from list below....... ▲▼

**2 Map centre**
(place name, post code, grid reference)

| | SHOW MAP CENTRE |

*Important:* Using nudge buttons on the right will move the location of your map

**3 Check full map area**    YOUR MAP COVERAGE

*Important:* Using nudge buttons on the right will move the location of your map

**4 Choice of supply**

Select From List.................. ▲▼

**5 Map key language**

Select From List................ ▲▼

**6 Cover image** (Integral Cover)    PICK AN IMAGE

**7 Add your Main title** (up to 16 characters)

| | ADD TO COVER |

**8 Add your Sub-title** (up to 32 characters)

| | ADD TO COVER |

**9 Please check your map is centred correctly before proceeding**

ADD TO BASKET

| Figure 5.3 | Customising maps according to customers' preferences |
|------------|------------------------------------------------------|
| | *Source*: Ordnance Survey OS Select (www.osselect.co.uk) |

Companies can also consider how the Internet can be used to change the range or combination of products offered. Some companies such as online fashion retailers may only offer a subset of products online. Alternatively, a company may have a fuller catalogue available online than is available through offline brochures. **Bundling** is a further alternative. For example, easyJet has developed a range of complementary travel-related services including flights, packages and car hire.

**Bundling**
Offering complementary services.

Finally, it should also be noted that information about the core features of the product becomes more readily available online, as pointed out by Allen and Fjermestad (2001). However, this has the greatest implications for price (downwards pressure caused by price transparency) and place and promotion (marketers must ensure they are represented favourably on the portal intermediaries) where the products will be compared with others in terms of core features, extended features and price.

### 2 Options for offering digital products

Companies such as publishers, TV companies and other media owners who can offer digital products such as published content, music or videos now have great flexibility to offer a range of product purchase options at different price points including:

- *Subscription.* This is a traditional publisher revenue model, but subscription can potentially be offered for different periods at different price points, e.g. 3 months, 12 months or 2 years.
- *Pay-per-view.* A fee for a single download or viewing session at a higher relative price than the subscription service. Music service Napster offers vouchers for download in a similar way to a mobile company 'pay-as-you-go' model. Travel publisher Lonely Planet enables visitors to a destination to download an introduction for a fraction of the price of a full printed guide. Technology publisher O'Reilly now offers 'Digital Shorts' which are concise guides about a particular product.
- *Bundling.* Different channels or content can be offered as individual products or grouped at a reduced price compared to pay-per-view.
- *Ad supported content.* There is no direct price set here, instead, the publisher's main revenue source is through adverts on the site (either CPM display advertising on-site using banner ads and skyscrapers) a fixed sponsorship arrangement or CPC, which stands for 'cost-per-click' more typical when using search ad network publishing such as Google Adsense (www.google.com/adsense.com) which accounts for around a third of Google's revenue. Other options include affiliate revenue from sales on third party sites or offering access to subscriber lists. The UK's most popular newspaper site, the *Guardian* (www.guardian.co.uk) once trialled an ad-free subscription service, but like many online publishers it has reverted to ad-supported content.

### 3 Options for changing the extended product

When a customer buys a new computer, it consists not only of the tangible computer, monitor and cables, but also the information provided by the computer salesperson, the instruction manual, the packaging, the warranty and the follow-up technical service. These are elements of the extended product. Chaffey and Smith (2008) suggest these examples of how the Internet can be used to vary the extended product:

- endorsements
- awards
- testimonies
- customer lists
- customer comments
- warranties
- guarantees

- money-back offers
- customer service (see people, process and physical evidence)
- incorporating tools to help users during their selection and use of the product.

Peppard and Rylander (2005) have researched how people assimilate information online when selecting products and point out it is important that the site replicates information about product selection that would normally be provided by interaction in other channels by a member of sales staff by phone or face-to-face. These facilities can be replicated online. For example, bank First Direct uses an interactive dialogue to recommend the best options on their savings mortgage products (Figure 5.4).

The digital value referred to by Ghosh (1998) will often be provided online without charge to encourage site visitors to engage with a brand on a first visit to a site or to encourage return visits, in which case it will be part of the extended product. He suggests that companies should provide free digital value to help build an audience which can then be converted from prospects into customers as part of permission marketing. He refers to this process as 'building a customer magnet'; today this would be known as a 'portal' or 'community'. There is good potential for customer magnets in specialised vertical markets served by business-to-business companies where there is a need for industry-specific information to assist individuals in their day-to-day work. For example, a customer magnet could be developed for the construction industry, agrochemicals, biotechnology or independent financial advisers. Examples include resource centres and communities at Tektronix (www.tektronix.com) and SAP (www.sap.com). Alternatively the portal could be branded as an 'extranet' that is only available to key accounts to help differentiate the service. Dell Premier is an example of such an extranet.

Extended product is not always provided free of charge. In other cases a premium may be charged for new services. Amazon (www.amazon.com) for instance is active in identifying

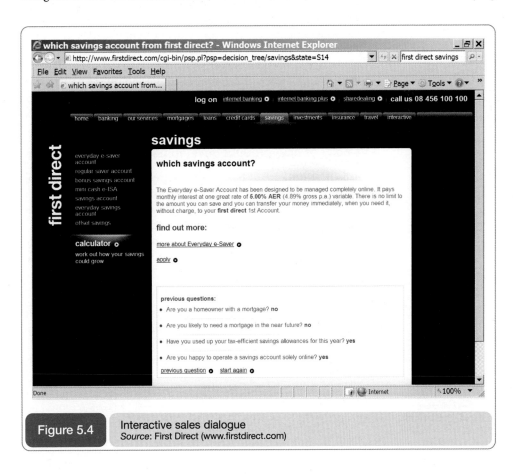

| Figure 5.4 | Interactive sales dialogue
*Source*: First Direct (www.firstdirect.com) |

new revenue sources through product innovation – for example it has always charged a premium for its wrapping service, but more recently has introduced related products including a credit card and offers Amazon Prime for customers who use the service frequently. For business audiences it offers advertising on its site or hosting and application support through Amazon Web Services.

## 4 Conducting research online

The Internet provides many options for learning about product preferences. It can be used as a relatively low-cost method of collecting marketing research, particularly about customer perceptions of products and services. Sawhney *et al.* (2005) have reviewed the options for using digital media for new product innovation where they contrast the traditional new product research process with a digitally augmented co-creation process. They suggest that online research tools should be evaluated according to how they can be used (1) front-end developments of ideation and concept against back-end developments involving product design and testing, and (2) the nature of collaboration – broad/high reach against deep/high richness.

Options for performing new product development research online include:

- *Online focus group*. A moderated focus group can be conducted to compare customers' experience of product use. Many companies now have permanent customer panels they can use to ask about new ideas.
- *Online questionnaire survey*. These typically focus on the site visitors' experience, but can also include questions relating to products.
- *Customer feedback or support forums*. Comments posted to the site or independent sites such as social networks may give suggestions about future product innovation. In Chapter 4 we showed how Dell created IdeaStorm (www.ideastorm.com) to encourage customers and partners to feedback on product ideas. Dell also integrates Opinion Lab (www.opinionlab.com) into its site to get 'voice of customer' feedback about particular pages, usability and support issues.
- *Web analytics*. A wealth of marketing research information is also available from response data from e-mail and search campaigns and the website itself, since every time a user clicks on a link offering a particular product, this indicates a preference for products and related offers. Such information can be used indirectly to assess customers' product preferences.

Approaches for undertaking these types of research are briefly reviewed in Chapter 10.

## 5 Velocity of new product development

Quelch and Klein (1996) note that the Internet can also be used to accelerate new product development since different product options can be tested online more rapidly as part of market research. Companies can use their own panels of consumers to test opinion more rapidly and often at lower costs than for traditional market research.

Another aspect of the velocity of new product development is that the network effect of the Internet enables companies to form partnerships more readily to launch new products.

## 6 Velocity of new product diffusion

Quelch and Klein (1996) also noted that the implication of the Internet and globalisation is that to remain competitive, organisations will have to roll out new products more rapidly to international markets. More recently, Malcolm Gladwell in his book *The Tipping Point* (2000) has shown how word-of-mouth communication has a tremendous impact on the rate of adoption of new products and we can suggest this effect is often enhanced or facilitated through the Internet. In Chapter 9, we will see how marketers seek to influence this effect through what is known as 'viral marketing'. Marsden (2004) provides a good summary of the implications of the **tipping point** for marketers. He says that 'using the science of social epidemics, *The Tipping Point* explains the three simple principles that underpin the

**Tipping point**

Using the science of social epidemics explains principles that underpin the rapid spread of ideas, products and behaviours through a population.

rapid spread of ideas, products and behaviours through a population'. He advises how marketers should help create a 'tipping point' for a new product or service, the moment when a domino effect is triggered and an epidemic of demand sweeps through a population like a highly contagious virus.

There are three main laws that are relevant from *The Tipping Point*:

### 1 The law of the few

This suggests that the spread of any new product or service is dependent on the initial adoption by 'connectors' who are socially connected and who encourage adoption through word-of-mouth and copycat behaviour. In an online context, these connectors may use personal blogs, e-mail newsletters and podcasts to propagate their opinions.

### 2 The stickiness factor

Typically, this refers to how 'glued' we are to a medium such as a TV channel or a website, but in this context it refers to attachment to the characteristics and attributes of a product or a brand. Gladwell stresses the importance of testing and market research to make the product effective. Marsden suggests that there are key cross-category attributes which are key drivers for product success and he commends the work of Morris and Martin (2000) which summarises these attributes as:

- *Excellence*: perceived as best of breed
- *Uniqueness*: clear one-of-a-kind differentiation
- *Aesthetics*: perceived aesthetic appeal
- *Association*: generates positive associations
- *Engagement*: fosters emotional involvement
- *Expressive value*: visible sign of user values
- *Functional value*: addresses functional needs
- *Nostalgic value*: evokes sentimental linkages
- *Personification*: has character, personality
- *Cost*: perceived value for money.

You can see that this list is also a useful prompt about the ideal characteristics of a website or online service.

### 3 The power of context

Gladwell suggests that like infectious diseases, products and behaviours spread far and wide only when they fit the physical, social and mental context into which they are launched. He gives the example of a wave of crime in the New York subway that came to an abrupt halt by simply removing the graffiti from trains and clamping down on fare-dodging. It can be suggested that products should be devised and tested to fit their context, situation or occasion of use.

---

**Activity 5.2**  **Assessing options online to vary product using the Internet**

**Purpose**

To illustrate the options for varying the product element of the marketing mix online.

**Activity**

Select one of the sectors below. Use a search engine to find three competitors with similar product offerings. List ways in which each has used the Internet to vary its core and extended product. Which of the companies do you think makes best use of the Internet?

- Computer manufacturers
- Management consultants
- Children's toy sector
- Higher education.

## The long tail concept

**Long tail concept**
A frequency distribution suggesting the relative variation in popularity of items selected by consumers.

The **long tail concept** is useful for considering the role of Product, Place, Price and Promotion online. The phenomenon, now referred to as the 'long tail', following an article by Anderson (2004), was arguably first applied to human behaviour by George Kingsley Zipf, professor of linguistics at Harvard who observed the phenomenon in word usage (see http://en.wikipedia.org/wiki/Zipf%27s_law). He found that if the variation in popularity of different words in a language is considered, there is a systematic pattern in the frequency of usage or popularity. Zipf's 'law' suggests that if a collection of items is ordered or ranked by popularity, the second item will have around half the popularity of the first one and the third item will have about a third of the popularity of the first one and so on. In general:

*The kth item is 1/k the popularity of the first.*

Look at Figure 5.5 which shows how the 'relative popularity' of items is predicted to decline according to Zipf's law from a maximum count of 1000 for the most popular item to 20 for the 50th item.

In an online context, application of this 'law' is now known as 'the long tail' thanks to Anderson (2004). It can be applied to the relative popularity of a group of websites or web pages or products on an individual site, since they tend to show a similar pattern of popularity. There are a small number of sites (or pages within sites) which are very popular (the head which may account for 80% of the volume) and a much larger number of sites or pages that are less popular individually, but still collectively important. Returning to the product context, Anderson (2004) argued that for a company such as Amazon, the long tail or Zipf's law can be applied to describe the variation in preferences for selecting or purchasing from a choice for products as varied as books, CDs, electronic items, travel or financial services. This pattern has also been identified by Brynjolfsson *et al.* (2003) who present a framework that quantifies the economic impact of increased product variety made available through electronic markets. They say:

*One reason for increased product variety on the Internet is the ability of online retailers to catalog, recommend, and provide a large number of products for sale. For example, the number of book titles available at Amazon.com is more than 23 times larger than the number of books on the shelves of a typical Barnes & Noble superstore, and 57 times greater than the number of books stocked in a typical large independent bookstore.*

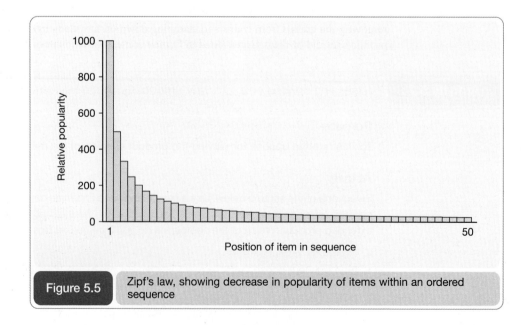

| Figure 5.5 | Zipf's law, showing decrease in popularity of items within an ordered sequence |

Looking at the issue from another perspective, they estimate that 40% of sales are from relatively obscure books with a sales rank of more than 100,000 (if you visit Amazon, you will see that every book has a sales rank from 1 for the most popular to over 1 million for the least popular). This indicates the importance of the long tail for online retailers like Amazon, since 40% of sales are from these less popular books which cannot be stocked in a conventional bookstore (a large real-world book store would typically hold about 100,000 books). In a Pricing context, another benefit for online retailers is that less popular products cannot be readily obtained in the real world, so Amazon can justify higher prices for these books. Brynjolfsson *et al.* (2003) estimated that average Amazon prices for an item in the top 100,000 is $29.26 and in less popular titles $41.60.

## The Internet and branding

**Branding**
The process of creating and evolving successful brands.

**Branding** and how a brand is developed and presented online is particularly important because a website visitor has limited physical cues to help form an opinion about a company and its services, such as talking to a sales representative or the ambiance of the physical store.

Erdem *et al.* (2002) noted in their study into the impact of brand credibility on consumer price sensitivity, that a credible brand signal helps to generate customer value by: (1) reducing perceived risk; (2) reducing information search costs, and (3) creating a favourable, trustworthy perception of the organisation.

**Brand**
The sum of the characteristics of a product or service perceived by a user.

Remember that branding involves much more than the name or logo associated with a company or products. A **brand** is described by Leslie de Chernatony and Malcolm McDonald in their classic 1992 book *Creating Powerful Brands* as:

> *an identifiable product or service augmented in such a way that the buyer or user perceives relevant unique added values which match their needs most closely. Furthermore, its success results from being able to sustain these added values in the face of competition.*

This definition highlights three essential characteristics of a successful brand which we need to relate to the online environment:

- brand is dependent on customer perception;
- perception is influenced by the added-value characteristics of the product;
- the added-value characteristics need to be sustainable.

To summarise, a brand is dependent on a customer's psychological affinity for a product, and is much more than the physical name or symbol elements of brand identity.

De Chernatony (2001) has evaluated the relevance of the brand concept on the Internet. He also believes that the main elements of brand values and brand strategy are the same in the Internet environment. However, he suggests that the classical branding model where consumers are passive recipients of value is challenged online. Instead he suggests that consumers on the Internet become active co-producers of value where consumers can contribute feedback through discussion groups to add value to a brand. De Chernatony argues for a looser form of brand control where the company facilitates rather than controls customer discussion.

**Brand experience**
The frequency and depth of interactions with a brand can be enhanced through the Internet.

A further method by which the Internet can change branding that was suggested by Jevons and Gabbott (2000) is that online, 'the first-hand experience of the brand is a more powerful token of trust than the perception of the brand'. In the online environment, the customer can **experience** or interact with the brand more frequently and to a greater depth. As Dayal *et al.* (2000) say, 'on the World Wide Web, the brand is the experience and the experience is the brand'. They suggest that to build successful online brands, organisations should consider how their proposition can build on these possible brand promises:

- *the promise of convenience* – making a purchase experience more convenient than the real-world one, or that with rivals;
- *the promise of achievement* – to assist consumers in achieving their goals, for example supporting online investors in their decision or supporting business people in their day-to-day work;
- *the promise of fun and adventure* – this is clearly more relevant for B2C services;
- *the promise of self-expression and recognition* – provided by personalisation services such as Yahoo! Geocities where consumers can build their own website;
- *the promise of belonging* – provided by online communities such as social networks.

Summarising the elements of online branding, de Chernatony (2001) suggests that successful online branding requires delivering three aspects of a brand: rational values, emotional values and promised experience (based on rational and emotional values). We return to the notion of brand promise at the start of Chapter 7 since this is closely related to delivering customer experience.

**Brand equity**

The assets (or liabilities) linked to a brand's name and symbol that add to (or subtract from) a service.

An alternative perspective on branding is provided by Aaker and Joachimsthaler (2000) who refer to brand equity, which they define as:

*a set of brand assets and liabilities linked to a brand, its name and symbol, that add to or subtract from the value provided by a product or service to a firm and/or to that firm's customers.*

So, brand equity indicates the value provided to a company, or its customers, through a brand. Assessing brand equity on the web needs to address the unique characteristics of computer-mediated environments as Christodoulides and de Chernatony (2004) have pointed out. These researchers set out to explore whether additional measures of brand equity were required online. Based on expert interviews they have identified the additional measures of brand equity which are important online, as summarised in Table 5.1. As we would expect, this includes attributes of the digital medium such as interactivity and customisation which combine to form relevance and a great online brand experience. Content is not stressed separately, which is surprising, although they do mention its importance under site design and it is also a key aspect of other attributes such as customisation, relevance and the overall experience. A more recent analysis of online brand equity which can be used to survey customers on the quality of brand experience for retail and service sites by Christodoulides *et al.* (2006) is presented in the introduction to Chapter 7.

| **Table 5.1** | Traditional measures of brand equity and online measures of brand equity |
|---|---|

| **Traditional measures of brand equity (Aaker and Joachimsthaler, 2000)** | **Online measures of brand equity (from Christodoulides and de Chernatony, 2004)** |
|---|---|
| • Price premium | • Online brand experience |
| • Satisfaction/loyalty | • Interactivity |
| • Perceived quality | • Customisation |
| • Leadership popularity | • Relevance |
| • Perceived value | • Site design |
| • Brand personality | • Customer service |
| • Organisational associations | • Order fulfilment |
| • Brand awareness | • Quality of brand relationships |
| • Market share | • Communities |
| • Market price and distribution coverage | • Engagement measured through web analytics (see Chapter 9) |

### Success factors for brand sites

In Chapter 1, we identified a 'brand website' as one of five classes of website or parts of sites which support different organisational goals. Examples include websites for presenting a consumer goods brand which cannot be purchased online such as a drink, deodorant or a household cleaning product. Although other types of sites we mentioned in Chapter 1 including transactional sites, relationship building sites, portals and social networks will all seek to provide a favourable brand experience. In the case of pure 'brand sites', the manager of the site needs to carefully think the best way the brand can engage with consumers given lack of content naturally associated with low-involvement products.

As Flores (2004) has suggested, it is unlikely that a brand site will be able to reach a large audience compared to a TV or radio ad. Consequently, to promote such a brand online the website will arguably be less important than other digital marketing approaches where consumers can engage with the brand on other sites including:

- display advertising on publisher sites or social networks;
- brand messages in paid search results on searches related directly or indirectly to the brand;
- sponsorship of sections or tools on publisher sites;
- editorial on publisher sites delivered through effective public relations;
- microsites on publisher sites – linked from display advertising and editorial.

**Brand advocate**
A customer who has favourable perceptions of a brand who will talk favourably about a brand to their acquaintances to help generate awareness of the brand or influence purchase intent.

For the site itself, it is not the quantity of visitors that is important, rather it is about the quality of visitors, since brand sites are most likely to attract brand advocates who can be important in influencing others to make them aware of the brand or trial the brand. As Ries and Ries (2000) have said, it is important that brand sites provide a home for the brand loyalists and advocates. It follows that brand owners should determine the type of content on a brand site which will encourage brand loyalists (and also the brand-neutral consumer) to visit and then return to the brand site. Flores (2004) has said that encouraging visitors to return is key and he suggests different aspects of a quality site experience to achieve this. Some of the methods he suggests to encourage visitors to return include:

- *Create a compelling, interactive experience including rich media which reflects the brand.* The research by Flores showed that a site which delivers an unsatisfactory experience will negatively affect brand perception. He notes that some brand sites which often contain rich media or video, although visually engaging may have poor usability or download speeds.
- *Consider how the site will influence the sales cycle by encouraging trial.* Trial will often be fulfilled offline so approaches such as samples, coupons or prize draws can be used. These response activators should be integrated throughout the site. For example, car brands will all have prominent options for taking a test drive, receiving a brochure or the option to win a car or a visit to a race circuit.
- *Developing an exchange (permission marketing) programme on your website to begin a 'conversation' with the most valuable customer segments.* Permission-based e-mail or text messages can be used to update consumers about new products or promotions.

Additionally we would stress the importance of achieving customer engagement with brand sites to encourage participation or co-creation of content. For example, brands can encourage users to share and submit their comments, stories, photos or videos. Once engaged in this way, visitors are more likely to return to a site to see other's comments.

Dorset Cereals (Figure 5.6, www.dorsetcereals.co.uk) gives a good example of how the opportunities for a consumer brand to engage its audiences have been well thought through. Some of the approaches used are indicated by the menu bar and other content and the associated goals can be inferred:

- *Our recipes.* Goals – increase product usage. Provide content for brand advocates.
- *Where to buy.* Goals – increase sales for new adoptions since product distribution is not as widespread as some brands.

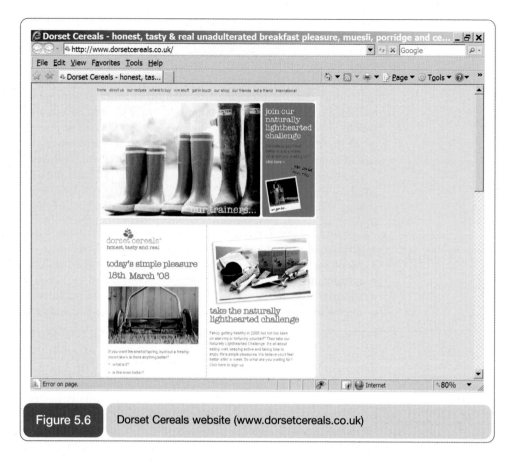

| Figure 5.6 | Dorset Cereals website (www.dorsetcereals.co.uk) |

- *Win stuff.* Goals: encourage trial and reward loyalists. The company has not used sampling to-date, but instead has run prize draws related to the rural nature of its brand, e.g. win a Land Rover, win trips to flower shows, photo competitions. The current featured promotion is the 'Naturally lighthearted challenge' which is a seven-day permission e-mail supported programme to eat more healthily.
- *Today's simple pleasure.* Goal: engage site visitors and encourage involve customers to keep brand 'front-of-mind' through a simple daily pleasures screensaver calendar.
- *Get in touch.* Goals: encourage feedback and dialogue.
- *Our shop.* Goals: Direct sales of cereal and branded merchandise such as cereal bowls.
- *Our friends.* Goals: Partner with related brands and sites which explain brand values.
- *Sell our cereals.* Goal: Find additional distributors.
- *Tell a friend.* Goal: Viral marketing (not incentivised).
- *International.* Goal: Show international availability.

Dou and Krishnamurphy (2007) have reviewed the attributes of product-related brand sites in comparison to service-brands. For the sites surveyed they found that many featured basic text information, implying they did not deliver compelling experiences.

### Brand identity

**Brand identity**
The totality of brand associations including name and symbols that must be communicated.

Aaker and Joachimsthaler (2000) also emphasise the importance of developing a plan to communicate the key features of the brand identity and increase brand awareness. Brand identity is again more than the name. These authors refer to it as a set of brand associations that imply a promise to customers from an organisation. See Mini case study 5.1 to see the different elements of brand identity which are effectively a checklist of what many e-tailers are looking to achieve.

### Brand names for online brands

Companies creating a new online brand or portal need to consider the characteristics of a successful brand name suggested by de Chernatony and McDonald (1992). Ideally, the name should be simple, distinctive, meaningful and compatible with the product. These principles can be readily applied to web-based brands. Examples of brands that fulfil most of these characteristics are CD WOW!, eBags and Travelocity. Others suggest that distinctiveness is most important: Amazon, Yahoo!, Expedia, Quokka.com (extreme sports), E*Trade, and FireandWater (HarperCollins) books.

Ries and Ries (2000) suggest two rules for naming online brands. (1) The Law of the Common Name – they say 'The kiss of death for an Internet brand is a common name'. This argues that common names such as Art.com or Advertising.com are poor since they are not sufficiently distinctive. (2) The Law of the Proper Name – they say 'Your name stands alone on the Internet, so you'd better have a good one'. This suggests that proper names are to be preferred to generic names, e.g. Handbag.com against Woman.com, or Moreover.com against Business.com. The authors suggest that the best names will follow most of these eight principles: short, simple, suggestive of the category, unique, alliterative, speakable, shocking and personalised. Although these are cast as 'immutable laws' there will of course be exceptions!

If you are registering a domain for a new company it is also worth remembering that search engines tend to favour sites in their listings which include the name of the service which is searched for within the domain name. For example, a domain name such as MyVoucherCodes (www.myvouchercodes.com) will tend to rank well for 'voucher codes' since the search engine will see sites linking to it which contains the words 'voucher codes'.

---

| Mini Case Study 5.1 | Napster.com's brand identity |
|---|---|

Aaker and Joachimsthaler (2000) suggest that the following characteristics of identity need to be defined at the start of a brand building campaign. Marketing communications can then be developed that create and reinforce this identity. Here, we will apply them to Napster, which is revisited in the main case study at the end of this chapter.

- *Brand essence (a summary of what the brand represents)*
  This is not necessarily a tag line, but for Napster it has been described as an 'All you can eat music service which is fun and affordable'
- *Core identity (its key features)*
  - choice – millions of tracks
  - value for money – under £10 per month subscription for as many tracks as you can listen to
  - easy-to-use – Napster runs as a separate application built for purpose
  - listen anywhere – on a PC or other computer, MP3 player or mobile phone
  - listen on anything – unlike iPod, Napster is compatible with most MP3 players rather than being tied into a specific hardware manufacturer
- *Extended identity*
  - personality – flaunts what is standard for existing music providers thanks to its heritage as a peer-to-peer file-sharing service
  - personalisation – Napster Radio based on particular genres or based on other songs you have downloaded
  - community – facility to share tracks with friends or other Napster members
  - symbols – Napster cat logo

- *Value proposition*
  - functional benefits – ease of use and personalisation
  - emotional benefits – community, non-conformist
  - self-expressive benefit – build your own collection of your tastes
- *Relationship*

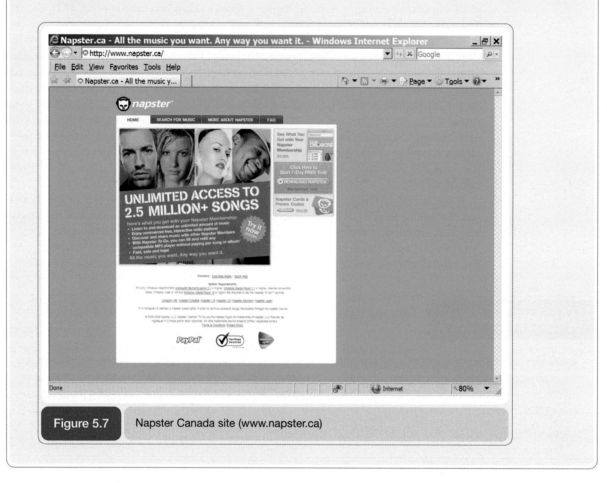

| Figure 5.7 | Napster Canada site (www.napster.ca) |

## The importance of brand online

The Internet presents a 'double-edged sword' to existing brands. We have seen that a consumer who already has knowledge of a brand is more likely to trust it. However, loyalty can be decreased because it encourages consumers to trial other brands. This is suggested by Figure 5.8. This trial may well lead to purchase of brands that have not been previously considered.

The BrandNewWorld (2004) survey showed that in some categories, a large proportion of buyers have purchased different brands from those they initially considered for example:

- large home appliances, 47%
- financial products and services, 39%
- holidays and travel, 31%
- mobile phones, 28%
- cars, 26%.

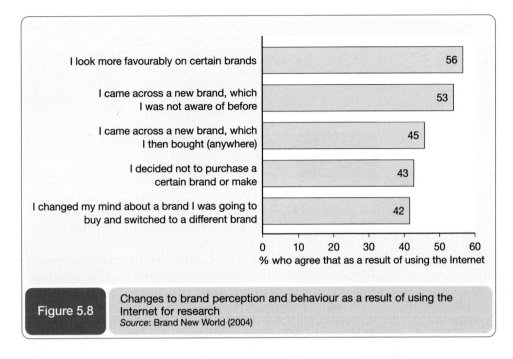

**Figure 5.8** Changes to brand perception and behaviour as a result of using the Internet for research
*Source*: Brand New World (2004)

But, for other types of products, existing brand preferences appear to be more important:

- clothing/accessories, 22%
- computer hardware, 21%
- garden/DIY products, 17%
- home furnishings, 6%.

The survey also suggested that experienced Internet users were more likely to switch brands (52% agreed they were more likely to switch after researching online) compared to less-experienced users (33%).

Of course, the likelihood of a consumer purchasing will depend upon their knowledge of the retailer brand or the product brand. Figure 5.9 shows that many customers will still buy an unknown manufacturer brand if they are familiar with the retailer brand. This is less true if they don't know the retailer. Significantly, if they don't know the retailer or the brand, it is fairly unlikely they will buy.

## Price

**Price variable**
The element of the marketing mix that involves defining product prices and pricing models.

**Pricing models**
Describe the form of payment such as outright purchase, auction, rental, volume purchases and credit terms.

The **Price element** of the marketing mix refers to an organisation's pricing policies which are used to define **pricing models** and, of course, to set prices for products and services. The Internet has dramatic implications for pricing in many sectors and there is a lot of literature in this area. Baker *et al.* (2000) and more recently Xing *et al.* (2006) noted two approaches that have been commonly adopted for pricing on the Internet: start-up companies have tended to use low prices to gain a customer base, while many existing companies have transferred their existing prices to the web. Other existing companies have used differential pricing with lower prices for some of their products online. This has been the approach followed by online electrical retailers such as Comet (www.comet.co.uk). The Pricing element mix will often relate to the Product element since online pricing depends on the range of products offered and the point at which a product is in its lifecycle. Extending the product range may allow these products to be discounted online. Some organisations have launched

| When buying online, I will buy a product if... | | | | |
|---|---|---|---|---|
| I am familiar with the *retailer* | Yes | Yes | No | No |
| I am familiar with the *product brand* | Yes | No | Yes | No |
| | 90% | 82% | 54% | 13% |

**Figure 5.9** The influence of brand knowledge on purchase. Matrix for question 'I will buy a product if ...'
*Source*: Brand New World (2004)

new products online which have a lower Price element, for example banks have launched 'eSavings' products where higher interest rates are offered to online customers. Alternatively, they may offer insurance products with a 10% online discount in order to encourage customers to use the digital channel. Often these agreements are dependent on the customer servicing their account online, which helps reduce the cost-base of the bank. This then relates to the service elements of the mix since service has to be delivered online.

Remember that lower prices may imply reducing the level of customer service to reduce costs and this can in turn lead to a poor repeat purchase rate. Remember that Amazon, one of the most successful online companies, established its brand through being known for its range of products and quality of service rather than having the lowest prices.

The main implications of the Internet for the price aspect of the mix, which we will review in this section, are:

1 increased price transparency and its implications on differential pricing;
2 downward pressure on price (including commoditisation);
3 new pricing approaches (including dynamic pricing, price testing and auctions);
4 alternative pricing structure or policies.

## 1 Increased price transparency

Quelch and Klein (1996) describe two contradictory effects of the Internet on price that are related to **price transparency**. First, a supplier can use the technology for **differential pricing**, for example, for customers in different countries. However, if precautions are not taken about price, the customers may be able to quickly find out about the price discrimination and they will object to it.

Pricing online has to take into account the concept of **price elasticity of demand**. This is a measure of consumer behaviour based on economic theory that indicates the change in demand for a product or service in response to changes in price. Price elasticity of demand is determined by the price of the product, availability of alternative goods from alternative suppliers (which tends to increase online) and consumer income. A product is said to be 'elastic' (or responsive to price changes) if a small change in price increases or reduces the demand substantially. A product is 'inelastic' if a large change in price is accompanied by a small amount of change in demand.

Although, intuitively, we would think that price transparency enabled through the Internet price comparison services such as Kelkoo, Pricerunner and Shopping.com, which leads to searching by product rather than by store level, would lead to common comparisons of price and the selection of the cheapest product – but the reality seems different. Pricing online is relatively inelastic. There are two main reasons for this. First, pricing is only one variable – consumers also decide on suppliers according to other aspects about the brand such as familiarity, trust and perceived service levels. Second, consumers often display **satisficing behaviour**. The term 'satisfice' was coined by Herbert Simon in 1957 when he said that

**Price transparency**
Customer knowledge about pricing increases due to increased availability of pricing information.

**Differential pricing**
Identical products are priced differently for different types of customers, markets or buying situations.

**Price elasticity of demand**
Measure of consumer behaviour that indicates the change in demand for a product or service in response to changes in price. Price elasticity of demand is used to assess the extent to which a change in price will influence demand for a product.

**Satisficing behaviour**
Consumers do not behave entirely rationally in product or supplier selection. They will compare alternatives, but then may make their choice given imperfect information.

people are only 'rational enough' and that they suspend or relax their rationality if they feel it is no longer required. This is called 'bounded rationality' by cognitive psychologists. In other words, although consumers may seek to minimise some variable (such as price) when making a product or supplier selection, most may not try too hard. Online, this is supported by research by Johnson *et al.* (2004) who showed that by analysing panel data from over 10,000 Internet households and three commodity-like products (books, compact discs and air travel services), the amount of online search is actually quite limited. On average, households visit only 1.2 book sites, 1.3 CD sites and 1.8 travel sites during a typical active month in each category. Of course, these averages will reflect a range of behaviour. This is consistent with previous research quoted by Marn (2000) which suggested that only around 8% of active online consumers are 'aggressive price shoppers'. Furthermore, he notes that Internet price bands have remained broad. Online booksellers' prices varied by an average of 33% and those of CD sellers by 25%.

**Aggregators**
An alternative term to *price comparison sites* or *comparison search engines (CSE).* Aggregators include product, price and service information comparing competitors within a sector such a financial services, retail or travel. Their revenue models commonly include affiliate revenues (CPA), pay-per-click advertising (CPC) and display advertising (CPM).

Retailers or other transactional e-commerce companies operating in markets where their products are readily reviewed online need to review their strategy towards the impact of aggregators which facilitate price comparison. One strategy for companies in the face of increased price transparency is to highlight the other features of the brand – such as the quality of the retail experience, fulfilment choice or customer service – to reduce the emphasis on cost as a differentiator. Another strategy is to educate the market about the limitations in aggregators such as incomplete coverage or limited information about delivery or service levels. This approach is highlighted by Mini case study 5.2 which shows the tensions between aggregators and the service provider brands they promote.

---

### Mini Case Study 5.2    The balance of power between brands and aggregator sites

A good example of the tensions between aggregators is shown by the public discussion between direct insurer DirectLine (www.directline.com) and aggregator MoneySupermarket (www.moneysupermarket.com). The *Guardian* (2007) reported on an ongoing spat which saw Direct Line disparaging comparison engines like Moneysupermarket, Confused.com and Go Compare in a multi-million TV campaign. It reported Roger Ramsden, strategy director for Royal Bank of Scotland insurance, which owns Direct Line as saying:

> Direct Line has never been available through a middleman of any sort and never will be, and that's what these [comparison] sites are. They are commercial operations rather than a public service, and the [advertising] campaign is responding to our customers who tell us they are unaware of this and find the sites confusing.

His assertion is partially true in that although MoneySupermarket covers approximately 80% of the motor insurance market, it does not list quotes from some large insurers such as Norwich Union or other insurers owned by the Royal Bank of Scotland including Direct Line, Churchill, Privilege and Tesco Personal Finance. In a counter argument, Richard Mason, director of Moneysupermarket.com, said that Direct Line's campaign:

> . . . smacks of complete desperation. We are the new kids on the block and Direct Line don't like it. They have lost their market share since we came on the scene – they were in a position where consumers thought they were competitive and kept renewing their policies. They spent hundreds of millions of pounds on advertising. But now consumers can find cheaper alternatives and are doing so in their droves.

Data from Hitwise (2006) supports MoneySupermarket's position. It suggests this site achieves around a third of its visits from price-sensitive searchers looking to compare by typing generic phrases such as 'car insurance', 'cheap car insurance' and 'compare car insurance'. It has also invested in traditional advertising through TV, print and outdoor media to increase brand awareness.

To the authors, this conflict shows the importance of companies that are featured within aggregators possessing a strong brand which can offer additional value in terms of customer service or trust. It also shows the continuing importance of offline advertising in shaping consumer perceptions of brands and to drive visitors directly to a destination site.

**Commoditisation**
The process whereby product selection becomes more dependent on price than on differentiating features, benefits and value-added services.

For business commodities, auctions on business-to-business exchanges can also have a similar effect of driving down price. Purchase of some products that have not traditionally been thought of as commodities may become more price sensitive. This process is known as **commoditisation**. Examples of goods that are becoming commoditised include electrical goods and cars.

---

### Activity 5.3    Assessing price ranges on the Internet

#### Purpose

To illustrate the concept of price transparency.

#### Activity

Visit a price comparison site such as Kelkoo (www.kelkoo.com) Pricerunner (www.pricerunner.com, Figure 5.10) or Shopzilla (www.shopzilla.com). Choose one of the products below and write down the range of prices from lowest to highest. What is the percentage premium charged for a product by the most expensive company?

- Low-involvement purchase – CD or book.
- Higher-involvement purchase – household appliance.

**Figure 5.10**    Pricerunner (www.pricerunner.com)

## 2 Downward pressure on price

The competition caused by price transparency and increased number of competitors is the main reason for downward pressure on price. Many aggregators or comparison sites have been set up which fuel this. For example, Figure 5.11 shows an example comparing four different supermarkets.

The Internet also tends to drive down prices since Internet-only retailers that do not have a physical presence do not have the overheads of operating stores and a retailer distribution network. This means that, in theory, online companies can operate at lower pricing levels than offline rivals. This phenomenon is prevalent in the banking sector where many banks have set up online companies or online only accounts offering better rates of interest on savings products. Online purchase discounts is a common approach in many markets.

Price elasticity of demand (see Box 5.2) assesses the extent to which a change in price will influence the demand for a product. It is calculated as the change in quantity demanded (expressed as a percentage) divided by the change in price as a percentage. Different products will naturally have different coefficients of price elasticity of demand depending on where they lie on the continuum of consumer tastes from relatively undifferentiated commodities to luxury, highly differentiated products where the brand perception is important.

**Pricing level**

The price set for a specific product or range of products

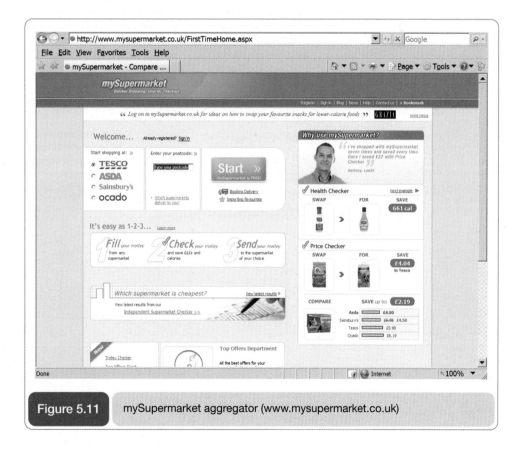

| Figure 5.11 | mySupermarket aggregator (www.mysupermarket.co.uk) |

Price elasticity of demand

The formula for the price elasticity of demand is:

$$Price\ elasticity\ of\ demand\ coefficient = \frac{(\%\ change\ in\ quantity\ demanded)}{(\%\ change\ in\ price)}$$

Price elasticity for products is generally described as:

- *Elastic (coefficient of price elasticity > 1).* Here, the percentage change in quantity demanded is greater than the percentage change in price. In elastic demand, the demand curve is relatively shallow and a small percentage increase in price leads to a reduction in revenue. On balance overall, when the price is raised, the total revenue of producers or retailers falls since the rise in revenue does not compensate for the fall in demand; and when the price is decreased, total revenue rises because the income from additional customers compensates in the decrease in revenue from reduced prices. Figure 5.12 shows the demand curve for a relatively elastic product (price elasticity = 1.67).
- *Inelastic demand (coefficient of price elasticity < 1).* Here, the percentage change in quantity demanded is smaller than the percentage change in price. In inelastic demand, the demand curve is relatively steep and a small percentage increase in price causes a small decrease in demand. On balance overall revenue increases as the price increases and falls as the price falls. Figure 5.13 shows the demand curve for a relatively inelastic product (price elasticity = 0.3125).

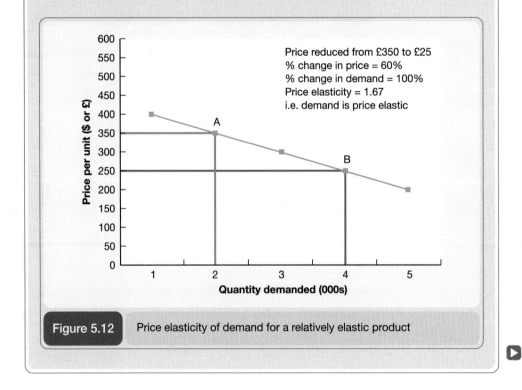

Price reduced from £350 to £25
% change in price = 60%
% change in demand = 100%
Price elasticity = 1.67
i.e. demand is price elastic

**Figure 5.12** Price elasticity of demand for a relatively elastic product

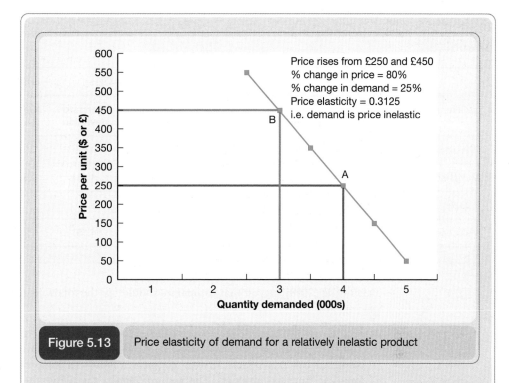

**Figure 5.13**    Price elasticity of demand for a relatively inelastic product

When the price elasticity coefficient is close to 1, this is described as unit elastic or unitary elastic. At the limits of elasticity, products will vary from:

- *Perfectly elastic* (*coefficient is not infinite*), effectively shown as a horizontal line on demand curve graphs such as Figure 5.12 where any increase in the price will cause demand (and revenue for the goods) to drop to zero.
- *Perfectly inelastic* (*coefficient of price elasticity is zero*), effectively shown as a vertical line on demand curve graphs such as Figure 5.13 where changes in the price do not affect the quantity demanded for the good.

When the price elasticity value is 1 of the demand for a good it is known as *unit elastic* (*or unitary elastic*).

Discounting of the most popular products is another pricing approach used by both online and traditional retailers to acquire customers or drive sales. For example, online booksellers may decide to offer a discount of 50% on the top 25 best-selling books in each category, for which no profit is made, but offer a smaller discount on less popular books to give a profit margin.

Xing *et al.* (2006) reported in their study of pricing levels for DVD merchants, summarised in Table 5.2, that traditional multichannel marketing companies tend to charge higher prices than pureplays or dot-com only companies, although pureplays will adjust their prices upwards more rapidly. However, they noted that this is market specific and when sales tax and shipping are taken into account, pureplays often charge more than multichannel merchants, as they found in a previous study of the consumer electronic market. They also found that **price dispersion** tended to be less for pureplays.

**Price dispersion**
The distribution or range of prices charged for an item across different retailers.

| Table 5.2 | A summary of the differences in pricing among DVD retailers from the research of Xing *et al.* (2006) |
|---|---|

| | All titles | | Popular titles | | Random titles | |
|---|---|---|---|---|---|---|
| **Retailer type** | **Average** | **Standard deviation** | **Average** | **Standard deviation** | **Average** | **Standard deviation** |
| Pureplay example – Amazon | 21.51 | 3.90 | 21.05 | 3.72 | 21.99 | 4.02 |
| Multichannel example – Borders | 22.95 | 4.44 | 22.57 | 4.01 | 23.34 | 4.81 |
| Pureplay average | 20.54 | 3.75 | 20.42 | 3.60 | 20.6 | 63.90 |
| Multichannel retailer average | 22.28 | 4.27 | 22.02 | 4.19 | 22.55 | 4.33 |

Baker *et al.* (2000) suggest that companies should use the following three factors to assist in pricing.

1 *Precision.* Each product has a price-indifference band, where varying price has little or no impact on sales. The authors report that these bands can be as wide as 17% for branded consumer beauty products, 10% for engineered industrial components, but less than 10% for some financial products. The authors suggest that while the cost of undertaking a survey to calculate price indifference is very expensive in the real world, it is more effective online. They give the example of Zilliant, a software supplier that, in a price discovery exercise, reduced prices on four products by 7%. While this increased volumes of three of those by 5–20%, this was not sufficient to warrant the lower prices. However, for the fourth product, sales increased by 100%. It was found that this was occurring through sales to the educational sector, so this price reduction was introduced for just customers in that sector.

2 *Adaptability.* This refers simply to the fact that it is possible to respond more quickly to the demands of the marketplace with online pricing. For some product areas, such as ticketing, it may be possible to dynamically alter prices in line with demand. Tickets.com adjusts concert ticket prices according to demand and has been able to achieve 45% more revenue per event as a result. The authors suggest that in this case, and for other sought-after items such as video games or luxury cars, the Internet can actually increase the price since there it is possible to reach more people.

3 *Segmentation.* This refers to pricing differently for different groups of customers. This has not traditionally been practical for B2C markets since at the point of sale, information is not known about the customer, although it is widely practised for B2B markets. One example of pricing by segments would be for a car manufacturer to vary promotional pricing, so that rather than offering every purchaser discount purchasing or cash-back, it is only offered to those for whom it is thought necessary to make the sale. A further example is where a company can identify regular customers and fill-in customers who only buy from the supplier when their needs can't be met elsewhere. In the latter case, up to 20% higher prices are levied.

What then are the options available to marketers given this downward pressure on pricing? We will start by looking at traditional methods for pricing and how they are affected by the Internet. Bickerton *et al.* (2000) identify a range of options that are available for setting pricing.

1   *Cost-plus pricing*. This involves adding on a profit margin based on production costs. As we have seen above, a reduction in this margin may be required in the Internet era.

2   *Target-profit pricing*. This is a more sophisticated pricing method that involves looking at the fixed and variable costs in relation to income for different sales volumes and unit prices. Using this method the breakeven amount for different combinations can be calculated. For e-commerce sales the variable selling cost, i.e the cost for each transaction, is small. This means that once breakeven is achieved each sale has a large margin. With this model differential pricing is often used in a B2B context according to the volume of goods sold. Care needs to be taken that differential prices are not evident to different customers. One company, through an error on their website, made prices for different customers available for all to see, with disastrous results.

3   *Competition-based pricing*. This approach is common online. The advent of price-comparison engines such as Kelkoo (www.kelkoo.com) for B2C consumables has increased price competition and companies need to develop online pricing strategies that are flexible enough to compete in the marketplace, but are still sufficient to achieve profitability in the channel. This approach may be used for the most popular products, e.g. the top 25 CDs, but other methods, such as target-profit pricing; will be used for other products.

4   *Market-oriented pricing*. Here the response to price changes by customers making up the market are considered. This is known as 'the elasticity of demand'. There are two approaches. *Premium pricing* (or *skimming the market*) involves setting a higher price than the competition to reflect the positioning of the product as a high-quality item. Penetration pricing is when a price is set below the competitors' prices to either stimulate demand or increase penetration. This approach was commonly used by dot-com companies to acquire customers. The difficulty with this approach is that if customers are price-sensitive then the low price has to be sustained – otherwise customers may change to a rival supplier. This has happened with online banks – some customers regularly move to reduce costs of overdrafts for example. Alternatively if a customer is concerned by other aspects such as service quality it may be necessary to create a large price differential in order to encourage the customer to change supplier.

Kotler (1997) suggests that in the face of price cuts from competitors in a market, a company has the following choices which can be applied to e-commerce:

- maintain the price (assuming that e-commerce-derived sales are unlikely to decrease greatly with price since other factors such as customer service are equally or more important);
- reduce the price (to avoid losing market share);
- raise perceived quality or differentiate product further by adding-value services;
- introduce new lower-priced product lines.

### 3 New pricing approaches (including auctions)

**Forward auctions**
Item purchased by highest bid made in bidding period.

**Reverse auctions**
Item purchased from lowest-bidding supplier in bidding period.

**Offer**
A commitment by a trader to sell under certain conditions.

**Bid**
A commitment by a trader to purchase under certain conditions.

Figure 5.14 summarises different pricing mechanisms. While many of these were available before the advent of the Internet and are not new, the Internet has made some models more tenable. In particular, the volume of users makes traditional or **forward auctions** (B2C) and **reverse auctions** (B2B) more tenable – these have become more widely used than previously. Emiliani (2001) and Dap (2003) have reviewed the implications of open and closed bid B2B reverse auctions in detail, and Mini case study 5.3 provides an example. To understand auctions it is important to distinguish between offers and bids. An **offer** is a commitment for a trader to sell under certain conditions, such as a minimum price. A **bid** is made by a trader to buy under the conditions of the bid, such as a commitment to purchase at a particular price. In a sealed-bid arrangement, suppliers submit their bids in response to an RFP posted to a website at a set time. In an open-bid arrangement, suppliers bid sequentially through a series of product lots or subgroups and can view their competitors' bids and respond in real time. A moving end-time (a 'soft close') is used for each lot, which means that any bid within the last minute of the closing time automatically extends the end time for a few minutes to allow other bidders to respond.

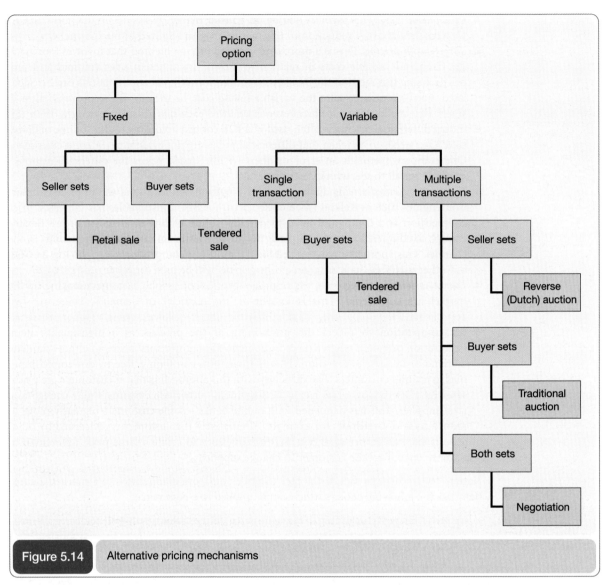

| Figure 5.14 | Alternative pricing mechanisms |
|---|---|

In a study of the consumer approach to auctions which assessed the type of value assessments and decision dynamics made at each stage of the auction, Ariely and Simonson (2003) suggested that participants in auctions do not always get the bargain they may be looking for. Their study of purchases of DVDs and electronic equipment found that:

*(a) due to a focus on the narrow auction context, consumers under-search and, consequently, overpay for widely available commodities (CDs, DVDs) and (b) higher auction starting prices tend to lead to higher winning bids, particularly when comparable items are not available in the immediate context.*

**Aggregated buying**
A form of customer union where buyers collectively purchase a number of items at the same price and receive a volume discount.

A further approach, not indicated in Figure 5.14, is **aggregated buying**. This approach was promoted by LetsBuyit.com, but the business model did not prove viable – the cost of creating awareness for the brand and explaining the concept was not offset by the revenue from each transaction.

Pitt *et al.* (2001) suggest that when developing a pricing strategy, the options will be limited by relative strengths of the seller and buyer. (See also Mini case study 5.3). Where the seller is more powerful then a negotiation may be more likely where the seller can counteroffer. Nextag.com provides such a service.

Marn (2000) suggests that the Internet can be used to test new pricing policies. For example, if a company wants to know the sales impact of a 3% price increase, it can try this on every 50th visitor to the site and compare the buy rates.

### Price testing and dynamic pricing

**Dynamic pricing**
Prices can be updated in real time according to the type of customer or current market conditions.

The Internet introduces new opportunities for **dynamic pricing** – for example, new customers could be automatically given discounted purchases for the first three items. Care has to be taken with differential pricing since established customers will be unhappy if significant discounts are given to new customers. Amazon trialled such a discounting scheme in 2000 and it received negative press and had to be withdrawn when people found out that their friends or colleagues had paid less. If the scheme had been a clear introductory promotion this problem may not have arisen.

Baye *et al.* (2007) reported that European electronics online retailer Pixmania (www.pixmania.com) used price experimentation to learn about its customers' price sensitivity. They noted that for a PDA, Pixmania adjusted its product price 11 times in a 14-week period, from a low of £268 to a high of £283, as part of a series of small experiments that enabled it to learn about the price sensitivities of its customers. This pricing strategy also provides an additional strategic benefit – unpredictability.

### Shipping fees

The setting of shipping fees can have a dramatic effect both on conversion rates and profitability according to research completed by Lewis *et al.* (2006). They note the popularity of free shipping offers when the basket size is above a certain amount, but also note that it can potentially cause profitability to fall if it is not set at the right level. They also suggest that different shipping fees could potentially be offered to different segments. Shipping fees can also be varied according to the time it takes for items to be delivered.

One further approach with innovation in treatment of shipping fees is to offer a loyalty programme in return for free express shipping – the basis of the Amazon Prime programme.

---

| Mini Case Study 5.3 | GlaxoSmithKline reduces prices through reverse auctions |

Healthcare company GlaxoSmithKline (GSK) started using online reverse auctions in 2000 to drive down the price of its supplies. For example, it bought supplies of a basic solvent for a price 15% lower than the day's spot price in the commodity market, and Queree (2000) reported that on other purchases of highly specified solvents and chemicals, SmithKline Beecham (prior to formation of GSK) regularly beat its own historic pricing by between 7 and 25%. She says:

*FreeMarkets, the company that manages the SmithKline Beecham auctions, quotes examples of savings achieved by other clients in these virtual marketplaces: 42% on orders for printed circuit boards, 41% on labels, 24% on commercial machinings and so on.*

The reverse auction process starts with a particularly detailed Request for Proposals (RFP) from which suppliers ask to take part, and then selected suppliers are invited to take part in the auction. Once the bidding starts, the participants see every bid, but not the names of the bidders. In the final stages of the auction, each last bid extends the bidding time by one more minute. One auction scheduled for 2 hours ran for 4 hours and 20 minutes and attracted more than 700 bids!

## 4 Alternative pricing structure or policies

Different types of pricing may be possible on the Internet, particularly for digital, down-loadable products. Software and music have traditionally been sold for a continuous right to use. As explained in more detail in the section on Product, the Internet offers new options such as payment per use, rental at a fixed cost per month, a lease arrangement and bundling with other products. The use of applications service providers (ASPs) to deliver service such as website traffic monitoring also gives new methods of volume pricing. Web analytics companies such as Indextools (www.indextools.com) and Webtrends (www.webtrendslive.com) charge in price bands based on the number of visitors to the purchaser's site.

Further pricing options which could be varied online include:

- basic price
- discounts
- add-ons and extra products and services
- guarantees and warranties
- refund policies
- order cancellation terms.

As a summary to the section on pricing, we summarise the research by Baye *et al.* (2007) which has many interesting examples of innovative online pricing approaches. They recommend that online retailers should ask the following questions when reviewing pricing online:

- *How many competitors are there at a point in time?* They suggest a product's markup should be increased when number of rivals falls and decreased when the number of rivals increases. They also recommend that since the identity of competitors online will differ from traditional offline rivals it is important to include key online competitors.
- *What is the position in the product lifecycle?* A product's markup should be decreased over its lifecycle or when new versions are introduced.
- *What is the price sensitivity or elasticity of a product?* They suggest continuously experimenting to learn from changes in the price sensitivity of a product.
- *What level is pricing set?* The optimal markup factor should be applied at the product rather than category or firm level based on price testing at the product level. They also note the variation of conversion rates and click-through fees from paid search engines and aggregators at the category or product level which makes it important to have micro-management of pricing.
- *Are rivals monitoring my price?* Be unpredictable if rivals are watching; exploit 'blind spots' if rivals are not watching.
- *Are we stuck in the middle?* A middle pricing point is sub-optimal particularly if prices can be set to target the lowest point in the market.

## Place

**Place variable**
The element of the marketing mix that involves distributing products to customers in line with demand and minimising cost of inventory, transport and storage.

The **Place** element of the marketing mix refers to how the product is distributed to customers. Typically, for offline channels, the aim of Place is to maximise the reach of distribution to achieve widespread availability of products while minimising the costs of inventory, transport and storage. In an online context, thanks to ease of navigating from one site to another, the scope of Place is less clear since Place also relates to Promotion and Partnerships. Take the example of a retailer of mobile phones. For this retailer to reach its potential audience to sell and distribute its product, it has to think beyond its own website to third-party websites where it can promote its services. Successful retailers are those that maximise their representation or visibility on third-party sites which are used by their target audiences. These third-party sites will include search engines, online portals reviewing mobile phones and product comparison sites. When thinking about representation on third-party sites, it is useful to think of the long-tail concept (Anderson, 2004) referenced in Figure 5.5. Across all Internet sites, there are a small number of sites including portals such as Google, MSN and Yahoo! which are very popular (the head which may theoretically account for 80% of the volume of visitors) and a much larger number of sites that are less popular individually, but still collectively important. Similarly within a category of sites, such as automotive, there will be a few very popular sites, and then many niche sites which are collectively important in volume and may be more effective at reaching a niche target audience. When considering Place and Promotion, it is important to target both the head and the tail to maximise reach and to attract quality visitors to the destination site.

The main implications of the Internet for the Place aspect of the mix, which we will review in this section, are:

1 place of purchase
2 new channel structures
3 channel conflicts
4 virtual organisations.

## 1 Place of purchase

Although the concept of place may seem peculiar for what is a global medium that transcends geographical boundaries, nevertheless marketers still have several options for managing the place of purchase. Allen and Fjermestad (2001) argue that the Internet has the greatest implications for place in the marketing mix since the Internet has a global reach. However, due to cost and time of international fulfilment together with issues of trust in the local country and the availability of phone support, most products are still sourced locally. The exception to this is digital products where there is no physical limitation on fulfilment – so, for example, Apple iTunes has proved successful in offering this service worldwide.

The web introduces new virtual places where products can be reviewed as part of the purchase process. The framework of Berryman *et al.* (1998), introduced in Chapter 2, is a simple framework for reviewing different places of promotion and/or distribution and purchase. However, McDonald and Wilson (2002) introduce two additional locations for purchase which are useful (Table 5.3):

**A** *Seller-controlled sites* are those that are the main site of the supplier company and are e-commerce-enabled.
**B** *Seller-oriented sites* are controlled by a third party but represent the seller and their competitors rather than providing a full range of options.
**C** *Neutral sites* are independent evaluator intermediaries or aggregators that enable price and product comparison and will result in the purchase being fulfilled on the target site.
**D** *Buyer-oriented sites* are controlled by third parties on behalf of the buyer.
**E** *Buyer-controlled sites* are typically restricted to business-to-business sites and usually involve either procurement posting on buyer-company sites or on those of intermediaries that have been set up in such a way that it is the buyer that initiates the market-making. This can occur through procurement posting, whereby a purchaser specifies what he or she wishes to purchase, this request being sent by e-mail to suppliers registered on the system and then offers are awaited. Aggregators are groups of purchasers who combine to purchase in bulk and thus benefit from a lower purchase cost.

Evans and Wurster (1999) have argued that there are three aspects of 'navigational advantage' that are key to achieving competitive advantage online. These three, which all relate to the Place elements of the mix, are:

- *Reach.* Evans and Wurster say: 'It [reach] means, simply, how many customers a business can connect with and how many products it can offer to those customers'. Reach can be increased by moving from a single site to representation with a large number of different intermediaries. Allen and Fjermestad (2001) suggest that niche suppliers can readily reach a much wider market due to search-engine marketing (Chapter 8). Evans and Wurster also suggest that reach refers to the range of products and services that can be offered since this will increase the number of people the company can appeal to.
- *Richness.* This is the depth or detail of information which is both collected about the customer and provided to the customer. The latter is related to the richness of product information and how well it can be personalised to be relevant to the individual needs.
- *Affiliation.* This refers to whose interest the selling organisation represents – consumers' or suppliers' – and stresses the importance of forming the right partnerships. This particularly applies to retailers. The authors suggest that successful online retailers will reward customers who provide them with the richest information on comparing competitive products. They suggest this tilts the balance in favour of the customer.

| Table 5.3 | Different places for virtual marketplace representation |
|---|---|

| Place of purchase | Examples of sites |
|---|---|
| A Seller-controlled | • Vendor sites, i.e. home site of organisation selling products, e.g. www.dell.com |
| B Seller-oriented | • Intermediaries controlled by third parties to the seller such as distributors and agents, e.g. Opodo (www.opodo.com) represents the main air carriers. Amazon marketplace where third-parties can sell products |
| C Neutral | • Intermediaries not controlled by buyer's industry, e.g. EC21 (www.ec21.com)<br>• Product-specific search engines, e.g. CNET (www.computer.com)<br>• Comparison sites, e.g. uSwitch (www.uswitch.com)<br>• Auction space, e.g. eBay (www.eBay.com) |
| D Buyer-oriented | • MySupermarket (www.mysupermarket.com)<br>• Priceline (www.priceline.com)<br>• Intermediaries controlled by buyers, e.g. the remaining parts of the Covisint network of motor manufacturers<br>• Discount sites for consumers such as voucher code sites, e.g. www.myvouchercodes.com and Cashback sites, e.g. GreasyPalm (www.greasypalm.com). |
| E Buyer-controlled | • Website procurement posting or reverse auctions on company's own site |

## Syndication

**Syndication**
Content or product information is distributed to third parties. Online this is commonly achieved through standard XML formats such as RSS.

Traditionally, **syndication** referred to articles or extracts from books being included in other publications such as newspapers and magazines. In an online context, this practice related to Place and partnerships needs to be reviewed for online content owners since there may be opportunities to generate additional revenue by re-publishing content on third-party sites, or it may be possible to increase exposure on partner sites and so generate awareness or visits to the company site. For example, through its Connect service, Amazon.com enables authors to publish a blog on their site based on an RSS feed (see Chapter 1) from their own blog, so increasing awareness of the blog.

But syndication also has implications for other companies, and in particular retailers, since syndication of information from their product catalogues to third-party aggregators is important to extend their reach. This is also possible through feeds which have a particular format, for example the Google Base format (http://base.google.com) is used to provide results from Google Product Search (www.google.com/products) whose results are integrated into the Google search results pages. Figure 5.15 shows how some companies have used standard data feeds to promote their products within Google Product Search.

Since integrating product data with a range of aggregators which will require formats can be time consuming, some companies such as Channel Advisor (www.channeladvisor.com), now offer a service to upload data and track results across a range of aggregators.

### Payment mechanisms – purchase place

Traditionally, online purchase will occur at the retailer through a partnership with an online secure payment provider such as Protx (www.protx.com) or Worldpay (www.worldpay.com). Effectively, the purchase transaction occurs on a different domain, but it is important that customers are reassured that the payment process is secure and to make it seamless.

More recently, more retailers are now offering payment mechanisms where the purchaser has already setup payment with another payment provider, of which Paypal (www.paypal.com) and Google Checkout (www.google.com/checkout) are dominant. This approach can assist with reassurance about privacy and security and increase purchase convenience and choice for the user, so these options also have to be reviewed.

**Figure 5.15**  Google Product Search (www.google.com/products)

**Localisation**
Tailoring of website information for individual countries or regions. Localisation can include simple translation, but also cultural adaptation.

## Localisation

Providing a local site, with or without a language-specific version and additional cultural adaptations, is referred to as localisation. A site may need to support customers from a range of countries with:

- different product needs
- language differences
- cultural adaptation.

Some approaches used for cultural adaptation and localisation are described further in Chapter 7 in the section on localisation.

---

**Activity 5.4** | **Place of purchase on the Internet**

**Purpose**

To illustrate the concept of representation and reach on the Internet.

**Activity**

For the same sector as you selected in Activity 5.2, find out which company has the best reach in terms of numbers of links from other sites. Go to a search engine such as Google and use the advanced search to find the number of sites that link to that site. Alternatively use the syntax: link:URL in the search box.

---

## 2 New channel structures

New channel structures enabled by the Internet have been described in detail in Chapters 2 and 4. The main types of phenomena that companies need to develop strategies for are:

- *Distintermediation*. Is there an option for selling direct? Selling direct can lead to the channel conflicts mentioned in the next section. When assessing this option there will be a number of barriers and facilitators to this change. Research by Mols (2001) in the banking sector in Denmark suggests that important factors are senior management support, a willingness to accept some cannibalisation of existing channels and perceived customer benefits.
- *Reintermediation*. The new intermediaries created through reintermediation described by Sarkar *et al.* (1996) should be evaluated for suitability for partnering in affiliate arrangements. These intermediaries, the aggregators mentioned earlier in this chapter such as Kelkoo, receive a commission on each click or sale resulting from a referral from their site.
- *Countermediation*. Should the organisation partner with another independent intermediary, or set up its own independent intermediary? For example, a group of European airlines have joined forces to form Opodo (www.opodo.com) which is intended to counter independent companies such as Lastminute.com (www.lastminute.com) and eBookers (www.ebookers.com) in offering discount fares.

The distribution channel will also be affected. For instance, grocery retailers have had to identify the best strategy for picking customers' goods prior to home delivery. Options include in-store picking (selection of items on customer orders) and regional picking centres. The former is proving more cost effective.

# 3 Channel conflicts

A significant threat arising from the introduction of an Internet channel is that while disintermediation gives a company the opportunity to sell direct and increase profitability on products, it can also threaten distribution arrangements with existing partners. Such channel conflicts are described by Frazier (1999), and need to be carefully managed. Frazier identifies some situations when the Internet should only be used as a communications channel. This is particularly the case where manufacturers offer an exclusive, or highly selective, distribution approach. To take an example, a company manufacturing expensive watches costing thousands of pounds will not in the past have sold direct, but will have used a wholesaler to distribute watches via retailers. If this wholesaler is a major player in watch distribution, then it is powerful and will react against the watch manufacturer selling direct. The wholesaler may even refuse to act as distributor and may threaten to distribute only a competitor's watches, which are not available over the Internet. Furthermore, direct sales may damage the product's brand or change its price positioning.

Further channel conflicts involve other stakeholders including sales representatives and customers. Sales representatives may see the Internet as a direct threat to their livelihood. In some cases, such as Avon cosmetics and Enyclopaedia Britannica, this has proved to be the case, with this sales model being partly or completely replaced by the Internet. For many B2B purchases, sales representatives remain an essential method of reaching the customer to support them in the purchase decision. Here, following training of sales staff, the Internet can be used as a sales support and customer education tool. Customers who do not use the online channels may also respond negatively if lower prices are available to their online counterparts. This is less serious than other types of channel conflict.

To assess channel conflicts it is necessary to consider the different forms of channel the Internet can take. These are:

- a communication channel only
- a distribution channel to intermediaries
- a direct sales channel to customers
- any combination of the above.

To avoid channel conflicts, the appropriate combination of channels must be arrived at. For example, Frazier (1999) notes that using the Internet as a direct sales channel may not be wise when a product's price varies considerably across global markets. In the watch manufacturer example, it may be best to use the Internet as a communication channel only.

Internet channel strategy will, of course, depend on the existing arrangements for the market. If a geographical market is new and there are no existing agents or distributors, there is unlikely to be channel conflict in that there is a choice of distribution through the Internet only or appointments of new agents to support Internet sales, or a combination of the two. Often SMEs will attempt to use the Internet to sell products without appointing agents, but this strategy will only be possible for retail products that need limited pre-sales and after-sales support. For higher-value products such as engineering equipment, which will require skilled sales staff to support the sale and after-sales servicing, agents will have to be appointed.

For existing geographical markets in which a company already has a mechanism for distribution in the form of agents and distributors, the situation is more complex, and there is the threat of channel conflict. The strategic options available when an existing reseller arrangement is in place have been described by Kumar (1999):

- *No Internet sales.* Neither the company nor any of its resellers makes sales over the Internet. This will be the option to follow when a company, or its resellers, feel that the number of buyers has not reached the critical mass thought to warrant the investment in an online sales capability.

- *Internet sales by reseller only.* A reseller who is selling products from many companies may have sufficient aggregated demand (through selling products for other companies) to justify the expenditure of setting up online sales. The manufacturer may also not have the infrastructure to fulfil orders direct to customers without further investment, whereas the reseller will be set up for this already. In this case it is unlikely that a manufacturer would want to block sales via the Internet channel.
- *Internet sales by manufacturer only.* It would be unusual if a manufacturer chose this option if it already had existing resellers in place. Were the manufacturer to do so, it would probably lead to lost sales as the reseller would perhaps stop selling through traditional channels.
- *Internet sales by all.* This option is arguably the logical future for Internet sales. It is also likely to be the result if the manufacturer does not take a proactive approach to controlling Internet sales.

Strategy will need to be reviewed annually and the sales channels changed as thought appropriate. Given the fast rate of change of e-commerce, it will probably not be possible to create a five-year plan! Kumar (1999) notes that history suggests that most companies have a tendency to use existing distribution networks for too long. The reason for this is that resellers may be powerful within a channel and the company does not want to alienate them, for fear of losing sales.

## 4 Virtual organisations

Benjamin and Wigand (1995) state that 'it is becoming increasingly difficult to delineate accurately the borders of today's organisations'. A further implication of the introduction of electronic networks such as the Internet is that it becomes easier to outsource aspects of the production and distribution of goods to third parties (Kraut *et al.*, 1998). This can lead to the boundaries within an organisation becoming blurred. Employees may work in any time zone, and customers are able to purchase tailored products from any location. The absence of any rigid boundary or hierarchy within the organisation should lead to a company becoming more responsive and flexible, and having a greater market orientation. Davidow and Malone (1992) describe the virtual corporation as follows:

> *To the outside observer, it will appear almost edgeless, with permeable and continuously changing interfaces between company, supplier and customer. From inside the firm, the view will be no less amorphous, with traditional offices, departments, and operating divisions constantly reforming according to need. Job responsibilities will regularly shift.*

**Virtual organisation and virtualisation**

A virtual organisation uses information and communications technology to allow it to operate without clearly defined physical boundaries between different functions. It provides customised services by outsourcing production and other functions to third parties.

Kraut *et al.* (1998) suggest the following features of a **virtual organisation**:

- Processes transcend the boundaries of a single form and are not controlled by a single organisational hierarchy.
- Production processes are flexible, with different parties involved at different times.
- Parties involved in the production of a single product are often geographically dispersed.
- Given this dispersion, co-ordination is heavily dependent on telecommunications and data networks.

Introna (2001) notes that a key aspect of the virtual organisation is strategic alliances or partnering. The ease of forming such alliances in the value network as described in Chapter 2 is one of the factors that has given rise to the virtual organisation.

**Virtualisation**

The process whereby a company develops more of the characteristics of a virtual organisation.

All companies tend to have some elements of the virtual organisation. The process whereby these characteristics increase is known as **virtualisation**. Malone *et al.* (1987) argued that the presence of electronic networks tends to lead to virtualisation since they enable the governance and co-ordination of business transactions to be conducted effectively at lower cost.

What are the implications for a marketing strategist of this trend towards virtualisation? Initially it may appear that outsourcing does not have direct relevance to market orientation. However, an example shows the relevance. Michael Dell relates (in Magretta, 1998) that Dell does not see outsourcing as getting rid of a process that does not add value, rather it sees it as a way of 'co-ordinating their activity to create the most value for customers'. Dell has improved customer service by changing the way it works with both its suppliers and its distributors to build a computer to the customer's specific order within just six days. This *vertical integration* has been achieved by creating a contractual vertical marketing system in which members of a channel retain their independence, but work together by sharing contracts.

So, one aspect of virtualisation is that companies should identify opportunities for providing new services and products to customers looking to outsource their external processes. The corollary of this is that it may offer companies opportunities to outsource some marketing activities that were previously conducted in-house. For example, marketing research to assess the impact of a website can now be conducted in a virtual environment by an outside company rather than by having employees conduct a focus group.

Referring to small and medium businesses, Azumah *et al.* (2005) indicate three levels of development towards what they term and e-organisation:

- 1/2-fusion organisations – minimum use of the Internet and network technologies.
- Fusion organisation – committed and intensive use of the Internet and network technologies.
- E-organisation – uses technologies as the core of the business for managing the entire business processes, from the point of receiving a customer order to processing the order and parts, and supplying and delivery.

Marshall *et al.* (2001) provide useful examples of different structures for the virtual organisation. These are:

- *Co-alliance model* – effort and risk are shared equally by partners.
- *Star alliance model* – here the effort and risk are centred on one organisation that subcontracts other virtual partners as required.
- *Value alliance model* – this is a partnership where elements are contributed across a supply chain for a particular industry. This is effectively the value network of Chapter 2.
- *Market alliance model* – this is similar to the value alliance, but is more likely to serve several different marketplaces.

Using the Internet to facilitate such alliances can provide competitive advantage to organisations operating in business-to-business markets since their core competences can be complemented by partnerships with third parties. This can potentially help organisations broaden their range of services or compete for work that on their own they may be unable to deliver. Such approaches can also be used to support business-to-consumer markets. For example, Dell can compete on price and quality in its consumer markets through its use of a star alliance model where other organisations are responsible for peripherals such as monitors or printers or distribution.

At a more practical level, electronic partnerships can be used to deliver the entire marketing mix referenced in this chapter through standardised data exchange interfaces which include:

- advertising through Paid Search networks (e.g. Google AdWords);
- promoting services through feeds on price comparison search engines (e.g. Kelkoo or Google Product Search);
- promoting services through affiliate networks (e.g. Commission Junction) or advertising networks (e.g. Google AdSense publishers programme);
- procuring expertise for short-term digital marketing work through an online web skills marketplace such as Elance (www.elance.com), Guru.com (www.guru.com) or Scriptlance (www.scriptlance.com);
- use of secure payment system services such as Paypal or Google Checkout;
- analysis of web performance through online web analytics services (e.g Google analytics).

You can see that Google has been active in providing services to support businesses across many of these different aspects of the selling process.

## Promotion

**Promotion variable**
The element of the marketing mix that involves communication with customers and other stakeholders to inform them about the product and the organisation.

The **Promotion** element of the marketing mix refers to how marketing communications are used to inform customers and other stakeholders about an organisation and its products. This topic is discussed in more depth in Chapters 8 and 9 – it is simply introduced here.

Promotion is the element of the marketing mix that is concerned with communicating the existence of products or services to a target market. Burnett (1993) defines it as:

> the marketing function concerned with persuasively communicating to target audiences the components of the marketing program in order to facilitate exchange.

A broader view of promotion is given by Wilmshurst (1993):

> Promotion unfortunately has a range of meanings. It can be used to describe the marketing communications aspect of the marketing mix or, more narrowly, as in sales promotion. In its very broad sense it includes the personal methods of communications, such as face to face or telephone selling, as well as the impersonal ones such as advertising. When we use a range of different types of promotion – direct mail, exhibitions, publicity etc. we describe it as the promotional mix.

The main elements of the promotional or communications mix and their online equivalents summarised by Chaffey and Smith (2008) are shown in Table 5.4.

| Table 5.4 | The main elements of the promotional mix |
| --- | --- |

| Communications tool | Online implementation |
| --- | --- |
| Advertising | Interactive display ads, pay-per-click search advertising |
| Selling | Virtual sales staff, site merchandising, chat and affiliate marketing |
| Sales promotion | Incentives such as coupons, rewards, online loyalty schemes |
| Public relations | Online editorial, blogs, feeds, e-newsletters, newsletters, social networks, links and viral campaigns |
| Sponsorship | Sponsoring an online event, site or service |
| Direct mail | Opt-in e-mail using e-newsletters and e-blasts (solus e-mails) |
| Exhibitions | Virtual exhibitions and whitepaper distribution |
| Merchandising | Promotional ad-serving on retail sites, personalised recommendations and e-alerts |
| Packaging | Virtual tours, real packaging is displayed online |
| Word-of-mouth | Viral, affiliate marketing, e-mail a friend, links |

Specification of the Promotion element of the mix is usually part of a communications strategy. This will include selection of target markets, positioning and integration of different communications tools. The Internet offers a new, additional marketing communications channel to inform customers of the benefits of a product and assist in the buying decision. These are different approaches for looking at how the Internet can be used to vary the Promotion element of the mix:

1 reviewing new ways of applying each of the elements of the communications mix – such as advertising, sales promotions, PR and direct marketing;
2 assessing how the Internet can be used at different stages of the buying process;

3  using promotional tools to assist in different stages of customer relationship management from customer acquisition to retention. In a web context this includes gaining initial visitors to the site and gaining repeat visits through these types of communications techniques:
   - reminders in traditional media campaigns why a site is worth visiting – such as online services and unique online offers and competitions;
   - direct e-mail reminders of site proposition – new offers;
   - frequently updated content – including promotional offers or information that helps your customer do their job or reminds them to visit.

The Promotion element of a marketing plan also requires three important decisions about investment for the online promotion or the online communications mix:

- *Investment in site promotion compared to site creation and maintenance.* Since there is often a fixed budget for site creation, maintenance and promotion, the e-marketing plan should specify the budget for each to ensure there is a sensible balance and the promotion of the site is not underfunded.
- *Investment in online promotion techniques in comparison to offline promotion.* A balance must be struck between these techniques. Typically, offline promotion investment often exceeds that for online promotion investment. For existing companies, traditional media such as print are used to advertise the sites, while print and TV will also be widely used by dot-com companies to drive traffic to their sites.
- *Investment in different online promotion techniques.* For example, how much should be paid for banner advertising as against online PR about online presence, and how much for search engine registration?

These issues are explored further in Chapter 8.

## People, process and physical evidence

The people, process and physical evidence elements of the mix are closely related and often grouped as 'the service elements'. They are significant since the level of perceived service will impact a customer's loyalty and the probability of their recommending the service. Since this issue is closely related to the online customer experience, we also look at issues of website performance and response to customer e-mails in Chapter 7, including review of frameworks such as WEBQUAL and E-SERVQUAL for assessing service effectiveness.

Some of the key issues in improving the delivery of service online have been summarised by Rayport *et al.* (2005). They identify these questions that senior executives and managers should ask to assess the combination of technology and human assistance that is used to deliver service. We have added some typical examples of applications for each type:

1  *Substitution.* Deploying technology instead of people (or the opposite situation), for example:
   - frequently asked questions section on a website;
   - in-site search engine;
   - interactive sales dialogue recommending relevant products (Figure 5.4) based on human response;
   - avatar offering answers to questions as in the Ikea Ask Anna feature;
   - automated e-mail response or a series of 'Welcome' e-mails educating customers about how to use a service;
   - using video to demonstrate products online.
2  *Complementarity.* Deploying technology in combination with people, for example:
   - call-back facility where the website is used to setup a subsequent call from contact centre;
   - online chat facility – the user chats through text on the website;
   - an employee using a WiFi-enabled hand-held device to facilitate easy rental car returns.

**3** *Displacement.* Outsourcing or 'off-shoring' technology or labour, for example:
- a fast-food chain centralising drive-through order taking in a remote call centre);
- the online chat or call-back systems referred to above can be deployed at a lower cost through outsourcing.

Note that this perspective doesn't stress another important aspect of the service elements of the online marketing mix, namely the participation by other customers in shaping a service through their feedback and the collaboration that occurs as customers will answer other customers questions in a forum.

We will now review the different elements of the service elements of the mix in more detail.

## People

**People variable**
The element of the marketing mix that involves the delivery of service to customers during interactions with customers.

The **People** element of the marketing mix relates to how an organisation's staff interact with customers and other stakeholders during sales and pre-and post-sales communications with them.

Chaffey and Smith (2008) make a similar point to Rayport *et al.* (2006) when they suggest that, online, the main consideration for the People element of the mix is the review of how staff involvement in the buying is changed, either through new roles such as replying to e-mails or online chat enquiries or through them being replaced through automated online services.

While the options for this form of customer service outlined above are straightforward, what is challenging is to implement the applications effectively. For example, if an FAQ doesn't have sufficient relevant answers or a call-back does not occur at the right time, then the result will be a dissatisfied customer who is unlikely to use a service again or will tell others about their experience either through ratings in shopping comparison engines (e.g. Figure 5.10) or sites created for this purpose such as Blagger (www.blagger.com).

To manage service, quality, organisations must devise plans to accommodate the five stages shown in Figure 5.16.

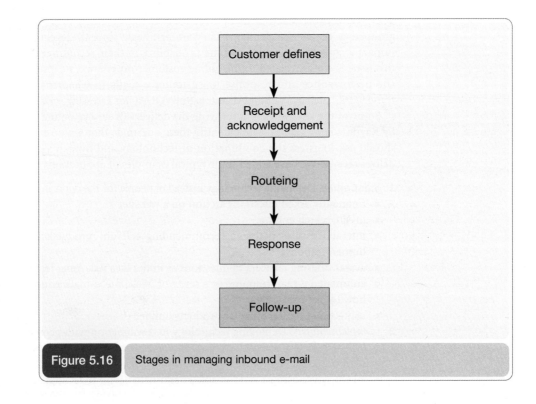

| Figure 5.16 | Stages in managing inbound e-mail |

### Stage 1: Customer defines support query

Companies should consider how easily the customer can find contact points and compose a support request on site. Best practice is clearly to find e-mail support options. Often, finding contact and support information on a website is surprisingly difficult. Standardised terminology on site is 'Contact Us', 'Support' or 'Ask a Question' (see Mini case study 5.4). Options should be available for the customer to specify the type of query on a web form or provide alternative e-mail addresses such as products@company.com or returns@company.com on site, or in offline communications such as a catalogue. Providing FAQs or automated diagnostic tools should be considered at this stage to reduce the number of inbound enquiries. Epson (www.epson.co.uk) provides an online tool to diagnose problems with printers and to suggest solutions.

Finally, the website should determine expectations about the level of service quality. For example, inform the customer that 'your enquiry will be responded to within 24 hours'.

**Avatars** are increasingly being used to reduce the need for enquiries such as 'Ask Anna' on the Ikea site. Research by Holzwarth *et al.* (2006) found that use of an avatar-based sales agent can lead to more satisfaction with the retailer, a more positive attitude toward the product and a greater purchase intent. They investigated the usage of 'attractive' versus 'expert' advisers dependent on the complexity of the purchase decision.

### Stage 2: Receipt of e-mail and acknowledgement

Best practice is that automatic message acknowledgement occurs. This is usually provided by autoresponder software. While many autoresponders only provide a simple acknowledgement, more sophisticated responses can reassure the customer about when the response will occur and highlight other sources of information.

### Stage 3: Routeing of e-mail

Best practice involves automated routeing or workflow. Routeing the e-mail to the right person is made easier if the type of query has been identified through the techniques described for Stage 1. It is also possible to use pattern recognition to identify the type of enquiry. For example, Nationwide (www.nationwide.co.uk) use Brightware's 'skill-based message routeing' so that messages are sent to a specialist adviser where specific enquiries are made. Such software can also be used at Stage 1 to give an autoresponse appropriate for the enquiry.

**Avatar**

A term used in computer-mediated environments to mean a 'virtual person'. Derived from the word's original meaning: '*n.* the descendant of a Hindu deity in a visible form; incarnation; supreme glorification of any principle'.

**Autoresponder or 'mailbots'**

Software tool or 'agent' running on web servers that automatically sends a standard reply to the sender of an e-mail message.

---

| Mini Case Study 5.4 | Online customer service at Barclays |
|---|---|

In 2005, Barclays deployed web self-service to answer customers' questions online and reduce the 100,000 monthly calls to its helpdesk. Accessible on every page, via 'Ask a question', the Barclays solution allows customers to ask questions and receive meaningful, accurate answers on any subject from credit card offers to information about how the company scores credit.

In the first 12 months, 'Ask a question' was used by 350,000 customers and answered more than half-a-million questions. Only 8% of customers escalated through to the call centre, pointing to high levels of customer satisfaction and resulting in improvements to call centre efficiency and quality of service. In 2007, more than two million customers used 'Ask a question' to find answers to their enquiries.

'Ask a question' is providing invaluable insight in the critical decision-making process about what concerns customers have and what products are of interest. For example, it identified a higher demand from personal banking customers for making foreign currency payments than was previously known to Barclays. This information is being used to inform the bank about customer trends and requirements, and for creating customer-driven website content.

It was apparent that website visitors who ask questions through web self-service were more than casual browsers but customers with genuine buying requirements. There was potential to increase sales conversion by putting the right information and product offer in front of these customers based on what they were asking about. 'Ask a question' was enhanced to incorporate ad-serving, which serves up targeted advertising and sales promotions in response to questions asked by customers via the bank's website. The adverts change automatically depending on their relevance to customer questions, or to products and services Barclays wants to promote. For example, when customers ask questions about foreign currency accounts, 'Ask a question' will provide a specific answer and display adverts for travel insurance, the use of debit cards abroad and foreign mortgages. As well as promoting products directly relevant to the customer's search, ad-serving is used to cross-promote related products and services. These ads provide customers with an appealing call to action that speeds sales completion and increases response rates.

Advertising products alongside search results is producing high conversion rates with 12% of customers responding to a product advertisement. 'Ask a question' is also improving usability, allowing customers to access all of the content relevant to them from a single click or question. By integrating ad-serving with 'Ask a question', Barclays have been able to achieve high levels of behavioural targeting that have previously only been available through expensive and complicated website analytics tools. Because advertisements and promotions are served in response to customer enquiries, there is no need for the system to log or track vast amounts of historical customer data to analyse and predict customer behaviour in order to deliver targeted information. This cuts the complexity of delivering targeted information and increases sales.

*Source*: Transversal (2008) *UK companies fail the multichannel customer service test*. Research report, March 2008, available online at www.transversal.com

### Stage 4: Compose response

Best practice is to use a library of pre-prepared templates for different types of query. These can then be tailored and personalised by the contact centre employee as appropriate. The right type of template can again be selected automatically using the software referred to in Stage 2. Through using such auto-suggestion, Nationwide has seen e-mail handling times reduced by 25% for messages requiring adviser intervention. Sony Europe identifies all new support issues and adds them with the appropriate response to a central knowledge base.

### Stage 5: Follow-up

Best practice is that if the employee does not successfully answer the first response, then the e-mail should suggest callback from an employee or a live chat. Indeed, to avoid the problem of 'e-mail ping-pong' where several e-mails may be exchanged, the company may want to proactively ring the customer to increase the speed of problem resolution, and so solve the problem. Finally, the e-mail follow-up may provide the opportunity for outbound contact and marketing, perhaps advising about complementary products or offers.

## Process

**Process variable**
The element of the marketing mix that involves the methods and procedures companies use to achieve all marketing functions.

The **Process** element of the marketing mix refers to the methods and procedures companies use to achieve all marketing functions – such as new product development, promotion, sales and customer service (as described in the previous section). The restructuring of the organisation and channel structures to accommodate online marketing which were described in the previous chapter are part of Process.

Customer contact strategies are a compromise between delivering quality customer service with the emphasis on customer choice and minimising the cost of customer contacts. Typical operational objectives that should drive the strategies and measure effectiveness are:

- to minimise average response time per e-mail and the range of response time from slowest to fastest. This should form the basis of an advertised service quality level.
- to minimise clear-up (resolution) time, for example number of contacts and elapsed time to resolution.
- to maximise customer satisfaction ratings with response.
- to minimise average staff time and cost per e-mail response.

Customer contact strategies for integrating web and e-mail support into existing contact centre operations usually incorporate elements of both of the following options:

- *Customer-preferred channel.* Here the company uses a customer-led approach where customers use their preferred channel for enquiry, whether it be phone call-back, e-mail or live chat. There is little attempt made to influence the customer as to which is the preferable channel. Note that while this approach may give good customer satisfaction ratings, it is not usually the most cost-effective approach, since the cost of phone support will be higher than customer self-service on the web, or an e-mail enquiry.
- *Company-preferred channel.* Here the company will seek to influence the customer on the medium used for contact. For example, easyJet encourages customers to use online channels rather than voice contact to the call centre for both ordering and customer service. Customer choice is still available, but the company uses the website to influence the choice of channel.

## Physical evidence

**Physical evidence variable**
The element of the marketing mix that involves the tangible expression it is purchased and used.

The **Physical evidence** element of the marketing mix refers to the tangible expression of a product and how it is purchased and used. In an online context, 'physical evidence' refers to the customer's experience of the company through the website. It includes issues such as site ease of use or navigation, availability and performance, which are discussed further in Chapter 7.

---

## Case Study 5 — The re-launched Napster changes the music marketing mix

This case about the online music subscription service Napster illustrates how different elements of the mix can be varied online. It also highlights success factors for developing an online marketing strategy since Napster's proposition, objectives, competitors and risk factors are all reviewed.

The Napster brand has had a varied history. Its initial incarnation was as the first widely used service for 'free' peer-to-peer (P2P) music sharing. The record companies mounted a legal challenge to Napster due to lost revenues on music sales which eventually forced it to close. But the Napster brand was purchased and its second incarnation offers a legal music download service in direct competition with Apple's iTunes.

### The original Napster

Napster was initially created between 1998 and 1999 by a 19-year-old called Shawn Fanning while he attended Boston's Northeastern University. He wrote the program initially as a way of solving a problem for a friend who wanted to find music downloads more easily online. The name 'Napster' came from Fanning's nickname.

The system was known as peer-to-peer since it enabled music tracks stored on other Internet user's hard disks in MP3 format to be searched and shared with other Internet users. Strictly speaking, the service was not a pure P2P since central services indexed the tracks available and their locations in a similar way to which instant messaging (IM) works.

The capability to try a range of tracks proved irresistible and Napster use peaked with 26.4 million users worldwide in February 2001.

It was not long before several major recording companies backed by the RIAA (Recording Industry Association of America) launched a lawsuit. Of course, such an action also gave Napster tremendous PR and more users trialled the service. Some individual bands also responded with lawsuits. The rock band Metallica found that a demo of their song '*I disappear*' began circulating on the Napster network and was eventually played on the radio. Other well-known artists who vented their ire on Napster included Madonna and Eminem by posting false 'cuckoo egg' files instead of music; Madonna asked the downloader: 'What the fuck do you think you're doing?'! However, not all artists felt the service was negative for them. UK band Radiohead pre-released some tracks of their album *Kid A* on to Napster and subsequently became number 1 in the US despite failing to achieve this previously.

Eventually, as a result of legal action, an injunction was issued on 5 March 2001 ordering Napster to cease trading of copyrighted material. Napster complied with this injunction, but tried to make a deal with the record companies to pay past copyright fees and to turn the service into a legal subscription service.

In the following year, a deal was agreed with German media company Bertelsmann AG to purchase Napster's assets for $8 million as part of an agreement when Napster filed for Chapter 11 bankruptcy in the United States. This sale was blocked and the website closed. Eventually, the Napster brand was purchased by Roxio, Inc. which used the brand to rebrand their PressPlay service.

Since this time, other P2P services such as Gnutella, Grokster and Kazaa have prospered and these have been more difficult for the copyright owners to pursue in court; however, many individuals have now been sued in the USA and Europe and the associations of these services with spyware and adware has damaged them, which has reduced the popularity of these services.

## New Napster in 2008

Fast forward to 2008 and Napster now has around 830,000 subscribers in the United States, Canada and the United Kingdom who pay up to £14.95 each month to gain access to about 1.5 million songs. The company is seeking to launch in other countries such as Japan through partnerships. Revenue for financial year 2008 is expected to exceed $125 million, representing growth of 17%.

The online music download environment has also changed with legal music downloading propelled through increasing adoption of broadband, the success of Apple iTunes and its portable music player the iPod, which by 2005 had achieved around half-a-billion sales.

Napster gains its main revenues from online subscriptions and permanent music downloads. The Napster service offers subscribers on-demand access to over one million tracks that can be streamed or downloaded as well as the ability to purchase individual tracks or albums on an *à la carte* basis. Subscription and permanent download fees are paid by end-user customers in advance via credit card, online payment systems or redemption of pre-paid cards, gift certifi-

cates or promotional codes. Napster also periodically licenses merchandising rights and resells hardware that its end-users use to store and replay their music.

BBC (2005) estimated that the global music market is now worth $33 billion (£18.3 billion) a year while the online music market accounted for around 5% of all sales in the first half of 2005. Napster (2005), quoting Forrester Research, estimates that United States purchases of downloadable digital music will exceed $1.9 billion by 2007 and that revenues from online music subscription services such as Napster will exceed $800 million by 2007.

BBC (2005) reports Brad Duea, president of Napster, as saying:

> The number one brand attribute at the time Napster was shut down was innovation. The second highest characteristic was actually 'free'. The difference now is that the number one attribute is still innovation. Free is now way down on the list. People are able to search for more music than was ever possible at retail, even in the largest megastore.

Napster is not currently a profitable company, although losses are declining. The SEC filings for 2008 reported a Net loss for the third quarter of fiscal 2008 narrowed to $2.8 million, compared to a net loss of $9.5 million in the previous year.

## The Napster proposition

Napster subscribers can listen to as many tracks as they wish which are contained within the catalogue of over one million tracks (the service is sometimes described as 'all you can eat' rather than 'à la carte'). Napster users can listen to tracks on any compatible device that includes Windows Digital Rights Management software, which includes MP3 players, computers, PDAs and mobile phones.

Duea describes Napster as an 'experience' rather than a retailer. He says this because of features available such as:

- Napster recommendations;
- Napster radio based around songs by particular artists;
- Napster radio playlists based on the songs you have downloaded;
- swapping playlists and recommendations with other users.

iTunes and Napster are probably the two highest profile services, but they have quite different models of operating. There are no subscribers to iTunes, where users purchase songs either on a per-track basis or in the form of albums. By mid-2005, over half-a-billion tracks had been purchased on Napster. Some feel that iTunes locks people into purchasing Apple hardware; as one would expect, Duea of Napster says that Steve Jobs of Apple 'has tricked people into buying a hardware trap'.

But Napster's subscription model has also been criticised since it is a service where subscribers do not 'own' the music unless they purchase it at additional cost, for example to burn it to CD. The music is theirs to play either on a PC or on a portable player, but for only as long as they continue to subscribe to Napster. So it could be argued that Napster achieves lock-in in another form and requires a different approach to music ownership than some of its competitors.

During 2007, Napster launched a wireless music service branded 'Napster Mobile'. In conjunction with Ericsson this offers ringtones, OTA (over-the-air) downloads and wallpapers via a variety of mobile carriers in the United States and Europe, including Cingular/ATT, O2 Ireland, TMN in Portugal, SunComm and Dobson. Using Napster Mobile, customers are able to purchase music downloads from the full music catalogue using their mobile phone handset and have the songs delivered OTA to their handsets with a copy sent to their PC as well.

## Napster strategy

Napster (2005) describe their strategy as follows. The overall objective is to become the 'leading global provider of consumer digital music services'. They see these strategic initiatives as being important to achieving this:

- *Continue to build the Napster consumer brand* – as well as increasing awareness of the Napster brand identity, this also includes promoting the subscription service which encourages discovery of new music. Napster say 'We market our Napster service directly to consumers through an integrated offline and online marketing program consistent with the existing strong awareness and perception of the Napster brand. The marketing message is focused on our subscription service, which differentiates our offering from those of many of our competitors. Offline marketing channels include television (including direct-response TV), radio and print advertising. Our online marketing program includes advertising placements on a number of websites (including affiliate partners) and search engines'.
- *Continue to innovate by investing in new services and technologies* – this initiative encourages support of a wide range of platforms from portable MP3 players, PCs, cars, mobile phones, etc. The large technical team in Napster shows the importance of this strategy. In the longer term, access to other forms of content such as video may be offered. Napster see their ability to compete depend substantially upon their intellectual property. They have a number of patents issued, but are also in dispute with other organisations over their patents.
- *Continue to pursue and execute strategic partnerships* – Napster has already entered strategic partnerships with technology companies (Microsoft and Intel), hardware companies (iRiver, Dell, Creative, Toshiba and IBM), retailers (Best Buy, Blockbuster, Radio Shack, Dixons Group, The Link, PC World, Currys, Target) and others (Molson, Miller, Energizer, Nestlé). Distribution partnerships with mobile providers are a key aspect of its strategy and Napster has pursued agreements in this area. In 2008, Napster launched their Mobile music service with Telecom Italia which serves more than 35 million subscribers; Entel PCS, the leading Chilean mobile operator with more than 5.5 million subscribers and in Japan Napster Mobile for NTT DoCoMo.
- *Continue to pursue strategic acquisitions and complementary technologies* – this is another route to innovation and developing new services.

## Customers

*The Register* (2005) reported that in the UK, by mid-2005, Napster UK's 750,000 users had downloaded or streamed 55 million tracks since the service launched in May 2004. The company said 80% of its subscribers are over the age of 25, and half of them have kids. Some three-quarters of them are male. Its subscribers buy more music online than folk who buy one-off downloads do and research shows that one in five of them no longer buy CDs, apparently.

Describing its marketing strategy Napster says in its SEC filing:

> We primarily focus our marketing efforts on online advertising, where we can most cost effectively reach our target audience of 25–40 year-olds, as well as strategic partnerships where we can market our service with complementary products. In the United Kingdom and Germany, we also market our paid Napster service directly to consumers through a predominately online marketing program, consistent with the existing strong awareness and perception of the Napster brand. The marketing message is focused on our subscription service, which differentiates our offering from many of our competitors. Our online marketing program includes advertising placements on a number of websites (including affiliate partners) and search engines.

## Distribution

Napster's online music services are sold directly to end-users through the website (www.napster.com). Affiliate networks and universities have procured site licences (in the US, a significant proportion of subscribers are university users). Prepaid cards are also available through retail partners such as Dixons in the UK, who also promote the service.

Napster also bundles its service with hardware manufacturers such as iRiver, Dell, Creative Labs, Gateway and Samsung.

## Competition

Napster see their competitors for online music services in the US as Apple Computer's iTunes, Amazon, RealNetworks, Inc.'s Rhapsody, Yahoo! Unlimited, Sony Connect, AOL Music, MusicNet and MusicNow. In the UK, in 2005, new services with a subscription model were launched by retailers HMV and Virgin. They expect other competitors such as MTV Networks to enter the market soon.

Napster believes that the main competitive factors affecting their market include programming and features, price and performance, quality of customer support and compatibility with popular hardware devices and brand.

## Employees

As of 31 March 2005, Napster had 135 employees, of whom 10 directly supported the online music service (maintaining content and providing customer care), 25

were in sales and marketing, 63 were in engineering and product development and 37 were in finance, administration and operations. The costs of managing these staff is evident in Table 5.5.

## Risk factors

In their annual report submission to the United States Securities and Exchange Commission, Napster is required to give its risk factors, which also give an indication of success factors for the business. Napster summarises the main risk factors as follows:

1  The success of our Napster service depends upon our ability to add new subscribers and reduce churn.
2  Our online music distribution business has lower margins than our former consumer software products business. Costs of our online music distribution business as a percentage of the revenue generated by that business are higher than those of our former consumer software products business. The cost of third-party content, in particular, is a substantial portion of revenues we receive from subscribers and end-users and is unlikely to decrease significantly over time as a percentage of revenue.
3  We rely on the value of the Napster brand, and our revenues could suffer if we are not able to maintain its high level of recognition in the digital music sector.

| Table 1.1 | Summary of Napster finances from Napster (2007) |
|---|---|

| | 2007 | 2006 | 2005 | 2004 | 2003 |
|---|---|---|---|---|---|
| | | (in thousands, except per share amounts) | | | |
| Net revenues | $ 111 081 | $ 94 691 | $ 46 729 | $ 11 964 | $ – |
| Cost of revenues | 78 646 | 69 208 | 37 550 | 10 530 | – |
| Gross margin | 32 435 | 25 483 | 9 179 | 1 434 | – |
| Operating expenses: | | | | | |
| Research and development | 11 045 | 13 137 | 12 112 | 11 952 | – |
| Sales and marketing | 34 213 | 51 741 | 39 249 | 15 701 | – |
| General and administrative | 24 311 | 20 881 | 23 953 | 22 055 | 18 591 |
| Restructuring charges | – | – | – | 1 119 | – |
| Amortisation of intangible assets | 271 | 1 265 | 1 936 | 2 172 | 666 |
| Total operating expenses | 69 840 | 87 024 | 77 250 | 52 999 | 19 257 |
| Loss from continuing operations | (37 405) | (61 541) | (68 071) | (51 565) | (19 257) |
| Other income, net | 4 018 | 2 811 | 1 091 | 634 | 914 |
| Loss before income tax benefit (provision) | (33 387) | (58 730) | (66 980) | (50 931) | (18 343) |
| Income tax benefit (provision) | (1 257) | 1 160 | 15 547 | 4 515 | 7 182 |
| Loss from unconsolidated entity | (1 991) | (289) | – | – | – |
| Loss from continuing operations, after income taxes | (36 635) | (57 859) | (51 433) | (46 416) | (11 161) |
| Income (loss) from discontinued operations, net of tax effect | (191) | 2 914 | 21 927 | 2 003 | (489) |
| Net loss | $ (36 826) | $ (54 945) | $ (29 506) | $ (44 413) | $ (11 650) |

4 We face significant competition from traditional retail music distributors, from emerging paid online music services delivered electronically such as ours, and from 'free' peer-to-peer services.

5 Online music distribution services in general are new and rapidly evolving and may not prove to be a profitable or even viable business model.

6 We rely on content provided by third parties, which may not be available to us on commercially reasonable terms or at all.

7 We must provide digital rights management solutions that are acceptable to both content providers and consumers.

8 Our business could be harmed by a lack of availability of popular content.

9 Our success depends on our music service's interoperability with our customers' music playback hardware.

10 We may not successfully develop new products and services.

11 We must maintain and add to our strategic marketing relationships in order to be successful.

12 The growth of our business depends on the increased use of the Internet for communications, electronic commerce and advertising.

13 If broadband technologies do not become widely available or widely adopted, our online music distribution services may not achieve broad market acceptance, and our business may be harmed.

14 Our network is subject to security and stability risks that could harm our business and reputation and expose us to litigation or liability.

15 If we fail to manage expansion effectively, we may not be able to successfully manage our business, which could cause us to fail to meet our customer demand or to attract new customers, which would adversely affect our revenue.

16 We may be subject to intellectual property infringement claims, such as those claimed by SightSound Technologies, which are costly to defend and could limit our ability to use certain technologies in the future.

## Finances

Despite growth in subscribers and revenue, Napster has experienced significant net losses since its inception and according to the SEC filing Napster (2005), 'we expect to incur net losses for at least the next twelve months and likely continue to experience net losses thereafter'. Since 1 April 2003, Napster have incurred approximately $97.8 million of after-tax losses from continuing operations. A summary of the finances is presented in Table 5.5.

*Sources*: BBC (2005), Napster (2005), Wikipedia (2005), *The Register* (2005), Wired (2002) and SEC

### Question

Evaluate how Napster has varied each element of the marketing mix to compete with traditional and online music retailers.

## Summary

1. Evaluating the opportunities provided by the Internet for varying the marketing mix is a useful framework for assessing current and future Internet marketing strategy.

2. *Product*. Opportunities for varying the core product through new information-based services and also the extended product should be reviewed.

3. *Price*. The Internet leads to price transparency and commoditisation and hence lower prices. Dynamic pricing gives the ability to test prices or to offer differential pricing for different segments or in response to variations in demand. New pricing models such as auctions are available.

4. *Place*. This refers to place of purchase and channel structure on the Internet. There are three main locations for e-commerce transactions: seller site, buyer site and intermediary. New channel structures are available through direct sales and linking to new intermediaries. Steps must be taken to minimise channel conflict.

5. *Promotion*. This aspect of the mix is discussed in more detail in Chapter 8.

6. *People, process and physical evidence*. These aspects of the mix are discussed in more detail in Chapters 6 and 7 where customer relationship management and service delivery are discussed.

## Exercises

### Self-assessment exercises

1. Select the two most important changes introduced by the Internet for each of the 7 Ps.
2. What types of product are most amenable to changes to the core and extended product?
3. Explain the differences in concepts between online B2C and B2B auctions.
4. Explain the implications of the Internet for Price.
5. What are the implications of the Internet for Place?

### Essay and discussion questions

1. 'The marketing mix developed as part of annual planning is no longer a valid concept in the Internet era.' Discuss.
2. Critically evaluate the impact of the Internet on the marketing mix for an industry sector of your choice.
3. Write an essay on pricing options for e-commerce.
4. Does 'Place' have any meaning for marketers in the global marketplace enabled by the Internet?

### Examination questions

1. Describe three alternative locations for transactions for a B2B company on the Internet.
2. Explain two applications of dynamic pricing on the Internet.
3. How does the Internet impact an organisation's options for core and extended (augmented) product?
4. Briefly summarise the implications of the Internet on each of these elements of the marketing mix:
   (a) Product
   (b) Price
   (c) Place
   (d) Promotion.
5. Explain the reasons why the Internet could be expected to decrease prices online.
6. How can an organisation vary its promotional mix using the Internet?

## References

Aaker, D. and Joachimsthaler, E. (2000) *Brand Leadership*. Free Press, New York.
Allen, E. and Fjermestad, J. (2001) E-commerce marketing strategies: a framework and case analysis, *Logistics Information Management*, 14(1/2), 14–23.
Anderson, C. (2004) The Long Tail. *Wired*. 12, 10, October, www.wired.com/wired/archive/12.10/tail.html.
Ariely, D. and Simonson, I. (2003) Buying, bidding, playing or competing, *Journal of Consumer Psychology*, 13 (1&2), 113–23.
Azumah, G., Loh, S. and McGuire, S. (2005) E-organisation and its future implication for SMEs *Production Planning & Control*, Vol. 16, No. 6, September 2005, 555–562

Baker, W., Marn, M. and Zawada, C. (2000) Price smarter on the Net, *Harvard Business Review*, February, 2–7.

Baye, M., Gatti, J., Kattuman, P. and Morgan, J. (2007) Dashboard for online pricing. *The California Management Review*, Fall 2007, 50, No 1, 202–216.

BBC (2005) Napster boss on life after piracy. *BBC*. By Derren Waters, 22 August. http://news.bbc.co.uk/1/hi/entertainment/music/4165868.stm.

Benjamin, R. and Wigand, R. (1995) Electronic markets and virtual value-chains on the information superhighway, *Sloan Management Review*, Winter, 62–72.

Berryman, K., Harrington, L., Layton-Rodin, D. and Rerolle, V. (1998) Electronic commerce: three emerging strategies, *McKinsey Quarterly*, No. 1, 152–9.

Bickerton, P., Bickerton, M. and Pardesi, U. (2000) *CyberMarketing*, 2nd edn, Butterworth-Heinemann, Oxford.

Bicknell, D. (2002) Banking on customer service, *e.Businessreview*, January, 21–2.

Booms, B. and Bitner, M. (1981) Marketing strategies and organisation structures for service firms. In J. Donnelly and W. George (eds), *Marketing of Services*. American Marketing Association, New York.

Brand New World (2004) www.brandnewworld.co.uk. Joint research by Anne Mollen (Cranfield School of Management) and AOL Europe.

Brynjolfsson, E., Smith, D. and Hu, Y. (2003) Consumer surplus in the digital economy: estimating the value of increased product variety at online booksellers, *Management Science*, 49(11), 1580–96, http://ebusiness.mit.edu/research/papers/176_ErikB_OnlineBooksellers2.pdf.

Burnett, J. (1993) *Promotional Management*. Houghton Mifflin, Boston.

Chaffey, D. and Smith, P.R. (2008) *E-marketing Excellence. Planning and Optimising Your Digital Marketing*, 3rd edn, Butterworth-Heinemann, Oxford.

Christodoulides, G. and de Chernatony, L. (2004) Dimensionalising on- and offline brands' composite equity, *Journal of Product and Brand Management*, 13(3), 168–79.

Christodoulides, G,, de Chernatony, L., Furrer, O., Shiu, E. and Temi, A. (2006) Conceptualising and measuring the equity of online brands, *Journal of Marketing Management*, September 2006, Vol. 22, Issue 7/8, 799–825.

Davidow, W.H. and Malone, M.S. (1992) *The Virtual Corporation. Structuring and Revitalizing the Corporation for the 21st Century*. HarperCollins, New York.

Dap, S. (2003) An exploratory study of the introduction of online reverse auctions, *Journal of Marketing*, Vol. 67 (July 2003), 96–107.

Dayal, S., Landesberg, H. and Zeissberg, M. (2000) Building digital brands, *McKinsey Quarterly*, No. 2.

de Chernatony, L. (2001) Succeeding with brands on the Internet, *Journal of Brand Management*, 8(3), 186–95.

de Chernatony, L. and McDonald, M. (1992) *Creating Powerful Brands*. Butterworth-Heinemann, Oxford.

Diamantopoulos, A. and Matthews, B. (1993) *Making Pricing Decisions: A Study of Managerial Practice*. Chapman & Hall, London.

Dou, W. and Krishnamurthy, S. (2007) Using brand websites to build brands online: a product versus service brand comparison. *Journal of Advertising Research*, June, 193–206.

Erdem, T., Swait, J. and Louviere, J. (2002) The impact of brand credibility on consumer price sensitivity, *International Journal of Research in Marketing* 19(1), 1–19.

Emiliani, V. (2001) Business-to-business online auctions: key issues for purchasing process improvement, *Supply Chain Management: An International Journal*, 5(4), 176–86.

Evans, P. and Wurster, T.S. (1999) Getting real about virtual commerce, *Harvard Business Review*, November, 84–94.

Fill, C. (2000) *Marketing Communications – Contexts, Contents and Strategies*, 3rd edn. Financial Times/Prentice Hall, Harlow.

Flores, L. (2004). 10 Facts about the value of brand websites. AdMap, February 2004, 26–8. Source: http://www.imediaconnection.com/content/wp/admap.pdf.

Frazier, G. (1999) Organising and managing channels of distribution, *Journal of the Academy of Marketing Science*, 27(2), 222–40.

Ghosh, S. (1998) Making business sense of the Internet, *Harvard Business Review*, March–April, 127–35.

Gladwell, M. (2000) *The Tipping Point: How Little Things can Make a Big Difference*. Little, Brown, New York.

Guardian (2007) Beware when you compare Harriet Meyer, Friday 22 June 2007, Guardian http://money.guardian.co.uk/insurance_/story/0,,2108482,00.html.

Harridge-March, S. (2004) Electronic marketing, the new kid on the block. *Marketing Intelligence and Planning*, 22(3), 297–309.

Hitwise (2006) Paid and organic search: profile of MoneySupermarket. Hitwise blog posting from http://weblogs.hitwise.com/heaher-hopkins/2006/09/paid_and_organic_search_profile.html.

Holzwarth, M., Janiszewski, C. and Neumann, M. (2006) The influence of avatars on online consumer shopping behavior, *Journal of Marketing*, Vol. 70 (October 2006), 19–36.

Introna, L. (2001) Defining the virtual organisation. In S. Barnes and B. Hunt (eds), *E-Commerce and V-Business: Business Models for Global Success*. Butterworth-Heinemann, Oxford.

Jevons, C. and Gabbott, M. (2000) Trust, brand equity and brand reality in Internet business relationships: an interdisciplinary approach, *Journal of Marketing Management*, 16, 619–34.

Johnson, E., Moe, W., Fader, P., Bellman, S. and Lohse, G. (2004) On the depth and dynamics of online search behavior, *Management Science*, 50(3), 299–308.

Kotler, P. (1997) *Marketing Management: Analysis, Planning, Implementation and Control*, 9th international edn. Prentice-Hall, Upper Saddle River, NJ.

Kraut, R., Chan, A., Butler, B. and Hong, A. (1998) Coordination and virtualisation: the role of electronic networks and personal relationships, *Journal of Computer Mediated Communications*, 3(4).

Kumar, N. (1999) Internet distribution strategies: dilemmas for the incumbent, *Financial Times*, Special issue on mastering information management, no. 7. Electronic Commerce (www.ftmastering.com).

Lautenborn, R. (1990) New marketing litany: 4Ps passes; C-words take over, *Advertising Age*, 1 October, 26.

Lewis, M., Singh, V. and Fay, S. (2006) An empirical study of the impact of nonlinear shipping and handling fees on purchase incidence and expenditure decisions, *Marketing Science*, Vol. 25, No. 1, January–February 2006, 51–64.

McCarthy, J. (1960) *Basic Marketing: A Managerial Approach*. Irwin, Homewood, IL.

McDonald, M. and Wilson, H. (2002) *New Marketing: Transforming the Corporate Future*. Butterworth-Heinemann, Oxford.

Magretta, J. (1998) The power of virtual integration. An interview with Michael Dell, *Harvard Business Review*, March–April, 72–84.

Malone, T., Yates, J. and Benjamin, R. (1987) Electronic markets and electronic hierarchies: effects of information technology on market structure and corporate strategies, *Communications of the ACM*, 30(6), 484–97.

Marn, M. (2000) Virtual pricing, *McKinsey Quarterly*, No. 4.

Marsden, P. (2004) Tipping point marketing: a primer, *Brand strategy*, April. Available at: www.viralculture.com/pubs/tippingpoint2.htm.

Marshall, P., McKay, J. and Burn J. (2001) Structure, strategy and success factors in the virtual organisation. In S. Barnes and B. Hunt (eds) *E-Commerce and V-Business. Business Models for Global Success*. Butterworth-Heinemann, Oxford.

McCarthy, J. (1960) *Basic marketing: a managerial approach*. Richard D. Irwin, Homewood, Illinois.

Mols, N. (2001) Organising for the effective introduction of new distribution channels in retail banking, *European Journal of Marketing*, 35(5/6), 661–86.

Morris, R.J. and Martin, C.L. (2000) Beanie Babies: a case study in the engineering of a high involvement/relationship-prone brand, *Journal of Product and Brand Management*, 9(2), 78–98.

Napster (2005) Annual Report, pubished at Investor relations site (http://invetor.napster.com).

Napster (2007) Annual Report, published at Investor relations site (http://investor.napster.com).

Nitish, S., Fassott, G., Zhao, H. and Boughton, P. (2006) A cross-cultural analysis of German, Chinese and Indian consumers' perception of website adaptation, *Journal of Consumer Behaviour*, 5: 56–68.

NMA (2008) Profile – Travis Katz, Author: Luan Goldie, *New Media Age magazine*, published 31.01.08.

Peppard, J. and Rylander, A. (2005) Products and services in cyberspace *International Journal of Information Management*, Vol. 25, No. 4.

Pitt, L., Berthorn, P., Watson, R. and Ewing, M. (2001) Pricing strategy and the Net, *Business Horizons*, March–April, 45–54.

Quelch, J. and Klein, L. (1996) The Internet and international marketing, *Sloan Management Review*, Spring, 61–75.

Queree, A. (2000) *Financial Times*, Technology Supplement, 1 March.

Rayport, J. and Sviokla, J. (1994) Managing in the marketspace, *Harvard Business Review*, July, 141–50.

Rayport, J., Jaworski, B. and Kyung, E. (2005) Best face forward: improving companies' service interfaces with customers, *Journal of Interactive Marketing*, 19(4), 67–80.

*The Register* (2005) Napster UK touts subscriber numbers. *The Register*. Tony Smith, 5 September. www.theregister.co.uk/2005/09/05/napster_numbers.

Ries, A. and Ries, L. (2000) *The 11 Immutable Laws of Internet Branding*. HarperCollins Business, London.

Sarkar, M., Butler, B. and Steinfield, C. (1996) Intermediaries and cybermediaries: A continuing role for mediating players in the electronic marketplace, *Journal of Computer Mediated Communication*, 1(3).

Sawhney, M., Verona, G. and Prandelli, E. (2005) Collaborating to create: The Internet as a platform for customer engagement in product innovation. *Journal of Interactive Marketing*, Volume 19, 4, Autumn 2005, 4–17.

Singh, N. and Pereira, A. (2005) The Culturally Customized Website: Customizing Websites for the Global Marketplace, Butterworth-Heinemann, Oxford, UK.

Smith, P.R. and Chaffey, D. (2005) *E-Marketing Excellence: at the Heart of EBusiness*, 2nd edn. Butterworth-Heinemann, Oxford.

Wikipedia (2005) Napster. Wikipedia. Wikipedia entry at http://en.wikipedia.org/wiki/Napster.

Wilmshurst, J. (1993) *Below the Line Promotion*. Butterworth-Heinemann, Oxford.

Wired (2002) The Day Napster Died. *Wired magazine*. Brad King, May 2002. www.wired.com/news/mp3/0,1285,52540,00.html.

Xing, X., Yang, S. and Tang, F. (2006) A comparison of time-varying online price and price dispersion between multichannel and dotcom DVD retailers. *Journal of Interactive Marketing*, 20, (2), 3–20.

## Further reading

Allen, E. and Fjermestad, J. (2001) E-commerce marketing strategies: a framework and case analysis, *Logistics Information Management*, 14(1/2), 14–23. Includes an analysis of how the 4 Ps are impacted by the Internet.

Baker, W., Marn, M. and Zawada, C. (2000) Price smarter on the Net, *Harvard Business Review*, February, 2–7. This gives a clear summary of the challenges and opportunities of Internet pricing.

Ghosh, S. (1998) Making business sense of the Internet, *Harvard Business Review*, March–April, 127–35. This paper gives many examples of how US companies have adapted their products to the Internet and asks key questions that should govern the strategy adopted.

Harridge-March, S. (2004) Electronic marketing, the new kid on the block. *Marketing Intelligence and Planning*, 22(3), 297–309. Like the Allen and Fjermestad (2001) paper, this gives a review of the impact of the Internet on different aspects of the marketing mix.

Kumar, N. (1999) Internet distribution strategies: dilemmas for the incumbent, *Financial Times*, Special issue on mastering information management, no. 7. Electronic Commerce (www.ftmastering.com). This article assesses the impact of the Internet on manufacturers and their distribution channels. The other articles in this special issue are also interesting.

Smith, P.R. and Chaffey, D. (2005) *E-Marketing Excellence: at the Heart of EBusiness*, 2nd edn. Butterworth-Heinemann, Oxford. Chapter 2 is devoted to applying the marketing mix to Internet marketing.

 ## Web links

- **Chris Anderson** has a blog site (www.thelongtail.com), the Long Tail, to support his book on the topic published in 2006 by Hyperion, New York.

- **CIM 10 minute guide to the marketing mix**. (http://www.cim.co.uk/mediastore/10_minute_guides/10_min_Marketing_Mix.pdf). A fairly detailed introduction to the marketing mix with further links.

- **ClickZ** (www.clickz.com). An excellent collection of articles on online marketing communications, US-focused. Relevant section for this chapter: Brand marketing.

- **Comparison Engines** (www.comparisonengines.com). A portal focusing on the latest techniques and developments for aggregators in the US and Europe.

- **The culturally customized website** (www.theculturallycustomizedwebsite.com). Resources supporting the authors' book of this title.

- **Gladwell.com** (www.gladwell.com). Author's site with extracts from *The Tipping Point* and other books.

- **Paul Marsden's** Viral Culture site (www.viralculture.com). Articles related to the tipping point and connected marketing.

# 6

# Relationship marketing using the Internet

## Learning objectives

After reading this chapter, the reader should be able to:

- Assess the relevance of the concepts of relationship, direct and database marketing on the Internet
- Evaluate the potential of the Internet to support one-to-one marketing, and the range of techniques and systems available to support dialogue with the customer over the Internet
- Assess the characteristics required of tools to implement one-to-one marketing

## Questions for marketers

Key questions for marketing managers related to this chapter are:

- How can the Internet be used to support the different stages of the customer lifecycle?
- How do I implement permission marketing?
- What do personalisation and mass customisation mean and how should I apply them in my marketing?

## Links to other chapters

This chapter is related to other chapters as follows:

- Chapter 4 introduces customer lifecycle-based segmentation models
- Chapter 7 has guidelines on how to develop the right customer experience to assist in forming and maintaining relationships
- Chapter 8 describes methods of acquiring customers for one-to-one marketing
- Chapters 10 and 11 give examples of relationship marketing in the business-to-consumer and business-to-business markets

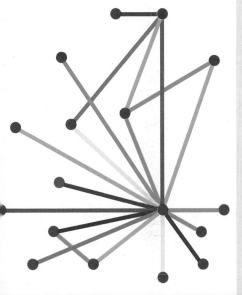

## Introduction

Building long-term relationships with customers is essential for any sustainable business, and this applies equally to online elements of a business. Failure to build relationships to gain repeat visitors and sales largely caused the failure of many dot-coms following huge expenditure on customer acquisition. Research summarised by Reichheld and Schefter (2000) showed that acquiring online customers is so expensive (he suggested 20–30% higher than for traditional businesses) that start-up companies may remain unprofitable for at least two to three years. The research also shows that by retaining just 5% more customers, online companies can boost their profits by 25% to 95%.

Over the last decade or more, relationship marketing, direct marketing and database marketing have combined to create a powerful new marketing paradigm. This paradigm is often referred to as **customer relationship management (CRM)**. A related approach is known as **one-to-one marketing** where, in theory, relationships are managed on an individual basis. But, owing to the costs of managing relationships on an individual level, many companies will apply CRM by using approaches which automate the tailoring of services to develop relationships with particular customer segments or groups, rather than individuals. These tailored messages can then be delivered by e-mail marketing or recommendations and promotions on the website. Delivering the relevant messages involves a company in developing a long-term relationship with each customer in order to better understand that customer's needs and then deliver services that meet these individual needs.

The interactive nature of the web combined with e-mail communications provides an ideal environment in which to develop customer relationships, and databases provide a foundation for storing information about the relationship and providing information to strengthen it by improved, personalised services. This online approach to CRM is often known as **e-CRM or electronic customer relationship management**, and it is on this we focus in this chapter.

Figure 6.1 summarises the linkages between CRM and existing marketing approaches. Direct marketing provides the tactics that deliver the marketing communications, and sometimes the product itself, to the individual customer. Relationship marketing theory provides the conceptual underpinning of CRM since it emphasises enhanced customer service through knowledge of the customer, and deals with markets segmented to the level of the individual. Database marketing provides the technological enabler, allowing vast quantities of customer-related data to be stored and accessed in ways that create strategic and tactical marketing opportunities.

**Customer relationship management**
A marketing-led approach to building and sustaining long-term business with customers.

**One-to-one marketing**
A unique dialogue occurs between a company and individual customers (or groups of customers with similar needs).

**Electronic customer relationship management**
Using digital communications technologies to maximise sales to existing customers and encourage continued usage of online services.

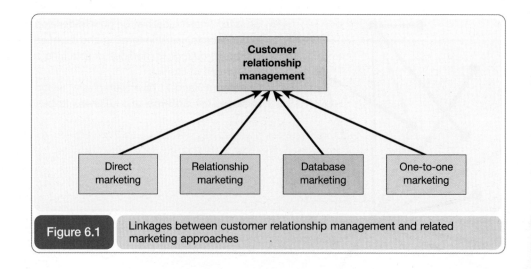

**Figure 6.1**    Linkages between customer relationship management and related marketing approaches

This chapter begins by introducing the key concepts of relationship marketing, customer engagement and e-CRM. We then review, in more detail how e-CRM can be implemented using techniques such as permission marketing, personalisation and e-mail.

| Digital marketing in practice | The EConsultancy interview |
|---|---|

### Timo Soininen, CEO, Sulake (Habbo Hotel)

#### Overview and main concepts covered

Timo Soininen is the CEO of Sulake Corporation, the Finnish digital media group that owns virtual world Habbo Hotel, as well as other online games and social networks.

We asked him about the risks and rewards for brands targeting online communities, as well as the company's plans for the future.

#### The interview

**Q: Where has Habbo got to in terms of active users?**

*Timo Soininen*: We've reached around 6.5 million unique monthly users on all the Habbo sites. Around 80 million player accounts have been created since the beginning, which was seven years ago now but feels like an eternity.

The biggest markets for us are North America, the UK, France, Spain and Latin America. We have a presence in 33 markets, where we have payment systems and localised sites, and the service is available in 11 languages.

**Q: What's behind that ratio between unique users and accounts? Is that level of churn typical in virtual worlds, and social networks for that matter?**

*Timo Soininen*: I think a lot of the virtual worlds differ from social networking services because in virtual worlds people typically have characters.

We are an anonymous service. We don't allow people to share their real-life data at all – for security reasons, obviously. The dynamics are different. Some users create multiple characters – a single user could easily have created two or three different characters.

**Q: Presumably a lot of people also experiment with the service and decide they don't want to continue.**

*Timo Soininen*: Yes. What also often happens is you hear about the service, you go on it to check it out and create a character, but decide later on that you want to start again once you have the hang of it. I'm sure that happens with social networks as well, but I'm not an expert on that.

**Q: You've had a lot of success attracting brands to the environment. What are the main things they need to watch out for?**

*Timo Soininen*: The starting point is that we have to think about the users – it is their place. Advertisers have to come in in a way that is respectful.

Just flashing banners at them will not work – you have to go in deep and understand the dynamics of the service. The key purpose is to get the brand involved and become a topic inside the community – something people talk about and share.

One of the main problems in Second Life is what I call the iceberg model. The real bit is below the surface. In the visible bit, 'Brand X' will create a virtual venue, but you can only fit a certain amount of people into a virtual venue.

What can be very scaleable, and what persuades brands to do repeat activities with us, is when you go deep into the community and become part of the users' rooms and activities, sponsoring a game or arranging a quest.

They become a topic inside the environment and really add value to the user. That, in a nutshell, is what you need to do.

**Q: Can you give a recent example of a successful campaign?**

*Timo Soininen*: We recently ran a very successful campaign in one market for Unilever's Rexona brand. We worked very closely with our producers and their brand team to choose elements that really fit in with the brand. It became huge.

We tailored the campaign to the brand and there was a really interesting debate about it between boys and girls. They added some very cool stuff to the environment.

**Q: What metrics do you provide to advertisers?**

*Timo Soininen*: The good thing about these worlds is that everything is measurable – you can track how many unique users you have reached, page views, friend recommendations, game plays and so on.

Unlike Second Life, we also have the magic thing called reach. We have a lot of users that are very responsive to this type of thing, if you do it well.

People are interested in the traditional metrics and how their brands have been affected, and we can deliver standard reports. You can also tweak the campaign as you go, if needed.

**Q: What do you think is needed to drive more adoption of payments in virtual worlds?**

*Timo Soininen*: The important thing is, up until now, buying stuff online has been relatively cumbersome. We have been using a multitude of payment systems, from premium SMS – which is very popular with teenagers but has very high commission levels from the operators – to e-banking, credit cards and physical scratchcards in kiosks. We have more than 160 payment channels.

What will inevitably happen is that in terms of mobile payments, as the IP world hits the market, we will see more mass adoption and it will become more convenient and secure for people to impulse-buy on the web.

We are also working with big players like Paypal in various markets, although it hasn't been massively successful with teenagers, at least for us. It's a surprisingly underdeveloped area, but we believe that you have to offer users as many payment options as possible in order to maximise revenue. You shouldn't force people into one form of payment – it limits your business.

**Q: What are your thoughts on Facebook's open source strategy? Are you ultimately looking at offering a similar platform to outside developers?**

*Timo Soininen*: There is some interesting stuff happening in the virtual world space. Raph Koster is building an open source-based platform for virtual worlds, and I think that's an interesting approach. But if you want to have a visually cohesive world, it's not easy. If you think about computer games like World of Warcraft, people create their own stuff, but there's a good chance the magic will be destroyed unless the tools are really elaborate and whatever is created can fit in with the environment.

We have been using very simplified pixel graphics, and have never been big fans of creating replicas of the real world as that basically destroys the illusion inside your head. Our approach, from the beginning, has been to give some props and tools to allow users to express themselves, and they have used them to create mash-ups. There is some pretty exciting stuff.

Third parties – not just users – will be able to create stuff, but it will be a mash-up of using web technologies and client technologies as well.

We are launching game tools that users can create themselves using props and functional items, and eventually will even allow them to create some of the props inside the environment. But you have to have very good quality control and moderation of what goes inside the environment. We've always been strict on the moderation angle.

**Q: Can you give us an overview of the reasons behind your purchase of [social networking service] IRC-Galleria earlier this year, and when we might see that coming to the UK?**

*Timo Soininen*: It's extremely successful and is one of the few social networking sites that earns a big chunk of its revenue from end-users, which gives us synergies and the potential to leverage their operational infrastructure quite easily. Also, there is something pretty interesting about it – it is one of the most active social networking sites in terms of user activity. Our plan is to rebrand it, work on the positioning and then start to go into international markets.

Facebook has been a gigantic success and continues to be, but we believe segmentation will start to happen more and more with social networking sites. There are a hell of a lot of sites out there, but we believe we will come to the market with a different angle from other players.

**Q: Can you give us an update on your move into mobile?**

*Timo Soininen*: We have had a product for Habbo working on mobile for a long time, but we have not yet decided to implement it.

The data pricing from the operators, especially for younger users, has been very expensive. Also, the higher-end devices that you need for a meaningful experience have not yet been available en masse. That is changing rapidly now. We also have recently launched what I think is one of the few virtual mobile worlds out there, called minifriday.com, and we have around 110,000 registered users in it already. Check it out. It's pretty cool. We will probably use the technology for another couple of projects.

*Source*: http://www.e-consultancy.com/news-blog/news;etter/3450/sulake-ceo-timo-soininen-discusses-habbo-hotel.html. E-consultancy.com provides information, training and events on best practice in online marketing and e-commerce management.

# Key concepts of relationship marketing

**Relationship marketing**
'Consistent application of up to date knowledge of individual customers to product and service design which is communicated interactively in order to develop a continuous and long term relationship which is mutually beneficial' (Cram, 1994).

**Mass marketing**
One-to-many communication between a company and potential customers, with limited tailoring of the message.

Relationship marketing is best understood within the context of the historical development of marketing. The Industrial Revolution, the large-scale production of more widely distributed, standardised products changed the nature of marketing. Whereas marketing had previously been largely by word of mouth and based on personal relationships, it became an impersonal mass-marketing monologue. During the twentieth century, differentiation of products and services became more important, and this highlighted the need for feedback from customers about the type of product features required. Sharma and Sheth (2004) have stressed the importance of this trend from mass marketing to what is now widely known as 'one-to-one' or 'customer-centric marketing' (although many would regard the latter as a tautology since the modern marketing concept places the customer at the heart of marketing activity). These authors give the example of the Dell model where each PC is manufactured and distributed 'on demand' according to the need of a specific customer. This is an example of what they refer to as 'reverse marketing' with the change in emphasis on marketing execution from product supply to customer need. Another aspect of this transformation is that online, web marketers can track the past behaviours of customers in order to customise communications to encourage future

**Customer-centric marketing**
The approach to Internet marketing function is based on customer behaviour within the target audience and then seeks to fulfil the needs and wants of each individual customer.

**Sense and respond communications**
Delivering timely, relevant communications to customers as part of a contact strategy based on assessment of their position in the customer lifecycle and monitoring specific interactions with a company's website, e-mails and staff.

purchases. This approach, which is another aspect of reverse marketing and also a key concept with e-CRM, can be characterised as '**sense and respond communications**'. The classic example of this is the personalisation facilities provided by Amazon where personal recommendations are provided. Another aspect of online reverse marketing is the Dell IdeaStorm (www.ideastorm.com) approach of soliciting customer feedback on potential new products.

## Benefits of relationship marketing

Relationship marketing is aimed at increasing customer loyalty or retention within a current customer base which is highly desirable for the following reasons:

- Effectively no acquisition costs (which are usually far higher than 'maintenance' costs).
- Less need to offer incentives such as discounts, or to give vouchers to maintain custom (although these may be desirable).
- Less price-sensitive (loyal customers are happy with the value they are getting).
- Loyal customers will recommend the company to others ('referrals').
- Individual revenue growth occurs as trust increases.

Rigby *et al.* (2000) have summarised a study by Mainspring and Bain & Company which evaluated the spending patterns and loyalty of consumers in online retail categories of clothing, groceries and consumer electronics. Their work shows that e-tailers could not breakeven on 'one-time' shoppers. For grocery e-tailers, customers have to be retained for 18 months for breakeven. The study also shows that repeat purchasers tend to spend more in a given time period and generate larger transactions. For example, online grocery shoppers spend 23% more in months 31–36 than in the first six months; this includes products in other categories (cross- and up-selling). A final effect is that repeat customers tend to refer more people, to bring in greater business. The impact of these referrals can be signficant – over a three-year period, in each product category, more than 50% additional revenue of the referrer was generated. Each referrer also has a lower acquisition cost.

| Table 6.1 | A summary of different concepts for the transactional and relationship paradigms |
|---|---|

| Transactional paradigm concept | Relationship paradigm concept | Comments and examples |
|---|---|---|
| Market segment | Individual customer | Raphel (1997) describes the success story of AMC Kabuki 8 movie theatres in San Francisco. Despite the competition from the giant multiplexes, AMC is flourishing because of its understanding of the cinematic preferences of its customers so they can be informed in advance of ticket sales. 'The most failure-prone fault-line in transactional marketing is the statistical customer – the hypothetical human who is composed of statistically averaged attributes drawn form research.' (Wolfe, 1998) |
| Duration of transaction | Lifetime relationship | The pursuit of customer loyalty 'is a perpetual one – more of a journey than a destination'. (Duffy, 1998) |
| Margin | Lifetime value | To support the Huggies product in the 1970s, Kimberley-Clark spent over $10m to construct a database that could identify 75% of the four million expectant mothers every year in the USA, using information obtained from doctors, hospitals and childbirth trainers. During the pregnancy, mothers received a magazine and letters with advice on baby care. When the baby arrived a coded coupon was sent, which was tracked to learn which mothers had tried the product. The justification was the lifetime value of these prospective customers, not the unit sale. (Shaw, 1996) |

| Transactional paradigm concept | Relationship paradigm concept | Comments and examples |
|---|---|---|
| Market share | Most-valued customers | Rather than waging expensive 'trench warfare' where profit and customer share objectives are linked automatically to overall market share, companies have now realised that, as 80% of their business often comes from 20% of their customers (the famous Pareto law), then retaining and delighting that 20% will be much more cost effective than trying to retain the loyalty of the 80%. Reichheld (1996) conducted research indicating that an increase in customer retention of 5% could improve profitability by as much as 125%. |
| Mass market monologue | Direct marketing dialogue | 'The new marketing requires a feedback loop.' (McKenna, 1993) |
| Passive consumers | Empowered clients | 'Transactional marketing is all about seduction and propaganda and it depends on a passive, narcotized receptor, the legendary "couch potato".' (Rosenfield, 1998) |

Table 6.1 summarises the differences between the two paradigms discussed in this section. Figure 6.20 shows that to build relationships and loyalty online, the quality of the online experience is significant. The topic of loyalty drivers is discussed further in Chapter 7.

## Differentiating customers by value

A core approach to relationship marketing is to focus our limited resources and marketing activities on the most valuable customers. Figure 6.2 gives a visual indication of this approach using the terminology suggested by Peppers and Rogers (2002). They identify three groups of customers with corresponding strategies as follows:

### 1 Most-valuable customers (MVCs)

These are the customers who contribute the most profit and are typically a small proportion of the total customer base as suggested by their position in the pyramid. These customers will likely have purchased more or higher-value products. The strategy for these customers focuses on retention rather than extension. In the case of a bank, personal relationship managers

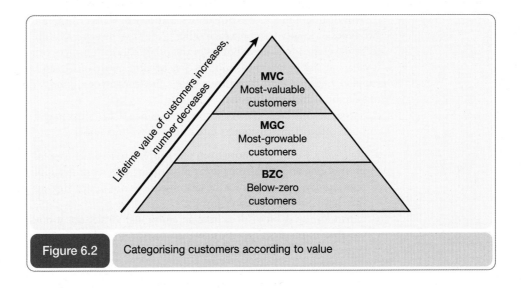

| Figure 6.2 | Categorising customers according to value |

would be appointed for customers in this category to provide them with guidance and advice and to make sure they remain loyal. Often this strategy will work best using direct personal contact as the primary communication channel, but using online marketing for support where the customer has a propensity to use online channels.

### 2 Most-growable customers (MGCs)

These are customers who show potential to become more valuable customers. They are profitable when assessed in terms of lifetime value, but the number of product holdings or lifetime value is relatively low compared with the MVCs.

Strategies for these customers centre on extension, through making recommendations about relevant products based on previous purchases. Encouraging similar re-purchases could also be part of this. Online marketing offers great opportunities to make personalised recommendations through the website and e-mail.

### 3 Below-zero customers (BZCs)

BZCs are simply unprofitable customers. The strategy for these customers may vary – they can be encouraged to develop towards MGCs, but more typically expenditure will be minimised if it is felt that it will be difficult to change their loyalty behaviour or the source of their being unprofitable. Again, digital media can be used as a lower-cost form of marketing expenditure to encourage these customers to make repeat purchases or to allow them to self-serve online.

## Customer loyalty

**Customer loyalty**
The desire on the part of the customer to continue to do business with a given supplier over time.

**Behavioural loyalty**
Loyalty to a brand is demonstrated by repeat sales and response to marketing campaigns.

**Emotional loyalty**
Loyalty to a brand is demonstrated by favourable perceptions, opinions and recommendations.

Another core facet of relationship marketing is its focus on increasing **customer loyalty**, particularly of the MVCs and MGCs. Sargeant and West (2001) describe loyalty as:

> *the desire on the part of the customer to continue to do business with a given supplier over time.*

To successfully develop retention strategies, it is useful to acknowledge that there are two types of loyalty, behavioural loyalty and emotional loyalty. **Behavioural loyalty** is the name given to behaviour that proves loyalty to the brand through sales. It means that the customer behaves in the way the brand wants, i.e. by spending money. Measures of behavioural loyalty include response rates to direct marketing to the customer base, 'share of wallet' and market share. **Emotional loyalty** acknowledges that perceptions and emotions drive behaviour. A customer who is emotionally loyal has empathy and attachment with a brand and company and is more likely to recommend it to potential customers.

This distinction, which is not always acknowledged, is critical to retention marketing. The two types of loyalty reinforce each other if they can be achieved together and strategies need to be developed to achieve both. On the other hand, customers who are only behaviourally loyal are at risk of lapsing as soon as they become aware of, or can readily switch to, another supplier. Likewise there is relatively little value from an emotionally loyal customer who does not exhibit behavioural loyalty!

Sargeant and West (2001) extend the concept of behavioural and emotional loyalty through categorising customers into one of these four types:

- *No loyalty.* Customers move from one supplier to another for reasons such as cost or price promotions or because they don't discern any difference in supplier.
- *Spurious loyalty.* In this case the customer does not switch supplier due to inertia although they have limited emotional loyalty.
- *Latent loyalty.* A buyer does have an emotional loyalty but it doesn't necessarily translate to behavioural loyalty – they may still 'shop around'.
- *True loyalty.* The behavioural pattern indicates a single favoured supplier or product in a given category.

# The relationship between satisfaction and loyalty

**Customer satisfaction**
The extent to which a customer's expectations of product quality, service quality and price are met.

Although the terms 'satisfaction' and 'loyalty' are sometimes used interchangeably, we have seen that they do not necessarily correspond. 'Customer satisfaction' refers to the degree a customer is happy about the quality of products and services. As a customer's satisfaction with products and/or services increases, so should their behavioural and emotional loyalty.

As we have seen, though, there may be customers with a high degree of satisfaction who don't exhibit behavioural loyalty and, conversely, customers who are behaviourally loyal may be at risk of defection since they are not satisfied. The implications are that it is important not only to measure satisfaction with online services, but loyalty also. In this way we are able to identify customers at risk of defection who are likely to choose an alternative and those in the zone of indifference. This is an important category of customer who, although they may have a high degree of satisfaction, is not necessarily loyal.

---

### Mini Case Study 6.1 — How car manufacturers use loyalty-based segmentation

An approach to reconciling customer satisfaction, loyalty, value and potential is to use a value-based segmentation. This modelling approach is often used by car manufacturers and other companies who are assessing strategies to enhance the future value of their customer segments. This approach involves creating a segmentation model combining real data for each customer about their current value and satisfaction, and modelled values for future loyalty and value. Each customer is scored according to these four variables:

- Current satisfaction
- Repurchase loyalty
- Current value
- Future potential

#### Table 6.2 — Loyalty-based segmentation for car manufacturer

| SLVP score | Nature of customer | Segment strategy |
|---|---|---|
| Moderate satisfaction and loyalty. Moderate current and future potential value | An owner of average loyalty who replaces their car every three to four years and has a tendency to repurchase from brand | Not a key segment to influence. But should encourage to subscribe to e-newsletter club and deliver targeted messages around time of renewal |
| High satisfaction, moderate loyalty. Low future and potential value | A satisfied owner but tends to buy second-hand and keeps cars until they have a high mileage | Engage in dialogue via e-mail newsletter and use this to encourage advocacy and make aware of benefits of buying new |
| Low satisfaction and loyalty. High current and future potential value | A dissatisfied owner of luxury cars who is at risk of switching | A key target segment who needs to be contacted to understand issues and reassure about quality and performance |

## Net Promoter Score

**Net Promoter Score** (NPS) is a measure of advocacy originally popularised by Reichheld (2006) in his book: 'the Ultimate Question' is essentially 'would you recommend us?' The aim is to work out techniques to maximise this NPS. Reichheld explains the main process for NPS as follows:

1 *Systematically categorise customers into promoters, passives or detractors. If you prefer, you can call them loyal advocates, fair-weather friends and adversaries.*
2 *Creating closed-loop processes so that the right employees will directly investigate the root causes that drive customers into these categories.*
3 *Making the creation of more promoters and fewer detractors a top priority so employees up and down the organisation take actions based on their findings from these root-cause investigations.*

In practice, consumers are asked 'Would you recommend [Brand/ Company X] to a friend or colleague?', answered on a scale between 0 (not at all likely) and 10 (extremely likely). The actual score is calculated by subtracting the percentage of detractors (those giving 0–6 answers) from promoters (9–10s). The middle section, between 7 and 8, are the so-called passives.

The concept of NPS is based on economic analysis of the customer base of a company. For Dell, Reichheld estimates that the average consumer is worth $210 (five year, Net Present Value), whereas a detractor costs the company $57 and a promoter generates $328. Online Dell uses software from Opinion Labs (www.opinionlabs.com) to both gather feedback and follow-up on negative experiences and so reduce the number of detractors with major negative sentiment.

So, the idea is that after surveying as many customers as possible (to make it representative) and show you are listening, to then work backwards to determine which aspects of the experience of interacting with a brand creates 'promoters' or 'detractors'. Some specific approaches that can be used to help manage NPS in the online environment are:

1 *Facilitating online advocacy*:
   ● Page template contains 'Forward/recommend to a friend' options.
   ● E-mail templates contain 'Forward to a friend option'.
   ● Facilitate customer feedback through a structured programme of e-mailing customers for their opinions and NPS evaluations and by making it easy for site owners to comment.
   ● Showcase positive experiences – for example, e-retail sites often contain options for rating and commenting on products.
   ● Involve customers more in shaping your web services and core product offerings, such as the approach used by Dell in their IdeaStorm site (www.ideastorm.com).
2 *Managing online detractors*:
   ● Use online reputation management tools (www.davechaffey.com/online-reputation-management-tools) for notification of negative (and positive) comments.
   ● Develop a process and identify resources for rapidly responding to negative comments using a natural and open approach.
   ● Assess and manage the influence of negative comments within the natural listings of search engines.
   ● Practice fundamental marketing principles of listening to customer comments about products and services and aim to rectify them to win back the situation!

An example of a comany that seeks feedback from customers and then makes this feedback available to all customers is shirt retailer Charles Tyrwhitt (Figure 6.3).

| Figure 6.3 | Independent feedback for Charles Tyrwhitt (www.ctshirts.co.uk), a shirts retailer |

Kirby and Samson (2007) have critiqued the use of the NPS in practice. For example, they ask:

> is an NPS of 40, consisting of 70% promoters and 30% detractors, the same as the same NPS consisting of 40% promoters and 0% detractors?

They also quote research by Kumar *et al.* (2007) which shows that while about three-quarters of US telecoms and financial service customers may intend to recommend when asked, only about one-third actually follow through and only about 13% of those referrals actually generate new customers. Keiningham *et al.* (2007) have assessed the value of recommendation metrics as determinants of customer lifetime value and also believe that the use of NPS could be misleading. They say the consequences of a simple focus on NPS are:

> the potential misallocation of customer satisfaction and loyalty resources due to flawed strategies that are guided by a myopic focus on customers' recommend intentions.

## Key concepts of electronic customer relationship management (e-CRM)

E-CRM or **electronic customer relationship management** involves creating strategies and plans for how digital technology and digital data can support CRM. Some specialists in e-commerce teams have this as their job title or in their job description. But what is e-CRM? This is what Smith and Chaffey (2005) say:

**Electronic customer relationship management**
Using digital communications technologies to maximise sales to existing customers and encourage continued usage of online services.

*What is e-CRM? Customer Relations Management with an 'e'? Ultimately, E-CRM cannot be separated from CRM, it needs to be integrated and seamlessly. However, many organisations do have specific e-CRM initiatives or staff responsible for e-CRM. Both CRM and e-CRM are not just about technology and databases, it's not just a process or a way of doing things, it requires, in fact, a complete customer culture.*

More specifically, we can say that important e-CRM challenges and activities which require management are:

- Using the *website for customer development* from generating leads through to conversion to an online or offline sale using e-mail and web-based information to encourage purchase.
- *Managing e-mail list quality* (coverage of e-mail addresses and integration of customer profile information from other databases to enable targeting).
- Applying *e-mail marketing* to support up-sell and cross-sell.
- *Data mining* to improve targeting.
- Providing online personalisation or *mass customisation* facilities to automatically recommend the 'next-best product'.
- Providing *online customer service facilities* (such as frequently asked questions, call-back and chat support).
- Managing *online service quality* to ensure that first-time buyers have a great customer experience that encourages them to buy again.
- Managing the *multichannel customer experience* as they use different media as part of the buying process and customer lifecycle.

## Customer engagement

**Customer engagement**
Repeated interactions that strengthen the emotional, psychological or physical investment a customer has in a brand.

**Media fragmentation**
Describes a trend to increasing choice and consumption of a range of media in terms of different channels such as web and mobile and also within channels, for example more TV channels, radio stations, magazines, more websites. Media fragmentation implies increased difficulty in reaching target audiences.

Forrester (2007) heralded customer engagement as 'Marketing's new key metric', given the rapidly increasing online media fragmentation. For customer engagement in an online context, it would be a mistake to limit understanding of engagement to that on a single occasion, according to whether someone dwells on the site for a significant time or whether they convert to sale or other outcome. Instead engagement really refers to the long-term ability of a brand to gain a customer's attention on an ongoing basis whether the engagement could occur on site, in third-party social networks or in e-mail or traditional direct communications. Consultant Richard Sedley of cScape (www.cscape.com) has developed the definition of customer engagement as 'Repeated interactions that strengthen the emotional, psychological or physical investment a customer has in a brand.'

Forrester (2007) has developed a framework to measure engagement through the customer lifecycle and also away from a brand's own site, such as on publisher sites or social networks.

According to Forrester, engagement has four parts which can be measured both online and offline:

- *Involvement.* Forrester says that online this includes website visits, time spent, pages viewed.
- *Interaction.* This is contributed comments to blogs, quantity/frequency of written reviews, and online comments as well as comments expressed in customer service. [We could add the recency, frequency and category of product purchases, and also ongoing engagement in e-mail marketing programmes as discussed later in this chapter, are all important here.]
- *Intimacy.* This is sentiment tracking on third-party sites including blogs and reviews, as well as opinions expressed in customer service calls.
- *Influence.* This is advocacy indicated by measures such as likelihood to recommend, brand affinity, content forwarded to friends, etc.

It should be measured by data collected both online and offline.

Forrester analyst Brian Haven says:

*Using engagement, you get a more holistic appreciation of your customers' actions, recognising that value comes not just from transactions but also from actions people take to influence others. Once engagement takes hold of marketing, marketing messages will become conversations, and dollars will shift from media buying to customer understanding.*

## Benefits of e-CRM

Using the Internet for relationship marketing involves integrating the customer database with websites to make the relationship targeted and personalised. Through doing this marketing can be improved as follows:

- *Targeting more cost-effectively*. Traditional targeting, for direct mail for instance, is often based on mailing lists compiled according to criteria that mean that not everyone contacted is in the target market. For example, a company wishing to acquire new affluent consumers may use postcodes to target areas with appropriate demographics, but within the postal district the population may be heterogeneous. The result of poor targeting will be low response rates, perhaps less than 1%. The Internet has the benefit that the list of contacts is *self-selecting* or pre-qualified. A company will only aim to build relationships with those who have visited a website and expressed an interest in its products by registering their name and address. The act of visiting the website and browsing content indicates a target customer. Thus the approach to acquiring new customers with whom to build relationships is fundamentally different as it involves attracting the customers to the website, where the company provides an offer to make them register.
- *Achieve mass customisation of the marketing messages* (and possibly the product). This tailoring process is described in a subsequent section. Technology makes it possible to send tailored e-mails at much lower cost than is possible with direct mail and also to provide tailored web pages to smaller groups of customers (microsegments).
- *Increase depth and breadth and improve the nature of relationship*. The nature of the Internet medium enables more information to be supplied to customers as required. For example, special pages such as Dell's Premier can be set up to provide customers with specific information. The nature of the relationship can be changed in that contact with a customer can be made more frequently. The frequency of contact with the customer can be determined by customers – whenever they have the need to visit their personalised pages – or they can be contacted by e-mail by the company.
- *A learning relationship can be achieved using different tools throughout the customer lifecycle.* For example: tools summarise products purchased on-site and the searching behaviour that occurred before these products were bought; online feedback forms about the site or products are completed when a customer requests free information; questions asked through forms or e-mails to the online customer service facilities; online questionnaires asking about product category interests and opinions on competitors; new product development evaluation – commenting on prototypes of new products.
- *Lower cost*. Contacting customers by e-mail or through their viewing web pages costs less than using physical mail, but perhaps more importantly, information needs to be sent only to those customers who have expressed a preference for it, resulting in fewer mail-outs. Once personalisation technology has been purchased, much of the targeting and communications can be implemented automatically.

## Marketing applications of CRM

A CRM system supports the following marketing applications:

1 *Sales force automation (SFA).* Sales representatives are supported in their account management through tools to arrange and record customer visits.
2 *Customer service management.* Representatives in contact centres respond to customer requests for information by using an intranet to access databases containing information on the customer, products and previous queries. It is more efficient and may increase customer convenience if customers are given the option of web self-service, i.e. accessing support data through a web interface.
3 *Managing the sales process.* This can be achieved through e-commerce sites, or in a B2B context by supporting sales representatives by recording the sales process (SFA).
4 *Campaign management.* Managing advertising, direct mail, e-mail and other campaigns.
5 *Analysis.* Through technologies such as data warehouses and approaches such as data mining, which are explained further later in the chapter, customers' characteristics, their purchase behaviour and campaigns can be analysed in order to optimise the marketing mix.

**Web self-service**

Customers perform information requests and transactions through a web interface rather than by contact with customer support staff.

## CRM technologies and data

Database technology is at the heart of delivering these CRM applications. Often the database is accessible through an intranet website accessed by employees or an extranet accessed by customers or partners providing an interface onto the entire customer relationship management system. E-mail is used to manage many of the inbound, outbound and internal communications managed by the CRM system. A workflow system is often used for automating CRM processes. For example, a workflow system can remind sales representatives about customer contacts or can be used to manage service delivery, such as the many stages of arranging a mortgage. The three main types of customer data held as tables in customer databases for CRM are typically:

1 *Personal and profile data.* These include contact details and characteristics for profiling customers, such as age and sex (B2C), and business size, industry sector and the individual's role in the buying decision (B2B).
2 *Transaction data.* A record of each purchase transaction including specific product purchased, quantities, category, location, date and time and channel where purchased.
3 *Communications data.* A record of which customers have been targeted by campaigns and their response to them (outbound communications). Also includes a record of inbound enquiries and sales representative visits and reports (B2B).

The behavioural data available through 2 and 3 are very important for targeting customers to more closely meet their needs.

Despite these benefits, it should be noted that in 2000 it was reported that around 75% of CRM projects failed in terms of delivering a return on investment or completion on time. This is not necessarily indicative of weaknesses in the CRM concept, rather it indicates the difficulty of implementing a complex information system that requires substantial changes to an organisation's processes and major impacts on the staff that conduct them. Such failure rates occur in many other information systems projects.

Read Mini case study 6.2 'Customer data management at Deutsche Bank' for an example of the practical realities of managing customer data in a large organisation.

| Mini Case Study 6.2 | Customer data management at Deutsche Bank |
| --- | --- |

Deutsche Bank is one of the largest financial institutions in Europe, with assets under management worth 100 billion euros (£60 billion). It operates in seven different countries under different names, although the company is considering consolidating into a single brand operating as a pan-European bank.

In 1999 its chairman, Dr Walther, said the company had to improve its cost-to-revenue ratio to 70% from 90% and add 10 million customers over the next four to eight years. That would be achieved by increasing revenues through growing customer value by cross- and up-selling, reducing costs through more targeted communications and by getting more new customers based on meaningful data analysis.

Central to this programme has been the introduction of an enterprise-wide database, analysis and campaign management system called DataSmart. This has brought significant changes to its marketing processes and effectiveness. Achieving this new IT infrastructure has been no mean feat – Deutsche Bank has 73 million customers, of which 800,000 are on-line and 190,000 who use its online brokerage service, it has 19,300 employees, 1250 branches and 250 financial centres, plus three call centres supporting Deutsche Bank 24, its telebanking service. It also has e-commerce alliances with Yahoo!, e-Bay and AOL.

'DataSmart works on four levels – providing a technical infrastructure across the enterprise, consolidating data, allowing effective data analyses and segmentations, and managing multichannel marketing campaigns', says Jens Fruehling, head of the marketing database automation project, Deutsche Bank 24. The new database runs on the largest Sun server in Europe with 20 processors, 10 gigabytes of RAM and 5 terabytes of data storage. It is also mirrored. The software used comprises Oracle for the database, Prime Response for campaign management, SAS for data mining, Cognos for OLAP reporting, plus a data extraction, transformation, modelling and loading tool.

'Before DataSmart, we had a problem of how to get data from our operating systems, where it was held in a variety of different ways and was designed only for use as transactional data. There are 400 million data sets created every month. We had a data warehouse which was good, but was not right for campaign management or data mining', says Fruehling.

The new data environment was developed to facilitate all of those things. It also brings in external data such as Experian's Mosaic. 'We have less information on new prospects, so we bought third party data on every household – the type of house, the number of householders, status, risk, lifestyle data, financial status, age, plus GIS coding', he says.

For every customer, over 1000 fields of data are now held. These allow the bank to understand customers' product needs, profile, risk, loyalty, revenue and lifetime value. That required a very sophisticated system. For every customer, there is also a whole bundle of statistical models, such as affinity for a product and channel, profitability overall and by type of product. 'These are calculated monthly so we can perform time-series analyses, so if their profitability is falling, we can target a mailing to them', says Fruehling. DataSmart has allowed Deutsche Bank to make some important changes in its marketing process, allowing it to operate more quickly and effectively. 'We have a sales support system called BTV in our branches to communicate with each bank manager. They can see the customer data and are able to add information, such as lists of customers who should be part of a branch campaign, who to include or exclude, and response analyses', he says.

Previously, typical marketing support activity involved segmenting and selecting customers, sending these lists through BTV for veto by branch managers, making the final selection, then sending those lists to BTV and the lettershop for production. 'There were many disconnects in that process – we had no campaign history, nothing was automated. Our programmers had to write SAS code for every selection, which is not the best way to work. We had no event-driven campaigns', says Fruehling.

An interface has been developed between PrimeVantage, BTV and each system supporting the seven key channels to market. Now the database marketing unit simply selects a template for one of its output channels. This has allowed Deutsche Bank to become more targeted in its marketing activities, and also faster. 'Regular selections are very important because local branches do our campaigns. We may have up to 20 separate mailings per week for different channels. That is now much more profitable', says Fruehling. Customer surveys are a central part of the bank's measurement culture and these have also become much easier to run.

'Every month we run a customer opinion poll on a sample of 10,000. Every customer is surveyed twice in a year. That takes half a day to run, whereas previously it took a week and 30 people using SAS. If a customer responds, their name is then suppressed; if they do not, they are called by the call centre', he says.

The bank's customer acquisition programme, called AKM, now uses up to 30 mailings per year with as many as 12 different target groups and very complex selection criteria. 'We flag customers using SAS and PrimeVantage recognises those flags', he says. 'We are now looking to move to a higher communications frequency so every customer gets a relevant offer.'

*Source*: European Centre for Customer Strategies case study (www.eccs.uk.com), 2001

### Question

Summarise the data types that Deutsche Bank collects and how they are used for customer relationship management.

## Customer lifecycle management

**Customer lifecycle**
The stages each customer will pass through in a long-term relationship through acquisition, retention and extension.

**Customer selection**
Identifying key customer segments and targeting them for relationship building.

**Customer acquisition**
Strategies and techniques used to gain new customers.

As was explained in Chapter 4 in the section on target marketing strategy and through Mini case study 4.2 on Euroffice, assessing and understanding the position of the customer in their relationship with an organisation is key to online marketing strategy. In this section we review methods of assessing the position of customers in the lifecycle and the use of 'sense and respond' communications to build customer loyalty at each stage of the customer lifecycle.

A high-level view of the classic **customer lifecycle** of select, acquire, retain, extend is shown in Figure 6.4.

1 **Customer selection** means defining the types of customers that a company will market to. It means identifying different groups of customers for which to develop offerings and to target during acquisition, retention and extension. Different ways of segmenting customers by value and by their detailed lifecycle with the company are reviewed.

2 **Customer acquisition** refers to marketing activities to form relationships with new customers while minimising acquisition costs and targeting high value customers. Service quality and selecting the right channels for different customers are important at this stage and throughout the lifecycle.

**Customer extension**
- 'Sense and respond '
- Cross-selling and up-selling
- Optimise service quality
- Use the right channels

**Customer retention**
- Understand individual needs
- Relevant offers for continued usage of online services
- Maximise service quality
- Use the right channels

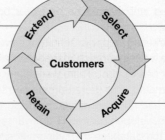

**Customer selection**
- Who do we target?
- What is their value?
- What is their lifecycle?
- Where do we reach them?

**Customer acquisition**
- Target the right segments
- Minimise acquisition cost
- Optimise service quality
- Use the right channels

| Figure 6.4 | The four classic marketing activities of customer relationship management |

**Customer retention**
Techniques to maintain relationships with existing customers.

**Customer extension**
Techniques to encourage customers to increase their involvement with an organisation.

3 **Customer retention** refers to the marketing activities taken by an organisation to keep its existing customers. Identifying relevant offerings based on their individual needs and detailed position in the customer lifecycle (e.g. number and value of purchases) is key.

4 **Customer extension** refers to increasing the depth or range of products that a customer purchases from a company. This is often referred to as 'customer development'.

There is a range of customer extension techniques that are particularly important to online retailers:

- *Re-sell.* Selling similar products to existing customers – particularly important in some B2B contexts as rebuys or modified rebuys.
- *Cross-sell.* Selling additional products which may be closely related to the original purchase, but not necessarily so.
- *Up-sell.* A subset of cross-selling, but in this case selling more expensive products.
- *Reactivation.* Customers who have not purchased for some time, or have lapsed can be encouraged to purchase again.
- *Referrals.* Generating sales from recommendations from existing customers – for example, member-get-member deals.

You can see that this framework distinguishes between customer retention and customer extension. Retention involves keeping the most valuable customers by selecting relevant customers for retention, understanding their loyalty factors that keep them buying and then developing strategies that encourage loyalty and cement the relationship. Customer extension is about developing customers to try a broader range of products to convert the most growable customers into the most valuable customers. You will also see that there are common features to each area – balancing cost and quality of service through the channels used according to the anticipated value of customers.

Peppers and Rogers (1997) recommend the following stages to achieve these goals, which they popularise as the 5 Is (as distinct from the 4 Ps):

- *Identification.* It is necessary to learn the characteristics of customers in as much detail as possible to be able to conduct the dialogue. In a business-to-business context, this means understanding those involved in the buying decision.
- *Individualisation.* Individualising means tailoring the company's approach to each customer, offering a benefit to the customer based on the identification of customer needs. The effort expended on each customer should be consistent with the value of that customer to the organisation.
- *Interaction.* Continued dialogue is necessary to understand both the customer's needs and the customer's strategic value. The interactions need to be recorded to facilitate the learning relationship.
- *Integration.* Integration of the relationship and knowledge of the customer must extend throughout all parts of the company.
- *Integrity.* Since all relationships are built on trust it is essential not to lose the trust of the customer. Efforts to learn from the customer should not be seen as intrusive, and privacy should be maintained. (See Chapter 3 for coverage of privacy issues related to e-CRM.)

## Permission marketing

**Permission marketing**
Customers agree (opt-in) to be involved in an organisation's marketing activities, usually as a result of an incentive.

**Permission marketing** is a significant concept that underpins online CRM throughout management of the customer lifecycle. 'Permission marketing' is a term coined by Seth Godin. It is best characterised with just three (or four) words:

*Permission marketing is …*
> *anticipated, relevant and personal [and timely].*

Godin (1999) notes that while research used to show we were bombarded by 500 marketing messages a day, with the advent of the web and digital TV this has now increased to over 3000 a day! From the marketing organisation's viewpoint, this leads to a dilution in the effectiveness of the messages – how can the communications of any one company stand out? From the customer's viewpoint, time is seemingly in ever-shorter supply, customers are losing patience and expect reward for their attention, time and information. Godin refers to the traditional approach as 'interruption marketing'. Permission marketing is about seeking the customer's permission before engaging them in a relationship and providing something in exchange. The classic exchange is based on information or entertainment – a B2B site can offer a free report in exchange for a customer sharing their e-mail address which will be used to maintain a dialogue; a B2C site can offer a screensaver in exchange.

From a practical e-commerce perspective, we can think of a customer agreeing to engage in a relationship when they check a box on a web form to indicate that they agree to receive further communications from a company (see Figure 3.5 for further examples). This approach is referred to as 'opt-in'. This is preferable to opt-out, the situation where a customer has to consciously agree not to receive further information.

The importance of incentivisation in permission marketing has also been emphasised by Seth Godin who likens the process of acquisition and retention to dating someone. Likening customer relationship building to social behaviour is not new, as O'Malley and Tynan (2001) note; the analogy of marriage has been used since the 1980s at least. They also report on consumer research that indicates that while marriage may be analogous to business relationships, it is less appropriate for B2C relationships. Moller and Halinen (2000) have also suggested that due to the complexity of the exchange, longer-term relationships are more readily formed for interorganisational exchanges. So, the description of the approaches that follow are perhaps more appropriate for B2B applications.

Godin (1999) suggests that dating the customer involves:

1 offering the prospect an *incentive* to volunteer;
2 using the attention offered by the prospect, offering a curriculum over time, teaching the consumer about your product or service;
3 reinforcing the *incentive* to guarantee that the prospect maintains the permission;
4 offering additional *incentives* to get even more permission from the consumer;
5 over time, using the permission to change consumer behaviour towards profits.

Notice the importance of incentives at each stage. The use of incentives at the start of the relationship and throughout it is key to successful relationships. As we shall see in a later section, e-mail is very important in permission marketing to maintain the dialogue between company and customer.

Writing for the *What's New in Marketing* e-newsletter, Chaffey (2004) has extended Godin's principles to e-CRM with his 'e-permission marketing principles':

- **Principle 1** – *Consider selective opt-in to communications.* In other words, offer choice in *communications preferences* to the customer to ensure more relevant communications. Some customers may not want a weekly e-newsletter, rather they may only want to hear about new product releases. Remember opt-in is a legal requirement in many countries. Four key communications preferences options, selected by tick box are:
  - Content – news, products, offers, events
  - Frequency – weekly, monthly, quarterly, or alerts
  - Channel – e-mail, direct mail, phone or SMS
  - Format – text vs HTML.
  Make sure though that through providing choice you do not overstretch your resources, or on the other hand limit your capabilities to market to customers (for example, if customers only opt-in to an annual communication such as a catalogue update) you still need to find a way to control the frequency and type of communications.

**Interruption marketing**
Marketing communications that disrupt customers' activities.

**Opt-in**
A customer proactively agrees to receive further information.

**Opt-out**
A customer declines the offer to receive further information.

- **Principle 2** – *Create a 'common customer profile'.* A structured approach to customer data capture is needed otherwise some data will be missed, as is the case with the utility company that collected 80,000 e-mail addresses, but forgot to ask for the postcode for geo-targeting! This can be achieved through a common customer profile – a definition of all the database fields that are relevant to the marketer in order to understand and target the customer with a relevant offering. The customer profile can have different levels to set targets for data quality (Level 1 is contact details and key profile fields only, Level 2 includes preferences and Level 3 includes full purchase and response behaviour).
- **Principle 3** – *Offer a range of opt-in incentives.* Many websites now have 'free–win–save' incentives to encourage opt-in, but often it is one incentive fits all visitors. Different incentives for different audiences will generate a higher volume of permission, particularly for business-to-business websites. We can also gauge the characteristics of the respondent by the type of incentives or communications they have requested, without the need to ask them.
- **Principle 4** – *Don't make opt-out too easy.* Often marketers make it too easy to unsubscribe. Although offering some form of opt-out is now a legal requirement in many countries due to privacy laws, a single click to unsubscribe is making it too easy. Instead, wise e-permission marketers such as Amazon use the concept of 'My Profile' or a 'selective opt-out'. Instead of unsubscribe, they offer a link to a 'communications preferences' web form to update a profile that includes the options to reduce communications, which may be the option taken rather than unsubscribing completely.
- **Principle 5** – *Watch, don't ask.* The need to ask interruptive questions can be reduced through the use of monitoring clicks to better understand customer needs and to trigger follow-up communications. Some examples:
  - monitoring click-through to different types of content or offer;
  - monitoring the engagement of individual customers with e-mail communications;
  - follow-up reminder to those who don't open the e-mail first time.
- **Principle 6** – *Create an outbound contact strategy.* Online permission marketers need a plan for the number, frequency and type of online and offline communications and offers. This is a **contact** or **touch strategy** which is particularly important for large organisations with several marketers responsible for e-mail communications. We describe contact strategies in more depth in the next section.

**Contact strategy**

Definition of the sequence and type of outbound communications required at different points in the customer lifecycle.

An example of permission marketing in practice, and how to set goals for permission, is provided in Chapter 9 in Mini-case study **9.2**, 'Beep-beep-beep-beep, that'll be the bank then'. In this campaign to promote a new interactive banking service, the campaign objectives and results (in brackets) were to:

- capture 5000 mobile phone numbers from customers (200% of plan);
- acquire 3000 e-mail addresses (176% of plan);
- raise awareness about the new service (31,000 customers view demonstration);
- create 1000 new registrations (576% of plan).

## 'Right touching' through online contact strategies

Given the difficulty in achieving customer engagement, with the increase in media fragmentation and the development of high attention media such as social networks, the need for developing a structured approach to communicating with customers across the lifecycle has become more urgent. Dave Chaffey (http://blog.right-touching.com) has emphasised the importance for companies to build and refine an integrated multichannel touch or contact strategy which delivers customised communications to consumers by search ads, e-mail and web recommendations and promotions.

Every customer interaction or response to a communication should be followed-up by a series of relevant communications delivered by the right combinations of channel (web, e-mail, phone, direct mail) to elicit a response or further dialogue. This is contextual marketing, where the aim is to deliver relevant messages which fit the current context of what the customer is interested in according to the searches they have performed, the type of content they have viewed or the products they have recently purchased.

---

**Box 6.1**

Right touching can be sumarised as:

A **Multichannel Communications Strategy**
**Customised** for Individual Prospects and Customers forming segments
Across a **defined customer lifecycle**
Which...
Delivers the **Right Message**
Featuring the **Right Value Proposition** (product, service or experience)
With the **Right Tone**
At the **Right Time** or context
With the Right **Frequency and Interval**
Using the Right **Media/Communications channels**
To achieve...
Right **balance of value between both parties**

---

A contact policy should be developed to manage and control communications so that they are at an acceptable level. The contact strategy should indicate the following:

- *Frequency* – e.g. minimum once per quarter and maximum once per month.
- *Interval* – e.g. there must be a gap of at least one week or one month between communications.
- *Content and offers* – we may want to limit or achieve a certain number of prize draws or information-led offers.
- *Links* – between online communications and offline communications.
- *A control strategy* – a mechanism to make sure these guidelines are adhered to, for example using a single 'focal point' for checking all communications before creation dispatch.

Examples of contact strategies for Euroffice and Tesco.com were discussed in Chapter 4. Table 6.3 gives a typical format for developing a contact strategy.

---

**Table 6.3** Example welcome contact strategy

| | Message type | Interval/trigger condition | Outcomes required | Medium for message/sequence |
|---|---|---|---|---|
| 1 | Welcome message | Guest site membership signup Immediate | • Encourage trial of site services<br>• Increase awareness of range of commercial and informational offerings | E-mail, post transaction page |
| 2 | Engagement message | 1 month inactive (i.e. < 3 visits) | • Encourage use of forum (good enabler of membership)<br>• Highlight top content | E-mail, home page, side panels deep in site |
| 3 | Initial cross-sell message | 1 month active | • Encourage membership<br>• Ask for feedback | E-mail |
| 4 | Conversion | 2 days after browsing content | • Use for range of services for guest members or full members | Phone or e-mail |

# Personalisation and mass customisation

**Personalisation**

Web-based personalisation involves delivering customised content for the individual, through web pages, e-mail or push technology.

The potential power of **personalisation** is suggested by these quotes from Evans *et al.* (2000) that show the negative effects of lack of targeting of traditional direct mail:

> *Don't like unsolicited mail ... haven't asked for it and I'm not interested.*
>
> Female, 25–34

> *Most isn't wanted, it's not relevant and just clutters up the table ... you have to sort through it to get to the 'real mail'.*
>
> Male, 45–54

> *It's annoying to be sent things that you are not interested in. Even more annoying when they phone you up ... If you wanted something you would go and find out about it.*
>
> Female, 45–54

**Mass customisation**

The creation of tailored marketing messages or products for individual customers or groups of customers typically using technology to retain the economies of scale and the capacity of mass marketing or production.

**Collaborative filtering**

Profiling of customer interest coupled with delivery of specific information and offers, often based on the interests of similar customers.

Personalisation and **mass customisation** can be used to tailor information content on a website, and opt-in e-mail can be used to deliver it to add value and at the same time remind the customer about a product. 'Personalisation' and 'mass customisation' are terms that are often used interchangeably. In the strict sense, personalisation refers to customisation of information requested by a site customer at an *individual* level. Mass customisation involves providing tailored content to a *group* or *individuals* with similar interests. It uses technology to achieve this on an economical basis. An example of mass customisation is when Amazon recommends similar books according to what others in a segment have offered, or if it sent a similar e-mail to customers who had an interest in a particular topic such as e-commerce.

Other methods of profiling customers include collaborative filtering and monitoring the content they view. With **collaborative filtering**, customers are openly asked what their interests are, typically by checking boxes that correspond to their interests. A database then compares the customer's preferences with those of other customers in its database, and then makes recommendations or delivers information accordingly. The more information a database contains about an individual customer, the more useful its recommendations can be. The best-known example of this technology in action can be found on the Amazon website (www.amazon.com), where the database reveals that customers who bought book X also bought books Y and Z.

Figure 6.5 summarises the options available to organisations wishing to use the Internet for mass customisation or personalisation. If there is little information available about the customer and it is not integrated with the website then no mass customisation is possible (A). To achieve mass customisation or personalisation, the organisation must have sufficient information about the customer. For limited tailoring to groups of customers (B), it is necessary to have basic profiling information such as age, sex, social group, product category interest or, for B2B, role in the buying unit. This information must be contained in a database system that is directly linked to the system used to display website content. For personalisation on a one-to-one level (C) more detailed information about specific interests, perhaps available from a purchase history, should be available.

An organisation can use Figure 6.5 to plan their relationship marketing strategy. The symbols $X_1$ to $X_3$ show a typical path for an organisation. At $X_1$ information collected about customers is limited. At $X_2$ detailed information is available about customers, but it is in discrete databases that are not integrated with the website. At $X_3$ the strategy is to provide mass customisation of information and offers to major segments, since it is felt that the expense of full personalisation is not warranted.

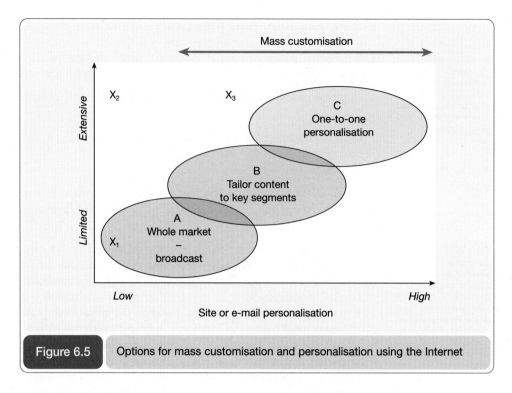

| Figure 6.5 | Options for mass customisation and personalisation using the Internet |

## Online and multichannel service quality

In the last part of Chapter 7, we review how the online presence can be managed in order to achieve online service quality, which is also a key element leading to customer satisfaction and loyalty.

## Approaches to implementing e-CRM

E-CRM uses common approaches or processes to achieve online customer acquisition and retention. Refer to Figure 6.6 for a summary of a common, effective process for permission-based online relationship building to achieve the different stages of the customer lifecycle.

In the following sections we proceed through the different stages in more detail.

### Stage 1: Attract new and existing customers to site

For new customers, the goal is to attract quality visitors who are likely to convert to the site using all the online and offline methods of site promotion described in Chapter 8 and 9, such as search engines, portals and banner advertisements. These promotion methods should aim to highlight the value proposition of the site and it is important to communicate a range of incentives such as free information or competitions (and others shown in top-left box of Figure 6.8) which are tailored for different personas. To encourage new users to use the one-to-one facilities of the website, information about the website, or incentives to visit it, can be built into existing direct marketing campaigns such as catalogue mailshots.

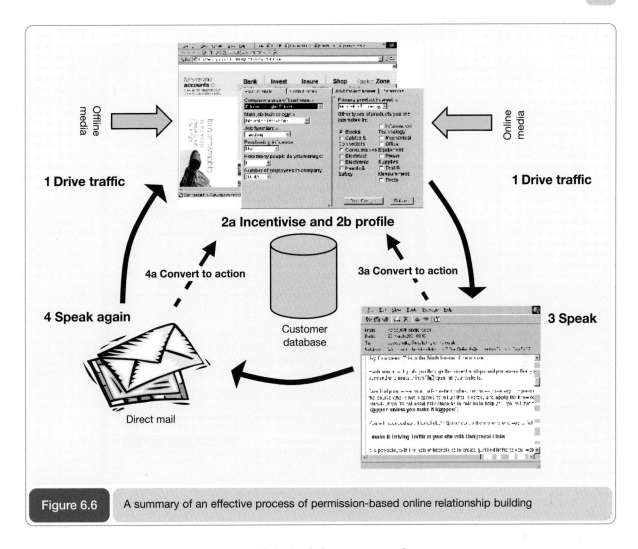

| Figure 6.6 | A summary of an effective process of permission-based online relationship building |

## Stage 2a: Incentivise visitors to action

**Lead generation offer**
Offered in return for customers providing their contact details and characteristics. Commonly used in B2B marketing where free information such as a report or a seminar will be offered.

**Sales generation offer**
Encourage product trial. A coupon redeemed against a purchase is a classic example.

The first time a visitor arrives at a site is the most important since if he or she does not find the desired information or experience they may not return. We need to move from using the customer using the Internet in pull mode, to the marketer using the Internet in push mode through e-mail and traditional direct mail communications. The quality and credibility of the site must be sufficient to retain the visitor's interest so that he or she stays on the site. To initiate one-to-one, offers or incentives must be prominent, ideally on the home page. It can be argued that converting unprofiled visitors to profiled visitors is a major design objective of a website. Two types of incentives can be identified: **lead generation offers** and **sales generation offers**.

Types of offers marketers can devise include information value, entertainment value, monetary value and privileged access to information (such as that only available on an extranet).

## Stage 2b: Capture customer information to maintain relationship

Capturing profile information is commonly achieved through an online form such as shown in Figure 6.7 which the customer must complete to receive the offer. It is important to design these forms to maximise their completion. Factors which are important are:

### Register for newsletter updates by email

Register your details with us to receive the latest travel deals and ideas direct to your inbox.

**You...**

Title:　　First Name:　　　　　Surname:

[Mr ▾]　[＿＿＿＿＿＿]　　[＿＿＿＿＿＿]

First line of address:　　　　Post Code:

[＿＿＿＿＿＿＿＿＿＿]　　[＿＿＿＿]

Email address:　　　　　　Mobile Number*:

[＿＿＿＿＿＿＿＿＿＿]　　[＿＿＿＿＿＿]

*In future, we may investigate innovative ways of communication with you by SMS, which could include exclusive access to competitions and offers. If you are interested in being part of this, please provide your mobile.

**Your preferences...**

How often would you prefer to receive updates?　　[Please select ▾]

| Please select |
| Weekly |
| Fortnightly |
| Monthly |
| Bi-Monthly |

What airport do you prefer to fly from?

**Do you have a particular interest** ?

☐ Summer Sun　　☐ Winter Sun　　☐ Ski

☐ City Breaks　☐ Lakes & Mountains　☐ Villas

☐ World Wide　☐ Accomodation Only　　☐ Auctions

☐ Flights　　☐ Cruises　　☐ Mobile Homes

**Data Protection Notice**

1. All details provided by you will be held by us and used in accordance with our Privacy Policy.
2. We may from time to time contact you **by post** with further information on the latest offers, brochures, products or services which we believe may be of interest to you, from Thomson (a division of TUI UK Limited), other hoiday divisions within and group companies of TUI UK limited.

| Figure 6.7 | Opt-in customer profiling form |

- *branding* to reassure the customer;
- *key profile fields* to capture the most important information to segment the customer for future communications, in this case postcode, airport and preferred activities (not too many questions should be asked);
- *mandatory fields* – mark fields which must be completed or, as in this case, only include mandatory figures;
- *privacy* – 'we will not share' is the magic phrase to counter the customer's main fear of their details being passed on. A full privacy statement should be available for those who need it;
- *KISS* – 'Keep it simple, stupid' is a well-known American phrase;
- *WIFM* – 'What's in it for me?' Explain why the customer's data is being captured; what benefits it will give them?;
- validation – of e-mail, postcode etc. checking data as far as possible to make it accurate.

As well as online data capture, it is important to use all customer touchpoints to capture information and keep it up-to-date since this affects the ability to target customers accurately. Figure 6.8 provides a good way for a company to review all the possible methods of capturing e-mail addresses and other profile information.

Apart from the contact information, the other important information to collect is a method of **profiling the customer** so that appropriate information can be delivered to them. For example, B2B company RS Components asks for:

- industry sector
- purchasing influence
- specific areas of product interest
- how many people you manage
- total number of employees in company.

**Customer profiling**
Using the website to find out a customer's specific interests and characteristics.

| | New customers | Existing customers |
|---|---|---|
| **Online touch points** | • Online incentive such as prize-draw (B2C) or white paper download (B2B)<br>• Viral marketing<br>• E-newsletter opt-in on site<br>• Registration to view content or submit content to a community forum<br>• Renting list, co-branded e-mail or advertising in third-party e-newsletter to encourage opt-in<br>• Co-registration with third party sites | • Capture e-mail when customer first registers or purchases online<br>• E-newsletter and other methods given on left |
| **Offline touch points** | • Direct mail offer perhaps driving visitors to web<br>• Trade shows or conference<br>• Paper response to traditional direct mail communication<br>• Phone response to direct mail or ad | • Paper order form, customer registration/product warranty form<br>• Sales reps – face-to-face<br>• Contact centre – by phone<br>• Point of sale for retailers |

**Figure 6.8**    Matrix of customer touch points for collecting and updating customer e-mail contact and other profile information

## Stage 3: Maintain dialogue using online communication

To build the relationship between company and customer there are three main Internet-based methods of physically making the communication. These are:

1 Send an e-mail to the customer.
2 Display specific information on the website when the customer logs in. This is referred to as 'personalisation'.
3 Use push technology such as RSS feeds to deliver information to the customer.

Dialogue will also be supplemented by other tools such as mailshots, phone calls or personal visits, depending on the context. For example, after a customer registers on the RS Components website, the company sends out a letter to the customer with promotional offers and a credit-card-sized reminder of the user name and password to use to log in to the site.

As well as these physical methods of maintaining contact with customers, many other marketing devices can be used to encourage users to return to a site. These include:

- loyalty schemes – customers will return to the site to see how many loyalty points they have collected, or convert them into offers. An airline such as American Airlines, with its Advantage Club, is a good example of this;
- news about a particular industry – for a business-to-business site;
- new product information and price promotions;
- industry-specific information to help the customer do his or her job;
- personal reminders – the US company 1-800-Flowers has reminder programmes that automatically remind customers of important occasions and dates;
- customer support – Cisco's customers log on to the site over one million times a month to receive technical assistance, check orders or download software. The online service is so well received that nearly 70% of all customer enquiries are handled online.

### The 'emotionally unsubscribed' e-mail list members

The inactive members of an e-mail list are sometimes called the 'emotionally unsubscribed'. They represent a significant issue in the management of customer e-mail marketing programmes. Although unsubscribe rates are usually low (for example, less than 0.1% per campaign) there can be upwards of 50% of a list who are 'emotionally unsubscribed', i.e. they are not actually subscribed but rarely open or click, suggesting that e-mail is not an effective communications channel. To avoid this and to maintain the dialogue, it is important ensure that the contact strategy has been planned and implemented to deliver relevant messages. Some other steps that can be taken to manage this issue include:

- Measure the level of activity in e-mail response at a more granular level, e.g. review open, click, purchase rates or other actions at different points in time compared to when the subscribers first signed up. Response rates from different segment types who have taken different actions can also be reviewed to see how engaging they find the e-newsletter.
- Test different frequencies. It may be appropriate to reduce frequency if customers become 'emotionally unsubscribed' and then e-mails received will have a large impact. List members can also be surveyed for their preferences, possibly as part of a reactivation campaign.
- Develop automated customer lifecycle e-mails which are part of the contact strategy which are relevant and tailored according to the interests of the subscriber. Lifecycle e-mails will include welcome e-mail contact strategies, reactivation e-mail strategies and other service messages such as customer feedback surveys.
- Ensure the fields that are used to customise messages are those that are most likely to be relevant. Often these won't be the obvious fields such as gender, but contextual information related to content or products which have been recently consumed, as shown by Figure 6.9.
- Use offline communications such as direct mail and phone where list members express a preference for these (and see Stage 4 below).

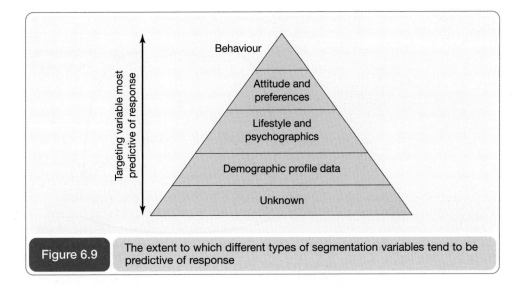

| Figure 6.9 | The extent to which different types of segmentation variables tend to be predictive of response |

## Stage 4: Maintain dialogue using offline communication

Direct mail or phone contact may still be cost-effective forms of communication since these can also be tailored and may have more 'cut-through' compared to an e-mail. With direct mail campaigns the aim may be to drive traffic to the website in a web response campaign using techniques such as:

- online competition
- online web seminar (webinar)
- sales promotion.

A further objective in stage 3 and stage 4 is to improve customer information quality. In particular, e-mails may bounce – in which case offline touch points as indicated in Figure 6.8 need to be planned to determine the latest addresses.

'Right touching' involves getting the balance right between the frequency of online communications (stage 3) and offline communications (stage 4) determined by how responsive customers are to different communications channels since stage 3 is a lower-cost route.

## The IDIC approach to relationship building

An alternative process for building customer relationships online has been suggested by Peppers and Rogers (1998) and Peppers *et al.* (1999). They suggest the IDIC approach as a framework for customer relationship management and using the web effectively to form and build relationships (Figure 6.10).

Examples of the application of IDIC within web marketing include:

- *Customer identification.* This stresses the need to identify each customer on their first site visit and subsequent visits. Common methods for identification are the use of cookies or asking a customer to log on to a site. Within e-mail marketing, it is possible to track individual responses with most e-mail marketing systems. In subsequent customer contacts, additional customer information should be obtained using a process known as '**drip irrigation**'. Since information will become out-of-date through time, it is important to verify, update and delete customer information. Figure 6.11 gives an example of a site where first-time visitors who don't possess a cookie are welcomed.
- *Customer differentiation.* This refers to building a profile to help segment customers. Appropriate services are then developed for each customer. Activities suggested are identifying the top customers, non-profitable customers, large customers who have ordered less in recent years and customers who buy more products from competitors.

**Drip irrigation**
Collecting information about customer needs through their lifetime.

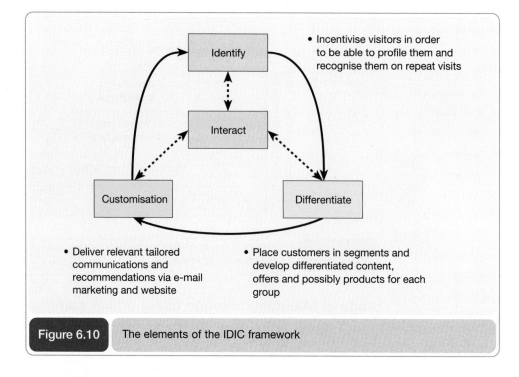

**Figure 6.10**    The elements of the IDIC framework

- *Customer interaction.* These are interactions provided on-site, such as customer service questions or creating a tailored product. More generally, companies should listen to the needs and experiences of major customers. Interactions should be in the customer-preferred channel, for example e-mail, phone or post.
- *Customer customisation.* This refers to dynamic personalisation or mass customisation of content or e-mails according to the segmentation achieved at the acquisition stage. This stage also involves further market research to find out if products can be further tailored to meet customers' needs. The company shown in Figure 6.11 uses the same panel to provide tailored messages for registered members.

## Techniques for managing customer activity and value

Within the online customer base of an organisation, there will be customers who have different levels of activity in usage of online services or in sales. A good example is a bank – some customers may use the online account once a week, others much less frequently and some not at all. Figure 6.12 illustrates the different levels of activity. A key part of e-CRM strategy is to define measures which indicate activity levels and then develop tactics to increase activity levels through more frequent use. An online magazine could segment its customers in this way, also based on returning visitors. Even for companies without transactional service a similar concept can apply if they use e-mail marketing – some customers will regularly read and interact with the e-mail and others will not.

Objectives and corresponding tactics can be set for:

- Increasing the number of new users per month and annually (separate objectives will be set for existing bank customers and new bank customers) through promoting online services to drive visitors to the website.
- Increasing the percentage of active users (an appropriate threshold can be used – for different organisations it could be set at 7, 30 or 90 days). Using direct communications, such as e-mail, personalised website messages, direct mail and phone communications to new, dormant and inactive users, increases the percentage of active users.

| Figure 6.11 | Identification and customisation on the CIPD site |
|---|---|
| | *Source*: CIPD (www.cipd.co.uk) |

- Decreasing the percentage of dormant users (once new or active – could be sub-categories) who have not used the service or responded to communications within a defined time period, such as three months.
- Decreasing the percentage of inactive users (or non-activated) users. These are those who signed up for a service such as online banking and had a username issued, but have not used the service.

You can see that corresponding strategies can be developed for each of these objectives.

Another key metric, in fact the *key* retention metric for e-commerce sites, refers to repeat business. The importance of retention rate metrics was highlighted by Agrawal *et al.* (2001). The main retention metrics they mention which influence profitability are:

- *repeat-customer base* – the proportion of the customer base that has made repeat purchases;
- *number of transactions per repeat customer* – this indicates the stage of development of the customer in the relationship (another similar measure is number of product categories purchased);
- *revenue per transaction of repeat customer* – this is a proxy for lifetime value since it gives average order value.

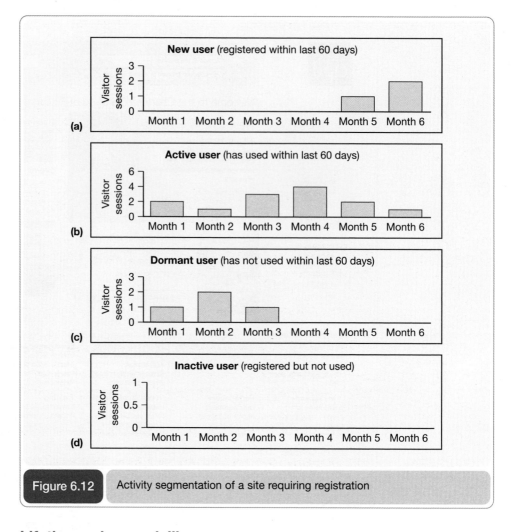

| Figure 6.12 | Activity segmentation of a site requiring registration |

## Lifetime value modelling

**Lifetime value**
Lifetime value is the total net benefit that a customer or group of customers will provide a company over their total relationship with a company.

An appreciation of **lifetime value (LTV)** is key to the theory and practice of customer relationship management.

Digital technology has enabled marketers to become more sophisticated in how they can identify and target valuable customers. Kumar *et al.* (2007) explain it this way:

> *By applying statistical models, they can predict not only when each customer is likely to make a future purchase but also what he or she will buy and through which channel. Managers can use these data to estimate a potential lifetime value for every customer and to determine whether, when and how to contact each one to maximise the chances of realising (and even increasing) his or her value.*

However, while the term is often used, calculation of LTV is not straightforward, so many organisations do not calculate it. You are referred to Kumar *et al.* (2007) for an explanation of LTV calculations. Lifetime value is defined as the total net benefit that a customer, or group of customers, will provide a company over their total relationship with the company. Modelling is based on estimating the income and costs associated with each customer over a period of time, and then calculating the net present value in current monetary terms using a discount rate value applied over the period.

There are different degrees of sophistication in calculating LTV. These are indicated in Figure 6.13. Option 1 is a practical way or approximate proxy for future LTV, but the true LTV is the future value of the customer at an individual level.

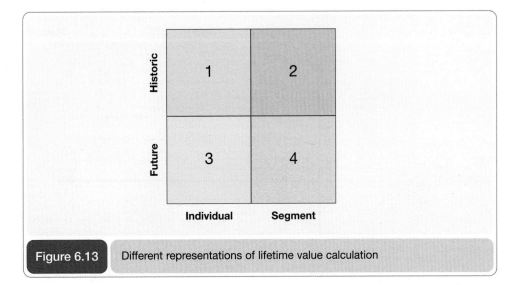

| **Figure 6.13** | Different representations of lifetime value calculation |

Lifetime value modelling at segment level (4) is vital within marketing since it answers the question:

*How much can I afford to invest in acquiring a new customer?*

If online marketers try to answer this from a short-term perspective, as is often the case – i.e. by judging it based on the profit from a single sale on an e-commerce site – there are two problems:

- We become very focused on short-term return on investment (ROI) and so may not invest sufficiently to grow our business.
- We assume that each new customer is worth precisely the same to us and we ignore differentials in loyalty and profitability between differing types of customer.

Lifetime value analysis enables marketers to:

- plan and measure investment in customer acquisition programmes;
- identify and compare critical target segments;
- measure the effectiveness of alternative customer retention strategies;
- establish the true value of a company's customer base;
- make decisions about products and offers;
- make decisions about the value of introducing new e-CRM technologies.

Figure 6.14 gives an example of how LTV can be used to develop a CRM strategy for different customer groups. Four main types of customers are indicated by their current and future value as bronze, silver, gold and platinum. Distinct customer groupings (circles) are identified according to their current value (as indicated by current value) and future value as indicated by lifetime value calculations. Each of these groups will have a customer profile signature based on their demographics, so this can be used for customer selection. Different strategies are developed for different customer groups within the four main value groupings. Some bronze customers, such as groups A and B, realistically do not have development potential and are typically unprofitable, so the aim is to reduce costs in communications and if they do not remain as customers this is acceptable. Some bronze customers, such as group C, may have potential for growth so for these the strategy is to extend their purchases. Silver customers are targeted with customer extension offers and gold customers are extended where possible, although they have relatively little growth potential. Platinum customers are the best customers, so it is important to understand the communication preferences of these customers and to not over-communicate unless there is evidence that they may defect.

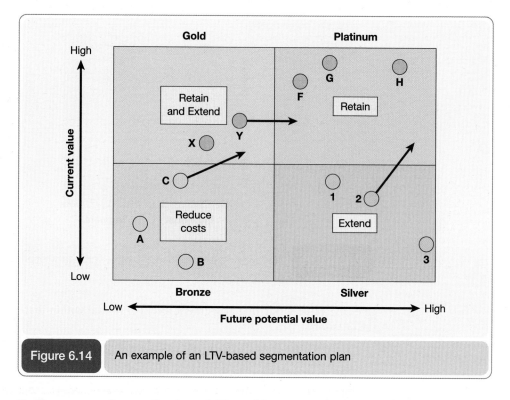

| Figure 6.14 | An example of an LTV-based segmentation plan |

To illustrate another application of LTV and how it is calculated, take a look at the last example in Activity 6.1.

| Activity 6.1 | Charity uses lifetime value modelling to assess returns from new e-CRM system |

A charity is considering implementing a new e-mail marketing system to increase donations from its donors. The charity's main role is as a relief agency which aims to reduce poverty through providing aid, particularly to the regions that need it most. Currently, its only e-mail activity is a monthly e-newsletter received by its 200,000 subscribers which features its current campaigns and appeals. It hopes to increase donations by using a more targeted approach based on previous customer behaviour. The e-mail system will integrate with the donor database which contains information on customer profiles and previous donations.

The company is considering three solutions which will cost between £50,000 and £100,000 in the first year. In the charity, all such investments are assessed using lifetime value modelling.

Table 6.4 is a lifetime value model showing customer value derived from using the current system and marketing activities.

**A** *Donors* – this is the number of initial donors. It declines each year dependent on the retention rate (row B).

**B** *Retention rate* – in lifetime value modelling this is usually found to increase year-on-year, since customers who stay loyal are more likely to remain loyal.

**C** *Donations per annum* – likewise, the charity finds that the average contributions per year increase through time within this group of customers.

| | Year 1 | Year 2 | Year 3 | Year 4 | Year 5 |
|---|---|---|---|---|---|
| **Table 6.4** — Lifetime value model for customer base for current system | | | | | |
| A Donors | 100,000 | 50,000 | 27,500 | 16,500 | 10,725 |
| B Retention | 50% | 55% | 60% | 65% | 70% |
| C Donations per annum | £100 | £120 | £140 | £160 | £180 |
| D Total donations | £10,000,000 | £6,000,000 | £3,850,000 | £2,640,000 | £1,930,500 |
| E Net profit (at 20% margin) | £2,000,000.0 | £1,200,000.0 | £770,000.0 | £528,000.0 | £386,100.0 |
| F Discount rate | 1 | 0.86 | 0.7396 | 0.636 | 0.547 |
| G NPV contribution | £2,000,000.0 | £1,032,000.0 | £569,492.0 | £335,808.0 | £211,196.7 |
| H Cumulative NPV contribution | £2,000,000.0 | £3,032,000.0 | £3,601,492.0 | £3,937,300.0 | £4,148,496.7 |
| I Lifetime value at net present value | £20.0 | £30.3 | £36.0 | £39.4 | £41.5 |

**D** *Total donations* – calculated through multiplying rows A and C.

**E** *Net profit (at 20% margin)* – LTV modelling is based on profit contributed by this group of customers, row D is multiplied by 0.2.

**F** *Discount rate* – since the value of money held at a point in time will decrease due to inflation, a discount rate factor is applied to calculate the value of future returns in terms of current day value.

**G** *NPV contribution* – this is the profitability after taking the discount factor into account to give the net present value in future years. This is calculated by multiplying row E by row F.

**H** *Cumulative NPV contribution* – this adds the previous year's NPV for each year.

**I** *Lifetime value at net present value* – this is a value per customer calculated by dividing row H by the initial number of donors in Year 1.

Based on preliminary tests with improved targeting, it is estimated that with the new system, retention rates will increase from 50% to 51% in the first year, increasing by 5% per year as currently. It is estimated that in Year 1 donations per annum will increase from £100 per annum to £120 per annum, increasing by £20 per year as currently.

### Question

Using the example of the lifetime value for the current donor base with the current system, calculate the LTV with the new system.

Kumar *et al.* (2007) note that the capability of a customer to generate value is divided into lifetime value of purchases (CLV) and what they term CRV, customer referral value. This concept is closely related to that of the 'net promoter score' identified earlier in the chapter, see page **338**. These authors stress that there is not a clear correlation between CLV and CRV. For example, in their study they found that customers with the highest CLV did not have the highest CRV. So they suggest that customers should be segmented according to both attributes and then tactics developed. For one company they studied, they identified four groupings of customers presented in a customer value matrix plotting average CRV at one year on the $x$ axis and average CLV after one year on the $y$ axis to give these segments:

- *Champions (top-right) – 21% of customers*, CLV=$370, CRV=$590
- *Misers (bottom-left) – 21% of customers*, CLV=$130, CRV=$64
- *Affluents (top-left) – 29% of customers*, CLV=$1219, CRV=$49
- *Advocates (bottom-right) – 29% of customers*, CLV=$180, CRV=$670

You can see that it would be worthwhile using different tactics for each segment to encourage recommendation or purchase – for example to migrate misers to affluents or advocates, and advocates and affluents to champions.

### Sense, respond, adjust – delivering relevant e-communications through monitoring customer behaviour

To be able to identify customers in the categories of value, growth, responsiveness or defection risk, we need to characterise them using information about them which indicates their purchase and campaign-response *behaviour*. This is because the past and current actual behaviour is often the best predictor of future behaviour. We can then seek to influence this future behaviour.

Digital marketing enables marketers to create a cycle of:

- monitoring customer actions or behaviours and then …
- reacting with appropriate messages and offers to encourage desired behaviours,
- monitoring response to these messages and continuing with additional communications and monitoring.

Or, if you prefer, simply:

*Sense → Respond → Adjust*

The sensing is done through using technology to monitor visits to particular content on a website or clicking on particular links in an e-mail. Purchase history can also be monitored, but since purchase information is often stored in a legacy sales system it is important to integrate this with systems used for communicating with customers. The response can be done through messages on-site or in e-mail and then adjustment occurs through further sensing and responding.

This 'sense and respond' technique has traditionally been completed by catalogue retailers such as Argos, Littlewoods Index or retailers such as Boots (see Mini case study 6.3) using a technique known as 'RFM analysis'. This technique tends to be little known outside retail circles, but e-CRM gives great potential to apply it in a range of techniques since we can use it not only to analyse purchase history, but also visit or log-in frequency to a site or online service and response rates to e-mail communications.

## Mini Case Study 6.3    Boots mine diamonds in their customer data

The high street retailer Boots launched its Advantage loyalty card in 1997. Today, there are over 15 million card holders of whom 10 million are active. Boots describes the benefits for its card holders as follows.

There are 23 analysts in the Customer Insight team, run by Helen James, who mine the data available about card users and their transactional behaviour. They use tools including MicroStrategy's DSS Agent and Andyne's GQL which are used for the majority of queries. IBM's Intelligent Miner for Data is used for more advanced data mining, such as segmentation and predictive modelling. Helen James describes the benefits of data mining as follows:

*From our traditional electronic point-of-sale data we knew what was being sold, but now [through data mining] we can determine what different groups of customers are buying and monitor their behaviour over time.*

The IBM case study gives these examples of the applications of data mining:

*What interests the analysts most is the behaviour of groups of customers. They are interested, for example, in the effect of Boots' marketing activity on customers – such as the impact of promotional offers on buying patterns over time. They can make a valuable input to decisions about layout, ranging and promotions by using market basket analysis to provide insight into the product purchasing repertoires of different groups of customers.*

Like others, Boots has made a feature of multi-buy promotional schemes in recent years with numerous 'three for the price of two' and even 'two for the price of one' offers. Using the card data the Insight team has now been able to identify four groups of promotion buyers:

- the deal seekers who only ever buy promotional lines;
- the stockpilers who buy in bulk when goods are on offer and then don't visit the store for weeks;
- the loyalists – existing buyers who will buy a little more of a line when it is on offer but soon revert to their usual buying patterns;
- the new market – customers who start buying items when on promotion and then continue to purchase the same product once it reverts to normal price.

'This sort of analysis helps marketeers to understand what they are achieving via their promotions, rather than just identifying the uplift. They can see whether they are attracting new long-term business or just generating short-term uplift and also the extent to which they are cannibalising existing lines,' says Helen. Analysing market basket trends by shopper over time is also providing Boots with a new view of its traditional product categories. Customers buying skin-care products, for example, often buy hair-care products as well so this is a good link to use in promotions, direct mail and in-store activity.

Other linkings which emerge from the data – as Helen says, quite obvious when one thinks about them – include films and suntan lotion; sensitive skin products – be they washing-up gloves, cosmetics or skincare; and films and photograph frames with new baby products. 'Like many large retailers we are still organised along product category lines,' she says, 'so it would never really occur to the baby products buyers to create a special offer linked to picture frames – yet these are the very thing which new parents are likely to want.'

'We're also able to see how much shoppers participate in a particular range,' says Helen. 'They may buy toothbrushes, but do they also buy toothpaste and dental floss?' It may well be more profitable to encourage existing customers to buy deeper in the range than to attract new ones.

Monitoring purchases over time is also helping to identify buying patterns which fuel further marketing effort. Disposable nappy purchases, for example, are generally limited by the number of packs a customer can carry. A shopper visiting Boots once a fortnight and buying nappies is probably buying from a number of supply sources, whereas one calling at the store twice a week probably gets most of her baby's nappy needs from Boots. Encouraging the first shopper to visit more often would probably also increase nappy sales. Boots combines its basic customer demographic data (data such as age, gender, number of children and postcode) with externally available data. However, according to Helen, 'the real power comes from being able to combine this with detailed purchase behaviour data – and this is now being used to fuel business decisions outside of the marketing arena.'

This helps Boots to understand the main drivers of customer value and identify which customers they should value and retain and which could be more valuable if they focused on them more.

*Lifestage analysis* provides insight into how a customer's value changes over their lifetime. Using it, Boots can identify which are the potentially valuable customers of the future. They can also see the point at which a customer might become less valuable and try to prevent this. It is also clear that some messages become very important at certain times (for example, vitamins to people over 35 who have realised they may not be immortal) and irrelevant at others (what mother is concerned about cosmetics within a couple of weeks of the birth of her child?). This informs the mix of messages the customer receives, for instance via direct mail.

*Attitudinal insight* from market research surveys and questionnaires gives Boots an understanding of the attitudes driving the behaviour they see on their database. It is pointless directing a lot of marketing effort at people whose attitudes mean that they are unlikely to become more valuable to Boots.

This diversity of data is being used to build up a multi-dimensional picture of customers that gets to the heart of what drives customer value both today and into the future. Analysis of attitudes and customer repertoires offers Boots pointers to influencing customer value in a positive way. This understanding of customers has many applications within Boots, from the way the Boots brand is communicated to specific cross-selling activities for store staff. One of the first applications of this segmentation was as a driver of the Boots relationship marketing programme enabled by the Advantage card.

The segmentation provides a framework for relationship marketing. Specific campaigns help Boots to deliver that framework. These could encourage customers to shop along different themes – summer holidays, Christmas shopping – and incentivise them to make a visit. They may simply raise awareness of a particular new product or service – Boots Health & Travel Cover launched in April is a good example of this. They could be an invitation to an exclusive shopping event where the customer can shop in peace and perhaps earn extra points as well.

To make all this happen Boots needed a campaign management system that could involve customers in the relationship marketing programme most relevant to them. The 'campaign management' component has been fully integrated within CDAS (Cross-domain Authentication Service) through a bespoke development by IBM. This means that direct marketing analysts are able to develop their target customer profiles without having to first create a separate extract of the data, and are also able to base these profiles on the full richness of information held within the database. Having defined these criteria, the system will automatically come up with a mailing list of matching card holders with no further intervention. The system not only automates the measurement of basic campaign response analysis, but also makes the list of customers actually mailed available within the analysis environment so that more sophisticated response analysis can be performed. 'The close integration of the campaign management system within the analytic environment of CDAS is one of its main strengths' – 'not only are we able to drive high response rates by tightly targeting relevant customer groups, but we are able to close the loop from initial customer analysis, through customer selection and campaign execution back to campaign response measurement and further campaign analysis.'

*Computer Weekly* (2001) Interactive Being. *Computer Weekly*, 2 May 2001, article by Lindsay Nicolle

### Recency frequency monetary value (RFM) analysis

RFM is sometimes known as FRAC, which stands for: Frequency, Recency, Amount, (obviously equivalent to monetary value), Category (types of product purchased – not included within RFM). We will now give an overview of how RFM approaches can be applied, with special reference to online marketing. We will also look at the related concepts of latency and hurdle rates.

### Recency

This is the recency of customer action, e.g. purchase, site visit, account access, e-mail response. Novo (2003) stresses the importance of recency when he says:

> *Recency, or the number of days that have gone by since a customer completed an action (purchase, log-in, download, etc., is the most powerful predictor of the customer repeating an action … Recency is why you receive another catalogue from the company shortly after you make your first purchase from them.*

Online applications of analysis of recency include monitoring through time to identify vulnerable customers, and scoring customers to preferentially target more responsive customers for cost savings.

### Frequency

Frequency is the number of times an action is completed in a period of a customer action, e.g. purchase, visit, e-mail response – for example 5 purchases per year, 5 visits per month, 5 log-ins per week, 5 e-mail opens per month, 5 e-mail clicks per year. Online applications of this analysis include combining with recency for 'RF targeting'.

### Monetary value

The monetary value of purchase(s) can be measured in different ways – for example average order value of £50, total annual purchase value of £5000. Generally, customers with higher monetary values tend to have a higher loyalty and potential future value since they have purchased more items historically. One example application would be to exclude these customers from special promotions if their RF scores suggested they were actively purchasing. Frequency is often a proxy for monetary value per year since the more products purchased, the higher the overall monetary value. It is possible, then, to simplify analysis by just using recency and frequency. Monetary value can also skew the analysis with high-value initial purchases.

### Latency

**Latency**
The average length of time that different customers types takes between different activities, e.g. log-ins, paying bills, first and second purchase.

**Latency** is a powerful concept, closely related to frequency – it is the average time between customer events in the customer lifecycle. Examples include the average time between website visits, second and third purchase and e-mail click-throughs. Online applications of latency include putting in place triggers that alert companies to customer behaviour outside the norm, for example increased interest or disinterest, and then to manage this behaviour using e-communications or traditional communications. For example, if a B2B or B2C organisation with a long interval between purchases found that latency decreased for a particular customer, then they may be investigating an additional purchase via e-mail or website (their recency and frequency would likely increase also). E-mails, phone calls or direct mail could then be used to target this person with relevant offers according to what they were searching for.

### Hurdle rate

**Hurdle rate**
The proportion of customers that fall within a particular level of activity. For example, the percentage of members of an e-mail list that click on the e-mail within a 90-day period, or the number of customers that have made a second purchase.

According to Novo (2003), '**hurdle rate**' refers to the percentage of customers in a group (such as in a segment or on a list) who have completed an action. It is a useful concept since it can be used to compare the engagement of different groups or to set targets to increase engagement with online channels as the examples below show:

- 20% of customers have visited in the past 6 months
- 5% of customers have made 3 or more purchases this year
- 60% of registrants have logged on to system this year
- 30% have clicked through on e-mail this year.

### Grouping customers into different RFM categories

In the examples above, each division for recency, frequency and monetary value is placed in an arbitrary position to place a roughly equal number of customers in each group. This approach is also useful since the marketer can set thresholds of value relevant to their understanding of their customers.

RFM analysis involves two techniques for grouping customers:

### 1 Statistical RFM analysis

This involves placing an equal number of customers in each RFM category using quintiles of 20% (10 deciles can also be used for larger databases) as shown in Figure 6.15. The figure also shows one application of RFM with a view to using communications channels more effectively. Lower-cost e-communications can be used to correspond with customers who use only services more frequently since they prefer these channels, while more expensive offline communications can be used for customers who seem to prefer traditional channels.

### 2 Arbitrary divisions of customer database

This approach is also useful since the marketer can set thresholds of value relevant to their understanding of their customers.

For example, RFM analysis can be applied for targeting using e-mail according to how a customer interacts with an e-commerce site. Values could be assigned to each customer as follows:

*Recency:*
1 – Over 12 months
2 – Within last 12 months
3 – Within last 6 months
4 – Within last 3 months
5 – Within last 1 month

*Frequency:*
1 – More than once every 6 months
2 – Every 6 months
3 – Every 3 months
4 – Every 2 months
5 – Monthly

*Monetary value:*
1 – Less than £10
2 – £10–£50
3 – £50–£100
4 – £100–£200
5 – More than £200

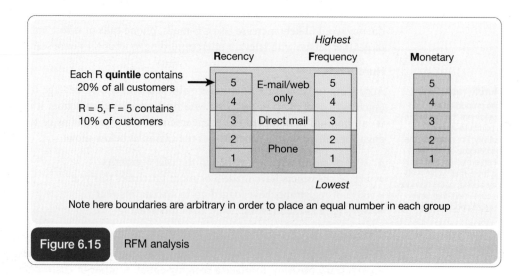

Note here boundaries are arbitrary in order to place an equal number in each group

**Figure 6.15**    RFM analysis

Simplified versions of this analysis can be created to make it more manageable – for example a theatre group uses these nine categories for its direct marketing:

*Oncers (attended theatre once):*
- Recent oncer          attended <12 months
- Rusty oncer           attended >12 but <36 months
- Very rusty oncer      attended in 36+ months

*Twicers:*
- Recent twicer         attended < 12 months
- Rusty twicer          attended >12 but < 36 months
- Very rusty twicer     attended in 36+ months

*2+ subscribers:*
- Current subscribers   booked 2+ events in current season
- Recent                booked 2+ last season
- Very rusty            booked 2+ more than a season ago

Another example, with real-world data, is shown in Figure 6.16. You can see that plotting customer numbers against recency and frequency in this way for an online company gives a great visual indication of the health of the business and groups that can be targeted to encourage more repeat purchases.

### Product recommendations and propensity modelling

**Propensity modelling**

The approach of evaluating customer characteristics and behaviour and then making recommendations for future products.

'**Propensity modelling**' is one name given to the approach of evaluating customer characteristics and behaviour, in particular previous products or services purchased, and then making recommendations for the next suitable product. However, it is best known as recommending the 'Next best product' to existing customers.

A related acquisition approach is to target potential customers with similar characteristics through renting direct mail or e-mail lists or advertising online in similar locations.

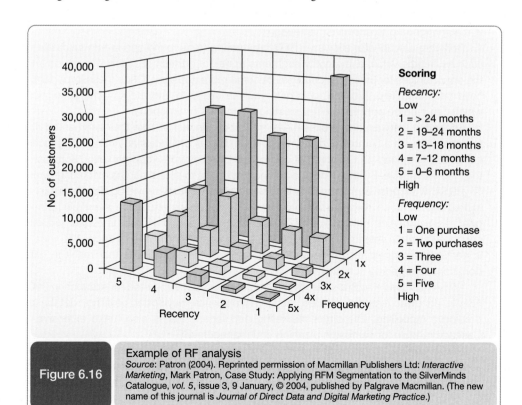

**Figure 6.16**

Example of RF analysis
*Source*: Patron (2004). Reprinted permission of Macmillan Publishers Ltd: *Interactive Marketing*, Mark Patron, Case Study: Applying RFM Segmentation to the SilverMinds Catalogue, *vol. 5*, issue 3, 9 January, © 2004, published by Palgrave Macmillan. (The new name of this journal is *Journal of Direct Data and Digital Marketing Practice*.)

The following recommendations are based on those in van Duyne *et al.* (2003):

1 *Create automatic product relationships* [i.e. Next best product]. A low-tech approach to this is, for each product, to group together products previously purchased together. Then for each product, rank product by number of times purchased together to find relationships.

2 *Cordon off and minimise the 'real estate' devoted to related products.* An area of screen should be reserved for 'Next best product prompts' for up-selling and cross-selling. However, if these can be made part of the current product they may be more effective.

3 *Use familiar 'trigger words'.* That is, familiar from using other sites such as Amazon. Such phrases include: 'Related products', 'Your recommendations', 'Similar', 'Customers who bought …', 'Top 3 related products'.

4 *Editorialise about related products.* That is, within copy about a product.

5 *Allow quick purchase of related products.*

6 *Sell related product during checkout.* And also on post-transaction pages, i.e. after one item has been added to the basket or purchased.

Note that techniques do not necessarily require an expensive recommendations engine except for very large sites.

---

### Mini Case Study 6.4    Charity PDSA refines its understanding of its members

The context for this case is provided by Robin Prouse who is the Training Manager of Apteco Ltd, (www.apteco.com) a company that specialises in analytical marketing software. He is in a unique position to understand the difficulties and challenges facing many organisations in making sense of their customer data and has worked with PDSA.

Robin says, 'The starting place for most organisations is to gather and organise their data in one place. Once the data is available and in a suitable software tool such as FastStats Discoverer, the question then arises, what do you do with it? Understanding and being able to visualise who your current customers are is the springboard to effective marketing.

Software functionality allows for RFM information to be found and in turn calculate valuable knowledge, such as lifetime value, and identify segments at risk of attrition or churn. When you know your customers, the opportunities for cross-sell or up-sell become more apparent. Once these important customer segments have been identified, profiling tools give you the ability to find the key characteristics of their members, which can then be applied to other existing customers or prospects.

Integrated software now makes it easier for the marketer to take their segmented data and present their message through a number of different channels. E-mail broadcasting is becoming increasingly popular and being able to upload your contact list and content directly from your marketing software adds another link to the marketing cycle. By capturing and adding responses to your data, the marketing cycle is made complete.'

PDSA (www.pdsa.org) is the UK's leading veterinary charity providing free veterinary care for the sick and injured pets of those unable to afford veterinary fees. The charity, which is entirely funded by public support, operates a UK-wide network of 47 PetAid hospitals and branches and also works through some 348 contracted private veterinary practices. PDSA also operates 180 charity shops UK-wide, but its main income is derived from direct marketing and relationship-building programs that result in gifts in wills, voluntary donations and trading activities.

PDSA has used FastStats Discoverer from Apteco since the product's launch in 2005. The charity relies heavily on Discoverer for detailed marketing analytics, supporter profiling, database segmentation and predictive modelling. The direct marketing and legacy teams also make extensive use of Discoverer's Cascade module for campaign planning and management.

PDSA holds a huge database of past transactional and promotional histories on nearly six million supporters. This data set is used to report lifetime value, patterns and trends in support, and for the identification of cross-sell and up-sell opportunities. In conjunction with third-party geo-demographic data, Discoverer has been used to build sophisticated legacy propensity models, donor profiles and channel attrition analysis.

As PDSA improves its online presence via its website, www.pdsa.org.uk and dedicated e-mail marketing campaigns, Discoverer has increasingly been used to monitor and classify donor e-mail addresses. This allows marketers to combine online knowledge with that contained in transactional and operational systems – linking offline lifetime value, demographics and product propensity models with online marketing permissions and click-through analysis.

## Loyalty schemes

Loyalty schemes are often used to encourage customer extension and retention. You will be familiar with schemes run by retailers such as the Tesco Clubcard or Nectar schemes or those of airlines and hotel chains. Such schemes are often used for e-CRM purposes as follows:

- initial bonus points for sign-up to online services or initial registration;
- points for customer development or extension – more points awarded to encourage second or third online purchase;
- additional points to encourage reactivation of online services;
- popular products are offered for a relatively low number of points to encourage repeat purchases.

If customers have lapsed in using online services, it is often necessary to contact them by direct mail or phone to make these offers.

As well as loyalty schemes operated by retailers and their partners, there are also some online-specific loyalty schemes which are operated independently. While early attempts at developing the online Beenz currency (www.beenz.com) failed, others such as iPoints (www.ipoints.com) have survived. New ones are still being launched – for example, Pigs Back has worked well in Ireland and was launched in the UK in 2005 (www.pigsback.co.uk). A more recent innovation is the growth in cashback intermediaries such as the UK site Greasypalm (www.greasypalm.co.uk, Figure 6.17) and the US site Fat Wallet (www.fatwallet.com). These are affiliate intermediary sites which share affiliate revenue with their loyal customers. Such sites are a threat to long-term profitability since affiliate marketing is usually intended to acquire new customers by paying out a sum to the affiliate. But because of the power of the cashback intermediaries who have developed a loyal customer base, online retailers may be forced to pay ongoing affiliate revenue out to customers who purchase more than once. Of course, the retailer can model the impact of these sites on customer lifetime value and profitability and then decide whether they wish to continue in a commercial agreement with them.

## Virtual communities and social networks

We have discussed some of the psychological reasons for the popularity of social networks in Chapter 2 in the section on consumer buyer behaviour (see page **86**, under Social interaction communication models) and in Chapter 9 we review some of the related Web 2.0 marketing techniques that can be used for customer acquisition. But in this section, we consider why social networks have developed and how they can be used to develop customer understanding and for relationship building.

**Virtual community**
An Internet-based forum for special-interest groups to communicate.

The reasons for the popularity of virtual communities today such as the social networks Bebo, Facebook, MySpace and Linked In can be traced back to the nineteenth century. The German sociologist Ferdinand Tonnies (1855–1936) made the distinction between public society and private community (Loomis, 1957). Tonnies employed the terms *Gemeinschaft* meaning community (informal, organic or instinctive ties typified by the family or neighbourhood) and *Gesellschaft* meaning society (formal, impersonal, instrumental, goal-orientated relations typified by big cities, the state and large organisations). Membership of Gemeinschaft is self-fulfilling (intrinsic motivation) whereas being a member of a Gesellschaft is a means to further individual goals (extrinsic motivation).

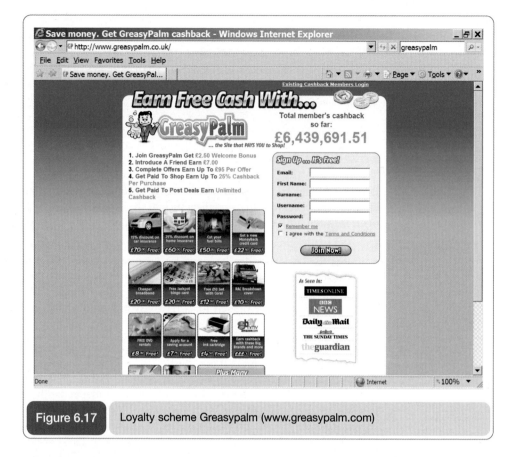

| Figure 6.17 | Loyalty scheme Greasypalm (www.greasypalm.com) |

Marshall McLuhan (1964) posited that 'cool' (meaning on-going and shared) and inclusive 'electric media' (meaning telephone and television, rather than books) would 'retribalise' human society into clusters of affiliation. Nicholas Negroponte (1995) predicted that in the near future 'we will socialise in digital neighbourhoods'. Manuel Castells (1996) has developed the concept of 'networked individualism', in which individuals build their networks on and off-line on the basis of values, interests and projects, and believes that 'our societies are increasingly structured around the bipolar opposition of the Net and the Self'.

Virtual communities are the emerging construct of the traditional social marketplaces where groups of people who share common interests and needs come together online. Most are drawn together by the opportunity to share a sense of community with like-minded individuals, regardless of where they live.

Virtual communities also provide opportunities for some companies to develop relationships with their customers. Since the publication of the article by Armstrong and Hagel in 1996 entitled 'The real value of online communities' and John Hagel's subsequent book (Hagel, 1997) there has been much discussion about the suitability of the web for virtual communities.

The power of the virtual communities, according to Hagel (1997), is that they exhibit a number of positive feedback loops (or 'virtuous circles'). Focused content attracts new members, who in turn contribute to the quantity and quality of the community's pooled knowledge. Member loyalty grows as the community grows and evolves. The purchasing power of the community grows and thus the community attracts more advertisers to fund it. The growing revenue potential attracts yet more vendors, providing more choice and attracting more members. As the size and sophistication of the community grow (while it still remains tightly focused) its data-gathering and profiling capabilities increase – thus enabling better-targeted marketing and attracting more vendors . . . and so on. In such positive feedback loops there is an initial start-up period of slow and uneven growth until critical mass in members, content, vendors and transactions is reached. The potential for growth is then exponential – until the limits of the focus of the community as it defines itself are reached.

From this description of virtual communities it can be seen that they provide many of the attributes for effective relationship marketing – they can be used to learn about customers and provide information and offers to groups of customers.

When deciding on a strategic approach to virtual communities, companies have two basic choices if they decide to use them as part of their efforts in relationship building. They can provide community facilities on the site, or they can monitor and become involved in relevant communities set up by other organisations.

If a company sets up a community facility on its site, it has the advantage that it can improve its brand by adding value to its site. Sterne (1999) suggests that minimal intrusion should occur, but it may be necessary for the company to seed discussion and moderate out some negative comments. It may also be instrumental in increasing word-of-mouth promotion of the site. The community will provide customer feedback on the company and its products as part of the learning relationship. However, the brand may be damaged if customers criticise products, so some moderation is required. Honda UK (www.honda.co.uk/car) provides a good example of a community created by their brand on their site. Rather than having a separate community section, the community is integrated within the context of each car as a 'second opinions' menu option in the context of each car. Interestingly, some negative comments are permitted to make the discussion more meaningful.

A potential problem with a company-hosted forum is that it may be unable to get sufficient people to contribute to a company-hosted community. But an example where initial recruitment of contributors and moderation has been used to grow the forum successfully is shown in Figure 6.18. Communities are best suited to high-involvement brands, such as a professional body like CIPD, or those related to sports and hobbies and business-to-business.

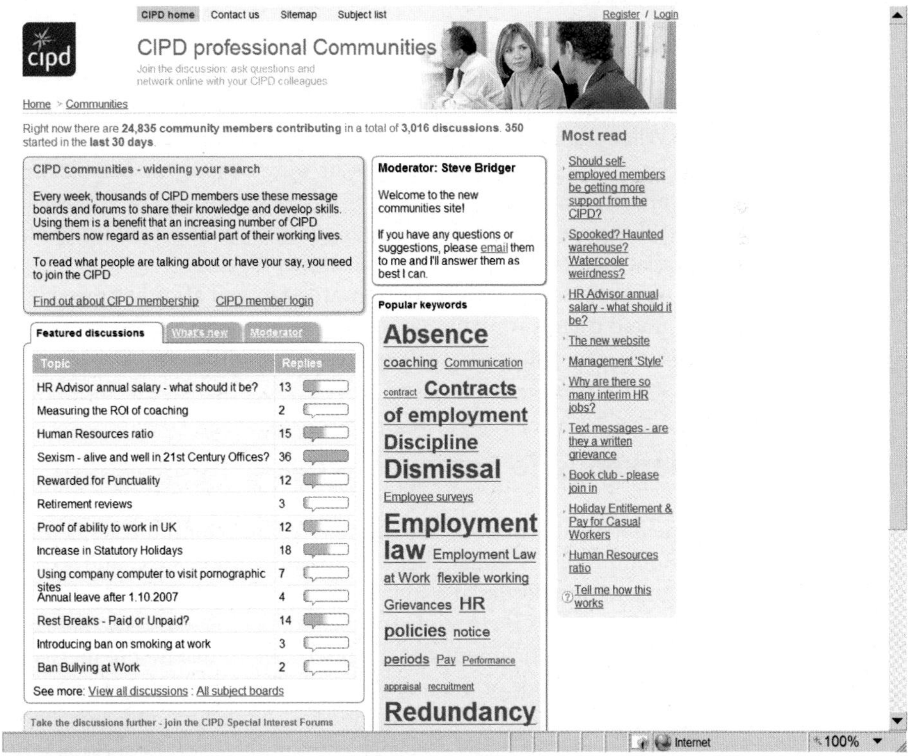

**Figure 6.18**   CIPD forums – a forum operated by a company to keep closer to its customers

What is the reality behind Armstrong and Hagel's original vision of communities? How can companies deliver the promise of community? The key to a successful community is customer-centred communication. It is a customer-to-customer (C2C) interaction (Chapter 1). Consumers, not businesses, generate the content of the site, e-mail list or bulletin board.

According to Durlacher (1999), depending on market sector, an organisation has a choice of developing different types of community: communities of purpose, position and interest for B2C, and of profession for B2B.

- *Purpose* – people who are going through the same process or trying to achieve a particular objective. Examples include those researching cars, e.g. at Autotrader (www.autotrader.co.uk), or stocks online, e.g. at the Motley Fool (www.motleyfool.co.uk). Price or product comparison services such as Bizrate (www.bizrate.com) are also in this category.
- *Position* – people who are in a certain circumstance, such as a health disorder, or in a certain stage of life, such as communities set up specifically for young people or old people. Examples are teenage chat site Habbo Hotel (www.habbohotel.com), 50 Connect, www.50connect.co.uk 'and MumsNet (www.mumsnet.com).
- *Interest* – this community is for people who share an interest or passion such as sport (www.thefootballforum.net), music (www.pepsi.com) or leisure (www.ukclimbing.com).
- *Profession* – these are important for companies promoting B2B services.

A further classification of communities is that of Armstrong and Hagel (1996) which is arguably less useful and identifies communities of transaction, communities of interest, communities of fantasy and communities of relationship.

What tactics can organisations use to foster community? Despite the hype and potential, many communities fail to generate activity, and a silent community isn't a community. Parker (2000) suggests eight questions organisations should ask when considering how to create a customer community:

1  What interests, needs or passions do many of your customers have in common?
2  What topics or concerns might your customers like to share with each other?
3  What information is likely to appeal to your customers' friends or colleagues?
4  What other types of business in your area appeal to buyers of your products and services?
5  How can you create packages or offers based on combining offers from two or more affinity partners?
6  What price, delivery, financing or incentives can you afford to offer to friends (or colleagues) that your current customers recommend?
7  What types of incentives or rewards can you afford to provide for customers who recommend friends (or colleagues) who make a purchase?
8  How can you best track purchases resulting from word-of-mouth recommendations from friends?

## Marketing to consumers using independent social networks

One potential benefit of marketing to virtual communities is that they are naturally formed around problems shared, benefits sought, interests etc. and so are naturally self-segmented. Segmentation occurs at a microscopic level – for example, the biggest community on eBay Neighbourhoods is currently (http://neighbourhoods.ebay.com/espresso-machines) which has developed for aficionados of quality coffee to debate the merits of various strains of coffee beans, of methods of preparation, of coffee machines and of brands such as Starbucks. Each species of bean, each processing mode, each machine and each brand will have its enthusiasts.

The owners of many specialist communities will be seeking advertising revenue (see Case study 8 on Facebook on page **493**), so they may accept links to merchants and display advertising if the match of product/service and community interests is close enough and the advertising doesn't divert from the community.

Google AdSense (Chapter 9) may be used to serve contextual ads to the community via the content network of Google. Google's Site Placement targeting tool can be useful for potential partner sites. Although social networks such as Facebook and MySpace use advertising as a revenue source, for the advertisers responses tend to be low because the focus of users is on interacting, not on the ads.

### Virtual worlds

Virtual worlds are immersive digital environments where members' avatars socialise (chat, shop, dance and date) in a 3D virtual user-built environment. Second Life (see Mini case study 6.4) is perhaps the best known. Typically though, these virtual worlds are not true communities in that they have not formed around a set of values or interests that forms a gravitational core of the community. Virtual buildings and sports arenas may have advertising hoardings etc. but these essentially ape the traditional marketing of the offline real world. As these virtual worlds are not drawn together by a common affiliation they do not form the neat self-defining marketing target of the virtual community.

---

**Mini Case Study 6.5**   How can Second Life be used for marketing?

Virtual community Second Life (www.slurl.com, Figure 6.19) has received much hype in the media. But how large is it and how can companies use it for marketing?

Most Second Life users have a basic account which includes access to events, shopping and building. A premium Second Life account, starting at $9.95 a month, enables users to get land on which they can build, display, entertain and live. You also receive extended support options, including the ability to submit a support ticket and engage in a text chat session with support teams. According to the figures available from Second Life (http://secondlife.com/whatis/economy.php), at the start of 2008 there were just 12 million people with a basic account and only around 90,000 with a premium account.

**Figure 6.19**   IBM Office within Second Life
*Source*: http://www-03.ibm.com/press/us/en/photo/22427.wss. Reprint courtesy of International Business Machines Corporation, copyright 2007 © International Business Machines Corporation.

### Branded stores

Many brands have set up virtual islands and stores in virtual world Second Life. With brands such as Coca-Cola, Sears, Dell, IBM and Calvin Klein attracting fewer than 500 visitors a week (see http://nwn.blogs.com/nwn/mixed_reality_headcount/index.html for the latest figures) it is clear that Second Life has a limited reach. One can only assume that the brands who have invested in a Second Life presence have done this to test for the future or possibly PR benefits.

However, IBM has partnered with Linden Labs, the creators of SL since they have identified 'many applications of virtual world technology for business and society in commerce, collaboration, education, training and more'. Figure 6.19 shows two IBM employees – represented by their 3D avatars having a discussion prior to a business meeting at the IBM Open Source and Standards office in the Second Life virtual world.

## Customer experience – the missing element required for customer loyalty

We have in this chapter shown how delivering relevant timely communications as part of permission marketing is important to developing loyalty. However, even the most relevant communications will fail if another key factor is not taken into account – this is the *customer experience*. If a first-time or repeat customer experience is poor due to a slow-to-download difficult-to-use site, then it is unlikely that loyalty from the online customer will develop. The relationship between the drivers of customer satisfaction and loyalty is shown in Figure 6.20. In the next chapter we review techniques used to help develop this experience.

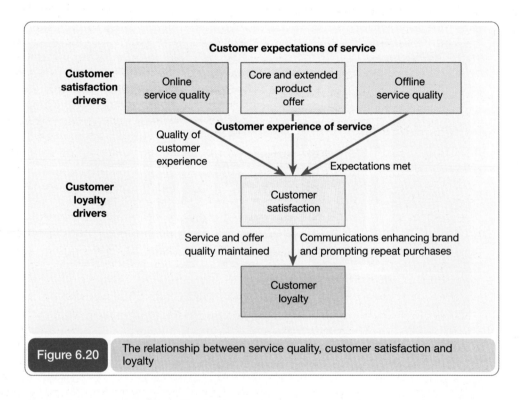

| Figure 6.20 | The relationship between service quality, customer satisfaction and loyalty |

## Case Study 6　　Dell gets closer to its customers online

Dell is a technology company, offering a broad range of product categories, including desktop computer systems, storage, servers and networking products, mobility products, software and peripherals, and services to manage IT infrastructure for large organisations. Dell are the number one supplier of personal computer systems in the United States, and the number two supplier worldwide.

### Dell proposition

The main Dell product offerings are:

1 *Desktop PCs* – Five lines of desktop computer systems are produced for different markets. For example, the OptiPlex line is designed to help business, government and institutional customers manage their total cost of ownership by offering stability, security and managed product transitions. The Dimensionline is designed for small businesses and home users requiring the latest features for their productivity and entertainment needs. The XPS tm and Alienware lines are targeted at customers who require the highest performance gaming or entertainment experience available. In July 2007, they introduced the Vostro tm line, which is designed to provide technology and services to suit the specific needs of small businesses.

2 *Servers and networking* – The PowerEdge tm line of servers is designed to offer customers affordable performance, reliability and scalability. Again different options are available for different markets include high performance rack, blade and tower servers for enterprise customers and lower priced tower servers for small organisations, networks and remote offices.

3 *Storage* – For example storage area networks, network-attached storage, direct-attached storage, disk and tape backup systems, and removable disk backup.

4 *Mobility* – Notebook computers are targeted at customers who require the highest performance gaming or entertainment experience available.

5 *Software and peripherals* – Office software and hardware including printers, televisions, notebook accessories, networking and wireless products, digital cameras, power adapters, scanners and other products.

6 *Enhanced services* – Dell's global services business offers tailored solutions that help customers lower the cost of their services environment and maximise system performance, efficiency and return on investment. These include: infrastructure consulting services; deployment services to install and integrate new systems; asset recovery and recycling services; training services; enterprise support services, and managed lifecycle services (outsourced IT management).

7 *Financial services* for business and consumer customers in the US through a joint venture between Dell and CIT Group, Inc.

### Dell business strategy

Dell's vision is to 'strive to provide the best possible customer experience by offering superior value; high-quality, relevant technology; customised systems; superior service and support; and differentiated products and services that are easy to buy and use'.

The core elements of the strategy which are evident in Dell's marketing communications are:

- *We simplify information technology for customers.* Making quality personal computers, servers, storage and services affordable is Dell's legacy. We are focused on making information technology affordable for millions of customers around the world. As a result of our direct relationships with customers, or 'customer intimacy', we are best positioned to simplify how customers implement and maintain information technology and deliver hardware, services and software solutions tailored for their businesses and homes.

- *We offer customers choice.* Customers can purchase systems and services from Dell via telephone, kiosks and our website, www.dell.com, where they may review, configure and price systems within our entire product line; order systems online; and track orders from manufacturing through shipping. We have recently launched a retail initiative and plan to expand that initiative by adding new distribution channels to reach additional consumers and small businesses through retail partners and value-added resellers globally.

- *Customers can purchase custom-built products and custom-tailored services.* Historically our flexible, build-to-order manufacturing process enabled us to turn over inventory every five days on average, thereby reducing inventory levels and rapidly bring the latest technology to our customers. The market and our competition has evolved and we are now exploring the utilisation of original design manufacturers and new distribution strategies to better meet customer needs and reduce product cycle times. Our goal is to introduce the latest relevant technology more quickly and to rapidly pass on component cost savings to a broader set of our customers worldwide.

- *We are committed to being environmentally responsible in all areas of our business*. We have built environmental consideration into every stage of the Dell product lifecycle – from developing and designing energy-efficient products, to reducing the footprint of our manufacturing and operations, to customer use and product recovery.

## Dell's sales and marketing

Dell sell products and services directly to customers through dedicated sales representatives, telephone-based sales and online at www.dell.com. Customer segments include large corporate, government, healthcare and education accounts, as well as small-to-medium businesses and individual consumers.

Dell stresses the importance of its direct business model in providing direct and continuous feedback from customers, thereby allowing them to develop and refine our products and marketing programmes for specific customer groups.

In its SEC filing, Dell emphasises how it listens to customers to develop relevant innovative technology and services they trust and value. Evidence for using the participative nature of Web 2.0 is that customers can offer suggestions for current and future Dell products, services and operations on an interactive portion of the Dell website called Dell IdeaStorm. It says: 'This constant flow of communication, which is unique to our direct business model, also allows us to rapidly gauge customer satisfaction and target new or existing products.'

For large business and institutional customers, Dell maintain a field sales force throughout the world. Dedicated account teams, which include field-based system engineers and consultants, form long-term relationships to provide our largest customers with a single source of assistance and develop specific tailored solutions for these customers. Dell also maintain specific sales and marketing programmes targeted at federal, state and local governmental agencies as well as specific healthcare and educational markets.

## Dell Premier

For its large organisational customers, Dell offers Premier (http://premier.dell.com), which is a secure, customisable procurement and support site or extranet designed to save organisations time and money through all phases of I/T product ownership. The main benefits of Dell Premier are described as:

- *Easy ordering* – a custom online store ensures access to your products at your price.
- *Easy tracking* – view real-time order status, online invoices and purchase history details.
- *Easy control* – custom access groups define what users can see and do within Premier.

## Marketing communications

Dell markets its products and services to small-to-medium businesses and consumers primarily by advertising on television and the Internet, advertising in a variety of print media and by mailing a broad range of direct marketing publications, such as promotional pieces, catalogues and customer newsletters. In certain locations we also operate Dell stores or kiosks, typically located within shopping centres, that allow customers to view our products in person and purchase online with the assistance of a Dell expert.

## Dell online communications

The management of the consumer site was presented to EConsultancy (2008). Dell has a three-stage order funnel:

- marketing communications execution measured by site visits;
- site merchandising measured by *consideration %* (site visits to e-store visits);
- store merchandising measured by *conversion %* (e-store visits to e-receipts).

The presenter explained how Dell aims to understand and act on customer behaviour based on identification of a series of consideration drivers – for example, the quality of online advertising; path quality through site; merchandising/offers – and conversion drivers – for example, configurator 'ease of use'; accessibility of decision support tools and consistency of message through the entire path.

Dell will invest in strategic improvements to the site to improve these levers – examples mentioned included new merchandising approaches such as customer ratings and reviews, videos, major 'path' or customer journey changes created through decision support tools to 'Help me choose'. There are also more tactical initiatives to help deliver the right message to each customer including customisation/personalisation, real estate optimisation and message balancing.

More tactical persuasion of site visitors is based on price moves/optimised price position to market and the mix of product features. A wide range of different offers need to be managed. Tactical promotions which are driven by promotional 'end dates' which are weekly or bi-weekly include varying:

- free shipping
- money-off discounts
- free upgrades (e.g. memory)
- free accessories
- finance offers
- service upgrades.

The presenter also noted how, across Europe, the promotional mix has to vary to reflect the differences in buying psychology. He summarises the main differences between customers as follows:

- UK – all about price
- CH – add value over price
- DE – all about high-end products in mix
- IT – design is important (!)
- DK – cheap is good
- NO – added value is key
- FR – tailored for France.

## Dell's use of digital media channels

The main digital media channels used by Dell.com in Europe are:

- Paid search through programmes such as Google AdWords are used to promote value through time-limited offers related to the phrase searched upon. For example, a Google search for 'cheapest Dell' displays an ad: 'Discount Dell Laptops www.dell.co.uk/laptop – Save up to £300 on selected Dell Laptops from £329. Buy online now!'

- Display advertising, for example advertising on technology websites, is particularly important for the corporate market.
- Affiliate marketing – used to protect the Dell brand by enabling affiliates to bid on terms such as 'Dell laptops' and to target niche audiences such as owners of gaming machines.
- E-mail marketing – an e-newsletter is used to keep in touch with existing customers and deliver targeted offers when their hardware may be renewed.

## Dell and indirect channels

Although the focus of Dell's business strategy has been selling directly to its customers, it also uses some indirect sales channels when there is a business need. In the US they sell products indirectly through third-party solution providers, system integrators and third-party resellers. During financial year 2008, Dell began offering Dimension desktop computers and Inspiron notebook computers in retail stores in the Americas and announced partnerships with retailers in the UK, Japan and China. Dell says: 'These actions represent the first steps in our retail strategy, which will allow us to extend our business model and reach customers that we have not been able to reach directly'.

*Source*: 2007 SEC Filing EConsultancy (2008)

### Question

Describe approaches used by Dell within their site design and promotion to deliver relevant offers for different types of online customers.

## Summary

1. The three areas of relationship marketing, direct marketing and database marketing have converged to create a powerful new marketing paradigm known as 'customer relationship management' (CRM).

2. Relationship marketing theory provides the conceptual underpinning of one-to-one marketing and customer relationship management since it emphasises enhanced customer service through customer knowledge.

3. The objective of CRM is to increase customer loyalty in order to increase profitability over customers' lifetime value (LTV). It is aimed at improving all aspects of the level of customer service.

4. CRM tactics can be based around the acquisition – retention – extension model of the ideal relationship between company and customer. Marketers can use 'sense and respond' techniques such as RFM analysis to target customers for retention and extension.

5. Direct marketing provides the tactics that deliver the marketing communications (and sometimes the product itself) to the individual customer. This approach is evolving rapidly with the advent of the Internet, the rise of call centres and advances in logistics.

6. Database marketing provides the technological enabler, allowing vast amounts of data to be stored and accessed in ways that create business opportunities.

7. Online relationship marketing is effective since it provides an interactive, multimedia environment in which the customer opts-in to the relationship.

8. Steps in implementing one-to-one on the Internet are:
   - Step 1 – Attract customers to site.
   - Step 2a – Incentivise in order to gain contact and profile information.
   - Step 2b – Capture customer information to maintain the relationship and profile the customer.
   - Step 3 – Maintain dialogue through using online communications to achieve repeat site visits.
   - Step 4 – Maintain dialogue consistent with customer's profile using direct mail.

9. Personalisation technologies enable customised e-mails to be sent to each individual (or related groups) and customised web content to be displayed or distributed using push technology.

10. Integration with databases is important for profiling the customer and recording the relationship.

11. Virtual communities have an important role to play in fostering relationships.

12. Marketers must be aware of the risk of infringing customer privacy since this is damaging to the relationship. Providing customers with the option to opt-in and opt-out of marketing communications is a legal requirement in many countries.

13. Internet-based one-to-one marketing needs to be integrated with traditional communications by mail and phone as described in Chapter 8.

## Exercises

### Self-assessment exercises

1. Why is the Internet a suitable medium for relationship marketing?

2. Explain 'personalisation' in an Internet marketing context.

3. What is meant by 'customer profiling'?

4. Explain the concept and benefits of the 'sense and respond' approach to customer communications.

5. How can customer concerns about privacy be responded to when conducting one-to-one marketing using the Internet?

6. Explain the relationship between database marketing, direct marketing and relationship marketing.

7. Explain the concept and applications of RFM analysis to different types of web presence.

8. How can a website integrate with telemarketing?

### Essay and discussion questions

1. Explain the factors that influence the development of multichannel customer contact strategies.
2. Compare and contrast traditional transaction-oriented marketing with one-to-one marketing using the Internet.
3. Write a report summarising for a manager the necessary stages for transforming a brochureware site to a one-to-one interactive site and the benefits that can be expected.
4. Explore the legal and ethical constraints on implementing relationship marketing using the Internet.

### Examination questions

1. Define and explain direct marketing within the Internet context.
2. What characteristics of the Internet make it so conducive to the direct marketing approach?
3. How does a company initiate one-to-one marketing with a company using the Internet?
4. Explain the concept of a 'virtual community' and how such communities can be used as part of relationship marketing.
5. Suggest three measures a company can take to ensure that a customer's privacy is not infringed when conducting one-to-one marketing.
6. What is the role of a database when conducting one-to-one marketing on the Internet?
7. What is 'web self-service'? What are typical challenges in managing this?
8. Explore opportunities and methods for personalising the interactive web session and adding value for that individual customer.

## References

Agrawal, V., Arjona, V. and Lemmens, R. (2001) E-performance: the path to rational exuberance, *McKinsey Quarterly*, No. 1, 31–43.

Armstrong, A. and Hagel, J. (1996) The real value of online communities, *Harvard Business Review*, May–June, 134–41.

Castells, M. (1996) *The Rise of the Network Society*, Blackwell, Oxford.

Chaffey, D. (2004) E-permission marketing. Chartered Institute of Marketing, *What's New in Marketing*, e-newsletter, Issue 25, (www.wnim.com).

Cram, T. (1994) *The Power of Relationship Marketing: Keeping Customers for Life*. Financial Times Management, London.

Duffy, D. (1998) Customer loyalty strategies, *Journal of Consumer Marketing*, 15(5), 435–48.

Durlacher (1999) UK online community, *Durlacher Quarterly Internet Report*, Q3, 7–11, London.

EConsultancy (2008) Dell case study. Online Marketing Masterclass, presented at the Royal Institute of British Architects, November 2008.

Evans, M., Patterson, M. and O'Malley, L. (2000) Bridging the direct marketing–direct consumer gap: some solutions from qualitative research, *Proceedings of the Academy of Marketing Annual Conference*, 2000, Derby, UK.

Forrester (2007) Marketing's New Key Metric: Engagement. Marketers must measure involvement, interaction, intimacy, and influence. *Forrester Analyst report*. Brian Haven, 8 August 2007.

Godin, S. (1999) *Permission Marketing*. Simon and Schuster, New York.

Hagel, J. (1997) *Net Gain: Expanding Markets through Virtual Communities*. Harvard Business School Press, Boston.

Keiningham, T., Cooil, B., Aksoy, L., Andreassen, T. and Weiner, J. (2007) The value of different customer satisfaction and loyalty metrics in predicting customer retention, recommendation and share-of-wallet, *Managing Service Quality*, Vol. 17, No. 4.

Kirby, K. and Samson, A. (2007) Customer advocacy metrics: the NPS theory in practice, *AdMap*, February 2008, 17–19.

Kumar, V., Petersen, J. and Leone, R. (2007) How valuable is word of mouth? *Harvard Business Review*, October 2007, Vol. 85 Issue 10, 139–146.

Loomis, C.P. (1957) *Community and Society: Gemeinschaft und Gesellschaft*, Michigan State University Press.

McKenna, R. (1993) *Relationship Marketing: Successful Strategies for the Age of the Customer*. Addison-Wesley, Reading, MA.

McLuhan, M. (1964) *Understanding Media*, Routledge, London.

Moller, K. and Halinen, A. (2000) Relationship marketing theory: its roots and direction, *Journal of Marketing Management*, 16, 29–54.

Negroponte, N. (1995) *Being Digital*, Hodder and Stoughton, London.

Novo, J. (2003) *Drilling Down: Turning customer data into profits with a spreadsheet*. Available from www.jimnovo.com.

O'Malley, L. and Tynan, C. (2001) Reframing relationship marketing for consumer markets, *Interactive Marketing*, 2(3), 240–6.

Parker, R. (2000) *Relationship Marketing on the Web*. Adams Streetwise, Cincinnati, OH.

Patron, M. (2004) Case study: applying RFM segmentation to the SilverMinds catalogue, *Interactive Marketing*, 5(3), 269–75.

Peppers, D. and Rogers, M. (1997) *Enterprise One-to-One: Tools for Building Unbreakable Customer Relationships in the Interactive Age*. Piatkus, London.

Peppers, D. and Rogers, M. (1998) *One-to-One Fieldbook*. Doubleday, New York.

Peppers, D. and Rogers, M. (2002) *One to One B2B: Customer Relationship Management Strategies for the Real Economy*. Cupstone, Oxford.

Peppers, D., Rogers, M. and Dorf, B. (1999) Is your company ready for one-to-one marketing? *Harvard Business Review*, January–February, 3–12.

Raphel, M. (1997) How a San Francisco movie complex breaks attendance records with database marketing, *Direct Marketing*, 59(11), 52–5.

Reichheld, F.F. (1996) *The Loyalty Effect*. Harvard Business School Press, Boston.

Reichheld, F. and Schefter, P. (2000) E-loyalty, your secret weapon, *Harvard Business Review*, July–August, 105–13.

Reicheld, F. (2006) *The Ultimate Question: Driving Good Profits and True Growth*. Harvard Business School Publishing.

Rigby, D., Bavega, S., Rastoi, S., Zook, C. and Hancock, S. (2000) The value of customer loyalty and how you can capture it. Bain and Company/Mainspring Whitepaper, 17 March. Published at www.mainspring.com.

Rosenfield, J.R. (1998) The future of database marketing, *Direct Marketing*, 60(10), 28–31.

Sargeant, A. and West, D. (2001) *Direct and Interactive Marketing*. Oxford University Press, Oxford.

Sharma, A., and Sheth, J. (2004) Web-based marketing: the coming revolution in marketing thought and strategy, *Journal of Business Research*, 57(7), 696–702.

Shaw, R. (1996) How to transform marketing through IT, *Management Today*, Special report.

Smith, P.R. and Chaffey, D. (2005) *E-Marketing Excellence: at the Heart of Business*, 2nd edn. Butterworth-Heinemann, Oxford.

Sterne, J. (1999) *World Wide Web Marketing*, 2nd edn. Wiley, New York.

Stone, M., Abbott, J. and Buttle, F. (2001) Integrating customer data into CRM strategy. In B. Foss and M. Stone (eds) *Successful Customer Relationship Marketing*. Wiley, Chichester.

van Duyne, D., Landay, J. and Hong, J. (2003) *The Design of Sites. Patterns, Principles, and Processes for Crafting a Customer-centered Web Experience*. Addison-Wesley, Reading, MA.

Wolfe, D.B. (1998) Developmental relationship marketing: connecting messages with mind, an empathetic marketing system, *Journal of Consumer Marketing*, 15(5), 449–67.

## Further reading

Chaffey, D. (2003) *Total E-mail Marketing*. Butterworth-Heinemann, Elsevier, Oxford. A detailed, practical guide to permission-based e-mail marketing.

Peppers, D., Rogers, M. and Dorf, B. (1999) Is your company ready for one-to-one marketing? *Harvard Business Review*, January–February, 3–12. A fairly detailed summary of the IDIC approach.

Reichheld, F. and Schefter, P. (2000) E-loyalty, your secret weapon, *Harvard Business Review*, July–August, 105–13. An excellent review of the importance of achieving online loyalty and approaches to achieving it.

Tapp, A. (2005) *Principles of Direct and Database Marketing*, 3rd edn. Financial Times/Prentice Hall, Harlow. A well-structured guide to best practice in direct and interactive marketing.

## Web links

- **ClickZ** (www.clickz.com). An excellent collection of articles on online marketing communications. US-focused. Relevant section for this chapter: CRM strategies.

- **CRM Today** (www.crm2day.com). A portal with articles about the practical aspects of deploying CRM technology.

- **Database Marketing Institute** (www.dbmarketing.com). Useful collection of articles on best practice.

- **Jim Novo** (www.jimnovo.com). A site by a US consultant that has a lot of detail on techniques to profile and target customers online.

- **MyCustomer** (www.mycustomer.com). Articles about the principles and technology of customer relationship management.

- **Net Promoter Score blog** (http://netpromoter.typepad.com/fred_reichheld). Multi-author blog and forum discussing the practicalities of implementing NPS.

- **Peppers and Rogers One-to-One marketing website** (www.1to1.com). A site containing a lot of information on the techniques and tools of relationship marketing.

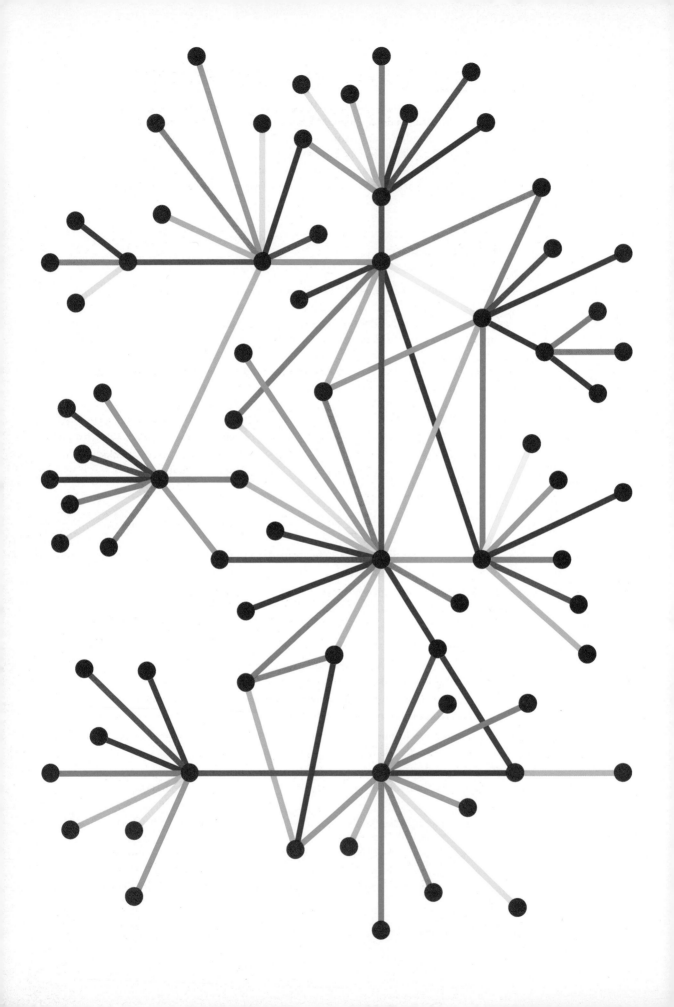

# Part 3

# Internet marketing: implementation and practice

In Part 3 particular issues of the execution of an Internet marketing strategy are described, including development of a website and ensuring a quality customer experience (Chapter 7), marketing communications to promote a site (Chapters 8 and 9) and the mainte-nance and evaluation of an online presence (Chapter 10). In Chapters 11 and 12, specific examples are given of how business-to-consumer and business-to-business companies are using the Internet.

## 7 Delivering the online customer experience p. 386

- Planning website design and build
- Initiation of the website project
- Researching site users' requirements
- Designing the user experience
- Development and testing of content
- Online retail merchandising
- Promoting the site
- Service quality

## 8 Campaign planning for digital media p. 445

- The characteristics of digital media
- Step 1. Goal setting and tracking for interactive marketing communications
- Step 2. Campaign insight
- Step 3. Segmentation and targeting
- Step 4. Offer, message development and creative
- Step 5. Budgeting and selecting the digital media mix
- Step 6. Integration into overall media schedule or plan

## 9 Marketing communications using digital media channels p. 502

1 Search engine marketing
2 Online public relations
3 Online partnerships including affiliate marketing
4 Interactive display advertising
5 Opt-in e-mail marketing and mobile text messaging
6 Viral and electronic word-of-mouth marketing
7 Offline promotion techniques

**10**

## Evaluation and improvement of digital channel performance p. 575

- Performance management for digital channels
- The maintenance process
- Responsibilities in website maintenance

**11**

## Business-to-consumer Internet marketing p. 618

- The consumer perspective: online consumer behaviour
- The retail perspective: e-retailing
- Implications for e-retail marketing strategy

**12**

## Business-to-business Internet marketing p. 648

- B2B trading environments and electronic marketplaces
- Online marketing efficiency gains
- Analysing the factors which influence the adoption of Internet technologies
- Digital marketing strategies

# 7

# Delivering the online customer experience

## Learning objectives

After reading this chapter, the reader should be able to:

● Describe the different stages involved in creating a new site or re-launching an existing site
● Describe the design elements that contribute to effective website content
● Define the factors that are combined to deliver an effective online customer experience

## Questions for marketers

Key questions for marketing managers related to this chapter are:

● Which activities are involved in building a new site or updating an existing site?
● What are the key factors of online service quality and site design that will encourage repeat visitors?
● Which techniques can I use to determine visitors' requirements?
● Which forms of buyer behaviour do consumers exhibit online?
● What are the accepted standards of site design needed for an effective site?

## Links to other chapters

Related chapters are:

● Chapters 4 and 5, which describe the development of the strategy and tactics that inform the design of the website
● Chapters 8 and 9, which describes approaches to promoting websites
● Chapter 10, which describes the analysis of a site and the maintenance of a site once it is created

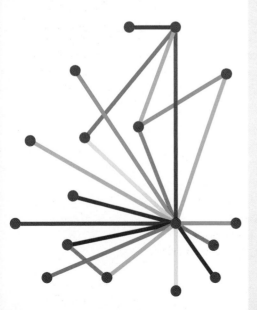

## Introduction

Developing the capability to create and maintain an effective online presence through a website is a key part of Internet marketing. 'Effective' means that the website and related communications must deliver relevance to its audience, whether this is through news content for a portal, product and service information for a business-to-business site, or relevant products and offers for an e-commerce site. At the same time, 'effective' means the website must deliver results for the company.

However, delivering relevant content for the audience is only part of the story. Interacting with web content is not a static experience, it is an interactive one. So Internet marketers also have to work hard to develop consumer trust and deliver a great experience for their audience. In their book *Managing the Customer Experience*, Shaun Smith and Joe Wheeler (2002) suggest that companies should ask afresh 'what experience must we provide to meet the needs and expectations of customers?' They note that some companies use online channels to replicate existing services, whereas others have extended the experience online. In Chapter 5, in the section on the contribution of branding as part of the Product element of the mix, we explained how it is important to provide a promise of what the online representation of the brand will deliver to customers. The concept of online brand promise is closely related to that of delivering online customer experience. In this chapter, we will explore different practical actions that companies can take to create and maintain satisfactory online experiences. An indication of the effort required to produce a customer-centric online presence is given by Alison Lancaster, at the time the head of marketing and catalogues at John Lewis Direct and currently marketing director at Charles Tyrrwhit (www.ctshirts.co.uk) who says:

**Online customer experience**
The combination of rational and emotional factors of using a company's online services that influences customers' perceptions of a brand online.

> A good site should always begin with the user. Understand who the customer is, how they use the channel to shop, and understand how the marketplace works in that category. This includes understanding who your competitors are and how they operate online. You need continuous research, feedback and usability testing to continue to monitor and evolve the customer experience online. Customers want convenience and ease of ordering. They want a site that is quick to download, well-structured and easy to navigate.

You can see that creating effective online experiences is a challenge since there are many practical issues to consider, which we present in Figure 7.1. This is based on a diagram by de Chernatony (2001) who suggested that delivering the online experience promised by a brand requires delivering rational values, emotional values and promised experience (based on rational and emotional values). The factors that influence the online customer experience can be presented in a pyramid form of success factors as is shown in Figure 7.1 (the different success factors reflect current best-practice and differ from those of de Chernatony). The diagram also highlights the importance of delivering service quality online, as has been indicated by Trocchia and Janda (2003). More recently, Christodoulides *et al.* (2006) have tested the importance of a range of indicators of online brand equity for online retail and service companies. This analysis was performed across these five dimensions of brand equity assessed by asking the questions below – they provide an excellent framework which can be applied to assess and benchmark the quality of brand experience for different types of website:

1 **Emotional connection**
   *Q1:* I feel related to the type of people who are [X]'s customers
   *Q2:* I feel as though [X] actually cares about me
   *Q3:* I feel as though [X] really understands me
2 **Online experience**
   *Q4:* [X]'s website provides easy-to-follow search paths
   *Q5:* I never feel lost when navigating through [X]'s website
   *Q6:* I was able to obtain the information I wanted without any delay

3 **Responsive service nature**

*Q7:* [X] is willing and ready to respond to customer needs

*Q8:* [X]'s website gives visitors the opportunity to 'talk back' to [X]

4 **Trust**

*Q9:* I trust [X] to keep my personal information safe

*Q10:* I feel safe in my transactions with [X]

5 **Fulfilment**

*Q11:* I got what I ordered from [X]'s website

*Q12:* The product was delivered by the time promised by [X]

**Web merchandising**

The aims of web merchandising are to maximise the sales potential of an online store for each visitor. This means connecting the right products, with the right offer to the right visitor, and remembering that the online store is part of a broader experience including online and offline advertising, in-store visits, customer service and delivery.

Figure 7.1 incorporates many of the factors that are relevant for a transactional e-retail site such as price and promotions which together form **web merchandising** (see the end of the chapter), but you can see that many of the rational and emotional values are important to any website. Some of the terms such as 'usability' and 'accessibility' (which are delivered through an effective website design) you may not be familiar with, but these will all be explained later in this chapter.

In Figure 7.1 these factors are all associated with using the website, but the online customer experience extends beyond this, and Internet marketing should also consider these issues:

- ease of locating the site through search engines (Chapter 8)
- services provided by partners online on other websites

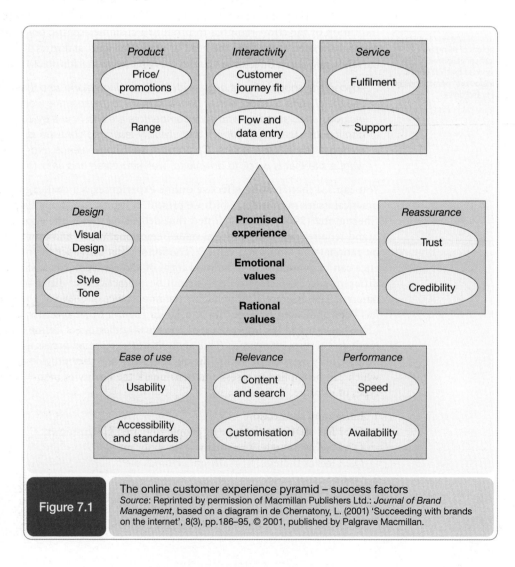

**Figure 7.1**   The online customer experience pyramid – success factors
*Source*: Reprinted by permission of Macmillan Publishers Ltd.: *Journal of Brand Management*, based on a diagram in de Chernatony, L. (2001) 'Succeeding with brands on the internet', 8(3), pp.186–95, © 2001, published by Palgrave Macmillan.

- quality of outbound communications such as e-newsletters
- quality of processing inbound e-mail communications from customers
- integration with offline communications.

Alternative frameworks, such as WEBQUAL and E-SERVQUAL, for assessing website effectiveness are covered in the section on service quality.

We start the chapter by considering how we create a website to deliver appropriate rational and emotional values since website design is a core part of creating the online customer experience. We also look at the stages in managing a project to improve the customer experience. Our coverage on website design is integrated with consideration of researching online buyer behaviour since an appropriate experience can only be delivered if it is consistent with customer behaviour, needs and wants. We then go on to review delivery of service quality online. This includes aspects such as speed and availability of the site itself which support the rational values, and also fulfilment and support which are a core part of the promised experience.

---

| Digital marketing in practice | The EConsultancy interview |

### Steve Nicholas, Assistant Director of E-commerce, Guess

#### Overview and main concepts covered

Steve talks about the challenges of multichannel retailing, especially for a well-known global brand in the fashion sector and one that has both wholesale and retail businesses to think about.

#### The interview

**Q: Can you summarise where Guess is in terms of multichannel retail?**

*Steve Nicholas*: In terms of multichannel, we're really in a good place from a merchandising and inventory perspective, because of the way we are set up.

We're set up with virtual inventory that is tied to our e-commerce site and retail stores, so we get an initial allocation that's strictly for e-commerce and can pull from a reserve in our North American warehouse.

The warehouse ships out about 80% of its merchandise to the stores and holds back around 20% for replenishment. E-commerce can pull from that 20% for hot selling items and quickly push out to our stores any not-so-hot selling items that may have been included in the initial e-commerce-only allocation.

In our US stores, we also have a store portal or merchandise locator, which store personnel can use to order from the website in the store. If a store does not have a particular size or colour, we can accommodate that customer's order through the e-commerce site, from the store register.

So in terms of inventory, we're in a solid position to accommodate the customer from a multichannel perspective.

From a broader, assortment perspective, we have a debate going on about whether the e-commerce site should represent 'Guess – the brand' or 'Guess – the retail stores'.

If you go to Guess.com and want to buy shoes, do you expect to see all the shoes that Guess as a company markets through its wholesale, licensee and retail businesses or just the shoes we are currently selling in our retail stores? It's a question of strategy really.

**Q: How does that affect how you market products online? Have you set up your site primarily as a place for consumers to research products, before buying in-stores?**

*Steve Nicholas*: Sure. Our website is a shop window for the latest and greatest products that we have available in our North American retail stores.

We use a company called Foresee Results, which creates custom online visitor surveys and matches up the data with the American Consumer Satisfaction Index to compare our visitors' satisfaction with that of the satisfaction of visitors to other websites. We continually rank near the top in terms of multichannel satisfaction scores.

From the surveys, we have visibility – we know that 69% of the people browsing on our site have made two or more purchases in our stores during the last year and 37% have made five or more. They view our site as an online catalogue to see what the new items are, and then go to the store to try it on and purchase.

**Q: Have you found affiliate marketing and other performance-based online marketing techniques difficult to reconcile with your branding aims?**

*Steve Nicholas*: We've just ventured into the affiliate world, launching an affiliate programme this summer. It's a bit too early to speak about the results from that, but it's a huge branding challenge for us.

Guess is such a well-known brand and we have to be very selective when picking our affiliate partners. We don't want the Guess name appearing just anywhere on the internet.

We are keeping it to affiliates that we feel are brand-appropriate and are covering the right demographic. We could be less selective, of course – picking affiliate partners and getting short-term incremental sales, but only at the expense, we feel, of long-term company success.

We're using them for traffic more than anything – and making sure we protect the brand always.

We have a Guess Factory division and e-commerce site and we are being less selective with affiliate partners for that.

**Q: You've yet to add transactional functionality to your UK and European sites. Is there any plan to?**

*Steve Nicholas*: At some point, yes. As a company, we have moved in the last few years from a wholesaler to a global retailer with a wholesale operation as well. So it's all part and parcel of that.

The relationships and infrastructure are not yet ready for us to sell online in the UK or other countries. That's not to say it won't happen in the next few years – it's just getting the structure right. We are looking at the opportunities.

**Q: We noticed you were running a free shipping offer on gbyguess.com. Could you talk through the financial thinking behind that?**

*Steve Nicholas*: On our websites, we don't really offer discounts or promote sale items – that's because we want to elevate the brand. Free shipping really becomes the only way for us to offer a discount, in a way.

We find that it really does work, and all the research we see suggests that it's the main thing customers want and that it really drives sales. Customers respond to it time and again. Of course, the other school of thought is that for many years customers have been expected to pay shipping, even with catalogue retailing, so why not turn it into a profit centre whenever you can? Everything is a balancing act.

We've done tests and found that our customers often respond better to free shipping than a discount offer – even if you give them percentage discounts much larger than the actual value of the free shipping.

**Q: You use Flash quite extensively on your site. Is it a must in the fashion sector, despite usability/accessibility issues?**

*Steve Nicholas*: It's another ongoing debate. There are sites that are fun to shop on and are interactive, but they aren't necessarily the best to shop on. More and more apparel e-commerce sites are definitely adding interactive elements.

**Q: Why don't you display shipping costs and payment options on the product listing page? If people have to visit the checkout to see this information then isn't it artificially 'boosting' dropout rates?**

*Steve Nicholas*: We've actually found that not doing that is unfavourable. Some decisions are more guided by branding and aesthetics than 'shop-ability'.

**Q: You keep items in the basket across multiple visits. What observations do you have on this as a driver of sales?**

*Steve Nicholas*: It is a deliberate ploy and a best practice, although I'm afraid I don't have the results to share as we have never conducted tests with a control group to truly understand the effects.

*Source*: http://www.e-consultancy.com/news-blog/newsletter/3415/steve-nicholas-assistant-director-of-e—commerce-at-guess.html

## Planning website design and build

In the past, it has been a common mistake among those creating a new website for the first time, to 'dive in' and start creative design and content creation without sufficient forward planning. Planning is necessary since design of a site must occur before creation of web pages – to ensure a good-quality site that does not need reworking at a later stage. The design process (Figure 7.2) involves analysing the needs of owners and users of a site and then deciding on the best way to build the site to fulfil these needs. Without a structured plan and careful design costly reworking is inevitable, as the first version of a site will not achieve the needs of the end-users or the business.

Of the stages shown in Figure 7.2, those of market research and design are described in most detail in this chapter since the nature of the website content is, of course, vital in providing a satisfactory experience for the customer which leads to repeat visits. Testing and promotion of the website are described in subsequent chapters. An alternative model can be found in a practical 'Internet marketing framework' presented by Ong (1995) and summarised by Morgan (1996).

The process of website development summarised in Figure 7.2 is idealised because, for efficiency, many of these activities have to occur in parallel. Figure 7.3 gives an indication of the relationship between these tasks, and how long they may take, for a typical website project. We will explain some of the specialist design terminology later in this chapter. The content planning and development stages overlap in that HTML and graphics development are necessary to produce the prototypes. As a consequence, some development has to occur while analysis and design are under way. The main development tasks which need to be scheduled as part of the planning process are as follows:

1 *Pre-development tasks.* For a new site, these include domain name registration and deciding on the company (ISP) to host the website. They also include preparing a brief setting out the aims and objectives of the site, and then – if it is intended to outsource the site – presenting the brief to rival agencies to bid for and pitch their offering.

2   *Analysis and design.* This is the detailed analysis and design of the site, and includes clarification of business objectives, market research to identify the audience and typical customer personas and user journeys and their needs, defining the information architecture of different content types and prototyping different functional and visual designs to support the brand.

3   *Content development and testing.* Writing the HTML pages, producing the graphics, database integration, usability and performance testing.

4   *Publishing or launching the site.* This is a relatively short stage.

5   *Pre-launch promotion or communications.* Search engine registration and optimisation is most important for new sites. Although search engines can readily index a new site, some place a penalty on new sites (sometimes known as 'the Google sandbox effect'), where the site is effectively on trial until is established. Briefing the PR company to publicise the launch is another example of pre-launch promotion.

6   *Ongoing promotion.* The schedule should also allow for promotion after site launch. This might involve structured discount promotions on the site, or competitions which are planned in advance. Many now consider search engine optimisation and pay-per-click marketing (Chapter 9) as a continuous process, and will often employ a third party to help achieve this.

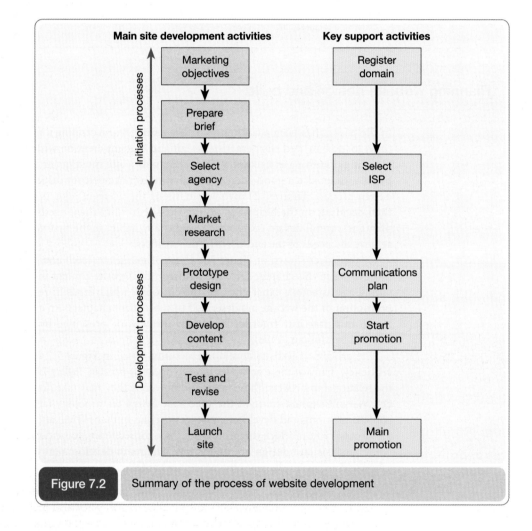

| Figure 7.2 | Summary of the process of website development |

| ID | Task name | Duration | Start |
|----|-----------|----------|-------|
| 1 | **Phase 1 - Scoping and planning** | **7 days** | **Fri 10/10/05** |
| 2 | Review documentation | 2 days | Fri 14/10/05 |
| 3 | Meet to agree requirements | 1 day | Wed 19/10/05 |
| 4 | Define and agree page template | 2 days | Thu 20/10/05 |
| 5 | Agree page template requirements | 0 days | Mon 24/10/05 |
| 6 | **Phase 2 - Persona development** | **9 days** | **Thu 20/10/05** |
| 7 | Set objectives and develop persona | 6 days | Thu 20/10/05 |
| 8 | Feedback and sign off | 3 days | Fri 28/10/05 |
| 9 | Agreed personas and scenarios | 0 days | Tue 01/11/05 |
| 10 | **Phase 3 - Brand design** | **23 days** | **Thu 20/10/05** |
| 11 | Initial brand design | 10 days | Thu 20/10/05 |
| 12 | Usability brand design | 10 days | Tue 01/11/05 |
| 13 | Revise brand design | 5 days | Tue 15/11/05 |
| 14 | Agreed brand design | 0 days | Mon 21/11/05 |
| 15 | **Phase 4 - Page layout/detailed design** | **64 days** | **Thu 03/11/05** |
| 16 | Refine wireframes | 0 days | Thu 03/11/05 |
| 17 | Usability wireframes | 4 days | Fri 11/11/05 |
| 18 | Create/revise page design | 40 days | Thu 17/11/05 |
| 19 | Agreed page design - Brand 1 | 0 days | Mon 28/11/05 |
| 20 | Agreed page design - Brand 2 | 0 days | Wed 14/12/05 |
| 21 | Agreed page design - Brand 3 | 0 days | Mon 16/01/06 |
| 22 | Agreed page design - Brand 4 | 0 days | Wed 01/02/06 |
| 23 | **Phase 5 - Page creation and delivery** | **58 days** | **Tue 29/11/05** |
| 24 | Brand 1 - Page creation and delivery | 12 days | Tue 29/11/05 |
| 25 | Brand 2 - Page creation and delivery | 12 days | Wed 14/12/05 |
| 26 | Brand 3 - Page creation and delivery | 12 days | Mon 16/01/06 |
| 27 | Brand 4 - Page creation and delivery | 12 days | Wed 01/02/06 |

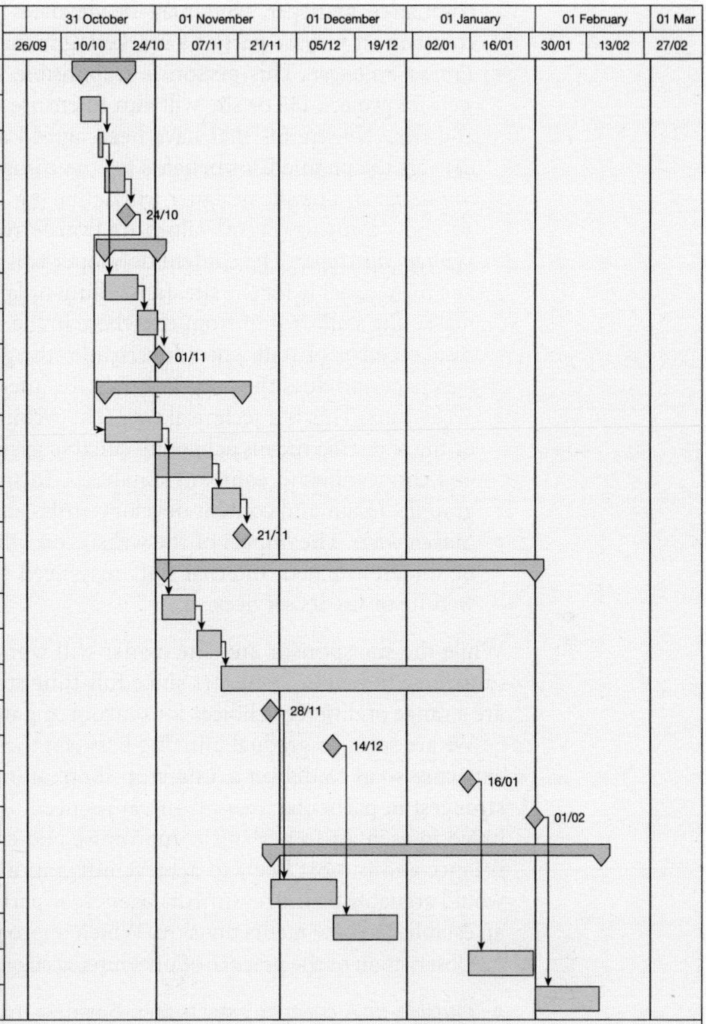

Project: Project Plan
Date: Fri 30/09/05

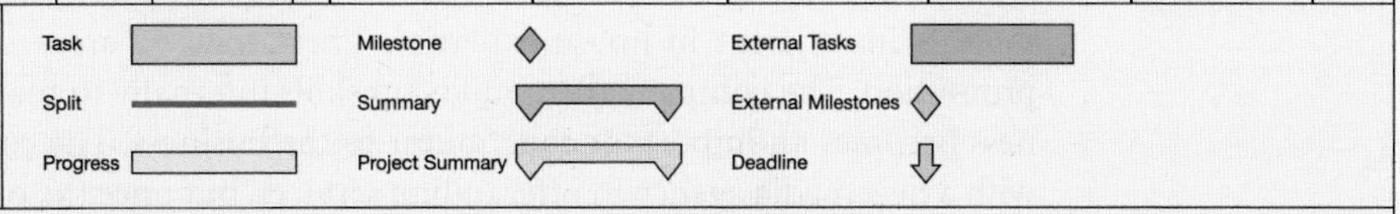

Legend: Task, Split, Progress, Milestone, Summary, Project Summary, External Tasks, External Milestones, Deadline

Page 1

**Figure 7.3**    Example of website development

## Who is involved in a website project?

The success of a website is dependent on the range of people involved in its development, and how well they work as a team. Typical profiles of team members follow:

- *Site sponsors.* These will be senior managers who will effectively be paying for the system. They will understand the strategic benefits of the system and will be keen that the site is implemented successfully to achieve the objectives they have set. Sponsors will also aim to encourage staff by means of their own enthusiasm and will stress why the introduction of the system is important to the business and its workers. This will help overcome any barriers to introduction of the website.

- *Site owner.* 'Ownership' will typically be the responsibility of a marketing manager or e-commerce manager, who may be devoted full-time to overseeing the site in a large company; it may be part of a marketing manager's remit in a smaller company.
- *Project manager.* This person is responsible for the planning and co-ordination of the website project. He or she will aim to ensure that the site is developed within the budget and time constraints that have been agreed at the start of the project, and that the site delivers the planned-for benefits for the company and its customers.
- *Site designer.* The site designer will define the 'look and feel' of the site, including its layout and how company brand values are transferred to the web.
- *Content developer.* The content developer will write the copy for the website and convert it to a form suitable for the site. In medium or large companies this role may be split between marketing staff or staff from elsewhere in the organisation who write the copy and a technical member of staff who converts it to the graphics and HTML documents forming the web page and does the programming for interactive content.
- *Webmaster.* This is a technical role. The webmaster is responsible for ensuring the quality of the site. This means achieving suitable availability, speed, working links between pages and connections to company databases. In small companies the webmaster may take on graphic design and content developer roles also.
- *Stakeholders.* The impact of the website on other members of the organisation should not be underestimated. Internal staff may need to refer to some of the information on the website or use its services.

While the site sponsor and site owner will work within the company, many organisations outsource the other resources since full-time staff cannot be justified in these roles. There are a range of different choices for outsourcing which are summarised in Activity 7.1.

We are seeing a gradual blurring between these different types of supplier as they recruit expertise so as to deliver a 'one-stop shop' or 'full-service agency', but they still tend to be strongest in particular areas. Companies need to decide whether to partner with the best of breed in each, or to perhaps compromise and choose the one-stop shop that gives the best balance and is most likely to achieve integration across different marketing activities – this would arguably be the new media agency, or perhaps a traditional marketing agency that has an established new media division. Which approach do you think is best?

Observation of the practice of outsourcing suggests that two conflicting patterns are evident:

- *Outside-in.* A company starts an e-business initiative by outsourcing some activities where there is insufficient in-house expertise. These may be areas such as strategy or online promotion. The company then builds up skills internally to manage these areas as e-business becomes an important contributor to the business. The company initially partnered with a new media agency to offer online services, but once the online contribution to sales exceeded 20% the management of e-commerce was taken inside. The new media agency was, however, retained for strategy guidance. An outside-in approach will probably be driven by the need to reduce the costs of outsourcing, poor delivery of services by the supplier or simply a need to concentrate a strategic core resource in-house.
- *Inside-out.* A company starts to implement e-business using existing resources within the IT department and marketing department in conjunction with recruitment of new media staff. They may then find that there are problems in developing a site that meets customers' needs or in building traffic to the site. At this point they may turn to outsourcing to solve the problems.

These approaches are not mutually exclusive and an outside-in approach may be used for some e-commerce functions, such as content development, while an inside-out approach is used for other functions such as site promotion. It can also be suggested that these approaches are not planned – they are simply a response to prevailing conditions. However, in order to cost e-business and manage it as a strategic asset it can be argued that the e-business manager should have a long-term picture of which functions to outsource and when to bring them in-house.

| Activity 7.1 | Options for outsourcing different e-marketing activities |
|---|---|

**Purpose**

To highlight the outsourcing available for e-business implementation and to gain an appreciation of how to choose suppliers.

**Activity**

A B2C company is trying to decide which of its e-business activities it should outsource. Select a single supplier that you think can best deliver each of these services indicated in Table 7.1. Justify your decision.

| Table 7.1 | Options for outsourcing different e-business activities |
|---|---|

| E-marketing function | Traditional marketing agency | Digital marketing agency | ISP or traditional IT supplier | Management consultants |
|---|---|---|---|---|
| 1  Strategy | | | | |
| 2  Design | | | | |
| 3  Content and service development | | | | |
| 4  Online promotion | | | | |
| 5  Offline promotion | | | | |
| 6  Infrastructure | | | | |

## Website prototyping and agile software development

**Prototype**

A preliminary version of part, or a framework of all, of a website, which can be reviewed by its target audience or the marketing team. Prototyping is an iterative process in which website users suggest modifications before further prototypes and the final version of the site are developed.

**Prototypes** are trial versions of a website that are gradually refined through an iterative process to become closer to the final version. Initial prototypes or 'mockups' may simply be paper prototypes, perhaps of a 'wireframe' or screen layout. These may then be extended to include some visuals of key static pages using a tool such as Adobe Photoshop. Finally, working prototypes will be produced as HTML code is developed. The idea is that the design agency or development team and the marketing staff who commissioned the work can review and comment on prototypes, and changes can then be made to the site to incorporate these comments. Prototyping should result in a more effective final site which can be developed more rapidly than a more traditional approach with a long period of requirements determination.

Each iteration of the prototype typically passes through the stages shown in Figure 7.4, which are:

1 *Analysis.* Understanding the requirements of the audience of the site and the requirements of the business, defined by business and marketing strategy (and comments input from previous prototypes).
2 *Design.* Specifying different features of the site that will fulfil the requirements of the users and the business as identified during analysis.
3 *Develop.* The creation of the web pages and the dynamic content of the website.
4 *Test and review.* Structured checks are conducted to ensure that different aspects of the site meet the original requirements and work correctly.

**Hard launch**

A site is launched once fully complete with full promotional effort.

**Soft launch**

A trial version of a site is launched with limited publicity.

When using the prototyping approach for a website, a company has to decide whether to implement the complete version of the website before making it available to its target audience (**hard launch**) or to make available a more limited version of the site (**soft launch**). If it is necessary to establish a presence rapidly, the second approach could be used. This also has the benefit that feedback can be solicited from users and incorporated into later versions.

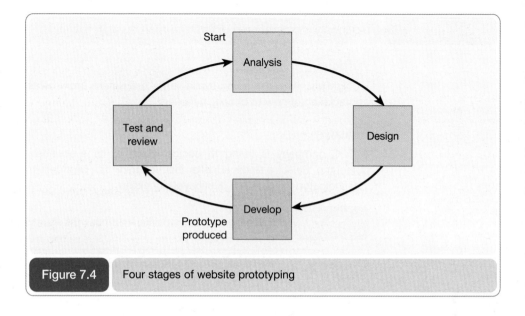

| Figure 7.4 | Four stages of website prototyping |

## Agile software development

**Agile development**

An iterative approach to developing software and website functionality with the emphasis on face-to-face communications to elicit, define and test requirements. Each iteration is effectively a mini-software project including stages of planning, requirements analysis, design, coding, testing and documentation.

**Scrum**

Scrum is a methodology that supports agile software development based on 15–30 day sprints to implement features from a product backlog. 'Scrum' refers to a daily project status meeting during the sprint.

Today, the concept of prototyping has been extended across the whole lifecycle for developing website functionality or software applications where it is known as **agile software development**. The goal of agile development is to be able to create stable releases more frequently than traditional development methodologies, i.e. new functionality will be introduced through several releases each month rather than a more significant release every few weeks, months or even years. The approach is sometimes known as 'permanent beta'. Another difference with agile development is the emphasis on face-to-face communication to define requirements rather than detailed requirements specifications.

**Scrum** is a methodology that supports agile software development. Scrum involves stakeholders including the *scrum master* who is effectively a project manager, the *product owner* who represents the stakeholders such as the business owners and customers and the *scrum team* which includes the developers.

Scrum is based on focused sprints of a 15–30 day period where the team creates an increment of potentially releasable software. Potential functionality for each sprint are agreed at a *sprint planning meeting* from the *product backlog*, a prioritised set of high-level requirements. The sprint planning meeting is itself iterative with the product owner stating their requirements from the product backlog and the technical team then determining how much of this they can commit to complete during the forthcoming sprint. The term 'scrum' refers to a daily project status meeting during the sprint. See http://www.softhouse.se/hploads/scrum_eng_webb.pdf for an overview of the process.

The principles of agile development are encapsulated in the *Agile Manifesto* (http://agile-manifesto.org/) which was agreed in 2001 by proponents of previous rapid development methodologies including the Dynamic Systems Development Methodology and Extreme Programming. The Agile Manifesto is useful in illustrating the principles of agile programming it contrasts with traditional approaches. The text of the manifesto is:

*We are uncovering better ways of developing software by doing it and helping others do it. Through this work we have come to value:*

- *Individuals and interactions over processes and tools*
- *Working software over comprehensive documentation*
- *Customer collaboration over contract negotiation*
- *Responding to change over following a plan*

*That is, while there is value in the items on the right, we value the items on the left more.*

# Initiation of the website project

**Initiation of the website project**
This phase of the project should involve a structured review of the costs and benefits of developing a website (or making a major revision to an existing website). A successful outcome to initiation will be a decision to proceed with the site development phase, with an agreed budget and target completion date.

Before the analysis, design and creation of the website, all major projects will have an initial phase in which the aims and objectives of the website are reviewed, to assess whether it is worthwhile investing in the website and to decide on the amount to invest. This is part of the strategic planning process described in Chapters 4 and 5. This provides a framework for the project that ensures:

- there is management and staff commitment to the project;
- objectives are clearly defined;
- the costs and benefits are reviewed in order that the appropriate amount of investment in the site occurs;
- the project will follow a structured path, with clearly identified responsibilities for different aspects such as project management, analysis, promotion and maintenance;
- the implementation phase will ensure that important aspects of the project, such as testing and promotion, are not skimped.

## Domain name registration

**Domain name registration**
The process of reserving a unique web address that can be used to refer to the company website, in the form of www.<company name>.com or www.<company name>.co.uk.

If the project involves a new site rather than an upgrade, it will be necessary to **register a new domain name**, more usually referred to as a 'web address' or 'uniform (or universal) resource locator' (URL).

Domain names are registered using an ISP or direct or hosting company through one of the domain name services, such as:

- *InterNIC* (www.internic.net). Registration for the .com, .org and .net domains.
- *Nominet* (www.nominet.org.uk). Registration for the .co.uk domain. All country-specific domains, such as .fr (France) or .de (Germany), have their own domain registration authority.
- *Nomination* (www.nomination.uk.com). An alternative registration service for the UK, allowing registration in the (uk.com) pseudo-domain.

The following guidelines should be borne in mind when registering domain names:

- *Register the domain name as early as possible.* This is necessary since the precedent in the emerging law is that the first company to register the name is the one that takes ownership if it has a valid claim to ownership.
- *Register multiple domain names* if this helps the potential audience to find the site. For example, British Midland may register its name as www.britishmidland.com and www.britishmidland.co.uk.
- *Use the potential of non-company brand names* to help promote a product. For example, a 1998 traditional media campaign for British Midland used www.iflybritishmidland.com as a memorable address to help users find its site.

The law related to the control of domain name purchase is covered in Chapter 3.

## Selecting an Internet service provider

**Internet service provider**
Company that provides home or business users with a connection to access the Internet. It can also host websites or provide a link from web servers to allow other companies and consumers access to a corporate website.

Selecting the right partner to host a website is an important decision since the quality of service provided will directly impact on the quality of service delivered to a company's customers. The partner that hosts the content will usually be an **Internet service provider (ISP)** or a specialist hosting provider such as rackspace (ww.rackspace.com) for the majority of small and medium companies, but for larger companies the web server used to host the content may be inside the company and managed by the company's IT department.

The quality of service of hosted content is essentially dependent on two factors: the performance of the website and its availability.

## The performance of the website

The important measure in relation to performance is the speed with which a web page is delivered to users from the time it is requested by clicking on a hyperlink (see Table 7.2 for examples). The length of time is dependent on a number of factors, some of which cannot be controlled (such as the number of users accessing the Internet), but primarily depends on the **bandwidth** of the ISP's connection to the Internet and the performance of the web server hardware and software. It also depends on the 'page weight' of the site's pages measured in kilobytes (which is dependent on the number and complexity of images and animations). Table 7.2 shows that the top five sites with the fastest download speeds have a much smaller page size compared with the slower sites from 95 to 100. However, viewing these slower sites over a broadband connection shows that this is perhaps less of an issue than in the days when the majority, rather than the minority, were dial-up Internet users.

**Bandwidth**
Indicates the speed at which data are transferred using a particular network medium. It is measured in bits per second (bps).

| Table 7.2 | Variation in download speed (across a 56.6 kbps modem) and page size for the highest five and lowest six of the top 100 UK sites for the week starting 6 October 2005 |
|---|---|

| Website | | Average download speed | Page size |
|---|---|---|---|
| 1 | Thomas Cook | 4.65 sec | 18.46 kb |
| 2 | British Airways | 5.15 sec | 23.46 kb |
| 3 | Next On-Line Shopping | 5.64 sec | 26.90 kb |
| 4 | EasyJet | 6.09 sec | 27.88 kb |
| 5 | NTL | 6.66 sec | 29.77 kb |
| 95 | Nokia UK | 37.60 sec | 180.98 kb |
| 96 | The Salvation Army | 37.68 sec | 171.07 kb |
| 97 | Rail Track | 38.14 sec | 111.00 kb |
| 98 | workthing.com | 38.77 sec | 187.35 kb |
| 99 | Orange | 40.01 sec | 194.16 kb |
| 100 | FT.com | 44.39 sec | 211.55 kb |

*Source*: Site Confidence (www.siteconfidence.co.uk)

A major factor for a company to consider when choosing an ISP is whether the server is *dedicated* to one company or whether content from several companies is located on the same server. A dedicated server is best, but it will attract a premium price.

## The availability of the website

The availability of a website is an indication of how easy it is for a user to connect to it. In theory this figure should be 100 per cent but sometimes, for technical reasons such as failures in the server hardware or upgrades to software, the figure can drop substantially below this.

The extent of the problem of e-commerce service levels was indicated by *The Register* (2004) in an article titled 'Wobbly shopping carts blight UK e-commerce'. The research showed that failure of transactions once customers have decided to buy is often a problem. As the article said, 'UK e-commerce sites are slapping customers in the face, rather than shaking them by the hand. Turning consumers away once they have made a decision to buy is commercial suicide'. The research showed this level of problems:

- 20% of shopping carts did not function for 12 hours a month or more.
- 75% failed the standard service level availability of 99.9% uptime.
- 80% performed inconsistently with widely varying response times, time-outs and errors – leaving customers at best wondering what to do next and at worst unable to complete their purchases.

Similarly, SciVisum, a web-testing specialist, found that three-quarters of Internet marketing campaigns are impacted by website failures, with 14 per cent of failures so severe that they prevented the campaign meeting its objectives. The company surveyed marketing professionals from 100 UK-based organisations across the retail, financial, travel and online gaming sectors. More than a third of failures were rated as 'serious to severe', with many customers complaining or being unable to complete web transactions. These are often seen by marketers as technology issues which are owned by others in the business, but marketers need to ask the right questions. The SciVisum (2005) research showed that nearly two-thirds of marketing professionals did not know how many users who were making transactions their websites could support, despite an average transaction value of £50 to £100, so they were not able to factor this into campaign plans. Thirty-seven per cent could not put a monetary value on losses caused by customers abandoning web transactions. A quarter of organisations experienced website overloads and crashes as a direct result of a lack of communication between the two departments.

SciVisum recommends that companies do the following:

- Define the peak visitor throughput requirements for each customer journey on the site. For example, the site should be able to support at the same time: approximately 10 checkout journeys per second, 30 add-to-basket journeys per second, 5 registration journeys per second, 2 check-my-order-status journeys per second.
- Service-level agreement. More detailed technical requirements need to be agreed for each of the transaction stages. Home-page delivery time and server uptime are insufficiently detailed.
- Set up a monitoring programme that measures and reports on the agreed journeys 24/7.

## Researching site users' requirements

**Analysis phase**
The identification of the requirements of a website. Techniques to achieve this may include focus groups, questionnaires sent to existing customers or interviews with key accounts.

**Analysis** involves using different marketing research techniques to find out the needs of the site audience. These needs can then be used to drive the design and content of the website.

Analysis is not a 'one-off' exercise, but is likely to be repeated for each iteration of the prototype. Although analysis and design are separate activities, there tends to be considerable overlap between the two phases. In analysis we are seeking to answer the following types of 'who, what, why, how' questions:

- Who are the key audiences for the site?
- Why should they use the site (what will appeal to them)?
- What should the content of site be? Which services will be provided?
- How will the content of the site be structured (information architecture)?
- How will navigation around the site occur?
- What are the main marketing outcomes we want the site to deliver (registrations, leads, sales)?

**User-centred design**
A design approach which is based on research of user characteristics and needs.

To help answer these questions, web designers commonly use an approach known as **user-centred design** which uses a range of techniques to ensure the site meets user needs.

A structured approach to user-centred design is defined in the standard: *ISO 13407: Human-centred design processes for interactive systems*. This was published in 1999 and also covers software and hardware systems.

**Persuasion marketing**

Using design elements such as layout, copy and typography together with promotional messages to encourage site users to follow particular paths and specific actions rather than giving them complete choice in their navigation.

Within this design process, usability and accessibility are goals which we will now study further. It is generally agreed that website designers also need to add persuasion marketing into the design mix; to create a design that is not only easy to use, but also delivers results for the business. This approach is essential since usability, which will often lead to giving the user choice, may conflict with using a website to meet business objectives which will often need to persuade customers to register or buy a product. Most websites should not give total business choice in which sections they use but, as with any marketing communication, should influence the recipient of the communication to encourage them to take particular actions or follow particular paths. You can see that this concept of user-centred design is similar to the concept of customer orientation or customer-centricity which we have covered in preceding chapters.

Consultant Bryan Eisenberg of Future Now (www.futurenowinc.com) is an advocate of persuasion marketing alongside other design principles such as usability and accessibility. He says:

> during the wireframe and storyboard phase we ask three critical questions of every page a visitor will see:
>
> 1  What action needs to be taken?
> 2  Who needs to take that action?
> 3  How do we persuade that person to take the action we desire?

## Usability

**Usability**

An approach to website design intended to enable the completion of user tasks.

**Usability** is a concept that can be applied to the analysis and design for a range of products which defines how easy they are to use. The British Standard/ISO Standard (1999): *Human Centred design processes for interactive systems* defines usability as:

> the extent to which a product can be used by specified users to achieve specified goals with effectiveness, efficiency and satisfaction in a specified context of use.

You can see how the concept can be readily applied to website design – web visitors often have defined *goals* such as finding particular information or completing an action such as booking a flight or viewing an account balance.

In Jakob Nielsen's classic book *Designing Web Usability* (Nielsen, 2000b), he describes usability as follows:

> An engineering approach to website design to ensure the user interface of the site is learnable, memorable, error free, efficient and gives user satisfaction. It incorporates testing and evaluation to ensure the best use of navigation and links to access information in the shortest possible time. A companion process to information architecture.

**Expert review**

An analysis of an existing site or prototype by an experienced usability expert who will identify deficiencies and improvements to a site based on their knowledge of web design principles and best practice.

**Usability/user testing**

Representative users are observed performing representative tasks using a system.

In practice, usability involves two key project activities. Expert reviews are often performed at the beginning of a redesign project as a way of identifying problems with a previous design. Usability testing involves:

1  identifying representative users of the site (see, for example, Table 7.3) and identifying typical tasks;
2  asking them to perform specific tasks such as finding a product or completing an order;
3  observing what they do and how they succeed.

For a site to be successful, the user tasks or actions need to be completed:

- *effectively* – web usability specialists measure task completion; for example, only 3 out of 10 visitors to a website may be able to find a telephone number or other piece of information.
- *efficiently* – web usability specialists also measure how long it takes to complete a task onsite, or the number of clicks it takes.

Jakob Nielsen explains the imperative for usability best in his 'Usability 101' (www.useit.com/alertbox/20030825.html). He says:

> On the Web, usability is a necessary condition for survival. If a website is difficult to use, people leave. If the homepage fails to clearly state what a company offers and what users can do on the site, people leave. If users get lost on a website, they leave. If a website's information is hard to read or doesn't answer users' key questions, they leave. Note a pattern here?

For these reasons, Nielsen suggests that around 10% of a design project budget should be spent on usability, but often actual spend is significantly less.

Some would also extend usability to including testing of the visual or brand design of a site in focus groups, to assess how well consumers perceive it reflects the brand. Often, alternative visual designs are developed to identify those which are most appropriate.

| Table 7.3 | Different potential audiences for a website | |
|---|---|---|
| **Customers vary by** | **Staff** | **Third parties** |
| New or existing prospects | New or existing | New or existing |
| Size of prospect companies (e.g. small, medium or large) | Different departments<br>Sales staff for different markets | Suppliers<br>Distributors |
| Market type (e.g. different vertical markets) | Location (by country) | Investors<br>Media |
| Members of buying process (decision makers, influencers, buyers) | Students | |
| Familiarity (with using the web, the company, its products and services or its website) | | |

Additional website design research activities include the use of *personas* and *scenario-based design* as introduced in Chapter 2.

## Web accessibility

**Accessibility**
An approach to site design intended to accommodate site usage using different browsers and settings – particularly required by the visually impaired and visitors with other disabilities including motor control, learning difficulties and deaf users. Users whose first language is not English can also be assisted.

**Web accessibility** is another core requirement for websites. It is about allowing all users of a website to interact with it regardless of disabilities they may have, or the web browser or platform they are using to access the site. The visually impaired are the main audience that designing an accessible website can help. However, increased usage of mobile or wireless access devices such as personal digital assistants (PDAs) and **GPRS** or 3G phones also make consideration of accessibility important.

The following quote shows the importance of accessibility to a visually impaired user who uses a screen-reader which reads out the navigation options and content on a website.

> For me being online is everything. It's my hi-fi, it's my source of income, it's my supermarket, it's my telephone. It's my way in.

**General Packet Radio Services (GPRS)**
A standard offering mobile data transfer and WAP access approximately 5 to 10 times faster than traditional GSM access.

(Lynn Holdsworth, screen-reader user, web developer and programmer)
Source: RNIB

**Accessibility legislation**
Legislation intended to protect users of websites with disabilities including visual disability.

Remember, as we explained in Chapter 3, that many countries now have specific **accessibility legislation** to which website owners are subject. This is often contained within disability and discrimination acts. In the UK, the relevant act is the Disability and Discrimination Act (DDA) 1995. Recent amendments to the DDA make it unlawful to discriminate against disabled people in the way in which a company recruits and employs people, provides services or provides education. Providing services is the part of the law that applies to website design. Providing accessible websites is a requirement of Part II of the Disability and Discrimination Act published in 1999 and required by law from 2002. In the 2002 code of practice there is a legal requirement for websites to be accessible. This is most important for sites which provide a service; for example, the code of practice gives this example:

> *An airline company provides a flight reservation and booking service to the public on its website. This is a provision of a service and is subject to the Act.*

Although there is a moral imperative for accessibility, there is also a business imperative to encourage companies to make their websites accessible. The main arguments in favour of accessibility are:

- *Number of visually impaired people.* In many countries there are millions of visually impaired people varying from 'colour blind' to partially sighted to blind. The number of web users with other disabilities is also significant.
- *Number of users of less popular browsers or variation in screen display resolution.* Microsoft Internet Explorer is now the dominant browser, but there are less well-known browsers which have a loyal following among the visually impaired (for example, screen-readers and Lynx, a text-only browser) and early-adopters (for example, Mozilla Firefox, Safari and Opera). If a website does not display well in these browsers, then you may lose these audiences. Complete Activity 7.2 to review how much access has varied since this book was first published.
- *More visitors from natural listings of search engines.* Many of the techniques used to make sites more usable also assist in search engine optimisation. For example, clearer navigation, text alternatives for images and site maps can all help improve a site's position in the search engine rankings.
- *Legal requirements.* In many countries it is a legal requirement to make websites accessible. For example, the UK has a Disability Discrimination Act that requires this.

Note, the compilation in Table 7.4 is from a site with a large proportion of technical users researching web design issues, which accounts for the high proportion of Firefox and higher resolution screen users. Each site needs to use web analytics systems such as Google Analytics to review the usage of their site by visitors using access devices with different screen resolutions. This can help identify an acceptable minimum screen resolution (for example, 1024 × 768) and the usage levels and hence support needed for specific devices such as an Appel iPhone or Sony PSP.

Guidelines for creating accessible websites are produced by the governments of different countries and non-government organisations such as charities. Internet standards organisations, such as the World Wide Web Consortium, have been active in promoting guidelines for web accessibility through the Website Accessibility Initiative (see www.w3.org/WAI). This describes common accessibility problems such as:

> *images without alternative text; lack of alternative text for imagemap hot-spots; misleading use of structural elements on pages; uncaptioned audio or undescribed video; lack of alternative information for users who cannot access frames or scripts; tables that are difficult to decipher when linearised; or sites with poor colour contrast.*

A fuller checklist for acessibility compliance for website design and coding using HTML is available from the World Wide Web Consortium (www.w3.org/TR/WCAG10/_full-checklist.html).

| Activity 7.2 | Allowing for the range in access devices |

One of the benefits of accessibility requirements is that they help website owners and web agencies consider the variation in platforms used to access websites.

**Questions**

1 Update the compilation in Table 7.4 to the latest values using Onestat.com or other data from web analytics providers.

2 Explain the variations. Which browsers and screen resolutions do you think should be supported?

| Table 7.4 | The range in browsers and screen resolutions |

| Web browser popularity | | | Screen resolution popularity | | |
|---|---|---|---|---|---|
| 1 | Microsoft IE | 58.5% | 1 | Higher resolution | 26% |
| 2 | Mozilla Firefox | 31% | 2 | 1024 × 768 | 54% |
| 3 | Apple Safari | 1.7% | 3 | 800 × 600 | 14% |
| 4 | Netscape | 1.5% | 4 | 640 × 480 | 0% |
| 5 | Opera | 1.5% | 5 | Unknown | 6% |

*Source*: W3 Schools (http://www.w3schools.com/browsers/browsers_stats.asp, January 2007)

There are three different priority levels which it describes as follows:

- *Priority 1 (Level A)*. A web content developer must satisfy this checkpoint. Otherwise, one or more groups will find it impossible to access information in the document. Satisfying this checkpoint is a basic requirement for some groups to be able to use web documents.
- *Priority 2 (Level AA)*. A web content developer should satisfy this checkpoint. Otherwise, one or more groups will find it difficult to access information in the document. Satisfying this checkpoint will remove significant barriers to accessing web documents.
- *Priority 3 (Level AAA)*. A web content developer may address this checkpoint. Otherwise, one or more groups will find it somewhat difficult to access information in the document. Satisfying this checkpoint will improve access to web documents.

So, for many companies the standard is to meet Priority 1, and Priority 2 or 3 where practical.

Some of the most important Priority 1 elements are indicated by these 'quick tips' from the WAI:

**Alt tag**

Appears after an image tag and contains a phrase associated with that image. For example: ‹img src="logo.gif" alt="Company name, company products"/›.

- *Images* and *animations*: use **alt tags** to describe the function of each visual.
- *Image* maps: use the client-side map and text for hot spots.
- *Multimedia*: provide captioning and transcripts of audio, and descriptions of video.
- *Hypertext links*: use text that makes sense when read out of context for example, avoid 'click here'.
- *Page organisation*: use headings, lists and consistent structure. Use CSS for layout and style where possible.
- *Graphs* and *charts*: summarise or use the longdesc attribute.
- *Scripts*, *applets* and *plug-ins*: provide alternative content in case active features are inaccessible or unsupported.
- *Frames*: use the noframes element and meaningful titles.
- *Tables*: make line-by-line reading sensible. Summarise.
- *Check your work*. Validate: use tools, checklist, and guidelines at www.w3.org/TR/WCAG.

Figure 7.5 is an example of an accessible site which still meets brand and business objectives while supporting accessibility through resizing of screen resolution, text resizing and alternative image text.

## Localisation

**Localisation**
Tailoring of website information for individual countries.

A further aspect of customer-centricity for website design is the decision whether to include specific content for particular countries. This is referred to as 'localisation'. A site may need to support customers from a range of countries with:

- different product needs;
- language differences;
- cultural differences – this approach is also referred to as 'cultural adaptation'.

Localisation will address all these issues. It may be that products will be similar in different countries and localisation will simply involve converting the website to suit another country. However, in order to be effective this often needs more than translation, since different promotion concepts may be needed for different countries. Note that each company prioritises different countries according to the size of the market, and this priority then governs the amount of work it puts into localisation.

Singh and Pereira (2005) provide an evaluation framework for the level of localisation:

- *Standardised websites (not localised)*. A single site serves all customer segments (domestic and international).
- *Semi-localised websites*. A single site serves all customers; however, contact information about foreign subsidiaries is available for international customers. Many sites fall into this category.

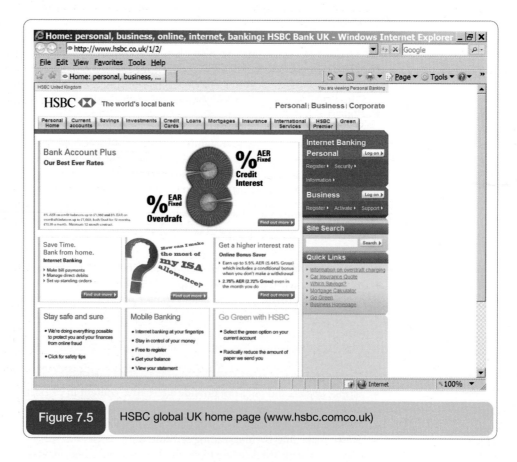

| Figure 7.5 | HSBC global UK home page (www.hsbc.comco.uk) |

- *Localised websites.* Country-specific websites with language translation for international customers, wherever relevant. 3M (www.3m.com) has adapted the websites for many countries to local language versions. It initially focused on the major websites.
- *Highly-localised websites.* Country-specific websites with language translation; they also include other localisation efforts in terms of time, date, zip code, currency formats, etc. Dell (www.dell.com) provides highly-localised websites.
- *Culturally customised websites.* Websites reflecting complete 'immersion' in the culture of target customer segments; as such, targeting a particular country may mean providing multiple websites for that country depending on the dominant cultures present. Durex (www.durex.com) is a good example of a culturally customised website.

Deciding on the degree of localisation is a difficult challenge for managers since while it has been established that local preferences are significant, it is often difficult to balance localisation costs against the likely increase or conversion rate through localisation. In a survey published in *Multilingual* (2008), localisation was seen as important with 88% of managers at multinational companies stating that localisation is a key issue and with 76% of them saying that it is important specifically for international customer satisfaction. Yet over half of these respondents also admitted that they allocate only between 1% and 5% of their overall budget for localisation.

An indication of the importance of localisation in different cultures has been completed by Nitish *et al.* (2006) for the German, Indian and Chinese cultures assessing localised websites in terms not only of content, but cultural values such as collectivism, individualism, uncertainty avoidance and masculinity. The survey suggests that without cultural adaptation, confidence or flow decreased so resulting in lower purchase intent.

A further aspect of localisation to be considered is search engine optimisation (SEO, see Chapter 9) since sites which have local language versions will be listed more prominently within the search engine results pages for local versions of the search engines. Many specialist companies have been created to help manage these content localisation issues for companies – for example, agency Web Certain maintains a forum advising on localisation (www.multilingual-seo.com).

One example of the effect of localisation on conversion rates is provided by MySpace CEO Mike Katz who stated in NMA (2008) that: 'All the 27 sites are localised, we don't believe that one size fits all. We know that from the first day we localise in any language, we triple our sign-ups on original users. In 2008, 45 million of the 130 million MySpace users were outside the US. New sites were planned for Russia, India, Poland and Korea, each requiring a local version of the MySpace model.

## Reviewing competitors' websites

Benchmarking of competitors' websites is vital in positioning a a website to compete effectively with competitors that already have websites. Given the importance of this activity, criteria for performing benchmarking have been described in Chapters 2 and 4.

Benchmarking should not only be based on the obvious tangible features of a website such as its ease of use and the impact of its design. Benchmarking criteria should include those that define the companies' marketing performance in the industry and those that are specific to web marketing as follows:

- *Financial performance* (available from About Us, investor relations and electronic copies of company reports) – this information is also available from intermediary sites such as finance information or share dealing sites such as Interactive Trader International (www.iii.com.uk) or Bloomberg (www.bloomberg.com) for major quoted companies.
- *Marketplace performance* – market share and sales trends and, significantly, the proportion of sales achieved through the Internet. This may not be available directly on the website, but may need the use of other online sources. For example, new entrant to European aviation easyJet (www.easyjet.com) achieved over two-thirds of its sales via the website and competitors needed to respond to this.

- *Business and revenue models* (see Chapter 5) – do these differ from other marketplace players?
- *Marketplace positioning* – the elements of the marketing mix covered in Chapter 5 including Product, Pricing and Place.
- *Marketing communications techniques* – is the customer value proposition of the site clear? Does the site support all stages of the buying decision from customers who are unfamiliar with the company through to existing customers? Are special promotions used on a monthly or periodic basis? Beyond the competitor's site, how do they promote their site? How do they make through use of intermediary sites to promote and deliver their services?
- *Services offered* – what is offered beyond brochureware? Is online purchase possible? What is the level of online customer support and how much technical information is available?
- *Implementation of services* – these are the practical features of site design that are described in this chapter, such as aesthetics, ease of use, personalisation, navigation, availability and speed.

A review of corporate websites suggests that, for most companies, the type of information that can be included on a website will be fairly similar. Many commentators, such as Sterne (2001), make the point that some sites miss out the basic information that someone who is unfamiliar with a company may want to know, such as:

- *Who are you?* 'About Us' is now a standard menu option.
- *What do you do?* What products or services are available?
- *Where do you do it?* Are the products and services available internationally?

## Designing the information architecture

**Information architecture**
The combination of organisation, labelling and navigation schemes constituting an information system.

Rosenfeld and Morville (2002) emphasise the importance of **information architecture** to an effective website design. They say:

> *It is important to recognise that every information system, be it a book or an intranet, has an information architecture. 'Well developed' is the key here, as most sites don't have a planned information architecture at all. They are analogous to buildings that weren't architected in advance. Design decisions reflect the personal biases of designers, the space doesn't scale over time, technologies drive the design and not the other way around.*

In their book, Rosenfeld and Morville give alternative definitions of an information architecture. They say it is:

**1** *The combination of organisation, labelling, and navigation schemes within an information system.*

**2** *The structural design of an information space to facilitate task completion and intuitive access to content.*

**3** *The art and science of structuring and classifying websites and intranets to help people find and manage information.*

**4** *An emerging discipline and community of practice focused on bringing principles of design and architecture to the digital landscape.*

**Site map**
A graphical or text depiction of the relationship between different groups of content on a website.

Essentially, in practice, creation of an information architecture involves creating a plan to group information logically – it involves creating a site structure which is often represented as a **site map**. Note, though, that whole books have been written on information architecture, so this is necessarily a simplification! A well-developed information architecture is very important to usability since it determines navigation options. It is also important for search engine optimisation (Chapter 8), since it determines how different types of content that users may search for are labelled and grouped.

A planned information architecture is essential to large-scale websites such as transactional e-commerce sites, media owner sites and relationship-building sites that include a large volume of product or support documentation. Information architectures are less important to small-scale websites and brand sites, but even here the principles can be readily applied and can help make the site more visible to search engines and more usable.

The benefits of creating an information architecture include:

- A defined structure and categorisation of information will support user and organisation goals, i.e. it is a vital aspect of usability.
- It helps increase 'flow' on the site – a user's mental model of where to find content should mirror that of the content on the website.
- Search engine optimisation – a higher listing in the search rankings can often be used through structuring and labelling information in a structured way.
- Applicable for integrating offline communications – offline communications such as ads or direct mail can link to a product or campaign landing page to help achieve direct response, sometimes known as 'web response'. A sound URL strategy, as explained in Chapter 8, can help this.
- Related content can be grouped to measure the effectiveness of a website as part of design for analysis, which is also explained below.

### Card sorting

Using card sorting is a way in which users can become actively involved in the development process of information architecture.

**Card sorting** or **web classification**

The process of arranging a way of organising objects on the website in a consistent manner.

Card sorting is a useful approach since websites are frequently designed from the perspective of the designer rather than the information user, leading to labels, subject grouping and categories that are not intuitive to the user. Card sorting or web classification should categorise web objects (e.g documents) in order to facilitate information task completion or information goals the user has set.

Robertson (2003) explains an approach to card sorting which identifies the following questions when using the technique to aid the process of modelling web classification systems:

- Do the users want to see the information grouped by subject, task, business or customer groupings, or type of information?
- What are the most important items to put on the main menu?
- How many menu items should there be, and how deep should it go?
- How similar or different are the needs of the users throughout the organisation?

Selected groups of users or representatives will be given index cards with the following written on them, depending on the aim of the card sorting process

- types of documents;
- organisational key words and concepts;
- document titles;
- descriptions of documents;
- navigation labels.

The user groups may then be asked to:

- Group together cards that they feel relate to each other.
- Select cards that accurately reflect a given topic or area.
- Organise cards in terms of hierarchy – high-level terms (broad) to low-level terms.

At the end of the session the analyst must take the cards away and map the results into a spreadsheet to find out the most popular terms, descriptions and relationships. If two or more different groups are used, the results should be compared and reasons for differences should be analysed.

### Blueprints

**Blueprint**

Shows the relationships between pages and other content components, and can be used to portray organisation, navigation and labelling systems.

According to Rosenfeld and Morville (2002), blueprints:

> show the relationships between pages and other content components, and can be used to portray organisation, navigation and labelling systems.

They are often thought of, and referred to, as 'site maps' or 'site structure diagrams' and have much in common with these, except that they are used as a design device clearly showing grouping of information and linkages between pages, rather than a page on the website to assist navigation.

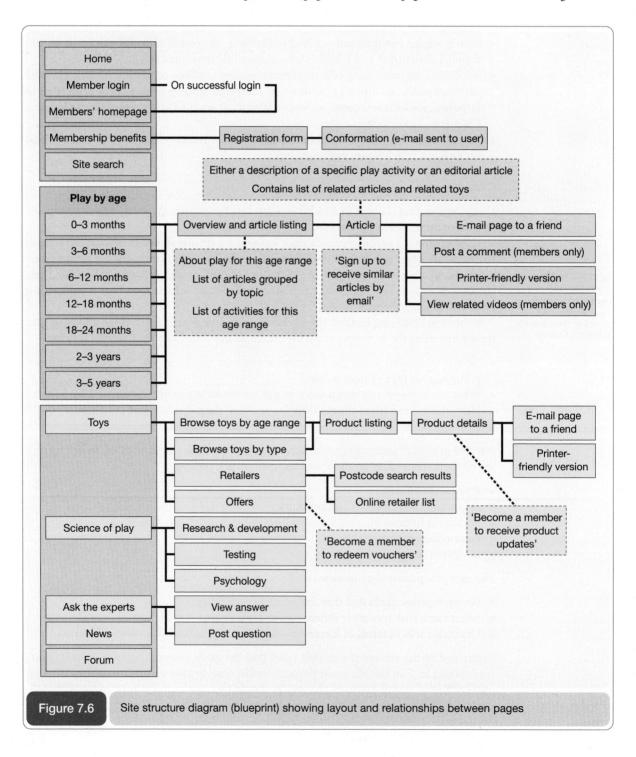

Figure 7.6    Site structure diagram (blueprint) showing layout and relationships between pages

Refer to Figure 7.6 for an example of a site structure diagram for a toy manufacturer website which shows the groupings of content and an indication of the process of task completion also.

## Wireframes

A related technique to blueprints is the wireframes which are used by web designers to indicate the eventual layout of a web page. Figure 7.7 shows that the wireframe is so called because it just consists of an outline of the page with the 'wires' of content separating different areas of content or navigation shown by white space.

Wodtke (2002) describes a wireframe (sometimes known as a 'schematic') as:

*a basic outline of an individual page, drawn to indicate the elements of a page, their relationships and their relative importance.*

A wireframe will be created for all types of similar page groups, identified at the blueprint (site map) stage of creating the information architecture.

Wireframes are then transformed into physical **site design page templates** which are now traditionally created using standardised **cascading style sheets (CSS)** which enable a standard look and feel to be enforced across different sections of the site.

The standards body W3C (www.w3.org) defines cascading style sheets as

*a simple mechanism for adding style (e.g. fonts, colors, spacing) to Web documents.*

**Wireframe**

Also known as 'schematics', a way of illustrating the layout of an individual web page.

**Site design page template**

A standard page layout format which is applied to each page of a website. Typically defined for different page categories (e.g. category page, product page, search page).

**Cascading style sheets**

A simple mechanism for adding style (e.g. fonts, colours, spacing) to web documents. CSS enables different style elements to be controlled across an entire site or section of site. Style elements that are commonly controlled include typography, background colour and images, and borders and margins.

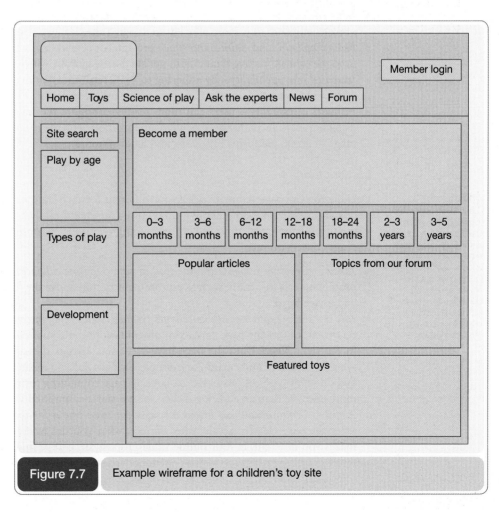

**Figure 7.7**    Example wireframe for a children's toy site

CSS enable different style elements to be controlled across an entire site or section of site. Style elements that are commonly controlled include:

- typography
- background colour and images
- borders and margins.

For example, CSS will use this syntax to enforce the standard appearance of body copy on a site:

```
body {
  margin:0;
  padding:0;
  color:#666666;
  background-color:#f3f3f3;
  font-family: Arial, 'Trebuchet MS', Verdana;
  font-size: 70%;
  background-repeat:repeat-x;
  background-position:top;
}
```

The benefits of CSS are:

- *Bandwidth* – pages download faster after initial page load since style definitions only need to be downloaded once as a separate file, not for each page.
- *More efficient development* – through agreeing site style and implementing in CSS as part of page templates, it is more efficient to design a site.
- *Reduces updating and maintenance time* – presentational markup is stored in one place separate from the content making it quicker to update the site globally with less scope for errors.
- *Increased interoperability* – by adhering to W3C recommendations; helps with support of multiple browsers.
- *Increases accessibility* – users can more readily configure the way a site looks or sounds using browsers and other accessibility support tools. The site is more likely to render on a range of access platforms like PDAs and Smart Phones.

### Landing pages

**Landing page**
A destination page when a user clicks on an ad or other form of link from a referring site. It can be a home page but more typically, and desirably, a landing page is a page with the messaging focused on the offer in the ad. This will maximise conversion rates and brand favourability.

Deciding on the page template design for different forms of landing pages is particularly important for site owners seeking to maximise conversion rate. Chaffey and Smith (2008) suggest these are typical aims and corresponding questions to consider for increasing landing page conversion rate:

- *Aim 1 – Generate response (online lead or sale & offline callback).* Does the page have a prominent call-to-action, such as a prominent button above the fold and repeated in text and image form?
- *Aim 2 – Engage different audience types (reduce bounce rate, increase value events, increase return rate).* Does the page have a prominent headline and subheads showing the visitor is in the right place? Does the page have scent-trail trigger messages, offers or images to appeal to different audiences? For example, Dell has links on its site to appeal to consumers and different types of businesses. A landing page containing form fields to fill in is often more effective than an additional click since it starts committed visitors on their journey.
- *Aim 3 – Communicate key brand messages (increase brand familiarity and favourability).* Does the page clearly explain who you are, what you do, where you operate and what makes you different. Is your online value proposition compelling? Do you use customer testimonials or ratings to show independent credibility? To help with this, use run-of-site messages (on all pages) across the top of the screen or in the left or right sidebars.

- *Aim 4 – Answer the visitor's questions (reduce bounce rates, increase conversion rates).* Different audiences will want to know different things. Have you identified personas (Chapter 4) and do you seek to answer their questions). Do you use FAQ or messages which say 'New to company'.
- *Aim 5 – Showcase range of offers (cross-sell).* Do you have recommendations on related or best selling products and do you show the full-range of your offering through navigation?
- *Aim 6 – Attract visitors through search engine optimisation (SEO).* How well do you rank for relevant search terms compared to competitors? Do your navigation, copy and page templates indicate relevance to search engines through on-page optimisation?

Blueprints illustrate how the content of a website is related and navigated while a wireframe focuses on individual pages; with a wireframe the navigation focus becomes where it will be placed on the page. Wireframes are useful for agencies and clients to discuss the way a website will be laid out without getting distracted by colour, style or messaging issues which should be covered separately as a creative planning activity.

**Storyboarding**

The use of static drawings or screenshots of the different parts of a website to review the design concept with user groups. It can be used to develop the structure – an overall 'map' with individual pages shown separately.

The process of reviewing wireframes is sometimes referred to as **storyboarding**, although the term is often applied to reviewing creative ideas rather than formal design alternatives. Early designs are drawn on large pieces of paper, or mock-ups are produced using a drawing or paint program.

At the wireframe stage, emphasis is not placed on use of colour or graphics, which will be developed in conjunction with branding or marketing teams and graphic designers and integrated into the site after the wireframe process.

According to Chaffey and Wood (2005), the aim of a wireframe will be to:

- integrate consistently available components on the web page (e.g. navigation, search boxes);
- order and group key types of components together;
- develop a design that will focus the user on to core messages and content;
- make correct use of white space to structure the page;
- develop a page structure that can be easily reused by other web designers.

Common wireframe or template features you may come across are:

- navigation in columns on left or right and at top or bottom;
- header areas and footer areas;
- 'slots' or 'portlets' – these are areas of content such as an article or list of articles placed in boxes on the screen. Often slots will be dynamically populated from a content management system;
- slots on the homepage may be used to:
  - summarise the online value proposition
  - show promotions
  - recommend related products
  - feature news, etc.
  - contain ads.

## Designing the user experience

**Design phase**

The design phase defines how the site will work in the key areas of website structure, navigation and security.

Once analysis has determined the information needs of the site, the site can be designed. **Design** is critical to a successful website since it will determine the quality of experience users of a site have; if they have a good experience they will return, if not they will not! A 'good experience' is determined by a number of factors such as those that affect how easy it is to find information: for example, the structure of the site, menu choices and searching facilities. It is also affected by less tangible factors such as the graphical design and layout of the site.

Achieving a good design is important before too many web pages are developed because, if time is taken to design a site, less time will be wasted later when the site is reworked. Large sites are usually produced by creating templates comprising the graphical and menu elements to which content is added.

As mentioned previously, design is not solely a paper-based exercise, but needs to be integrated into the prototyping process. The design should be tested by review with the client and customer to ensure it is appropriate. The design of site layout, navigation and structure can be tested in two different ways. First, early designs can be paper-based – drawn by the designer on large pieces of paper – or 'mock-ups' can be produced on screen using a drawing or paint program. This process is referred to as 'storyboarding'. Second, a working, dynamic prototype can be produced in which users can select different menu options on-screen that will take them to skeleton pages (minus content) of different parts of the site.

Since the main reason given in Table 7.6 (page 431) for returning to a website is high-quality content, it is important to determine, through analysis, that the content is correct. However, the quality of content is determined by more than the text copy. It is important to achieve high-quality content through design. To help in this it is useful to consider the factors that affect quality content. These are shown in Figure 7.8. All are determined by the quality of the information.

## Developing customer-oriented content

Nigel Bevan (1999a) says:

> Unless a website meets the needs of the intended users it will not meet the needs of the organisation providing the website. Website development should be user-centred, evaluating the evolving design against user requirements.

**User-centred design**

Design based on optimising the user experience according to all factors, including the user interface, which affect this.

How can this customer-oriented or user-centred content be achieved? User-centred design starts with understanding the nature and variation within the user groups. According to Bevan (1999a), issues to consider include:

- Who are the important users?
- What is their purpose for accessing the site?
- How frequently will they visit the site?
- What experience and expertise do they have?
- What nationality are they? Can they read your language?
- What type of information are they looking for?
- How will they want to use the information: read it on the screen, print it or download it?
- What type of browsers will they use? How fast will their communication links be?
- How large a screen or window will they use, with how many colours?

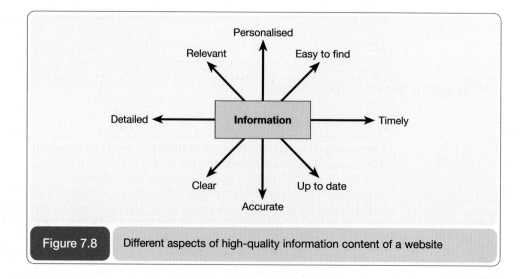

| Figure 7.8 | Different aspects of high-quality information content of a website |

Rosenfeld and Morville (2002) suggest four stages of site design that also have a user-centred basis:

1 Identify different audiences.
2 Rank importance of each to business.
3 List the three most important information needs of audience.
4 Ask representatives of each audience type to develop their own wish lists.

We noted in Chapter 2 that customer persona and scenario analysis is a powerful technique of understanding different audiences which can be used to inform and test website design.

### Evaluating designs

A test of effective design for usability is dependent on three areas according to Bevan (1999b):

- *Effectiveness* – can users complete their tasks correctly and completely?
- *Productivity (efficiency)* – are tasks completed in an acceptable length of time?
- *Satisfaction* – are users satisfied with the interaction?

## Marketing-led site design

**Marketing-led site design**

Site design elements are developed to achieve customer acquisition, retention and communication of marketing messages.

We have seen that there are many guidelines on how to approach website design from user- or customer orientation. The marketing aims of the site should, however, always be remembered. Marketing-led site design is informed by marketing objectives and tactics. A common approach is to base the design on achieving the performance drivers of successful Internet marketing referred to in Chapter 4 and the loyalty drivers referred to at the start of this chapter. Design will be led by these performance drivers as follows:

- *Customer acquisition* – the online value proposition must be clear. Appropriate incentives for customer acquisition such as those described in Chapter 6 must be devised.
- *Customer conversion* – the site must engage first-time visitors. Call to action for customer acquisition and retention offers must be prominent with benefits clearly explained. The fulfilment of the offer or purchase must be as simple as possible to avoid attrition during this process.
- *Customer retention* – appropriate incentives and content for repeat visits and business must be available (see Chapter 6).
- *Service quality* – this has been covered in this chapter. Service quality is affected by site navigation, performance, availability and responsiveness to enquiries.
- *Branding* – the brand offer must be clearly explained and interaction with the brand must be possible.

## Elements of site design

Once the requirements of the user and marketer are established we turn our attention to the design of the human–computer interface. Nielsen (2000b) structures his book on web usability according to three main areas, which can be interpreted as follows:

1 *site design and structure* – the overall structure of the site;
2 *page design* – the layout of individual pages;
3 *content design* – how the text and graphic content on each page is designed.

### Site design and structure

The structures created by designers for websites will vary greatly according to their audience and the site's purpose, but we can make some general observations about approaches to site design and structure and their influence on consumers. For example, Rosen and Purinton

(2004) have assessed the design factors which influence a consumer (based on questionnaires of a group of students). They believe there are some basic factors that determine the effectiveness of an e-commerce site. They group these factors as follows:

- *Coherence* – simplicity of design, easy to read, use of categories (for browsing products or topics), absence of information overload, adequate font size, uncrowded presentation.
- *Complexity* – different categories of text.
- *Legibility* – use of 'mini home page' on every subsequent page, same menu on every page, site map.

You can see that these authors suggest that simplicity in design is important. Another example of research into website design factors supports the importance of design. Fogg *et al.* (2003) asked students to review sites to assess the credibility of different suppliers based on the website design. They considered these factors most important:

| | |
|---|---|
| Design look | 46.1% |
| Information design/structure | 28.5% |
| Information focus | 25.1% |
| Company motive | 15.5% |
| Usefulness of information | 14.8% |
| Accuracy of information | 14.3% |
| Name recognition and reputation | 14.1% |
| Advertising | 13.8% |
| Bias of information | 11.6% |
| Tone of the writing | 9.0% |
| Identity of site sponsor | 8.8% |
| Functionality of site | 8.6% |
| Customer service | 6.4% |
| Past experience with site | 4.6% |
| Information clarity | 3.7% |
| Performance on a test | 3.6% |
| Readability | 3.6% |
| Affiliations | 3.4% |

However, it should be borne in mind that such generalisations can be misleading based on the methodology used. Reported behaviour (e.g. through questionnaires or focus groups) may be quite different from actual observed behaviour. Leading e-retail sites (for example Amazon.com and eBay.com) and many media sites typically have a large amount of information and navigation choices available on-screen since the site designers know from testing alternative designs that consumers are quite capable of finding content relevant to them, and that a wider choice of links means that the user can find the information they need without clicking through a hierarchy. When performing a real-life product search, in-depth information on the products and reviews of the product are important in making the product decision and are one of the benefits that online channels can give. Although design look is top of the list of factors presented by Fogg *et al.* (2003), you can see that many of the other factors are based on the quality of information.

In the following coverage, we will review the general factors which designers consider in designing the style, organisation and navigation schemes for the site.

### Site style

An effective website design will have a style that is communicated through use of colour, images, typography and layout. This should support the way a product is positioned or its brand.

### Site personality

The style elements can be combined to develop a personality for a site. We could describe a site's personality in the same way we can describe people, such as 'formal' or 'fun'. This personality has to be consistent with the needs of the target audience (Figure 7.9). A business audience often requires detailed information and prefers an information-intensive style such as that of the Cisco site (Figure 7.12) (www.cisco.com). A consumer site is usually more graphically intensive. Before the designers pass on their creative designs to developers, they also need to consider the constraints on the user experience, such as screen resolution and colour depth, browser used and download speed.

### Graphic design

Graphic design of websites represents a challenge since designers of websites are severely constrained by a number of factors:

- *The speed of downloading graphics* – designers need to allow for home users who view sites using a slow modem across a phone line and who are unlikely to wait minutes to view a website.
- *The screen resolutions of the computer* – designing for different screen resolutions is necessary, since some users with laptops may be operating at a low resolution such as 640 × 480 pixels, the majority at a resolution of 800 × 600 pixels, and a few at higher resolutions of 1064 × 768 pixels or greater.

| Figure 7.9 | A personality that appeals to a youthful audience at www.i-to-i.com |

- *The number of colours on screen* – some users may have monitors capable of displaying 16 million colours giving photo-realism, while other may have only 256 colours.
- *The type of web browser used* – different browsers, such as Microsoft Internet Explorer and Netscape Navigator, and different versions of browsers, such as version 4.0 or 5.0, may display graphics or text slightly differently or may support different plug-ins (see the section in Chapter 9 on testing).

As a result of these constraints, the design of websites is a constant compromise between what looks visually appealing and modern, and what works for the older browsers with slower connections. This is often referred to as the 'lowest common denominator problem' since this is what the designer must do – design for the old browsers, using slow links and low screen resolutions. One method for avoiding the 'lowest common denominator problem' is to offer the user a 'high-tech' or 'low-tech' choice: one for users with fast connections and high screen resolutions, and another for users who do not have these. This facility is mainly seen offered on sites produced by large companies since it requires more investment to effectively duplicate the site.

Despite these constraints, graphic design is important in determining the feel or character of a site. The graphic design can help shape the user's experience of a site and should be consistent with the brand involved.

### Site organisation

**Information organisation scheme**

A structure chosen to group and categorise information.

In their book *Information Architecture for the World Wide Web*, Rosenfeld and Morville (2002) identify several different **information organisation schemes**. These can be applied for different aspects of e-commerce sites, from the whole site through to different parts of the site.

Rosenfeld and Morville (2002) identify the following information organisation schemes:

- *Exact.* Here information can be naturally indexed. If we take the example of books, these can be alphabetical – by author or title; chronological – by date; or for travel books, for example, geographical – by place. Information on an e-commerce site may be presented alphabetically, but it is not suitable for browsing.
- *Ambiguous.* Here the information requires classification – again taking the examples of books, the Dewey Decimal System is an ambiguous classification scheme since librarians classify books into arbitrary categories. Such an approach is common on an e-commerce site since products and services can be classified in different ways. Other ambiguous information organisation schemes that are commonly used on websites are where content is broken down by topic, by task or by audience. The use of metaphors is also common, a metaphor being where the website corresponds to a familiar real-world situation. Microsoft Windows Explorer, where information is grouped according to Folders, Files and Trash is an example of a real-world metaphor. The use of the shopping basket metaphor is widespread within e-commerce sites. It should be noted though that Nielsen (2000b) believes that metaphors can be confusing if the metaphor isn't understood immediately or is misinterpreted.
- *Hybrid.* Here there will be a mixture of organisation schemes, both exact and ambiguous. Rosenfeld and Morville (2002) point out that using different approaches is common on websites, but this can lead to confusion because the user is not clear what mental model is being followed. We can say that it is probably best to minimise the number of information organisation schemes.

### Site navigation schemes

**Site navigation scheme**

Tools provided to the user to move between different information on a website.

**Flow**

Describes how easy it is for users of a site to move between the different pages of content of the site.

Devising a site that is easy to use is critically dependent on the design of the **site navigation scheme**. Hoffman and Novak (1997) and many subsequent studies (e.g. Rettie, 2001; Smith and Sivakumar, 2004) have stressed the importance of the concept of **flow** in governing site usability. The concept of 'flow' was first brought to prominence by Mihaly Csikszentmihalyi, a psychology professor at the University of Chicago. In his book, *Flow: The Psychology of Optimal Experience*, he explains his theory that people are most happy when they are in a state of flow – a Zen-like state of total oneness with the activity at hand. In an online marketing context, 'flow' essentially describes how easy it is for users to find the information or experiences they need as they move from one page of the site to the next, but it also includes other interactions such as filling in on-screen forms. Rettie (2001) has suggested that the quality of navigation is one of the prerequisites for flow, although other factors are also important. They include quick download time, alternative versions, auto-completion of forms, opportunities for interaction, navigation which creates choices, predictable navigation for control and segmenting content by Internet experience.

It can be suggested that there are three important aspects to a site that is easy to navigate. These are:

- *Consistency.* A site will be easier to navigate if the user is presented with a consistent user interface when viewing the different parts of the site. For example, if the menu options in the support section of the site are on the left side of the screen, then they should also be on the left when the user moves to the 'news section' of the site.
- *Simplicity.* Sites are easier to navigate if there are limited numbers of options. It is usually suggested that two or possibly three levels of menu are the most that are desirable. For example, there may be main menu options at the left of the screen that take the user to the different parts of the site, and at the bottom of the screen there will be specific menu options that refer to that part of the site. (Menus in this form are often referred to as 'nested'.)
- *Context.* Context is the use of 'signposts' to indicate to users where they are located within the site – in other words, to reassure users that they are not 'lost'. To help with this, the website designer should use particular text or colour to indicate to users which part of the site they are currently using. Context can be provided by the use of JavaScript 'rollovers', where the colour of the menu option changes when the user positions the mouse over the menu option and then changes again when the menu option is selected. Many sites also have a site-map option that shows the layout and content of the whole site so the user can understand its structure. When using a well-designed site it should not be necessary to refer to such a map regularly.

**Navigation**

Describes how easy it is to find and move between different information on a website. It is governed by menu arrangements, site structure and the layout of individual pages.

**Narrow and deep navigation**

Fewer choices, more clicks to reach required content.

**Broad and shallow navigation**

More choices, fewer clicks to reach required content.

**Deep linking**

Jakob Nielsen's term for a user arriving at a site deep within its structure.

Most **navigation** systems are based upon a hierarchical site structure. When creating the structure, designers have to compromise between the two approaches shown in Figure 7.10. The **narrow and deep** approach has the benefit of fewer choices on each page, making it easier for the user to make their selection, but more clicks are required to reach a particular piece of information. The **broad and shallow** approach requires fewer clicks to reach the same piece of information, but the design of the screen potentially becomes cluttered. Figures 7.10(a) and 7.11 depict the narrow and deep approach and Figures 7.10(b) and 7.12 the broad and shallow approach. Note that in these cases the approaches are appropriate for both non-technical and technical audiences. A rule of thumb is that site designers should ensure it only takes three clicks to reach any piece of information on a site. This implies the use of a broad and shallow approach on most large sites. Lynch and Horton (1999) recommend a broad and shallow approach and note that designers should not conceive of a single home page where customers arrive on the site, but of different home pages according to different audience types. Each of the pages in the second row of Figure 7.10(b) could be thought of as an example of a home page which the visitors can bookmark if the page appeals to them. Nielsen (2000b) points out that many users will not arrive on the home page, but may be referred from another site or according to a print or TV advert to a particular page such as www.b2b.com/jancomp. He calls this process '**deep linking**' and site designers should ensure that navigation and context are appropriate for users arriving on these pages.

As well as compromises on depth of links within a site, it is also necessary to compromise on the amount of space devoted to menus. Nielsen (1999) points out that some sites devote so much space to navigation bars that the space available for content is limited. Nielsen suggests that the designer of navigation systems should consider the following information that a site user wants to know:

- *Where am I?* The user needs to know where they are on the site and this can be indicated by highlighting the current location and clear titling of pages. This can be considered as *context.* *Consistency* of menu locations on different pages is also required to aid cognition. Users also need to know where they are on the web. This can be indicated by a logo, which by convention is at the top or top-left of a site.

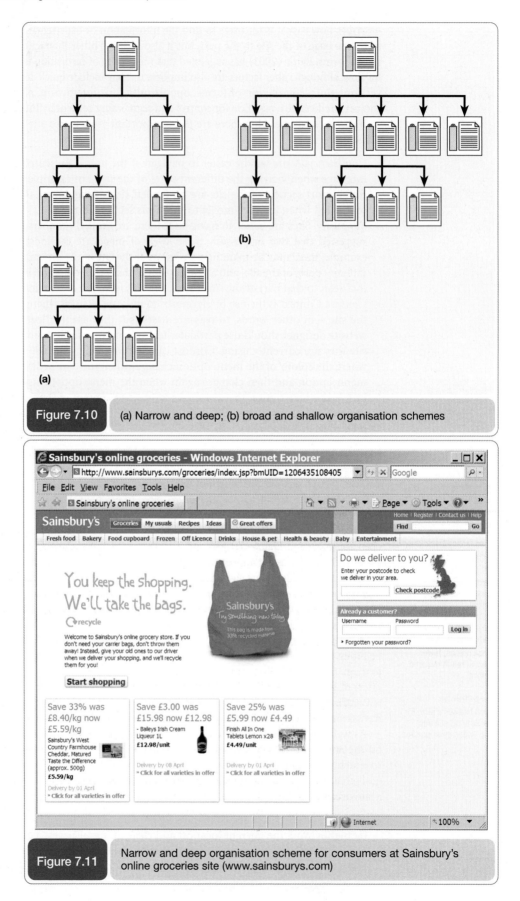

| Figure 7.10 | (a) Narrow and deep; (b) broad and shallow organisation schemes |

| Figure 7.11 | Narrow and deep organisation scheme for consumers at Sainsbury's online groceries site (www.sainsburys.com) |

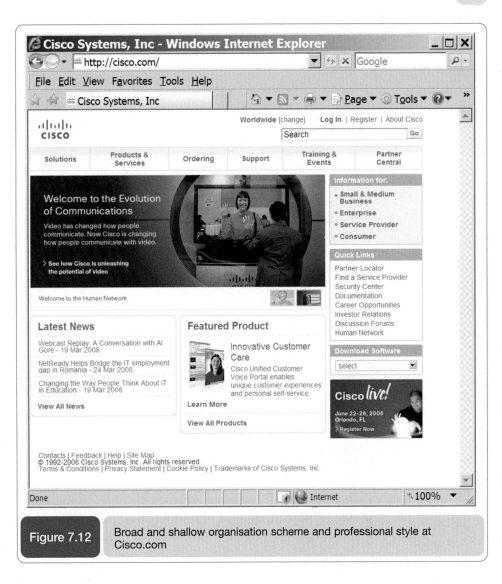

Figure 7.12    Broad and shallow organisation scheme and professional style at Cisco.com

- *Where have I been?* This is difficult to indicate on a site, but for task-oriented activities such as purchasing a product it can show the user that they are at the $n$th stage of an operation, such as making a purchase.
- *Where do I want to go?* This is the main navigation system which gives options for future operations.

To answer these questions, clear succinct labelling is required. Widely used standards such as Home, Main page, Search, Find, Browse, FAQ, Help and About Us are preferable. But for other particular labels it is useful to have what Rosenfeld and Morville (2002) call 'scope notes' – an additional explanation. These authors also argue against the use of iconic labels or pictures without corresponding text since they are open to misinterpretation and take longer to process.

Since using the navigation system may not enable the user to find the information they want rapidly, alternatives have to be provided by the site designers. These alternatives include search, advanced search, browse and site map facilities. Whatis.com (www.whatis.com) illustrates these features well.

### Menu options

Designing and creating the menus to support navigation present several options, and the main ones are briefly described here.

#### 1 Text menus, buttons or images

The site user can select menus by clicking on different objects. They can click on a basic text hyperlink, underlined in blue, by default. It should be noted that these will be of different sizes according to the size the user has selected to display the text. The use of text menus only may make a site look primitive and reduce its graphic appeal. Rectangular or oval buttons can be used to highlight menu options more distinctly. Images can also be used to show menu options. For instance, customer service could be denoted by a picture of a help desk. While these are graphically appealing it may not be obvious that they are menu options until the user positions the mouse over them. A combination of text menu options and either buttons or images is usually the best compromise. This way users have the visual appeal of buttons or images, but also the faster option of text – they can select these menus if they are waiting for graphical elements to load, or if the images are turned off in the web browser. However, icons should have the advantage that their understanding is not language-dependent.

#### 2 Rollovers

'Rollover' is the term used to describe colour changes – where the colour of the menu option changes when the user positions the mouse over the menu option, and then changes again when the menu option is selected. Rollovers are useful in that they help achieve the context referred to in the previous section, by highlighting the area of the site the user is in.

#### 3 Positioning

Menus can be positioned at any of the edges of the screen, with left, bottom or top being conventional for Western cultures. The main design aim is to keep the position consistent between different parts of the site.

#### 4 Frames

Frames are a feature of HTML which enable menus to be positioned at one side of the screen in a small area (frame), while the content of the page is displayed in the main frame. Frames have their advocates and detractors, but they are still used on some sites (e.g. www.tesco.com) which require particular functionality. Detractors point to poor display speed, difficulties in indexing content in search engines and inflexibility in positioning.

#### 5 Number of levels

In a hierarchical structure there could be as many as ten different levels, but for simplicity it is normal to try to achieve a site structure with a nesting level of four or fewer. Even in an electronic commerce shopping site with 20,000 products it should be possible to select a product within four menu levels. For example:

- level 1 – drink
- level 2 – spirits
- level 3 – whisky
- level 4 – brand X.

#### 6 Number of options

Psychologists recommend having a limited number of choices within each menu. If a menu has more than seven, it is probably necessary to add another level to the hierarchy to accommodate the extra choices.

## Page design

The page design involves creating an appropriate layout for each page. The main elements of a particular page layout are the title, navigation and content. Standard content, such as copyright information, may be added to every page as a footer. Issues in page design include:

- *Page elements.* We have to consider the proportion of a page devoted to content compared to all other material such as headers, footers and navigation elements. The location of these elements also needs to be considered. It is conventional for the main menu to be at the top or on the left. The use of a menu system at the top of the browser window allows more space for content below.
- *The use of frames.* This is generally discouraged since it makes search engine registration more difficult, and makes printing and bookmarking more difficult for visitors.
- *Resizing.* A good page layout design should allow for the user to change the size of text or work with different monitor resolutions.
- *Consistency.* Page layout should be similar for all areas of the site unless more space is required – for example for a discussion forum or product demonstration. Standards of colour and typography can be enforced through cascading style sheets.
- *Printing.* Layout should allow for printing or provide an alternative printing format.

## Content design

The home page is particularly important in achieving marketing actions – if the customers do not understand or do not buy into the proposition of the site, then they will leave. Gleisser (2001) states that it is important to clarify what he refers to as 'the essentials': who we are, what we offer, what is inside and how to contact us.

A study of the advertising impact of website content design has been conducted by Pak (1999). She reviewed the techniques used on websites to communicate the message to the customer in terms of existing advertising theory. The study considered the creative strategy used, in terms of the rational and emotional appeals contained within the visuals and the text. As would be expected intuitively, the appeal of the graphics was more emotional than that for the text; the latter used a more rational appeal. The study also considered the information content of the advertisements using classification schemes such as that of Resnik and Stern (1977). The information cues are still relevant to modern website design. Some of the main information cues, in order of frequency of use, were:

- performance (what does the product do?)
- components/content (what is the product made up of?)
- price/value
- implicit comparison
- availability
- quality
- special offers
- explicit comparisons.

Aaker and Norris (1982) devised a framework in which the strategy for creative appeal is based on emotion and feeling, and that for rational and cognitive appeal is based on facts and logic.

Copywriting for the web is an evolving art form, but many of the rules for good copywriting are as for any media. Common errors we see on websites are:

- too much knowledge assumed of the visitor about the company, its products and services;
- using internal jargon about products, services or departments – using undecipherable acronyms.

Web copywriters also need to take account of the user reading the content on-screen. Approaches to dealing with the limitations imposed by the customer using a monitor include:

- writing more concisely than in brochures;
- chunking, or breaking text into units of 5–6 lines at most, which allows users to scan rather than read information on web pages;
- use of lists with headline text in larger font;
- never including too much on a single page, except when presenting lengthy information such as a report which may be easier to read on a single page;
- using hyperlinks to decrease page sizes or help achieve flow within copy, either by linking to sections further down a page or linking to another page.

Chaffey and Smith (2008) summarise the essentials of good copywriting for the web under the mnemonic 'CRABS', which stands for chunking, relevance, accuracy, brevity and scannability.

Hofacker (2000) describes five stages of human information processing when a website is being used. These can be applied to both page design and content design to improve usability and help companies get their message across to consumers. Each of the five stages summarised in Table 7.5 acts as a hurdle, since if the site design or content is too difficult to process then the customer cannot progress to the next stage. It is useful to consider the stages in order to minimise these difficulties.

| Table 7.5 | A summary of the characteristics of the five stages of information processing described by Hofacker (2000) | |
|---|---|---|
| **Stage** | **Description** | **Applications** |
| 1 Exposure | Content must be present for long enough to be processed | Content on banner ads may not be on screen long enough for processing and cognition |
| 2 Attention | User's eyes will be drawn towards headings and content, not graphics and moving items on a web page (Nielsen, 2000b) | Emphasis and accurate labelling of headings is vital to gain a user's attention. Evidence suggests that users do not notice banner adverts, suffering from 'banner blindness' |
| 3 Comprehension and perception | The user's interpretation of content | Designs that use common standards and metaphors and are kept simple will be more readily comprehended |
| 4 Yielding and acceptance | Is information (copy) presented accepted by customers? | Copy should refer to credible sources and present counter arguments as necessary |
| 5 Retention | As for traditional advertising, this describes the extent to which the information is remembered | An unusual style or high degree of interaction leading to flow and user satisfaction is more likely to be recalled |

Gleisser (2001) surveyed website designers to identify consensus on what were success factors in website design. The results of this research are used to summarise this section:

- *The home page essentials.* Segmentation, targeting and positioning play a key role in informing design. The essentials are who we are, what we offer, what is inside and how to contact us.
- *Cater for the needs of anticipated users.* Websites should be quick to download and easy to navigate. Users may not be able to incorporate the latest technical capabilities, such as plug-ins, so these should be used with care.

- *Update the website frequently.* This is to encourage repeat visitors and keep customers informed of new products and offers.
- *Gathering customer information.* The website should be used as part of a 'push' marketing strategy which includes gathering customer information and better targeting of direct marketing using a range of media.

## Development and testing of content

It is not practical to provide details of the methods of developing content – for two reasons. First, to describe all the facilities available in web browsers for laying out and formatting text, and for developing interactivity, would require several books! Second, the programming standards and tools used are constantly evolving, so material is soon out-of-date.

**Development**
The creation of a website by programmers. It involves writing the HTML content, creating graphics and writing any necessary software code such as JavaScript or ActiveX (programming).

**Testing**
Involves different aspects of the content such as spelling, validity of links, formatting on different web browsers and dynamic features such as form filling or database queries.

### Testing content

Marketing managers responsible for websites need to have a basic awareness of website **development** and **testing**. We have already discussed the importance of usability testing with typical users of the system. In brief, other necessary testing steps include:

- test that the content displays correctly on different types and versions of web browsers;
- test plug-ins;
- test all interactive facilities and integration with company databases;
- test spelling and grammar;
- test adherence to corporate image standards;
- test to ensure all links to external sites are valid.

Testing often occurs on a separate test web server (or directory) or *test environment*, with access to the test or prototype version being restricted to the development team. When complete, the website is released or published to the main web server or *live environment*.

### Tools for website development and testing

A variety of software programs are available to help developers of websites. Some of these tools are listed below to illustrate the range of skills a website designer will need; an advanced website may be built using tools from each of these categories since even the most advanced tools may not have the flexibility of the basic tools.

### Basic text editors

Text editors are used to edit HTML tags. For example, '<Bstrong>Products</Bstrong>' will make the enclosed text display bold within the web browser. Such tools are often available at low-cost or zero – including the Notepad editor included with Windows. They are very flexible and all website developers will need to use them at some stage in developing content since more automated tools may not provide this flexibility and may not support the latest standard commands. Entire sites can be built using these tools, but it is more efficient to use the more advanced tools described below and then use the editors for 'tweaking' content.

### Specialised HTML and graphics editors

Specialised HTML and graphics editing tools provide facilities for adding HTML tags automatically. For example, adding the Bold text tag <B> </B> to the HTML document will happen when the user clicks the bold tag. Some of these editors are WYSIWYG. Examples of standard tools include Microsoft FrontPage Express (www.microsoft.com) and the more sophisticated and widely used tool Dreamweaver (www.macromedia.com).

More advanced tools include *content management systems* which are today essential for any site which is frequently updated to support marketing. This topic is discussed further in Chapter 9. They provide advanced content editing facilities, but also provide tools to help manage and test the site, including graphic layouts of the structure of the site – making it easy to find, modify and re-publish the page. Style templates can be applied to produce a consistent 'look and feel' across the site. Tools are also available to create and manage menu options.

Examples of graphics tools include:

- Adobe Photoshop (extensively used by graphic designers, www.adobe.com);
- Macromedia Flash and Director-Shockwave (used for graphical animation).

## Online retail merchandising

For online retail site owners, merchandising is a crucial activity, in the same way it is for physical retail store owners. In both cases, the aims are similar – to maximise sales potential for each store visitor. Online, this means presenting relevant products and promotions to site visitors which should help boost key measures of site performance such as conversion rate and average order value. You will see that many of these approaches are related to the concept of **findability**. Some of the most common approaches used are:

**Findability**

An assessment of how easy it is for a web user to locate a single content object or to use browse the navigation and search system to find content. Like usability it is assessed through efficiency – how long it takes to find the content and effectiveness – how satisfied the user is with the experience and relevance of the content they find.

- *Expanding navigation through synonyms.* Through using a range of terms which may apply to the same product, the product may become easier to find if a site visitor is searching using a particular expression.
- *Applying faceted navigation or search approaches.* Search results pages are important in online merchandising since conversion rates will be higher if relevant products and offers are at the top of the list. **Faceted navigation** enables website users to 'drill-down' to easily select a relevant product by selecting different product attributes (Figure 7.13).
- *Featuring the bestselling products prominently.* Featuring strongest product lines prominently is a common approach, with retailers such as Firebox (Figure 4.21) showing 'Top 10' or 'Top 20' products.

**Faceted navigation**

Enables users to rapidly filter results from a product search based on different ways of classifying the product by their attributes or features. For example by brand, by sub-product category, by price bands.

- *Use of bundling.* The classic retail approaches of buy-one-get-one-free (BOGOFF) is commonly applied online through showcasing complementary products. For example, Amazon discounts two related books it offers. Related products are also shown on the product page or in checkout, although care has to be taken here since this can reduce conversion rates.
- *Use of customer ratings and reviews.* Reviews can be important in influencing sales. Research from online ratings service Bazaar Voice showed that for one of its clients, CompUSA, the use of reviews achieved:
  - 60% higher conversion
  - 50% higher order value
  - 82% more page views per visitor.
  Mini case study 7.1 'figleaves.com uncovers customer feedback to increase conversion' shows another example.
- *Use of product visualisation systems.* These systems enable web users to zoom in and rotate on products. Research by Scene7 (2008) summarised in Figure 7.14 shows the popularity and effectiveness ratings for these techniques.

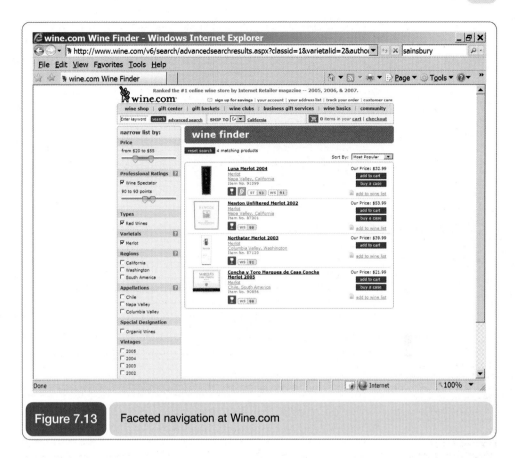

**Figure 7.13**    Faceted navigation at Wine.com

**Rich Internet applications**

Interactive applications which provide options such as product selectors or games. They may incorporate video or sound also. Typically built using technologies such as Adobe Flash, Ajax, Flex, Java or Silverlight.

Some of these techniques use Web 2.0 approaches with interactive **rich Internet applications (RIA).** The research reports on an assessment of the measures that are used to assess the deployment of these applications which give a useful indication of how online merchandising approaches are evaluated. The full breakdown of effectiveness measures is:

- increased engagement (clicks/usage) = 63.3%
- increased conversion rate = 60.2% (reduced abandonment, 35.5%)
- increase revenues = 47.2%
- qualitative feedback = 41%
- increase repeat purchase = 29.6%
- increase average order size = 28.4%
- reduce returns = 18.

Moe (2003) and other researchers have suggested that, in theory, it should be possible to use web analytics to profile customers in real time using cluster analysis to assess the buying mode they are in – for example, buying, searching, or browsing. This information can then be used to deliver the most relevant merchandising. While this is possible in theory, it seems limited in practice. Although companies do use Google Adwords to direct users to the most appropriate landing page for a particular search term they enter.

Weathers and Makienko (2006) have also investigated the effect of merchandising on online store success rate based on a study of users of review site Bizrate.com. They found that features to enable searching for products were particularly important, as was a choice of ordering options.

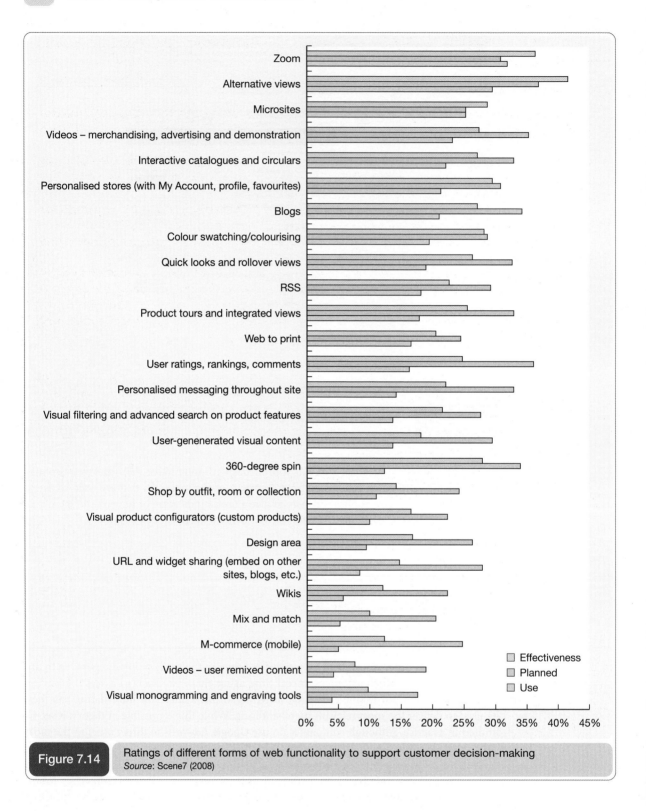

Figure 7.14   Ratings of different forms of web functionality to support customer decision-making
*Source*: Scene7 (2008)

## Mini Case Study 7.1    figleaves.com uncovers customer feedback to increase conversion

figleaves.com (Figure 7.15) explains its online value proposition as follows:

- *figleaves.com is the world's largest online seller of branded intimate apparel. The retailer offers branded underwear, swimwear, exercisewear, nightwear and hosiery for men and women.* [Core proposition and audience]
- *While the choice is huge, it couldn't be easier to find what you are looking for. You can shop by brand, size, price, colour, style or occasion; or, if you know exactly what you are looking for, we will take you directly to it in one click.* [Ease of use/findability]
- *You can easily return goods if they don't fit or if they don't meet your expectation. It's our famous 'no hassle' returns policy. If you're in the UK we even pay the returns postage.* [Returns policy]
- *What's more, you can check out your purchases at home – no queuing for or embarrassing moments in luridly lit changing rooms.* [Unique channel-specific advantage of online service]
- *Underwear makes a great gift for both men and women. If you are buying for a loved one then we can send your present in a beautiful gift box along with a personalised message. Alternatively, you can send a gift certificate so that the recipient can choose exactly what they want themselves.* [Gifting]
- *We know how much you appreciate speedy delivery – in-stock items are usually dispatched within 24 hours.* [Delivery]

## Figure 7.15    Example of customer ratings at figleaves.com.

This research by Bazaarvoice shows the value of using customer reviews:

- Overall, products with reviews have a 12.5% higher conversion rate than those without.
- Products with 20+ reviews have an 83.85% higher conversion than those products without reviews. Note that products prompting the most reviews tend to be the bestsellers and thus are generally higher converting.
- Analysing the session conversion for the same products before and after going live, the same products with reviews have a 35.27% higher overall session conversion rate.
- Conversion was not negatively affected for products without reviews.
- The look-to-book ratio is four times lower (better) for products with reviews compared to those without.
- Overall look-to-book is 32.6% higher (worse) for products without reviews.
- Since going live, products with reviews have seen a significant decrease (better) in the look-to-book ratio.
- Products without reviews saw no significant decrease.

*Source*: Bazaar Voice case study (http://bazaarvoice.com/cs_rr_conversion_figleaves.html)

## Promote site

Promotion of a site is a significant topic that will be part of the strategy of developing a website. It will follow the initial development of a site and is described in detail in Chapter 9. Particularly important issues that must be considered during the course of site design are search engine optimisation and the experience delivered on landing pages where the visitor arrives not on the home page, but deeper within the site.

## Service quality

Delivering service quality in e-commerce can be assessed through reviewing existing marketing frameworks for determining levels of service quality. Those most frequently used are based on the concept of a 'service-quality gap' that exists between the customer's expected level of service (from previous experience and word-of-mouth communication) and their perception of the actual level of service delivery. We can apply the elements of service quality on which Parasuraman *et al.* (1985) suggest that consumers judge companies. Note that there has been heated dispute about the validity of this SERVQUAL instrument framework in determining service quality – see, for example, Cronin and Taylor (1992). Despite this it is still instructive to apply these dimensions of service quality to customer service on the web (see, for example, Chaffey and Edgar (2000), Kolesar and Galbraith (2000), Zeithaml *et al.* (2002) and Trocchia and Janda (2003)):

- *tangibles* – the physical appearance of facilities and communications;
- *reliability* – the ability to perform the service dependably and accurately;
- *responsiveness* – a willingness to help customers and provide prompt service;
- *assurance* – the knowledge and courtesy of employees and their ability to convey trust and confidence;
- *empathy* – providing caring, individualised attention.

As well as applying these academic frameworks, organisations can use benchmarking services such as Foresee (www.foreseeresults.com) based on the American Customer Satisfaction Index methodology which assess satisfaction scores based on the gap between expectations and actual service.

It should also be remembered that the level of service selected by an online transactional service is based on the relationship between the costs to serve, the value of the product and the likelihood of the channel to increase conversion. Figure 7.16 shows the typical situation for a bank. Typically costs to serve increase to the top-right of the diagram, as does the capability to convert through a more extended dialogue and the value generated from sale. The figure shows a general pattern, but the options are often not mutually exclusive – for example, phone contact may be available for all levels, but emphasised for the most complex products. We introduced some of these methods of delivering service in Chapter 5:

1 *Straight-through processing*. Transaction typically occurs without intervention from staff for a relatively simple product such as a savings account.
2 *Call-backs*. The customer has the option to specify the bank call if there is anything they are unclear on.
3 *Live chat*. Online discussion between service representative and the client. This may be invoked proactively if analysis suggests the customer is having difficulty in deciding.
4 *Co-browsing*. Sharing of screen to walk through application process.
5 *Phone*. Typically this has the highest cost, but often the highest conversion rate.

Two of the most significant frameworks for assessing online service quality are:

- WEBQUAL (Loiacono *et al.*, 2000) which considers 14 dimensions. It has been criticised for relating too much to functional design issues rather than service issues. The dimensions are:
  1 *Information quality* – the concern that information provided is accurate, updated, and appropriate.
  2 *Functional fit to task* – the extent to which users believe that the website meets their needs.
  3 *Tailored communications* – communications can be tailored to meet the user's needs.
  4 *Trust* – secure communication and observance of information privacy.
  5 *Response time* – time to get a response after a request or an interaction with a website.
  6 *Ease of understanding* – easy to read and understand.
  7 *Intuitive operations* – easy to operate and navigate.
  8 *Visual appeal* – the aesthetics of the site.
  9 *Innovativeness* – the creativity and uniqueness of the website.
  10 *Emotional appeal* – the emotional affect of using the website and intensity of involvement.

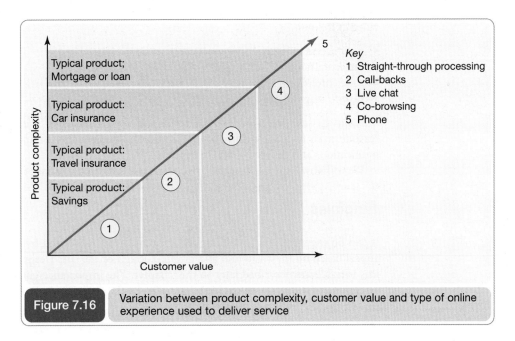

| Figure 7.16 | Variation between product complexity, customer value and type of online experience used to deliver service |

11 *Consistent image* – the website does not create dissonance for the user by an image incompatible with that projected by the firm through other media.

12 *Online completeness* – allowing all or most necessary transactions to be completed online (for example, purchasing over the website).

13 *Relative advantage* – equivalent to or better than other means of interacting with the company.

14 *Customer service* – the response to customer inquiries, comments and feedback when such response requires more than one interaction.

- E-SERVQUAL (Zeithaml *et al.*, 2002) which contains seven dimensions. The first four are classified as the core service scale, and the latter three dimensions are regarded as a recovery scale, since they are only relevant when online customers have questions or problems:

  1 *Efficiency* refers to the ability of the customers to get to the website, search for information or transact as requires.

  2 *Fulfilment* involves the accuracy of service promises, including products in-stock availability and delivering the products in the promised time.

  3 *Reliability* is associated with the technical functioning of the site, including availability and performance.

  4 *Privacy* is related to assurance that shopping behaviour data are not shared and that credit card information is secure.

  5 *Responsiveness* refers to the ability of e-tailers to provide appropriate support information to customers when requested.

  6 *Compensation* involves returns facilities for refunds and return shipping and handling costs.

  7 *Contact* is the ability of customers to talk to a live service agent online.

Both are useful frameworks which can still be applied to evaluate online service quality today, although arguably they omit the importance of accessibility, findability techniques, multichannel integration and customer reviews and ratings (as discussed in the later section on merchandising as a determinant of satisfactory experience).

Online marketers should assess what customers' expectations are in each of these areas, and identify where there is an **online service–quality gap** between the customer expectations and what is currently delivered.

**Online service–quality gap**
The mismatch between what is expected and delivered by an online presence.

Research across industry sectors suggests that the quality of service is a key determinant of loyalty. Feinberg *et al.* (2000) report that when reasons why customers leave a company are considered, over 68% leave because of 'poor service experience', with other factors such as price (10%) and product issues (17%) less significant. Poor service experience was subdivided as follows:

- poor access to the right person (41%)
- unaccommodating (26%)
- rude employees (20%)
- slow to respond (13%).

This survey was conducted for traditional business contacts, but it is instructive since these reasons given for poor customer service have their equivalents online through e-mail communications and delivery of services on-site.

We will now examine how the five determinants of online service quality apply online.

## Tangibles

It can be suggested that the tangibles dimension is influenced by ease of use and visual appeal based on the structural and graphic design of the site. Design factors that influence this variable are described later in this chapter. The importance customers attach to these different aspects of service quality is indicated by the compilation in Table 7.6 which considers the reasons why customers return to a site.

| Table 7.6 | Ten key reasons for returning to a site |
|-----------|-----------------------------------------|

| Reason to return | Percentage of respondents |
|------------------|:-------------------------:|
| 1  High-quality content | 75 |
| 2  Ease of use | 66 |
| 3  Quick to download | 58 |
| 4  Updated frequently | 54 |
| 5  Coupons and incentives | 14 |
| 6  Favourite brands | 13 |
| 7  Cutting-edge technology | 12 |
| 8  Games | 12 |
| 9  Purchasing capabilities | 11 |
| 10  Customisable content | 10 |

*Source*: Forrester Research poll of 8600 online households, 1998

## Reliability

The reliability dimension is dependent on the availability of a website – in other words, how easy it is to connect to the website as a user. Many companies fail to achieve 100% availability and potential customers may be lost for ever if they attempt to use the site when it is unavailable.

Reliability of e-mail response is also a key issue. Chaffey and Edgar (2000) reported on a survey of 361 UK websites across different sectors. Of those in the sample, 331 (92%) were accessible at the time of the survey and, of these, 299 provided an e-mail contact point. E-mail enquiries were sent to all of these 299 websites; of these, 9 undeliverable mail messages were received. It can be seen that, at the time of the survey, service availability was certainly not universal. Surprisingly, more recent surveys suggest some improvement, but still indicate a poor quality of service overall. Transversal (2005), the provider of the MetaFAQ software to answer customers' responses online, found the following reliability of response:

- *Average number of questions answered*
  - travel 1.2 out of 10
  - telecoms 1 out of 10
  - average all companies 2.1 out of 10
- *Percentage of companies that responded to e-mail*
  - travel 40%
  - telecoms 70%
  - average 56%
- *Average e-mail response time*
  - travel 42 hours
  - telecoms 32 hours
  - average 33 hours.

The problem was still apparent in a similar survey completed by Transversal in 2008 with fewer than half (46%) of the routine customer service questions e-mailed to 100 leading organisations answered adequately.

## Responsiveness

The same 2005 survey showed that responsiveness was poor overall: of the 290 successfully delivered e-mails, a 62% response rate occurred within a 28-day period. For over a third of companies there was zero response!

Of the companies that did respond, there was a difference in responsiveness (excluding immediately delivered automated responses) from 8 minutes to over 19 working days! While the mean overall was 2 working days, 5 hours and 11 minutes, the median across all sectors (on the basis of the fastest 50% of responses received) was 1 working day and 34 minutes. The median result suggests that response within one working day represents best practice and could form the basis for consumer expectations.

In the 2008 survey, the average time to respond to e-mail was nearly 4 days (46 hours), with 28% of organisations not even replying at all. But some companies responded with useful answers within 10 minutes. Transversal believe that the figures show a major deterioration since 2006, when e-mail successfully answered 60% of queries and kept customers waiting less time – on average 33 hours – for a reply.

Responsiveness is also indicated by the performance of the website – the time it takes for a page request to be delivered to the user's browser as a page impression. Data from monitoring services such as Keynote (www.keynote.com) indicate that there is a wide variability in the delivery of information and hence service quality from web servers hosted at ISPs, and companies should be careful to monitor this and specify levels of quality with suppliers in service-level agreements (SLAs). Table 7.2 shows the standard set by the best-performing sites and the difference compared to the worst-performing sites.

This issue is also significant in terms of promotion costs, since in 2008 Google introduced an assessment of site response time into its 'Quality Score' for assessing suitability (see Chapter 9 for details). The result is that for ads that are otherwise similar, the slower performing site will pay more for an equivalent position or its position will be lower for a similar bid amount!

## Assurance

In an e-mail context, assurance can best be considered as the quality of response. In the survey reported by Chaffey and Edgar (2000), of 180 responses received, 91% delivered a personalised human response, with 9% delivering an automated response which did not address the individual enquiry; 40% of responses answered or referred to all three questions, with 10% answering two questions and 22% one. Overall, 38% did not answer any of the specific questions posed!

### Multichannel communications preferences

Upton (2008) reports on research where 1000 UK consumers aged 18+ were surveyed to identify the role and importance of customer services and communications for online businesses. Despite the growing popularity of e-mail as a communication tool, 53% of those interviewed still prefer to communicate with businesses over the telephone, particularly for service enquiries, compared with 48% for e-mail and 16% for traditional mail. However, when asked about their experiences, three out of ten UK consumers stated they found it difficult to locate contact details on websites.

Surprisingly, 53% of consumers consider three minutes waiting time a satisfactory period to speak with an agent over the telephone. Consumers particularly disliked ringing a contact centre only to be met with a computerised answering service. As Upton notes, replacing a skilled operator with an automated service might save money in the short term – however, in the long term companies risk losing brand advocacy and sales. Additionally, customers believe 24 hours is a respectable amount of time to wait for a response when contacting a business via e-mail.

He concludes:

*Overall the research shows that in this era of multi-communication, consumers are no longer allied to any particular mode of communication. They will select the most convenient or appropriate channel even if the retailer trades solely online.*

*As a result, brands need to provide their contact centre agents with the tools to seamlessly combine different communication channels such as telephone, e-mail, v-mail, web chat and SMS to communicate with the consumer and meet their expectations of service.*

*Agents also need to have real-time access to all past interactions with a customer. This should include text transcriptions of conversations and e-mails, scanned copies of letters received and despatched, as well as call recordings, comments and outcomes ensuring that the agent is fully briefed on the existing relationship that the customer has with the brand. Importantly, this information can be further used to tailor all future contact with the customer, delivering greater levels of customer satisfaction. By employing the customer's preferred channel of communication, which has been identified using the data from real conversations with individuals, it is possible to meet customer expectations, and as a result maximise retention and brand advocacy.*

A further assurance concern of e-commerce websites is the privacy and security of customer information (see Chapter 3). A company that adheres to the UK Internet Shopping Is Safe (ISIS) (www.imrg.org/isis) or TRUSTe principles (www.truste.org) will provide better assurance than one that does not. For security, 'hacker safe' accreditation is available from Scan Alert (www.scanalert.com) who are owned by McAfee security products. This involves automated daily scans to test site security.

Chaffey and Smith (2008) suggest that the following actions can be used to achieve assurance in an e-commerce site:

- provide clear and effective privacy statements;
- follow privacy and consumer protection guidelines in all local markets;
- make security of customer data a priority;
- use independent certification bodies;
- emphasise the excellence of service quality in all communications.

## Empathy

Although it might be considered that empathy requires personal human contact, it can still be achieved, to an extent, through e-mail. Chaffey and Edgar (2000) report that of the responses received, 91% delivered a personalised human response, with 29% passing on the enquiry within their organisation. Of these 53, 23 further responses were received within the 28-day period; 30 (or 57%) of passed-on queries were not responded to further.

Provision of personalisation facilities is also an indication of the empathy provided by the website, but more research is needed as to customers' perception of the value of web pages that are dynamically created to meet a customer's information needs.

An alternative framework for considering how service quality can be delivered through e-commerce is to consider how the site provides customer service at the different stages of the buying decision – discussed in Chapter 2 in the section on online consumer behaviour. Thus, quality service is not only dependent on how well the purchase itself is facilitated, but also on how easy it is for customers to select products and on after-sales service, including fulfilment quality. The Epson UK site (www.epson.co.uk) illustrates how the site can be used to help in all stages of the buying process. Interactive tools are available to help users select a particular printer, diagnose and solve faults, and technical brochures can be downloaded. Feedback is solicited on how well these services meet customers' needs.

It can be suggested that for managers wishing to apply a framework such as SERVQUAL in an e-commerce context there are three stages appropriate to managing the process:

1 *Understanding expectations.* Customer expectations for the e-commerce environment in a particular market sector must be understood. The SERVQUAL framework can be used with market research and benchmarking of other sites to understand requirements such as responsiveness and empathy. Scenarios can also be used to identify customer expectations of using services on a site.

2 *Setting and communicating the service promise.* Once expectations are understood, marketing communications can be used to inform the customers of the level of service. This can be achieved through customer service guarantees or promises. It is better to under-promise than over-promise. A book retailer who delivers a book in 2 days when 3 days were promised will earn the customer's loyalty better than the retailer who promises 1 day but delivers in 2! The enlightened company may also explain what it will do if it doesn't meet its promises – will the customer be recompensed? The service promise must also be communicated internally and combined with training to ensure that the service is delivered.

3 *Delivering the service promise.* Finally, commitments must be delivered through on-site service, support from employees and physical fulfilment. Otherwise, online credibility is destroyed and a customer may never return.

Tables 7.7 and 7.8 summarise the main concerns of online consumers for each of the elements of service quality. Table 7.7 summarises the main factors in the context of SERVQUAL and Table 7.8 presents the requirements from an e-commerce site that must be met for excellent customer service.

| Table 7.7 | Online elements of service quality | | |
|---|---|---|---|
| **Tangibles** | **Reliability** | **Responsiveness** | **Assurance and empathy** |
| Ease of use | Availability | Download speed | Contacts with call centre |
| Content quality | Reliability | E-mail response | Personalisation |
| Price | E-mail replies | Call-back | Privacy |
| | | Fulfilment | Security |

| Table 7.8 | Summary of requirements for online service quality | |
|---|---|---|
| **E-mail response requirements** | **Website requirements** |
| • Defined response times and named individual responsible for replies | • Support for customer-preferred channel of communication in response to enquiries (e-mail, phone, postal mail or in person) |
| • Use of autoresponders to confirm query is being processed | • Clearly indicated contact points for enquiries via e-mail mailto: and forms |
| • Personalised e-mail where appropriate | • Company internal targets for site availability and performance |
| • Accurate response to inbound e-mail by *customer-preferred channel*: outbound e-mail or phone call-back | • Testing of site usability and efficiency of links, HTML, plug-ins and browsers to maximise availability |
| • Opt-in and opt-out options must be provided for promotional e-mail with a suitable offer in exchange for a customer's provision of information | • Appropriate graphic and structural site design to achieve ease of use and relevant content with visual appeal |
| • Clear layout, named individual and privacy statements in e-mail | • Personalisation option for customers |
| | • Specific tools to help a user to answer specific queries such as interactive support databases and frequently asked questions (FAQ) |

*Source*: Chaffey and Edgar (2000)

# The relationship between service quality, customer satisfaction and loyalty

Figure 7.17 highlights the importance of online service quality. If customer expectations are not met, customer satisfaction will be poor and repeat site visits will not occur, which makes it difficult to build online relationships. Note, however, that online service quality is also dependent on other aspects of the service experience including the offline component of the service, such as fulfilment, and the core and extended product offer including pricing. If the customer experience is satisfactory, it can be suggested that customer loyalty will develop.

Reichheld and Schefter (2000) suggest that it is key for organisations to understand not only what determines service quality and customer satisfaction, but also loyalty or repeat purchases. From their research, they suggest five 'primary determinants of loyalty' online:

- quality customer support;
- on-time delivery;
- compelling product presentations;
- convenient and reasonably priced shipping and handling;
- clear trustworthy privacy policies.

Figure 7.17 shows a more recent compilation of consumers' opinions of the importance of these loyalty drivers in the online context. It can be seen that it is the after-sales support and service which are considered to be most important – the ease of use and navigation are relatively unimportant.

Of course, the precise nature of the loyalty drivers will differ between companies. Reichheld and Schefter (2000) reported that Dell Computer has created a customer experience council that has researched key loyalty drivers, identified measures to track these and put in place an action plan to improve loyalty. The loyalty drivers and their summary metrics were:

- Driver: *order fulfilment*. Metrics: *ship to target* – percentage that ship on time exactly as the customer specified.
- Driver: *product performance*. Metrics: *initial field incident rate* – the frequency of problems experienced by customers.
- Driver: *post-sale service and support*. Metrics: *on-time, first-time fix* – the percentage of problems fixed on the first visit by a service representative who arrives at the time promised.

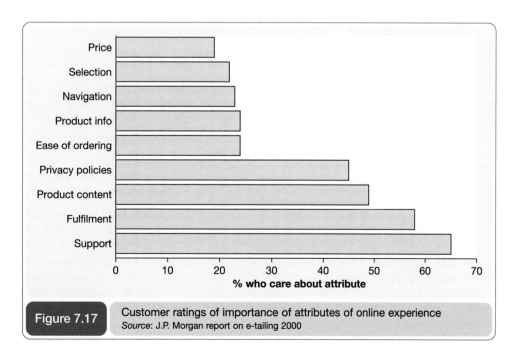

| Figure 7.17 | Customer ratings of importance of attributes of online experience |
| --- | --- |
| | *Source*: J.P. Morgan report on e-tailing 2000 |

Rigby *et al.* (2000) assessed repeat-purchase drivers in grocery, clothing and consumer electronics e-tail. It was found that the key loyalty drivers were similar to those of Dell, including correct delivery of order, but other factors such as price, ease of use and customer support were more important.

To summarise this section, and in order to more fully understand the online expectations of service quality, complete Activity 7.3.

---

| Activity 7.3 | An example of factors determining online service quality |
| --- | --- |

**Purpose**

To understand the elements of online service quality.

**Activity**

Think back to your experience of purchasing a book or CD online. Alternatively, visit a site and go through the different stages. Write down your expectations of service quality from when you first arrive on the website until the product is delivered. There should be around ten different stages.

---

| Case Study 7 | Refining the online customer experience at dabs.com |
| --- | --- |

This case study highlights the importance placed on website design as part of the customer experience by dabs.com which is one of the UK's leading Internet retailers of IT and technology products from manufacturers such as Sony, Hewlett-Packard, Toshiba and Microsoft.

## Company background and history

Dabs.com was originally created by entrepreneur David Atherton in partnership with writer Bruce Smith (the name 'Dabs' comes from the combined initials of their two names). Their first venture, Dabs Press, was publishing technology books. Although David and Bruce remain firm friends, Dabs has been 100% owned by David since 1990 but was purchased by telecoms company BT in April 2006 for an undisclosed sum. Dabs.com is a wholly owned subsidiary of BT, but the Dabs branding remains on its site. BT has used the Dabs website design and catalogue system for its own BT Shop (www.shopbt.com). Turnover for the 2006 financial year was £160 million (£15 million from elsewhere in Europe) with a gross profit of £24 million.

Dabs Direct was launched in 1990 as a mail-order firm which mainly promoted itself through ads in home technology magazines such as *Personal Computer World* and *Computer Shopper*.

Dabs.com was launched in 1999 at the height of the dot-com boom, but unlike many dot-com start-up businesses, dabs.com was based on an existing offline business.

In its first year, dabs.com was loss-making with £1.2 million lost in 2000–1; this was partly due to including free delivery as part of the proposition to acquire new customers.

In 2003, the company opened its first 'bricks and mortar' store at Liverpool John Lennon Airport and it has also opened an operation in France (www.dabs.fr). The French site remains, but the retail strategy has now ended since margins were too low, despite a positive effect in building awareness of the brand in retail locations.

## Strategy

The importance that dabs.com owners place on customer experience and usability is suggested by their mission statement, which places customer experience at its core together with choice and price. Dabs.com's mission is:

*to provide customers with a quick and easy way of buying the products they want, at the most competitive prices around, delivered directly to their door.*

Growth has been conservatively managed, since as a privately held company dabs.com has to grow profitably rather than take on debts. Dabs.com has reviewed the potential of other European countries for distribution and may select a country where broadband access is high, such as Sweden or the Netherlands. Countries such as Italy where consumers traditionally prefer face-to-face sales would not be early candidates to target for an opening.

Dabs.com targets the B2B market as well as the consumer market, offering a different version of the site for business users. According to *New Media Age* (2008) 60% of sales are from this source.

In terms of products, dabs.com has focused on computers and related products but is considering expanding into new categories or even ranges. Initially these will be related to what computer users need while they are working.

## Dabs.com performance

In 2005, dabs.com, a £200 million company with 235 staff, holding 15,000 lines for a customer base of almost 1.5 million and processing around 5000 customer orders every day. Dabs.com has 8 million visits a month from around 750,000 unique users. Its catalogue contains 20,000 products with laptops, LCD monitors and external hard drives among the main sales lines. The company launched Dabs.fr in France in 2004.

NCC (2005) reports that dabs.com believes that what its customers require is a dynamic site that provides comprehensive information on its product ranges, delivery charges, returns policy, financing services and rewards scheme. It also provides dabs.tv, a video service that allows customers to see more complex products in greater detail.

Jonathan Wall, Dab's marketing director, sees security as important as part of the customer experience and to protect the business, he says:

> We were one of the first e-businesses to adopt Visa's 'Verified by Visa' 3D secure payment authentication system and we've also implemented MasterCard's SecureCode variant. We've always worked closely with both credit card companies and it's a concern that dates back to our mail order side. The threat of being attacked and defrauded is always in the forefront of our thoughts.

## Delivery

To ensure delivery as promised, Jonathan Wall explains the importance dabs.com attach to IT:

> We invest as much in our highly automated warehouse as we do in our marketing. Our systems use a sophisticated combination of dynamic bins and unique product numbering. Many of the management team come from technical backgrounds. Our back office system was written in OpenVMS by our IT director. Our sales processing system was written in-house.

## Staffing

According to NCC (2005), staff skills are viewed as important from technology staff, to product buyers. Wall says:

> We pay a higher than average salary, and that means we get a higher level of staff. And we really see the effect of that in the way our buyers and merchandisers approach the market.

Dabs.com ended offline sales in September 2001, after online sales reached half of turnover. This enabled it to reduce costs. Although its consumer sales are online, dabs.com does retain a call centre for customer service and account management services for its business clients who spend £15,000 or more per year. Excellence in customer service is also seen as part of the customer experience and helps dabs.com reduce complaints to trading standards officers compared to some of its online rivals, such as eBuyer.com.

Dabs.com published these customer service statistics in March 2008 for the previous 28 days:

- average wait time for chats: 10 seconds
- average e-mail response time: 5 hours (based on working hours)

## The 2003 site update

In 2003, dabs.com achieved a year-on-year profits rise from £2.5m to £5.1m and sales rise from £150m to £200m. It predicted that growth will continue, with sales reaching £350m in 2005. Dabs has about one million unique visitors monthly and adds a further 30,000 new users every month. This success has been achieved in just four years from the launch of its first transactional site in 1999. The site reassures each visitor by the scale of its success. On 5 December it read:

- 1,098,412 customers
- 37,093 orders in December
- 21,289 products available for sale.

Dabs's marketing director, Jonathan Wall, talking to *IT Week* (2003), explained how the initial growth occurred and how future growth will be sustained: 'We dominate the PC hobbyist/IT professional sector, but our business must evolve. We want to cast our net further so that we are appealing to people who are interested in technology as a whole. New customers need a new approach. We have built a new environment and a new website for this target audience.'

In mid-2003 dabs.com launched a site to help it achieve sales to the new audience. Research was used to help develop the new site. The usability of the existing website was tested and the new concept was also shown to a focus group. After analysing the responses Dabs created a pilot site, which the same focus group then approved. In total, the new site took 10 months to develop and represented an investment of £750,000.

## The 2005 site update

NCC (2005) says Wall makes the business case for the new site as follows:

> Our new site will take us right up there to the top of the field – you have to try to stay ahead. We'll have guided navigation, still quite rare on a UK site, which will help customers to find what they're looking for more intuitively. Early e-commerce customers knew that they specifically wanted a Sony Vaio laptop, for example. New customers just know that they want a laptop that's small and fast and costs less than £1000. Guided navigation means they can search according to a product's attributes rather than specific brands and models.

Since the average selling price of laptops is going down, slim margins are decreased further. Wall says: 'Selling electronic equipment on the web has traditionally been passive but by redesigning our site we'll be able to show customers what extra £50 spent on a laptop will buy them.'

Although the previous site was updated only two years ago, he describes the need to keep ahead of competitors as 'a cat and mouse thing'. But new site advances must be combined with competitive prices, Wall says:

> Online customers are price-loyal, not retailer-loyal. The customer is only as loyal as the cheapest price they can pay for a product. It means your competitors are only ever one click away. We have to do everything to keep our customers on our site. Getting them to pay that price to you, rather than your competitor, means that you'll need to exploit the constantly-evolving benefits of digital technology to make their buying experience on your site as fluent and satisfactory as possible.

## On-site search capabilities

A feature of the new site is improved on-site search capabilities from Endeca, which powers the search of Walmart and Circuit City sites in the US. Search is important to increasing conversion rates, and so increasing sales, since if a user is not presented with a relevant product when they search, they are likely to try another retailer. The search capability should strike a balance between delivering too many results and too few. Channel Register (2005) reports that dabs.com hopes to increase conversion rate by up to 50% by updating the site's search and navigation features. The current conversion rate is 3.5% and it is hoped this will be increased to nearer 5%.

Endeca's new search allows users to select products by attributes including price, brand and even size and weight. This method of narrowing down the search should result in the customer being left to choose from a list of 10 or 20 products rather than hundreds.

Another aspect of the business case for the new site is to ensure the customer makes the right decision since product returns are costly for dabs.com and annoying for the customer.

Dabs.com marketing director Jonathan Wall explained: 'When we launched the website in 1999 people knew what they wanted. Now we find a large tranche of customers might know the type of product they want to buy but not which model they want. The new site is about guiding them through the process.'

## Accessibility

Since dabs.com has tech-savvy customers, it has to support them as they adopt new ways of browsing. Dabs.com found that by 1995 nearly a fifth of its users were using the Mozilla Firefox browser, so a further requirement for the new site was to make it accessible to users browsing with a range of browsers such as Firefox, Opera and Apple's Safari.

## Marketing communications

Marketing communications approaches used by dabs.com are summarised in Chapter 8 in Mini case study 8.6 (see page 478) 'Electronic retailers cut back on their e-communications spend'. For customer acquisition, the main communications tools that are used are:

- paid sSearch engine marketing (the main investment)
- referrals from affiliates (this has been reduced)
- online display advertising on third-party sites (limited)
- PR
- sponsorship (shirt sponsorship for premiership team Fulham).

*New Media Age* (2008) reports that Dabs now has one full-time person managing its search campaigns. Its head of online marketing also spends 20% of her time on this area. The company also uses bid management software to allow it to manage its keyword base of 100,000 terms and to improve return on investment.

Dabs.com uses affiliate marketing less than previously. Marketing director Jonathan Wall speaking to *New Media Age* (2008) believes that the major affiliate sites that many of his rivals use, while still important, have had their heyday. He says:

> I think most sites noticed things getting harder, on prices and demand, from the summer onwards. We were finding that the big affiliate shopping portals weren't delivering the traffic they used to, so we revamped our e-mail strategy. We work a lot harder to make the e-mails more appealing and we put up a lot

*of original content about products we know our audience will find interesting. The result has been the retention of 90% of customers opted-in to an e-mail that has gone from once to twice a week.*

*Sources*: Channel Register (2005), *IT Week* (2003), NCC (2005)

## Question

1. The management of dabs.com has invested in several major upgrades to its online presence in order to improve the online customer experience. Assess the reasons for the need to invest in site upgrades by referring to the dabs.com example. To what extent do you think major, regular site upgrades are inevitable?

2. Compare the quality of the online customer experience of dabs.com by visiting the site and those of its competitors, such as www.ebuyer.com and www.euroffice.com. Explain the categories of criteria you have used to make your assessment.

## Summary

1. An effective online customer experience is dependent on many factors, including the visual elements of the site design and how it has been designed for usability, accessibility and performance.

2. Careful planning and execution of website implementation is important, in order to avoid the need for extensive reworking at a later stage if the design proves to be ineffective.

3. Implementation is not an isolated process; it should be integrated with the Internet marketing strategy. Analysis, design and implementation should occur repeatedly in an iterative, prototyping approach based on usability testing that involves the client and the users to produce an effective design.

4. A feasibility study should take place before the initiation of a major website project. A feasibility study will assess:
   - the costs and benefits of the project;
   - the difficulty of achieving management and staff commitment to the project;
   - the availability of domain names to support the project;
   - the responsibilities and stages necessary for a successful project.

5. The choice of host for a website should be considered carefully since this will govern the quality of service of the website.

6. Options for analysis of users' requirements for a website include:
   - interviews with marketing staff;
   - questionnaire sent to companies;
   - usability and accessibility testing;
   - informal interviews with key accounts;
   - focus groups;
   - reviewing competitors' websites.

7. The design phase of developing a website includes specification of:
   - the information architecture, or structure, of the website using techniques such as site maps, blueprints and wireframes;
   - the flow, controlled by the navigation and menu options;
   - the graphic design and brand identity;
   - country-specific localisation;
   - the service quality of online forms and e-mail messages.

## Exercises

### Self-assessment exercises

1. Explain the term 'prototyping' in relation to website creation.
2. What tasks should managers undertake during initiation of a web page?
3. What is 'domain name registration?'
4. List the factors that determine website 'flow'.
5. Explain the structure of an HTML document and the concept of 'tags'.
6. List the options for designing website menu options.
7. What is a 'hierarchical' website structure?
8. What are the factors that control the performance of a website?

### Essay and discussion questions

1. Discuss the relative effectiveness of the different methods of assessing the customers' needs from a website.
2. Select three websites of your choice and compare their design effectiveness. You should describe design features such as navigation, structure and graphics.
3. Explain how strategy, analysis, design and implementation of a website should be integrated through a prototyping approach. Describe the merits and problems of the prototyping approach.
4. When designing the interactive services of a website, such as online forms and e-mails to customers, what steps should the designer take to provide a quality service to customers?

### Examination questions

1. What is website prototyping? Give three benefits of this approach.
2. What controls on a website project are introduced at the initiation phase of the project?
3. A company is selecting an ISP. Explain:
   (a) what an ISP is;
   (b) which factors will affect the quality of service delivered by the ISP.
4. How are focus groups used to gain understanding of customer expectations of a website?
5. Name, and briefly explain, four characteristics of the information content of a site that will govern whether a customer is likely to return to that website.
6. When the graphic design and page layout of a website are being described, what different factors associated with type and set-up of a PC and its software should the designer take into account?
7. What is meant by 'opt-in'? Why should it be taken into account as part of website design?

## References

Aaker, D. and Norris, N. (1982) Characteristics of TV commercials perceived as informative, *Journal of Advertising*, 25(2), 22–34.

Bevan, N. (1999a) Usability issues in website design. *Proceedings of the 6th Interactive Publishing Conference*, November. Available online at www.usability.serco.com.

Bevan, N. (1999b) Common industry format usability tests. *Proceedings of UPA'98*, Usability Professionals Association, Scottsdale, Arizona, 29 June–2 July 1999. Available online at www.usability.serco.com.

BSI (1999) BS 13407 Human-centred design processes for interactive systems. British Standards Institute.

Chaffey, D. and Edgar, M. (2000) Measuring online service quality, *Journal of Targeting, Analysis and Measurement for Marketing*, 8(4) (May), 363–78.

Chaffey, D. and Smith, P.R. (2008) *E-marketing Excellence. Planning and Optimizing your Digital Marketing – at the Heart of E-Business*, 3rd edn. Butterworth-Heinemann, Oxford.

Chaffey, D. and Wood, S. (2005) *Business Information Management*. Financial Times/Prentice Hall, Harlow.

Channel Register (2005) Dabs.com in £500k makeover, Channel Register, www.channelregister.co.uk, John Leyden, 2 September.

Christodoulides, G., de Chernatony, L., Furrer, O., Shiu, E. and Temi, A. (2006) Conceptualising and measuring the equity of online brands. *Journal of Marketing Management*, September, Vol. 22 Issue 7/8, 799–825.

Cronin, J. and Taylor, S. (1992) Measuring service quality: a re-examination and extension, *Journal of Marketing*, 56, 55–63.

de Chernatony, L. (2001) Succeeding with brands on the Internet, *Journal of Brand Management*, 8(3), 186–95.

Feinberg, R., Trotter, M. and Anton, J. (2000) At any time – from anywhere – in any form. In D. Renner (ed.) *Defying the Limits, Reaching New Heights in Customer Relationship Management*. Report from Montgomery Research Inc., San Francisco, CA, http://feinberg.crmproject.com.

Fogg, B., Soohoo, C., Danielson, D., Marable, L., Stanford, J. and Tauber, E. (2003) How do people evaluate a website's credibility? A Consumer WebWatch research report, prepared by Stanford Persuasive Technology Lab.

Gleisser, G. (2001) Building customer relationships online: the website designer's perspective, *Journal of Consumer Marketing*, 18(6), 488–502.

Hofacker, C. (2000) *Internet Marketing*. Wiley, New York.

Hoffman, D.L. and Novak, T.P. (1997) A new marketing paradigm for electronic commerce, *The Information Society*, Special issue on electronic commerce, 13, 43–54.

*IT Week* (2003) E-shop adds to attractions. By David Neal, *IT Week* 12 September, 24, www.itweek.co.uk.

Kolesar, M. and Galbraith, R. (2000) A services-marketing perspective on e-retailing, *Internet Research: Electronic Networking Applications and Policy*, 10(5), 424–38.

Loiacono, E., Watson, R. and Goodhue, D. (2000) 'WEBQUAL: a measure of website quality', in *Marketing Theory and Applications*, Vol. 13, K. Evans and L. Scheer (eds), American Marketing Association, Chicago, 2002, 432–439.

Lynch, P. and Horton, S. (1999) *Web Style Guide: Basic Design Principles for Creating Websites*. Yale University Press, New Haven, CT.

Morgan, R. (1996) An Internet marketing framework for the World Wide Web, *Journal of Marketing Management*, 12, 757–75.

Moe, W. (2003) Buying, searching, or browsing: differentiating between online shoppers using in-store navigational clickstream. *Journal of Consumer Psychology*, 13 (1/2), 29.

*Multilingual* (2008) Localizing a localizer's website: the challenge. Jan/Feb 2008, 30–33.

NCC (2005) dabs.com benefits from innovative approach. *Principia*. NCC members magazine. Issue 37, May/June. www.nccmembership.co.uk/pooled/articles/BF_WEBART/view.asp?Q=BF_WEBART_162441.

*New Media Age* (2008) Vertical focus: consumer electronics, *New Media Age*, 28 February 2008.

Nielsen, J. (1999) Details in study methodology can give misleading results. Jakob Nielsen's Alertbox, 21 February, www.useit.com/alertbox/990221.html.

Nielsen, J. (2000a) Novice vs. expert users, Jakob Nielsen's Alertbox, 6 February. www.useit.com/alertbox/20000206.html.

Nielsen, J. (2000b) *Designing Web Usability*. New Riders Publishing, USA.

Nitish, S., Fassott, G., Zhao, H. and Boughton, P. (2006) A cross-cultural analysis of German, Chinese and Indian consumers' perception of website adaptation, *Journal of Consumer Behaviour*, 5: 56–68.

NMA (2008) Profile – Travis Katz, Author: Luan Goldie, *New Media Age*, published 31 January 08.

Ong, C. (1995) Practical aspects of marketing on the WWW, MBA Dissertation, University of Sheffield, UK.

Pak, J. (1999) Content dimensions of web advertising: a cross national comparison, *International Journal of Advertising*, 18(2), 207–31.

Parasuraman, A., Zeithaml, V. and Berry, L. (1985) A conceptual model of service quality and its implications for future research, *Journal of Marketing*, 49, Fall, 48.

*The Register* (2004) Wobbly shopping carts blight UK e-commerce, The Register.Co.uk, 4 June.

Reichheld, F. and Schefter, P. (2000) E-loyalty, your secret weapon, *Harvard Business Review*, July–August, 105–13.

Resnik, A. and Stern, A. (1977) An analysis of information content in television advertising, *Journal of Marketing*, January, 50–3.

Rettie, R. (2001) An exploration of flow during Internet use, *Internet Research*, 11(2), 103–13.

Rigby, D., Bavega, S., Rastoi, S., Zook, C. and Hancock, S. (2000) The value of customer loyalty and how you can capture it. Bain and Company/Mainspring whitepaper, 17 March. Published at www.mainspring.com.

Robertson, J. (2003) Information design using card sorting. Step Two. Available online at www.steptwo.com.au/papers/cardsorting/index.html.

Rosen, D. and Purinton, E. (2004) Website design: viewing the Web as a cognitive landscape, *Journal of Business Research*, 57(7), 787–94.

Rosenfeld, L. and Morville, P. (2002) *Information Architecture for the World Wide Web*, 2nd edn. O'Reilly, Sebastopol, CA.

Scene 7 (2008) Scene7 ondemand survey: Web 2.0 experience 2008 and Beyond, January 2008.

SciVisum (2005) Internet campaign effectiveness study, press release, July, www.scivisum.co.uk.

Singh, N. and Pereira, A. (2005) *The Culturally Customized Website, Customizing Websites for the Global Marketplace*, Butterworth-Heinemann, Oxford, UK.

Smith, D. and Sivakumar, K. (2004) Flow and Internet shopping behavior: a conceptual model and research propositions, *Journal of Business Research*, 57(10), 1199–208.

Smith, S. and Wheeler, J. (2002) *Managing the Customer Experience*. Financial Times/Prentice Hall, London.

Sterne, J. (2001) *World Wide Web Marketing*, 3rd edn. Wiley, New York.

Transversal (2005) UK companies fail online customer service test. Transversal press release, 17 March, http://transversal.com/html/news/viewpress.php?article=42.

Upton, N. (2008) Online customer service. *What's New in Marketing* E-newsletter, Issue 66, February 2008. Available online at www.wnim.com.

Trocchia, P. and Janda, S. (2003) How do consumers evaluate Internet retail service quality? *Journal of Services Marketing*, 17(3).

Wodtke, C. (2002) *Information Architecture: Blueprints for the Web*. New Riders, IN.

Weathers, D. and Makienko, I. (2006) Assessing the relationships between e-tail success and product and website factors, *Journal of Interactive Marketing*, Vol. 2, 41–54.

Zeithaml, V., Parasuraman, A. and Malhotra, A. (2002) Service quality delivery through websites: a critical review of extant knowledge, *Academy of Marketing Science*, 30(4), 368.

## Further reading

Bevan, N. (1999) Usability issues in website design, *Proceedings of the 6th Interactive Publishing Conference*, November. Available online at www.usability.serco.com. Accessible lists of web-design pointers.

Noyes, J. and Baber, C. (1999) *User-centred Design of Systems*. Springer-Verlag, Berlin. Details the user-centred design approach.

Preece, J., Rogers, Y. and Sharp, H. (2002) *Interaction Design*. Wiley, New York. Clearly describes a structured approach to interaction design, including web interaction.

## Web links

### Accessibility

- **EConsultancy** (www.e-consultancy.com/topic/accessibility) Channel provides buyers guides and suppliers within this category.
- **Royal National Institute for the Blind** (www.rnib/org.uk/accessibility) web accessibility guidelines.
- **W3C** (www.w3.org/WAI) Guidelines and resources from the World Wide Web Consortium (W3C).

### Information architecture

- **Boxes and Arrows** (www.boxesandarrows.com) A great collection of best practice articles and discussions about IA topics such as controlled vocabularies.
- **Peter Morville** (www.semanticstudios.com/publications). Blog of the author of the classic information architecture book. In-depth best practice articles.
- **Louis Rosenfeld site** (www.louisrosenfield.com) Rosenfeld is also author of the classic Information Architecture book.
- **Jesse James Garrett** (http://jjg.net/ia) Design expert JJG's Articles on IA.
- **Step Two** (www.steptwo.com.au) This design company has introductory outlines and more detailed articles on information architecture and other aspects of usability.

### Usability

- **UsabilityNet** (www.usabilitynet.org) A portal about usability with good links to other sites and an introduction to usability terms and concepts.
- **Usability.Gov** (www.usability.gov) A comprehensive US portal site covering every aspect of usability, from planning and analysing to designing, followed by testing and refining.
- **UseIt** (www.useit.com/alertbox). Ten years on, it is still worth subscribing for Jakob Nielsen's often trenchant views on web design, which are typically based on his user research.
- **UIE** (www.uie.com/articles) Jared Spool's user interface engineering articles provide good best practice summary articles.
- **Yahoo! Developer Network Design Pattern library** (http:developer.yahoo.com/ypatterns/index.php) These contain many common usability elements from breadcrumbs to buttons, so this should be on the bookmark list of all involved with web design.

### Web development

- **Web Developers Handbook** (www.alvit.de/handbook) One of the best resources summarising all web development how-to resources and blogs.
- **Sitepoint** (www.sitepoint.com) online publisher with a range of blog articles in all web design categories.
- **Crea8asiteforums** (www.cre8asiteforums.com/forums) Popular forum covering many aspects of website design.
- **Webby Awards** (www.webbyawards.com) Best practice. The Oscars for the web – international.

### Web standards

- **A List Apart** (www.alistapart.com) Explores the design, development and meaning of web content, with a special focus on web standards and best practices.
- **Web Standards Project (WASP)** (www.webstandards.org) – a consortium that promotes web standards.
- **The World Wide Web Consortium** (www.w3.org) – the global standards body prominent in defining web standards.
- **Zeldman.com** (www.zeldman.com) The blog of web standards advocate, Jeffrey Zeldman.

# 8

# Campaign planning for digital media

## Learning objectives

After reading this chapter, the reader should be able to:

- Assess the difference in communications characteristics between digital and traditional media
- Identify the main success factors in managing a digital campaign
- Understand the importance of integrating online and offline communications
- Relate promotion techniques to methods of measuring site effectiveness

## Questions for marketers

Key questions for marketing managers related to this chapter are:

- How do the characteristics of digital media differ from those of traditional media?
- How should I plan an online marketing campaign?
- How do I choose the best mix of online and offline communications techniques?

## Links to other chapters

Related chapters are:

- Chapter 1 describes the 6 Is, a framework that introduces the characteristics of Internet marketing communications
- Chapter 2 introduces portals and search engines – one of the methods of online traffic building discussed in this chapter
- Chapter 3 introduces some of the legal and ethical constraints on online marketing communications
- Chapter 4 provides the strategic basis for Internet marketing communications
- Chapter 7 describes on-site communications
- Chapter 9 reviews the different digital media channels in detail
- Chapter 10 considers the measurement of communications effectiveness

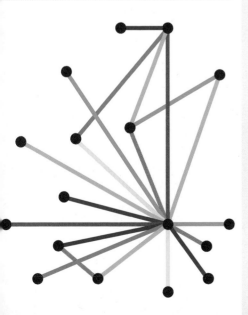

## Introduction

A company that has developed an effective online customer experience as discussed in Chapter 7 is only part-way to achieving successful Internet marketing outcomes. In the days of the dot-com boom a common expression was: 'If you build it, they will come'. This famous line proved true of a baseball stadium built in the 1989 film *Field of Dreams*, but unfortunately, it doesn't apply to websites. Berthon *et al.* (1998) make the analogy between online communications and a trade fair. Here, there will be many companies at different stands promoting their products and services. Effective promotion and achieving visibility of the stand is necessary to attract some of the many show visitors to that stand. Similarly, if you want to maximise quality visitors within a target audience to a website to acquire new customers online, Internet marketers have to select the appropriate online and offline marketing communications such as search engine marketing, display advertising and affiliate advertising which were introduced in Figure 1.9 (page 29). This is a major challenge since there are tens of millions of websites with many pages, each vying to attract an audience – Google indexes over 20 billion pages.

### Goals of interactive marketing communications

**Continuous e-communications activities**
Long-term use of e-marketing communications intended to generate site visitors for customer acquisition (such as search engine, affiliate marketing and online sponsorship) and retention (for example, e-newsletter marketing).

Planning for how digital media are used includes both short-term campaigns to support a particular goal such as launching a new product, promoting a sale or encouraging prospects to attend an event, and longer-term **continuous e-communications activities** which review the best mix of communications to use to drive visitors to a site to achieve the main outcomes for the site such as product sales (for a retailer), lead generation (for a business-to-business company), engagement with a brand or subscriptions or ad revenue (for an online publisher).

Chaffey and Smith (2008) refer to the relevance of timing for traffic building. They say:

*Some e-marketers may consider traffic building to be a continuous process, but others may view it as a specific campaign, perhaps to launch a site or a major enhancement. Some methods tend to work best continuously; others are short term. Short-term campaigns will be for a site launch or an event such as an online trade show.*

A similar sentiment is expressed in Mini case study 8.1 on the Alliance & Leicester which refers to use of 'drip' as against 'burst' communications.

---

| Mini Case Study 8.1 | Full rather than a burst online presence for Alliance & Leicester |
|---|---|

Speaking to *New Media Age* (2006), Graham Findlay, Customer Acquisition Manager at bank Alliance & Leicester, highlighted the importance of continuous e-communications when he said:

*A big part of my team's job is to continually monitor traffic to and from our sites. We work to maintain the bank's profile. Some of our competitors don't always have a full online presence, settling instead for bursts of activity. That's certainly not our strategy.*

This sentiment is backed up through investment in search and affiliate marketing. The article reported that Alliance & Leicester have increased their search engine marketing budget from 2001: £10,000 to £3 million in 2006 as part of a £13 million budget. About search he says:

*I believe there's volume to be made from search and it's only right that a direct bank like us features in the top listings through search.*

Four typical objectives and tactics of developing an interactive or digital marketing communications programme are:

- *Traffic building goals.* Use online digital media and offline promotion to drive quality visitors or traffic to a website which convert to the outcomes required (sales, lead, newsletter sign-up) at an acceptable cost.
- *Conversion and engagement goals.* Use on-site communications to deliver an effective, relevant message to the visitor which helps shape customer perceptions or achieve a required marketing outcome.
- *Third-party site reach goals.* Reach, influence and engage with prospective customers on third-party media sites such as online news and magazines sites, portals and social networks.
- *Multichannel marketing goals.* Integrate all communications channels to help achieve multichannel marketing objectives by supporting mixed-mode buying.

## The structure of this chapter

We begin Chapter 8 by reviewing the unique characteristics of digital media which must be applied for success in online campaigns. We then look at the different practical aspects of communications which must be reviewed as part of planning and managing a digital campaign and integrating it with traditional media. These are the sections of this chapter and the main questions we will be answering.

1 *Goal setting and tracking* – which specific goals should be set for online campaigns and how do we measure success? What response mechanisms will be most effective?
2 *Campaign insight* – which data about customer and competitor behaviour is available to inform our decision?
3 *Segmentation and targeting* – how can we target and reach our different audiences?
4 *Offer and message development* – how do we specify our offer and key messages?
5 *Budgeting and selecting the digital media mix* – how should we set the budget and invest in different forms of digital media?
6 *Integration into overall media schedule* or plan – how should we plan the media schedule which incorporates different waves of online and offline communications?

In Chapter 9, we will review the success factors for the main digital media channels shown in Figure 1.9 which make up the tactics of a digital marketing campaign. When a visitor is directed to a site from another third-party site via a digital media channel, the origin is known as a referrer or referring site. The main categories of digital media include:

- *Search engine marketing.* The two key search marketing techniques are paid placements or sponsored links using pay-per-click (PPC) marketing, and placements in the natural or organic listings using Search Engine Optimisation (SEO).
- *Online PR.* Maximising favourable mentions of a company, brand, product or websites on third-party sites such as social networks or blogs that are likely to be visited by their target audience. Also includes responding to negative mentions and conducting public relations via a site through a press centre or blog, for example.
- *Online partnerships.* Creating and managing long-term arrangements to promote your online services on third-party websites or through e-mail communications. Different forms of partnership include link building, affiliate marketing, aggregators such as price comparison sites like Moneysupermarket (www.moneysupermarket.com), online sponsorship and co-branding.
- *Interactive advertising.* Use of online display ads such as banners and rich media ads to achieve brand awareness and encourage click-through to a target site.

---

**Online site promotion**

Internet-based technique used to generate website traffic.

**Offline site promotion**

Traditional techniques such as print and TV advertising used to generate website traffic.

**Mixed-mode buying**

The customer's purchase decision is influenced by a range of media such as print, TV and Internet.

**Digital media channel**

Online communications technique used to achieve goals of brand awareness, familiarity, favourability, and to influence purchase intent by encouraging users of digital media to visit a website to engage with the brand or product and ultimately to purchase online or offline through traditional media channels such as by phone or in-store.

**Referrer** or **referring site**

The source of a visitor to a site delivered via a digital media channel. Typically a specific site, e.g. Google AdWords, or a media site or an individual ad placement on the site.

- *Opt-in e-mail marketing.* Renting e-mail lists or placing ads in third-party e-newsletters or the use of an in-house list for customer activation and retention.
- *Viral and social marketing.* Viral marketing is effectively online word of mouth – messages are forwarded to help achieve awareness and, in some cases, drive response.

---

**Digital marketing in practice** | **The EConsultancy interview**

## Matthew Finch, Warner Breaks, on silver surfers

### Overview and main concepts covered

Warner Breaks' Matthew Finch has over eight years experience in the online world, starting out as a developer before moving into e-commerce, online marketing and strategy. He oversees online marketing for Warner Breaks, where he has significantly increased online sales and received a number of awards for campaigns.

Here, Matthew talks about targeting older Internet users – an untapped opportunity for many online marketers.

### The interview

**Q: There's bags of research out there about growing internet usage by older users. Is this what you have experienced at Warner Breaks?**

*Matthew Finch*: Warner Breaks predominately appeals to the 50+ market. We have certainly seen a rise in website visitors over the past two years from older users.

However, we are seeing a split between pre-retired and post-retired. There has certainly been a significant rise in Internet usage in the 50 to 65 pre-retirement group, where many of these people have exposure to computers and the Internet through their jobs. In comparison, we are finding that the 65+ post-retired group are less likely to come online, unless driven by a younger household member.

We have also seen the way our users interact with online marketing is changing, with greater engagement and response to display, search and e-mail marketing by older users.

**Q: How has this affected your overall marketing strategy?**

*Matthew Finch*: Online sales of Warner Breaks have grown considerably over the past couple of years. We have found online marketing a highly effective direct response channel, delivering a very strong cost-per-acquisition. As a result we have significantly increased our investment in online marketing.

However, traditional offline marketing is still essential to this audience, as many of our post-retired audience are not online. We will continue to invest in TV, press and direct mail.

The key to our success in 2007 and beyond is integration between offline and online, delivering integrated campaigns and supporting messaging.

**Q: What work have you been doing to attract and retain older customers online?**

*Matthew Finch*: We have invested significantly in display advertising and affiliate marketing to reach new customers and, of course, search marketing.

E-mail marketing has increased significantly over the past 12 months as we find our customers are highly receptive to communication by e-mail, delivering very impressive open rates and CTR.

**Q: What are the key things you need to do to make your site more user-friendly and accessible for silver surfers?**

*Matthew Finch:* We are doing a lot of work in this area. We have improved the layout of our website with consistent navigation, clear separation of text and images, and plenty of white space.

We will further improve accessibility with variable font sizes, support for screen-readers and better consideration for colour blindness.

**Q: Is this demographic being well covered by agencies, ad networks and affiliate networks?**

*Matthew Finch:* I have yet to find a single ad network or affiliate network that can deliver high volume in this demographic. We tend to find users spread across a diverse range of sites, so we deliver a broad media plan. We find that age-targeting with ISP and web mail sites such as Yahoo! and MSN is particularly effective.

**Q: Are there any trends in online behaviour among older users that you need to be aware of, or is it consistent with other age groups?**

*Matthew Finch:* I wouldn't say there are any particular trends. I think it is about ensuring the messaging is relevant and engaging, and not too gimmicky. There needs to be a clear benefit to the user, beyond just a wow factor that appeals to younger audiences. We have had great success with viral competitions, where we keep the execution simple, with an incentive to forward on to a friend.

**Q: Are any social networks or portals important to target for this age group?**

*Matthew Finch:* It has been well documented that people in this age group are increasingly using social networks such as Myspace and YouTube. We have created a Flickr group to allow our customers to share holiday photos, which has been well received. We do have more plans to engage more with social networks over the next 12 months.

User review sites are very important; with all of our hotels receiving regular comments on Tripadvisor. We are planning to launch customer reviews on our website later in the year. We have yet to use price comparison sites, as our product offer is unique so not comparable with other holiday companies.

**Q: Do concerns about security affect your ability to complete transactions online? What can you do to reassure customers?**

*Matthew Finch:* From focus group research and our own web stats, we see that many older users are still not comfortable with transacting online, preferring to research through the website but make the final purchase over the phone.

**Q: Can you give us any other interesting examples about online marketing at any of your properties/divisions?**

*Matthew Finch:* This year we have begun using video within our display advertising, which delivers a CTR of over 1%.

We have also developed highly targeted e-mail marketing, delivering different communication to segments of our customer base. In many cases this produces open rates of over 50%.

*Source*: http://www.e-consultancy.com/news-blog/newsletter/3361/warner-breaks-mat-finch-on-silver-surfers.html#1

## The characteristics of digital media

Through understanding the key interactive communications characteristics enabled through digital media we can exploit these media while guarding against their weaknesses. In this section, we will describe eight key changes in the media characteristics between traditional and digital media. Note that the 6 Is in Chapter 1 (page 31) provide an alternative framework that is useful for evaluating the differences between traditional media and new media.

### 1 From push to pull

**Push media**

Communications are broadcast from an advertiser to consumers of the message, who are passive recipients.

**Pull media**

The consumer is proactive in selection of the message through actively seeking out a website.

Traditional media such as print, TV and radio are push media – one-way streets where information is mainly unidirectional, from company to customer unless direct response elements are built in. In contrast, the web is an example of pull media. This is its biggest strength and its biggest weakness. It is a strength since pull means that prospects and customers only visit a website when it enters their head to do so, when they have a defined need – they are proactive and self-selecting. But this is a weakness since online pull means marketers have less control than in traditional communications where the message is pushed out to a defined audience. What are the e-marketing implications of the pull medium? First, we still need to provide the physical stimuli to encourage visits to websites. This may mean traditional ads, direct mail, physical reminders or encouraging word-of-mouth. Second, we need to ensure our site is optimised for search engines – it is registered and is ranked highly on relevant keyword searches. Third, e-mail is important – this is an online push medium, and it should be a priority objective of website design to capture customers' e-mail addresses in order that opt-in e-mail can be used to push relevant and timely messages to customers.

### 2 From monologue to dialogue to trialogue

**Interactivity**

The medium enables a dialogue between company and customer.

Creating a dialogue through interactivity is the next important feature of the web and digital media such as mobile and interactive TV which provide the opportunity for two-way interaction with the customer. This is a key distinguishing feature of the medium according to Peters (1998), and Deighton (1996) proclaimed the interactive benefits of the Internet as a means of developing long-term relationships with customers as described in Chapter 6. For example, if a registered customer requests information, or orders a particular product, it will be possible for the supplier to contact them in future using e-mail or personalised web messages with details of new offers related to their specific interest.

Walmsley (2007) believes that the main impact of digital media has not been to find new ways to connect brands to consumers as originally anticipated, but in connecting those consumers to each other. In the age of trialogue; brands need to reinterpret themselves as facilitators. Walmsley believes this trialogue will influence every aspect of marketing, from product design through to product recommendation. An example where product design is influenced is Threadless.com, the online T-shirt store, which only carries designs its users have uploaded, and manufactures only those that get a critical mass of votes (see Figure 8.1).

**Trialogue**

The interaction between company, customer and other customers facilitated through online community, social networks, reviews and comments.

But digital dialogues have a less obvious benefit also – intelligence. Interactive tools for customer self-help can help collect intelligence – clickstream analysis recorded in web analytics systems can help us build up valuable pictures of customer preferences.

### 3 From one-to-many to one-to-some and one-to-one

Traditional push communications are one-to-many, from one company to many customers, often the same message to different segments and often poorly targeted. With digital media 'one-to-some' – reaching a niche or micro-segment becomes more practical – e-marketers can afford to tailor and target their message to different segments through providing different site

**Figure 8.1** Threadless (www.threadless.com)

content or e-mail for different audiences through **mass customisation** and **personalisation** (Chapter 6). Note that many brochureware sites do not take full advantage of the Internet and merely use the web to replicate other media channels by delivering a uniform message.

Potentially, digital media provide a one-to-one communication (from company to customer) rather than the one-to-many communication (from company to customers) that is traditional in marketing using the mass media, such as newspapers or television. Figure 8.2 illustrates the interaction between an organisation (O) communicating a message (M) to customers (C) for a single-step flow of communication. It is apparent that for traditional mass marketing in (a) a single message ($M_1$) is communicated to all customers ($C_1$ to $C_5$).

Hoffman and Novak (1997) believe that this change is significant enough to represent a new model for marketing, or a new 'marketing paradigm'. They suggest that the facilities of the Internet, including the web, represent a computer-mediated environment in which the interactions are not between the sender and receiver of information, but with the medium itself. They say:

> consumers can interact with the medium, firms can provide content to the medium, and in the most radical departure from traditional marketing environments, consumers can provide commercially-oriented content to the media.

This situation is shown in Figure 8.2(c). This potential has not yet been fully developed since many companies are still using the Internet to provide standardised information to a general audience.

### 4 From one-to-many to many-to-many communications

Digital media also enable many-to-many communications. Hoffman and Novak (1996) noted that new media are many-to-many media. Here customers can interact with other customers via a website, in independent communities or on their personal websites and blogs. We will see in the section on online PR that the implications of many-to-many communications are a loss of control of communications requiring monitoring of information sources.

## 5 From 'lean-back' to 'lean-forward'

Digital media are also intense media – they are lean-forward media in which the website usually has the visitor's undivided attention. This intensity means that the customer wants to be in control and wants to experience flow and responsiveness to their needs. First impressions are important. If the visitor to your site does not find what they are looking for immediately, whether through poor design or slow speed, they will move on, probably never to return.

## 6 The medium changes the nature of standard marketing communications tools such as advertising

In addition to offering the opportunity for one-to-one marketing, the Internet can be, and widely still is, used for one-to-many advertising. On the Internet the brand essence and key concepts from the advertiser arguably becomes less important, and typically it is detailed

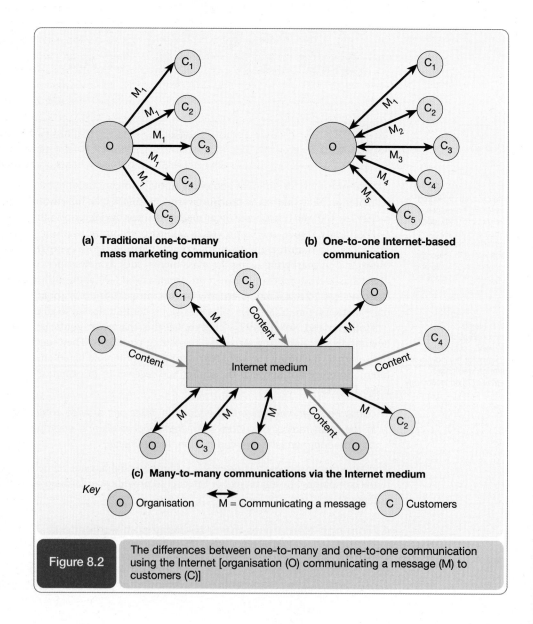

(a) Traditional one-to-many mass marketing communication

(b) One-to-one Internet-based communication

(c) Many-to-many communications via the Internet medium

Key

O Organisation      M = Communicating a message      C Customers

**Figure 8.2**   The differences between one-to-many and one-to-one communication using the Internet [organisation (O) communicating a message (M) to customers (C)]

information and independent opinions the user is seeking. The website itself can be considered as similar in function to an advertisement (since it can inform, persuade and remind customers about the offering, although it is not paid for in the same way as a traditional advertisement). Berthon *et al.* (1996) consider a website as a mix between advertising and direct selling since it can also be used to engage the visitor in a dialogue. Constraints on advertising in traditional mass media, such as paying for time or space, become less important. The wastage in traditional advertising where ads are either ignored or are not relevant for an audience is reduced in online marketing and search marketing in particular. In pay-per-click (PPC) advertising, display of ads can be controlled according to user need based on what searchers are looking for and cost is only incurred where interest is indicated by a click. Affiliate marketing is also a **pay-per-performance communications** technique where cost is only incurred where there is a response. Consumers are looking for information online all the time, so advertising in search engines in traditional short *campaign-based* bursts is inappropriate for most companies – *continuous* representation is needed.

**Pay-for-performance communications**
The wastage from traditional media buys can be reduced online through advertising models where the advertisers only pay for a response (cost-per-click) as in pay-per-click search marketing or for a lead or sale as in affiliate marketing.

Peters (1998) suggests that communication via the new medium is differentiated from communication using traditional media in four different ways. First, *communication style* is changed with *immediate*, or synchronous, transfer of information through online customer service being possible. Asynchronous communication, where there is a time delay between sending and receiving information as through e-mail, also occurs. Second, *social presence* or the feeling that a communications exchange is sociable, warm, personal and active may be lower if a standard web page is delivered, but can be enhanced, perhaps by personalisation. Third, the consumer has more *control of contact*; and fourth the user has control of *content*, for example through personalisation facilities or posting their own content where practical.

Although Hoffman and Novak (1996) point out that with the Internet the main relationships are not *directly* between sender and receiver of information, but with the web-based environment, the classic communications model of Schramm (1955) can still be used to help understand the effectiveness of marketing communication using the Internet. Figure 8.3 shows the model applied to the Internet. Four of the elements of the model that can constrain the effectiveness of Internet marketing are:

- *encoding* – this is the design and development of the site content or e-mail that aims to convey the message of the company, and is dependent on understanding of the target audience;
- *noise* – this is the external influence that affects the quality of the message; in an Internet context this can be slow download times, the use of plug-ins that the user cannot use or confusion caused by too much information on-screen;
- *decoding* – this is the process of interpreting the message, and is dependent on the cognitive ability of the receiver, which is partly influenced by the length of time they have used the Internet;
- *feedback* – this occurs through online forms and through monitoring of on-site behaviour through log files (Chapter 9).

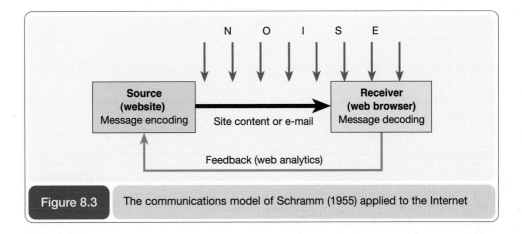

| Figure 8.3 | The communications model of Schramm (1955) applied to the Internet |

## 7 Increase in communications intermediaries

If we contrast traditional advertising and PR with digital media, there is an increase in options to reach audiences online through a potentially large number of media. Traditional radio channels, newspapers and print titles have migrated online, but in addition there are a vast number of online-only publishers including horizontal portals (Chapter 2) such as search engines and vertical portals such as industry-specific sites. The concept of the long tail (Chapter 5) also applies to websites in any sector. There are a handful of key sites, but many others can also be used to reach customers. The online marketer needs to select the most appropriate of this plethora of sites which customers visit to drive traffic to their website.

## 8 Integration

Although digital media have distinct characteristics compared to traditional media, it does not follow that we should concentrate our communications solely on digital media. Rather we should combine and integrate traditional and digital media according to their strengths. We can then achieve synergy – the sum being greater than the parts. Most of us still spend most of our time in the real world rather than the virtual world and multichannel customers' journeys involve both media, so offline promotion of the proposition of a website is important. It is also important to support mixed-mode buying. For example, a customer wanting to buy a computer may see a TV ad for a certain brand which raises awareness of the brand and then see a print advert that directs them across to the website for further information. However, the customer does not want to buy online, preferring the phone, but the site allows for this by prompting with a phone number at the right time. Here all the different communications channels are mutually supporting each other.

Similarly, inbound communications to a company need to be managed and are crucial to the health of a brand, as stated by Schultz and Schultz (2004). Consider when the customer needs support for an error with their system. They may start by using the on-site diagnostics, which do not solve the problem. They then ring customer support. This process will be much more effective if support staff can access the details of the problem as previously typed in by the customer to the diagnostics package.

We conclude this section with our summary of some of the main differences between traditional and digital media (Table 8.1) and a review of how consumers perceive the Internet in comparison to traditional media (Mini case study 8.2).

| Table 8.1 | Summary of differences in characteristics of traditional media and digital media (note that rows 10–12 are similarities between the two media types) |
|---|---|

| Traditional media | Digital media |
|---|---|
| 1 Push emphasis (e.g. TV and print ads and direct mail) | Pull emphasis. Relevance to context (search engine marketing (SEM)) |
| 2 One-way communications | Dialogue and interactivity and trialogue through user-generated content (UGC) |
| 3 Targeting cost constrained by media placements | Micro-targeting and personalisation through SEM and media placements on niche sites |
| 4 Limited customer-to-customer interactions | Participation: communities and social networks |
| 5 Static campaigns – once campaigns have been booked with a media agency it is difficult to adjust them | Dynamic campaigns where it is possible to test alternative creative and targeting and then revise during campaign according to performance |
| 6 Burst campaigns maximise ad impact over a short-term period | Continuous campaigns where a permanent presence is required in online media (e.g. in SEM and aggregators) |
| 7 Limited media-buying opportunities with high degree of wastage | Limitless media-buying opportunities with pay-per-performance options |

| | |
|---|---|
| 8 Detailed response measurement often limited to qualitative research | Potentially measurable at micro-level through web analytics and ad tracking systems |
| 9 Pre-testing | Can also test and refine during campaign |
| 10 Most communications to reach audience via media owners | Media owners are still important but communications also possible via website and non-media owned blogs and social networks |
| 11 Integrated communications vital | Integrated communications vital |
| 12 Not cheap, quick or easy | Not cheap, quick or easy |

---

## Mini Case Study 8.2    Consumer perceptions of the Internet and different media

Branthwaite *et al.* (2000) conducted a global qualitative project covering 14 countries across North and South America, East and West Europe, Asia and Australia to investigate consumer perceptions of the Internet and other media. In order to reflect changing media habits and anticipate future trends, a young, dynamic sample were selected in the 18–35 age range, with access to the Internet, who were regular users of all four media. Consumers' perceptions of the Internet, when asked to explain how they felt about the Internet in relation to different animals, were as follows:

> *The dominant sense here was of something exciting, but also inherently malevolent, dangerous and frightening in the Internet.*

The positive aspect was expressed mainly through images of a bird but also a cheetah or dolphin. These captured the spirit of freedom, opening horizons, versatility, agility, effortlessness and efficiency. Even though these impressions were relative to alternative ways of accomplishing goals, they were sometimes naive or idealistic. However, there was more scepticism about these features from those with substantial experience or great naivety.

Despite their idealism and enthusiasm for the Internet, these users found a prevalent and deep-rooted suspicion of the way it operated. The malevolent undertones of the Internet came through symbols of snakes or foxes predominantly, which were associated with cunning, slyness and unreliability. While these symbols embodied similar suspicions, the snake was menacing, intimidating, treacherous and evasive, while the fox was actively deceptive, predatory, surreptitious, plotting and persistent. For many consumers, the Internet was felt to have a will of its own in the form of the creators of the sites (the ghosts in the machine). A snake traps you and then tightens its grip. A fox is mischievous.

In comparison with other media, the Internet was described as follows:

> *The Internet seemed less like a medium of communication than the others, and more like a reservoir of information.*

This distinction was based on differences in the mode of operating: other media communicated to you whereas with the Internet the user had to actively seek and extract information for themselves. In this sense, the Internet is a recessive medium that sits waiting to be interrogated, whereas other media are actively trying to target their communications to the consumer.

This meant that these users (who were not addicted or high Internet users) were usually task-orientated and focused on manipulating their way around (tunnel vision). The more inexperienced you were, the more concentration was needed, but irritation or frustration was never far away for most people.

Everywhere, regardless of experience and availability, the Internet was seen as a huge resource, with futuristic values, that indicated the way the world was going to be. It was respected for its convenience and usefulness. Through the Internet you could learn, solve problems, achieve goals, travel the world without leaving your desk and enter otherwise inaccessible spaces. It gave choice and control, but also feelings of isolation and inadequacy. There was an onus on people wherever possible to experience this medium and use it for learning and communicating.

The most positive attitudes were in North America. Slick and well-structured websites made a positive impression and were a valuable means of securing information through the links to other sites and to carry out e-commerce. However, even here there was frustration with slow downloading and some uncooperative sites. In other countries, there was concern at the irresponsibility of the medium, lack of seriousness and dependability. There was desire for supervisory and controlling bodies (which are common for print and TV). Banner ads were resented as contributing to the distractions and irritations. Sometimes they seemed deliberately hostile by distracting you and then getting you lost. Internet advertising had the lowest respect and status, being regarded as peripheral and trivial.

In the least-economically advanced countries, the Internet was considered a divisive medium which excluded those without the resources, expertise or special knowledge.

Table 8.2 and Figure 8.4 present the final evaluation of the Internet against other media

| Table 8.2 | Comparison of the properties of different media |
| --- | --- |

|  | TV | Outdoor | Print | Internet |
| --- | --- | --- | --- | --- |
| Intrusiveness | High | High | Low | Low |
| Control/selectivity of consumption | Passive | Passive | Active, selective | Active, selective |
| Episode attention span | Long | Short | Long | Restless, fragmented |
| Active processing | Low | Low | High | High |
| Mood | Relaxed, seeking exceptional gratification | Bored, under-stimulated | Relaxed, seeking interest, stimulation | Goal-orientated, needs-related |
| Modality | Audio/visual | Visual | Visual | Visual (auditory increasing) |
| Processing | Episodic, superficial | Episodic/semantic | Semantic, deep | Semantic, deep |
| Context | As individual in interpersonal setting | Solitary (in public space) | Individual, personal | Alone, private |

*Source*: Branthwaite *et al.* (2000)

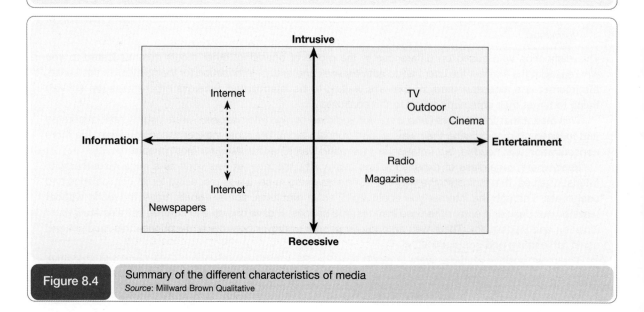

| Figure 8.4 | Summary of the different characteristics of media<br>*Source*: Millward Brown Qualitative |
| --- | --- |

## Step 1. Goal setting and tracking for interactive marketing communications

Digital marketers should develop communications objectives for different timescales:

- *Annual marketing communications objectives.* For example, achieving new site visitors or gaining qualified leads could be measured across an entire year since this will be a continuous activity based on visitor building through search engines and other campaigns. Annual budgets are set to help achieve these objectives.
- *Campaign-specific communications objectives.* Internet marketing campaigns such as to support a product launch through online advertising and viral marketing. Specific objectives can be stated for each in terms of gaining new visitors, converting visitors to customers and encouraging repeat purchases. Campaign objectives should build on traditional marketing objectives, have a specific target audience and have measurable outcomes which can be attributed to the specific campaign.

### Terminology for measuring digital campaigns

There are a bewildering series of terms used to set goals and track the effectiveness of digital campaigns, so we start this section by explaining the main measures you will encounter in models for campaign planning and reports from online campaigns. Figure 8.5 shows different measures from least sophisticated to more sophisticated as shown under the following headings.

**Visitor session (visit)**
A series of one or more page impressions, served to one user, which ends when there is a gap of 30 minutes or more between successive page impressions for that user

**Unique visitor**
Individual visitor to a site measured through cookies or the IP address on an individual computer.

#### 0 Volume measures including clicks, visitor session and unique visitors

Traffic volume is usually measured as the number of click-throughs or visits to a site (**visitor sessions**) to a site or alternatively **unique visitors**. If possible, unique visitors is preferable to using page views or hits as a measure of effectiveness, since it represents opportunities to communicate with individuals but, as we will explain in Chapter 10, it may be technically difficult to calculate 'uniques' accurately as measurement is based on cookies. A more sophisticated measure is reach (%) or online audience share. This is only possible using panel data/audience data tools such as www.netratings.com, www.comscore.com or www.hitwise.com.
*Example*: An online bank has one million unique visitors per month.

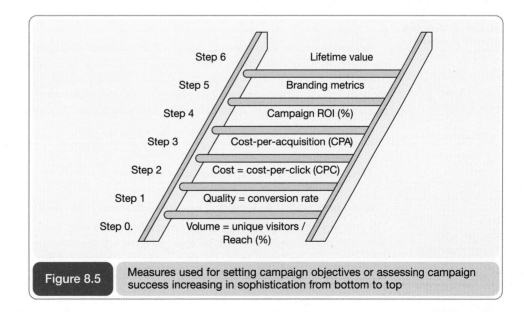

| Figure 8.5 | Measures used for setting campaign objectives or assessing campaign success increasing in sophistication from bottom to top |

**Visit** or **session conversion rate**

An indication of the capability of a site in converting visitors to defined outcomes such as registration. Calculated by dividing the number of conversion events by the number of visitor sessions within a time period.

## 1 Quality measures including conversion rates to action and bounce rate

Traffic volume measures give no indication of whether the audience referred to the site engages with it, so we need quality measures to show us this. Conversion rate is the best known quality measure which shows what proportion of visitors from different sources within a defined time period convert to specific marketing outcomes on the web, such as lead, sale or subscription.

*Example*: 10% of visitors convert to an outcome such as logging in to their account, or asking for a quote for a product.

Conversion rates can be expressed in two different ways – at the visit level (**visit** or **session conversion rate**) or the unique visitor level (**visitor conversion rate**).

Eric Peterson (2004) explains it this way:

*the denominator you use [to calculate conversion rate] will depend on whether you're trying to understand how people behave during visits or the people themselves. If you're interested in people [and the overall buying process] use unique visitors, if you're interested in behaviour [on a single visit] use visits.*

**Visitor conversion rate**

An indication of the capability of a site in converting visitors to defined outcomes such as registration. Calculated by dividing the number of conversion events by the number of unique visitors within a defined time period.

*Examples*:

$$Visit\ conversion\ rate = \frac{10\ conversion\ events}{1000\ visits} = 1\%$$

For an e-retailer this is the order conversion rate:

$$Order\ conversion\ rate = \frac{10\ sales}{1000\ visits} = 1\%$$

$$Visitor\ conversion\ rate = \frac{10\ conversion\ events}{800\ visits} = 1.25\%$$

For an e-retailer, this can be called the buyer conversion rate, also known as the browse-to-buy ratio or for a travel company 'look to book':

$$buyer\ conversion\ rate = \frac{10\ sales}{800\ unique\ visitors} = 1.25\%$$

**Bounce rate**

Proportion of visitors to a page or site who exit after visiting a single page only, usually expressed as a percentage.

A related measure that is useful to monitor during campaigns is the **bounce rate** which indicates the proportion of referred visitors to a page or site who exit after visiting a single page only, usually expressed as a percentage (i.e. that arrive at the site and bounce off it since they don't discover relevance!)

Reviewing bounce or engagement rates can improve the effectiveness of landing pages and the quality of referrers to a page. The benefit of using bounce rates rather than conversion rates is that there is a much wider variation in bounce rates for a page (i.e. typically 20% to 80%, compared to sub-10%), which enables problems with individual referrers, keywords or landing page conversions to be more readily identified. Bounce rates are calculated as follows:

$$Bounce\ rate\ \% = \frac{100 \times single\ page\ visits\ to\ a\ page\ (or\ site)}{all\ visits\ starting\ on\ page\ (or\ site)}$$

*Engagement rate % = (100 − bounce rate %)*

## 2 Media cost measures including cost-per-click and cost-per-thousand

**Cost-per-click**

The cost of each click from a referring site to a destination site, typically from a search engine in pay-per-click search marketing.

**Cost-per-thousand**

The cost of placing an ad viewed by 1000 people.

The cost of visitor acquisition is usually measured as the **cost-per-click (CPC)** specific to a particular digital media channel, such as pay-per-click search engine marketing, since it is difficult to estimate for an entire site with many visitors referred from offline advertising. *Example*: £2 CPC (500 clicks delivered from Google Adwords costing £1000).

**Cost-per-thousand (CPM)** is usually used as the currency when buying display ad space, for example, £10 CPM will mean that the ad will be served to 1000 visitors (technically visitor sessions). An effective CPM can also be calculated for other media channels, such as pay-per-click advertising, for comparison.

### 3 Acquisition cost measures including cost-per-action or acquisition

A digital campaign will not be successful if it meets its objectives of acquiring site visitors and customers but the cost of achieving this is too high. So it is essential to have specific objectives and measures for the cost of using different digital media channels to drive visitors to the site and convert to transaction. This is stated as the **cost-per-acquisition (CPA)** (sometimes cost-per-action). Depending on context and market, CPA may refer to different outcomes. Typical cost targets include:

- cost-per-acquisition – of a visitor;
- cost-per-acquisition – of a lead;
- cost-per-acquisition – of a sale (most typical form of CPA, also known as CPS).

To control costs, it is important for managers to define a target **allowable cost-per-acquisition** such as £30 for generating a business lead or £50 for achieving sign-up to a credit card. When the cost of visitor acquisition is combined with conversion to outcomes this is the cost of (customer) acquisition.

*Example*: £20 CPA (for £2 CPC, 10% conversion with one-in-ten visits resulting in sale).

### 4 Return on investment (ROI) measures

Return on investment is used to assess the profitability of any marketing activity, or indeed any investment. You will also know that there are different forms of ROI, depending on how profitability is calculated. Here we will assume it is just based on sales value or profitability based on the cost per click and conversion rate.

$$\text{ROI} = \frac{\text{profit generated from referrer}}{\text{amount spent on advertising with referrer}}$$

A related measure, which does not take profitability into account is return on advertising spend (ROAS) which is calculated as follows:

$$\text{ROAS} = \frac{\text{total revenue generated from referrer}}{\text{amount spent of advertising with referrer}}$$

### 5 Branding measures

These tend to be most relevant to interactive advertising or sponsorship. They are the equivalent of offline advertising metrics, i.e. brand awareness (aided and unaided), ad recall, brand favourability and purchase intent.

### 6 Lifetime value-based ROI measures

Here the value of gaining the customer is not just based on the initial purchase, but the lifetime value (and costs) associated with the customer. This requires more sophisticated models which can be most readily developed for online retailers and online financial services providers. The technique for the calculation of LTV was outlined in Chapter 6.

*Example*: A bank uses a net present value model for insurance products which looks at the value over 10 years but whose main focus is on a 5-year result and takes into account:

- acquisition cost
- retention rates
- claims
- expenses.

This is valuable since it helps give them a realistic 'allowable cost per sale' which is needed to get return over 5 years. They track this in great detail – for example, they will know the ROI of different Google Adwords keywords and will then select keyphrase and bid strategies accordingly.

Figure 8.6 shows an example of an online ad campaign for an insurance product placing many of the core volume, quality and cost measures covered in this section in context. Here an opportunity or lead is when a quote is requested. Note that the cost of acquisition is high, but this does not take into account the synergies of online advertising with offline campaigns, i.e. those who are influenced by the ad, but do not click through immediately.

## Examples of digital campaign measures

**Traffic building**
Using online and offline site promotion techniques to generate visitors to a site.

**SMART**
Specific, Measurable, Actionable, Relevant and Time-related.

As mentioned in the introduction to this chapter, an interactive marketing communications plan usually has four main goals. Here are example objectives associated with each:

1   *Traffic building goals.* Use online digital media and offline promotion to drive quality visitors or traffic to a website which convert to the outcomes required (sales, lead, newsletter sign-up) at an acceptable cost – this activity is commonly referred to as 'traffic building'.
    Examples of SMART traffic building objectives which can be expressed as visitors, visits or sales:
    - Achieve 100,000 unique visitors or 200,000 visitor sessions within one year (the technical methods of calculating these terms are covered in Chapter 10).
    - Deliver 20,000 online sales at an average order value of £50 and a cost-per-acquisition of £10.
    - Convert 30% of existing customer base to active use (at least once every 90 days) of online service.
    - Achieve 10% 'share of searches' within a market.

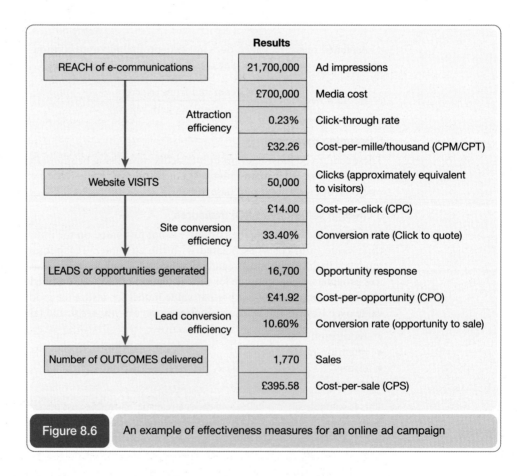

| | Results | |
|---|---|---|
| REACH of e-communications | 21,700,000 | Ad impressions |
| | £700,000 | Media cost |
| Attraction efficiency | 0.23% | Click-through rate |
| | £32.26 | Cost-per-mille/thousand (CPM/CPT) |
| Website VISITS | 50,000 | Clicks (approximately equivalent to visitors) |
| | £14.00 | Cost-per-click (CPC) |
| Site conversion efficiency | 33.40% | Conversion rate (Click to quote) |
| LEADS or opportunities generated | 16,700 | Opportunity response |
| | £41.92 | Cost-per-opportunity (CPO) |
| Lead conversion efficiency | 10.60% | Conversion rate (opportunity to sale) |
| Number of OUTCOMES delivered | 1,770 | Sales |
| | £395.58 | Cost-per-sale (CPS) |

**Figure 8.6**    An example of effectiveness measures for an online ad campaign

2 *Conversion or engagement goals.* Use on-site communications to deliver an effective message to the visitor which helps influence perceptions or achieves a required marketing outcome. The message delivered on-site will be based on traditional marketing communications objectives for a company's products or services. For example:

- encourage trial (for example, achieve 4% conversion of new unique visitors to registration or downloads of a music service such as iTunes or Napster);
- build in-house permission-based list (grow e-mail database by 10,000 during year through data capture activities);
- encourage engagement with content (conversion of 20% of new unique visitors to product information area);
- persuade customer to purchase (conversion of 5% of unique new visitors);
- encourage further purchases (conversion of 30% of first-time buyers to repeat purchasers within a 6-month period).

3 *Third-party site reach goals.* Reach, influence and engage with prospects customers on third-party sites such as online news and magazines sites, portals and social networks.

- Reach a targeted audience of 500,000 during the campaign.
- Create awareness of a product or favourability towards a brand (measured through brand research of brand awareness, brand favourability or purchase intent through using an online brand-tracking service such as Dynamic Logic, www.dynamiclogic.com).

4 *Multichannel marketing goals.* Integrate all communications methods to help achieve marketing objectives by supporting mixed-mode buying.

Examples of mixed-mode buying objectives:

- Achieve 20% of sales achieved in the call centre as a result of website visits.
- Achieve 20% of online sales in response to offline adverts.
- Increase average amount spent in store for every active site visitor from £3 to £4.
- Reduce contact-centre phone enquiries by 15% by providing online customer services.

A good example of developing SMART objectives is provided in Chapter 9 in Mini case study 9.2 'Beep-beep-beep-beep, that'll be the bank then' (see page **555**). In this campaign to promote a new interactive banking service the campaign objectives and results were to:

- capture 5000 mobile phone numbers from customers (200% of plan);
- acquire 3000 email addresses (176% of plan);
- raise awareness about the new service (31,000 customers view demonstration);
- create 1000 new registrations (576% of plan).

This example shows the importance of capturing and maintaining up-to-date customer details such as e-mail addresses and mobile phone numbers.

It is also worth noting that communications objectives will differ according to the stage of development of an e-commerce service. Rowley (2001) suggests that the general goals of these four stages are:

- *Contact* – promoting corporate image, publishing corporate information and offering contact information. Content.
- *Interact* – embed information exchange. Communication.
- *Transact* – online transactions and interaction with trading partners. Commerce.
- *Relate* – two-way customer relationship. Community.

Four similar levels of intensity of promotional activity are also identified by van Doren *et al.* (2000).

As well as the 'hard' measures, digital campaigns present great opportunities to learn about:

- *Factors that influence response* – marketers should try to build in tests to inform future campaigns.
- *Customer characteristics* – interactive media make it relatively easy to profile customers by relating response back to their characteristics if these are held in an integrated database.

- *Individual customer preferences and opinions* – monitor response by tracking click response behaviour, but do record this information where it can be related to the individual customer and used for future targeting! Ask questions about their characteristics and preferences on web response forms or on forums

Examples of strategic objectives for Internet marketing are also discussed in Chapter 4 – these overlap with these communications objectives.

## Conversion marketing value objectives

Although traffic-building objectives and measures of effectiveness are often referred to in terms of *traffic quantity*, such as the number of visitors or page impressions, it is the *traffic quality* that really indicates the success of interactive marketing communications (e.g. van Doren *et al.*, 2000; Chaffey and Smith, 2008). The bounce rate measure described above is an excellent method of assessing the quality of traffic from different sources or referrers.

A conversion-based approach like that shown in Figure 8.7 is essential to setting realistic online objectives. Take, for example, the objectives of a campaign for a B2B services company such as a consultancy company, where the ultimate objective is to achieve 1000 new clients using the website in combination with traditional media to convert leads to action. To achieve this level of new business, the marketer will need to make assumptions about the level of conversion that is needed at each stage of converting prospects to customers. This gives a core objective of 1000 new clients and different critical success factors based on the different conversion rates.

Traffic quality is determined by whether the visitors are within the target audience for the website and whether they have a current need or propensity for the services or content on the site. It follows that digital media channels that have the best capability to target users who are currently seeking products, for example search engine marketing, will be most effective in converting visitors. So for more goal setting it is useful to set goals based on conversion models for individual media channels such as online advertising and search engine marketing which will have different conversion rates.

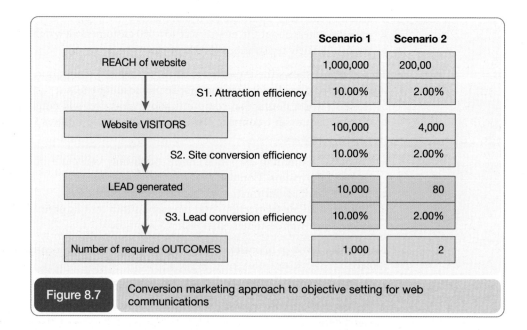

| | Scenario 1 | Scenario 2 |
|---|---|---|
| REACH of website | 1,000,000 | 200,00 |
| S1. Attraction efficiency | 10.00% | 2.00% |
| Website VISITORS | 100,000 | 4,000 |
| S2. Site conversion efficiency | 10.00% | 2.00% |
| LEAD generated | 10,000 | 80 |
| S3. Lead conversion efficiency | 10.00% | 2.00% |
| Number of required OUTCOMES | 1,000 | 2 |

**Figure 8.7**    Conversion marketing approach to objective setting for web communications

## Objective setting and measurement for non-transactional sites

Often, it is only the e-retailers, financial services or travel companies who have data on the full range of measures in Figures 8.5 or 8.6 since this is essential for proving the ROI of online marketing campaigns such as display ads or pay-per-click search. If there are no products available for sale online, such as a luxury car manufacturer or a high-value B2B service offering white paper downloads, then it is less clear how to calculate ROI.

**Value event scoring**
Value events are outcomes that occur on the site as indicated by visits to different page or content types which suggest that marketing communications are effective. Examples include leads, sales, newsletter registrations and product page views. They can be tagged and scored using many web analytics systems, for example Google refers to them as conversion goals.

To get the most from campaigns which don't result in sale online and optimise their effectiveness, it is useful to put a value or points score on different outcomes, for example in the case of the car manufacturer, values could be assigned to brochure requests (5 points or £20), demonstration drive requests (20 points or £100) or simply visits to the site involving reviewing product features information (1 point or £1). This approach is known as **value event scoring**.

Through knowing the average percentage of online brochure requests or demo drive requests that convert to sales, and the average order value for customers referred from the website, then the value of these on-site outcomes can be estimated. This is only an estimate, but it can help inform campaign optimisation, by showing which referring sites, creative or PPC keywords and pages visited on the site which are most likely to generate desirable outcomes. Mini-case study 8.3 gives an example of different types of events for a photo sharing site.

---

| Mini Case Study 8.3 | Spanish photo sharing website measures value events |

Fotonatura (www.fotonatura.org), a Spanish photo sharing website, uses these micro-conversion goals in Google Analytics which give an overall conversion rate of 1.72%:

- Goal 1 – Registration (503 conversions)
- Goal 2 – Photo publication (3788 conversions)
- Goal 3 – Premium service registration (9 conversions)
- Goal 4 – Camera sales page (1049 conversions)

*Source*: Kaushik (2008)

---

### Campaign response mechanisms

Digital media have increased the choice of response mechanisms. We will look at online and offline response mechanisms that need to be considered for both online and offline campaign media. Reviewing response mechanisms is important since too narrow may limit response, but too broad and unfocused may not give the right types of response – marketers need to emphasise the response types most favourable to the overall success of the campaign. Policies for response mechanism across campaigns should be specified by managers to ensure the right approach is used across all campaigns.

Remember also that brands such as fast moving consumer goods brands do not have to drive visitors to their own site; through advertising and creating interactive microsites on third-party sites, they can potentially be more effective in reaching their audience who are more likely to spend their time on online media sites than on destination brand sites.

### Online response mechanism

The required response mechanisms should be specified in the digital campaign plan and the number of responses from each modelled. Figure 8.8 suggests the typical options of outcomes to online campaign media. From the creative such as a display ad, pay-per-click ad or rented e-mail newsletter, there are four main options.

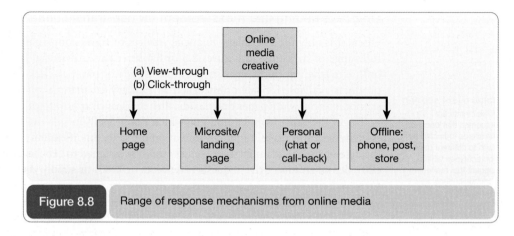

**Figure 8.8** Range of response mechanisms from online media

**1 Home page**

In the majority of cases, investment in online media will be wasted if visitors are driven from the media site to the home page of the destination website. Typically it is appealing to many audiences and offering too much choice – it won't effectively reinforce the message of the online creative or convert to further action.

**2 Microsite/landing page**

A focused landing page or specially created microsite can more effectively convert visitors to the action to help gain a return on the online campaign investment. A URL strategy is used to make the page easy to label in offline creative. This specifies how different types of content on a site will be placed in different folders or directories of a website (this can also help with search engine optimisation). For example, if you visit the BBC site (www.bbc.co.uk) look at how the web address details vary as you move from one section to another such as News or Sport. An individual destination page on a website may be labelled, for example, www.company.com/ products/insurance/car-insurance. A further example is where site owners have to make a decision how to refer to content in different countries, either in the form:

*http://<country-name>.<company-name>.com*

or the more common

*http://www.<companyname.com>.com/<country-name>*

Campaign URLs or CURLs are commonly used today, the idea being that they will be more memorable than the standard company address and blend in with the campaign concept. For example, an insurer used the CURL www.quotemehappy.com, a mortgage provider www.hateyourmortgage.com and a phone company www.sleeptomorrow.com, which are memorable elements of the campaign.

**3 Personal (chat or call-back)**

In this case the creative or the landing page encourages campaign respondents to 'talk' directly with a human operator. It is usually referred to as a 'call-back service' and integrates web and phone. Buttons or hyperlinks encourage a call-back from a telephone operator or an online chat. The advantage of this approach is that it engages the customer more and will typically lead to a higher conversion-to-sale rate since the customer's questions and objections are more likely to be answered and the personal engagement is more likely to encourage a favourable impression.

#### 4  Offline: phone, post or store

Because part of a campaign is run online does not mean that offline responses should be excluded. Offline response mechanisms should not be discarded unless the cost of managing them cannot be justified, which is rarely the case. Figure 8.9 gives an example of best practice offering a range of response mechanisms.

### Offline response goals for multichannel integration

We also need to include the right response mechanism for the offline media element of the campaigns such as TV ads, print ads or direct-mail pieces. The permission-based **web response model** (Hughes, 1999) is one that is frequently used today in direct marketing (Chapter 6). For example, this process could start with a direct mail drop or offline advert. The website is used as the direct response mechanism, hence 'web response'. Ideally, this approach will use targeting of different segments. For example, a Netherlands bank devised a campaign targeting six different segments based on age and income. The initial letter was delivered by post and contained a PIN (personal identification number) which had to be typed in when the customer visited the site. The PIN had the dual benefit that it could be used to track responses to the campaign, while at the same time personalising the message to the consumer. When the PIN was typed in, a 'personal page' was delivered for the customer with an offer that was appropriate to their particular circumstances.

The need for marketers to still support a range of communications channels as part of multichannel integration is suggested in Mini case study 8.4 'Disasters Emergency Committee uses a range of media to gain donations'.

**Web response model**

The website is used as a response mechanism for offline campaign elements such as direct mail or advertising.

| Figure 8.9 | Alternative response mechanisms at IVA Expert |

| Mini Case Study 8.4 | Disasters Emergency Committee uses a range of media to raise funds |

There are few people who did not see the images of the human and physical devastation caused by the earthquake on the ocean floor near Sumatra, Indonesia and subsequent tsunami on 26 December 2004. These images and reports were the catalyst for unprecedented levels of individual and corporate philanthropy. From a communications perspective, it is a useful indication of channel preferences. Over £350 million was donated to the Disasters Emergency Committee (DEC) Tsunami Earthquake Appeal through a range of channels shown in Figure 8.10.

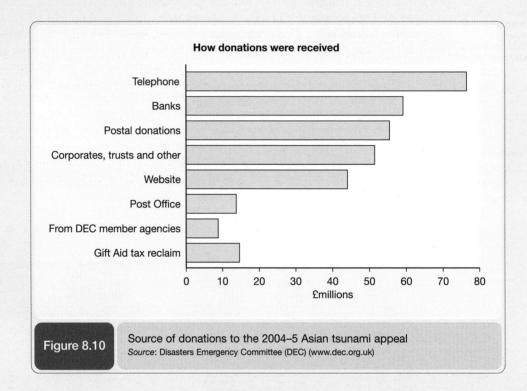

| Figure 8.10 | Source of donations to the 2004–5 Asian tsunami appeal<br>*Source*: Disasters Emergency Committee (DEC) (www.dec.org.uk) |

While the Internet was a source of many donations, it is perhaps surprising that the volume of online donations is not higher and it shows the continued popularity of traditional communications channels. The popularity of the web in comparison to e-mail and SMS is also striking as indicated by these details of donations:

- *Telephone*: Over £75 million was donated through the DEC appeal telephone line. Overall the appeal received a total of 1.7 million calls via the automated system at peak times and over 100 volunteers answered 12,500 live calls.
- *Online*: On New Year's Eve, with the help of major Internet service providers, the world record for online donations was broken with over £10 million donated in 24 hours. Overall £44 million was donated online by over half a million web users.
- *Text messaging*: Major UK mobile phone operators raised £1 million by joining forces and offering a free donation mechanism – enabling people to text their gifts.
- *Interactive TV*: The Community Channel raised over £0.5 million from donors using the 'red button' on interactive TV.

### Which planet are you on?

Consider the options for online promotion of a fast moving consumer goods brand (FMCG) such as coffee (e.g. Nescafe, www.nescafe.co.uk), tomato ketchup (e.g., Heinz, www.heinzketchup.com), or toiletries (e.g., Andrex, www.andrexpuppy.co.uk). The challenge is obvious – it is difficult to reach a large audience similar to using mass media such as TV, magazines or outdoor. Such destination sites will only attract a limited number of visitors, such as brand loyalists (who it is important to engage since these are often key advocates of these products) or students researching the brands! Another approach which can drive more volume is to use on-pack promotions or direct response TV and print campaigns that encourage consumers to enter competitions and engage into e-mail or text message dialogue in keeping with their profile. The 2005 Walkers Crisps (www.walkers.co.uk) 'Win With Walkers' competition is a good example of this. Walkers gave away an iPod Mini every five minutes (8700 in total) to texters who responded to messages on 600 million packets of crisps. The campaign was supported by a £1.5 million advertising push, featuring ex-footballer Gary Lineker. In September alone, 5% of the UK population entered, which must explain why I didn't win when I texted in at four in the morning!

The final approach, which is required to achieve reach volume is to advertise on third-party sites. Figure 8.11 show the options with an analogy made to the different groups of planets in the Solar System and the arrows indicate which approach is selected to achieve reach or traffic building. Typically, the smaller the site (which forms the long tail), the more accurate targeting is possible, but demographic targeting is possible on large portals. For example, McDonalds advertises on MSN Hotmail based on the profile of the user and Ford uses AOL to reach family-oriented purchasers.

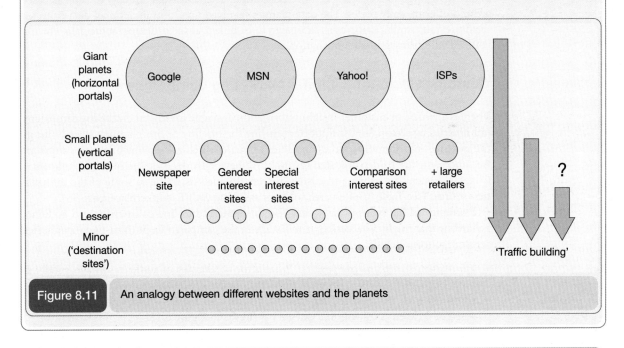

**Figure 8.11**   An analogy between different websites and the planets

## Step 2. Campaign insight

Research into the marketplace context of a campaign is core to a planned approach. When a company is working with an agency, the marketer at the client company will incorporate initial campaign insight into a brief. This will give agency staff valuable information about the audience and marketplace for a proposition. The agency may then access more detailed insight during the campaign.

Fill (2007) describes this stage of communications planning as context analysis. He identifies these aspects of context which should be researched:

- *Customer context* including dimensions of segment characteristics; levels of awareness, perception and attitudes towards the brand or organisation; level of involvement; types of perceived risk and influence of different members of the decision-making unit.
- *Business context* including corporate and marketing strategy and plans; brand/organisation analysis and competitor analysis.
- *Internal context* including financial constraints; organisation identity; culture, value and beliefs; marketing expertise; agency availability and suitability.
- *External context* including key stakeholders; communications and needs; social, political, economic, legal and technological restraints and opportunities.

So, the context analysis references all existing plans such as business and marketing plans, internal and external information sources. Information from these will be collated and put into a campaign brief.

More detailed campaign insight will be accessed and analysed once the agency or internal team are working on the campaign. Large agencies use 'data planners' or 'customer communications planners' to review all available external data sources such as market, audience and internal data on customer profiles, past campaign results on the most effective channels in generating product sales to assist clients in strategic development and execution of campaigns. This data is then used to inform campaign targeting and media selection.

For example, a brief might specify that an FMCG client wants to run an online promotional campaign, with the goal of stimulating trial of products and adding to a prospect database through encouraging online registration. The campaign strategy or offer is based around offering daily prizes. The data planner involved uses all transactional data collected from previous similar campaigns campaign to be linked to socio-demographic data which is coupled with transactional information.

## Customer insight for digital marketing campaigns

There is a wealth of customer insight information available for digital marketing campaigns, but it varies by sector. So it is important during the briefing or pre-planning stage to list all the possible information sources and then evaluate which are worthwhile, since some are free and some are paid syndicated research. We have introduced some of the techniques in Chapter 2, such as persona and customer scenario analysis, and also some of the information sources (see Table 2.3, Research tools for assessing your E-marketplace, page 56).

Examples of the types of customer insight related to online competitor and audience behaviour that might be accessed at this stage in the campaign from third-party syndicated research sources include:

- *Site audience reach and composition.* What is the breakdown of audiences by age, gender or socio-economic group on different sites? This data is available from online audience panel providers such as Nielsen Netrating, Comscore and Hitwise. An example showing the reach of different sites within a category is shown in Figure 8.12.
- *Online buying behaviour and preferences.* For example, from the Forrester Internet User Monitor or the BMRB Internet Monitor or TGI.net. In the UK, TGI.net gives information on typical product preferences for a particular site – for example, the percentage of the audience whose last holiday was a city break. Additional surveys can be conducted via publisher sites.
- *Customer media consumption.* The usage of different offline and online media for different target demographics can be accessed from sources such as Hitwise.
- *Customer search behaviour.* The proportion of different phrases and their importance can be used to inform messaging. The example in Figure 8.13 shows the importance of the word 'cheap' in searches for flight and how it varies through time, which could be used to inform messaging within a paid search or display ad campaign.

| Rank | Website – (Show domain) | Market Share | |
|------|-------------------------|--------------|---|
| 1 | YouTube | 42.93% | |
| 2 | Crunchyroll.com | 7.95% | |
| 3 | IMEEM | 4.94% | |
| 4 | Windows Media | 3.76% | |
| 5 | Tudou.com | 3.15% | |
| 6 | Veoh | 2.87% | |
| 7 | MetaCafe | 2.58% | |
| 8 | Yahoo! Video Streaming | 1.80% | |
| 9 | Google Video | 1.62% | |
| 10 | Megavideo | 1.50% | |

Period: w/ending 20 October 2007

**Figure 8.12**   Top 10 entertainment–multimedia websites by share of visits in Singapore
*Source*: Hitwise blog posting (http://weblogs.hitwise.com/sandra-hanchard/2007/10/)

- *Competitor campaign activity*. The activity of current advertising campaigns and previous seasonal campaigns. For example, in the UK, this is available from Thomson Intermedia.
- *Competitor performance*. This will give information on the audience size (reach) and composition of competitor sites and services like Hitwise can show which marketing techniques such as search engine marketing or affiliate marketing are successful in driving visitors to a competitor since referring sites and search terms can be accessed.

Wertime and Fenwick (2008) suggest a similar technique to persona development for campaigns which they describe as a 'participant print'. The main elements of the participant print are:

- *General profile*. This is basic demographic and psychographic information about customers. It may also include insight from previous online campaigns and activities such as search keywords and propensity to respond for different demographic groups (response rates).
- *Digital profile*.
  - *Digital usage habits*. The authors say this includes the usage of different digital media channels, types of sites used and digital platforms they use.
  - *Content consumption preferences*. This includes favoured sources of information related to the product category from portals specific to the product, comparison sites and specialist blogs.
  - *Content creation profile*. This reviews the propensity of the group to participate online. For example, in contests where they upload photos or ringtones, blogs or forums they comment on including neutral sites and competitor sites.
- *Individual profiles*. This is information about existing prospects and customers including profile information from customer databases, content preferences from web analytics and qualitative research with customers about their their needs, wants and how they prefer to use digital channels.

An example of the type of in-depth research available is the IPA Touchpoints survey which covers both surveyed usage of websites and other media, and opinions including why they use particular media. Hussein (2006) describes the purpose of this – he says the aim is to enable campaign planners to identify relevant target markets (demographic groups, attitudinal groups, activity groups, and so on) and fully understand them in terms of:

| Rank | 2006 | 2007 |
|------|------|------|
| 1 | flights to australia | flights to australia |
| 2 | cheap flights to australia | flights to new york |
| 3 | flights to new york | cheap flights to new york |
| 4 | flights to tenerife | flights to tenerife |
| 5 | cheap flights to new york | cheap flights to australia |
| 6 | cheap flights to tenerife | flights to new zealand |
| 7 | flights to canada | flights to canada |
| 8 | flights to cyprus | flights to thailand |
| 9 | flights to lanzarote | flights to florida |
| 10 | flights to dublin | cheap flights to tenerife |
| 11 | flights to new zealand | flights to cyprus |
| 12 | cheap flights to cyprus | flights to amsterdam |
| 13 | flights to florida | flights to dublin |
| 14 | flights to malaga | flights to lanzarote |
| 15 | flights to USA | flights to paris |
| 16 | cheap flights to canada | flights to las vegas |
| 17 | cheap flights to malaga | cheap flights to canada |
| 18 | flights to paris | flights to dubai |
| 19 | flights to prague | flights to malaga |
| 20 | cheap flights to spain | cheap flights to cyprus |

**Figure 8.13** Top flight destination searches, four weeks ending 29 December 2006 vs 2007
*Source*: Hitwise UK

- how they spend their day (shopping, work, travelling);
- who they spend it with (friends, family, work colleagues);
- what they believe in (views and opinions on life, brands, media, advertising);
- what is important to them (time spent on activities, family values);
- how, when, where and why they consume particular media.

Further information on marketplace analysis, including links to the main data sources for digital campaign insights, are provided in Table 2.3.

## Step 3. Segmentation and targeting

Campaign targeting strategy defines the target audience or type of people which you need to reach with your campaign communications. It's about defining, selecting and reaching specific audiences online. Targeting methods vary according to the market, campaign and e-communications tools involved. The key targeting issues to define for the online elements of a campaign are:

- Quality of insight about customer or prospect available to assist with targeting.
- Range of variables or parameters used to target – e.g. audience characteristics, value, needs and behaviours.
- Identifying the targeting attributes or variables which will influence response.
- Specific targeting approaches available for the key e-communications tools – e.g. online advertising, search engine marketing and e-mail marketing.

The targeting approaches used for acquisition and retention campaigns will naturally depend on established segmentations and knowledge about customers. We have also discussed targeting approaches from a strategic basis in Chapters 4 and 6. From a campaign point of view, Table 8.3 shows some of the main targeting variables which can be reviewed in digital campaign planning.

| Table 8.3 | A range of targeting and segmentation approaches for a digital campaign |

| Targeting variable | Examples of online targeting attributes |
| --- | --- |
| 1  Relationship with company | New contacts (prospects), existing customers, lapsed customers |
| 2  Demographic segmentation | B2C: Age, gender, social group, geographic location |
| | B2B: Company size, industry served, individual members of decision-making unit |
| 3  Psychographic or attitudinal segmentation | Attitudes to risk and value when buying, e.g. early adopter, brand loyal or price conscious |
| 4  Value | Assessment of current or historical value and future value |
| 5  Lifecycle stage | Position in lifecycle, related to value and behaviour, i.e. time since initial registration, number of products purchased, categories purchased in |
| 6  Behaviour | <ul><li>Search term entered into search engine</li><li>Responsiveness to different types of offers (promotion or product type)</li><li>Responsiveness to campaigns in different channels (channel preference)</li><li>Purchase history in product categories including recency, frequency and monetary value (Chapter 6)</li></ul> |

Let's look at each targeting variable in a little more depth.

1 *Relationship with company.* Campaigns will often be intended to target new contacts *or* existing contacts. But remember, some communications – such as e-newsletters and e-mail campaigns – will reach both. Marketers have to consider whether it will be cost-effective to have separate communications for new, existing and lapsed contacts – or to target each of these groups in the same communications but using different content aimed at each.

When visitors click through to your website from online and offline campaigns, copy should be presented that recognises the relationship or, again, provide a range of content to recognise each different relationship. Visit Microstrategy (www.microstrategy.com) to see how its registration page establishes the relationship.

2 *Demographic segmentation.* This is typically based on age, gender or social group. Online demographics are often used as the basis for which sites to purchase display advertising or for renting e-mail lists. Demographics can also be used to limit or focus who pay-per-click search ads are displayed to.

3 *Psychographic or attitudinal segmentation.* This includes attitudes to risk and value when buying, e.g. early adopter, brand loyal or price conscious. It is less straightforward to target on these attributes of a consumer since it is easier to buy media based on demographic breakdown. However, certain sites may be more suitable for reaching a particular psychographic audience. The psychographic characteristics of the audience are still an important part of the brief, to help develop particular messages.

It is possible to collect attitudinal information on a site and add it to the customer profile. For example, Wells Fargo asks investors to select:

- the type of investment preferred (individual stocks or mutual funds); and
- what type of investor best describes you? (aggressive growth to more cautious).

4 *Value.* The higher value customers (indicated by higher average order value and higher modelled customer lifetime values) will often warrant separate communications with different offers. Sometimes digital channels are not the best approach for these customers – relationship managers will want direct contact with their most valuable customers; while digital channels are used to communicate more cost-effectively with lower value customers. It is also worth considering reducing the frequency of e-mails to this audience.

5  *Lifecycle stage.* This is very useful where customers follow a particular sequence in buying or using a service, such as online grocery shopping or online banking. As explained in Chapter 6, automated, event-triggered e-mail marketing can be developed for this audience. For example, bank First Direct uses a six-month welcome strategy based on e-mail and direct mail communications. For other campaigns, the status of a customer can be used for targeting – for example not-purchased or used service, purchased once, purchased more than five times and active, purchased more than five times and inactive, etc.

6  *Behavioural.* Behavourial targeting is one of the big opportunities provided by digital marketing. It involves assessing customers' past actions in following links, reading content, using online services or buying products, and then follows up on these with a more relevant message based on the propensity to act based on the previous action.

Online options for behavioural targeting can be illustrated by a travel company such as lastminute.com:

- *Pay-per-click search engine marketing* makes targeting possible according to the type of keyphrase typed when a potential customer searches for information. A relevant ad specific to a holiday destination the prospect is looking for 'e.g. Hotel New York' can then be shown.
- *Display advertising* makes behavioural targeting possible since cookies can be used to track visitors across a site or between sites and display relevant ads. If a site user visits the travel section of a newspaper site, then the ad about 'lastminute' can be served as they visit other content on this site, or potentially on other sites.
- *E-mail marketing* can be targeted based on customer preferences indicated by links they have clicked on. For example, if a user has clicked a link on a holiday in North America, then a targeted e-mail can be delivered relevant to this product or promotion. More sophisticated analysis based on RFM analysis (Chapter 6) can also be used.

When reviewing the options for which variables to use to target, the campaign planner must keep in mind that those selected for targeting should be those which are most likely to influence the level of response for the campaign. It is possible to target on may variables, but the incremental benefit of targeting on additional variables many not be worth the cost and effort. Figure 6.9 (page 355) indicates the general improvement in campaign response dependent on the type of targeting variables used. This approach is used by travel company Travelocity in their e-mail marketing. Speaking at the 2006 Internet Retailing Forum they described how they concentrate their efforts on behaviour suggesting purchase intent, i.e. when a visitor to their site clicks on a particular type of holiday, e-mails sent to the customer should be updated to reflect that.

## Step 4. Offer, message development and creative

Many digital campaigns have direct response as the primary objective. Defining the right offer is vital to achieving these response objectives. But there are also likely to be brand objectives, to communicate the 'big idea' or concept behind the campaign or to position the brand.

In an online environment, there is very little time for the message to be delivered. Eye-tracking studies suggest average gaze or dwell times for a whole page may be around 10 seconds as suggested by Table 8.4, but individual fixation times on page elements such as page headlines or ads are much lower, so it is important the message is succinct and powerful.

| Table 8.4 | Variation in fixation time for different websites |
| --- | --- |

| Web page name | Visual complexity level | Average gaze time (seconds) | First fixation | Longest fixation | Scanpath shape |
| --- | --- | --- | --- | --- | --- |
| BBC UK | Complex | 10.3 | Upcoming show picture | Upcoming show picture | U, Z |
| Computer Science Manchester | Complex | 10.1 | Wide graphic/ picture | Wide graphic/ picture | Z |
| Gene Ontology | Complex | 12.5 | Title | Title | C, I |
| IMG Group | Complex | 11.4 | Horizontal menu | Right menu | Z, U |
| Vodafone UK | Complex | 11.3 | Flashing image | Flashing image | * |
| Google Results | Simple | 9.3 | Results | Logo, search keyword | Z, U |
| John Rylands Library Catalogue | Simple | 6.0 | Horizontal menu | Search source | Z |
| MINT Group | Simple | 9.1 | Logo | Logo | U |
| Peve Group | Simple | 8.9 | Centre graphic | Centre graphic | Z, I |

*Source*: Harper (2006)

So given the limit page dwell times and fixations, a clear primary message is needed in the different forms of digital media where it is delivered:

- *Paid search* – within the headline of the ad.
- *Natural search* – within the <title> tag and meta description tag (see Chapter 9).
- *E-mail marketing* – within the subject line and the headline or title of the e-mail supported by images as shown in Figure 8.14.
- *Display ads* – within the opening frame and possibly repeated in all frames.

The primary message should deliver relevance according to the context, so within paid search the primary message should be consistent with the search term entered by the user and should highlight the value proposition clearly. To successfully communicate our offer and message, we also need to ensure that the creative and copy helps achieve the five stages of information processing shown in Table 7.5 i.e. Exposure, Attention, Comprehension and Perception, Yielding and Acceptance, and Retention (page 422). Similarly, we also need to deliver a response as shown by well-known AIDA mnemonic which stands for:

- **A** wareness / **A** ttention
- **I** nterest
- **D** esire
- **A** ction.

Having captured attention and developed interest with a primary offer and message, the creative needs to stimulate desire and action with the secondary offer and message, which:

- reassures prospects by giving a little more evidence of the offer or product benefits;
- convinces the sceptic and encourages them to click;
- can appeal to different types of person to the primary offer;
- again, should have a clear call-to-action.

Jenkinson (2003) proposes that every marketing communication should contain a blend of five elements related to customer experience, with the significance or intensity of each element varying. He believes that this is useful for briefing the communication requirements

| Figure 8.14 | Clear primary, time-limited message in an e-mail communication |
| --- | --- |
| | *Source*: Euroffice (www.euroffice.co.uk) |

from different communications media. The elements of this 'CODAR' framework are illustrated by the example in Figure 8.15.

- *Idea forming.* Generating ideas in the consumer's or client's mind, such as the brand promise, a value proposition or brand values.
- *Relationship building.* Building a relationship including affinity, emotional bonding, brand know-how or expertise, and database and/or personal knowledge about the customer.
- *Sales activation.* Stimulating the customer towards further investigation, trial or purchase.
- *Help.* Providing service and assistance to the customer relevant to their needs and wants – from informing the customer about availability of new technology/product to consultancy in the purchase process, in use status reporting, or resolution of a post purchase problem.
- *Product experience.* Using and interacting with the brand's deliverables, including store and website design, product availability, information such as a bank statement, value or pleasure in use.

Many lessons from direct marketing can be applied to digital communications. In his book, *Commonsense Direct Marketing*, Drayton Bird (2000) identified 'twenty-five pointers before you write a word or sketch a layout'. Here are the most relevant ones to be considered when developing online creative work:

- **What is the objective?**
  Gather names? Produce qualified leads? Make firm sales? Get free trials?
- **Are you clear on the positioning?**
  What will your message tell the prospect about your product or service? Does it fit in with the positioning?

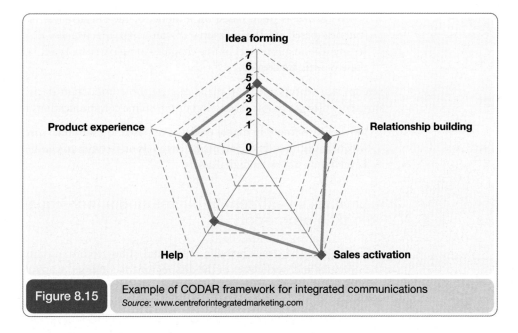

| Figure 8.15 | Example of CODAR framework for integrated communications |
|---|---|
| | Source: www.centreforintegratedmarketing.com |

- **Who are you selling to?**
  What are their hopes, fears, likes, dislikes, needs? Are they male or female? Young or old, rich or poor? Until you know these facts, you will not know what tone to adopt, let alone what to say.
- **What is it? And what does it do?**
  Obvious, but...
- **What need in your prospect does your product or service fulfil?**
  How many of the nine basic human motivations are relevant to potential customers of your product or service: make money, save money, save time and effort, help their families, feel secure, impress others, gain pleasure, improve themselves and belong to a group?
- **What makes it so special?**
  Interrogate your product or service. How does it differ from the alternatives? These are its features.
- **What benefits are you offering?**
  What it does rather than what it is.
- **What do you consider the most important benefit to be?**
  Ideally a unique benefit, but certainly the most appealing combination of benefits.

## Step 5. Budgeting and selecting the digital media mix

Traditional approaches such as those suggested by Kotler *et al.* (2001) can be used to set overall communications budgets. For example:

- *Affordable method* – the communications budget is set after subtracting fixed and variable costs from anticipated revenues.
- *Percentage-of-sales methods* – the communications budget is set as a percentage of forecast sales revenues.
- *Competitive parity methods* – expenditure is based on estimates of competitor expenditure. For example, e-marketing spend is typically 10–15% of the marketing budget.
- *Objective and task method* – this is a logical approach where budget is built up from all the tasks required to achieve the objectives in the communications plan. This is a bottom-up

approach that is often based on a model of the effectiveness of different digital media channels based on the measures of campaign effectiveness described in the objective setting section at the start of this chapter. Complete Activity 8.1 below to understand how these models are created.

Digital marketing campaign plans require three important decisions to be made about investment for the online promotion or the online communications mix. These are:

1 Level of investment in digital media as opposed to traditional media.
2 Mix of investment in digital media channels or e-communications tools.
3 Level of investment in digital assets.

## 1 Level of investment in digital media techniques in comparison to offline promotion

A balance must be struck between online and offline communications techniques based on the strengths and weaknesses of the different media options. A useful framework for considering the media characteristics which influence decisions on which to invest in has been developed by Coulter and Starkis (2005). Offline media are often superior in generating attention, stimulating attention and gaining credibility. Online media tend to be better at engagement due to personalisation, interaction and support of word-of-mouth. The offer can also often be fulfilled online for products that can be bought online. However, there are limits to the number of people that can be reached through online media (a limit to number searching on particular terms) and the cost is not necessarily always lower in competitive markets as shown in Mini case study 8.5.

---

| Activity 8.1 | A framework for selecting media |
| --- | --- |

Coulter and Starkis (2005) identify these factors for media selection. We have added comments.

**Quality**

1 *Attention-getting capability (Attention)* – ability of an ad placed in this specific media to 'grab the customer's attention' due to the nature of that media.
2 *Stimulating emotions (Stimulation)* – ability of an ad placed in this specific media to convey emotional content and/or elicit emotional responses.
3 *Information content and detail (Content)* – ability of an ad placed in this specific media to convey a large amount of information and/or product description.
4 *Credibility/prestige/image (Credibility)* – ability of a specific media to lend prestige to a product through association (i.e. because that product is advertised within the media).
5 *Clutter* – degree to which it is difficult for a product advertised within a specific media to 'stand out' due to the large number of competitive offerings/messages.

[*Comment*: We would stress the capability of the media to generate a response, which is dependent on the combination of factors mentioned here that relate to brand awareness and influence. For online media, certain media such as pay-per-click search marketing tends to be more responsive than media buys of ads on portals since there is less clutter and the relevance is higher since the web user is searching.]

## Time

1 *Short lead time* – degree to which an ad can be created and/or placed within a specific media in a relatively short period of time.
2 *Long exposure time* – degree to which the communication recipient is able to examine the advertising message within a specific media for an extended period of time.

[*Comment*: The ability to dynamically alter an ad during a campaign to select the best performing creative for each placement is particularly important online – for example optimising different creative executions of a display ad or a Google AdWords ad.]

## Flexibility

1 *Appeal to multiple senses (Appeal)* – degree to which an ad placed within this specific media can communicate via sight, sound, taste, touch, and/or smell concurrently.
2 *Personalisation* – degree to which an advertising message placed within this specific media can be customised in order to target a specific individual or group of individuals.
3 *Interactivity* – degree to which the customer can respond to information conveyed in an advertisement placed within this specific media.

## Coverage

1 *Selectivity* – degree to which an ad placed within this specific media is able to target a specific group of people.
2 *Pass-along audience (Pass-along)* – degree to which an ad placed within this specific media is seen by those other than the original message recipient.

[*Comment*: This is the viral marketing effect.]
3 *Frequency/repeat exposure (Frequency)* – degree to which any single ad placed within this specific media may be seen by any one particular individual on more than one occasion.

[*Comment*: Online this capability is available through behavioural targeting of display ads where cookies can be used to serve ads to the same person and develop the message with each new exposure if appropriate.]

4 *Average media reach (Reach)* – degree to which an ad placed within this specific media reaches a relatively wide audience.

## Cost

1 *Development/production cost (Development cost)* – relative cost of developing or producing an ad for this specific media.
2 *Average media delivery cost (Delivery cost)* – average cost-per-thousand associated with this specific media.

[*Comment*: We should also ad cost-per-response which is dependent on the click-through rate for each media and placement.]

The relative importance of these characteristics and the investment in different digital media will be dependent on the product and the type of campaign – whether it is direct-response-oriented or brand-oriented – and the scale of budget.

Figure 8.16 (page 479) outlines typical options that companies have during a campaign, quarterly or annually. Which do you think would be the best option for an established company as compared to a dot-com 'pureplay' company? It seems that in both cases, offline promotion investment often exceeds that for online promotion investment. However, some pureplays do invest the majority of their budget in paid search and affiliate marketing, although they are likely to find there are limits to growth that this will impose. There are also increases to buying digital media suggested by Mini case study 8.6 which need to be considered. For existing companies, traditional media such as print are used to advertise the sites, while print and TV will also be widely used by dot-com companies to drive traffic to their sites.

**Econometric modelling**
A quantitative technique to evaluate the past influence or predict the future influence on a dependent variable (typically sales in a marketing context) of independent variables which may include product price, promotions and the level and mix of media investments.

## Econometric modelling

Econometrics or econometric modelling is an established approach to understanding the contribution of different media in influencing consumers and ultimately generating sales and profit. It can also be used in a predictive way to plan for future campaigns. It is increasingly used in integrated campaigns to assess the appropriate media mix (see Cook (2004) for further explanation).

---

### Mini Case Study 8.6    E-retailers cut-back on their digital communications spend.

Technology e-retailer dabs.com has traditionally used the following as their main communications tools:

- search engine marketing (the main investment)
- referrals from affiliates (this has been reduced)
- online display advertising on third party sites (limited)
- PR.

Jonathan Wall, Dabs marketing director, explains how dabs.com reappraised their use of e-communications tools. He said:

> We stopped all our affiliate and price-comparison marketing in February because we wanted to see what effect it had on our business and if we were getting value for money. It was proving a very expensive channel for us and we've found [stopping] it has had virtually no effect, because we're seeing that people will still go to Kelkoo to check prices and then come to our site anyway. It's like they're having a look around first and then coming to a brand they know they can trust. We're continuing with paid-for search on Google, but that's all we're doing with online marketing at the moment.

NMA (2005) also reported that Empire Direct had adopted a similar approach to its communication mix reporting that its co-founder and sales and marketing director Manohar Showan had revealed that the company has significantly moved from online to offline advertising. He said:

> We've moved a lot more into national papers and specialist magazines – two years ago, if you'd asked me where we marketed and advertised ourselves, I would have said the majority was online. But now it's turned right round and online's the minority.

NMA (2005b) believes that the reason for this is not a mistrust of the very medium it's using to take sales but, instead, the result of a growing realisation that its acquisition costs were swelling online. Showan says:

> We were very keen advocates of affiliate marketing and pay-per-click search. The trouble was we had to pay for every click and we were finding that the cost of acquiring each new customer was getting more and more. One big issue was that we were finding people would come to us through affiliates just to check information on a product they'd already bought, so we were basically paying for customers to find out how to hook up their new VCR. We still have affiliates – our main one is Kelkoo – and we still bid for clicks on Google, but not as much as we used to. One of the things we were finding with the search engines is that, with our own search optimisation and because so many people were coming to our site, we were normally very high up the list just through normal searching. In our experience, particularly with Google, if people can see what they want in the main list, they don't look to the right-hand side of the page.

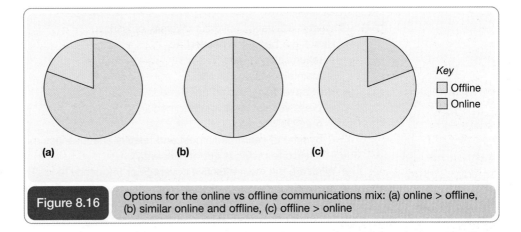

| Figure 8.16 | Options for the online vs offline communications mix: (a) online > offline, (b) similar online and offline, (c) offline > online |

One of its main benefits is its ability to separate the effects of a range of influences such as offline or online media usage or other variables such as price, promotions used and to quantify these individual effects. A simple example might be for the sales of a drinks brand:

*Sales* = 100 +

> + 2.5 × own TVRs (television ratings)
>
> – 1.4 × own price
>
> + 1.6 × competitor price
>
> + 1.0 × distribution
>
> – 0.8 × temperature
>
> – 1.2 × competitor TVRs

These relationships are typically identified using multiple linear regression models where a single dependent variable (typically sales) is a function of one or more explanatory or independent variables such as price, temperature, level of promotion.

Econometric models are developed from historic time-series data which record fluctuations dependent on different variables including seasonal variables, but most importantly, variations in media spend levels and the mix of media. In econometrics, sales fluctuations are expressed in terms of the factors causing them.

| Box 8.1 | Econometrics applications according to the Institute of Practitioners in Advertising |

1 *Overall communication effectiveness (payback)*. This is the aggregate response of consumers to an advertising campaign over the entire period of its influence. Effects can often be reported by individual media. Sometimes it is also possible to quantify secondary effects where advertising increases (say) distribution, that in turn generates additional sales.
2 *Comparative campaign effects*. Econometric modelling can help to determine which campaign is the most potent influence on sales or other key measures.

3 *Efficiency*. Efficiency covers a diversity of issues:
- How big a budget is needed to:
  - reach sales targets
  - maintain adstock levels.
- How advertising should be flighted:
  - press vs television vs other media
  - burst vs drip
  - by time of year (media cost and relative effectiveness may be issues)
  - relative to previous activity (recency).
- What are the most effective coverage or frequency levels?
- Are particular weights of advertising more effective per unit of advertising – i.e. at what point does diminishing returns set in? The issue of diminishing marginal returns to scale with respect to advertising weight is one of the aspects of efficiency most often raised. It can imply ratings becoming less effective per additional rating point. It could refer to costs or responses that differ by region or time of year. All imply a resource allocation issue where econometrics can be helpful.

4 *Cross-brand effects: portfolio, umbrella and halo*. In some markets operators have a portfolio of products that may even be direct competitors – for example brewing or financial products. Advertising one of these could positively or adversely affect others. Thorough evaluation of advertising should investigate both the effects on the advertised brand and its stablemates.

5 *Competitive effects*. Competitive effects can be measured:
- on your own brand;
- on the competitor by modelling their sales (also showing your brand's effects on them).

Once the relative effects of own and competitive media activity are understood it becomes possible to calculate the budget levels required to offset competitive actions.

*Source*: Summarised from IPA (2004) *Econometrics Explained* by Louise Cook and Mike Holmes, edited by Les Binet

## 2 Selecting the right mix of digital media communications tools

When selecting the mix of digital media for a campaign or longer-term investments, marketers will determine the most appropriate mix based on their knowledge built up through experience of previous campaigns and taking input from their advisers such as experienced colleagues or agency partners.

Varianini and Vaturi (2000) have suggested that many online marketing failures have resulted from poor control of media spending. The communications mix should be optimised to minimise the cost of acquisition. If an online intermediary has a cost acquisition of £100 per customer while it is gaining an average commission on each sale of £5 then, clearly, the company will not be profitable unless it can achieve a large number of repeat orders from the customer.

Agrawal *et al.* (2001) suggest that e-commerce sites should focus on narrow segments that have demonstrated their attraction to a business model. They believe that promotion techniques such as affiliate deals with narrowly targeted sites and e-mail campaigns targeted at segments grouped by purchase histories and demographic traits are 10 to 15 times more likely than banner ads on generic portals to attract prospects who click through to purchase. Alternatively, pay-per-click ads on Google may have a higher success rate.

When this experience isn't there, which is often the case with new digital media opportunities, it is important to do a more structured evaluation including factors such as the ability of each medium to influence perceptions, drive a response, the cost of response and the quality of response – are respondents more likely to convert to the ultimate action such as sale? What is their likely lifetime value? For example some digital media channels such as affiliates are more likely to attract customers with a lower lifetime value who are more likely to switch suppliers.

Media planning and buying agency Zed Media have produced a useful summary of how a media mix might typically vary according to budget (see Figure 8.17).

The figure shows that for a direct response campaign with limited budget, investment in controllable, targeted media which typically have a lower cost-per-acquisition such as affiliates and paid search should be the main focus. If more budget is available, it may not be possible to buy further keywords or there may be benefits from generating awareness of the offering through more display advertising.

With a brand campaign where the focus is on generating awareness, the recommendations of Zed Media are reversed where they recommend that, even at lower budgets, more investment should be made in display advertising.

Deciding on the optimal expenditure on different communication techniques will be an iterative approach since past results should be analysed and adjusted accordingly. Marketers can analyse the proportion of the promotional budget that is spent on different channels and then compare this with the contribution from purchasing customers who originated using the original channel. This type of analysis, reported by Hoffman and Novak (2000) and shown in Table 8.5, requires two different types of marketing research. First, **tagging** of customers can be used. Here, we monitor, using specifically coded URLs or cookies, the numbers of customers who are referred to a website through different online techniques such as search engines, affiliate or banner ads, and then track the money they spend on purchases.

**Tagging**
Tracking of origin of customers and their spending patterns.

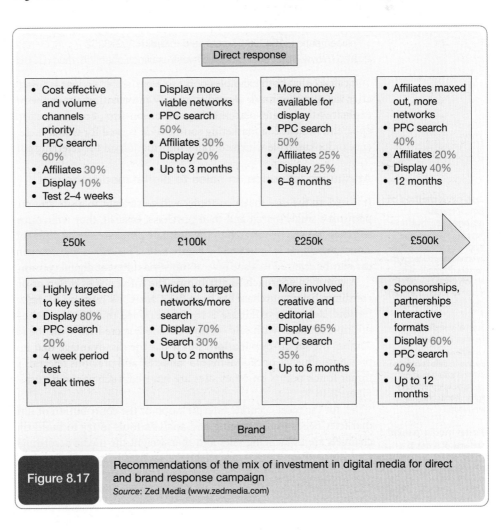

**Figure 8.17**    Recommendations of the mix of investment in digital media for direct and brand response campaign
*Source*: Zed Media (www.zedmedia.com)

| Table 8.5 | Relative effectiveness of different forms of marketing communications for a B2C company | | |
|---|---|---|---|

| Medium | Budget % | Contribution % | Effectiveness |
|---|---|---|---|
| Print (off) | 20% | 10% | 0.5 |
| TV (off) | 25% | 10% | 0.25 |
| Radio (off) | 10% | 5% | 0.5 |
| PR (off) | 5% | 15% | 3 |
| Word of mouth (off) | 0% | 25% | Infinite |
| Banners (on) | 20% | 20% | 1 |
| Affiliate (on) | 20% | 10% | 0.5 |
| Links (on) | 0% | 3% | Infinite |
| Search engine registration (on) | 0% | 2% | Infinite |

Here are two examples of tracking tags placed on the referring hyperlink within the HTML code (e.g. <a href= "tracking tag URL shown below">Text or image prompting the user to link</a>). Such a tracking tag can be placed within a pay-per-click ad campaign, or a banner on an affiliate or display ad site:

1 http://www.ingdirect.co.uk/xos/aboutoursavingsaccount.asp?ct=1&siteid=339931;& placementid=11847966;&creativeid=0&adid=20323252
2 http://www.firstdirect.com/saveinvest/esavings.shtml?fd_msc=CC085

You can see that both examples point to a particular savings landing page. The 'query string' after the question mark is used to specify information about the referrer. In item 1, this is explicit with the site, placement (position on site), creative treatment and ad number all apparent. In item 2, a marketing source code is used for which there will be a separate reference or lookup table which contains information on the referring ad.

### Attributing influence on sales to digital media channel

**Last-click method of digital media channel attribution**

The site which referred a visitor immediately before purchase is credited with the sale. Previous referrals influenced by other customer touch points on other sites are ignored.

**Digital media de-duplication**

A single referrer of a visit leading to sale is credited with the sale based on the last-click method of digital media channel attribution.

**Digital media 'assist'**

A referrer of a visit to a site before the ultimate sale is credited with the sale, often through a weighting system.

It is seldom the case that a customer will go straight to a site and purchase, or that they will perform a single search and then purchase. Instead, they will commonly perform multiple searches and will be referred to the ultimate purchase site by different types of site. This consumer behaviour is indicated by Figure 8.18. This shows that someone looking to purchase a car may be referred to a site several times via different digital communications channels.

A common approach to attributing the influence of different online media a customer consumes before purchase has been the 'Last-click method of digital media channel attribution'. Referring to Figure 8.18, you can see this has the benefit that we don't credit multiple affiliates with sale – only Affiliate 2 is credited with the sale, a process known as 'Digital media de-duplication'. But it has the disadvantage that it simplifies the reality of previous influence or digital media 'assists' and previous referrals influenced by other customer touch points on other sites are ignored, such as the natural search or display ad in Figure 8.18.

So, for the most accurate interpretation of the contribution of different media, the online marketer needs to use tagging and analysis tools to try to build the best picture of which channels are influencing sales and then weight the media accordingly. For example, a more sophisticated approach is to weight the responsibility for sale across several different referrers according to a model – so just considering the affiliates, Affiliate 1 might be credited with 30% of the sales value and Affiliate 2 with 70% for example. This approach is useful since it indicates the value of display advertising – a common phenomenon is the halo effect

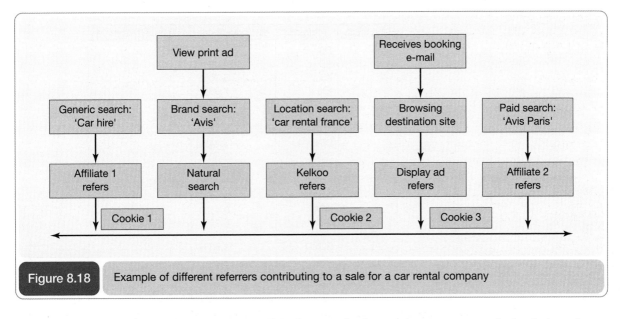

| Figure 8.18 | Example of different referrers contributing to a sale for a car rental company |

where display ads indirectly influence sales by creating awareness and stimulating sale at a later point in time. These are sometimes known as 'viewthrough' or post impression effects.

These allocation approaches won't be possible if agencies are using different tracking tools and reporting separately on different media channels – for example, the ad agency reports on display advertising, the search agency on pay-per-click, the affiliate manager on affiliate sales. Instead it is important to use a unified tracking system which typically uses common tags across all media channels. Common unified tracking solutions that consider all media are available from the likes of Atlas, Doubleclick Dart and some of the larger media agencies.

Further sophistication of tracking will be worthwhile for companies investing millions in digital media in order to understand the customer journey and the contribution of media. A useful analysis to perform is in the form shown in Figure 8.19. This anonymised example shows the importance of display ads, for example, and how different channels support each other.

It can then be worthwhile understanding the role of individual channels better, and in particular paid search. Marketers need to understand how consumers use different types of terms as shown in Table 8.6 which shows the repeated use of different types of search terms for a single customer (other digital channels such as affiliates are ignored here). The two columns on the right show how it is unrealistic to attribute the sale to the last search since the influence of the assists isn't shown.

| Table 8.6 | Example of weighted allocation of different searches |

| User id | Search query | Sale? | Value attributed: last click method | Value attributed: weighted method |
|---------|--------------|-------|-------------------------------------|-----------------------------------|
| 123 | Mobile phone (generic search) | No | £0 | £40 |
| 123 | Best camera phone (category generic search) | No | £0 | £40 |
| 123 | Nokia phone (product search) | No | £0 | £40 |
| 123 | Nokia N91 Orange (product + supplier search) | No | £0 | £40 |
| 123 | E-retailer brand name (branded search) | Yes | £200 | £40 |

| Channels | Sequence | % Conversions | Channel allocation |
|---|---|---|---|
| 2 | DS | 34.01% | 74.75% |
|  | SD | 20.98% |  |
|  | XS | 8.35% |  |
|  | SX | 7.33% |  |
|  | DX | 2.24% |  |
|  | XD | 1.83% |  |
| 3 | DDS | 7.74% | 18.53% |
|  | SDS | 5.30% |  |
|  | SXS | 3.05% |  |
|  | DXD | 1.02% |  |
|  | DXS | 0.81% |  |
|  | XSX | 0.41% |  |
|  | SDX | 0.20% |  |
| 4 | SDSD | 1.63% | 4.48% |
|  | DSDS | 1.43% |  |
|  | DXDX | 0.41% |  |
|  | DSDX | 0.20% |  |
|  | DSXD | 0.20% |  |
|  | DXDS | 0.20% |  |
|  | DXSD | 0.20% |  |
|  | SDSX | 0.20% |  |
| 5 | DSDSD | 1.02% | 1.43% |
|  | SDSDS | 0.41% |  |
| 6 | DSDSDS | 0.20% | 0.61% |
|  | SDSDSD | 0.20% |  |
|  | SDSDXS | 0.20% |  |
| 7 | DSDSDSD | 0.20% | 0.20% |

**Figure 8.19** Example of the sequence of visits to a site in generating conversions where two or more digital media channels were involved (Codes for channels: D = Display, S = Search, X = Aggregator)

Achieving and measuring repeat visits is worthwhile since according to Flores and Eltvedt (2005) on average, purchase intent sees a double digit increase after someone has been to a site more than once.

For some promotional techniques, tagging of links on third-party sites will not be practical. These will be grouped together as unattributed referrers. For word-of-mouth referrals, we have to estimate the amount of spend for these customers through traditional market research techniques such as questionnaires or asking at point of sale. The use of tagging enables much better insights on the effectiveness of promotional techniques than is possible in traditional media, but due to its complexity it requires a large investment in staff time and tracking software to achieve it. It is also very dependent on cookie deletion rates.

To see how a budget can be created for a digital campaign, complete Activity 8.2.

## 3 Level of investment in digital assets

**Digital asset**
The graphical and interactive material that supports a campaign displayed on third-party sites and on microsites. Includes display ads, e-mail templates, video, audio and other interactive media such as Flash animations.

The **digital assets** are the creative that support a campaign such as that shown in Mini case study 8.7, they include:

- display ad or affiliate marketing creative such as banners and skyscrapers;
- microsites;
- e-mail templates;
- video, audio and other interactive media such as Flash animations, games or screensavers which form a microsite.

| Activity 8.2 | Creating a digital campaign budget |
|---|---|

### Purpose

To illustrate the type of budget created internally or by digital marketing agencies. Figure 8.20 shows an extract.

### Activity

Download the spreadsheet from www.davechaffey.com/Spreadsheets to understand how the different calculations relate to each other. Try changing the cost of media (blue cells) and different click-through rates (blue cells) for which typical values are shown for a competitive retail product. View the formulas to see how the calculations are made.

How would you make this model more accurate (i.e. how would you break down each digital media channel further?)

| Input parameter table | | |
|---|---|---|
| Overall budget | £10,000 | Blue cells = input variables – vary these for 'what-if' analysis |
| Average order value | £50 | Orange cells = output variables (calculated – do not overtype) |
| Gross profit margin | 30.0% | |

| | | Advertising | | Search | | Partners | |
|---|---|---|---|---|---|---|---|
| | | Ad buys (CPM) | Ad network (CPM) | Paid search (CPC) | Natural search | Affiliates (CPA) | Aggregators |
| Media cost | Setup / creative / Mgt costs | £0 | £0 | £0 | £0 | £0 | £0 |
| | CPM | £10.0 | £10.0 | £4.0 | £0.4 | £10.0 | £20.0 |
| | CPC | £5.0 | £5.0 | £0.20 | £0.20 | £5.0 | £10.0 |
| | Media costs | £10,000 | £10,000 | £30,000 | £10,000 | £10,000 | £10,000 |
| | Total cost setup and media | £10,000 | £10,000 | £30,000 | £10,000 | £10,000 | £10,000 |
| | Budget % | 10% | 10% | 30% | 10% | 10% | 10% |
| Media impressions and response | Impressions or names | 1,000,000 | 1,000,000 | 7,500,000 | 25,000,000 | 1,000,000 | 500,000 |
| | CTR | 0.2% | 0.2% | 2.0% | 0.2% | 0.2% | 0.2% |
| | Clicks or site visits | 2,000 | 2,000 | 150,000 | 50,000 | 2,000 | 1,000 |
| Conversion to opportunity (lead) | Conversion rate to opportunity | 100.0% | 100.0% | 100.0% | 100.0% | 100.0% | 100.0% |
| | Number of opportunities | 2,000 | 2,000 | 150,000 | 50,000 | 2,000 | 1,000 |
| | Cost per opportunity | £5.0 | £5.0 | £0.2 | £0.2 | £5.0 | £10.0 |
| Conversion to sales | Conversion rate to sale | 100.0% | 100.0% | 100.0% | 100.0% | 50.0% | 100.0% |
| | Number of sales | 2,000 | 2,000 | 150,000 | 50,000 | 1,000 | 1,000 |
| | % of sales | 1.0% | 1.0% | 72.7% | 24.2% | 0.5% | 0.5% |
| | Cost per sale (CPA) | £5.0 | £5.0 | £0.2 | £0.2 | £10.0 | £10.0 |
| Revenue | Total revenue | £100,000 | £100,000 | £7,500,000 | £2,500,000 | £50,000 | £50,000 |
| Costs | Cost of goods sold | £70,000 | £70,000 | £5,250,000 | £1,750,000 | £35,000 | £35,000 |
| | Media costs | £10,000 | £10,000 | £30,000 | £10,000 | £10,000 | £10,000 |
| | Total costs (inc media) | £80,000 | £80,000 | £5,280,000 | £1,760,000 | £45,000 | £45,000 |
| Profitability | Profit | £20,000 | £20,000 | £2,220,000 | £740,000 | £5,000 | £5,000 |
| | Return on investment | 25.0% | 25.0% | 42.0% | 42.0% | 11.1% | 11.1% |

| Figure 8.20 | Spreadsheet template for digital campaign budgeting (extract) |
|---|---|

| Mini Case Study 8.7 | Lynx uses microsite to promote its 'Get More' campaign |
|---|---|

In 2004 a new deodorant brand, Lynx Pulse, used online games, screensavers, viral e-mails, video clips and soundtracks, to extend the brand experience – from applying deodorant to interacting with the brand – for 1.4 million unique users.

A similar approach was repeated in 2008 using a similar range of digital assets in the 'Get In There' campaign which was part of a long-term 'Lynx Effect' brand concept supported at a campaign specific URL (www.lynxeffect.com, Figure 8.21). Rather than a short-term campaign, to maximise the impact the brief was to 'create a consistent long-term presence for the Lynx-Axe brand online'. Another difference from previous campaigns was the greater use of video and user generated content.

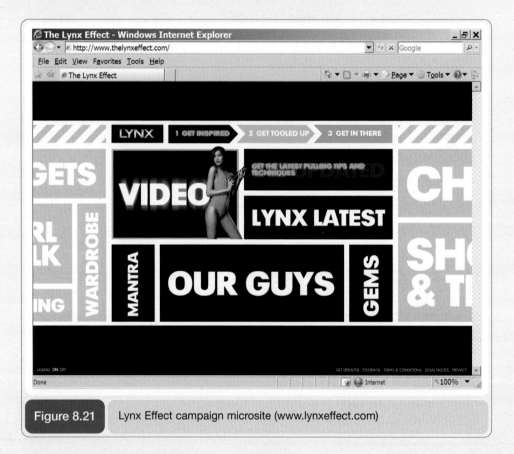

| Figure 8.21 | Lynx Effect campaign microsite (www.lynxeffect.com) |
|---|---|

The reason for the campaign was highlighted by Karen Hamilton, regional VP of marketing, Lynx-Axe Europe explained the thinking behind the campaign to NMA (2008) when she said:

> With our new campaign we feel we now have a digital presence that not only continues to give young guys the edge in the mating game but also provides us with an ongoing platform to deliver cutting-edge digital creativity. With Get In There, BBH came to us with a big idea that's rooted in the heart of our brand and understands the role of digital in our target audience's life. We have specifically created a large amount of exciting, diverse and tailored content that works across many different platforms.

For the agency Jonathan Bottomley, planning director, BBH said:

> Get In There is a rallying cry from the brand to get guys away from their computers, out of the chat rooms and to start meeting real girls rather than virtual girls.

*The idea had to break into the heart of guys' digital lives, so we created an extended network of linked content to sit on partner sites that guys visit all the time: YouTube, FHM, Flickr, Bebo. At the heart of the network is lynxeffect.com, which provides guys with tips, tools and widgets that they can use to approach girls. The idea is to give them an 'in', something to break the ice so that the fear of wondering what to say is reduced.*

*There are killer weapons, such as the Lynx FX soundboard, which you can download to your mobile phone to turn it into a pulling machine. There are downloadable business cards, magic tricks and e-mail tools, all of which are refreshed regularly. For guys in need of inspiration, hidden camera footage showcases the exploits of the Lynx Guys, characters who are getting in there with the ladies, trying to show how its done.*

As with traditional media, there is a tension between spend on the advertising creative and the media space purchased to run the executions. There is a danger that if spend on media is too high, then the quality of the execution and the volume of digital assets produced will be too low.

## Step 6. Integration into overall media schedule or plan

**Integrated marketing communications**
The co-ordination of communications channels to deliver a clear, consistent message.

In common with other communications media, digital media are most effective when they are deployed as part of an **integrated marketing communications** approach. Kotler *et al.* (2001) describe integrated marketing communications as:

> *the concept under which a company carefully integrates and co-ordinates its many communications channels to deliver a clear, consistent message about the organisation and its products.*

The characteristics of integrated marketing communications have been summarised by Pickton and Broderick (2001) as the 4 Cs of:

- *Coherence* – different communications are logically connected.
- *Consistency* – multiple messages support and reinforce, and are not contradictory.
- *Continuity* – communications are connected and consistent through time.
- *Complementary* – synergistic, or the sum of the parts is greater than the whole!

The 4 Cs also act as guidelines for how communications should be integrated.

Further guidelines on integrated marketing communications from Pickton and Broderick (2001) that can be usefully applied to Internet marketing are the following.

- Communications planning is based on *clearly identified marketing communications objectives* (see later section).
- Internet marketing involves the *full range of target audiences* (see the section on developing customer-oriented content in Chapter 7). The full range of target audiences is the customer segments plus employees, shareholders and suppliers.
- Internet marketing should involve *management of all forms of contact*, which includes management of both outbound communications, such as banner advertising or direct e-mail, and inbound communications such as e-mail enquiries.
- Internet marketing should utilise a *range of promotional tools*. These are the digital media channels illustrated in Figure 1.9 (page 29).
- *A range of media* should be used to deliver the message about the website. Marketing managers need to consider the most effective mix of media to drive traffic to their website. The different techniques can be characterised as traditional offline marketing communications or new online communications. The objective of employing these techniques is to

acquire new traffic on an e-commerce site using the techniques summarised in Figure 1.9. Many of these techniques can also be used to drive customers to a site for retention.

- The communications plan should involve careful selection of the *most effective promotional and media mix*. This is discussed at the end of the chapter.

Additionally, we can say that integrated marketing communications should be used to support customers through the entire buying process, across different media.

## Planning integrated marketing communications

The Account Planning Group (www.apg.org.uk), in its definition of media planning, highlights the importance of the role of media planning when they say that the planner:

*needs to understand the customer and the brand to unearth a key **insight** for the communication/solution [Relevance].*

*As media channels have mushroomed and communication channels have multiplied, it has become increasingly important for communication to cut through the cynicism and **connect** with its audience [Distinctiveness].*

*...the planner can provide the edge needed to ensure the solution reaches out through the clutter to its **intended audience** [Targeted reach].*

*...needs to **demonstrate** how and why the communication has performed [Effectiveness].*

More specifically, Pickton and Broderick (2001) state that the aim of marketing communications media planning as part of integrated marketing communications should be to:

- *Reach* the target audience;
- determine the appropriate *Frequency* for messaging;
- achieve *Impact* through the creative for each media.

### Media-neutral planning (MNP)

**Media-neutral planning**
An approach to planning ad campaigns to maximise response across different media according to consumer usage of these media.

The concept of **media-neutral planning (MNP)** has been used to describe an approach to planning integrated marketing campaigns including online elements. Since it is a relatively new concept, it is difficult to describe absolutely. To read a review of the different interpretations see Tapp (2005) who notes that there are three different aspects of planning often encompassed with media-neutral planning:

- *Channel planning*, i.e. which route to market shall we take: retail, direct, sales partners etc. (we would say this emphasis is rare).
- *Communications-mix planning*, i.e. how do we split our budget between advertising, direct marketing, sales promotions and PR.
- *Media planning*, i.e. spending money on TV, press, direct mail and so on.

In our view, MNP is most usually applied to the second and third elements and the approach is based on reaching consumers across a range of media to maximise response. For example, Crawshaw (2004) says:

*The simple reason we would want media-neutral communications is so that we can connect the right message with our target audience, at the right time and place to persuade them to do what we want. This will lead to powerful, effective, value for money communications that solve clients' business challenges.*

A customer-centric media-planning approach is key to this process, Anthony Clifton, Planning Director at WWAV Rapp Collins Media Group, is quoted by the Account Planning Group as saying (quoted in Crawshaw, 2004):

*Real consumer insight has to be positioned at the core of the integrated planning process and the planner must glean a complete understanding of the client's stake holders, who they are, their mindset, media consumption patterns and relationship with the business – are they 'life-time' consumers or have they purchased once, are they high value or low value customers etc. This requires lifting the bonnet of the database, segmentation and market evaluation.*

## Key activities in media selection and planning

The starting point for media planning, selection and implementation is to have clearly defined campaign objectives:

- For direct response campaigns, the most important are response volume, quality and cost.
- For campaigns where awareness and branding are the main outcomes, branding metrics become important.

Pickton and Broderick (2001) identify six activities in media implementation:

- *Target audience selection.* These are, of course, the individuals to whom the communications are directed and whom you must reach with your media. These individuals are often confused with the target market that buys and uses the products. For both consumer and business markets, the two can be quite different.
- *Media objectives.* Objectives related to achieving the right reach, frequency and impact of communications. You will always have a cost constraint – a media budget with which to achieve these objectives.
- *Media selection.* Allocating the media budget to the most appropriate classes of media and then choosing the best individual media vehicles. You might decide to allocate a proportion of spend to the media class 'interactive advertising', and then select the right vehicles such as MSN, Yahoo! and smaller vertical portals.
- *Media scheduling.* Determining the most appropriate times for advertising to take place across different media, selecting the sequence and timing of outbound communications such as e-mail and direct mail.
- *Media buying.* Buying the media – obtaining the best deals in terms of getting the right audience of the right size for the right expenditure.
- *Media evaluation.* The vital need to measure, analyse and act on your results.

A particularly important aspect for online media is that this evaluation and adjustment can – and should – occur during the campaign, in order to identify the best placements and creatives and to refine the ongoing media plan.

### Learning from cross-media optimisation studies

**Cross-media optimisation studies**
Studies to determine the optimum spend across different media to produce the best results.

Many **cross-media optimisation studies (XMOS)** have shown that the optimal online spend for low-involvement products is surprisingly high at 10–15% of total spend. Although this is not a large amount, it compares to previous spend levels below 1% for many organisations. XMOS research is designed to help marketers and their agencies answer the (rather involved) question 'What is the optimal mix of advertising vehicles across different media, in terms of frequency, reach and budget allocation, for a given campaign to achieve its marketing goals?'

The mix between online and offline spend is varied to maximise campaign metrics such as reach, brand awareness and purchase intent. Table 8.7 summarises the optimal mix identified for four famous brands. For example, Dove (1AB, 2004) found that increasing the level of interactive advertising to 15% would have resulted in an increase in overall branding metrics of 8%. The proportion of online is small, but remember that many companies are spending less than 1% of their ad budgets online, meaning that offline frequency is too high and they may not be reaching many consumers.

| Table 8.7 | Optimum media mix suggested by XMOS studies | | |
|-----------|------|----------|--------|
| **Brand** | **TV** | **Magazine** | **Online** |
| Colgate | 75% | 14% | 11% |
| Kleenex | 70% | 20% | 10% |
| Dove | 72% | 13% | 15% |
| McDonald's | 71% | 16% (radio) | 13% |

*Source*: Interactive Advertising Bureau (www.iab.net/xmos)

The reasons for using and increasing the significance of online in the media mix are similar to those for using any media mix as described by Sissors and Baron (2002):

- *Extend reach* – adding prospects not exposed by a single medium/other media.
- *Flatten frequency distribution* – if audiences viewing TV ads are exposed too many times, there is a law of diminishing returns and it might prove better to reallocate that budget to online media.
- *Reach different kinds of audiences.*
- *Provide unique advantages in stressing different benefits* – based on the different characteristics of each medium.
- *Allow different creative executions to be implemented.*
- *Add gross impressions if the other media is cost efficient.*
- *Reinforce messages by using different creative stimuli.*

Briggs *et al.* (2005) give the example of the launch of a new model of car. Their XMOS study provides these insights:

- Advertising works, but the price of some media has been bid up to make it inefficient compared to alternatives.
- TV generates the greatest level of absolute reach and produces high levels of purchase-consideration impact, but is less cost effective compared to magazine and online.
- Magazines and online category-related sites are similar in their impact, being very selective and efficiently delivering 'in-market' prospects.
- Electronic roadblocks are the most cost-efficient,and can produce significant daily reach (40% or more); however, they are not as scalable as TV.
- While roadblocks delivered 40% reach in a day, TV can deliver nearly twice the level in a single day.
- Due to changing media habits of consumers, Ford's campaign could be fine tuned to increase sales by 5% without spending a dollar more.

For integrated communications to be successful, the different techniques should be successfully integrated through time as part of a campaign or campaigns.

Figure 8.22 shows how communications can be planned around a particular event. (SE denotes 'search engine'; C1 and C2 are campaigns 1 and 2.) Here we have chosen the launch of a new version of a website, but other alternatives include a new product launch or a key seminar. This planning will help provide a continuous message to customers. It also ensures a maximum number of customers are reached using different media over the period.

In keeping with planning for other media, Pincott (2000) suggests there are two key strategies in planning integrated Internet marketing communications. First, there should be a media strategy which will mainly be determined by how to reach the target audience. This will define the online promotion techniques described in this chapter and where to advertise online. Second, there is the creative strategy. Pincott says that 'the dominant online marketing paradigm is one of direct response'. However, he goes on to suggest that all site promotion will also influence perceptions of the brand.

Finally, here are five questions about integration you must ask when creating a campaign:

1 *Consistent branding and messaging.* Is the branding and messaging sufficiently similar (coherent) throughout the campaign?

2 *Varying the offer, messaging and creative through the campaign.* Is offer and messaging varied sufficiently through the campaign? With each different medium and wave of the campaign, it can improve results to subtly vary the offer, message and creative. This might appear to conflict with the first guideline, but the two can be compatible, since:
 - different treatments and offers will appeal to different people and achieve different results;
 - if each communication in a campaign is identical, then future campaign waves will be ignored;
 - escalating or improving offers during a campaign can achieve better response.

3 *Frequency (number) and interval of communications.* Are you exposing the audience sufficiently or too much to your messages? This is a difficult balance to strike. In our view, some marketers often undercommunicate for fear of overcommunicating!

 With online media buys, it's also important to think about frequency as well as reach. Increases in frequency will usually increase awareness as for any medium – though direct response will usually peak quite quickly before ebbing away.

 If you have defined touch strategies that mandate a minimum or maximum number of communications within a period – and the interval between them – you should check that your plans fit in with these or that they do not constrain your campaign.

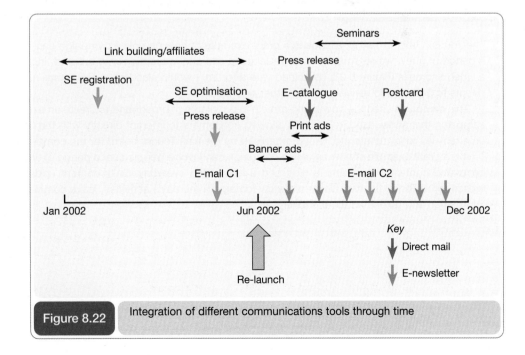

| Figure 8.22 | Integration of different communications tools through time |

4 *Sequencing of communications.* You have the option to:
- launch your campaigns online first;
- launch your campaigns offline first;
- launch your campaigns simultaneously online and offline.

Here are some examples where your online and offline activities might not launch simultaneously:
- a campaign for an event promotion starts with a direct mail or an e-mail;
- e-communications are reserved as contingency – in case offline response volumes are not high enough;
- a promotion is launched online first (notified by e-mail) to appeal to loyal customers;
- an unusual ad execution is launched online first to create a buzz;
- a press release is announced first online so that it can be transmitted by particular advocates;
- a timed or limited offer is launched online, because timing of receipt can be more accurately assured.

5 *Optimising timing.* Do communications get delivered and received at the optimal time? For online display advertising, PPC and e-mail marketing there are specific times of the day, days of the week or times of the month that your message will work best.

As a final example for this chapter, Mini case study 8.8 features many of the aspects of a great online campaign which take advantage of the online media. This campaign is:

- *Immersive* – uses rich media video clips and interactive maps to engage visitors.
- *Sustained* – runs over a period of two weeks to build campaign inertia and encourage ongoing engagement.
- *Participative* – visitors can feedback comments through the blog.
- *Integrated* – initial interest generated through print campaign and mailings to customer data.

---

| Mini Case Study 8.8 | The Tourism Ireland Taxi Challenge campaign |
|---|---|

The Tourism Ireland Taxi Challenge is a great example of how an online campaign can involve people over a period of a few weeks to get people revisiting a site and interacting with a brand. Includes integration of a video microsite (Figure 8.23) combined with a forum. I would also like to see e-mail reminders pushed to people to get them to revisit and offer other promotions.

This campaign used the power and growth in popularity of broadband to create an experiential marketing campaign that showcased Ireland and allowed consumers to interact directly with the brand. It was based on a ten-day road trip around Ireland organised by the Irish Tourist board for the competition winners.

It is a great example of how an online campaign can involve people over a period of time. It includes user-generated content with a simple blog and a new video everyday. Daily content updates gave people a reason for revisiting the site. Users can view footage of the day's activities, leave comments, browse tourist information and download the trip itinerary.

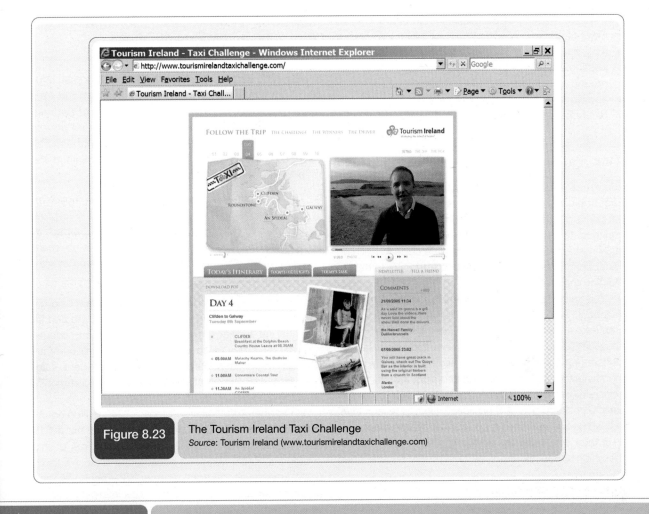

Figure 8.23 | The Tourism Ireland Taxi Challenge
*Source*: Tourism Ireland (www.tourismirelandtaxichallenge.com)

## Case Study 8    A short history of Facebook

### Context

This case is about the social network FaceBook. According to its owners:

*Facebook is a social utility that helps people communicate more efficiently with their friends, family and co-workers. The company develops technologies that facilitate the sharing of information through the social graph, the digital mapping of people's real-world social connections. Anyone can sign up for Facebook and interact with the people they know in a trusted environment.*

The case illustrates some of the challenges for an owner of a social network managing growth and decline in usage. It also highlights the challenges for partners and advertisers considering working with a social network.

The case is presented as key events during the development of Facebook.

### Facebook launched and extended – 4 February 2004

Facebook was founded while Mark Zuckerberg was a student at Harvard University. Initially membership was limited to Harvard students. The initial viral effect of the software was indicated by the fact that more than half of the undergraduate population at Harvard registered on the service within the first month!

Zuckerberg used open source software PHP and the MySQL database to create the original 'TheFacebook.com' site and these technologies are still in use today. When Facebook first launched in February 2004, there were just three things that users could do on the site, although they are still core to the functionality of the site. Users could create a profile with their picture and information, view other people's profiles, and add people as friends.

Since 2004, Facebook has introduced other functionality to create the Facebook experience. Some of the most significant of these include:

- a wall for posting messages
- news feeds
- messages
- posting of multiple photos and videos
- groups
- applications
- facebook or social ads.

## Intellectual property dispute – September 2004 and ongoing

There has been an ongoing dispute on ownership of Facebook since another Harvard-originated social networking site – 'HarvardConnection', which later changed its name to Connect U – alleged in September 2004 that Zuckerberg had used source code to develop Facebook when they originally contracted him to help in building their site.

It is also alleged that another system predated Facebook. Aaron J. Greenspan, a Harvard student in 2003, created a simple web service that he called houseSYSTEM. It was used by several thousand Harvard students for a variety of online college-related tasks – six months before Facebook started and eight months before ConnectU went online. Mark Zuckerberg was briefly an early participant. No suit has been filed by Greenspan, instead he has published a book about his experience.

It later expanded to include any university student, then high school students, and eventually anyone aged 13 and over.

## Brand identity established – 23 August 2005

In August, Facebook bought the domain name face-book.com from the Aboutface Corporation for $200,000 and dropped 'the' from its name.

## International expansion – 11 December 2005

Throughout 2005, Facebook extended its reach into different types of colleges and by the end of 2005 included most small universities and junior colleges in the United States, Canada and Mexico. It was also made available in many universities in the UK and Ireland, and by December Australia and New Zealand were added to the Facebook network, bringing its size to more than 2000 colleges and over 25,000 high schools.

## Initial concerns about privacy of member data – 14 December 2005

Two MIT students downloaded over 70,000 Facebook profiles from four schools (MIT, NYU, the University of Oklahoma and Harvard) using an automated script, as part of a research project on Facebook privacy.

## Facebook receives $25 million in funding – April 2006 and Microsoft invests – October 2007

In May 2005 Facebook received a $13 million cash infusion from venture firm Accel Partners, followed in April 2006 by a further $25 million from a range of partners including Greylock Partners, Meritech Capital Partners and investor Peter Thiel, the co-founder of PayPal. Facebook spokesman Chris R. Hughes explained the rationale for the investment when he said:

> This investment supports our goal to build an industry-leading company that will continue to grow and evolve with our users. We're committed to building the best utility to enable people to share information with each other in a secure and trusted environment.

Paul S. Madera, Meritech's managing director, said his firm was impressed by Facebook's rapid growth and its potential for further expansion in the coveted college-age market. 'They've been designated by their community as the chosen community portal,' Madera said. 'This is a company that the entire venture community would love to be a part of.'

In October 2007 Microsoft took a $240 million equity stake in Facebook. This stake was based on a $15 billion valuation of Facebook. Under the terms of this strategic alliance, Microsoft became the exclusive third-party advertising platform partner for Facebook, and began to sell advertising for Facebook internationally as well as in the United States.

## New feed functionality launched – September 2006

New information feeds were launched in mid-2006 and these show the challenges of balancing the benefit of new functionality against disrupting existing user habits. Writing in the Facebook blog in September 2006 Mark Zuckerberg said:

> We've been getting a lot of feedback about Mini-Feed and News Feed. We think they are great products, but we know that many of you are not immediate fans and have found them overwhelming and cluttered.
>
> Other people are concerned that non-friends can see too much about them. We are listening to all your suggestions about how to improve the product; it's brand new and still evolving.

Later, in an open letter on the blog dated 8 September 2006, Zuckerberg said:

*We really messed this one up. When we launched News Feed and Mini-Feed we were trying to provide you with a stream of information about your social world. Instead, we did a bad job of explaining what the new features were and an even worse job of giving you control of them. I'd like to try to correct those errors now.*

Categorising friends into different types (Friends Lists – December 2007) is one approach that has helped to manage this.

## Facebook Platform for applications launched – 24 May 2007

The Facebook Platform provides an API (application programming interface) which enables software developers to create applications that interact with core Facebook features. The Facebook developer's resource (http://developers.facebook.com) explains there are three main components used to build FB apps:

1 *Interface (API)*. The Facebook API uses a REST-based interface. This means that our Facebook method calls are made over the Internet by sending HTTP GET or POST requests to our REST server. With the API, you can add social context to your application by utilising profile, friend, photo and event data.
2 *Query (FQL)*. Facebook Query Language, or FQL, allows you to use an SQL-style interface to more easily query the same data that you can access through other Facebook API methods.
3 *Facebook Markup (FBML)*. FBML Enables you to build full Facebook Platform applications that deeply integrate into a user's Facebook experience. You can hook into several Facebook integration points, including the Profile, Profile Actions, Canvas, News Feed and Mini-Feed.

By January 2008, over 18,000 applications had been built on Facebook Platform with 140 new applications added per day. More than 95% of Facebook members have used at least one application built on Facebook Platform.

According to the Facebook Applications Directory (http://www.facebook.com/apps/) listing in February 2008, the most popular FB applications were:

1 FunWall. Videos, Photos, Graffiti, Greeting Cards, Flash Embeds and more! 2,254,075 daily active users
2 Who's in your Top Friends? Add your Best Friends to your profile! 1,956,803 daily active users
3 Super Wall Share videos, pictures, graffiti and more with your friends! 915,832 daily active users
4 Bumper Sticker, Stick your friends with funny stickers! 891,230 daily active users

5 Friends for Sale! Buy and sell your friends as pets! 585,153 daily active users.
6 Scrabulous. Play Scrabulous (Scrabble) within Facebook – 632,372 daily active users.
7 Texas HoldEm Poker. Play Texas HoldEm with your FB friends – 557,671 daily active users.
8 Movies. Compare your taste in movies with friends – 528,996 daily active users.
9 Compare People. Find out who stands where in various categories: cutest, sexiest, smartest and many more. 428,432 daily active users.
10 Are YOU Interested? FUN application to see who is interested in YOU! 486,459 daily active users.

Some applications have been accused of FB application spam, i.e. 'spamming' users to request that the application be installed.

Facebook Platform for mobile applications was launched in October 2007. Although many Facebook users already interacted with their friends through mobile phones.

## Facebook passes 30 million active users – July 2007

Facebook active users passed 30 million according to the Facebook blog in July 2007. Mashable (http://mashable.com/2007/07/10/facebook-users-2) reported that this represented a doubling in the first part of 2007).

Data produced by querying the Facebook ad targeting tool (www.facebook.com/ads), completed in November 2007 by blogger PK Francis, suggests that the majority of Facebook users in many countries are female: http://midnightexcess.wordpress.com/2007/11/23/facebook-member-stats-an-update.

In terms of user engagement metrics, Facebook (http://www.facebook.com/press/info.php?statistics) shows:

- some 68 million active users.
- An average of 250,000 new registrations per day since January 2007.
- It is the sixth-most trafficked site in the United States (comScore).
- More than 65 billion page views per month.
- More than half of active users return daily.
- People spend an average of 20 minutes on the site daily (comScore).

## Advertisers assess reputational damage – Summer 2007

In August 2007, the BBC announced that six major mainly financial services firms (First Direct, Vodafone, Virgin Media, the AA, Halifax and the Prudential) had withdrawn advertisements from the networking website Facebook after they appeared on a British National Party page.

At a similar time, bank HSBC was forced to respond to groups set up on Facebook criticising them for their introduction of new student banking charges (although not until the case had been featured in the national media).

## Facebook Ads launched – 7 November 2007

Some of the features of Facebook Ads (www.facebook.com/ads/) include:

- Targeting by age, gender, location, interests and more.
- Alternative payment models – cost-per-click (CPC) or impression based (CPM).
- 'Trusted Referrals' or 'Social Ads' – ads can also be shown to users whose friends have recently engaged with a company Facebook page or engaged with the company website through Facebook Beacon.

At the time of the launch the Facebook blog made these comments, which indicate the delicate balance in getting the balance right between advertising revenue and user experience. They said, first of all, what's not changing:

- *Facebook will always stay clutter-free and clean.*
- *Facebook will never sell any of your information.*
- *You will always have control over your information and your Facebook experience.*
- *You will not see any more ads than you did before this.*

Then, what is changing:

- *You now have a way to connect with products, businesses, bands, celebrities and more on Facebook.*
- *Ads should be getting more relevant and more meaningful to you.*
- *You now have the option to share actions you take on other sites with your friends on Facebook.*

These were originally implemented as 'social ads' and were based on a piece of technology known as 'Beacon' that tracks purchases or reviews made by Facebook users on outside sites, then reports these purchases to those users' friends.

Commercial companies or more commonly not-for-profit organisations (e.g. http://www.facebook.com/joinred) can also create their own Facebook pages (currently free). Facebook users can express their support by adding themselves as a fan, writing on the company Wall, uploading photos and joining other fans in discussion groups. When users become Fans, they can optionally agree to be kept up-to-date about developments which then appear in their news feeds.

## Privacy concerns sparked by 'Beacon technology' – November 2007

Facebook received a lot of negative publicity on its new advertising format related to the 'Beacon' tracking system which Mark Zuckerberg was forced to respond to on the Facebook blog (5 December 2007). He said:

*About a month ago, we released a new feature called Beacon to try to help people share information with their friends about things they do on the web. We've made a lot of mistakes building this feature, but we've made even more with how we've handled them. We simply did a bad job with this release, and I apologise for it. While I am disappointed with our mistakes, we appreciate all the feedback we have received from our users. I'd like to discuss what we have learned and how we have improved Beacon.*

*When we first thought of Beacon, our goal was to build a simple product to let people share information across sites with their friends. It had to be lightweight so it wouldn't get in people's way as they browsed the web, but also clear enough so people would be able to easily control what they shared. We were excited about Beacon because we believe a lot of information people want to share isn't on Facebook, and if we found the right balance Beacon would give people an easy and controlled way to share more of that information with their friends.*

*But we missed the right balance. At first we tried to make it very lightweight so people wouldn't have to touch it for it to work. The problem with our initial approach of making it an opt-out system instead of opt-in was that if someone forgot to decline to share something, Beacon still went ahead and shared it with their friends. It took us too long after people started contacting us to change the product so that users had to explicitly approve what they wanted to share. Instead of acting quickly, we took too long to decide on the right solution. I'm not proud of the way we've handled this situation and I know we can do better.'*

## New friends list functionality launched – December 2007

A criticism levelled at Facebook has been the difficulty in separating out personal friends and business acquaintances.

In December 2007, Facebook launched a significant new functionality called Friend Lists to enhance the user experience. Friend Lists enables users to create named groups of friends in particular categories, e.g. business or personal, and these private lists can be used to message people, send group or event invitations, and to filter updates from certain groups of friends.

## December 2007/January 2008 – First drop in numbers using Facebook and new data centres to manage growth in users

Application spam has been considered one of the possible causes for the drop in visitors to Facebook starting from the beginning of 2008, when the website's growth fell from December 2007 to January 2008, its first drop since the website first launched.

To put this in context, the Facebook blog reported at the end of 2007 that nearly two million new users from around the world sign up for Facebook each week. This creates technical challenges – the blog reported that at end of 2007 full capacity was reached in their California datacentres. They explained that in the past they had handled this problem by purchasing a few dozen servers, but this time they had run out of physical space in the datacentres for new machines. But now Facebook assigns a user logging on to a relevant data centre – users in Europe and the eastern half of the US are connected direct to a new Virginia data centre whenever they're browsing the site and not making any changes, otherwise users are connected to California.

## Facebook expands internationally – February 2008

Despite the hype generated among English speakers, Facebook only announced the launch of a Spanish site in February 2008 with local language versions planned for Germany and France. It seems that Facebook will inevitably follow the path taken by other social networks such as MySpace in launching many local language versions.

*Sources*: Facebook (www.facebook.com), Facebook press room (http://www.facebook.com/press.php), Facebook blog (http://blog.facebook.com). Wikipedia (2008) Wikipedia Pages for Facebook (http://en.wikipedia.org/wiki/Facebook) and Mark Zuckerberg (http://en.wikipedia.org/wiki/Mark_Zuckerberg)

### Questions

1 As an investor in a social network such as Facebook, which financial and customer-related metrics would you use to assess and benchmark the current business success and future growth potential of the company?
2 Complete a situation analysis for Facebook focusing on an assessment of the the main business risks which could damage the future growth potential of the social network.
3 For the main business risks to Facebook identified in your answer to Question 2, suggest approaches the company could use to minimise these risks

### Summary

1. The main categories of digital media channels are:
   - *Search engine marketing* – search engine optimisation (SEO) improves the position in the natural listings, and pay-per-click marketing features a company in the sponsored listings.
   - *Online PR* – including techniques such as link-building, blogging, RSS and reputation management.
   - *Online partnerships* – including affiliate marketing (commission-based referral), co-branding and sponsorship.
   - *Online advertising* – using a range of formats including banners, skyscrapers and rich media such as overlays.
   - *E-mail marketing* – including rented lists, co-branded e-mails, event-triggered e-mails and ads in third-party e-newsletters for acquisition, and e-newsletters and campaign e-mails to house lists.
   - *Viral marketing* – developing great creative concepts which are transmitted by online word-of-mouth.

2. Key characteristics of interactive communications are the combination of push and pull media, user-submitted content, personalisation, flexibility and, of course, interactivity to create a dialogue with consumers.

3. We reviewed these elements of a digital marketing communications plan:
   - Step 1. Goal setting and tracking. These can include goals for campaign volume (unique visitors and visits), quality (conversion to value events), cost (including cost-per-acquisition) and profitability.
   - Step 2. Campaign insight. Information to feed into the campaign plan includes potential site audience reach and compositions, online buying behaviour and preferences, customer search behaviour and competitor campaign activity.
   - Step 3. Segmentation and targeting. Key segmentation approaches are relationship with company, demographic segmentation, psychographic or attitudinal segmentation, value, lifecycle stage and behaviour.
   - Step 4. Offer and message development includes identification of primary and secondary offers.
   - Step 5. Budgeting and selecting the digital media mix should be based on conversion models reviewing all the digital media channels.
   - Step 6. Integration into overall media schedule or plan. The principles of integration include coherence, consistency, continuity and complementarities.

## Exercises

### Self-assessment exercises

1. Review the reasons why continuous marketing activity involving certain digital media channels is preferable to more traditional burst or campaign-based activity.
2. Describe the unique characteristics of digital media in contrast to traditional media.
3. Give example goals for an online acquisition campaign in terms of response rates or engagement with creative, cost and overall campaign effectiveness.
4. Review the options for targeting particular audience groups online with different digital media.
5. How should a company decide on the relative investment between digital media and traditional media in a marketing campaign?
6. What are the options for integrating different types of digital media channels with traditional media?
7. How can different forms of customer insight be used to inform campaign execution?
8. What are the issues that a marketer should consider when defining their offer and message for an online campaign?

### Essay and discussion questions

1. Discuss the analogy of Berthon et al. (1998) that effective Internet promotion is similar to a company exhibiting at an industry trade show attracting visitors to its stand.
2. Select a company of your choice and assess the effectiveness of the integration between their traditional communications, digital media channels and their website.
3. Select a recent campaign from a charity and with reference to their website campaign pages, identify how they should set campaign goals and review effectiveness.
4. How should companies decide on the granularity of targeting in digital media campaigns? Select two digital media channels to illustrate your examples.

## Examination questions

1. Outline the range of goals that should be used to define success criteria for an online marketing campaign.

2. Using an example from a business-to-business company, describe the options available for targeting an audience through an e-mail newsletter.

3. Explain why integration between online and traditional media will make a campaign more effective overall.

4. Describe different options for testing the effectiveness of competing offers online.

5. Which do you think are the three most important changes in campaign communications introduced by the emergence of digital media channels?

6. Which considerations would determine the suitability of incorporating a mobile 'text-to-win' promotion into an offline campaign?

7. In which ways is the long tail concept relevant to campaign planning?

8. How should a confectionary brand assess the success of a campaign microsite in uplift of branding metrics?

## References

Agrawal, V., Arjona, V. and Lemmens, R. (2001) E-performance: the path to rational exuberance, *McKinsey Quarterly*, No. 1, 31–43.

Atlas DMT (2004) The Atlas rank report: how search engine rank impacts traffic [not dated]. Atlas DMT Research (www.atlassolutions.com).

Berthon, P., Lane, N., Pitt, L. and Watson, R. (1998) The World Wide Web as an industrial marketing communications tool: models for the identification and assessment of opportunities, *Journal of Marketing Management*, 14, 691–704.

Berthon, P., Pitt, L. and Watson, R. (1996) Resurfing $W^3$: research perspectives on marketing communication and buyer behaviour on the World Wide Web, *International Journal of Advertising*, 15, 287–301.

Bird, D. (2000) *Commonsense Direct Marketing*, 4th edn, Kogan Page, London, UK.

Branthwaite, A., Wood, K. and Schilling, M. (2000) The medium is part of the message – the role of media for shaping the image of a brand. *ARF/ESOMAR Conference*, Rio de Janeiro, Brazil, 12–14 November.

Briggs, R., Krishnan, R. and Borin, N. (2005) Integrated multichannel communication strategies: evaluating the return on marketing objectives – the case of the 2004 Ford F-150 launch, *Journal of Interactive Marketing Communications*. Volume 19, Number 3/Summer 2005.

Chaffey, D. (2006) *Total E-mail Marketing*, 2nd edn. Butterworth–Heinemann, Elsevier, Oxford.

Chaffey, D. and Smith, P.R. (2008) E-marketing Excellence: *Planning and Optimising Your Digital Marketing*. 3rd, Butterworth–Heinemann, Oxford.

Cook, L. (2004) Econometrics and integrated campaigns. *AdMap*, June 2004, 37–40.

Coulter, K. and Starkis, J. (2005) Development of a media selection model using the analytic network process, *International Journal of Advertising*, 24(2), 193–215.

Crawshaw, P. (2004) Media neutral planning – what is it? Online article, Account Planning Group (www.apg.org.uk). No date given.

Deighton, J. (1996) The future of interactive marketing, *Harvard Business Review*, November–December, 151–62.

Fill, C. (2007) *Marketing Communications: Engagement, Strategies and Practice*, FT, Prentice Hall, Harlow, UK.

Flores, L and Eltvedt H. (2005) Beyond advertising – lesson about the power of brand new websites to build and expand brands ESOMAR, Montreal 2005. ESOMAR, Online Conference, Montreal, June 2005.

Harper, S. (2006) Pilot Eye Tracking Study, University of Manchester, School of Computer Science web research summary. Available at: http://hcw.cs.manchester.ac.uk/research/vicram/studies/eyetracking.php.

Hoffman, D.L. and Novak, T.P. (1996) Marketing in hypermedia computer-mediated environments: conceptual foundations, *Journal of Marketing*, 60 (July), 50–68.

Hoffman, D.L. and Novak, T.P. (1997) A new marketing paradigm for electronic commerce, *The Information Society*, Special issue on electronic commerce, 13 (Jan–Mar), 43–54.

Hoffman, D.L. and Novak, T.P. (2000) How to acquire customers on the web, *Harvard Business Review*, May–June, 179–88. Available online at: http://ecommerce.vanderbilt.edu/papers.html.

Hughes, A. (1999) Web Response – Modern 1:1 marketing. *Database Marketing Institute* article, www.dbmarketing.com/articles/Art196.htm.

Hussein, I. (2006) IPA TouchPoints, *AdMap*, July–August, 46–48.

IAB (2004) XMOS Research Case Studies. Published at: http://www.iab.net/insights_research/1672/1678/1690.

iMediaConnection (2003) Interview with ING Direct VP of Marketing, Jurie Pietersie, www.mediaconnection.com/content/1333.asp.

IPA (2004) Econometrics Explained by Louise Cook and Mike Holmes, Edited by Les Binet. A whitepaper published by the Institute of Practitioners in Advertising at www.ipa.co.uk.

Jenkinson, A. (2003) Seeboard. A case study from the Centre for Integrated Marketing, www.centreforintegratedmarketing.com.

Kaushik (2008) Excellent Analytics Tip #13: Measure Macro AND Micro Conversions. Blog post, 26 March 2008 by Avinash Kaushik, http://www.kaushik.net/avinash/.

Kotler, P., Armstrong, G., Saunders, J. and Wong, V. (2001) *Principles of Marketing*, 3rd European edn. Financial Times/Prentice Hall, Harlow.

New Media Age (2005) Perfect Match by Greg Brooks, *New Media Age*, 29 September. www.nma.co.uk.

*New Media Age* (2006) Banking on Search. *New Media Age*, 16 March 2006.

NMA (2008) Ad Watch – Lynx makes successful pass at digital with Get In There, *New Media Age*, 14–15, published: 7 February 2008.

Novak, T. and Hoffman, D. (1997) New metrics for new media: towards the development of web measurement standards, *World Wide Web Journal*, 2(1), 213–46.

Peters, L. (1998) The new interactive media: one-to-one but to whom? *Marketing Intelligence and Planning*, 16(1), 22–30.

Petersen, E. (2004) *Web Measurement Hacks. Tips and Tools to Help Optimize your Online Business.* O'Reilly, Sebastapol, CA. www.oreilly.com/catalog/webmeasurehks/chapter/index.html.

Pickton, A. and Broderick, D. (2001) *Integrated Marketing Communications*. Financial Times/Prentice Hall, Harlow.

Pincott, G. (2000) Website promotion strategy. White paper from Millward Brown Intelliquest. Available online at www.intelliquest.com.

Rowley, J. (2001) Remodelling marketing communications in an Internet environment, *Internet Research: Electronic Networking Applications and Policy*, 11(3), 203–12.

Schramm, W. (1955) How communication works. In *The Process and Effects of Mass Communications*, W. Schramm (ed.), 3–26. University of Illinois Press, Urbana, IL.

Schultz, D. and Schultz, H. (2004). *Integrated Marketing Communications: the Next Generation.* Wiley, New York.

Sissors, J., and Baron, R. (2002) *Advertising Media Planning*, 6th edn. McGraw-Hill, Chicago.

Tapp, A. (2005) Clearing up media neutral planning, *Interactive Marketing*, 6(3), 216–21.

van Doren, D., Flechner, D. and Green-Adelsberger, K. (2000) Promotional strategies on the World Wide Web, *Journal of Marketing Communications*, 6, 21–35.

Varianini, V. and Vaturi, D. (2000) Marketing lessons from e-failures, *McKinsey Quarterly*, No. 4, 86–97.

Walmsley, A. (2007) New media; the age of the trialogue, *The Marketer*, September, 12.

Wertime, K. and Fenwick, I. (2008) *DigiMarketing – The Essential Guide to New Media and Digital Marketing*. John Wiley and Sons, Singapore.

## Further reading

Fill, C. (2005) *Marketing Communications – Contexts, Contents and Strategies*, 4th edn. Financial Times/Prentice Hall, Harlow. The entire book is recommended for its integration of theory, concepts and practice.

Novak, T. and Hoffman, D. (1997) New metrics for new media: towards the development of web measurement standards, *World Wide Web Journal*, 2(1), 213–46. This paper gives detailed, clear definitions of terms associated with measuring advertising effectiveness.

Wertime, K. and Fenwick, I. (2008) *DigiMarketing – The Essential Guide to New Media and Digital Marketing*. John Wiley and Sons, Singapore.

Zeff, R. and Aronson, B. (2001) *Advertising on the Internet*, 3rd edn. Wiley, New York. A comprehensive coverage of online banner advertising and measurement techniques and a more limited coverage of other techniques such as e-mail-based advertising.

## Web links

Links on specific digital media channels such as e-mail marketing and search engine marketing are at the end of Chapter 9.

Sites focusing on approaches to running interactive marketing campaigns

- **ClickZ** (www.clickz.com/experts/). Has columns on different aspects of interactive communications including media planning.
- **DaveChaffey.com** (www.davechaffey.com). A blog of links and articles about developments in interactive communications structured according to the chapters in this book.
- **iMediaConnection** (www.imediaconnection.com). Media site reporting on best practice in online advertising.
- **US Internet Advertising Bureau** (www.iab.net). The widest range of studies about Internet advertising effectiveness. In UK: www.iabuk.net.
- **Journal of Computer Mediated Communications** (http://www.blackwell-synergy.com/loi/jcmc). A free online peer-reviewed journal describing developments in interactive communications.
- **Media Buyer Planner** (www.buyerplanner.com). Developments in media planning with strong focus on online media.
- **Marketing Sherpa** (www.marketingsherpa.com). Articles and links on Internet marketing communications including e-mail and online advertising.
- **World Advertising Research Centre** (www.warc.com) Covers offline and online media. Mainly subscription service, but with some free resources.

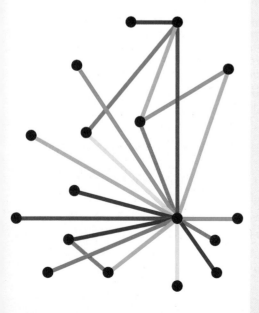

# 9

# Marketing communications using digital media channels

## Learning objectives

After reading this chapter, the reader should be able to:

● Distinguish between the different types of digital media channels
● Evaluate the advantages and disadvantages of each digital media channel for marketing communications
● Assess the suitability of different types of digital media for different purposes

## Questions for marketers

Key questions for marketing managers related to this chapter are:

● Which digital communications media should we select for different types of campaign?
● Which are the success factors which will make our campaigns more effective?

## Links to other chapters

Related chapters are:

● Chapter 8 introduces digital communications. The section towards the end of the chapter on 'Selecting the right mix of digital media communications tools' in 'Step 5. Budgeting and selecting the digital media mix', is particularly relevant
● Chapter 10 also considers the measurement of communications effectiveness

# Introduction

**Digital media channel**

Online communications technique such as search engine marketing, affiliate marketing and display advertising used to engage web users on third-party sites; encourage them to visit an organisation's site or purchase through traditional channels such as by phone or in-store.

Digital marketing managers use many different **digital media channels**, such as affiliate marketing, e-mail marketing and search engine marketing, to attract visitors to their website. They also have options such as display advertising and widget marketing for communicating brand values to visitors of third-party websites. Companies also have to consider the role of traditional communications disciplines such as advertising, direct mail and PR in generating awareness and favourability about brands and in encouraging site visits.

Choosing the most effective digital communications techniques and refining them to attract visitors and new customers at an efficient cost is now a major marketing activity, both for online business and multichannel businesses. In this chapter, we explain the differences between the different digital media options and review the strengths, weaknesses and success factors for using the communications techniques.

## How is this chapter structured?

This chapter is structured around the six main digital media channels we have identified in Table 9.1 (Figure 1.9 on page 29 portrays a graphical summary). To enable easy comparison of the different techniques and to assist with assignments and revision, we have structured each section the same way:

- *What is it?* A description of the digital media channel.
- *Advantages and disadvantages?* A structured review of the benefits and drawbacks of each channel.
- *Best practice in planning and management.* A summary of the issues such as targeting, measurement and creative which need to be considered when running a campaign using each digital channel. This expands on the coverage given in the previous chapter on these issues.

As you read each section, you should compare the relative strengths and weaknesses of the different techniques. In the final section, we summarise their strengths and weaknesses for different applications.

| Table 9.1 | Summary of different digital media channels | |
|---|---|---|
| **Digital media channel** | **Description** | **Different communications techniques** |
| Search engine marketing (SEM) | Gaining listings in the search engine results pages of the major search engines, Google, Yahoo!, Live and Ask and local variants. Also includes advertising on third-party publisher sites which are part of the search content networks | • Search Engine Optimisation (SEO) listing in the natural listing which does not attract a fee per click. Based on on page optimisation and link-building<br>• Pay-per-click (advertising) sponsored listings using Google AdWords for example<br>• Product or keyword feeds can be incorporated into search results (Yahoo! Search Submit) or to aggregators |
| Online public relations (E-PR) | Maximising favourable mentions of your company, brands, products or websites on third-party sites such as social networks or blogs that are likely to be visited by your target audience. Also includes monitoring and, where necessary, responding to negative mentions and conducting public relations via a site through a press centre or blog, for example | • Syndicating content (e.g. press releases), gaining positive mentions, managing reputation on third-party sites, particularly forums and social networks<br>• Use of blogs and feeds |

| Digital media channel | Description | Different communications techniques |
|---|---|---|
| Online partnerships including affiliate marketing | Creating and managing long-term arrangements to promote your online services on third-party websites or through e-mail communications. Different forms of partnership include link building, affiliate marketing, aggregators such as price comparison site like Moneysupermarket (www.moneysupermarket.com), online sponsorship and co-branding | • Commission-based affiliate marketing<br>• Creating long-term partnership relationships such as sponsorship, link-building or editorial |
| Interactive display advertising | Use of online display ads such as banners and rich media ads to achieve brand awareness and encourage click-through to a target site | • Site-specific media buys<br>• Use of ad networks<br>• Behavioural targeting |
| Opt-in e-mail marketing | Using legal, permission-based e-mailing to prospects or customers who have agreed to receive e-mails from an organisation. E-mails to communicate with prospects can be rented from a publisher or other list owner or companies can build up their own 'house list' containing customer or prospect details | • Acquisition e-mail activity including list rental, co-branded campaigns, advertising on e-newsletters<br>• Retention and growth activity, e.g. house list for e-newsletters and customer e-mail campaigns<br>• Automatic or event-triggered e-mail campaign activity |
| Viral and electronic word-of-mouth marketing | Viral marketing is effectively online word of mouth – compelling brand-related content is forwarded or discussed electronically, for example, in social networks or discussed offline to help achieve awareness and, in some case, drive response. Strong link with online PR activity | • Creating 'viral agents' or compelling interactive content<br>• Encouraging transmission of viral messages<br>• Using customer advocacy effect<br>• Widget marketing |

## Digital marketing in practice    The EConsultancy interview

### Nick Robertson, CEO, ASOS, on the tension between affiliate and brand marketing

#### Overview and main concepts covered

ASOS CEO Nick Robertson was at the centre of a 'firestorm' in 2007 when he labelled some affiliates as 'grubby' after closing down their affiliate programme. Nick explains the reasons behind his decision to close down the ASOS affiliate programme. The e-tailer certainly doesn't seem to have been hampered by its decision ...

#### The interview

**Q: Can you throw some light on the issues you were having with your affiliate programme when you ditched it, and clarify what you meant by your comments about affiliates?**

*Nick Robertson:* The problems we were having were that we were paying commissions on sales we would have generated ourselves.

About a year-and-a-half to two years ago, we took a view – and it was a very harsh view – that by culling our affiliate programme and paying no commissions on sales, we might dent our top line slightly but we would be considerably more profitable. We would re-invest that profit into brand marketing to drive top-line sales, on which we would not be paying commission.

Let me put it into perspective. We had an affiliate programme and we had an affiliate manager that the affiliates loved. I'm hardly surprised, because we made those affiliates a bloody fortune. We had a 60-day cookie period and 12–15% commissions.

When you get bigger, you find that … your customers are travelling around the web and are picking up these cookies left, right and centre. We found we were paying commissions on sales to customers who would have come to us anyway. They might not have come straight away but they were familiar with ASOS, they knew ASOS, but they just had to click on some other sites and we would have to pay commissions on them.

We have been proved absolutely right – more than right. It hasn't dented our top-line sales at all. Look at the figures. Look at the top-line growth of Figleaves, Firebox, Iwantoneofthose or NET-A-PORTER. These are sites that spend considerable amounts of money on affiliate marketing and we are outstripping the growth of all of them.

**Q: Why didn't you just reduce the cookie period?**

***Nick Robertson:*** Because we were still paying commissions. We did end up reducing it from 60 days to 30 days to one week, I think.

To be honest, what was happening was that it was taking so long to police it. You'd have affiliates who would ask to be involved in the programme and register one site, and then, funnily enough, just use the codes to open up a completely different site.

We would run a discount promotion with a magazine like *Grazia*, a tactical marketing initiative, and that discount would be widely used all over the Internet. These were affiliates who we had told not to generate traffic on the back of discount codes.

It got to the point where it was a full-time policing job just to stop the unethical and against-the-rules practices that these affiliates were employing. What happened was the bad affiliates tarnished the good affiliates and we just culled the lot. And we haven't looked back. I'm not in any hurry to introduce a new affiliate programme.

I'd like someone to show me a site out there that's growing not just in terms of top-line sales but also in terms of profit [through affiliate marketing]. With some sites, it's ridiculous. They have an average basket of £25 or so and are paying 15% affiliate commission – they are losing money on those sales so what is the point? They might as well not process those sales. It is costing you to get it out of the door. The only fashion retailer that makes a 15% return on sales is Next plc.

**Q: Why do you feel the brand marketing you've been investing in has served you better, despite the fact that it isn't as targeted or measurable?**

***Nick Robertson:*** The fashion industry is about image. That is the way of the world and you can't get away from it. That's why we spend millions upon millions of pounds promoting our brand image. Why is Topshop spending huge amounts of money with Kate Moss?

What was happening was the affiliates out there had no conception of that. My banners weren't replaced. My products would be out of stock because they wouldn't bother using the feeds. It was a horror story. Here was me trying to build a brand. It wasn't all of them, but a lot of them.

**Q: What quality of traffic are you getting through magazine advertising?**

***Nick Robertson:*** Every metric about ASOS is going through the roof – not just customer numbers, but average basket size, profile, age, everything is going in the direction we want it to. Why? Because we spend a lot of money building the brand.

I'm not going to pay commissions to people when we would have got the genuine sales anyway. I have 2m [prospective] customers a month coming in. Where is the affiliate programme? Who is driving this traffic? They are coming direct.

> *Q:* **Are you actually going to re-launch the programme?**
>
> *Nick Robertson*: Right now, I have better uses for my marketing money. In the forsee-
> able future, no. I'm struggling to come up with reasons why we would. The bigger we
> get, the more questionable it is. Seventy per cent of our products are unique, so you
> can't get them anywhere else.
>
> *Source*: http://www.e-consultancy.com/news-blog/newsletter/3223/asos-ceo-speaks-out-on-grubbygate.html.

## Search engine marketing

**Search engine marketing**

Promoting an organisation through search engines to meet its objectives by delivering relevant content in the search listings for searchers and encouraging them to click through to a destination site. The two key techniques of SEM are *search engine optimisation (SEO)* to improve results from the natural listings, and *paid-search marketing* to deliver results from the sponsored listings within the search engines.

**Navigational search**

Searchers use a search engine such as Google to find information deeper within a company site by appending a qualifier such as a product name to the brand or site name. Organisations need to check that relevant pages are available in the search results pages for these situations.

Search engine marketing (SEM) is vital for generating quality visitors to a website as suggested by Figure 9.1. We all now naturally turn to a search engine such as Google, Yahoo! and MSN Search or other regional search engine when we are seeking a new product, service of entertainment. We also turn to search when we are familiar with a brand, shortcutting site navigation by searching for a brand, appending a brand name to a product or typing a URL into Google, which is surprisingly common, accounting for over 50% of paid search expenditure according to Atlas (2007). This is known as 'navigational search'. Given the obvious importance of reaching an audience during their consideration process for a product or when they are locating a brand, search engine marketing (SEM) has become a fiercely competitively area of digital marketing.

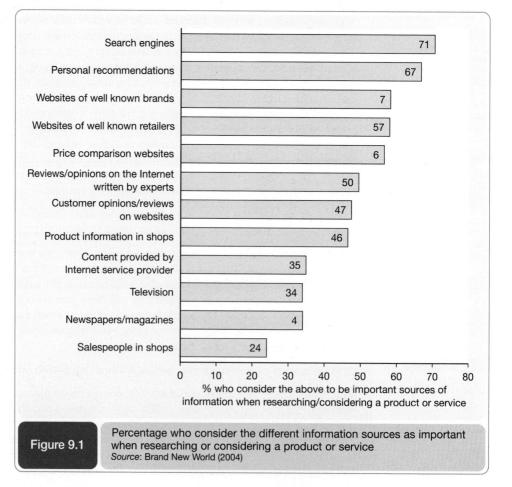

**Figure 9.1**  Percentage who consider the different information sources as important when researching or considering a product or service
*Source*: Brand New World (2004)

There are two main types of SEM which are quite distinct in the marketing activities needed to manage them, so we will study them separately, although in practice they should be integrated:

**Search engine optimisation**
A structured approach used to increase the position of a company or its products in search engine natural or organic results listings for selected keywords or phrases.

1 **Search engine optimisation** (SEO) involves achieving the highest position or ranking practical in the **natural** or **organic listings** shown in Figure 9.2 as the main body of the **search engine results pages (SERPS)** across a range of specific combination of keywords (or keyphrases) entered by search engine users.

As well as listing pages which the search engine determines as relevant for the search performed based on the text it contains and other factors, such as links to the page, the SERPs also contain other tools which searchers may find useful. Google terms these tools part of a strategy known as **universal search**. For example, Figure 9.2 shows a link to different price comparison services. Other tools include links to other databases such as Google Product Search, Google Scholar or YouTube videos.

2 **Paid search marketing or pay-per-click (PPC)** is similar to conventional advertising; here a relevant text ad with a link to a company page is displayed when the user of a search engine types in a specific phrase. A series of text ads usually labelled as 'sponsored links' are displayed above, or to the right of, the natural listings as in Figure 9.2. Although many searchers prefer to click on the natural listings, a sufficient number do click on the paid listings (typically around a quarter or a third of all clicks) such that they are highly profitable for companies such as Google and a well-designed paid search campaign can drive a significant amount of business for the search companies.

**Natural** or **organic listings**
The pages listing results from a search engine query which are displayed in a sequence according to relevance of match between the keyword phrase typed into a search engine and a web page according to a ranking algorithm used by the search engine.

**Search engine results pages**
The page(s) containing the results after a user types a keyphrase into a search engine. SERPS contain both natural or organic listings and paid or sponsored listings.

**Universal search**
The natural listings incorporate other relevant results from vertical searches related to a query, such as video, books, scholar, news, sitelinks and images.

**Paid search marketing (pay-per-click) marketing**
A relevant text ad with a link to a company page is displayed on the SERPs when the user of a search engine types in a specific phrase. A fee is charged for every click of each link, with the amount bid for the click mainly determining its position. Additionally, PPC may involve advertising through a content network of third-party sites (which may be on a CPC, CPM or CPA basis).

**Figure 9.2**

Search engine results pages in Google (www.google.co.uk) illustrating the natural and paid listings
*Source*: Reprinted by permission of Google, Inc. Google™ search engine is a trademark of Google, Inc.

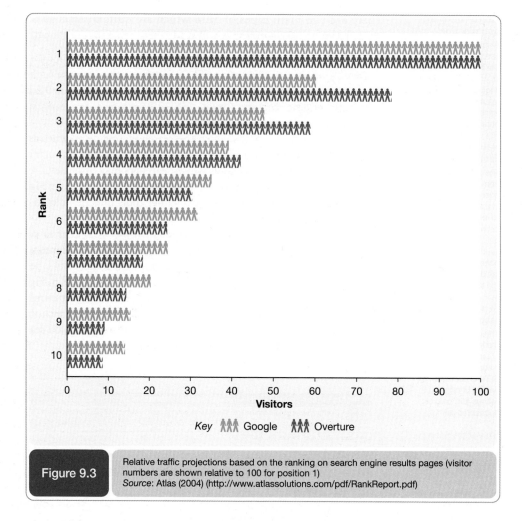

| Figure 9.3 | Relative traffic projections based on the ranking on search engine results pages (visitor numbers are shown relative to 100 for position 1)<br>*Source*: Atlas (2004) (http://www.atlassolutions.com/pdf/RankReport.pdf) |

The importance of effective search engine marketing is suggested by Figure 9.3 which shows that the higher the rank of a company and products in the search engine results pages (SERPs) the more visitors will be received. It is widely thought that it is essential to be in the top three sites listed in the results from a search, but the figure and Box 9.1 'Understanding consumer search engine behaviour' show that some visitors can still be delivered from lower rankings.

| Box 9.1 | Understanding consumer search engine behaviour |

Search marketing firm iProspect conducted research on how we search by commissioning Jupiter Research to survey 2400 US searchers about their behaviour. Some of the key findings digital marketers need to be aware of are as follows:

- **Searchers value brand credibility**. 36% of search engine users believe that the companies whose websites are returned at the top of the search results are the top brands in their field.
- **Many searchers don't look beyond the first page**. 41% of search engine users who continue their search when not finding what they seek, will change engines or change their search term if they don't find what they seek on the first page of search results. This figure was 28% in 2002.

- **Search term refinement**. 82% of search engine users re-launch an unsuccessful search using the same search engine as they used for their initial search, but add more keywords to refine the subsequent search. This figure was just 68% in 2002.
- **Searchers prefer natural listings**. Between 60% and 80% of clicks are on the natural rather than paid listings depending on the term. Note that separate audience panel research by Comscore (2008) has shown that the paid click rate in Google is around 25% for search results pages with around 50% of searches containing paid ads.

*Source*: iProspect research, 2006 (www.iprospect.com)

## What is SEO?

Improving positions in the natural listings is dependent on marketers understanding the process whereby search engines compile an index by sending out spiders or robots to crawl around sites that are registered with that search engine (Figure 9.4). The figure shows that the technology harnessed to create the natural listings involves these main processes:

**Spiders** or **robots**
Spiders are software processes, technically known as robots, employed by search engines to index web pages of registered sites on a regular basis. They follow links between pages and record the reference URL of a page for future analysis.

1 Crawling. The purpose of the crawl is to identify relevant pages for indexing and assess whether they have changed. Crawling is performed by **robots** (bots) which are also known as **spiders**. These access web pages and retrieve a reference URL of the page for later analysis and indexing.

   Although the terms 'bot' and 'spider' give the impression of something physical visiting a site, the bots are simply software processes running on a search engine's server which request pages, follow the links contained on that page and so create a series of page references with associated URLs. This is a recursive process, so each link followed will find additional links which then need to be crawled.

2 *Indexing*. An index is created to enable the search engine to rapidly find the most relevant pages containing the query typed by the searcher. Rather than searching each page for a query phrase, a search engine 'inverts' the index to produce a lookup table of documents containing particular words.

   The index information consists of phases stored within a document and also other information characterising a page such as the document's title, meta description, PageRank, trust or authority, spam rating, etc. For the keywords in the document, additional attributes will be stored such as semantic markup (<h1>, <h2> headings denoted within HTML), occurrence in **link anchor text**, proximity, frequency or density and position in document, etc.

**Link anchor text**
The text used to form the blue underlined hyperlink viewed in a web browser defined in the HTML source. For example: Visit Dave Chaffey's web log is created by the HTML code: <A HREF 5 "http://www.davechaffey. com">Visit Dave Chaffey's web log</A>.

3 *Ranking or scoring*. The indexing process has produced a lookup of all the pages that contain particular words in a query, but they are not sorted in terms of relevance. Ranking of the document to assess the most relevant set of documents to return in the SERPs occurs in real time for the search query entered. First, relevant documents will be retrieved from a runtime version of the index at a particular data centre, then a rank in the SERPs for each document will be computed based on many ranking factors, of which we highlight the main ones in later sections.

4 *Query request and results serving*. The familiar search engine interface accepts the searcher's query. The user's location is assessed through their IP address and the query is then passed to a relevant data centre for processing. Ranking then occurs in real time for a particular query to return a sorted list of relevant documents and these are then displayed on the search results page.

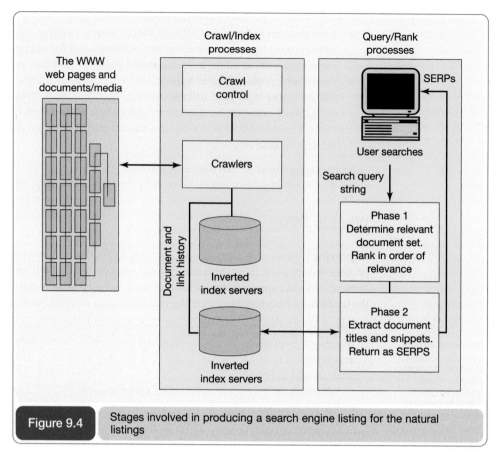

| Figure 9.4 | Stages involved in producing a search engine listing for the natural listings |
|---|---|

**On-page optimisation**

Writing copy and applying markup such as the <title> tag and heading tag <h1> to highlight to search engine relevant keyphrases within a document.

**External link building**

A proactive approach to gain quality links from third-party sites.

**Internal link architecture**

Structuring and labelling links within a site's navigation to improve the results of SEO.

**Backlink**

Hyperlink which links to a particular web page (or website). Also known as an inbound link. Google PageRank and Yahoo! WebRank are methods of enumerating this.

### Search engine ranking factors

Google has stated that it uses more than 200 factors or signals within its search ranking algorithms. These include positive ranking factors which help boost position and negative factors or filters which are used to remove search engine spam from the index where SEO companies have used unethical approaches such as automatically creating links to mislead the Google algorithms.

The two most important factors for good ranking positions in all the main search engines are:

- *Matching between web page copy and the keyphrases searched.* The main factors to optimise on are keyword density, keyword formatting, keywords in anchor text and the document meta-data including page title tags. The SEO process to improve results in this area is known as on-page optimisation. We will cover some of details of best practice for this process in a topic later in this section.
- *Links into the page (inbound or backlinks).* Google counts each link to a page from another page or another site as a vote for this page. So pages and sites with more external links from other sites will be ranked more highly. The quality of the link is also important, so if links are from a site with a good reputation and relevant context for the keyphrase, then this is more valuable. Internal links are also assessed in a similar way. The processes to improve this aspect of SEO are external link building and internal link architecture.

## Advantages and disadvantages of SEO

### Advantages of SEO

The main benefits of SEO are:

- *Highly targeted.* Visitors are searching for particular products or services so will often have a high intent to purchase – they are qualified visitors.
- *Potentially low cost visitors.* There are no media costs for ad display or click-through. Costs arise solely from the optimisation process where agencies are paid to improve positions in the search results.
- *Dynamic.* The search engine robots will crawl the home page of popular sites daily, so new content is included relatively quickly for the most popular pages of a site (less so for deep links).

### Disadvantages of SEO

Despite the targeted reach and low cost of SEO, it is not straightforward as these disadvantages indicate:

- *Lack of predictability.* Compared with other media SEO is very unreliable in terms of the return on investment – it is difficult to predict results for a given investment.
- *Time for results to be implemented.* The results from SEO may take months to be achieved, especially for new sites.
- *Complexity and dynamic nature.* The search engines take hundreds of factors into account, yet the relative weightings are not published, so there is not a direct correlation between marketing action and results – 'it is more of an art than a science'. Furthermore the ranking factors change through time.
- *Ongoing investment.* Investment needed to continue to develop new content and generate new links.
- *Poor for developing awareness in comparison with other media channels.* Searchers already have to be familiar with a brand or service to find it. However, it offers the opportunity for less well-known brands to 'punch above their weight' and to develop awareness following click-through.

Remember, though, that search engine marketing is only one online digital communications tool. For established brands, we commonly see from web analytics that more than half of site visitors arrive at a site not through search engines, but directly through typing in the web address or following a bookmark (web analytics tools label these as 'no referrer'). The volume of direct visitors shows the power of branding, PR and offline communications in driving visitor traffic. In 2003, Statmarket (www.statmarket.com) reported that direct navigation accounted for 65% of site visits worldwide, with 21% following links and just 14% arriving by search engines. For first time visits, however, search marketing is generally found to be over 20%.

## Best practice in planning and managing SEO

In this section we will review six of the main approaches used to improve the results from SEO. You will see that SEO is a technical discipline and that the techniques used change through time. For this reason SEO is often outsourced to a specialist SEO agency, although some companies believe they can gain an edge through having an internal specialist who understands the company's customers and markets well. You will see, though, that some of the on-page optimisation techniques recommended in this section are relatively straightforward and it is important to control brand and proposition messages. Content editors and reviewers within a company therefore need to be trained to understand these factors and incorporate them into their copywriting.

## 1. Search engine submission

While some unscrupulous search marketing companies offer to register you in the 'Top 1000 search engines', in reality registering in the top 5–10 search engines of each country an organisation operates in (see compilations at SearchEngineWatch, www.searchenginewatch. com/reports) will probably account for more than 95% of the potential visitors. Most existing companies will be automatically included in the search index since the search engine robots will follow links from other sites that link to them.

**Search engine submission**
The process of informing search engines that a site should be indexed for listing in the search engine results pages.

For new companies, achieving **search engine submission** is now straightforward – for example, in Google there is an 'Add a URL' page (e.g. www.google.com/addurl.html). Unfortunately it can take time for a site to be ranked highly in search results even if it is the index: Google allegedly places new sites in a review status sometimes referred to as the *Google sandbox effect*. However, Google search engineers deny the existence of this and explain it is a natural artifact produced by new sites having limited links, history and so reputation. Either way, it is important to remember this constraint when creating startup companies or separate unlined microsites for a campaign since you may have to reply on paid search to gain SERPS visibility.

## 2 Index inclusion

**Index inclusion**
Ensuring that as many of the relevant pages from your domain(s) are included within the search engine indexes you are targeting to be listed in.

Although a search engine robot may visit the home page of a site, it will not necessarily crawl all pages or assign them equal weight in terms of PageRank or relevance. So when auditing sites as part of an SEO initiative, SEO agencies will check how many pages are included within the search engine index for different search engines. This is known as **index inclusion**.

Potential reasons for not gaining complete index inclusion include:

- Technical reasons why the search robots do not crawl all the pages, such as the use of SEO-unfriendly content management system with complex URLs.
- Pages identified as spam or of less importance (what used to be known as the supplemental index in Google), perhaps due to a hierarchical structure.
- If you are a multinational company with different content sites for different countries, then it is challenging to deliver the relevant content for local audiences with use of regional domains tending to work best.

Companies can check the index inclusion through:

- Reviewing web analytics data which will show the frequency with which the main search robots crawl a site.
- Using web analytics referrer information to find out which search engines a site's visitors originate from, and the most popular pages.
- Checking the number of pages that have been successfully indexed on a site. For example, in Google the search 'inurl:www.davechaffey.com' or site:www.davechaffey.com lists all the pages of Dave's site indexed by Google and gives the total number in the top-right of the SERPs.

## 3 Keyphrase analysis

**Keyphrase (keyword phrase)**
The combination of words users of search engines type into a search box which form a search query.

The key to successful search engine marketing is achieving **keyphrase** relevance since this is what the search engines strive for – to match the combination of keywords typed into the search box to the most relevant destination content page. Notice that we say 'keyphrase' (short for 'keyword phrase') rather than 'keyword' since search engines such as Google attribute more relevance when there is a phrase match between the keywords that the user types and a phrase on a page. Despite this, many search companies and commentators talk about optimising your 'keywords' and, in our opinion, pay insufficient attention to keyphrase analysis.

Key sources for identifying the keyphrases your customers are likely to type when searching for your products include your market knowledge, competitors' sites, keyphrases from visitors who arrive at your site (from web analytics), the internal site search tool and the keyphrase analysis tools from vendors such as Overture (now Yahoo Search Marketing) listed at www.davechaffey.com/seo-keyword-tools. When completing keyphrase analysis we need to understand different qualifiers that users type in. For example, this list of seven different types of keyphrases with different qualifiers is taken from an Overture representative talking at Search Engine Strategies in 2004. We have added examples for 'car insurance':

- *Comparison/quality* – compare car insurance
- *Adjective* (price/product qualifiers) – cheap car insurance, woman car insurance
- *Intended use* – high mileage car insurance
- *Product type* – holiday car insurance
- *Vendor* – churchill car insurance
- *Location* – car insurance UK
- *Action request* – buy car insurance.

You can see some of these types of keyphrases by using the Overture keyterm suggestion tool. For example at a single point in time, for a single month in the UK, the most popular phrases related to car insurance were:

1 Car insurance, 1,423,350.
2 Cheap car insurance, 71,979.
3 Car insurance quote, 32,857.
4 Woman car insurance, 21,087.
5 Young driver car insurance, 17,175.
6 Performance car insurance, 12,379.
7 Car insurance uk, 11,719.
8 AA car insurance, 7,956.
9 Online car insurance quote, 7,423.
10 Car insurance company, 7,186.

These data suggest the importance of ranking well for high-volume keyphrases such as 'cheap car insurance' and 'car insurance uk'.

### 4 On-page optimisation

Although each search engine has its own algorithm with many weighting factors that change through time, fortunately there are common factors in the match between search terms entered and the occurrence of the words on the page that influence search engine rankings.

#### Occurrence of search term in body copy

The number of times the keyphrase is repeated in the text of the web page is a key factor in determining the position for a keyphrase. Copy can be written to increase the number of times a word or phrase is used (technically, its keyphrase density) and ultimately boost position in the search engine. Note though that search engines carry out checks that a phrase is not repeated too many times such as 'cheap flights... cheap flights... cheap flights... cheap flights... cheap flights... cheap flights... cheap flights... cheap flights...' or the keyword is hidden using the same colour text and backgound and will not list the page if this keyphrase density is too high or it believes 'search engine spamming' has occurred.

Although the most basic test of relevance for search engines is the number of times the phrase appears on the page, there are many other factors that can also be applied. In its guidance for Webmasters, Google states:

> *Google goes far beyond the number of times a term appears on a page and examines all aspects of the page's content (and the content of the pages linking to it) to determine if it's a good match for your query.*

These other factors include

- frequency (which must be not too excessive, i.e. less than 2–4%);
- occurrence in headings <h1>, <h2>;
- occurrence in anchor text of hyperlinks;
- markup such as bold;
- density (the number of times);
- proximity of phrase to start of document and the gap between individual keywords;
- alternative image text (explained below);
- document meta-data (explained below).

### Alternative image text

Graphical images can have hidden text associated with them that is not seen by the user (unless graphical images are turned off or the mouse is rolled-over the image) but will be seen and indexed by the search engine. For example, text about a company name and products can be assigned to a company logo using the 'ALT' tag or attribute of the image tag as follows:

&lt;img name="Logo" src="logo.gif" alt="Car insurance"&gt;

Due to search engine spamming this factor is assigned limited relevance, although it is still worthwhile for images that link to another page within the site. However, it is best practice to use this approach for significant images since it is also required by accessibility law and screen-readers used by the blind and visually impaired read-out the ALT tags.

### Document meta-data

'Meta' refers to information 'about' the page which characterises it. The three most important types of meta-data are the document <title> tag, the document 'descriptions' meta tag and the document 'keywords' meta tag. These need to be unique for each page on a site(s) otherwise the search engine may assess the content as duplicate and some pages may be down-weighted in importance. Let's look at it in a little more detail:

1 *The document title.* The <title> tag is arguably the most important type of meta-data since each search engine places significant weighting on the keyphrases contained within it AND it is the call-to-action hyperlink on the search engine results page (Figure 9.2). If it contains powerful, relevant copy you will get more clicks and the search engine will assess relevance relative to other pages which are getting fewer clicks.

2 *The 'description' meta tag.* A meta tag is an attribute of the page within the HTML <head> section which can be set by the content owner. The 'description' meta tag denotes the information which will typically be displayed in the search engine results page. If it is absent or too short relevant 'snippets' will be used from within the body copy, but it is best to control messages.

   So, the page creator can modify this to make a stronger call-to-action in the search engine listings as in this case:

   *&lt;meta name="description" content="Direct Line offers you great value car insurance by cutting out the middleman and passing the savings directly on to you. To find out if you could save, why not get a car insurance quote? Breakdown Cover Insurance also available."&gt;*

To see how relevant and unique your <title> and meta descriptions are, use the Google 'site': syntax with a keyphrase – this will return all the pages on your site about a particular topic. For example,

&lt;seo site:davechaffey.com&gt;

To view meta tags for a site, select View, Source or Page Source in your browser.

3 *The 'keywords' meta tag.* The meta keywords meta tag is used to summarise the content of a document based on keywords. Some unscrupulous SEOs can still be heard to say to potential clients ('we will optimise your meta tags'). But this is not significant today since

the keywords meta tag is relatively unimportant as a ranking factor (Google has never used them), although these keywords may be important to internal search engines. For example:

*<meta name="keywords" content="Car insurance, Home insurance, Travel insurance, Direct line, Breakdown cover, Mortgages personal loans, Pet insurance, Annual holiday insurance, Car loans, uk mortgages, Life insurance, Critical illness cover">*

### 5 External linking

Boosting externals links is vital to SEO in competitive markets – on-page optimisation is insufficient, although it is less easy to control and often neglected. The founders of Google realised that the number of links into a page and their quality was a great way of determining the relevance of a page to searchers, especially when combined with the keyphrases on that page (Brin and Page, 1998). Although the Google algorithm has been upgraded and refined continuously since then, the number and quality of external links is still recognised as the most important ranking factor and this is similar for other search engines.

Generally, the more links a page has from good quality sites, the better its ranking will be. **PageRank** helps Google deliver relevant results since it counts each link from another site as a vote. However, not all votes are equal – Google gives greater weight to links from pages which themselves have a high PageRank and where the link anchor text or adjacent text contains text relevant to the keyphrase. Google's PageRank algorithm is what initially made it successful, but it was published by the founders and now a similar technique is used by all the main search engines. It has been refined to identify sites that are 'authority sites' for a particular type of search. For keyphrases where there is a lot of competition, such as 'car insurance', the quantity and quality of inbound links may even be more important than keyphrase density in determining ranking.

**PageRank**
A scale between 0 to 10 used by Google to assess the importance of websites according to the number of inbound links or backlinks.

While natural links will be generated if content is useful, a proactive approach to link-building is required in competitive markets. Chaffey and Smith (2008) recommend these steps to help boost your external links.

1 *Identify and create popular content and services.* By creating more valuable content and then showcasing them within your navigation, or grouping it within a few pages such as a 'Useful Resources' or a more extensive 'Resource Centre', you can encourage more people to link to your content naturally, or approach them and suggest they link or bookmark not only to the home page, but directly to the useful tools that have been created.
2 *Identify potential partner sites.* There are several options to find partner sites. It is helpful to try to identify the types of sites that you may be able to link with, for example:
   - directories of links (often less valuable)
   - traditional media sites
   - niche online-only media sites
   - trade associations
   - manufacturers, suppliers and other business partners
   - press release distribution sites
   - bloggers including customers and partners
   - social networks.

   Directory type sites can be searched for by searching on different keyphrases such as <keyphrase> + directory or 'Add URL'. Alternatively, you can use the Yahoo Site Explorer (https://siteexplorer.search.yahoo.com) or paid tools such as Advanced Link Manager to find links from competitors.
3 *Contact partner sites.* A typical sequence is:
   - Step 1 – write e-mail encouraging link (or phone call to discuss from someone inside the company will often work best);
   - Step 2 – follow-up link;
   - Step 3 – setup links.

Today, Google assesses not just the number of links into a page, but also uses the concepts of quality based on PageRank and hubs and authorities to assess the quality or relevance of a page about a particular topic. Google also won't follow links which it deems to be unnatural, either because it identifies them as SPAM or they have the rel="nofollow" attribute such as ads purchased links or comments in forum (because of comment spam). This approach was originally described by Google engineers Bharat and Mihaila (1999). Essentially, a hub page (actually referred to as 'Expert page' in the paper) is a page which contains many quality outbound links about a particular topic. An authority page, referred to as a 'target' in the paper, contains many inbound links about a topic. Expert pages (hubs) are given more weighting to identify authority pages. The context or theme of the linking page is also very important, with the search engines needing to determine hubs and authorities based on an assessment of the context of the link for the page based on the phrases it contains.

### 6 Internal link structures

Many of the principles of external link building can also be applied to links within sites. The most important principle is to include keyphrases used by searchers within the anchor text of a hyperlink to point to relevant content. It's also important to consider how to increase the number of internal links to pages which you want to rank well. A meshed structure with lots of interlinks can work better than a simple hierarchy.

PageRank varies for pages across a site. The home page is typically highest, with each page deeper within the site having a lower PageRank. There are several implications of this. First, it is helpful to include the most important keyphrases you want to target on the homepage or at the second level in the site hierarchy. Second pages that feature in the main or secondary navigation (text link menus referencing the keyphrase in the anchor text are best) are more likely to rank highly than pages deeper in the site that don't have many internal backlinks because they are not in the menu. Third, you need to review whether there are pages deeper within the site which feature products or services that are important, and which you need to rank for. If so, you need to find a method of increasing the number of backlinks (internal or external), perhaps by including a link to them in the footer or sidebars of the site which are separate from the main navigation. Google webmaster tools has reports on internal and external links which are excellent diagnostic tools.

To summarise the complexities of SEO, we present a compilation of the most important ranking factors based on a panel of experts defined by SEOMoz (2007) Google Search Engine Ranking Factors v2, published at www.seomoz.org/article/search-ranking-factors, 2 April 2007.

### On-page optimisation ranking factor importance

- Title attribute of document = 4.9/5
- Meta name description = 2/5
- Meta name keywords = 1/5
- Keyword frequency and density = 3.7/5
- Keyword in headings – h1 = 3.1, h2 = 2.8
- Keyword in document name = 2.8

### Off-page optimisation ranking factor importance

- More backlinks (higher PageRank)= 4/5
- Page assessed as a hub (based on pattern of outbound links) = 3.5/5
- Page assessed as an authority (based on pattern of backlinks) = 3.5/5
- Link anchor text contains keyword = 4.4/5
- Link velocity (rate at which changes) = 3.5/5

## Paid search marketing

Although SEO has proved a popular form of digital marketing, paid search marketing is still of great relevance since it gives much more control on the appearance in the listings subject to the amount bid and the relevance of the ad.

Each of the main search engines has its own paid advertising programme:

- Google Adwords (http://adwords.google.com)
- Yahoo! Search Marketing (http://searchmarketing.yahoo.com, formerly Overture)
- Microsoft adCenter (http://adcenter.microsoft.com)
- MIVA Pay Per Click, Pay Per Call and Pay Per Text (www.miva.com)

### What is paid search marketing?

We explained the principles of paid search marketing or sponsored links in the introduction to the section on search engine marketing (page 506). Although we said that the main model for paying for sponsored listings in the search engines is pay-per-click marketing, we have called this section paid search marketing since there are, increasingly, other options for payment on what is known as the content network.

### Paid search content network

**Content network**

Sponsored links are displayed by the search engine on third-party sites such as online publishers, aggregators or social networks. Ads can be paid for on a CPC, CPM or a CPA basis. There are also options for graphical or video ads as well as text-based ads.

**Contextual ad**

Ad relevant to page content on third-party sites brokered by search ad networks.

**Trusted feed**

An automated method of putting content into a search engine index or an aggregator database.

Paid listings are also available through the 'content network' of the search engines such as Google Adsense and Yahoo! Content Match. These contextual ads are automatically displayed according to the page content (see www.davechaffey.com for examples). They can be paid for on a CPC, CPM or CPA (pay-per-action) basis and include not only text ads but also options for graphical display ads or video ads. Google generates around a third of its revenue from the content network, so there is a significant amount of expenditure on the network.

### Trusted feeds

Trusted feeds are not significant to search advertising for most organisations, so we will only cover them briefly. In trusted feeds, the ad or search listings content is automatically uploaded to a search engine from a catalogue or document database in a fixed format which often uses the XML data exchange standard (see www.w3.org/XML). This technique is mainly used by retailers that have large product catalogues for which prices and product descriptions may vary, and so potentially become out-of-date in the SERPs. A related technique is paid-for inclusion (PFI). Here, PPC ads are placed within the search listings of some search engines interspersed with the organic results. In paid inclusion, the advertiser specifies pages with specific URLs for incorporation into the search engine organic listings. There is typically a fixed set-up fee and then also a PPC arrangement when the ad is clicked on. A crucial difference with other PPC types is that the position of the result in the search engine listings is not paid according to price bid, but through the normal algorithm rules of that search engine to produce the organic listings. The service most commonly used for PFI is Yahoo! Sitematch. Note that Google does not offer trusted feed in its main search results at the time of writing but it does offer a free XML feed to its main Google Product Search (formerly Froogle) comparison engine.

### What controls position in paid search?

In early pay-per-click programs, the relative ranking of sponsored listings was typically based on the highest bidded cost-per-click for each keyword phrase. So it was a pure auction arrangement with the cost-per-click dependent on the balance of the extent of competition in the marketplace against the revenue or profit that can be generated dependent on conversion rates to sale and retention. The variation in bid amounts for clients of one search bid management tool are shown in Table 9.2.

| Table 9.2 | Variation in cost-per-click in different categories for US paid search campaigns, January 2008 |
|---|---|

| Category | CPC ($) |
|---|---|
| All finance | 2.70 |
| Credit | 2.95 |
| Mortgage | 2.61 |
| Auto finance | 1.68 |
| Travel | 0.65 |
| Automotive | 0.57 |
| Retail | 0.36 |
| Dating | 0.40 |

*Source*: Efficient Frontier

**Quality score**
An assessment in paid search by Google AdWords (and now other search engines) of an individual ad triggered by a keyword which, in combination with the bid amount, determines the ranking of the ad relative to competitors. The primary factor is the click-through rate for each ad, but quality score also considers the match between the keyword and the occurrence of the keyword in the text, historical click-through rates, the engagement of the searcher when they click-through to the site and the speed at which the page loads.

Contrary to what many web users may believe, today it is not necessarily the company which is prepared to pay the most per click who will get top spot. The search engines also take the relative click-through rates of the ads dependent on their position (lower positions naturally have lower click-through rates) into account when ranking the sponsored links, so ads which do not appear relevant, because fewer people are clicking on them, will drop down or may even disappear off the listing. The analysis of CTR to determine position is part of the **quality score**, a concept originally developed by Google but now integrated as part of the Microsoft Live and Yahoo! search networks.

### The quality score

Understanding the quality score is the key to successful paid search marketing. You should consider its implications when you structure the account and write copy. Google developed the quality score because they understood that delivering *relevance* through the sponsored links was essential to their user's experience, and their profits. In their AdWords help system, they explain:

*The AdWords system works best for everybody; advertisers, users, publishers and Google too when the ads we display match our users' needs as closely as possible. We call this idea 'relevance'.*

*We measure relevance in a simple way: Typically, the higher an ad's quality score, the more relevant it is for the keywords to which it is tied. When your ads are highly relevant, they tend to earn more clicks, move higher in Ad Rank and bring you the most success.*

A summary formula for the Google quality score is:

*Quality score = (keyword's click-through rate, ad text relevance, keyword relevance, landing page relevance and other methods of assessing relevance)*

So, higher click-through rates achieved through better targeted creative copy are rewarded as is relevance of the landing page (Google now sends out AdBots-Google to check them out). More relevant ads are also rewarded through ad text relevance, which is an assessment of the match of headline and description to the search term. Finally, the keyword relevance is the match of the triggering keyword to the search term entered.

If you have ever wondered why the number of paid ads above the natural listings varies from none to three, then it's down to the quality score – you can only get the coveted positions for keywords which have a sufficiently high quality score – you can't 'buy your way to the top' as many think.

## Advantages and disadvantages of paid search marketing

Paid search listings, or sponsored links, are very important to achieve visibility in all search engines when an organisation is in a competitive market. If, for example, a company is promoting online insurance, gambling or retail products, there will be many companies competing using the search engine optimisation techniques described in the previous section. Sometimes, the companies that are appearing at the top of the listing will be small companies or affiliates. Such companies are less constrained by branding guidelines and may be able to use less ethical search engine marketing techniques which are close to search engine spamming. Furthermore, smaller organisations can be more nimble, they can respond faster to changes in search engine ranking algorithms, sometimes referred to as the 'Google dance', by changing the look and feel or structure of their site.

As a result, many companies with an established paid search programme may generate more visits from paid search than SEO, although this wouldn't be true for companies that are class leaders in SEO.

### Advantages of paid search marketing

The main benefit of paid search marketing are:

- *The advertiser is not paying for the ad to be displayed.* As we explained at the start of Chapter 8, wastage is much lower with paid search compared to traditional advertising. Cost is only incurred when an ad is clicked on and a visitor is directed to the advertiser's website. Hence it's a cost-per-click (CPC) model! However, there are increasingly options for paid search marketing using other techniques – Google also offers CPM (site targeting) and CPA (pay-per-action) options on its content network where contextual ads are displayed on third-party sites relevant to the content on a page.
- *PPC advertising is highly targeted.* The relevant ad with a link to a destination web page is only displayed when the user of a search engine types in a specific phrase (or the ad appears on the content network, triggered by relevant content on a publisher's page), so there is limited wastage compared to other media. Users responding to a particular keyphrase or reading related content have high intent or interest and so tend to be good-quality leads.
- *Good accountability.* With the right tracking system, the ROI for individual keywords can be calculated.
- *Predictable.* Traffic, rankings and results are generally stable and predictable in comparison with SEO.
- *Technically simpler than SEO.* Position is based on combination of bid amount and quality score. Whereas SEO requires long-term, technically complex work on page optimisation, site re-stucturing and link building.
- *Speed.* PPC listings get posted quickly, usually in a few days (following editor review). SEO results can take weeks or months to be achieved. Moreover, when a website is revised for SEO, rankings will initially drop while the site is re-indexed by the search engines.
- *Branding.* Tests have shown that there is a branding effect with PPC, even if users do not click on the ad. This can be useful for the launch of products or major campaigns.

### Disadvantages of paid search marketing

However, there disadvantages to be managed:

- *Competitive and expensive.* Since pay-per-click has become popular, some companies may get involved in bidding wars that drive bids up to an unacceptable level. Some phrases such as 'life insurance' can exceed £10 per click.
- *Inappropriate.* For companies with a lower budget or a narrower range of products on which to generate lifetime value, it might not be cost effective to compete.

- *Requires specialist knowledge.* PPC requires a knowledge of configuration, bidding options and of the reporting facilities of different ad networks. Internal staff can be trained, but they will need to keep up-to-date with changes to the paid search services.
- *Time consuming.* To manage a PPC account can require daily or even hourly checks on the bidding in order to stay competitive. This can amount to a lot of time. The tools and best practice varies frequently, so keeping up-to-date is difficult.
- *Irrelevant.* Sponsored listings are only part of the search engine marketing mix. Many search users do not click on these because they don't trust advertisers, although these are mainly people involved in marketing!

## Best practice in planning and managing paid search marketing

With PPC, as for any other media, media buyers carefully evaluate the advertising costs in relation to the initial purchase value or lifetime value they feel they will achieve from the average customer. As well as considering the cost-per-click (CPC), you need to think about the conversion rate when the visitor arrives at your site. Clearly, an ad could be effective in generating click-throughs or traffic, but not achieve the outcome required on the website such as generating a lead or online sale. This could be because there is a poor-incentive call-to-action or the profile of the visitors is simply wrong. One implication of this is that it will often be more cost effective if targeted microsites or landing pages are created specifically for certain keyphrases to convert users to making an enquiry or sale. These can be part of the site structure, so clicking on a 'car insurance' ad will take the visitor through to the car insurance page on a site rather than a home page.

Table 9.3 shows how cost-per-click differs between different keywords that on generic (e.g. 'car insurance') and specific (e.g. 'women's car insurance'). It also shows the impact of different conversion rates on the overall CPA. The table also shows the cost of PPC search in competitive categories and why companies will strive to maximise their quality score to help reduce costs.

The cost per customer acquisition (CPA) can be calculated as follows:

$$Cost\ per\ acquisition = \frac{100}{conversion\ rate\ \%} \times cost\text{-}per\text{-}click$$

Given the range in costs, two types of strategy can be pursued in PPC search engine advertising. If budget permits, a premium strategy can be followed to compete with the major competitors who are bidding the highest amounts on popular keywords. Such a strategy is based on being able to achieve an acceptable conversion rate once the customers are driven through to the website. A lower-cost strategy involves bidding on lower-cost, less popular phrases. These will generate less traffic, so it will be necessary to devise a lot of these phrases to match the traffic from premium keywords.

| Table 9.3 | Estimates of cost-per-click for achieving top position within Google Adwords for keywords in Google UK, 2008 | | | | |
|---|---|---|---|---|---|
| **Keywords** | **Clicks/day** | **Avg. CPC** | **Cost/day** | **CPA @ 25% conversion** | **CPA @ 10% conversion** |
| 'car insurance' | 1323 | €15.6 | €20,640 | €62 | €156 |
| 'cheap car insurance' | 199 | €14.6 | €2905 | €58 | €146 |
| 'woman car insurance' | 4 | €11.6 | €46 | €46 | €116 |

*Source*: Based on Google Adwords™ advertising programme Traffic Estimator

## Optimising pay-per-click

Each PPC keyphrase ideally needs to be managed individually in order to make sure that the bid (amount per click) remains competitive in order to show up in the top of the results. Experienced PPC marketers broaden the range of keyphrases to include lower-volume phrases. Since each advertiser will typically manage thousands of keywords to generate click-throughs, manual bidding soon becomes impractical.

Some search engines include their own bid management tools, but if an organisation is using different pay-per-click schemes, it makes sense to use a single tool to manage them all. It also makes comparison of performance easier too. Bid management software such as Atlas One Point (www.atlasonepoint.com) and BidBuddy (www.bidbuddy.co.uk) can be used across a range of PPC services to manage keyphrases across multiple PPC ad networks and optimise the costs of search engine advertising. The current CPC is regularly reviewed and your bid is reduced or increased to maintain the position you want according to different strategies and ROI limits, with amounts capped such that advertisers do not pay more than the maximum they have deposited.

As more marketers have become aware of the benefits of PPC, competition has increased and this has driven up the cost-per-click (CPC) and so reduced its profitability.

Although pay-per-click marketing does not initially appear as complex as search engine optimisation, in reality, there are many issues to consider. For example, the EConsultancy (2008b) guide to pay-per-click marketing identifies these paid search strategy issues which paid search marketers and their agencies must address.

1 **Targeting**
   - *Search ad network strategy.* Which of the search networks mentioned above do you use? Which are used in different countries?
   - *Content network strategy.* How do you treat the content network? Do you disable it? Create separate campaigns? Target specific sites using the Placement tool? Develop different creative? Use placement targeting in Google?
   - *Campaign structure strategy.* Campaign structure is important to ensure that searches using a specific search term trigger the relevant ad creative. Are AdGroups small enough to deliver a message relevant for the keyphrase entered?
   - *Keyword matching strategy.* How is creative targeted using the combination of broad match and negative match, phrase match and exact match?
   - *Search-term targeting strategy.* What are the strategies for targeting different types of keyphrases such as brand, generic, product-specific and different qualifiers (cheap, compare, etc.)?

2 **Budget and bid management**
   - *Budgeting strategy.* Is budget set as maximum cost-per-click (CPC) at the appropriate level to deliver satisfactory return on investment? Is daily budget sufficient that ads are served at full delivery (always present)?
   - *Listing position strategy.* Which positions are targeted for different keywords?
   - *Bidding strategies.*
   - *Dayparting strategy.* Are ads delivered continuously through the day and week or are different certain days and times targeted (e.g. office hours, evening after Ad breaks)?
   - *Bid management tool strategy.* Is a tool used to automate bidding? Which?

3 **Creative testing and campaign optimisation**
   - *Ad creative and copy strategy.* How are the 95 characters forming ad headlines, description and creative used to encourage click-through (and reduce click-through from unqualified visitors if necessary)? Is alternative copy tested? How are ads tested?
   - *Destination or landing page strategy.* How are landing pages improved?
   - *Campaign review and optimisation strategy.* What is the workflow for reviewing and improving success? Which reports are used? How often are they reviewed? By who? Which tests are used? What are the follow-ups?
   - *Specialist and innovative paid search techniques.* These include local, international, pay-per-call, mobile search.

4 **Communications integration.**
- *SEO integration strategy.* How is SEO integrated with paid search to maximise ROI?
- *Affiliate integration strategy.* How is affiliate marketing integrated with paid search to maximise ROI?
- *Marketing campaign integration strategy.* How is budget and creative changed during offline campaigns?

### Beware of the fake clicks!

Whenever the principle of PPC marketing is described to marketers, very soon a light bulb switches on and they ask, 'So we can click on competitors and bankrupt them?' Well, actually, no. The PPC ad networks detect multiple clicks from the same computer (IP address) and say they filter them out. However, there are techniques to mimic multiple clicks from different locations, such as software tools and even services where you can pay a team of people across the world to click on these links. It is estimated that in competitive markets 1 in 5 of the clicks may be fake. While this can be factored into the conversion rates you will achieve, ultimately this could destroy PPC advertising so the search engines work hard to eliminate it.

## Online public relations

### What is online public relations (E-PR)?

**Public relations**

The management of the awareness, understanding and reputation of an organisation or brand, primarily achieved through influencing exposure in the media.

The web has become a very important element of **public relations (PR)**. Mike Grehan, a UK search engine marketing specialist, explains (Grehan, 2004):

> *Both online and off, the process is much the same when using PR to increase awareness, differentiate yourself from the crowd and improve perception. Many offline PR companies now employ staff with specialist online skills. The web itself offers a plethora of news sites and services. And, of course, there are thousands and thousands of newsletters and zines covering just about every topic under the sun. Never before has there been a better opportunity to get your message to the broadest geographic and multi-demographic audience. But you need to understand the pitfalls on both sides to be able to avoid.*

Online PR activity is closely associated with improving results from many of the other communications techniques described in this chapter, in particular SEO (link-building), partnership marketing and viral marketing/word-of-mouth marketing. Furthermore, online PR has witnessed much innovation of Web 2.0-based approaches such as blogs, feeds, social networks and widgets which we will explore in this section.

But let's start with an understanding of traditional public relations – itself somewhat intangible. As you will know, 'PR' and 'public relations' are often used interchangeably. Unfortunately, PR is also an abbreviation for 'press release' or 'press relations'. Of course, the scope of PR is much wider than press releases. The UK Institute of PR (IPR, 2003) defines PR as:

> *the management of reputation – the planned and sustained effort to establish and maintain goodwill and mutual understanding between an organisation and its publics.*

The 'publics' referred to include the range of organisations a company interacts with and is dependent on. These include investors, customers, employees, suppliers, government organisations and non-governmental organisations such as charities.

The Public Relationships Consultants Association (PRCA, 2005) defines PR as:

> *the managed process of communication between one group and another ... [it] is the method of defining messages and communicating them to target audiences in order to influence a desired response.*

You can see that the PRCA definition is more action-oriented, in fact not dissimilar to definitions for direct marketing. IPR (2003) notes that public relations involves activities such as

> *media relations, corporate communications, community relations, corporate social responsibility issues and crisis management, investor relations, public affairs and internal communications.*

From a marketing communications and traffic building perspective, the main activities we are interested in are media relations which are used to influence those in the marketplace. While websites are important tools for promoting investor relations and CSR (corporate social responsibility), this is not our main focus here. The definition of PR activities above omits activities that can directly reach the consumer such as 'buzz marketing', although the media often have a role in that.

**Online PR** or E-PR leverages the network effect of the Internet. Remember that Internet is a contraction of 'interconnected networks'! Mentions of a brand or site on other sites are powerful in shaping opinions and driving visitors to your site. The main element of online PR is maximising favourable mentions of an organisation, its brands, products or websites on third-party websites which are likely to be visited by its target audience. Furthermore, as we noted in the section on search engine optimisation, the more links there are from other sites to your site, the higher your site will be ranked in the natural or organic listings of the search engines. Minimising unfavourable mentions, for example monitoring and influencing conversations in blogs and social networks through **online reputation management**, is also an aspect of online PR.

## Differences between online PR and traditional PR

Ranchhod *et al.* (2002) identify four key differences between online PR and traditional PR.

- *The audience is connected to organisations.* Previously, there was detachment – PR people issued press releases which were distributed over the newswires, picked up by the media, and then published in their outlets. These authors say:

  > *the communication channel was uni-directional. The institutions communicated and the audiences consumed the information. Even when the communication was considered a two-way process, the institutions had the resources to send information to audiences through a very wide pipeline, while the audiences had only a minuscule pipeline for communicating back to the institutions.*

- *The members of the audience are connected to each other.* Through publishing their own websites or e-newsletters or contributing to reviews or discussions on others, information can be rapidly distributed from person to person and group to group. The authors say:

  > *Today, a company's activity can be discussed and debated over the Internet, with or without the knowledge of that organisation. In the new environment everybody is a communicator, and the institution is just part of the network.*

- *The audience has access to other information.* Often in the past, the communicator was able to make a statement that it would be difficult for the average audience member to challenge – the Internet facilitates rapid comparison of statements. The authors say:

  > *It takes a matter of minutes to access multiple sources of information over the Internet. Any statement made can be dissected, analysed, discussed and challenged within hours by interested individuals. In the connected world, information does not exist in a vacuum.*

- *Audiences pull information.* This point is similar to the last one. Previously there were limited channels in terms of television and press. Today there are many sources and channels of information – this makes it more difficult for the message to be seen. The authors say:

  > *Until recently, television offered only a few channels. People communicated with one another by post and by phone. In these conditions, it was easy for a public relations practitioner to make a message stand out.*

---

**Online public relations (E-PR)**
Maximising favourable mentions of your company, brands, products or websites on third-party websites which are likely to be visited by your target audience. Online PR can extend reach and awareness of a brand within an audience and will also generate backlinks vital to SEO. It can also be used to support viral or word-of-mouth marketing activities in other media.

**Online reputation management**
Controlling the reputation of an organisation through monitoring and controlling messages placed about the organisation.

For the marketer or PR professional, managing PR, the main differences are:

- *Less easy to control.* There are many more places a brand can be discussed online, such as in blogs and forums, compared to traditional media where there are a smaller number of media outlets with news filtered through journalists and other editorial staff.
- *More options to create own stories.* Since a company will have its own site, press centre, feeds and blogs, it is possible to bypass other media owners to some extent.
- *Need for faster response.* It is often said that 'bad news travels fast'. This has been facilitated online and a 'blogstorm' can soon arise where many bloggers are critical of a brand's action. Rapid response teams are needed.
- *Easier to monitor.* Since Google and online reputation management tools index many pages, it is arguably easier to identify when a brand is discussed online.

## Advantages and disadvantages of online public relations

### Advantages of online public relations

The advantages of the proactive online public relations techniques which seek to build a buzz around a campaign or to gain favourable mentions and links on third-party sites are:

- *Reach.* E-PR can be a relatively low-cost method of directly reaching a niche audience or a mass audience if the brand is amenable to stories that are of interest to publishers. This is often the case for new online brands and startups such as Zopa (www.zopa.com). If buzz around an online campaign orchestrated through online PR is successful then additional reach and impact may also be generated by traditional media such as TV, print and radio. Audiences may also be reached indirectly via journalists who read blogs or subscribe to feeds of news stories as described shortly to find out the latest breaking stories.
- *Cost.* The costs for online PR are the agency or internal staff fees for developing the online PR plan, concepts and content. Since there are no media placement costs, this can be cost effective.
- *Credibility.* Independent comments that are made by a person independent from a company are considered more authentic and can so help raise trust about an online provider such as a retailer. A survey by Brand New World (2004a) ranked the following information sources in order of importance when researching or considering a product or service:
  - 71%: search engines
  - 67%: personal recommendations
  - 57%: websites of well-known retailers
  - 56%: price-comparison websites
  - 50%: reviews/opinions on the internet written by experts
  - 47%: customer opinions/reviews on websites
  - 46%: product information in shops
  - 38%: content provided by your internet service provider
  - 34%: television
  - 34%: newspaper/magazines
  - 24%: salespeople in shops.

  You can see that personal recommendations are particularly important and seem to be trusted more than content sites giving reviews and opinions (although these are still given credence by many web users).
- *Search engine optimisation.* E-PR can help generate backlinks to a site which are favourable for SEO, often from large sites such as online newspapers or magazines which have good link equity.
- *Brand-enhancement and protection.* Favourable stories can enhance the reputation of a brand among its target audience. But since unfavourable media mentions may damage a brand, monitoring and response to these is a necessity for most brands.

### Disadvantages of online public relations

The main disadvantage of E-PR is that it is not a controlled discipline like online advertising techniques such as pay-per-click marketing or display advertising where the returns generated will be known for a given expenditure. In other words, it could be considered a high-risk investment.

Many marketers are also wary of creating blogs or forums on their sites which may solicit negative comments. However, there are counter-arguments to this, namely that it is best to control and be involved with a discussion about a brand on the site rather than when it is less controlled on third-party sites. For example, brands such as Dell (www.ideastorm.com) and Honda enable web users to make comments about their brands so this shows they are listening to customer comments and gain valuable sentiment which can feed into new product development ideas.

## Best practice in planning and managing online public relations

In this section we will review the different types of online PR activities and techniques to improve results from these activities. The main activities which can be considered to be specifically involved with online PR include:

- Communicating with media (journalists) online.
- Link building.
- Web 2.0 content including blogs, podcasting, RSS feeds and widgets.
- Managing how your brand is presented on third-party sites.
- Creating a buzz – online viral marketing.

### Communicating with media (journalists) online

Communicating with media (journalists) online uses the Internet as a new conduit to disseminate press releases through e-mail and on-site. Options to consider for a company include: setting up a press-release area on the website; creating e-mail alerts about news that journalists and other third parties can sign up to; submitting your news stories or releases to online news feeds. Examples include of feeds include PR Newswire: (www.prnewswire.com), Internetwire (www.internetwire.com/iwire/home), PressBox (www.pressbox.co.uk); PRWeb (www.prweb.com), Business Wire (www.businesswire.com). Press releases can be written for search engine optimisation (SEO). Figure 9.5 gives an example of one service that has been set up to assist with managing PR online.

An increasing number of journalists rely on blogs and feeds for finding sources for stories. A Euro RSCG Magnet (2005) study showed that over half of journalists used blogs to inform their stories, with around 25% using them for their day-to-day work. Of course, the figure is higher in tech-sectors. Charles Arthur (www.charlesarthur.com), contributor to the Guardian Online in a posting 'Why I'm not reading PR e-mails to get news stories any more', says:

> I'm not going to read things that are obviously press releases because the possibility of it just being annoying or irrelevant is too great; I'm going to go to my aggregator instead, because I've chosen every feed there for its potential interest. I pay more attention to my RSS feeds because they're sources I've chosen, rather than the e-mails I get from PR companies.

**Link building**
A structured activity to include good quality hyperlinks to your site from relevant sites with a good page rank.

### Link building

Link building is a key activity for SEO. It can be considered to be an element of online PR since it is about getting your brand visible on third-party sites and creating backlinks related to your site.

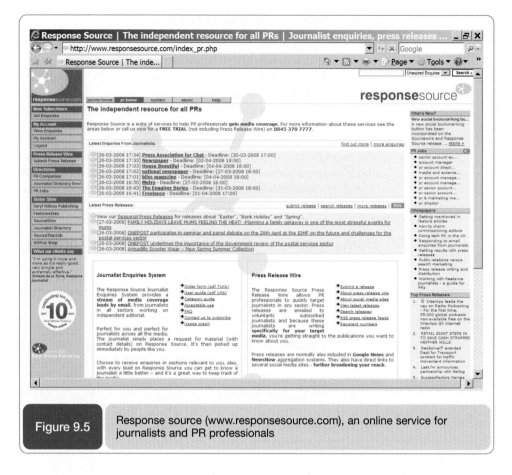

Figure 9.5    Response source (www.responsesource.com), an online service for journalists and PR professionals

**Reciprocal link**
Link agreed between yourself and another organisation.

Link building needs to be a structured effort to achieve as many quality links into a website as possible from referring websites (these commonly include **reciprocal links** which tend to be less valuable from an SEO perspective than one-way links). We have also seen that your position in the search engine results pages will be higher if you have quality links into relevant content on your site (not necessarily the home page).

McGaffin (2004) provides a great introduction to implementing a structured link building programme. The main principle of link building is as follows, McGaffin says: 'Create great content, link to great content and great content will link to you.' He describes how you should review existing links, link to competitors, set targets and then proactively enquire to suitable site owners for links.

Chaffey and Smith (2008) suggest similar steps to McGaffin. They describe several options to find partner sites which can also be helpful for students completing case study-based assignments since it will enable them to find related sites within an online marketplace analysis (Chapter 2). First, it is helpful to try to identify the different types of sites that you may be able to link with, for example:

- directories of links (often less valuable)
- traditional media sites
- niche online-only media sites
- trade associations
- manufacturers, suppliers and other business partners
- press release distribution sites
- bloggers including customers and partners
- social networks.

Second, identify sites, for example by:

- Google Searches on keyphrases related to site, to identify directory-type sites, search for these phrases on Google for different keyphrases:
  1  <keyphrase> + directory
  2  <keyphrase> + 'Add URL'
  3  <keyphrase> + 'Submit site'
  4  <keyphrase> + 'Add Listing'
  5  <keyphrase> + 'Links'
  6  <keyphrase> + 'Where to buy' / 'Stores' / 'Suppliers'
- Use Yahoo Site Explorer to find links from competitors or intermediaries. Enter a URL into https://siteexplorer.search.yahoo.com and then select Show Inlinks 'Except from this sub-domain'.
- Use Google-related syntax. Once seed sites have been identified, the Google 'related:' syntax can be used to find additional links. The Google-related syntax typically identifies sites which share links in common. So competitor sites or media sites may both be present.

---

| Box 9.2 | Reviewing the links into a site |
|---------|-------------------------------|

You can use the syntax link:site in Google to see examples of links into a page on a site as judged by Google, e.g. www.davechaffey.com. But note that this also includes internal links and is not comprehensive. A better option to display links is the Yahoo! Site explorer tool (https://siteexplorer.search.yahoo.com). For alerts of new links or new mentions on other sites, Google Alert (www.googlealert.com) or Google's own alerts (www.google.com/alerts) are useful tools.

---

### Web 2.0 atomised content including blogs, podcasting, mashups, RSS feeds, social networks and widgets

**Web 2.0 concept**
A collection of web services that facilitate interaction of web users with sites to create user-generated content and encouraging behaviours such as community or social network participation, mashups, content rating, use of widgets and tagging.

Many specialist online PR techniques such as blogs, podcasting and RSS feeds, are collectively referred to as Web 2.0 which we introduced in the first chapter. Web 2.0 represents a revolution in web usage where previously passive consumers of content become active contributors. In Web 2.0 the web itself is merely a platform for interacting with content.

### Blogs and blogging

'Blogs' give an easy method of regularly publishing web pages which are best described as online journals, diaries or news or events listings. Many blogs provide commentary or news on a particular subject; others function as more personal online diaries. A typical blog combines text, images and links to other blogs, web pages and other media related to its topic. The capability for readers to leave comments in an interactive format is an important part of many blogs. Feedback (traceback) comments from other sites are also sometimes incorporated. Frequency can be hourly, daily, weekly or less frequently, but several updates daily is typical.

**Blog**
An online diary or news source prepared by an individual or a group of people. From 'Web log'.

An example of a useful blog which can keep marketing professionals up-to-date about Internet marketing developments is www.marketingvox.com which is coupled with daily e-mail digests of stories posted. Another example, with articles summarising the latest development in digital marketing structured according to the chapters of a book, is Davechaffey.com (www.davechaffey.com). Business blogs are created by people within an organisation. They can be useful in showing the expertise of those within the organisation, but need to be carefully controlled to avoid releasing damaging information. An example of a business blog used to showcase the expertise of its analysts is the Jupiter Research Analyst Weblogs (http://weblogs.jupiterresearch.com). Technology company Sun Microsystems has several hundreds of bloggers and has a policy to control them to make positive comments.

There are many free services which enable anyone to blog (for example www.blogger.com which was purchased by Google in 2003). Blogs were traditionally accessed through online tools (e.g. www.bloglines.com, www.blogpulse.com) or software readers (www.rssreader.com) but were incorporated into mainstream software in 2005–6.

The main tools which are free or paid for online services to create blogs for individual or companies, in approximate order of popularity, are:

1 *Movable Type* (www.movabletype.org) from Six Apart is a download for management on your servers. Paid service.
2 *Typepad* (www.typepad.com) also from Six Apart who also offer this as an online service, like most of those below, which is easier for smaller business. Paid service.
3 *Blogger* (www.blogger.com) purchased by Google some time ago – the best free option?
4 *Wordpress* (www.wordpress.com) – open source alternative. Highly configurable. Used by many personal bloggers.
5 *Other open source CMS more often used for corporate sites, e.g. Plone, Drupal* and *Mambo* or corporate content management systems such as Microsoft Office SharePoint server.

The blogging format enables the content on a website to be delivered in different ways. For example, the EConsultancy blog has a lot of rich content related to Internet marketing which can be delivered in different ways:

• *By topic* (in categories or topics to browse) – example, online PR category.
• *By tag* (more detailed topics – each article will be tagged with several tags to help them appear in searches) – example, 'blogs and blogging' tag (Figure 9.6).
• *By author* (features from different columnists who can be internal or external) – example, guest column from Andrew Girdwood on SEO.
• *By time* (all posts broken down by the different methods above are in reverse date order).

This shows the importance of having a search feature on the blog for readers to find specifics – this is usually a standard feature.

These features are useful from a usability viewpoint since they help visitors locate what is most relevant to them. They are also useful for SEO, since they provide pages focused on a particular topic, e.g. online PR, which are regularly updated with fresh content. That said, there are many basic blogs which don't have any other option than breaking down by archives.

### Tagging and folksonomies

**Tagging**
Users or web page creators categorise content on a site through adding descriptive terms. A common approach in blog posts.

A defining characteristic of Web 2.0 is '**tagging**' whereby users add their own metadata to content they produce, consume and share. On Flickr (www.flickr.com) and Del.icio.us (del.icio.us) for example, any user can attach tags to digital media items (files, bookmarks, images). The aggregation of tags creates an organic, free-form, 'bottom-up' taxonomy. The information architect Thomas van derWal coined the term or 'folksonomy' derived from the idea of a 'folk-taxonomy' (Fitzgerald, 2006). **Folksonomies** are flat (that is, they have no hierarchy, and show no parent–child relationships) and, critically, are completely uncontrolled. A key implication of their lack of structure is that they do not support functions such as drill-down searching and cross-referencing. A key implication of their 'anything goes' approach is the potential for highly idiosyncratic classifications. The growth of folksonomies has generated a great deal of discussion regarding their potential to interfere with 'official' taxonomies and thus to generate 'search noise'. However, there is also much discussion of the potential for folksonomies to co-exist with and complement the 'official' taxonomies (Johnston, 2008).

**Folksonomy**
A contraction of 'folk taxonomy', a method of classifying content based on tagging that has no hierarchy, i.e. without parent–child relationships.

### Social bookmarking

**Social bookmarking**
Web users keep a shared version of favourite sites ('Favorites') online. This enables the most popular sites in a category to be identified.

Sites like Digg, Google, Reddit, StumbleUpon, De.icio.us, Netscape, Newsvine and Yahoo! allow users store, organise, search and manage bookmarks of web pages on the Internet rather than on their PC. With such **social bookmarking** systems, users save links to web pages that they want to remember and/or share on bookmark hosting sites. These bookmarks are usually public but can be saved privately, shared only with specified people or groups, shared only inside certain networks, or some other combination of public and private domains. Those with permission can usually view these bookmarks chronologically, by popularity (Figure 9.7), by category or tags, or via a search engine.

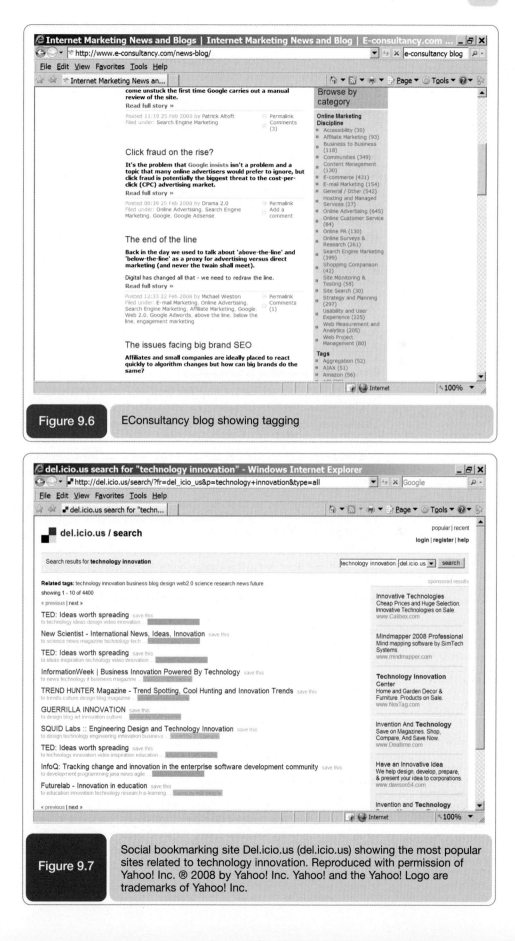

**Figure 9.6**   EConsultancy blog showing tagging

**Figure 9.7**   Social bookmarking site Del.icio.us (del.icio.us) showing the most popular sites related to technology innovation. Reproduced with permission of Yahoo! Inc. ® 2008 by Yahoo! Inc. Yahoo! and the Yahoo! Logo are trademarks of Yahoo! Inc.

Most social bookmark services encourage users to organise their bookmarks with informal tags instead of the traditional browser-based system of folders, although some services feature categories/folders or a combination of folders and tags. They also enable viewing bookmarks associated with a chosen tag, and information about the number of users who have bookmarked them. Some social bookmarking services also draw inferences from the relationship of tags to create clusters of tags or bookmarks.

**Podcast**

Individuals and organisations post online media (audio and video) which can be viewed in the appropriate players including the iPod which first sparked the growth in this technique.

Podcasts are related to blogs since they can potentially be generated by individuals or organisations to voice an opinion either as audio (typically MP3) or less commonly currently as video (video podcasts). They have been successfully used by media organisations such as the BBC which has used them for popular programmes such as film reviews or discussions and for live recordings such as the Beethoven symphonies that received over 600,000 downloads in June 2005 alone. Virgin Radio has also used podcasting, but cannot broadcast music (due to copyright restrictions), only the presenters! A big challenge for achieving visibility for podcasts is that content can only currently be recognised by tags and it is difficult to assess quality without listening to the start of a podcast. All the main search engines are working on techniques to make searching of voice and video content practical. In the meantime, some start-ups such as Odeo (www.odeo.com) and Blinkx (www.blinkx.com) are developing solutions.

In a business-to-business context, network provider Cisco (www.cisco.com) has used video podcasts for its Interaction network, which is used to sell the benefits of its services to small and medium businesses.

### Photo, video and slide sharing sites

Photo sharing sites which are popular include Flickr (a Yahoo! service), Picasa (a Google service), Photobucket , Webshots Community, Kodak Gallery, ImageShack and SnapFish. These again rely on tagging to enable users to find related shots they are interested in and can be used to create mashups using widgets to embed the object into a blog or other site (see below for explanation of these terms). Some online campaigns for high-involvement products such as cars or holidays now invite customers to submit their own pictures via services such as Flickr to build ongoing interest in a campaign.

Video sharing sites include YouTube, Google Videos, Jumpcut, Grouper, Revver, Blip.TV, VideoEgg and Daily Motion. These sites have very similar features to photo sharing sites but some add more features in the form of subscriptions to channels and offer code to embed the players on social networks or blogs. Massive global downloading of clips such as 'Star Wars Kid' and 'Lonely Girl' reasonate with Andy Warhol's predication that everyone will be famous for15 minutes. Through YouTube, Google have signed deals with content providers such as BBC, CBS, Universal Music and Sony BMG. Other provides such as Viacom, Turner Broadcasting, the National Hockey League, CNN and Warner Bros have also announced partnership with the peer-to-peer video distributer. Joost is intended as a full-screen experience with longer-form content, more like regular TV. There is a centralised portion of the network that acts as the initial distribution point. Once the video has been distributed to a wide enough audience, the P2P portion of the technology takes over to ensure quick acquisition. Unlike web-based services, such as YouTube, which encourage users to upload and share their own video creations, Joost is focused on professional content owners – small or independent film-makers – and so is not strictly Web 2.0.

Another way of accessing academic content is through slide sharing sites such as SlideShare.net.

**Really Simple Syndication feed**

Blog, news or other content is published by an XML standard and syndicated for other sites or read by users in RSS reader software services. Now typically shortened to 'feed', e.g. news feed or sports feed.

### Really Simple Syndication feeds

Really Simple Syndication (RSS) is closely related to blogging where blog, news or any type of content such as a new podcast is received by subscribers using a feed reader. It offers a method of receiving news in a feed that uses a different broadcast method from e-mail, so is not subject to the same conflicts with spam or spam filters. Many journalists now subscribe to RSS feeds from sources such as the BBC (http://news.bbc.co.uk/2/hi/help/3223484.stm) which publishes RSS feed for different types of content on its site.

An RSS document, now more commonly called a 'feed', 'web feed' or 'channel' contains either a summary of content from an associated website or the full text and images. RSS makes it possible for people to keep up with their favourite websites in an automated manner that is more convenient than checking them manually. RSS content can be read using software called an 'RSS reader', 'feed reader' or an 'aggregator'. While some RSS aggregators, such as Bloglines, are web-based, others such as RSS Reader are desktop clients, while others are integrated directly into a web browser or e-mail reader. RSS is now being used to syndicate not just notices of new blog entries, but also all kinds of data updates including stock quotes, weather data and photo availability.

## Mashups

**Mashup**

Websites, pages or widgets that combine the content or functionality of one website or data source with another to create something offering a different type of value to web users from the separate types of content or functionality.

**Mashups** (a term originally referring to the pop music practice, notably hip-hop, of producing a new song by mixing two or more existing pieces) are sites or widgets that combine the content or functionality of one website with another to create something offering a different type of value to web users from the other types of content or functionality. In practice they provide a way of sharing content between sites and stitching together sites through exchanging data in common XML-based standards such as RSS.

Examples of mashups include:

- Chicagocrime.org took police data for crime incidents and plotted them on street maps from Google Maps so that visitors could check in advance whether it was the sort of place you might get mugged, and when.
- Housingmaps.com combines Google Maps with Craigslist apartment rental and home purchase data to create an interactive housing search tool.
- Personal content aggregators such as Netvibes (www.netvibes.com), iGoogle (www.google.com/ig) or Pageflakes (www.pageflakes.com) often incorporate news stories from feeds and other data such as the latest e-mails or social network alerts. These are effectively a personal mashup.
- Backstage.bbc.co.uk is the BBC's developer network to encourage innovation and support new talent. Content feeds are available for people to build with on a non-commercial basis.

You can see that the integration of maps with different data sources is a common type of mashup. Figure 9.8 shows a typical mashup based on Google maps (here from Feedjit.com) which integrates data from different sources, in this case Google Maps data and a location lookup based on visitor IP address.

Syndicated feeds such as live news feeds can also be incorporated into third-party sites as another form of mashup. These can be filtered using tools such as Yahoo! Pipes to select content most relevant for the site on which the feed is incorporated.

## Social networks

**Social network**

A site that facilitates peer-to-peer communication within a group or between individuals through providing facilities to develop user-generated content (UGC) and to exchange messages and comments between different users.

We have described **social networks** in more depth in other chapters including Chapters 1, 2 and 6. From an online PR perspective, social networking sites can be valuable in these ways:

- They can be used to assess the 'Zeitgeist', i.e. what current trends and opinions are being discussed which can then be built into PR campaigns.
- They can assist in recommendations about products. For example, Hitwise research (Hitwise, 2007) suggests that a high proportion of visits to fashion retail stores such as Top Shop were preceded by usage of social networks, suggesting that some visits are prompted by discussions.
- They can be used to solicit feedback about product experiences and brand perception, either by explicit requests or observing what is discussed. *New Media Age* (2008) quotes Miles Sturt, head of customer experience satisfaction at Nokia, saying buzz research can have an impact on the next model the company makes, rather than the one after: 'It gives us feedback on new handsets within three or four weeks, instead of the four to six months it takes to sit people down for market research interviews. That's important because our

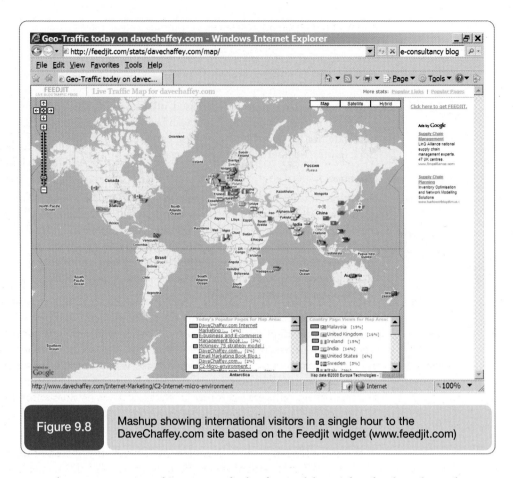

| Figure 9.8 | Mashup showing international visitors in a single hour to the DaveChaffey.com site based on the Feedjit widget (www.feedjit.com) |

product teams start working on a refresh of a model straight after launch, so they can apply feedback to the next version of a handset rather than wait a few months for conventional market research that may have to wait for the launch after that.' While Sohail Godall, consumer research executive in the European marketing intelligence team at Samsung, agrees that buzz can be plugged directly into product development, he says: 'What has really helped us is monitoring our products' buzz levels. More specifically, which features are doing well against our competitors and which aren't performing as strongly, such as phone camera quality and MP3 playback.'

But, as we note in the section on managing reputation, it is important to monitor comments and respond as appropriate.

### Widgets

**Widget**

A badge or button incorporated into a site or social network space by its owner, with content or services typically served from another site making a widget effectively a mini-software application or web service. Content can be updated in real time since the widget interacts with the server each time it loads.

**Widgets** are different forms of tools made available on a website or on a user's desktop. They are a relatively new concept associated with Web 2.0. They either provide some functionality, like a calculator, or they provide real-time information, for example on news or weather.

Site owners can encourage partners to place them on their sites and this will help educate people about your brand, possibly generating backlinks for SEO purposes and also engaging with a brand when they're not on the brand owner's site. Widgets offer partner sites the opportunity to add value to their visitors through the gadget functionality or content, or to add to their brand through association with you (co-branding).

Widgets are often placed in the left or right sidebar, or in the body of an article. They are relatively easy for site owners to implement, usually a couple of lines of Javascript, but this does depend on the content management system.

The main types of widgets are:

- *Web widgets.* Web widgets have been used for a long time as part of affiliate marketing, but they are getting more sophisticated by enabling searches on a site, real-time price updates or even streaming video.
- *Google gadgets.* Different content can be incorporated into a personalised Google 'iGoogle' homepage.
- *Desktop and operating system gadgets.* Vista, the new Microsoft operating system, makes it easier to create and enable subscription to these widgets and place them into sidebars.
- *Social media widgets.* These encourage site visitors to subscribe to RSS or to bookmark the page on their favourite social media site like Delicious, Digg and Technorati.
- *Facebook applications.* Facebook have opened up their API (application programming interface) to enable developers to create small interactive programs that users can add to their space to personalise it. Charitable site Just Giving has a branded app with several hundred users.

### Atomisation (Web 2.0)?

**Atomisation**

Atomisation in a Web 2.0 context refers to a concept where the content on a site is broken down into smaller fundamental units which can then be distributed via the web through links to other sites. Examples of atomisation include the stories and pages in individual feeds being syndicated to third-party sites and widgets.

**Atomisation** is a way of summarising a significant trend in Web 2.0 which incorporates some of the marketing techniques we have reviewed here such as posts on social networks, feeds and widgets.

Atomisation traditionally means fine particles of powder or liquid, but in a Web 2.0 context it describes how the content on a website can be broken down into smaller components and then released onto the web where they can be aggregated together with other content to provide content and services valuable for other site owners and visitors.

For site owners, options to consider for the application of atomisation include:

- Providing content RSS feeds in different categories through their content management system. For example, the BBC effectively provides tens of thousands of newsletters on their site at the level of detail or granularity to support the interest of their readers i.e. separate feeds at different levels of aggregation, e.g. sport, football, premier league football or a fan's individual team.
- Separating out content which should be provided as data feeds of new stories or statistics into widgets on other sites. For example, the 2007-launched UK retail statistics widget dashboard for iGoogle.
- Development of web services which update widgets with data from their databases. A classic example is the Just Giving widget (www.justgiving.com) where money raised by a charity donor is regularly updated.
- Creating badges which can be incorporated within blogs or social networks by their fans or advocates. The membership body CIPD does this well through their 'link to us' programme (www.cipd.co.uk/absite/bannerselect.htm) which encourages partners to add banners or text links to their site to link with the CIPD site. Similarly, Hitwise encourages retailers to link it through its Top 10 Award programme (an award for the Top 10 most popular websites across each of the 160+ Hitwise industries by market share of visits).
- Reviewing whether widgets or feeds from other companies can be included within their content to provide value for their users.

### Managing how your brand is presented on third-party sites

Many of the Web 2.0 techniques explained in the previous section such as feeds, mashups and widgets can be used to present a brand positively on third-party sites through syndication of content or interactive services.

But an important additional part of managing online PR is to set up monitoring services of mentions of brands on social networks and other third-party sites. It is also necessary to have the resources to deal with negative PR as part of online reputation management. Microsoft's PR agency reputedly has a 'rapid response' unit that can respond to online PR. Examples of alerting services include Googlealert (www.googlealert.com), Google Alerts (www.google.com/alerts) and paid services such as Market Sentinel (www.marketsentinel.com), Mark Monitor (www.markmonitor.com), Nielsen Buzzmetrics, (www.buzzmetrics.com), Reputation Intelligence (www.reputationintelligence.com) and Brand Intelligence (www.brandintelligence. com). Mini case study 9.1 'Profiting from buzz' indicates how these services work.

---

**Mini Case Study 9.1**    Profiting from buzz

The explosion in blogging, user reviews and feedback online has spawned 'buzz' specialists who report on sentiment towards a brand. For example, established US market research company Nielsen has a Nielsen Online division which combines its NetRatings audience panel and BuzzMetrics to produce 'brand maps' which show clients such as Microsoft, P&G and Toyota how they (and competitors) are viewed on relevant issues.

*New Media Age* (2007) quotes Jonathan Carson, president of BuzzMetrics at Nielsen Online, as saying:

*There are billions of conversations online that we can tap into. Brands want to know whether the volume of discussion about them is going up or down and whether the sentiment is good or bad. For example, Nielsen Online showed US broadcasters that* Lost *and* Desperate Housewives *would be hits because of the buzz they generated before they aired. It allowed them to focus on promoting those shows above others that weren't being talked about.*

Alan Ault, MD of buzz research company WaveMetrix, comments that buzz metrics requires human interpretation to gauge the significance of the feedback generated by software scanning the web for positive, neutral and negative comments. He says:

*The fact you've been talked about 2% more than last month and maybe sentiment is up 1% doesn't mean a lot. It has to be interpreted and weighted towards reliable sources, as any research would be.*

He suggests caution in paying too much attention to blogs, but instead specialist forums which are about a particular topic.

---

### Creating a buzz – online viral marketing

From a practical point of view, online viral marketing often involves generating word-of-mouth and links through to a website, so it can be considered part of online PR. However, since it takes many forms it is covered separately in a later section of this chapter.

---

## Online partnerships including affiliate marketing

We showed in Chapter 5 that partnerships are an important part of today's marketing mix. The same is true online. Resources must be devoted to managing your online partners. Many large organisations have specific staff to manage these relationships. In smaller organisations partnership management is often neglected, which is a missed opportunity. There are three key types of online partnerships which need to be managed: link building (covered in the previous section), affiliate marketing and online sponsorship. All should involve a structured approach to managing links through to a site. The main and most important form of partnership marketing for transactional e-commerce sites which we review in this section is affiliate marketing. We also review options for online sponsorship. Other forms of digital marketing communications reviewed in this chapter, which are often free in terms of the visitors generated, can also be considered as partner marketing, for example online PR, link-building and use of Web 2.0 syndication.

## Affiliate marketing

Affiliate marketing divides marketers and agencies as to its value. The discussion, as is indicated by Case study 9 (see page **505**), revolves around the value of affiliate marketing in generating incremental sales. There is no doubt that affiliates can generate more sales at a controlled cost, the question is whether these sales would have occurred anyway if a brand is well known. For example, Amazon has an affiliate programme but it could be argued that its brand is so well known and it has such a large customer base that it would receive most sales anyway. However, Amazon has run its programme for over 10 years and although it has reduced commissions, it is still running and is used to promote new product offerings such as music downloads.

### What is affiliate marketing?

**Affiliate marketing**
A commission-based arrangement where referring sites (publishers) receive a commission on sales or leads by merchants (retailers or other transactional sites). Commission is usually based on a percentage of product sale price or a fixed amount for each sale (CPA or cost per acquisition), but may also sometimes be based on a per-click basis, for example when an aggregator refers visits to merchants.

**Affiliate marketing** is the ultimate form of marketing communications since it is what is known as a 'pay-per-performance marketing' method – it's a commission-based arrangement where the merchant only pays when they make the sale or get a lead. Compare this to the wastage with traditional advertising or direct mail! It can also drive a volume of business in a range of sectors – many banks, travel companies and online retailers get more than 10% of their sales from a well-run affiliate marketing programme. It's not so suitable though for business products or lower-priced consumer products since it will not be sufficiently profitable for the affiliates, and it may be difficult to recruit sufficient affiliates.

Figure 9.9 summarises the affiliate marketing process. You can see that the when a visitor to an affiliate site (who may be an online publisher or aggregator) clicks through to a merchant site, this prospect will be tracked through a cookie placed on the visitor's PC. If the prospect later transacts within an agreed period, usually 1, 7, 30, 60 or 90 days, the affiliate will be credited with the sale through an agreed amount (percentage of sale or fixed amount).

Digital marketers need to be selective in choosing the right forms of affiliate marketing – not all may be desirable. These are the options of affiliate marketing models for you to consider.

- *Aggregators.* These are the major comparison sites like Kelkoo, Shopzilla, USwitch and Moneysupermarket. These aren't strictly affiliates since some, such as Kelkoo and Shopzilla, charge on a cost-per-click, but USwitch and Moneysupermarket are CPA based. Google Product Search (formerly Froogle) uses a similar model, but is a free option for retailers to submit a feed for which products may then be featured in the top of the Google SERPs.
- *Review sites.* For example CNet software or hardware reviews, or maybe startups like Reevoo or Review Centre. These all link to merchants based on cost-per-click or cost-per-acquisition deals.

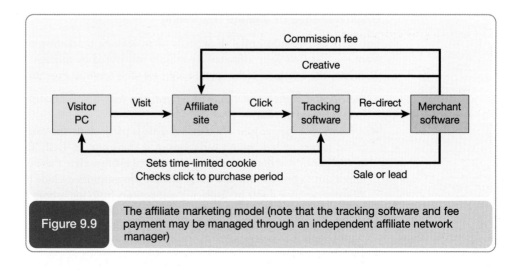

| Figure 9.9 | The affiliate marketing model (note that the tracking software and fee payment may be managed through an independent affiliate network manager) |

- *Rewards sites.* These split the commission between the reward site and their visitors. Examples are GreasyPalm or QuidCo.
- *Voucher code sites.* MyVoucherCodes or Hot UK Deals are typical. If you have some great deals to entice first-time shoppers you should generate business, although many search by well-known brand.
- *Uber-bloggers.* Martin Lewis's MoneySavingExpert.com is an incredibly popular site due to his PR efforts and great content. Although he has no ads, he is an affiliate for many sites he recommends.
- *Everyone else.* They don't tend to be high volume super-affiliates like all the above, but they're collectively important and you can work them via affiliate networks like Commission Junction or Tradedoubler. They often specialise in SEO or PPC.

## Advantages and disadvantages of affiliate marketing

### Advantages of affiliate marketing

Many of the benefits of affiliate marketing are closely related to search engine marketing since affiliates are often expert at deploying SEO or PPC to gain visibility in the search results pages. The main benefits of affiliate marketing are:

- *SERPS visibility.* Gain more visibility in the paid and natural listings of the SERPs (increase 'share of search' page).
- *Reach different audiences.* Can use different affiliates to target different audiences, product categories and related phrases.
- *Responsiveness to marketplace changes.* Affiliates may be more responsive than your in-house or agency teams in terms of algorithm changes for SEO or changes in bidding approaches for PPC. They are also great at identifying gaps in your search strategy. For example, they may be quicker at advertising on new products, or may use keyphrase variants that you haven't considered.
- *Target generic phrases in SERPs.* Enables you to reach customers through generic phrases (e.g. 'clothing') at a relatively low cost if the affiliates secure better positions in natural listings.
- *Increase reach in SERPs.* Increase the reach of your brand or campaign since affiliate ads and links featuring you will be displayed on third-party sites.
- *Generate awareness.* Can be used to generate awareness of brand or new products for which a company is not well known.
- *Diversity risk.* Use of affiliates reduces the risk caused by temporary or more fundamental problems with your SEM management or other digital marketing programmes.
- *Pay-per-performance.* The costs of acquisition can be controlled well.

### Disadvantages of affiliate marketing

But there can be substantial drawbacks to an affiliate marketing programme which arise from the fact that your affiliates are mainly motivated by money. It follows that some of them may use unethical techniques to increase their revenue. Potential disadvantages are:

- *Incremental profit or sales may be limited.* You may be cannibalising business you would have achieved anyway.
- *Affiliates may exploit your brand name.* This is particularly the case where affiliates exploit brand names by bidding on variations of it (for example 'Dell', 'Dell Computers' or 'Dell laptop') or by gaining a presence in the natural listings. Here there is already awareness. It is important to prevent this and many affiliate programmes exclude brand bidding, although affiliates can have a role in displacing competitors from the listings for brand terms.
- *May damage brand reputation.* Your ads may be displayed on sites inconsistent with your brand image, such as gambling or pornography sites. Alternatively, creative may be out-of-date which could be illegal.

- *Programme management fees.* If using an affiliate network to manage your campaigns they may take up to 30% of each agreed affiliate commission as additional 'network override'.
- *Programme management time.* Affiliate marketing is found on forming and maintaining good relationships. This cannot be done through the agency alone – marketers within a company need to speak to their top affiliates.

## Best practice in planning and managing affiliate marketing

In this section we will review how affiliate networks can be used to improve the results from affiliate marketing and the main controls on affiliate marketing, i.e. commission, cookie periods and creative. It is important that these parameters are clearly defined in the affiliate agreement to reduce the likelihood of abuse.

### Affiliate networks

**Affiliate network**

Third-party brokers also known as affiliate managers who manage recruitment of affiliates and infrastructure to manage a merchant's affiliate programme in the form of links, tracking and payment of a range of affiliates.

To manage the process of finding affiliates, updating product information, tracking clicks and making payments many companies use an **affiliate network** or affiliate manager such as the US/European networks Commission Junction (www.cj.com), Link Share (www.link-share.com) or Trade Doubler (www.tradedoubler.com, mainly European). Since the affiliate network takes a cut on each sale, many merchants also try to setup separate relationships with preferred affiliates, often known as 'super affiliates'.

Since many of the important affiliates are members of more than one affiliate network programme, it is usually found that it is not worthwhile for a merchant to join more than two affiliate networks. They also need to be careful that several affiliates are not credited for multiple sales since this quickly becomes unprofitable for the merchant.

Affiliate marketing is often thought to apply solely to e-retailers where the affiliate is paid if there is a purchase on the merchant site. In fact, payment can occur for any action which is recorded on the destination site, for example through a 'thank you' post-transaction page after filling a form. This could be a quote for insurance, trial of a piece of software or registration for download of a paper. However, the majority of affiliate activity is within consumer sectors such as travel, finance and retail rather than business-to-business.

The value of affiliate networks in managing the relationships between merchants and publishers is such that it is rare for merchants to bypass them and so avoid the network override, although Amazon is one example of a merchant with their own programme.

### Commission

In affiliate marketing, it is vital that commission is set at such a level that it incentivises affiliates to preferentially promote a merchants' products, while at the same time being profitable.

**Earnings per click**

A relative measure of the effectiveness of a site or section of a site in generating revenue for the site owner through affiliate marketing for every 100 outbound clicks generated.

The affiliates or publishers are naturally obsessive about their **earnings per click (EPC)**. This is average earnings per click and is usually measured across 100 clicks.

EPC is a crucial measure in affiliate marketing since an affiliate will compare merchants on this basis and then usually decide to promote those with the highest EPC, which will be based on the commission levels and the conversion rates to sale for different merchants.

A merchant will set commission levels according to a product's awareness level within a merchant's portfolio of products or how much they feel they need to promote them. It will also be worth increasing commissions when there is a favourable promotion on a product since affiliates will then promote it, knowing that their EPC is more likely to increase. Less well-known products or newly launched products will often have more favourable commissions. For example at the time of writing, Tesco.com used affiliates for different products with different commission as follows:

- e-diets commission from £12 on 1–9 sales to £20 on 61+ sales
- wine at 2% on lowest tier to 3% on the Gold tier of sales of >£2500
- grocery and utilities – flat fee of £5 for first-time purchase only.

### Cookie expiry period

Affiliates' EPC will also depend on the cookie expiry period agreed on the time between a visitor clicks the affiliate link and the sale is accredited to the affiliate. Common times are 7, 30 or 90 days. A longer cookie period will result in a higher EPC. Prussakov (2007) recommends that 60 to 90 days is often best to incentivise affiliates in competitive markets with a longer decision-making period. Merchants don't typically want to pay multiple affiliates for a single sale. Instead, it is usually the last referring affiliate that is credited or a mix between the first and last. So a good tracking system is required to resolve this.

### Creative and links

Managing the creative which affiliates use to promote a merchant is a challenge since creative needs to be up-to-date in line with different promotions or it may be misleading, or even illegal. So this needs to be monitored by the affiliate manager. Many merchants now provide live product feeds to affiliate networks in order to keep their promotions and product pricing up-to-date.

There are risks of brand damage through affiliates displaying creative on content which a merchant might feel was not complementary to their brand (for example, a gambling site). This needs to be specified in the affiliate agreement – sites need to be reviewed carefully before affiliates are permitted to join a specific programme and additional sites used by each affiliate should be monitored.

Another form of brand or trademark abuse is when an affiliate bids on a merchant's brand name such that they may receive credit for a sale when a prospect was already aware of the merchant, as explained in Chapter 3 in the legal section. The limits of this should also be specified within the affiliate agreements and monitored carefully.

## Online sponsorship

Online sponsorship is not straightforward. It's not just a case of mirroring existing 'real-world' sponsorship arrangements in the 'virtual world', although this is a valid option. There are many additional opportunities for sponsorship online which can be sought out, even if you don't have a big budget at your disposal.

Ryan and Whiteman (2000) define online sponsorship as:

*the linking of a brand with related content or context for the purpose of creating brand awareness and strengthening brand appeal in a form that is clearly distinguishable from a banner, button or other standardised ad unit.*

For the advertiser, online sponsorship has the benefit that their name is associated with an online brand that the site visitor is already familiar with. So, for users of a publisher site, with whom they are familiar, sponsorship builds on this existing relationship and trust.

Paid-for sponsorship of another site, or part of it, especially a portal, for an extended period is another way to develop permanent links. Co-branding is a lower-cost method of sponsorship and can exploit synergies between different companies. Note that sponsorship does not have to directly drive visitors to a brand site – it may be more effective if interaction occurs on the media owner's microsite.

A great business-to-business example of online sponsorship is offered by WebTrends which sponsors the customer information channel on ClickZ.com (www.clickz.com/experts). They combined this sponsorship with different ads each month offering e-marketers the chance to learn about different topics such as search marketing, retention and conversion marketing through detailed white papers and a 'Take 10' online video presentation by industry experts which could be downloaded by registered users. The objective of these ads was to encourage prospects to subscribe to the WebTrends WebResults e-newsletter and to assess purchase intent at sign-up enabling follow-up telemarketing by regional distributors. WebTrends reported the following results over a single year of sponsorship:

- list built to 100,000 WebResults total subscribers
- 18,000 Take 10 presentations
- 13,500 seminar attendees.

A study by Performance Research (2001) compared differences in the perception of the online audience to banner ads and sponsorships. Respondents were shown a series of web page screens; for each, half of the respondents were shown a similar version with a banner advertisement, and the remaining half were shown a nearly identical image with web sponsorship identifications (such as 'Sponsored by', 'Powered by' and 'in association with'). The results were illuminating. Of the 500 respondents, ratings for different aspects of perception were:

- trustworthy (28% for sponsorships to 15% for ads)
- credible (28% to 16%)
- in tune with their interests (32% to 17%)
- likely to enhance site experience (33% to 17%)
- more likely to consider purchasing a sponsor's product or service (41% to 23%)
- less obtrusive (66% to 34%).

### Co-branding and contra-deals

**Co-branding** of sites or e-mails are closely related to online sponsorship. These '**contra-deals**', as they are sometimes referred to, typically occur where there is an association between two brands and they are complementary but not competitive.

For example, one online publisher may offer subscribers the chance to sign-up with newsletters from a another company, a process known as 'co-registration'.

Co-branding can be a cost-effective form of online marketing, but specific resource such as 'online partnership manager' has to be put in place to set up and manage the relationships between partners. This will often be part of an affiliate manager's role.

**Co-branding**

An arrangement between two or more companies who agree to jointly display content and perform joint promotion using brand logos, e-mail marketing or banner advertisements. The aim is that the brands are strengthened if they are seen as complementary. Co-branding is often a reciprocal arrangement which can occur without payment as part of a wider agreement between partners.

**Contra-deals**

A reciprocal agreement in the form of an exchange where payment doesn't take place. Instead services or ad space to promote another company as part of co-branding occurs.

---

## Interactive display advertising

### What is display advertising?

**Display (interactive) advertising**

Display ads are paid ad placements using graphical or *rich media ad units* within a web page to achieve goals of delivering brand awareness, familiarity, favourability and purchase intent. Many ads encourage interaction through prompting the viewer to interact or rollover to play videos, complete an online form or to view more details by clicking through to a site.

**Display advertising** involves an advertiser paying for an advertising placement on third-party sites such as publishers or social networks. The process usually involves **ad serving** from a different server from that on which the page is hosted (ads can be served on destination sites in a similar way). Ad serving uses a specialist piece of software, possibly mounted on an independent server such as Doubleclick (now owned by Google). In 2008, Google launched its free Ad manager service (www.google.com/admanager) to help site owners sell, schedule, optimise revenue, serve ads and measure directly-sold and network-based inventory.

Advertising is used on a range of sites in order to drive traffic to an organisation's **destination site**, or alternatively a **microsite** or nested ad-content on the media owner's site or on the destination site. The destination page from a banner ad will usually be designed as a specifically created direct-response page to encourage further action. For example, the nappy supplier Huggies placed an advertisement on a childcare site that led the parents clicking on this link to more detailed information on Huggies contained on the site and encouraging them opt-in to a loyalty programme.

**Ad serving**
The term for displaying an advertisement on a website. Often the advertisement will be served from a web server different from the site on which it is placed.

**Destination site**
The site reached on click-through.

**Microsite**
A small-scale destination site reached on click-through which is part of the media owner's site.

**Run-of-site**
Cost per 1000 ad impressions. CPM is usually higher for run-of-site advertisements where advertisements occur on all pages of the site.

**Results-based payment**
Advertisers pay according to the number of times the ad is clicked on.

**XMOS (cross-media optimisation studies)**
Research designed to help marketers and their agencies answer the question 'What is the optimal mix of advertising vehicles across different media, in terms of frequency, reach and budget allocation, for a given campaign to achieve its marketing goals?' The mix between online and offline spend is varied to maximise campaign metrics such as reach, brand awareness and purchase intent.

Display advertising is still colloquially known as banner advertising, but practitioners such as the trade body, the Internet Advertising Bureau (www.iab.net and www.iabuk.net), media owners such as publishers, advertisers and their agencies now commonly refer to 'display advertising'. This reflects the increasing range of ad formats we will discuss below.

## Purchasing ad placements

When media is purchased, it is either purchased on a specific site such as *The Times* or *New York Times*, or it is purchased across several sites, which are known as an ad network.

Banner advertising is purchased for a specific period. It may be purchased for the ad to be served on:

- the **run-of-site** (the entire site)
- a section of site
- according to keywords entered on a search engine.

Traditionally, the most common payment is according to the number of customers who view the page as a cost-per-thousand (CPM) ad or page impressions. Typical CPM is in the range £10–£30. Other options that benefit the advertiser if they can be agreed are per-click-through or per-action such as a purchase on the destination site. Although initially media owners were able to control charging rates and largely used a per exposure model with the increase in unused ad inventory, there has been an increase in **results-based payment** methods particularly within ad networks.

## Advantages and disadvantages of display advertising

Robinson *et al.* (2007) have noted that the two primary goals of online display advertising are first, using display adverts as a form of marketing communication used to raise brand awareness; and second, as a direct response medium focused on generating a response. Cartellieri *et al.* (1997) refer to a wider range of goals for online campaigns including:

- *Delivering content.* This is the typical case where a click-through on a banner advertisement leads through to a destination site giving more detailed information on an offer. This is where a direct response is sought.
- *Enabling transaction.* If a click-through leads through to a merchant such as a travel site or an online bookstore this may lead directly to a sale. A direct response is also sought here.
- *Shaping attitudes.* An advertisement that is consistent with a company brand can help build brand awareness.
- *Soliciting response.* An advertisement may be intended to identify new leads or as a start for two-way communication. In these cases an interactive advertisement may encourage a user to type in an e-mail address or other information.
- *Encouraging retention.* The advertisement may be placed as a reminder about the company and its service and may link through to on-site sales promotions such as a prize draw.

These objectives are not mutually exclusive, and more than one can be achieved with a well-designed ad campaign.

### Advantages of online advertising

- *Direct response.* Display advertising can generate an immediate direct response via click-through to a website enabling transaction for retail products for example.
- *Enhancing brand awareness and reach.* The visual imagery of a display ad can generate awareness about a brand, product or need. This is less practical in search engine marketing where searchers are already seeking a specific brand, product or need, although there are opportunities to make searchers aware of other, unknown suppliers. We also saw at the end of Chapter 8 that **XMOS studies** showed that online was useful for reaching audiences whose consumption of traditional media has decreased.

**Media multiplier** or **halo effect**

The role of one media channel on influencing sale or uplift in brand metrics. Commonly applied to online display advertising, where exposure to display ads may increase click-through rates when the consumer is later exposed to a brand through other media, for example sponsored links or affiliate ads. It may also improve conversion rates on a destination sites through higher confidence in the brand or familiarity with the offer.

- *Media-multiplier or halo effect.* Repeated exposure to ads online, particularly in association with other media, can increase brand awareness and ultimately purchase intent. Furthermore, practitioners report a media multiplier or halo effect of buying online ads which can help increase the response rates from other online media. For example, if a web user has been exposed to banner ads, this may increase their response to paid search ads and may also increase their likelihood of converting on a site since brand awareness and trust may be higher.

  This is suggested by research reported by MAD (2007) in the travel market which involved asking respondents what their response to an online ad that appealed to them would be. Surely it would be a click? In fact the results broke down as follows:

  – search for a general term relating to the advertisement (31 per cent)
  – go straight to advertisers site (29 per cent)
  – search for the advertiser's name (26 per cent)
  – click on banner to respond (26 per cent)
  – visit a retail store (4%).

  Of course, this methodology shows us reported behaviour rather than actual behaviour, but it is still significant that more than twice as many people are being driven to a search engine by banner advertising than by clicking directly on the banner! The research concludes that paid search marketing needs to be optimised to work with banner advertising, by anticipating searches that are likely to be prompted by the banner and ensure a higher rank for search results. For example, a brand featuring a Cyprus holiday offer will generate generic search terms like 'package holiday Cyprus' rather than brand searches.

  Abraham (2008) has also shown that online ads can stimulate offline sales. For one retailer with a turnover of $15 billion, research showed that over a three-month period, sales increased (compared to a control group) by 40% online and by 50% offline among people exposed to an online search – and display – ad campaign promoting the entire company. Because its baseline sales volumes are greater in physical stores than on the Internet, this retailer derived a great deal more revenue benefit offline than the percentages suggest.

- *Achieving brand interactions.* Many modern display ads comprise two-parts – an initial visual encouraging interaction through a rollover and then another visual or application encouraging interaction with a brand. This enables advertisers to calculate an interaction rate (IR) to assess the extent to which viewers interact with a brand ad.

- *Targeting.* Media buyers can select the right site or channel within a site to reach the audience (e.g. a specialist online car magazine or review site or the motoring channel within an online newspaper or TV channel site). Audiences can also be targeted via their profile through serving personalised ads, or ad in e-mail if visitors have registered on a site.

  Behavioural re-targeting options is used in an ad network to preferentially serve an ad to someone who seems to have an interest in a topic from the content they consume. Effectively the ad follows the viewer around the site. For example, if someone visits the car section of a site, then the ad is served to them when they view other sections of the site. Re-targeting can work across an ad-network too and can even be sequential, where the messages are varied for an individual the more times they are exposed to the ad. Search re-targeting offers the option to display an ad after a visitor has searched on a particular term such as a car marque. Tracking of individuals is achieved through use of cookies.

- *Cost.* There are opportunities to buy online media at a cheaper rate compared to traditional media, although this is less true in focused, competitive markets such as financial services where there is limited premium inventory for media buyers to purchase.

  Ad networks from suppliers such as Blue Lithium or 24-7 Media give advertisers the options of advertising across a network of sites to reach a particular demographic, e.g. female 18–25, but at a lower cost than media buys on a specific site since the actual site used for the ad placement isn't known (hence these are sometimes known as '*blind network buys*'). Lower CPMs are achievable and in some cases CPC or CPA payment options are available. Site owners such as publishers use ad networks since it gives them a method of gaining fees from unused ad inventory which has not sold at premium rates.

- *Dynamic updates to ad campaigns.* In comparison with traditional media, where media placements have to be bought weeks or months in advance, online ads are more flexible since it is possible to place an advertisement more rapidly and make changes during the campaign. Experienced online advertisers build in flexibility to change targeting through time. Best practice is to start wide and then narrow to a focus – allow 20% budget for high-performing ad placements (high CTR and conversion).

  In an iMediaConnection (2003) interview with ING Direct VP of Marketing, Jurie Pieterse, the capability to revise creative is highlighted:

  > *Another lesson we learned is the importance of creative. It's critical to invest in developing various creative executions to test them for best performance and constantly introduce new challengers to the top performers. We've also learned there's no single top creative unit – different creative executions and sizes perform differently from publisher to publisher.*

- *Accountability.* As we will discuss later in the section, it is readily possible to measure reach, interaction and response to ads. However, it is more difficult to measure brand impact.

### Disadvantages of online advertising

- *Relatively low click-through rates.* When discussing online ads, many web users will state they ignore ads and find them intrusive. Published click-through rates support this, with most compilations showing response rates of around 0.1 to 0.2%, but with rich media formats such as video ads attracting higher click-through rates. This phenomenon is known among practitioners as banner blindness (see for example, Nielsen (2007). The first 468 × 68 pixel banner ad was placed on Hotwired in 1995 and the call-to-action 'Click here!' generated a clickthrough of 25%. Since then, the click-through rate (CTR) has fallen dramatically with many consumers suffering from 'banner blindness' – they ignore anything on a website that looks like an ad. Remember though, that for reasons such as awareness generation and the media multiplier effect, digital marketers should not dismiss online advertising as ineffectual based on click-through rates alone. Figure 9.10 shows a more recent compilation.
- *Relatively high costs or low efficiency.* When the low response rates are combined with relatively high costs of over £10 per thousand, this makes online ads an inefficient medium.
- *Brand reputation.* Brands can potentially be damaged in the consumers' mind if they are associated with some types of content such as gambling, pornography or racism. It is difficult to monitor precisely which content an ad is served next to when millions of impressions are bought across many sites, this is particularly the case when using ad networks.

---

**Page** and **ad impressions** and **reach**

One page impression occurs when a member of the audience views a web page. One ad impression occurs when a person views an advertisement placed on the web page. Reach defines the number of unique individuals who view an advertisement.

**CPM (cost-per-thousand)**

The cost of placing an ad viewed by 1000 people.

## Best practice in planning and managing display ad campaigns

In this section we will review how measurement, targeting and creative can be used to improve the results from display ad campaigns.

### Measurement of display effectiveness

Figure 9.11 summarises the different terms used for measuring banner ad effectiveness. Each time an advertisement is viewed is referred to as an **advertisement** or **ad impression**. 'page impressions' and 'page views' are other terms used. Since some people may view the advertisement more than one time, marketers are also interested in the **reach**, which is the number of unique individuals who view the advertisement. This will naturally be a smaller figure than that for ad impressions. Cost of ads is typically based on **CPM** or cost-per-thousand (*mille*) ad impressions as with other media. However, the popularity of CPC search advertising and CPA affiliate deals mean that these are options too.

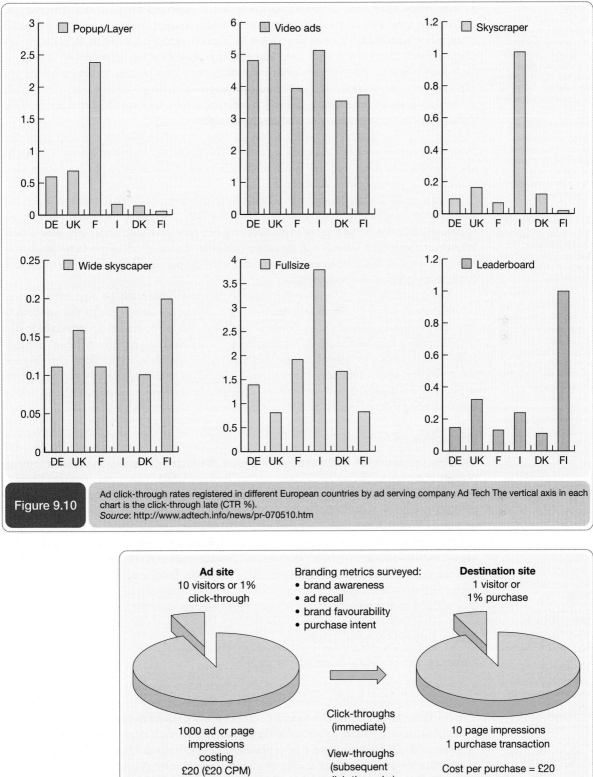

**Figure 9.10**

Ad click-through rates registered in different European countries by ad serving company Ad Tech The vertical axis in each chart is the click-through late (CTR %).
*Source*: http://www.adtech.info/news/pr-070510.htm

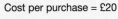

**Figure 9.11**    Basic model for interactive display advertising

**Interaction rate**
The proportion of ad viewers who interact with an online ad through rolling over it. Some will be involuntary depending on where the ad is placed on screen, so it is highly dependent on placement.

**Website auditors**
Auditors accurately measure the usage of different sites in terms of the number of ad impressions and click-through rates.

**Effective frequency**
The number of exposures or ad impressions (frequency) required for an advertisement to become effective.

**Click-through** and **click-through rate**
A click-through (ad click) occurs each time a user clicks on a banner advertisement to direct them to a web page that contains further information. The click-through rate is expressed as a percentage of total ad impressions, and refers to the proportion of users viewing an advertisement who click on it. It is calculated as the number of click-throughs divided by the number of ad impressions.

**View-through**
Indicates when a user views an ad and subsequently visits a website.

**Interstitial ads**
Ads that appear between one page and the next.

**Overlay**
Typically an animated ad that moves around the page and is superimposed on the website content.

As with other digital media, direct response to ads is measured through click-through rate. **Interaction rate (IR)** is a form of measurement that is unique to display ads. It refers to the many ads which encourage the site visitor to interact through a prompt to 'rollover' and another Flash creative will be loaded which may offer a clear brand message rendered in large font, a response form such as an insurance quote or a request to obtain a SIM or a game or poll. The engagement of the ad campaign for different placements can then be assessed through the interaction rate which will typically be ten times higher than the click-through rate if the targeting, offer and creative is right.

When payment is made according to the number of viewers of a site it is important that the number of viewers be measured accurately. To do this independent **website auditors** are required. The main auditing body in the UK is the Audit Bureau of Circulation Electronic, ABCelectronic (www.abce.org.uk).

There is much discussion about how many impressions of an advertisement an individual has to see for it to be effective. Novak and Hoffman (1997) note that for traditional media it is thought that fewer than three exposures will not give adequate recall. For new media, because of the greater intensity of viewing a computer screen, recall seems to be better with a smaller number of advertisements compared with old media. The technical term for adequate recall is '**effective frequency**'.

When a user clicks on the advertisement, he or she will normally be directed to further information, viewing of which will result in a marketing outcome. Usually the user will be directed through to part of the corporate website that will have been set up especially to deal with the response from the advertisement. When a user clicks on an advertisement immediately this is known as a '**click-through**', but adserving systems (using cookies) also measure **view-through** which indicates when a user views an ad and subsequently visits a website within a defined period, such as 30 days. This increases overall response, but it should be borne in mind that users may have visited the site in response to other stimuli.

## Interactive ad formats

As well as the classic 468 × 60 rotating GIF banner ad which is decreasing in popularity, media owners now provide a choice of larger, richer formats which web users are more likely to notice. Research has shown that message association and awareness building are much higher for flash-based ads, rich-media ads and larger-format rectangles (multipurpose units, MPUs) and skyscrapers. Other online ad terms you will hear include '**interstitials**' (intermediate adverts before another page appears) and the more common '**overlays**' (formerly more often known as '*superstitials*' or '*overts*') that appear above content and, of course, '*pop-up windows*' that are now less widely used because of their intrusion. Online advertisers face a constant battle with users who deploy pop-up blockers or less commonly ad-blocking software, but they will persist in using rich-media formats where they generate the largest response.

## Interactive ad targeting options

Online ads can be targeted through placing ads:

- *On a particular type of site (or part of site)* which has a specific visitor profile or type of content. So a car manufacturer can place ads on the home page of Handbag.com to appeal to a young female audience. A financial services provider can advertise in the money section of the site to target those interested in these products. To reach large mass-market audiences, advertisers can place an ad on a large portal home page such as MSN which has millions of visitors each day (sometimes known as a 'road-block' if they take all ad inventory).
- *To target a registered user's profile.* A business software provider could advertise on the FT to target registrants' profiles such as finance directors or IT managers.
- *At a particular time of day or week.*

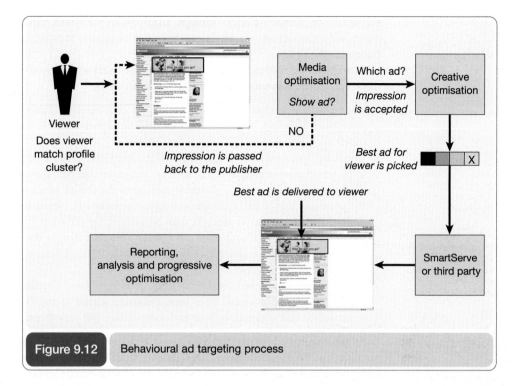

**Figure 9.12**   Behavioural ad targeting process

**Behavioural ad targeting**

Enables an advertiser to target ads at a visitor as they move elsewhere on the site or return to the site, thus increasing the frequency or number of impressions served to an individual in the target market.

- *To follow users' behaviour.* Behavioural ad targeting is all about relevance – dynamically serving relevant content, messaging or ad which matches the interests of a site visitor according to inferences about their characteristics. These inferences are made by anonymously tracking the different types of pages visited by a site user during a single visit to a site or across multiple sessions. Other aspects of the environment used by the visitor can also be determined, such as their location, browser and operating system. For example, FT.com using software from Revenue Science can identify users in eight segments: Business Education, Institutional Investor, Information Technology, Luxury and Consumer, Management, Personal Finance, Travel and Private Equity. The targeting process is shown in Figure 9.12. First the ad serving system detects whether the visitor is in the target audience (media optimisation), then creative optimisation occurs to serve the best ad for the viewer type.

## Ad creative

As with any form of advertising, certain techniques will result in a more effective advertisement. Robinson *et al.* (2007) conducted research on the factors which increased click-through response to banner ads. The main variables they (and previous studies they reference include):

- banner size
- message length
- promotional incentive
- animation
- action phrase (commonly referred to as a call-to-action)
- company brand/logo.

The relatively new video ad formats have also proved effective in increasing response rates (as indicated by Figure 9.10).

Their research indicated that the design elements which made the most effective banner ads included a larger size, longer message, absence of promotional incentives and the presence of information about casino games. Surprisingly, the inclusion of brand name was not favourable in increasing click-through, although, as we noted, this may be because the ad generates a subsequent search on the brand. Please note that this study was restricted to online gambling ads.

Anecdotal discussions by the authors with marketers who have advertised online indicate the following are also important and worth considering:

- *Appropriate incentives are needed to achieve click-through.* Banner advertisements with offers such as prizes or reductions can achieve higher click-through rates by perhaps as much as 10 per cent.
- *Creative design needs to be tested extensively.* Alternative designs for the advertisement need to be tested on representatives of a target audience. Anecdotal evidence suggests that the click-through rate can vary greatly according to the design of the advertisement, in much the same way that recall of a television advertisement will vary in line with its concept and design. Different creative designs may be needed for different sites on which advertisements are placed. Zeff and Aronson (2001) note that simply the use of the words 'click here!' or 'click now' can dramatically increase click-through rates because new users do not know how banners work!
- *Placement of advertisement and timing need to be considered carefully.* The different types of placement options available have been discussed earlier in the chapter, but it should be remembered that audience volume and composition will vary through the day and the week.

Different styles of ad creative can be viewed by visiting the Ad Gallery of an ad serving company such as Tangozebra (www.tangozebra.com) or Eyeblaster (www.eyeblaster.com), or an ad review site such as Banner Blog (www.bannerblog.com.au, Figure 9.13) which features ads from many countries.

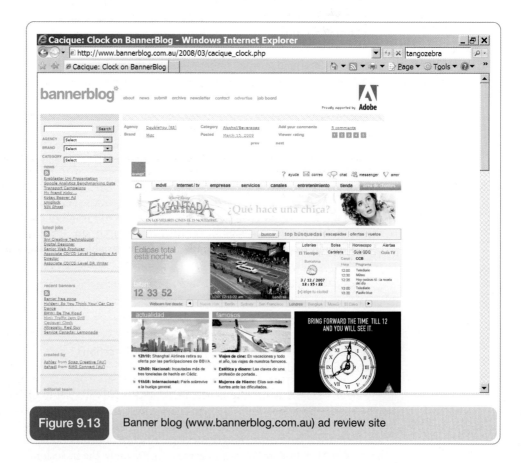

Figure 9.13    Banner blog (www.bannerblog.com.au) ad review site

## Opt-in e-mail marketing and mobile text messaging

We have grouped email marketing with text messaging since these are both 'push media' which share much in terms of their applications for prospect and customer communications. In this coverage we concentrate on e-mail marketing since mobile marketing was covered in Chapter 3.

### What is e-mail marketing?

When devising plans for e-mail marketing communications, marketers need to plan for:

**Outbound e-mail marketing**
E-mails are sent to customers and prospects from an organisation.

**Inbound e-mail marketing**
Management of e-mails from customers by an organisation.

- **Outbound e-mail marketing**, where e-mail campaigns are used as a form of direct marketing to encourage trial and purchases and as part of a CRM dialogue.
- **Inbound e-mail marketing**, where e-mails from customers, such as service enquiries, are managed (this was discussed in Chapters 3 and 5 and isn't discussed further in this chapter).

The applications of outbound e-mail marketing communications broadly break down into customer acquisition and retention activities. e-mail activities within organisation tend to focus on customer acquisition as these ratings (on a 5-point scale) on the relative merits of different applications of e-mail by Chittenden and Rettie (2003) suggest:

- customer retention (4.5)
- sales promotion (4.4)
- gathering customer data (3.0)
- lead generation (3.0)
- brand awareness (2.7)
- customer acquisition (2.1).

### Opt-in e-mail options for customer acquisition

For acquiring new visitors and customers to a site, there are three main options for e-mail marketing. From the point of view of the recipient, these are:

- *Cold e-mail campaign.* In this case, the recipient receives an opt-in e-mail from an organisation that has rented an e-mail list from a consumer e-mail list provider such as Experian (www.experian.com), Claritas (www.claritas.com) or IPT Limited (www.myoffers.co.uk) or a business e-mail list provider such as Mardev (www.mardev.com), Corpdata (www.corpdata.com) or trade publishers and event providers such as VNU. Although they have agreed to receive offers by e-mail, the e-mail is effectively cold. For example, a credit card provider could send a cold e-mail to a list member who is not currently their member. It is important to use some form of 'statement of origination', otherwise the message may be considered spam. Cold e-mails tend to have higher CPAs than other forms of online marketing, but different lists should still be evaluated.
- *Co-branded e-mail.* Here, the recipient receives an e-mail with an offer from a company they have a reasonably strong affinity with. For example, the same credit card company could partner with a mobile service provider such as Vodafone and send out the offer to their customer (who has opted in to receive e-mails from third parties). Although this can be considered a form of cold e-mail, it is warmer since there is a stronger relationship with one of the brands and the subject line and creative will refer to both brands. Co-branded e-mails tend to be more responsive than cold e-mails to rented lists since the relationship exists and fewer offers tend to be given.

- *Third-party e-newsletter.* In this visitor acquisition option, a company publicises itself in a third-party e-newsletter. This could be in the form of an ad, sponsorship or PR (editorial) which links through to a destination site. These placements may be set up as part of an interactive advertising ad buy since many e-newsletters also have permanent versions on the website. Since e-newsletter recipients tend to engage with them by scanning the headlines or reading them if they have time, e-newsletter placements can be relatively cost effective.

Viral marketing, which is discussed in the next main section, also uses e-mail as the mechanism for transferring messages.

## Opt-in e-mail options for prospect conversion and customer retention (house list)

**Opt-in**
An individual agrees to receive e-mail communications.

**House list**
A list of prospect and customer names, e-mail addresses and profile information owned by an organisation.

E-mail is most widely used as a prospect conversion and customer retention tool using an **opt-in house list** of prospects and customers that have given permission to an organisation to contact them. For example, Lastminute.com has built a house list of over 10 million prospects and customers across Europe. Successful e-mail marketers adopt a strategic approach to e-mail and develop a contact or touch strategy which plans the frequency and content of e-mail communications as explained in Chapters 4 and 6. Some options for in-house e-mail marketing include:

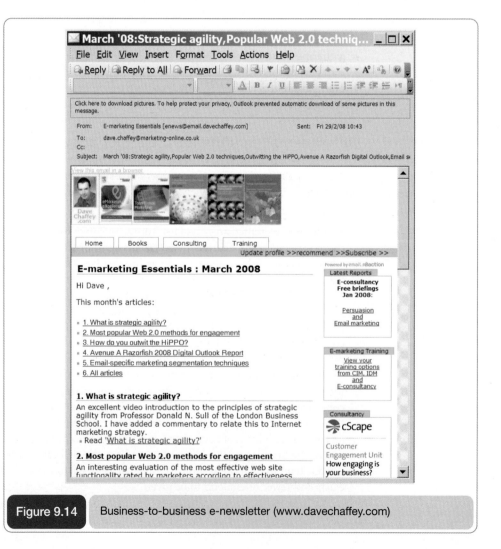

**Figure 9.14**    Business-to-business e-newsletter (www.davechaffey.com)

- *Conversion e-mail.* Someone visits a website and expresses interest in a product or service by registering and providing their e-mail address, although they do not buy. Automated follow-up e-mails can be sent out to persuade the recipient to trial the service. For example, betting company William Hill found that automated follow-up e-mails converted twice as many registrants to place their first bet compared to registrants who did not receive an e-mail.
- *Regular e-newsletter type.* Options are reviewed for different frequencies such as weekly, monthly or quarterly with different content for different audiences and segments. These are commonly used to update consumers on the latest products or promotions or business customers on developments within a market (Figure 9.14).
- *House-list campaign.* These are periodic e-mails to support different objectives such as encouraging trial of a service or newly launched product, repeat purchases or reactivation of customers who no longer use a service.
- *Event-triggered.* These tend to be less regular and are sent out perhaps every three or six months when there is news of a new product launch or an exceptional offer.
- *E-mail sequence.* Software can send out a series of e-mails with the interval between e-mails determined by the marketer.

The popularity of applying different e-mail marketing tactics is shown in Figure 9.15.

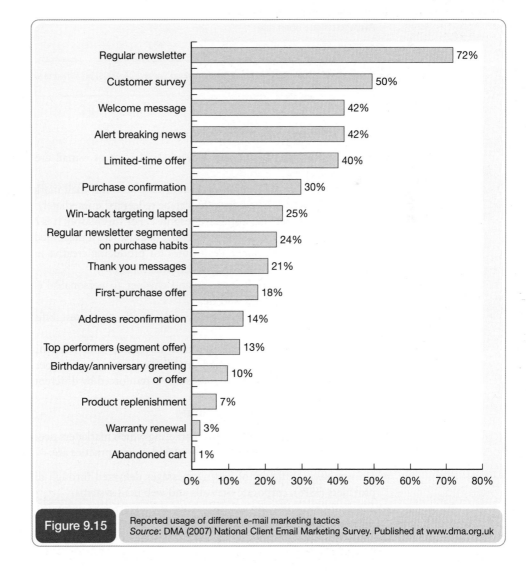

**Figure 9.15**  Reported usage of different e-mail marketing tactics
*Source:* DMA (2007) National Client Email Marketing Survey. Published at www.dma.org.uk

## Advantages and disadvantages of e-mail marketing

### Advantages of e-mail marketing

We saw in Chapter 6 that permission-based e-mail is an effective tool for building relationships with customers online. Despite the increase in spam, such that the vast majority of e-mails are spam or viruses (most estimates exceed 80%), e-mail can still drive good response levels as indicated by Table 9.4, particularly for in-house lists (retention e-mail marketing) indicated in the figure. Owing to its advantages, in many countries such as the UK (DMA, 2007) the volume of e-mail marketing has exceeded direct mail volumes. However, no one is suggesting direct mail will disappear since it will typically have a higher impact than e-mail marketing and the two work best when integrated.

| Table 9.4 | Typical response rates to e-mail marketing campaigns | |
| --- | --- | --- |
| | **Acquisition e-mail** | **Retention e-mail** |
| Average hard bounce rate | 6% | 2% |
| Average unique open rate | 22% | 29% |
| Average unique click-through rate | 7% | 11% |

*Source*: DMA (2006). National Email Benchmarking Survey, Q4, 2006, published at www.dma.org.uk

The main advantages of e-mail marketing are:

- *Relatively low cost of fulfilment.* The physical costs of e-mail are substantially less than direct mail.
- *Direct response medium encourages immediate action.* E-mail marketing encourages click-through to a website where the offer can be redeemed immediately – this increases the likelihood of an immediate, impulsive response. For this reason, it is one of the best methods of attracting existing customers to return to a site (it's a push media).
- *Faster campaign deployment.* Lead times for producing creative and the whole campaign lifecycle tends to be shorter than traditional media.
- *Ease of personalisation.* It is easier and cheaper to personalise e-mail than for physical media and also than for a website.
- *Options for testing.* It is relatively easy and cost effective to test different e-mail creative and messaging.
- *Integration.* Through combining e-mail marketing with other direct media that can be personalised, such as direct mail, mobile messaging or web personalisation, campaign response can be increased as the message is reinforced by different media.

### Disadvantages of e-mail marketing

Some of the disadvantages of e-mail marketing which marketers need to manage as they run their campaigns so that they are closely related to best practice are:

- *Deliverability.* Difficulty of getting messages delivered through different Internet service providers (ISPs), corporate firewalls and web mail systems.
- *Renderability.* Difficulty of displaying the creative as intended within the in-box of different e-mail reading systems.
- *E-mail response decay.* E-mail recipients are most responsive when they first subscribe to an e-mail. It is difficult to keep them engaged.

- *Communications preferences.* Recipients will have different preferences for e-mail offers, content and frequency which affect engagement and response. These have to be managed through communications preferences.
- *Resource intensive.* Although e-mail offers great opportunities for targeting, personalisation and more frequent communications, additional people and technology resources are required to deliver these.

## Best practice in planning and managing e-mail marketing

In this section we will review how measurement, targeting and creative can be used to improve the results from e-mail marketing.

### E-mail service providers

**E-mail service providers**

Provide a web-based service used by marketers to manage their e-mail activities including hosting e-mail subscription forms, broadcast and tracking.

**E-mail service providers (ESPs)** are a popular method companies use to manage their e-mail marketing. ESPs provides a web-based service used by marketers to manage their e-mail activities with less recourse to an agency. Rather than buying software that you host and manage on your server, the software is effectively used on a subscription basis, with a cost based on number of e-mails sent and runs on another company's server. The ESP manages four key capabilities including hosting of forms for managing e-mail subscriptions and landing pages, the broadcast tools for dispatching the e-mails and a database containing the prospect or customer profiles. They also provide tracking of effectiveness as shown by the example in Figure 9.16.

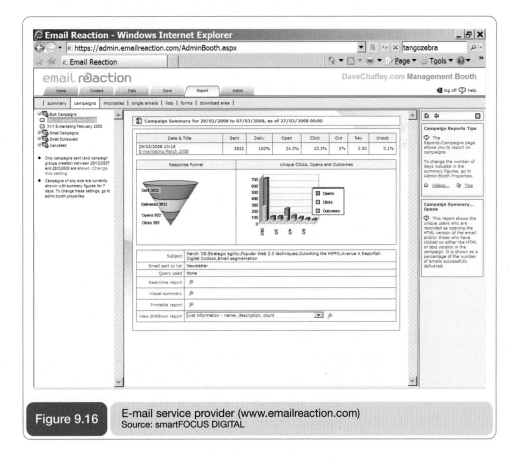

Figure 9.16  E-mail service provider (www.emailreaction.com)
Source: smartFOCUS DIGITAL

### Measuring e-mail marketing

Figure 9.16 shows that the key measures for e-mail marketing are:

- *Delivery rate* (here indicated by 'non-bounce rate'). E-mails will bounce if the e-mail address is no longer valid or a spam filter blocks the e-mail.
- *Open rate.* This is measured for HTML messages through downloaded images. It is an indication of how many customers open an e-mail, but is not accurate since some users have preview panes in their e-mail readers which load the message even if is deleted without reading, and some e-mail readers such as Outlook Express now block images by default (this has resulted in a decline in open rates through time). Open rates for particular types of e-mail address, e.g. Hotmail.com, is also an indication of deliverability problems.
- *Click-through or click rate.* This is the number of people who click through on the e-mail of those delivered (strictly unique clicks rather than total clicks). You can see that response rates are quite high at around 10%.

Additionally, and most important, are the marketing outcomes or value events (Chapter 8) such as sales and leads achieved when an e-mail recipient clicks through to the website. Retailers will also have additional methods of comparing e-mail campaigns such as revenue/profit per e-mail or thousand e-mails and average order value (AOV).

### E-mail marketing success factors

Effective e-mail marketing shares much in common with effective direct e-mail copy. Chaffey (2006) uses the mnemonic CRITICAL for a checklist of questions that can be used to improve the response of e-mail campaigns. It stands for:

- *Creative.* This assesses the design of the e-mail including its layout, use of colour and image and the copy (see below).
- *Relevance.* Does the offer and creative of the e-mail meet the needs of the recipients? This is dependent on the list quality and targeting variables used.
- *Incentive* (or offer). The WIFM factor ('What's in it for me?') for the recipient. What benefit does the recipient gain from clicking on the hyperlink(s) in the e-mail? For example, a prize draw is a common offer for B2C brands.
- *Targeting and timing.* Targeting is related to the relevance. Is a single message sent to all prospects or customers on the list or are e-mails with tailored creative, incentive and copy sent to the different segments on the list? Timing refers to when the e-mail is received: the time of day, day of the week, point in the month and even the year; does it relate to any particular events? There is also the relative timing – when it is received compared to other marketing communications – this depends on the integration.
- *Integration.* Are the e-mail campaigns part of your integrated marketing communications? Questions to ask include: are the creative and copy consistent with my brand? Does the message reinforce other communications? Does the timing of the e-mail campaign fit with offline communications?
- *Copy.* This is part of the creative and refers to the structure, style and explanation of the offer together with the location of hyperlinks in the e-mail.
- *Attributes (of the e-mail).* Assess the message characteristics such as the subject line, from address, to address, date/time of receipt and format (HTML or text). Send out Multipart/MIME messages which can display HTML or text according to the capability of the e-mail reader. Offer choice of HTML or text to match users' preferences.
- *Landing page (or microsite)* – These are terms given to the page(s) reached after the recipient clicks on a link in the e-mail. Typically, on click-through the recipient will be presented with an online form to profile or learn more about them. Designing the page so the form is easy to complete can affect the overall success of the campaign.

A relevant incentive, such as free information or a discount, is offered in exchange for a prospect providing their e-mail address by filling in an online form. Careful management of e-mail lists is required since, as the list ages, the addresses of customers and their profiles will change, resulting in many bounced messages and lower response rates. Data protection law also requires the facility for customers to update their details.

## Practical issues in managing e-mail marketing

**Deliverability**
Refers to ensuring e-mail messages are delivered and aren't blocked by spam filters because the e-mail content or structure falsely identifies a permission-based e-mail as a spammer, or because the sender's IP address has a poor reputation for spam.

**Renderability**
The capability of an e-mail to display correctly formatted in different e-mail readers.

Two of the main practical challenges for e-mail marketers or their agencies to manage are **deliverability** and **renderability**.

E-mail marketers have to ensure their e-mails are delivered given the increase in efforts by ISPs and web-e-mail companies to reduce spam into their end-users in-boxes due to the volume of spam. E-mail marketers do not want to be identified as a 'False positive' where permission-based e-mails may be bounced or placed into junk-mail boxes or simply deleted if the receiving system assesses that they are spam.

Web-based e-mail providers such as Hotmail and Yahoo! Mail have introduced standard authentication techniques known as Sender ID and Domain Keys which e-mail marketers should use to make sure the e-mail broadcaster is who they say they are and doesn't spoof their address as many spammers do. E-mail providers also assess the reputation of the e-mail broadcasters using services such as SenderScore (www.senderscore.org) based on the number of complaints and quality of e-mails sent.

It is also important that e-mail marketers do not use keywords in their e-mails which may identify them as spam. For example, e-mail filter such as Spam Assassin (www.spamassin.org) have these types of rules which are used to assess spam:

- SUB_FREE_OFFER — Subject starts with 'Free'
- SUBJECT_DRUG_GAP_VIA — Subject contains a gappy version of 'viagra'
- TO_ADDRESS_EQ_REAL — To: repeats address as real name
- HTML_IMAGE_RATIO_04 — BODY: HTML has a low ratio of text to image area
- HTML_FONT_BIG — BODY: HTML tag for a big font size

Although the word 'free' in a subject line may cause a problem, this is only one part of the signature of a spam, so it may still be possible to use this word if the reputation of the sender is good. Figure 9.17 shows an example of a service for email marketers to check they are not likely to be assessed as a spammer.

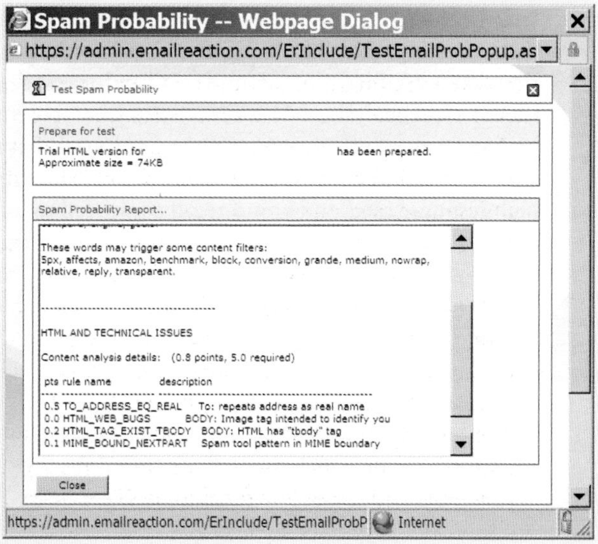


Figure 9.17 Service for email marketers from www.emailreaction.com
*Source*: smartFOCUS DIGITAL

Renderability refers to how the e-mail appears in different e-mail readers. Often images are blocked by readers in an effort to defeat spammers who use the fact that images are downloaded as the user views the e-mail to detect that the e-mail is a valid address. So e-mails that are only made up of images with no text are less likely to be effective than hybrid messages combining text and images. Formatting can also differ in different readers, so designers of e-mails have to test how e-mails render in common e-mail readers such as Hotmail and Yahoo! Mail.

A further challenge is trying to achieve ongoing engagement with list members. Some approaches that are commonly used include:

● Develop a welcome programme where over the first three to six months targeted automatically-triggered e-mails to educate subscribers about your brand, products and deliver targeted offers.
● Use offers to re-activate list-members as they become less responsive.
● Segment list members by activity (responsiveness) and age on list and treat differently, either by reducing frequency or using more offline media.
● Follow-up on bounces using other media to reduce problems of dropping deliverability.
● Best practice when renting lists is to request only e-mails where the opt-in is within the most recent six to nine months when subscribers are most active.

### List management

E-mail marketers need to work hard to improve the quality of their list as explained in Chapter 6. DMA (2008) report that companies often fail to collect the most recent address with UK companies having e-mail addresses for only 50% of their database. Respondents believed that the data and its selection accounted for over half of a campaign's success. The creative and offer are still considered significant while timing is viewed as having the least impact, accounting for just 10% of the success of an e-mail campaign. The report noted that the majority of respondents gather new e-mail addresses through organic website traffic with offline (paper-based) activity accounting for 40% and telemarketing for 31%.

## Mobile text messaging

We have concentrated our coverage on e-mail marketing in this section since the amount of marketing investment and levels of activity in e-mail marketing is much higher than mobile text messaging because it seems that receiving permission-based e-mails is more acceptable than receiving what may be perceived as an intrusive text message on a mobile device. Additionally, it enables more complex, visual messages to be delivered. However, Rettie *et al.* (2005) in an analysis of 26 text marketing campaigns (5401 respondents) demonstrated surprising levels of effectiveness. Her team found that overall acceptability of SMS advertising was 44%, significantly higher than the acceptability of telemarketing and found relatively high response rates and brand recall compared to direct mail and e-mail marketing.

| Mini Case Study 9.2 | Beep-beep-beep-beep, that'll be the bank then – driving sales through mobile marketing |
|---|---|

Say and Southwell (2006) creators of the text message banking system at First Direct (part of the HSBC Group, describe how if mobile marketing is carefully used with a trusted brand it can be effective. Their use of mobile marketing started in 2001 with product offer campaigns encouraging mobile users to log-on to the bank, call the contact centre or receive a direct mail pack for more information. Since there was a delay between requesting a direct mail pack and receiving one, a more responsive mechanism was for customers who replied to a text message with their e-mail address to immediately receive an e-mail with a link to a website featuring more information and an application form.

First Direct also use mobile short codes within their offline advertising encouraging those who read ads in newspapers about a product, for example, to follow-up on them immediately.

Short codes were also used for promotions. In one example, a 'text to win TXT2WIN' approach was used where customers were sent an e-mail or a direct mail pack with information about a new Internet Banking Plus account aggregation service (Figure 9.18) plus details of a prize draw to win a holiday or ticket to a football match. To enter the competition, customers were asked to review an online demonstration, find an answer to a question, and text the answer to a shortcode number with their name, postcode and e-mail address.

The campaign objectives and results (in brackets) were to:

- capture 5000 mobile phone numbers from customers (200% of plan);
- acquire 3000 e-mail addresses (176% of plan);
- raise awareness about the new service (31,000 customers view demonstration);
- create 1000 new registrations (576% of plan).

This case shows the need for text message marketing to be carefully integrated with other direct channels such as web, e-mail and phone. It also shows the importance of capturing and maintaining up-to-date customer details such as e-mail addresses and mobile phone numbers.

*Source*: Say and Southwell (2006).

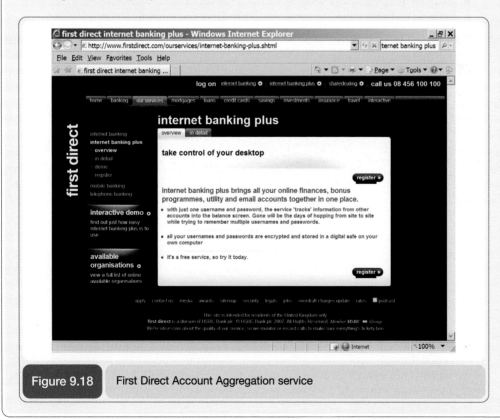

| Figure 9.18 | First Direct Account Aggregation service |
|---|---|

## Viral and electronic word-of-mouth marketing

### What is viral marketing and word-of-mouth?

**Viral marketing** harnesses the network effect of the Internet and can be effective in reaching a large number of people rapidly as a marketing message is rapidly transmitted in the same way as a natural virus or a computer virus. It is effectively an online form of word-of-mouth communications which is sometimes also known as 'buzz marketing'. The two main forms of online viral marketing are through passalong-e-mails or discussions within social networks. When planning integrated campaigns, it is important to note that the online viral affect can be amplified through offline media mentions or advertising either on TV and radio or in print.

**Word-of-mouth (WOM) marketing** is an established concept closely related to viral marketing, but broader in context. The Word-of-Mouth Marketing Association (www.womma.org/wom101) explain how WOM can be harnessed:

> word-of-mouth can be encouraged and facilitated. Companies can work hard to make people happier, they can listen to consumers, they can make it easier for them to tell their friends, and they can make certain that influential individuals know about the good qualities of a product or service.

They go on to explain that all word-of-mouth marketing techniques are based on the concepts of customer satisfaction, two-way dialogue and transparent communications. The basic elements are:

- educating people about your products and services;
- identifying people most likely to share their opinions;
- providing tools that make it easier to share information;
- studying how, where and when opinions are being shared;
- listening and responding to supporters, detractors and neutrals.

WOMMA identify different approaches for facilitating WOM. The ones that are most relevant to online marketing are:

- *Buzz marketing.* Using high-profile entertainment or news to get people to talk about your brand.
- *Viral marketing.* Creating entertaining or informative messages that are designed to be passed along in an exponential fashion, often electronically or by e-mail.
- *Community marketing.* Forming or supporting niche communities that are likely to share interests about the brand (such as user groups, fan clubs and discussion forums); providing tools, content and information to support those communities.
- *Influencer marketing.* Identifying key communities and opinion leaders who are likely to talk about products and have the ability to influence the opinions of others.
- *Conversation creation.* Interesting or fun advertising, e-mails, catch phrases, entertainment or promotions designed to start word-of-mouth activity.
- *Brand blogging.* Creating blogs and participating in the blogosphere, in the spirit of open, transparent communications; sharing information of value that the blog community may talk about.
- *Referral programmes.* Creating tools that enable satisfied customers to refer their friends.

Positive WOM is believed to increase purchase intent. For example, Marsden *et al.* (2005) found that brands such as HSBC, Honda and O2 with a greater proportion of advocates measured through Net Promoter Score (NPS, Chapter 6) tended to be more successful. They recommend ten ways to encourage word-of-mouth, most of which can be facilitated online:

- *Implement and optimise referral programmes.* Reward customers for referring new customers, and reward the referee as well as the referrer.
- *Set up brand ambassador schemes.* Recruit brand fans as ambassadors who receive exclusive merchandise/offers to share with their contacts.
- *Use tryvertising.* A combination of 'try' or 'trial' and 'advertising', this is a twist on product sampling. The idea is that rather than provide free samples or trials to anyone in a target market, tryvertising involves sampling on a selective and exclusive basis to lead users – ideally with new products or services before they become widely available.
- *Use causal marketing.* Associate your brand with a good cause that builds on brand values (e.g. Nike anti-racism in sport).
- *Measure your Net Promoter Score (NPS).* Track your NPS (see page 338 for further details) at all brand touchpoints to find out what you are doing right, and what needs to be improved.
- *Start an influencer outreach programme.* Reach out to the 10% who tell the other 90% what to try and buy with special offers and programmes.
- *Harness the power of empowered involvement.* Create advocacy – let your lead clients, customers or consumers call the shots on your innovation and marketing with VIP votes and polls.
- *Focus innovation on doing something worth talking about.* Do something new that delivers an experience that exceeds expectations.

In an online context, word-of-mouth marketing is important since there is great potential for facilitating electronic word-of-mouth. It is very important for online marketers to understand how WOM can be generated and influenced since research, such as that conducted by Forrester (2007) quoted in the section on online public relations, shows that recommendations from friends, family or even other online consumers are trusted and are a major consideration in product and supplier selection.

### E-mail forwarding or passalong viral marketing

E-mail forwarding is a common online activity. For example, research quoted by Dee *et al.* (2007) showed that for a US sample, around 60% of web users frequently forward on by e-mail anything they think may be of interest to friends, family or colleagues. Phelps *et al.* (2004) have explored some of the motivations for forwarding e-mails and they found that 'Respondents reported experiencing positive emotions when they sent passalong e-mails. They might feel excited, helpful, happy or satisfied'. For a message to be forwarded it had to meet the conditions of it being important or containing something that the sender thought the other person would like and even those most likely to forward had to be in the right mood and have the time.

Chaffey and Smith (2008) distinguish between these types of viral e-mail mechanisms:

- *Passalong e-mail viral.* This is where e-mail or word-of-mouth alone is used to spread the message. This is classic viral marketing such as those showcased on the Viral Bank (www.viralbank.com) which involve an e-mail with a link to a site such as a video or an attachment. Towards the end of a commercial e-mail it does no harm to prompt the first recipient to forward the e-mail to interested friends or colleagues. Even if only one in 100 responds to this prompt, it is still worth it. The dramatic growth of Hotmail, reaching 10 million subscribers in just over a year, was effectively down to passalong as people received e-mails with a signature promoting the service. Word-of-mouth helped too.

    Passalong or forwarding has worked well for video clips, either where they are attached to the e-mail or where the e-mail contains a link to download the clip. If the e-mail has the 'WOW!' factor, of which more later, a lot more than one in a 100 will forward the e-mail. This mechanism is what most people consider to be viral, but there are the other mechanisms that follow too.

- *Web-facilitated viral (e-mail prompt).* Here, the e-mail contains a link/graphic to a web page with 'e-mail a friend' or 'e-mail a colleague'. A web form is used to collect the e-mail address to which the e-mail should be forwarded, sometimes with an optional message. The company then sends a separate message to the friend or colleague.
- *Web-facilitated viral (web prompt).* Here it is the web page such as a product catalogue or white paper which contains a link/graphic to 'e-mail a friend' or colleague. A web form is again used to collect data and an e-mail is subsequently sent.
- *Incentivised viral.* This is distinct from the types above since the e-mail address is not freely given. This is what we need to make viral really take off. By offering some reward for providing someone else's address we can dramatically increase referrals. A common offer is to gain an additional entry for a prize draw. Referring more friends gains more entries to the prize draw. With the right offer, this can more than double the response. The incentive is offered either by e-mail (the second option above) or on a web page (the third option). In this case, there is a risk of breaking privacy laws since the consent of the e-mail recipient may not be freely given. Usually only a single follow-up e-mail by the brand is permitted. So you should check with the lawyers if you are considering this.
- *Web-link viral.* But online viral isn't just limited to e-mail. Links in discussion group postings or blogs which are from an individual are also in this category. Either way, it's important when seeding the campaign to try to get as many targeted online and offline mentions of the viral agent as you can.

### Social network-related viral marketing

Dee *et al.* (2007) also note the importance of social networks in influencing perceptions about brands, products and suppliers. Their research shows large differences in gender and age on the types of products discussed, but recommendations on restaurants, computers, movies and vehicles are popular in all categories.

Microsoft (2007), which part owns Facebook, has developed these approaches for taking advantage of social networking either through buying ad space, creating a brand space or brand channels that enable consumers to interact with or promote a brand:

- *Understand consumers' motivations for using social networks.* Ads will be most effective if they are consistent with the typical lifestage of networkers or the topics that are being discussed.
- *Express yourself as a brand.* Use the web to show the unique essence of your brand, but think about how to express a side of the brand that it is not normally seen.
- *Create and maintain good conversations.* Advertisers who engage in discussions are more likely to resonate with the audience, but once conversations are started they must be followed through.
- *Empower participants.* Social network users use their space and blogs to express themselves. Providing content or widgets to associate themselves with a brand may be appealing. For example, in the first six months of launching charity donation widgets, 20,000 have been used online and they became one of the biggest referrers to the JustGiving website and driving more people to fundraising pages to make donations (JustGiving, 2007).
- *Identify online brand advocates.* Use reputation management tools to identify influential social network members who are already brand advocates. Approach the most significant ones directly. Consider using contextual advertising such as Microsoft content ads or Google Adsense to display brand messages within their spaces when brands are discussed.
- *The Golden Rule: behave like a social networker.* Microsoft recommend this simple fundamental principle which will help the content created by advertisers to resonate with social networkers: behave like the best social networkers through:
  - being creative
  - being honest and courteous (ask permission)
  - being individual
  - being conscious of the audience
  - updating regularly.

| Mini Case Study 9.3 | Fragrance brand uses social network widgets to target an older audience |
|---|---|

Unilever brand Impulse developed a campaign site to interact with the fragrance brand, with information about the ranges, a 'mixology' section and a talk with TV presenter Dave Berry.

Although Impulse has traditionally been aimed at teenagers, this campaign targeted an older audience.

Site visitors were able to watch the TV ad and buy a limited edition bag by illustrator Daisy de Villeneuve by entering their details on the site or texting to a shortcode to buy the Impulse-branded bag for £2.

As part of the campaign theme of matchmaking, social networkers were able to download a 'MySparks' widget to their MySpace profile which could be customised to tell other members how well they 'spark' with others. Impulse also ran a campaign across Yahoo! Movies offering users tickets to exclusive film screenings.

*Source: New Media Age* (2007)

## Advantages and disadvantages of viral marketing

The advantages and disadvantages of viral marketing are shared with those with online PR as covered earlier in the chapter. However, it can be argued that the risk in investment in viral marketing is higher since it is difficult to predict the success of a particular viral agent.

### Advantages of viral marketing

The main advantage of viral marketing is that an effective viral agent can reach a large audience in a cost-effective way. We have also seen how consumers rate the opinions of their peers, friends and family highly, so they can be highly influential. Kumar *et al.* (2007) have discussed the potential value that can be generated through customer referrals in several case studies.

### Disadvantages of viral marketing

The main disadvantage is that this is a high-risk marketing communications technique, since it requires significant initial investment in the viral agent and seeding. However, there is no guarantee that the campaign will 'go viral', in which case the investment will be wasted.

Of course, although positive viral marketing can spread rapidly, so can negative sentiments about a company, which we referred to in the section on online reputation management (see page **534**).

## Best practice in planning and managing viral marketing

Much discussion of practice in viral and word-of-mouth marketing centres around how and who to reach to achieve influence. Some, such as Malcom Gladwell and Seth Godin in their popular books *The Tipping Point* and *Unleashing the Ideavirus* have suggested that influentials are important. Godin (2001) writes about the importance of what he terms 'the ideavirus' as a marketing tool. He describes it as 'digitally augmented word-of-mouth'. What differences does the ideavirus have from word-of-mouth? First, transmission is more rapid, second, transmission tends to reach a larger audience, and third, it can be persistent – reference to a product on a service. Godin emphasises the importance of starting small by seeding a niche audience he describes as a 'hive' and then using advocates in spreading the virus – he refers to them as 'sneezers'. Traditionally, marketers would refer to such a grouping as 'customer advocates' or 'brand loyalists'.

Others believe that the role of influencers in achieving word-of-mouth can be overstated. Balter and Butman, in their book, *Grapevine*, say:

*Everybody talks about products and services, and they talk about them all the time. Word-of-mouth is NOT about identifying a small subgroup of highly influential or well-connected people to talk up a product or service. It's not about mavens or bees or celebrities or people with specialist knowledge. It's about everybody.*

While the influencers will have a greater impact, academics, Watts and Dodds (2007) concur, arguing that the 'influentials hypothesis' is based on untested assumptions and in most cases does not match how diffusion operates in the real world. He comments that 'most social change is driven not by influentials, but by easily influenced individuals influencing other easily influenced individuals'.

The role of social media in influencing consumers is discussed further in Chapter 2 in the section on consumer behaviour (see page **57**).

### Viral marketing in practice

Chaffey and Smith (2008) say that in practice a viral campaign requires a clever idea, a game, a shocking idea or a highly informative idea which makes compulsive viewing. It can be a video clip, a TV ad, a cartoon, a funny picture, a poem, song, political message or a news item. It is so amazing, it makes people want to pass it on. A good example is shown in the Subservient Chicken, originally launched to promote a new chicken meal by Burger King. Subservient Chicken (Figure 9.19) responds to commands typed in by users. It has circulated around millions of users worldwide and is one of the most successful viral campaigns in terms of passalong.

This is a challenge for commercial companies since to be successful, it will need to challenge convention and this may not fit well with the brand.

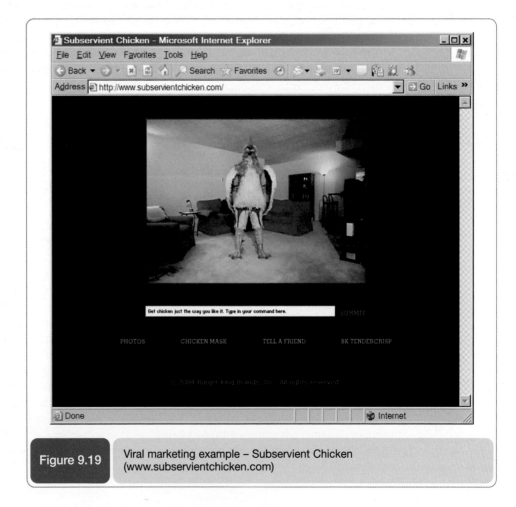

| Figure 9.19 | Viral marketing example – Subservient Chicken (www.subservientchicken.com) |

To make a viral campaign effective, Justin Kirby of viral marketing specialists DMC (www.dmc.co.uk) suggests these three things are needed (Kirby, 2003):

- *Creative material – the 'viral agent'*. This includes the creative message or offer and how it is spread (text, image, video).
- *Seeding*. Identifying websites, blogs or people to send e-mail to start the virus spreading. Seeding can also be completed by e-mail to members of a house list or renting a list with the likely audience.
- *Tracking*. To monitor the effect, to assess the return from the cost of developing the viral agent and seeding.

## Offline promotion techniques

The importance of offline communications in driving visitors to a website is well-known by site owners who find that greater levels of investment in offline advertising using TV, print or radio results in greater visitor numbers to websites. This can be tracked by web analytics which shows an increase in searches containing the brand or campaign name or the web address or direct visitors who enter the site URL into the address bar.

Research has identified that there is a clear correlation between investment in offline advertising and visits to a website. For example, Hitwise (2006) found in a study of brands including BSkyB, Orange and the AA that searches on brand terms and URLs increased when offline media investment was combined with online. For example, when Sky's media campaign included both online and offline advertising (in September to November of 2005) the strongest result was achieved online with searches for the Sky brand increasing +20% and searches for the Sky URL more than doubling. When offline ran without the integration of online in March 2006, the same lift in searches was not evident. This research also shows the need for significant offline spend with Sky spending around 20% online with print, TV and radio still remaining significant (see Figure 9.20).

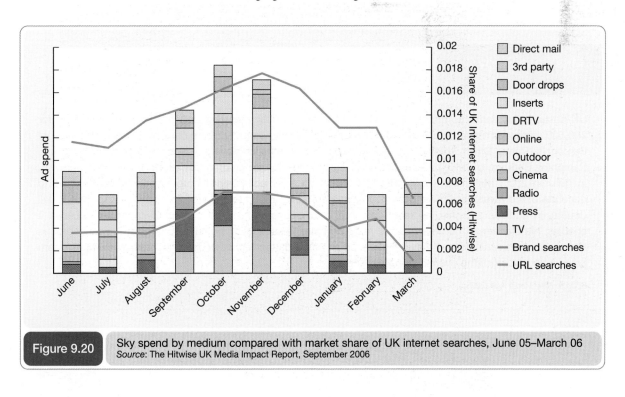

| Figure 9.20 | Sky spend by medium compared with market share of UK internet searches, June 05–March 06
*Source*: The Hitwise UK Media Impact Report, September 2006 |

The linkage between advertising and search has also been investigated by Graham and Havlena (2007) who additionally studied the role of advertising in generating word-of-mouth discussion online. They found 'strong evidence that advertising does stimulate increased visitation to the websites of advertised brands – an indicator of consumer interest and involvement with a brand'.

Online website promotion techniques such as search engine marketing and banner advertising often take prominence when discussing methods of traffic building. But we start with using offline communications to generate site visitors since it is one of the most effective techniques to generate site traffic and the characteristics of offline media are such (Figure 8.4, page 456) that they often have a higher impact and are more creative, which can help explain the online value proposition. 'Offline promotion' refers to using communications tools such as advertising and PR delivered by traditional media such as TV, radio and print in order to direct visitors to an online presence.

**Offline promotion**
Using traditional media such as TV, radio and print to direct visitors to an online presence.

Despite the range of opportunities for using new online communications tools, traditional communications using offline media such as TV, print and direct mail and others shown in Figure 1.9 (page 29) remain the dominant form of investment in marketing communications for most. Even organisations which transact a large proportion of their business online continue to invest heavily in offline communications. EConsultancy (2008a) research into advanced adopters showed that even here the average expenditure on digital media channels as a proportion of communications budget was only 23%. Consider the travel sector where both travel suppliers such as BA, Thomson and easyJet and intermediaries such as Expedia and Opodo transact an increasing proportion of their sales online, but are still reliant on offline communications to drive visitors to the web to transact.

When the web analytics data about referring visitors is assessed, for most companies who are not online-only businesses, we find that over half the visitors are typically marked as 'No referrer'. This means that they visited the site direct by typing in the web address into the address bar in response to awareness of the brand generated through real-world communications (others may have bookmarked the site or clicked through from a search engine).

So offline communications are effective at reaching an audience to encourage them to visit a site, but are also useful as a way of having an impact or explaining a complex proposition as, Mini case study 9.4 shows.

| Mini Case Study 9.4 | Offline communications vital for finding the perfect partner at Match.com |
|---|---|

UK-based online dating company Match.com has over 1.5 million members and in 2004 was responsible for 200,000 marriages around the world. Match.com and partner company uDate.com compete against Yahoo! Personals, Dating Direct, traditional players and a host of smaller players. Given the intense competition, Samantha Bedford, UK MD, believes it is essential to invest in offline communications for continued growth. In Autumn 2005, Match.com spent over £3 million on a TV advertising campaign since they wanted to generate brand awareness given that they estimate that by 2008 the value of the online dating market will double. In addition to achieving reach and brand awareness, offline advertising is important because it enables Match.com to communicate a fairly complex message to potential customers. Focus groups showed that many singles felt they did not need an online dating service and did not realise how Match.com could help as part of the overall dating experience.

*Source: New Media Age (2005a)*

## Advantages and disadvantages of using offline communications to support e-commerce

Offline communications work; they are effective in achieving four critical things:

- *Reach,* since newspaper, TV and postal communications are used by virtually all consumers.
- *Brand awareness* through using high-impact visuals.
- *Emotional connection* with brand again through visuals and sounds.
- *Explanation* of the online value proposition for a brand.

A further benefit is that for any given objective, integrated marketing communications received through different media are more effective in achieving that objective. We mentioned this cumulative reinforcement effect of integrated marketing communications when referring to the 4 Cs of coherence, consistency, continuity and complementarities earlier in the chapter. Having said this, the disadvantages of using offline communications to encourage online channel usage compared to many online communications tools are obvious. In general the disadvantages of offline communications are:

- *Higher cost.* Return on investment tends to be higher for online communications such as search engine optimisation, pay-per-click marketing or affiliate marketing.
- *Higher wastage.* The well-known expression about 'half my advertising is wasted, but I don't know which half' may be true about offline marketing, but it isn't true online if the right tracking processes are in place.
- *Poorer targeting.* Targeting by behaviour, location, time, search keyword, site and site content is readily possible online. This tends to be more targeted compared to most offline media (apart from direct marketing).
- *Poorer accountability.* It is straightforward to track response online – offline it is expensive and error-prone.
- *Less detailed information.* The detailed information to support a decision can only be cost-effectively delivered online.
- *Less personalised.* Although direct mail can be personalised, personalisation is more straightforward online.
- *Less interactive experience.* Most offline communications are one-way – interaction is possible online with the right creative.

## Incidental and specific advertising of the online presence

**Incidental offline advertising**
Driving traffic to the website is not a primary objective of the advert.

**Specific offline advertising**
Driving traffic to the website or explaining the online proposition is a primary objective of the advert.

Two types of offline advertising can be identified: incidental and specific. Reference to the website is **incidental** if the main aim of the advert is to advertise a particular product or promotion and the website is available as an ancillary source of information if required by the viewer. Traditionally, much promotion of the website in the offline media by traditional companies has been incidental – simply consisting of highlighting the existence of the website by including the URL at the bottom of an advertisement. Reference to the website is **specific** if it is an objective of the advert to explain the proposition of the website in order to drive traffic to the site to achieve direct response. Here the advert will highlight the offers or services available at the website, such as sales promotions or online customer service. Amazon commonly advertises in newspapers to achieve this. Naturally, this approach is most likely to be used by companies that only have an online presence, but existing companies can develop straplines to use which explain the website value proposition (as Mini case study 4.3 'BA asks 'have you clicked yet?', page 249 illustrates well). Many state 'Visit our website!!', but clearly a more specific strapline can be developed which describes the overall proposition of the site ('detailed information and product guides to help you select the best product for you') or is specific to the campaign ('we will give you an instant quote online, showing how much you save with us').

### Offline response mechanisms

The different response mechanics such as web response and URL strategy which we discussed in Chapter 8 in the section on campaign response mechanisms have to be used to maximise response since this helps to direct potential customers to the most appropriate content on the website. Different URLs are also useful for measuring the response of offline media campaigns since we can measure the number of visitors arriving directly at the URL by entering the domain name.

## Public relations

Public relations can be an important tool for driving traffic to the website if changes to online services or online events are significant or if a viral campaign is discussed online. The days of the launch of a website being significant are now gone, but if a site is re-launched with significant changes to its services, this may still be worthy of mention. Many newspapers have regular features listing interesting entertainment or leisure sites or guides to specific topics such as online banking or grocery shopping. Trade magazines may also give information about relevant websites.

Jenkins (1995) argues that one key objective for public relations is its role in transforming a negative situation into a positive achievement. The public relations transfer process he suggests is as follows:

- from ignorance to knowledge;
- from apathy to interest;
- from prejudice to acceptance;
- from hostility to sympathy.

These are, of course, goals of online PR which was discussed in more detail earlier in this chapter.

## Direct marketing

Direct marketing can be an effective method of driving traffic to the website. As mentioned earlier, a web response model can be used where the website is the means for fulfilling the response, but a direct mail campaign is used to drive the response. Many catalogue companies will continue to use traditional direct mail to mail-out a subset of their offering, with the recipient tempted to visit the site through the fuller offering and incentives such as competitions or web-specific offers.

## Other physical reminders

Since we all spend more time in the real rather than the virtual world, physical reminders explaining why customers should visit websites are significant. What is in customers' hands and on their desk top will act as a prompt to visit a site and counter the weakness of the web as a pull medium. This is perhaps most important in the B2B context where a physical reminder in the office can be helpful. Examples, usually delivered through direct marketing, include brochures, catalogues, business cards, point-of-sale material, pens, postcards, inserts in magazines and password reminders for extranets.

## Word-of-mouth marketing

It is worth remembering that, as we stated in the section on viral and word-of-mouth marketing, word-of-mouth plays an important role in promoting sites, particularly consumer sites where the Internet is currently a novelty. Opinion Research Corporation International,

ORCI (1991), reported on a study among US consumers that showed that the typical Internet consumer tells 12 other people about his or her online shopping experience. This compares with the average US consumer, who tells 8.6 additional people about a favourite film and another 6.1 people about a favourite restaurant! It has been said that if the online experience is favourable then a customer will tell 12 people, but if it is bad they will tell twice as many, so word-of-mouth can be negative also. Parry (1998) reported that for European users, word-of-mouth through friends, relatives and colleagues was the most important method by which users found out about websites, being slightly more important than search engines and directories or links from other sites.

Thus the role of opinion leaders and multi-step communications with target audiences receiving information about the Internet experience from opinion leaders, the mass media and the Internet, appear to be perhaps even more important in relation to the Internet than for other media. Dichter (1966) summarised how word-of-mouth communications work. To exploit such communications, it is necessary for marketers to use appropiate techniques to target and adapt the message for the opinion leaders when a product or service is at an early stage of diffusion (Rogers, 1983). Viral marketing (see later) will often target these opinion leaders to become advocates in initial contacts.

---

| Activity 9.1 | Selecting the best digital media channel mix techniques |
|---|---|

Suggest the best mix of online (and offline) promotion techniques to build traffic for the following situations:

1. Well-established B2C brand with high brand awareness.
2. Dot-com start-up.
3. Small business aiming to export.
4. Common B2C product, e.g. household insurance.
5. Specialist B2B product.

---

| Case Study 9 | Innovation at Google |
|---|---|

### Context

In addition to being the largest search engine on planet Earth, mediating the searches of tens of billions of searches daily, Google is an innovator. All online marketers should follow Google to see the latest approaches it is trialling.

### Google's mission

Google's mission is encapsulated in the statement 'to organise the world's information … and make it universally accessible and useful'. Google explains that it believes that the most effective, and ultimately the most profitable, way to accomplish their mission is to put the needs of users first. Offering a high-quality user experience has led to strong word-of-mouth promotion and strong traffic growth.

Putting users first is reflected in three key commitments illustrated in the Google SEC filing:

1 *We will do our best to provide the most relevant and useful search results possible, independent of financial incentives. Our search results will be objective and we will not accept payment for inclusion or ranking in them.*

2 *We will do our best to provide the most relevant and useful advertising. Advertisements should not be an annoying interruption. If any element on a search result page is influenced by payment to us, we will make it clear to our users.*

3 *We will never stop working to improve our user experience, our search technology and other important areas of information organisation.*

The range of Google services is well known:

- Google web search.
- Movie, music and weather information.
- News, finance, maps, image, book and groups information.
- Google image search.
- Google book search.
- Google scholar.
- Google base. Allows content owners to submit content that they want to share on Google websites.
- Google webmaster tools. Provides information to webmasters to help them enhance their understanding of how their websites interact with the Google search engine. Content owners can submit sitemaps and geotargeting information through Google Webmaster Tools to improve search quality.
- Google Co-op and Custom Search. Tailored version of the search engine.
- Google Video and YouTube.
- Google Docs. Edit documents, spreadsheets, and presentations from anywhere using a browser.
- Google Calendar.
- Gmail.
- Google Reader. This is a free service that lets users subscribe to feeds and receive updates from multiple websites in a single interface. Google Reader also allows users to share content with others, and function with many types of media and reading-styles.
- Orkut – a social network.
- Blogger. A web-based publishing tool that lets web users publish blogs.
- Google Desktop. Search own local content.
- Picasa. A free service that allows users to view, manage and share their photos.
- Google GEO – Google maps, Earth and local.
- Google Checkout provides a single login for buying online. On 1 February 2008, Google began charging merchants who use Google Checkout 2% of the transaction amount plus $0.20 per transaction to the extent these fees exceed ten times the amount they spend on AdWords advertising.
- Google Mobile, Maps, Mobile, Blogger and Gmail are all available on mobile devices.

For 2007, Google spent around 12.8% of its revenue in research and development. An increase from less than 10% in 2005.

## Google revenue models

Google generated approximately 99% of its revenues in 2007 from its advertisers with the remainder from its enterprise search products where companies can install search technology through products such as the Google Appliance and Google Mini.

Google AdWords, the auction-based advertising program that enables advertisers, is the main source of revenue. Advertisers pay on a 'pay-per-click' cost basis within the search engines and within other services such as Gmail, but with cost-per-thousand payment options available on Google Networks members' websites. Google has introduced classified-style ad programmes for other media, including:

- Google Audio Ads (ads are placed in radio programmes)
- Google Print Ads
- Google TV Ads
- Google Video Ads, user-initiated click-to-play video ads.

So, Google's revenues are critically dependent on how many searches it achieves in different countries and the proportion of searchers who interact with Google's ads. Research by Comscore (2008) suggests around 25% of searches result in an ad click where sponsored search results are included (around 50% of searches). Of course, Google is also looking to increase the number of advertisers and invests heavily in this through trade communications to marketers. Increased competition to advertise against a search term will result in increased bid amounts and so increased revenue for Google.

International revenues accounted for approximately 48% of total revenues in 2007, and more than half of user traffic came from outside the US. In 2007, 15% of ad revenue was from the UK alone.

Some 35% of Google's revenue is from the Network of content partners who subscribe to the Google Adsense programme. From the inception of the Google Network in 2002 through the first quarter of 2004, the growth in advertising revenues from Google Network members' websites exceeded that from Google's own websites, which had a negative impact on our operating margins.

## Risk factors

Some of the main risk factors that Google declares include:

1 **New technologies could block Google ads.** Ad-blocking technology could, in the future, adversely affect Google's results, although there has not been widespread adoption of these ad blocking approaches.
2 **Litigation and confidence loss through click fraud.** Click fraud can be a problem when competitors click on a link, but this is typically small scale. A larger

problem for Google to manage is structured click fraud where site owners on the Google content network seek to make additional advertising feeds.

3 **Index spammers could harm the integrity of web search results.** This could damage Google's reputation and cause users to be dissatisfied with Google's products and services. Google says:

*There is an ongoing and increasing effort by 'index spammers' to develop ways to manipulate our web search results. For example, because our web search technology ranks a web page's relevance based in part on the importance of the websites that link to it, people have attempted to link a group of websites together to manipulate web search results.*

*Source*: SEC, 2008

At 31 December 2007, Google had 16,805 employees, consisting of 5788 in research and development, 6647 in sales and marketing, 2844 in general and administrative and 1526 in operations. All of Google's employees are also equity holders, with significant collective employee ownership. As a result, many employees are highly motivated to make the company more successful. Google's engineers are encouraged to spend up to 10% of their time identifying new approaches.

### Question

Explain how Google generates revenue and identify future levels of revenue given some of the risk factors are for future revenue generation.

## Summary

1. Online promotion techniques include:
   - *Search engine marketing* – search engine optimisation (SEO) improves position in the natural listings and pay-per-click marketing features a company in the sponsored listings.
   - *Online PR* – including techniques such as link building, blogging, RSS and reputation management.
   - *Online partnerships* – including affiliate marketing (commission-based referral), co-branding and sponsorship.
   - *Online advertising* – using a range of formats including banners, skyscrapers and rich media such as overlays.
   - *E-mail marketing* – including rented lists, co-branded e-mails, event-triggered e-mails and ads in third-party e-newsletters for acquisition, and e-newsletters and campaign e-mails to house lists.
   - *Viral marketing* – developing great creative concepts which are transmitted by online word-of-mouth.

2. Offline promotion involves promoting the website address, highlighting the value proposition of the website and achieving web response through traditional media advertisements in print or on television.

3. Interactive marketing communications must be developed as part of integrated marketing communications for maximum cost effectiveness.

4. Key characteristics of interactive communications are the combination of push and pull media, user-submitted content, personalisation, flexibility and, of course, interactivity to create a dialogue with consumers.

5. Objectives for interactive communications include direct sales for transactional sites, but they also indirectly support brand awareness, favourability and purchase intent.

6. Important decisions in the communications mix introduced by digital media include:
   - the balance between spend on media and creative for digital assets and ad executions;
   - the balance between spend in traditional and offline communications;
   - the balance between investment in continuous and campaign-based digital activity;
   - the balance of investment in different interactive communications tools.

Table 9.5 provides a summary of the strengths and weaknesses of the tools discussed in this chapter.

| Table 9.5 | Summary of the strengths and weaknesses of different communications tools for promoting an online presence | |
|---|---|---|
| **Promotion technique** | **Main strengths** | **Main weaknesses** |
| Search engine optimisation (SEO) | Highly targeted, relatively low cost of PPC. High traffic volumes if effective. Considered credible by searchers | Intense competition, may compromise look of site. Complexity of changes to ranking algorithm |
| Pay-per-click (PPC) marketing | Highly targeted with controlled cost of acquisition. Extend reach through content network | Relatively costly in competitive sectors and low volume compared with SEO |
| Trusted feed | Update readily to reflect changes in product lines and prices | Relatively costly, mainly relevant for e-retailers |
| Online PR | Relatively low cost and good targeting. Can assist with SEO through creation of backlinks | Identifying online influencers and setting up partnerships can be time-consuming. Need to monitor comments on third-party sites |
| Affiliate marketing | Payment is by results (e.g. 10% of sale or leads goes to referring site) | Costs of payments to affiliate networks for setup and management fees. Changes to ranking algorithm may affect volume from affiliates |
| Online sponsorship | Most effective if low-cost, long-term co-branding arrangement with synergistic site | May increase awareness, but does not necessarily lead directly to sales |
| Interactive advertising | Main intention to achieve visit, i.e. direct response model. But also role in branding through media multiplier effect | Response rates have declined historically because of banner blindness |
| E-mail marketing | Push medium – can't be ignored in user's inbox. Can be used for direct response link to website. Integrates as a response mechanism with direct mail | Requires opt-in for effectiveness. Better for customer retention than for acquisition? Inbox cut-through – message diluted among other e-mails. Limits on deliverability |
| Viral and word-of-mouth marketing | With effective viral agent, possible to reach a large number at relatively low cost. Influencers in social networks significant | Difficult to create powerful viral concepts and control targeting. Risks damaging brand since unsolicited messages may be received |
| Traditional offline advertising (TV, print, etc.) | Larger reach than most online techniques. Greater creativity possible, leading to greater impact | Targeting arguably less easy than online. Typical high cost of acquisition |

# Exercises

## Self-assessment exercises

1. Briefly explain and give examples of online promotion and offline promotion techniques.

2. Explain the different types of payment model for banner advertising.

3. Which factors are important in governing a successful online banner advertising campaign?

4. How can a company promote itself through a search engine?

5. Explain the value of co-branding.

6. How can online PR help to promote a new product?

7. How should websites be promoted offline?

8. What do you think the relative importance of these Internet-based advertising techniques would be for an international chemical manufacturer?
   (a) Display advertising.
   (b) Paid search marketing.
   (c) Affiliate marketing.

## Essay and discussion questions

1. Discuss the analogy of Berthon *et al.* (1998) that effective Internet promotion is similar to a company exhibiting at an industry trade show attracting visitors to its stand.

2. Discuss the merits of the different models of paying for banner advertisements on the Internet for both media owners and companies placing advertisements.

3. Explain the factors that control the position of a company's products and services in the search engine results pages of a search engine such as Google.

4. Compare the effectiveness of different methods of online advertising including display advertisements, paid search marketing and affiliate marketing.

## Examination questions

1. Give three examples of digital media channels and briefly explain their communications benefits.

2. Describe four different types of site on which online display advertising for a car manufacturer's site could be placed.

3. Click-through is one measure of the effectiveness of online advertising.
   (a) What is 'click-through'?
   (b) Which factors are important in determining the click-through rate of a banner advertisement?
   (c) Is click-through a good measure of the effectiveness of online advertising?

4. What is meant by co-branding? Explain the significance of co-branding.

5. What are 'meta-tags'? How important are they in ensuring a website is listed in a search engine?

6. Name three alternative tupes of e-mail marketing that can be used for promotion of a particular website page containing a special offer.

7. Briefly evaluate the strengths and weaknesses of affiliate marketing for a well-known retailer.

8. Which techniques can be used to promote a website in offline media?

## References

Abraham, M. (2008) The off-line impact of online ads, *Harvard Business Review*, April 2008, Vol. 86 Issue 4, 28–28.

Atlas (2004) The atlas rank report: how search engines rank impacts traffic [not dated]. Atlas DMT Research (www.atlassolutions.com).

Atlas (2007) Paying for navigation: the impact of navigational behavior on paid search, Research report by Nico Brooks, Director, Search Strategy, Published 2007 at (www.atlassolutions.com).

Balter, D. and Butman, J. (2005) *Grapevine: The New Art of Word-of-Mouth Marketing*. New York: Portfolio, 2005.

Berthon, P., Lane, N., Pitt, L. and Watson, R. (1998) The World Wide Web as an industrial marketing communications tool: models for the identification and assessment of opportunities, *Journal of Marketing Management*, 14, 691–704.

Bharat, K. and Mihaila, G. (1999) Hilltop: a search engine based on expert documents. Poster of the WWW9 Conference, Amsterdam, 15–19 May 2000. Available online from: http://scholar.google.co.uk/scholar?&q=intitle%3A%22Hilltop%3A+A+Search%33.

Brand New World (2004) Joint research by Anne Mollen (Cranfield Scchool of Management) and AOL Europe. www.brandnewworld.co.uk.

Brand New World (2004a), joint research by Anne Mollen (Cranfield School of Management) and AOL Europe: How the internet is changing consumers' attitudes to brands and what marketers and advertisers can do about it.

Brin, S. and Page, L (1998) The anatomy of a large-scale hypertextual web search engine, *Computer Networks and ISDN Systems*, Volume 30, Issue 1–7 (April 1998), 107–117, published at: http://www-db.stanford.edu/~backrub/google.html.

Cartellieri, C., Parsons, A., Rao, V. and Zeisser, M. (1997) The real impact of Internet advertising, *McKinsey Quarterly*, No. 3, 44–63.

Chaffey, D. (2006) *Total E-mail Marketing*, 2nd edn. Butterworth–Heinemann, Elsevier, Oxford.

Chaffey, D. and Smith, P.R. (2008) *E-marketing Excellence*, 3rd edn. Butterworth–Heinemann Elsevier, Oxford.

Chittenden, L. and Rettie, R. (2003) An evaluation of e-mail marketing and factors affecting response. *Journal of Targeting, Measurement and Analysis for Marketing*, March 2003; 11, 3, 203–217.

Comscore (2008) Why Google's surprising paid click data are less surprising. By Magid Abraham, 28 February 2008, Published at: http:www.comscore.com/blog/2008/02/why_googles_surprising_paid_click_data_are_less_surprising.html.

Dee, A., Bassett, B. and Hoskins, J. (2007) Word-of-mouth research: principles and applications. *Journal of Advertising Research*, Dec 2007, Vol. 47, Issue 4, 387–97.

Dichter, E. (1966) How word-of-mouth advertising works, *Harvard Business Review*, 44 (November–December), 147–66.

DMA (2006) UK National Email Benchmarking Report, Q4 2006. Published at www.dma.org.uk.

DMA (2007) UK National Client Email Marketing Survey., 2007. Published at www.dma.org.uk.

DMA (2008) UK National Client Benchmarking Report, 2008. Published at www.dma.org.uk.

EConsultancy (2007) Search Engine Optimisation Best Practice Guide. Author: Dave Chaffey. Available from www.e-consultancy.com.

EConsultancy (2008a) Managing Digital Channels Research Report. Author: Dave Chaffey. Available from www.e-consultancy.com.

EConsultancy (2008b) Paid Search Marketing, Best Practice Guide. Author: Dave Chaffey. Available from www.e-consultancy.com.

Euro RSCG Magnet (2005) Great thoughts turning information into knowledge. Online article. New York, NY, 20 June 2005. Available from: http://www.eurorscgpr.com/index/php?s=_thought.

Fitzgerald, M. (2006) 'The Name Game: tagging tools let users describe the world in their own terms as taxonomies become folksonomies', *CIO Magazine*, 1 April, 2006.

Forrester (2007) Consumer Trends Survey North America – leveraging user-generated content. January 2007. Brian Haven.

Godin, S. (2001) *Unleashing the Ideavirus*. Available online at: www.ideavirus.com.

Graham, J., Havlena, W. (2007) Finding the 'missing link': advertising's impact on word of mouth, web searches, and site visits. By: Graham, Jeffrey, Havlena, William, *Journal of Advertising Research*, Dec 2007, 47 (4), 427–35.

Grehan, M. (2004) Increase your PR by increasing your PR. Article in *E-marketing News* e-newsletter, November. Source: www.e-marketing-news.co.uk/november.html#pr.

Hitwise (2006) UK media impact report, Analyst Heather Hopkins. Available online at www.hitwise.com.

Hitwise (2007) Social networks can drive traffic – case study of ASOS and TopShop. Blog posting by analyst Heather Hopkins, 1 March 2007, http://weblogs.hitwise.com/heather-hopkins/2007/03/social_networks_can_drive_taf.html.

iMediaConnection (2003) Interview with ING Direct VP of Marketing, Jurie Pietersie, www.mediaconnection.com/content/1333.asp.

IPR (2003) Unlocking the potential of PR. A best practice report. *IPR and DTI*. Available from the Institute of PR (www.ipr.org.uk).

iProspect (2006) iProspect search engine user behavior study (April 2006). Available at www.iprospect.com.

Jenkins, F. (1995) *Public Relations Techniques*, 2nd edn. Butterworth–Heinemann, Oxford.

Johnston, K. (2008) Folksonomies, collaborative filtering and e-business: is Enterprise 2.0 one step forward and two steps back?, *European Journal of Knowledge Management*, Volume 5, Issue 4, 411–418.

JustGiving (2007) Justgiving Widget version 2.0. Blog posting, 24 July 2007. http://justgiving.typepad.com/charities/2007/07/justgiving-widg.html.

Kirby, J. (2003) Online viral marketing: next big thing or yesterday's fling? *New Media Knowledge*. Published online at www.newmediaknowledge.co.uk.

Kumar, V., Petersen, J. and Leone, R. (2007) How valuable is word of mouth? *Harvard Business Review*, October 2007, Vol. 85, Issue 10, 139–146.

MAD (2007) How online display advertising influences search volumes. Published: 4 June 2007 00:00. MAD Network (*Marketing Week*), Centaur Communications. http://technologyweekly.mad.co.uk/Main/InDepth/SearchEngineMarketing/Articles/f66d813eeab74e93ad8f252ae9c7f02a/How-online-display-advertising-influences-search-volumes.html.

Marsden, P. Samson, A. and Upton, N. (2005) Advocacy drives growth, *Brand Strategy*, Dec 2005/Jan 2006, Issue 198.

McGaffin, K. (2004) *Linking Matters: how to create an effective linking strategy to promote your website*. Published at www.linkingmatters.com.

MessgeLabs Intelligence (2008) *MessageLabs Intelligence Monthly* report, January 2008, published at http://messagelabs.co.uk/intelligence/aspx.

Microsoft (2007) Word of the web guidelines for advertisers: understanding trends and monetising social networks. Research report available from http://advertising.microsoft.com.

*New Media Age* (2005a) Perfect match. By Greg Brooks, *New Media Age*, 29 September. www.nma.co.uk.

*New Media Age* (2005b) Product placement. By Sean Hargrave, *New Media Age*, 12 May.

*New Media Age* (2005c) Unilever unifies global brand under new sites. By Claire Armitt, *New Media Age*, October.

*New Media Age* (2007) Unilever uses social networks to reach older teenage girls, Luan Goldie, Published: 26 July 2007.

*New Media Age* (2008) Measuring Buzz. Author: Sean Hargrave, Published: 17 January 2008.

Nielsen, J. (2007) Banner blindness: old and new findings, http://www.usit.com/alertbox/ banner-blindness.html. Jakob Nielsen's Alertbox, published online, 20 August 2007.

Novak, T. and Hoffman, D. (1997) New metrics for new media: towards the development of web measurement standards, *World Wide Web Journal*, 2(1), 213–46.

ORCI (1991) Word-of-mouth drives e-commerce, Survey summary, May. Opinion Research Corporation International, www.opinionresearch.com.

Parry, K. (1998) *Europe gets wired. A survey of Internet use in Great Britain, France and Germany, Research Report 1998*. KPMG Management Consulting, London.

Performance Research (2001) *Performance research study: 'Mastering sponsorship online'*. www.performanceresearch.com/web-based-sponsorships.htm.

Phelps, L., Lewis, R., Mobilio, L., Perry, D. and Niranjan, R. (2004) Viral marketing or electronic word-of-mouth advertising: examining consumer responses and motivations to pass along, *Journal of Advertising Research*, Dec 2004, Vol. 44, Issue 4, 333–348.

PRCA (2005) Website definition of PR. The Public Relationships Consultants Association, www.prca.org.uk.

Prussakov, E. (2007) *A practical guide to affiliate marketing. Quick reference for affiliate managers and merchants*. Self-published.

Ranchhod, A., Gurau, C. and Lace, J. (2002) Online messages: developing an integrated communications model for biotechnology companies, *Qualitative Market Research: An International Journal*, 5(1), 6–18.

Rettie, R., Grandcolas, U. and Deakins, B. (2005) Text message advertising: response rates and branding effects, *Journal of Targeting, Measurement & Analysis for Marketing*, Jun 2005, Vol. 13 Issue 4, 304–312.

Robinson, H., Wysocka, A. and Hand, C. (2007) Internet advertising effectiveness: the effect of design on click-through rates for banner ads, *International Journal of Advertising*, 26(4), 527–541.

Rogers, E. (1983) *Diffusion of Innovations*, 3rd edn. Free Press, New York.

Ryan, J. and Whiteman, N. (2000) Online advertising glossary: sponsorships. *ClickZ Media Selling channel*. 15 May.

Say, P. and Southwell, J. (2006) Case study: Beep-beep-beep-beep, that'll be the bank then — Driving sales through mobile marketing, *Journal of Direct, Data and Digital Marketing Practice*, Vol. 7, No. 3, 262–5.

SEC (2008) Annual report filing on form 10–K to US Securities and Exchange Commission (SEC) for Google Inc., 15 February 2008.

SEOMoz (2007) Google search engine ranking factors v2, published at www.seomoz.org/ articl/search-ranking-factors, 2 April 2007.

Statmarket (2003) Statmarket press release: search engine referrals nearly double worldwide, according to WebSiteStory, 12 March. Available online at www.statmarket.com.

Watts, D. and Dodds, S. (2007) Influentials, networks and public opinion formation. *Journal of Consumer Research* 34, 4 (2007): 441–58.

Zeff, R. and Aronson, B. (2001) *Advertising on the Internet*, 3rd edn. Wiley, New York.

## Further reading

Bala, I. and Davenport, T. (2008) Reverse engineering google's innovation machine. *Harvard Business Review*, April 2008, Vol. 86, Issue 4, 58–68.

Fill, C. (2005) *Marketing Communications – Contexts, Contents and Strategies*, 4th edn. Financial Times/Prentice Hall, Harlow. The entire book is recommended for its integration of theory, concepts and practice.

Novak, T. and Hoffman, D. (1997) New metrics for new media: towards the development of web measurement standards, *World Wide Web Journal*, 2(1), 213–46. This paper gives detailed, clear definitions of terms associated with measuring advertising effectiveness.

Zeff, R. and Aronson, B. (2001) *Advertising on the Internet*, 3rd edn. Wiley, New York. A comprehensive coverage of online banner advertising and measurement techniques and a more limited coverage of other techniques such as e-mail-based advertising.

## Web links

### General digital media channel-related e-mail newsletters and portals

- **ClickZ Experts** (www.clickz.com/experts). Has columns on e-mail marketing, e-mail marketing optimisation and e-mail marketing case studies.
- **Dave Chaffey Digital Marketing Strategy Guides** (www.davechaffey.com/guides). A summary of strategy and tools available for the full range of digital marketing channels.
- **E-consultancy.com** (www.e-consultancy.com). Best practice sections on different e-communications tools and newsletter features interviews with e-commerce practitioners.
- **Marketing Sherpa** (www.marketingsherpa.com). Articles and links on Internet marketing communications including e-mail and online advertising.

### E-mail-related advice sites

- **Direct Marketing Association UK** (www.dma.org.uk). Best practice guidelines and benchmarks of response rates.
- **E-mail Experience Council** (www.emailexperience.org). A US organisation with compilations of practical tips on e-mail marketing.
- **E-mail Marketing Tools** (www.davechaffey.com/email-tools). A compilation of tools for managing e-mail broadcast and deliverability.

### Affiliates and aggregator advice sites

- **A4UForum** (www.a4uforum.co.uk). Used by affliates to discuss approaches and compare programmes.
- **Affiliate marketing blog** (http://blog.affiliatetip.com). Practical tips and the latest developments from affiliate Shawn Collins.
- **Comparison Engines** (www.comparisonengines.com). A blog focusing on developments in shopping comparison intermediaries.

### Internet advertising research sites

- **Atlas Solutions Institute** (http://www.atlassolutions.com). Microsoft owned ad-serving and tracking provider with research about consumer behaviour and optimising ad effectiveness.
- **Doubleclick** (http://www.doubleclick.com/insight/research). Google owned ad-serving and tracking provider with research about consumer behaviour and optimising ad effectiveness.
- **EyeBlaster** (www.eyeblaster.com) is one of the main providers of rich media ad-serving technologies. Its galleries have good examples.
- **iMediaConnection** (www.imediaconnection.com). Media site reporting on best practice in online advertising.

- **US Internet Advertising Bureau** (www.iab.net). The widest range of studies about Internet advertising effectiveness. In UK: www.iabuk.net.

- **Tangozebra** (www.tangozebra.co.uk) is a UK-based provider of ad-serving technology which showcases many of the most recent ad campaigns by industry category.

- **World Advertising Research Centre** (www.warch.com). Mainly subscription service, but some free resources.

### Search-engine-related links

- **Google Webmaster tools** (www.google.com/webmasters) provides a useful set tools for sites verified by their owners including index inclusion, linking and ranking for different phrases indifferent locations.

- **Dave Chaffey's keyword suggestion tools** (www.davechaffey.com/seo-keyword-tools). The latest version of a range of free and paid tools for natural and paid search.

- **Reputation management** (www.davechaffey.com/online-reputation-management-tools).

- **Search Engine Watch** (www.searchenginewatch.com). A complete resource on SEO and PPC marketing. See Search Engine Land (www.searchengineland.com) for more commentary.

- **Webmasterworld** (www.webmasterworld.com). A forum, where search practitioners discuss best practice.

### Viral marketing/Word-of-mouth research sites

- **Mashable** (www.mashable.com). Site focusing on developments and statistics related to social networks.

- **Viral and Buzz Marketing Network** (www.vbma.net). A European-oriented community of academics and professionals for discussion of the applications of connected marketing

- **Word-of-mouth marketing association** (www.womma.org). A US-oriented community of word-of-mouth marketing specialists.

- **O'Reilly Radar** (http://radar.oreilly.com). Commentary on the development of Web 2.0 approaches technologies from publishers O'Reilly, whose founder Tim O'Reilly coined the term Web 2.0.

- **Widget blog** (http://blog.snipperoo.com/). Blog focusing on developments in widgets and gadgets.

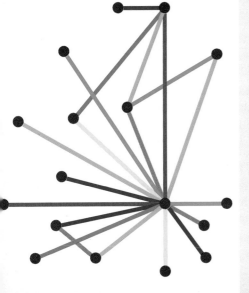

# 10

# Evaluation and improvement of digital channel performance

## Learning objectives

After reading this chapter, the reader should be able to:

● Identify the tasks necessary when managing an online presence
● Understand terms used to measure and improve site effectiveness
● Develop an appropriate process to collect measures for Internet marketing effectiveness

## Questions for marketers

Key questions for marketing managers related to this chapter are:

● How much resource do I need to put into maintaining and monitoring the site?
● What processes should I use to maintain the website?
● How do I measure the effectiveness of web marketing?

## Links to other chapters

This chapter should be read in conjunction with these chapters:

● Chapter 4 describes the development of an Internet marketing strategy. The aim of measurement is to quantify whether the objectives of this strategy have been achieved
● Chapter 7 describes how to set up a website, and should be read before this chapter to introduce the reader to the concepts of website development
● Chapter 8 describes methods of promoting a website. It should be read before this chapter since one aspect of measuring the effectiveness of Internet marketing is aimed at assessing the different promotional methods

## Introduction

Companies that have a successful approach to online marketing often seem to share a common characteristic. They attach great importance and devote resources to monitoring the success of their online marketing putting in place the processes to continuously improve the performance of their digital channels. This culture of measurement is visible in the UK bank Alliance and Leicester, which in 2004 reported that they spent over 20% of their £80 million marketing communications budget on online marketing. Stephen Leonard, head of e-commerce, described their process as 'Test, Learn, Refine' (*Revolution*, 2004). Graeme Findlay, senior manager, customer acquision of e-commerce at A&L explains further:

> *Our online approach is integrated with our offline brand and creative strategy, with a focus on direct, straightforward presentation of strong value-led messages. Everything we do online, including creative, is driven by an extensive and dynamic testing process.*

Seth Romanow, Director of Customer Knowledge at Hewlett-Packard, speaking at the 2004 E-metrics summit, described their process as 'Measure, Report, Analyse, Optimise'. Amazon refers to their approach as 'the culture of metrics' (see Case study 10). Jim Sterne, who convenes an annual event devoted to improving online performance (www.emetrics.org), has summarised his view on the required approach in his book *Web Metrics* (Sterne, 2002) as 'TIMITI', which stands for Try It! Measure It! Tweak It! – i.e. online content should be reviewed and improved continuously rather than as a periodic or ad-hoc process. The importance of defining an appropriate approach to measurement and improvement is such that the term '**web analytics**' has developed to describe this key Internet marketing activity. A web analytics association (www.waa.org) has been developed by vendors, consultants and researchers in this area to manage best practice. Eric Petersen, an analyst specialising in web analytics, defines it as follows (Peterson, 2004):

**Web analytics**

Techniques used to assess and improve the contribution of e-marketing to a business, including reviewing traffic volume, referrals, clickstreams, online reach data, customer satisfaction surveys, leads and sales.

> *Web analytics is the assessment of a variety of data, including web traffic, web-based transactions, web server performance, usability studies, user submitted information [i.e. surveys] and related sources to help create a generalised understanding of the visitor experience online.*

You can see that – in addition to what are commonly referred to as 'site statistics' about web traffic – sales transactions, usability and researching customers' views through surveys are also included. We believe, though, that the definition can be improved further, it suggests analysis for the sake of it, whereas the business purpose of analytics should be emphasised. The definition could also refer to comparison of site visitor volumes and demographics relative to competitors using panels and ISP collected data.

A more recent definition from the Web Analytics Association (WAA, www.web analyticsassociation.org) in 2005 is:

> *web analytics is the objective tracking, collection, measurement, reporting and analysis of quantitative Internet data to optimise websites and web marketing initiatives.*

To succeed in a measured approach to improving results from Internet marketing we suggest that there are four main organisational prerequisites, which are broken down as shown in Figure 10.1 into the quality of the web analytics processes including defining the right improvement measures and purchasing the right tools and the management processes – such as putting in place a process where staff review results and then modify their marketing activities accordingly. In this chapter, we will review both approaches.

This chapter is in two parts – the first part is about performance management, where we review the approach to improving performance through assessing appropriate measures, tools and the right process to apply them as suggested by Figure 10.1. In the second part, we

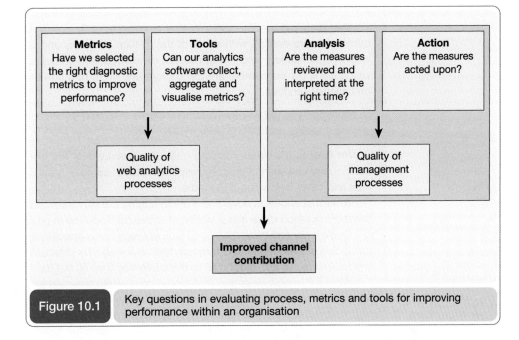

**Figure 10.1** Key questions in evaluating process, metrics and tools for improving performance within an organisation

review some of the issues involved with maintaining an online presence, looking at the tools and process for keeping a website up-to-date.

## Justin Basini, Head of Brand Marketing, Capital One

### Overview and main concepts covered

Capital One's European head of brand marketing Justin Basini talks about the challenges of resourcing and measuring multichannel campaigns, as well as ways in which the web has affected how consumers research and buy financial services.

### The interview

*Q*: **Can you start off with an overview of your web marketing strategy?**

*Justin Basini*: We are moving much more to a multichannel approach. We see the web as an integrated part of the marketing mix and an increasingly important part of it. Within that context, there are two things we see the web being good for.

The first thing is in building our brand and creating richer, web-based experiences for consumers so they can reassess our brand and start to form an opinion of Capital One.

One example is a campaign we ran last year, for wemakechangingeasy.com, which had a microsite with lots of hosted content on it with podcasts and so on. We've also just started a campaign for our new World Mastercard with a microsite that will host a lot of content.

Those efforts are to ensure we present a branded face that's over and above traffic generation to our own website.

The second aspect is traffic generation and response. Historically, we've had a lot of success in our businesses driving response through the Internet, and helping people to select the right product on our website.

That breaks down into three areas – our own advertising efforts, through which we form tight partnerships with some of the affiliate networks and larger players; search engine optimisation; and being present on comparison sites like Moneysupermarket, which we know consumers are using more and more to guide their product selection on financial services.

**Q: Have you gained any interesting insights into how your customers react with different online and offline channels?**

*Justin Basini*: It's been changing quite significantly over the last few years. Much of the industry has seen depressed response rates in some of the offline media, like direct mail and other below-the-line media.

What that shows is consumers are changing the way they consume marketing and are moving much more into a phase of active participation in product choice.

That's a general trend, but if you look at credit cards specifically, the market for new cardholders was dominated three or four years ago by direct mail applications. The model was 'send out direct mail to the customer, they fill out the form and get a card'.

What we're now seeing is that model completely reversed into an inbound model, where the customer will go on the web, read newspapers and visit consumer groups and comparison sites to inform themselves about products. We now acquire vastly more applications through the Internet than we do through direct mail.

The consumer is becoming more active and is demanding a greater level of knowledge than before, and the Internet is facilitating that much more than before.

The way you need to respond to that is to build a web experience that integrates through the channels. Campaign integration is something we are pushing very hard – creating a full suite of services that takes the consumer from awareness through to application as seamlessly as possible.

**Q: How has your move towards campaign integration affected how online marketing sits within your organisational structure and how it's resourced?**

*Justin Basini*: We're moving much more to a model of campaign execution, where we try to understand what the consumer wants from each campaign and build teams and agency partners around that.

I believe that at some level, the future of marketing will be like that – you structure things for individual campaigns in order to be able to flex to the different consumer demands, rather than staffing rigidly by channel, which creates channel-based marketing programmes. If you have 30 people doing direct mail, guess what? You get a lot of direct mail.

If you base your resourcing more on campaigns and what the consumer wants you to do, hopefully you get the right mix.

**Q: What are the main challenges that that model poses? What do you need to watch out for?**

*Justin Basini*: You have to be flexible, and there is one main thing to watch out for – you need to make sure you retain your channel-specific knowledge.

You don't want the people in the company that are really knowledgeable about TV advertising – or Internet or direct mail – to be subsumed by a campaign view. You need to combine that knowledge with a consumer view, and that's when you hit the sweet-spot.

One key area to be flexible in is making sure that your resourcing is as responsive to the consumer, from a campaign perspective, as possible.

That means you need to give yourself time and forward-plan a lot more. We've found we have to pre-think campaigns a lot more than we did in the past. You need to create this rolling cycle of campaign delivery.

**Q: What KPIs are you using for your different marketing programmes?**

*Justin Basini*: To track our brand, we are using what I call a triangulation approach. The reason I moved us to that is in my experience, companies I have worked for have been too focused on one study.

With the classic Millward Brown tracker, where you go to the market once a month – and I'm not criticising it at all, classic quantitative brand track is superb – you need to combine it with two other things.

You need to combine in it with a longer-term view – a 12-to-24-month view – of where things are going in the market, and intense qualitative research to decode the numbers you are seeing. We use a range of KPIs built off that approach to see how our brand is performing in the market.

And from the response side, we use a range of KPIs – cost-to-acquire, cost-per-application and looking at the efficiencies of each of the marketing channels – to make sure we are optimising all the time.

**Q: You touched on this previously, but there is obviously a lot of discussion happening on blogs, forums and other sites about credit card companies, products, charges and so on. Are you engaging in any reputation monitoring or online PR yet?**

*Justin Basini*: We are starting to think more about that space, so we are aware of it. We don't have a formal monitoring process currently in place, but we are aware of what is going on.

In the future, as noise grows in that area and we can get more interesting feedback from consumers about our products, I think that will be a rich area for insight.

*Source*: http://www.EConsultancy.com/news-blog/newsletter/3440/q-amp-a-with-capital-one-s-head-of-brand-marketing-justin-basini.html

## Performance management for digital channels

To improve results for any aspect of any business, performance management is vital. As Bob Napier, Chief Information Office, Hewlett-Packard was reported to have said back in the 1960s,

> *You can't manage what you can't measure.*

The processes and systems intended to monitor and improve the performance of an organisation, and specific management activities such as Internet marketing are widely known as 'performance management systems' and are based on the study of performance measurement systems.

Many organisations now have an established online presence, but there are many unanswered questions about the process by which the marketing performance of this presence is evaluated and how it is modified with a view to improving its performance. Adams *et al.* (2000), for example, asked managers to name their priorities for improvements to e-business performance measurement systems. Results differed for different types of organisation, reflecting the stage of evolution in their measurement. For bricks-and-mortar companies, developing or introducing a more comprehensive measurement system and enhancing

**Performance management system**
A process used to evaluate and improve the efficiency and effectiveness of an organisation and its processes.

**Performance measurement system**
The process by which metrics are defined, collected, disseminated and actioned.

analysis capabilities to establish what really drives business performance was most important. For clicks-and-mortar, integrating new systems with legacy systems and benchmarking against best practice were most important. Finally, dot-coms, as start-ups, were concerned with improving clickstream analysis and customer tracking and profiling, and improving the entire company's performance measurement system.

Although we have stated that measurement is an important part of maintaining a website, it is worth noting that the reality is that measurement is often neglected when a website is first created. Measurement is often highlighted as an issue once the first version of a site has been 'up and running' for a few months, and employees start to ask questions such as 'How many customers are visiting our site, how many sales are we achieving as a result of our site and how can we improve the site to achieve a return on investment?' The consequence of this is that performance measurement is something that is often built into an online presence retrospectively. Of course, it is preferable if measurement is built into site management from the start since then a more accurate approach can be developed, and it is more readily possible to apply a technique known as 'design for analysis' (DFA). Here, the site is designed so companies can better understand the types of audience and their decision points. For example, for Dell (www.dell.com), the primary navigation on the home page is by business type. This is a simple example of DFA since it enables Dell to estimate the proportion of different audiences to their site and, at the same time, connect them with relevant content.

Other examples of DFA include:

- Breaking up a long page or form into different parts, so you can see which parts people are interested in.
- A URL policy (see Chapter 8) used to recommend entry pages for printed material.
- Group content by audience type or buying decision and setting up content groups of related content within web analytics systems.
- Measure attrition at different points in a customer journey, e.g. exit points on a five-page buying cycle.
- A single exit page to linked sites.

In this section, we will review approaches to performance management by examining three key elements of an Internet marketing measurement system. These are, first, the *process* for improvement, secondly, the measurement framework which specifies groups of relevant Internet marketing metrics and, finally, an assessment of the suitability of tools and techniques for collecting, analysing, disseminating and actioning results. We will review three stages of creating and implementing a performance management system.

## Stage 1: Creating a performance management system

The essence of *performance management* is suggested by the definition for performance *measurement* used by Andy Neely and co-workers of Cranfield School of Management's Centre for Business Performance. They define performance measurement as (Neely *et al.*, 2002):

> *the process of quantifying the efficiency and effectiveness of past actions through acquisition, collation, sorting, analysis, interpretation and dissemination of appropriate data.*

Performance management extends this definition to the process of analysis and actioning change in order to drive business performance and returns. Online marketers can apply many of the approaches of business performance management to Internet marketing. As you can see from the definition, performance is measured primarily through information on process effectiveness and efficiency as introduced in Chapter 4 in the section on objective setting, where we noted that it is important to include both effectiveness and efficiency measures.

---

**Clickstream analysis**
Reviewing the online behaviour of site visitors based on the sequence of pages that they visit, the navigation and promotion they respond to, the ultimate outcomes and where they leave the site.

**Design for analysis**
The required measures from a site are considered during design to better understand the audience of a site and their decision points.

**Internet marketing metrics**
Measures that indicate the effectiveness of Internet marketing activities in meeting customer, business and marketing objectives.

**Effectiveness**
Meeting process objectives, delivering the required outputs and outcomes. 'Doing the right thing.'

**Efficiency**
Minimising resources or time needed to complete a process. 'Doing the thing right.'

The need for a structured performance management process is clear if we examine the repercussions if an organisation does not have one. These include: poor linkage of measures with strategic objectives or even absence of objectives; key data not collected; data inaccuracies; data not disseminated or analysed; or no corrective action. Many of the barriers to improvement of measurement systems reported by respondents in Adams *et al.* (2000) also indicate the lack of an effective process. The barriers can be grouped as follows:

- *senior management myopia* – performance measurement not seen as a priority, not understood or targeted at the wrong targets – reducing costs rather than improving performance;
- unclear responsibilities for delivering and improving the measurement system;
- *resourcing issues* – lack of time (perhaps suggesting lack of staff motivation), the necessary technology and integrated systems;
- *data problems* – data overload or of poor quality, limited data for benchmarking.

These barriers are reinforced by the survey by Cutler and Sterne (2000) which describes the main obstacles to metrics development as lack of qualified personnel (31%), data overload (19%) and lack of technical resources (software) (19%).

To avoid these pitfalls, a co-ordinated, structured measurement process such as that shown in Figure 10.2 is required. Figure 10.2 indicates four key stages in a measurement process. These were defined as key aspects of annual plan control by Kotler (1997). Stage 1 is a goal-setting stage where the aims of the measurement system are defined – this will usually take the strategic Internet marketing objectives as an input to the measurement system. The aim of the measurement system will be to assess whether these goals are achieved and specify corrective marketing actions to reduce variance between target and actual key performance indicators. Stage 2, performance measurement, involves collecting data to determine the different metrics that are part of a measurement framework as discussed in the next section. Stage 3, performance diagnosis, is the analysis of results to understand the reasons for variance from objectives (the 'performance gap' of Friedman and Furey, 1999) and selection of marketing solutions to reduce variance. The purpose of stage 4, corrective action, according to Wisner and Fawcett (1991), is:

> to identify competitive position, locate problem areas, assist the firm in updating strategic objectives and making tactical decisions to achieve these objectives and supply feedback after the decisions are implemented.

In an Internet marketing context, corrective action is the implementation of these solutions as updates to website content, design and associated marketing communications. At this

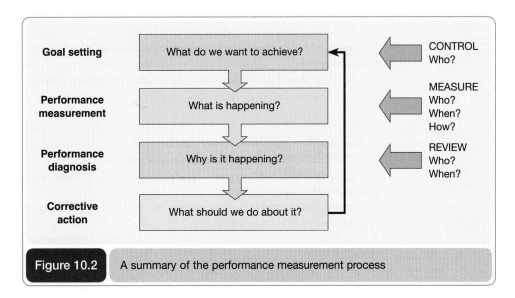

**Figure 10.2**    A summary of the performance measurement process

stage the continuous cycle repeats, possibly with modified goals. Bourne *et al.* (2000) and Plant (2000) suggest that in addition to reviewing objectives, the suitability of the metrics should also be reviewed and revised.

## Stage 2: Defining the performance metrics framework

Measurement for assessing the effectiveness of Internet marketing can be thought of as answering these questions:

1 Are corporate objectives identified in the Internet marketing strategy being met?
2 Are marketing objectives defined in the Internet marketing strategy and plan achieved?
3 Are marketing communications objectives identified in the Internet marketing plan achieved?
4 How efficient are the different promotional techniques used to attract visitors to a site?

These measures can also be related to the different levels of marketing control specified by Kotler (1997). These include strategic control (question 1), profitability control (question 1), annual-plan control (question 2) and efficiency control (question 3).

Efficiency measures are more concerned with minimising the costs of online marketing while maximising the returns for different areas of focus such as acquiring visitors to a website, converting visitors to outcome or achieving repeat business.

Chaffey (2000) suggests that organisations define a measurement framework or create a management dashboard which defines groupings of specific metrics used to assess Internet marketing performance. He suggests that suitable measurement frameworks will fulfil these criteria:

- Include both macro-level effectiveness metrics which assess whether strategic goals are achieved and indicate to what extent e-marketing contributes to the business (revenue contribution and return on investment). This criterion covers the different levels of marketing control specified by Kotler (1997), including strategic control, profitability control and annual-plan control.
- Include micro-level metrics which assess the efficiency of e-marketing tactics and implementation. Wisner and Fawcett (1991) note that organisations typically use a hierarchy of measures and they should check that the lower-level measures support the macro-level strategic objectives. Such measures are often referred to as '*performance drivers*', since achieving targets for these measures will assist in achieving strategic objectives. E-marketing performance drivers help optimise e-marketing by attracting more site visitors and increasing conversion to desired marketing outcomes. These achieve the marketing efficiency control specified by Kotler (1997). The research by Agrawal *et al.* (2001), who assessed companies on metrics defined in three categories of attraction, conversion and retention as part of an e-performance scorecard, uses a combination of macro- and micro-level metrics.
- Assess the impact of the e-marketing on the satisfaction, loyalty and contribution of key stakeholders (customers, investors, employees and partners) as suggested by Adams *et al.* (2000).
- The framework must be flexible enough to be applied to different forms of online presence, whether business-to-consumer, business-to-business, not-for-profit or transactional e-tail, CRM-oriented or brand-building. Much discussion of e-marketing measurement is limited to a transactional e-tail presence. Adams *et al.* (2000) note that a 'one-size-fits-all' framework is not desirable.
- Enable comparison of performance of different e-channels with other channels as suggested by Friedman and Furey (1999).
- The framework can be used to assess e-marketing performance against competitors' or out-of-sector best practice.

When identifying metrics it is common practice to apply the widely used SMART mnemonic and it is also useful to consider three levels – business measures, marketing measures and specific Internet marketing measures (see the objective setting section in Chapter 4).

There is a framework of measures, shown in Figure 10.3, which can be applied to a range of different companies. Metrics for the categories are generated as objectives from Internet marketing planning which then need to be monitored to assess the success of strategy and its implementation. As explained in Chapter 4, objectives can be devised in a top-down fashion, starting with strategic objectives for business contribution and marketing outcomes leading to tactical objectives for customer satisfaction, behaviour and site promotion. An alternative perspective is bottom-up – using granular conversion models such as those reviewed in Chapters 4 and 8, goals set for site promotion and on-site customer behaviour can be used to set realistic goals for marketing outcomes and business contribution. In Chapter 4, we reviewed two alternative frameworks (see Tables 4.6 and 4.9) which can also be used for creating a performance dashboard.

## Channel promotion

**Channel promotion**
Measures that assess why customers visit a site – which adverts they have seen, which sites they have been referred from.

**Referrer**
The site that a visitor previously visited before following a link.

These measures consider where the website users originate – online or offline, and what are the sites or offline media that prompted their visit. Log file analysis can be used to assess which intermediary sites customers are referred from and which keywords they typed into search engines when trying to locate product information. Promotion is successful if traffic is generated that meets objectives of volume and quality as explained in Chapter 8. Quality will be determined by whether visitors are in the target market and have a propensity for the service offered (through reviewing conversion and bounce rates for different referrers). Differences in costs of acquiring customers via different digital media channels also need to be assessed. In Chapter 8 we explore the issue of allocating sales to the appropriate digital media in section 2 'Selecting the right mix of digital media communications tools' of Step 5 (see page **480**). 'Budgeting and selecting the digital media mix'.

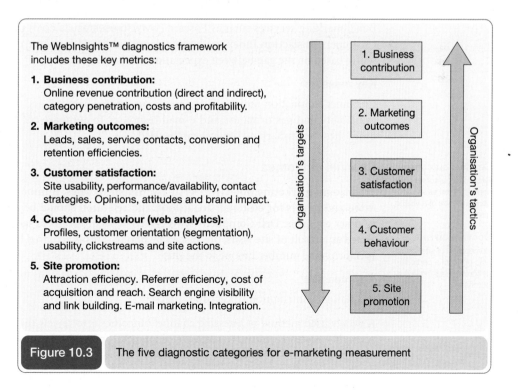

The WebInsights™ diagnostics framework includes these key metrics:

1. **Business contribution:**
   Online revenue contribution (direct and indirect), category penetration, costs and profitability.

2. **Marketing outcomes:**
   Leads, sales, service contacts, conversion and retention efficiencies.

3. **Customer satisfaction:**
   Site usability, performance/availability, contact strategies. Opinions, attitudes and brand impact.

4. **Customer behaviour (web analytics):**
   Profiles, customer orientation (segmentation), usability, clickstreams and site actions.

5. **Site promotion:**
   Attraction efficiency. Referrer efficiency, cost of acquisition and reach. Search engine visibility and link building. E-mail marketing. Integration.

Organisation's targets

Organisation's tactics

1. Business contribution
2. Marketing outcomes
3. Customer satisfaction
4. Customer behaviour
5. Site promotion

**Figure 10.3**  The five diagnostic categories for e-marketing measurement

### Key measure

Referral mix. For each referral source such as paid search or display ads it should be possible to calculate:

- percentage of all referrals or sales (and influence in achieving sale last click or assist);
- cost-per-acquisition (CPA) or cost-per-sale (CPS);
- contribution to sales or other outcomes.

**Channel buyer behaviour**

Describes which content is visited and the time and duration.

## Channel buyer behaviour

Once customers have been attracted to the site we can monitor content accessed, when they visit and how long they stay, and whether this interaction with content leads to satisfactory marketing outcomes such as new leads or sales. If visitors are incentivised to register on-site it is possible to build up profiles of behaviour for different segments. Segments can also be developed according to their source and content accessed. It is also important to recognise return visitors for whom cookies or login are used. In Chapter 6 we saw how hurdle rates can be used to assess activity levels for return visits, e.g. 30% of customers return to use the online service with 90 days.

### Key ratios

- Bounce rates for different pages, i.e. proportion of single page visits.
- Home page views/all page views e.g. 20% = (2000/10,000).
- Stickiness: page views/visitor sessions e.g. 2 = 10,000/5000.
- Repeats: visitor sessions/visitors e.g. 20% = 1000/5000

**Stickiness**

An indication of how long a visitor stays on-site.

**Channel satisfaction**

Evaluation of the customer's opinion of the service quality on the site and supporting services such as e-mail.

## Channel satisfaction

Customer satisfaction with the online experience is vital in achieving the desired channel outcomes, although it is difficult to set specific objectives. Online methods such as online questionnaires, focus groups and interviews can be used to assess customers' opinions of the website content and customer service and how it has affected overall perception of brand. Benchmarking services such as Foresee (www.foreseeresults.com) based on the American Customer Satisfaction Index methodology are published for some industries. These assess scores based on the gap between expectations and actual service.

### Key measure

Customer satisfaction indices. These are discussed in Chapter 7 and include ease of use, site availability and performance, and e-mail response. To compare customer satisfaction with other sites, benchmarking services can be used.

**Channel outcomes**

Record of customer actions taken as a consequence of a visit to a site.

**Conversion rate**

Percentage of site visitors who perform a particular action such as making a purchase.

## Channel outcomes

Traditional marketing objectives such as number of sales, number of leads, conversion rates and targets for customer acquisition and retention should be set and then compared to other channels. Dell Computer (www.dell.com) records on-site sales and also orders generated as a result of site visits, but placed by phone. This is achieved by monitoring calls to a specific phone number unique to the site.

### Key measure

- Channel contribution (direct and indirect).

A widely used method of assessing channel outcomes is to review the conversion rate, which gives an indication of the percentage of site visitors who take a particular outcome. For example:

- Conversion rate, visitors to purchase = 2% (10,000 visitors, of which 200 make purchases).
- Conversion rate, visitors to registration = 5% (10,000 visitors, of which 500 register).

**Attrition rate**
Percentage of site visitors lost at each stage in making a purchase.

A related concept is the **attrition rate** which describes how many visitors are lost at each step of a conversion funnel from landing page to checkout. Figure 10.4 shows that for a set time period, only a proportion of site visitors will make their way to product information, a small proportion will add an item to a basket and a smaller proportion still will actually make the purchase. A key feature of e-commerce sites is that there is a high attrition rate between a customer adding an item to a basket and subsequently making a purchase. It is surmised that this is due to fears about credit card security, and that customers are merely experimenting.

**Channel profitability**
The profitability of the website, taking into account revenue and cost and discounted cash flow.

## Channel profitability

A contribution to business profitability is always the ultimate aim of e-commerce. To assess this, leading companies set an Internet contribution target of achieving a certain proportion of sales via the channel. When easyJet (www.easyjet.com) launched its e-commerce facility in 1998, it set an Internet contribution target of 30% by 2000. They put the resources and communications plan in place to achieve this and their target was reached in 1999. Assessing contribution is more difficult for a company that cannot sell products online, but the role of the Internet in influencing purchase should be assessed. Discounted cash flow techniques are used to assess the rate of return over time.

### Multichannel evaluation

The frameworks we have presented in this chapter are explained in the context of an individual channel, but with the contribution of the channel highlighted as percentage sales or profitability. But as Wilson (2008) has pointed out, there is a need to evaluate how different channels support each other. Wilson says:

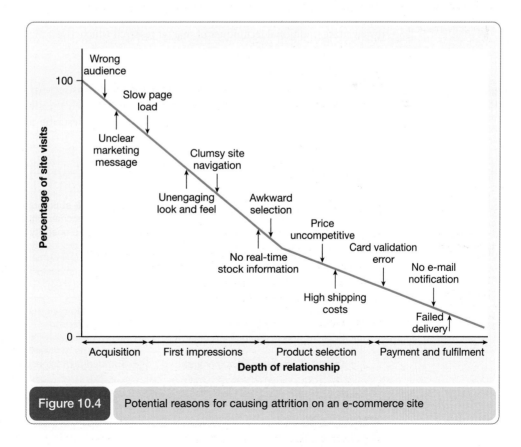

| Figure 10.4 | Potential reasons for causing attrition on an e-commerce site |

*Traditional metrics have been aligned to channels, measuring resource input or leads in at one end and the value of sales generated by the channel at the other end. For companies that have been operating in a single channel environment, this might have been relatively efficient – but it no longer works when the organisation diversifies to a multichannel approach.*

He suggests the most important aspect of multichannel measurement is to measure 'channel cross-over effects'. This involves asking, for example: 'How can the impact of a paid search campaign be measured if it is as likely to generate traffic to a store, salesforce or call centre as to a website?' and 'How can the impact of a direct mail campaign be tracked if it generates website traffic as well as direct responses?'

An example of a balanced scorecard style dashboard developed to assess and compare channel performance for a retailer is presented in Figure 10.5.

## Stage 3: Tools and techniques for collecting metrics and summarising results

Organisations need to select the most appropriate tools for collecting and reporting metrics which meet requirements such as reporting of marketing performance, accuracy, analysis and visualisation tools, integration with other marketing information systems (import, export and integration using XML standards), ease of use, configuration (e.g. creation of custom dashboards and e-mail alerts), support quality, cost of purchase, configuration and ongoing support.

Techniques to collect metrics include the collection of site-visitor activity data such as that stored in web analytics systems and in site log files; the collection of metrics about outcomes such as online sales or e-mail enquiries and traditional marketing research techniques such as questionnaires and focus groups which collect information on the customer's experience on the website. We start by describing methods for collecting site-visitor activity data and then review more traditional techniques of market research which assess the customer experience.

### Collecting site-visitor activity data

**Site-visitor activity data**

Information on content and services accessed by e-commerce site visitors.

**Site-visitor activity data** captured in web analytics systems records the number of visitors on the site and the paths or clickstreams they take through the site as they visit different content. There are a wide variety of technical terms to describe this activity data which Internet marketers need to be conversant with.

---

**Results (6)**
- Revenue
- Multichannel contribution
- Degree multichannel sells up
- Costs per channel
- Degree of sweating assets
- Multichannel infrastructure costs

**Customers & stakeholders (5)**
- Overall customer satisfaction
- Customer propensity to defect
- Customer propensity to purchase
- Customer percepton of added value
- Integration of customer experience

**Core processes (3)**
- Productive multichannel usage
- Price (relative to competitors/other channels)
- Quality of integrated customer view

**People and knowledge (4)**
- Staff satisfaction
- Appropriate behaviours 'Living the brand'
- Willingness to diversify/extend the brand
- Knowledge of target customer

**Figure 10.5**  Multichannel performance scorecard example for a retailer
*Source*: Wilson (2008)

In the early days of Internet marketing, in the mid-1990s, this information was typically collected using log files. The server-based log file is added to every time a user downloads a piece of information (a **hit**) and is analysed using a **log file analyser** as illustrated by Figure 3.8. Examples of transactions within a log file are:

*www.davechaffey.com – [05/Oct/2006:00:00:49 -000] 'GET /index.html HTTP/1.0' 200 33362*

*www.davechaffey.com – [05/Oct/2006:00:00:49 -000] 'GET /logo.gif HTTP/1.0' 200 54342*

Despite their wide use in the media, hits are not a useful measure of website effectiveness since if a page consists of 10 graphics, plus text, this is recorded as 11 hits. **Page impressions** or **page views** and **unique visitors** are better measures of site activity. Auditing companies such as ABC electronic (www.abce.org.uk), which audit sites for the purpose of proving the number of visitors to a site to advertisers, use unique visitors and page impression as the main measures.

An example of visitor volume to a website using different measures based on real, representative data for one month is presented in Figure 10.6. You can see how hits are much higher than page views and unique visitors and are quite misleading in terms of the 'opportunities to see' a message. We can also learn from the ratio between some of these measures – the figure indicates:

- *Pages per visit (PPV)* – the average number of pages viewed per visitor to a site (this is indicative of engagement with a site since the longer a visitor stays on a 'sticky site', the higher this value will be). PPV is a more accurate indication of stickiness than duration on a site in minutes since this figure is skewed upwards by visitors who arrive on a site and are inactive before their session times out at 30 minutes.
- *Visits per (unique) visitor (VPV)* – this suggests the frequency of site visits. Readers will realise that this value is dependent on the period that data are collected over. These data are reported for a month during which time one would not expect many returning visitors. So it is often more relevant to present these data across a quarter or a year.

Other information giving detailed knowledge of customer behaviour that can be reported by any web analytics package include:

- top pages;
- entry and exit pages;
- path or clickstream analysis showing the sequence of pages viewed;
- country of visitor origin (actually dependent on the location of their ISP);
- browser and operating system used;
- referring URL and domain (where the visitor came from).

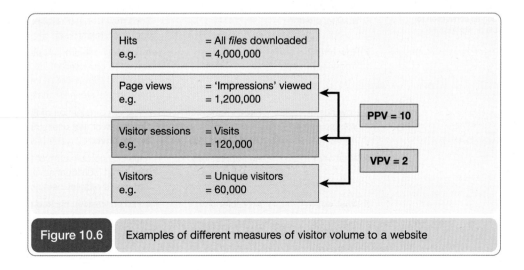

**Figure 10.6**     Examples of different measures of visitor volume to a website

### Comparing apples to oranges?

With hundreds of different web analytics tools being used on different sites, it is important that there are standards for measuring visitor volumes. In particular, there are different techniques for measuring unique visitors which can be measured through IP addresses, but this is more accurate if it is combined with cookies and browser types. International standards bodies such as the Web Analytics Association (www.webanalyticsassociation.org) and UK organisations such as ABCelectronic (www.abce.org.uk) and JICWEB (www.jicwebs.org) have worked to standardise the meaning and data collection methods for different measures. See Table 10.1 below, or visit these sites for the latest precise definition of the terms in this section. Media buyers are particularly interested in accurate audited figures of media sites and organisations such as ABCelectronic are important for this.

### AB and multivariate testing

Often site owners and marketers reviewing the effectiveness of a site will disagree and the only method to be certain of the best-performing design or creative alternatives is through designing and running experiments to evaluate the best to use. Matt Round, then Director of Personalisation at Amazon, speaking at the E-metrics summit in 2004, said the Amazon philosophy, described further in Case study 10.2 is

*Data trumps intuition.*

AB testing and multivariate testing are two measurement techniques that can be used to review design effectiveness to improve results.

### AB testing

**AB testing**

A/B or AB testing refers to testing two different versions of a page or a page element such as a heading, image or button for effectiveness. The alternatives are served alternately with the visitors to the page randomly split between the two pages. Changes in visitor behaviour can then be compared using different metrics such as click-through rate on page elements like buttons or images, or macro-conversion rates, such as conversion to sale or sign-up.

In its simplest form, A/B or **AB testing** refers to testing two different versions of a page or a page element such as a heading, image or button. Some members of the site are served alternately, with the visitors to the page randomly split between the two pages. Hence it is sometimes called 'live split testing'. The goal is to increase page or site effectiveness against key performance indicators including click-through rate, conversion rates and revenue per visit.

| Table 10.1 | Terminology for key website volume measures | |
|---|---|---|
| **Measure** | **Measure** | **Definition** |
| 1 How many? 'audience reach' | Unique users | A unique and valid identifier [for a site visitor]. Sites may use (i) IP + User – Agent, (ii) cookie and/or (iii) registration ID |
| 2 How often? 'frequency metric' | Visit | A series of one or more page impressions, served to one user, which ends when there is a gap of 30 minutes or more between successive page impressions for that user |
| 3 How busy? 'volume metric' | Page impression | A file, or combination of files, sent to a valid user as a result of that user's request being received by the server |
| 4 What see? | Ad impressions | A file or a combination of files sent to a valid user as an individual advertisement as a result of that user's request being received by the server |
| 5 What do? | Ad clicks | An ad impression clicked on by a valid user |

Source: ABCe (www.abce.org.uk)

**Control page**
The page against which subsequent optimisation will be assessed. Typically a current landing page. When a new page performs better than the existing control page, it becomes the control page in subsequent testing. Also known as 'champion-challenger'

When completing AB testing it is important to identify a realistic baseline or **control page** (or audience sample) to compare against. This will typically be an existing landing page. Two new alternatives can be compared to previous control which is known as an ABC test. Different variables are then applied as in Table 10.2.

| Table 10.2 | AB test example | |
|---|---|---|
| **Test** | **A (Control)** | **B (Test page)** |
| Test 1 | Original page | New headline, existing button, existing body copy |
| Test 2 | Original page | Existing headline, new button, existing body copy |
| Test 3 | Original page | Existing headline, existing button, new body copy |

An example of the power of AB testing is an experiment Skype performed on their main topbar navigation, where they found that changing the main menu options 'Call Phones' to 'Skype Credit' and 'Shop' to 'Accessories' gave an increase of 18.75% revenue per visit (Skype were speaking at the 2007 E-metrics summit). That's significant when you have hundreds of millions of visitors! It also shows the importance of being direct with navigation and simply describing the offer available rather than the activity.

### Multivariate testing

Multivariate testing is a more sophisticated form of AB testing which enables simultaneous testing of pages for different combinations of page elements that are being tested. This enables selection of the most effective combination of design elements to achieve the desired goal.

An example is shown of a multivariate test is shown in Mini case study 10.1.

| Mini Case Study 10.1 | Multivariate testing at National Express Group increases conversion rates |
|---|---|

The National Express Group is the leading provider of travel solutions in the UK. Around one billion journeys a year are made worldwide on National Express Group's bus, train, light rail and express coach and airport operations. A significant proportion of ticket bookings are made online through the company's website at www.nationalexpress.com.

The company uses multivariate testing provider Maxymiser to run an experiment to improve conversion rate of a fare-selection page which was the penultimate step in booking (Figure 10.7). The analysis team identified a number of subtle alterations to content (labelled A to E) and calls to action on the page with the aim of stimulating visitor engagement and driving a higher percentage of visitors through to successful conversion without changing the structure of the page or National Express brand identity. In order to aid more effective up-sell to insurance add-ons, changes to this call to action were also proposed.

It was decided that a multivariate test would be the most effective approach to determine the best performing combination of content. The variants jointly developed by Maxymiser and the client were tested with all live site visitors and the conversion rate of each combination monitored. 3500 possible page combinations were tried and during the live test the underperforming combinations were taken out to maximise conversion rates at every stage.

At the end of the testing period, after reaching statistical validity, results gave the best combination of elements showing a 14.11% increase in conversion rates for the page, i.e. 14.11% more visitors were sent through to the fourth and final step in the registration process, immediately hitting bottom line revenue for National Express (Figure 10.8).

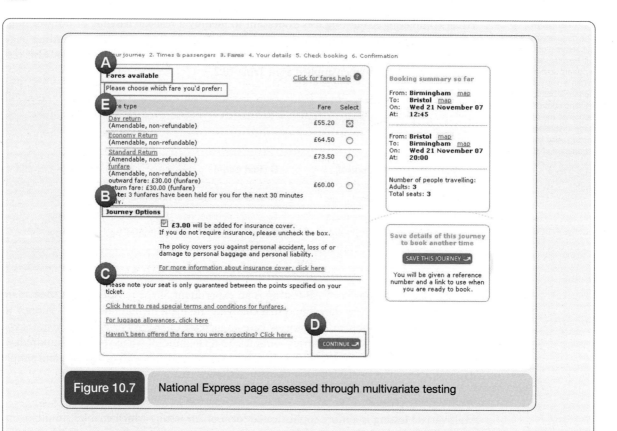

**Figure 10.7** National Express page assessed through multivariate testing

| Content combination | Maxybox A | Maxybox B | Maxybox C | Maxybox D | Maxybox E | Lift on control |
|---|---|---|---|---|---|---|
| **1** | Variant 3 | Variant 2 | Variant 4 | Variant 3 | Variant 1 | 14.11% |
| **2** | Variant 3 | Variant 3 | Variant 4 | Default | Default | 14.09% |
| **3** | Variant 6 | Variant 3 | Variant 4 | Default | Default | 11.15% |
| **4** | Variant 3 | Variant 3 | Variant 2 | Default | Variant 3 | 10.57% |
| **Default content** | Variant 3 | Variant 2 | Default | Default | Default | 0.00% |

Conversion rate uplift by page combination:

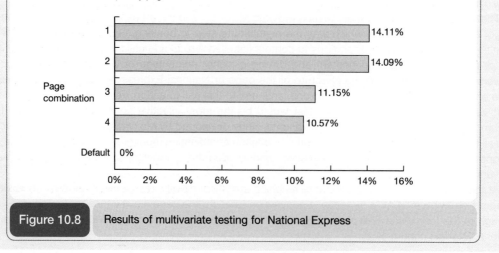

**Figure 10.8** Results of multivariate testing for National Express

## Clickstream analysis and visitor segmentation

Clickstream analysis refers to detailed analysis of visitor behaviour in order to identify improvements to the site. Each web analytics tool differs slightly in its reports and terminology, but all provide similar reports to help companies assess visitor behaviour and diagnose problems and opportunities. Table 10.3 gives an indication of the type of questions asked by web analyst and consultant Dave Chaffey (www.davechaffey.com) when reviewing clients' sites.

| Table 10.3 | A summary of how an analyst will interpret web analytics data. GA is terminology for Google Analytics (www.google.com/analytics), one of the most widely used tools |
|---|---|

| Analyst question | Typical web analytics report terminology | Diagnosis analyst used to improve performance |
|---|---|---|
| How successful is the site at achieving engagement and outcomes? | Conversion goals (GA) Bounce rates (GA) Pages/visit (GA) | • Is engagement and conversion consistent with other sites in sector? • What are maximum engagement and conversion rates from different referrers? |
| Where are visitors entering the site? | Top entry pages Top landing pages (GA) | • How important is home page compared to other page categories and landing pages? Does page popularity reflect product popularity? • Review messaging/conversion paths are effective on these pages • Assess source of traffic, in particular keywords from search engines and apply elsewhere |
| What are the sources of visitors (referrers)? | Referrers Traffic sources Filters set up to segment visitors | • Are the full range of digital media channels relevant for a company represented? • Is the level of search engine traffic consistent with the brand reputation? • What are the main link partners driving free traffic (potential for more?) |
| What is the most popular content? | Top content (GA) | • Is page popularity as expected? Are there problems with findability caused by navigation labelling? • Which content is most likely to influence visitors to outcome? • Which content is most popular with returning visitors segment? |
| Which are the most popular findability methods? | Site search (GA) | • How popular are different forms of navigation, e.g. top menu, sidebar menus, etc? • What are the most popular searches? Where do searches tend to start? Are they successfully finding content or converting to sale? |
| Where do visitors leave the site? | Top exit pages (GA) | • Are these as expected (home page, About Us page, transaction completion)? • Are there error pages (e.g. 404 not found) which cause visitors to leave? |
| Which clickstreams are taken? | Path analysis Top paths (GA) | • How can attrition in conversion funnels be improved? • What does forward path analysis show are the most effective calls-to-action? • What does reverse path analysis indicate about the pages which influence sales? |

### Path analysis

Aggregate clickstreams are usually known within web analytics software as forward or reverse paths. This is a fairly advanced form of analysis, but the principle is straightforward – you seek to learn from the most popular paths.

Viewed at an aggregate level across the site through 'top paths' type reports, this form of clickstream analysis often doesn't appear that useful. It highlights typically paths which are expected and can't really be influenced. The top paths are often:

- Home page : Exit
- Home page : Contact Us : Exit
- News page : Exit

Clickstream analysis becomes more actionable when the analyst reviews clickstreams in the context of a single page – this is forward path analysis or reverse path analysis.

### On-site search effectiveness

On-site search is another crucial part of clickstream analysis on many sites since it is a key way of finding content, so a detailed search analysis will pay dividends. Key search metrics to consider are:

- number of searches;
- average number of searches per visitor or searcher;
- % of searches returning zero results;
- % of site exits from search results;
- % of returned searches clicked;
- % of returned searches resulting in conversion to sale or other outcome;
- most popular search terms – individual keyword and keyphrases.

### Visitor segmentation

Segmentation is a fundamental marketing approach, but is often difficult within web analytics to relate customer segments to web behaviour because the web analytics data isn't integrated with customer or purchase data, although it is possible in the most advanced systems such as Omniture, Visual Sciences and WebTrends.

However, all analytics systems have a capability for segmentation and it is possible to create specific filters or profiles to help understand one type of site visitor behaviour. Examples include:

- First time visitors or returning visitors.
- Visitors from different referrer types including:
  - Google natural;
  - Google paid;
  - Strategic search keyphrases, brand keyphrases, etc.;
  - Display advertising.
- Converters against non-converters.
- Geographic segmentation by country or region (based on IP addresses).
- Type of content accessed, e.g. are some segments more likely to convert? For example, speaking at Ad Tech London '06, MyTravel reported that they segment visitors into:
  - site flirt (two pages or fewer);
  - site browse (two pages or more);
  - saw search results;
  - saw quote;
  - saw payment details;
  - saw booking confirmation details.

**Forward path analysis**
Reviews the combinations of clicks that occur from a page. This form of analysis is most beneficial from important pages such as the home page, product and directory pages. Use this technique to identify: messaging/ navigation combinations which work best to yield the most clicks from a page. These approaches can then be deployed elsewhere on the site or page. Work poorly and yield a relatively small percentage of clicks from a page.

**Reverse path analysis**
Reverse path analysis indicates the most popular combination of pages and/or calls-to-action which lead to a page. This is particularly useful for transactional pages such as the first checkout page on a consumer site; a lead generation or contact us page on a business-to-business site; an e-mail subscription page or a call-me back option.

## Collecting site outcome data

'Site outcome data' refers to a customer performing a significant action which is of value to the marketer. This is usually a transaction that is recorded. It involves more than downloading a web page, and is proactive. Key marketing outcomes include:

- registration to site or subscriptions to an e-mail newsletter;
- requests for further information such as a brochure or a request for a call-back from a customer service representative;
- responding to a promotion such as an online competition;
- a sale influenced by a visit to the site;
- a sale on-site.

An important aspect of measures collected offline is that the marketing outcomes may be recorded in different media according to how the customer has performed mixed-mode buying. For example, a new customer enquiry could arrive by e-mail, fax or phone. Similarly, an order could be placed online using a credit card, or by phone, fax or post. For both cases what we are really interested in is whether the website influenced the enquiry or sale. This is a difficult question to answer unless steps are put in place to answer it. For all contact points with customers staff, need to be instructed to ask how they found out about the company, or made their decision to buy. Although this is valuable information it is often intrusive, and a customer placing an order may be annoyed to be asked such a question. To avoid alienating the customer, these questions about the role of the website can be asked later, perhaps when the customer is filling in a registration or warranty card. Another device that can be used to identify use of the website is to use a specific phone number on the website, so when a customer rings to place an order it is known that the number was obtained from the website. This approach is used by Dell.

## Selecting a web analytics tool

There is a bewildering range of hundreds of web analytics tools, varying from shareware packages with often primitive reporting through to complex systems which may cost hundreds of thousands of dollars a year for a popular site. Given this, it is difficult for the Internet marketer to select the best tool or tools to meet their needs. One of the first issues to consider is the different types of measures that need to be integrated within the performance management system. Figure 10.9 gives an indication of the types of data that need to be integrated; these include operational data, tactical and strategic data.

### Operational data

Data would be ideally collected and reported within a single tool at this level, but unfortunately to obtain the best reporting it is often necessary to resort to four different types of tools/data source:

- Referrer data from acquisition campaigns such as search marketing or online advertising. Separate tools are often also required for retention e-mail marketing.
- Site-centric data about visitor volume and clickstream behaviour on the website.
- Customer response and profile data.
- Transactional data about leads and sales which are often obtained from separate legacy systems.

### Tactical data

These data are typically models of required response such as:

- Reach models with online audience share data for different demographic groupings from sources such as Hitwise and Netratings.
- Lifetime value models which are created to assess profitability of visitors to the site from different sources and so need to integrate with operational data.

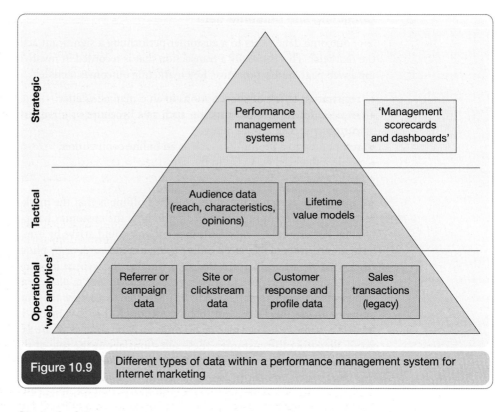

| Figure 10.9 | Different types of data within a performance management system for Internet marketing |

### Strategic data

Performance management systems for senior managers will give the big picture presented as scorecards or dashboards showing the contribution of digital channels to the organisation in terms of sales, revenue and profitability for different products. These data indicate trends and relative performance within the company and to competitors such that the Internet marketing strategy can be reviewed for effectiveness. The efficiency of the processes may be indicated through, for example, the cost of acquisition of customers in different markets and their conversion and retention rates.

An important requirement of a web analytics tool is that it should seek to integrate all these different data sources. The other main requirements of a web analytics tool to consider include:

- reporting of marketing performance (many are technical tools which do not clearly report on results from a marketing perspective);
- accuracy of technique;
- analysis tools;
- integration with other marketing information systems (export);
- ease of use and configuration;
- cost, which often varies according to site visitor volumes and number of system users;
- suitability for reporting on e-marketing campaigns.

Many online tracking tools were originally developed to report on the performance of the site and the pages accessed rather than specifically to report on e-marketing campaigns. It is therefore important that companies have an excellent campaign-reporting capability. When online marketers are reviewing the capability of tools, they should be able to answer these questions:

- *Can the tool track through from point entry on site through to outcome?* For example, to outcomes such as registration, lead or sale? Integration with data to reflect actual leads or sales in a legacy system should also be reported.
- *Can the tool track and compare a range of online media types?* These were explained in Chapter 8 – for example, interactive (banner) ads, affiliates, e-mail marketing, natural and paid search.

- *Can return-on-investment models be constructed?* For example, by entering costs and profitability for each product.
- *Can reports be produced at both a detailed level and a summary level?* This enables comparison of performance for different campaigns and different parts of the business.
- *Is there capability to track click-throughs at an individual respondent level for e-mail campaigns?* This is important for follow-up marketing activities such as a phone call, direct mail or e-mail after an e-mail list member has expressed interest in a product through clicking on a promotion link.
- *Are post-view responses tracked for ads?* Cookies can be used to assess visitors who arrive on the site at a later point in time, rather than immediately.
- *Are post-click responses tracked for affiliates?* Similarly, visitors from affiliates may buy the product not on their first visit, but on a later visit.
- *Do e-mail campaign summaries give unique clicks as well as total clicks?* If an e-mail communication such as a newsletter contains multiple links, then total clicks will be higher.
- *Is real-time reporting available?* Is immediate access to campaign performance data available (this is usually possible with browser or tag-based campaign tracking solutions)?
- *Are cross-campaign and cross-product or content reporting available?* Is it readily possible to compare campaigns and sales levels across different products or different parts of the site rather than an aggregate?

Accuracy is another important aspect of web analytics tool and managers need to be aware of some of the weaknesses of web analytics tools based on log file analysis. Perhaps the worst are the problems of undercounting and overcounting. These are reviewed in Table 10.4.

A relatively new approach to the problems of undercounting and overcounting of server-based log file analysis described in Table 10.4 is to use a different *browser-based* or *tag-based* measurement system that records access to web pages every time a page is loaded into a user's web browser through running a short script, program or tag inserted into the web page. The key benefit of the browser-based approach is that it is potentially more accurate than server-based approaches. Figure 10.10 indicates how the browser-based approach works.

An example of the output reporting from a web analytics service is shown in Figure 10.11.

| Table 10.4 | Inaccuracies caused by server-based log file analysis |
| --- | --- |

| Sources of undercounting | Sources of overcounting |
| --- | --- |
| Caching in user's web browsers (when a user accesses a previously accessed file, it is loaded from the user's cache on their PC) | Frames (a user viewing a framed page with three frames will be recorded as three page impressions on a server-based system) |
| Caching on proxy servers (proxy servers are used within organisations or ISPs to reduce Internet traffic by storing copies of frequently used pages) | Spiders and robots (traversing of a site by spiders from different search engines is recorded as page impressions. These spiders can be excluded, but this is time-consuming) |
| Firewalls (these do not usually exclude page impressions, but they do assign a single IP address for the user of the page, rather than referring to an individual's PC) | Executable files (these can also be recorded as hits or page impressions unless excluded) |
| Dynamically generated pages, generated 'on the fly', are difficult to assess with server-based log files | |

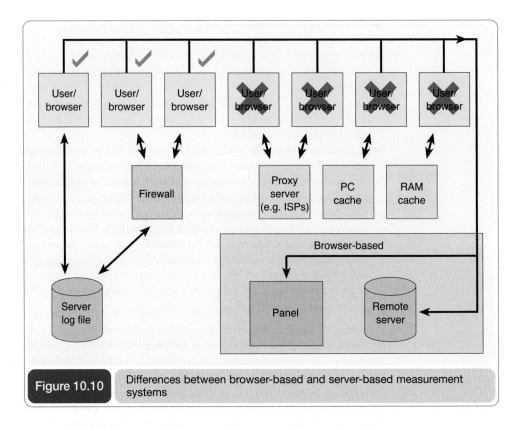

**Figure 10.10** Differences between browser-based and server-based measurement systems

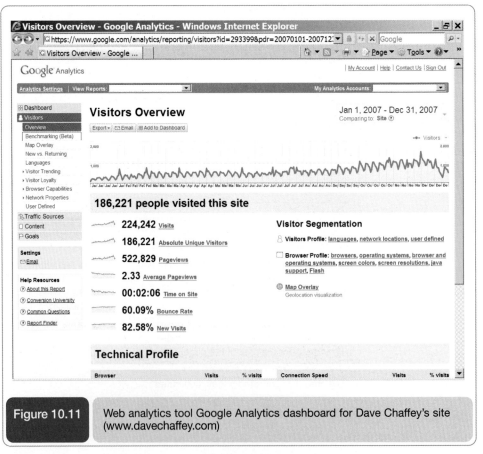

**Figure 10.11** Web analytics tool Google Analytics dashboard for Dave Chaffey's site (www.davechaffey.com)

### Specialist web analysis tools

In addition to standard web analytics tools such as that shown in Figure 10.11, other tools have more capability for integration of data and analysis of individual user sessions to identify and diagnose problems with a particular page. For example Speed Trap (www.speed-trap.com, Figure 10.12) and Tealeaf Technologies (www.tealeaf.com) offer these capabilities.

### Marketing research using the Internet

**Marketing research** will help determine the influence of a website and related communications on customer perception of the company and its products and services. The options for conducting survey research include interviews, questionnaires and focus groups. They are summarised in Table 10.5. Each of these techniques can be conducted offline or online. Offline methods are especially appropriate for companies with a smaller number of customers who can be easily accessed, for example by sales staff. When surveys such as interviews are conducted they may not solely concern the impact of the website, but questions about this could be part of a wider survey on customer perception of the company or its product.

This type of measurement will use the traditional techniques of survey-based marketing research, which seek to collect primary data by gathering descriptive information about people's attitudes, preferences or buying behaviour.

**Internet-based market research**
The use of online questionnaires and focus groups to assess customer perceptions of a website or broader marketing issues.

The techniques that are appropriate for conducting this type of research will need to target a sample of people who actively use the website. The best place to find these customers is on the website! As a result, online focus groups and questionnaires administered online are becoming more common. The use of **Internet-based market research** is relatively new, so there is little research on what works and what does not. However, some general comments can be made for the different survey types.

**Figure 10.12**    Speed Trap web analytics tool

| Table 10.5 | A comparison of different online metrics collection and research methods |

| Technique | Strengths | Weaknesses |
|---|---|---|
| Server-based log file analysis of site activity | • Directly records customer behaviour on site plus where they were referred from<br>• Low cost | • Not based around marketing outcomes such as leads or sales<br>• Size – even summaries may be over 50 pages long<br>• Does not directly record channel satisfaction<br>• Undercounting/overcounting<br>• Misleading unless interpreted carefully |
| Browser-based site activity data | • Greater accuracy than server-based analysis<br>• Counts all users, cf. panel approach | • Relatively expensive method<br>• Similar weaknesses to server-based technique apart from accuracy<br>• Limited demographic information |
| AB and multivariate testing | • Structured experiments to review influence of on page variables (e.g. messaging and buttons) to improve conversion from a website | • Often requires cost of a separate tool or module from standard web analytics package<br>• Content management systems or page templates may not support AB/multivariate testing |
| Panel activity and demographic data | • Provides competitor comparisons<br>• Gives demographic profiling representative<br>• Avoids undercounting and overcounting | • Depends on extrapolation from data-limited sample that may not be representative |
| Outcome data, e.g. enquiries, customer e-mails | • Records marketing outcomes | • Difficulty of integrating data with other methods of data collection when service collected manually or in other information systems |
| Online questionnaires Customers are prompted randomly – every *n*th customer or after customer activity or by e-mail | • Can record customer satisfaction and profiles<br>• Relatively cheap to create and analyse | • Difficulty of recruiting respondents who complete accurately<br>• Sample bias – tend to be advocates or disgruntled customers who complete |
| Online focus groups Synchronous recording | • Relatively cheap to create | • Difficult to moderate and co-ordinate<br>• No visual cues, as from offline focus groups |
| Mystery shoppers Example is customers are recruited to evaluate the site, e.g. www.emysteryshopper.com | • Structured tests give detailed feedback<br>• Also tests integration with other channels such as e-mail and phone | • Relatively expensive<br>• Sample must be representative |

### Questionnaires

Malhotra (1999) suggests that Internet surveys using questionnaires will increase in popularity since the cost is generally lower, they can be less intrusive and they have the ability to target specific populations. Questionnaires often take the form of pop-up surveys. The key issues are:

**A** *Encouraging participation.* Techniques that can be used are:

- interruption on entry – a common approach where every 100th customer is prompted;
- continuous, for example click on a button to complete survey;
- on registration on-site the customer can be profiled;
- after an activity such as sale or customer support, the customer can be prompted for their opinion about the service;
- incentives and promotions (this can also be executed on independent sites);
- by e-mail (an e-mail prompt to visit a website to fill in a survey or a simple e-mail survey).

**B** *Stages in execution.* It is suggested that there are five stages to a successful questionnaire survey:

1 attract (button, pop-up, e-mail as above);
2 incentivise (prize or offer consistent with required sample and audience);
3 reassure (why the company is doing it – to learn, not too long and that confidentiality is protected);
4 design and execute (brevity, relevance, position);
5 follow-up (feedback).

**C** *Design.* Grossnickle and Raskin (2001) suggest the following approach to structuring questionnaires:

- easy, interesting questions first;
- cluster questions on same topic;
- flow topic from general to specific;
- flow topic from easier behavioural to more difficult attitudinal questions;
- easy questions last, e.g. demographics or offputting questions.

Typical questions that can be asked for determining the effectiveness of Internet marketing are:

- *Who is visiting the site?* For example, role in buying decision? Online experience? Access location and speed? Demographics segment?
- *Why are they visiting?* How often do they visit? Which information or service? Did they find it? Actions taken? (Can be determined through web analytics.)
- *What do they think?* Overall opinion? Key areas of satisfaction? Specific likes or dislikes? What was missing that was expected?

### Focus groups

Malhotra (1999) notes that the advantage of online focus groups is that they can be used to reach segments that are difficult to access, such as doctors, lawyers and professional people. This author also suggests that costs are lower, they can be arranged more rapidly and can bridge the distance gap when recruiting respondents. Traditional focus groups can be conducted, where customers are brought together in a room and assess a website; this will typically occur pre-launch as part of the prototyping activity. Testing can take the form of random use of the site or, more usefully, the users will be given different scenarios to follow. It is important that focus groups use a range of familiarities (Chapter 8). Focus groups tend to be relatively expensive and time consuming, since rather than simply viewing an advertisement, the customers need to actually interact with the website. Conducting real-world focus groups has the benefit that the reactions of site users can be monitored; the scratch of the head and the fist hitting the desk cannot be monitored in the virtual world!

### Mystery shoppers

Real-world measurement is also important since the Internet channel does not exist in isolation. It must work in unison with real-world customer service and fulfilment. Chris Russell of eMysteryShopper (www.emysteryshopper.com), a company that has completed online customer service surveys for major UK retailers and travel companies, says 'we also needed to make sure that the bricks-and-mortar customer service support was actually supporting what the clicks-and-mortar side was promising. There is no doubt that an e-commerce site has to be a complete customer service fulfilment picture, it can't just be one bit working online that is not supported offline'. An eMysteryShopper survey involves shoppers not only commenting on site usability, but also on the service quality of e-mail and phone responses together with product fulfilment. Mystery shoppers test these areas:

- site usability
- e-commerce fulfilment
- e-mail and phone response (time, accuracy)
- impact on brand.

## The maintenance process

As part of the process of continuous improvement in online marketing, it is important to have a clearly defined process for making changes to the content of a website. This process should be understood by all staff contributing content to the site, with their responsibilities clearly identified in their job descriptions. To understand the process, consider the main stages involved in publishing a page. A simple model of the work involved in maintenance is shown in Figure 10.13. It is assumed that the needs of the users and design features of the site have already been defined when the site was originally created, as described in Chapter 7. The model only applies to minor updates to copy, or perhaps updating product or company information. The different tasks involved in the maintenance process are as follows:

1 *Write.* This stage involves writing the marketing copy and, if necessary, designing the layout of copy and associated images.

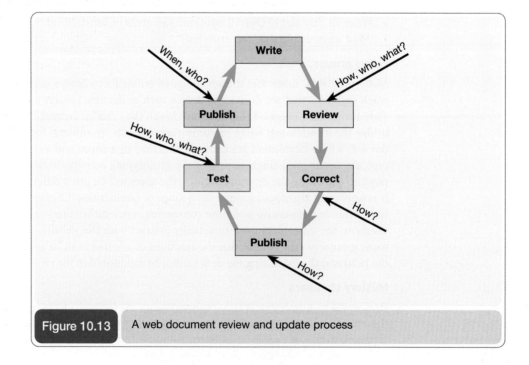

| Figure 10.13 | A web document review and update process |

**2** *Review.* An independent review of the copy is necessary to check for errors before a document is published. Depending on the size of organisation, review may be necessary by one person or several people covering different aspects of content quality such as corporate image, copy-editing text to identify grammatical errors, marketing copy, branding and legality.

**3** *Correct.* This stage is straightforward and involves updates necessary as a result of stage 2.

**4** *Publish (to test environment).* The publication stage involves putting the corrected copy on a web page that can be checked further. This will be in a test environment that can only be viewed from inside a company.

**5** *Test.* Before the completed web page is made available over the World Wide Web a final test will be required for technical issues such as whether the page loads successfully on different browsers.

**6** *Publish (to live environment).* Once the material has been reviewed and tested and is signed off as satisfactory, it will be published to the main website and will be accessible by customers.

## How often should material be updated?

Website content needs to be up-to-date, in line with customer expectations. The web is perceived as a dynamic medium and customers are likely to expect new information to be posted to a site straight away. If material is inaccurate or 'stale' then the customer may not return to the site.

After a time, the information on a web page naturally becomes outdated and will need to be updated or replaced. It is important to have a mechanism defining what triggers this update process and leads to the cycle of Figure 10.13. The need for material to be updated has several facets. For the information on the site to be accurate it clearly needs to be up-to-date. Trigger procedures should be developed such that when price changes or product specifications are updated in promotional leaflets or catalogues, these changes are also reflected on the website. Without procedures of this type, it is easy for there to be errors on the website. This may sound obvious, but the reality is that the people contributing the updates to the site will have many other tasks to complete, and the website could be a low priority.

A further reason for updating the site is to encourage repeat visits. For example, a customer could be encouraged to return to a business-to-business site if there is some industry news on the site. This type of content needs to be updated regularly according to the type of business, from daily, weekly to monthly. Again, a person has to be in place to collate such news and update the site frequently. Some companies such as RS Components have monthly promotions, which may encourage repeat visits to the site. It is useful to emphasise to the customer that the information is updated frequently. This is possible through simple devices such as putting the date on the home page, or perhaps just the month and year for a site that is updated less frequently.

As part of defining a website update process, and standards, a company may want to issue guidelines that suggest how often content is updated. This may specify that content is updated as follows:

- within two days of a factual error being identified;
- a new 'news' item is added at least once a month;
- when product information has been static for two months.

## Responsibilities in website maintenance

Maintenance is easy in a small company with a single person updating the website. That person is able to ensure that the style of the whole site remains consistent. For a slightly larger site, with perhaps two people involved with updating, the problem more than doubles since communication is required to keep things consistent. For a large organisation with many different departments and offices in different countries, site maintenance becomes very difficult, and production of a quality site is only possible when there is strong control to establish a team who all follow the same standards. Sterne (2001) suggests that the essence of successful maintenance is to have clearly identified responsibilities for different aspects of updating the website. The questions to ask are:

- Who owns the process?
- Who owns the content?
- Who owns the format?
- Who owns the technology?

We will now consider these in more detail, reviewing the standards required to produce a good-quality website and the different types of responsibilities involved. Review of new site functionality is a strategic issue and was covered in Chapter 4.

## Who owns the process?

One of the first areas to be defined should be the overall process for agreeing new site content and updating the site. But who agrees this process? For the large company it will be necessary to bring together all the interested parties, such as those within the marketing department and the site developers – who may be an external agency or the IT department. Within these groupings there may be many people with an interest such as the marketing manager, the person with responsibility for Internet or new-media marketing, a communications manager who places above-the-line advertising, and product managers who manage the promotion of individual products and services. All of these people should have an input in deciding on the process for updating the website. What, then, is this process? The process will specify responsibilities for different aspects of site management and detail the sequence in which tasks occur for updating the site. A typical update process is outlined in Figure 10.13. If we take a specific example we can illustrate the need for a well-defined process. Imagine that a large organisation is launching a new product – promotional literature is to be distributed to customers, the media are already available, and the company wants to add information about this product to the website. A recently recruited graduate is charged with putting the information on the site. How will this process actually occur? The following process stages need to occur:

1 Graduate reviews promotional literature and rewrites copy on a word processor and modifies graphical elements as appropriate for the website. This is the *write* stage in Figure 10.13.
2 Product and/or marketing manager reviews the revised web-based copy. This is part of the *review* stage in Figure 10.13.
3 Corporate communications manager reviews the copy for suitability. This is also part of the *review* stage in Figure 10.13.
4 Legal adviser reviews copy. This is also part of the *review* stage in Figure 10.13.
5 Copy revised and corrected and then re-reviewed as necessary. This is the *correct* stage in Figure 10.13.
6 Copy converted to web format and then published. This will be performed by a technical person such as a site developer, who will insert a new menu option to help users navigate to the new product. This person will add the HTML formatting and then upload the file using FTP to the test website. This is the first *publish* stage in Figure 10.13.
7 The new copy on the site will be reviewed by the graduate for accuracy, and needs to be tested on different web browsers and screen resolutions if it uses a graphical design different from the standard site template. This type of technical testing will need to be

carried out by the webmaster. The new version could also be reviewed on the site by the communications manager or legal adviser at this point. This is part of the *test* stage in Figure 10.13.

8 Once all interested parties agree the new copy is suitable, the pages on the test website can be transferred to the live website and are then available for customers to view. This is the second *publish* stage in Figure 10.13.

Note that in this scenario review of the copy at stages 2 to 4 happens before the copy is actually put onto the test site at stage 6. This is efficient in that it saves the technical person or webmaster having to update the page until the copy is agreed. An alternative would be for the graduate to write the copy at stage 1 and then the webmaster publishes the material before it is reviewed by the various parties. Each approach is equally valid.

Content management systems with workflow capabilities are now commonly used to help achieve review of page updates. Revised copy for a page can be automatically e-mailed to all reviewers and then the comments received by e-mail can be collated.

To conclude this section, refer to Activity 10.1 which shows a typical website update process and considers possible improvements.

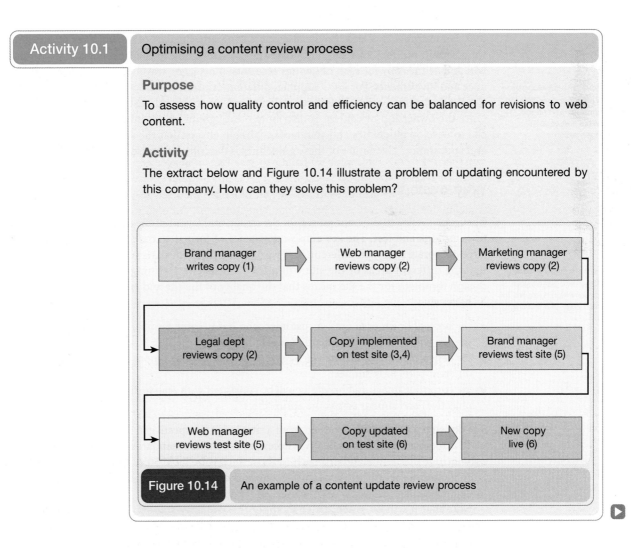

| Activity 10.1 | Optimising a content review process |

**Purpose**

To assess how quality control and efficiency can be balanced for revisions to web content.

**Activity**

The extract below and Figure 10.14 illustrate a problem of updating encountered by this company. How can they solve this problem?

Brand manager writes copy (1) → Web manager reviews copy (2) → Marketing manager reviews copy (2)

Legal dept reviews copy (2) → Copy implemented on test site (3,4) → Brand manager reviews test site (5)

Web manager reviews test site (5) → Copy updated on test site (6) → New copy live (6)

**Figure 10.14**    An example of a content update review process

---

**Problem description**

From the moment the brand manager identifies a need to update copy for their product, the update might happen as follows: brand manager writes the copy (half a day), one day later the web manager reviews the copy. Three days later the marketing manager checks the copy, seven days later the legal department checks the copy, two days later the revised copy is implemented on the test site and two days later the brand manager reviews the test site. The next day the web manager reviews the website, followed by updating and final review, before the copy is added to the live site two days later and over a fortnight from when a relatively minor change to the site was identified!

---

## Who owns the content?

For a medium-to-large site where the content is updated regularly, as it should be, it will soon become impossible for one person to update all the content. It is logical and practical to distribute the responsibility for owning and developing different sections of the site to the people in an organisation who have the best skills and knowledge to develop that content. For example, in a large financial services company, the part of the business responsible for a certain product area should update the copy referring to their products. One person will update the copy for each of savings accounts, mortgages, travel insurance, health insurance and investments. For a PC supplier, different **content developers** will be required for the product information, financing, delivery information and customer service facilities. Once the ownership of content is distributed throughout an organisation, it becomes crucial to develop guidelines and standards that help ensure that the site has a coherent 'feel' and appearance. The nature of these guidelines is described in the sections that follow.

**Content developer**
A person responsible for updating web pages within part of an organisation

## Who owns the format?

The format refers to different aspects of the design and layout of the site, commonly referred to as its 'look and feel'. The key aim is consistency of format across the whole website. For a large corporate site, with different staff working on different parts of the site, there is a risk that the different areas of the site will not be consistent. Defining a clear format or **site design template** for the site means that the quality of the site and customer experience will be better since:

**Site design template**
A standard page layout format which is applied to each page of a website.

- *the site will be easier to use* – a customer who has become familiar with using one area of the site will be able to confidently use another part of the site;
- *the design elements of the site will be similar* – a user will feel more at home with the site if different parts look similar;
- the corporate image and branding will be consistent with real-world branding (if this is an objective) and similar across the entire site.

Site design templates were reviewed from a site design perspective in Chapter 7.

To achieve a site of this quality it is necessary for written standards to be developed. These may include different standards such as those shown in Table 10.6. The standards adopted will vary according to the size of the website and company. Typically, larger sites, with more individual content developers, will require more detailed standards.

Note that it will be much easier to apply these quality standards across the site if the degree of scope for individual content developers to make changes to graphics or navigation is limited and they concentrate on changing text copy. To help achieve consistency, the software used to build the website should allow templates to be designed that specify the menu structure and graphical design of the site. The content developers are then simply adding text- and graphics-based pages to specific documents and do not have to worry about the site design.

## Who owns the technology?

The technology used to publish a website is important if a company is to utilise fully the power of the Internet. Many standards, such as those in Table 10.6, need to be managed in addition to the technology.

| Table 10.6 | Website standards | |
|---|---|---|
| **Standard** | **Details** | **Applies to** |
| Site structure | Will specify the main areas of the site, for example products, customer service, press releases, how to place content and who is responsible for each area | Content developers |
| Navigation | May specify, for instance, that the main menu must always be on the left of the screen with nested (sub-) menus at the foot of the screen. The home button should be accessible from every screen at the top left corner of the screen. See Lynch and Horton (1999) for guidelines on navigation and site design | Website designer/ webmaster usually achieves these through site templates |
| Copy style and page structure | General guidelines, for example reminding those writing copy that web copy needs to be briefer than its paper equivalent and ranking factors for SEO (Chapter 9). Where detail is required, perhaps with product specifications, it should be broken up into chunks that are digestible on-screen. Copy and page structure should also be written for search engine optimisation to keyphrases (Chapter 8) | Individual content developers |
| Testing standards | Check site functions for:<br>• different browser types and versions<br>• plug-ins<br>• invalid links<br>• speed of download of graphics<br>• spellcheck each page | Website designer/ webmaster |
| Corporate branding | Specifies the appearance of company logos and the colours and typefaces used to convey the brand message | Website designer/ webmaster and graphic design |
| Process | Web page or updating an existing page. Who is responsible for reviewing and updating? | All |
| Performance | Availability and download speed figures | Staff managing the server |

As well as issues of integrating systems, there are detailed technical issues for which the technical staff in the company need to be made responsible. These include:

- availability and performance of the website server;
- checking HTML for validity and correcting broken links;
- managing different versions of web pages in the test and live environments and content management.

## Content management

**Content management**
Software tools for managing additions and amendments to website content.

**Content management** refers to when software tools (usually browser-based software running on a server) permit business users to contribute web content, while an administrator keeps control of the format and style of the website and the approval process. These tools are used to organise, manage, retrieve and archive information content throughout the life of the site.

Content management systems (CMS) provide these facilities:

- *Structure authoring* – the design and maintenance of content structure (sub-components, templates, etc.), web page structure and website structure.
- *Link management* – the maintenance of internal and external links through content change and the elimination of dead links.
- *Search engine visibility* – the content within the search engine must be stored and linked such that it can be indexed by search engine robots to add it to their index. This was not possible with some first-generation content management systems, but is typical of more recent content management systems.
- *Input and syndication* – the loading (spidering) of externally originating content and the aggregation and dissemination of content from a variety of sources.
- *Versioning* – the crucial task of controlling which edition of a page, page element or the whole site is published. Typically this will be the most recent, but previous editions should be archived and it should be possible to roll back to a previous version at the page, page element or site level.
- *Security and access control* – different permissions can be assigned to different roles of users and some content may only be available through log-in details. In these cases, the CMS maintains a list of users. This facility is useful when a company needs to use the same CMS for an intranet, extranet or public Internet site which may have different levels of permission.
- *Publication workflow* – content destined for a website needs to pass through a publication process to move it from the management environment to the live delivery environment. The process may involve tasks such as format conversion (e.g. to PDF or to WAP), rendering to HTML, editorial authorisation and the construction of composite documents in real time (personalisation and selective dissemination).
- *Tracking and monitoring* – providing logs and statistical analysis of use to provide performance measures, tune the content according to demand and protect against misuse.
- *Navigation and visualisation* – providing an intuitive, clear and attractive representation of the nature and location of content using colour, texture, 3D rendering or even virtual reality.

From this list of features you can see that modern CMSs are complex and many CMSs are expensive investments. Some open-source CMSs are available, without the need to purchase a licence fee, which have many of the features explained in this section. One example is Plone (www.plone.org) which is used by large organisations' websites such as NASA. Dave Chaffey uses Plone to manage the contents for updates to this book which readers can find on his website (www.davechaffey.com).

### Initiatives to keep content fresh

It is often said that up-to-date content is crucial to site 'stickiness', but fresh content will not happen by accident, so companies have to consider approaches that can be used to control the quality of information. Generic approaches that we have seen which can work well are:

- assign responsibility for particular content types of site sections;
- make the quality of web content produced part of employees' performance appraisal;
- produce a target schedule for publication of content;
- identify events which trigger the publication of new content, e.g. a new product launch, price change or a press release;
- identify stages and responsibilities in updating – who specifies, who creates, who reviews, who checks, who publishes;
- measure the usage of content through web analytics or get feedback from site users;
- audit and publish content to show which is up-to-date.

---

| Case Study 10 | Learning from Amazon's culture of metrics |
|---|---|

## Context

Why a case study on Amazon? Surely everyone knows who Amazon are and what they do? Yes, well, that's maybe true, but this case goes under the surface to review some of the 'insider secrets' of Amazon's success.

Like eBay, Amazon.com was born in 1995. The name reflected the vision of Jeff Bezos, to produce a large-scale phenomenon like the Amazon river. This ambition has proved justified since just 8 years later, Amazon passed the $5 billion sales mark – it took Wal-Mart 20 years to achieve this.

Amazon is now a global brand with over 76 million active customers accounts and order fulfilment to more than 200 countries. Despite this volume of sales, at 31 December 2007 Amazon employed approximately 17,000 full-time and part-time employees.

In September 2007, it launched Amazon MP3, à la carte DRM-free MP3 music downloads, which now includes over 3.1 million songs from more than 270,000 artists.

## Vision and strategy

In their 2008 SEC filing, Amazon describe the vision of their business as to:

> Relentlessly focus on customer experience by offering a wide selection of merchandise, low prices and convenience.

The vision is to offer Earth's biggest selection and to be Earth's most customer-centric company. Consider how these core marketing messages summarising the Amazon online value proposition are communicated both on-site and through offline communications.

Amazon.com adopts what is calls '*An Everyday Low Pricing*' strategy, where it's objective is '*not to discount a small number of products for a limited period of time, but to offer low prices everyday and apply them broadly across our entire product range*'.

Of course, achieving customer loyalty and repeat purchases has been key to Amazon's success. Many dot-coms failed because they succeeded in achieving awareness, but not loyalty. Amazon achieved both. In their SEC filing they stress how they seek to achieve this. They say:

> We work to earn repeat purchases by providing easy-to-use functionality, fast and reliable fulfilment, timely customer service, feature-rich content, and a trusted transaction environment. Key features of our websites include editorial and customer reviews; manufacturer product information; web pages tailored to individual preferences, such as recommendations and notifications; 1-Click® technology; secure payment systems; image uploads; searching on our websites as well as the Internet; browsing; and the ability to view selected interior pages and citations, and search the entire contents of many of the books we offer with our 'Look Inside the Book' and 'Search Inside the Book' features. Our community of online customers also creates feature-rich content, including product reviews, online recommendation lists, wish lists, buying guides, and wedding and baby registries.

In practice, as is the practice for many online retailers, the lowest prices are for the most popular products, with less popular products commanding higher prices and a greater margin for Amazon. Free shipping offers are used to encourage increase in basket size since customers have to spend over a certain amount to receive free shipping. The level at which free shipping is set is critical to profitability and Amazon has changed it as competition has changed and for promotional reasons.

Amazon communicate the fulfilment promise in several ways including presentation of latest inventory availability information, delivery date estimates, and options for expedited delivery, as well as delivery shipment notifications and update facilities.

This focus on the customer has translated to excellence in service with the 2004 American Customer Satisfaction Index giving Amazon.com a score of 88 which was at the time the highest customer satisfaction score ever recorded in any service industry, online or offline.

Round (2004) notes that Amazon focuses on customer satisfaction metrics. Each site is closely monitored with standard service availability monitoring (for example, using Keynote or Mercury Interactive) site availability and download speed. Interestingly it also monitors per-minute site revenue upper/lower bounds – Round describes an alarm system rather like a power plant where if revenue on a site falls below $10,000 per minute, alarms go off! There are also internal performance service-level agreements for web services where $t$% of the time, different pages must return in $x$ seconds.

## Customers

Amazon defines what it refers to as three consumer sets: customers, seller customers and developer customers. There are over 76 million customer accounts, but just 1.3 million active seller customers in its marketplaces and Amazon is seeking to increase this. Amazon is unusual for a retailer in that it identifies 'developer customers' who use its Amazon Web Services, which provide access to technology infrastructure such as hosting that developers can use to develop their own web services.

Members are also encouraged to join a loyalty programme, Amazon Prime – a fee-based membership programme in which members receive free or discounted express shipping in the United States, the United Kingdom, Germany and Japan.

## Competition

In its SEC (2008) filing Amazon describes the environment for its products and services as 'intensely competitive'. It views its main current and potential competitors as: (1) physical-world retailers, catalogue retailers, publishers, vendors, distributors and manufacturers of its products, many of which possess significant brand awareness, sales volume and customer bases, and some of which currently sell, or may sell, products or services through the Internet, mail order or direct marketing; (2) other online e-commerce sites; (3) a number of indirect competitors, including media companies, web portals, comparison shopping websites and web search engines, either directly or in collaboration with other retailers; and (4) companies that provide e-commerce services, including website development, third-party fulfilment and customer service.

Amazon believes the main competitive factors in its market segments include 'selection, price, availability, convenience, information, discovery, brand recognition, personalised services, accessibility, customer service, reliability, speed of fulfilment, ease of use, and ability to adapt to changing conditions, as well as our customers' overall experience and trust in transactions with us and facilitated by us on behalf of third-party sellers'.

For services offered to business and individual sellers, additional competitive factors include the quality of their services and tools, their ability to generate sales for third parties they serve and the speed of performance for their services.

## From auctions to marketplaces

Amazon auctions (known as 'zShops') were launched in March 1999, in large part as a response to the success of eBay. They were promoted heavily from the home page, category pages and individual product pages.

Today, competitive prices of products are available through third-party sellers in the 'Amazon Marketplace' which are integrated within the standard product listings. The strategy to offer such an auction facility was initially driven by the need to compete with eBay, but now the strategy has been adjusted such that Amazon describe it as part of the approach of low pricing. Amazon stocks around 26% of its units through sellers, so enabling it to extend its range.

Although it might be thought that Amazon would lose out on enabling its merchants to sell products at lower prices, in fact Amazon makes greater margin on these sales since merchants are charged a commission on each sale and it is the merchant who bears the cost of storing inventory and fulfilling the product to customers. As with eBay, Amazon is just facilitating the exchange of bits and bytes between buyers and sellers without the need to distribute physical products.

## How 'the culture of metrics' started

A common theme in Amazon's development is the drive to use a measured approach to all aspects of the business, beyond the finance. Marcus (2004) describes an occasion at a corporate 'boot-camp' in January 1997 ▶

when Amazon CEO Jeff Bezos 'saw the light'. 'At Amazon, we will have a Culture of Metrics', he said while addressing his senior staff. He went on to explain how web-based business gave Amazon an 'amazing window into human behaviour'. Marcus says:

> Gone were the fuzzy approximations of focus groups, the anecdotal fudging and smoke blowing from the marketing department. A company like Amazon could (and did) record every move a visitor made, every last click and twitch of the mouse. As the data piled up into virtual heaps, hummocks and mountain ranges, you could draw all sorts of conclusions about their chimerical nature, the consumer. In this sense, Amazon was not merely a store, but an immense repository of facts. All we needed were the right equations to plug into them.

James Marcus then goes on to give a fascinating insight into a breakout group discussion of how Amazon could better use measures to improve its performance. Marcus was in the Bezos group, brainstorming customer-centric metrics. Marcus (2004) summarises the dialogue, led by Bezos:

> 'First, we figure out which things we'd like to measure on the site', he said. 'For example, let's say we want a metric for customer enjoyment. How could we calculate that?'
>
> There was silence. Then somebody ventured: 'How much time each customer spends on the site?'
>
> 'Not specific enough', Jeff said.
>
> 'How about the average number of minutes each customer spends on the site per session', someone else suggested. 'If that goes up, they're having a blast.'
>
> 'But how do we factor in purchase?' I [Marcus] said feeling proud of myself. 'Is that a measure of enjoyment?'
>
> 'I think we need to consider frequency of visits, too', said a dark-haired woman I didn't recognise. 'Lot of folks are still accessing the web with those creepy-crawly modems. Four short visits from them might be just as good as one visit from a guy with a T-1. Maybe better.'
>
> 'Good point', Jeff said. 'And anyway, enjoyment is just the start. In the end, we should be measuring customer ecstasy.'

It is interesting that Amazon was having this debate about the elements of RFM analysis (described in Chapter 6) in 1997, after already having achieved $16 million of revenue in the previous year. Of course, this is a minuscule amount compared with today's billions of dollars turnover. The important point was that this was the start of a focus on metrics, which can be seen through the description of Matt Round's work later in this case study.

## From human to software-based recommendations

Amazon has developed internal tools to support this 'Culture of Metrics'. Marcus (2004) describes how the 'Creator Metrics' tool shows content creators how well their product listings and product copy are working. For each content editor, such as Marcus, it retrieves all recently posted documents including articles, interviews, booklists and features. For each one it then gives a conversion rate to sale plus the number of page views, adds (added to basket) and repels (content requested, but the back button then used). In time, the work of editorial reviewers, such as Marcus, was marginalised since Amazon found that the majority of visitors used the search tools rather than read editorial and they responded to the personalised recommendations as the matching technology improved (Marcus likens early recommendations techniques to 'going shopping with the village idiot').

## Experimentation and testing at Amazon

The 'Culture of Metrics' also led to a test-driven approach to improving results at Amazon. Matt Round, speaking at E-metrics 2004 when he was director of personalisation at Amazon, describes the philosophy as 'data trumps intuitions'. He explained how Amazon used to have a lot of arguments about which content and promotion should go on the all-important home page or category pages. He described how every category VP wanted top-centre and how the Friday meetings about placements for next week were getting 'too long, too loud and lacked performance data'.

But today 'automation replaces intuitions' and real-time experimentation tests are always run to answer these questions since actual consumer behaviour is the best way to decide upon tactics.

Marcus (2004) also notes that Amazon has a culture of *experiments* of which A/B tests are key components. Examples where A/B tests are used include new home page design, moving features around the page, different algorithms for recommendations, changing search relevance rankings. These involve testing a new treatment against a previous control for a limited time of a few days or a week. The system will randomly show one or more treatments to visitors and measure a range of parameters such as units sold and revenue by category (and total), session time and session length. The new features will usually be launched if the desired metrics are statistically significantly better. Statistical tests are a challenge though as distributions are not normal (they have a large mass at zero, for example, of no purchase). There are other challenges since multiple A/B tests are running every day and A/B tests may overlap and so conflict. There are also longer-term effects where some features are 'cool' for the first two weeks and the opposite effect where changing navigation may degrade performance temporarily. Amazon also finds that as its users evolve in their online experience, the way they act online has changed. This means that Amazon has to constantly test and evolve its features.

## Technology

It follows that the Amazon technology infrastructure must readily support this culture of experimentation and this can be difficult to achieve with standardised content management. Amazon has achieved its competitive advantage through developing its technology internally and with a significant investment in this which may not be available to other organisations without the right focus on the online channels.

As Amazon explains in SEC (2005):

*using primarily our own proprietary technologies, as well as technology licensed from third parties, we have implemented numerous features and functionality that simplify and improve the customer shopping experience, enable third parties to sell on our platform, and facilitate our fulfilment and customer service operations. Our current strategy is to focus our development efforts on continuous innovation by creating and enhancing the specialised, proprietary software that is unique to our business, and to license or acquire commercially-developed technology for other applications where available and appropriate. We continually invest in several areas of technology, including our seller platform; A9.com, our wholly-owned subsidiary focused on search technology on www.A9.com and other Amazon sites; web services; and digital initiatives.*

Round (2004) describes the technology approach as 'distributed development and deployment'. Pages such as the home page have a number of content 'pods' or 'slots' which call web services for features. This makes it relatively easy to change the content in these pods and even change the location of the pods on-screen. Amazon uses a flowable or fluid page design, unlike many sites, which enables it to make the most of real-estate on-screen.

Technology also supports more standard e-retail facilities. SEC (2005) states:

*We use a set of applications for accepting and validating customer orders, placing and tracking orders with suppliers, managing and assigning inventory to customer orders, and ensuring proper shipment of products to customers. Our transaction-processing systems handle millions of items, a number of different status inquiries, multiple shipping addresses, gift wrapping requests and multiple shipment methods. These systems allow the customer to choose whether to receive single or several shipments based on availability and to track the progress of each order. These applications also manage the process of accepting, authorising and charging customer credit cards.*

## Data-driven automation

Round (2004) said that 'Data is king at Amazon'. He gave many examples of data-driven automation including customer channel preferences, managing the way content is displayed to different user types, such as new releases and top-sellers, merchandising and recommendation (showing related products and promotions) and also advertising through paid search (automatic ad generation and bidding).

The automated search advertising and bidding system for paid search has had a big impact at Amazon. Sponsored links were initially done by humans, but this was unsustainable due to the range of products at Amazon. The automated program generates keywords, writes ad creative, determines best landing page, manages bids, measures conversion rates, profit per converted visitor and updates bids. Again the problem of volume is there: Matt Round described how the book *How to Make Love like a Porn Star* by Jenna Jameson received tens of thousands of clicks from pornography-related searches, but few actually purchased the book. So the update cycle must be quick to avoid large losses.

There is also an automated e-mail measurement and optimisation system. The campaign calendar used to be manually managed with relatively weak measurement and it was costly to schedule and use. A new system:

- automatically optimises content to improve customer experience;
- avoids sending an e-mail campaign that has low click-through or a high unsubscribe rate;
- includes inbox management (avoid sending multiple e-mails/week);
- has a growing library of automated e-mail programs covering new releases and recommendations.

But there are challenges if promotions are too successful if inventory isn't available.

## Your recommendations

'Customers Who Bought X ... also bought Y' is Amazon's signature feature. Round (2004) describes how Amazon relies on acquiring and then crunching a massive amount of data. Every purchase, every page viewed and every search is recorded. So there are now two new versions: 'Customers who shopped for X also shopped for ...', and 'Customers who searched for X also bought ...'. They also have a system codenamed 'Goldbox' which is a cross-sell and awareness raising tool. Items are discounted to encourage purchases in new categories!

He also describes the challenge of techniques for sifting patterns from noise (sensitivity filtering), and clothing and toy catalogues change frequently so recommendations become out-of-date. The main challenges though are the massive data size arising from millions of customers, millions of items and recommendations made in real time.

## Partnership strategy

As Amazon grew, its share price growth enabled partnership or acquisition with a range of companies in different sectors. Marcus (2004) describes how Amazon partnered with Drugstore.com (pharmacy), Living.com (furniture), Pets.com (pet supplies), Wineshopper.com (wines), HomeGrocer.com (groceries), Sothebys.com (auctions) and Kozmo.com (urban home delivery). In most cases, Amazon purchased an equity stake in these partners, so that it would share in their prosperity. It also charged them fees for placements on the Amazon site to promote and drive traffic to their sites. Similarly, Amazon charged publishers for prime position to promote books on its site which caused an initial hue-and-cry, but this abated when it was realised that paying for prominent placements was widespread in traditional booksellers and supermarkets. Many of these new online companies failed in 1999 and 2000, but Amazon had covered the potential for growth and was not pulled down by these partners, even though for some, such as Pets.com, it had an investment of 50%.

Analysts sometimes refer to 'Amazoning a sector', meaning that one company becomes so dominant in an online sector such as book retail such that it becomes very difficult for others to achieve market share. In addition to developing, communicating and delivering a very strong proposition, Amazon has been able to consolidate its strength in different sectors through its partnership arrangements and through using technology to facilitate product promotion and distribution via these partnerships. The Amazon retail platform enables other retailers to sell products online using the Amazon user interface and infrastructure through their 'Syndicated Stores' programme. For example, in the UK, Waterstones (www.waterstones.co.uk) is one of the largest traditional bookstores. It found competition with online so expensive and challenging, that eventually it

entered a partnership arrangement where Amazon markets and distributes its books online in return for a commission online. Similarly, in the US the large book retailer Borders uses the Amazon merchant platform for distributing its products. Toy retailer Toys'R'Us have a similar arrangement. Such partnerships help Amazon extend its reach into the customer-base of other suppliers, and of course, customers who buy in one category such as books can be encouraged to purchase into other areas such as clothing or electronics.

Another form of partnership referred to above is the Amazon Marketplace which enables Amazon customers and other retailers to sell their new and used books and other goods alongside the regular retail listings. A similar partnership approach is the Amazon 'Merchants@' programme which enables third-party merchants (typically larger than those who sell via the Amazon Marketplace) to sell their products via Amazon. Amazon earns money either through fixed fees or sales commissions per unit. This arrangement can help customers who get a wider choice of products from a range of suppliers with the convenience of purchasing them through a single checkout process.

Finally, Amazon has also facilitated formation of partnerships with smaller companies through its affiliates programme. Internet legend records that Jeff Bezos, the creator of Amazon, was chatting to someone at a cocktail party who wanted to sell books about divorce via her website. Subsequently, Amazon.com launched its Associates Program in July 1996 and it is still going strong. Googling www.google.com/search?q=www.amazon.com +-site%3Awww.amazon.com for sites that link to the US site, shows over four million pages, many of which will be affiliates. Amazon does not use an affiliate network which would take commissions from sale, but thanks to the strength of its brand has developed its own affiliate programme. Amazon has created tiered performance-based incentives to encourage affiliates to sell more Amazon products.

## Marketing communications

In their SEC filings Amazon states that the aims of their communications strategy are (unsurprisingly) to:

- Increase customer traffic to our websites.
- Create awareness of our products and services.
- Promote repeat purchases.
- Develop incremental product and service revenue opportunities.
- Strengthen and broaden the Amazon.com brand name.

Amazon also believe that their most effective marketing communications are a consequence of their focus on continuously improving the customer experience. This then creates word-of-mouth promotion which is effective in acquiring new customers and may also encourage repeat customer visits.

As well as this, Marcus (2004) describes how Amazon used the personalisation enabled through technology to reach out to a difficult-to-reach market which Bezos originally called 'the hard middle'. Bezos's view was that it was easy to reach 10 people (you called them on the phone) or the ten million people who bought the most popular products (you placed a superbowl ad), but more difficult to reach those in between. The search facilities in the search engine and on the Amazon site, together with its product recommendation features meant that Amazon could connect its products with the interests of these people.

Online advertising techniques include paid search marketing, interactive ads on portals, e-mail campaigns and search engine optimisation. These are automated as far as possible, as described earlier in the case study. As previously mentioned, the affiliate programme is also important in driving visitors to Amazon, and Amazon offers a wide range of methods of linking to its site to help improve conversion. For example, affiliates can use straight text links leading direct to a product page and they also offer a range of dynamic banners which feature different content such as books about Internet marketing or a search box.

Amazon also use co-operative advertising arrangements, better known as 'contra-deals', with some vendors and other third parties. For example, a print advertisement in 2005 for a particular product such as a wireless router with a free wireless laptop card promotion was to feature a specific Amazon URL in the ad. In product fulfilment packs, Amazon may include a leaflet for a non-competing online company such as Figleaves.com (lingerie) or Expedia

| Table 10.7 | Financial results summary for Amazon for year ended 31 December 2007 |
| --- | --- |

| | (All figures in millions) | | |
| --- | --- | --- | --- |
| | **2007** | **2006** | **2005** |
| Net sales | $14835 | $10711 | $8490 |
| Cost of sales | 11482 | 8255 | 6451 |
| Gross profit | 3353 | 2456 | 2039 |
| Operating expenses (1): | | | |
| Fulfilment | 1292 | 937 | 745 |
| Marketing | 344 | 263 | 198 |
| Technology and content | 818 | 662 | 451 |
| General and administrative | 235 | 195 | 166 |
| Other operating expense, net | 9 | 10 | 47 |
| Total operating expenses | 2698 | 2067 | 1607 |
| Income from operations | 655 | 389 | 432 |
| Interest income | 90 | 59 | 44 |
| Interest expense | (77) | (78) | (92) |
| Other income (expense), net | (1) | (4) | 2 |
| Remeasurements and other | (7) | 11 | 42 |
| Total non-operating income (expense) | 5 | (12) | (4) |
| Income before income taxes | 660 | 377 | 428 |
| Provision for income taxes | 184 | 187 | 95 |
| Income before cumulative effect of change in accounting principle | 476 | 190 | 333 |
| Cumulative effect of change in accounting principle | – | – | 26 |
| Net income | $476 | $190 | $359 |

*Sources*: Internet Retailer (2003), Marcus (2004), Round (2004), SEC (2005), SEC (2008)

(travel). In return, Amazon leaflets may be included in customer communications from the partner brands.

The associates programme directs customers to Amazon websites by enabling independent websites to make millions of products available to their audiences with fulfilment performed by Amazon or third parties. Amazon pays commissions to hundreds of thousands of participants in the associates programme when their customer referrals result in product sales. In addition, they offer everyday free shipping options worldwide and recently announced Amazon.com Prime in the US, their first membership programme in which members receive free two-day shipping and discounted overnight shipping. Although marketing expenses do not include the costs of free shipping or promotional offers, Amazon views such offers as effective marketing tools.

## Questions

1  By referring to the case study, Amazon's website for your country and your experience of Amazon offline communications evaluate how well Amazon communicates their core proposition and promotional offers.
2  Using the case study, characterise Amazon's approach to marketing communications.
3  Explain what distinguishes Amazon in its uses of technology for competitive advantage.
4  How does the Amazon 'culture of metrics' differ from that in other organisations from your experience.

## Summary

1.  A structured measurement programme is necessary to collect measures to assess a website's effectiveness. Action can then be taken to adjust the website strategy or promotional efforts. A measurement programme involves:
    *   Stage 1: Defining a measurement process.
    *   Stage 2: Defining a metrics framework.
    *   Stage 3: Selecting of tools for data collection, reporting and analysis.

2.  Measures of Internet marketing effectiveness can be categorised as assessing:
    *   *Level 1: Business effectiveness* – these measure the impact of the website on the whole business, and look at financial measures such as revenue and profit and promotion of corporate awareness.
    *   *Level 2: Marketing effectiveness* – these measure the number of leads and sales achieved via the Internet and effect of the Internet on retention rates and other aspects of the marketing mix such as branding.
    *   *Level 3: Internet marketing effectiveness* – these measures assess how well the site is being promoted, and do so by reviewing the popularity of the site and how good it is at delivering customer needs.

3.  The measures of effectiveness referred to above are collected in two main ways – online and offline – or in combination.

4.  Online measures are obtained from a web-server log file or using browser-based techniques. They indicate the number of visitors to a site, which pages they visit and where they originated from. These also provide a breakdown of visitors through time or by country.

5.  Offline measures are marketing outcomes such as enquiries or sales that are directly attributable to the website. Other measures of the effectiveness are available through surveying customers using questionnaires, interviews and focus groups.

6.  Maintaining a website requires clear responsibilities to be identified for different roles. These include the roles of content owners and site developers, and those ensuring that the content conforms with company and legal requirements.

7. To produce a good-quality website, standards are required to enforce uniformity in terms of:
   - site look and feel
   - corporate branding
   - quality of copy.

## Exercises

### Self-assessment exercises

1. Why are standards necessary for controlling website maintenance? What aspects of the site do standards seek to control?
2. Explain the difference between hits and page impressions. How are these measured?
3. Define and explain the purpose of test and live versions of a website.
4. Why should content development be distributed through a large organisation?
5. What is the difference between online and offline metrics?
6. How can focus groups and interviews be used to assess website effectiveness?
7. Explain how a web log file analyser works. What are its limitations?
8. Why is it useful to integrate the collection of online and offline metrics?

### Essay and discussion questions

1. 'Corporate standards for a website's format and update process are likely to stifle the creative development of a site and reduce its value to customers.' Discuss.
2. 'There is little value in the collection of online metrics recorded in a web-server log file. For measurement programmes to be of value, measures based on marketing outcomes are more valuable.' Discuss.
3. You have been appointed manager of a website for a car manufacturer and have been asked to refine the existing metrics programme. Explain, in detail, the steps you would take to develop this programme.
4. The first version of a website for a financial services company has been live for a year. Originally it was developed by a team of two people, and was effectively 'brochure-ware'. The second version of the site is intended to contain more detailed information, and will involve contributions from 10 different product areas. You have been asked to define a procedure for controlling updates to the site. Write a document detailing the update procedure, which also explains the reasons for each control.

### Examination questions

1. Why are standards necessary to control the process of updating a website? Give three examples of different aspects of a website that need to be controlled.
2. Explain the following terms concerning measurement of website effectiveness:
   (a) hits;
   (b) page impressions;
   (c) referring pages.
3. Measurement of websites concerns the recording of key events involving customers using a website. Briefly explain five different types of event.

4. Describe and briefly explain the purpose of the different stages involved in updating an existing document on a commercial website.

5. Distinguish between a test environment and a live environment for a website. What is the reason for having two environments?

6. Give three reasons explaining why a website may have to integrate with existing marketing information systems and databases within a company.

7. You have been appointed manager of a website and have been asked to develop a metrics programme. Briefly explain the steps you would take to develop this programme.

8. If a customer can be persuaded to register his or her name and e-mail address with a website, how can this information be used for site measurement purposes?

## References

Adams, C., Kapashi, N., Neely, A. and Marr, B. (2000) Managing with measures. Measuring e-business performance. *Accenture white paper*. Survey conducted in conjunction with Cranfield School of Management.

Agrawal, V., Arjona, V. and Lemmens, R. (2001) E-performance: the path to rational exuberance, *McKinsey Quarterly*, No. 1, 31–43.

Bourne, M., Mills, J., Willcox, M., Neely, A. and Platts, K. (2000) Designing, implementing and updating performance measurement systems, *International Journal of Operations and Production Management*, 20(7), 754–71.

Chaffey, D. (2000) Achieving Internet marketing success, *The Marketing Review*, 1(1), 35–60.

Cutler, M. and Sterne, J. (2000) E-metrics. Business metrics for the new economy. *Netgenesis white paper*.

Friedman, L. and Furey, T. (1999) *The Channel Advantage*. Butterworth-Heinemann, Oxford.

Grossnickle, J. and Raskin, O. (2001) *The Handbook of Online Marketing Research: Knowing your Customer Using the Net*. McGraw-Hill, New York.

Internet Retailer (2003) The new Wal-Mart? *Internet Retailer*, Paul Demery.

Kotler, P. (1997) *Marketing Management – Analysis, Planning, Implementation and Control*. Prentice-Hall, Englewood Cliffs, NJ.

Lynch, P. and Horton, S. (1999) *Web Style Guide. Basic Design Principles for Creating websites*. Yale University Press, New Haven, CT.

Malhotra, N. (1999) *Marketing Research: An Applied Orientation*. Prentice-Hall, Upper Saddle River, NJ.

Marcus, J. (2004) *Amazonia. Five Years at the Epicentre of the Dot-com Juggernaut*. The New Press, New York.

Neely, A., Adams, C. and Kennerley, M. (2002) *The Performance Prism. The Scorecard for Measuring and Managing Business Success*. Financial Times/Prentice Hall, Harlow.

Petersen, E. (2004) *Web Analytics Demystified*. Self-published. Available from www.webanalyticsdemystified.com.

Plant, R. (2000) *e-Commerce: Formulation of Strategy*. Prentice-Hall, Upper Saddle River, NJ.

*Revolution* (2004) Alliance and Leicester banks on e-commerce, by Philip Buxtone, *Revolution* (www.revolutionmagazine.com).

Round, M. (2004) Presentation to E-metrics, London, May 2005. www.emetrics.org.

SEC (2005) United States Securities and Exchange Commission submission Form 10-K from Amazon. For the fiscal year ended 31 December 2004.

SEC (2008) United States Securities and Exchange Commission Submission Form 10-K from Amazon. For the fiscal year ended 31 December 2007.

Sterne, J. (2001) *World Wide Web Marketing*, 3rd edn. Wiley, New York.

Sterne, J. (2002) *Web Metrics: Proven Methods for Measuring Website Success*. Wiley, New York.

Wilson, H. (2008) *The Multichannel Challenge*. Butterworth-Heinemann, Oxford, UK. Copyright Elsevier.

Wisner, J. and Fawcett, S. (1991) Link firm strategy to operating decisions through performance measurement, *Production and Inventory Management Journal*, Third Quarter, 5–11.

## Further reading

Berthon, P., Pitt, L. and Watson, R. (1998) The World Wide Web as an industrial marketing communication tool: models for the identification and assessment of opportunities, *Journal of Marketing Management*, 14, 691–704. This is a key paper assessing how to measure how the Internet supports purchasers through the different stages of the buying decision.

Friedman, L. and Furey, T. (1999) *The Channel Advantage*. Butterworth–Heinemann, Oxford. Chapter 12 is on managing channel performance.

Sterne, J. (2001) *World Wide Web Marketing*, 3rd edn. Wiley, New York. Chapter 11 is entitled 'Measuring your success'. It mainly reviews the strengths and weaknesses of online methods.

## Web links

### Web analytics resources

- **ABCe** (www.abce.org.uk). Audited Bureau of Circulation is standard for magazines in the UK. This is the electronic auditing part. Useful for definitions and examples of traffic for UK organisations.

- **EConsultancy** (www.e-consultancy.com) site has a section on web analytics including buyers' guides to the tools available.

- **E-metrics** (www.emetrics.org). Jim Sterne's site has many resources for online marketing metrics.

- **Web Analytics Association** (WAA, www.webanalyticsassociation.org). The site of the trade association for web analytics has useful definitions, articles and forums on this topic.

- **Web Analytics Demystified** (www.webanalyticsdemystified.com). A site to support Eric Petersen's books with a range of content.

### Web analytics expertise

- **Avinash Kaushik's blog** (www.kaushik.net). Avinash is an expert in web analytics and his popular blog shows how web analytics should be used to control and improve return on e-marketing investments.

- **EpikOne** (www.epikone.com/resources). A specialist web analytics blog and e-book by Justin Cutroni giving guidance on how to tailor Google Analytics.

- **Neil Mason of Applied Insights** (www.applied-insights.co.uk). Blog featuring Neil's insights related to measurement and control of e-marketing.

- **Jim Sterne of Target Marketing** (www.targeting.com). Leading commentator on the topic.

## Online marketing research resources

1  Digests of published market research data:
   - ClickZ Internet research (www.clickz.com/stats)
   - Market Research.com (www.marketresearch.com)
   - MR Web (www.mrweb.co.uk)

2  Directories of MR companies:
   - British Market Research Association (www.bmra.org.uk)
   - Market Research Society (www.mrs.org.uk)
   - International MR agencies (www.greenbook.org)

3  Traditional market research agencies
   - MORI (www.mori.com/emori)
   - NOP (www.nopworld.com)
   - Nielsen (www.nielsen.com)

4  Government sources:
   - European government (http://europa.eu.int/comm/eurostat)
   - OECD (www.oecd.org)
   - UK government (www.open.gov.uk, www.ons.gov.uk)
   - US government (www.stat-usa.gov)

5  Online audience data:
   - Comscore (www.comscore.com)
   - Hitwise (www.hitwise.com)
   - Mori (www.mori.com/emori)
   - Netratings (www.netratings.com)
   - NOP World (www.nopworld.com)

# Business-to-consumer Internet marketing

## Learning objectives

After reading this chapter, the reader should be able to:

- understand online shopping behaviour, and more specifically how consumer profiles and online experiences shape and influence the extent to which individuals are likely to engage with the online trading environment
- explain the development of e-retailing and describe various types of online retailing activities and strategies
- begin to develop an understanding from a retailer's perspective of the strategic implications of trading online in consumer markets.

## Questions for marketers

Key questions for marketing managers related to this chapter are:

- Who are our customers and how are web shopping experiences affecting future online behaviour?
- What are customer expectations of web-based service delivery?
- Which factors affect demand for online business-to-consumer services?
- What are the key decisions that a consumer-facing organisation should consider when developing an e-retail strategy?

## Links to other chapters

This chapter builds on concepts and frameworks introduced earlier in the book. The main related chapters are as follows:

- Chapter 2, which provides an introduction to the characteristics of Internet consumer behaviour
- Chapter 4, which introduces strategic approaches to exploiting the Internet
- Chapter 6, which examines customer relationship management issues
- Chapter 7, covering issues relating to successful site development and operations

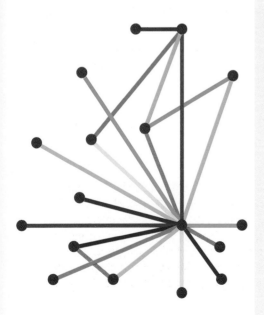

## Introduction

Business-to-consumer (B2C) markets have made a significant contribution to the commercial development of the Internet encouraging wide-scale use of computer networks by a diverse and increasingly global range of consumers. According to researchers in the US, more than 875 million consumers worldwide shopped on the Internet in 2007, and the growth is set to continue; indeed in financial terms UK analysts' predictions suggest that online retail sales will reach £78 billion a year by 2010 (IMRG, 2008) nearly double the online sales recorded in 2007. The Internet provides access to a digital trading environment, which facilitates market exchanges using a growing number of access points and types of fixed and mobile technologies. As the Internet has become more widely accessible, online trading has presented customer-facing businesses with many opportunities and challenges. The success levels of Internet-based retailers has been eagerly watched and tracked by analysts around the globe as an indicator of the potential of this virtual trading environment to change fundamentally the way all businesses trade with their customers. Online success in consumer markets is not guaranteed but during the last decade many new and established retail companies have developed successful online operations: Argos, Tesco, Marks & Spencer, Currys, Screwfix Direct, Next and Figleaves.com.

This chapter explores some of the key issues having an impact on the growth and development of online B2C markets and begins by focusing on first the consumers: who they are; their expectations; how online experiences affect the motivation to shop online; and then retailers: the meaning and scope of the term *e-retailing* and the different ways in which digital and Internet technologies are used to create a virtual *retail channel*. The chapter concludes with a discussion of the factors affecting the development of successful e-retail strategies.

### Key themes and concepts

This chapter considers online B2C markets from two distinct perspectives:

- **The consumer perspective** – the first part of the chapter focuses on the online consumer, namely his/her profile, which has been found to strongly influence the extent to which particular consumers shop online and also online shopping experiences, which are likely to shape online shopping intentions.
- **The retailer perspective** – the second part of the chapter examines the development of e-retailing, types of online strategies, factors likely to affect how retailers develop e-retailing activities, managerial and strategic challenges.

This chapter provides illustrative case studies, examples of consumer and retailer behaviour and graphics as supporting material. Academic articles are used to support underlying theoretical issues and concepts.

## The consumer perspective: online consumer behaviour

Levels of consumer demand for online shopping and services might ultimately determine the size of e-retail markets and when or if a market saturation point will be reached for online purchasing. Various influences, such as whether the consumer has access to the Internet, levels of competency in use of the technology and the perceived benefits of Internet shopping, have been identified as key factors likely to impact on whether an individual shops online.

Internet retailing, or e-retailing as it will be referred to for the rest of this chapter, offers the consumer an experience very different from shopping in the high street: web-based stores can be open continuously around the clock; interactive promotions, which can be highly customised and permission-based; dynamic pricing enables real-time prices, which reflect current market demand e.g., eBay auctions; comparison shopping is much easier and quicker online than in the physical world. Indeed, many consumers, even if they do not intend to buy online, turn to the Internet to find information about a product in the early part of the buying decision-making process. An example of an online brand, which facilitates comparison of products and prices, is Kelkoo.com. The origins of the name from the French phrase 'Quel coût?' can be interpreted as 'At what price?' or even 'What a bargain'. The Kelkoo portal was taken over by Yahoo in 2004 to reportedly enable advertisers to have better target marketing opportunities but retains the brand identity and continues to aid pre-purchase product comparisons.

As a result of the innovative characteristics of the virtual shopping environment, the online consumer experience can become an elective and very goal-orientated activity whereby consumers go to the Internet to seek the particular products and services they wish to buy. Perea *et al.* (2004) highlight that while consumers are increasingly shopping online it is not clear what drives them to shop in this way. They suggest there are various factors, including ease of use, enjoyment and consumer traits, which will determine whether an individual will become an avid Internet shopper. So who are the customers who shop online?

## Who are the online customers?

Many researchers have written about online consumer behaviour and a very wide array of factors and variables have been cited as influencing the extent to which individuals are likely to shop online. Hoffman *et al.* (2004), focused on the impact of demographics, and highlighted inequities of Internet access based on race and gender. Source *et al.* (2005) looked at age and found that 'while older shoppers search for significantly fewer products than their younger counterparts they actually purchase as much as the younger consumer'. Doherty and Ellis-Chadwick (2006) suggest the large body of literature looking at online consumer behaviour variables can be grouped into two broad categories: studies of *consumer profiles* and studies of *consumer experiences*.[1]

### The consumer profile

A consumer's profile can strongly influence where, when and how an individual shops online and also have important marketing implications. We can break the consumer profile down into two distinct sub-categories: classification variables and character variables.

*Classification variables* are those personal attributes which tend to remain static throughout an individual's lifetime or evolve slowly over time. These variables are particularly useful for marketers as they can help to *identify* particular consumers and target groups. Moreover, according to Jobber (2007), profile segmentation variables can be used to group consumers together in a meaningful way so they can be reached by suitable media communications. See Table 11.1 for a list of classification variables and possible implications for online target marketing. It is also important to consider the overall size of the target market and the extent to which it is viable to spend company resources accessing and developing market share. Now read Mini case 11.1 and consider the importance of geographical distribution of Internet user populations and try to consider how understanding the nature of online markets and how they are changing might help the development of successful online target marketing strategies.

---

1 The discussion of the consumer profile is based on review of Internet Retailing literature by Doherty and Ellis-Chadwick (2006).

| Table 11.1 | Consumer profile: classification variables |
| --- | --- |

| Profile variable | Online marketing impact |
| --- | --- |
| Age | Age can affect levels of access to technology, computer literacy and, eventually, the extent to which individuals use the Internet as part of their shopping routines. In the UK, of the 16 to 24 age group, 90% had accessed the Internet within the 3 months prior to interview, compared with 24% of the 65+ age group (Office for National Statistics, 2007). |
| Education | At the higher end of the educational spectrum (university and college graduates) the Internet is considered as essential if not indispensible. However, the digital divide is persistent and Internet access is lower in areas with poorer educational achievement and lower-income schools. |
| Employment status | Employment places time constraints on online shopping behaviour, i.e. when and where individuals can access online shopping channels. |
| Gender | Male consumers still tend to make more purchases and buy higher ticket items online than females although the gap between is narrowing significantly. In the UK, 71% of males compared with 62% of females accessed the Internet during 2007. |
| Geography | Location is an important consideration: where people live can affect the potential size of the online market; Asia now has the largest number of Internet users, followed by the European Union (EU). Interestingly the USA no longer has the highest number of Internet users (see Mini case 11.1 for further discussion of access and user populations). |
| Household size | Household size has the potential to affect the number of people involved in purchasing decisions and the direction of influence. For example, research has shown that in Europe children and teenagers can have a strong influence on purchasing based on their levels of computing competency. |
| Household type | Household type has the potential to affect product and service requirements; major shifts towards single person households in the UK (11% increase since 1971 to 29%) has led to a shift in purchasing patterns and times of purchasing. Online, such households can create logistical difficulties when delivering bulky and perishable goods. Interestingly over three-quarters of all households with children have access to the Internet as opposed to just over half of households without children. |
| Income | Income affects purchasing power and also influences whether individuals have access to the Internet. In the UK, AB, C1, C2 social-economic groups are significantly more likely to have access to the Internet and to subsequently shop online than groupings D, E. Income is positively related to a tendency to shop online. |
| Mobility | Mobility affects channel access; less mobile targets may be encouraged to shop online. This also applies to macro-populations, which are poorly served by public and private transport. |
| Race and ethnicity | Race and ethnicity affects access to technology and economic circumstances. In the US, the number of African–Americans with Internet access is increasing to over 50% but this sector of the population lags behind the Caucasians and Hispanics. |

This table has been compiled from information and statistics from Hoffman *et al.* (2004), Office for National Statistics (2007) and from Internet usage and world population data (30 September 2007) from www.internetworldstats.com/stats.html.

Mini Case Study 11.1    Consumer access and online user populations

Access to the Internet is an important consideration as it affects the distributions of user populations. The point of access can be fixed or mobile and, say, be at home or work. In the UK, according to the Office for National Statistics (2007), the most common place to access the Internet was at home (87%), although 44% have accessed it at work, 19% at another person's home, 12% at a place of education and 4% at a public library. Table 11.2 shows Internet access in conjunction with global population statistics to provide insight into worldwide Internet penetration.

Table 11.2    World Internet usage and population statistics

| World regions | Population (2007 est.) | Population % of world | Internet user, data | % Population (penetration) | Usage % of world | Usage growth 2000–2007 |
|---|---|---|---|---|---|---|
| Africa | 933,448,292 | 14.2% | 43,995,700 | 4.7% | 3.5% | 874.6% |
| Asia | 3,712,527,624 | 56.5% | 459,476,825 | 12.4% | 36.9% | 302.0% |
| Europe | 809,624,686 | 12.3% | 337,878,613 | 41.7% | 27.2% | 221.5% |
| Middle East | 193,452,727 | 2.9% | 33,510,500 | 17.3% | 2.7% | 920.2% |
| North America | 334,538,018 | 5.1% | 234,788,864 | 70.2% | 18.9% | 117.2% |
| Latin American/ Caribbean | 556,606,627 | 8.5% | 115,759,709 | 20.8% | 9.3% | 540.7% |
| Oceania/ Australia | 34,468,443 | 0.5% | 19,039,390 | 55.2% | 1.5% | 149.9% |
| World totals | 6,574,666,417 | 100.0% | 1,244,449,601 | 18.9% | 100.0% | 244.7% |

In Africa, Internet penetration per head of population is less than 5%, which is most likely due to access to technology both at an individual and an organisation level. There has been fairly limited development of the Internet infrastructure in Africa because of geographical extremes, political instability and controls, and lack of financial investment. In Asia, especially China in the early days, consumer adoption of the Internet was severely restricted by political factors. However, recently these markets have become more liberalised and subject to less restrictions, which has resulted in rapid growth in user populations. It is interesting to note that Asia now has more individual Internet users than anywhere else in the world; almost double the number in Northern America.  The impact of the changing user base is that more websites are becoming available in the native languages of the users and in the future English may not continue as the dominant language of the web.

However, North America continues to have the highest overall Internet penetration (70.2% of the population) of the seven continents, which is unsurprising given it is where consumer access to the Internet originated and arguably offers much lower barriers to access than any other parts of the globe, e.g., free local telephone rates, widespread use of computers. But, it should be noted, there is variation in penetration rates among specific groups of North American users based on race, gender, age, with African–Americans being the least likely to be online.  Hoffman et al. (2004) also argue that although the Internet is becoming indispensible, inequities exist: 'an essential part of everyday life – and indispensable in many ways – for many individuals in our society, Internet access remains elusive'.

In Europe the difference in Internet adoption is noticeable between the well-developed northern countries, which have a higher level of penetration per head of population than southern European and former eastern block countries. Iceland continues to have the highest levels of Internet access with almost

90% of the population being connected. It is possible that national and individual wealth accounts for much of the variation in access in European countries (see Table 11.3). With the exception of Ireland, which is currently twenty-first in the Internet penetration population rankings, the top countries in terms of GDP per capita are also at the top of the rankings in terms of Internet penetration.

| Table 11.3 | Wealth of nations compared to Internet penetration: Europe |

| Country | Population | GDP per capita[1] | % Population[2] (Internet penetration) | Internet population ranking in Europe |
|---|---|---|---|---|
| Luxembourg | 463,273 | $87,955 | 68.00% | 6th |
| Norway | 4,657,321 | $72,306 | 67.40% | 8th |
| Iceland | 299,076 | $54,858 | 86.30% | 1st |
| Ireland | 4,104,354 | $52,400 | 50.20% | 21st |
| Switzerland | 7,523,024 | $51,771 | 67.80% | 7th |
| Denmark | 5,438,698 | $50,965 | 69.20% | 5th |
| Sweden | 9,107,795 | $42,383 | 75.60% | 2nd |
| Netherlands | 16,447,682 | $40,571 | 73.30% | 4th |
| Finland | 5,275,491 | $40,197 | 62.30% | 10th |
| United Kingdom | 60,363,602 | $39,213 | 62.30% | 11th |

1 International Monetary Fund, World Economics Outlook Database, April 2007.
2 Internet Usage and World Population Statistics are for 20 September 2007, http://www.internetworld stats,com/stats.htm

The Internet infrastructure spans the globe but analysis of the penetration of user populations shows there are major variations in levels of access depending on where consumers live. Furthermore, even within nations with high levels of Internet access there are high levels of variability. Overall, the key trend is that the Internet user base continues to grow and as a result global Internet penetration is increasing. Currently in nations with well-established technological infrastructures, penetration appears to stabilise at around 60 to 65% of the population.

Market development has been cited as a major reason why retailers seek to develop online shopping websites. Many retailers see potential to increase sales through the development of international markets. However, if companies are to succeed in such market expansion they will need to develop understanding of the make-up of the international markets they intend to target, the distribution of potential online shoppers and the cultural implications.

*Source*: Based on Ellis-Chadwick (2008)

*Character variables* are less straightforward to understand and identify as they comprise any attributes of a consumer's perceptions, beliefs and attitudes, which might influence online behaviour and also shape an individual's intentions to shop online – e.g. innovativeness, enjoyment, skills and experience and emotions. It is important to recognise that character variables are more likely to develop, change and be significantly modified over time by online shopping experiences than classification variables. For example, if a consumer has negative beliefs about, say, privacy and security of online transactions, which are due to *lack of computer skills* these *beliefs* are likely to shape negative *attitudes* towards the Internet and reduce the *intention* to shop online. Conversely, if a consumer *believes* the Internet is, say, *easy to use,* they are more likely to have a positive *attitude* towards the idea of online shopping and ultimately have an increased *intention* to shop online. Each stance may be continually reinforced by positive or negative feedback from online shopping experiences. See Figure 11.1 for a model of how character variables interact.

Consumers' beliefs about a range of variables might ultimately shape their attitudes towards the Internet and their purchasing intentions. Examples include:

- *Security and privacy of information* – customers have an expectation that if they are prepared to provide detailed personal and financial information it will be stored securely. If this is not the case, personal belief, attitudes and intentions to shop online are likely to be negatively affected when a case of fraudulent credit card use or stolen identity occurs.
- *Risk* – online consumers are buying into a trading situation laden with uncertainty and a lack of cues to reinforce trading relationships and risk. Bauer (1960) identified six key types of risk likely to affect consumers: financial, product performance, social, psychological, physical and time/convenience loss. Online sales effectiveness can be increased significantly if the perception of risk is reduced. Willingness to purchase is considered to be inversely affected by perceived risk. Stone and Gronhaug (1993) state that 'risk is the subjective expectation of a loss'.
- *Trust* – is a potential outcome of risk reduction. Trust needs to be increased and perceived risk decreased for consumers to develop positive beliefs in the organisation's online reputation. Dimensions of trust include service provider expertise, product performance, firm reputations, satisfaction (with past interactions) and similarity. It should be noted that some researchers have suggested that not all online customers respond in the same manner. Newholm *et al.* (2004) conclude that e-retailers should adopt a differential approach to building trust and raise the point that types of customers and products can significantly affect how retailers should develop approaches for handling risk and trust. Indeed 'bargain hunters' are inherently risk takers and in this case it becomes the propensity to engage in risk taking, rather than being risk averse. eBay's Online auctions have seen

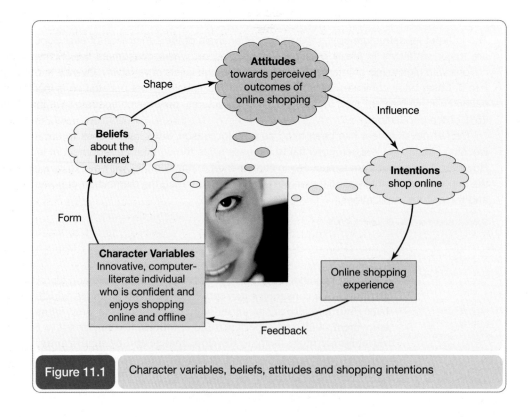

| Figure 11.1 | Character variables, beliefs, attitudes and shopping intentions |

a massive upsurge in the number of sales of second-hand goods, which are traded between unknown buyers and sellers. Each party has limited knowledge of the other's past trading performance, the levels of service quality or the condition of the goods and/or services on offer and yet millions of buyers are willing to gamble large sums of money in pursuit of goods. The high level of purchasing activity has not gone unnoticed by retailers as many now offer goods for sale within the eBay platform.

- *Perceived usefulness* – is positively associated with the intention to purchase and is defined as the extent to which an individual perceives that a new technology will enhance or improve his/her performance. Applied to online shopping, usefulness relates to the amount of time and effort required to learn how to shop online measured against the levels of service excellence provided by the retailer (Perea *et al.*, 2004).
- *Ease of use* – is an individual's perception that using a new technology will be free of effort and has been found to have particular influence in the early stages of a user's experience with a new technology (Davis, 1993).

In summary, *classification* and *character* variables have both been found to play an important role in predicting how consumers might behave over time, but it should be acknowledged that only character variables will be significantly affected by online shopping experiences (Doherty and Ellis-Chadwick, 2006). For example, gender may influence the extent to which an individual might shop online but gender will not be changed by online shopping experiences.

## The consumers' online shopping experiences

The actual experience of online shopping has been found to have an effect on consumers' overall assessment of the online shopping process (Doherty and Ellis-Chadwick, 2006). Positive experiences in terms of convenience, service delivery, website security have all been found to increase customer satisfaction (Szymanski and Hise, 2000). Website design, ease of navigation, good levels of service and good value products have been found to increase consumer loyalty and also found to enhance the customer experience (Wolfinbarger and Gilly, 2003). E-retailers should aim to understand how customer expectations have been raised. Some of the key areas where customers have high expectations are:

- *Delivery* – the critical link between an online order and the delivery of the product is often referred to as the final or last mile. The last mile, including product transportation, is frequently considered the most important element of the order fulfilment process, i.e. 89% of online shoppers rate on-time delivery high in importance and 85% of buyers who receive their order on time would shop at the Internet merchant again. Thus, delivery-related issues have been shown to have a high level of importance to online shoppers (Esper *et al.*, 2003).
- *Timeliness* – the speed of digital communications has raised customer expectations in terms of response times and they expect a speedy shopping experience. It is no longer acceptable to take three or four days to respond to an online customer enquiry; an online customer expects that the response will be instantaneous or at least within a couple of hours. Additionally, they expect to be able to order goods and services at any time.
- *Availability* – the Internet creates a sales environment, which is not restricted by space constraints, therefore there is an increased expectation that not only will there be a wider range of goods for sale online but also the goods will be readily available for immediate delivery.
- *Convenience* – it should be easier and quicker to compare prices online; there should be easy access to a wide range of retailers without the inconvenience of having to travel to a number of different locations.
- *Customer service* – customer value is the foremost driver of competitive advantage in the Internet shopping environment and customer service can be measured by the consumer

in terms of price savings, service excellence, time savings and experiential values such as entertainment, visual stimulation/reward, levels of interaction. Positive response to such factors can lead to heightened loyalty (Lee and Overby, 2004). Online customer loyalty has also been well researched. Srinivasan *et al.* (2002) identified several variables as being unique to online consumer markets. Read about the various dimensions of customer loyalty and how they can be translated into website features in Table 11.4.

It is important to understand that the increase in customer expectations can have quite wide-reaching organisational implications. The gap between customer expectations of the online offer and the actual performance can have a significant impact on online performance. Now read Mini case study 11.2 which explores the relationship between experiences and online success. Note that the similar E-SERVQUAL and WEBQUAL frameworks are described towards the end of Chapter 7.

---

### Mini Case Study 11.2 — eTailQ

There has been a great deal of academic research looking at the relationship between quality and online success in consumer markets. Wolfinbarger and Gilly (2003) used the idea that quality is related to customer satisfaction and retention and ultimately customer loyalty. The study identified four dimensions of e-tailing and in doing so enabled the development of a reliable scale for the measurement of online retail quality called eTailQ. The four key dimensions identified by the study can help managers to understand customer judgements of a company website and how customers shape their attitudes based on their experiences of visiting say a retailer's website. The four dimensions in rank order of importance are:

1 **Website design:**
   - Easy navigation
   - Appropriate levels of information
   - Effective information search facility
   - Straightforward ordering
   - Appropriate personalisation
   - Appropriate product selection
2 **Fulfilment/reliability:**
   - Accurate display aimed at ensuring alignment between customer expectations and realisation
   - Delivery of the right product within promised time frame
3 **Customer service:**
   - Responsiveness to enquiries
   - Helpful
   - Willing service
   - Immediacy of response
4 **Privacy/security:**
   - Secure payment facilities
   - Secure and private personal information

Customer judgement of the quality of the website visit is an important part of the customer's online experience and the outcome of the evaluation process could determine whether the customer (a) is sufficiently *satisfied* to return and make another purchase, (b) develops *loyalty* intentions and subsequently recommends a site to friends and family, (c) develops a positive relationship with the brand.

| Table 11.4 | Loyalty variables |
|---|---|

| Loyalty variable | Website feature |
|---|---|
| Customisation | Personally, tailored product ranges, for example lists of regular grocery purchases, favourite products, brands, etc. |
| Contact interactivity | Two-way communications that demonstrate the dynamic nature of the online buyer/supplier customer relationship. |
| Cultivation | E-mail offers relating to past purchases, informing customers when there is a discount sale on items similar to their previous purchases. |
| Care | Real-time stock-out information/order tracking. Shoppers are looking for evidence that the retailer has paid attention to detail throughout the purchasing process. |
| Community | Product reviews from satisfied customers. Include a facility allowing and encouraging exchange of opinions among shoppers. |
| Choice | Online shoppers expect greater choice online. Therefore, the retailer needs to offer either wide or deep (or both) product and/or service choice. |
| Convenience | Easy access to required information and a simple transaction interface. Over-designed and cognitively complex sites tend to lose visitors before they make a purchase. |
| Character | Symbols, graphics, style, colours, themes can be used to reinforce brand image and convey brand personality. |

*Source*: Based on Srinivasan *et al.*, 2002

In summary, consumer demand for online shopping continues to grow at a rapid rate. As the Internet infrastructure expands and develops, more parts of the world are able to have access to the technology, which enables them to shop online. Political and economic development is also playing a part in enabling certain parts of the world to take part in the e-commence revolution.

At an individual level more is now known about online consumer behaviour and for retail managers and marketers the key to online success is developing better understanding of the *consumer's profile* and the *consumer's experiences of online shopping*. It is important to remember that online shoppers tend to have different profiles and characteristics to offline shoppers, which shape their shopping intentions. Online shoppers tend to be younger, wealthier, better educated, have higher 'computer literacy' and more disposable income than the offline shopper. It is also important when planning e-retail strategies to consider that as the Internet becomes a more mainstream shopping channel there are likely to be a greater range of cultural differences as wider sectors of the global populations have greater access to online shopping channels. The next part of the chapter explores B2C markets from the retailer's perspective and looks at how organisations are developing the online shopping provision.

# The retail perspective: e-retailing

This section explores online shopping from the retailer's perspective. More specifically, it considers the development of the online trading environment and e-retailing activities, trading formats and strategies and the strategic implications of trading online in consumer markets.

## Development of e-retailing

In the early 1990s, when the development of the Internet as a trading environment began with the first exchanges of commercial e-mail, traditional retailers had little interest in trading online. As this new virtual environment expanded and became more widely known as the 'information superhighway', business communities began to consider the commercial opportunities of trading in a digital environment. However, for many retailers it was considered as a remote 'geekish' environment used solely by computer experts and scientists. It was not until the mid-1990s that larger retail companies began to consider how the Internet might impact on trade in the future and the challenges they might face.

In 1995, few retailers considered the Internet to be important as a channel to market but given the potential of Internet technologies to radically reconfigure the underlying processes of retailing, and because of the highly dynamic and innovative nature of the electronic marketplace, some companies began to test out online trading. Tesco began selling chocolates and flowers, and soon afterwards Sainsbury's and Dixons launched websites. Retailers in well-developed nations, particularly in the US and northern Europe, have spent recent years working out how to best use this new digital phenomenon to support and develop retail trading.

Since 2001 many retailers have accepted the Internet as a durable trading environment and have set about working out how to shape their companies to cope with the demands of trading and interacting in a virtual environment. Difficulties to overcome have been logistics, distribution and how to ensure standards of online customer service. But for companies that have been able to resolve these issues there has been the potential to develop sustained competitive advantage and customer value (for further discussion see Case study 11, page **638**).

By 2008 most retailers consider it essential to have a website and a growing number also offer their customers the option to shop online. Online retailing has become increasingly popular and important to retailers and consumers around the world. In the UK, during the last ten years, the online shopping spend has increased from around 0.07% to 7% of total annual retail sales. Moreover, recent evidence suggests that consumers' appetite for online shopping is growing rapidly as the Internet has become increasingly accessible, convenient and secure. In the UK, millions of customers now shop online, spending an average of over €800 each in 2006 (Verdict Research, 2007). In the case of Tesco.com, Internet sales have increased to over £1bn annually and profits close to £60m. Tesco offers online shoppers throughout the UK a full range of over ten thousand of products online, which can be found in its high street stores, plus a comprehensive and expanding range of non-food goods through the recently established Tesco Direct.

It is interesting to consider, given such levels of online retail success, why all retailers are not following the Tesco model and offering customers similar levels of, say, product choice service and support online as they do in their offline stores. Sainsbury's, for example, offers online shopping services to around 83% of the UK but there are limits to the product range; Waitrose (in conjunction with Ocado) supply a wide range of products online but shopping delivery services are restricted (by location) to around 40% of the UK population. By contrast, Wm Morrison do not offer any form of online shopping (Ellis-Chadwick *et al.*, 2007).

This variability in levels of online service and product choice offered by UK grocery retailers (reportedly, some of the most well-developed online shopping services in the world) prompts investigation into the types of formats and operational strategies that retailers adopt when trading online.

# E-retail formats and operational strategies

The introduction of online shopping has made classifying retailers by operational formats an increasingly complex task. Traditionally, retailers are classified by: types of retail organisation, e.g., multiples, independent, co-operative; format, e.g., store-based, home-based and each of these features of the operation can also be modified by the breadth and depth of product range offered, target markets served and number of outlets operated. Arguably, online shopping formats have evolved as part of the *natural* progression of the retail life cycle. Davidson *et al.*, (1976) introduced the idea of the retail lifecycle to explain the evolution of forms of retailing over time. Based on the premise that styles of retail operation have a lifecycle in much the same way products do and will start from an *introductory* phase where the operational style is innovative, and then move through into a *growth* stage as the business expands, into a *maturity* stage where the company begins to see greater profitability and then finally into *decline* stage, where the business is overtaken by more innovative competitors offering different retail styles and operational formats.

In the case of online shopping, the retail lifecycle only gives us part of the picture as it does not take into account environmental influences. Online shopping has emerged in part as a response to the competitive pressures which are the underlying drivers in the retail lifecycle model, and in part due to the rapid development of digital *technology* which has had a profound effect on all businesses, not just retailers, by creating a whole new trading arena. We will now look at *operational categories* and *operational strategies* to build up a picture of the choices that retail marketing strategists face when building and developing an online operation.

## Operational categories

To begin to understand the operational styles and strategies of online retailers it is important to consider three main operational categories:

- *Bricks-and-clicks retailers* are generally long-established retailers operating from bricks-and-mortar stores in, say, the high street and then the Internet is integrated into their businesses either strategically or tactically as a marketing tool or a sales channel. According to Dennis *et al.* (2004) online shoppers prefer shopping at websites operated by established high-street retailers as they understand what a brand means in terms of value and the physical part of the operation gives an increased sense of security.
- *Clicks-and-mortar retailers* tend to be virtual merchants and design their operating format to accommodate consumer demands by trading online supported by a physical distribution infrastructure. Virtual channels have distinct advantages over traditional marketing channels in that they potentially reduce barriers to entry. The location issue, considered to be the key determinant of retail patronage (Finn and Louviere, 1990), is in the physical sense reduced, along with the need for sizeable capital investment in stores. The best-known virtual merchant using this format is Amazon.com, the world's largest online bookstore.
- *Pureplay retailers* – 'clicks-only' or virtual retailers operate entirely online. In reality it is almost impossible for a business to operate online without a point of access to the Internet. Therefore, generally speaking, the term 'pureplay' refers to retailers who do not have fixed-location stores and or own physical operational support systems, e.g. distribution warehouses. While this category has produced some very innovative retailers, in reality few retailers actually outsource all warehousing, picking, packing, shipping, returns and replenishment requirement. Figures 11.2 and 11.3 show screenshots from the home pages of Play.com, which is a leading online retailer of DVDs, music, video games, books, electronics, gadgets and ringtones, and Expedia.co.uk, which is a travel portal that enables travellers to engage in activities from 'kite surfing in Miami to a wine tour of Tuscany, from a pub crawl in Dublin to safari in Cape Town – add some spice to your holiday with Expedia. With over 3000 activities, attractions, services and more at your fingertips! You can choose to book it alone or add it when you tailor make your package with us'.[1] Perhaps the key difference

---

[1] Expedia.co.uk http://www.expedia.co.uk/daily/activities/default.aspx?rfrr=-13007)

between these two companies is that one sells products and the other services. In the case of services, the customer takes themselves to the point of consumption rather than having goods delivered to their door. Other companies which fit this category are those which sell products in digitised form (Dennis *et al.*, 2004). The example of digitised products and the services industry is discussed in more detail in Chapter 12.

In addition to these three operational categories, there are new types of business which are targeting consumer markets. The growth in importance of *intermediaries* has led to the use of the term 'reintermediation' (see Chapter 1). In this case companies, not traditionally service shoppers, use the Internet and the web to connect buyers and sellers through the web and by e-mail. Manufacturers of consumer goods have also seen the opportunities offered by using the Internet as a sales channel to regain some of their power lost to the retailers in the past by the shortening of distribution channels. The process of disintermediation works by the manufacturer excluding the retailer altogether and marketing directly to the customer, thus shortening the value chain and/or the supply chain by trading electronically and shifting the balance of power closer to the end-consumer. Early examples of disintermediation originated within the banking industry, when it was noticed that information technology and industry regulation had reduced the need for retail banks as intermediaries.

## E-retailing operational strategies

The Internet trading environment is largely still in its introduction phase and as a result e-retailing is still evolving. It is possible that virtual merchants (brick-and-clicks, pureplays, intermediaries) could prove to be highly successful, established retailers operating from fixed-location stores but could find themselves increasingly being replaced by new Internet-based retail formats. The implications are considerable, as the provision of online shopping is beginning to fundamentally alter the way that consumers shop, and in doing so revolutionise the retail environment.

| Figure 11.2 | Play.com (www.play.com) |

**Figure 11.3**    Expedia UK (www.expedia.co.uk)

Dutch researchers Weltevreden and Boschma (2007) have developed a typology which categorises potential operational strategies that retailers might adopt and develop into information-based and sales-based (Table 11.5).

### Information only strategies (adapted from Weltevreden *et al.*, 2005)

- *Billboards strategy*: retailers use this type of website to provide information primarily to make customers aware of the company's existence. The site will not provide specific product information and only gives limited details about services offered.
- *Brochure strategy*: this type of website acts as a showcase providing information with a little more detail of specific products, say, new product lines.
- *Catalogue strategy*: this type of website provides detailed product information but offers little in terms of additional services.
- *Service strategy*: this type of website provides customers with access to a range of support services which can help build and develop customer relationships, e.g. searchable database of customer support information.

| Table 11.5 | Internet operational strategies | | | | | |
|---|---|---|---|---|---|---|

| Strategy | Product information | Synergies/ additional services | Online sales physical channel(s) | Physical outlets | Website resembles | Physical outlets have limited functions |
|---|---|---|---|---|---|---|
| Billboard | None | None/limited | No | Yes | – | No |
| Brochure | Limited | None/limited | No | Yes | – | No |
| Catalogue | Extensive | None/limited | No | Yes | – | No |
| Service | Limited/extensive | Extensive | No | Yes | – | No |
| Export | Extensive | None/limited | Yes | Yes | No similarity | No |
| Mirror | Extensive | None/limited | Yes | Yes | Strong similarity | No |
| Synergy | Extensive | Extensive | Yes | Yes | Similarity | No |
| Anti-mirror | Extensive | None/limited | Yes | Yes | Similarity | Yes |
| Virtual | Extensive | Limited/extensive | Yes | No | – | – |

*Source*: Adapted from Weltevreden *et al.* (2005)

### Online sales strategies

- *Export strategy*: in this case retailers sell online but the operation has no linkages to the physical retail presence the retailer may have in the high street. This strategy is sometimes adopted when entering a new market and can limit risk for a well-established brand.
- *Mirror strategy*: in this case a website has the look and feel of a retailer's offline operation but there are no linkages between the online and offline channel. The website is almost like an additional store.
- *Synergy strategy*: in this case there are strong links between the online and offline operations, e.g. cross-promotions, returns of goods ordered online can be taken back into the physical store.
- *Anti-mirror strategy*: here the website has become the dominant sales channel and physical stores are used to support the web operation rather than the other way around.
- *Virtual strategy*: the retailer either gives up the physical presence or does not develop one. It should be noted that in this case the distinction between category and strategy becomes blurred.

Perhaps the key question is how do retailers select the right strategy to adopt? There is a pattern of retail adoption, whereby retailers move from information-based strategies to online sales strategies. A five-year study examining the extent of Internet adoption in the UK by Ellis-Chadwick *et al.* (2002) found that traditional retailers are increasingly likely to begin by having an information-based website and then develop services before offering online sales. European retailers are seen as being advanced in their use of computer-based technologies, so it comes as no surprise that some retail companies were quick to explore the commercial potential of the Internet. But it has taken time for companies to assess and develop a strategic significance for their online activities. Typically, a newly established retail website aims to cover a range of business objectives but is likely to show limited evidence of targeting of content towards specific online consumers; corporate information for investors has often been presented alongside details of consumer promotions and graduate recruitment features. However, as the web usage develops, the focus and strategic contribution of the online channels change. Figure 11.4 suggests how the strategic focus might change over time.

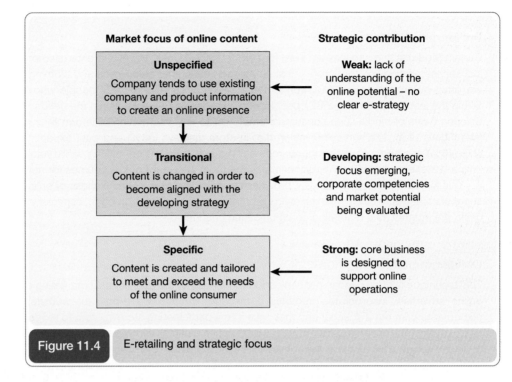

**Market focus of online content**          **Strategic contribution**

**Unspecified**

Company tends to use existing company and product information to create an online presence

**Weak:** lack of understanding of the online potential – no clear e-strategy

**Transitional**

Content is changed in order to become aligned with the developing strategy

**Developing:** strategic focus emerging, corporate competencies and market potential being evaluated

**Specific**

Content is created and tailored to meet and exceed the needs of the online consumer

**Strong:** core business is designed to support online operations

| Figure 11.4 | E-retailing and strategic focus |

**Retail channel**

Retailers' use of the Internet as both a communication and a transactional channel concurrently in business-to-consumer markets.

**Share of voice**

The relative advertising spend of the different competitive brands within the product category. Share of voice is calculated by dividing a particular brand's advertising spend by the total category spend (De Pelsmacker *et al.*, 2004).

As retailers develop their usage of the Internet for providing information, customer services and online sales it becomes a **retail channel**. This term was introduced by Doherty *et al.* (1999) to describe companies' multi-purpose adoption of the Internet, using it as both a communication and transactional channel concurrently in business-to-consumer markets. Traditionally the term *channel* describes the flow of a product from source to end-user. This definition implies a passive unidirectional system whereby the manufacturer or producer markets through a wholesaler or retailer to the consumer. Recent developments in information technology are changing this orientation by enabling retailers to focus their marketing efforts on managing customers more effectively (Mulhern, 1997). Therefore, the Internet brings the customer even closer to the retailers via a new combined marketing and distribution channel, in effect an interactive *retail channel*. This move may also suggest a shift towards a bidirectional retailer–consumer relationship, in which more power accrues to the customer (Hagel and Armstrong, 1997). As a result of the technological capacity e-retailers are becoming increasingly creative with how they are using the Internet and associated digital technologies to serve the needs of their online customers. Now read Mini case study 11.3 'The offline impact of online marketing'.

| Mini Case Study 11.3 | The offline impact of online marketing |

Increasingly, companies are keen to understand the effect and impact of their promotional spend, and particularly how different marketing communication tools perform. As with broadcast media advertising, it can be difficult to assess the impact of Internet marketing initiatives on offline sales. Traditionally, in the retail sector, it is not common practice to track the reasons why consumers arrive in a particular store to make their purchase. However, according to Hewitt (2004) the Internet is 'not just a great promotion vehicle, it's also the tracking source that enables us to close the loop and see what happened after the visitor left the website and went shopping'. He suggests several ways in which retailers might use the Internet to follow their customers' offline purchasing behaviour. Tactics to gather information include the following.

## Pre-purchase Internet surveys

Certain products and services are ideal for selling online (books, travel and entertainment tickets) and financial services, whereas other products such as cars, consumer electronics and clothing are researched but not often purchased online. AOL conducted a series of surveys of 1004 people who had purchased TVs within the last six months and 521 people who intended to buy a TV within the next six months to find the differing types of media such consumers employed to find information to inform their purchasing decision (see Figure 11.5). The surveys revealed that in-store displays (58%) and past experience/previous ownership (48%) are the most important sources of TV purchase decision making, while retailer flyers (13%) and online (12%) are ranked by TV purchasers as the most important media sources for new TV information.

This kind of survey is useful as it provides an indication of the effectiveness of online promotion. It also suggests that it is necessary to link online promotion with in-store promotion, especially if retailers are solely using the Internet as a marketing communication channel.

## Online coupon redemption

This technique is often used in the early adoption stages of the Internet as a marketing communication. The online advertiser incorporates/promotes a discount coupon via e-mail (or website) and requests the customer to print out a voucher and then take it to a participating store in order to redeem the discount (e.g. see Figure 11.6 concerning McArthur Glen Designer Outlets). On redemption of the printed voucher the retailer is able to analyse the impact of the online promotion on the offline purchasing behaviour and in doing so develops an understanding of their return on investment in online advertising.

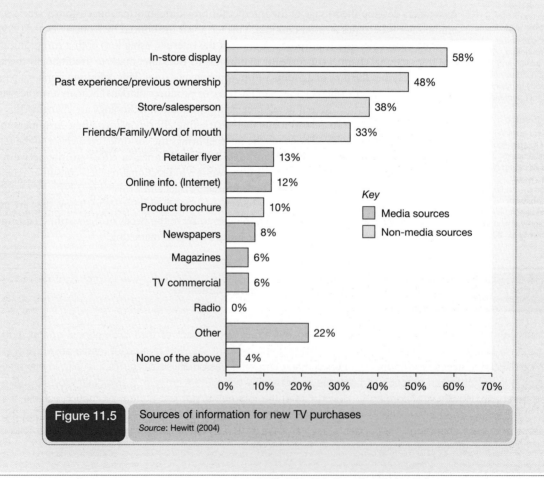

| Figure 11.5 | Sources of information for new TV purchases |
|---|---|
| | *Source*: Hewitt (2004) |

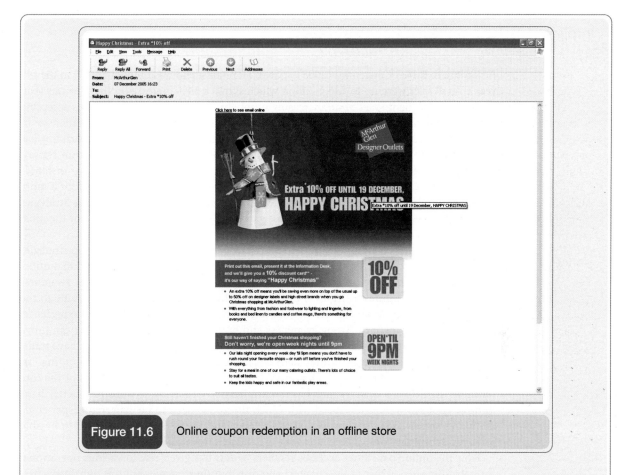

| Figure 11.6 | Online coupon redemption in an offline store |

## Online rebate/gift with purchase

In this instance the retailer tracks the online customer's information through the use of cookies and offers some form of discount or gift offer with purchase. Generally, the customer will be required to register online.

Just as consumer use of the Internet has been growing rapidly during the last decade, so too has the use of the Internet as a medium to communicate a company's marketing messages. Research has shown the Internet as having an increasing share of voice when compared with other media. Furthermore, a survey conducted by IAB (2008) found that consumer advertisers still make a strong contribution to the online advertising spend. The strategic implications of such findings are that retailers should be developing measurement techniques to determine the effectiveness of the online media on the offline spend.

## Consumer advertiser spend surges in 2007

Internet advertising grew by 41% in the first half of 2007. Classified advertising saw a significant growth of 72% and now represents nearly 21% of all Internet advertising spend. Internet display advertising (banners, skyscrapers and rich media) have a 21% share and paid-for search advertising (search engine listings, which are paid for based on click-through rates) accounts for over 57% of the total spend of online advertising. The significant growth in this final category is attributable to online research: 'In July 2007 Internet users carried out 1.4 billion search queries and over 80% of these resulted in a click-through to a website. Advertisers recognise that search plays a valuable role in building brands, selling products and creating a competitive advantage online.' (IAB, 2008). Key drivers for the continuing strong growth of online advertising spend are cited as the widespread adoption of broadband as a means of accessing the Internet, online evolution of the user base, whereby more in terms of numbers and types of users now have access to the Internet, the rise of social networking sites and more widespread and more efficient use of measurement and web analytics by advertisers.

Based on Internet Advertising Bureau (2008)

## Implications for e-retail marketing strategy

According to IMRG Capgemini (2008), 15% of all retail spend was online in 2007; in the full year e-retail sales were up to £46.6 billion which shows a 54% increase on the previous year. For the retailer the impact of an increasing number of consumers and businesses accepting the Internet and other forms of digital media as a stable channel to market is an increase in customer expectations, which creates competitive pressures and challenges. In part, this has been caused by new market entrants that have established their market position by, say, offering very wide and deep product choice, dynamic demand-driven pricing or instantaneous real-time purchase and delivery. The result is retailers are required to adopt a more dynamic and flexible approach to dealing with these raised expectations. Allegra Strategies (2005) identified a number of performance gaps and Table 11.6 presents some of the most significant gaps and the managerial implications.

For the e-retailers it is important to identify any performance gaps and develop strategies which help to close them. For example, in the case of logistics, research has found that utilising carriers (road haulage, air freight) that have higher levels of positive consumer awareness with appropriate online strategies (i.e. offering a choice of carriers) can contribute to the consumer's willingness to buy and overall satisfaction with the online buying experience. Therefore, development of strong awareness and brand image among consumers can prove to be a beneficial strategy for both the e-retailer and the carrier, since consumers have traditionally carried out the home delivery function themselves (i.e. shopping in 'brick-and-mortar' retail stores). Of course, this in itself raises the expectations of the care taken by the delivery agent, which has the implication of having to introduce better handling of goods as well as the speed with which the goods need to be delivered (Esper *et al.*, 2003). A further consideration is that the retailer and the chosen carrier need to be able jointly to satisfy the consumer so that they may benefit from co-branding.

How the online consumer accesses retailers' goods has given rise to various operational formats (discussed earlier in the chapter) and distribution strategies but this only forms part of the retailers e-strategy. Nicholls and Watson (2005) discuss the importance of creating e-value in order to develop profitable and long-term strategies and agree that logistics and fulfilment is a core element of online value creation but at two other important platforms: firm structure, and marketing and sales.

*Firm structure* can be used strategically depending on organisational capabilities and technology infrastructure. Porter (2001) described the emergence of integration and the potential impact on e-value chains. Integration can ensure faster decision making, more flexibility and attract suitable e-management specialists and capital investment (Nicholls and Watson, 2005). In the case of the UK grocery sector, larger retailers have adopted different approaches towards structuring their online operations. See Case study 11 for a detailed discussion of how ASDA, Morrisons, Sainsbury, Tesco and Waitrose have each adopted different strategic pathways to the development of online activities.

*Marketing and sales* can be used in customer-centric value creation strategies in the form of interactive marketing communications strategies (see Chapter 9 for a detailed discussion) and revenue streams. Indeed according to Dennis *et al.* (2004) there are four revenue stream business models, which in turn are based on advertising, merchandising and sales, transaction fees and subscriptions.

Strategic implications for retailers wishing to be successful online are far reaching and require a retailer to develop a carefully informed strategy, which is guided by a business model that can satisfy corporate objectives through the deriving value from corporate capabilities while effectively meeting the expectations of the online consumer. The target market and the product category can have a significant influence on success.

In conclusion, it is now widely acknowledged that there is a need for a company to have a coherent e-retail strategy underpinned by a clear vision of how to create sustained competi-

**Resource**

A resource is defined as a physical asset over which an organisation has control. This narrow definition allows resources to be clearly distinguished from capabilities (Beard and Sumner, 2004).

| Table 11.6 | Performance gaps and managerial implications |
|---|---|

| Performance gap | Commentary | Managerial implications |
|---|---|---|
| The disparity between brand strength and website offer | • The gap between Internet use and the lack of website development means there is still the potential to capture browse and buy behaviour | • Companies need to develop websites to meet consumer expectations capture this behaviour<br>• A failure to do so will result in lost sales as consumers browse and/or buy elsewhere, i.e. the effect is both 'on' and 'off' line |
| The disparity between brand strength offline and online | • Retailer brand strength is frequently not reflected online. This may dilute current brand perception and leaves an opening for competitors to establish a stronger online brand presence even if they are weaker 'offline' | • The first 'dot-com' wave was concerned with establishing first mover advantage. This second wave is concerned with 'bricks-and-mortar' retailers establishing their brand strengths online, i.e. a 'brand' wave<br>• Any lack of investment will deliver mind share advantages to competitors even if they have a lesser brand. In this second wave it will be difficult to recover a competitive position once any brand advantage has been lost |
| A lack of alignment between the nature of the online competitive environment and the maturity of consumer demand | • The most advanced entrants are from overseas or national catalogue companies, the larger retailers (to a variable extent) and specialist niche companies | • The market is still at an early stage in many retail categories. There remains a potential competitive advantage for a 'bricks-and-mortar' retailer to 'grab this window of opportunity' |
| Inertia in decision making | • There is a 'battle for budgets' within retailers, i.e. retrench and invest in core business at the expense of new channels<br>• Some retail cultures run counter to non-traditional means of 'doing business' | • Barriers to customer contact need to be removed. Budgetary constraints are misaligned where the cost of doing nothing means lost opportunity at best, and at worst lost competitive advantage<br>• The maturing outsourcing market may unblock the cost–benefit perception |

*Source*: Allegra Strategies (2005)

**Capabilities**
Capabilities are intangible and are developed from the combined and co-ordinated behaviour and activities of an organisation's employees, and it is therefore 'embedded in the organisation and processes' (Makadok, 2001). The definition of a capability is an organisation's ability to 'perform a set of co-ordinated tasks, utilising organisational resources, for the purposes of achieving a particular end result'.

tive advantage if a business is to gain the maximum benefits from operating online. An online retailer's strategy is likely to be affected by the category and operational strategy it adopts, the type of products and services it sells and the market segments it chooses to serve. Traditional offline retailers will need to defend their existing market share as new entrants online are increasingly shaping the future of the Internet as a retail environment. Retailers need to ensure that the value created by e-retailing is additional rather than a redistribution of profitability. It has been suggested that by removing the physical aspects of the retail offer the Internet increases competition.

The consumers' appetite for purchasing groceries online has increased dramatically in recent years. During the first half of 2007 Tesco.com online sales grew by 35% to £748 million and over the Christmas period Tesco.com and Tesco Direct collectively handled over 2 million orders (Tesco plc, 2007). But it is not just the customers who are getting enthusiastic about the Internet; retailers are also increasingly realising the Internet's commercial potential through its ability to present and store information, facilitate two-way communication with customers, collect market research data, promote goods and services and ultimately to support the online ordering of merchandise. The Internet currently provides an extremely rich and flexible new retail channel that the major supermarkets in the UK are keen to exploit (Doherty et al., 2003).

Now that more consumers are using the Internet to do their grocery shopping, retailers are beginning to think more strategically about how they can use the technology to deliver a sustainable competitive advantage (Nicholls and Watson, 2005). The Internet is now viewed as a significant new weapon in any organisation's competitive armoury, but there is still a significant amount of debate about how its competitive potential might best be realised. In the past the focus has tended to be how Internet technologies could be used to deliver efficiencies and cut costs, but now the view is that competitive advantage is more likely to be achieved through differentiation than cost leadership. This case examines how leading grocery retailers in the UK are seeking to developing a sustainable competitive position from an IT investment, such as a retail website using resource-based theory.

## Resourced-based theory

Barney (1991) suggests the resource-based view of the firm means that organisations should invest in those resources and capabilities that they believe will lead to successfully gaining a sustainable competitive advantage.

## Improving competitive positioning through resource-based theory

A retailer's IT-oriented resources can be thought of in terms of its physical computing assets: software and information system applications, as well as the hardware and physical computing infrastructure. The ability of such physical information technologies to support the

attainment of competitive advantage has been recognised for many years and companies such as Boots and Ryan Air are examples of companies that have gained a sustained competitive advantage directly through the development and implementation of an innovative piece of software (Ward and Peppard, 2002). In addition to physical computing resources, a retailer's 'capability' to deliver effective information systems, equally has the potential to deliver a sustained competitive advantage because of the skills, competences and relationships necessary to effectively manage information systems and technologies.

Consideration of the application of resource-based theory to create competitive advantage from the introduction of IT suggests that there may be three ways in which a grocery retailer might attain a sustainable competitive advantage from the introduction of an Internet-based shopping channel:

- *IT resources*. If a retailer can develop a website that offers distinctively better functionality and services than its competitors, then it may achieve a direct competitive advantage through its IT resources.
- *IS capabilities*. A retailer may also be able to gain a sustainable improved competitive advantage by having superior IS capabilities that allow it to keep in front of the competition by being able to develop and enhance its website, in ways that are important to the customer, on an ongoing basis.
- *Resource complementarity*. If a retailer's website is leveraged through the deployment of complementary resources, such as service, brand image, customer loyalty or logistics, the organisation may be able to gain a competitive advantage from its online channel, even if its website is no better than that of its competitors.

## Resource-based theory and UK grocery retailers

Resource-based theory forms the basis of the analysis which is used to explore the strategic pathways followed by the UK's five leading grocery retailers in their development of web-based sales channels. Together these five retailers account for over 95 per cent of online grocery sales in the UK and were chosen because grocery retailing is one of the most complex and demanding forms of online retailing.

## ASDA/Wal-Mart

During the 1990s ASDA was in a difficult financial position, losing market share and struggling with unsuccessful diversification into furniture and carpets, and as a result stated the company would not be pursuing 'faddish' activities such as Internet retailing (Owen, 2003). However, in November 2000 ASDA@home, an online shopping service, was launched selling a limited range of goods from 32 stores (ASDA plc, 2000). Initially, picking of goods was done within the store by specially trained staff while plans were in place for the building of depots in key locations when the service would be used by a sufficient number of customers. However, in 2002 ASDA closed two of its online operations distribution centres, in Croydon and Watford, after the system was dogged by technical difficulties. The online shopping service continued but used the operational model conceived by Tesco: supplying customers directly from their nearest participating store. Since 2004, ASDA has focused on increasing the coverage of its online service provision beyond 40% in order to be able to offer online shopping to more areas of the UK. The planned expansion comes in response to losing market share to Tesco.com and Sainsbury's, with lack of coverage cited as a key factor. ASDA has reportedly invested over £7m in developing its online operation, as it is seen to represent an ideal way of expanding ASDA's market coverage without buying further outlets. Emphasis has been given to improving customer satisfaction by increasing the number of delivery slots and product availability, as well as improving the site's usability. The group's e-commerce director emphasised the importance of customer satisfaction when he commented: '...giving great customer service is our top priority – that's why we poll hundreds of customers every week. The last survey shows that 97% of our customers are happy with the service', (ASDA plc, 2005). Currently, the company is aiming to geographically expand online retailing, offering services from 157 of its 310 outlets. A selected range of products will be offered including food, health and beauty, household and electrical goods, and domestic appliances. Andy Bond, the group's CEO, suggested the market expansion approach was in response to a re-evaluation of online marketing and admitted that the company had made mistakes with regard to Internet shopping stating '...we were slow to understand how big a market and how big a customer demand there was for dotcom.' (IMRG, 2006). Currently, ASDA accounts for approximately 16% of the UK's online grocery shopping market (ComScore Networks, 2006).

## Sainsbury plc

In 1995, Sainsbury's promoted the Wine Direct mail order service in response to Tesco's announcement that they were about to launch the first online wine ordering service in the UK (Sainsbury plc, 1995). By 1997, online services were expanded and customers were invited to create online shopping lists and home shopping was tried from seven stores. By the end of 1998 the online service provision was expanded to over 30 stores. For Sainsbury's, e-commerce was not considered as simply an additional shopping channel but as rather an integrated part of their retailing services where customers can have access to a significant amount of information, and thereby enhancing a customer's shopping experience. Reportedly, the company's e-business strategy was devised to support core business activities by building excellence. Sainsbury's aimed to develop and own the best online portals by providing information, interaction and transactional services and delivering quality service through offers, online ordering and delivery. In 2000, Sainsbury's announced a series of e-commerce initiatives to improve the e-commerce activities across the group. These initiatives range from business-to-business solutions aiming to reduce costs, streamline systems and improve product availability, to improved business-to-customers solutions such as the re-launch of its website, the opening of a highly automated picking centre to serve customers living within the M25 area and their intention to create a joint venture with Carlton TV for interactive shopping (Sainsbury plc, 2000). This was not the approach adopted by its main rival Tesco, which adopted the store-based system to deliver the products to the customers, Sainsbury's was the first to move into dedicated picking centres as it was considered to be the best solution for serving customers without jeopardising its offline service. According to Dino Adriano, the group's CEO: 'our extensive experience over the past three-and-a-half years, combined with that of US food retailers, indicates that the feasibility of store-based home shopping services is not a sustainable long-term proposition. We have learnt a lot from our R&D about the economics of home shopping and while a store-based system is operable in principle, it is neither viable nor capable of dealing with significant volume without affecting the quality of services being offered to shoppers in-store' (Sainsbury plc, 1999). However, in 2001 expansion of the online shopping service to provide almost 50% national coverage was facilitated by using a combination of warehouse and in-store picking systems. By 2002, Sainsbury's was established as second in the UK online shopping market with 71% coverage. In 2004, expansion of store-based picking helped to streamline logistical costs and reduce the cost of order fulfilment, which contributed to the online shopping service breaking even. This was an important milestone in the company's e-commerce strategy as achieving profitability was one of Sainsbury's strategic aims for the service in 2004. Further cost-cutting initiatives were subsequently introduced closing the automated picking centre, but the expansion of online service was put on hold in 2005 due to the group's difficult financial situation and the introduction of a three-year recovery plan aiming to improve the supermarket's overall performance (Sainsbury plc, 2005). Currently, 'Sainsbury's Online' operates from 97 stores, selling an extended range of food and grocery products and claims to cover 83% of the UK. Reportedly, Sainsbury's accounts for approximately 14% of the UK's online grocery market.

## Tesco plc

Tesco's chief executive, Terry Leahy, was quoted in *The Sunday Times* as saying: 'We will be the world's biggest online grocery retailer and we intend to become the UK's No.1 e-commerce business' (Lorenz and Nuki, 1999). A goal quickly achieved, as by the end of 2000 Tesco offered a wide range of products to 90% of the UK population. The online shopping service Tesco.com was established soon afterwards and operated as an independent subsidiary to Tesco plc and was cited as an important part of the organisation's future strategy. (See Tesco Company reports 2001 to 2007 at www.tesco corporate.com.) Tesco.com was the first UK grocery online shopping service to break even at the end of 2000. Additionally in 2000, the online services diversified offering many non-food product ranges and financial services. Tesco's online expansion was seen as a countermove against Wal-Mart's recent acquisition of ASDA, whose bigger physical presence potentially increased Tesco's vulnerability at the time. However, the Internet was seen as the ideal way to bypass space restrictions. According to Tesco's CEO, its net strategy enabled Tesco to match Wal-Mart by expanding virtually. 'On the Internet we are not constrained by space as the store can be as large as we like' (Tesco plc, 2000). To support its logistical operations, the management team developed a sophisticated semi-automated in-store picking service, supported by local refrigerated delivery vans using existing facilities rather than building high-tech dedicated warehouses. A strategic advantage of this approach was faster geographical expansion of the online shopping services and a distinct advantage of extended national

coverage of Tesco's online shopping service provision. At this time, Tesco offered its online shopping services to 91% of the UK population using 300 of its stores to support the operation, as well as starting to launch its Tesco.com model outside the UK with Ireland being the first country where online services rolled out. Tesco.com also began to develop specialised services for niche home markets, e.g. the blind and partially sighted. This venture was acknowledge as being significant by the Royal National Institute for the Blind who gave Tesco their new 'See It Right' award for developing 'Tesco Access' (Tesco plc, 2001). By 2003, 96% of the UK population could shop online with Tesco.com giving the company 65% of the UK online grocery shopping market and further diversification of product ranges, e.g. financial services and telecoms. In the same year Tesco expanded its online shopping services to overseas markets in the Far East: South Korea – Homeplus.co.kr (Tesco plc, 2003). Tesco.com constantly focused on upgrading its technology in order to streamline services, provide innovative features and extend the range of points at which customers can access online shopping. Sales continued to grow strongly in the year – up by 31.9%, to reach almost £1 billion and profits increased by 54.9% to £56.2 million. In addition, the company is readjusting its service model to adjust for the growth of Tesco.com by opening dedicated online warehouses in areas where online shopping thrives. These warehouses are designed to the same standards as their bricks-and-mortar superstores aiming to eliminate operational difficulties. Diversification and expansion of the online product portfolio and customer services continues with the addition of a series of innovations such as DVDs to your door – a rental service; energy utilities – thousands of customers save money on their gas and electricity bills; getting healthy online by using the e-diets service to help customers to tailor their eating plans to what's right for them, taking into account lifestyles, food preferences and health recommendations; and Internet telephony. Currently, Tesco is focusing on the development of Tesco Direct, which offers customers a wide range of non-food goods as well as launching a range of own-brand computer software. Currently, Tesco accounts for approximately 66% of the UK's online shopping market.

## Waitrose

In 1998, Waitrose began offering Waitrose@work, an office-based ordering system targeting a specific niche market. The success of this operation led the company to look for further ways to extend the Internet to provide online services for consumer markets. This aim was fulfilled by following a unique strategic pathway. Contrary to its main rivals, Waitrose did not develop its own e-commerce oper- ▶

ating platform but instead acquired a 40% share in an LMS e-commerce grocery business. This acquisition helped to expand online service provision and eventually created a new online brand: Ocado, a warehouse-based grocery shopping operation (John Lewis Partnership plc, 2001). In 2002, Waitrose Deliver was introduced and it offered online purchasing from 33 Waitrose stores. According to Sir Stuart Hampson, Waitrose's chairman: 'We were able to forge a marriage with a partner who had developed a technologically advanced operating platform but which lacked the product to give its credibility' (Hampson, 2006). The sophisticated technology behind the service differentiated Ocado and reportedly enabled it to offer the very best customer service available in home delivered grocery shopping anywhere in the UK. By 2005 Ocado, covered 40% of the UK in terms of geographical coverage and continued to maintain that warehouse-based order fulfilment is more reliable than a store-based format (Rigby, 2005). In 2005, Waitrose and Ocado continued with the policy of market expansion as its key strategic pathway by adding more areas, namely the Midlands and North West. Currently, even though Ocado's number of weekly deliveries continue to rise and online trade is growing at an annual rate of around 30%, the operation continues to show losses on the Partnership's balance sheet (John Lewis Partnership plc, 2008).

## Wm Morrisons

The company is reportedly the fourth largest supermarket group in the UK since its merger with Safeway (Osborne, 2003). However, Morrisons did not launch its website until 2003 and in doing so only operated as an information resource offering access to corporate information, company history, PR information and a recruitment feature. The company continued to add information to the website but to date does not include any transactional features or e-mail facilities. In 2006, Morrisons developed their 'festival of football website' which is quoted as being new territory for the company. Nevertheless, the web is becoming an integral part of marketing initiatives and the company is gauging customer responses in order to determine how the company's web-based activity will be developed in the future. In the past, the chairman was adamant that Morrisons would not deliver to homes but currently the company's whole internet strategy is under review with the web becoming an integral part of its marketing initiatives. According to Richard Burgess, Morrison's Marketing Communication Manager, the company is now looking forward to gauging customer response and will use this as a benchmark for how our web-based activity will move forward in the future (Morrisons plc, 2006).

In conclusion, profiling each of the case study retailers has mapped out the strategic pathways chosen for the development of their online service provision, and provided some insight into how each retailer has arrived at its current level of service provision, in terms of geographical spread, strategic and operational approaches. In general terms, Tesco appears to have manoeuvred itself into a position of market leadership that is not dissimilar to the one that it enjoys in the traditional grocery sector but this has been achieved by a five-year period of experimentation with online shopping, making use of various combinations of resources and capabilities. In the meantime, the other four leading UK grocery retailers have been far from idle, Sainsbury's has been the closest contender with the other three retailers all making significant improvements to their web-based offering in recent years.

## Questions

1  By referring to the case study, map out the strategic pathways adopted by ASDA, Sainsbury's, Tesco and Waitrose, and highlight the resources and competencies which helped each company to develop as an online grocery retailer.
2  Discuss the extent to which Tesco has achieved a competitive advantage through superior IT resources.
3  Explain why the creation of a sustained competitive advantage becomes more difficult to achieve as competitive rivalry increases.
4  Visit the websites of ASDA/WALMART, Morrisons, Sainsbury's, Tesco and Waitrose and explore each company site noting down novel and common features – e.g. recipes, customer surveys, promotional information, store locator, extent of product range. Now summarise how each of the sites differ in terms of the services offered.

Adapted from Ellis-Chadwick *et al*. (2007)

## Summary

1. This chapter has focused on e-tailing from two perspectives: the consumer and the retailer. In doing so the chapter has raised questions about the different types of customer that shop online and the various types of retail strategies used to create an online presence.

2. Online consumer behaviour is influenced by a number of factors, which shape and influence an individual's intention to shop online and have important managerial implications for retailers when developing target marketing strategies and looking for market development opportunities.

3. The online customer profile is made up of two distinct sub-categories: classification variables, and character variables, which are ultimately used to interpret the meaning of any online shopping experiences.

4. Online consumer behaviour is made up of a set of beliefs about the Internet, that are shaped from attitudes which influence an individual's intention to shop online. Over time an individual's behaviour can be modified by positive and negative online shopping experiences.

5. Websites that do not deliver a *good* online experience are unlikely to succeed. E-retailers need to develop a sound understanding of who their customers are and how best to deliver satisfaction via the Internet. In the future, more retailers may begin to develop more strategically focused websites, integrated into support systems.

6. Trading via the Internet challenges e-retailers to pay close attention to the online markets they want to serve and to understand that there are differences between the on- and offline customer expectations.

7. Website quality is important as it is a key determinant of customer satisfaction and eventually customer loyalty.

8. Given current levels of growth in adoption from both consumers and retailers, the Internet is developing into a well-established retail channel that provides an innovative and interactive medium for communications and transactions between e-retail businesses and online consumers.

9. The Internet and web present opportunities for companies to adopt different online retail formats to satisfy their customer needs, which may include a mix of Internet and physical-world offerings, e.g. bricks-and-mortar and pureplay retailers.

10. Retailers have developed a range of different strategies for using the web to interact with consumers from electronic billboards providing information to highly integrated online shopping and communication channels.

11. The virtual environment created by the Internet and associated technologies is a growing trading platform for retailing. This arena is increasing both in terms of the number of retail businesses that are online and the extent to which the Internet is being integrated into almost every aspect of a retailer's operations. As a result retailers must choose how they can best employ the Internet in order to serve their customers, rather than whether to adopt the Internet at all.

12. There are strategic advantages to be gained from deploying Internet technologies efficiently and effectively. Leading grocery retailers in the UK have demonstrated some of the opportunities for creating a sustained competitive advantage online based on various applications of IT resources and associated company capabilities.

## Exercises

**'Going shopping online'** (based on consumer decision behaviour presented by Jobber (2007))

Select a product or service of your choice that you are about to, or would like to be able to, purchase. Visit as many websites as required until you find a product or service that could meet your needs if you were to make a purchase. Make sure you take note of all the sites you visit, the amount of time spent on each site and the type of information you might need to help you make your product/service choice.

Now try to analyse your online shopping experience using by answering the following questions:

| Questions | Possible solutions |
|---|---|
| 1. The problem you were seeking to solve | (a) If you were looking for a new pair of stylish sports shoes your problem could be defined as *an image* problem<br>(b) If looking for a train ticket to get to work when your car is being serviced your problem could be defined as a *lack of transport* problem |
| 2. The extent of your information searching | How many websites did you visit? Did you think about consulting other sources of information? During this phase of the  buying process we tend to build up an *awareness set* of possible brands which might solve our purchasing problem |
| 3. The choice criteria which informed your decision making | The next step is to reduce the possible options into a set of product choices you might actually consider purchasing. Then we screen our reduced choices using *choice criteria* to identify the final choice. You might have used, price or reliability to do this evaluation – alternatively you might have considered time (for example, where looking for a train ticket to get to work when your car is being serviced your problem could be defined as a 'lack of transport' problem) |
| 4. The purchase solution  (your preferred product or service) | |
| 5. Evaluate the websites you have visited in terms of how easy it was to find the information you needed to make your purchasing decision | |

## Self-assessment exercises

1. Make a list of classification variables, which a retailer might use when trying to identify an online target market for (a) high-tech training shoes, (b) organic beauty products.

2. Explain the difference between 'classification' and 'character' variables.

3. Describe three different strategies an e-retailer might develop when creating an online presence.

4. Describe the different types of formats an online retailer might follow.

5. From a resource-based view, explain the difference between 'resources' and 'capabilities'.

**Essay and discussion questions**

1. Discuss whether you consider that all products on sale in the high street can be sold as easily via the Internet.

2. Select three websites that demonstrate the different ways in which a retailer might use the Internet to interact with its customers. Compare the contents of the websites and explain what the potential benefits are for the customers of each of the sites.

**Examination questions**

1. It was once predicted that the Internet would replace high street stores and that within ten years the majority of retail purchases would be made online. However, while online shopping is continuing to grow year-on-year it still represents a small part of the total retail spend. Explain why the early predictions have not been met from either the perspective of the consumer or the retailer.

2. Tesco.com, has established a position of being the world's leading online grocer with an estimated sales turnover of £401m and profits up 37% to £21m (as at 21 September 2005). However, Iceland was the first UK retailer to offer nationwide delivery of a range of groceries ordered via the web yet they have ceased to offer this service.

   Discuss why Tesco.com been able to establish such a dominant market position.

# References

Allegra (2005) Allegra Strategies Limited, London WC2N 5BW.

ASDA plc (2000) 'ASDA begins to roll out nationwide home shopping service', press release, available at: www.walmartsfacts.com/articles/3549.aspx (accessed February, 2008).

ASDA plc (2005) 'ASDA on target to double size of home shopping service by end of 2005', 31 May, www.walmartsfacts.com (accessed February, 2008).

Barney, J.B. (1991) From resources and sustained competitive advantage, *Journal of Management*, 17 (1), 99–120.

Bauer, R. (1960) Consumer behaviour as risk taking, *Proceedings of the American Marketing Association*, December, 389–98.

Beard, J.W. and Sumner, M. (2004) 'Seeking strategic advantage in the post-net era: viewing ERP systems from the resource-based perspective', *Journal of Strategic Information Systems*, 13 (2), 129–50.

ComScore Networks (2006) 'Tesco captures four times more online orders than closest competitor during first seven months of 2006', press release, 22 August, available at: www.conscore.com/press/release.asp?press=986 (accessed February 2008).

Davis, F.D. (1993) 'User acceptance of information technology: system characteristics and behavioural aspects'. *International Journal of Man–Machine Studies*, 38 (3), 475–87.

Davidson, W., Bates, A. and Bass, S. (1976) The Retail Life Cycle, *Harvard Business Review*, 54 (6), 89–96.

Dennis, C., Fenech, T. and Merrilees, B. (2004) *E-retailing*. Routledge, Taylor and Francis Group, London.

De Pelsmacker, P., Geuens, M. and Van den Bergh, J. (2004) *Marketing Communications: a European Perspective*, 2nd edn. Financial Times/Prentice Hall, Harlow.

Doherty, N.F., Ellis-Chadwick, F.E. and Hart, C.A. (1999) Cyber retailing in the UK: the potential of the Internet as a retail channel, *International Journal of Retail and Distribution Management*, 27(1), 22–36.

Doherty, N.F., Ellis-Chadwick, F.E. and Hart, C.A. (2003) 'An analysis of the factors affecting the adoption of the internet in the UK retail sector', *Journal of Business Research*, 56 (11), 887–97.

Doherty, N.F. and Ellis-Chadwick, F.E. (2006) 'New perspective in Internet retailing: a review and strategic critique of the field', *Int J of Retail and Distribution Management*, 24, (4/5), 389–411.

Ellis-Chadwick, F. (2008) *International Journal of Business Environments* [IN PRESS].

Ellis-Chadwick, F.E., Doherty, N.F. and Anastasakis, L. (2007) 'E-strategy in the UK retail grocery market: a resource-based analysis', *International Journal of Managing Service Quality*, Vol. 17, no. 6, 703–727.

Ellis-Chadwick, F.E., Doherty, N.F. and Hart, C. (2002) Signs of change? A longitudinal study of Internet adoption by UK retailers, *Journal of Retailing and Consumer Services*, 9(2).

Esper, T., Jensen, T., Turnipseed, F. and Burton, S. (2003) The last mile: an examination of effects of online retail delivery strategies on consumers, *Journal of Business Logistics*, 24 (2), 177.

Finn, A. and Louviere, J. (1990) Shopping centre patronage models; fashioning a consideration set segmentation solution, *Journal of Business Research*, 21, 277–88.

Hagel, J. III and Armstrong, A.G. (1997) *Net Gain – Expanding Markets through Virtual Communities*. Harvard Business School Press, Boston.

Hampson, S. (2006) 'Clicks and mortar – the development store in the internet age', Anniversary Manufacturers & Commerce Lecture at the Royal Society for the Encouragement of Arts, Manufacturers and Commerce (RSA), 18 May, available at: www.johnlewispartnership.co.uk/Display.aspx?MasterId=e21b533a-ab0a-45e3-984d-7c20a716503b&NavigationId=563 (accessed February 2008).

Hewitt, D. (2004) You can tell how you're selling offline. www.imediaconnection.com/content/2892.asp (accessed February 2008).

Hoffman, D., Novak, T. and Venkatesh, A. (2004) 'Has the Internet become indispensable?' *Communications of the ACM'* July 2004/Vol. 47, No. 7, 37–42.

IAB (2008) Interactive advertising bureau (2008) 'UK Internet advertising expenditure grows 38% year on year to reach £2.8 billion in 2007, www.iabuk.net/en/1/pwcad spendstudy080408.mxz (accessed July 2008).

IMRG (2006) 'ASDA to expand online shopping', Interactive Media in Retail Group News Release, 6 November, available at: www.imrg.org/ItemDetail.aspx?clg=News&cid=nws&pid=News_Asda&language=en-GB (accessed February 2008).

IMRG Capgemini (2008) E-retailing Excellence, Interactive Media in Retail Group 88 Kingsway, London WC2B 6AA, http://www.imrg.org/ItemDetail.aspx?clg-InfoItems&cid=pr&pid=pr_IMRG_Index_Jan08&language=en-GB (accessed February 2008).

Jobber, D. (2007) *Principles and Practice of Marketing*. McGraw-Hill Companies, London.

John Lewis Partnership plc (2001) 'The John Lewis Partnership: Report & Accounts 2001', available at: www.johnlewispartnership.co.uk/Display.aspx?&MasterId=3a870a7d-6317-4f49-9ede-138f44473e9e&NavigationId=578 (accessed February 2008).

John Lewis Partnership plc (2003) 'John Lewis Partnership plc Annual Report and Accounts 2003', available at: www.johnlewispartnership.co.uk/Display.aspx?&MasterId=3a870a7d-6317-4f49-9ede-138f44473e9e&NavigationId=578 (accessed February 2008).

John Lewis Partnership plc (2007) 'John Lewis Partnership plc Annual Report and Accounts 2007', available at: www.johnlewispartnership.co.uk/Display.aspx?&MasterId=3a870a7d-6317-4f49-9ede-138f44473e9e&NavigationId=578 (accessed February 2008).

John Lewis Partnership plc (2008) 'John Lewis Partnership plc Annual Report and Accounts 2008', available at: www.johnlewispartnership.co.uk/Display.aspx?&MasterId=3a870a7d-6317-4f49-9ede-138f44473e9e&NavigationId=578 (accessed February 2008).

Lee, E. and Overby, J. (2004) Creating value for online shoppers: implications for satisfaction and loyalty, *Journal of Consumer Satisfaction and Loyalty*, 17, 54–68.

Lorenz, A. and Nuki, P. (1999) 'Tesco takes on high street in web revolution', *The Sunday Times*, No. 19, September, B3.

Makadok, R. (2001) 'Towards a synthesis of the resource-based and dynamic-capability views of rent creation', *Strategic Management Journal*, Vol. 22 No. 5, 387–401.

Morrisons plc (2006) Morrisons unveil new summer football website, available at: www.morrisons.co.uk/1547.asp (accessed February 2008).

Mulhern, F.J. (1997) Retail marketing: from distribution to integration, *International Journal of Research in Marketing*, 14, 103–24.

Newholm, T., McGoldrick, P., Keeling, K., Macaulay, L. and Doherty, J. (2004), Multi-story trust and online retailer strategies, *The International Review of Retail, Distribution and Consumer Research*, October, 14 (4), 437–56.

Nicholls, A. and Watson, A. (2005) 'Implementing e-value strategies in UK retailing', *International Journal of Retail and Distribution Management*, 33 (6) 426–43.

Office for National Statistics (2007) Internet access 2007: Households and Individuals http://www.statistics.gov.uk/pdfdir/inta0807.pdf (accessed February 2008).

Osbourne, (2003) 'Morrison pops Safeway in the basket', *Daily Telegraph*, 10 January 2003, p. 35.

Owen, G. (2003) 'Corporate strategy in food retailing: 1980–2002', available at: http://cep.lse.ac.uk/seminarpapers/24-05-04%20_%20Background%20paper%20by%20Geoffrey%20Owen.pdf (accessed February 2008).

Perea, T., Dellaret, B. and Ruyter, K. (2004) What drives consumers to shop online? A literature review, *International Journal of Service and Industry Management*, 15 (1), 102–21.

Porter, M. (2001) Strategy and the Internet, *Harvard Business Review*, March, 62–78.

Rigby, E. (2005) 'Tesco to open online grocery warehouse', *Financial Times*, No. 27 October, 22.

Sainsbury plc (1995) 'J Sainsbury plc Annual Review 1995 and Summary Financial Statement', available at: www.isainsburys.co.uk/files/reports/ar1995.pdf (accessed February 2008).

Sainsbury plc (1999) 'Sainsbury's to open UK's largest food picking centre for home shopping network', 17 May, available at: www.isainsburys.co.uk/index.asp?PageID=424&subsection=%Year=1999%NewsID=55 (accessed February 2008).

Sainsbury plc (2000) 'J Sainsbury plc Annual Report and Accounts 2000', available at: www.isainsburys.co.uk/files/reports/ar2000/ar2000rev.pdf (accessed February 2008).

Sainsbury plc (2005) 'J Sainsbury plc Annual Review and Summary Financial Statement 2005', available at: www.jsainsburys.co.uk/ar05/files/review05.pdf (accessed February 2008).

Source, P., Perotti, V. and Widrick, S. (2005) Attitude and age differences in online buying, *International Journal of Retail and Distribution Management*, 33 (2), 122–32.

Srinivasan, S., Anderson, R. and Ponnavolu, K. (2002) Customer loyalty in e-commerce: an exploration of its antecedents and consequences, *Journal of Retailing*, 78, 41–50.

Stone, R. and Gronhaug, K. (1993) Perceived risk: further considerations for the marketing discipline, *European Journal of Marketing*, 27(3), 39–50.

Szymanski, D. and Hise, R. (2000) 'E-satisfaction: an initial examination', *Journal Retailing*, Vol. 76, No. 3, 309–322.

Tesco plc (2000) 'Tesco plc Annual Review and Summary Financial Statement 2000', available at: www.tescocorporate.com/../../../fig/TESCO_REVIEW_2000.pdf (accessed February 2008).

Tesco plc (2001) 'First RNIB web access award goes to Tesco', 22 May.

Tesco plc (2003) 'Tesco plc Annual Review and Summary Financial Statement 2003', available at: www.tescocorporate.com/../../../fig/tesco_review_2003.pdf (accessed February 2008).

Tesco plc (2008) Christmas trading statement http://www.tescocorporate.com/images/Christmas%20Trading%20Statement%20January%202000_0.pdf (accessed February 2008).

Tesco plc (2007) Interim report Every little helps http://www.tescocorporate.com/images/Tesco%20interim_3.pdf (accessed February 2008).

Verdict Research (2007) *UK e-retail 2007*, Verdict Research Limited, Charles House, 108–110 Finchley Road, London NW3 5JJ.

Ward, J. and Peppard, J. (2002) *Strategic Planning for Information Systems*, John Wiley & Sons, Chichester.

Weltevreden, J.W.J., Atzema, O.A.L.C and Boschma, R.A. (2005) The adoption of the Internet by retailers: a new typology of strategies, *Journal of Urban Technology* **12** (3) (2005), 59–87.

Weltevreden, J. and Boschma, R. (2008) Internet strategies and performance of Dutch retailers *Journal of Retailing and Consumer Services*, 15 (3), 63–178.

Wolfinbarger, M. and Gilly, M. (2003) eTailQ: dimensionalising, measuring and predicting eTail quality, *Journal of Retailing*, 79, 183–98.

## Further reading

Dennis, C., Fenech, T. and Merrilees, B. (2004) *E-retailing*. Routledge, Taylor and Francis Group, London.

Mohammed, R., Fisher, R., Jaworski, B. and Addison, G. (2004) *Internet Marketing 2 edn with E-commerce*. McGrawHill, Maidenhead.

## Web links

- **ASDA WALMART Plc** (http://www.asda-corporate.com/about-asda/history.asp)
- **Expedia** (www.expedia.co.uk)
- **John Lewis Partnership** (www.johnlewispartnership.co.uk)
- **J Sainsbury Plc Corporate site** (http://www.jsainsburys.co.uk)
- **Office for National Statistics (2007)** (http://www.statistics.gov.uk/cci/nugget.asp?id=8)
- **Play.com** (www.play.com)
- **Tesco plc Interim Results 2000 to 2007** (www.tescocorporate.com)
- **World Internet Users and Population Statistics** (www.internetworldstats.com/stats.htm)
- **Wm Morrisons plc** (http://www.morriosons.co.uk/Corporate/)

# 12

# Business-to-business Internet marketing

## Learning objectives

After reading this chapter, the reader should be able to:

- Explain the meaning of the electronic market place and discuss the advantages and disadvantages of trading in electronic markets
- Understand the implications for organisations seeking to operate efficiently and effectively online
- Identify the factors which are likely to influence whether an organisation operating in B2B markets is trading online
- Discuss how organisations are using Internet technologies as part of their online marketing strategies

## Questions for marketers

Key questions for marketing managers related to this chapter are:

- What are the advantages and disadvantages of belonging to an electronic marketplace?
- What are your organisation's sources of competitive advantage and are they applicable in online markets?
- How can your organisation benefit from creating online efficiency and online effectiveness?
- What are the key factors likely to influence whether your organisation develops a billboard website, a fully-integrated transactional website and/or a market place trading portal?
- What is the strategic focus of your organisation's digital marketing strategy?

## Links to other chapters

This chapter should be read in conjunction with these chapters:
- Chapter 2 The Internet micro-environment
- Chapter 3 The Internet macro-environment
- Chapter 4 Internet marketing strategy
- Chapter 5 The Internet and the marketing mix
- Chapter 11 Business-to-consumer Internet marketing

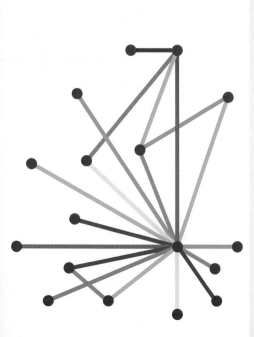

## Introduction

It has been suggested that Internet technologies can significantly change how businesses trade and also have the capacity to affect levels of profitability and success. However, leading business writers cannot agree on the level of influence: Porter (2001) strongly argued the Internet to be 'a complement to, not a cannibal of, traditional ways of competing'. Tapscott (1997) and Evans and Wurster (2000) argue that business is completely different as a result of trading online as the Internet creates a radically different trading environment. So perhaps the crux of the debate is that on the one hand organisations should look at Internet and web technologies as being essential to support operations and improve services (in their chosen field of operations) or on the other hand organisations should consider the Internet as a *new virtual world* of opportunities, where there are few established rules and limitations. There are examples to substantiate both sides of the debate. New market entrants have reshaped consumer markets and taken market share from existing companies by developing innovative market positions using seemingly unorthodox approaches, for example:

- Amazon.com established its position as the world's largest bookseller using competitors' and suppliers' inventories;
- eBay built its digital empire by facilitating online auctions and in doing so positioned the company as a global consumer-to-consumer trading arena;
- Google positioned itself as the most effective search engine by freely giving away its core service to end users.

However, in the banking and airline industries Internet technologies have been used to enhance and streamline existing well-established services. In the case of banking, a major advantage of trading via the Internet is that it does not restrict banks to physical locations or geographical areas. Internet technology allows established banks to target new markets with existing services and products and in doing so add customer value. In addition to creating and sustaining a market advantage, banks are also introducing new technology, to reduce the costs of operations and administration. Similarly in the case of the airline industry, where significant improvements have been made to passenger services, e.g. Scandinavian Airlines offer check-in procedures online. Indeed, many business services can be tailored to be delivered online and in doing so reduce costs, offer marketing opportunities and result in an overall enhanced business operation in terms of efficiency and effectiveness. Consequently, for businesses trading online it is important to ensure there is a clear understanding of the potential impact of the online trading environment. Kalaignanam *et al.* (2008) highlight that 'a business can leverage the potential of the Internet to enhance the *effectiveness* of its competitive strategy as well as the *efficiency* of its operations' and it is therefore important for marketing managers to be fully aware of where sources of competitive advantage can be found. This chapter focuses on B2B electronic market places, the issues affecting the development of online marketing strategies and the factors affecting the development of fully integrated online operations in B2B markets.

### Key themes and concepts

This chapter explores business-to business (B2B) use of the Internet by focusing on:

- electronic marketplaces
- the significance of efficiency and effectiveness to businesses trading online
- factors that influence B2B adoption of the Internet
- development of business strategies.

## B2B trading environments and electronic marketplaces

### Types of organisational markets

Traditionally, there are three main types of organisational markets in which businesses primarily trade with businesses: industrial, reseller and government. In Europe, the economic activity a company engages in allows it to be classified using Standard Industry Codes (SIC), European and international, to ensure consistency in classification of organisations by activity (Central Statistical Office, 1992). These codes were first introduced in 1948 but are regularly updated to reflect changes over time and to accommodate new products and new industries. The codes facilitate the identification of activity sectors and different types of trading markets. Analysis of the main organisational markets reveals variations in company size, trading requirements, investments and trading potential.

- *Industrial markets* generally comprise organisations which are heavily dependent on raw materials and actually producing tangible goods – e.g. agriculture and hunting and forestry, fishing, heavy manufacturing, engineering, vehicles industry, electricity and gas supply and construction. Due to the capital investment required in many industrial sectors, markets tend to be dominated by a small number of very large companies. This is particularly noticeable in areas of manufacturing that require major capital funding and investment (e.g. ship building and the manufacture of chemicals). It should be noted that this does not mean all manufacturers operate on a vast scale. In the case of specialist engineering companies, they can be quite numerous, small in size and widely dispersed. Business.com (Figure 12.1) provides a directory service to locate businesses in specific vertical industrial markets and its revenue model is based on the placement of pay-per-click adverts.

| Figure 12.1 | Business.com (www.business.com) |

- *Reseller markets* are made up of organisations that buy products and services in order to resell them – e.g. wholesalers, retailers, hotels and restaurants, transport, storage, communications, financial institutions, estate agents and letting. This covers a very diverse collection of organisations and as a result company size and market sector structures vary considerably.
- *Government markets* consist of government agencies and bodies that buy goods and services to carry out specific functions and provide particular services – e.g. public administration, education, health services, armed forces, community, social and personal services activities. Government agencies control vast funds of public money generated from direct and indirect taxation. In many instances, purchasing requirements exceed those of large private commercial organisations.

Initially, the B2B sector was slow to realise the potential of the Internet, deterred by threats of lack of security, lack of strategic vision among other factors. However, now organisations in all types of industrial markets are realising the advantage of being able to link customers to trading information and the opportunity to transact online. The UK government, for example, is using the Internet and the web to modernise and improve many public services by providing more web-based *customer* service information as well as introducing sophisticated back-office e-procurement systems. Additionally, the government has set targets, which state that 100% of government services should be capable of being accessed online by 2005. Directgov is a portal site which provides information and access to a wide range of central government services.

As more and more organisations from all types of industrial markets have begun to develop web-based operations, B2B markets have been growing rapidly in recent years and the opportunities for trading have been expanding exponentially.

## Growth, volume and dispersion of B2B electronic markets

In the first instance, questions about growth and the rise of electronic networks and the information revolution primarily focused on reseller markets (B2C Internet marketing is discussed in detail in Chapter 11) and some commentators asked whether the online trading environment was 'merely another revolution in retailing formats' (Evans and Wurster, 2000). However, this turned out not to be a true reflection. Indeed, as commercial adoption of the Internet expanded it emerged that information was at the heart of value creation and competitive advantage, which ultimately opened up opportunities for trading. Evans and Wurster (2000) suggested the reason for the importance of information was that:

- the traditional principles of business strategy continued to apply in electronic markets in much the same way as in offline markets;
- the objects of strategy, such as business units, industrial supply chains, customer relationships, organisational structure, etc., were held together by a glue and this glue is information.

But the important difference between online and offline markets was determined by the fact that the glue gets dissolved by new technologies and as a result formalised and well-established business structures and supply chains are changed and can begin to fragment, thereby creating opportunities for new types of organisations offering new products and services to enter online markets. It soon became apparent that the online trading environment was much more than an innovative retail format, and all types of organisations would be affected to some extent by the adoption of new Internet technologies. A benchmarking study by the DTI (2004) found in the UK approximately 90% of businesses had access to the Internet (in companies with over 50 employees the percentage is approaching 100%), this trend in adoption has continued and the majority now at least have a website providing company information and contact details. The most important point from the report was the change in emphasis in the key measure of ITC adoption from connectivity and access to the Internet (how many businesses are online) to how is the technology used to deliver real value for businesses (what are they doing online). Many B2B organisations began to consider not whether they *should* be online but how best to *gain advantage* from adoption of Internet technologies. Initially, many managers focused on how to reduce operating costs and develop more integrated supply-side systems through the use of the Internet. The introduction and development of e-procurement systems proved to be a valuable area of business activity in which to reduce costs through, say, the reduction of the cost of invoicing. However, this initiative, although highly beneficial, was primarily an *internal* organisational benefit and the integration of systems opened the door to pursue *external* trading opportunities. Many innovative business models have developed as a result of widespread adoption of Internet technologies in B2B markets. For example, in the industrial market *e-auctions* are used by General Electric (GE) to trade with both established and non-established suppliers. The model is a web-based electronic bidding mechanism that operates in a similar way to those held in traditional auction rooms and tendering processes. In the GE case the aim is to drive costs down via a competitive, open-bidding process. The downward movement of prices is sometimes referred to as a 'reverse auction' as opposed to a bidding situation where prices are driven upwards. GE purchasing managers do not always select the lowest bid as they will assess the potential risks associated with the supplier: say, the ability to fulfil the order, quality and requirements for after-sales service issues, rejection rates and quality of goods. An emergent benefit of this model is that e-auctions allow companies to monitor competitive pricing, which helps the organisation reduce total costs.

In government markets, *e-sourcing* systems are used by the BBC. The BBC has taken a very proactive and innovative approach towards adoption of Internet technologies to facilitate the expansion of external trading opportunities. In this case the adoption of e-sourcing systems, services and technology has become the key mechanism for conducting procurements using e-tendering, e-evaluation and e-auctions. The e-sourcing is very successful as it ensures open, auditable and streamlined interaction with suppliers and creates opportunities for more interaction from different suppliers through advertising contract opportunities. There are benefits for both buyers and suppliers as the technology systems enable submission of tenders in a secure web-based environment. Operationally, gains are achieved through streamlining and cost reduction as the system allows geographically dispersed teams of evaluators to assess the contract bids efficiently, eliminating the need for paper, print and distribution, leading to better informed decision making. Additionally, e-auctions enable the BBC to operate a very visible transparent mechanism for suppliers to make competing offers and, perhaps more importantly, enables the procurement function to achieve best value for the licence payer (BBC, 2008). Inter-trading between organisations within and across different types of organisational markets has largely been responsible for the growth and development of e-market places.

While e-auctions focus on the sales side of purchasing, e-fulfilment focuses on the delivery of goods in a timely and appropriate fashion and is central to the re-engineering of the supply chain. According to a survey, 'fulfilment' will be an area of significant growth for businesses operating online. However, over 80% of organisations cannot fulfil international orders of tangible goods because of the complexities of shipping, although there are some geographical locations (e.g. parts of Europe and Asia) that are better served by local warehouse support networks than others. Time will inevitably establish the validity of the proposition that online purchasing practices are sustainable business models.

While considering buying and selling in B2B markets it is also important to remember that there are differences between B2B and B2C markets which have implications for the growth and development of online markets. According to Jobber (2007), in organisational markets there are typically fewer customers who are likely to buy goods in bulk quantities and the buyer organisations tend to be larger and subsequently of great value to the supplier. What are the implications of this? Firstly, with fewer buyers the existence of suppliers and customers tends to be well known and it can be a very straightforward process to change over to web-based communications and trading. Choice criteria vary: impulse purchases, and those based on emotional motives are rare in organisational buying situations as buyers tend to be professionals who use technical and economic choice criteria to inform their decision making. This means that efforts to promote brands are different to those used for consumer brands and price setting tends to involve more negotiation between the seller and the buyer.

## E-marketplaces

**Electronic marketspace**
A virtual marketplace such as the Internet in which no direct contact occurs between buyers and sellers.

Rayport and Sviokla (1995) introduced the term **electronic marketspace** and suggested the Internet created a new environment which had significant implications for the way in which businesses trade. The speed of development of computer, network and Internet technologies played a key role in the rapid expansion of the marketspace and subsequently the commercial practice of electronic trading. It should be remembered, however, that electronic trading *per se* is not a new phenomenon; commercial exchanges have taken place using electronic data interchange (EDI) and dedicated data links between organisations for several decades. Nevertheless, what is new is Internet technologies. Communication standards and protocols create a virtual trading environment where any organisation with a computer and access to the Internet has the potential to trade in global markets.

Many different types of e-marketplaces emerged as a result of being based on different business models. Perhaps the most straightforward way to classify e-marketplaces is by type of user for example:

- *B2B independent e-marketplace* – an online platform operated by a third party which is open to buyers or sellers in a particular industry. By registering on an independent e-marketplace, members can access classified advertisements and requests for quotations or bids in a particular industrial sector. In Chapter 2 (Figure 2.23) we looked at how Alibaba.com, one of the biggest online marketplaces, had developed. Members will typically be expected to pay a fee or make some form of payment. Eventoclick.com is an example of a European e-marketplace which assists companies of any size with their outsourcing services, from accommodation, restaurants, travel agencies, translators, through catering services, marketing to merchandising and classified advertising (Figure 12.2). This portal is of Spanish origin and has nearly 20,000 registered users.
- *Buyer-oriented e-marketplace* – an example of a portal which is normally run by a consortium of buyers in order to establish an efficient purchasing environment. Joining as a buyer, this type of market place can help lower, say, administrative costs or improve bargaining power with suppliers. As a supplier, an organisation can use a buyer-oriented e-marketplace to advertise and this can prove to be highly effective as the buyers will tend to be from a particular target segment.
- *Supplier-oriented e-marketplace* – sometimes known as a supplier directory, this is established and operated by a group of suppliers who are seeking to establish an efficient sales channel via the Internet to a large number of buyers. They are usually searchable by the product or service being offered. Supplier directories benefit buyers by providing information about suppliers for markets and regions they may not be familiar with. Sellers can use these types of marketplace to be found and to get leads. For example, Agrelma (agrelma.com, Figure 12.3) brings together producers of fruit, vegetable, olive oil, cheese and many other food products. Key seller groups are producers, exporters and wholesalers, the portal has a global focus but is based in Italy. Over 3500 companies are registered with the portal.

Vertical and horizontal e-marketplaces provide online access to businesses vertically up and down every segment of a particular industry sector such as automotive, chemical, construction or textiles. Buying or selling using a vertical e-marketplace can increase operating efficiency and help to decrease supply chain costs, inventories and cycle time. A horizontal e-marketplace connects buyers and sellers across different industries or regions. You can use a horizontal e-marketplace to purchase indirect products such as office equipment or stationery. An example of a vertical market is VertMarkets (www.vertmarkets.com) (Figure 12.4).

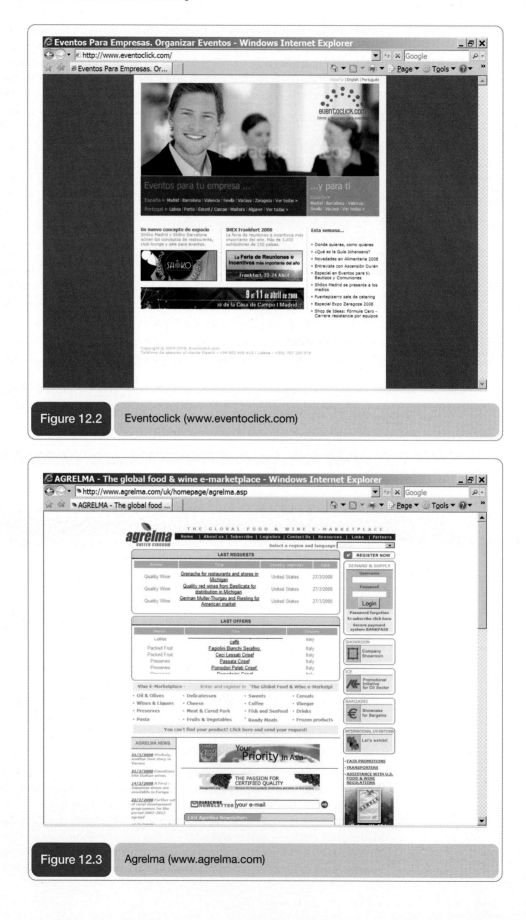

**Figure 12.2** Eventoclick (www.eventoclick.com)

**Figure 12.3** Agrelma (www.agrelma.com)

This is an American company which provides industry-specific online sales and marketing products and services to small and medium sized suppliers. VertMarkets has created a trading platform which brings together buyers and sellers in over 60 wide-ranging industry-specific marketplaces, including chemical processes, metal tooling and supermarket distribution. In total, VertMarkets create market opportunities for businesses in eight distinct industry groups, such as information technology, public sector, life sciences, and food and beverages.

In addition to e-market places there are *online exchanges* or *trading hubs*, which are websites where buyers and sellers trade goods and services online and vary according to the size and number of companies using them and the type of commodity traded. There are already successful exchanges in markets as diverse as energy, textiles and logistics. Like online auctions, online exchanges allow trading between B2B organisations. Key growth factors for this type of trading environment are that large companies can use the exchanges to reduce stock holdings while small companies can bid collectively to earn volume discounts or to jointly deliver a large contract. The operational procedures can vary – for example, in some online exchanges suppliers are invited to provide a quote whereas in others buyers are invited to bid for specific products and services. In addition, there are commodity exchanges, where the price of a standardised commodity such as energy or telecoms bandwidth continuously changes as a result of changes in supply and demand. There are some important considerations for managers thinking about entering into online exchanges:

- Are all the required major suppliers already signed up to the exchange?
- Does the exchange operate a comprehensive list of products and services to facilitate price comparison?
- Could belonging to an exchange destabilise existing customer/supplier relationships?
- Does our organisation have adequate systems in place to support order fulfilment?

**Figure 12.4**    VertMarkets (www.vertmarkets.com)

- What will be the effect of making information about prices and stock levels available to competitors, as well as potential customers?
- What are the cost comparisons between operating through an online exchange and existing sales and procurement systems?

An example of a trading hub is GlobalNetXchange. GNX is an e-business solution and service within the global retail industry. The e-market is owned by a consortium of large retail organisations from around the world: Sears, Carrefour, Oracle, Coles Myer Ltd, KarstadtQuelle AG, The Kroger Co., METRO AG, Pinault-Printemps-Redoute, J Sainsbury plc and Federated Department Stores. GNX solutions connect retailers, manufacturers and their trading partners to reduce costs and improve efficiency by streamlining and automating critical sourcing and supply chain processes. Since the launch in 2000, several major companies have registered with GNX including Colgate Palmolive, Goodyear, Johnson & Johnson, Lever Fabergé, Marks & Spencer, Michelin, Philips, Procter & Gamble, Sears and Unilever. The site is available in Chinese, German, English, Italian, Japanese, Portuguese, French and Spanish (E-market Services, 2008).

This section has considered the growth and development of B2B online markets and different types of e-markets and online hubs. For Internet marketing managers there are some generic issues to consider when trading through these types of market portals. For buyers, e-market sites can lower prices, lower search and order costs, but for sellers, market share and value can become eroded over a relatively short period of time when trading in such electronic markets.

Nevertheless, e-marketplaces and online exchanges have grown in importance because of the potential to improve economic efficiency, reduce margins between price and cost, and speed up complicated business deals. Improving efficiency is important to all businesses but *doing things right*, in other words being efficient, is only part of the story as it is also important for an organisation to *do the right thing* – in other words be effective.

## Online marketing efficiency gains

According to Brown (1987), the critical difference between efficiency and effectiveness is that 'the former is cost-focused and the latter is customer-focused'. A highly successful company will be able to score highly on both levels whereas an ineffective and inefficient company is likely to go out of business very quickly (Table 12.1). Kalaignanam *et al.* (2008) explain how a marketing strategy can be affected by the appropriateness of the amount, types and pattern of deployment of marketing resources used by a business to create a successful market position and create competitive advantage. In other words, if the marketing resources are suitable and well deployed then the marketing strategy should be highly effective. Additionally, these authors suggest that marketing operations efficiency can be viewed as the ratio of the amount of marketing output generated to the amount of marketing resource inputs employed to implement a marketing strategy. We will now examine the factors which affect the effectiveness of marketing strategies and the efficiency of marketing operations in B2B markets.

| Table 12.1 | How efficiency and effectiveness combine to determine business success | |
| --- | --- | --- |
| | **Ineffective** | **Effective** |
| **Inefficient** | Goes out of business quickly | Survives |
| **Efficient** | Dies slowly | Does well and continues to be successful |

*Source:* Jobber, 2007

For many years, it has been recognised that the Internet's power, scope and interactivity provide businesses with a unique opportunity to transform their businesses. As online market-places have evolved, the Internet has begun to change aspects of the way many businesses trade. The Internet has:

- become an important channel for promoting relationships with customers and other partners (Ansari and Mela, 2003);
- affected all of the elements of the marketing mix – promotion becomes highly interactive, pricing flexible and dynamic, products digital, and place virtual communication strategies of firms (Zettelmeyer, 2000);
- influenced the structure of the competitive market and increased trading opportunities with new partners (Varadarajan and Yadav, 2002);
- increased the capacity to deliver tangible gains through economic efficiencies (Vijayasarathy and Tyler, 1997).

## How organisations make efficiency gains

Kalaignanam *et al.* (2008) have suggested there are three distinct areas where efficiency gains in marketing operations:

- *Decision information costs* – efficiencies can result from using information to facilitate decision making and reduce information processing costs.
- *Quality costs* are incurred to ensure that the products or operations conform to specifications. Internet technology can be used to significantly reduce these through gains in efficiency – e.g. if a product does not conform to standards, the customer is likely to return the goods, which has implications for staffing, quality control and can even lead to a breakdown in customer relations.
- *Factor costs* increase in proportion to the level of activity. Traditionally, they are used in the context of production activities encompassing material and labour costs. Factor costs in marketing operations comprise labour costs, material costs and miscellaneous costs (e.g. travel and rentals).

Organisations can use the interactivity of Internet technologies to improve the efficiency of their marketing by focusing on these three types of costs.

Kalaignanam *et al.* (2008) also suggest three areas of marketing activities where significant efficiency gains can be made:

1 **Post-sales customer relationship management**
   - *Buyer–seller relationships.* Relationships deepen as more and more companies become comfortable with trading in the online environment, and there is more standardisation of communication platforms through the use of Internet technologies. Buyers and sellers develop closer relationships and often work together in a very co-operative manner to achieve benefits for both parities using the Internet.
   - *Electronic billing* – some industries (e.g. telephone, utilities banking) serve very large customer bases (B2B and B2C) and many of the transactions are typically repeated, for instance quarterly gas bills. For such companies invoicing cost and the production of printed bills is expensive and therefore there is great potential for cost reduction through the application of electronic billing and automated payments.
   - *Self-service technologies* – the airline industry is making significant changes to its cost base and in doing so improving levels of customer service by introducing self-service bag drops, the online check-in and getting flyers to print their own boarding cards. When linked to customer retention strategies (e.g. frequent flyer programmes) the capital cost for the installations of self-service technologies can quickly be redeemed.
   - *Online product registrations* – warranties are an important cue for buyers of the value of products and services; moreover, extended warranty schemes can aid customer retention

rates and are responsible for a significant percentage of profits in certain industries – but operating such schemes can be very costly. Processing claims against warranties is labour-intensive and time consuming. Organisations can make significant cost savings through online product registration and warranty claim processing.

- *Online technical support* – in B2B markets customer relationship management is critically important. In high-tech industries much time can be spent dealing with teething problems resulting from the installation of a new software package. If the supplier can set up a system that can diagnose problems electronically then operating cost can be significantly reduced. Hewlett Packard and Dell are examples of companies where significant cost savings have been made as a result of using the website to distribute technical manuals and provide customer support.

2 **Market research**

- *Online surveys* – these can be highly effective at reducing costs. Material costs and the cost of posting can be reduced to virtually nothing. The cost of process is also reduced as the need for data input personnel is eliminated, and there is, potentially, improved quality due to reduction of data input errors. It should be noted that there are some additional upfront costs, e.g. designing the survey and supporting databases. Business analysts for Eastman Kodak Co. found that online surveys are completed more quickly compared to conventional surveys and are more successful in gathering a large sample.

- *Online focus groups* – by conducting electronic focus groups involving geographically dispersed participants, businesses can reduce information processing costs and factor costs but there are potential issues of generalisability and potential bias.

3 **Knowledge sharing**

- *New product development* (NPD) *knowledge sharing*. Product development cycles are generally becoming shorter and time to market much faster. The knowledge required for successfully implementing NPD projects often resides in different parts of the business, e.g. accounting, R&D, marketing or production. Consequently, an opportunity exists to leverage the Internet to facilitate sharing of intra-organisational knowledge. The Internet can be integrated into different stages of NPD for information gathering and transfer, both within and outside the organisation – e.g., customers, competitors and channel members.

- *Online advertising knowledge sharing*. The ability to digitise advertising content (e.g. artwork, audio and video files) and share it through online databases among departments within the organisation and with advertising agencies enables streamlining of brand management and considerable savings. In the case of Coca-Cola huge efficiency gains were made by making available via the Internet over 100 years worth of corporate marketing and advertising icons. This provided easy access for anyone developing new marketing communication projects. Further benefits and efficiencies were gained by centralised storing and updating, and managing and disseminating best advertising practices. The system comprises downloadable video, photographs and marketing and advertising icons. A key benefit of the online knowledge system is that it enhances productivity gains by reusing existing brand knowledge.

- *Online sales knowledge*. Sharing information about sales leads has in the past been an inefficient, inaccurate and time-consuming activity and can result in duplication of effort. However, prospecting and qualifying sales leads and cross-referencing customers through an Internet-based contact management system can help eliminate redundancy and waste and significantly streamline the sales function. An example of other efficiencies related to the sales function occurs at trade shows. The promotional expenditure is the second largest area of spend in a business marketing communications budget and can account for as much as a quarter of the total show budget. Cost efficiencies can be made by using the Internet for pre-announcement of the show promotions, cross-promoting with other advertising and communication campaigns, using e-mail customer invitations.

- *Online service knowledge.* The Internet can be used to act as a platform to enhance the efficiency of intra-organisational learning through establishing problem–solution exchanges, e.g. online customer conflict-resolution centres.
- *Addressability.* The Internet can be used to find users and update customer databases, which can result in great efficiencies in targeting and the profitability of direct mail campaigns. Online communications offer an opportunity to create highly tailored, fast communications that can deliver high information content at comparatively low cost (Gattiker *et al.*, 2000).

The extent to which an organisation can take advantage of these potential efficiency gains is related to the extent of adoption and integration of Internet technologies. For companies with fully integrated systems there are many opportunities to make operation efficiency gains. But it is also important to remember that organisations have to be effective as well efficient if they are to enjoy long-term success online. It is important for organisations to establish effective customer relationships. The next section considers the factors which determine an organisation's levels of adoption of Internet technologies, which will also tend to determine its capacity to operate efficiently and effectively online.

## Analysing the factors which influence the adoption of Internet technologies

Some organisations have wholeheartedly embraced the use of Internet technologies whereas others 'have been far more timid either developing small scale, experimental applications or completely ignoring the Internet's potential altogether' (Ellis-Chadwick *et al.*, 2002). Table 12.2 summarises the key factors cited as affecting levels of business adoption of the Internet. It is possible to identify four key dimensions within these factors, which are likely to significantly affect online marketing planning and ultimately the effectiveness and efficiency of an organisations Internet operations. The dimensions (based on Ellis-Chadwick, 2008) are:

- *Financial dimension* – Businesses are beginning to consider carefully the Internet's potential to deliver economic gains. Ashworth *et al.* (2005) have stressed the importance of financial factors and how the extent to which business can benefit from economics of scale is likely to influence rates of Internet adoption. Businesses are also likely to evaluate the cost of operations, the availability of operational and development funding and the time line of online profitability. The outcome of analysis of financial variables is likely to critically affect the extent to which a business trades online, offers interactive services or invests in using the Internet to support its operations.
- *Operational dimension* – Grewal *et al.* (2004) highlighted the importance of the suitability of product range and the impact of logistical complexities of getting goods to buyers at acceptable costs and within an appropriate time frame as key determinants of whether businesses offer the Internet as a channel choice. For successful development of the online channel, businesses also need to have in place a suitable technological infrastructure, and a supportive and technologically integrated supply chain. A business's assessment of operational variables is likely to impact not only on the extent of development of online retail provision but also on the level of the online service provision. Other factors, which can be considered under the operational dimension, are company size and maturity and the choice of online format. Analysis of the operational factors is likely to influence the extent to which a business integrates online and offline channels.
- *Market dimension* – A business's perceptions and understanding of online market potential are cited as important indicators of the level and range of development of online market provision. Businesses tend to develop understanding of the market potential by assessing the suitability of the customer base (Grewal *et al.*, 2004). However, researchers suggest it is also important to understand the customer experience in a multichannel trading environment if the online channel is to be seriously developed. From this viewpoint, businesses should assess customers'

| Table 12.2 | Summary of the factors affecting adoption of the Internet |
|---|---|

| Factors influencing adoption | O'Keefe et al. (1998) | Doherty et al. (2003) | Grewal et al. (2004) | Lunce et al. (2006) | Ashworth et al. (2005) | Verdict (2007) | Lee and Kim (2007) |
|---|---|---|---|---|---|---|---|
| Capabilities and resources | ✓ | ✓ | | | ✓ | | ✓ |
| Channel – relative advantage | | ✓ | | | | | ✓ |
| Choice of online format | | | ✓ | | | | |
| Company size | ✓ | | | ✓ | | | |
| Cost of operating sustainable online retail operations – economies of scale | ✓ | ✓ | ✓ | | ✓ | | |
| Ease of access, use and convenience | | | ✓ | ✓ | | ✓ | |
| Economies of scale innovativeness | | | | | ✓ | | ✓ |
| Internal expertise | ✓ | ✓ | ✓ | | ✓ | | ✓ |
| Level and type of information provision | | | ✓ | | | | |
| Levels of customer service | ✓ | | ✓ | | | ✓ | ✓ |
| Logistical infrastructure complexities | | ✓ | ✓ | | ✓ | | ✓ |
| Maturity of online market positioning | | | | ✓ | | | |
| Perceived and actual levels of security | | ✓ | ✓ | | | | ✓ |
| Product category and range | ✓ | | ✓ | ✓ | | ✓ | |
| Size and maturity of target market | ✓ | ✓ | | ✓ | ✓ | | |
| Strategic vision and commitment | ✓ | ✓ | | | ✓ | ✓ | ✓ |
| Sufficient financial capital | | | | ✓ | ✓ | | |
| Suitability of customer base | ✓ | ✓ | ✓ | | | | ✓ |
| Suitable technological infrastructure | | ✓ | | | | | ✓ |
| Supply chain management issues | | | | | ✓ | ✓ | |

*Source*: Gunawan *et al*, 2008

perceived ease of use, convenience and levels of security in order to develop a realistic assessment of the market potential. Perceptions of online market potential, knowledge of markets served and market opportunities are likely to influence the extent to which businesses see the Internet as a new virtual world of trading opportunities.

- *Strategic dimension* – According to Doherty *et al.* (2003), strategic vision and leadership are critical to the development of a businesses use of Internet and web technologies. However, a clear vision needs to be supported by appropriate competencies and capabilities (Lee and Kim, 2007), say, suitable technological and Internet marketing expertise (Lee and Brandyberry, 2003), appropriate technological, financial and operational resources for a business to use the Internet effectively and efficiently to support its trading activities, develop a competitive positioning and capitalise on the opportunities created by trading in the new virtual world.

The implications are that for organisations wishing to engage successfully in developing transactional operations online there is a need to have certain factors in place. Perhaps most importantly well-resourced strategic leadership that can navigate a course, which not only creates a clear online positioning but also a sustainable competitive advantage, that is leveraged by maximising operational efficiencies and strategic effectiveness. But in addition, there should be evidence of a rich and fertile target market consisting of buyers who are motivated to buy online.

## Digital marketing strategies

The final part of the chapter considers B2B Internet marketing strategies. It should be noted that it is not the aim of this section to revisit the process of planning online marketing strategies (which is discussed in Chapter 4), but to consider how Internet marketing strategies might be used and integrated into organisational planning activities.

So far this chapter has focused on e-marketplaces, the issues of online efficiency and effectiveness and the factors which affect levels of organisational adoption of the Internet. In essence, each of these sections forms an integral part of the online strategic planning process. According to Nicholls and Watson (2005), many organisations are developing a better understanding of the importance of strategic thinking and how it can lead to development of successful online trading. In the past, companies have been accused of a lack of strategic planning, which was ultimately said to be the cause of their online failures (Porter, 2001). During the dot-com boom many companies were accused of a lack of strategic planning, which was ultimately said to be the cause of their business failures. E-strategy has been discussed at various levels from business re-engineering, new approaches to marketing planning to analysing and measuring specifics of web-based activities.

From a strategic planning perspective, Teo and Pian (2003) found that the level of Internet adoption has a significant positive relationship with an organisation's capacity to develop competitive advantage. This is in line with the earlier discussions of the factors, which affect levels of adoption. The implications are that organisations should seriously consider how to develop maximum capacity to benefit from the online trading environment. Organisations that hesitate are likely to be superseded by existing or new competitors. While in the current climate this sounds rather obvious, the business potential that can be derived from adopting Internet technologies is not always immediately clear. This situation helps to reinforce the importance of digital marketing planning as it can help to ensure that organisations reduce the risk of losing their competitive edge by missing out on the benefits of new technology. On the plus side, there are increasing opportunities to benefit from innovation, growth, cost reduction, alliance and differentiation advantages through planned adoption and development of Internet and digital technologies as more trading partners become part of the digital marketspace.

According to Nicholls and Watson (2005), in order to develop an online strategy it is critically important to use Internet technologies effectively and it is also vital to analyse the operational situation. Furthermore, it is important to assess the degree to which the offline and online management infrastructure, marketing and logistics functions are integrated.

Figure 12.5 shows a model of e-value creation with key areas, which affect strategy development: the organisation's core strategic objectives, its business characteristics, internal resources and competencies. Different objectives need to be supported by different organisational structures and marketing strategies – e.g. greater cost reduction is likely to be achieved if technologies are integrated throughout the organisation. The characteristics of the organisation are likely to have a significant impact on Internet strategies – e.g. small companies will have to consider carefully how to resource a fully transactional website and handle the logistics. Currently, a good deal of emphasis is placed on the supply-side of e-commerce strategies. Streamlining of procurement systems through the use of Internet technologies can make significant cost reductions, which can produce cost saving, managerial efficiencies in the purchasing function and financial benefits.

Mini case study 12.1 gives an example of a B2B services company that has taken a strategic approach to customer-centric strategy.

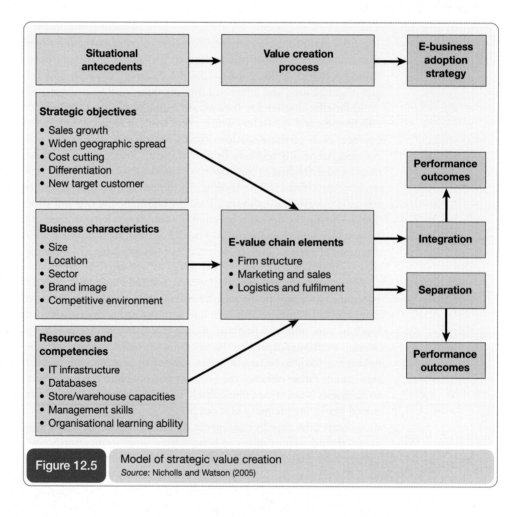

**Figure 12.5**  Model of strategic value creation
*Source*: Nicholls and Watson (2005)

| Mini Case Study 12.1 | Customer-centric strategy at Thomson Financial |
| --- | --- |

The Thomson Corporation is a global provider of integrated information-based solutions to business and professional customers. Thomson serve professionals in the fields of law, tax, accounting, financial services, scientific research and healthcare. Thomson Financial (www.thomson.com/solutions/financial/) provides information and software tools that help its customers make better decisions, faster.

Harrington and Tjan (2008) identified these steps in developing an online customer strategy for Thomson Financial.

### Step 1. Map out your real market

Initially, in 2001, Thomson were using third-party reports to estimate market size. The approximately $15 billion financial-information market was divided into three categories: firms on the buy side, firms on the sell side, and corporate clients.

Using a more sophisticated approach the market was broken down into segments of users. Eight segments were identified and then, using a range of data including competitor reports, interviewing customers, Thomson Financial mapped out their share for each.

### Step 2. Understand the customers' objectives and work flow

The next step involved finding out exactly how products were being used by different personas. For example, gathering information not only on the activities of a bank's head of research, who bought the product, but also on the behaviour of analysts doing research for their clients.

Thomson Financial used a combination of traditional survey methods and less traditional methods such as 'day in the life' observations of customers to chart users' activities. Key to this research was an approach called 'three minutes.' What were end users of a product or service doing three minutes before they used it and three minutes after? What were they doing for the next three minutes? Thomson kept asking that until we got a view of the full day. The aim was to make Thomson products part of as much of that day as practical.

### Step 3. Develop products that provide what users value most

Once Thomson had a picture of users' needs, candidates for new features that would address unmet needs were identified. Candidate features and information were based on the biggest pain points for end users – which aspects of their jobs were so problematic that customers would pay to make them better? To determine this, Thomson surveyed more than 1200 investment managers, for instance, to find out the features those users valued most in the aggregate. Then they performed a conjoint analysis in which investment managers were asked to make trade-offs among attributes that might enhance the product. This gave a truer picture of their preferences. They saw that within the investment manager group there were three distinct clusters of needs: basic users, advanced users and real-time-focused users. The three clusters valued some but not all of the same things. They then concentrated future development efforts on creating three versions of our solution, each aimed at meeting the needs of one cluster.

### Step 4. Keep the focus on users

Thomson highlight the importance of ongoing research and introduction of new functionality when they say:

> we are continually evaluating and refining our customer strategy. Implementing it requires a flexible go-to-market plan, which we enable by including sales and product development people right up front in the research; by employing effective customer feedback loops that are built into a periodic review process; and by gradually scaling up the strategy across segments and businesses.

In summary, it is perhaps reasonable to suggest that organisations are beginning to consider use of the Internet from a much more strategic perspective. Organisations operating in B2B sectors are generally well-placed to implement online strategies due to having well-established long-standing trading relationships with customers and members of the supply chain.

| Case Study 12 | B2B adoption of the Internet: Inspirational Cosmetics |
|---|---|

Internet adoption by organisations is, according to research, a process which involves different stages and each of the stages is affected by a number of variables. The stages summarised by Aguila-Obra and Padilla-Meléndez (2006) and the variables are shown in Tables 12.3 and 12.4.

Businesses at the initiation stage are likely to have a very basic level of Internet use but will move towards developing a very basic website and e-mail. By the time the adoption stage is achieved businesses are likely to have their own server in place. Changes to operations and managerial structure will have begun to take place by the time the routinisation stage is reached. Finally, when the infusion stage is reached many changes will have occurred including the development of different organisational units for managing the technology.

In addition to the impact of organisational, external and technology factors, firm size has an impact on the stage and speed of development. In other words the bigger the firm the more likely it is to have its own website and supporting technology infrastructure. Moreover, the larger the firm the greater the level and intensity of the business activity and the greater the number of employees involved.

(Discussion of Factors and Stages based on Aguila-Obra and Padilla-Melendez (2006)

Inspirational Cosmetics (IC) is a recently developed subsidiary of the giant pharmaceutical corporation Multichemical. IC is based in Stockholm and produces a range of high-quality cosmetic products and surgical applications. The company specialises in developing products for the 'anti-ageing' market. IC was established when the parent company, Multichemical, acquired a small Swedish company called Abbalaars, which produced highly effective anti-ageing creams from organically grown plants. The organisational structure of IC has been developed using a combination of local and international expertise. Local producers continue to supply high-quality organic materials for the production of facial creams. These producers are located all around Sweden and vary in size, in terms of number of employees from 5 to 500. The 'think global, act local' approach to the company development has also been applied to the development of the technology infrastructure. Multichemical provides an Internet infrastructure, which is capable of supporting a highly sophisticated range of Internet strategies. However, Abbalaars made limited use of the Internet internally: the company had a computer network linking all parts of the business but externally the website was a static site giving contact details and a short company history. IC has recently appointed an e-commerce director, Henrik Bjornesson, whose responsibility it is to develop online sales revenues and improve communications within the supply chain.

| Table 12.3 | Factors and variables affecting Internet adoption |
|---|---|

| Factors affecting adoption | Variables |
|---|---|
| External factors | • Organisational environment<br>• Industry competition<br>• External support<br>• Internet user expectations<br>• Global electronic markets |
| Technology factors | • Benefits of technology adoption<br>• Barrier to technology adoption<br>• Comparative advantage<br>• Cost<br>• Technology infrastructure |
| Organisational factors | • Perceived costs<br>• Internal resources<br>• Skills and expertise<br>• Levels of investment<br>• Business objectives<br>• Organisational structure |
| Firm size | • Small<br>• Medium<br>• Large |

*Source*: Based on Aguila-Obra and Padilla-Meléndez (2006)

| Table 12.4 | Stages of internet adoption and influencing factors |
| --- | --- |

| Stage | Influencing factors |
| --- | --- |
| Initiation | Firms tend to have limited access to technology resources and are unlikely to have internal computer network but firms at this stage are looking at opportunities created by the web. Investment and financial cost are key at this stage |
| Adoption/adaptation | Firms will already have made an investment in technology but still need external support as they are beginning to use the web.<br>Managerial expertise and external networks are key here |
| Acceptance/routinisation | Firms are likely to have a fairly well-established technology infrastructure and are likely to be using the Internet and the web extensively for internal and external communications |
| Infusion | By this stage the firms have largely become self-sufficient in terms of operating and developing Internet and web technologies. Managerial skill will also be very well developed |

*Source*: Based on Aguila-Obra and Padilla-Meléndez (2006)

## Questions

1 Assess the stage of the Internet adoption for:
  - Multichemical.
  - Inspirational Cosmetics.
  - The organic growers (suppliers).
2 Explain which factor and variables Henrik Bjornesson is most likely to consider when deciding how to achieve the business goals set by Rosemary Dulwich, the CEO of Inspirational Cosmetics.

3 Consider the likely stage of adoption of the suppliers of organic produce. Suggest ways in which Inspirational Cosmetics might develop its use of the Internet with these suppliers.

## Summary

1. This chapter has examined B2B use of Internet technologies and in doing so it has considered the e-markets, the importance of efficiency and effectiveness to organisations operating online, the factors which affect adoption and has briefly looked at online marketing strategies.

2. Discussions of the concepts of efficiency and effectiveness have revealed many areas where organisations can look to make gains and in doing so improve their overall competitive positioning.

3. The chapter also examined B2B e-markets and considered the importance of e-markets in terms of growth and dispersion of use of Internet technologies across different industrial sectors.

4. We explored different types of e-market places and provided case examples of different types of e-market portals.

5. We summarised the factors that affect internet adoption and suggested ways in which these factors cluster together into separate dimensions of influencing factors: financial, market, operational and strategic.

6. Digital marketing strategies are not always integrated into a business's wider planning activities. However, this is becoming more important as organisations increasingly integrate Internet technologies into the buying and selling activities.

## Exercises

### Self-assessment exercises

1. Evaluate and compare the factors likely to affect (a) a construction company, (b) an insurance brokerage contemplating setting up a transactional website aiming to develop online market share.

2. Explain the difference between online market efficiency and online market effectiveness.

### Essay and discussion questions

1. Discuss why a business operating in an industrial market might be cautious about putting new product specifications on the company website.

2. Discuss to what extent trading online alters relationships between trading partners.

3. Explain how Internet technologies can contribute to the development of online business strategies.

### Examination question

1. Discuss the extent to which B2B e-marketplaces are fundamentally different to traditional offline markets.

## References

Aguila-Obra, A.R.D. and Padilla-Meléndez, A. (2006) 'Organisational factors affecting Internet technology adoption, *Internet Research*, 16(1) 91–110.

Ansari, A. and Mela, C.F. (2003) E-customisation, *J Mark Res* **40** (2003) 131–145 May.

Ashworth, C. Schmidt, R. Pioche, E. and Hallsworth, A. (2005) An approach to sustainable 'fashion' e-retail: A five stage evolutionary strategy for clicks-and-mortar and pureplay enterprises. *Journal of Retailing and Consumer Service*, Vol. 13, No. 4, 289–299.

BBC (2008) Supplying the BBC: e-commerce, http://www.bbc.co.uk/supplying/ecommerce.shtml (accessed March 2008).

Brown, R. (1987) Marketing: A function and a philosophy. *Quarterly Review of Marketing* 12(3) 25–50.

Central Statistical Office (1992) *Introduction to Standard Industrial Classification of Economic Activities* SIC(92). CSO Publications, London.

Doherty, N.F. and Ellis-Chadwick, F.E. (2003) The relationship between retailers' targeting and e-commerce strategies: an empirical analysis, *Internet Research*, Vol. 13, No. 3, 170–182.

Doherty, N.F., Ellis-Chadwick, F.E. and Hart, C.A. (1999) Cyber retailing in the UK: the potential of the Internet as a retail channel, *International Journal of Retail and Distribution Management*, 27(1), 22–36.

DTI (2004) *Business in the Information Age: The International Benchmarking Study 2004*. www.thecma.com/accounts/CMA/documents/Nov2004/ibs2004.pdf.

Ellis-Chadwick, F.E. (2008) Online retailing: open all hours? *International Journal of Business Environments*, Vol. 2, No. 2.

Ellis-Chadwick, F.E., McHardy, P. and Wiesehofer, H. (2002) Online customer relationships in the European financial services sector: a cross-country investigation, *International Journal of Financial Services Marketing*, 6(4).

E-market Services Significant E-marketplaces http://www.emarketservices.com/start/Knowledge/E_business_Issues/E_marketplace_development/index.html?cl=ems (accessed January 2008).

E-market services (2008) http://www.emarketservices.com/.

Evans, P. and Wurster, T.S. (2000) *Blown to Bits: How the New Economics of Information Transforms Strategy*. Harvard Business School, USA.

Gattiker, U.E., Perlusz, S. and Bohmann, K. (2000) Using the Internet for B2B activities: a review and further direction for research, *Internet Research Electronic Networking Application and Policy*, 10(2), 126–40.

Grewal, Iyer G. and Levy, M. (2004) Internet retailing: enablers, limiters and market consequences, *Journal of Business Research*, Vol. 57, No. 7, 703–713.

Gunawan, G., Ellis-Chadwick, F. and King, M. (2008) 'An empirical study of the uptake of performance measurement by internet retailers', *Internet Research*, Vol. 18, Issue 4, 361–81.

Harrington, R. and Tjan, A. (2008) Transforming strategy one customer at a time. *Harvard Business Review*, March 2008, Vol. 86, Issue 3, 62–72.

Jobber, D. (2007) *Principles and Practice of Marketing*, 5th edn. McGraw-Hill.

Kalaignanam, K., Kushwaha, T. and Varadarajan, P. (2008) Marketing operations efficiency and the Internet: an organizing framework, *Journal of Business Research*, Volume 61, Issue 4, 300–308.

Lee and Brandyberry, A. (2003) The e-tailer's dilemma, *ACM SIGMIS Database*, Vol. 34, No. 2.

Lee, S. and Kim, K-J. (2007) Factors affecting the implementation success of Internet-based information systems, *Computers in Human Behaviour*, Vol. 23, Issue 4, 1853–1880, July.

Lunce, S., Lunce, L., Kawai, Y. and Maniam, B. (2006) Success and Failure of Pureplay Organisations: Webvan versus Peapod, a comparative analysis.

Nicholls, A. and Watson, A. (2005) Implementing e-value strategies in UK retailing, *International Journal of Retail and Distribution Management*, 33(6), 426–43.

O'Keefe, R. M., O'Connor, G. and Kung, H. J. (1998) Early adopters of the Web as a retail medium: small company winners and losers, *European Journal of Marketing*, Vol. 32, No 7/8, 629–643.

Porter, M. (2001) Strategy and the Internet, *Harvard Business Review*, March, 62–78.

Rayport, J. and Sviokla, J. (1995) Exploiting the virtual value chain, *Harvard Business Review*, November – December, 75–87.

Tapscott, D. (1997) *Growing Up Digital*. McGraw-Hill, New York.

Teo, T. and Pian, Y. (2003) A contingency perspective on Internet adoption and competitive advantage, *European Journal of Information Systems*, 12(2), 78–92.

Varadarajan, R.P. and Yadav, M.S. (2002) Marketing strategy and the Internet: an organising framework, *J Acad Mark Sci*, **30** (2002), 296–313, Fall.

Verdict Research (2007) *UK e-retail 2007*, Verdict Research limited, Charles House, 108–110 Finchley Road, London, NW3 5JJ.

Vijayasarathy, L. and Tyler, M. (1997) Adoption factors and electronic data interchange use: a survey of retail companies. *International Journal of Retail Distribution and Management*, Vol. 25, No. 9, 286–292.

Wrigley, N. and Lowe, M.S. (eds) (2001) *Retailing, Consumption and Capital*. Addison Wesley Longman, Harlow, 90–115.

Zettelmeyer, F. (2000) Expanding the internet: pricing and communications strategies when firms compete on multiple channels, *J Mark Res*, 37 (2000), 292–308, August.

## Further reading

Benyon Davies (2004) *E-business*, Palgrave Macmillan.

Chaffey (2009) *E-business and E-commerce Management*, 4th edn, Pearson Education.

Harris, L. and Dennis, C. (2008) *Marketing the E-business*, 2nd edn, Routledge.

Laundon and Traver (2007) *E-commerce: Business, Technology, Society*, 4th edn, Prentice Hall.

**3G** Third generation of mobile phone technology.

**4G** Fourth-generation wireless, expected to deliver wireless broadband at 20–40 Mbps (about 10–20 times the current rates of ADSL broadband service).

## A

**A/B testing** A/B or AB testing refers to testing two different versions of a page or a page element such as a heading, image or button. The alternatives are served alternately with the visitors to the page randomly split between the two pages. Hence, it is sometimes called 'live split testing'. Changes in visitor behaviour can then be compared using different metrics such as click-through rate on page elements like buttons or images, or macro-conversion rates, such as conversion to sale or sign-up. AB testing is aimed at increasing page or site effectiveness against key performance indicators including click-through rate, conversion rates and revenue per visit. Since it does not consider combinations of variables tested, for best uplift multivariate testing is increasingly used.

**Above the fold** A term, derived from printed media, which is used to indicate whether a banner advertisement or other content is displayed on a web page without the need to scroll. This is likely to give higher click-through, but note that the location of the 'fold' within the web browser is dependent on the screen resolution of a user's personal computer.

**Access platform** A method for customers to access digital media.

**Access provider** A company providing services to enable a company or individual to access the Internet. Access providers are divided into Internet service providers (ISPs) and online service providers (OSPs).

**Accessibility** An approach to site design intended to accommodate site usage using different browsers and settings particularly required by the visually impaired and visitors with other disabilities including motor control, learning difficulties and deafness. Users whose first language is not English can also be assisted.

**Accessibility legislation** Legislation intended to assist users of websites with disabilities including visual disability.

**Acquisition** *See* **Customer acquisition**.

**Active Server Page (ASP)** A type of HTML page (denoted by an .asp file name) that includes scripts (small programs) that are processed on a web server before the web page is served to the user's web browser. ASP is a Microsoft technology that usually runs on a Microsoft Internet Information Server (usually on Windows NT). The main use of such programs is to process information supplied by the user in an online form. A query may then be run to provide specific information to the customer such as delivery status on an order, or a personalised web page.

**ActiveX** A programming language standard developed by Microsoft that permits complex and graphical customer applications to be written and then accessed from a web browser. ActiveX components are standard controls that can be incorporated into websites and are then automatically downloaded for users. Examples are graphics and animation or a calculator form for calculating interest on a loan or a control for graphing stock prices. A competitor to Java.

**Ad creative** The design and content of an ad.

**Ad impression** Similar in concept to a page impression; describes one viewing of an advertisement by a single member of its audience. The same as ad view, a term that is less commonly used.

**Ad inventory** The total number of ad impressions that a website can sell over time (usually specified per month).

**Ad network** Ad networks from suppliers such as Blue Lithium or 24-7 Media give advertisers the options of advertising across a network of sites to reach a particular demographic, e.g. female 18–25, but at a lower cost than targeting a single site since the actual site used for the ad placement isn't known (hence these are sometimes known as 'blind network buys').

**Ad rotation** When advertisements are changed on a website for different user sessions. This may be in response to ad targeting or simply displaying different advertisements from those on a list.

**Ad serving** The term for displaying an advertisement on a website. Often the advertisement will be served from a web server different from the site on which it is placed. For example, the server URL for displaying the advertisement is http://ad.doubleclick.net.

**Ad space** The area of a web page that is set aside for banner advertising.

**Ad view** Similar in concept to a page impression; describes one viewing of an advertisement by a single member of its audience. The same as ad impression, the term that is more commonly used.

**Advertisement** Advertisements on websites are usually banner advertisements positioned as a masthead on the page.

**Advertising broker** *See* **Media broker**.

**Advertising networks** A collection of independent websites of different companies and media networks, each of which has an arrangement with a single advertising broker (*see* **Media broker**) to place banner advertisements.

**Affiliate** A company promoting a merchant typically through a commission-based arrangement either direct or through an affiliate network.

**Affiliate marketing** A commission-based arrangement where referring sites (publishers) receive a commission on sales or leads by merchants (retailers). Commission is usually based on a percentage of product sale price or a fixed amount for each sale (CPA or cost-per-acquisition), but may also sometimes be based on a per-click basis, for example when an aggregator refers visits to merchants.

**Affiliate networks** Third-party brokers also known as affiliate managers who manage recruitment of affiliates and infrastructure to manage a merchant's affiliate programme in the form of links, tracking and payment of a range of affiliates.

**Agents** Software programs that can assist people to perform tasks such as finding particular information such as the best price for a product.

**Aggregators** An alternative term to *price comparison sites*. Aggregators include product, price and service information comparing competitors within a sector such a financial services, retail or travel. Their revenue models commonly include affiliate revenues (CPA), pay-per-click advertising (CPC) and display advertising (CPM).

**Aggregated buying** A form of customer union where buyers collectively purchase a number of items at the same price and receive a volume discount.

**Agile software development** An iterative approach to developing software and website functionality with the emphasis on face-to-face communications to elicit, define and test requirements. Each iteration or scrum is effectively a mini-software project including stages of planning, requirements analysis, design, coding, testing and documentation.

**Allowable cost-per-acquisition** A target maximum cost for generating leads or new customers profitably.

**Alt tags** Alt tags appear after an image tag and contain a phrase associated with that image. For example: <img src="logo.gif" alt="Company name, company products"/>.

**Analysis phase** The identification of the requirements of a website. Techniques to achieve this may include focus groups, questionnaires sent to existing customers or interviews with key accounts.

**Anchor text (also known as link text)** The (usually) clickable text element representing a hyperlink. Or more prosaically, the body copy that is hyperlinked.

**Animated banner advertisements (animated GIFs)** Early banner advertisements featured only a single advertisement, but today they will typically involve several different images, which are displayed in sequence to help to attract attention to the banner and build up a theme, often ending with a call to action and the injunction to click on the banner. These advertisements are achieved through supplying the ad creative as an animated GIF file with different layers or frames, usually a rectangle of $468 \times 60$ pixels. Animated banner advertisements are an example of rich-media advertisements.

**Announcements** *See* **Site announcements**.

**Archie** A database containing information on what documents and programs are located on FTP servers. It would not be used in a marketing context unless one were looking for a specific piece of software or document name.

**Asymmetric encryption** Both parties use a related but different key to encode and decode messages.

**Atomisation** Atomisation in a Web 2.0 context refers to a concept where the content on a site is broken down into smaller fundamental units which can then be distributed via the web through links to other sites. Examples of atomisation include the stories and pages in individual feeds being syndicated to third-party sites and widgets.

**Attrition rate** Percentage of site visitors who are lost at each stage in making a purchase.

**Audit (external)** Consideration of the business and economic environment in which the company operates. This includes the economic, political, fiscal, legal, social, cultural and technological factors (usually referred to by the acronym STEP or SLEPT).

**Audit (internal)** A review of website effectiveness.

**Auditors** *See* **Site auditors**.

**Authentication** *See* **Security methods**.

**Autoresponders** Software tools or agents running on web servers that automatically send a standard reply to the sender of an e-mail message. This may provide information for a standard request sent to, say, price_list@company_name.com, or it could simply state that the message or order has been forwarded to the relevant person and will be answered within two days. (Also known as mailbots.)

**Availability** *See* **Security methods**; **Site availability**.

**Avatar** A term used in computer-mediated environments to mean a 'virtual person'. Derived from the word's original meaning: '*n*. the descendant of a Hindu deity in a visible form; incarnation; supreme glorification of any principle'.

**Average order value (AOV)** The average amount spent for a single checkout purchase on a retail site for a particular customer group, e.g. first time purchasers.

# B

**Backbones** High-speed communications links used to enable Internet communications across a country and internationally.

**Backlinks** Hyperlinks which link to a particular web page (or website). Also known as inbound links. Google PageRank and Yahoo! WebRank are methods of enumerating this.

**Balanced scorecard** A framework for setting and monitoring business performance. Metrics are structured according to customer issues, internal efficiency measures, financial measures and innovation.

**Bandwidth** Indicates the speed at which data are transferred using a particular network medium. It is measured in bits per second (bps).

- kbps (one kilobit per second or 1000 bps; a modem operates at up to 56.6 kbps).
- Mbps (one megabit per second or 1,000,000 bps; company networks operate at 10 or more Mbps).
- Gbps (one gigabit per second or 1,000,000,000 bps; fibre-optic or satellite links operate at Gbps).

**Banner advertisement** A typically rectangular graphic displayed on a web page for purposes of brand building or driving traffic to a site. It is normally possible to perform a click-through to access further information from another website. Banners may be static or animated (*see* **Animated banner advertisements**).

**Behavioural ad targeting** Enables an advertiser to target ads at a visitor as they move elsewhere on the site or return to the site, thus increasing the frequency or number of impressions served to an individual in the target market.

**Behavioural loyalty** Loyalty to a brand is demonstrated by repeat sales and response to marketing campaigns.

**Behavioural traits of web users** Web users can be broadly divided into directed and undirected information seekers.

**Bid** A commitment by a trader to purchase under certain conditions.

**Blog** Personal online diary, journal or news source compiled by one person, an internal team or external guest authors. Postings are usually in different categories. Typically comments can be added to each blog posting to help create interactivity and feedback.

**Bluecasting** Bluecasting involves messages being automatically pushed to a consumer's bluetooth-enabled phone or they can pull or request audio, video or text content to be downloaded from a live advert. In the future ads will be able to respond to those who view them.

**Bluejacking** Sending a message from a mobile phone or transmitter to another mobile phone which is in close range via Bluetooth technology.

**Blueprints** Show the relationships between pages and other content components; can be used to portray organisation, navigation and labelling systems.

**Bluetooth** A standard for wireless transmission of data between devices over short ranges (less than 10m), e.g. a mobile phone or a PDA.

**Botnet** Independent computers, connected to the Internet, are used together, typically for malicious purposes through controlling software. For example, they may be used to send out spam or for a denial of service attack where they repeatedly access a server to degrade its software. Computers are often initially infected through a virus when effective anti-virus measures are not in place.

**Bounce rate** Proportion of visitors to a page or site that exit after visiting a single page only, usually expressed as a percentage.

**Brand** The sum of the characteristics of a product or service perceived by a user.

**Brand advocate** A customer who has favourable perceptions of a brand who will talk favourably about a brand to their acquaintances to help generate awareness of the brand or influence purchase intent.

**Brand equity** The brand assets (or liabilities) linked to a brand's name and symbol that add to (or subtract from) a service.

**Brand experience** The frequency and depth of interactions with a brand can be enhanced through the Internet.

**Brand identity** The totality of brand associations including name and symbols that must be communicated.

**Branding** The process of creating and evolving successful brands.

**Bricks-and-mortar** A traditional organisation with limited online presence.

**Broad band shallow navigation** More choices, fewer clicks to reach required content.

**Broadband technology** A term referring to methods of delivering information across the Internet at a higher rate by increasing bandwidth.

**Brochureware** A website in which a company has simply transferred ('migrated') its existing paper-based promotional literature onto the Internet without recognising the differences required by this medium.

**Broker** *See* **Media broker**.

**Browser** *See* **Web browser**.

**Bundling** Offering complementary services.

**Business model** A summary of how a company will generate revenue, identifying its product offering, value-added services, revenue sources and target customers.

**Business-to-business (B2B)** Commercial transactions between an organisation and other organisations (inter-organisational marketing).

**Business-to-business exchanges or marketplaces** Virtual intermediaries with facilities to enable trading between buyers and sellers.

**Business-to-consumer (B2C)** Commercial transactions between an organisation and consumers.

**Buy-side e-commerce** E-commerce transactions between a purchasing organisation and its suppliers.

## C

**Call centre** A location for inbound and outbound telemarketing.

**Call-back service** A direct response facility available on a website to enable a company to contact a customer by phone at a later time as specified by the customer.

**Campaign-based e-communications** E-marketing communications that are executed to support a specific marketing campaign such as a product launch, price promotion or a website launch.

**Campaign URL (CURL)** A web address specific to a particular campaign.

**Capabilities** Capabilities are intangible and are developed from the combined and coordinated behaviour and activities of an organisation's employees, and it is therefore 'embedded in the organisation and processes' (Makadok, 2001 – see Chapter 11). The definition of a capability is an organisation's ability to 'perform a set of co-ordinated tasks, utilising organisational resources, for the purposes of achieving a particular end result'

**Card sorting** The process of setting up a way of organising objects on the website in a consistent manner.

**Cascading style sheets** A simple mechanism for adding style (e.g. fonts, colours, spacing) to web documents. CSS enables different style elements to be controlled across an entire site or section of site. Style elements that are commonly controlled include typography, background colour and images, and borders and margins.

**Catalogue** Catalogues provide a structured listing of registered websites in different categories. They are similar to an electronic version of *Yellow Pages*. Yahoo! and Excite are the best known examples of catalogues. (Also known as directories.) The distinction between search engines and catalogues has become blurred since many sites now include both facilities as part of a portal service.

**Certificate** A valid copy of a public key of an individual or organisation together with identification information. It is issued by a trusted third party (TTP) or certification authority (CA).

**Certification authority (CA)** An organisation issuing and managing certificates or public keys and private keys to individuals or organisations together with identification information.

**Change management** Controls to minimise the risks of project-based and organisational change.

**Channel buyer behaviour** Describes which content is visited and the time and duration.

**Channel conflicts** A significant threat arising from the introduction of an Internet channel is that while disintermediation gives the opportunity for a company to sell direct and increase the profitability of products it can also threaten existing distribution arrangements with existing partners.

**Channel marketing strategy** Defines how a company should set specific objectives for a channel such as the Internet and vary its proposition and communications for this channel.

**Channel outcomes** Record customer actions taken as a consequence of a visit to a site.

**Channel profitability** The profitability of a website, taking into account revenue and cost and discounted cash flow.

**Channel promotion** Measures that assess why customers visit a site – which adverts they have seen, which sites they have been referred from.

**Channel satisfaction** Evaluation of the customer's opinion of the service quality on the site and supporting services such as e-mail.

**Channel structure** The configuration of partners in a distribution channel.

**Clicks-and-mortar** A business combining online and offline presence.

**Clicks-only or Internet pureplay** An organisation with principally an online presence.

**Clickstream** A record of the path a user takes through a website. Clickstreams enable website designers to assess how their site is being used.

**Clickstream analysis** Reviewing the online behaviour of site visitors based on the sequence of pages that they visit, the navigation and promotion they respond to, the ultimate outcomes and where they leave the site.

**Click-through** A click-through (ad click) occurs each time a user clicks on a banner advertisement to direct them to a web page that contains further information.

**Click-through rate** Expressed as a percentage of total ad impressions, and refers to the proportion of users viewing an advertisement who click on it. It is calculated as the number of click-throughs divided by the number of ad impressions.

**Click-tracking Java** technology can be used to track movements of individual users to a website.

**Client–server** The client–server architecture consists of client computers such as PCs sharing resources such as a database stored on a more powerful server computer.

**Co-branding** An arrangement between two or more companies where they agree to jointly display content and perform joint promotion using brand logos, e-mail marketing or banner advertisements. The aim is that the brands are strengthened if they are seen as complementary. Co-branding is often a reciprocal arrangement which can occur without payment as part of a wider agreement between partners.

**Cold list** Data about individuals that are rented or sold by a third party.

**Collaborative filtering** Profiling of customer interest coupled with delivery of specific information and offers, often based on the interests of similar customers.

**Commoditisation** The process whereby product selection becomes more dependent on price than on differentiating features, benefits and value-added services.

**Common Gateway Interface (CGI)** A method of processing information on a web server in response to a customer's request. Typically a user will fill in a web-based form and the results will be processed by a CGI script (application). Active Server Pages (ASPs) are an alternative to a CGI script.

**Competitive intelligence (CI)** A process that transforms disaggregated information into relevant, accurate and usable strategic knowledge about competitors, position, performance, capabilities and intentions.

**Competitor analysis** Review of Internet marketing services offered by existing and new competitors and adoption by their customers.

**Competitor benchmarking** A structured analysis of the online services, capabilities and performance of an organisation within the areas of customer acquisition, conversion, retention and growth.

**Computer telephony integration** The integration of telephony and computing to provide a platform for applications that streamline or enhance business processes.

**Confidentiality** *See* **Security methods**.

**Consumer-to-business (C2B)** Consumers approach the business with an offer.

**Consumer-to-consumer (C2C)** Informational or financial transactions between consumers, but usually mediated through a business site.

**Consumer behaviour** Research into the motivations, media consumption preferences and selection processes used by consumers as they use digital channels together with traditional channels to purchase online products and use other online services.

**Contact** or **touch strategy** Definition of the sequence and type of outbound communications required at different points in the customer lifecycle.

**Content** Content is the design, text and graphical information that forms a web page. Good content is the key to attracting customers to a website and retaining their interest or achieving repeat visits.

**Content developer** A person responsible for updating web pages within part of an organisation.

**Content management** Software tools for managing additions and amendments to website content.

**Content network** Sponsored links are displayed by the search engine on third-party sites such as online publishers, aggregators or social networks. Ads can be paid for on a CPC, CPM or a CPA basis. There are also options for graphical or video ads in addition to text-based ads.

**Contextual ads** Ads relevant to page content on third-party sites brokered by search ad networks.

**Continuous e-communications activities** Long-term use of e-marketing communications intended to generate site visitors for customer acquisition (such as search engine, and affiliate marketing and online sponsorship) and retention (for example, e-newsletter marketing).

**Contra-deals** A reciprocal agreement in the form of an exchange where payment doesn't take place. Instead services or ad space to promote another company as part of co-branding occurs.

**Control page** The page against which subsequent optimisation will be assessed. Typically a current landing page. When a new page performs better than the existing control page, it becomes the control page in subsequent testing. Also known as 'champion-challenger'.

**Convergence** A trend in which different hardware devices such as televisions, computers and telephones merge and have similar functions.

**Conversion marketing** Using marketing communications to maximise conversion of potential customers to actual customers.

**Conversion rate** Proportion of visitors to a site, or viewers of an advert, who take an action such as registration or checkout. *See* **Visit conversion rate** and **Visitor conversion rate**.

**Cookies** Cookies are small text files stored on an end-user's computer to enable websites to identify the user. They enable a company to identify a previous visitor to a site, and build up a profile of that visitor's behaviour. *See* **Persistent cookies**, **Session cookies**, **First-party cookies**, **Third-party cookies**.

**Core product** The fundamental features of the product that meet the user's needs.

**Core tenants** A shopping centre or mall is usually a centrally owned managed facility. In the physical world, the management will aim to include in the mall stores that sell a different but complementary range of merchandise and include a variety of smaller and larger stores. The core tenants or 'anchor stores' as they are often called are the dominant large-scale store operators that are expected to draw customers to the centre.

**Cost models for Internet advertising** These include per-exposure, per-response and per-action costs.

**Cost-per-acquisition (CPA)** The cost of acquiring a new customer. Typically limited to the communications cost and refers to cost per sale for new customers. May also refer to other outcomes such as cost-per-quote or enquiry.

**Cost-per-click (CPC)** The cost of each click from a referring site to a destination site, typically from a search engine in pay-per-click search marketing.

**Cost-per-targeted mille (CPTM)** Cost per targeted thousand for an advertisement. (*See* **Targeting**.)

**Cost per thousand (CPM)** Cost per 1000 ad impressions.

**Countermediation** Creation of a new intermediary by an established company.

**Cracker** A malicious meddler who tries to discover sensitive information by poking around computer networks.

**Cross-media optimisation studies (XMOS)** Studies to determine the optimum spend across different media to produce the best results.

**Cross-selling** Persuading existing customers to purchase products from other categories than their typical purchases.

**Customer acquisition** Strategies and techniques used to gain new customers.

**Customer-centric marketing** An approach to marketing based on detailed knowledge of customer behaviour within the target audience which seeks to fulfil the individual needs and wants of customers.

**Customer communications channels** The range of media used to communicate directly with a customer.

**Customer engagement** Repeated interactions that strengthen the emotional, psychological or physical investment a customer has in a brand.

**Customer experience** *See* **Online customer experience**.

**Customer extension** Techniques to encourage customers to increase their involvement with an organisation.

**Customer insight** Knowledge about customers' needs, characteristics, preferences and behaviours based on analysis of qualitative and quantitative data. Specific insights can be used to inform marketing tactics directed at groups of customers with shared characteristics.

**Customer journey** A description of modern multichannel buyer behaviour as consumers use different media to select suppliers, make purchases and gain customer support.

**Customer lifecycle** The stages each customer will pass through in a long-term relationship through acquisition, retention and extension.

**Customer loyalty** The desire on the part of the customer to continue to do business with a given supplier over time. *See* **Behavioural loyalty** and **Emotional loyalty**.

**Customer orientation** Providing content and services on a website consistent with the different characteristics of the audience of the site.

**Customer profiling** Using the website to find out customers' specific interests and characteristics.

**Customer relationship management (CRM)** A marketing-led approach to building and sustaining long-term business with customers.

**Customer retention** Techniques to maintain relationships with existing customers.

**Customer satisfaction** The extent to which a customer's expectations of product quality, service quality and price are met.

**Customer scenarios (user journeys)** Alternative tasks or outcomes required by a visitor to a website. Typically accomplished in a series of stages of different tasks involving different information needs or experiences.

**Customer segments** Groups of customers sharing similar characteristics, preferences and behaviours who are targeted with different propositions as part of *target marketing strategy*.

**Customer selection** Identifying key customer segments and targeting them for relationship building.

**Customer touch-points** Communications channels with which companies interact directly with prospects and customers. Traditional touch-points include face-to-face (in-store or with sales representatives), phone and mail. Digital touch-points include web services, e-mail and, potentially, mobile phone.

**Cybermediaries** Intermediaries who bring together buyers and sellers or those with particular information or service needs.

**Cyberspace and cybermarketing** These terms were preferred by science-fiction writers and tabloid writers to indicate the futuristic nature of using the Internet, the prefix 'cyber' indicating a blurring between humans, machines and communications. The terms are not frequently used today since the terms Internet, intranet and World Wide Web are more specific and widely used.

# D

**Data controller** Each company must have a defined person responsible for data protection.

**Data fusion** The combining of data from different complementary sources (usually geodemographic and lifestyle or market research and lifestyle) to 'build a picture of someone's life' (M. Evans (1998) From 1086 to 1984: direct marketing into the millennium, *Marketing Intelligence and Planning*, 16(1), 56–67).

**Data subject** The legal term to refer to the individual whose data are held.

**Data warehousing and data mining** Extracting data from legacy systems and other resources; cleaning, scrubbing and preparing data for decision support; maintaining data in appropriate data stores; accessing and analysing data using a variety of end-user tools; and mining data for significant relationships. The primary purpose of these efforts is to provide easy access to specially prepared data that can be used with decision support applications such as management reports, queries, decision support systems, executive information systems and data mining.

**Database marketing** The process of systematically collecting, in electronic or optical form, data about past, current and/or potential customers, maintaining the integrity of the data by continually monitoring customer purchases, by enquiring about changing status, and by using the data to formulate marketing strategy and foster personalised relationships with customers.

**Decryption** The process of decoding (unscrambling) a message that has been encrypted using defined mathematical rules.

**Deep linking** Jakob Nielsen's term for a user arriving at a site deep within its structure or where search engines index a mirrored copy of content normally inaccessible by search engine spiders.

**Deliverability** Deliverability refers to ensuring e-mail messages are delivered and aren't blocked by spam filters because the e-mail content or structure falsely identifies a permission-based e-mail as a spammer, or because the sender's IP address has a poor reputation for spam.

**Demand analysis** Quantitative determination of the potential usage and business value achieved from online customers of an organisation. Qualitative analysis of perceptions of online channels is also assessed.

**Demand analysis for e-commerce** Assessment of the demand for e-commerce services among existing and potential customer segments using the ratio Access : Choose : Buy online.

**Demographic characteristics** Variations in attributes of the population such as age, sex and social class.

**Denial of service attack** Also known as a distributed denial of service (DDOS) attack, this involves a hacker group taking control of many 'zombie' computers attached to the Internet whose security has been compromised. This 'botnet' is then used to make many requests to a target server, so overloading it and preventing access to other visitors.

**Design for analysis (DFA)** The required measures from a site are considered during design to better understand the audience of a site and their decision points.

**Design phase (of site construction)** The design phase defines how the site will work in the key areas of website structure, navigation and security.

**Destination site** Frequently used to refer to the site that is visited following a click-through on a banner advertisement. Could also apply to any site visited following a click on a hyperlink.

**Destination store** A retail store in which the merchandise, selection, presentation, pricing or other unique features act as a magnet for the customer.

**Development phase (of site construction)** 'Development' is the term used to describe the creation of a website by programmers. It involves writing the HTML content, creating graphics, and writing any necessary software code such as JavaScript or ActiveX (programming).

**Differential advantage** A desirable attribute of a product that is not currently matched by competitor offerings.

**Differential pricing** Identical products are priced differently for different types of customers, markets or buying situations.

**Digital assets** The graphical and interactive material that support a campaign displayed on third-party sites and on microsites, they include display ads, e-mail templates, video, audio and other interactive media such as Flash animations.

**Digital audio broadcasting (DAB) radio** Digital radio with clear sound quality with the facility to transmit text, images and video.

**Digital brand** A digital brand is a brand identity used for a product or company online that differs from the traditional brand. (Also known as an online brand.)

**Digital cash** An electronic version of cash in which the buyer of an item is typically anonymous to the seller. (Also referred to as virtual or electronic cash or e-cash.)

**Digital certificates (keys)** A method of ensuring privacy on the Internet. Certificates consist of keys made up of large numbers that are used to uniquely identify individuals. *See* **Public key**.

**Digital marketing** This has a similar meaning to 'electronic marketing' – both describe the management and execution of marketing using electronic media such as the web, e-mail, interactive TV, IPTV and wireless media in conjunction with digital data about customers' characteristics and behaviour.

**Digital media** Communications are facilitated through content and interactive services delivered by different digital technology platforms including the Internet, web, mobile phone, interactive TV, IPTV and digital signage. *See* **Digital media channels**.

**Digital media 'assists'** A referrer of a visit to a site before the ultimate sale is credited with the sale, often through a weighting system.

**Digital media channels** Online communications techniques such as search engine marketing, affiliate marketing and display advertising used to engage web users on third-party sites; encouraging them to visit an organisation's site or purchase through traditional channels such as by phone or in-store.

**Digital media de-duplication** A single referrer of a visit leading to sale is credited with the sale based on the last-click method of digital media channel attribution.

**Digital radio** All types of radio broadcast as a digital signal.

**Digital signage** The use of interactive digital technologies within billboard and point of sale ads. For example, videos and bluetooth interaction.

**Digital signatures** The electronic equivalent of written signatures which are used as an online method of identifying individuals or companies using public-key encryption.

**Digital television** Information is received and displayed on a digital television using binary information (0s and 1s), giving options for better picture and sound quality and providing additional information services based on interactivity. *See* **Interactive digital TV**.

**Direct marketing** Marketing to customers using one or more advertising media aimed at achieving measurable response and/or transaction.

**Direct response** Usually achieved in an Internet marketing context by call-back services.

**Directed information seeker** Someone who knows what information he or she is looking for.

**Directories** Directory websites provide a structured listing of registered websites in different categories. They are similar to an electronic version of *Yellow Pages*. Yahoo! and Excite are the best known examples of directories. (Also known as catalogues.)

**Disintermediation** The removal of intermediaries such as distributors or brokers that formerly linked a company to its customers.

**Display advertising** Paid ad placements using graphical or *rich media ad units* within a web page to achieve goals of delivering brand awareness, familiarity, favourability and purchase intent. Many ads encourage interaction through prompting the viewer to interact or *rollover* to play videos, complete an online form or to view more details by clicking through to a site.

**Disruptive technologies** New technologies that prompt businesses to reappraise their strategic approaches.

**Distribution channels** The mechanism by which products are directed to customers either through intermediaries or directly.

**Domain name** The web address that identifies a web server. *See* **Domain name system**.

**Domain name registration** The process of reserving a unique web address that can be used to refer to the company website.

**Domain name system** The domain name system (DNS) provides a method of representing Internet Protocol (IP) addresses as text-based names. These are used as web addresses. For example, www.microsoft.com is the representation of site 207.68.156.58. Domain names are divided into the following categories:

- Top-level domain name such as *.com* or *.co.uk*. (Also known as Global (or generic) top-level domain names (gLTD).)

- Second-level domain name. This refers to the company name and is sometimes referred to as the 'enterprise name', e.g. *novell.com*.

- Third-level or sub-enterprise domain name. This may be used to refer to an individual server within an organisation, such as *support.novell.com*.

**Doorway pages** Specially constructed pages which feature keywords for particular product searches. These often redirect visitors to a home page.

**Download** The process of retrieving electronic information such as a web page or e-mail from another remote location such as a web server.

**Drip irrigation** Collecting information about customer needs through their lifetime.

**Dynamic pricing** Prices can be updated in real time according to the type of customer or current market conditions.

**Dynamic web page** A page that is created in real time, often with reference to a database query, in response to a user request.

# E

**Early adopters** Companies or departments that invest in new marketing techniques and technologies when they first become available in an attempt to gain a competitive advantage despite the higher risk entailed than that involved in a more cautious approach.

**Early (first) mover advantage** An early entrant into the marketplace.

**Earnings-per-click (EPC)** A relative measure of the effectiveness of a site or section of a site in generating revenue for the site owner through affiliate marketing for every 100 outbound clicks generated.

**E-business** *See* **Electronic business.**

**E-cash** *See* **Digital cash.**

**E-commerce** *See* **Electronic commerce.**

**Econometric modelling** A quantitative technique to evaluate the past influence or predict the future influence on a dependent variable (typically sales in a marketing context) of independent variables which may include product price, promotions and the level and mix of media investments.

**Effective cost-per-thousand (eCPM).** A measure of the total revenue a site owner can achieve through advertising or other revenue options. eCPM is calculated as advertising revenue achieved for every 1000 pages that are served for the whole site or a section. *See* EPC.

**Effective frequency** The number of exposures or ad impressions (frequency) required for an advertisement to become effective.

**Effectiveness** Meeting process objectives, delivering the required outputs and outcomes. 'Doing the right thing.'

**Efficiency** Minimising resources or time needed to complete a process. 'Doing the thing right.'

**E-government** The use of Internet technologies to provide government services to citizens.

**Electronic business (e-business)** All electronically mediated information exchanges, both within an organisation and with external stakeholders, supporting the range of business processes.

**Electronic cash** *See* **Digital cash.**

**Electronic commerce (e-commerce)** All financial and informational electronically mediated exchanges between an organisation and its external stakeholders. (*See* **Buy-side e-commerce** and **Sell-side e-commerce.**)

**Electronic commerce transactions** Transactions in the trading of goods and services conducted using the Internet and other digital media.

**Electronic customer relationship management** Using digital communications technologies to maximise sales to existing customers and encourage continued usage of online services.

**Electronic data interchange (EDI)** The exchange, using digital media, of standardised business documents such as purchase orders and invoices between buyers and sellers.

**Electronic mail (e-mail)** Sending messages or documents, such as news about a new product or sales promotion between individuals. A primitive form of push channel. E-mail may be inbound or outbound.

**Electronic mail advertising** Advertisements contained within e-mail such as newsletters.

**Electronic mall** *See* **Virtual mall.**

**Electronic marketing** Achieving marketing objectives through use of electronic communications technology.

**Electronic marketspace** A virtual marketplace such as the Internet in which no direct contact occurs between buyers and sellers.

**Electronic shopping or ES test** This test was developed by de Kare-Silver to assess the extent to which consumers are likely to purchase a particular retail product using the Internet.

**Electronic tokens** Units of digital currency that are in a standard electronic format.

**E-mail marketing** Typically applied to outbound communications from a company to prospects or customers to encourage purchase or branding goals. E-mail marketing is most commonly used for mailing to existing customers on a house-list, but can also be used for mailing prospects on a rented or co-branded list. E-mails may be sent as part of a one-off campaign or can be automated event-based triggered e-mails such as a Welcome strategy which can be broadcast based on rules about intervals and customer characteristics. *See* **Inbound e-mail** and **Outbound e-mail.**

**E-mail service providers (ESPs)** Provide a web-based service used by marketers to manage their e-mail activities including hosting e-mail subscription forms, broadcast and tracking.

**E-marketing** *See* **Electronic marketing.**

**Emergent strategy** Strategic analysis, strategic development and strategy implementation are interrelated and are developed together.

**Emotional loyalty** Loyalty to a brand is demonstrated by favourable perceptions, opinions and recommendations.

**Encryption** The scrambling of information into a form that cannot be interpreted. Decryption is used to make the information readable.

**Enterprise application integration** The middleware technology that is used to connect together different software applications and their underlying databases is now known as 'enterprise application integration (EAI).

**Entry page** The page at which a visitor enters a website. It is identified by a log file analyser. *See* **Exit page** and **Referring site**.

**Environmental scanning and analysis** The process of continuously monitoring the environment and events and responding accordingly.

**E-retail** According to Dennis *et al.* (2004), see Chapter 11, the business of e-retailing is defined as the sale of goods and services via the Internet or other electronic channels for individual consumers. This definition includes all e-commerce and related activities that ultimately result in transactions.

**Ethical standards** Practices or behaviours which are morally acceptable to society.

**Evaluating a website** *See* **Website measurement**.

**Exchange** *See* **Business-to-business exchanges or marketplaces**.

**Exit page** The page from which a visitor exits a website. It is identified by web analytics services.

**Expert reviews** An analysis of an existing site or prototype, by an experienced usability expert who will identify deficiencies and improvements to a site based on their knowledge of web design principles and best practice.

**Exposure-based payment** Advertisers pay according to the number of times the ad is viewed.

**Extended product** Additional features and benefits beyond the core product.

**Extension** *See* **Customer extension**.

**External link building** A proactive approach to gain quality links from third-party sites.

**Extranet** Formed by extending an intranet beyond a company to customers, suppliers, collaborators or even competitors. This is password-protected to prevent access by general Internet users.

# F

**Faceted navigation** Used to enable users to rapidly filter results from a product search based on different ways of classifying the product by their attributes or features. For example by brand, by sub-product category, by price bands.

**Feed or RSS feed** Blog, news or other content is published by an XML standard and syndicated for other sites or read by users in RSS reader services such as Google Reader, personalised home pages or e-mail systems. RSS stands for *really simple syndication*.

**File Transfer Protocol (FTP)** A standard method for moving files across the Internet. FTP is available as a feature of web browsers that is sometimes used for marketing applications such as downloading files like product price lists or specifications. Standalone FTP packages such as WSFTP are commonly used to update HTML files on web servers when uploading revisions to the web server.

**Findability** An assessment of how easy it is for a web user to locate a single content object or to use browse navigation and search system to find content. Like usability it is assessed through efficiency – how long it takes to find the content – and effectiveness – how satisfied the user is with the experience and relevance of the content they find.

**Firewall** A specialised software application mounted on a server at the point where a company is connected to the Internet. Its purpose is to prevent unauthorised access into the company by outsiders. Firewalls are essential for all companies hosting their own web server.

**First-party cookies** Served by the site currently in use – typical for e-commerce sites.

**Flow** Describes a state in which users have a positive experience from readily controlling their navigation and interaction on a website.

**Focus groups** Online focus groups have been conducted by w3focus.com. These follow a bulletin board or discussion group form where different members of the focus group respond to prompts from the focus group leaders.

**Folksonomy** A contraction of 'folk taxonomy', a method of classifying content based on tagging that has no hierarchy (i.e. without parent–child relationships).

**Form** A method on a web page of entering information such as order details.

**Forward auctions** Item purchased by highest bid made in bidding period.

**Forward path analysis** Forward path analysis reviews the combinations of clicks that occur from a page. This form of analysis is most beneficial when it is forward from important pages such as the home page, product and directory pages. This technique is used to identify messaging/navigation combinations which work best to yield the most clicks from a page. Similar, effective messaging approaches can then be deployed elsewhere on the site.

**Frame** A technique used to divide a web page into different parts such as a menu and separate content.

# G

**Global (or generic) top-level domain names (gLTD)** The part of the domain name that refers to the category of site. The gLTD is usually the rightmost part of the domain name such as .co.uk or .com.

**Globalisation** The increase of international trading and shared social and cultural values.

**Gopher** Gopher is a directory-based structure containing information in certain categories.

**GPRS** This is approximately five times faster than GSM and is an 'always-on' service which is charged according to usage. Display is still largely text-based and based on the WAP protocol.

**Graphic design** All factors that govern the physical appearance of a web page.

**Graphics Interchange Format (GIF)** A graphics format used to display images within web pages. An interlaced GIF is displayed gradually on the screen, building up an image in several passes.

**GSM** The digital transmission technique standard used widely for mobile voice data.

# H

**Halo effect** The role of one media channel on influencing sale or uplift in brand metrics. Commonly applied to online display advertising, where exposure to display ads may increase clickthrough rates when the consumer is later exposed to a brand through other media, for example sponsored links or affiliate ads. It may also improve conversion rates on a destination sites through higher confidence in the brand or familiarity with the offer.

**Hacker** Someone who enjoys exploring the details of programmable systems and how to stretch their capabilities.

**Hard launch** A site is launched once fully complete with full promotional effort.

**Hit** A hit is recorded for each graphic or page of text requested from a web server. It is not a reliable measure for the number of people viewing a page. A page impression is a more reliable measure denoting one person viewing one page.

**Home page** The index page of a website with menu options or links to other resources on the site. Usually denoted by <web address>/index.html.

**House list** A list of prospect and customer names, e-mail addresses and profile information owned by an organisation.

**HTML (Hypertext Markup Language)** A standard format used to define the text and layout of web pages. HTML files usually have the extension .HTML or .HTM.

**HTTP (Hypertext Transfer Protocol)** A standard that defines the way information is transmitted across the Internet.

**Hurdle rate** The proportion of customers that fall within a particular level of activity. For example, the percentage of members of an e-mail list that click on the e-mail within a 90-day period, or the number of customers that have made a second purchase.

**Hype cycle** A graphic representation of the maturity, adoption and business application of specific technologies.

**Hyperlink** A method of moving between one website page and another, indicated to the user by text highlighted by underlining and/or a different colour. Hyperlinks can also be achieved by clicking on a graphic image such as a banner advertisement that is linked to another website.

# I

**Identity theft** The misappropriation of the identity of another person, without their knowledge or consent.

**I-Mode** A mobile access platform that enables display of colour graphics and content subscription services.

**Inbound customer contact strategies** Approaches to managing the cost and quality of service related to management of customer enquiries.

**Inbound e-mail** E-mail arriving at a company.

**Inbound e-mail marketing** Management of e-mails from customers by an organisation.

**Inbound Internet-based communications** Customers enquire through web-based form and e-mail (*see* **Web self-service**).

**Inbound link.** See backlink.

**Incidental offline advertising** Driving traffic to the website is not a primary objective of the advert.

**Index inclusion** Ensuring that as many of the relevant pages from your domain(s) are included within the search engine indexes you are targeting to be listed in.

**Infomediary** An intermediary business whose main source of revenue derives from capturing consumer information and developing detailed profiles of individual customers for use by third parties.

**Information architecture** The combination of organisation, labelling and navigation schemes constituting an information system.

**Information organisation schemes** The structure chosen to group and categorise information.

**Initiation of the website project** This phase of the project should involve a structured review of the costs and benefits of developing a website (or making a major revision to an existing website). A successful outcome to initiation will be a decision to proceed with the site development phase, with an agreed budget and target completion date.

**Insertion order** A printed order to run an advertisement campaign. It defines the campaign name, the website receiving the order and the planner or buyer giving the order, the individual advertisements to be run (or who will provide them), the sizes of the advertisements, the campaign start and end dates, the CPM, the total cost, discounts to be applied, and reporting requirements and possible penalties or stipulations relative to the failure to deliver the impressions.

**Integrated marketing communications** The co-ordination of communications channels to deliver a clear, consistent message.

**Integrity** *See* **Security methods**.

**Intellectual property rights (IPRs)** Protect the intangible property created by corporations or individuals that is protected under copyright, trade secret and patent laws.

**Interactive banner advertisement** A banner advertisement that enables the user to enter information.

**Interactive digital TV (iDTV)** Television displayed using a digital signal delivered by a range of media – cable, satellite, terrestrial (aerial). Interactions can be provided through phone line or cable service.

**Internal link architecture** Structuring and labelling links within a site's navigation to improve the results of SEO.

**Internet Protocol Television (IPTV)** Digital television service delivered using Internet protocol, typically by a broadband connection. IPTV can be streamed for real-time viewing or downloaded before playback.

**Interactivity** The medium enables a dialogue between company and customer.

**Interaction rate (IR)** The proportion of ad viewers who interact with an online ad through rolling over it. Some will be involuntary depending on where the ad is placed on screen, so it is highly dependent on placement.

**Intermediaries** Online sites that help bring together different parties such as buyers and sellers.

**Internet** The physical network that links computers across the globe. It consists of the infrastructure of network servers and communication links between them that are used to hold and transport the vast amount of information on the Internet.

**Internet-based market research** The use of online questionnaires and focus groups to assess customer perceptions of a website or broader marketing issues.

**Internet contribution** An assessment of the extent to which the Internet contributes to sales is a key measure of the importance of the Internet to a company.

**Internet EDI** Use of electronic data interchange standards delivered across non-proprietary Internet protocol networks.

**Internet governance** Control of the operation and use of the Internet.

**Internet marketing** The application of the Internet and related digital technologies in conjunction with traditional communications to achieve marketing objectives.

**Internet marketing metrics** *See* **Metrics for Internet marketing**.

**Internet marketing strategy** Definition of the approach by which Internet marketing will support marketing and business objectives.

**Internet pureplay** An organisation with the majority of its customer-facing operations online, e.g. Egg.

**Internet Relay Chat (IRC)** A communications tool that allows a text-based 'chat' between different users who are logged on at the same time. Of limited use for marketing purposes except for special-interest or youth products.

**Internet service provider (ISP)** Company that provides home or business users with a connection to access the Internet. It can also host websites or provide a link from web servers to allow other companies and consumers access to a corporate website.

**Interruption marketing** Marketing communications that disrupt customers' activities.

**Interstitial ads** Ads that appear between one page and the next.

**Intranet** A network within a single company that enables access to company information using the familiar tools of the Internet such as web browsers and e-mail. Only staff within a company can access the intranet, which will be password-protected.

## J

**Java** A programming language standard supported by Sun Microsystems, which permits complex and graphical customer applications to be written and then accessed from a web browser. An example might be a form for calculating interest on a loan. A competitor to ActiveX.

**Joint Photographics Experts Group (JPEG)** A compressed graphics standard specified by the JPEG. Used for graphic images typically requiring use of many colours, such as product photographs where some loss of quality is acceptable. The format allows for some degradation in image quality to enable more rapid download.

# K

**Key performance indicators (KPIs)** Metrics used to assess the performance of a process and/or whether goals set are achieved.

**Keyphrase (keyword phrase)** The combination of words users of search engines type into a search box which form a search query.

# L

**Lagging performance indicator** A metric which indicates past performance. Corrective action can then be applied to improve performance.

**Landing page** A destination page when a user clicks on an ad or other form of link from a *referring site*. It can be a home page, but more typically and desirably a landing page is a page with the messaging focused on the offer in the ad. This will maximise conversion rates and brand favourability.

**Last-click method of digital media channel attribution** The site which referred a visitor immediately before purchase is credited with the sale. Previous referrals influenced by other customer touch-points on other sites are ignored.

**Latency** The average length of time that different customer types takes between different activities, e.g. log-ins, paying bills, first and second purchase.

**Lead** Details about a potential customer (prospect). (*See* **Qualified lead**.)

**Leading performance indicator** A measure which is suggestive of future performance and so can be used to take proactive action to shape future performance.

**Lead generation offers** Offered in return for customers providing their contact details and characteristics. Commonly used in B2B marketing where free information such as a report or a seminar will be offered.

**Lifetime value (LTV)** The total net benefit that a customer or group of customers will provide a company over their total relationship with a company.

**Link anchor text** The text used to form the blue, underlined hyperlink viewed in a web browser defined in the HTML source. For example: Visit Dave Chaffey's web log is created by the HTML code: <A HREF="http://www.davechaffey.com">Visit Dave Chaffey's web log</A>

**Link building** A proactive approach to gain quality links from third-party sites.

**List broker** Will source the appropriate e-mail list(s) from the list owner.

**List owner** Has collected e-mail addresses which are offered for sale.

**Live website** Current site accessible to customers, as distinct from test website.

**Localisation** Designing the content of the website in such a way that it is appropriate to different audiences in different countries.

**Log file** A file stored on a web server that records every item downloaded by users.

**Log file analysers** Web analytics tools that are used to build a picture of the amount of usage of different parts of a website based on the information contained in the log file.

**Long tail concept** A frequency distribution suggesting the relative variation in popularity of items selected by consumers.

**Loyalty techniques** Customers sign up to an incentive scheme where they receive points for repeat purchases, which can be converted into offers such as discounts, free products or cash. (Also known as online incentive schemes.)

# M

**Macro-environment** Broader forces affecting all organisations in the marketplace including social, technological, economic, political and legal aspects.

**Mailbots** *See* **Autoresponders**.

**Maintenance process** The work involved in running a live website such as updating pages and checking the performance of the site.

**Malware** Malicious software or toolbars, typically downloaded via the Internet, which act as a 'trojan horse' by executing other unwanted activites such as keylogging of user passwords or viruses which may collect e-mail addresses.

**Marketing-led site design** Site design elements are developed to achieve customer acquisition, retention and communication of marketing messages.

**Marketing intermediaries** Firms that can help a company to promote, sell and distribute its products or services.

**Marketing mix** The series of seven key variables – Product, Price, Place, Promotion, People, Process and Physical evidence – that are varied by marketers as part of the customer offering.

**Marketing planning** A logical sequence and a series of activities leading to the setting of marketing objectives and the formulation of plans for achieving them.

**Marketplace** *See* **Business-to-business exchanges or marketplaces**.

**Marketsite** eXchange, eHub, metamediaries are terms used to refer to complex websites that facilitate trading exchanges between companies around the globe.

**MarketSite™** is a trade mark of commerceOne and considered as the leading e-marketplace operating environment.

**Marketspace** A virtual marketplace such as the Internet in which no direct contact occurs between buyers and sellers. (Also known as electronic marketspace.)

**Markup language** *See* **HTML, XML**.

**Mashup** Websites, pages or widgets that combine the content or functionality of one website or data source with another to create something offering a different type of value to web users from the separate types of content or functionality.

**Mass customisation** The ability to create tailored marketing messages or products for individual customers or a group of similar customers (a bespoke service), yet retain the economies of scale and the capacity of mass marketing or production.

**Mass marketing** One-to-many communication between a company and potential customers, with limited tailoring of the message.

**Measurement** *See* **Website measurement**.

**Media broker** A company that places advertisements for companies wishing to advertise by contacting the media owners.

**Media buyer** The person within a company wishing to advertise who places the advertisement, usually via a media broker.

**Media buying** The process of purchasing media to meet the media plan requirements at the lowest costs.

**Media fragmentation** Describes a trend to increasing choice and consumption of a range of media in terms of different channels such as web and mobile and also within channels, for example more TV channels, radio stations, magazines, more websites. Media fragmentation implies increased difficulty in reaching target audiences.

**Media multiplier** or **halo effect** The role of one media channel on influencing sale or uplift in brand metrics. Commonly applied to online display advertising, where exposure to display ads may increase click-through rates when the consumer is later exposed to a brand through other media, for example sponsored links or affiliate ads. It may also improve conversion rates on a destination sites through higher confidence in the brand or familiarity with the offer.

**Media-neutral planning (MNP)** An approach to planning ad campaigns to maximise response across different media according to consumer usage of these media.

**Media owners** The owners of websites (or other media such as newspapers) that accept advertisements.

**Media planning** The process of selecting the best combination of media to achieve marketing campaign objectives. Answers questions such as 'How many of the audience can I reach through different media?', 'On which media (and ad vehicles) should I place ads?', 'Which frequency should I select?', 'How much money should be spent in each medium?'

**Media site** Typical location where paid-for ads are placed.

**Merchandising** *See* **Web merchandising**.

**Meta-data** Literally, data about data – a format describing the structure and content of data.

**Meta search engines** Meta search engines submit keywords typed by users to a range of search engines in order to increase the number of relevant pages since different search engines may have indexed different sites. An example is the meta-crawler search engine or www.mamma.com.

**Meta-tags** Text within an HTML file summarising the content of the site (content meta-tag) and relevant keywords (keyword meta-tag), which are matched against the keywords typed into search engines.

**Metrics for Internet marketing** Measures that indicate the effectiveness of Internet marketing activities in meeting customer, business and marketing objectives.

**Micro-environment** Specific forces on an organisation generated by its stakeholders.

**Micropayments (microtransactions)** Digital cash systems that allow very small sums of money (fractions of 1p) to be transferred, but with lower security. Such small sums do not warrant a credit card payment, because processing is too costly.

**Microsite** Specialised content that is part of a website that is not necessarily owned by the organisation. If owned by the company it may be as part of an extranet. (*See* **Nested ad content**.)

**Microsoft Internet Information Server (IIS)** Microsoft IIS is a web server developed by Microsoft that runs on Windows NT.

**Mixed-mode buying** The process by which a customer changes between online and offline channels during the buying process.

**Mobile commerce** The use of wireless devices such as mobile phones for informational or monetary transactions.

**Multichannel marketing** Customer communications and product distribution are supported by a combination of digital and traditional channels at different points in the buying cycle.

**Multichannel marketing strategy** Defines how different marketing channels should integrate and support each other in terms of their proposition development and communications based on their relative merits for the customer and the company.

**Multichannel prioritisation** Assesses the strategic significance of the Internet relative to other communications channels and then deploys resources to integrate with marketing channels.

# N

**Narrow and deep navigation** Fewer choices and more clicks to reach required content.

**Natural or organic listings** The pages listing results from a search engine query which are displayed in a sequence according to relevance of match between the keyword phrase typed into a search engine and a web page according to a ranking algorithm used by the search engine.

**Navigation** The method of finding and moving between different information and pages on a website. It is governed by menu arrangements, site structure and the layout of individual pages.

**Navigational search** Searchers use a search engine such as Google to find information deeper within a company site by appending a qualifier such as a product name to the brand or site name. Organisations need to check that relevant pages are available in the search results pages for these situations.

**Nested ad content** This refers to the situation when the person undertaking the click-through is not redirected to a corporate or brand site, but is instead taken to a related page on the same site as that on which the advertisement is placed. (Sometimes referred to as microsite.)

**Net Promoter Score** A measure of the number of advocates a company (or website) has who would recommend it compared to the number of detractors.

**Non-repudiability** *See* **Security methods**.

**Notification** The process whereby companies register with the data protection register to inform about their data holdings.

# O

**Offer** An incentive in direct marketing or a product offering.

**Offline site promotion** Traditional techniques such as print and TV advertising used to generate website traffic.

**Offline web metric** Offline measures are those that are collated by marketing staff recording particular marketing outcomes such as an enquiry or a sale. They are usually collated manually, but could be collated automatically.

**On-page optimisation** Writing copy and applying markup such as the <title> tag and heading tags <h1> to highlight to search engines relevant keyphrases within a document.

**One-to-one marketing** A unique dialogue that occurs directly between a company and individual customers (or less strictly with groups of customers with similar needs). The dialogue involves a company in listening to customer needs and responding with services to meet these needs.

**Online brand** *See* **Digital brand**.

**Online branding** How online channels are used to support brands that, in essence, are the sum of the characteristics of a product or service as perceived by a user.

**Online customer experience** The combination of rational and emotional factors in using a company's online services that influences customers' perceptions of a brand online.

**Online incentive schemes** *See* **Loyalty techniques**.

**Online intermediary sites** Websites that facilitate exchanges between consumer and business suppliers.

**Online promotion contribution** An assessment of the proportion of customers (new or retained) who are reached by online communications and are influenced as a result.

**Online PR (e-PR)** Maximising favourable mentions of your company, brands, products or websites on third-party websites which are likely to be visited by your target audience. Online PR can extend reach and awareness of a brand within an audience and will also generate backlinks vital to SEO. It can also be used to support viral or word-of-mouth marketing activities in other media.

**Online reputation management** Controlling the reputation of an organisation through monitoring and controlling messages placed about the organisation.

**Online revenue contribution** An assessment of the direct contribution of the Internet or other digital media to sales, usually expressed as a percentage of overall sales revenue.

**Online service providers (OSPs)** An OSP is sometimes used to distinguish large Internet service providers (ISPs) from other access providers. In the UK, AOL, Freeserve, VirginNet and LineOne can be considered OSPs since they have a large amount of specially developed content available to their subscribers. Note that this term is not used as frequently as ISP, and the distinction between ISPs and OSPs is a blurred one since all OSPs are also ISPs and the distinction only occurs according to the amount of premium content (only available to customers) offered as part of the service.

**Online service-quality gap** The mismatch between what is expected and delivered by an online presence.

**Online site promotion** Internet-based techniques used to generate website traffic.

**Online social network** A service facilitating the connection, collaboration and exchange of information between individuals.

**Online value proposition (OVP)** A statement of the benefits of online services that reinforce the core proposition and differentiate from an organisation's offline offering and that of competitors.

**Online web metrics** Online measures are those that are collected automatically on the web server, often in a server log file.

**Operational effectiveness** Performing similar activities better than rivals. This includes efficiency of processes.

**Opt-in** A customer proactively agrees to receive further information.

**Opt-in e-mail** The customer is only contacted when he or she has explicitly asked for information to be sent (usually when filling in an on-screen form).

**Opt-out** A customer declines the offer to receive further information.

**Opt-out e-mail** The customer is not contacted subsequently if he or she has explicitly stated that he or she does not want to be contacted in future. Opt-out or unsubscribe options are usually available within the e-mail itself.

**Outbound e-mail** E-mail sent from a company.

**Outbound e-mail marketing** E-mails are sent to customers and prospects from an organisation.

**Outbound Internet-based communications** The website and e-mail marketing are used to send personalised communications to customers.

**Outsourcing** Contracting an outside company to undertake part of the Internet marketing activities.

**Overlay** Typically an animated ad that moves around the page and is superimposed on the website content.

**Overt** Typically an animated ad that moves around the page and is superimposed on the website content.

## P

**Page impression** One page impression occurs when a member of the audience views a web page. (*See* **Ad impression** and **Reach**.)

**PageRank** A scale between 0 to 10 used by Google to assess the importance of websites according to the number of inbound links or backlinks.

**Page request** The process of a user selecting a hyperlink or typing in a uniform resource locator (URL) to retrieve information on a specific web page. Equivalent to page impression.

**Page view** *See* **Page impression**.

**Paid search marketing (pay-per-click PPC)** A relevant text ad with a link to a company page is displayed on the SERPs when the user of a search engine types in a specific phrase. A fee is charged for every click of each link, with the amount bid for the click mainly determining its position. Additionally, PPC may involve advertising through a content network of third-party sites (which may be on a CPC, CPM or CPA basis).

**Pay-for-performance communications** The wastage from traditional media buys can be reduced online through advertising models where the advertisers only pays for a response (cost-per-click) as in pay-per-click search marketing or for a lead or sale as in affiliate marketing.

**Payment systems** Methods of transferring funds from a customer to a merchant.

**People variable** The element of the marketing mix that involves the delivery of service to customers during interactions with those customers.

**Performance drivers** Critical success factors that determine whether business and marketing objectives are achieved.

**Performance management system** A process used to evaluate and improve the efficiency and effectiveness of an organisation and its processes.

**Performance measurement system** The process by which metrics are defined, collected, disseminated and actioned.

**Performance metrics** Measures that are used to evaluate and improve the efficiency and effectiveness of business processes.

**Performance of website** Performance or quality of service is dependent on its availability and speed of access.

**Permission marketing** Customers agree (opt in) to be involved in an organisation's marketing activities, usually as a result of an incentive.

**Persistent cookies** Cookies that remain on a computer after a visitor session has ended. Used to recognise returning visitors.

**Personal data** Any information about an individual stored by companies concerning their customers or employees.

**Personalisation** Web-based personalisation involves delivering customised content for the individual through web pages, e-mail or push technology.

**Personas** A thumbnail summary of the characteristics, needs, motivations and environment of typical website users.

**Persuasion marketing** Using design elements such as layout, copy and typography together with promotional messages to encourage site users to follow particular paths and specific actions rather than giving them complete choice in their navigation.

**Phishing** Obtaining personal details online through sites and e-mails masquerading as legitimate businesses.

**Phone-me** A call-back facility available on the website for a company to contact a customer by phone at a later time, as specified by the customer.

**Physical evidence variable** The element of the marketing mix that involves the tangible expression of a product and how it is purchased and used.

**Pixel** The small dots on a computer screen that are used to represent images and text. Short for 'picture element'. Used to indicate the size of banner advertisements.

**Place variable** The element of the marketing mix that involves distributing products to customers in line with demand and minimising cost of inventory, transport and storage.

**Plug-in** A program that must be downloaded to view particular content such as an animation.

**Podcasts** Individuals and organisations post online media (audio and video) which can be viewed in the appropriate players (including the iPod which first sparked the growth in this technique). The latest podcast updates can be automatically delivered by *Really Simple Syndication*.

**Portal** A website that acts as a gateway to information and services available on the Internet by providing search engines, directories and other services such as personalised news or free e-mail.

**Portfolio analysis** Evaluation of value of current e-commerce services or applications.

**Positioning** Customers' perception of the product and brand offering relative to those of competitors.

**Prescriptive strategy** The three core areas of strategic analysis, strategic development and strategy implementation are linked together sequentially.

**Price comparison sites** *See* **Aggregators**.

**Price dispersion** The distribution or range of prices charged for an item across different retailers.

**Price elasticity of demand** Measure of consumer behaviour that indicates the change in demand for a product or service in response to changes in price.

**Pricing level** The price set for a specific product or range of products.

**Price transparency** Customer knowledge about pricing increases due to increased availability of pricing information.

**Price variable** The element of the marketing mix that involves defining product prices and pricing models.

**Pricing model** Describes the form of payment such as outright purchase, auction, rental, volume purchases and credit terms.

**Primary persona** A representation of the typical site user.

**Privacy** A moral right of individuals to avoid intrusion into their personal affairs. (*See* **Security methods**.)

**Privacy and Electronic Communications Regulations Act** A law intended to control the distribution of e-mail and other online communications including cookies.

**Privacy statement** Information on a website explaining how and why individuals' data are collected, processed and stored.

**Process variable** The element of the marketing mix that involves the methods and procedures companies use to achieve all marketing functions.

**Product variable** The element of the marketing mix that involves researching customers' needs and developing appropriate products. (*See* **Core product** and **Extended product**.)

**Profiling** *See* Customer profiling.

**Promotion (online and offline)** Online promotion uses communication via the Internet itself to raise awareness about a site and drive traffic to it. This promotion may take the form of links from other sites, banner advertisements or targeted e-mail messages. Offline promotion uses traditional media such as television or newspaper advertising and word-of-mouth to promote a company's website.

**Promotion variable** The element of the marketing mix that involves communication with customers and other stakeholders to inform them about the product and the organisation.

**Propensity modelling** A name given to the approach of evaluating customer characteristics and behaviour and then making recommendations for future products.

**Prosumer** 'Producer + consumer'. The customer is closely involved in specifying their requirements in a product.

**Prototypes and prototyping** A prototype is a preliminary version of part (or a framework of all) of a website that can be reviewed by its target audience, or the marketing team. Prototyping is an iterative process where website users suggest modifications before further prototypes are made and the final version of the site is developed.

**Proximity marketing** Marketing messages are delivered in real time according to customers' presence based on the technology they are carrying, wearing or have embedded. Bluecasting is the best-known example.

**Psychographic segmentation** A breakdown of customers according to different characteristics.

**Public key** A unique identifier of a buyer or a seller that is available to other parties to enable secure e-commerce using encryption based on digital certificates.

**Public-key encryption** An asymmetric form of encryption in which the keys or digital certificates used by the sender and receiver of information are different. The two keys are related, so only the pair of keys can be used together to encrypt and decrypt information.

**Public-key infrastructure (PKI)** The organisations responsible for issuing and maintaining certificates for public-key security together form the PKI.

**Public relations** The management of the awareness, understanding and reputation of an organisation or brand, primarily achieved through influencing exposure in the media.

**Pull media** The consumer is proactive in selection of the message through actively seeking out a website.

**Push media** Communications are broadcast from an advertiser to consumers of the message, who are passive recipients.

**Push technology** The delivery of web-based content to the user's desktop without the need for the user to visit a site to download information. E-mail can also be considered to be a push technology. A particular type of information is a push channel.

# Q

**Qualified lead** Contact and profile information for a customer with an indication of the level of their interest in product categories.

**Quality score** An assessment in paid search by Google AdWords (and now other search engines) of an individual ad triggered by a keyword which, in combination with the bid amount, determines the ranking of the ad relative to competitors. The primary factor is the click-through rate for each ad, but quality score also considers the match between the keyword and the occurrence of the keyword in the text, historical click-through rates, the engagement of the searcher when they click-through to the site and the speed at which the page loads.

**Quick Response (QR) code** A QR code is a two-dimensional matrix bar code. QR codes were invented in Japan where they are a popular type of two-dimensional code used for direct response.

# R

**Reach** The number of unique individuals who view an advertisement.

**Really Simple Syndication (RSS)** Blog, news or other content is published by an XMLstandard and syndicated for other sites or read by users in RSS reader software services.

**RealNames** A service for matching company names and brands with web addresses.

**Reciprocal links** Links which are agreed between yourself and another organisation.

**Referrer** The site that a visitor previously visited before following a link.

**Referring sites** A log file may indicate which site a user visited immediately before visiting the current site. (*See* **Click-through**, **Destination site** and **Exit page**.)

**Referrer or referring site** The source of a visitor to site delivered via a digital media channel. Typically a specific site, e.g. Google AdWords or a media site or an individual ad placement on the site.

**Registration (individuals)** The process whereby an individual subscribes to a site or requests further information by filling in contact details and his or her needs using an electronic form.

**Registration (of domain name)** The process of reserving a unique web address that can be used to refer to the company website.

**Reintermediation** The creation of new intermediaries between customers and suppliers providing services such as supplier search and product evaluation.

**Relationship marketing** Consistent application of up-to-date knowledge of individual customers to product and service design, which is communicated interactively in order to develop a continuous, mutually beneficial and long-term relationship.

**Renderability** The capability of an e-mail to display correctly formatted in different e-mail readers.

**Repeat visits** If an organisation can encourage customers to return to the website then the relationship can be maintained online.

**Representation** The locations on the Internet where an organisation is located for promoting or selling its services.

**Repurposing** Developing for a new access platform, such as the web, content which was previously used for a different platform.

**Resource analysis** Review of the technological, financial and human resources of an organisation and how they are utilised in business processes.

**Resources** Resources are defined as physical assets over which an organisation has control. This narrow definition of resources allows them to be clearly distinguished from capabilities (Beard and Sumner, 2004 – see Chapter 11).

**Results-based payment** Advertisers pay according to the number of times the ad is clicked on.

**Retail channel** Retailers' use of the Internet as both a communication and a transactional channel concurrently in business-to-consumer markets.

**Retail format** This is the general nature of the retail mix in terms of range of products and services, pricing policy, promotional programmes, operating style or store design and visual merchandising; examples include mail-order retailers (non-store-based) and department-store retailers.

**Retention** *See* **Customer retention**.

**Return on advertising spend (ROAS)** This indicates amount of revenue generated from each referrer. ROAS = Total revenue generated from referrer/Amount spent on advertising with referrer.

**Return on investment (ROI)** This indicates the profitability of any investment, or in an advertising context for each referring site.

ROI = Profit generated from investment/Cost of investment.

ROI = Profit generated from referrers/Amount spent on advertising with referrer.

**Return path** An interaction where the customer sends information to the iDTV provider using a phone line or cable.

**Revenue models** Describe methods of generating income for an organisation.

**Reverse auctions** Item purchased from lowest-bidding supplier in bidding period.

**Reverse path analysis** indicates the most popular combination of pages and/or calls-to-action which lead to a page. This is particularly useful for transactional pages such as the first checkout page on a consumer site; a lead generation or contact-us page on a business-to-business site; an e-mail subscription page; a call-me back option.

**Rich media** Advertisements that are not static, but provide animation, audio, sound or interactivity as a game or form to be completed. An example of this would be a banner display advertisement for a loan in which a customer can type in the amount of loan required, and the cost of the loan is calculated immediately.

**Rich Internet Applications (RIA)** Interactive applications which provide options such as product selectors or games. They may incorporate video or sound also. Typically built using technologies such as Adobe Flash, Ajax, Flex, Java or Silverlight.

**Robot** A tool, also known as a spider, that is employed by search engines to index web pages of registered sites on a regular basis. *See* **Spider**.

**Run-of-site** A situation where a company pays for banner advertisements to promote its services across a website.

## S

**Sales generation offers** Offers that encourage product trial. A coupon redeemed against a purchase is a classic example.

**Sales promotions** The Internet offers tremendous potential for sales promotions of different types since it is more immediate than any other medium – it is always available for communication, and tactical variations in the details of the promotion can be made at short notice.

**Satisficing behaviour** Consumers do not behave entirely rationally in product or supplier selection. They will compare alternatives, but then may make their choice given imperfect information.

**Saturation of the Internet** Access to the Internet will reach saturation as home PC ownership reaches a limit, unless other access devices become popular.

**Scenario-based analysis** Models of the future environment are developed from different starting points.

**Scenario of use** A particular path or flow of events or activities performed by a visitor to a website.

**Scripts** Scripts can run either on the user's browser (client-side scripts) (*see* **Web browser**) or on the web server (server-side scripts).

**Scrum** A methodology that supports agile software development based on 15–30 day sprints to implement features from a product backlog. 'Scrum' refers to a daily project status meeting during the sprint.

**Search engine** Specialised website that uses automatic tools known as spiders or robots to index web pages of registered sites. Users can search the index by typing in keywords to specify their interest. Pages containing these keywords will be listed, and by clicking on a hyperlink the user will be taken to the site.

**Search engine listing** The list of sites and descriptions returned by a search engine after a user types in keywords.

**Search engine marketing (SEM)** Promoting an organisation through search engines to meet its objectives by delivering relevant content in the search listings for searchers and encouraging them to click-through to a destination site. The two key techniques of SEM are *search engine optimisation (SEO)* to improve results from the natural listings and *paid-search marketing* to deliver results from the sponsored listings within the search engines through pay-per-click (PPC) paid-search engine marketing and through content-network paid-search marketing (which may be on a PPC basis or on a CPM basis). SEM is about connecting the searchers with information which will help them find what they are looking for and will help site owners generate revenue or disseminate information.

**Search engine optimisation (SEO)** A structured approach used to increase the position of a company or its products in search engine natural or organic results listings (the main body of the search results page) for selected keywords or phrases.

**Search engine ranking** The position of a site on a particular search engine.

**Search engine results pages (SERPs)** The page(s) containing the results after a user types in a keyphrase into a search engine. SERPs contain both natural or organic listings and paid or sponsored listings.

**Search engine submission** The process of informing search engines that a site should be indexed for listing in the search engine results pages.

**Secure Electronic Transaction (SET)** A standard for public-key encryption intended to enable secure e-commerce transactions, lead-developed by Mastercard and Visa.

**Secure HTTP** Encrypted HTTP.

**Secure Sockets Layer (SSL)** A commonly used encryption technique for scrambling data such as credit card numbers as they are passed across the Internet from a web browser to a web server.

**Security methods** When systems for electronic commerce are devised, or when existing solutions are selected, the following attributes must be present:

- *Authentication* – are parties to the transaction who they claim to be? This is achieved through the use of digital certificates.

- *Privacy and confidentiality* – are transaction data protected? The consumer may want to make an anonymous purchase. Are all non-essential traces of a transaction removed from the public network and all intermediary records eliminated?

- *Integrity* – checks that the message sent is complete, i.e. that it is not corrupted.

- *Non-repudiability* – ensures sender cannot deny sending message.

- *Availability* – how can threats to the continuity and performance of the system be eliminated?

**Seeding** The viral campaign is started by sending an e-mail to a targeted group that are likely to propagate the virus.

**Segmentation** Identification of different groups within a target market in order to develop different offerings for each group.

**Sell-side e-commerce** E-commerce transactions between a supplier organisation and its customers.

**Sense and respond communications** Delivering timely, relevant communications to customers as part of a contact strategy based on assessment of their position in the customer lifecycle and monitoring specific interactions with a company's website, e-mails and staff.

**Server log file** *See* **Online web metrics**.

**Service quality** The level of service received on a website. Dependent on reliability, responsiveness and availability of staff and the website service.

**Serving** Used to describe the process of displaying an advertisement on a website (ad serving) or delivering a web page to a user's web browser. (*See* **Web server**.)

**Session** *See* **Visitor session**.

**Session cookie** A cookie used to manage a single visitor session.

**Share of search** The audience share of Internet searchers achieved by a particular audience in a particular market.

**Share of voice** The relative advertising spend of the different competitive brands within the product category.

**Share of voice (SOV)** is calculated by dividing a particular brand's advertising spend by the total category spend.

**Short code** Five-digit numbers combined with text that can be used by advertisers or broadcasters to encourage consumers to register their interest. They are typically followed-up by an automated text message from the advertiser with the option to opt in to further information by e-mail or to link through to a WAP site.

**Short Message Service (SMS)** The formal name for text messaging.

**Site** *See* **Website**.

**Site announcements** Usually used to describe the dissemination of information about a new or revised website.

**Site auditors** Auditors accurately measure the usage for different sites as the number of ad impressions and click-through rates. Auditors include ABC (Audit Bureau of Circulation) and BPA (Business Publication Auditor) International.

**Site availability** An indication of how easy it is to connect to a website as a user. In theory this figure should be 100 per cent, but for technical reasons such as failures in the server hardware or upgrades to software, sometimes users cannot access the site and the figure falls below 90 per cent.

**Site design page template** A standard page layout format which is applied to each page of a website. Typically defined for different page categories (e.g. category page, product page, search page).

**Site map** A graphical or text depiction of the relationship between different groups of content on a website.

**Site measurement** *See* **Website measurement**.

**Site navigation scheme** Tools provided to the user to move between different information on a website.

**Site re-launch** Where a website is replaced with a new version with a new 'look and feel'.

**Site statistics** Collected by log file analysers, these are used to monitor the effectiveness of a website.

**Site 'stickiness'** An indication of how long a visitor stays on a site. Log file analysers can be used to assess average visit times.

**Site visit** One site visit records one customer visiting the site. Not equivalent to User session.

**Site-visitor activity data** Information on content and services accessed by e-commerce site visitors.

**Sitemapping tools** These tools diagram the layout of the website, which is useful for site management and can be used to assist users.

**Situation analysis** Collection and review of information about an organisation's external environment and internal processes and resources in order to inform its strategies.

**SMART metrics** SMART metrics must be:

- Specific
- Measurable
- Actionable
- Relevant
- Timely.

**Smartcards** Physical cards containing a memory chip that can be inserted into a smartcard reader before items can be purchased.

**Social exclusion** Part of society is excluded from the facilities available to the remainder.

**Social bookmarking** Web users keep a shared version of favourite sites ('Favorites') online. This enables the most popular sites in a category to be identified.

**Social network** A site that facilitates peer-to-peer communications within a group or between individuals through providing facilities to develop user-generated content (UGC) and to exchange messages and comments between different users.

**Soft launch** A trial version of a site launched with limited publicity.

**Soft lock-in** Electronic linkages between supplier and customer increase switching costs.

**Software agents** *See* **Agents**.

**Spam** Unsolicited e-mail (usually bulk mailed and untargeted).

**Spamming** Bulk e-mailing of unsolicited mail.

**Specific offline advertising** Driving traffic to the website or explaining the online proposition is a primary objective of the advert.

**Spider** Spiders are software processes, technically known as robots, employed by search engines to index web pages of registered sites on a regular basis. They follow links between pages and record the reference URL of a page for future analysis.

**Splash page** A preliminary page that precedes the normal home page of a website. Site users can either wait to be redirected to the home page or can follow a link to do this. Splash pages are not now commonly used since they slow down the process of customers finding the information they need.

**Sponsorship** Sponsorship involves a company paying money to advertise on a website. The arrangement may involve more than advertising. Sponsorship is a similar arrangement to co-branding.

**Stage models** Models for the development of different levels of Internet marketing services.

**Stages in website development** The standard stages of creation of a website are initiation, feasibility, analysis, design, development (content creation), testing and maintenance.

**Static (fixed) web page** A page on the web server that is invariant.

**STEP** A framework for assessing the macroenvironment, standing for Social, Technological, Economic and Political (including legal).

**Storyboarding** Using static drawings or screenshots of the different parts of a website to review the design concept with customers or clients.

**Strategic agility** The capability to innovate and so gain competitive advantage within a marketplace by monitoring changes within an organisation's marketplace and then to efficiently evaluate alternative strategies and then select, review and implement appropriate candidate strategies.

**Strategic analysis** Collection and review of information about an organisation's internal processes and resources and external marketplace factors in order to inform strategy definition.

**Strategic positioning** Performing different activities from rivals or performing similar activities in different ways.

**Strategic windows** Opportunities arising through a significant change in environment.

**Strategy formulation** Generation, review and selection of strategies to achieve strategic objectives.

**Strategy process model** A framework for approaching strategy development.

**Streaming media** Sound and video that can be experienced within a web browser before the whole clip is downloaded.

**Streaming media server** A specialist server used to broadcast audio (e.g. podcasts) or video (e.g. IPTV or webcast presentations). Served streams can be unicast (a separate copy of stream is served for each recipient), multicast (recipients share streams) or peer-to-peer where the media is shared between different recipient's computers using a Bitorrent or Kontiki approach.

**Style guide** A definition of site structure, page design, typography and copy defined within a company. (*See* **Graphic design**.)

**Subject access request** A request by a data subject to view personal data from an organisation.

**Superstitials** Pop-up adverts that require interaction to remove them.

**Surfer** An undirected information seeker who is often looking for an experience rather than information.

**Symmetric encryption** Both parties to a transaction use the same key to encode and decode messages.

**Syndication** Content or product information is distributed to third parties. Online this is commonly achieved through standard XML formats such as RSS.

# T

**Tagging** Tracking of the origin or referring site or of visitors to a site and their spending patterns. Also tagging refers to where users or web page creators categorise content on a site through adding descriptive terms. A common approach in blog posts.

**Target marketing strategy** Evaluation and selection of appropriate segments and the development of appropriate offers.

**Targeting (through banner advertisers)** Advertising networks such as DoubleClick offer advertisers the ability to target advertisements dynamically on the World Wide Web through their 'DART' targeting technology. This gives advertisers a means of reaching specific audiences.

**Technology convergence** A trend in which different hardware devices such as TVs, computers and phone merge and have similar functions.

**Telemarketing using the Internet** Mainly used for inbound telemarketing, including sales lines, carelines for goods and services and response handling for direct response campaigns.

**Telnet** A program that allows remote access to data and text-based programs on other computer systems at different locations. For example, a retailer could check to see whether an item was in stock in a warehouse using a telnet application.

**Template** *See* **Site design page template**.

**Test website** A parallel version of the site to use before the site is made available to customers as a live website.

**Testing content** Testing should be conducted for plug-ins; for interactive facilities and integration with company databases; for spelling and grammar; for adherence to corporate image standards; for implementation of HTML in different web browsers; and to ensure that links to external sites are valid.

**Testing phase** Testing involves different aspects of the content such as spelling, validity of links, formatting on different web browsers and dynamic features such as form filling or database queries.

**Third-party cookies** Served by another site to the one being viewed – typical for portals where an ad network will track remotely or where the web analytics software places a cookie.

**Tipping point** Using the science of social epidemics explains principles that underpin the rapid spread of ideas, products and behaviours through a population.

**Trademark** A trademark is a unique word or phrase that distinguishes your company. The mark can be registered as plain or designed text, artwork or a combination. In theory, colours, smells and sounds can also be trademarks.

**Traffic-building campaign** The use of online and offline promotion techniques such as banner advertising, search engine promotion and reciprocal linking to increase the audience of a site (both new and existing customers).

**Transactional sites** Sites that support online sales.

**Transaction log file** A web server file that records all page requests.

**Transfer Control Protocol/Internet Protocol (TCP/IP)** The passing of data packets around the Internet occurs via TCP/IP. For a PC to be able to receive web pages or for a server to host web pages it must be configured to support this protocol.

**Trialogue** The interaction between company, customer and other customers facilitated through online community, social networks, reviews and comments.

**Trusted feed** A trusted feed is an automated method of putting content into a search engine index or an aggregator database.

**Trusted third parties (TTPs)** Companies with which an agreement has been reached to share information.

# U

**Undirected information seeker** A person who does not know what information they are looking for – a surfer.

**Uniform (universal) resource locator (URL)** Text that indicates the web address of a site. A specific domain name is typed into a web browser window and the browser will then locate and load the website. It is in the form of: http://www.domain-name.extension/filename.html.

**Unique visitors** Individual visitors to a site measured through cookies or IP addresses on an individual computer.

**Universal search** The *natural listings* incorporate other relevant results from vertical searches related to a query, such as video, books, scholar, news, sitelinks and images.

**Unsubscribe** An option to opt out from an e-mail newsletter or discussion group.

**Upload** The transfer of files from a local computer to a server. Usually achieved using FTP. E-mail or website pages can be uploaded to update a remote server.

**Up-selling** Persuading existing customers to purchase more expensive products (typically related to existing purchase categories).

**URL strategy** A defined approach to how content is labelled through placing it in different directories or folders with distinct web addresses.

**Usability** An approach to website design intended to enable the completion of user tasks.

**Usability/user testing** Representative users are observed performing representative tasks using a system.

**Usenet newsgroup** An electronic bulletin board used to discuss a particular topic such as a sport, hobby or business area. Traditionally accessed by special newsreader software, these can now be accessed via a web browser from www.deja.com.

**User-centred design** Design based on optimising the user experience according to all factors, including the user interface, which affect this.

**User journey** *See* **Customer scenarios**.

**User session** Used to specify the frequency of visits to a site. Not equivalent to site visit.

# V

**Validation** Validation services test for errors in HTML code which may cause a web page to be displayed incorrectly or for links to other pages that do not work.

**Value chain** A model that considers how supply chain activities can add value to products and services delivered to the customer.

**Value event scoring** Value events are outcomes that occur on the site as indicated by visits to different page or content types which suggest marketing communications are effective. Examples include, leads, sales, newsletter registrations and product page views. They can be tagged and scored using many web analytics systems, for example Google refers to them as conversion goals.

**Value network** The links between an organisation and its strategic and non-strategic partners that form its external value chain.

**Value proposition of site** The benefits or value of a website that are evident to its users.

**Vertical portals** These are generally business-to-business sites that will host content to help participants in an industry to get their work done by providing industry news, details of business techniques, and product and service reviews.

**View** *See* **Page impression**.

**View-through** A view-through indicates when a user views an ad and subsequently visits a website.

**Viral marketing** A marketing message is communicated from one person to another, facilitated by different media, such as word of mouth, e-mail or websites. Implies rapid transmission of messages is intended.

**Viral referral** An 'e-mail a friend or colleague' component to an e-mail campaign or part of website design.

**Virtual cash** *See* **Digital cash**.

**Virtual community** An Internet-based forum for special-interest groups to communicate using a bulletin board to post messages.

**Virtual mall** A website that brings together different electronic retailers at a single virtual (online) location. This contrasts with a fixed-location infrastructure – the traditional arrangement where retail organisations operate from retail stores situated in fixed locations such as real-world shopping malls. (Also known as electronic mall.)

**Virtual merchants** Retailers such as Amazon that only operate online – they have no fixed-location infrastructure.

**Virtual organisation** An organisation that uses information and communications technology to allow it to operate without clearly defined physical boundaries between different functions. It provides customised services by outsourcing production and other functions to third parties.

**Virtual private network** Private network created using the public network infrastructure of the Internet.

**Virtualisation** The process whereby a company develops more of the characteristics of a virtual organisation.

**Visit conversion rate** An indication of the capability of a site in converting visitors to defined outcomes such as registration. Calculated by dividing the number of conversion events by the number of visitor sessions within a time period.

**Visitor conversion rate** An indication of the capability of a site in converting visitors to defined outcomes such as registration. Calculated by dividing the number of conversion events by the number of unique visitors within a defined time period.

**Visitor session (visit)** A series of one or more page impressions, served to one user, which ends when there is a gap of 30 minutes or more between successive page impressions for that user.

# W

**Walled garden** A limited range of e-commerce services on iDTV (compared to the Internet).

**WAP** WAP is a technical standard for transferring information to wireless devices, such as mobile phones.

**Web 2.0 concept** A collection of web services that facilitate interaction of web users with a site to create user-generated content and encouraging certain behaviours online such as community or social network participation and user-generated content, mashups, content rating, use of widgets and tagging.

**Web 3.0 concept** Next-generation web incorporating high-speed connectivity, complex cross-community interactions and an intelligent or semantic web where automated applications can access data from different online services to assist searchers perform complex tasks of supplier selection.

**Web accessibility** Designing websites so that they can be used by people with visual impairment whatever browser/access platform they use.

**Web addresses** Web addresses refer to particular pages on a web server, which is hosted by a company or organisation. The technical name for web addresses is uniform or universal resource locators (URLs).

**Web analytics** Techniques used to assess and improve the contribution of e-marketing to a business, including reviewing traffic volume, referrals, clickstreams, online reach data, customer satisfaction surveys, leads and sales.

**Web Application Protocol (WAP)** A standard that enables mobile phones to access text from websites.

**Web browsers** Browsers such as Mozilla Firefox and Microsoft Internet Explorer provide an easy method of accessing and viewing information stored as HTML web documents on different web servers.

**Webmaster** A webmaster is responsible for ensuring the quality of a website. This means achieving suitable availability, speed, working links between pages and connections to company databases. In small companies the webmaster may be responsible for graphic design and content development.

**Web merchandising** The aims of web merchandising are to maximise sales potential of an online store for each visitor. This means connecting the right products, with the right offer to the right visitor, and remembering that the online store is part of a broader experience including online and offline advertising, in-store visits, customer service and delivery.

**Web radio** Internet radio is when existing broadcasts are streamed via the Internet and listened to using plug-ins such as Real Media or Windows Media Player.

**Web response model** The website is used as a response mechanism for offline campaign elements such as direct mail or advertising.

**Web self-service** Content and services provided by an organisation to replace or complement in-store or phone customer enquiries in order to reduce costs and increase customer convenience.

**Web servers** Web servers are used to store the web pages accessed by web browsers. They may also contain databases of customer or product information, which can be queried and retrieved using a browser.

**Website auditors** Auditors accurately measure the usage of different sites in terms of the number of ad impressions and click-through rates.

**Website content** Accessible on the World Wide Web that is created by a particular organisation or individual. The location and identity of a website is indicated by its web address (URL) or domain name. It may be stored on a single server in a single location, or a cluster of servers.

**Website measurement** The process whereby metrics such as page impressions are collected and evaluated to assess the effectiveness of Internet marketing activities in meeting customers, business and marketing objectives.

**Wide Area Information Service (WAIS)** An Internet service that has been superseded by the World Wide Web.

**Widget** A badge or button incorporated into a site or social network space by its owner, with content or services typically served from another site making widgets effectively a mini-software application or web service. Content can be updated in real time since the widget interacts with the server each time it loads.

**Wi-Fi ('wireless fidelity')** A high-speed wireless local-area network enabling wireless access to the Internet for mobile, office and home users.

**Wireframe** Also known as 'schematics', a way of illustrating the layout of an individual web page.

**Wireless Markup Language (WML)** Standard for displaying mobile pages such as transferred by WAP.

**Word-of-mouth marketing** According to the Word-of-Mouth Marketing Association it is giving people a reason to talk about your products and services, and making it easier for that conversation to take place. It is the art and science of building active, mutually beneficial consumer-to-consumer and consumer-to-marketer communications.

**World Wide Web** A medium for publishing information on the Internet. It is accessed through web browsers, which display web pages and can now be used to run business applications. Company information is stored on web servers, which are usually referred to as websites.

# X

**XML** An advanced markup language giving better control than HTML over format for structured information on web pages.

**XMOS (cross-media optimisation studies)** XMOS research is designed to help marketers and their agencies answer the question 'What is the optimal mix of advertising vehicles across different media, in terms of frequency, reach and budget allocation, for a given campaign to achieve its marketing goals?' The mix between online and offline spend is varied to maximise campaign metrics such as reach, brand awareness and purchase intent.

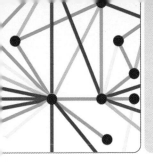

# Index

WITHDRAWN